Paralegal Today

The Legal Team at Work

Sixth Edition

Roger LeRoy Miller
Mary Meinzinger

DEVELOPING PARALEGAL SKILLS

ETHICS WATCH

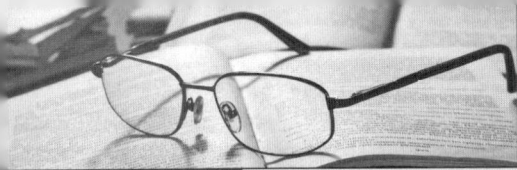

PRACTICE FOCUS

FEATURED CONTRIBUTORS

Paralegal Today

The Legal Team at Work

Sixth Edition

Roger LeRoy Miller
Mary Meinzinger

DELMAR
CENGAGE Learning™

Australia • Brazil • Japan • Korea • Mexico • Singapore • Spain • United Kingdom • United States

Paralegal Today: The Legal Team at Work, Sixth Edition
Roger LeRoy Miller and Mary Meinzinger

Vice President, Careers & Computing: Dave Garza

Director of Learning Solutions: Sandy Clark

Senior Acquisitions Editor: Shelley Esposito

Director, Development-Career and Computing: Marah Bellegarde

Managing Editor: Larry Main

Senior Product Manager: Melissa Riveglia

Editorial Assistant: Diane Chrysler

Senior Market Development Manager: Erin Brennan

Senior Brand Manager: Kristin McNary

Senior Production Director: Wendy Troeger

Production Manager: Mark Bernard

Senior Content Project Manager: Betty L. Dickson

Art Director: Riezebos Holzbaur Group

Senior Technology Project Manager: Joe Pliss

Media Editor: Deborah Bordeaux

For product information and technology assistance, contact us at
Cengage Learning Customer & Sales Support, 1-800-354-9706.
For permission to use material from this text or product,
submit all requests online at **www.cengage.com/permissions**.
Further permissions questions can be e-mailed to
permissionrequest@cengage.com.

Library of Congress Control Number: 2012941386
ISBN-13: 978-1-1335-9107-8
ISBN-10: 1-1335-9107-8

Delmar Learning
5 Maxwell Drive
Clifton Park, NY 12065-2919
USA

Cengage Learning is a leading provider of customized learning solutions with office locations around the globe, including Singapore, the United Kingdom, Australia, Mexico, Brazil, and Japan. Locate your local office at:
international.cengage.com/region

Cengage Learning products are represented in Canada by Nelson Education, Ltd.

To learn more about Delmar, visit **www.cengage.com/delmar**

Purchase any of our products at your local college store or at our preferred online store **www.ichapters.com**

Notice to the Reader
Publisher does not warrant or guarantee any of the products described herein or perform any independent analysis in connection with any of the product information contained herein. Publisher does not assume, and expressly disclaims, any obligation to obtain and include information other than that provided to it by the manufacturer. The reader is expressly warned to consider and adopt all safety precautions that might be indicated by the activities described herein and to avoid all potential hazards. By following the instructions contained herein, the reader willingly assumes all risks in connection with such instructions. The reader is notified that this text is an educational tool, not a practice book. Since the law is in constant change, no rule or statement of law in this book should be relied upon for any service to any client. The reader should always refer to standard legal sources for the current rule or law. If legal advice or other expert assistance is required, the services of the appropriate professional should be sought. The publisher makes no representations or warranties of any kind, including but not limited to, the warranties of fitness for particular purpose or merchantability, nor are any such representations implied with respect to the material set forth herein, and the publisher takes no responsibility with respect to such material. The publisher shall not be liable for any special, consequential, or exemplary damages resulting, in whole or part, from the readers' use of, or reliance upon, this material.

Printed in the United States
1 2 3 4 5 6 7   16 15 14 13 12

To MaryKay and Jim,

You both continue to
inspire all of us.
Keep it up for another
thirty years.

R.L.M.

To the paralegal students
at Madonna University.
You are my inspiration.
May this book be yours.

M.M.

Contents in Brief

Contents

3 Key Elements of the Law   433

Featured Contributor: Nancy R. Gallo, "Paralegals in Family Law Practice" 526

In the Office: Protecting Client Information and Client Interests 533

Developing Paralegal Skills: Preparing for Property-Settlement Negotiations 537

Ethics Watch: Wills and Paralegal Supervision 540

Developing Paralegal Skills: Drafting a Client's Will 542

Going Green: Stay Home 542

Technology and Today's Paralegal: Online Help for Estate Planning 545

Practice Focus: Helping Clients with Estate Planning 546

In the Office: Productive Meetings 554

Developing Paralegal Skills: Reserving a Corporate Name 560

Technology and Today's Paralegal: Online Incorporation 562

Practice Focus: Protecting Limited Liability 565

Featured Contributor: Angela Schneeman, "Going Corporate" 568

Going Green: Out to Lunch? 570

Developing Paralegal Skills: A Case of *Respondeat Superior* 571

Ethics Watch: Dispensing Legal Advice 574

Developing Paralegal Skills: Assisting with a Workers' Compensation Claim 575

Appendices

Preface

The economic slowdown that has dominated headlines and Americans' lives in recent years heralds a new era in this country. It means all firms are attempting to reduce costs. Americans, as producers and consumers, have figured out new ways to live without spending as much as they used to. It follows that when people must seek the help of attorneys, they expect those attorneys to proceed in the most cost-effective way. Consequently, paralegals are being asked to do more work than ever before. It is not surprising that the paralegal occupation has been rapidly growing. We have tried to impart the excitement that surrounds the burgeoning paralegal profession throughout the pages of this textbook. This new edition was designed to be both accessible and motivational. Its many practical features and striking design encourage learning.

Paralegal Today, Sixth Edition, is filled with pedagogical aids that guarantee students will maintain their interest in this subject. We use real-world examples, plus numerous boxed features. Those of you who have used the text before already know that it has perhaps the most extensive supplements package ever offered.

All of the basic areas of paralegal studies are covered in *Paralegal Today,* including careers, ethics and professional responsibility, pretrial preparation, trial procedures, criminal law, legal interviewing and investigation, legal research and analysis, computer-assisted legal research, and legal writing. The book also provides in-depth coverage of substantive law, including bankruptcy, contracts, intellectual property, torts, product liability, real property, estates, business organizations, and family law. In addition, there are a number of features that we describe in this preface.

Two New Features

This edition of *Paralegal Today* breaks ground with two new features that you will find in every chapter.

- *Social Media Today*—Personal use of Facebook, Twitter, and other forms of social media has become common. Many people spend significant time on social media and rely on these tools as primary methods of communication. It has become increasingly apparent that whatever we post on social media reflects on us, whether positively or negatively. The wise user is aware that it is not just our friends who can see what we post; employers and others can scour the Internet for social media history to learn a lot about us. Because of the permanence of our digital footprint, we must think of the long-term consequences of people seeing what we disseminate. The same is true for professional organizations such as law firms. Increasingly, law firms and corporations seek to project a favorable image to the world through social media tools. Each chapter has tips about the prudent use of social media, and several chapters discuss the active use of social media in the practice of law.

- *Practice Focus*—The nature of the legal profession is evolving because of ever-improving technology and new forms of competition. In this feature, we see how law firms and paralegals are being affected by such change. Since change cannot be avoided, legal professionals who adapt to the new environment will be best prepared to keep up with the times.

social MEDIA TODAY

When you are posting on Facebook, assume that your comments will be published in your local newspaper and read by the managing partner of your firm over breakfast.

PRACTICE focus

PROFESSIONAL RESPONSIBILITY AND VIRTUAL PARALEGALS

One growing area for paralegals is "virtual paralegals." Unlike paralegals employed directly by law firms, virtual paralegals contract their services to attorneys, law firms, corporations, agencies, and others as independent contractors. Paralegals in virtual careers cite the increased flexibility in their schedules as a major benefit, as well as the ability to work from home. Lauren Hidden of the International Virtual Assistants Association believes virtual positions will increase as firms seek to reduce costs, saying, "The future is very bright" for virtual paralegals.

Like more traditional paralegals, virtual paralegals can only work under the direct supervision of a licensed attorney. The attorney's responsibility to supervise the virtual paralegal's work is no different from his or her responsibility to supervise a paralegal employed by the same firm. What is different is that the virtual paralegal typically works with greater independence.

One important step you can take to address potential ethics issues while working as a virtual paralegal is to draft your own ethics policy, including procedures and processes to ensure that you do not violate state ethics rules for the state in which your supervising attorney is licensed. This requires paralegals working in different states to be able to assure an attorney elsewhere that they are familiar with the appropriate rules.

Draft such a policy conservatively, ensuring that you avoid any action that might put an attorney in violation of state ethics rules or even create the appearance of professional impropriety. Look carefully at the ABA's *Model Guidelines for the Utilization of Legal Assistant Services* for guidance in drafting a policy. Also, review specific guidelines from the bar association in any state in which you may provide services.

A Practical, Realistic Approach

There sometimes exists an enormous gulf between classroom learning and on-the-job realities. We have tried to bridge this gulf in *Paralegal Today*, Sixth Edition, by offering a text full of practical advice and "hands-on" activities. Exercises at the end of each chapter provide opportunities for your students to apply the concepts and skills discussed in the chapter. Many of the book's other key features, which you will read about shortly, were designed to give students a glimpse of the types of situations and demands they may encounter on the job as professional paralegals. A special introduction to the student, which appears before Chapter 1, contains practical advice and tips on how to master the legal concepts and procedures presented in this text—advice and tips that your students can also apply later, on the job.

Paralegal Today, Sixth Edition, also realistically portrays paralegal working environments and on-the-job challenges. Each chapter, for example, describes challenges to a paralegal's ethical obligations. These realistic situations give students a better understanding of how seemingly abstract ethical rules affect the tasks performed by attorneys and paralegals in the legal workplace.

Technology

We have attempted to make sure that *Paralegal Today*, Sixth Edition, is the most up-to-date text available in today's marketplace. To that end, we have included in this edition materials and features indicating how the latest developments in technology are affecting the law, the legal workplace, and paralegal tasks. These features and materials will help your students learn how to take advantage of technology to enhance their quality and productivity as paralegals.

A Chapter on Online Legal Research

Chapter 8 is devoted to online legal research. It shows students how to do legal research and investigation using the legal databases provided by Westlaw® and Lexis®, as well as some less well-known and less costly online information sources.

TECHNOLOGY AND
today's paralegal

MORE CAREER OPPORTUNITIES FOR TECH-SAVVY PARALEGALS

Paralegals possessing superior technological skills are in demand. Knowing the basics—document creation, spreadsheets, database management, and online legal research—is essential. Also knowing how to utilize social media such as LinkedIn, Facebook, and Google+ is becoming increasing important. Finally, the use of smartphones and tablets has become part of the life of many paralegals. Here we review some skills that paralegals should master to secure their future in the job market.

MASTER DOCUMENT-CREATION SKILLS

A Feature Focusing on Technology

The *Technology and Today's Paralegal* feature appears in each chapter. These updated features focus on how technology is affecting a specific aspect of paralegal work or on how paralegals can use technology to their benefit. For example, in Chapter 2 (Career Opportunities), the feature looks at the career opportunities available for tech-savvy paralegals. Titles of some other *Technology and Today's Paralegal* features include the following:

- Cases of First Impression and the Internet (Chapter 5).
- Who Bears the Costs of Electronic Discovery? (Chapter 10).
- Courtroom Technology (Chapter 12).
- Identity Theft, Spam, and Related Legal Issues (Chapter 14).
- Online Help for Estate Planning (Chapter 17).

ON THE web

The Federal Rules of Civil Procedure are available online at **www.law.cornell.edu**. Select "Federal Rules," which provides Federal Rules of Civil Procedure and other federal rules.

Margin Web Sites

All chapters include several instances of a margin feature titled *On the Web*. This feature suggests Web sites that students should know about and that provide further information on the topic being discussed in the text.

USING INTERNET RESOURCES

1. On the Internet, access LAW MATCH, an online résumé bank, at **www.lawmatch.com**. How do you use it? Would you post your résumé there? Why or why not? If you are currently looking for a position, try posting your résumé at that site.

2. Visit the Web site for *Paralegal Today* magazine at **www.paralegaltoday.com**. You will find many useful

Chapter-Ending Internet Exercises

To help your students navigate the Web and find various types of information online, we have included at the end of each chapter one or more Internet exercises in a section titled *Using Internet Resources*. Each exercise directs the student to a specific Web site and asks a series of questions about the materials available at that site.

The Organization of This Textbook

As paralegal instructors know, materials should be presented in such a way that students can build their skills and knowledge base block by block. This is difficult because, no matter where you begin, you will need to refer to some information that has not yet been presented to the student. For example, if you try to explain on the first or second day of class what paralegals do, you will necessarily have to mention terms that may be unfamiliar to the students, such as *deposition* or *substantive law* or *procedural law*. In this text, the authors have attempted, when possible, to organize the topics covered in such a way that the student is not mystified by terms and concepts not yet discussed.

Content Presentation

No one way of organizing the coverage of topics in a paralegal text will be suitable for every instructor, but we have attempted to accommodate your needs as much as possible by organizing the text into three basic parts.

- Part 1 (Chapters 1–6) focuses primarily on the paralegal profession—its origins and development, the wide array of paralegal careers, the requirements and procedures that students can expect to encounter in the legal workplace, and the threshold ethical responsibilities of the profession. Part 1 also discusses the structure of the American legal system—the sources of law and the courts.

- Part 2 (Chapters 7–13) looks in detail at legal procedures and paralegal skills. The student learns about the basic procedural requirements in civil and criminal litigation, as well as the skills involved in conducting interviews and investigations, legal research and analysis, and legal writing.

- Part 3 (Chapters 14–19) focuses on substantive law. The areas of law treated in this part of the text include torts, product liability, consumer law, contracts, intellectual property, insurance, real property, estates, family law, business organizations, employment, bankruptcy, and environmental law. Additionally, the chapters covering substantive law include many numbered, highlighted examples to provide real-world illustrations of the legal concepts being discussed.

A Flexible Arrangement

We believe that this organization of the materials allows the greatest flexibility for instructors. Although to a certain extent each chapter in the text builds on information contained in previous chapters, the chapters and parts can also be used independently. In other words, instructors who wish to alter the presentation of topics to fit their course outlines, or who wish to use only selected chapters or parts, will find it relatively easy to do so.

Key Features

In addition to the *Technology and Today's Paralegal* feature and the new *Practice Focus* and *Social Media Today* features, which we have already discussed, every chapter in this text has the following features. Each feature is set apart and used both to instruct and to pique the interest of your paralegal students.

Developing Paralegal Skills

The *Developing Paralegal Skills* feature presents hypothetical examples of paralegals at work to help your students develop crucial paralegal skills. The feature includes checklists and practical tips. Some examples are the following:

- Working for a Public Defender (Chapter 2).
- Checking the Accident Scene (Chapter 11).
- Locating Assets (Chapter 12).
- Preparing Graphic Presentations (Chapter 13).
- Preparing a Proof of Claim (Chapter 19).

DEVELOPING paralegal skills

THE DANGERS OF THE UNAUTHORIZED PRACTICE OF LAW

Every state restricts the "practice of law" to licensed attorneys. State bar associations take this restriction seriously, and they aggressively enforce unauthorized practice of law rules against anyone the bar suspects is infringing on attorneys' control of the practice of law.

Unfortunately, the definition of the "practice of law" is unclear, making it a trap for the unwary. The ABA defines it as "the rendition of services for others that call for the professional judgment of a lawyer." In essence, "practicing" law includes giving legal advice, preparing legal documents, and representing a client in court.

Of course, paralegals routinely do the first two of these. Each is perfectly legal as long as these activities are done under the supervision of a licensed attorney. For example, you will often have to relay legal advice from the attorney to the client. To protect yourself, you must make clear that the advice comes from the lawyer, not you. You can avoid unauthorized practice problems by:

- Being clear that everyone understands you are a paralegal in all communications and meetings by:

1. Including your title when signing letters, emails, and other documents and on your business cards.
2. Introducing yourself with your title in meetings.
3. Disclosing your status when communicating with a court.

- Ensuring that activities that might be construed to be the "practice of law" are supervised by a licensed attorney by:

1. Making sure that an attorney reviews and signs off on all legal documents you prepare.
2. Explicitly stating that the attorney is the source of any legal advice when relaying advice to a client by stating, "I asked Attorney Smith about that and she said . . . ."

- Informing yourself about your state's unauthorized practice rules by:

1. Researching court decisions, regulations, and state bar opinions on the topic.
2. Contacting your state paralegal associations and state bar for information and publications on the topic.

Taking care to follow such guidelines will protect the law firm you work for and will protect you, your career, and your firm's clients.

ETHICS WATCH

SOCIAL EVENTS AND CONFIDENTIALITY

Assume that you are at a party with some other paralegals. You tell a paralegal whom you know quite well of some starting news—that a client of your firm, a prominent city official, is being investigated for drug dealing. Although your friend promises to keep this information strictly confidential, she nonetheless tells her husband, who tells a coworker, who in turn tells a friend, and so on. Soon, the news has reached the press, and the resulting media coverage results in irreparable harm to the official's reputation in the community.

Revealing the juicy gossip breached your obligation to the client. If it can be proved that the harm is the direct result of your breach of the duty of confidentiality, the official could sue you and the attorney and the firm for whom you work for damages.

In this situation, you would have violated the NFPA *Model Code of Ethics and Professional Responsibility*, Section 1.5(f), which states: "A paralegal shall not engage in any indiscreet communications concerning clients." This behavior would also have violated the ABA *Model Guidelines for the Utilization of Paralegal Services*, Guideline 6: "A lawyer is responsible for taking reasonable measures to ensure that all client confidences are preserved by a paralegal." Finally, you would have violated the NALA *Code of Ethics and Professional Responsibility*, Canon 7: "A paralegal must protect the confidences of a client."

Featured Contributor

SECURING CLIENT INFORMATION IN THE DIGITAL AGE

Anita Whitby

BIOGRAPHICAL NOTE

Anita Whitby is a business law attorney and Park University faculty member. She has extensive experience as a course developer and teacher of legal studies and business law courses. Ms. Whitby is also a textbook reviewer for Cengage Learning and serves on the advisory board for the series known as *Annual Editions: Business Ethics*. Her current research interests include data privacy ethics, intellectual property, and immersive online learning.

The Digital Age has ushered in an array of electronic devices and technology to help streamline law offices. However, the use of such electronic devices and technology presents serious ethical issues. The following best practices will help paralegals avoid common pitfalls associated with the use of popular devices and technology.

E-MAIL ENCRYPTION

When the topic of e-mail security comes up, we often think about it in terms of Trojans attacking a computer network. However, it is the act of sending unsecured e-mail communication that is the main source of client

data breaches. Communicating with clients via e-mail may seem harmless, but it must be done with extra precaution. Whether you are using a laptop or smartphone, be sure to use encryption software for client communication. Encryption ensures that client information is protected. Because the communication cannot be "unlocked" without a "key," misdirected communication is not in danger of being disclosed to a third party.

CLIENT WORKPLACE E-MAIL & CONFIDENTIALITY

What if a client prefers to communicate via e-mail? The American Bar Association recently issued an ethics opinion regarding the attorney's

IN THE office

AM I CLEAR?

E-mail is a common form of communication, but it causes problems when not used properly. E-mails are the equivalent of letters or memos. When we write a letter or a memo, we usually read it more than once and think carefully about what we're saying. Too many times, we treat e-mails as if they were oral communications—that is, we write in a chatty and imprecise manner. Before sending any e-mail to a client, print it, read it, be sure it is addressed to the right party, and edit it. Remember that the matter you're discussing is important to the client, and your communication should be professional and clear. You should always follow office e-mail procedures carefully. If your firm uses social media for office communications, you should also use discretion when you create such communications. You are often judged on how carefully you communicate.

Ethics Watch

The Ethics Watch feature typically takes a student into a hypothetical situation that clearly presents an ethical problem. All are tied to specific ethical principles of the NALA, NFPA, or ABA. When possible, students are told what they should and should not do in the particular situations discussed. In some instances, consultation with a supervising attorney is necessary. Some examples are the following:

- Paralegal Expertise and Legal Advice (Chapter 1).
- Social Events and Confidentiality (Chapter 4).
- Letters and the Unauthorized Practice of Law (Chapter 9).
- Communicating with Jurors (Chapter 12).

Featured Contributor Articles

Each chapter contains a contributed article written by an educator or an expert in the field. These articles offer your students practical tips on some aspect of paralegal work relating to the topic covered in the chapter. Some examples are the following:

- "Learning Well and Finding Your Place," by Kristine M. Condon, who is the coordinator of a paralegal studies program in Illinois and an experienced paralegal (Chapter 1).
- "Why Mediation May Be the Best Legal Alternative," by P. Darrel Harrison, an attorney and mediator who is an instructor and program director for an ABA-approved paralegal program in San Diego (Chapter 6).
- "Strategies for Protecting Intellectual Property" by Deborah E. Bouchoux, a paralegal educator at Georgetown University and author of *Intellectual Property* and other educational books (Chapter 15).
- "Paralegals in Family Law Practice," by Nancy R. Gallo, professor and coordinator of legal studies at Sussex County Community College, New Jersey, and author of a textbook on family law (Chapter 17).

In the Office

First introduced in the Fifth Edition, this feature offers a practical perspective about working in the law-office environment. The culture of law offices varies, but successful paralegals conduct themselves professionally and pay attention to details that make them invaluable. Examples of *In the Office* include:

- Use Time Wisely (Chapter 1)
- Watch Those Deadlines! (Chapter 6)
- Efficiency in Research (Chapter 7)
- Time Management (Chapter 9)
- Online Privacy (Chapter 14)

Other Special Pedagogical Features

In the Sixth Edition, we have included a number of special pedagogical features, as discussed below.

Chapter Outlines

On every chapter-opening page, a *Chapter Outline* lists the first-level headings within the chapter. These outlines allow you and your students to tell at a glance what topics are covered in the chapters.

Chapter Objectives

In every chapter, just following the *Chapter Outline*, we list five or six chapter objectives. Your students will know immediately what is expected of them as they read each chapter.

Margin Web Sites

As already mentioned, *On the Web* features appear in the page margins throughout the text. This feature directs students to specific Web sites for further information on the topics being discussed.

Vocabulary and Margin Definitions

Legal terminology is often a major challenge for beginning paralegal students. We use an important pedagogical device—margin definitions—to help your students understand legal terms. Whenever an important term is introduced, it appears in colored type and is defined. In addition, the term is listed and defined in the margin of the page, alongside the paragraph in which the term appears (see the examples on the right).

At the end of each chapter, all terms that have appeared in colored type within the chapter are listed in alphabetical order in a section called *Key Terms and Concepts*. Your students can examine this list to make sure that they understand all of the important terms introduced in the chapter. For easy reference and review, each term in the list is followed by the number of the page on which it was defined.

All terms in colored type are also listed and defined in the *Glossary* at the end of the text. Spanish equivalents to many important legal terms in English are provided in a separate glossary in Appendix J.

reprimand
A disciplinary sanction in which an attorney is rebuked for misbehavior. Although a reprimand is the mildest sanction for attorney misconduct, it is serious and may significantly damage the attorney's reputation in the legal community.

suspension
A serious disciplinary sanction in which an attorney who has violated an ethical rule or a law is prohibited from practicing law in the state for a specified or an indefinite period of time.

Chapter Summaries

We have included a chapter summary in table form at the conclusion of each chapter in the Sixth Edition. Each summary conveys important concepts from the chapter. This visually appealing format facilitates the student's review of the chapter contents.

Exhibits and Forms

When appropriate, we present exhibits illustrating important forms or concepts relating to paralegal work. Many exhibits are filled in with hypothetical data. Exhibits and forms in *Paralegal Today*, Sixth Edition, include those listed below:

- A Sample Client Bill (Chapter 3).
- Exclusive and Concurrent Jurisdiction (Chapter 6).
- A Sample Demand Letter (Chapter 9).
- Memorandum in Support of a Motion to Suppress (Chapter 13).

Chapter Summary

Ethics and Professional Responsibility

THE REGULATION OF ATTORNEYS

Attorneys are regulated by licensing requirements and by the ethical rules of their state. The purpose of attorney regulation is to protect the public against incompetent legal professionals and unethical attorney behavior.

1. *Who are the regulators?*—Lawyers establish the majority of rules governing their profession through state bar associations and the American Bar Association (ABA), which has established model rules and guidelines relating to professional conduct. Other key participants in the regulation of attorneys are state supreme courts, state legislatures, and (occasionally) the United States Supreme Court.

2. *Licensing requirements*—Licensed attorneys generally must be graduates of a law school and have passed a state bar examination and an extensive personal background check.

3. *Ethical Codes and Rules*—Most states have adopted a version of either the 1969 *Model Code of Professional Responsibility* or the 1983 revision of the *Model Code*, called the *Model Rules of Professional Conduct*, both of which were published by the ABA. The *Model Rules* are often amended by the ABA to keep up-to-date with the realities of modern law practice. Most states have adopted laws based on the *Model Rules*.

4. *Sanctions for violations*—The *Model Code* and *Model Rules* spell out the ethical and professional duties governing attorneys and the practice of law. Attorneys who violate these duties may be subject to reprimand, suspension, or disbarment. Additionally, attorneys (and paralegals) face potential liability for malpractice or for violations of criminal statutes.

ATTORNEY ETHICS AND PARALEGAL PRACTICE

Some of the ethical rules governing attorney behavior pose difficult problems for paralegals, so paralegals should consult their state's ethical code to learn the specific rules for which they will be accountable. The following rules apply in most states.

1. *Duty of competence*—This duty is violated whenever a client suffers harm as a result of the attorney's (or paralegal's) incompetent action or inaction.
   a. Breaching the duty of competence may lead to a lawsuit against the attorney (and perhaps against the paralegal) for negligence. This may arise from faulty research, missed deadlines, or mistakes in documents.
   b. Attorneys must adequately supervise a paralegal's work to ensure that this duty is not breached.

2. *Confidentiality of information*—All information relating to a client's representation must be kept in confidence and not revealed to third parties who are not authorized to know the information.
   a. Paralegals should be careful both on and off the job not to discuss client information with third parties. Breaches of confidentiality can include unauthorized persons overhearing telephone conversations or personal comments, or faxes being sent to parties not intended to see them.

Continued

Chapter-Ending Materials for Review and Study

Every chapter contains numerous chapter-ending pedagogical materials. These materials are designed to provide a wide variety of assignments for your students. The chapter-ending pedagogy begins with the *Key Terms and Concepts*, followed by the chapter summaries, which we have already mentioned. These are followed by the materials described below.

Questions for Review

Every chapter includes a number of relatively straightforward questions for review. These questions are designed to test the student's knowledge of the basic concepts discussed in the chapter.

Ethical Questions

Because of the importance of ethical issues in paralegal training, we have also included one or more ethical questions at the end of each chapter. Each question presents a hypothetical situation, which is followed by one or two questions about what the paralegal should do to solve the dilemma.

Practice Questions and Assignments

The hands-on approach to learning paralegal skills is emphasized in the practice questions and assignments. There are several of these questions and assignments at the end of each chapter. A particular situation is presented, and the student is asked to actually carry out an assignment.

Questions for Critical Analysis

Every chapter has several questions for critical analysis. These questions are designed to elicit critical evaluation and discussion of issues relating to the topics covered in the chapter.

Projects

There are one or more projects at the end of every chapter. These are specific work tasks that your students can perform. Often, these projects involve obtaining information from sources that paralegals may deal with on the job, such as a library, a court, a prosecutor's office, or a police department.

Group Projects

Each chapter provides an assignment designed to promote teamwork, usually for groups of four students, with specific instructions for each student's tasks.

Using Internet Resources

As already mentioned, concluding the chapter-ending materials in each chapter is a section titled *Using Internet Resources*. The Internet exercises presented in these sections are designed to familiarize students with useful Web sites and with the extensive array of resources available online.

Appendices

To make this text a reference source for your students, we have included the appendices listed below.

A NALA's *Code of Ethics and Professional Responsibility*

B NALA's *Model Standards and Guidelines for Utilization of Paralegals*

C NFPA's *Model Code of Ethics and Professional Responsibility and Guidelines for Enforcement*

D NALS *Code of Ethics and Professional Responsibility*

E Paralegal Associations

F Information on NALA's CP Program

G Information on NFPA's PCC and PACE® Examinations

H Information on NALS Certification

I The Constitution of the United States

J Spanish Equivalents for Important Legal Terms in English

For Users of the Fifth Edition

Those of you who have used the Fifth Edition of *Paralegal Today* will probably want to know some of the major changes that have been made for the Sixth Edition. Generally, all of the major elements in the Fifth Edition—including the text, exhibits, features, and end-of-chapter pedagogy—have been rewritten, revised, or updated as necessary to reflect new laws, procedures, and technological developments. To keep the book at a manageable size, coverage of less critical material has been reduced in favor of adding new developments and pedagogical features. *Today's Professional Paralegal* has been deleted in favor of the new feature *Practice Focus*, but no key material in the previous feature has been lost. The explosion in social media, both in personal use and increasingly in the workplace, is integrated into the book both by the multiple *Social Media Today* tips that are in every chapter as well as substantive discussions in various chapters about the use of social media such as Google+ and Facebook in law practice. We think that we have improved the text greatly, thanks to many suggestions from users of previous editions as well as from other paralegal educators and legal professionals.

Significant Revisions to Chapters

In the process of making the changes discussed above, we have also revised every chapter to enhance readability. To that end, we have deleted or summarized material not critical to the purpose of the text or the course. Here, we summarize some other major changes in each chapter.

- **Chapter 1** (Today's Professional Paralegal)—This chapter introduces the new *Practice Focus* feature (as well as the *Social Media Today* tips). The *Practice Focus* (A Client-Centered Perspective) explains the different missions that types of legal work address and discusses which legal services are most likely to promote long-term client loyalty. A new *Featured Contributor*, Kristine Condon, explains "Learning Well and Finding Your Place."

- **Chapter 2** (Career Opportunities)—This chapter has been updated with the newest data on salaries and job opportunities in the paralegal profession. A new subsection in the text, "Using Social Media Properly," discusses how the digital shadow created by social media impacts the market value of a legal professional.

- **Chapter 3** (The Inner Workings of the Law Office)—Text has been added regarding the storage of law files on "the cloud" and the security issues involved. Discussion of document retention, including e-mail retention, has been expanded. There is a new subsection in the chapter, "Communication by Social Media," that covers the need for clear guidelines within firms for successful use of these tools.

- **Chapter 4** (Ethics and Professional Responsibility)—A new *Featured Contributor*, Anita Whitby, discusses "Securing Client Information in the Digital Age." The *Practice Focus* added here concerns "Professional Responsibility and Virtual Paralegals," as more practicing attorneys use virtual paralegals due to the flexibility and lower overhead costs. There is new discussion about paralegal registration, education, and certification.

- **Chapter 5** (Sources of American Law)—The coverage of statutory and common law has been revised, along with other text matter, as suggested by reviewers. The *Practice Focus* on "Practicing Administrative Law: Disability Claims" gives students exposure to the possibility of employment related to administrative law, either within an agency or through legal representation of clients.

- **Chapter 6** (The Court System and Alternative Dispute Resolution)—The *Technology and Today's Paralegal* feature has been revised to update discussion about "Courts in the Internet Age." The *Practice Focus* feature then expands on the use of electronics in the courtroom. A new *Featured Contributor*, P. Darrel Harrison, explains "Why Mediation May Be the Best Legal Alternative."

- **Chapter 7** (Legal Research and Analysis)—This chapter begins Part 2 of the text, Legal Procedures and Paralegal Skills. It was revised with the assistance of a legal research instructor at a law school to ensure timeliness and accuracy. New cases are used to illustrate details of citations and how to read the parts of cases. The use of new information strategies in outsourcing of legal research, such as by "crowd sourcing," is discussed in the *Practice Focus*.

- **Chapter 8** (Contemporary Online Legal Research)—Because of the rapid changes in online research and the familiarity of students today with online processes, this chapter has been greatly revised to recognize the central role paralegals play in research. Besides Lexis and Westlaw, lower-cost competitors are discussed, as are unpriced services, such as Google Scholar and certain legal blogs.

- **Chapter 9** (Legal Writing: Form and Substance)—The chapter has been edited for relevance with the assistance of a legal writing instructor and includes new material on avoiding confusion through clear legal writing. There is increased focus on the steps in the legal writing process starting at the beginning of an assignment.

- **Chapter 10** (Civil Litigation: Before the Trial)—New material on "Effective E-Discovery" is presented in the *Practice Focus*. Pretrial motions are given enhanced coverage, and the sequence in presentation of such material has been changed to reduce the likelihood of confusion by students.

- **Chapter 11** (Conducting Interviews and Investigations)—A new *Featured Contributor,* Jennifer Allen, details "Ten Strategies for Effective Interviews and Investigations." There is also a new discussion of the use of digital shadows in the investigation of potential witnesses.

- **Chapter 12** (Trial Procedures)— Technology is advancing rapidly. The text explains how social media can be used in helping to enforce delinquent court judgments and in other areas of legal practice. As noted in the *Practice Focus,* more courts are allowing new technologies that are changing how trials proceed.

- **Chapter 13** (Criminal Law and Procedures)—The ways in which social media are used in crime detection are discussed in the text. This includes the steps needed to ensure that such information can meet the standards required of proper evidence. While some aspects of court procedure do not take advantage of new technologies, as explained in the *Practice Focus,* "CSI Comes to the Courtroom," many new tools are being used in criminal procedures.

- **Chapter 14** (Tort Law, Product Liability, and Consumer Law)—This is the first chapter in Part 3, Key Elements of the Law. The coverage of various torts has been clarified for greater student comprehension. In the coverage of product liability law, the *Practice Focus* explains "Handling Product-Related Claims." Consumer law coverage of deceptive practices has been improved, and new examples have been added.

- **Chapter 15** (Contracts and Intellectual Property Law)—This chapter has been revised and updated. There is a new discussion of advertisements and contract law, an area often confusing to students. More examples have been added to illustrate the law in practice. There is also new discussion of how damages are measured in contract cases.

- **Chapter 16** (Real Property and Insurance Law)—The material in this chapter has been restructured for greater relevance to areas of law that frequently involve paralegals, including new text on certain areas of insurance. The *Practice Focus* covers the particular complexities in commercial real estate transactions.

- **Chapter 17** (Family Law and Estates)—Here there is a new discussion of the roles paralegals may play in dealing with domestic abuse issues. There is expanded coverage of nontraditional marriages and relationships, including surrogacy motherhood. The new *Practice Focus* concerns how paralegals can help clients with estate planning.

- **Chapter 18** (Business Organizations and Employment Law)—Text discussion now includes restrictive covenants in employment and how firms can be proactive in limiting potential liability in employment discrimination suits. There is also expanded discussion of disability discrimination. More detail on some aspects of the formation of business entities is provided.

- **Chapter 19** (Bankruptcy and Environmental Law)—The *Practice Focus* covers "Skills Needed to Assist Bankruptcy Clients" and details steps in the bankruptcy process.

Supplemental Teaching/Learning Materials

Paralegal Today, Sixth Edition, is accompanied by what is likely the largest number of teaching and learning supplements available for any text of its kind. We understand that instructors face a difficult task in finding the time necessary to teach the materials that they wish to cover during each term. In conjunction with a number of our colleagues, we have developed supplementary teaching materials that we believe are the best obtainable today. Each component of the supplements package is described below.

Paralegal CourseMate

Paralegal Today: The Legal Team at Work, Sixth Edition, has a Paralegal CourseMate available. Paralegal CourseMate includes:

- an interactive eBook, with highlighting, note-taking, and search capabilities
- interactive teaching and learning tools, including:
  - Quizzing
  - Case studies
  - Chapter objectives
  - Flashcards
  - Web links
  - Crossword puzzles
  - PowerPoint® presentations
  - Videos
  - Video questions
  - Additional questions
  - Engagement Tracker, a first-of-its-kind tool that monitors student engagement in the course
  - And more!

To learn more about this resource and to access free demo CourseMate resources, go to **www.cengagebrain.com**, and search by this book's ISBN (9781133591078). To access CourseMate materials that you have purchased, go to **login.cengagebrain.com**, enter your access code, and create an account or log into your existing account.

Instructor's Manual

The Instructor's Manual has been greatly revised to incorporate changes in the text and to provide comprehensive teaching support. The Instructor's Manual contains the following:

- A sample course syllabus.
- Detailed lecture outlines.
- Teaching suggestions.
- Answers to end-of-chapter and CourseMate questions.
- Testbank (doubled in size for this edition) and answer key.

Instructor Resources

Spend less time planning and more time teaching. With Delmar Cengage Learning's Instructor Resources to Accompany *Paralegal Today: The Legal Team at Work,* preparing for class and evaluating students have never been easier!

This invaluable instructor CD-ROM allows you "anywhere, anytime" access to all of your resources.

- The **Instructor's Manual** contains various resources for each chapter of the book.
- The **Computerized Testbank** in ExamView makes generating tests and quizzes a snap. With over 2,500 questions and different styles to choose from, you can create customized assessments for your students with the click of a button. Add your own unique questions and print rationales for easy class preparation.
- Customizable **PowerPoint® Presentations** focus on key points for each chapter. (PowerPoint® is a registered trademark of the Microsoft Corporation.)

To access additional course materials (including CourseMate), please go to **login.cengage. com**, then use your SSO (single sign-on) login to access the materials.

WebTUTOR™

The WebTUTOR™ supplement allows you, as the instructor, to take learning beyond the classroom. This online courseware is designed to complement the text and benefit students and instructors alike by helping to better manage your time, prepare for exams, organize your notes, and more. WebTUTOR™ allows you to extend your reach beyond the classroom.

WebPage

Come visit our Web site at **www.paralegal.delmar.cengage.com**, where you will find valuable information such as hot links and sample materials to download, as well as other Delmar Cengage Learning products.

Supplements At-a-Glance

SUPPLEMENT:	WHAT IT IS:	WHAT'S IN IT:
Paralegal CourseMate CourseMate	Online interactive teaching and learning tools and an interactive eBook. Go to **login.cengage.com** to access.	Interactive teaching and learning tools, including: • Quizzing • Case studies • Chapter objectives • Flashcards • Web links • Crossword puzzles • PowerPoint® presentations • Videos • Video questions • Additional questions • Interactive eBook • Engagement Tracker
Online Instructor Companion Site	Resources for the instructor accessible via Cengage Single Sign-On	• Instructor's manual with a course syllabus, lecture outlines, teaching suggestions, answers to end-of-chapter and CourseMate questions, and testbank and answer key • Computerized Testbank in ExamView, with many questions and styles to choose from to create customized assessments for your students • PowerPoint® presentations
Instructor Resources CD-ROM INSTRUCTOR RESOURCES	Resources for the instructor, available on CD-ROM	• Instructor's manual with a course syllabus, lecture outlines, teaching suggestions, answers to end-of-chapter and CourseMate questions, and test bank and answer key • Computerized Testbank in ExamView, with many questions and styles to choose from to create customized assessments for your students • PowerPoint® presentations
WebTutor™ WebTUTOR	WebTUTOR™ supplemental courseware is the best way to use the Internet to turn everyone in your class into a front-row student. It complements Cengage Learning paralegal textbooks by providing interactive reinforcement that helps students grasp complex concepts. WebTUTOR™ allows you to know quickly what concepts your students are or aren't grasping.	• Automatic and immediate feedback from quizzes and exams • Online exercises that reinforce what students have learned • Flashcards • Greater interaction and involvement through online discussion forums

Please note that the Internet resources are of a time-sensitive nature and URL addresses may often change or be deleted.

Acknowledgments for Previous Editions

Numerous careful and conscientious individuals have helped us in this undertaking from the beginning. We continue to be indebted to those whose contributions helped to make previous editions of *Paralegal Today* a valuable teaching/learning text. We particularly thank the following paralegal educators for their insightful criticisms and comments:

Laura Barnard
Lakeland Community College, OH

Lia Barone
Norwalk Community College, CT

Carol Brady
Milwaukee Area Technical College, WI

Rhonda Brashears
Certified Paralegal, TX

Debra Brown
Coastline Community College, CA

Chelsea Campbell
Lehman College, NY

Linda S. Cioffredi
Woodbury College, VT

Jeptha Clemens
Northwest Mississippi Community
    College, MS

Arlene A. Cleveland
Pellissippi State Technical Community
    College, TN

Lynne D. Dahlborg
Suffolk University, MA

Kevin R. Derr
Pennsylvania College of Technology, PA

Bob Diotalevi
Florida Gulf Coast University, FL

Donna Hamblin Donathan
Marshall University Community
    College, OH

Dora Dye
City College of San Francisco, CA

Wendy B. Edson
Hilbert College, NY

Jameka Ellison
Everest University, FL

Leslie Sturdivant Ennis
Samford University, AL

Pamela Faller
College of the Sequoias, CA

Gary Glascom
Cedar Crest College, PA

Dolores Grissom
Samford University, AL

Paul D. Guymon
William Rainey Harper College, IL

Sharon Halford
Community College of Aurora, CO

Vera Haus
McIntosh College, NH

Linda Wilke Heil
Central Community College, NE

Jean A. Hellman
Loyola University, IL

Melinda Hess
College of Saint Mary, NE

Louise Hoover
Rockford Business College, IL

Marlene L. Hoover
El Camino College, CA

Susan J. Howery
Yavapai College, AZ

Jill Jasperson
Utah Valley State College, UT

Melissa M. Jones
Samford University, AL

Deborah Winfrey Keene
Lansing Community College, MI

Jennifer Allen Labosky
Davidson County Community College, NC

Dora J. Lew
California State University, East Bay, CA

Mary Hatfield Lowe
Westark Community College, AR

Gerald A. Loy
Broome Community College, NY

Paula Montlary
Florida Career College, FL

Linda Mort
Kellogg Community College, MI

Constance Ford Mungle
Oklahoma City University, OK

H. Margaret Nickerson
William Woods College, MO

Martha G. Nielson
University of California, San Diego, CA

Elizabeth L. Nobis
Lansing Community College, MI

Joy D. O'Donnell
Pima Community College, AZ

Anthony Piazza
David N. Myers College, OH

Francis D. Polk
Ocean County College, NJ

Ruth-Ellen Post
Rivier College, NH

Elizabeth Raulerson
Indian River Community College, FL

Kathleen Mercer Reed
University of Toledo, OH

Lynn Retzak
Lakeshore Technical Institute, WI

Evelyn L. Riyhani
University of California, Irvine, CA

Melanie A. P. Rowand
California State University, East Bay, CA

Vitonio F. San Juan
University of La Verne, CA

Susan F. Schulz
Southern Career Institute, FL

Sean Scott
St. Petersburg College, FL

Joanne Spillman
Westwood College Online, CO

John G. Thomas III
North Hampton County Community
    College, PA

Derek Thomson
Bryant and Stratton College, NY

Loretta Thornhill
Hagerstown Community College, MD

Julia Tryk
Cuyahoga Community College, OH

Stonewall Van Wie III
Del Mar College, TX

Lorrie Watson
Orangeburg Calhoun Technical College,
    SC

Acknowledgments for the Sixth Edition

During the preparation of the Sixth Edition of *Paralegal Today*, several professionals offered us penetrating criticisms, comments, and suggestions for improving the text. While we haven't been able to comply with every request, the reviewers listed below will see that many of their suggestions have been taken to heart.

Lora C. Clark
Pitt Community College, NC

Terri L. Lindors
Globe University, Broadview University,
    Minnesota School of Business, MN

Roger Stone
Hilbert College, NY

Anita Whitby
Park University, MO

We also are grateful to the following *Featured Contributors* to *Paralegal Today*, Sixth Edition, for enhancing the quality of our book with their tips and illuminating insights into paralegal practice:

Jennifer J. Allen
Davidson County Community College, NC

Deborah E. Bouchoux
Georgetown University, DC

Jo-Christy Brown
Attorney, TX

S. Whittington Brown
Attorney, AR

Loretta Calvert
Volunteer State Community College, TN

Kristine M. Condon
Kankakee Community College, IL

Matt Cornick
Clayton State University, GA

Regina G. Dowling
University of Hartford, CT

Wendy B. Edson
Hilbert College, NY

Nancy R. Gallo
Sussex County Community College, NJ

P. Darrel Harrison
San Diego Miramar College, CA

Daniel F. Hinkel
Corporate Counsel, GA

Steven C. Kempisty
Bryant & Stratton College, NY

Anita Whitby
Park University, MO

William Putman
Paralegal Educator/Author, NM

Linda J. Wolf
Paralegal, TX

Angela Schneeman
Paralegal and Author, MN

E. J. Yera
Attorney, FL

Beth Walston-Dunham
Paralegal Educator/Author, MO

In preparing this text, we were also the beneficiaries of the expertise brought to the project by the editorial and production staff of Delmar Cengage Learning. Our Senior Acquisitions Editor, Shelley Esposito, successfully guided the project through each phase and put together a supplements package that is without parallel in the teaching and learning of paralegal skills. Melissa Riveglia, our Senior Product Manager, was also incredibly helpful in putting together the teaching/learning package. We also wish to thank Betty Dickson, Senior Content Project Manager, for her assistance throughout the production process. Additionally, we wish to thank Mark Linton, our Senior Marketing Manager, and Diane Chrysler, Editorial Assistant, for their valuable contributions to the project.

A number of other individuals contributed significantly to the quality of *Paralegal Today,* Sixth Edition. We wish to thank Roger Meiners for his assistance in creating what we believe is the best introductory paralegal text on the market today. We also thank Suzanne Jasin for her special efforts on the project. Finally, we are indebted to the staff at Parkwood Composition, our compositor, whose ability to generate the pages for this text quickly and accurately made it possible for us to meet our ambitious printing schedule.

We know that we are not perfect. If you or your students have suggestions on how we can improve this book, write to us. That way, we can make *Paralegal Today* an even better book in the future. We promise to answer every single letter that we receive.

Roger LeRoy Miller
Mary Meinzinger

Skill Prep

A Paralegal Skills Module

What's Inside

After reading this skills module, you will be better prepared to . . .

- Make good choices
  (College Prep, p. xli)

- Manage your time
  (Time Prep, p. xliii)

- Be engaged in your studies
  (Study Prep, p. xlv)

- Study for quizzes and exams
  (Test Prep, p. xlix)

- Read your textbook efficiently
  (Read Prep, p. li)

- Write quality papers
  (Write Prep, p. liii)

- Make a presentation
  (Presentation Prep, p. lviii)

Welcome!

With this course and this textbook, you've begun what we hope will be a stimulating and thought-provoking journey into the study of law. In this course, you will learn about the paralegal profession, the basic structure of the legal system, and substantive law, such as torts and criminal law. You'll also learn about procedural issues, such as civil litigation and criminal procedure. This book will help you develop paralegal skills, including legal research and writing, interviewing, and investigation. Building your base of knowledge will get you well on your way to a great future as a paralegal.

We have developed this skills module to help you get the most out of this course and textbook. Whether you are a recent high school graduate moving on to college or a working professional continuing your education, what you want most when you study is RESULTS. You want to become familiar with the issues and ideas presented in this textbook so that you can talk about them during class and remember them as you prepare for exams and assignments. Natural talent alone will not ensure your success as a paralegal; you also must develop effective study skills and good work habits. This study skills module is designed to help you do just that. With tips on lifestyle decisions, time management, how to be more engaged when you study, how to get the most out of your textbook, how to prepare for quizzes and exams, how to write papers, and how to prepare and deliver a presentation, this guide will help you develop the skills you need to be the best learner you can be.

COLLEGE *Prep*

It takes several things to succeed in a college class—especially concentration and commitment to your studies. To do this, you need energy. When you are full of energy, time seems to pass quickly, and it is easier to get things done. As you know, when you don't have energy, time feels as if it is dragging, and even your favorite activities can feel like a burden. To have the energy you need to be a great college learner, it is important to make good lifestyle choices. You need to get enough sleep, eat well, take care of yourself, and maintain good relationships. An important part of being a successful student is paying attention to what goes on in your life so that you have all the ingredients you need to maintain your focus and energy.

Here are some suggestions to help you keep up your energy so that you can succeed in everything you do.

- Too often, we become so busy with other aspects of our lives that we neglect our health. It is crucial that you eat a balanced diet, exercise regularly, and get enough sleep. If you don't take care of your physical well-being, other areas of your life will suffer. Research shows that people who are physically active learn better in school.

- Hearing is not the same thing as listening. Many people are not good listeners. People often hear what they want to hear. We all filter information through our own experiences and interests. When talking with friends, instructors, or family members, focus carefully on what they say, as you may learn something unexpected. A good paralegal listens well to attorneys' instructions and to clients as well.

- Be very careful about what you post on the Internet. A good rule of thumb is, "Don't post anything that you wouldn't want the world to know." Many employers search the Internet for information concerning potential employees, and one embarrassing photo, comment, or tweet can have long-term negative consequences. Law firms are particularly careful about hiring people with good character.

- Most people who succeed have a plan: they know what they want to accomplish and when. Do you have a life plan for after college? If not, you can start by making a list of your lifetime goals, even though they may change later on. You can also create a career plan that includes a list of skills you will need to succeed. Then, in addition to your classes, choose outside activities that will help you develop the skills that can lead to a good job.

- Whenever we do something new, whether in college or in other areas of life, we usually aren't very good at it. We can always benefit from feedback from those who are accomplished in that area, such as instructors or people working in a given field. Therefore, welcome feedback that is offered to you, and if it isn't given, ask for it.

©Supri Suharjoto/www.shutterstock.com

Most people who succeed have a plan.

If you don't take care of your physical well-being, other areas of your life will inevitably suffer.

- Do you want to become a better writer? Your college probably has a writing center with resources to help you with your writing assignments. If not, you should be able to find a tutor who will help you figure out what you are trying to communicate and how to put it effectively on paper. Clear writing is a critical skill for paralegals.

- Filing systems are an easy way to keep track of your money. First, label file folders for different categories related to your personal finances, such as paycheck stubs, bank statements, and receipts from purchases. If you find you need another category, just set up a new folder. Paralegals must have excellent file systems. Do it in your own life and it will come naturally on the job.

- Do you want to become a better public speaker? Consider using your campus's audiovisual resources to sharpen this essential skill. Record yourself giving a presentation and then critique your performance. Invite a few friends to give their reaction, too. Join a school organization such as a debate or drama club to gain confidence in front of a live audience. Being comfortable talking to strangers is a much-needed skill for most paralegals.

- Be thankful for the people who care about you. Your family and good friends are a precious resource. When you have problems, don't try to solve them by yourself.

Don't focus on disappointments. Talk to the people in your life who want you to succeed and be happy, and listen to their advice.

- No doubt you have seen people jump to conclusions that were not correct. Critical thinking is a crucial skill for paralegals, and, as with any other skill, you will get better at it with practice. Whether you are considering a friend's argument, a test question, a major purchase, or a personal problem, carefully weigh the evidence, balance strengths and weaknesses, and make a reasoned decision.

- Rather than worrying about approval from others, seek approval from the person who matters the most—yourself. Your conscience will tell you when you are doing the right thing. Don't let worries about what others think run—or ruin—your life.

TIME *Prep*

Doing well in college-level courses involves a lot of work. You have to go to class, read the textbook, pay attention to lectures, take notes, complete homework assignments, write papers, and take exams. On top of that, there are other things in your life that call for your time and attention. You have to take care of your home, run daily errands, take care of family, spend time with friends, work a full- or part-time job, and find time to unwind. With all that you're involved in, knowing how to manage your time is critical if you want to succeed as a learner.

The key to managing your time is knowing how much time you have and using it well. At the beginning of every term, you should evaluate how you use your time. How much time do you spend working? Caring for your home and family? Watching TV or movies? Studying? Keep a record of what you do hour by hour for a full week. Once you see where all your time goes, you can decide which activities you might change in order to manage your time more effectively. If you think you are busy in college, wait until you are a practicing paralegal! Then time management will be even more critical.

Here are some other helpful tips on how to make the most of your time.

- Plan your study schedule in advance. At the beginning of each week, allocate time for each subject that you need to study. If it helps, put your schedule on a calendar computer program for efficient daily planning. Learning to schedule tasks you need to complete and recording upcoming deadlines will serve you well when you are a paralegal.

- Don't be late for classes, meetings, or other appointments. If you find that you have trouble being on time, adjust your planning to arrive ten minutes early to all engagements. That way, even if you are "late" you will still be on time. It is critical to learn to be prompt for clients and court matters.

- To reduce the time spent looking for information on the Internet, start with a clear idea of your research task. Use a trusted search engine and focus only on the subject at hand. Do not allow yourself to be sidetracked by other activities such as checking e-mail or social networking.

- Set aside a little time each day to assess whether you are on track to meet the requirements in all your classes, whether that involves studying for a test, writing a paper, or completing a group project. Don't let deadlines "sneak up" on you. A calendar program or app can help you keep track of target dates and can even give you friendly reminders.

- Nothing wastes more time—or is more aggravating—than having to redo schoolwork that was somehow lost on your computer. Back up all of your important files periodically. You can copy them onto an external hard drive or a USB flash drive.

- Concentrate on doing one thing at a time. Multitasking is a trap we often fall into that leads to doing several things quickly but poorly. When you are studying, don't carry on a text conversation with a friend or have one eye on the Internet.

- Set goals for yourself, not only with schoolwork but also with responsibilities in other areas of your life. If you tell yourself, "I will have this task done by Monday at noon and that other task finished before dinner on Wednesday," you will find it much easier to balance the many demands on your time.

- Regularly checking e-mail and text messages not only interrupts the task at hand, but is also an easy excuse for not working. Set aside specific times of the day to check and answer e-mail, and, when necessary, make sure that your cell phone is off or

Concentrate on doing one thing at a time.

To manage your time well, you need to know where it is going.

out of reach. A reply text can wait until you complete your work.

- Sometimes, a task is so large that it seems impossible, making it more tempting to put off. When given a large assignment, break it into a series of small assignments. Then, make a list of the assignments, and as you finish each one, give yourself the satisfaction of crossing it off your list.

- Many of us have a particular time of day when we are most alert, whether early morning, afternoon, or night. Plan to do schoolwork during your most efficient time, and set aside other times of the day for activities that do not require serious concentration.

- Slow down! Some people think they are getting more work done by rushing, but that often leads to poor decisions, mistakes, and errors of judgment, all of which waste time. Work well, not quickly, and you will save time.

- In marketing, *to bundle* means to combine several products. In time management, it means combining two activities to free up some time. For example, if you need to exercise and want to socialize, bundle the two activities by doing activities with your friends. Take along some schoolwork when you head to the laundromat—you can get a lot done while you're waiting for the spin cycle. Or, you can record class lectures (ask the professor for permission) so that you can review class material while you're running errands.

- Develop a habit of setting time limits for tasks, both in and out of school. You will find that with a time limit in mind, you will waste less time and work more efficiently, a prized skill among paralegals.

- Most e-mail systems have free calendar features that allow you to send e-mail reminders to yourself concerning assignments, tests, and other important dates.

- A Chinese adage goes, "The longest journey starts with a single step." If you are having trouble getting started on a project or assignment, identify the first task that needs to be done. Then do it! This helps avoid time-wasting procrastination.

Bundling, or combining two activities, will help you save time.

STUDY *Prep*

What does it take to be a successful student? Success does not depend on how naturally smart you are. Successful students and paralegals aren't born, they're made. What this means is that even if you don't consider yourself naturally "book smart," you can do well in this course by developing study skills that will help you understand, remember, and apply key concepts in school and on the job.

There are five things you can do to develop good study habits:

- Be engaged
- Ask questions
- Take notes
- Make an outline
- Mark your text

Be Engaged

If you've ever heard elevator music, you know what easy listening is like—it stays in the background. You don't pay attention to it and you probably forget it after a few minutes. That is *not* what you should be doing in class. You have to be engaged. Being *engaged* means listening to discover (and remember) something. In other words, listening is more than just hearing. Not only do you have to hear what the professor is saying in class, you have to pay attention to it. And as you listen with attention, you will hear what your instructor believes is important. One way to make sure that you are listening attentively is to take notes. Doing so will help you focus on the professor's words and will help you identify the most important parts of the lecture.

We study best when we are free from distractions.

Ask Questions

If you are really engaged in a course, you will ask a question or two whenever you do not understand something. You can also ask a question to get your instructor to share her or his opinion on a subject. However you do it, true engagement requires you to be a participant in your class. The more you participate, the more you will learn (and the more your instructor will know who you are!).

Take Notes

Note taking has a value in and of itself, just as outlining does. The physical act of writing makes you a more efficient learner, since you must think about what you are writing. In addition, your notes provide a guide to what your instructor thinks is important. That means you will have a better idea of what to study before the next exam if you have a set of notes that you took during class. Paralegals usually take notes while listening to work instructions, doing research, or talking to clients or witnesses. It is a skill that increases the quality and accuracy of results.

Make an Outline

As you read through each chapter of this textbook, you might make an outline—a simple method for organizing information. You can create an outline as part of your reading or at the end of your reading. Or you can make an outline when you reread a section before moving on to the next one. The act of physically writing an outline helps us retain the material, thereby giving us a better chance of earning a higher grade. Even if you make an outline that is no more than the headings in this text, you will be studying more efficiently than you would be otherwise.

To make an effective outline, you have to be selective. Outlines that contain all the information in the text are not very useful. Your objectives in outlining are, first, to identify the main concepts and, then, to add details that support those main concepts.

Your outline should consist of several levels written in a standard format. The most important concepts are assigned Roman numerals;

Legal "Shorthand"

Members of the legal profession usually use abbreviations and symbols as part of a shorthand system to allow for greater efficiency when taking notes. Rather than writing out common legal terms, here are some of the shorthand abbreviations and symbols often used:

Δ or **D**	defendant
π or **P**	plaintiff
≈	similar to
≠	not equal to, not the same as
∴	therefore
a/k/a	also known as
atty	attorney
b/c or **b/cz**	because
b/p	burden of proof
cert	*certiorari*
dely	delivery
dep	deposition
disc	discovery
JML	judgment as a matter of law
JNOV	judgment *non obstante veredicto* (notwithstanding the verdict)
JOP	judgment on the pleadings
juris or **jx**	jurisdiction
K	contract
mtg	mortgage
n/a	not applicable
neg	negligence
PL	paralegal
Q	as a consequence, consequently
re	regarding
§ or **sec**	section
s/b	should be
S/F	Statute of Frauds
S/L	statute of limitations

You can expand on this list by creating and using other symbols or abbreviations. Once you develop a workable shorthand system, routinely use it in the classroom and then carry it over to your job. Most organizations you will work for will also use symbols and abbreviations, which you can add to your shorthand system.

the second most important, capital letters; the third most important, numbers; and the fourth most important, lowercase letters. Here is a quick example from part of Chapter 12:

I. Trial Procedures

    A. Preparing for Trial

    B. Contacting and Preparing Witnesses

        1. Contacting Witnesses and Issuing Subpoenas

        2. Preparing Witnesses for Trial

            a. Tell Witnesses What to Expect

            b. Role Playing

            c. Numerous Details

    C. Exhibits and Displays

    D. The Trial Notebook

Mark Your Text

Because you own your textbook for this course, you can greatly improve your learning by marking your text. By doing so, you will identify the most important concepts of each chapter, reinforce your knowledge as you mark, and at the same time make a handy study guide for reviewing material at a later time.

Different Ways of Marking

The most common form of marking is to underline important points. The second most common method is to use a felt-tipped highlighter, or marker, in yellow or some other transparent color. Marking also includes circling, numbering, using arrows, jotting brief notes, or any other method that allows you to remember things when you go back to skim the pages in your textbook prior to an exam.

Why Marking Is Important

Marking is important for the same reason that outlining is—it helps you to organize the information in the text. It allows you to become an active participant in the mastery of the material. Researchers have shown that the physical act of marking, just like the physical acts of note taking and outlining, helps you better retain the material. The clearer the material is organized in your mind, the more you'll remember. Studies indicate that active readers (those who engage with the text by outlining or marking) typically do better on exams. One reason this may be true is that outlining and/or marking require sharper concentration, and greater concentration facilitates greater recall.

Two Points to Remember When Marking

Read one section at a time before you do any extensive marking. You can't mark a section until you know what is important, and you can't know what is important until you read the whole section. Don't mark too extensively. Just as an outline cannot contain everything that is in a text (or, with respect to note taking, in a lecture), marking the whole book isn't useful. If you do mark the whole book, when you go back to review the material, your markings will not help you remember what was important.

The key to marking is *selective* activity. Mark each page in a way that allows you to see the most important points at a glance. You can follow up your marking by adding information to your subject outline.

With these skills in hand, you will be well on your way to becoming a great student. Here are a few more hints that will help you develop effective study skills.

- Put a check mark next to material that you do not understand. After you have completed an entire chapter, take a break. Then, work on better comprehension of the checkmarked material.

- As a rule, do schoolwork as soon as possible when you get home after class. The longer you wait, the more likely you will be distracted by television, video games, phone calls from friends, or social networking.

- Many students are tempted to take class notes on a laptop computer. This is a bad idea for two reasons. First, it is hard to copy diagrams or take other "artistic" notes on a computer. Second, it is easy to get distracted by checking e-mail or surfing the Web. (Notice, too, how many people look over the shoulders of other students who are surfing the Web rather than paying attention.)

- We study best when we are free from distractions such as the Internet, phones, and our friends. That's why your school library is often the best place to work. Set aside several hours a week of "library time" to study where you can concentrate in peace and quiet. When you are working as a paralegal, being able to devote quiet attention to material is a key skill.

- Reward yourself for studying! From time to time, allow yourself a short break so you can surf the Internet, go for a jog, take a nap, or do something else that you enjoy. These interludes will refresh your mind and enable you to study longer and more efficiently.

- When you are given a writing assignment, make sure you allow yourself enough time to revise and polish your final draft. Good writing takes time—you likely will need to revise a paper several times before it's ready to be handed in.

- A neat study space is important. Staying neat forces you to stay organized. When your desk is covered with piles of papers, notes, and textbooks, things are being lost even though you may not realize it. The only work items that should be on your desk are those that you are working on that day.

- Often, studying involves pure memorization. To help with this task, create flash (or note) cards. On one side of the card, write the question or term. On the other side, write the answer or definition. Then, use the cards to test yourself on the material.

- Mnemonic (ne-*mon*-ik) devices are tricks that increase our ability to memorize. A well-known mnemonic device is the phrase ROY G BIV, which helps people remember the colors of the rainbow—red, orange, yellow, green, blue, indigo, violet. You can create your own mnemonics for whatever you need to memorize. The more fun you have coming up with mnemonics for yourself, the more useful they will be.

- Take notes twice. First, take notes in class. Then, when you get back home, rewrite your notes. The rewrite will act as a study session by forcing you to think about the material. Invariably, it will lead to questions that are crucial to the study process.

- By turning headings or subheadings in all of your textbooks into questions—and then answering them—you will increase your understanding of the material.

- Multitasking while studying is generally a bad idea. You may think that you can review your notes and watch television at the same time, but your ability to study will almost certainly suffer. It's OK to give yourself Internet or TV breaks from schoolwork, but do not combine the two.

TEST *Prep*

You have worked hard reading your textbook, paying close attention in class, and taking good notes. Now it's test time, when that hard work pays off. To do well on an exam, of course, it is important that you learn the concepts in each chapter as thoroughly as possible; however, there are additional strategies for taking exams. You should know which reading materials and lectures will be covered. You should also know in advance what type of exam you are going to take—essay or objective or both. (Objective exams usually include true/false, fill-in-the-blank, matching, and multiple-choice questions.) Finally, you should know how much time will be allowed for the exam. By taking these steps, you will reduce any anxiety you feel as you begin the exam, and you'll be better prepared to work through the entire exam.

Follow Directions

Students are often in a hurry to start an exam, so they don't bother to read the instructions. The instructions can be critical, however. In a multiple-choice exam, for example, if there is no indication that there is a penalty for guessing, then you should never leave a question unanswered. Even if only a few minutes are left at the end of an exam, you should guess on the questions about which you are uncertain.

Additionally, you need to know the weight given to each section of an exam. In a typical multiple-choice exam, all questions have equal weight. In other types of exams, particularly those with essay questions, different parts of the exam carry different weights. You should use these weights to apportion your time accordingly. If the essay portion of an exam accounts for 20 percent of the total points on the exam, you should not spend 60 percent of your time on the essay.

Finally, you need to make sure you are marking the answers correctly. Some exams require a No. 2 pencil to fill in the dots on a machine-graded answer sheet. Other exams require underlining or circling. In short, you have to read and follow the instructions carefully.

Objective Exams

An objective exam consists of multiple-choice, true-false, fill-in-the-blank, or matching questions that have only one correct answer. Students usually commit one of two errors when they read objective-exam questions: (1) they read things into the questions that do not exist, or (2) they skip over words or phrases. Most test questions include key words such as:

- all
- never
- always
- only

If you miss any of these key words, you may answer the question wrong even if you know the information. Consider the following example:

> True or False? All cases in which one person kills another person are considered murder.

In this instance, you may be tempted to answer "True," but the correct answer is "False," because the charge of murder is only brought in cases in which one person *intentionally* killed another. In cases in which a person unintentionally killed another, the charge is manslaughter.

Whenever the answer to an objective question is not obvious, start with the process of elimination. Throw out the answers that are clearly incorrect. Typically, the easiest way to eliminate incorrect answers is to look for those that are meaningless, illogical, or inconsistent. Often, test

Grades aren't a matter of life and death, and worrying about them can have a negative effect on your performance.

authors put in choices that make perfect sense and are indeed true, but they are not the answer to the question under study.

If you follow the above tips, you will be well on your way to becoming an efficient, results-oriented student. Here are a few more suggestions that will help you get there.

- Instructors usually lecture on subjects they think are important, so those same subjects are also likely to be on the exam. This is another reason to take extensive notes in class.

- Review your lecture notes immediately after each class, when the material is still fresh in your mind. Then, review each subject once a week, giving yourself an hour to go back over what you have learned. Reviews make tests easier because you will feel comfortable with the material.

- At times, you will find yourself studying for several exams at once. When this happens, make a list of each study topic and the amount of time needed to prepare for that topic. Then, create a study schedule to reduce stress and give yourself the best chance for success.

- When preparing for an exam, you might want to get a small group together (two or three other students) for a study session. Discussing a topic out loud can improve your understanding of that topic and will help you remember the key points that often come up on exams.

- Some professors make old exams available, either by posting them online or putting them on file in the library. Old tests can give you an idea of the kinds of questions the professor likes to ask. You can also use them to take practice exams.

- Cramming just before the exam is a dangerous proposition. Cramming tires the brain unnecessarily and adds to stress, which can severely hamper your testing performance. If you've studied wisely, have confidence that you will recall the information when you need it.

- Be prepared. Make a list of everything you will need for the exam, such as pens or pencils, a watch, and a calculator. Arrive at the

Cramming just before the exam is a dangerous proposition.

exam early to avoid having to rush, which will only add to your stress. Good preparation helps you focus on the task at hand.

- Be sure to eat before taking a test. Having some food in your stomach will give you the energy you need to concentrate. Don't go overboard, however. Too much food or heavy foods will make you sleepy during the exam.

- When you first receive your exam, look it over quickly to make sure that you have all the pages. If you are uncertain, ask your professor or exam proctor. This initial scan may uncover other problems as well, such as illegible print or unclear instructions.

- If the test requires you to read a passage and then answer questions about that passage, read the questions first. This way, you will know what to look for as you read.

- With essay questions, look for key words such as "compare," "contrast," and "explain." These will guide your answer. If you have time, make a quick outline. Most importantly, get to the point without wasting your time (or your professor's) with statements such as "There are many possible reasons for . . . ."

- When you finish a test early, your first instinct may be to hand it in and get out of the classroom as quickly as possible. It is always a good idea, however, to review your answers. You may find a mistake or an area where some extra writing will improve your grade.

- Grades aren't a matter of life and death, and worrying too much about a single exam can have a negative effect on your performance. Keep exams in perspective. If you do poorly on one test, it's not the end of the world. Rather, it should motivate you to do better on the next one.

READ *Prep*

This textbook is the foundation for your introduction to paralegal studies. It contains key concepts and terms that are important to understanding law and the practice of law. This knowledge will be important not only for you to succeed in this course but for your future paralegal career. For this reason, it is essential that you develop good reading skills so that you can get the most out of this textbook and other class materials.

All students know how to read, but reading for a college-level course goes beyond being able to recognize words on a page. Students must read to learn. Read a chapter with the goal of understanding its key points and how it relates to other chapters. In other words, you have to be able to explain what you read. To do this, you need good reading habits and skills, which are necessary for success as a paralegal.

Reading for Learning Requires Focus

Reading (and learning from) a textbook is not like reading a newspaper, magazine, or novel. The point of reading for learning isn't to get through the material as fast as you can or to skip parts to get to the stuff you think is most interesting. A textbook is a source of deep information about a subject. The goal of reading a textbook is to learn as much of that information as you can. This kind of reading requires concentration. When you read to learn, you have to make an effort to focus on the book and tune out other distractions so that you can comprehend and remember the information you have read.

How to read this book:
1. Preview
2. Read in detail
3. Review

Reading for Learning Takes Time

When reading your textbook, you need to go slow. The most important part of reading for learning is not how many pages you get through or how fast you get through them. Instead, the goal is to learn the key concepts that are presented in each chapter. To do that, you need to read slowly, carefully, and with great attention. It will be the same on the job—careful reading is essential in legal work.

Reading for Learning Takes Repetition

Even the most well-read scholar will tell you that it's difficult to learn from a textbook just by reading through it once. To read for learning, you have to read assigned material a number of times. This doesn't mean, though, that you just sit and read the same section three or four times. Instead, you should follow a preview-read-review process. Here's a good guide to follow:

The First Time

The first time you read a section of the book, you should preview it. During the preview, pay attention to how the chapter is formatted. Look over the title of the chapter, the section headings, and highlighted or bolded words. This will give you a good preview of the important ideas in the chapter. You should also pay close attention to any graphs, illustrations, or figures that are used in the chapter, since these provide a visual illustration of important concepts. You should also give special attention to the first and last sentence of each paragraph. First sentences usually introduce the main point of the paragraph, while last sentences usually sum up what was presented in the paragraph.

The goal of previewing is to identify the main idea of the section. Of course, you may not be able to come up with a detailed answer yet, but that's not the point of previewing. Instead, the point is to develop some general ideas about what the section is about so that when you do read it in full, you know what to look for.

The Second Time

After the preview, you'll want to read through the passage in detail. During this phase, it is important to read with a few questions in mind: What is the main point of this paragraph? What does the author want me to learn from this? How does this relate to what I read before? Keeping these questions in mind will help you be an attentive reader who is actively focusing on the main ideas of the passage.

After you have completed a detailed read of the chapter, take a break so that you can rest your mind (and your eyes). When you resume studying, you should write up a summary or paraphrase of what you just read. You don't need to produce a detailed, lengthy summary of the whole chapter. Instead, try to come up with a brief paraphrase that covers the most important ideas of the chapter. This paraphrase will help you remember the main points of the chapter, allow you to check the accuracy of your reading, and provide a good guide for later review.

The Third Time (and Beyond)

After you've finished a detailed reading of the chapter, you should take the time to review the chapter (at least once, but maybe even two, three, or more times). During this step, you should review each paragraph and the notes you made, asking this question: "What was this paragraph about?" At this point, you'll want to answer the question in some detail, drawing on what you learned during your first two readings.

Reading with others is also a great way to review the chapter. After completing the reading individually, group members should meet and take turns sharing what they learned from their reading. Explaining the material to others will reinforce and clarify what you already know. It also provides an opportunity to learn from others.

Gaining another perspective on a passage will increase your knowledge, since different people will key in on different things during a reading.

Whether you're reading your textbook for the first time or reviewing it for the final exam, here are a couple of tips that will help you be an attentive and attuned reader.

1. Set Aside Time and Space

To read effectively, you need to be focused and attentive, and that won't happen if your phone is buzzing with text messages every two minutes, if the TV is on in the background, or if you're surrounded by friends or family. Similarly, you won't be able to focus on your book if you're trying to read in a room that is too hot or too cold, or sitting in an uncomfortable chair. So when you read, find a quiet, comfortable place that is free from distractions where you can focus on one thing—learning from the book.

2. Take Frequent Breaks

Reading your textbook shouldn't be a test of endurance. Rest your eyes and your mind by taking a short break every twenty to thirty minutes. The concentration you need to read attentively requires lots of energy, and you won't have enough energy if you don't take frequent breaks. Studies indicate that hard concentration can rarely go beyond thirty minutes, as our minds need small rest breaks.

3. Keep Reading

Effective reading is like playing sports or a musical instrument—practice makes perfect. The more time that you spend reading, the better you will be at learning from your textbook. Your vocabulary will grow, and you'll have an easier time learning and remembering information in all your courses.

WRITE *Prep*

A key part of succeeding as a student is learning how to write well. Whether writing papers, presentations, essays, or even e-mails to your instructor, you have to be able to put your thoughts into words and do so with force, clarity, and precision. In this section, we outline a three-phase process that you can use to write virtually anything.

1. Getting ready to write
2. Writing a first draft
3. Revising your draft

Phase 1: Getting Ready to Write

First, make a list. Divide the ultimate goal—a finished paper—into smaller steps that you can tackle right away. Estimate how long it will take to complete each step. Start with the date your paper is due and work backwards to the present. For example, if the due date is December 1 and you have about three months to write the paper, give yourself a cushion and schedule November 20 as your target completion date. Plan what you want to get done by November 1, and then list what you want to get done by October 1.

How to Pick a Topic

To generate ideas for a topic, any of the following approaches work well:

- **BRAINSTORM WITH A GROUP.** There is no need to create in isolation. You can harness the energy and the natural creative power of a group to help you.

- **SPEAK IT.** To get ideas flowing, start talking. Admit your confusion or lack of clear ideas. Then just speak. By putting your thoughts into words, you'll start thinking more clearly.

- **USE FREE WRITING.** Free writing, a technique championed by writing teacher Peter Elbow, is also very effective when trying to come up with a topic. There's only one rule in free writing: Write without stop-

ping. Set a time limit—say, ten minutes—and keep your fingers dancing across the keyboard the whole time. Ignore the urge to stop and rewrite. There is no need to worry about spelling, punctuation, or grammar during this process.

Refine Your Idea

After you've come up with some initial ideas, it's time to refine them:

- **SELECT A TOPIC AND WORKING TITLE.** Using your instructor's guidelines for the paper or speech, write down a list of topics that interest you. Write down all of the ideas you think of in two minutes. Then choose one topic. The most common pitfall is selecting a topic that is too broad. "Trial Procedure" is not a useful topic for your paper. Instead, consider something narrow that can be accomplished with some detail, such as "Motions for Judgment Notwithstanding the Verdict."

- **WRITE A THESIS STATEMENT.** Clarify what you want to say by summarizing it in one concise sentence. This sentence, called a *thesis statement,* refines your working title. A thesis is the main point of the paper; it is a declaration of some sort. You might write a thesis statement such as "Motions for judgment notwithstanding the verdict (JNOV) have a low success rate but are an essential tool in obtaining a favorable outcome for a client."

Set Goals

Effective writing flows from a purpose. Think about how you'd like your reader or listener to respond after considering your ideas.

- If you want to persuade someone to your point of view, make your writing clear and logical. Support your assertions with evidence.

- If your purpose is to move the reader into action, explain exactly what steps to take and offer solid benefits for doing so.

To clarify your purpose, state it in one sentence—for example, "The purpose of this paper is to discuss and analyze how motions for JNOV are constructed and presented at trial."

Begin Research

In the initial stage, the objective of your research is not to uncover specific facts about your topic. That comes later. First, you want to gain an overview of the subject. You must first learn enough about such motions and how they are used to be able to explain them to others.

Make an Outline

An outline is a kind of map. When you follow a map, you avoid getting lost. Likewise, an outline keeps you from wandering off topic. To create your outline, follow these steps:

1. Review your thesis statement and identify the three to five main points you need to address in your paper to support your thesis that such motions are worth filing.

2. Next, look closely at those three to five major points or categories and think about what minor points or subcategories you want to cover in your paper. Your major points are your big ideas; your minor points are the details you need to fill in under each of those ideas.

3. Ask for feedback. Have your instructor or a classmate review your outline and offer suggestions for improvement. Did you choose the right categories and subcategories? Do you need more detail anywhere? Does the flow from idea to idea make sense?

Do In-Depth Research

Three-by-five-inch index cards are an old-fashioned but invaluable tool for in-depth research. Simply write down one idea or piece of information per card. This makes it easy to organize—and reorganize—your ideas and information. Organizing research cards as you create them saves time. Use rubber bands to keep *source cards* (cards that include the bibliographical information for a source) separate from *information cards* (cards that include nuggets of information from a source) and to maintain general categories.

When creating your cards, be sure to:

- Copy all of the information correctly.
- Always include the source and page number on information cards.

- Be neat and organized. Write legibly, using the same format for all of your cards.

In addition to source cards and information cards, generate *idea cards*. If you have a thought while you are researching, write it down on a card. Label these cards clearly as containing your own ideas.

Phase 2: Writing a First Draft

To create your draft, gather your index cards and confirm that they are arranged to follow your outline. Then write about the ideas in your notes. It's that simple. Look at your cards and start writing. Write in paragraphs, with one idea per paragraph. As you complete this task, keep the following suggestions in mind:

- **REMEMBER THAT THE FIRST DRAFT IS NOT FOR KEEPS.** You can worry about quality later; your goal at this point is simply to generate lots of words and lots of ideas.

- **WRITE FREELY.** Many writers prefer to get their first draft down quickly and would advise you to keep writing, much as in free writing. Of course, you may pause to glance at your cards and outline. The idea is to avoid stopping to edit your work.

- **BE YOURSELF.** Let go of the urge to sound "official" or "scholarly," and avoid using unnecessary big words or phrases. Instead, write in a natural voice. Address your thoughts not to the teacher but to an intelligent student or someone you care about. Visualize this person, and choose the three or four most important things you'd say to her about the topic.

- **MAKE WRITING A HABIT.** Don't wait for inspiration to strike. Make a habit of writing at a certain time each day.

- **GET PHYSICAL.** While working on the first draft, take breaks. Go for a walk. Speak or sing your ideas out loud. From time to time, practice relaxation techniques and breathe deeply.

- **HIDE IT IN YOUR DRAWER FOR A WHILE.** Schedule time for rewrites before you begin, and schedule at least one day between revisions so that you can let the material sit. The brain needs that much time to disengage itself from the project.

Phase 3: Revising Your Draft

During this phase, keep in mind the saying, "Write in haste; revise at leisure." When you are working on your first draft, the goal is to produce ideas and write them down. During the revision phase, however, you need to slow down and take a close look at your work. One guideline is to allow 50 percent of writing time for planning, researching, and writing the first draft. Then use the remaining 50 percent for revising.

There are a number of especially good ways to revise your paper:

1. Read it out loud.

The combination of voice and ears forces us to pay attention to the details. Is the thesis statement clear and supported by enough evidence? Does the introduction tell your reader what's coming? Do you end with a strong conclusion that expands on what's in your introduction rather than just restating it?

2. Have a friend look over your paper.

This is never a substitute for your own review, but a friend can often see mistakes you miss. Remember, when other people criticize or review your work, they are not attacking you. They're just commenting on your paper. With a little practice, you will learn to welcome feedback because it is one of the fastest ways to approach the revision process.

3. Cut.

Look for excess baggage. Avoid at all costs and at all times the really, really terrible mistake of using way too many unnecessary words, a mistake that some student writers often make when they sit down to write papers for the various courses in which they participate at the fine institutions of higher learning that they are fortunate enough to attend. (Example: The previous sentence could be edited to "Avoid unnecessary words.") Also, look for places where two (or more sentences) could be rewritten as one. Resist the temptation to think that by cutting text you are losing something. You are actually gaining—a clearer, more polished product. For maximum efficiency, make the larger cuts first—sections, chapters, pages. Then go for the smaller cuts—paragraphs, sentences, phrases, words.

4. Paste.

In deleting both larger and smaller passages in your first draft, you've probably removed some of the original transitions and connecting ideas. The next task is to rearrange what's left of your paper or speech so that it flows logically. Look for consistency within paragraphs and for transitions from paragraph to paragraph and section to section.

5. Fix.

Now it's time to look at individual words and phrases. Define any terms that the reader might not know, putting them in plain English whenever you can. In general, focus on nouns and verbs. Using too many adjectives and adverbs weakens your message and adds unnecessary bulk to your writing. Write about the details, and be specific. Also, check your writing to ensure that you are:

- Using the active voice. Write "*The research team began the project*" rather than (passively) "*A project was initiated.*"

- Writing concisely. Instead of "*After making a timely arrival and perspicaciously observing the unfolding events, I emerged totally and gloriously victorious,*" be concise with "*I came, I saw, I conquered.*"

- Communicating clearly. Instead of "*The speaker made effective use of the television medium, asking in no uncertain terms that we change our belief systems,*" you can write specifically, "*The reformed criminal stared straight into the television camera and shouted, 'Take a good look at what you're doing! Will it get you what you really want?'*"

6. Prepare.

In a sense, any paper is a sales effort. If you hand in a paper that is wearing wrinkled jeans, its hair tangled and unwashed and its shoes untied, your instructor is less likely to buy it. To avoid this situation, format your paper following accepted standards for margin widths, endnotes, title pages, and other details. Ask your instructor for specific instructions on how to cite the sources used in writing your paper. You can find useful guidelines in the *MLA Handbook for Writers of Research Papers*, a book from the Modern Language Association. If you cut and paste material from a Web page directly into your paper, be sure to place that material in quotation marks and cite the source. Before referencing an e-mail message, verify the sender's identity. Remember that anyone sending e-mail can pretend to be someone else. Use quality paper for the final version of your paper. For an even more professional appearance, bind your paper with a plastic or paper cover.

7. Proofread.

As you ease down the home stretch, read your revised paper one more time. This time, go for the big picture and look for the following using this proofreading checklist:

- A clear thesis statement.

- Sentences that introduce your topic, guide the reader through the major sections of your paper, and summarize your conclusions.

- Details—such as quotations, examples, and statistics—that support your conclusions.

- Lean sentences that have been purged of needless words.

- Plenty of action verbs and concrete, specific nouns.

- Finally, look over your paper with an eye for spelling and grammar mistakes. Use contractions sparingly if at all. Use your word processor's spell-check, by all means, but do not rely on it completely as it will not catch everything.

When you are through proofreading, take a minute to savor the result. You've just witnessed something of a miracle—the mind organizing diverse ideas into a creative work of art! That's the *aha!* in writing.

Academic Integrity: Avoiding Plagiarism

Using another person's words, images, or other original creations without giving proper credit is called *plagiarism*. Plagiarism amounts to taking someone else's work and presenting it as your own—the equivalent of cheating on a test. The consequences of plagiarism can range from a failing grade to expulsion from school. Plagiarism can be unintentional, as some students don't understand the research process. Sometimes they leave writing until the last minute and don't take the time to organize their sources of information. Also, some people are raised in cultures where identity is based on group membership rather than individual achievement. These students may find it hard to understand how creative work can be owned by an individual.

To avoid plagiarism, ask an instructor where you can find your school's written policy on this issue. Don't assume that you can resubmit a paper you wrote for another class for a current class; many schools will regard this as plagiarism even though you wrote the paper. The basic guidelines for preventing plagiarism are to cite a source for each phrase, sequence of ideas, or visual image created by another person. While ideas cannot be copyrighted, the specific way that an idea is *expressed* can be. You also need to list a source for any idea that is closely identified with a particular person. The goal is to clearly distinguish your own work from the work of others. There are several ways to ensure that you do this consistently:

- **IDENTIFY DIRECT QUOTES.** If you use a direct quote from another writer or speaker, put that person's words in quotation marks. If you do research online, you might find yourself copying sentences or paragraphs from a Web page and pasting them directly into your notes. This is the same as taking direct quotes from your source. To avoid plagiarism, identify such passages in an obvious way.

- **PARAPHRASE CAREFULLY.** Paraphrasing means restating the original passage in your own words, usually making it shorter and simpler. Students who copy a passage word for word and then just rearrange or delete a few phrases are running a serious risk of plagiarism. Remember to cite a source for paraphrases, just as you do for direct quotes. When you use the same sequence of ideas as one of your sources— even if you have not paraphrased or directly quoted—cite that source.

- **NOTE DETAILS ABOUT EACH SOURCE.** For books, details about each source include the author, title, publisher, publication date, location of publisher, and page number. For articles from print sources, record the article title and the name of the magazine or journal as well. If you found the article in an academic or technical journal, also record the volume and number of the publication. A librarian can help identify these details. If your source is a Web page, record as many identifying details as you can find—author, title, sponsoring organization, URL, publication date, and revision date. In addition, list the date that you accessed the page. Be careful when using Web resources, as not all Web sites are considered legitimate sources. Wikipedia, for instance, may not be regarded as a legitimate source for certain information;

the National Institute of Justice's Web site, however, is acceptable.

- **CITE YOUR SOURCES AS ENDNOTES OR FOOT-NOTES TO YOUR PAPER.** Ask your instructor for examples of the citation format to use. You do not need to credit wording that is wholly your own, nor do you need to credit general ideas, such as the suggestion that people use a to-do list to plan their time. But if you borrow someone else's words or images to explain an idea, do give credit.

PRESENTATION *Prep*

In addition to reading and writing, your success as a student will depend on how well you can communicate what you have learned. Most often, you'll do so in the form of presentations. Many people are intimidated by the idea of public speaking, but it really is just like any other skill—the more often you do it, the better you will get. Developing a presentation is similar to writing a paper. Begin by writing out your topic, purpose, and thesis statement. Then carefully analyze your audience by using the strategies listed below.

If your topic is new to listeners . . .

- Explain why your topic matters to them.
- Relate the topic to something that they already know and care about.
- Define any terms that they might not know.

If listeners already know about your topic . . .

- Acknowledge this fact at the beginning of your speech.
- Find a narrow aspect of the topic that may be new to listeners.
- Offer a new perspective on the topic, or connect it to an unfamiliar topic.

If listeners disagree with your thesis . . .

- Tactfully admit your differences of opinion.
- Reinforce points on which you and your audience agree.
- Build credibility by explaining your qualifications to speak on your topic.
- Quote experts who agree with your thesis—people whom your audience is likely to admire.
- Explain to your audience that their current viewpoint has costs for them and that a slight adjustment in their thinking will bring significant benefits.

If listeners might be uninterested in your topic . . .

- Explain how listening to your speech can help them gain something that matters deeply to them.
- Explain ways to apply your ideas in daily life.

Remember that audiences generally have one question in mind: *"So what?"* They want to know that your presentation relates to their needs and desires. To convince people that you have something worthwhile to say, think of your main topic or point. Then see if you can complete this sentence: "I'm telling you this because . . . ."

Organize Your Presentation

Consider the length of your presentation. Plan on delivering about one hundred words per minute. Aim for a lean presentation—enough words to make your point but not so many as to make your audience restless. Leave your listeners wanting more. When you speak, be brief and then be seated. Presentations are usually organized in three main parts: the introduction, the main body, and the conclusion.

1. The introduction.

Rambling presentations with no clear point or organization put audiences to sleep. Solve this problem by making sure your introduction conveys the point of your presentation. The following introduction, for example, reveals the thesis and indicates exactly what's coming. It conveys that the speech will have three distinct parts, each in logical order:

> Prison overcrowding is a serious problem in many states. I intend to describe prison conditions around the country, the challenges these conditions create, and how various states are addressing the issue.

Some members of an audience will begin to drift during any speech, but most people pay attention for at least the first few seconds.

Highlight your main points in the beginning sentences of your speech. People might tell you to open your introduction with a joke, but humor is tricky. You run the risk of falling flat or offending somebody. Save jokes until you have plenty of experience and know your audiences well. Also avoid long, flowery introductions in which you tell people how much you like them and how thrilled you are to address them. If you lay it on too thick, your audience won't believe you. Get down to business, which is what the audience wants. Draft your introduction, and then come back to it after you have written the rest of your presentation. In the process of creating the main body and conclusion, your thoughts about the purpose and main points of your speech might change.

2. The main body.

The main body of your speech accounts for 70 to 90 percent of your presentation. In the main body, you develop your ideas in much the same way that you develop a written paper. Transitions are especially important in presentations. Give your audience a signal when you change points. Do so by using meaningful pauses, verbal emphasis, and transitional phrases: "On the other hand, until the public realizes what is happening to children in these countries . . ." or "The second reason police officers use *Miranda* cards is . . . ." In long presentations, recap from time to time. Also, make it a point to preview what's to come. Hold your audience's attention by using facts, descriptions, expert opinions, and statistics.

3. The conclusion.

At the end of the presentation, summarize your points and draw your conclusion. You started with a bang; now finish with drama. The first and last parts of a presentation are the most important. Make it clear to your audience when you have reached the end. Avoid endings such as, "This is the end of my presentation. Are there any questions?" A simple standby is "So, in conclusion, I want to reiterate three points: First . . ." When you are finished, stop speaking. Although this sounds quite obvious, a good presentation is often ruined by a speaker who doesn't know when, or how, to wrap things up.

Support Your Presentation with Notes and Visuals

To create speaking notes, you can type out your presentation in full and transfer key words or main points onto a few three-by-five-inch index cards. Number the cards so that if you drop them, you can quickly put them in order again. As you finish the information on each card, move it to the back of the pile. Write information clearly and

Speeches are usually organized in three main parts: the introduction, the main body, and the conclusion.

- Use fewer visuals rather than more. For a fifteen-minute presentation, a total of five to ten slides is usually enough.
- Limit the amount of text on each visual. Stick to key words presented in short sentences or phrases and in bulleted or numbered lists.
- Use a consistent set of plain fonts. Make them large enough for all audience members to see.
- Stick with a simple, coherent color scheme. Use light-colored text on a dark background or dark text on a light background.

in letters large enough to be seen from a distance. The disadvantage of the index card system is that it involves card shuffling, so some speakers prefer to use outlined notes.

You can also create supporting visuals. Presentations often include visuals such as PowerPoint slides or handwritten flip charts. These visuals can reinforce your main points and help your audience understand how your presentation is organized. They also serve to trigger your memory about what you should say to flesh out the bullet points in your visuals. Use visuals to *complement* rather than *replace* speech. If you use too many visuals or if they are too complex, your audience might focus on them and forget about you.

Overcome Fear of Public Speaking

Surveys indicate that the fear of public speaking is the number one fear for many people. For those who harbor this fear, being overlooked by an audience in favor of visuals may be exactly what they hope for! Ideally, though, while many of us may not be able to eliminate fear of public speaking entirely, we can take steps to reduce and manage it. The following tips will help you conquer any fear you might feel at the thought of public speaking.

PREPARE THOROUGHLY Research your topic thoroughly. Knowing your topic inside and out can create a baseline of confidence. To make a strong start, memorize the first four sentences that you plan to deliver, and practice them many times. Delivering them flawlessly when you're in front of an audience can build your confidence for the rest of your speech.

ACCEPT YOUR PHYSICAL SENSATIONS You have probably experienced the physical sensations that are commonly associated with stage fright: dry mouth, a pounding heart, sweaty hands, muscle jitters, shortness of breath, and a shaky voice. One immediate way to deal with such sensations is simply to notice them. Tell yourself, "Yes, my hands are clammy. Yes, my stomach is upset. Also, my face feels numb." Trying to deny or ignore such facts can increase your fear. In contrast, when you fully accept sensations, they start to lose power. While speakers often feel nervous, they do not look that nervous. Members of the audience are there to listen and are sympathetic.

FOCUS ON CONTENT, NOT DELIVERY If you view presentations simply as an extension of a one-to-one conversation, you will realize that the goal is not to perform but to communicate your ideas to an audience just as you would explain them to a friend. This can reduce your fear of speaking. Instead of thinking about yourself, focus on your message. Your audience is more interested in what you have to say than in how you say it. Forget about giving a "speech." Just give people valuable ideas and information that they can use.

Practice Your Presentation

The key to successful public speaking is practice.

- **USE YOUR "SPEAKER'S VOICE."** When you practice, do so in a loud voice. Your voice sounds different when you talk loudly, and this fact can be unnerving. Get used to it early on. People do not like to strain to hear what you have to say.

- **PRACTICE IN THE ROOM IN WHICH YOU WILL DELIVER YOUR PRESENTATION.** Ideally, you will be able to practice your presentation in the room in which it will be given. If that is not possible, at least visit the site ahead of time so you are comfortable with your surroundings. Also make sure that the materials you will need for your presentation, including any audiovisual equipment, will be available when you need them and that you know how to use them.

- **MAKE A RECORDING.** Many schools have video recording equipment available for student use. Use it while you practice and then view the finished recording to evaluate your presentation. Pay special attention to your body language—how you stand, your eye contact, and how you use your hands.

- **LISTEN FOR REPEATED WORDS AND PHRASES.** Examples of unwanted filler words include *you know, kind of,* and *really,* plus *uh, umm,* and *ah.* To get rid of them, try to notice them every time they pop up in your daily speech.

- **KEEP PRACTICING.** Avoid speaking word for word, as if you were reading a script. When you know your material well, you can deliver it in a natural way. Practice your presentation until you could deliver it in your sleep, then run through it a few more times. You do not want to hide behind a computer monitor or stare at your script while you read it. You know the material, so you only need visual triggers on PowerPoint slides or note cards.

Deliver Your Presentation

Before you begin, get the audience's attention. If people are still filing into the room or adjusting their seats, they're not ready to listen. Wait for the audience to settle into their seats before you begin.

For a great presentation, keep these tips in mind:

DRESS FOR THE OCCASION The clothing you choose to wear on the day of your presentation delivers a message that's as loud as your words. Consider how your audience will be dressed, and then choose a wardrobe based on the impression you want to make. It shows respect for the audience to be dressed professionally.

Talking about Practice

When practicing your presentation, you'll need to do more than just read through it silently. While it's good to use practice sessions to memorize the contents of your speech, these sessions are also important times to work on how you use your voice and body as you speak. To make your practice time efficient and beneficial, follow the two-step process shown below and repeat it two or three (or more) times until you're ready to deliver a professional, polished presentation.

1. Practice

- If possible, practice your presentation in the room where you will be actually giving it. If this is not possible, make your practice setting as similar to the actual setting as possible.

- Record your practice so that you can analyze it later.

- Working from your outline or notes, go through the entire presentation without stopping. If you make mistakes, try to fix them as you go along.

2. Review

Watch the recording of your first practice and ask yourself:

- Did I leave out important ideas?

- Did I focus too much on one point and not enough on others?

- Did I talk too fast or too slowly?

- Did I speak clearly?

- Was my body language distracting or helpful?

- Did I maintain good eye contact?

After watching the recording, write down three or four specific changes that you will make to improve your presentation.

PROJECT YOUR VOICE   When you speak, do it loudly enough to be heard. Avoid leaning over your notes or a computer monitor.

MAINTAIN EYE CONTACT   When you look at people, they become less frightening. Remember, too, that it is easier for the audience to listen to someone when that person is looking at them. Find a few friendly faces around the room, and imagine that you are talking to each of these people individually.

NOTICE YOUR NONVERBAL COMMUNICATION, YOUR BODY LANGUAGE   Be aware of what your body is telling your audience. Contrived or staged gestures will look dishonest. Hands in pockets, twisting your hair, chewing gum, or leaning against a wall will detract from your speech and make you appear less polished.

WATCH THE TIME   You can increase the impact of your words by keeping track of the time during your presentation. It's better to end early than to run late.

PAUSE WHEN APPROPRIATE   Beginners sometimes feel they have to fill every moment with the sound of their voice. Release that expectation. Give your listeners a chance to make notes and absorb what you say.

HAVE FUN   Chances are that if you lighten up and enjoy your presentation, so will your listeners.

Reflect on Your Presentation

Review and reflect on your performance. Did you finish on time? Did you cover all of the points you intended to cover? Was the audience attentive? Did you handle any nervousness effectively? Welcome evaluation from others. Most of us find it difficult to hear criticism about our speaking. Be aware of resisting such criticism, and then let go of your resistance. Listening to feedback will increase your skill.

The Paralegal Profession

Today's Professional Paralegal

Chapter Outline

Introduction	What Do Paralegals Do?	Paralegal Skills and Attributes
What Is a Paralegal?	Paralegal Education	The Future of the Profession

After completing this chapter, you will know:

- What a paralegal is.
- What kinds of tasks paralegals perform.
- The names of the professional associations of paralegals.

- The education and training available to paralegals.
- Whether paralegals must be certified or licensed.
- Key skills and attributes of the professional paralegal.

Introduction

If you are considering a career as a paralegal, be prepared to be part of an exciting and growing profession. Over time, law firms have been giving greater responsibilities to paralegals. The opportunities for paralegals to work outside of law firms (in corporations or government agencies, for example) are also expanding. As the profession has grown, the average paralegal salary has increased. According to one 2012 survey, experienced paralegals earned average compensation of $73,200.[1]

How do you know if you want to become part of this dynamic profession? The first step in finding out is to become familiar with what a paralegal is, what kinds of work paralegals do, and what education and skills are needed. These topics are covered in this chapter. In Chapter 2, you will learn about where paralegals work, how much they earn, and how they got their jobs. As you read through the chapters in this book, remember that this is only an introduction to the profession and the starting point of your education. You should supplement what you learn in the classroom by talking and networking with paralegals in various professional environments. After all, in today's competitive job market, whom you know can sometimes be as important as what you know in getting the job you desire.

What Is a Paralegal?

In this book, we use the terms *paralegal* and *legal assistant,* as is often done in the legal community, although the term paralegal is becoming dominant. Some people or groups may prefer one label to the other, but such disagreement does not mean that the labels describe different job duties. Indeed, some persons who are trained professional paralegals may be called something else entirely at their workplace, such as *legal technician* or *legal research specialist.*

Definition of Paralegal

After years of disagreement, two of the major organizations involved reached a consensus on the definition of paralegal. The **American Bar Association (ABA)**, which is a national association for attorneys, and the **National Association of Legal Assistants (NALA)**, which is the largest national organization of paralegals, jointly agree to the following definition:

> A **legal assistant**, or **paralegal**, is a person qualified by education, training, or work experience who is employed or retained by a lawyer, law office, corporation, governmental agency or other entity and who performs specifically delegated substantive legal work, for which a lawyer is responsible.[2]

The **National Federation of Paralegal Associations (NFPA)**, which is the second largest paralegal association, prefers the term *paralegal.*[3] Members of NFPA were concerned by the fact that many attorneys refer to their secretaries as legal assistants and wanted to distinguish the role of paralegals as professionals. The NFPA gives the following definition for *paralegal:*

> A Paralegal is a person, qualified through education, training or work experience to perform substantive legal work that requires knowledge of legal concepts and is customarily, but not exclusively, performed by a lawyer. This person may be retained or employed by a lawyer, law office, governmental agency or other entity or may be authorized by administrative, statutory or court authority to perform this work. Substantive shall mean work requiring recognition, evaluation, organization, analysis, and communication of relevant facts and legal concepts.[4]

Another major organization, the **American Association for Paralegal Education (AAfPE)**, provides the following definition:

> Paralegals perform substantive and procedural legal work as authorized by law, which work, in the absence of the paralegal, would be performed by an attorney.

American Bar Association (ABA)
A voluntary national association of attorneys. The ABA plays an active role in developing educational and ethical standards for attorneys and in pursuing improvements in the administration of justice.

National Association of Legal Assistants (NALA)
One of the two largest national paralegal associations in the United States; formed in 1975. NALA is actively involved in paralegal professional development.

paralegal or legal assistant
A person qualified by education, training, or work experience who is employed or retained by a lawyer, law office, corporation, governmental agency, or other entity and who performs specifically delegated substantive legal work, for which a lawyer is responsible.

National Federation of Paralegal Associations (NFPA)
One of the two largest national paralegal associations in the United States; formed in 1974. NFPA is actively involved in paralegal professional development.

American Association for Paralegal Education (AAfPE)
A national organization of paralegal educators; the AAfPE was established in 1981 to promote high standards for paralegal education.

Paralegals have knowledge of the law gained through education, or education and work experience, which qualifies them to perform legal work. Paralegals adhere to recognized ethical standards and rules of professional responsibility.[5]

Expanding Roles

Regardless of which term is used, paralegals or legal assistants today perform many functions that traditionally were performed by attorneys. The paralegal's work falls somewhere between that of an attorney and that of a legal secretary. Paralegals perform substantive legal work that they are trained to perform through education, experience, or (usually) both.

What Do Paralegals Do?

Paralegals assist attorneys in many ways. The following is a sampling of some of the tasks that legal assistants typically perform in a law office. Keep in mind that today's paralegals work in many nontraditional settings, including corporations, government agencies, courts, insurance companies, real estate firms, and almost any other entity that uses legal services. Throughout this book, you will read about the specific tasks that paralegals perform in different settings.

A Sampling of Paralegal Tasks

Typically, legal assistants perform the following duties:

- *Conduct client interviews and maintain contact with clients*—provided that the client is aware of the status and function of the legal assistant and the legal assistant does not give legal advice (see the *Ethics Watch* feature on the facing page).

- *Locate and interview witnesses*—to gather relevant facts and information about a lawsuit, for example.

- *Conduct legal investigations*—to obtain, organize, and evaluate information from sources such as police reports, medical records, photographs, court documents, experts' reports, technical manuals, and product specifications.

- *Calendar and track important deadlines*—such as the date by which a certain document must be filed with the court or the date by which the attorney must respond to a settlement offer.

- *Organize and maintain client files*—to keep the documents in each client's file accessible.

- *Conduct legal research*—to identify, analyze, and summarize the appropriate laws, court decisions, or regulations that apply to a client's case.

- *Draft legal documents*—such as legal correspondence, interoffice memoranda, contracts, wills, mortgages, and documents to be filed with the court.

- *File legal documents with courts*—such as complaints, answers, and motions.

- *Summarize witness testimony*—such as when depositions (sworn testimony) are taken of individuals out of court or when the parties have given written statements.

- *Coordinate litigation proceedings*—communicate with opposing counsel, court personnel, and other government officials; prepare necessary documents for trial; and schedule witnesses.

- *Attend legal proceedings*—such as trials, depositions, real estate closings, executions of wills, and court or administrative hearings.

- *Use computers and technology*—to perform many of the above tasks.

No matter what task is being performed, paralegals have an obligation to meet high ethical standards. You will see the *Ethics Watch* feature in every chapter in the text-book, and ethical obligations will be reviewed in detail in Chapter 4.

Paralegals' Duties Vary

The specific tasks that paralegals perform vary dramatically depending on the size of the office, the kind of law that the firm practices, and the amount of experience or expertise the paralegal has. If you work in a one-attorney office, for example, you may also perform certain secretarial functions. Your tasks include conducting legal research and investigating the facts, photocopying documents, keying data into the computer, and answering the telephone while the secretary is out to lunch.

If you work in a larger law firm, you usually have more support staff (secretaries, file clerks, and others) to whom you can delegate tasks. Your work may also be more specialized, so you work on only certain types of cases. If you work in a law firm's real estate department, for example, you may deal only with legal matters relating to that area of law.

Although paralegal duties vary, the tasks that paralegals report spending the most time performing are drafting legal documents, handling client relations, and conducting legal research.

ETHICS WATCH

PARALEGAL EXPERTISE AND LEGAL ADVICE

Paralegals often gain a great deal of knowledge in specific areas of law. If you specialize in environmental law, for example, you will become knowledgeable about environmental claims. In working with a client on a matter involving an environmental agency, you might be tempted to advise the client on which type of action would be most favorable to him or her. Never do so. Only attorneys may give legal advice, and paralegals who give legal advice risk penalties for the unauthorized practice of law. Whatever legal advice is given to the client must come directly from the attorney.

If you speak to a client, the advice must reflect exactly (or nearly exactly) what the attorney said with no modification and must be communicated to the client as directed by the attorney. After consulting with your supervising attorney, for example, you can say to the client that the attorney "advises that you do all that you can to settle the claim as soon as possible."

The rule prohibiting the unauthorized practice of law is stated in Section 1.8 of the NFPA *Model Code of Ethics and Professional Responsibility:* "A paralegal shall comply with the applicable legal authority governing the unauthorized practice of law in the jurisdiction in which the paralegal practices." It is also required by the NALA *Code of Ethics and Professional Responsibility* Canon 4: "A paralegal must use discretion and professional judgment commensurate with knowledge and experience but must not render independent legal judgment in place of an attorney."

Featured Contributor

LEARNING WELL AND FINDING YOUR PLACE

Kristine M. Condon

BIOGRAPHICAL NOTE

Kristine M. Condon is the Program Coordinator of the ABA-approved Paralegal/Legal Assistant Studies Program at Kankakee Community College, a program she established in 2001. She began her legal career as a deputy clerk to the Illinois Supreme Court as it established the first "paperless" office in the Illinois court system. She was the computer training director for a top-ten Chicago-based law firm and a senior trainer for the American Medical Association.

Ms. Condon is also a member of the Campaign for Legal Services Committee of Prairie State Legal Services, a provider of low-cost civil legal services to the poor and the elderly in Kankakee County, and has published in the *Paralegal Educator,* the magazine of AAfPE.

© Cengage Learning 2014

"The justice wants to see you in his chambers."

I couldn't imagine what I had done wrong, yet I must have done something to be summoned. It was my first job out of paralegal school, in the plum job of my legal career as a deputy clerk with my state's highest court. Daily contact with three of the Court's seven members, including the chief justice, was part of my routine. I thought I had been a model employee. Was my paralegal career over before it really started?

I made my way down the hall to the chambers of a justice who was the longest-serving member of the Court. He had served as the dean of a Chicago-area law school. As the county's top prosecutor, he had secured the conviction of one of the nation's most notorious mass murderers. Yet his kind appearance and gentle demeanor belied his storied career. He greeted me warmly and asked me to sit.

Paralegals and Technology

Many legal assistants have become the technology experts at law firms. Because lawyers are busy with the practice of law, paralegals are often in the best position to know the firm's needs. Increasingly, paralegals take a leading role in reviewing and recommending new, specialized legal software programs and online databases.

Needless to say, computer skills and technical knowledge are highly valued. Paralegals use software packages for internal case management to organize client files, manage calendars, share research, record reference materials, and track the number of hours to be billed to clients. Attorneys and paralegals use time and billing software to manage expenses, generate bills, calculate accounts receivable, and produce financial reports. Legal databases available on the Internet allow paralegals to perform sophisticated legal research at their desks. When cases that involve many documents must be prepared for trial, litigation support software can help retrieve, categorize, and index the various materials for presentation.

These technologies are discussed in the appropriate chapters throughout this book. Technology is one of the foremost areas of expanding paralegal

social MEDIA TODAY

Choose your social technology tools with an eye to which programs your coworkers and clients use. If everyone at your firm uses Twitter, you should too. If they are on LinkedIn, you should be too.

"Are you familiar with these?" He gestured to a library bookcase filled with volumes of court opinions authored by his predecessors. I was. He made his way to a specific volume and thumbed to a well-worn page. He said, "This volume contains the opinion in Abraham Lincoln's first case before our Court."[1]

He continued: "Kris, Lincoln didn't have the tools we have today to argue before this Court, including paralegals. On some days, your job may be even more difficult as a paralegal than it would be as a lawyer, because we're asking you to anticipate everything we might possibly need. But Lincoln found his place in our profession by learning well as he studied the law. We want you to know that we're confident you learned well during your own schooling. You'll find your place here."

That was it. A conversation of a few minutes changed how and what I did for my career with the Court then and in the paralegal classroom now. How do *you* demonstrate to your employer that you learned well and have found your place as a paralegal? Here's what I learned.

- **Come prepared.** Try to anticipate what your supervisor might need from your research and determine the time commitment involved.

- **Expect the unexpected.** Anticipate the amount of time needed for a project and add 10% to provide for the unexpected.

- **Be ethical without exception.** Your friends may think cases are fodder for lunch conversation. Don't ever give in to the temptation. Nonlawyers are subject to the same ethical guidelines as the attorneys for whom they work.

---

1. *Scammon v. Cline*, 3 Ill. 456, 2 Scam. 456, 1840 WL 2967 (1840).

- **Know where and how to find the answers.** I never told a justice or an attorney, "I don't know." If they asked, I'd say, "I don't know at the moment, but I know how to find it." And then I did.

- **Be mindful of cost.** My mistakes and expenses were paid for by a client: the taxpayer. In the case of online research, I often began my basic work in print and shifted to online when I had a solid lead to research.

- **Use a variety of sources.** In the Web 2.0 era, it is malpractice not to check a complete list of online sources, legal and non-legal. The amount of digital content on the Internet is massive; it's your job as the paralegal to search for the relevant sources.

- **Check, check, and double-check.** Use notification tools, such as KeyCite Alert and Shepard's Online, to make sure your authority stays current from the time you draft until the time you submit.

- **Stay current with trends in a field.** Some students think reviewing weekly legal publications is a waste of time, until an interviewer asks them whether they've read the latest bar journal article on that topic.

- **Pay attention to the details of mechanics and citation.** Legal writing requires a high degree of precision—beyond good grammar, spelling, and punctuation. Court rules are court rules. Know them inside and out, especially as they apply to formatting, citing, and preparing legal documents.

Probably the most important lesson my justice imparted to me that day early in my career was that I needed to understand the past to anticipate the future. After all, even Lincoln could not have anticipated the explosive growth of the legal profession and the increasingly important role paralegals play in shaping it. Take advantage of every opportunity to learn well in your paralegal education—and you, too, will find your place.

---

responsibility, and those entering the profession should know that technological skills will greatly enhance their marketability.

Paralegal Education

The first paralegals were competent legal secretaries who learned through on-the-job training how to perform more complex legal tasks given to them by the attorneys for whom they worked. No formal paralegal education programs existed until the late 1960s. Once attorneys realized that using paralegals was cost-effective and benefited both the client and the firm (as you will read in Chapter 3), paralegal education programs expanded.

According to the ABA's Standing Committee on Paralegals, there are now more than a thousand paralegal training programs operating in the United States. A great deal of variety exists in the quality of the education provided. Of course, your formal education is only part of becoming a successful legal professional as the *Featured Contributor* discusses above.

Educational Options

The role of formal paralegal education has become increasingly important in the growth and development of the paralegal profession. Many colleges, universities, and business and private schools now offer programs. Generally, paralegal education programs fall into one of five categories:

- Two-year community college programs, leading to an associate of arts degree or a paralegal certificate. Such programs usually require the completion of about 60 semester hours and include some general education requirements.

- Four-year bachelor's degree programs with a major or minor in paralegal studies. A bachelor's degree in paralegal studies usually requires about 120 semester hours, with 50 to 60 of these hours spent on general education courses. A person may select a minor field that enhances her or his desirability in the job market. Conversely, a student who majors in another field—for example, nursing—and obtains a minor in paralegal studies will also be very marketable to potential employers.

- Certificate programs offered by private institutions, usually three to eighteen months in length. Typically, these programs require a high school diploma or the equivalent for admission.

- Postgraduate certificate programs, usually three to twelve months in length, resulting in the award of a paralegal certificate. These programs require applicants to have already earned a bachelor's degree in order to be admitted; some also require applicants to have achieved a certain grade point average.

- Master's degree programs, usually two years in length, which are offered by several universities. These programs prepare students to work as paralegals, paralegal supervisors, or law office administrators. Some programs offer specific concentrations—for example, dispute resolution or intellectual property. To be admitted to a master's degree program, a student must have a bachelor's degree.

Because those seeking to become paralegals have diverse educational backgrounds, capabilities, and work experience, no one program is best for everyone. Deciding which program is most appropriate depends on personal needs and preferences.

Curriculum—A Blend of Substantive and Procedural Law

substantive law
Law that defines the rights and duties of individuals with respect to each other's conduct and property.

procedural law
Rules that define the manner in which the rights and duties of individuals are enforced.

A legal assistant's education includes the study of both substantive law and procedural law. **Substantive law** includes all laws that define, describe, regulate, and create legal rights and obligations. For example, a law prohibiting employment discrimination on the basis of age falls into the category of substantive law. **Procedural law** establishes the methods of enforcing the rights established by substantive law. Questions about what documents need to be filed to begin a lawsuit, when the documents should be filed, which court will hear the case, and which witnesses will be called are all procedural law questions. In brief, substantive law defines our legal rights and obligations; procedural law specifies which methods, or procedures, must be employed to enforce those rights and obligations.

The Role of the AAfPE and ABA in Paralegal Education

The American Association for Paralegal Education (AAfPE) was formed by educators in 1981 to promote high standards for paralegal education. The AAfPE and the ABA are the two major organizations responsible for developing the standards and curriculum for paralegal education programs across the nation. California was the first state to require a paralegal to meet certain minimum educational requirements. Although most states do not have such requirements, many employers either require or prefer job candidates with a certain level of education. Some employers select only graduates from established programs. A searchable database of schools offering paralegal programs is available at the AAfPE Web site, **www.aafpe.org**, in the "Find a School" menu.

In 1974, the ABA established a set of educational standards for paralegal training programs. Since then, the ABA guidelines have been revised to keep pace with changes in the profession. Paralegal schools are not required to be approved by the ABA. Rather, ABA approval is a voluntary process that gives extra credibility to the schools that successfully apply for it. Programs that meet the ABA's quality standards and that are approved by the ABA are referred to as **ABA-approved programs**. Of the paralegal education programs in existence, approximately 275 have received ABA approval.

Certification

Certification refers to formal recognition by a professional group or state agency that a person has met the standards of ability specified by that group. Generally, this means passing an examination given by the organization and meeting certain requirements with respect to education and/or experience. Note that the term *certification,* as used here, does not refer to receiving a paralegal certificate. You may obtain a paralegal certificate after completing school, but you will not be considered a *certified paralegal* unless you complete the NALA, NFPA, NALS, AAPI, or state certification process. These certification programs are discussed in the following paragraphs. No state *requires* paralegals to be certified. Although most employers also do not require certification, earning a voluntary certificate from a professional society or the state can offer a competitive advantage in the labor market and lead to a higher salary (see Chapter 2).

NALA and NFPA Certification

Paralegals who meet the background qualifications set by NALA are eligible to take a two-day, comprehensive examination to become a **Certified Legal Assistant (CLA)** or, for those who prefer to use the term *paralegal,* a **Certified Paralegal (CP)**. NALA also sponsors the **Advanced Paralegal Certification (APC)** program (before 2006, this was called the Certified Legal Assistant Specialty, or CLAS). The APC program provides a series of Internet-based courses composed of text lessons, slides, exercises, and interactive tests. NALA offers APC certification to those who are already CLAs or CPs and want to demonstrate special competence in a particular field of law. Appendix F provides more detailed information on NALA certification and requirements.

Paralegals who have at least two years of work experience and who have met specific educational requirements can take the Paralegal Advanced Competency Exam (PACE) through NFPA. The PACE is broken down into two tests, one on general issues and ethics and one on specialty areas. Those who pass the examination use the designation **Registered Paralegal (RP)**. Further information on the PACE program is provided in Appendix G of this book.

Certification by Other Paralegal Organizations

NALS (the association for legal professionals) offers three different certifications:

- Paralegals who have completed an accredited curriculum course or who have one year of work experience may take the basic certification exam (ALS) for legal professionals.

- Paralegals who have three years of work experience or who have earned a prior certification may take the advanced certification exam (PLS) for legal professionals.

ABA-approved program
A legal or paralegal educational program that satisfies the standards for paralegal training set forth by the American Bar Association.

certification
Formal recognition by a private group or a state agency that a person has satisfied the group's standards of ability, knowledge, and competence; ordinarily accomplished through the taking of an examination.

ON THE web

Learn more about the APC program at the NALA Web site at **www.nala.org**. From the "Certification" menu, select "Advanced Paralegal Certification." For information on NFPA's PACE program, go to **www.paralegals.org**. From the menu, select "PACE/RP."

Certified Legal Assistant (CLA) or Certified Paralegal (CP)
A legal assistant whose legal competency has been certified by the National Association of Legal Assistants (NALA) following an examination that tests the legal assistant's knowledge and skills.

Advanced Paralegal Certification (APC)
A credential awarded by the National Association of Legal Assistants to a Certified Paralegal (CP) or Certified Legal Assistant (CLA) whose competency in a legal specialty has been certified based on an examination of the paralegal's knowledge and skills in the specialty area.

Registered Paralegal (RP)
A paralegal whose competency has been certified by the National Federation of Paralegal Associations (NFPA) after successful completion of the Paralegal Advanced Competency Exam (PACE).

- Paralegals who have five years of work experience may take an examination to obtain Professional Paralegal (PP) certification, which was developed by paralegals.

The American Alliance of Paralegals, Inc. (AAPI), also provides a Paralegal Certification Program for paralegals who possess at least five years of work experience and have met specific educational requirements.

State Certification

Several states, including California, Florida, Louisiana, North Carolina, Ohio, and Texas, have implemented voluntary, state-specific certification programs. Details for state programs can be found on the Internet; for example, for Texas, see **www.tbls.org**. Some state bar associations have information on certification as well. For example, for Ohio, see **www.ohiobar.org**. Other states are considering implementing such programs. Generally, paralegal organizations (such as NALA) are in favor of *voluntary* certification and oppose *mandatory* (legally required) certification or state licensing (as you will read in Chapter 4).

Continuing Legal Education

continuing legal education (CLE) programs
Courses through which attorneys and other legal professionals extend their education beyond school.

Paralegals, like attorneys, often supplement their formal education by attending **continuing legal education (CLE) programs**. CLE courses, which are offered by state bar associations, commercial providers, law schools, and paralegal associations, are usually seminars and workshops that focus on specific topics or areas of law. Such programs are a good way to learn more about a specialized area of law or keep up to date on the latest developments in the law and in technology. Many employers encourage their paralegals to take CLE courses and often pay some or all of the costs involved.

Additionally, some paralegal organizations require their members to complete a certain number of CLE hours per year as a condition of membership. Both NALA and NFPA require certified paralegals to take CLE courses annually to maintain their certification status. The NFPA requires certified paralegals to complete twelve hours of continuing education every two years. California requires a minimum number of CLE hours from *all* persons who work as paralegals. Paralegals in California are required to complete four CLE hours in legal ethics every three years and four CLE hours in substantive law every two years.[6]

ON THE web

NALA provides an online campus for continuing legal education (CLE) at **www.nala.org**. From the menu, select "Continuing Education." For information on NFPA's online CLE offerings, go to **www.paralegals.org**. From the menu, select "CLE."

Paralegal Skills and Attributes

As noted earlier, paralegals now perform many tasks that lawyers customarily performed. Thus, the demands on paralegals to be professional and efficient have increased. To be successful, a paralegal must not only possess specific legal knowledge, but should also exhibit certain aptitudes and personality traits. For example, paralegals need to be able to think logically and to analyze complex issues of law and conflicting descriptions of fact. Some general characteristics that paralegals should have (or try to develop) are discussed below.

Analytical Skills

Paralegals are often responsible for gathering and analyzing certain types of data. A corporate paralegal, for example, may be required to analyze new government regulations to see how they affect the corporation. A paralegal working for the Environmental Protection Agency may be responsible for collecting and analyzing data on toxic waste disposal and drafting a memo on the matter.

Legal professionals need to be able to break down complex theories and fact patterns into smaller, more easily understandable components. That is how lawyers formulate arguments and judges decide cases. The process of legal analysis is critical to the paralegal's duties, especially when the paralegal is engaged in factual investigation, trial preparation, and legal research and writing. Analytical reasoning will be discussed in greater depth in Chapters 7 and 9 of this book. For now, it is important that you focus on developing a step-by-step approach to tackling each new subject or task that you encounter. Making analytical thinking a habit will improve your proficiency as a legal assistant.

Communication Skills

Good communication skills are critical to people working in the legal area. The legal profession is a "communications profession" because effective legal representation depends to a great extent on how well a legal professional communicates with clients, witnesses, judges, juries, opposing attorneys, and others. Poor communication can damage a case, destroy a client relationship, and harm the legal professional's reputation. Good communication, in contrast, wins cases, clients, and sometimes promotions.

Communication skills include reading, speaking, listening, and writing. We look briefly at each of these here. Although we focus on communication skills in the law office setting, realize that good communication skills are essential to success in any work environment.

Reading Skills

Reading skills involve more than just being able to understand the meaning of written letters and words. Reading skills also involve understanding the *meaning* of a sentence, paragraph, section, or page. As a legal professional, you need to be able to read and comprehend many different types of written materials, including statutes and court decisions. You need to be familiar with legal terminology and concepts so that you know the meaning of these legal writings. You also need to

social MEDIA TODAY

Consider using a "listening" tool to monitor your online presence. Find the tool that delivers the best performance for the dollar—a free tool that finds just 20 percent of the mentions of you is less valuable than a pay tool that captures 90 percent of online mentions of you.

Excellent reading skills are a plus in any profession, but they are especially important in the legal arena. As a paralegal, you must not only be able to read well, but also be able to interpret what you are reading, whether it be a statute, a court's decision, or a contract's provision. What other important skills should every paralegal acquire?

© Yuri Arcurs/www.Shutterstock.com

develop the ability to read documents *carefully* so that you do not miss important distinctions, such as the difference in meaning that can result from the use of *and* instead of *or*. The importance of proofreading as a reading skill is highlighted in the *Developing Paralegal Skills* feature below.

Speaking Skills

Paralegals must be able to speak well. In addition to using correct grammar, legal assistants need to be precise and clear in communicating ideas or facts to others. For example, when you discuss facts learned in an investigation with your supervising attorney, your oral report must explain exactly what you found, or it could mislead the attorney. A miscommunication in this context could have serious consequences if it leads the attorney to take an action that harms the client's interests.

Oral communication also has a nonverbal dimension—that is, we communicate our thoughts and feelings through gestures, facial expressions, and other "body language." For example, if your body language suggests you are uncomfortable with a client, the client will be less responsive to your questions.

Interpersonal Skills

Good listening skills are an important part of paralegal work. Instructions must be followed carefully. To understand instructions, you must listen to them carefully.

DEVELOPING
paralegal skills

PROOFREADING LEGAL DOCUMENTS

Geena Northrop, a paralegal, works for a solo practitioner (a one-attorney law firm). Among her many duties, she handles some legal writing for the attorney. Geena has learned that when creating a legal document, writing the document is only half the job. The rest is proofreading—and not just once. One proofreading is simply not enough to catch every error. Geena has adopted the motto of one of the instructors in her paralegal program: "Proof, proof, and proof again!"

Today, she has set aside some time to proofread carefully a last will and testament that her supervising attorney and she created for a client. Geena prints out a copy of the document for proofreading purposes, because she has learned that it is difficult to proofread a document only on a computer screen. Moreover, style and formatting problems are often not as evident on a screen as they are on hard copy.

Her first step in proofreading the document is to make sure that the document reflects all of the relevant information from her notes. Geena reviews her notes point by point from the client interview and from her later discussion with the attorney about the will. She compares the notes to the document.

All looks well in this respect, so she proceeds to her second step in proofreading: checking style and format. Are all

of the headings in the correct size and font? Is the spacing between headings consistent? Are all of the paragraphs properly indented? She finds a couple of problems and marks her hard copy to make the appropriate changes. She then reads the document word for word to ensure that there are no grammatical problems, spelling errors, or typos. Finally, she revises the document on her computer, prints it out, and takes it to the attorney for his review.

CHECKLIST FOR PROOFREADING LEGAL DOCUMENTS

- When you create a legal document, do not assume that one proofreading will be sufficient to catch all problems or errors that the document may contain.

- Read through the document again to make sure that the style and formatting elements are consistent throughout.

- Print out the document, and go through the contents line by line to make sure that it includes all required or relevant information.

- Reading a document out loud can be an effective way to catch errors.

- Finally, read through the document word for word to ensure that it is free of grammatical errors, misspelled words, and typos.

DEVELOPING
paralegal skills

INTERVIEWING A CLIENT

Brenda Lundquist is a paralegal in a one-attorney firm. She has many responsibilities, including interviewing prospective divorce clients. Using a standard set of forms, Brenda meets with a prospective client and obtains information about the reasons for the divorce, finances and assets, and desired custody arrangements. This information is needed to assist the supervising attorney in determining whether to take the case. The information will also help Brenda in preparing the documents to be filed with the court should the attorney decide to represent the client. Brenda enjoys the work because she likes helping people, and often people who are getting divorced need both emotional and legal support.

CHECKLIST FOR CLIENT INTERVIEWS

- Plan the interview in advance.
- Print out forms and checklists to use during the interview.
- Introduce yourself as a paralegal or legal assistant.
- Explain the purpose of the interview to the client.
- Communicate your questions precisely.
- Listen carefully and be supportive, as necessary.
- Summarize the client's major concerns.
- Give the client a "time line" for what will happen in the legal proceedings.

Asking follow-up questions helps to clarify anything that you do not understand. In addition, repeating the instructions not only ensures that you understand them but also gives the attorney a chance to add anything he or she may have forgotten. Listening skills are particularly important in the interviewing context. In Chapter 11, you will read in detail about various listening skills and techniques that will help you conduct effective interviews. If you can relate well to the person whom you are interviewing, your chances of obtaining useful information are increased (see the *Developing Paralegal Skills* feature above for more on interviews).

Similarly, there will also be times when you will have to deal with people in your office who are under a great deal of stress. You may have to deal with people you consider to be "difficult." The more effectively you can respond to these people in ways that promote positive working relationships, the more productive you will be as a member of a legal team.

Writing Skills

Good writing skills are crucial to your success. Legal assistants draft letters, memoranda, and a variety of legal documents. Letters to clients, witnesses, court clerks, and others must be clear and well organized and must follow the rules of grammar and punctuation. Legal documents must also be free of errors. Lawyers are generally attentive to details and they expect legal assistants to be equally so. Remember, you represent your supervising attorney when you write. You will learn more about writing skills in Chapter 9.

Computer Skills

In all workplaces today, computer skills are essential. At a minimum, you will be expected to have experience with document creation and to have some data-entry skills. Paralegals well versed in the technology now widely used will have an edge in the job market. Some of the best-paying paralegal positions are held by paralegal specialists who know how to use sophisticated software, such as database-management systems, and how to adapt new technology, such as social media tools, to the workplace so as to improve efficiency.

We cannot stress enough that to become a successful paralegal, the best thing you can do during your training is to become as knowledgeable as possible about online communications. Throughout this book, you will read about how technology is being applied to all areas of legal practice. You will also learn how you can use technology to perform various paralegal tasks and to keep up to date on the law. (See this chapter's *Technology and Today's Paralegal* feature below for some online resources for paralegals.) As technology continues to advance, high-tech paralegals will increasingly be in demand.

Organizational Skills

Being a well-organized person is a plus for a legal assistant. Law offices are busy places. There are phone calls to be answered and returned, witnesses to get to court and on the witness stand on time, documents to be filed, and checklists and procedures to be followed. If you are able to organize files, create procedures and checklists, and keep things running smoothly, you will be doing a great service to the legal team and to clients.

TECHNOLOGY AND
today's paralegal

ONLINE RESOURCES FOR PARALEGALS

There are many career resources available online. To keep your skills up to date and to stay on top of developments in the law, you should regularly check such resources.

PARALEGAL ASSOCIATIONS

Many paralegals belong to the National Association of Legal Assistants (NALA) or to the National Federation of Paralegal Associations (NFPA). Both organizations offer excellent gateways for paralegal resources. NALA's Web site (**www.nala.org**) displays information on many professional certification and continuing education programs. It also provides links to state and local affiliated organizations. The NFPA Web site (**www.paralegals.org**) offers a continuing education calendar, a gateway to legal research sites, and a variety of career advice. *Legal Assistant Today*, a magazine for paralegals, also has a Web site (**www.paralegaltoday.com**) that features salary data, job listings, continuing education information, and downloadable forms.

AMERICAN BAR ASSOCIATION

The ABA is not just for lawyers! The Standing Committee on Paralegals provides career information, continuing education, directories, a gateway to blogs by paralegals, and information on paralegal education standards. The ABA also hosts its annual "Techshow," a large conference that teaches legal professionals the latest ways to use technology to best advantage.

BRYAN GARNER'S LEGAL WRITING SITE

America's most celebrated legal writing guru, Southern Methodist University law professor Bryan Garner, is best known for his books, *The Elements of Legal Style*, *Garner's Modern American Usage*, and *Legal Writing in Plain English*. He is the current editor of the famous *Black's Law Dictionary*. Garner's Web site, *LawProse, Inc.* (**www.lawprose.org**), offers a bibliography of articles on legal writing, the schedule of his legal writing seminars, and a way to subscribe to his "usage tip of the day."

THE PARALEGAL GATEWAY

The Paralegal Gateway (**www.paralegalgateway.com**) focuses on job advice, examples of successful résumés and interviews, and networking tools. It also offers links to continuing education resources and legal humor.

LEGAL NEWS

There is a wide range of online newsletters and Web sites on specific areas of law produced by law firms. The LawProf blog network (**www.lawprofessorblogs.com**) provides many subject-specific blogs (blawgs) by law professors that offer up-to-the-minute commentary on new cases, statutes, and news from trustworthy sources.

If you work in a nontraditional setting, such as for a corporation or for the government, you will similarly find that good organizational skills are the key to success. No matter where you work, you will need to organize files, data, and—most importantly—your time, as discussed in the *In the Office* feature below.

If organization comes naturally to you, you are ahead of the game. If not, now is the time to learn and practice organizational skills. You will find plenty of opportunities to do this as a paralegal student—by organizing your notebooks, devising an efficient tracking system for homework assignments, and creating a study or work schedule and following it. Other suggestions for organizing your time and work, both as a student and as a paralegal on the job, are included in the **Skill Prep: A Paralegal Skills Module** before Chapter 1. Many books offer guidelines on how to efficiently organize your work, your time, and your life in general.

The Ability to Keep Information Confidential

One of the requirements of being a paralegal is the ability to keep client information confidential. The word *requirement* is used because being able to keep confidences is not just a desirable attribute in a paralegal, but a mandatory one.

As you will read in Chapter 4, attorneys are ethically and legally obligated to keep all information relating to the representation of a client strictly confidential unless the client consents to the disclosure of the information. The attorney may disclose this information only to people who are also working on behalf of the client and who therefore need to know it. Paralegals share in this duty. If a paralegal reveals confidential client information to anyone outside the group working on the client's case, the lawyer (and the paralegal) may face consequences if the client suffers harm as a result. The law firm could be sued and the paralegal dismissed.

Keeping client information confidential means that you, as a paralegal, cannot divulge such information even to your spouse, family members, or closest friends. You should not talk about a client's case in hallways, elevators, or any areas in which others may overhear your conversation. You must be careful when handling client documents that you do not expose them to outsiders. Keeping work-related information confidential is an essential part of being a responsible and reliable paralegal.

IN THE office

USE TIME WISELY

Paralegals often work on many cases at once. To be responsive to job requirements and to meet the needs of clients, set aside a little time each day to review the demands on your time. Think about what must be done that day as well as what must be completed over time to meet deadlines. Make a list of what you need to accomplish. The list might be built into your calendaring software. Each morning, reevaluate what you got done the day before. If work was not completed, think about why. When working on multiple cases, it is critical to understand what must be accomplished on each case so that one deadline does not "sneak up" on you while you are paying attention to another. Consider adopting a time-management system. There are computer programs and apps to help you stay organized. Find one that works for you.

Professionalism

Paralegals should behave professionally at all times. That means you must be responsible and reliable in order to earn the respect and trust of the attorneys and clients with whom you work. It also means you must put aside any personal bias or emotion that interferes with your representation of a client or assessment of a case. Paralegals need to be honest and assertive in letting others know what things paralegals can and cannot do (for example, they cannot give legal advice). This is particularly important because not everyone is sure what legal assistants are, and some people may have misconceptions about the role paralegals play.

As a paralegal, you will find that you are judged not only by your actions and words but also by your appearance, attitude, and other factors. When deadlines approach and the pace of office work becomes somewhat frantic, it can be difficult to meet the challenge of acting professionally. When the pressure is on, it is important to remain calm and focus on completing your task quickly and accurately to ensure quality work. If you are interrupted by a client's call or another attorney, be aware that the way you react to that interruption is likely to affect whether others view you as professional. Try to be courteous and respectful during such interruptions. The paralegal must be detail oriented and accurate, even when working under pressure. As the *Practice Focus* feature below discusses, legal professionals must be client focused in order to be successful.

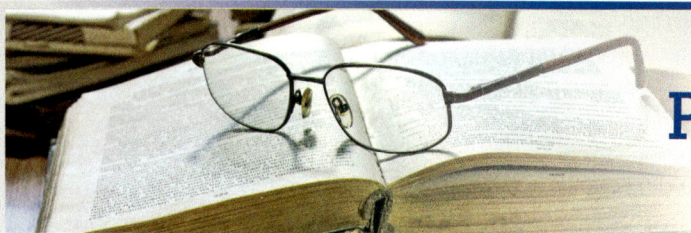

PRACTICE focus

A CLIENT-CENTERED PERSPECTIVE

As you navigate your career as a professional paralegal, think about how the business of law is evolving so that you can make the best choices for your career. Legal commentator Jordan Furlong of the Web site **Law21.ca** provides a way of how to think of legal work from a client perspective.

MISSION CRITICAL

• The most secure work is when a firm provides clients with *mission critical* legal services. That is, the things you and your supervising attorney do are ones that require legal training, demand high-quality legal work, and are essential to the client's business. This business is likely to stay in the hands of a law firm with an established reputation. Paralegals in such firms are likely to be engaged in less routine work and do more legal research.

• Next, clients have *ordinary course of business* needs. These actions require a lawyer but don't require as much creative work. In this area, clients are mostly concerned with how much the ser-

vice costs and that the law firm has effective processes in place to guarantee quality. Firms that use well-trained paralegals to cut costs and ensure quality will have an advantage.

• The third level of legal need is for *commodity* work. This is routine work that does not require as much legal training. Clients will be constantly seeking ways to bring down costs for this type of work, and paralegals can succeed by spotting opportunities to standardize form production or take other steps that cut costs.

HOW TO SUCCEED

The increasingly competitive environment for the practice of law means that successful professionals need more than raw intelligence. Professor William Henderson of Indiana University's College of Law analyzes trends in law practice. He argues that legal professionals increasingly need to be personable, collaborative, entrepreneurial, service oriented, and interested in contributing to the well-being of the law firm. If you develop these skills, you are more likely to succeed in the competitive, ever-evolving world of law practice.

The Future of the Profession

The paralegal profession is a dynamic, changing, and expanding field within the legal arena. Legal assistants continue to assume a growing range of duties in the nation's legal offices and perform many of the same tasks as lawyers. According to the U.S. Department of Labor, the employment of paralegals should grow "much faster than average" and "formally trained paralegals should have the best employment opportunities."[7] It is estimated that between 2008 and 2018, paralegal positions will have increased by 28 percent. Growth is occurring because law firms and other employers with legal staffs are hiring more paralegals to lower the cost—and increase the availability and efficiency—of legal services.

Those entering the profession today will find a broader range of career options than ever before. In addition, they will have the opportunity to help chart the course the profession takes in the future. The paralegal profession has become a popular career choice for many, so competition for jobs will continue, but formally trained and skilled paralegals will have excellent employment potential.

KEY TERMS AND CONCEPTS

ABA-approved program   9

Advanced Paralegal Certification (APC)   9

American Association for Paralegal Education (AAfPE)   3

American Bar Association (ABA)   3

certification   9

Certified Legal Assistant (CLA)   9

Certified Paralegal (CP)   9

continuing legal education (CLE) programs   10

legal assistant   3

National Association of Legal Assistants (NALA)   3

National Federation of Paralegal Associations (NFPA)   3

paralegal   3

procedural law   8

Registered Paralegal (RP)   9

substantive law   8

Chapter Summary

Today's Professional Paralegal

WHAT IS A PARALEGAL?

The terms *paralegal* and *legal assistant* mean the same to some people. The terms *legal technician* or *legal research specialist* may be used in some workplaces. Paralegals perform many of the tasks traditionally handled by attorneys. A paralegal is a person qualified by education, training, or work experience who is employed or retained by a law office, corporation, governmental agency, or other entity and who performs specifically delegated substantive legal work, for which a lawyer is responsible.

WHAT DO PARALEGALS DO?

1. *Typical tasks*—Legal assistants typically perform many of the following duties: interviewing and maintaining general contact with clients and witnesses, locating and interviewing witnesses, conducting legal investigations, calendaring and tracking important deadlines, organizing and maintaining client files, conducting legal research, drafting legal documents, filing legal documents with courts, summarizing witness testimony, coordinating litigation proceedings, attending legal proceedings, and using computers and technology.

2. *Duties often vary*—Paralegals perform different functions depending on where they work and on their abilities and experience. Duties also vary according to the size of a law firm and the kind of law practiced by the firm. Paralegals commonly spend the bulk of their time performing document management, client relations, and research.

PARALEGAL EDUCATION

Higher education and paralegal education programs have become increasingly important in the growth and development of the profession.

1. *Educational options*—Colleges, universities, and private institutions offer a wide variety of programs to train paralegals, ranging in length from three months to four years.

2. *Curriculum*—Paralegal education includes coverage of substantive law and of procedural law, as paralegals are involved in most aspects of the legal process.

3. *ABA and AAfPE paralegal education*—The American Bar Association (ABA) sets voluntary educational standards for paralegal training programs. ABA-approved programs are those that meet with the ABA's approval. ABA approval is a voluntary process; paralegal programs are not required to be approved by the ABA. AAfPE promotes high standards in paralegal education.

3. *Paralegals and technology*—Technology is the number-one area of expanding paralegal responsibility. Paralegals skilled in using technologies to assist them in performing their duties will excel in the profession.

4. *Certification*—The term certification refers to formal recognition by a professional group or state agency that an individual has met certain standards of proficiency specified by that group. Generally, this means passing an examination and meeting certain requirements with respect to education and/or experience. Paralegals may be certified by NALA, NFPA, or a state agency. Currently, no state requires paralegal certification.

5. *Continuing legal education (CLE)*—Continuing legal education courses are offered by state bar associations and paralegal associations. Such programs provide a way to learn more about a specialized area of law or keep up to date on the latest developments in law and technology.

PARALEGAL SKILLS AND ATTRIBUTES

Because paralegals today perform many of the tasks that lawyers used to perform, the demands on paralegals to be professional and efficient have increased.

1. *Analytical skills*—These include gathering and analyzing information relevant to legal matters.

2. *Communication skills*—Ability to communicate effectively with clients, witnesses, and others in the legal process is necessary. Understanding a matter and communicating about it involves reading, speaking, listening, and writing.

3. *Computer skills*—As more and more legal research is done online, and since computers are used in the production of most legal documents, being familiar with the tools available makes a paralegal more successful and competitive.

4. *Organizational skills*—Paralegals keep track of numerous legal documents and other matters related to cases and the functioning of a law office, so being well organized is a requirement of the profession.

5. *Keeping confidence*—As paralegals have knowledge of confidential legal matters, and help represent clients, protecting information from exposure to others is a requirement of the job.

6. *Professionalism*—In legal work, responsibility and trust are key. Legal professionals are judged on the basis of actions, words, and attitude.

FUTURE OF THE PROFESSION

The role of paralegals in law continues to grow as the providers of legal services have learned the effectiveness of qualified non-attorney professionals.

QUESTIONS FOR REVIEW

1. What is a paralegal? Is there any difference between a paralegal and a legal assistant?

2. What types of educational programs and training are available to paralegals? Must a person meet specific educational requirements to work as a paralegal?

3. What role does the American Bar Association play in paralegal education?

4. What does *certification* mean? What is a CLA or a CP? What is the APC program? What does PACE stand for?

5. List and describe the skills that are useful in paralegal practice. Do you have these skills?

ETHICAL QUESTIONS

1. Richard attends a six-month paralegal course and earns a certificate. In the West Coast city where he lives, certified paralegals—those with a CP or a CLA designation—are in great demand in the job market. Richard responds to a newspaper advertisement for a certified paralegal, indicating that he is one. Has Richard done anything unethical? What is the difference between a certificate and certification?

2. Paula Abrams works as a paralegal for a small law firm that specializes in tax law. Recently, Paula purchased some new tax-return software and was trained in how to use it. Last week, Paula used the software to prepare tax returns for the Benedetto family. Paula saved the forms on a disk. She then retrieved the Benedetto forms and used them for the Marshalls' tax return. Paula entered much of the Marshalls' tax information into the computer. Mr. Marshall had not provided the children's Social Security numbers to Paula, though, so she decided to add the Social Security numbers later. In the meantime, Paula left the Benedetto children's Social Security numbers on the form.

   In the tax-season rush, Paula inadvertently neglected to enter the children's Social Security numbers on the Marshalls' tax return. Several months later, the Marshalls received a letter from the Internal Revenue Service stating that their exemptions had been denied because their children's Social Security numbers had been claimed on someone else's tax return. How might this situation be resolved? What other kinds of ethical problems might result from using computer-generated forms?

PRACTICE QUESTIONS AND ASSIGNMENTS

1. Refer to Appendix E at the end of this book (or go to www.nala.org or www.paralegals.org) and find the answers to the following questions:

   a. Is there an affiliate of the National Association of Legal Assistants or the National Federation of Paralegal Associations in your city? Where is the nearest affiliate of either of these organizations located?

   b. Are there any regional or local paralegal associations in your area? If so, what are their names, street and e-mail addresses, and phone numbers?

2. Using the material on paralegal skills presented in the chapter, identify which of the following are skills that a paralegal should have, and explain why.

   a. Reading skills.
   b. Interpersonal skills.
   c. Marketing skills.
   d. Oral communication skills.
   e. Math skills.
   f. Computer skills.
   g. Management skills.

QUESTION FOR CRITICAL ANALYSIS

Tom and Sandy are having coffee after their first paralegal class. The instructor discussed the ongoing debate within the profession about whether to use the term *paralegal* or *legal assistant*. Tom says he agrees with NFPA that the term *paralegal* is preferable because no one will confuse paralegals with legal secretaries. Sandy, who has been working as a legal secretary for the last few years, is offended by Tom's remarks. What label do you prefer—*legal assistant* or *paralegal*—and why? Is it an important issue, in your opinion?

PROJECT

Arrange an interview with an experienced paralegal, such as a graduate of your program or another paralegal whom you may know. Ask the paralegal what he or she thinks are the most important skills and characteristics that paralegals should have.

GROUP PROJECT

This project asks the group to review information on the Web sites of NALA (www.nala.org) and NFPA (www.paralegals.org) about the organizations' certification programs. The members of the group will do the following tasks to complete the project:

- Student one will determine and summarize the requirements of the NALA certification exams.

- Student two will determine and summarize the requirements of the NFPA certification exams.

- Student three will compile the results in a chart or graph in Powerpoint or Excel.

- Student four will present the results to the class.

USING INTERNET RESOURCES

1. Browse through the materials on the Web sites of the National Association of Legal Assistants, or NALA (at www.nala.org), and the National Federation of Paralegal Associations, or NFPA (at www.paralegals.org). Pay particular attention to each organization's introduction or organizational overview, the benefits of membership, and the categories of membership offered by each of these organizations. How do they compare? Are there significant differences between the philosophy of and the benefits offered by the organizations?

2. Go to the Web site for Delmar Cengage Learning at www.cengage.com/community/paralegal and select "State Specific Resources." You will find links to relevant state-specific Web sites and to sites that furnish legal forms for individual states. Click on your state's Web links, and browse through the resources available. List the Web sites you find, and briefly describe the kind of information available at each site and how this information might be used by a paralegal. Can you access your state's bar association? Is there a way to view any of your state's codes (laws) or judicial opinions? Does the state attorney general or secretary of state have a Web site listed? If you do not see all of these resources for your state, try running an Internet search for your state's government to see if you can locate the needed resource(s).

END NOTES

1. www.salary.com.

2. Source: www.nala.org. This information is subject to updates and edits at any time.

3. The members of NFPA voted to remove the term *legal assistant* from their definition of *paralegal* in 2002. The American Association for Paralegal Education (AAfPE) took a similar position that year.

4. Reprinted by permission of the National Federation of Paralegal Associations, Inc. (NFPA®) www.paralegals.org.

5. Reprinted by permission of the American Association for Paralegal Education.

6. California Business and Professions Code, Sections 6450–6456. Enacted in 2000. California Advanced Specialist (CAS) certification is also available as a specialty exam through NALA to paralegals who possess CLA or CP certification. For more information on this state-specific NALA certification, see Appendix F.

7. See www.bls.gov/OCO. (From the "Professional" menu, select "Legal," then "Paralegals and legal assistants.")

CourseMate The available CourseMate for this text has an interactive eBook and interactive learning tools, including flash cards, quizzes, and more. To learn more about this resource and access free demo CourseMate resources, go to www.cengagebrain.com, and search for this book. To access CourseMate materials that you have purchased, go to login.cengagebrain.com.

Career Opportunities

Chapter Outline

Introduction

Where Paralegals Work

Paralegal Specialties

Paralegal Compensation

Planning Your Career

Locating Potential Employers

Marketing Your Skills

Enhancing Your Career

After completing this chapter, you will know:

- What types of firms and organizations hire paralegals.

- Some areas of law in which paralegals specialize.

- How much paralegals can expect to earn.

- How to search for an employer.

- How to present yourself to prospective employers.

- How to prepare a career plan and pursue it.

- How to use social media to promote your career.

Introduction

ON THE web

For helpful information on all aspects of paralegal careers, go to the National Association of Legal Assistants' Web site at **www.nala.org** and the National Federation of Paralegal Associations' Web site at **www. paralegals.org**.

Paralegals enjoy a wide range of employment opportunities in both the private and the public sectors. They are in demand at law firms because they help provide competent legal services at a lower cost to clients. Furthermore, although most legal assistants work in law offices, almost any business that uses legal services can make use of paralegals. Corporations, insurance companies, banks, and real estate agencies regularly employ legal assistants. In addition, the government has created positions for paralegals at many agencies. Paralegals now work in many court systems, county offices, and legal-services clinics across the nation.

This chapter provides you with a starting point for planning your career. In the pages that follow, you will read about where paralegals work and what compensation paralegals receive. You will also learn about the steps you will need to follow to plan your career, locate potential employers, and find a job.

Where Paralegals Work

Paralegal employers fall into a number of categories. This section describes the general characteristics of each of the major types of working environments. Regardless of where you work, on-the-job stress is a potential problem, as discussed in the *In the Office* feature on page 24.

Law Firms

social MEDIA TODAY

You need to differentiate yourself from everyone else online by providing unique, relevant, high-quality content on a regular basis. You should network with a purpose, not just share fun things.

When paralegals first established themselves in the legal community in the 1960s, they worked in law firms. Today, law firms continue to hire more paralegals than do any other organizations. Two-thirds of all paralegals work in law firms. Law firms vary in size from the small, one-attorney office to the huge "megafirm" with hundreds of attorneys. As you can see in Exhibit 2.1 below, most paralegals work in settings that employ fewer than twenty-five attorneys.

Working for a Small Firm

Many paralegals begin their careers working for one attorney or small law practices with just a few attorneys. To some extent, this is because small law firms (those with twenty-five or fewer attorneys) simply outnumber large ones. It may also be due to geographic location. For example, a paralegal who lives in a small community may find that his or her only option is to work for a small legal practice.

FIRM SIZE MATTERS. Working for a small firm offers many advantages to the beginning paralegal. If the firm is a general law practice, you will have the opportunity to gain experience in many different facets of the law. You will be able to learn whether you enjoy working in one area (such as family law) more than another (such as personal-injury law) in the event that you later decide to specialize. Some paralegals also prefer the more personal and less formal environment that often

EXHIBIT 2.1
Paralegal Employment and Salary by Size of Firm or Legal Department

The data in this exhibit comes from survey data reported in Paralegal Today.

Number of Attorneys	Percentage of Paralegals	Average Salary
1	14%	$40,796
2–5	29%	$44,261
6–10	18%	$55,530
11–25	17%	$55,098
26–50	13%	$54,635
51–100	6%	$71,837
Over 100	3%	$63,268

© Cengage Learning 2014

Paralegals who work for large firms often need to research statutes, court cases, or regulations in the firm's law library. Notebook computers, tablet devices, and smartphones facilitate the ease with which paralegals can do research and communicate with attorneys, clients, and others. What are the pros and cons of working for a large law firm?

exists in a small law office, as well as the variety of tasks and greater flexibility that characterize this setting.

Small size may also involve disadvantages, however. Paralegals who work for small firms may have less support staff to assist them. This means that if you work in a small law office, your job may involve a substantial amount of secretarial or clerical work.

THINK ABOUT COMPENSATION DIFFERENTIALS.   Compensation is another topic of potential concern. Small firms pay, on average, slightly lower salaries than do larger firms, as shown in Exhibit 2.1 on the facing page. Generally, the larger the firm, the higher the paralegal salaries will be. Small firms also may provide fewer employee benefits, such as pension plans and health benefits. At the same time, however, a small firm may be in a convenient location, may not insist on an expensive wardrobe, and may offer free parking.

Working for a Large Firm

In contrast to the (typically) more casual environment of the small law office, larger law firms usually are more formal. If you work for a larger firm, your responsibilities will probably be limited to specific, well-defined types of tasks. For example, you may work for a department that handles (or for an attorney who handles) only certain types of cases, such as real estate transactions. Office procedures and employment policies will also be more clearly defined and may be set forth in a written employment manual.

The advantages of the large firm often include greater opportunities for promotions and career advancement, higher salaries and better benefits packages, more support staff for paralegals, and more sophisticated technology that affords greater access to research resources.

You may see certain characteristics of large law firms as either advantages or disadvantages, depending on your personality and preferences. For example, if you favor the more specialized duties and more formal working environment of a large law firm, then you will view these characteristics as advantages. If you prefer to handle a greater variety of tasks and enjoy the more personal atmosphere of the small law office, then you might think the specialization and formality of a large law firm are disadvantages.

ON THE web

You can obtain a host of information on specific law firms by going to their Web pages. For example, go to the Web site for Wachtell, Lipton, Rosen & Katz at **www.wlrk.com**

IN THE office

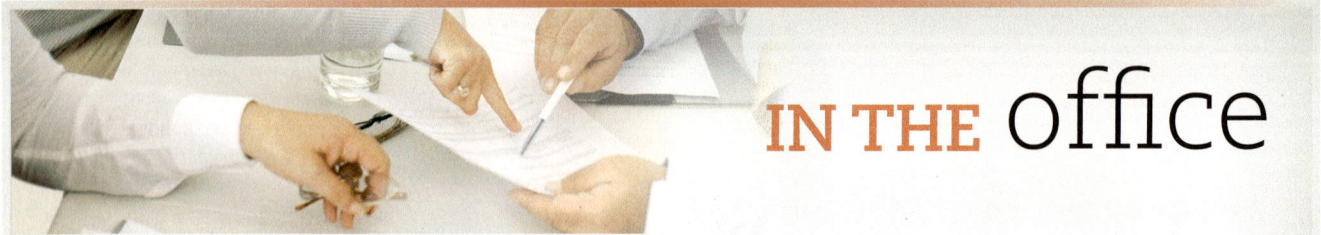

STRESS PROBLEMS

Stress can cause health problems. It is also related to making mistakes at work. When that happens, even more stress is generated. Errors increase when we rush to meet deadlines and have our minds on many things at once.

How can you reduce stress that may result in sloppy work and missed deadlines?

1. Be candid about your workload when a supervisor adds new work.

2. Prioritize your tasks. Determine, perhaps by consulting with your supervising attorney, which projects take priority.

3. Consider asking your supervisor to assign another person in the office to help you.

4. Keep in mind that being aware of stress is a key step in learning to deal with it in an effective way.

Being organized and clear about responsibilities will increase your productivity, concentration, and performance. It will also reduce the likelihood of stress building up in the office.

social MEDIA TODAY

LinkedIn is a key legal professional site. At last count, 96 percent of all attorneys are on it. When you sign up for LinkedIn, do not immediately send an invitation to everyone in your contact list—build your network carefully.

Corporations and Other Business Organizations

As already mentioned, many paralegals work in business environments outside of law firms. Almost any business that uses legal services may hire paralegals. An increasing number of paralegals work for corporate legal departments. Most large firms hire in-house attorneys to handle corporate legal affairs. Some large corporations have hundreds of attorneys on their payrolls. Paralegals who are employed by corporations usually work under the supervision of in-house attorneys.

Paralegals in a corporate setting perform a variety of functions, such as organizing meetings and maintaining necessary records, drafting employee contracts and benefit plans, and preparing financial and other reports for the corporation. Paralegals often are responsible for monitoring and reviewing government regulations to help ensure that the corporation operates within the law. When the corporation is involved in a lawsuit, paralegals may be assigned duties related to that lawsuit. (For more information on the duties of corporate paralegals, see Chapter 18.)

Nearly one-fifth of all paralegals work in corporate environments. Paralegals who are employed by corporations frequently receive higher salaries than those working for law firms. In addition, paralegals who are employed by corporations may work more regular hours. Unlike paralegals in law firms, corporate paralegals typically have not been required to generate a specific number of "billable hours" per year (hours billed to clients for paralegal services performed, to be discussed in Chapter 3).

Government

Paralegals employed by government agencies work in a variety of settings and often specialize in one aspect of the law. Agencies also usually provide excellent benefits.

Administrative Agencies

Most paralegals who work for the government work for administrative agencies, such as the federal Environmental Protection Agency (EPA) or a state environmental resources department. Paralegals who work for government agencies may conduct legal research and analysis, investigate welfare eligibility or disability claims, examine documents (such as loan applications), and engage in many other tasks. Within the federal government, the U.S. Department of Justice employs the largest number of paralegals, followed by the Social Security Administration and the Department of the Treasury.

Your best source of information about employment positions in a particular administrative agency is the agency itself. You can find the names and telephone numbers of federal agencies, as well as a description of their functions, in the *United States Government Manual,* which is available in your library. This information is also available online.

Paralegals who work for government agencies normally work regular hours and tend to work fewer total hours per year (have more vacation time) than paralegals in other environments. Like paralegals in corporations, they may not have to worry about billable hours, although other measures of productivity are likely to be used. Additionally, paralegals who work for the government usually enjoy comprehensive employment benefits.

Legislative Offices

Legislators in the U.S. Congress and in some state legislatures typically have staff members to help them with their duties. These duties often include legal research and writing, and paralegals sometimes perform such services. For example, a senator who plans to propose an amendment to a certain law may ask a paralegal on her or his staff to research the legislative history of that law carefully (to discern the legislature's intention when passing the law—see Chapters 5 and 7) and write up a summary of that history.

Law Enforcement Offices and Courts

Many paralegals work for government law enforcement offices and institutions. As you will read in Chapter 13, which discusses criminal law and procedures, a person accused of a crime is prosecuted by a *public prosecutor.* Public prosecutors (such as district attorneys, state attorneys general, and U.S. attorneys) are government officials who are paid by the government. Accused persons may be defended by private attorneys or, if they cannot afford to hire a lawyer, by *public defenders*—attorneys paid for by the state to ensure that criminal defendants are not deprived of their constitutional right to be represented by counsel. Both public prosecutors and public defenders rely on paralegals for assistance.

Paralegals also find work in other government settings, such as federal or state court administrative offices. Court administrative work ranges from recording and filing court documents (such as the documents filed during a lawsuit—see Chapter 10) to working for a small claims court (a court that handles claims below a specified amount—see Chapter 6). Paralegals also work for bankruptcy courts (see page 30 for a discussion of bankruptcy law).

Legal Aid Offices

Legal aid offices provide legal services to those who find it difficult to pay for legal representation. Most legal aid is government funded, although some support comes from private foundations.

Many paralegals who work in this capacity find their jobs rewarding, even though they usually receive lower salaries than they would in other settings. In part, this is because of the nature of the work—helping needy individuals. Additionally, paralegals in legal aid offices generally assume a wider array of responsibilities than they would in a traditional law office. For example, some federal and state administrative agencies, including the Social Security Administration, allow paralegals to represent clients in agency hearings and judicial proceedings. As you will read in Chapter 4, paralegals normally are not allowed to represent clients—only attorneys can do so. Exceptions to this rule exist when a court or agency permits nonlawyers to represent others in court or in administrative agency hearings.

Freelance Paralegals

freelance paralegal
A paralegal who operates his or her own business and provides services to attorneys on a contract basis. A freelance paralegal works under the supervision of an attorney, who assumes responsibility for the paralegal's work product.

A number of experienced paralegals operate as freelancers. **Freelance paralegals** (also called *independent contractors* or *contract paralegals*) own their own business and perform specified types of legal work for attorneys on a contract basis. Attorneys who need temporary legal assistance sometimes contract with freelance paralegals to work on particular projects. In addition, attorneys who need legal assistance but cannot afford to hire full-time paralegals might hire freelancers to work on a part-time basis. (The suggestions offered later in this chapter on how you can find work as a paralegal apply to freelance jobs as well.)

Freelancing has both advantages and disadvantages. Because freelancers are their own bosses, they can set their own schedules. Thus, they enjoy a greater degree of flexibility in their working hours. In addition, depending on the nature of their projects, they may work at home or in attorneys' offices. With flexibility, however, comes added responsibility. A freelance paralegal's income depends on the ability to promote and maintain business. If there are no clients for the month, there will be no income. Also, freelancers do not enjoy job benefits such as employer-provided group medical insurance.

legal technician or **independent paralegal**
A paralegal who offers services directly to the public without attorney supervision. Independent paralegals assist consumers by supplying them with forms and procedural knowledge relating to simple or routine legal procedures.

Realize that freelance paralegals work under attorney supervision. Freelancers are not to be confused with **legal technicians**—often called **independent paralegals**—who do *not* work under the supervision of an attorney and who provide (sell) legal services directly to the public. These services include helping members of the public obtain and fill out forms for certain types of legal transactions, such as bankruptcy filings and divorce petitions. As you will read in Chapter 4, legal technicians run the risk of violating state statutes prohibiting the unauthorized practice of law.

Paralegal Specialties

While many paralegals perform a wide range of legal services, others have found it satisfying to specialize in one area of law. Some areas of law in which paralegals report that they work at least some of the time are litigation (52 percent), corporate law (9 percent), contract law (13 percent), and real estate law (11 percent). Other specialties exist, and some are listed in Exhibit 2.2 below. Here, we discuss just a few of the areas in which paralegals may specialize, but remember that increasingly, in all practice settings, being able to use technology efficiently is a great asset, as discussed in the *Technology and Today's Paralegal* feature on page 28.

EXHIBIT 2.2
Average Compensation by Specialty

The authors compiled this exhibit using data from Paralegal Today.

Area of Legal Specialty	Average Compensation
Administrative	$39,250
Bankruptcy	$45,380
Contracts	$48,100
Corporate	$61,413
Criminal	$42,820
Employment	$47,289
Environmental	$57,633
Family	$39,078
Insurance	$55,371
Intellectual property	$67,300
Litigation	$53,615
Medical malpractice	$53,191
Personal injury (plaintiff)	$47,680
Probate (wills and estates)	$39,750
Real estate	$45,614
Workers' compensation	$36,200

Litigation

Working a lawsuit through the court system is called **litigation**. Paralegals who specialize in assisting attorneys in the litigation process are called **litigation paralegals**. Litigation paralegals work in general law practices, small litigation firms, litigation departments of larger law firms, and corporate legal departments. Litigation paralegals often specialize in a certain type of litigation, such as personal-injury litigation (which will be discussed shortly) or product liability cases (which involve injuries caused by defective products).

Work performed by litigation paralegals varies with the substantive law area being litigated. It also varies according to whether it is done on behalf of **plaintiffs** (those who bring lawsuits) or **defendants** (those against whom lawsuits are brought). Some litigation paralegals investigate cases, review documents containing evidence, interview clients and witnesses, draft documents to file with the courts, and prepare for hearings and trials. You will read in detail about litigation procedures and the important role played by paralegals in the litigation process in Chapters 10 through 12.

litigation
The process of working a lawsuit through the court system.

litigation paralegal
A paralegal who specializes in assisting attorneys in the litigation process.

plaintiff
A party who initiates a lawsuit.

defendant
A party against whom a lawsuit is brought.

Corporate Law

Corporate law consists of the laws that govern the formation, financing, merger and acquisition, and termination of corporations, as well as the rights and duties of those who own and run corporations. You will read in Chapter 18 about the meaning of these terms and the tasks that corporate paralegals typically perform.

Paralegals who specialize in corporate law may work in the legal department of a corporation, or for a law firm that specializes in corporate law. Corporate paralegals often perform such tasks as prepare and file documents with a state agency to set up corporations and to keep them in good standing, maintain corporate records, organize and schedule shareholders' meetings in accordance with state law, and prepare stock certificates. As you see on the facing page in Exhibit 2.2, which lists the average compensation by specialty, paralegals who work in corporate law generally receive higher salaries than paralegals in some other settings. In addition, corporate paralegals who further narrow their expertise to a concentration such as mergers are among the highest-paid paralegals today.

corporate law
Law that governs the formation, financing, merger and acquisition, and termination of corporations, as well as the rights and duties of those who own and run the corporation.

ON THE web

If you are looking for a job in a corporate legal department, Hoovers Online offers company and contact information for many public and private companies worldwide at **www.hoovers.com**

Contract Law

A number of paralegals work in contract law. As you will read in Chapter 15, a **contract** is an agreement (based on a promise or an exchange of promises) that can be enforced in court. Paralegals who specialize in contracts may work for a corporation's legal department, for a large law firm, or for a government agency.

The work of paralegals in contract law often involves preparing contracts and forms, and reviewing contracts to determine whether a party to the contract has complied with the contract's terms. In a lawsuit for breach of contract, for example, a paralegal might be asked to look closely at the terms and do some factual investigation to find out whether the contract has been breached (broken). Contract specialists also may conduct research in the law governing contracts, either before a contract is formed or during litigation concerning the contract's provisions. Note that because contracts are so common in our legal environment, many paralegals—not just contract specialists—are involved with work relating to contracts.

contract
An agreement (based on a promise or an exchange of promises) that can be enforced in court.

Real Estate Law

At law, **real estate**, or *real property,* consists of land and all things permanently attached to the land, such as houses, buildings, and trees. Because of the value of real estate (for most people, a home is the most expensive purchase they will ever make) and the complexities of the transaction, attorneys frequently assist persons or companies that buy or sell real property to make sure that nothing important is overlooked.

real estate
Land and things permanently attached to the land, such as houses, buildings, and trees.

TECHNOLOGY AND
today's paralegal

MORE CAREER OPPORTUNITIES FOR TECH-SAVVY PARALEGALS

Paralegals possessing superior technological skills are in demand. Knowing the basics—document creation, spreadsheets, database management, and online legal research—is essential. Also knowing how to utilize social media such as LinkedIn, Facebook, and Google+ is becoming increasing important. Finally, the use of smartphones and tablets has become part of the life of many paralegals. Here we review some skills that paralegals should master to secure their future in the job market.

MASTER DOCUMENT-CREATION SKILLS

Good document-creation skills are an asset. The faster you can accurately type text or key in data on a computer, the more work you can complete in a shorter time—and, consequently, the more valuable you are to an employer. This is true whether you are creating documents, scheduling court dates, managing calendars, or performing legal research. Make sure your touch-typing skills (typing without looking at the keys) are superior. Practice entering numbers as well as letters so that you can accurately key in court dates and deadlines in calendaring programs and figures in billing programs. Inexpensive or free typing programs are available on the Internet.

BE PROFICIENT WITH OFFICE SOFTWARE

Most law firms use a variety of software applications, including billing programs, e-mail, calendaring, and legal research applications. To be competitive, paralegals should be skilled at using these programs. For example, paralegals are often responsible for keeping track of the deadlines for filing court documents, along with court filing fees and requirements. Local court rules specify the filing dates and fees for different kinds of cases, but these rules change regularly. Failure to submit documents by their due dates can result in a court's dismissing the case or a client's dismissing the firm. Moreover, missed deadlines are a leading cause of malpractice (professional negligence) lawsuits filed by clients against attorneys.

Calendaring software helps ensure that attorneys do not miss important dates and calculates required fees based on the local court rules. Such software could suit the needs of a small law firm that handles only local cases, but it might not be adequate if the firm handles cases in numerous counties or states. The firm may use an online calendaring service instead. A paralegal who knows about such applications could suggest that the firm use these and other services that enhance productivity.

Look for calendaring "apps" for Android-based smartphones and for iPhones and iPads. Some of the apps can be integrated and synched with software that you may have in your office.

TAKE ON NEW CHALLENGES

Evolving technologies provide avenues for paralegals to advance their positions and become indispensable to their firms. For example, many courts now allow documents to be filed electronically. Paralegals are often responsible for making sure that these documents are in the proper electronic format and that they include hyperlinks to relevant resources.

Courts also allow electronic discovery—that is, prior to a trial, a party can obtain evidence in electronic form from the opposing party's e-mails, computers, iPhones, and other equipment. Some law firms also take video depositions (testimony from witnesses) when witnesses are unable to appear in person. Paralegals with skill in locating and obtaining electronic evidence or with the ability to film and produce videos are likely to be in demand.

TECHNOLOGY TIP

Along with technological advances come certain legal questions that are considered by the courts. For example, how long does electronic evidence need to be retained on an online or offline computer system? Who should be required to pay for the discovery of electronic evidence? A paralegal who understands the various legal issues surrounding the use of new technologies and who knows how the courts in the area are resolving these disputes will likely become a key member of the legal team.

Paralegals who specialize in real estate may find employment in a number of environments, including small law firms that specialize in real estate transactions, real estate departments in large law firms, corporations or other business firms that frequently buy or sell real property, banking institutions (which finance real estate purchases), title companies, and real estate agencies. As we will discuss in Chapter 16, paralegals working in real estate law often draft contracts for the sale of real estate, draft mortgage agreements, draft and record deeds, and schedule closings on the sale of property.

Personal-Injury Law

Much litigation involves claims brought by persons who have been injured in automobile accidents or other incidents as a result of the negligence of others. *Negligence* is a **tort**, or civil wrong, that occurs when a person's carelessness causes harm to another. Someone who has been injured as a result of another's negligence is entitled under tort law to obtain compensation from the wrongdoer. (Tort law, including negligence, will be discussed in Chapter 14.)

Paralegals who specialize in personal-injury litigation often work for law firms that concentrate in this field. Legal assistants working in this capacity obtain and review medical and employment records to calculate the client's lost income. These items are needed to ascertain the plaintiff's damages in a personal-injury lawsuit. Personal-injury paralegals are also hired by insurance companies to investigate claims. Defendants in personal-injury cases are typically covered by insurance (automobile or other), and a defendant's insurance company has a duty to defend an insured customer who is being sued.

Insurance Law

Insurance is a contract by which an insurance company (the insurer) promises to pay a sum or give something of value to another (either the insured or the beneficiary of the insurance policy) to compensate the other for a specified loss. Insurance may provide compensation for the injury or death of the insured or another, for damage to the insured's property, or for other losses, such as those resulting from lawsuits. Paralegals who specialize in insurance law may work for law firms that defend insurance companies in litigation brought against the companies. They may also work directly for insurance companies or for companies that buy large amounts of insurance, such as hospitals.

Paralegals with an insurance concentration may review government insurance regulations and monitor an insurance firm's compliance with these regulations. They may also be asked to review insurance contracts, undertake factual and legal investigations relating to insurance claims, or provide litigation assistance in lawsuits involving the insurance company. Paralegals are often asked to help in litigation involving insurance. For example, a paralegal may be asked to provide investigative or litigation assistance for a client who is bringing a lawsuit or defending against a personal-injury, malpractice, or other litigation in which insurance is an important factor.

Employment and Labor Law

As will be discussed in Chapter 18, laws governing employment relationships are referred to collectively as *employment and labor law*. This body of law includes laws governing health and safety in the workplace, labor unions and union-management relations, employment discrimination, sexual harassment, wrongful termination, pension plans, retirement and disability income, employee privacy rights, the minimum wage, and overtime wages.

Paralegals who are experienced in these issues may work for law firms, businesses, or government agencies. Some paralegals specialize in just one aspect of employment law, such as workers' compensation. Under **workers' compensation statutes**, employees who are injured on the job are compensated from state funds or insurance funds (obtained from taxes or insurance premiums paid by employers). Paralegals assist persons injured on the job in obtaining compensation from the state workers' compensation program. As mentioned earlier, some government agencies allow paralegals to represent clients during agency hearings, which are conducted to settle disputes, or during negotiations with the agencies.

---

tort
A civil wrong not arising from a breach of contract; a violation of a legal duty that causes harm to another.

social MEDIA TODAY

When you are posting on Facebook, assume that your comments will be published in your local newspaper and read by the managing partner of your firm over breakfast.

insurance
A contract by which an insurance company (the insurer) promises to pay a sum of money or give something of value to another (either the insured or the beneficiary) to compensate for a specified loss.

ON THE web

Some law firms that specialize in labor and employment issues post newsletters on the Web. One such firm is Ogletree Deakins, which you can access at **www. ogletreedeakins.com**

workers' compensation statutes
State laws establishing an administrative procedure for compensating workers for injuries that arise in the course of their employment.

Many state workers' compensation boards allow paralegals to represent clients in such hearings.

Frequently, working in employment law involves interacting with numerous administrative agencies, such as the Occupational Safety and Health Administration and the Equal Employment Opportunity Commission. Each governmental agency has its own set of rules and legal procedures. Paralegals who work in employment or labor law must be familiar with the relevant federal and state agencies, as well as with their specific roles in resolving disputes. We will cover employment law in Chapter 18 and administrative agencies in Chapter 5.

Estate Planning and Probate Administration

Estate planning and probate administration have to do with the transfer of an owner's property, or *estate*, on the owner's death. Through **estate planning**, the owner decides, *before* death, how his or her property will be transferred to others. The owner may make a **will** to designate the persons to whom his or her property is to be transferred. If someone contests the validity of the will, it must be **probated** (proved) in a **probate court**. Depending on the size and complexity of the estate, it may take months—in some cases, over a year—for the probate court to approve the property distribution and for the property to be transferred to the rightful heirs.

Because the probate process is time consuming and expensive, many people engage in estate planning to avoid probate. For example, a person may establish a **trust** agreement, a legal arrangement in which the ownership of property is transferred to a third person (the *trustee*) to be used for the benefit of another (the beneficiary). Paralegals often are responsible for interviewing clients to obtain information necessary to draft wills and trust agreements, for gathering information on debts and assets, and for locating heirs if necessary (see Chapter 17). A paralegal who is sensitive and caring toward clients, yet professional and conscientious in explaining and working out procedures, is well suited for this specialty.

Bankruptcy Law

Bankruptcy law allows debtors to obtain relief from their debts. Bankruptcy law is federal law, and bankruptcy proceedings take place in federal courts (see the discussion of the federal court system in Chapter 6). The twin goals of bankruptcy law are (1) to protect a debtor by giving him or her a fresh start and (2) to ensure that creditors who are competing for a debtor's assets are treated fairly. Bankruptcy law provides for several types of relief, and both individuals and business firms may petition for bankruptcy. Both large and small firms practice bankruptcy law and hire paralegals who specialize in this area.

Bankruptcy law, to be discussed in Chapter 19, imposes many strict requirements, which means that paralegals working in this field may have detailed responsibilities. The paralegal might be responsible for interviewing debtors to obtain information about their income, assets, and debts. This often involves verifying the accuracy of information provided by debtors and ensuring that debtors have completed required credit counseling. The paralegal may also review the validity of creditors' claims and prepare the documents that must be submitted to the bankruptcy court.

Intellectual Property Law

Intellectual property consists of the products of individuals' minds—products that result from creative processes. Those who create intellectual property acquire certain rights over the use of that property. Literary works, such as books, and artistic works, such as songs, are protected by *copyright law*. *Trademark law* protects firms' distinctive marks or logos. Inventions are protected by *patent law*. Firms may also have *trade secrets*, such as the formula to make Coca-Cola. The owner of intellectual property rights may sell the rights to another, may collect royalties on the use of the property (such as a popular song) by others, and may prevent unauthorized

estate planning
Making arrangements, during a person's lifetime, for the transfer of that person's property to others on the person's death. Estate planning often involves executing a will or establishing a trust fund to provide for others, such as a spouse or children, on a person's death.

will
A document directing how and to whom the maker's property and obligations are to be transferred on his or her death.

probate
The process of "proving" the validity of a will and ensuring that the instructions in a valid will are carried out.

probate court
A court that probates wills; usually a county court.

trust
An arrangement in which title to property is held by one person (a trustee) for the benefit of another (a beneficiary).

bankruptcy law
The body of federal law that governs bankruptcy proceedings. The twin goals of bankruptcy law are (1) to protect a debtor by giving him or her a fresh start and (2) to ensure that creditors competing for a debtor's assets are treated fairly.

intellectual property
Property that results from intellectual, creative processes. Copyrights, patents, and trademarks are examples of intellectual property.

publishers from reproducing the property (such as a novel). Chapter 15 will provide more detail about laws governing intellectual property.

Some law firms (or departments of large law firms) specialize in intellectual property law, such as patent law. Other firms provide a variety of legal services, of which intellectual property law is a part. In addition, corporate legal departments may be responsible for registering copyrights, patents, or trademarks with the federal government.

Paralegals who specialize in intellectual property research existing patents and trademarks. They also assist in compiling patent applications in accordance with detailed regulations, draft documents necessary to apply for trademark and copyright protection, and assist in litigating disputes. Because of the expertise required, paralegal intellectual property specialists are paid more than average (see Exhibit 2.2 on page 26). This is an especially good practice area for paralegals with a science background. In fact, anyone, including a paralegal, with three years of undergraduate science courses can apply to the U.S. Patent and Trademark Office to become a registered patent agent and thus be qualified to prepare patent applications.

Environmental Law

Environmental law consists of all laws that have been created to protect the environment. Environmental law involves the regulation of air and water pollution, natural resource management, endangered species protection, hazardous waste disposal and the clean-up of hazardous waste sites, pesticide control, and nuclear power regulation.

Employers of paralegal specialists in environmental law include administrative agencies (such as the federal Environmental Protection Agency, state natural resource departments, and local zoning boards), environmental law departments of large law firms, law firms that specialize in environmental law, and corporations. For example, a company may employ a paralegal as an *environmental coordinator* to help maintain compliance with regulations, oversee company environmental programs, and obtain permits to use land in certain ways. Paralegals working in law firms that handle environmental matters often assist in litigation concerning alleged violations of environmental laws. They perform tasks similar to those described previously for litigation and personal-injury paralegals.

Family Law

Family law, as the term implies, deals with family matters, such as marriage, divorce, alimony, child support, and child custody. We will discuss it in detail in Chapter 17. Family law is governed mostly by state statutes, so if you specialize in this type of law, you will need to become familiar with your state's requirements.

As a family law specialist, you might work for a small family law practice, for a family law department in a large law firm, or with a state or local agency, such as a community services agency that assists persons who need help with family-related problems. As a paralegal working in family law, you might research and draft documents that are filed with the court in divorce and adoption proceedings. You might also perform investigations into assets and the grounds for divorce. Paralegals in this area often have extensive contact with clients and need to be skilled at extracting information from sometimes emotionally distraught persons. Those with a background or interest in social work or counseling are particularly well suited to this specialty.

Criminal Law

Law is sometimes classified into the two categories of civil law and criminal law. **Civil law** is concerned with the duties that exist between persons or between citizens and their governments, excluding the duty not to commit crimes. Contract law, for example, is part of civil law. Tort law, which has to do with the infringement by one

---

social MEDIA TODAY

Various forms of social media can play significant roles in coordinating teams spread out geographically. If you are working with paralegals and lawyers in other locations, consider coordinating your work through social media tools.

environmental law
All state and federal laws or regulations enacted or issued to protect the environment and preserve environmental resources.

family law
Law relating to family matters, such as marriage, divorce, child support, and child custody.

civil law
Law dealing with the definition and enforcement of private rights, as opposed to criminal matters.

person of the legally recognized rights of another (see Chapter 14), is an area of civil law.

Criminal law, in contrast, is concerned with wrongs committed against the public as a whole. Criminal acts are prohibited by federal, state, or local statutes (criminal law and procedures will be discussed in Chapter 13). In a criminal case, the government seeks to impose a penalty (a fine or jail time) on a person who is alleged to have committed a crime. In a civil case, one party tries to make the other party comply with a duty or pay for the damage caused by the failure to so comply.

Paralegals who specialize in criminal law may work for public prosecutors, public defenders (which is discussed in the *Developing Paralegal Skills* feature below), or criminal defense attorneys. A legal assistant working for the prosecutor's office, for example, might draft search or arrest warrants. A paralegal working for the defense attorney (public or private) might obtain police reports, conduct research, and draft documents to be filed with the court, such as a document arguing that the police violated the defendant's constitutional rights. Although criminal law and civil law are quite different, the trial process is comparable, and paralegals perform similar types of tasks (investigation, summarizing witness testimony, and so forth) in preparation for litigation.

Additional Specialty Areas

The above listing of specialty areas is by no means exhaustive. Opportunities for paralegals exist in many other capacities. As the U.S. population ages, for example, more attorneys are focusing on serving the needs of older clients. **Elder law** is the term used to describe this broad specialty. Paralegals who work in this practice area may be asked to assist in a variety of tasks, including those relating to estate planning (discussed earlier), age-discrimination claims, financial arrangements for long-term care, Medicare and Medicaid, abuse suffered by elderly persons, and the visitation rights of grandparents.

---

criminal law
Law that governs and defines those actions that are crimes and that subjects persons convicted of crimes to punishment imposed by the government (a fine or jail time).

elder law
A relatively new legal specialty that involves serving the needs of older clients, such as estate planning and making arrangements for long-term care.

DEVELOPING
paralegal skills

WORKING FOR A PUBLIC DEFENDER

Michele Sanchez works as a paralegal for the public defender's office in her county. Today, she has been assigned to go to the county jail to meet with a new client, Geraldine Silverton. Silverton had been arrested for child abuse after her child's school notified the police. According to school officials, the child had bruises all over his body. The child also told his teacher that his mother frequently "beat him up" for no reason at all.

The client, Silverton, is upset and tells Michele that "no way in the world would she harm her boy." Silverton claims that her son was hurt when he fell off the trampoline in their backyard and that he's just "making up" the abuse story to get attention.

Silverton demands to be released from jail immediately. Michele makes a note of Silverton's concerns and then explains the scheduling for the bail hearings.

TIPS FOR MEETING WITH A NEW CLIENT

- Review the police report before meeting with the client.
- During the interview with the client, ask the client for his or her side of the story.
- Listen carefully and supportively to the client, and communicate with empathy.
- Do not appear to judge the client.

Nurses have found profitable and challenging work as paralegals. A paralegal who is also a trained nurse is able to evaluate legal claims involving injuries, such as those involved in personal-injury, medical malpractice, or product liability lawsuits. A relatively new specialty area among nurses—and within the legal profession—is that of the **legal nurse consultant (LNC)**. An LNC consults with legal professionals and others on medical aspects of legal claims or issues. LNCs usually work independently (offering their services on a contract basis) and are typically well paid for contract services—up to $200 per hour. Some LNCs work for law firms, insurance companies, government offices, and risk management departments of companies as salaried employees. The American Association of Legal Nurse Consultants offers a certification program in which nurses who meet the eligibility criteria (including educational credentials and sufficient experience as a legal nurse) and pass an examination can become certified as LNCs.

Paralegal Compensation

What do paralegals earn? This is an important question for anyone contemplating a career as a paralegal. You can obtain some idea of what paralegals make, on average, from paralegal compensation surveys. Following a discussion of these surveys, we look at some other components of paralegal compensation, including job benefits and compensation for overtime work.

Compensation Surveys

Paralegal income is affected by a number of factors. We have already covered the effects of the size of the firm or legal department (see Exhibit 2.1 on page 22) and the specialty area in which the paralegal practices (see Exhibit 2.2 on page 26). Another income-determining factor is the paralegal's years of experience. Typically, as shown in Exhibit 2.3 below, more experienced paralegals enjoy higher rates of compensation. This is particularly noticeable when a paralegal has worked for the same employer for a long period of time.

Another major factor that affects paralegal compensation is geographical location. Exhibit 2.3, like earlier exhibits, illustrates *national* averages. Exhibit 2.4 on the next page, by contrast, shows *regional* averages. As you can see, paralegals who work in San Francisco enjoy higher levels of compensation than paralegals in many other cities. Remember, though, that these figures represent averages and can therefore be deceptive. For examples, a paralegal working in a suburb of Chicago may not earn as much as a paralegal who works in downtown Chicago.

Keep in mind, too, that salary statistics do not tell the whole story. Although paralegals earn more in California than in Nebraska, the cost of living is higher in California than in Nebraska. This means that your real income—the amount you can purchase with your income—may, in fact, be the same in both states despite the differences in salary. If you are comparing job offers in different cities, be sure to consider the cost of living as well as the pay being offered. Salary statistics also do not reveal another important component of compensation—job benefits.

legal nurse consultant (LNC)
A nurse who consults with legal professionals and others about medical aspects of legal claims or issues. Legal nurse consultants normally must have at least a bachelor's degree in nursing and significant nursing experience.

ON THE web

To learn more about the American Association of Legal Nurse Consultants and its certification programs, go to **www.aalnc.org**

Position Classification	Average Compensation
Paralegal I	$47,023
Paralegal II	$53,825
Paralegal III	$62,251
Paralegal IV	$71,974
Paralegal Supervisor	$71,137
Paralegal Manager	$84,998

© Cengage Learning 2014

EXHIBIT 2.3
Average Paralegal Compensation by Experience

Data compiled by authors from salary.com. See that Web site for definition of the different paralegal positions.

EXHIBIT 2.4
Average Paralegal Salary by City

Authors compiled data from salary.com.

City	Median Salary
San Francisco	$64,545
Dallas	$53,545
Orlando	$50,442
Chicago	$57,179
New York	$62,729

social MEDIA TODAY

Social media technologies are about connecting and sharing information, which means privacy is an important issue. Make sure you understand who can see the material you post and how to control it. Facebook has numerous privacy settings, for example, as does Google+.

bonus
An end-of-the-year payment to a salaried employee in appreciation for that employee's overtime work, diligence, or dedication to the firm.

Job Benefits

Part of your total compensation package as an employee will consist of job benefits. These benefits may include paid holidays, sick leave, group insurance coverage (life, disability, medical, dental), pension plans, and possibly others. Benefits packages vary from firm to firm. One employer may pay the entire premium for your health insurance, for example, while another employer may require you to contribute part of the cost. Usually, the larger the firm, the greater the value of the benefits package. When evaluating any job offer, you need to consider the benefits that you will receive and what these benefits are worth to you. You will read more about the importance of job benefits later in this chapter in the context of evaluating a job offer.

Salaries versus Hourly Wages

Most paralegals are salaried employees. In other words, they receive a specified annual salary regardless of the number of hours they work. Others are paid an hourly wage rate for every hour worked. Paralegals are frequently asked to work overtime, and how they are compensated for overtime work usually depends on whether they are salaried employees or are paid hourly wages. Many firms compensate their salaried paralegals for overtime work through year-end **bonuses**, which are payments made to employees in recognition of their devotion to the firm and the high quality of their work. Paralegals often receive annual bonuses ranging from around $2,000 to around $5,000, depending on years of experience, firm size, and so forth. Some firms allow salaried employees to take compensatory time off work (for example, an hour off for every hour worked beyond usual working hours). Employees who are paid an hourly wage rate are normally paid overtime wages. In such cases, there may be no bonus or only a small one.

Planning Your Career

Career planning involves three key steps. The first step is defining your long-term goals. The second involves coming up with short-term goals and adjusting them to meet the realities of the job market. We look at these two steps in this section. (For some tips on how to succeed in your career, see this chapter's *Featured Contributor* feature beginning on page 36.) Later in this chapter, we discuss the third step: reevaluating your career after you have had some on-the-job experience as a paralegal.

Defining Your Long-Term Goals

From the beginning, you want to define, as clearly as possible, your career goals. This requires some personal reflection and self-assessment. What are you looking for in a career? Why do you want to become a paralegal? Is income the most important factor? Is job satisfaction (doing the kind of work you like) the most important factor? Is the environment in which you work the most important factor? What profession could best utilize your talents and skills? Asking yourself these and other broad questions about your personal preferences and values will help you define more clearly your overall professional goals.

Your Goals May Change

Do not be surprised to find that your long-term goals change over time. As you gain experience as a paralegal and your life circumstances alter, you may decide that your long-term goals are no longer appropriate. For example, the level of career involvement that suits you as a single person may not be appropriate should you marry and have children. Similarly, later in life, when your children leave home, you may have different goals with respect to work.

Explore New Challenges

Also, at the outset of your career, you cannot know what opportunities might arise in the future. Career planning is an ongoing challenge for everyone. Throughout your career as a paralegal, you will probably meet other paralegals who have made career changes. A high percentage of paralegals, for example, decided on the field after several years of working in another profession, such as nursing, law enforcement, business administration, or accounting. Changes within the profession, your own experiences, and new opportunities affect the career choices before you. The realities you face during your career are likely to play a significant role in modifying your long-term goals.

Short-Term Goals and Job Realities

Long-term goals are just that—goals that we hope to achieve over many years or even a lifetime. Short-term goals are the steps we take to realize our long-term goals. As an entry-level paralegal, one of your short-term goals is simply to find a job.

Ideally, you will find a job that provides you with a salary consistent with your training and abilities, a level of responsibility that is comfortable (or challenging) for you, and excellent job benefits. The realities of the job market are not always what we wish them to be, however. You should be prepared for the possibility that you might not find the "right" employer or the "perfect" job when you first start. You may be lucky from the outset, but it may take several attempts before you find the employer and the job that best suit your needs, skills, and talents.

Remember that even if you do not find the perfect job right away, you can gain valuable skills and experience in *any* job environment—skills and experience that can help you achieve long-term goals in the future. In fact, you might want to "try on" jobs at different-sized firms and in different specialty areas to see how they "fit" with your particular needs.

Locating Potential Employers

Looking for a job is time consuming and requires attention to detail, persistence, and creativity. Your paralegal education is preparing you, among other things, to do investigative research. The investigative skills that you will use on the job as a paralegal are the ones that you should apply when looking for a job.

Where do you begin your investigation? How can you find out what paralegal jobs are available in your area or elsewhere? How do you know which law firms practice the type of law that interests you? The following suggestions will help you answer these questions.

Networking

Career opportunities often go unpublished. Many firms post notices within their own organizations before publishing online or in the "Help Wanted" section of a newspaper or periodical. This opens doors to their own employees before the general public. It also spares employers from having to wade through many applications for a vacant position. If you have connections within an organization, you may be told that a position is opening up before other candidates are aware that an opportunity exists.

social
MEDIA TODAY

Investing a little time each day in your online presence can make you a recognized expert online, yielding career benefits for years to come.

Featured Contributor

PLAN AND PURSUE YOUR DESIRED CAREER

Linda J. Wolf, ACP

BIOGRAPHICAL NOTE

Linda J. Wolf, ACP, earned her bachelor's degree in journalism and political science from Baylor University. She worked as a news editor for the *Waco Tribune Herald* before moving to Dallas. She began her paralegal career with the intellectual property boutique firm of Richards, Medlock & Andrews. The firm was acquired by Sidley Austin LLP in 1996. She continues to specialize in intellectual property and is also responsible for managing the library in the Dallas office.

Wolf earned her CLA/CP credential and her CLAS in intellectual property. She has served NALA in many capacities, including as chair of the NALA Certifying Board, as president, and as representative on the ABA's Approval Commission for paralegal programs. She is a charter member of the Paralegal Division of the State Bar of Texas and a founding member of the first NALA affiliate in Dallas, the North Texas Paralegal Association.

In tough economic times, it is good to remind ourselves that our profession was born out of the recession of the 1960s and 1970s. History teaches us that a bad economy is fertile ground for people with vision and focus. So there is no better time to be a paralegal, as long as we remember a few golden rules.

For those of us who are veteran paralegals, we need to constantly hone and develop our skill sets to help set us apart in the competitive climate that we currently find ourselves. None of us can sit back on our laurels and assume our jobs are safe. How do we stay on top? First, ask yourself, What would make you better at your career? What would help you stand out from the crowd? For me, it was the choice to take

some chemistry courses when I found myself working for a lawyer with a chemical engineering degree at an intellectual property boutique firm. Find courses and programs in areas of law that interest you and take them. When you do so, you prove to your employer that regardless of your accomplishments to date, you are serious about learning. Plus, those educational offerings will help you stay on top of your game.

TAKE CONTROL OF YOUR CAREER

If you don't like to do e-discovery, then take courses that will enable you to migrate out of litigation and into your new area of law. But go about it the right way. Don't wake up one morning and decide you

---

networking
Making personal connections and cultivating relationships with people in a certain field, profession, or area of interest.

More paralegals find employment through networking than through any other means. For paralegals, **networking** is the process of making personal connections with the other paralegals, paralegal instructors, attorneys, and others who are involved in (or who know someone who is involved in) the paralegal or legal profession. Online networking, such as that provided by LinkedIn (**www.linkedin.com**), is becoming popular as well. Professional organizations and internships offer important networking opportunities.

Join a Professional Association

Students can form a network of paralegal connections through affiliation with professional associations and student clubs. You have already learned about NALA and NFPA, the two largest national associations for legal assistants. Other organizations of paralegals exist across the country. Some such organizations are listed in Appendix E at the end of this book. See if your local paralegal association allows students to be members. If it does, attend meetings and get to know other paralegals who may know of job opportunities in your area. Persons involved with want to do bankruptcy. Allow yourself time to dream about what your ideal job would be, and then develop a plan to create that perfect career for yourself. For instance, a good friend of mine worked in litigation for many years and realized that what she really wanted to do was work for the school district. She literally created her ideal career by educating her school board on why they needed a paralegal and how she could help them.

Keep your eyes open to new opportunities. Several years ago, the National Association of Legal Assistants (NALA) offered an institute in Social Security benefits administration during the annual educational conference. It was taught by an administrative law judge and was very successful. Because of the nature of the work, some paralegals who attended the Institute saw an opportunity to take that training and turn it into a second career after they retired. They saw an opportunity where none existed before.

PROMOTE YOURSELF

Remember to market yourself within your firm or company. Don't wait for the work to come to you—go out and find it. Attorneys have to market themselves within the company or firm, so why would it be any different for paralegals? If you are looking to segue into a different practice group within your firm or company, let a trusted adviser know that you are looking for new challenges. And if you've recently acquired new skills or knowledge, make sure you let management know. We do ourselves a grave injustice when we fail to market ourselves.

For those who are new to the profession, networking is the first key to success. If you haven't found a job yet, use all the networking tools at your fingertips to make contacts. Join the local and state associations, which all have job banks. Join NALA and participate in the conference center, where members can exchange ideas and share job-hunting tips. Take advantage of all the special networking tools such as LinkedIn, Plaxo, Facebook, and Classmates to connect with people who might be able to help you.

Once you have found a job, those connections can be a tremendous help. If you need help finding someone who can translate Russian, for example, you can reach out to your colleagues through your networking tools to see if anyone can recommend a resource for you. This is particularly helpful if you happen to work in a rural area, or in a narrow field of law.

KEEP ON TOP OF A GROWING FIELD

Regardless of your experience level, there are plenty of wonderful opportunities for paralegals in the job market. The Department of Labor lists our profession as one of the fastest growing professions in the United States today, with over 250,000 paralegals across the country. It will continue to grow. The Bureau of Labor Statistics projects that the profession will swell to 325,000 in the coming years.

So keep up with trends, stay on top of your education, and stay connected with your colleagues and you'll always be in demand.

"... networking is the first key to success."
"... market yourself ..."

other groups—such as the International Paralegal Management Association, or IPMA (an association of individuals who manage legal assistants), and the **state bar association** (a state-level association of attorneys)—can also provide valuable inside knowledge of potential job openings.

Network during Internships

Most paralegal education programs include an internship in which students are placed temporarily in a law firm or other work setting. The people you meet and deal with in these settings often turn out to be beneficial to you in finding future employment. In many cases, an intern who has performed well is offered a full-time position after graduation. Even if you are not interested in working for the firm with which you do your internship, be careful not to "burn your bridges." The legal community is relatively small, and lawyers are more inclined to hire paralegals about whom their colleagues have made positive remarks. Many online social networks, such as Facebook and Google+, are now being used by professionals to provide and obtain work-related information.

state bar association
An association of attorneys within a state. In most states, an attorney must be a member of the state bar association to practice law in the state.

Volunteer

You can develop your skills and build your professional network by volunteering with a local legal aid group or other organization that provides legal advice and assistance. Many attorneys volunteer for such work, so you may make a valuable connection while you help. You will also gain worthwhile experience, and will demonstrate to potential employers that you are willing and able to cooperate with other professionals in aiding others.

Finding Available Jobs

trade journal

A newsletter, magazine, or other periodical that provides a certain trade or profession with information (products, trends, or developments) relating to that trade or profession.

Your next effort should be to locate sources that list paralegal job openings. Classified ads in the newspaper were used traditionally, but not as much these days. **Trade journals** and similar publications, such as your local or state bar association's journal, newsletter, or Web site, may list openings for legal professionals. Increasingly, employers advertise job openings in online publications and turn to online databases to find prospective employees. Today the best starting point when launching your search is probably the Internet.

Identifying Possible Employers

You should also identify firms and organizations for which you might like to work and submit an employment application to them. In a well-organized job search, locate and contact organizations that offer the benefits, salary, opportunities for advancement, work environment, and legal specialty of your choice. Even though these employers may not have vacancies in your field at the moment, you want your job application to be immediately available when an opening occurs. Most firms, if they are interested in your qualifications, will keep your application on file for six months or so and may contact you if a position becomes available. As the *Ethics Watch* feature on the facing page discusses, be truthful about your background.

It is a good idea to begin compiling employer information for your job search while you are still completing your studies. Many of the resources you will need are available at the college you attend or through your paralegal program (and increasingly, online).

Legal Directories

Legal directories provide lists of attorneys, their locations, and their areas of practice. The *Martindale-Hubbell Law Directory,* which you can find at most law libraries (and online at **www.martindale.com**), lists the names, addresses, telephone numbers, areas of legal practice, and other data for many lawyers and law firms around the country. It is an excellent resource for paralegals interested in working for law firms or corporate legal departments. *West's Legal Directory* is another valuable source of information. It is on the Internet at **lawyers.findlaw.com**. The directory contains a detailed listing of U.S. attorneys and law firms, state and federal attorneys and offices, and corporate legal departments and general counsel.

Job-Placement Services

Throughout your job search, make full use of your school's placement service. Many colleges with paralegal programs provide job-placement services, and ABA-approved schools are required to provide ongoing placement services. Placement offices have personnel trained to assist you in finding a job, as well as in preparing job-search tools, such as your résumé and a list of potential employers.

A growing trend is to use legal staffing or placement companies (also known as *recruiters*) to locate employment. Usually, the employer pays the fees for the placement company's services, and the company recruits candidates for the paralegal position and arranges interviews. Placement services can be located through paralegal program directors, local paralegal associations, and state bar associations, as well as on the Web.

social MEDIA TODAY

Do not automatically accept "friend" requests in social media from people you do not know—limit who has access to your information.

ETHICS WATCH

THE IMPORTANCE OF INTEGRITY

When looking for a job, be honest with others about your skills and experience. Even though you may want to impress a prospective employer, never give in to the temptation to exaggerate your qualifications. For example, suppose that you are working for a law firm during your internship and would really like to be hired by the firm in the future as a paralegal. In conversations with people in the firm, don't try to impress them by making misleading statements about your qualifications or skills. For instance, suppose you tell your supervisor that your GPA was 3.8 when in fact it was 3.4. This "little white lie" may come back to haunt you in the future. If the firm offers you a permanent job, it will likely check your credentials, including your college or professional school transcripts. Any misrepresentation, no matter how minor it may seem, could doom your chances of being hired. Professional responsibility requires, among other things, that you be honest and pay close attention to detail—not only on the job but also when you are looking for a job.

This scenario is consistent with the NFPA *Model Code of Ethics and Professional Responsibility,* Section 1.3, "A paralegal shall maintain a high standard of professional conduct," and "A paralegal shall avoid impropriety and the appearance of impropriety and shall not engage in any conduct that would adversely affect his/her fitness to practice."

Legal staffing companies place paralegal employees in both temporary (called "contract") and full-time (called "direct-hire") positions. Temporary contract employees are often used when a regular employee needs to take leave or when a special project requires additional paralegals, such as in large-scale litigation cases. Contract jobs can last from a few days to over a year. Long-term contract opportunities can provide valuable work experience in a particular specialty. Direct-hire positions typically provide long-term employment with salary and benefits, which are not provided in most temporary employment contracts.

Marketing Your Skills

Once you have located potential employers, the next step is to market your skills and yourself effectively. Marketing your skills involves three stages: the application process, interviewing for jobs, and following up on job interviews.

Keep in mind throughout your job search that each personal contact you make, whether it results in employment or not, has potential for your future. A firm may not hire you today because you lack experience or because it has no openings, but it may hire you a year from now. Therefore, keep track of the contacts you make during your search, be patient, and be professional. You may be surprised how many doors will open for you—if not today, then tomorrow.

The Application Process

When looking for paralegal employment, you need to assemble and present professional application materials. The basic materials you should create are a résumé, a cover letter, a list of professional references, and a portfolio. The following discussion explains each of these and gives some practical tips on how to create them.

The Résumé

For most job applications, you must submit a personal *résumé* that summarizes your employment and educational background. Your résumé is an advertisement, and you should invest the time to make that advertisement effective. Because personnel officers in law firms, corporations, and government agencies may receive many résumés for each position they advertise, your résumé should create the best possible impression if you want to gain a competitive edge over other job seekers.

Either generate your résumé yourself, using a computer and a laser printer, or have a professional résumé-preparation service do it for you. Format each page so that the reader is able to scan it quickly and catch the highlights. You might vary the type size, but never use a type size or style that is difficult to read.

What to Include in Your Résumé

Your name, address, telephone number, e-mail address, and Web site address, if you have one, belong in the heading of your résumé. The body of the résumé should be simple, brief, and clear. As a general rule, it should contain only information relevant to the job that you are seeking. A one-page résumé is usually sufficient, unless two pages are required to list relevant educational background and work experience. Exhibit 2.5 on the facing page shows a sample résumé of a person with paralegal experience, and Exhibit 2.6 on page 42 shows one of a person without such experience. Note that you should avoid placing your name and address in the upper left-hand corner, as this area is often stapled.

PROVIDE DETAILS.   Divide your résumé into logical sections with headings as shown in the exhibits. Whenever you list dates, such as educational and employment dates, list them chronologically in reverse order. In other words, list your most recent educational or work history first. When discussing your education, list the names, cities, and states of the colleges or universities you have attended and the degrees you have received. You may want to indicate your major and minor concentrations such as "Major: Paralegal Studies" or "Minor: Political Science." When listing your work experience, specify your responsibilities in each position. Also include any relevant volunteer work that you have done.

Scholarships or honors should also be indicated. If you have a high grade point average (GPA), you should include the GPA in your résumé. Under the heading "Selected Accomplishments," you might indicate your ability to speak more than one language, or note that you possess another special skill, such as expertise in online research.

NO WORK EXPERIENCE?   What if you are an entry-level paralegal and have no work experience to highlight? What can you include on your résumé to fill out the page? If you are facing this situation, add more information on your educational background and experience. You can list specific courses that you took, student affiliations, or particular skills—such as computer competency—that you acquired during your paralegal training.

Do Not Include Personal Data

Avoid including personal data (such as age, marital status, number of children, gender, or hobbies) in your résumé. Employers are prohibited by law from discriminating against employees or job candidates on the basis of race, color, gender, national origin, religion, age, or disability. You can help them fulfill this legal obligation by not including in your résumé any information that could serve as a

---

social
MEDIA TODAY

Join the professional associations in your practice area through LinkedIn and other social media sites. This is a great place to begin to develop your online reputation by posting helpful commentary.

EXHIBIT 2.5
A Sample Résumé of a Person with
Paralegal Experience

ELENA LOPEZ

1131 North Shore Drive
Nita City, NI 48804
Telephone: (616) 555-0102 • E-mail: elopez@nitanet.net

EMPLOYMENT OBJECTIVE

A position as a paralegal in a private law firm that specializes in personal-injury practice.

EDUCATION

2009   Professional Training
Midwestern Professional School for Paralegals, Green Bay, WI
Focus: Litigation Procedures, Legal Investigation, Torts, Arbitration and
Mediation, Case Preparation, and Trial. GPA 3.8.

2006   Bachelor of Arts degree
University of Wisconsin, Madison, WI 53706. Political Science major. GPA 3.1.

PARALEGAL EXPERIENCE

- Caldwell Legal Clinic, Nita City, NI
  Paralegal: June 2009 to the present.
  Responsibilities: Legal research and document review; drafting discovery
  documents, including interrogatories, deposition summaries, and requests for
  admissions; and trial preparation in personal-injury cases.

- Legal Aid Society, Green Bay, WI
  Paralegal: June 2006 to May 2009.
  Responsibilities: Part-time assistance to legal aid attorneys in their representation
  of indigent clients in matters such as divorce, abuse, child custody, paternity, and
  landlord-tenant disputes.

- University of Wisconsin, Madison, WI
  Research Assistant: Political Science Department, January 2004 to May 2006.
  Responsibilities: Research on the effectiveness of federal welfare programs in
  reducing poverty in the United States.

AFFILIATIONS

Paralegal Association of Wisconsin
National Association of Legal Assistants

basis for discrimination. For the same reason, you would be wise not to include a photograph of yourself with your résumé. Also, most prospective employers are not interested in information on personal preferences, pastimes, or hobbies.

Proofread Your Results

Carefully proofread your résumé. Use the spelling checker and grammar checker on your computer, but do not totally rely on them. Have a friend or instructor review your résumé for punctuation, syntax, grammar, spelling, and content. If you find an error, you need to fix it, even if it means having new résumés printed. A mistake on your résumé tells the potential employer that you are a careless worker, and this message may ruin your chances of landing a job.

The Cover Letter

To encourage a recruiter to review your résumé, you need to capture his or her attention with a *cover letter* that accompanies the résumé. Because the cover letter is usually your first contact with an employer, it should be written carefully. It should

EXHIBIT 2.6
A Sample Résumé of a Person without Paralegal Experience

MARCUS BOHMAN

335 W. Alder Street

Gresham, CA 90650

Home Phone: (562) 555-6868 • Mobile: (562) 555-2468 • E-mail: mboh44@gresham.net

---

OBJECTIVE

To obtain a paralegal position in a firm that specializes in real estate transactions.

QUALIFICATIONS

I am a self-motivated, certified paralegal (CLA 2013) with knowledge and background in real estate and a strong academic record (3.7 GPA). In addition to the education listed below, I have completed several courses on real estate financing and possess excellent accounting skills.

EDUCATION

2013	*Bachelor of Arts Degree*—ABA-Approved Program University of La Verne, Legal Studies Program, La Verne, CA Major: Paralegal Studies; Minor: Business Management Emphasis on Real Property and Land-Use Planning, Legal Research and Writing.

EMPLOYMENT

2012–2013	*Intern, Hansen, Henault, Richmond & Shaw* Researched and drafted numerous real estate documents, including land sale contracts, commercial leases, and deeds. Scheduled meetings with clients. Participated in client interviews and several real estate closings. Filed documents with county.
2007–2012	*Office Assistant, Eastside Commercial Property* Maintained files and handled telephone inquiries at commercial real estate company. Coordinated land surveys and obtained property descriptions.
2006–2007	*Clerk, LandPro Title Company* Coordinated title searches and acted as a liaison among banks, mortgage companies, and the title company.
2004–2007	*Clerk, San Jose County Recorder's Office* Handled inquiries from the public and provided instruction to those seeking to look up records via microfiche.

---

be brief, perhaps only two or three paragraphs in length. Exhibit 2.7 on the facing page shows a sample cover letter. When possible, you should learn the name of the person in charge of hiring (by phone or e-mail, if necessary) and direct your letter to that person. If you do not know that person's name, use a generic title, such as "Human Resources Manager" or "Legal Assistant Manager."

CONTENT IS KEY. Your cover letter should point out a few things about yourself and your qualifications for the position that might persuade a recruiter to examine your résumé. As a recently graduated paralegal, for example, you might draw attention to your academic standing at school, your eagerness to specialize in the same area of law as the employer (perhaps listing some courses relating to that specialty), and your willingness to relocate to the employer's city. Your job is to convince the recruiter that you are a close match to the mental picture that he or she has of the perfect candidate for the job. Make sure that the reader knows when and where you can be reached. Often this is best indicated in the closing paragraph of the letter, as shown in Exhibit 2.7 on the facing page.

EXHIBIT 2.7
A Sample Cover Letter

ELENA LOPEZ

1131 North Shore Drive
Nita City, NI 48804
Telephone: (616) 555-0102 • E-mail: elopez@nitanet.net

August 22, 2013

Allen P. Gilmore, Esq.
Jeffers, Gilmore & Dunn
553 Fifth Avenue, Suite 101
Nita City, NI 48801

Dear Mr. Gilmore:

I am responding to your advertisement in the *Vegas Law Journal* for a paralegal to assist you in personal-injury litigation. I am confident that I possess the skills and qualifications that you seek.

As you can see from the enclosed résumé, I received my paralegal certificate from Midwestern Professional School for Paralegals after obtaining a Bachelor of Arts degree from the University of Wisconsin. My paralegal courses included litigation procedures, legal research, legal investigation, and legal writing, and I graduated with a G.P.A. of 3.8.

After completing school, I obtained a position with a legal aid office, where I worked for several years and honed my legal research and writing skills. My current position with Caldwell Legal Clinic has provided me with valuable experience in preparing personal-injury cases for trial. I enjoy this area of law and hope to specialize in personal-injury litigation.

I am excited about the possibility of meeting with you to learn more about the position that you have available. A list of professional references is provided in my resume, and a brief writing sample is attached for your perusal.

Please contact me to schedule an interview. You can contact me by phone after 3.00 P.M., Monday through Friday. I look forward to hearing from you.

Sincerely yours,

Elena Lopez

Elena Lopez

Enclosures

As with your résumé, read through your letter several times and have someone else read it also to make sure that it is free from mistakes and easily understood. You should use the same type of paper for your cover letter as you use for your résumé.

HARD COPY IS BEST.   What about e-mailing your cover letter and résumé to prospective employers? This is a difficult question. On the one hand, e-mail is much faster than regular mail or express delivery services. On the other hand, an e-mail résumé does not look as nice. While some firms are accustomed to receiving applications by e-mail, others are not, and attorneys generally prefer traditional résumés.

If the job you are applying for was advertised online or if the employer provided an e-mail address for interested job candidates to use, then e-mail is probably appropriate. Generally, though, job candidates who submit applications by e-mail should also send, by regular mail, printed copies of their letters and résumés.

List of Professional References

If a firm is interested in your application, you will probably be asked for a list of references—people the firm can contact to obtain information about you and your abilities. An instructor who has worked closely with you, an internship supervisor who has knowledge of your work, or a past employer who has observed your problem-solving ability would all make excellent references. You should have at least three professionally relevant references, but more than five references are rarely necessary. Avoid using the names of family members, friends, or others who are clearly biased in your favor.

List your references on a separate sheet of paper, making sure to include your name, address, and telephone number at the top of the page, in the same format as on your résumé. For each person included on the list, include his or her current institutional affiliation or business firm, address, telephone number, fax number, and e-mail address. Make it easy for prospective employers to contact and communicate with your references.

PERMISSION IS REQUIRED.   When creating your list of references, always remember the following rule: never list a person's name as a reference unless you have that person's permission to do so. After all, it will not help you win the position you seek if one of your references is surprised by a call. Such events raise a red flag and indicate that you are not concerned with details.

Obtaining permission from legal professionals to use them as references also gives you an opportunity to discuss your plans and goals with them, and they may be able to advise you and assist you in your networking. Additionally, it gives you a chance to discuss with them the kinds of experience and skills in which a prospective employer may be interested.

BUILD YOUR CONTACTS.   Start building your list of possible references early in your studies. Dressing professionally in class, volunteering, arriving on time for class, being prepared, and turning in professional work for assignments are all ways to make a good impression on a professor. Keep in touch with those you want to use as references later. The more they know about you, the more effective they will be as a reference.

Your Professional Portfolio

When a potential employer asks you for an interview, have your *professional portfolio* ready to give to the interviewer. The professional portfolio should contain another copy of your résumé, a list of references, letters of recommendation written by previous employers or instructors, samples of legal documents that you have composed, college or university transcripts, and any other relevant professional information, such as proof of professional certification or achievement. This collection of documents should be well organized and professionally presented. Depending on the size of your portfolio, a cover sheet, a table of contents, and a commercial binder may be appropriate.

SHOW WHAT YOU CAN DO.   The interviewer may be interested in your research and writing skills. Therefore, your professional portfolio should contain several samples of legal writing. If you are looking for your first legal position, go through your paralegal drafting assignments and pull out those that reflect your best work and that relate to the job skills you wish to demonstrate. Working with an instructor or other mentor, revise and improve those samples for inclusion in the portfolio. You might also use documents that you drafted while an intern or when working as a paralegal. These documents make excellent writing samples because they involve real-life circumstances. Be careful, however, and always remember, on any sample document, to completely black out (or "white out") any identifying reference to a client unless you have the client's permission to disclose his or her identity or if the information is not confidential.

Always include a résumé, as well as a list of references, in your professional portfolio, even though you already sent your résumé to the prospective employer with your cover letter. Interviewers may not have the résumé at hand at the time of the interview, and providing a second copy with your professional portfolio is a thoughtful gesture on your part.

FOCUS ON YOUR KEY ATTRIBUTE. Some interviewers may examine your professional portfolio carefully. Others may keep it to examine later, after the interview. Still others may not be interested in it at all. If there is a particular item in your portfolio that you would like the interviewer to see, make sure you point it out before leaving the interview.

Digital Marketing

An important part of marketing yourself is ensuring that you have a presence online that helps potential employers evaluate your skills. Consider building a professional-looking personal Web page that highlights your skills and presents a professional image. Use a conservative, business attire photograph and describe your skills and education. Provide examples of professional writing, such as links to articles you have written in a firm newsletter or a recent writing sample from your paralegal program. A personal Web site enables you to expand on the limited profile information on sites such as LinkedIn.

Your personal Web site, like your entire online presence, needs to demonstrate that you are a serious professional, able to handle the demands of a career that involves confidential information and disputes. Employers seek to narrow the search to fill a job opening to a small number of candidates. Hence, they are likely to drop a candidate from the pool if his or her personal Web site features unprofessional photographs or focuses on parties.

As a paralegal, you will have access to personal information about your firm's clients, which can include business information worth millions of dollars. Law firms and other employers want to be sure that they can rely on their staff to be professional. Your digital image must convey that you can do that.

The Interview

After an employer has reviewed your cover letter and résumé, the employer may contact you to schedule an interview. Interviews with potential employers may be the most challenging (and stressful) part of your search for employment.

Every interview will be different. Some will go well, but you will lose out to another candidate. Nonetheless, you have made a good contact, and you may be able to use this interviewer as a resource for information about other jobs. Remember what went right about the interview, and try to build on those positive aspects at the next one. While some interviews may go poorly despite your best efforts, good lessons can still be learned from disappointing experiences.

You will find that some interviewers are more skilled at interviewing than others. Some have a talent for getting applicants to open up, while others are confrontational and put the already nervous candidate on the defensive. Still others may be unprepared for the interview. They may not have had time to compare applicants' qualifications with the job requirements, for example. Some employers now use a problem-focused interview technique to see how you would respond to a work situation.

As the person being interviewed, you have no control over who will interview you or what the style may be. You do, however, have control over your preparations for the interview. The following discussion will help you with these preparations.

Before the Interview

You can do many things prior to the interview to improve your chances of getting the job. First, do your "homework." Learn as much about the employer as possible. Check with your instructors or other legal professionals to find out if they are familiar with the firm or the interviewer. To see what you can learn about the firm and its members, check the employer's Web site, if there is one, and consult relevant directories, such as legal and company directories, as well as business publications.

When you are called for an interview, learn the full name of the interviewer so that you will be able to address him or her by name during the interview and properly address a follow-up letter. During the interview, use Mr. or Ms. in addressing the interviewer unless directed by the interviewer to be less formal.

THINK ABOUT WHAT MAY BE ASKED.   Anticipate and review the questions that you might be asked during the interview. Then prepare (and possibly rehearse with a friend) your answers to these questions. For example, if you did not graduate from high school with your class but later received a general equivalency diploma (GED), you might be asked why you dropped out of school. If you have already prepared an answer for this question, it may save you the embarrassment of having to decide, on the spot, how to reduce a complicated story to a brief sentence or two.

You should also prepare yourself to be interviewed by a "team" of legal professionals, such as an attorney, a paralegal, and perhaps others from the firm. Some prospective employers invite others who will be working with a new paralegal to participate in the interviewing process.

Promptness is extremely important. Plan to arrive for the interview at least ten minutes early, and allow plenty of extra time to get there. If the firm is located in an area that is unfamiliar to you, make sure that you know how to get there, how long it will take, and, if you are driving, whether parking is available nearby.

LOOK PROFESSIONAL.   Appearance is also important. Wear a relatively conservative suit or dress to the interview, and limit your use of jewelry or other accents. You can find further tips on how to prepare for a job interview by checking online career sites or by looking at books dealing with careers and job hunting.

At the Interview

During the interview, pay attention and listen closely. Interviewers ask questions to learn whether a candidate will fit comfortably into the firm, whether the candidate is organized and competent and will satisfactorily perform the job, and whether the candidate is reliable and will work hard to master the tasks presented. Your answers should be directly related to the questions, and you should not stray from the point. If you are unsure of what the interviewer means by a certain question, ask for clarification.

Interviewers use certain question formats to elicit certain types of responses. Four typical formats for questions are the following:

- *Closed-ended questions*—to elicit simple "Yes" or "No" answers.

- *Open-ended questions*—to invite you to discuss, in some detail, a specific topic or experience.

- *Hypothetical questions*—to learn how you might respond to situations that could arise during the course of your employment.

- *Pressure questions*—to see how you deal with uncomfortable situations or unpleasant discussions.

You will learn more about question formats in Chapter 11, where we discuss some techniques that paralegals use when interviewing clients.

SOME TOPICS ARE NOT APPROPRIATE.   Certain questions are illegal or objectionable. These include questions about your marital status, family, religion, race, color, national origin, age, health or disability, or arrest record. You do not have to answer

EXHIBIT 2.8
Objectionable or Illegal Questions and Possible Responses

Q. Are you married?

A. If you are concerned that my social life will interfere with work, I can assure you that I keep the two very separate.

Q. Do you have any children yet?

A. That question leads me to believe that you would be concerned about my ability to prioritize my job and other responsibilities. Is that something that you are worried about?

Q. Are you or your husband a member of the Republican Party?

A. That is a private matter. Please realize that my family and political life will not interfere with my ability to do excellent work for your firm.

Q. You're quite a bit more mature than other applicants. Will you be thinking of retiring in the next ten years?

A. I don't understand how my age relates to my ability to perform this job.

© Cengage Learning 2014

such questions unless you choose to do so. Exhibit 2.8 above shows some examples of how you might respond to these types of questions. Note that because of record-keeping requirements imposed by the federal Equal Employment Opportunity Commission, an employer is likely to ask you to fill out a form that details your race, age, and other personal facts. This information is needed for the record but is not to be discussed in the interview process.

BE READY TO RESPOND. As odd as it may seem, one of the most difficult moments is when the interviewer turns the inquiry around by asking, "Now then, do you have any questions?" Be prepared for this. Before the interview, take time to list your concerns. Bring the list to the interview with you. Questioning the interviewer gives you an opportunity to learn more about the firm and how it uses paralegal services. Questioning the interviewer also reveals how you might interview a client on behalf of the firm. Exhibit 2.9 below lists some sample questions that you might ask the interviewer. You should not raise the issue of salary at the first interview unless you are offered the job. It is also not wise to ask early in the process about vacation time. The employer wants someone eager to work, not to take time off.

EXHIBIT 2.9
Questioning the Interviewer

Questions that you might want to ask the interviewer include the following:

- What method does the firm use to assign duties to paralegals?
- How do paralegals function within the organization?
- What clerical support is available for paralegals?
- Does the job involve travel? How will travel expenses be covered?
- What computer technology is used by the firm?
- Does the firm support paralegal continuing education and training programs?
- Will client contact be direct or indirect?
- Does the firm have an in-house library and access to computerized research services that paralegals can use?
- Will the paralegal be assigned work in a given specialty, such as real estate or family law?
- When does the job begin?
- What method is used to review and evaluate paralegal performance?
- How are paralegals supervised, and by whom?
- Are paralegals classified as exempt employees by this firm?
- Is there a written job description or employee policy manual for the job that I may review?

© Cengage Learning 2014

After the Interview

You should not expect to be hired as the result of one interview, although occasionally this does happen. Often, two and even three interviews take place before you are offered a job. After leaving the interview, jot down a few notes to provide a refresher for your memory should you be called back for a second (or third) interview. You will impress the interviewer if you are able to "pick up where you left off" from a discussion initiated several weeks earlier. Also, list the names and positions of the people you met during the interview process.

The Follow-Up/Thank-You Letter

A day or two after the interview, but not longer than a week later, you should send a *follow-up letter* to the interviewer. In this brief letter, you can mention again your availability and interest in the position, thank the interviewer for his or her time in interviewing you, and perhaps refer to a discussion that took place during the interview.

You may have left the interview with the impression that the meeting went poorly. But the interviewer may have a different sense of what happened at the meeting. Interviewers have different styles, and what you interpreted to be a bad interview may just have been a reflection of that interviewer's style. You simply have no way of being certain, so follow through and make yourself available for the job or at least for another meeting. For an example of a follow-up letter, see Exhibit 2.10 on the facing page.

Job-Hunting Files

In addition to keeping your professional portfolio materials up to date, you need to construct a filing system to stay on top of your job-search activities. Create a separate file for each potential employer, and keep copies of your letters, including e-mail messages, to that employer in your file, along with any responses. You might also want to keep lists or notes for addresses, telephone numbers, e-mail addresses, dates of contacts, advantages and disadvantages of employment with the various firms that you have contacted or by which you have been interviewed, topics discussed at interviews, and the like. Then, when you are called for an initial or repeat interview, you will have information on the firm at your fingertips. Always keep in mind that when looking for paralegal employment, your "job" is finding work as a paralegal—and it pays to be efficient.

Your files will also provide you with an excellent resource for networking even after you have a permanent position. The files may also provide useful information for a career change in the future.

Salary Negotiations

Sometimes a firm states a salary or a salary range in its advertisement for a paralegal. During a first interview, a prospective employer may offer that information as well. In other situations, an applicant does not know what the salary for a certain position will be until he or she is offered the job.

When you are offered a job, be prepared for the prospective employer to indicate a salary figure and ask you if that figure is acceptable to you. If it is acceptable, then you have no problem. If you think it is too low, then the situation becomes more delicate. When you have no other job offer and really need a job, you may not want to foreclose this job opportunity by saying that the salary is too low. You might instead tell the prospective employer that the job interests you and that you will consider the offer seriously. Also, remember that salary is just one factor in deciding what a job is worth to you. In addition to salary, you need to consider job benefits and other factors, including those listed in Exhibit 2.11 on page 50.

GATHER INFORMATION BEFOREHAND. Some prospective employers do not suggest a salary or a salary range but rather ask the job applicant what kind of salary he or she had in mind. You can prepare for this question by researching paralegal

EXHIBIT 2.10
A Sample Follow-Up Letter

ELENA LOPEZ

1131 North Shore Drive
Nita City, NI 48804
Telephone: (616) 555-0102 • E-mail: elopez@nitanet.net

September 3, 2013

Allen P. Gilmore, Esq.
Jeffers, Gilmore & Dunn
553 Fifth Avenue, Suite 101
Nita City, NI 48801

Dear Mr. Gilmore:

Thank you for taking time out of your busy schedule to meet with me last Thursday about your firm's paralegal position. I very much enjoyed our discussion, as well as the opportunity to meet some of your firm's employees.

I am extremely interested in the possibility of becoming a member of your legal team and look forward to the prospect of meeting with you again in the near future.

Sincerely yours,

Elena Lopez

Elena Lopez

© Cengage Learning 2014

salaries in the area. You can find information on salaries by checking local, state, and national paralegal compensation surveys. Check first with your local paralegal association to see if it has collected data on local paralegal salaries. You might also find helpful information in your school's placement office.

Suppose that you have found in your research that paralegals in the community usually start at $39,000 but that many with your education and training start at $46,000. If you ask for $48,000, then you may be unrealistically expensive—and the job offer may be lost. If you ask for $46,000, then you are still "in the ballpark"—and you may win the job.

RESPOND CAREFULLY.   Negotiating salaries can be difficult. On the one hand, you want to obtain a good salary and do not want to underprice your services. On the other hand, overpricing your services may extinguish an employment opportunity or eliminate the possibility of working for an otherwise suitable employer. Your best option might be to state a salary range that is acceptable to you. That way, you are not pinned down to a specific figure. Note, though, that if you indicate an acceptable salary range, you invite an offer of the lowest salary—so the low end of the salary range should be the threshold amount that you will accept.

Enhancing Your Career

Once you have gained several years' experience working as a paralegal, you can undertake the third step in career planning: reevaluating your career goals and reassessing your abilities based on your accumulated experience. Paralegals who want to advance in their careers normally have three options: (1) being promoted or transferring to another department or branch office of the firm; (2) moving to another firm, and perhaps another specialty; and (3) going back to school for additional education. Let us consider some factors that will come into play and how you can be proactive in constructing your career.

Career Paths

Large firms often provide career paths for their paralegal employees. Moving from the entry-level position of *legal-assistant clerk* to the position of *legal-assistant manager*, for example, may be one career track within a large law firm. A career track with a state government agency might begin at a *legal-technician* level and advance to a *legal-specialist* level.

Creating Opportunities

Smaller firms usually have no specific career path or opportunities for promotion and advancement. If you are the only paralegal in a small law firm, there will be no career path for you to follow. In this situation, you might stay with the firm and create your own position or career ladder. Moving up the ladder is often a matter of bringing in someone new to assist you with your responsibilities.

EXHIBIT 2.11
Salary Negotiations: What Is This Job Worth to You?

BENEFITS

What benefits are included? • Will the benefits package include medical insurance? • Life insurance? • Disability insurance? • Dental insurance? • What portion, if any, of the insurance premium will be deducted from your wages? • Is there an employee pension plan? • How many paid vacation days will you have? • Will the firm cover your paralegal association fees? • Will the firm assist you with tuition and other costs associated with continuing paralegal education? • Will the firm assist with day-care arrangements and/or costs? • Will you have access to a company car? • Does the firm help with parking expenses (important in major cities)?

CAREER OPPORTUNITIES

Does the position offer you opportunities for advancement? You may be willing to accept a lower salary now if you know that it will increase as you move up the career ladder.

COMPENSATION

Will you receive an annual salary or be paid by the hour? • If you will receive an annual salary, will you receive annual bonuses? • How are bonuses determined? • Is the salary negotiable? (In some large firms and in government agencies, it may not be.)

COMPETITION

How stiff is the competition for this job? If you really want the job and are competing with numerous other candidates for the position, you might want to accept a lower salary just to land the job.

JOB DESCRIPTION

What are the paralegal's duties within the organization? Do you have sufficient training and experience to handle these duties? • Are you underqualified or overqualified for the job? • Will your skills as a paralegal be utilized effectively? • How much overtime work will likely be required? • How stressful will the job be?

JOB FLEXIBILITY

How flexible are the working hours? • If you work eight hours of overtime one week, can you take a (paid) day off the following week? • Can you take time off during periods when the workload is less?

LOCATION

Do you want to live in this community? • What is the cost of living in this area? Remember, a $50,000 salary in New York City, where housing and taxes are very expensive, may not give you as much real income as a $38,000 salary in a smaller community in the Midwest.

PERMANENCE

Is the job a permanent or a temporary position? Usually, hourly rates are higher for temporary assistance than for permanent employees.

TRAVEL

Will you be required to travel? • If so, how often or extensively? • How will travel expenses be handled? Will you pay them and then be reimbursed by the employer?

Are you prevented from taking on more complicated tasks (which you are capable of performing) because of your heavy workload, much of which could be handled by a paralegal with less experience? Suggest a plan to your employer that shows how you can provide more valuable legal services if you delegate some of your existing responsibilities to a new employee. One of the advantages of working for a small firm is the lack of any set, formal structure for promotions. If the firm is expanding, the paralegal may have significant input into how and to whom responsibilities will be assigned as new people are hired.

You can also create opportunities by acquiring additional education. If you are interested in a particular specialty area, course work in that area, in addition to your existing paralegal training and experience, may help land a job that can advance your career. Alternatively, you might decide to work toward an advanced degree, such as a master's in business administration (MBA), to create new career opportunities. Some paralegals opt to go to law school and become attorneys. Whatever your decision, remember that the structure of law practice will continue to evolve, as the *Practice Focus* feature below explains.

Using Social Media Properly

Social media will be a key factor in determining your success in your paralegal career. Your online reputation, often called your *digital shadow,* will affect how future employers, your current employer, clients, opposing counsel, and others see you. You should assume that all your postings to Facebook, Twitter, Google+, LinkedIn, and other social media can be seen by everyone with whom you interact. Make sure that nothing you post diminishes your reputation.

PRACTICE focus

CHANGING TECHNOLOGY AND THE PRACTICE OF LAW

Technology continues to reshape the practice of law and the roles of lawyers, paralegals, and related professionals. The first wave of legal technology made legal professionals more productive at doing the jobs they were already doing. Document-creation software made it easier to draft documents. Computerized form banks helped speed document production for real estate closings or other transactions, and computer-based legal research (discussed in Chapter 8) brought legal researchers access to nearly all legal documents.

The second technology wave is bringing outsourcing to lawyers and other specialists outside of the United States, who typically work for lower rates. SunLexis is a company in India that provides litigation consulting for law firms, businesses, and individuals for up to two-thirds less than American lawyers charge. Among the services the firm offers are e-discovery (discussed in Chapter 10)

and document review services. Such firms can take over routine or tedious tasks from U.S.-based law firms, but they cannot provide legal advice or do other functions that require a law license.

This growing industry operates to make existing law firms more efficient. For paralegals, these firms offer opportunities to play a greater role in managing areas such as discovery, rather than engaging as much in traditional activities such as document review.

The third wave is the rise of social media in the law. Many firms are just beginning to explore how to use social media in the practice of law. Industry leaders are focusing on increasing productivity within the firm through internal social networks and marketing their services through external social media activities like Twitter and Facebook. To succeed in your career as a paralegal, invest in keeping current on the latest social media tools so you can assist in your firm's efforts and also market yourself. Remember to review your online presence on a regular basis and keep on top of the latest developments in social media tools.

Digital Shadow

You influence how people perceive your digital shadow. Social media expert Scott Klososky (**www.klososky.com**) pioneered the idea of online reputation management. In *Manager's Guide to Social Media,* he explains that your reputation isn't something that just happens to you or that you have no influence over. If you invest effort in creating an online reputation, you will see positive results. If you do not pay attention to what exists online, people will form their perception based on their searches.

You can invest in your digital shadow in four important ways:

1. Perhaps most important is what you do not do. Do not engage in heated arguments, post unprofessional photos, reveal personal information, suggest you do not work hard, or disparage your employer. A lawyer at a large New York firm accidentally sent an e-mail to his firm's entire practice group bragging about his two-hour sushi lunch and lack of productivity.

2. Keep your profiles on career sites such as LinkedIn and social sites such as Facebook consistent and up-to-date.

3. Monitor your online presence using a range of tools such as Google Alerts and Socialmention.com.

4. Create content online that will give a positive impression of you. Write professionally and clearly, post regularly, and share useful information.

Manage How Others See You

By being proactive and managing your digital shadow, you can enhance your future career prospects and help ensure that those you deal with both online and offline have a positive impression of your professionalism, your abilities, and your work ethic. As you have seen already, there are tips on effective use of social media in the margins throughout this book to give you further ideas about being connected productively in our online world.

Other Options to Consider

There are many other alternatives. You may apply for a job with another firm that offers you a better position or more advancement opportunities. You might apply for a position that has become available in a branch office of your firm. You might volunteer to speak to paralegal classes. In so doing, you establish new contacts and contribute to paralegal professional development. Researching and writing law-related articles for your paralegal association's newsletter or trade magazine improves your professional stature in the legal community as well. Any of these activities will increase your visibility both inside and outside the firm. These activities are part of networking. The people you meet may offer you employment opportunities that you did not even know existed.

KEY TERMS AND CONCEPTS

bankruptcy law　30	family law　31	plaintiff　27
bonus　34	freelance paralegal　26	probate　30
civil law　31	independent paralegal　26	probate court　30
contract　27	insurance　29	real estate　27
corporate law　27	intellectual property　30	state bar association　37
criminal law　32	legal nurse consultant (LNC)　33	tort　29
defendant　27	legal technician　26	trade journal　38
elder law　32	litigation　27	trust　30
environmental law　31	litigation paralegal　27	will　30
estate planning　30	networking　36	workers' compensation statutes　29

Chapter Summary

Career Opportunities

WHERE PARALEGALS WORK

1. *Law firms*—More than two-thirds of paralegals work in law firms—most of them in firms employing fewer than twenty attorneys. A small firm allows a legal assistant to gain experience in a number of areas of law and to work in a less formal environment. Paralegals in small firms often earn less than those in large firms, however, and often must perform secretarial duties. Paralegals working for large firms tend to specialize in a few areas of law, enjoy better employee benefits, and have more support staff.

2. *Corporations and other businesses*—About one-fifth of legal assistants work in corporations. Corporate legal departments may have hundreds of attorneys and paralegals on staff. Paralegals working for corporations work regular hours, do not have to be concerned with billable hours (discussed in Chapter 3), and generally receive above-average salaries. They may specialize in certain aspects of corporate law. In addition, paralegals work in many other public and private institutions, such as insurance companies, banks, real estate companies, title insur-

ance companies, legal-software companies, and law schools.

3. *Government*—Paralegals work in many government administrative agencies, such as the Social Security Administration. Other employment opportunities exist with legislative offices, public prosecutors' offices, public defenders' offices, and federal and state courts.

4. *Legal aid offices*—Some paralegals find it rewarding to work in legal aid offices, which provide legal services to those who find it difficult to pay for legal representation. These offices are largely funded by the government, but some support comes from private foundations.

5. *Freelance paralegals*—Some experienced paralegals own their businesses and work for attorneys on a contract basis. This work can have more flexible working hours and often can be done from a home office. The success (and income) of a paralegal in this area depends on the person's skill, business sense, and motivation.

PARALEGAL SPECIALTIES

Many paralegals specialize in one or two areas of law. The five areas in which the largest numbers of paralegals currently specialize are litigation, corporate law, contract law, real estate law, and personal-injury law. Other areas in which a legal assistant can specialize include insurance law, employment and labor law, estate planning and probate administration, bankruptcy law, intellectual property law, environmental law, family law, criminal law, elder law, and legal nurse consulting.

PARALEGAL COMPENSATION

Salaries and wage rates for paralegal employees vary. Factors affecting compensation include location, firm size, years of experience, and type of employer (law firm, corporation, or government agency). When evaluating a job, paralegals should consider not only salary or wages but also job benefits, such as insurance coverage, sick/vacation/holiday leave, and pension plans.

PLANNING YOUR CAREER

Career planning involves three steps: defining your long-term career goals, devising short-term goals and adjusting those goals to fit job realities, and reevaluating your career and career goals after you have had some on-the-job experience.

Continued

LOCATING POTENTIAL EMPLOYERS

When looking for employment, paralegals should apply the investigative skills that they learned in their paralegal training.

1. *Networking*—Many jobs come through networking with other professionals. You can begin networking while you are a student. If your local paralegal association allows students to become members, join the association. Knowing others in the legal community is a great asset when looking for a job.

2. *Finding available jobs*—You can locate potential employers by reviewing published and posted information about law firms and other possible employers. Advertisements can be found in trade journals, in newspapers, on the Internet, and at your school's placement office. Check legal directories for lists of law offices.

3. *Job-placement services*—

   a. **SCHOOL PLACEMENT SERVICES**—Paralegals should stay in contact with their school's placement office, which is often staffed with personnel trained to assist paralegals with job hunting.

   b. **LEGAL STAFFING OR PRIVATE PLACEMENT COMPANIES**—Paralegals may locate employment through private placement companies. Usually, the employer pays the placement company's fees, and the company recruits candidates for the position and schedules interviews. Placements may be for temporary or long-term positions. Paralegals can find out about job-placement companies through school program directors, local paralegal associations, state bar associations, or the Web.

MARKETING YOUR SKILLS

1. *The application process*—Prepare a professional résumé to outline your educational and work background. Do not include personal details. The cover letter that accompanies your résumé represents you, so draft it carefully. You should also have available a professional portfolio and a list of persons who have agreed to be professional references.

2. *The interview*—Do background research on a firm prior to your interview. Think through the answers you will give to likely questions, and be prepared to ask questions that indicate your interest and knowledge. After an interview, make notes of relevant issues so you can discuss them if called back.

3. *The follow-up/thank-you letter*—After an interview, send a personalized thank-you letter expressing continued interest.

4. *Job-hunting files*—Keep your records organized as you look for work by creating a filing system for all your job-search activities.

5. *Salary negotiations*—Some employers will ask you to specify an acceptable salary. Be prepared to give a salary or a salary range, depending on the job requirements. Research information about the salaries paralegals earn in your area.

ENHANCING YOUR CAREER

Career goals change over time, as do job opportunities. Advancing in your career may mean educating your employer about your abilities so that you can take on more responsibility, looking for a job in a different department or branch office of the same firm or with another firm, or attending continuing education programs. Skillful use of social media creates links and impressions about your ability. Participating in paralegal professional organizations or in paralegal education is a way to achieve higher visibility in the profession and to learn of new professional opportunities.

QUESTIONS FOR REVIEW

1. Name and describe five types of organizations that hire paralegals. Where do most paralegals work?

2. List and briefly describe each of the paralegal specialties discussed in this chapter. Which specialty area or areas interest you the most? Why?

3. How can paralegals locate potential employers? What is networking? How might networking help paralegals find jobs?

4. Of the methods suggested in this chapter for locating potential employers, which method do you think would be the most effective? Why?

ETHICAL QUESTION

Dennis Walker works at a very busy law firm. On his desk, besides a computer and telephone, there are stacks of work, leaving only enough room for a small work space in the center of the desk. His floor is likewise stacked high with legal documents. Dennis constantly misses deadlines and is often in trouble for turning work in late or doing work incorrectly. Dennis has tried to get organized but feels that it is impossible to do so because he has such a heavy workload. What are Dennis's ethical obligations in this situation?

PRACTICE QUESTIONS AND ASSIGNMENTS

1. In addition to the traditional law firm, for what types of employers do paralegals work?

2. What are some advantages and disadvantages of working for a small law firm? What are some advantages and disadvantages of working for a large law firm? Which would you prefer to do? Why?

QUESTION FOR CRITICAL ANALYSIS

What are your long-term career goals? Do your short-term goals relate logically to the attainment of your long-term goals? Why or why not? Compose one to two paragraphs explaining your long-term goals and how your short-term goals relate to them. Write these paragraphs as if you would share them with a potential employer.

PROJECTS

1. Locate the *Martindale-Hubbell Law Directory* or the *West Legal Directory* in your library or online. Find three law firms in your locale that practice areas of law in which you are interested. Record the names and addresses of the firms. Also try to find the names of the hiring partners or human resources managers whom you could contact about a job in the future. Start your job file today!

2. Draft a résumé for yourself using the ones in this chapter for guidance. Think of your strong suits that should be highlighted. Also, write a cover letter that introduces yourself in a favorable manner.

GROUP PROJECT

The group selects a legal specialty discussed in this chapter. Students one and two research the legal specialty by finding an article about it from a paralegal publication or Web site. They also write a one-page summary of the article, including the pros and cons of working in this specialty. Student three interviews a paralegal who works in this practice area, and likewise discusses the pros and cons of the specialty during the interview. Student four summarizes the results of both the research and the interview and presents the results to the class.

USING INTERNET RESOURCES

1. On the Internet, access LAW MATCH, an online résumé bank, at **www.lawmatch.com**. How do you use it? Would you post your résumé there? Why or why not? If you are currently looking for a position, try posting your résumé on that site.

2. Visit the Web site for *Paralegal Today* magazine at **www.paralegaltoday.com**. You will find many useful articles about the paralegal profession, education, and employment. Select an article about paralegal education, and write a three-paragraph summary of the article. Print and attach the first page of the article to submit with your summary.

CourseMate The available CourseMate for this text has an interactive eBook and interactive learning tools, including flash cards, quizzes, and more. To learn more about this resource and access free demo CourseMate resources, go to **www.cengagebrain.com**, and search for this book. To access CourseMate materials that you have purchased, go to **login.cengagebrain.com**.

The Inner Workings of the Law Office

Chapter Outline

Introduction

The Organizational Structure of Law Firms

Law Office Management and Personnel

Employment Policies

Filing Procedures

Law Firms and Financial Procedures

Communications

Law Office Culture and Politics

After completing this chapter, you will know:

- How law firms are organized and managed.

- Some typical policies and procedures governing paralegal employment.

- The importance of an efficient filing system in legal practice and some typical filing procedures.

- How clients are billed for legal services.

- How law office culture and politics affect the paralegal's working environment.

Introduction

The wide variety of environments in which paralegals work makes it impossible to predict exactly how the firm where you will work will be run. Typically, though, the way in which that firm operates will relate, at least in part, to the firm's form of business organization. Because most paralegals are employed by private law firms, this chapter focuses on the organization, management, and procedures characteristic of these firms.

First, we look at how the size and structure of a law firm affect the paralegal's working environment. As you would imagine, the working environment in a firm owned and operated by one attorney is significantly different from that in a large law firm with two or three hundred attorneys. Different still is the working climate of a large corporate enterprise or a government agency.

We then look at other aspects of the working environment of paralegals. Typically, a law firm will have specific policies and procedures relating to employment conditions, filing systems, billing and timekeeping procedures, and financial procedures. We conclude the chapter with a brief discussion of law office culture and politics.

The Organizational Structure of Law Firms

Law firms range in size from one-attorney firms to megafirms with hundreds of attorneys. Regardless of their size, law firms typically organize as sole proprietorships, partnerships, LLPs, or professional corporations. As the conditions for law practice change, however, the structure of firms evolves, as discussed in the *Practice Focus* feature below. Because the way in which a business is organized affects the office environment, we next look briefly at each of these three major organizational forms. These organizational forms and others will be discussed in greater detail in Chapter 18.

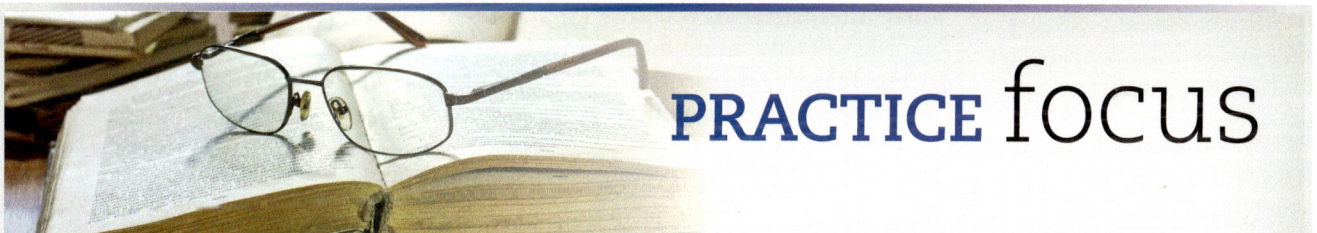

PRACTICE focus

EVOLVING LAW PRACTICE

The practice of law changes as the needs of clients change. For example, the world financial crisis that began in 2007 caused law firms that focus on business issues to change various aspects of their operations. In the past, many law firms aspired to be full-service firms, offering nearly every area of practice within the firm. Others sought to be boutique firms, staying small and focusing on a highly specialized practice.

Recently, some firms that strove to be one-stop-shops have transferred entire areas of their legal practice to competitors. For example, the worldwide law firm CMS Cameron McKenna transferred its immigration practice to Fragomen, Del Rey, Bernsen and Loewy, LLP. The Fragomen firm is itself very large, listed in *American Lawyer* magazine's "AMLAW 200" ranking of the 200 largest firms.

The Fragomen firm is highly focused on a single area of practice: immigration. It might be called a super-boutique firm. With over 200 lawyers, it is much larger than its nearest competitor, a firm with just 35 lawyers. Fragomen handles a high volume of cases, with more than 50,000 immigration transactions a year, primarily on a fixed-fee basis. The firm uses technology extensively and has been a leader in the application of computers to the practice of law. Its paralegals have access to a digital best-practices library of flowcharts that show how each transaction should be handled.

Particularly important for paralegals, the Fragomen firm uses more than 500 paralegals, with a paralegal-to-lawyer ratio of more than 2 to 1, and hundreds more of other non-attorney professionals. As more firms adopt the Fragomen model, opportunities for paralegals are likely to increase.

Sole Proprietorships

The **sole proprietorship** is the simplest business form and is often used by attorneys when they first set up legal practices. In a sole proprietorship, one individual—the sole proprietor—owns the business. The sole proprietor is entitled to any profits made by the firm but is also personally liable for all of the firm's debts or obligations. **Personal liability** means that the owner's personal assets (such as a home, savings or investment accounts, and other property) may have to be sacrificed to pay business obligations if the business fails. Because of the liability risk faced by a sole proprietor, most are organized as a Professional Corporation (P.C.) or another form, as discussed below.

Solo Practitioner

An attorney who practices law as a sole proprietor is often called a *sole (solo) practitioner*. To save on office overhead expenses, a sole practitioner may share an office with other attorneys. A paralegal may split time among sole practitioners who share an office and staff.

Wide Experience

Working for a sole practitioner with a general practice is a good way for a paralegal to learn about law office procedures because the paralegal will typically perform a wide variety of tasks. Many sole practitioners hire one person to act as secretary, paralegal, administrator, and manager. Paralegals holding this kind of position would probably handle many tasks: receiving and date-stamping the mail, printing out e-mails, organizing and maintaining the filing system, interviewing clients and witnesses, bookkeeping (receiving payments from clients, preparing and sending bills to clients, and the like), conducting investigations and legal research, drafting legal documents, assisting the attorney in trial preparation and perhaps in the courtroom, and other jobs, including office administration.

Working for a sole practitioner is a good way to find out which area of law you most enjoy because you will learn about procedures relating to many different areas. Alternatively, if you work for a sole practitioner who specializes in one area of law, you will have an opportunity to develop expertise in that area. In sum, working in a small law firm gives you an overview of law office procedures and legal practice that will help you throughout your career.

Partnerships

Most law firms are organized as partnerships, limited liability partnerships, or professional corporations. In a **partnership**, two or more people do business jointly as **partners**. A partnership may consist of just a few attorneys or over a hundred attorneys. In a partnership, each partner owns a share of the business and shares in the firm's profits or losses.

In smaller partnerships, the partners may participate equally in managing the partnership. They will likely meet to make decisions about clients, policies, procedures, and other matters important to the firm. In larger partnerships, managerial decisions are usually made by a committee of partners, one of whom may be designated as the **managing partner**.

Partnerships (and professional corporations, which are discussed below) frequently employ other attorneys who are not partners in the firm and thus do not share in the profits. Typically, these other attorneys are called **associate attorneys**. They are usually less experienced attorneys and may be invited to become partners after working for the firm for several years. Sometimes, firms hire **staff attorneys**, who work for the firm but will never become partners. Staff attorneys differ from *contract attorneys,* who provide services for busy firms on a project basis. Many firms also hire **law clerks**—law students who work for the firm during the summer or part-time during the school year to gain practical legal experience. Law clerks who

---

sole proprietorship

The simplest form of business organization, in which the owner is the business. Anyone who does business without creating a formal business entity has a sole proprietorship.

personal liability

An individual's personal responsibility for debts or obligations. The owners of sole proprietorships and partnerships are personally liable for the debts and obligations incurred by their businesses. If their firms go bankrupt or cannot meet debts, the owners will be personally responsible for the debts.

partnership

An association of two or more persons to carry on, as co-owners, a business for profit.

partner

A person who operates a business jointly with one or more other persons. Each partner is a co-owner of the business firm.

managing partner

The partner in a law firm who makes decisions relating to the firm's policies and procedures and who generally oversees the business operations of the firm.

associate attorney

An attorney working for a law firm who is not a partner and does not have an ownership interest in the firm. Associates are usually less experienced attorneys and may be invited to become partners after working for the firm for several years.

staff attorney

An attorney hired by a law firm as an employee. A staff attorney has no ownership rights in the firm and will not be invited to become a partner in the firm.

law clerk

A law student working as an apprentice with a law firm to gain practical experience.

meet with the approval of the members of the firm are often offered positions as associates when they graduate and pass the bar exam.

Liability of Partners

Like sole proprietors, attorneys in a partnership are personally liable for the debts and obligations of the business if the business fails. In addition, a partner can be held personally responsible for the misconduct or debts of another partner. For example, suppose a client sues a partner in the firm for malpractice and wins a large judgment. The firm carries malpractice insurance, but it is insufficient to pay the obligation. The court will order the attorney who committed the wrongful act to pay the balance due. Once the responsible attorney's personal assets are exhausted, the assets of the other (innocent) partners can be used to pay the judgment. This unlimited personal liability of partners is a disadvantage for law firms organized as partnerships.

Limited Liability Partnership (LLP)

In recent years, a form of partnership called the **limited liability partnership (LLP)** became available to firms. The LLP normally allows professionals to avoid personal liability for the malpractice of other partners. Although LLP statutes vary from state to state, generally state law limits the liability of partners in some way. For example, Delaware law protects each innocent partner from the "debts and obligations of the partnership arising from negligence, wrongful acts, or misconduct." You will read more about LLPs in Chapter 18. Note that professionals who are not attorneys can also organize as an LLP and that this form of business provides certain tax advantages as well as limits to the partners' liability.

limited liability partnership (LLP)
A business organizational form designed for professionals who normally do business as partners in a partnership. The LLP limits the personal liability of partners.

Professional Corporations

A **professional corporation (P.C.)** is a corporation formed by licensed professionals, such as lawyers or physicians. Like other kinds of corporations, it is owned by **shareholders**, so called because they have purchased the corporation's stock, or shares, and thus own a share of the business. The shareholders share in the profits and losses of the firm in proportion to how many shares they own. Their personal liability, unlike that of partners, may or may not be limited to the amount of their investments, depending on the circumstances and on state law. Limited personal liability is one of the key advantages of this corporate form of business.

In many respects, the professional corporation is run like a partnership, and the distinction between these two forms of business organization is often more a legal formality than an operational reality. Because of this, attorneys who organize their business as a professional corporation are nonetheless sometimes referred to as partners. For simplicity, in this chapter we will refer to anyone who has ownership rights in the firm as a partner.

professional corporation (P.C.)
A corporation formed by licensed professionals, such as lawyers or physicians. The liability of shareholders is often limited to the amount of their investments.

shareholder
One who purchases corporate stock, or shares, and who thus becomes an owner of the corporation.

Law Office Management and Personnel

When you take a job as a paralegal, you will want to quickly learn the relative status of the office personnel. Particularly, you will want to know who has authority over you and to whom you are accountable. You will also want to know who is accountable to you—whether you have an assistant or a secretary (or share an assistant or a secretary with another paralegal), for example. In a small firm, you will have no problem learning this information. If you work for a larger law firm, the lines of authority may be more difficult to perceive. Your supervisor will probably instruct you on the relative status of the firm's personnel. If you are not sure about who has authority over whom and what kinds of tasks are performed by various employees, you should ask your supervisor.

Professionalism and Courtesy

Regardless of formal lines of authority, it is important to be courteous and professional with all your colleagues. You may outrank a partner's secretary on paper, but if the partner and secretary have a long history of working together, the partner is likely to pay close attention to the secretary's views.

The lines of authority and accountability vary from firm to firm, depending on the firm's size and its management preferences. A sample organizational chart for a relatively small law partnership is shown in Exhibit 3.1 below. The decision makers in the firm represented by that chart are the partners. Next in authority are the associate attorneys and law clerks. The paralegals are supervised by both the attorneys (in regard to legal work) and the office manager (in regard to office procedural and paralegal staffing matters). In larger firms, there may be a **legal-assistant manager** or **paralegal manager**, who coordinates paralegal staffing and programs relating to paralegal educational and professional development.

Besides attorneys and paralegals, law firm employees include administrative personnel. In large firms, the partners may hire a **legal administrator** to run the business end of the firm. The legal administrator might delegate some authority to an office manager and other supervisory employees.

Variety of Support Staff

In small and medium-size firms, such as those represented in Exhibit 3.1, an **office manager** handles the administrative aspects of the firm. The legal administrator or office manager typically is in charge of docketing (calendaring) legal work undertaken by the attorneys; establishing and overseeing filing procedures; implementing new legal technology, such as new docketing software; ordering and monitoring supplies; and generally making sure that the office runs smoothly and that office procedures are established and followed. In a small firm, the office manager might also handle client billing procedures. The firm represented in Exhibit 3.1 has an accountant to perform this function.

The **support personnel** in a large law office may include secretaries, receptionists, bookkeepers, file clerks, messengers, and others. Depending on their functions and specific jobs, support personnel may fall under the supervision of any number of other personnel in the firm. In a very small firm, just one person—the legal secretary, for example—may perform all of the above-mentioned functions. No matter the size of the office, the need for accuracy and organization is great, as described in the *In the Office* feature on the facing page.

---

legal-assistant manager
or paralegal manager
An employee in a law firm who is responsible for overseeing the paralegal staff and paralegal professional development.

legal administrator
An administrative employee of a law firm who manages day-to-day operations. In smaller law firms, legal administrators are usually called office managers.

office manager
An administrative employee who manages the day-to-day operations of a firm. In larger law firms, office managers are usually called legal administrators.

support personnel
Employees who provide clerical, secretarial, or other support to the legal, paralegal, and administrative staff of a law firm.

EXHIBIT 3.1
A Sample Organizational Chart for a Law Partnership

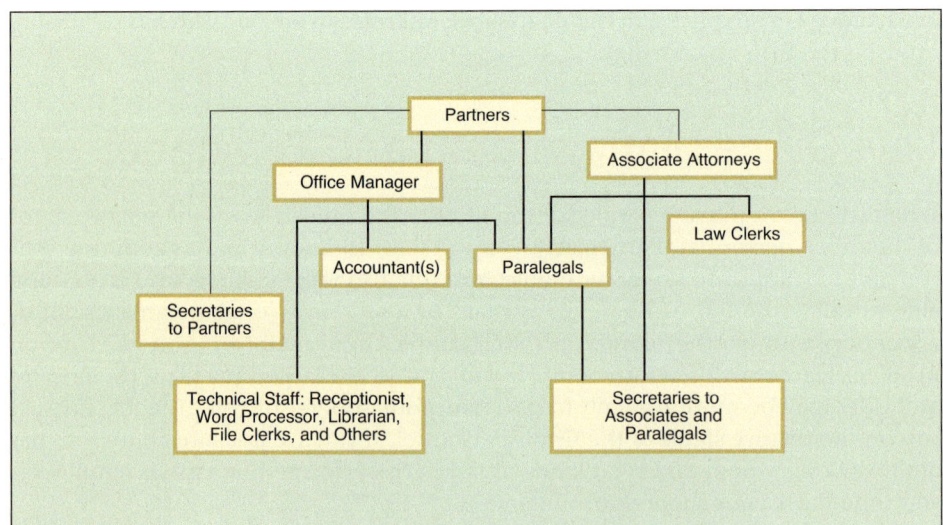

© Cengage Learning 2014

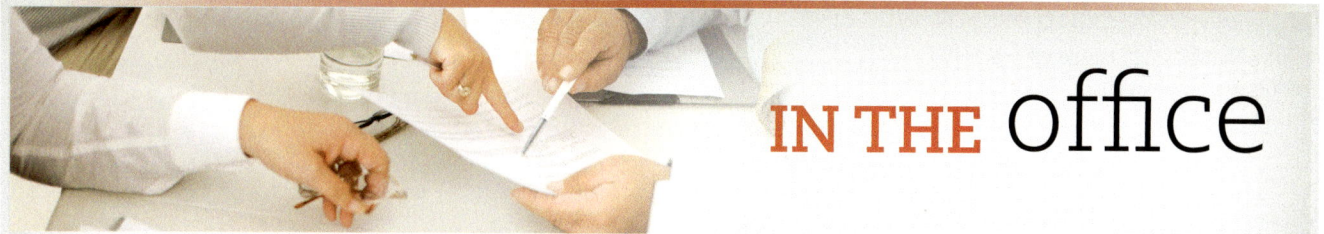

KEEP YOUR PRIORITIES IN ORDER

Staff members in a law office are frequently under pressure to meet deadlines. A paralegal can get caught between attorneys with competing demands or even between the demands of cases being handled by one supervising attorney who is under pressure. Do not let conflicts for your time build up. Discuss which tasks should be accomplished first. Identify conflicts between you and your supervisor about the best use of your limited time. Other people may forget, or may not know about, work you have to accomplish and may unintentionally be unreasonable in their expectations. Clear communications about what is needed, when work is due, and what gets priority will help you to avoid appearing unresponsive.

Employment Policies

Employees of a law firm, which include all personnel other than the partners or those who work for the firm on a contract basis, are subject to the firm's employment policies. A firm's policies governing employment may be published in an **employment manual** in larger firms. In smaller firms, these policies are often unwritten. In either case, when you take a job as a paralegal, or perhaps before you accept a position, you will want to become familiar with the firm's basic conditions of employment.

There will be a policy, for example, on how much vacation time you are entitled to during the first year, second year, and so on. Other policies will govern which holidays are observed by the firm, how much sick leave you can take, when you are expected to arrive at work, and what will serve as grounds for the employer to terminate your employment.

Employment policies vary from firm to firm. A leading concern of paralegals (and employees generally) is how much they will be paid, how they will be paid (that is, whether they will receive salaries or hourly wages), and what job benefits they will receive. These issues were discussed in Chapter 2, so we will not examine them here. Rather, we look at some other areas of concern to paralegals, including performance evaluations and termination procedures.

employment manual
A firm's handbook or written statement that specifies the policies and procedures that govern the firm's employees and employer-employee relationships.

Performance Evaluations

Many law firms conduct periodic performance evaluations to determine if employees will receive raises. Usually, performance is evaluated annually, but some firms conduct evaluations every six months, and some conduct them even more often for new employees.

Know What Is Expected of You

Because paralegal responsibilities vary from firm to firm, no one evaluation checklist applies to every paralegal. Some of the factors that may be considered during a performance evaluation are indicated in Exhibit 3.2 on the following page. Note, though, that performance evaluations are often much longer and more detailed than the list shown in the exhibit. For example, each major item in that list may have several subheadings and perhaps further subheadings under those. Normally, under each item is a series of options—ranging from "excellent" to "unsatisfactory" or something similar—for the supervisor or attorney to check.

EXHIBIT 3.2
Factors That May Be Considered in a Performance Evaluation

1. **RESPONSIBILITY**
   Making sure that all tasks are performed on time and following up on all pending matters.

2. **EFFICIENCY**
   Obtaining good results in the least amount of time possible.

3. **PRODUCTIVITY**
   Producing a sufficient quantity of work in a given time period.

4. **COMPETENCE**
   Knowledge level and skills.

5. **INITIATIVE**
   Applying intelligence and creativity to tasks and making appropriate recommendations.

6. **COOPERATION**
   Getting along well with others on the legal team.

7. **PERSONAL FACTORS**
   Appearance, grooming habits, friendliness, and poise.

8. **DEPENDABILITY**
   Arriving at work consistently on time and being available when needed.

When you begin work as a paralegal, you should learn at the outset exactly what your duties will be and what performance is expected of you. This way, you will be able to prepare for your first evaluation from the moment you begin working. You will not have to wait six months or a year before you learn that you were supposed to be doing something different.

Be Prepared

Make sure that you prepare for the evaluation and conduct yourself professionally at all times. Be your own advocate. This is especially important in larger offices, where you may not be well known to the supervisor doing your evaluation. Keep track of your accomplishments, such as the number of billable hours per week or month that you normally generate, so that you can point them out to your supervisor. If you were part of a team that worked many extra hours to win a big case for the firm, mention it during the evaluation. Make your supervisor aware of ways in which you save the firm money or contribute to the firm's success. If you master a new software program or pass the CLA (or CP) or PACE exam, tell your supervisor.

Get the Most from Your Performance Evaluation

Both paralegals and their employers can benefit from the discussions that take place during a performance evaluation. In the busy workplace, you may not have much time to talk with your supervisor about issues that do not relate to immediate work needs. Even if you do find a moment, you may feel awkward bringing up the topic of your performance or discussing a workplace problem. Performance evaluations are designed to allow both sides to exchange views on such matters.

During reviews, you will learn how the firm rates your performance. You can gain valuable feedback from your supervisor, learn more about your strengths and weaknesses, and identify the areas in which you need to improve your skills. Do not react negatively to criticisms of your performance. Even during an evaluation you are being evaluated. Adopting a positive outlook and showing that you appreciate constructive criticism will impress your supervisor.

You can also use the evaluation to give your supervisor feedback on the workplace. This is especially useful if you believe you are capable of handling more complex tasks than you are being assigned. Attorneys sometimes underutilize paralegals because they do not know their capabilities. If you suggest ways in which your knowledge could be put to better use, you may earn more challenging and rewarding responsibilities. Also, if you and your supervising attorney never seem to have the time to meet face-to-face for an evaluation, consider writing up your own evaluation and presenting it to him or her for review.

social MEDIA TODAY

Your firm needs a social media strategy because its competitors already have one. Many of its customers, current employees, and almost all of its future employees expect one.

Employment Termination

Policy manuals almost always deal with the subject of employment termination. A policy manual will likely specify what kind of conduct can serve as a basis for firing employees. For example, the manual might specify that if an employee is absent more than twelve days a year for two consecutive years, the employer has grounds to terminate the employment relationship. The manual will also probably describe termination procedures.

For example, the firm might require that it be notified one month in advance if an employee decides to leave the firm; if the employee fails to give such notice, he or she may lose accumulated vacation time or other benefits on termination. Leaving without notice will also make it harder to get a positive recommendation from the firm when you seek another position. Do not burn your bridges with an employer.

Employment Discrimination

Traditionally, employment relationships have been governed by the common law doctrine of employment at will. Under this doctrine, employers may hire and fire employees "at will"—that is, for any reason or no reason, and employees can leave a job for any or no reason. There are some exceptions to this doctrine, and state and federal statutes also regulate many aspects of the employment relationship.

Under state and federal anti-discrimination laws, employers may not refuse to hire job applicants, refuse to promote employees, or fire employees because of the employee's age, gender, or race, for example. Such laws regulating employment relationships will be discussed in Chapter 18, but it should be mentioned here that large law firms usually have special procedures that must be followed with respect to claims of employment discrimination.

For example, an employee who experiences sexual harassment—a form of gender-based discrimination that is prohibited by federal and state laws—may be required by the firm's harassment policy to follow formal complaint procedures to attempt to resolve the issue. If an employee fails to follow the required procedures, the firm may be able to avoid legal responsibility for the harassment. Similarly, if an employer does not have established procedures in place for dealing with discrimination, the employer may find it difficult to avoid liability for the discriminatory treatment by supervisors or others against an employee.

Filing Procedures

Every law firm, regardless of its size or structure, has some kind of established filing procedures. Efficient procedures are vital because the paperwork generated is substantial, and important documents must be safeguarded yet be readily retrievable when needed. The need to protect client information is stressed in the *Developing Paralegal Skills* feature on the next page. If a client file is misplaced or lost, the client may suffer costly harm.

Additionally, documents must be filed in such a way as to protect client confidentiality. The duty of confidentiality is discussed in Chapter 4, but it deserves mention here because of the extent to which it frames all legal work and procedures. This is particularly true of filing procedures. All information received from or about clients, including files and documents, is considered confidential. A breach of confidentiality by a paralegal or other employee can cause the law firm to incur extensive liability.

If you work for a small firm, filing procedures may be informal and you may need to assume the responsibility for organizing and developing an efficient and secure filing system. Larger firms normally have specific procedures concerning the creation, maintenance, use, and storage of office files. If you take a job with a large firm, a supervisor will probably train you in office procedures, including filing. Although the trend today, particularly in larger firms, is toward computerized

GOING **green**

FEWER CDs

Most computer programs require purchasers to buy a license for every computer on which the programs are installed. Rather than buy programs on discs, you can generally buy them online and download them with site licenses. Registration allows you to download a program again if you change to a new computer. That helps cut down on the production of more CDs and packaging materials.

DEVELOPING
paralegal skills

CONFIDENTIALITY AND CLIENT INFORMATION

One of the most important professional obligations of a paralegal is to treat all of your clients' information as confidential. The obligation to treat information as confidential has been long recognized by the common law, and some jurisdictions even provide criminal sanctions for professionals who violate this duty.

As a general rule, never share *any* information about your clients—even the fact that they are clients—with anyone outside your firm. Don't share "war stories" from work with friends or relatives if doing so could reveal information about the client. Never leave *any* information about your clients where others might see it.

To protect client confidentiality, you should:

- Keep all identifiable information about clients off the cover of files.
- Never leave a file unattended for even a short time in a publicly accessible location such as a library table or courtroom.

- Make sure all client files are removed from internal workspaces where outsiders might be present, such as conference rooms.
- Do not allow outsiders access to firm computer systems or networks.
- Use only secure networks or encrypted communications systems for transmission of confidential information. Most wireless networks in airports or Internet cafés are *not* secure.
- Password protect all electronic devices on which confidential matters are stored, such as smartphones that receive e-mails.
- Secure your computer when you leave your desk.

The obligation to maintain confidentiality continues even after a file is closed. Your firm should have document-retention policies that set out how long closed files are kept and how they are to be destroyed. Be sure to follow your firm's policies carefully. An excellent guide to such policies is available at **www.americanbar.org**. In the "search" box, type Lee Nemchek and it will take you to articles on this important topic.

filing systems, many firms create "hard copies" to ensure that files are not lost if computer systems crash.

Generally, law offices maintain several types of files. Typically, a law firm's filing system will include client files, work product files and reference materials, and forms files (as well as personnel files, which we do not discuss here).

Client Files

To illustrate client filing procedures, we present below the phases in the "life cycle" of a hypothetical client's file. The name of the client is Katherine Baranski. She has just retained (hired) one of your firm's attorneys to represent her in a lawsuit that she is bringing against Tony Peretto. Because Baranski is initiating the lawsuit, she is referred to as the *plaintiff*. Peretto, because he has to defend against Baranski's claims, is the *defendant*. The name of the case is *Baranski v. Peretto*. Assume that you will be working on the case and that your supervising attorney has just asked you to open a new case file. Assume also that you have already verified, through a "conflicts check" (to be discussed in Chapter 4), that no conflict of interest exists.

Opening a New Client File

The first step that you (or a secretary, at your request) will take in opening a new file is to assign the case a file number. For reasons of both efficiency and confidentiality, many firms identify their client files by numbers or some kind of numerical and/or alphabetical sequence instead of the clients' names. The *Baranski v. Peretto* case file might be identified by the letters BAPE—the first two letters of the plaintiff's name followed by the first two letters of the defendant's name.

Increasingly, law firms are using computerized databases to record and track case titles and files. For example, some firms use file labels containing bar codes that contain attorney codes, subject-matter codes, the client's name and file number, and so forth. The databases are also used for contract and billing information.

Typically, law firms maintain a master client list on which clients' names are entered alphabetically and cross-referenced to the clients' case numbers. If file numbers consist of numerical sequences, there is also a master list on which the file numbers are listed in numerical order and cross-referenced to the clients' names.

Adding Subfiles

As the work on the *Baranski* case progresses and more documents are generated or received, the file will expand. To ensure that documents will be easy to locate, you will create subfiles. One subfile might be created for client documents (such as a contract, will, stock certificate, or photograph) that the firm needs for reference or for evidence at trial. As correspondence relating to the *Baranski* case is generated, you will probably add a correspondence subfile. You will also want a subfile for your or the attorney's notes on the case, including research results.

As you will read in Chapters 10 through 12, litigation involves several stages. As the *Baranski* litigation progresses through these stages, subfiles for documents relating to each stage will be added to the *Baranski* file. Many firms find it useful to color-code or add tabs to subfiles so that they can be readily identified. Often, in large files, an index of each subfile's contents is created and attached to the inside cover of the subfile.

Documents are typically filed within each subfile in reverse chronological order, with the most recently dated document on the top. Usually, to safeguard the documents, they are punched at the top with a two-hole puncher so they can be secured within the file with a clip. Note, though, that an original client document should not be punched or altered in any way. It should always be left loose within the file (or paper-clipped to a copy of the document that *is* punched and secured in the file). For example, if you were holding in the file a property deed belonging to a client, you would not want to alter that document in any way.

File Use and Storage

Often, files are stored in a file room or area. Most firms have some kind of procedure for employees to follow when removing files from the storage area. A firm might require the office staff to replace a removed file with an "out card" indicating the date, the name of the file, and the name or initials of the person who removed it.

Note that documents should not be removed from a client file or subfile. Rather, the entire file or subfile should be removed for use. This ensures that important documents will not be separated from the file and possibly mislaid or lost. Many paralegals make copies of documents in the file for their use. For example, if you are working on the *Baranski* case and need to review certain documents in the file, you might remove them from the file temporarily, copy them, and immediately return the original documents and the file to storage.

Files and the Cloud

The latest information technology trend is "cloud-based computing." That means files and programs are stored online and so are accessible from any computer, smartphone, or tablet connected to the Internet. Law firms are cautious about giving up physical control of confidential information, because they worry about protecting clients' rights to the attorney-client privilege. Be sure to clear any use of cloud storage on your personal devices such as smartphones, tablets, and laptops with your firm. Do not put business information in your iCloud-connected Apple device or on a cloud storage site such as Dropbox without discussing it with your firm.

Even the fact that your firm is representing a client may be something the client wants kept confidential. Storing something as simple as contact information in a

social
MEDIA TODAY

Hackers can be hired almost as easily as a plumber. Never leave a laptop or iPad containing confidential information unattended in a public place. Never work on confidential files outside a secure environment.

mobile phone cloud "app" could result in revealing the fact of a relationship with the law firm. Be particularly cautious about leaving your portable devices logged on to cloud apps while using public wireless networks or in public places where electronic eavesdropping may occur.

Closing a File

Assume that the *Baranski* case has been settled out of court and that no further legal work on Baranski's behalf needs to be done. For a time, her file will be retained in the inactive files, but when it is fairly certain that no one will need to refer to it very often, if ever, it will be closed. Closed files are often stored in a separate area of the building or even off-site. Traditionally, many larger law firms stored the contents of old files on microfilm. Today, firms can use scanning technology to scan file contents for storage on on-site hard drives and off-site servers.

Specific procedures for closing files vary from firm to firm. Typically, when a case is closed, original documents provided by the client (for example, a deed to property) are returned to the client. Other materials, such as extra copies of documents or cover letters, are destroyed.

Destroying Old Files

Law firms do not have to retain client files forever, and at some point, the *Baranski* case file will be destroyed. Old files are normally destroyed by shredding so that confidentiality is preserved. Because shredded files can be pieced back together, many firms hire companies that have equipment guaranteed to destroy such materials so recovery is impossible. Law firms use great care when destroying client files because a court or government agency may impose a heavy fine on a law firm that destroys a file that should have been retained for a longer time. How long a particular file must be retained depends on many factors, including the nature of the client's legal matters and governing statutes, such as the statute of limitations.

Statutes of limitations limit the time period during which specific types of legal actions may be brought to court. Statutes of limitations for legal-malpractice actions vary from state to state—from six months to ten years after the attorney's last contact with the client. When the statute of limitations in your state expires is an important factor in determining how long to retain a client file, because an attorney or law firm will need the information contained in the client's file to defend against a malpractice action. If the file has been destroyed, the firm will not be able to produce any documents or other evidence to refute the plaintiff's claim.

Retention Policy

Your firm will have a document retention policy, and you should become very familiar with it. These are firm-wide policies on retaining documents related to particular matters. Importantly, these include policies on the retention of e-mails. Learn how your firm archives e-mails and what your responsibilities are with respect to maintaining those archives. In many cases, e-mails sent through firm computer systems (including smartphones provided by your firm) may be archived even if you delete them.

E-Mail Policy

Not only must you be careful to comply with firm policies on retaining e-mails, but any inappropriate use of a work-related e-mail account or device may leave evidence on servers or in archives. For example, a California firefighter found himself in trouble after his employer discovered his use of a work-provided two-way pager to send explicit text messages to his girlfriend. He did that while on duty. The employer uncovered the improper use by reviewing archived records of messages on the pager company's servers. The matter ended up before the U.S. Supreme Court. It held that the employer was entitled to know if employer-provided equipment was being used inappropriately.

statute of limitations
A statute setting the maximum time period within which certain actions can be brought to court or rights enforced. After the period of time has run, no legal action can be brought.

Work Product Files and Reference Materials

Many law firms keep copies of research projects, legal memoranda, and various case-related documents prepared by the firm's attorneys and paralegals so these documents can be referred to in future projects. In this way, legal personnel do not have to start all over again when working on a claim similar to one dealt with in the past.

Traditionally, hard copies of work product files, or legal-information files, were filed in the firm's law library with other reference materials and publications. Today, work product documents and research materials are often generated on computers and stored on DVDs, hard drives, or other data-storage devices. Often, in large firms, these materials are kept in a central data bank that is accessible by the firm's personnel. As the *Ethics Watch* feature below reminds us, backing up files is also critical in law firms.

Forms Files

Every law firm keeps on hand various forms that it commonly uses. These forms are usually stored in a **forms file**. A forms file might include forms for retainer agreements (to be discussed shortly), for filing lawsuits in specific courts, for bankruptcy

forms file
A reference file containing copies of the firm's commonly used legal documents and informational forms. The documents in the forms file serve as models for drafting new documents.

ETHICS WATCH

BACK UP YOUR WORK

Using computers on a routine basis we easily forget—while the computer system is working—that a power failure or other problem can occur at any time. Should this happen, all current work that has not been saved to a hard drive can be lost. Protect yourself and your firm by having backup copies of all your work, and also have a contingency plan, such as a second computer available to use. File backup can be done both in the office on external hard drives as well as off-site through a service that automatically keeps your files secure in case a catastrophe, such as a fire, destroys the office. There are many automatic backup systems such as Time Machine for Apple products and NovaBACKUP for PCs.

Backing up your work frequently is particularly important and can "save the day" if the computer system crashes or fails to the extent that data on the hard drive cannot be retrieved. If you routinely back up documents, you may save yourself hours of valuable time that could be required to re-create a document or file. You will also save yourself and the firm from the problem of deciding who will pay—the client or the law firm—for the extra time spent re-creating work. Moreover, with backups available, your employer will never be without a crucial document when it's needed. Another important precaution you can take to prevent loss of work is to have a crash-saving program available to recover lost data. (Of course, if your office computer system is connected to a server system, you will have online backup.)

This practice is consistent with the NFPA *Model Code of Ethics and Professional Responsibility*, which we will discuss in Chapter 4. Section 1.2 of the code states: "A paralegal shall maintain a high standard of professional conduct." Section 1.5 states: "A paralegal shall preserve all confidential information provided by the client or acquired from other sources before, during, and after the course of the professional relationship." Be sure to learn and follow your firm's backup policy.

ON THE web

For a sampling of the types of legal forms available on the Web, check the following sites: **www.lectlaw.com** and **www.legaldocs.com**.

petitions, for real estate matters, and for many other types of legal matters. Often, to save time, copies of documents relating to specific types of cases are kept for future reference. Then, when the attorney or paralegal works on a similar case, those documents can serve as models, or guides. (These forms may also be kept in a work product file, as just mentioned.)

Forms files are almost always computerized. Computerized forms have simplified legal practice by allowing legal personnel to generate customized documents within minutes. Forms for many standard legal transactions are available from legal-software companies on CD-ROMs and DVDs. They are also available online at Web sites, as you will read in Chapter 8.

Law Firms and Financial Procedures

In the business of law, the product is legal services, which are sold to clients. A major concern of any law firm is to have a clear policy on fee arrangements and efficient procedures to ensure that each client is billed appropriately for the time and costs associated with serving that client. Efficient billing procedures require that attorneys and paralegals keep accurate records of the time that they spend working on a given client's case or other legal matter.

Tiers of Firms

Law firms differ a great deal in their fee structures. Exhibit 3.3 below shows the general levels of attorney billing rates. At the top are the elite law firms in the biggest cities like New York and London. These firms primarily focus on complicated business transactions, international deals, and tax matters. The next tier consists of firms that dominate regional markets, such as in Cleveland, Ohio, or San Diego, California. These firms often work with large companies but are more likely to

EXHIBIT 3.3
General Structure of Law Firms and Providers of Legal Services and Typical Hourly Billing Rate for Attorney Services

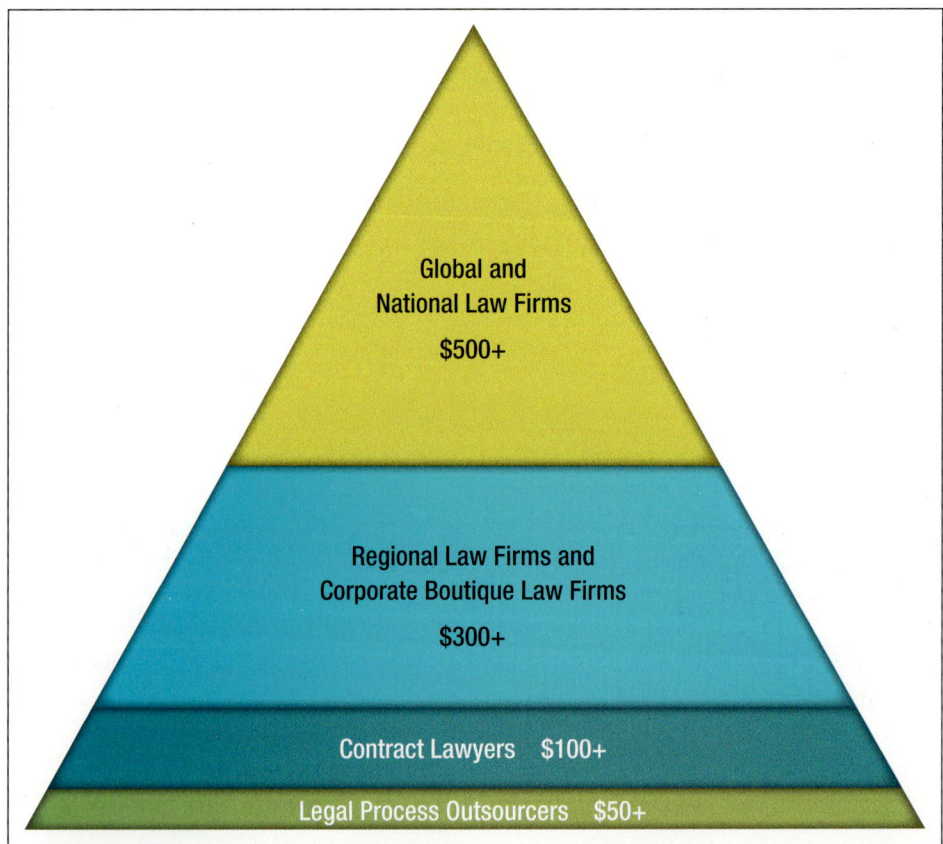

Global and National Law Firms
$500+

Regional Law Firms and Corporate Boutique Law Firms
$300+

Contract Lawyers $100+

Legal Process Outsourcers $50+

© Cengage Learning 2014

specialize, such as in insurance defense. Just below these firms are the boutique firms handling specialized areas like patents or immigration for high-end clients. Below that come smaller firms with smaller clients.

At the bottom are the legal process outsourcers. This level includes firms that specialize in routine matters requiring the least legal training. These firms often use professionals in India, where wages are much lower, to conduct document review or analyze thousands of e-mails as part of discovery.

Fee Arrangements

A major ethical concern of the legal profession has to do with the reasonableness of attorneys' fees and the ways in which clients are billed for legal services. Among other things, state ethical codes governing attorneys require legal fees to be reasonable. The American Bar Association's *Model Rules of Professional Conduct* (to be discussed in Chapter 4) holds that the fees charged by lawyers must be reasonable. The rule then lists the factors that should be considered in determining the reasonableness of a fee. The factors include the time and labor required to perform the legal work, the fee customarily charged in the locality for similar legal services, and the experience and ability of the lawyer performing the services.

Normally, fee arrangements are discussed and agreed on at the outset of any attorney-client relationship. Most law firms require each client to agree, in a signed writing called a **retainer agreement**, to whatever fee arrangements have been made. (Some states also require, by law, that fee arrangements be stated in writing.) The agreement specifies that the client is retaining (hiring) the attorney and/or firm to represent the client in a legal matter and states that the client agrees to the fee arrangements set forth in the agreement. Exhibit 3.4 on the following page shows a sample retainer agreement.

Basically, there are three types of fee arrangements: fixed fees, hourly fees, and contingency fees. We examine here each of these types of fees, as well as some alternative fee arrangements. In addition, some legal claims entitle a plaintiff who wins to have the defendant pay a reasonable attorney's fee to the plaintiff's lawyer. For example, many states provide for a losing defendant in a contracts case to pay the plaintiff's attorney's fees and costs. To collect requires that the lawyer be able to document his or her time and expenses.

Fixed Fees

The client may agree to pay a **fixed fee** for a specified legal service. Certain procedures, such as incorporation and simple divorce filings, are often handled on a fixed-fee basis because the attorney can reasonably estimate how much time will be involved in completing the work. Charging fixed fees is increasingly popular with clients who like knowing how much a matter will cost in advance.

Hourly Fees

With the exception of litigation work done on a contingency-fee basis (discussed below), most law firms charge clients hourly rates for legal services. Hourly rates vary widely from firm to firm. Some litigation firms charge high rates ($700 an hour or more) for their services because of their reputation for obtaining favorable settlements or court judgments for their clients. In contrast, an attorney just starting up a practice as a sole practitioner will have to charge a lower, more competitive rate (perhaps $100 per hour) to attract clients.

Law firms also bill clients for hourly rates for paralegal services. Because the hourly rate for paralegals is lower than that for attorneys, clients benefit from attorneys' use of paralegal services. Generally, the billing rate for paralegal services depends on the size and location of the firm. According to a compensation survey conducted by *Paralegal Today* in 2012, billing rates for paralegals begin at about $60 per hour and may exceed $155 per hour. About 40 percent of all billing for paralegal services ranged between $96 and $135 per hour.

---

social
MEDIA TODAY

Social media help build teams, so finding ways to use social tech tools can enhance your ability to work with the other paralegals and attorneys in your firm. Don't rely on others. Look for opportunities to make your team more effective through social media.

---

retainer agreement
A signed document stating that the attorney or the law firm has been hired by the client to provide certain legal services and that the client agrees to pay for those services.

---

fixed fee
A fee paid to the attorney by his or her client for having provided a specified legal service, such as the creation of a simple will.

EXHIBIT 3.4
A Sample Retainer Agreement

RETAINER AGREEMENT

I, Katherine Baranski, agree to employ Allen P. Gilmore and his law firm, Jeffers, Gilmore & Dunn, as my attorneys to prosecute all claims for damages against Tony Peretto and all other persons or entities that may be liable on account of an automobile accident that caused me to sustain serious injuries. The accident occurred on August 4, 2013, at 7:45 A.M., when Tony Peretto ran a stop sign on Thirty-eighth Street at Mattis Avenue and, as a result, his car collided with mine.

I agree to pay my lawyers a fee that will be one-third (33 percent) of any sum recovered in this case, regardless of whether the sum is received through settlement, lawsuit, arbitration, or any other way. The fee will be calculated on the sum recovered, after costs and expenses have been deducted. The fee will be paid when any money is actually received in this case. I agree that Allen P. Gilmore and his law firm have an express attorney's lien on any recovery to ensure that their fee is paid.

I agree to pay all necessary costs and expenses, such as court filing fees, court reporter fees, expert witness fees and expenses, travel expenses, long-distance telephone and facsimile costs, and photocopying charges. I understand that these costs and expenses will be billed to me by my attorney on a monthly basis and that I am responsible for paying these costs and expenses, even if no recovery is received.

I agree that this agreement does not cover matters other than those described above. This agreement does not cover an appeal from any judgment entered, any efforts necessary to collect money due because of a judgment entered by a court, or any efforts necessary to obtain other benefits, such as insurance.

I agree to pay a carrying charge amounting to the greater of five dollars ($5.00) or four percent (4%) per month on the average daily balance of bills on my account that are thirty (30) days overdue. If my account is outstanding by more than sixty (60) days, all work by the attorney shall cease until the account is paid in full or a monthly payment plan is agreed on.

This contract is governed by the law of the state of Nita.

I AGREE TO THE TERMS AND CONDITIONS STATED ABOVE:

Date: __2 / 4 / 2014__   *Katherine Baranski*
                          Katherine Baranski

I agree to represent Katherine Baranski in the matter described above. I will receive no fee unless a recovery is obtained. If a recovery is obtained, I will receive a fee as described above.

I agree to notify Katherine Baranski of all developments in this matter promptly, and I will make no settlement of this matter without her consent.

I AGREE TO THE TERMS AND CONDITIONS STATED ABOVE:

Date: __2 / 4 / 2014__   *Allen P. Gilmore*
                          Allen P. Gilmore
                          Jeffers, Gilmore & Dunn
                          553 Fifth Avenue
                          Suite 101
                          Nita City, NI 48801

Note that although your services might be billed to the client at a certain hourly rate—say, $100—the firm will not actually pay you $100 an hour in wages. The billable rate for paralegal services, as for attorney services, takes into account the firm's expenses for overhead (rent, utilities, employee benefits, supplies, and the like).

Contingency Fees

contingency fee
A legal fee that consists of a specified percentage (such as 30 percent) of the amount the plaintiff recovers in a civil lawsuit. The fee is paid only if the plaintiff wins the lawsuit (recovers damages).

A common practice among litigation attorneys, especially those representing plaintiffs in certain types of cases (such as personal-injury or negligence cases) is to charge the client on a contingency-fee basis. A **contingency fee** is contingent (dependent) on the outcome of the case. If the plaintiff wins the lawsuit and recovers damages or settles out of court, the attorney is entitled to a percentage of the amount recovered (refer to Exhibit 3.4 on the facing page for an example of a contingency-fee retainer agreement). If the plaintiff loses the lawsuit, the attorney gets nothing—although the client normally reimburses the attorney for the costs and expenses involved in preparing for trial (costs and expenses are discussed below, in regard to billing procedures).

FIXED PERCENTAGE.   Often, the attorney's contingency fee is one-fourth to one-third of the amount recovered. The agreement may provide for modification of the amount depending on how and when the dispute is settled. For example, an agreement that provides for a contingency fee of 33 percent of the amount recovered for a plaintiff may state that the amount will be reduced to a lower percentage if the case is settled out of court.

LIMITS ON FEES.   The law restricts the use of contingency-fee agreements to certain types of cases. An attorney can request a contingency fee only in civil matters, not in criminal cases. In a civil case, the plaintiff is often seeking monetary damages from the defendant to compensate the plaintiff for injuries suffered. In criminal cases, as you will read in Chapter 13, the government is seeking to punish the defendant for a wrongful act committed against society as a whole. If the defendant is found not guilty of the charges, he or she will not receive monetary damages that the attorney could share.

Attorneys are also typically prohibited (by state law) from entering into contingency-fee agreements in divorce cases and probate cases (see Chapter 17) and in workers' compensation cases (see Chapter 18). States usually prohibit contingency fees in these civil cases because lawmakers have determined that allowing attorneys to share in the proceeds recovered would be contrary to public policy.

Alternative Fee Arrangements

Some attorneys offer alternative fee arrangements to their clients. One alternative billing practice, called "task-based billing," is similar to a fixed-fee arrangement: fixed fees are charged for specific types of tasks that are involved in a legal matter. For example, the attorney might charge a flat fee for conducting a pretrial deposition (in which a party to a lawsuit or a witness gives sworn testimony—see Chapter 10). Another alternative billing practice is sometimes referred to as "value billing." When this arrangement is used, the fees charged to the client vary depending on the results of the representation—whether a lawsuit is lost, won, or settled, for example.

Client Trust Accounts

Law firms often require new clients to pay a **retainer**—an initial advance payment to the firm to cover part of the fee and costs that will be incurred on the client's behalf (such as travel expenses, fax charges, and the like). Some businesses keep an attorney on retainer. This means that the client pays the attorney a fixed amount every month or year, and the attorney handles all normal legal business that arises during that time. Retainer arrangements allow businesses to make legal costs predictable over time.

Funds received as retainers, as well as any funds received on behalf of a client (such as a payment to a client to settle a lawsuit), are placed in a special bank account. This account is usually referred to as a client **trust account** (or escrow account). The *Developing Paralegal Skills* feature on the next page reviews trust account procedure. It is extremely important that the funds held in a trust account be used *only* for expenses relating to the costs of serving that client's needs. Software programs designed for law offices simplify holding multiple accounts.

In many states, certain trust accounts come under the requirements of Interest on Lawyers' Trust Accounts (IOLTA) programs. All states have IOLTA programs,

---

social MEDIA TODAY

Tools such as Socialmention, klout, or twittalyzer offer a way to measure your online presence. Regularly checking your influence can help you adapt your use of social media tools.

---

retainer

An advance payment made by a client to a law firm to cover part of the legal fees and/or costs that will be incurred on that client's behalf.

---

trust account

A bank account in which one party (the trustee, such as an attorney) holds funds belonging to another person (such as a client); a bank account into which funds advanced to a law firm by a client are deposited. Also called an *escrow account*.

DEVELOPING
paralegal skills

CREATING A TRUST ACCOUNT

Louise Larson has been hired to work for Don Jones. Don is just starting his own solo practice of law after years of working with a medium-sized law firm in which he had nothing to do with the firm's financial management. Louise's first assignment is to establish a client trust accounting system.

Don and Louise review the ethical rules regarding client property and funds. These rules require that client funds not be commingled with the lawyer's funds. "It's too easy to 'borrow' from a client's funds when they are in the lawyer's own bank account," explains Don. "Therefore," Don continues, "the first thing we need to do is open a checking account for client trust funds." Don and Louise then discuss what needs to be done in order to open the

trust account and what other bookkeeping procedures will be involved in creating a client trust accounting system.

CHECKLIST FOR CREATING A CLIENT TRUST ACCOUNT

- Obtain and prepare the necessary forms from the bank in which the account will be maintained.
- Devise a bookkeeping method for tracking all fees and expenses for a particular case and/or client.
- Retain all deposit slips and canceled checks.
- Keep a record of payments made to clients.
- Decide who will have access to the account.

and most states' lawyers are required to participate. Client funds are deposited in an IOLTA account when the amount is small or is to be held for a short time. In either case, the interest that could be earned for the client is less than the cost of maintaining a separate client account. The funds are instead placed in a single, pooled, interest-bearing trust account. Banks forward the interest earned on the account to the state IOLTA program, which uses the money to fund charitable causes, mostly to support legal assistance for the poor.

Misuse of client funds constitutes a breach of the firm's duty to its client. An attorney's personal use of the funds, for example, can lead to disciplinary action and possible disbarment, as well as criminal penalties. *Commingling* (mixing together) a client's funds with the firm's funds also constitutes abuse and is one of the most common ways in which attorneys breach their professional obligations. If you handle a client's trust account, you should be especially careful to document your use of the funds to protect yourself and your firm against the serious problems that may arise if there are any problems with the account.

Billing and Timekeeping Procedures

As a general rule, a law firm bills its clients monthly. Each client's bill reflects the amount of time spent on the client's matter by the attorney or other legal personnel. Client billing serves an obvious financial function (collecting payment for services rendered). It also serves a communicative function (keeping the client informed of the work being done on a case), as discussed later in this chapter.

Generally, client bills are prepared by a legal secretary or a bookkeeper or, in larger firms, by someone in the accounting department. The bills are based on the fee arrangements made with the client and the time slips collected from the firm's attorneys and paralegals. The time slips (discussed below) indicate how many hours are to be charged to each client and at what hourly rate.

ON THE web

You can obtain information on selected time-and-billing software at the following Web sites: **www.pclaw.com**, **www. sagetimeslips.com**, and **www. tussman.com**.

A paralegal keeps track of the time she spent in the law office library. Later, she will enter the information into her firm's computerized billing program. Why is accuracy in time tracking so important for both the paralegal and the law firm?

Courtesy of © PhotoDisc, Inc.

Billable Hours

The *legal fees* billed to clients are based on the number of billable hours generated for work requiring legal expertise. **Billable hours** are the hours or fractions of hours that attorneys and paralegals spend in client-related work that requires legal expertise and that can be billed directly to clients. The *costs* billed to clients include expenses incurred by the firm (such as court fees, travel expenses, express-delivery charges, and copying costs) on the client's behalf. If an attorney is retained on a contingency-fee basis, the client is not billed monthly for legal fees. The client is normally billed monthly for any costs incurred on the client's behalf, however.

billable hours
Hours or fractions of hours that attorneys and paralegals spend in work that requires legal expertise and that can be billed directly to clients.

Billing Programs

Typically, a preliminary draft of the client's bill is given to the attorney responsible for that client's account. After the attorney reviews and possibly modifies the bill, the final bill is generated and sent to the client. Exhibit 3.5 on the following page illustrates a sample client bill. Most law firms have computerized billing procedures and use time-and-billing software designed specifically for law offices. Time-and-billing software is based on traditional timekeeping and billing procedures. Familiarity with essential features of such programs, combined with knowledge of the basic principles and procedures involved in client billing, will help you understand whatever type of time-and-billing software your employer may use.

Documenting Time and Expenses

Accurate timekeeping by attorneys and paralegals is crucial because clients cannot be billed for time spent on their behalf unless that time is documented. Traditionally, **time slips** have been used to document time spent by attorneys and paralegals working for a client. Today, time slips are incorporated into timekeeping software programs. We look here at *Timeslips*, a commonly used time-and-billing software program created by Sage Software.

time slip
A record documenting, for billing purposes, the hours (or fractions of hours) that an attorney or a paralegal worked for each client, the date on which the work was done, and the type of work done.

Jeffers, Gilmore & Dunn
553 Fifth Avenue
Suite 101
Nita City, NI 48801

BILLING DATE: February 28, 2014

Thomas Jones, M.D.
508 Oak Avenue
Nita City, NI 48801

RE: Medical-Malpractice Action Brought against Dr. Jones,
           File No. 15789

DATE	SERVICES RENDERED	PROVIDED BY	HOURS SPENT	TOTAL
1/30/14	Initial client consultation	APG (attorney)	1.00	$200.00
1/30/14	Client interview	EML (paralegal)	1.00	74.00
1/30/14	Document preparation	EML (paralegal)	1.00	74.00
2/5/14	Interview: Susanne Mathews (nurse)	EML (paralegal)	1.50	111.00
	TOTAL FOR LEGAL SERVICES			$459.00

DATE	EXPENSES			
2/5/14	Hospital charges for a copy of the medical documents			$75.00
	TOTAL FOR EXPENSES			$75.00
	TOTAL BILL TO CLIENT			$534.00

In the slip entry form shown in Exhibit 3.6 on the facing page, the user enters his or her name, the task being billed for, the client for whom the work is being performed, the case referenced, and a description of the task. The user then either enters the time spent on the task or turns on an automated stopwatch timer—shown in Exhibit 3.7 on the facing page—to track the time spent on the task. Tasks can also be recorded as recurring, and rates can be adjusted according to any special agreements. Notice that in Exhibit 3.6 the time is noted to the minute. While we refer to "hourly billing," the time recorded in client bills should also be expressed in parts of hours, not rounded to whole hours.

Costs incurred on behalf of clients have traditionally been entered on **expense slips**. Expenses are now usually entered into the billing program on a form similar to the time slip entry form shown in Exhibit 3.6. The form records a line-by-line description of each expense, along with the quantity and price of each item purchased on behalf of the client.

Billable versus Nonbillable Hours

The time recorded in timekeeping software is charged either to a client (billable hours) or to the firm (nonbillable hours). As mentioned, billable time generally includes the hours that attorneys and paralegals spend in client-related work that requires legal expertise. For example, the time you spend researching or investigating a client's claim is billable time. So is the time spent conferring with or about a

expense slip

A slip of paper on which any expense, or cost, that is incurred on behalf of a client (such as the payment of court fees or long-distance telephone charges) is recorded.

EXHIBIT 3.6
Timeslips Slip Entry Form

Screen shots are reprinted with the permission of Sage Software, Inc. Timeslips is the registered trademark of Sage Software, Inc.

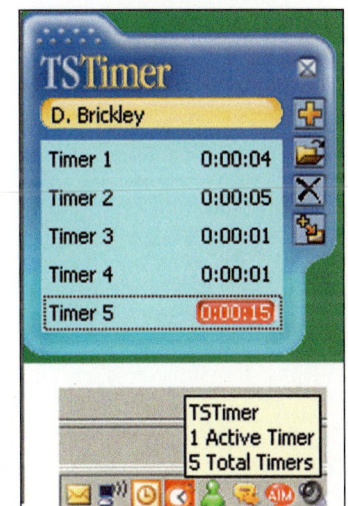

client, drafting documents on behalf of a client, interviewing clients or witnesses, and traveling on a client's behalf (to and from the courthouse to file documents, for example).

Time spent on other tasks, such as administrative work, staff meetings, or performance reviews, is nonbillable time. For example, suppose that you spend thirty minutes photocopying forms for the forms file, time sheets, or a procedures manual for the office. That thirty minutes is not considered billable time. In *Timeslips*, the user designates whether the task being recorded is billable, as you can see in the "Billing status" box in Exhibit 3.6 above.

Generally, law firms have a legitimate reason for wanting to maximize their billable hours: the financial well-being of a law firm depends to a great extent on how many billable hours are generated by its employees. Nonbillable time ultimately cuts into the firm's profits. Therefore, the more billable hours generated by the firm's legal professionals, the more profitable the business will be.

The Pressure to Generate Billable Hours

Attorneys and paralegals face pressure to produce billable hours for the firm. As a paralegal, you may be subject to this pressure and must learn how to handle it. Depending on the firm, a paralegal may be expected to generate between 800 and 2,000 billable hours per year. For example, suppose that your employer expects you to produce 1,800 billable hours per year. Discounting vacation time and holidays (assuming a two-week vacation and ten paid holidays), this equates to 37.5 hours weekly. If you work 40 hours a week, you will have only 2.5 hours a week for such nonbillable activities as interoffice meetings, performance reviews, coffee breaks, reorganizing your work area, and chatting with others in the office.

Ethics and Client Billing Practices

Because attorneys have a duty to charge their clients "reasonable" fees, legal professionals must be careful in their billing practices. They must not "pad" their clients' bills by including more billable hours than actually worked on behalf of those

EXHIBIT 3.7
Timeslips Timer

Screen shots are reprinted with the permission of Sage Software, Inc. Timeslips is the registered trademark of Sage Software, Inc.

double billing
Billing more than one client for the same billable time period.

clients. They also must avoid **double billing**—billing more than one client for the same time.

Double Billing

Sometimes, situations arise in which it is difficult to determine which client should be billed for a particular segment of time. For example, suppose that you are asked to travel to another city to interview a witness in a case for Client A. You spend three hours traveling in an airplane to get to that city. On the plane, you spend two hours summarizing a document relating to a case for Client B. Who should pay for those two hours, Client A, Client B, or both? In this situation, you could argue—as many attorneys do in similar circumstances—that you generated five billable hours, three on Client A's work, since travel time was required for Client A, and two on Client B's case. This is an example of how double billing can occur.

Double billing also occurs when a firm bills a new client for work that was done for a previous client. For example, suppose that an attorney is working on a case for Client B that is very similar to a case handled by the firm a year ago for Client A. The firm charged Client A $2,000 for the legal services. Because much of the research, writing, and other work done on Client A's case can transfer over to Client B's case, the firm is able to complete the work for Client B in half the time.

In this situation, would it be fair to bill Client B $2,000 also? After all, $1,000 of that amount represents hours spent on Client A's case (and for which Client A has already been billed). At the same time, would it be fair to Client A to bill Client B less for essentially the same services? Would it be fair not to allow the firm to profit from cost efficiencies generated by overlapping work? Could the firm split the savings created by the overlapping research ($1,000) with Client B by billing Client B $1,500 instead of $2,000?

The American Bar Association's Response to Double Billing

The American Bar Association (ABA) addressed double billing in a formal ethical opinion. In that opinion, the ABA stated that attorneys are prohibited from charging more than one client for the same hours of work. Additionally, the ABA rejected the notion that the firm, and not the client, should benefit from cost efficiencies created by the firm's work for previous clients. "The lawyer who has agreed to bill solely on the basis of time spent is obliged to pass the benefit of these economies on to the client."

Although ABA opinions are not legally binding on attorneys unless they are adopted by the states as law, they do carry significant weight in the legal community. Courts, for example, have tended to follow the ABA's position in resolving fee disputes. Typically, a court will not award attorneys' fees that it finds to be "excessive, redundant, or otherwise unnecessary."[1] States will sanction or even disbar an attorney for double billing a client.[2]

Communications

Excellent communication skills are a must for law firms to develop and retain clients, to function efficiently as a firm, and to help you develop as a paralegal. (See this chapter's *Featured Contributor* feature on pages 78 and 79 for tips on effective communication.)

Traditional Communications

Sending monthly bills to clients is one way to keep attorney-client communication channels open. Monthly billing may be inadequate to keep clients informed. The American Bar Association states that a part of professional conduct required of attorneys is to keep their clients reasonably informed about the status of legal matters. This means the attorney, perhaps with the assistance of a paralegal, provides the client with adequate information so they understand the elements of the law. The clients should also know about any legal proceedings that could come about as a result of a particular matter. Attorneys must also respond to inquiries from clients.

As a paralegal, you need to be aware that keeping clients reasonably informed about the progress being made on their cases goes beyond courtesy—it is a legal duty of attorneys. The meaning of "reasonably informed" varies depending on the client and on the nature of the work being done by the attorney. In some cases, a phone call every week or two will suffice to keep the client informed. In other cases, the attorney may ask the paralegal to draft a letter to a client explaining the status of the client's legal matter. Some firms have regular monthly mailings to update clients on the status of their cases. Generally, you should discuss with your supervising attorney how each client should be kept informed of the status of that client's case. (See the *Technology and Today's Paralegal* feature on page 80.)

Copies of all letters and e-mails to a client should, of course, be placed in the client's file. The file should also contain a written record of each phone call made to or received from a client. That way, there is a "paper trail" in the event it is ever necessary to provide evidence of communication with the client. (This is a good practice for all phone calls relating to a client's matter.) You will learn about the various forms of letters that attorneys send to clients in Chapter 9. Increasingly, attorneys and paralegals communicate with clients via e-mail. Because every paralegal will receive and reply to numerous e-mails, e-mail format and organization is an issue in how a firm functions and is regarded by clients.

Communication by Social Media

The practice of law is an inherently cooperative environment. As a paralegal, you will be working as part of a team with your supervising attorney, the client, and many other professionals. The new social media tools excel at facilitating collaboration and can help your team. As social media gurus David Thomas and Mike Barlow note in *The Executive's Guide to Enterprise Social Media Strategy*, one of the most important uses of social media is for internal communication among employees. Some of the most constructive ways social media are being used in the legal environment include:

- Private client spaces created to keep clients up to date on case developments.
- Internal **wikis** where knowledge can be shared.
- Collaborative spaces, secure behind firewalls, where a legal team can share documents.
- Internal community calendars to keep the legal team posted on where team members are and what they are doing, as well as progress on specific tasks.
- Firm-specific Twitter-like services for secure communication among the legal team.
- Firm Twitter feeds and other external social media that build the firm's digital shadow and help attract clients.

As a paralegal, you may be called on to play important roles in developing or implementing a social media strategy. This can be an assignment where you can demonstrate your value to the firm. The authors of *Social Media at Work: How Networking Tools Propel Organizational Performance*, all experts from networking giant Oracle Corp., point out that people seen as trailblazers today will soon be seen as the wise sages of social media's power within organizations.

Clear Policies

Establishing a clear policy governing how the firm and its employees will use social media tools is an important element of a social media strategy, just as it is with more traditional communications. Any policy should be clear and concise, and

---

social MEDIA TODAY

Be as cautious with social media as you are with e-mail. Just as you wouldn't open an e-mail attachment from someone you didn't know, be careful about clicking on links from tweets, as malware can be carried through Web links in tweets.

---

wiki
A Web page that can be added to and modified by anyone or by authorized users who share the site. The most famous example is Wikipedia.

Featured Contributor

TEN TIPS FOR EFFECTIVE COMMUNICATION

Wendy B. Edson

BIOGRAPHICAL NOTE

Wendy B. Edson received her master's degree in library science (M.L.S.) from the University of Rhode Island and served as law librarian at a Buffalo, New York, law firm. Later, she joined the Paralegal Studies faculty at Hilbert College, in Hamburg, New York, and helped to develop an ABA-approved bachelor's degree program.

As chairperson of the Paralegal Studies Department, Ms. Edson teaches paralegalism and legal ethics, legal research and writing, Internet research, and alternative dispute resolution (ADR). She also developed and coordinates the internship program. Edson reviews and publishes on the topics of paralegal education and legal research and writing. She has lectured to legal professionals on legal research, teaching skills, internships, legal ethics, and ADR. A contributor to AAfPE materials and programs, Edson also served as a volunteer mediator for the family courts in her area.

Words! They are the building blocks of human communication. Whether words are exchanged face to face—or by e-mail, phone, fax, or letter—communication is a two-way street. But how do we become skilled at maneuvering the two-way traffic of interpersonal communication? As in driving, we need to follow the "rules of the road." The rules of the road in regard to communication traffic are embodied in the following ten tips.

1. **Establish Communication Equality.** Communication equality does not require that individuals hold equal status in an office or organization but requires that each party believe in *equal rights* to speak and listen. Observe someone whom you consider to be a good communicator. You will note that he or she demonstrates equality by actively listening and responding appropriately to whoever is speaking. Workplace problems often reflect communication ailments rooted in inequality. A firm belief in communication equality, despite job titles, will help to create a cooperative, productive working environment.

2. **Plan for Time and Space.** Effective communication requires time. Imagine your reaction to a request to work overtime if your supervising attorney took thirty seconds to order you to do the work versus taking two minutes to explain the reason for the request and listening to your response. In the first situation, the attorney saved one and a half minutes but scored "zero" in terms of communication skills. In today's rushed world, it is easy to overlook the importance of communication skills in morale building and creating a cooperative, efficient workforce.

Effective communicators are aware of how the physical environment in which a conversation takes place can affect the communication process. Communication is always enhanced when the parties have reasonable privacy and are not continually interrupted. Another important factor is physical comfort.

Choosing an inappropriate time and place for communication denies the importance of the matters being discussed and may send the wrong message to both the speaker and the listener.

3. **Set the Agenda.** Skilled communicators prepare an *agenda*—whether written or mental—of matters to be discussed in order of their priority. Frequently, both parties bring their respective agendas to a discussion, which means that priorities may need to be negotiated. A subordinate who brings up the topic of desired vacation time when the supervisor is preoccupied with a major project clearly demonstrates that his or her priorities are different from those of the supervisor.

Successful communication requires that the parties first negotiate a *common agenda*—that is, determine jointly the agenda for a particular discussion or meeting and what topics should take priority. Then, the topics can be dealt with one by one, in terms of their relative importance, to the satisfaction of both parties.

should include "dos" as well as "don'ts" to encourage appropriate use of the tools. The policy should include specific instructions and examples so that those unfamiliar with social media can understand what is permitted or not. The Web site

Agenda awareness prevents parties from jumping from topic to topic without successfully resolving anything.

4. **Fine-Tune Your Speaking Skills.**   Observe an individual whom you consider to be a good speaker, whether before a group of persons or on a one-on-one basis. What skills does that individual demonstrate? Effective speakers work hard to express thoughts clearly; sometimes, they refer to notes or lists to refresh their memories. Skilled speakers also try to communicate accurately and to talk about matters that they know will interest their listeners. They cultivate *communication empathy*—the sincere effort to put themselves in their listeners' shoes. As you speak to others, pause occasionally and ask yourself: "Would I enjoy listening to what I am saying and how I am saying it?"

5. **Cultivate Listening Skills.**   Listening is not just refraining from speaking while another person is talking but is an *active process*—the other half of the communication partnership. An active listener does not interrupt the speaker. If you sense that the speaker is engaging in a monologue, you can use responsive behavior—including body language, attentiveness, and appropriate remarks—to steer the conversation back to a dialogue without cutting off the speaker.

An active listener realizes that listening is an investment in effective communication. By truly responding to what is being said, rather than regarding listening time as insignificant or as a time to plan his or her own remarks, the skilled listener establishes a bond of trust with the speaker. Active listeners avoid preconceived ideas about topics being discussed and assume that they do not know all the answers.

6. **Watch for Body Language.**   Body language is nonverbal communication that reflects our emotional state. Physical positions, such as leaning forward or away from the speaker while listening, can reinforce or negate our spoken responses. Body attitudes, whether relaxed (comfortable posture, leaning forward, uncrossed arms and legs, relaxed neck and shoulders) or tense (stiff posture, backing away, crossed arms and legs, rigid neck and shoulders), vividly illustrate our responses before we utter a word. Eye contact is one of the most important tools in the body language tool kit for communication. Interviewers, social workers, and police officers have learned that steady and responsive eye contact means sincerity and credibility.

7. **Put Note Taking in Perspective.**   Overinvolvement in note taking detracts from the communication process because opportunities to listen actively, speak responsively, and be sensitive to body language are reduced. The speaker may ramble while the listener records the ramblings in extensive notes.

When it is necessary to take notes, it is helpful to establish some rapport with the speaker or listener before launching the note-taking process. Alternatively, follow-up notes can be a workable solution to the problem. The note taker can devote the interview time to communication and, after the interview, record his or her general impressions of the interview and identify specific issues that need to be discussed further.

8. **Recognize the Role of Criticism.**   *Constructive criticism* focuses on specific actions or behaviors rather than personalities. It is objective rather than subjective. Criticism that is stated calmly and objectively ("We need to rewrite the section on holographic wills") is much more palatable for the person being criticized than is criticism in the form of a personal attack ("You did a terrible job"). By placing emphasis on actions instead of personalities, the parties can more easily work toward a satisfactory solution. If both the critic and the person being criticized can remain calm and can separate actions from personalities, then criticism will usually produce the desired result and *mutual* satisfaction.

9. **Aim for Satisfactory Closure.**   Closure means "wrapping up" the communication. Successful communicators know that handling closure properly can leave a participant with a good feeling even if the solution was not exactly what he or she initially desired. Summarizing the discussion and checking for agreement or a need for further discussion will encourage all participants to follow the tenth tip.

10. **Commit to Communicate.**   Excellent speakers and listeners have positive, self-confident attitudes that problems can be solved if the "rules of the road" are followed. Skilled communicators cultivate open minds, self-knowledge, and the ability to tolerate differences and empathize with others. They are committed to exercising their rights and responsibilities as speakers and listeners in the communication process.

"Eye contact is one of the most important tools in the body language tool kit for communication."

socialmediagovernance.com has many examples of policies used at a wide range of companies. Remember that client confidentiality is critically important in law firms, so any communications policy must address that issue.

TECHNOLOGY AND
today's paralegal

ONLINE COMMUNICATIONS

E-mail is a standard communication tool for businesses, including law firms. The reason e-mail is so popular is simple: it is a quick, easy-to-use, and inexpensive way to communicate. In large law firms and corporate enterprises, as well as in government agencies, e-mail messages have largely replaced the printed interoffice memos of the past as well as many letters. (As you have seen in this chapter, social media tools are starting to replace e-mail as a communications method *within* firms.)

APPLY PROFESSIONAL STANDARDS TO E-MAIL COMMUNICATIONS

Because e-mail is transmitted instantly, it may be difficult to remember that it is also a *written communication*. People using e-mail tend to adopt a casual, conversational tone and to ignore the traditional rules of writing, such as sentence structure, spelling, and capitalization. E-mail is still mail, however, and it should reflect the same professional tone and quality that you use in the firm's paper correspondence. If you want to convey a message to someone (especially a client), you need to use clear and effective language.

There are several things you can do to ensure that your e-mail messages are professional and error free. First, use a spell checker. Typos, misspellings, punctuation errors, and grammatical problems detract from the message and can easily be avoided. Make sure that you also proofread your e-mail carefully because programs will not catch all errors. Many times, it is helpful to print out an important message, let it sit for a while, and review it later when you can see it from a fresh perspective.

Make sure that you use the same form as you would in an ordinary letter (see Chapter 9), with perhaps a few variations—adding your e-mail address below your name in the closing and the word *confidential* at the top (when appropriate), for example. Many law firms have standard signature blocks that warn recipients that e-mails are confidential. Do not use quotes or pictures in your signature block. Those belong in your personal e-mail, not in work e-mails.

TIPS FOR FORMATTING E-MAIL MESSAGES

Because e-mail often looks different on the recipient's computer screen than it does on your screen, keep the format simple. Use double spacing between paragraphs rather than indenting with tabs, and do not underline or boldface text (these features often do not transmit clearly from one e-mail system to another). If the message concerns a legal matter and is being sent to a client's workplace or a shared e-mail address, be careful about how you identify the subject of the e-mail. For example, you could write "documents ready for signature" rather than "bankruptcy petition complete."

Send attachments in PDF rather than in Word files or similar document-creation programs. That avoids problems in opening documents if recipients do not have the same program, and it prevents differences in platforms from altering the format.

TECHNOLOGY TIP

Always print out a copy of your e-mail and retain it in the client's file so that a record exists. Be sure that any e-mail you send discloses your status as a paralegal (to avoid liability for the unauthorized practice of law). Request recipients to verify that important messages have been received (such as when you are notifying a person of a court date). E-mail systems often have a function that allows senders to request a "return receipt" to confirm that the message you sent was received. You should respond to incoming e-mail promptly so that the sender knows that you have received the e-mail. Finally, make sure that you know the policies of your firm regarding confidential e-mail. If used carefully, e-mail can be an efficient way to fulfill your duties and communicate with the firm's clients.

Law Office Culture and Politics

As a paralegal, you will find that each law firm you work for is unique. Even though two firms may be the same size and have similar organizational structures, they will have different cultures, or "personalities." The culture of a given legal workplace is ultimately determined by how the firm's owners (the partners, for example) define the fundamental goals of the firm.

Formality versus Reality

Each firm has a political infrastructure that may have little to do with the lines of authority and accountability spelled out in the firm's employment manual or other formal policy statement. An up-and-coming younger partner in the firm, for example, may exercise more authority than one of the firm's older partners who is about to retire. There may be rivalry among associate attorneys for promotion to partnership status, and you may be caught in the middle of their competition. In such cases, you may find yourself tempted to take sides, which could jeopardize your own future with the firm.

Unfortunately, paralegals have little way of knowing about the culture and politics of a given firm until they have worked for the firm awhile. Of course, if you know someone who works for or who has worked for a given firm and you value that employee's opinion, you might gain some advance knowledge about the firm's environment. Otherwise, when you start to work for a firm, you will need to learn for yourself about interoffice politics. One way to do this is to listen carefully whenever a co-worker discusses the firm's staff, and ask discreet questions to elicit information from co-workers about office politics and unwritten policies. This way, you can both prepare yourself to deal with these issues and protect your own interests. After you've worked for the firm for a time, you will be in a position to judge whether the company you have chosen is really the right firm for you.

Issues in Office Culture

Some of the things you should think about when investigating a law firm's culture include:

- Turnover—because it is costly to train new employees, no firm wants to constantly replace its staff. If a firm has high turnover, that will tell you that many employees may be unsatisfied with their work environment. Ask how long the average employee has been at the firm to get a sense of turnover.

- Competitive compensation—are employees paid based on seniority or are there rewards for exceptional performance?

- Creative benefits—does the firm offer more than the usual package of medical and retirement benefits? Is telecommuting or flex-time possible? Are there provisions for emergency backup child care?

- Does the firm provide candid assessments of performance?

- How does the firm mentor new employees?

- What is the firm's philosophy of management?

- What are the firm's goals?

- What is the firm vision and brand?

- What does it take to be successful at the firm?

You can ask about these issues in a job interview. You can also learn about many of them by looking at the firm's Web site before your interview. Interviewers are often impressed by job applicants who have taken the time to research the firm they are interviewing with, so be sure to learn as much as you can about the firm before the interview. Your career services office may be able to help with this, and legal directories are often good sources of information on law firms. Note also that firm culture does not remain static but changes over time as new employees are hired and older employees retire or move to new opportunities.

social
MEDIA TODAY

Posting negative comments about your employer or a client can haunt you, as many firms run alerts based on online mentions of their names.

KEY TERMS AND CONCEPTS

associate attorney   58

billable hours   73

contingency fee   70

double billing   76

employment manual   61

expense slip   74

fixed fee   69

forms file   67

law clerk   58

legal administrator   60

legal-assistant manager   60

limited liability partnership (LLP)   59

managing partner   58

office manager   60

paralegal manager   60

partner   58

partnership   58

personal liability   58

professional corporation (P.C.)   59

retainer   71

retainer agreement   69

shareholder   59

sole proprietorship   58

staff attorney   58

statute of limitations   66

support personnel   60

time slip   73

trust account   71

wiki   77

Chapter Summary

The Inner Workings of the Law Office

THE ORGANIZATIONAL STRUCTURE OF LAW FIRMS

Law firms can be organized in the following ways:

1. *Sole proprietorship*—In a sole proprietorship, one attorney owns the business and is entitled to all the firm's profits. That individual also bears the burden of any losses and is personally liable for the firm's debts.

2. *Partnership*—In a partnership, two or more lawyers jointly own the firm and share in the firm's profits and losses. Attorneys who are employed by the firm but who are not partners (such as associates and staff attorneys) do not share in the profits and losses of the firm.

Generally, partners are subject to personal liability for all of the firm's debts or other obligations. In many states, firms can organize as *limited liability partnerships,* in which partners are not held personally liable for the malpractice of other partners in the firm.

3. *Professional corporation*—In a professional corporation (P.C.), two or more individuals jointly own the business as shareholders. The owner-shareholders of the corporation share the firm's profits and losses (as partners do) but are not personally liable for the firm's debts or obligations beyond the amount they invested in the P.C.

LAW OFFICE MANAGEMENT AND PERSONNEL

Each law firm has a unique system of management and lines of authority. Generally, the owners of the firm (partners, for example) oversee and manage all other employees. Law firm personnel include associate attorneys; law clerks; paralegals; administrative personnel, who are supervised by the legal administrator or the office manager; and support personnel, including receptionists, secretaries, file clerks, and others.

EMPLOYMENT POLICIES

Employment policies relate to compensation and employee benefits, performance evaluations, employment termination, and other rules of the workplace, such as office hours. Frequently (particularly in larger firms), the policies of the firm are spelled out in an employment manual or other writing. Paralegals must be sure to know their specific responsibilities. Most large firms have policies and procedures that apply to evaluation, promotion, and termination at the firm.

FILING PROCEDURES

Every law firm follows certain filing procedures. In larger firms, these procedures may be written down. In smaller firms, procedures may be more casual and based on habit or tradition.

1. *Client files*—Confidentiality is a major concern and a fundamental policy of every law firm. A breach of confidentiality by anyone in the law office can subject the firm to extensive legal liability. The requirement of confidentiality shapes, to a significant extent, filing procedures. A typical law firm has client files, work product files and reference materials, forms files, and personnel files.

    Proper file maintenance is crucial to a smoothly functioning firm. An efficient filing system helps to ensure that important documents will not be misplaced and will be available when needed. Filing procedures must also maximize client confidentiality and the safekeeping of documents.

2. *Work product files*—Law firms often keep copies of all research materials, support materials related to cases, and legal memoranda. Maintenance of backup files is a requirement.

3. *Form files*—Firms often use standard form files that may have been prepared internally or have been professionally prepared by a service.

LAW FIRMS AND FINANCIAL PROCEDURES

A major concern of any law firm is to have a clear policy on fee arrangements and efficient billing procedures so that each client is billed appropriately.

1. *Tiers of Firms*—Top-level firms, which are generally full-service firms in major cities, generally have the highest billing rates, followed by major regional firms. Boutique firms and others fill the needs of different groups of clients.

2. *Fee arrangements*—Types of fee arrangements include fixed fees, hourly fees, and contingency fees. Clients who pay hourly fees are billed monthly for the time spent by attorneys and other legal personnel on the clients' cases or projects, as well as all costs incurred on behalf of the clients.

3. *Client trust accounts*—Law firms are required to place all funds received from a client into a special account called a client trust account. This is to ensure that the client's money remains separate from the firm's money. It is important that the funds held in the trust account be used only for expenses relating to the costs of serving that client's needs.

4. *Billing and timekeeping*—Firms require attorneys and paralegals to document how they use their time. Because the firm's income depends on the number of billable hours produced by employees, firms usually require attorneys and paralegals to generate a certain number of billable hours per year. Double billing presents a major ethical problem for law firms.

COMMUNICATIONS

Attorneys have a duty to keep their clients informed. Paralegals should be aware that this is a legal duty and that they play a significant role in meeting this duty. Sending billing statements to clients is one way to communicate; phone calls, letters, and e-mail messages are other ways to keep clients informed. Firms use a mix of traditional communications and new forms of social media to keep in touch with clients and to help generate new business. Firms need clear policies about communications within the firm and about how the firm presents itself to the outside world.

LAW OFFICE CULTURE AND POLITICS

Each office has its own culture, or personality, which is largely shaped by the attitudes of the firm's owners and the qualities they look for when hiring employees. Each firm also has a political infrastructure that is not apparent to outsiders. Office culture and politics make a great difference in terms of job satisfaction and comfort. Wise paralegals learn as soon as possible from co-workers or others about these aspects of the law office.

QUESTIONS FOR REVIEW

1. What are the basic organizational structures of law firms?

2. What is the difference between an associate and a partner? Who handles the administrative tasks of a law firm? Who supervises the work performed by paralegals?

3. What kinds of files do law firms maintain? What general procedures are typically followed in regard to client files?

4. How does a law firm arrange its fees with its clients? What ethical obligations do attorneys have with respect to legal fees?

5. How do lawyers and legal assistants keep track of their time? What is the difference between billable and nonbillable hours? What is a client trust account?

ETHICAL QUESTIONS

1. Sam Martin, an attorney, receives a settlement check for a client's case. It is made out jointly to Sam and his client. Sam endorses the check and instructs his paralegal to deposit it into his law firm's bank account, instead of the client's trust account, because he wants to take out his fee before he gives the client his portion of the money. Can Sam do this? Why or why not? What should Sam's paralegal do?

2. Tom Baker, a paralegal, has been doing research for a client using Westlaw (a computerized legal research database discussed in Chapter 8). Tom's supervising attorney tells him that the Westlaw charges Tom just incurred on behalf of an individual client should be billed to that client and a second client as well, since the Westlaw research applies in both cases. The second client is a large and prosperous corporation. What ethical violation has occurred? What should Tom do?

PRACTICE QUESTIONS AND ASSIGNMENTS

1. Using the material presented in the chapter, identify the following law practices by their organizational structure:

   a. Bill James is an attorney who practices law on his own. He owns his legal practice, the building in which he works, and most of the office furniture. He leases his office equipment. Bill has one secretary and one paralegal who work for him.

   b. Roberta Wagner owns a law firm with Joe Rosen. They own equal interests in the firm, participate equally in the firm's management, and share jointly in its profits and losses. Wagner & Rosen has three associates, six secretaries, and three paralegals who work for the firm.

   c. Randall Smith and Susan Street own a law firm together as shareholders. They employ eight associate attorneys, twelve secretaries, and five legal assistants.

2. Identify the type of billing that is being used in each of the following examples:

   a. The client is billed $200 per hour for a partner's time, $150 per hour for an associate attorney's time, and $125 per hour for a paralegal's time.

   b. The attorney's fee is one-third of the amount that the attorney recovers for the client, either through a pretrial settlement or through a trial.

   c. The attorney charges $250 to change the name of a client's business firm.

3. Louise Lanham hires John J. Roberts, an attorney with the law firm of Sands, Roberts & Simpson, located at 1000 Plymouth Road, Phoenix, Arizona, to represent her in a divorce. She agrees to pay attorney Roberts a rate of $200 per hour and to pay a paralegal rate of $100 per hour. She also agrees to pay all costs and expenses, such as filing fees, expert-witness fees, court-reporter fees, and other fees incurred in the course of her representation. Using Exhibit 3.4, *A Sample Retainer Agreement*, on page 70, draft a retainer agreement between Louise Lanham and John J. Roberts.

QUESTIONS FOR CRITICAL ANALYSIS

1. Do you think that performance evaluations are beneficial? What would happen if performance evaluations were not used? What types of information are included in them? What would you include to make them better?

2. Why are efficient and confidential filing systems and procedures particularly necessary in law offices, more so than in other types of businesses? What might happen without them?

3. Why is it so important for members of a legal team to meticulously keep track of their hours? Why are some hours billable and others not? What happens if accurate billing records are not kept? Why are client trust funds required? Why are these accounts so important? What can happen if client funds are misused?

4. James Johnson is a sole practitioner. His office is about an hour's drive from the federal district court in which he files many of his lawsuits. He used to talk on his cell phone to clients as he traveled the two hours to and from the courthouse. He would then bill the client on whose behalf he was going to the courthouse for two hours and the clients with whom he talked on the phone for increments of the same two hours. When the American Bar Association issued its rule prohibiting double billing, he was concerned that the rule would drive him out of business. Johnson feels that there should be different billing rules for lawyers in large firms and lawyers in small practices, such as his. What do you think?

5. Many law firms require their legal assistants to meet a quota of billable hours. Often, legal assistants can generate the number of billable hours required per week only by working more than the number of hours that they are paid to work. This can lead to the temptation to "pad the bill." Can you think of ways to meet the quota without breaching ethical standards?

PROJECTS

1. Research legal periodicals, such as *Legal Assistant Today* and the ABA's *Journal of Law Practice Management,* for articles on document/case management software. Write a one-page paper summarizing your findings. Be sure to describe how the software works and how its features and cost compare with other software on the market. Print and attach a copy of the articles to your paper.

2. Search the Internet for information on law practice management software. You will find that many sites give a description of their software and how much it costs. Some will provide a demonstration. Write a one-page paper that describes how the software works, its key features and those of the alternatives, and compare what is offered. Be sure to include the URLs of the Web sites used to obtain information.

GROUP PROJECT

In this project the group will research the use of social media by law firms and present its findings to class. Student one will research for what purpose law firms use social media and what the pros and cons of using social media are. Student two will research statistics on how many law firms use social media. Student three will research statistics on which social media sites law firms use and what the trends are among law firms for using various sites. Student four will summarize and compile the results of the research and will present the group's findings to the class.

USING INTERNET RESOURCES

1. Find legal forms on the Internet by going to the following Web site: **www.legaldocs.com**. Make a general list of the types of forms that are available. Are they free? If not, how much do the forms cost? How can they be purchased? What methods of payment are accepted?

2. Research time-and-billing software on the Internet by going to the following Web site: **www.sagetimeslips.com**. Click "Product Overview" to read about the latest version of *Timeslips*. What are some of the features of this software? Is it limited to one type of billing arrangement, or is it flexible? Can it create reports? What else can it do? Select "Free Trial" from the Products and Services menu if you want to try out the program for yourself.

END NOTES

1. *EEOC v. Clear Lake Dodge*, 60 F.3d 1146 (5th Cir. 1995).

2. See, for example, *Kentucky Bar Association v. Emerson*, 276 S.W.3d 823 (Ky., 2009) (attorney suspended from practice of law for failing to provide client with detailed billing).

CourseMate The available CourseMate for this text has an interactive eBook and interactive learning tools, including flash cards, quizzes, and more. To learn more about this resource and access free demo CourseMate resources, go to **www.cengagebrain.com**, and search for this book. To access CourseMate materials that you have purchased, go to **login.cengagebrain.com**.

Ethics and Professional Responsibility

Chapter Outline

After completing this chapter, you will know:

- Why and how legal professionals are regulated.

- Some important ethical rules governing the conduct of attorneys.

- How the rules governing attorneys affect paralegal practice.

- The kinds of activities that paralegals are and are not legally permitted to perform.

- Some of the pros and cons of regulation, including the debate over paralegal licensing.

Introduction

Paralegals preparing for a career in today's legal arena have a variety of career options. Regardless of which career path you follow, you should have a firm grasp of your state's ethical rules governing the legal profession. When you work under the supervision of an attorney, you and the attorney become team members. You work together on behalf of clients and share in the ethical and legal responsibilities arising as a result of the attorney-client relationship.

In preparing for a career as a paralegal, you must know what these responsibilities are, why they exist, and how they affect you. The first part of this chapter is devoted to the regulation of attorneys because the ethical duties imposed on attorneys affect paralegals as well. If a paralegal violates a rule governing attorneys, that may result in serious consequences for the client, for the attorney, and for the paralegal. Attorneys are subject to direct regulation by the state.

Paralegals are subject to less regulation, although states may impose more rules if believed desirable. Paralegals are regulated indirectly both by attorney ethical codes and by state laws that prohibit nonlawyers from practicing law. As the paralegal profession develops, professional paralegal organizations, the American Bar Association, and state bar associations continue to issue guidelines that serve to indirectly regulate paralegals.

The Regulation of Attorneys

self-regulation

The regulation of the conduct of a professional group by members of the group. Self-regulation involves establishing ethical or professional standards of behavior with which members of the group must comply.

According to Webster's dictionary, to regulate means "to control or direct in agreement with a rule." To a significant extent, attorneys engage in **self-regulation** because they play critical roles in establishing the majority of the rules governing their profession. One of the hallmarks of a profession is the establishment of minimum standards and levels of competence for its members. The accounting profession, for example, has established such standards, as have physicians, engineers, and members of most other professions.

Attorneys are also regulated by the state, because the rules of behavior established by the legal profession are adopted and enforced by state authorities. First, by establishing educational and licensing requirements, state authorities ensure that anyone practicing law is competent to do so. Second, by defining specific ethical requirements for attorneys, the states protect the public against unethical attorney behavior that may affect clients' welfare. Because the rules limiting who can practice law ("unauthorized practice of law" statutes) are largely written and enforced by lawyers, they also serve to assist lawyers by limiting competition from other groups, such as paralegals. We will discuss these requirements and rules shortly. Before we do, however, let's look at how these rules are created and enforced.

Who Are the Regulators?

Key participants in determining what rules should govern attorneys and the practice of law, as well as how these rules should be enforced, are bar associations, state supreme courts, state legislatures, and, in some cases, the United States Supreme Court. Procedures for regulating attorneys vary, of course, from state to state. What follows is a general discussion of some of the key regulators.

Bar Associations

Lawyers determine the requirements for entering the legal profession and the rules of conduct they will follow. Traditionally, lawyers have joined together in professional groups (bar associations) at the local, state, and national levels to discuss issues affecting the legal profession and to decide on standards of professional conduct.

In all states, to be admitted to practice, a prospective attorney must pass the state bar examination. Although membership in local and national bar associations is voluntary, membership in the state bar association (called a "unified bar") is mandatory in many states. Many lawyers are also members of the American Bar Association (ABA), the voluntary national bar association discussed in Chapter 1. As you will read shortly, the ABA plays a key regulatory role by proposing model (uniform) codes, or rules of conduct, for adoption by the various states.

State Supreme Courts

Typically, the state's highest court, often called the state supreme court, is the ultimate regulatory authority in a state. That court's judges decide what conditions (such as licensing requirements, discussed below) must be met before an attorney can practice law within the state and under what conditions that privilege will be suspended or revoked. In many states, the state supreme court works closely with the state bar association. For example, the association may recommend rules and requirements to the court. If the court agrees, it can order these rules to become state law. Under the authority of the courts, state bar associations often handle regulatory functions, including disciplinary proceedings against attorneys who fail to comply with professional requirements.

State Legislatures

State legislatures regulate the legal profession by passing laws affecting attorneys—statutes prohibiting the unauthorized practice of law, for example. In a few states, the states' highest courts delegate significant regulatory responsibilities to the state legislatures.

The United States Supreme Court

Occasionally, the United States Supreme Court decides issues relating to attorney conduct. For example, until a few decades ago, state ethical codes, or rules governing attorney conduct, prohibited lawyers from advertising their services to the public. These restrictions on advertising were later determined by the United States Supreme Court to be an unconstitutional limitation on attorneys' rights to free speech. Although there are still restrictions on what attorneys can say in advertisements, lawyer ads on television, billboards, radio, and the Internet are common.

Licensing Requirements

The **licensing** of attorneys, which gives them the right to practice law, is accomplished at the state level. Each state has different requirements that individuals must meet before they are allowed to practice law and give legal advice.

Basic Requirements

Generally, however, there are three basic requirements:

1. In most states, prospective attorneys must have a bachelor's degree from a university or college and must have graduated from an accredited law school (in many states, the school must be accredited by the ABA), which requires an additional three years of study.

2. A prospective attorney must pass a state bar examination—a rigorous examination that tests the candidate's knowledge of the law. The examination covers both state law (law applicable to the particular state in which the attorney is taking the exam and wishes to practice) and multistate law (law applicable in most states, including federal law). In addition, most states require prospective lawyers to pass the Multistate Professional Responsibility Exam on ethics rules.

3. The candidate must pass an extensive personal background investigation to verify that he or she is a responsible individual and otherwise qualifies to

social MEDIA TODAY

Check with your employer about its policy with respect to mentioning your place of employment on personal social media sites. Some firms do not want employees to mention the firm name on sites like LinkedIn or Facebook.

licensing
A government's official act of granting permission to an individual, such as an attorney, to do something that would be illegal in the absence of such permission.

engage in an ethical profession. An illegal act committed by the candidate in the past might disqualify the individual from being permitted to practice law. Only when these requirements have been met can an individual be admitted to the state bar and legally practice law within the state. In addition, each federal court requires admission to practice before an attorney can appear in a case filed there. This generally requires a sponsor and an application, but no test.

Licensing and UPL

Licensing requirements for attorneys are part of a long history of restrictions on entry into the legal profession. Beginning in the 1850s, restrictions on who could (or could not) practice law were put in place by state statutes prohibiting the **unauthorized practice of law (UPL)**. Court decisions relating to unauthorized legal practice also date to this period. By the 1930s, almost all states had enacted legislation prohibiting anyone but licensed attorneys from practicing law. Many of the regulatory issues facing the legal profession—and particularly paralegals—are directly related to these UPL statutes.

unauthorized practice of law (UPL)
The performance of actions defined by a legal authority, such as a state legislature, as constituting the "practice of law" without authorization to do so.

🖱 **ON THE** web

For a collection of ethics articles and laws, as well as links to other ethics sources, go to **www. legalethics.com**.

Ethical Codes and Rules

The legal profession is also regulated through ethical codes and rules adopted by each state—in most states, by order of the state supreme court. These codes of professional conduct evolved over time. A major step toward ethical regulation was taken in 1908, when the ABA approved the *Canons of Ethics,* which consisted of thirty-two ethical principles. In the following decades, various states adopted these canons as law. (Canons are generally accepted principles.)

Today's state ethical codes are based, for the most part, on later revisions of the ABA canons: the *Model Code of Professional Responsibility* (published in 1969) and the *Model Rules of Professional Conduct* (first published in 1983 to replace the *Model Code* and revised many times since then). Although most states have adopted laws based on the *Model Rules,* the *Model Code* is still in effect in some states. New York still uses the *Model Code,* for example, while California and Maine have developed their own rules. You should become familiar with the set of rules that is in effect in your state.

The *Model Code of Professional Responsibility*

The ABA *Model Code of Professional Responsibility,* often referred to simply as the *Model Code,* consists of nine canons (major principles). In the *Model Code,* each canon is followed by sections entitled "Ethical Considerations" (ECs) and "Disciplinary Rules" (DRs). The ethical considerations are "aspirational" in character—that is, they suggest ideal conduct, not necessarily behavior that is required by law. For example, Canon 6 ("A lawyer should represent a client competently") is followed by EC 6–1, which states (in part) that a lawyer "should strive to become and remain proficient in his practice." In contrast, disciplinary rules are mandatory in character—an attorney may be subject to disciplinary action for breaking one of the rules. For example, DR 6–101 (which follows Canon 6) states that a lawyer "shall not . . . neglect a legal matter entrusted to him."

The *Model Rules of Professional Conduct*

The 1983 revision of the ABA *Model Code*—referred to as the *Model Rules of Professional Conduct* or, more simply, as the *Model Rules*—represented a thorough revamping of the code. The *Model Rules* replaced the canons, ethical considerations, and disciplinary rules of the *Model Code* with a set of rules organized under eight general headings. Each rule is followed by comments shedding additional light on the rule's application and how the rule compares with the *Model Code*'s treatment of the same issue.

Because the 1983 *Model Rules* serve as models for the ethical codes of most states, we use the 1983 rules as the basis for our discussion in this text. It is important to note, however, that the ABA's ethics commission periodically updates and revises the *Model Rules* as necessary in light of the realities of modern law practice. For example, the ABA's ethics commission has revised the *Model Rules* to address new ethical concerns raised by technological developments (such as client confidentiality using e-mail). To view the ABA *Model Rules of Professional Conduct,* go to **www.americanbar.org**.

ON THE web

You can access the *Model Rules of Professional Conduct,* along with an explanation of various changes to the rules, on the ABA's Web site at **www.americanbar.org**. From the "Resources for Lawyers" menu, select "Ethics and Professionalism." On that page, select "Model Rules of Professional Conduct."

Sanctions for Violations

Attorneys who violate the rules governing professional conduct are subject to disciplinary proceedings brought by the state bar association, state supreme court, or state legislature—depending on the state's regulatory scheme. In most states, unethical attorney actions are reported (by clients, legal professionals, or others) to the ethics committee of the state bar association, which is obligated to investigate each complaint. For serious violations, the state bar association or the court initiates disciplinary proceedings against the attorney.

Formal Sanctions

Sanctions imposed for violations range from a **reprimand** (a formal "scolding" of the attorney—the mildest sanction[1]), to **suspension** (a more serious sanction in which the attorney is prohibited from practicing law in the state for a given period of time, such as one month or one year, or for an indefinite period of time), to **disbarment** (revocation of the attorney's license to practice law in the state—the most serious sanction).

Civil Liability

In addition to these sanctions, attorneys may be subject to civil liability for negligence. As will be discussed in Chapter 14, *negligence* (called **malpractice** when committed by a professional, such as an attorney) is a tort (a wrongful act) that is committed when an individual fails to perform a legally recognized duty. Tort law allows one who is injured by another's wrongful or careless act to bring a civil lawsuit against the wrongdoer for **damages** (compensation in the form of money). A client may bring a lawsuit against an attorney only if the client has suffered harm because of the attorney's failure to perform a legal duty.

If a paralegal's breach of a professional duty causes a client to suffer substantial harm, the client may sue not only the attorney but also the paralegal. Although law firms' liability insurance policies typically cover paralegals as well as attorneys, these policies do not cover paralegals working on a contract (freelance) basis. Just one lawsuit could ruin a freelance paralegal financially—as well as destroy that paralegal's reputation in the legal community. (Hence, obtaining liability insurance is important for freelance paralegals as well as for independent paralegals.)

Attorneys and paralegals are also subject to potential criminal liability under federal and state criminal statutes prohibiting fraud, theft, and other crimes.

Attorney Ethics and Paralegal Practice

Because most state codes are guided by the *Model Rules of Professional Conduct,* the rules discussed in this section are drawn from the *Model Rules.* Keep in mind, though, that your own state's code of conduct is the governing authority on attorney conduct in your state.

As a paralegal, one of your foremost professional responsibilities is to carefully follow the rules in your state's ethical code. You will want to obtain a copy of your state's ethical code and become familiar with its contents. A good practice is to keep

reprimand
A disciplinary sanction in which an attorney is rebuked for misbehavior. Although a reprimand is the mildest sanction for attorney misconduct, it is serious and may significantly damage the attorney's reputation in the legal community.

suspension
A serious disciplinary sanction in which an attorney who has violated an ethical rule or a law is prohibited from practicing law in the state for a specified or an indefinite period of time.

disbarment
A severe disciplinary sanction in which an attorney's license to practice law in the state is revoked because of unethical or illegal conduct.

malpractice
Professional misconduct or negligence—the failure to exercise due care—on the part of a professional, such as an attorney or a physician.

damages
Money awarded as a remedy for a civil wrong, such as a breach of contract or a tort (wrongful act).

A paralegal discusses a potential conflict of interest with her supervising attorney. Attorneys and paralegals must be careful to avoid violating the ethical rules of the legal profession, because violations of the rules can have serious professional and financial consequences. What are some ways that you can avoid violating your state's code of ethical conduct?

© Lisa S./www.Shutterstock.com

the code near at hand in your office. It is also helpful to develop a relationship with a trusted mentor at your firm for advice on such issues.

Professional duties—and the possibility of violating them—are involved in almost every task you will perform as a paralegal. Even if you memorize every rule governing the legal profession, you can still quite easily violate a rule unintentionally (few people breach professional duties intentionally). To minimize the chances that you accidentally violate a rule, you need to know not only what the rules are but also how they apply to the day-to-day realities of your job. In general, avoiding financial dealings and social relationships with clients helps you avoid violating ethical obligations.

The rules relating to competence, confidentiality, and conflict of interest deserve special attention here because they pose particularly difficult ethical problems for paralegals. Other important rules that affect paralegal performance—including the duty to charge reasonable fees, the duty to protect clients' property, and the duty to keep the client reasonably informed—will be discussed elsewhere in this text as they relate to special topics.

The Duty of Competence

Rule 1.1 of the *Model Rules* concerns one of the most fundamental duties of attorneys—the duty of competence. The Bar Association focuses on the requirement that licensed attorneys provide able representation to their clients. Competency in law requires knowledge of the subject, careful research to ensure being up-to-date, and proper preparation for representation whether in court or not. Most legal representation occurs out of court but requires the same knowledgeable approach.

Competent legal representation is the most basic requirement of the profession. **Breaching** (failing to perform) this duty may subject attorneys to one or more of the sanctions discussed earlier. As a paralegal, you share in this duty when you undertake work on an attorney's behalf.

How the Duty of Competence Can Be Breached

Most breaches of the duty of competence are inadvertent. Often, breaches of the duty of competence have to do with inadequate research, missed deadlines, and errors in legal documents filed with the court.

INADEQUATE RESEARCH.   Paralegals frequently do both legal and factual research for attorneys. Depending on the situation, an attorney's first step after meeting with a new client is often to have a paralegal research the facts involved, such as who did what to whom, when, where, and how. If the paralegal fails to discover a relevant fact and the attorney then relies on the paralegal's research in advising the client, the result could be a breach of the duty of competence.

Similarly, a paralegal conducting legal research might breach the duty of competence by failing to find or report a specific court decision that controls the outcome of a client's case. For example, suppose that a paralegal performs initial research into the law surrounding a particular dispute and reports her findings to the attorney. Then, while the paralegal is working on unrelated cases over the next few months, a state court rules on a case with issues very similar to those involved in the client's dispute. If the paralegal or the attorney does not go back and confirm that the initial research results are still accurate, a ruling that would influence the client's case could be overlooked. This would breach the attorney's duty of competence to the client.

Although attorneys are ultimately responsible for competent representation, paralegals play an important role in providing accurate information to their attorneys. If you are ever unsure of the accuracy of your research results, make sure to let the attorney know of your doubts. Also, keep good notes recording each step you took in conducting research so that you know what still needs to be done. These measures will help prevent accidental breaches of the duty of competence.

MISSED DEADLINES.   Paralegals often work on several cases at once. Keeping track of every deadline in every case can be challenging. Organization is the key to making sure that all deadlines are met. All dates relating to actions and events for every case or client should be entered on a calendar. Larger firms typically use computerized calendaring and "tickler" (reminder) systems. Even the smallest firm normally has calendar procedures and tickler systems in place.

Besides making sure that all deadlines are entered into the appropriate systems, you should also have your own personal calendar for tracking dates that are relevant to the cases on which you are working—and then make sure that you consistently use it. Check your calendar every morning or at some other convenient time. Also, check frequently with your attorney about deadlines that he or she may not have mentioned to you.

ERRORS IN DOCUMENTS.   Breaches of the duty of competence can involve errors in documents. For example, incorrect information might be included (or crucial information omitted) in a legal document to be filed with the court. If the attorney fails to notice the error before signing the document, and the document is delivered to the court, a breach of the duty of competence has occurred. Depending on its effect, this breach may expose the attorney and the paralegal to liability for negligence. To prevent these kinds of violations, be especially careful in drafting and proofreading documents.

breach
To violate a legal duty by an act or a failure to act.

social
MEDIA TODAY

Online media expert Scott Klososky notes that many organizations are in chaos with social media because of the rapid growth in these tools. If your firm does not have a social media policy, consider volunteering to help develop one.

Generally, if you are ever unsure about what to include in a document, when it must be completed or filed with the court, how extensively you should research a legal issue, or any other aspect of an assignment, ask your supervising attorney for clarification. Make sure that your work is adequately overseen by an attorney to reduce the chances that it will contain costly mistakes or errors. Whether communicating by e-mail or in person, clear communication is critical, as the *In the Office* feature below addresses.

Attorney's Duty to Supervise

Rule 5.3 of the *Model Rules* defines the responsibilities of attorneys to nonlawyer assistants. Attorneys may hire personnel to assist them, but they must supervise their assistants. A reason for the supervision is that attorneys must help ensure that their staff members behave in accord with the standards of the profession. The rule also specifies the circumstances under which a lawyer is held responsible for conduct by a nonlawyer that violates the standards set out for attorneys. The lawyer is responsible, for example, if she orders the conduct or ratifies (approves of) it, with knowledge of the specific conduct. Lawyers who have managerial authority in a law firm or have supervisory authority over a nonlawyer can also be held responsible for the nonlawyer's unethical conduct if they knew about it and failed to take any action to prevent it.

This rule applies not only to lawyers who work in private law firms but also to lawyers in corporate legal departments, government agencies, and elsewhere. In addition, in the statements outlining attorneys' responsibilities toward nonlawyer employees in this area, the ABA commission changed the word *should* to *must*. Attorneys *must* both instruct and supervise nonlawyer employees concerning appropriate ethical conduct and can be held personally responsible for the ethical violations of their subordinates.

Inadequate Supervision

Because attorneys are legally responsible for their assistants' work, it may seem logical to assume that attorneys will take time to direct that work carefully. In fact, paralegals may find it difficult to ensure that their work is adequately supervised. For one thing, most attorneys and paralegals are very busy. Making sure that all paralegals' tasks are properly overseen can be time consuming. At the same time, attorneys—especially if they know their paralegals are competent—often do not

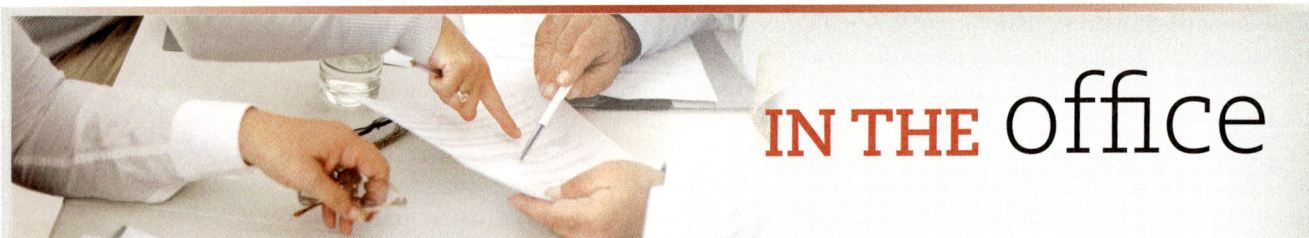

IN THE office

AM I CLEAR?

E-mail is a common form of communication, but it causes problems when not used properly. E-mails are the equivalent of letters or memos. When we write a letter or a memo, we usually read it more than once and think carefully about what we're saying. Too many times, we treat e-mails as if they were oral communications—that is, we write in a chatty and imprecise manner. Before sending any e-mail to a client, print it, read it, be sure it is addressed to the right party, and edit it. Remember that the matter you're discussing is important to the client, and your communication should be professional and clear. You should always follow office e-mail procedures carefully. If your firm uses social media for office communications, you should also use discretion when you create such communications. You are often judged on how carefully you communicate.

take the time to read every document the paralegals draft. Nonetheless, as a paralegal, you have a duty to assist your supervising attorney in fulfilling his or her ethical obligations, including the obligation to supervise your work.

If you ever believe that your attorney is not adequately supervising your work, there are several things you can do:

- Improve communications with the attorney—generally, the more you initiate communication with your supervising attorney, the more likely the attorney will take an active role in directing your activities.

- Ask the attorney for feedback on your work. Sometimes, it helps to place reminders on your calendar to discuss particular issues or questions with the attorney. When the opportunity to talk arises, these issues or questions will be fresh in your mind.

- Attach a note to a document that you have prepared for the attorney, requesting him or her to review the document (or revised sections of the document) carefully before signing it.

Ensuring proper supervision to protect yourself is highlighted in the *Developing Paralegal Skills* feature below.

Confidentiality of Information

Rule 1.6 of the *Model Rules* concerns attorney-client confidentiality. This rule is one of the oldest and most important rules of the legal profession. It would be difficult for a lawyer to properly represent a client without such a rule. A client must be able to confide in the attorney so that the attorney can best represent the client's interest. Because confidentiality is one of the easiest rules to violate, a thorough understanding of the rule is essential.

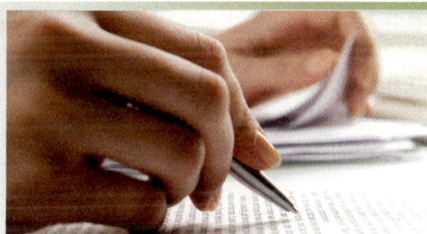

DEVELOPING
paralegal skills

ADEQUATE SUPERVISION

Michael Patton's supervising attorney, Muriel Chapman, asks him to prepare two complaints (the documents filed with the court to initiate a lawsuit) and gives him specific information needed for the two different cases. Muriel is scheduled to attend a deposition (a pretrial procedure in which testimony is given under oath) in another matter this afternoon and has asked Michael to finish the complaints and file them with the court today. Muriel tells Michael to use a complaint from a previous client's case as a model for creating the new complaints, replacing that client's information as necessary.

Michael finishes the work at 3:00 P.M. while Muriel is attending the deposition in the conference room. Michael needs to file the complaints at the courthouse by 5:00 P.M., but, knowing the adequate supervision rule, does not want to file the documents before Muriel has reviewed them. He decides that he must interrupt the deposition so that Muriel can look over the complaints before they are filed with the court. He flags a few passages that he is unsure about and proceeds into the conference room. Muriel asks the opposing counsel to take a short break so she can step out of the room to review the documents that he has prepared.

TIPS FOR OBTAINING ADEQUATE SUPERVISION

- Always request your supervising attorney to review your work.

- Use notes or ticklers as reminders to ask for a review.

- Make the review as convenient as possible for your supervising attorney and mark anything that needs particular attention.

- Discuss any ethical concerns with the attorney.

- Be persistent.

- Complete your work in a timely fashion so the attorney can review it.

The general rule of confidentiality is that all information relating to representation of a client must be kept confidential. There are exceptions to the rule, which we discuss shortly.

Note that the rule simply states that a lawyer may not reveal "information relating to representation of a client." Does this mean that if a client tells you that he is the president of a local company, you have to keep that information confidential, even when it is common knowledge? For example, could you tell your spouse, "Mr. X is the president of XYZ Corporation"? It may seem permissible, because that fact is so widely known. But in so doing, you must not indicate, by words or conduct, that Mr. X is a client of your firm. Mr. X may not want it known that he is talking to a lawyer at a law firm. People who learn that Mr. X has been at the law firm may think "something is up," which is likely to be true. Confidence has been breached.

Consider another example. Suppose that one evening at dinner you told your spouse that you had met Mr. X that day. Your spouse might reasonably assume that your firm was handling some legal matter involving Mr. X and might repeat that to other people. Because it may be difficult to decide what information is or is not confidential, a good rule of thumb is to regard all information about a client or a client's case as confidential.

Exceptions to the Confidentiality Rule

Rule 1.6, Confidentiality of Information, provides for certain exceptions to the confidentiality rule, each of which we look at here.

CLIENT GIVES INFORMED CONSENT TO THE DISCLOSURE.   The rule indicates that an attorney can reveal confidential information if the client gives informed consent to the disclosure. The attorney must fully explain the risks and alternatives involved in the disclosure for the consent to be informed.

For example, suppose that an attorney is drawing up a will for a client, and the client is leaving a particular property to her only son and not leaving a share of that property to her daughter. The daughter calls and wants to know how her mother's will reads. The attorney cannot divulge this confidential information to the daughter because the client has not consented to such disclosure. Now suppose that the attorney explains to the client that if her daughter does not learn about the provisions of the will until after her mother's death, it is more likely that she will contest it in court. After the attorney and client discuss the various alternatives and the risks of each, the client can give informed consent to the attorney to disclose information to her daughter.

IMPLIEDLY AUTHORIZED DISCLOSURES.   The ABA rules allow attorneys to make disclosures of information that are presumed necessary to represent clients. This exception is clearly necessary. Legal representation of clients necessarily involves the attorney's assistants who must have access to the confidential information to do their jobs. If a paralegal is working on the client's case, for example, he must know what the client told the attorney about the legal matter and must have access to information in the client's file concerning the case.

DISCLOSURES TO PREVENT HARM.   The *Model Rules* recognize that there are certain circumstances in which an attorney should be allowed to disclose confidential information when it is necessary to prevent harm to persons or property. Rule 1.6 specifically lists four exceptions to the confidentiality rule for this purpose:

1. An attorney is allowed to reveal a client's information to prevent reasonably certain death or substantial bodily harm. For example, suppose that the client confides in the attorney that he assaulted and nearly killed several people recently. The attorney is not allowed to disclose this information. If that client then tells the attorney that he is going to attack a specific person in the future, however, the attorney can disclose this information to prevent reasonably certain bodily harm to the person. This is addressed further in the *Developing Paralegal Skills* feature on the facing page.

social MEDIA TODAY

Don't misrepresent facts or tell lies of omission online. Doing so in front of millions of online viewers virtually ensures you will be caught.

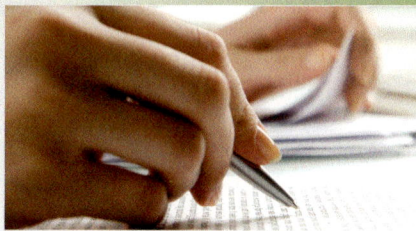

DEVELOPING
paralegal skills

WHAT IF YOU LEARN YOUR CLIENT IS PLANNING TO COMMIT A CRIME?

Communications between a client and his or her attorney, including those with the attorney's paralegal, are usually covered by the attorney-client privilege, discussed on pages 99 through 103. Privileged statements may not be disclosed without the client's consent. When the client makes statements that suggest he or she is going to commit a crime, however, the privilege does not apply.

For example, in one criminal case, the defendant told his lawyer that he was going to attempt to bribe one or more witnesses against him and that if he was unable to do so, he would "whack" the witnesses.[a] Later the defendant also threatened the lawyer.

The lawyer reported these threats to the district attorney and withdrew as the defendant's counsel. The defendant's new lawyer tried to have the first lawyer's testimony about the threats excluded, but failed. Because the defendant had threatened a criminal act (assaulting the witnesses and lawyer) that could involve serious bodily harm or death, the California appeals court held that privilege did not apply.

State rules on privilege differ, and you should make sure that you understand the range of crimes covered by your state's laws. All states exempt threats of death or serious injury, and such statements should be reported immediately. In addition, some states require reporting of certain criminal acts.

a.   *People v. Dang*, 93 Cal.App.4th 1293, 113 Cal.Rptr.2d 763 (2001).

2. In certain situations, an attorney can disclose confidential information to prevent a client from committing a crime or fraud. The crime or fraud must be reasonably certain to result in substantial injury to the financial interests or property of another. Also, the client must have used or be using the attorney's services to perpetrate the crime or fraud. If both these conditions are present, then the attorney can disclose information to the extent necessary to enable the affected person to contact the appropriate authorities.

3. If a client used the attorney to help commit a crime or fraud, and the crime or fraud will likely cause injury to the financial interests or property of another, the attorney can disclose confidential information to the extent necessary to prevent or reduce that injury.

4. An attorney can also disclose confidential information to establish a defense to a criminal charge in a controversy between the attorney and the client based on conduct involving the client, or to respond to allegations in any proceeding regarding the attorney's representation of the client.

DISCLOSURES TO ENSURE COMPLIANCE WITH *MODEL RULES*.   If a lawyer is unsure what is required to comply with the *Model Rules of Professional Conduct* in a particular situation, the lawyer can seek legal advice from another lawyer without violating confidentiality. For example, suppose that an attorney who is representing a corporation becomes suspicious that the corporation is engaged in fraud. The attorney is not sure what her professional responsibilities are in that particular situation, so she can seek confidential legal advice to assist her in complying with the *Model Rules*.

DEFENDING AGAINST A CLIENT'S LEGAL ACTION.   An attorney may also disclose confidential information if the information is necessary to establish a defense in an action brought by a client against the attorney. For example, if the client sues the attorney for malpractice, the lawyer might need to reveal confidential information to prove that he was not negligent. Note, though, that the attorney is permitted to disclose confidential information only to the extent that it is essential to defend the lawsuit.

DISCLOSURES TO COMPLY WITH COURT ORDER OR OTHER LAW.   An attorney may also reveal information relating to the representation of a client if ordered to do so by a court or other governmental entity. For example, suppose that one of the attorney's clients in a divorce case was allegedly hiding valuable assets from his wife. In that situation, a court could require the attorney to reveal any confidential information from the client related to the hidden assets. The attorney should first attempt to persuade the client to disclose the location and value of the assets. Nevertheless, the attorney can reveal as much information as he thinks reasonable to satisfy the needs of the court or other governmental entity.

Violations of the Confidentiality Rule

Paralegals, like other professionals, spend a good part of their lives engaged in their work. Naturally, they are tempted to discuss their work with family members, coworkers, and friends. As a paralegal, a great temptation you will face is the desire to discuss an interesting case with someone you know.

You can deal with this temptation in two ways: you can decide never to discuss anything concerning your work, or you can limit your discussion to issues and comments that will not reveal the identity of clients. The latter approach is more realistic for most people, but it requires great care. Something you say may reveal a client's identity, even though you are not aware of it. (See the *Ethics Watch* feature on the facing page.) Developing a reputation for being discreet will enhance your career by encouraging attorneys and clients to confide in you.

CONVERSATIONS OVERHEARD BY OTHERS.   Violations of the confidentiality rule can happen by oversight. Suppose that you and a secretary in your office are working on the same case and continue, as you walk to the elevator, a conversation that you have been having about the case. In the hall or on the elevator, your conversation could be overheard, and the confidential information revealed could have an adverse effect on your client's interests. It is important to avoid the possibility of unwittingly revealing confidential information to **third parties** in such situations. Therefore, never discuss confidential information when you are in common areas.

ELECTRONIC COMMUNICATIONS AND CONFIDENTIALITY.   Whenever you talk to or about a client on the telephone, make sure that your conversation will not be overheard by a third party. You may be sitting in your private office, but if your door is open, someone may overhear the conversation. Even employees of the firm should not hear information about cases they are not working on.

Paralegals should take special care when using cell phones. Although conversations on digital cell phones are difficult to intercept, there is still a security risk. No doubt you have overheard other people talking on their phones as if other people could not hear. Some violations of confidentiality are low-tech, such as talking on the phone in the open, while others are more sophisticated. The *Featured Contributor* on pages 100 and 101 provides more details about electronic security issues.

OTHER WAYS OF VIOLATING THE CONFIDENTIALITY RULE.   There are many other ways in which you can reveal confidential information without intending to do so. A file or document sitting on your desk, if observed by a third party, may reveal the identity of a client or enough information to suggest the client's identity. A computer screen, if visible to those passing by your desk, could convey information to someone who is not authorized to know that information. You might be speaking to an expert witness about rescheduling a meeting and accidentally let something about the case slip out.

Alternatively, you might be friendly with a paralegal at an opposing attorney's office because the two attorneys have worked on many cases together. You are on the phone trying to work out a date for an important meeting. This paralegal suggests a date, and you tell her that the attorney for whom you work is scheduled to

---

third party
A person or entity not directly involved in an agreement (such as a contract), legal proceeding (such as a lawsuit), or relationship (such as an attorney-client relationship).

ETHICS WATCH

SOCIAL EVENTS AND CONFIDENTIALITY

Assume that you are at a party with some other paralegals. You tell a paralegal whom you know quite well of some startling news—that a client of your firm, a prominent city official, is being investigated for drug dealing. Although your friend promises to keep this information strictly confidential, she nonetheless tells her husband, who tells a coworker, who in turn tells a friend, and so on. Soon, the news has reached the press, and the resulting media coverage results in irreparable harm to the official's reputation in the community.

Revealing the juicy gossip breached your obligation to the client. If it can be proved that the harm is the direct result of your breach of the duty of confidentiality, the official could sue you and the attorney and the firm for whom you work for damages.

In this situation, you would have violated the NFPA *Model Code of Ethics and Professional Responsibility,* Section 1.5(f), which states: "A paralegal shall not engage in any indiscreet communications concerning clients." This behavior would also have violated the ABA *Model Guidelines for the Utilization of Paralegal Services,* Guideline 6: Attorneys may utilize paralegals, but the attorneys must take proper steps to be sure that client confidentiality is protected. Finally, you would have violated the NALA *Code of Ethics and Professional Responsibility,* Canon 7: "A paralegal must protect the confidences of a client."

be in court on a specific client's case that day. If you name the client, or indicate that the attorney will be arguing a particular type of motion in the case, you may breach the duty of confidentiality. As the *Technology and Today's Paralegal* feature on page 102 emphasizes, there are many aspects to confidentiality.

Confidentiality and the Attorney-Client Privilege

All information relating to a client's representation is considered confidential information. Some confidential information also qualifies as privileged information, or information subject to the **attorney-client privilege**.

The attorney-client privilege can be vitally important during the litigation process. As you will read in Chapter 10, prior to a trial each attorney is permitted to obtain information relating to the case from the opposing attorney and other persons, such as witnesses. This means that attorneys must exchange certain information relating to their clients. An attorney need not provide privileged information, however—unless the client consents to the disclosure or a court orders it. Similarly, if an attorney is called to the witness stand during a trial, the attorney may not disclose privileged information unless the court orders him or her to do so.

What Kind of Information Is Privileged?

State statutes and court cases define what constitutes privileged information. Generally, any communications concerning a client's legal rights or problems fall under the attorney-client privilege. Suppose that an attorney's client is a criminal

attorney-client privilege
A rule of evidence requiring that confidential communications between a client and his or her attorney (relating to their professional relationship) be kept confidential, unless the client consents to disclosure.

Featured Contributor

SECURING CLIENT INFORMATION IN THE DIGITAL AGE

© Cengage Learning 2014

Anita Whitby

BIOGRAPHICAL NOTE

Anita Whitby is a business law attorney and Park University faculty member. She has extensive experience as a course developer and teacher of legal studies and business law courses. Ms. Whitby is also a textbook reviewer for Cengage Learning and serves on the advisory board for the series known as *Annual Editions: Business Ethics.* Her current research interests include data privacy ethics, intellectual property, and immersive online learning.

The Digital Age has ushered in an array of electronic devices and technology to help streamline law offices. However, the use of such electronic devices and technology presents serious ethical issues. The following best practices will help paralegals avoid common pitfalls associated with the use of popular devices and technology.

E-MAIL ENCRYPTION

When the topic of e-mail security comes up, we often think about it in terms of Trojans attacking a computer network. However, it is the act of sending unsecured e-mail communication that is the main source of client data breaches. Communicating with clients via e-mail may seem harmless, but it must be done with extra precaution. Whether you are using a laptop or smartphone, be sure to use encryption software for client communication. Encryption ensures that client information is protected. Because the communication cannot be "unlocked" without a "key," misdirected communication is not in danger of being disclosed to a third party.

CLIENT WORKPLACE E-MAIL & CONFIDENTIALITY

What if a client prefers to communicate via e-mail? The American Bar Association recently issued an ethics opinion regarding the attorney's

defendant, for example. The client tells the attorney that she was actually in the vicinity of the crime site at the time of the crime, but to her knowledge, no one noticed her presence there. This is privileged information that the attorney may disclose only with the client's consent or on a court's order to do so.

WORK PRODUCT.   Certain materials relating to an attorney's preparation of a client's case for trial are protected as privileged information under what is known as the **work product** doctrine. Usually, information concerning an attorney's legal strategy for conducting a case is classified as work product and, as such, may be subject to the attorney-client privilege. Legal strategy includes the legal theories that the attorney plans to use in support of the client's claim, how the attorney interprets the evidence relating to the claim, and the like.

Certain evidence gathered by the attorney to support the client's claim, however, such as financial statements relating to the client's business firm, would probably not be classified as work product.

CAUTION ADVISED.   Because it is often difficult to tell what types of information (including work product) qualify as privileged, paralegals should consult with their supervising attorneys whenever issues arise that may require that such a distinction be made. It is important to note that like any other confidential information relating to

---

work product
An attorney's mental impressions, conclusions, and legal theories regarding a case being prepared on behalf of a client. Work product normally is regarded as privileged information.

duty to caution clients about communicating sensitive information via workplace e-mail. A prime example is the client who communicates with the law firm through a workplace computer. In this situation, the client does not have an expectation of privacy because the employer's e-mail system is being used. A paralegal should notify the supervising attorney when there is a potential issue about the manner in which a client is communicating sensitive information to the firm.

E-MAIL "RECALL"

Security breaches can result from something as simple as sending an e-mail to the wrong recipient. The e-mail "recall" feature can be used, but the "recall" feature does not work for e-mails that have already been opened. In addition, the recall feature does not always function properly due to firewalls and other network settings. Therefore, a paralegal must be diligent in verifying the correct recipients before e-mail communications are sent. You can opt to use e-mail software that delays outgoing communication for a short period of time before it is sent. That gives extra time to address issues that may arise.

METADATA

Because documents contain metadata, a paralegal must be certain that sensitive information has been properly redacted. Saving a document in PDF format does not "scrub" it of revisions that may have been made.

Also, if you use an older version of Adobe software, you may mistakenly believe that it is sufficient to use the markup feature to "strike out" sensitive data. That works when the document is in print form. However, the underlying data still exists in electronic versions of the document and can be readily accessed. Therefore, be sure that electronic documents have been "scrubbed" of metadata. Newer versions of Adobe software allow users to highlight the material and then apply redactions to the document. You can be certain that a document is free of metadata by simply scanning a hard copy of the document and then using that "clean" version of the electronic document for dissemination.

WI-FI HOTSPOTS & WIRELESS PHONES

An often overlooked security danger involves the use of wireless devices to transmit e-mails, texts, and other communication via public Wi-Fi. These networks are unsecured. They should not be used to communicate confidential information. Use a secure mobile hotspot instead. It allows multiple Wi-Fi devices to connect to a secured mobile broadband network.

Wireless phone communication is also of concern because, like public Wi-Fi, it is not always secure. Third parties can use scanners to intercept cell phone calls. Many clients are unaware of the risks or have to be reminded of the potential for an unintended disclosure of their confidential information.

". . . many clients are unaware of the risks. . ."

a client's case, privileged information is subject to the exceptions to the confidentiality rule discussed above. You should be alert for inadvertent disclosures by opposing counsel or paralegals. If you think someone on the other side of a case has disclosed confidential information to you, immediately tell your supervising attorney.

When the Attorney-Client Privilege Arises

The attorney-client privilege comes into existence the moment a client communicates with an attorney concerning a legal matter. People sometimes mistakenly assume that there is no duty to keep client information confidential unless an attorney agrees to represent a client and the client signs an agreement. This is not so. The privilege—and thus the duty of confidentiality—arises even if the lawyer decides not to represent the client and even when the client is not charged any fee. Thus, mentioning to a friend that a high-profile party called your firm seeking legal representation, and the firm declined to take the case, could violate the privilege.

Duration of the Privilege

The client is the holder, or "owner," of the privilege, and only the client can waive (set aside) the privilege. Unless waived by the client, the privilege lasts indefinitely. In other words, the privilege continues even though the attorney has completed the client's legal matter and is no longer working on the case.

TECHNOLOGY AND
today's paralegal

ELECTRONIC COMMUNICATIONS AND CONFIDENTIALITY

Almost everyone has had the experience of sending an e-mail to the wrong recipient or accidentally using "reply to all" instead of "reply" and so broadcasting a personal message to a group. Similarly, some law firm employees have sent inappropriate e-mails concerning personal behavior to lists including partners and clients.

Careless communications can be more than simply embarrassing when they occur in a legal environment: Confidential information could be disclosed and privilege lost. Such an incident can damage the sender's employment prospects, the interests of the client, and the reputation of the firm. This is a problem that goes beyond the workplace. Personal Web pages or social networking messages with inappropriate content may be seen by employers, opponents, or clients.

There are three major issues for paralegals to consider when using electronic communications or social media at work and at home:

1. Is a work-related communication truly confidential, or could an opposing party discover it during litigation?

2. Is a communication an appropriate use of the employer's property?

3. What sort of personal information is appropriate to share with the world through Facebook, Twitter, and other services?

CONFIDENTIALITY

Just labeling an e-mail or text message "confidential" does not mean that it will be treated as confidential. Simply adding nonprivileged material to a privileged communication won't protect the non-privileged portion. Your firm should have a policy about when it is appropriate to send confidential information electronically and when it is not. Seek guidance from your supervising attorney if you have any doubt about the appropriateness of transmitting confidential information.

PERSONAL USE OF BUSINESS SYSTEMS

Many employers, including law firms, provide employees with communication devices and services, such as smartphones, tablet devices, and laptop computers. Firms often allow some personal use of these devices but retain the right to monitor and audit the content of the e-mails, messages, and Web traffic on them. Be sure to check your employer's policies on appropriate use of such devices before making personal use, such as for personal e-mail, of firm-provided hardware or services. Some firms will not want you to list the firm name on LinkedIn or other networking site profiles, for fear of encouraging other firms to raid their employees.

There are limits on employers' abilities to monitor personal communications, however. The United States Supreme Court held that a pager text-messaging service could provide an employer with the content of employees' text messages, but emphasized the extent of the measures the employer took to ensure that it did not violate the employees' privacy in reviewing personal use of the employer-provided electronic device.[a] Think carefully about how you are using employer-provided communications devices and systems. Make sure your use is within your employer's policies.

TECHNOLOGY TIP ABOUT ONLINE PERSONAL INFORMATION

Remember, when you post the details of your latest date or pictures of your vacation online, your employer or clients may stumble across those postings simply by Googling your name. Even if you change a Facebook page later, caching by search engines means that an embarrassing picture or post could linger in cyberspace for years. The bottom line: don't post pictures or text online that you would feel uncomfortable showing to your boss. Assume employers and prospective employers will search your name online.

---

a.   *City of Ontario, Calif. v. Quon*, 130 S.Ct. 2619 (2010).

Privileged information is confidential information. If such information is disclosed to others, it is no longer confidential and can no longer be considered privileged. This is another reason why it is so important to guard against accidental violations of the confidentiality rule: if the rule is violated, information that otherwise might have been protected by the attorney-client privilege can be used against the client's interests.

Consider what would happen if a paralegal inadvertently sent, by e-mail, a confidential document to opposing counsel instead of to the client. The document, because it contained the attorney's analysis of confidential client information, might be classified as privileged information under the work product doctrine. The disclosure of the information to the opposing counsel destroyed its confidential character—and therefore any possibility that it might be protected as privileged information.

Conflict of Interest

A **conflict of interest** arises when representing one client injures the interests of another client. Model Rules 1.7, 1.8, 1.9, 1.10, and 1.11 pertain to conflict-of-interest situations. The general rule is that an attorney should not represent a client if doing so would be directly adverse to another client, or if there is a significant risk that the attorney's ability to consider, recommend, or carry out an appropriate course of action for the client would be materially (significantly) limited as a result of the attorney's other responsibilities or interests. A classic example of a conflict of interest exists when an attorney simultaneously represents two adverse parties in a legal proceeding. Clearly, in such a situation, the attorney's loyalties must be divided.

conflict of interest
A situation in which two or more duties or interests come into conflict, as when an attorney attempts to represent opposing parties in a legal dispute.

Simultaneous Representation

If an attorney reasonably believes that representing two parties in a legal proceeding will not adversely affect either party's interest, then the attorney is permitted to do so—but only if both parties give informed consent. Normally, attorneys avoid this kind of situation because what might start out as a simple, uncontested proceeding could evolve into a legal battle.

Divorce proceedings, for example, may begin amicably but end up in heated disputes over property division. If the husband and wife employ only one attorney, the attorney then faces a conflict of interest: assisting one party will necessarily be adverse to the interests of the other. Because of the potential for a conflict of interest in divorce proceedings, some courts do not permit attorneys to represent both spouses.

Similar conflicts arise when the "family attorney" is asked to handle a family matter and the family members eventually disagree on what the outcome should be. Consider a situation in which two adult children request the family lawyer to handle the procedures required to settle their deceased parent's estate. The will favors one child, and the other child decides to challenge the will's validity. The attorney cannot represent both sides without facing a conflict of interest.

Attorneys representing corporate clients may face conflicts of interest when corporate personnel become divided on an issue. For example, assume that Carl Finn, an attorney, represents ABC Corporation. Finn typically deals with the corporation's president, Julie Johnson, when giving legal assistance and advice. At times, however, Finn deals with other corporate personnel, including Seth Harrison, the corporation's accountant. Harrison and Johnson disagree on several major issues, and eventually Johnson arranges to have Harrison fired. Harrison wants attorney Finn to represent him in a lawsuit against the corporation for wrongful termination of his employment. Finn would have a conflict of interest. He could not represent Harrison. He can continue to represent ABC, however.

Former Clients

A conflict of interest may involve former clients. The ABA rules express particular caution when a lawyer may be in a position to represent a new client in a matter that would conflict with the interests of a former client. In such instances, at a minimum, the attorney must notify the former client of the matter and, if needed, obtain written consent. The rule regarding former clients is closely related to the rule on preserving the confidentiality of a client. The rationale behind the rule is that an attorney, in representing a client, is entrusted with certain information that may be unknown to others. That information should not be used against the client—even after the *representation* has ended.

JOB CHANGES AND FORMER CLIENTS.   The rule concerning former clients does not prohibit an individual attorney or paralegal from working at a firm or agency that represents interests contrary to those of a former client. If that were the situation, many of those who have worked for large firms would find it hard to change jobs. The rules depend on the specific circumstances. In some situations, when a conflict of interest results from a job change, the new employer can avoid violating the rules governing conflict of interest through the use of screening procedures. That is, the new employer can erect an **ethical wall** around the new employee so that the new employee remains ignorant about the case that would give rise to the conflict of interest.

WALLING-OFF PROCEDURES.   Law offices usually have procedures for "walling off" an attorney or other legal professional from a case when a conflict of interest exists. The firm may announce in a memo to all employees that a certain attorney or paralegal should not have access to specific files, for example, and may set out procedures to be followed to ensure that access to those files is restricted. Computer documents relating to the case may be protected by passwords or in some other way. Commonly, any hard-copy files relating to the case are flagged with a sticker to indicate that access to the files is restricted.

Firms normally take great care to establish and uphold such restrictions because if confidential information is used in a way harmful to a former client, the former client may sue the firm for damages. In defending against such a suit, the firm must show that it took reasonable precautions to protect that client's interests. The *Developing Paralegal Skills* feature below summarizes how steps are taken to build an ethical wall.

ethical wall
A term that refers to the procedures used to create a screen around a legal employee to shield him or her from information about a case in which there is a conflict of interest.

ON THE web

To read an article by NFPA's ethics coordinator entitled "The Ethical Wall: Its Application to Paralegals," go to **www.paralegals.org**. Select "Positions & Issues" from the menu, and then select "Ethics" to find a link to the article.

DEVELOPING
paralegal skills

BUILDING AN ETHICAL WALL

Lana Smith, a paralegal, has been asked by her supervising attorney to set up an ethical wall because a new attorney, Chandra Piper, has been hired from the law firm of Nunn & Bush. While employed by Nunn & Bush, Piper represented the defendant, Seski Manufacturing, in the ongoing case of *Tymes v. Seski Manufacturing Co.* Smith's firm—and Piper's new employer—represents the plaintiff, Joseph Tymes, in that case. Consequently, Piper's work for Nunn & Bush creates a conflict of interest, which Piper has acknowledged in a document signed under oath. Smith makes a list of the walling-off procedures to use to ensure that the firm does not violate the rules on conflict of interest.

CHECKLIST FOR BUILDING AN ETHICAL WALL

- Prepare a memo to the office manager regarding the conflict and the need for special arrangements to ensure that Piper will have no involvement in the *Tymes* case.

- Prepare a memo to the team representing Tymes to inform them of the conflict of interest and the special procedures to be followed.

- Prepare a memo to the firm giving the case name, the nature of the conflict, the parties involved, and instructions to maintain a blanket of silence with respect to Chandra Piper.

- Arrange for Piper's office to be on a different floor from the team (if possible) to demonstrate, if necessary, that the firm took steps to separate Piper and the team and to prevent them from having access to one another's files.

- Arrange with the office manager for computer passwords to be issued to the team members so that access to computer files on the *Tymes* case is available only to team members.

- Place "ACCESS RESTRICTED" stickers on the files for the *Tymes* case.

- Develop a security procedure for signing out and tracking the case files in the *Tymes* case to prevent inadvertent disclosure of the files to Piper or her staff members.

Other Conflict-of-Interest Situations

Several other situations may give rise to conflicts of interest. Gifts from clients may create conflicts of interest, because they tend to bias the judgment of the attorney or paralegal. Some types of gifts are specifically prohibited. For example, the *Model Rules* prohibit an attorney from preparing documents (such as wills) for a client if the client gives the attorney or a member of the attorney's family a gift in the will. Note that as a paralegal, you may be offered gifts from appreciative clients at Christmas or other times. Generally, such gifts pose no ethical problems. If a client offers you a gift that has substantial value, however, you should discuss the issue with your supervising attorney.

Attorneys also need to be careful about taking on a client whose case may create an "issue conflict" for the attorney. Generally, an attorney cannot represent a client on a substantive legal issue if the client's position is contrary to that of another client being represented by the lawyer—or the lawyer's firm.

Occasionally, conflicts of interest may arise when two family members who are both attorneys or paralegals are involved in the representation of adverse parties in a legal proceeding. Because there is a risk that the family relationship will interfere with professional judgment, generally an attorney should not represent a client if an opposing party to the dispute is being represented by a member of the attorney's family (such as a spouse, parent, child, or sibling). If you, as a paralegal, are married to or living with another paralegal or an attorney, you should inform your firm of this fact if you ever suspect that a conflict of interest might result from your relationship. Similarly, if you discover that you may have a financial interest in the outcome of a lawsuit that your firm is handling (such as owning stock in a company involved in a lawsuit in which a party is represented by the firm), you should notify the attorney of the potential conflict.

Conflicts Checks

Whenever a potential client consults with an attorney, the attorney will want to make sure that no potential conflict of interest exists before deciding whether to represent the client. Running a **conflicts check** is a standard procedure in every law office and one that is frequently undertaken by paralegals. Before you can run a conflicts check, you need to know the name of the prospective client, the other party or parties that may be involved in the client's legal matter, and the legal issue involved.

Normally, every law firm has some established procedure for conflicts checks, and in larger firms there is usually a computerized database containing the names of former clients and the other information you will need in checking for conflicts of interest.

conflicts check
A procedure for determining whether an agreement to represent a potential client will result in a conflict of interest.

The Indirect Regulation of Paralegals

Paralegals are regulated *indirectly* in several ways. Clearly, the ethical codes for attorneys just discussed indirectly regulates the conduct of paralegals. Additionally, paralegal conduct is evaluated on the basis of standards and guidelines created by paralegal professional groups that create best practices but do not have the force of law, as well as guidelines for the utilization of paralegals developed by the American Bar Association and various states.

Paralegal Ethical Codes

Paralegals are becoming increasingly self-regulated. Recall from Chapter 1 that the two major national paralegal associations in the United States—the National Federation of Paralegal Associations (NFPA), and the National Association of Legal Assistants (NALA)—were formed to define and represent paralegal professional interests on a national level. Shortly after they were formed, both of these associations adopted codes of ethics defining the ethical responsibilities of paralegals.

ON THE web

You can find NFPA's *Model Code of Ethics and Professional Responsibility and Guidelines for Enforcement* on the Web at **www. paralegals.org**. Select "Positions & Issues" from the menu. Then select "Model Code of Ethics."

NFPA's Code of Ethics

In 1977, NFPA adopted its first code of ethics, called the *Affirmation of Responsibility*. The code has since been revised several times and, in 1993, was renamed the *Model Code of Ethics and Professional Responsibility*. In 1997, NFPA revised the code, particularly its format, and took the step of appending to its code a list of enforcement guidelines setting forth recommendations on how to discipline paralegals who violate ethical standards promulgated by the code. The full title of NFPA's current code is the *Model Code of Ethics and Professional Responsibility and Guidelines for Enforcement*.

Exhibit 4.1 below presents the rules from Section 1 of the code, entitled "NFPA Model Disciplinary Rules and Ethical Considerations." For reasons of space, only the rules are included in the exhibit, not the ethical considerations that follow each rule. The ethical considerations are important to paralegals, however, because they explain what conduct the rule prohibits. The full text of NFPA's code (including the rules, ethical considerations, and guidelines for enforcement) is presented in Appendix C of this book.

NALA's Code of Ethics

In 1975, NALA issued its *Code of Ethics and Professional Responsibility*, which, like NFPA's code, has since undergone several revisions. Exhibit 4.2 on the facing page presents NALA's code in its entirety. Note that NALA's code, like the *Model Code of Professional Responsibility* discussed earlier in this chapter, presents ethical precepts as a series of "canons." (Prior to the 1997 revision of its code, NFPA also listed its ethical standards as "canons.")

Compliance with Paralegal Codes of Ethics

Paralegal codes of ethics state the ethical responsibilities of paralegals generally, but they particularly apply to members of paralegal organizations that have adopted the codes. Any paralegal who is a member of an organization that has adopted one of these codes is expected to comply with the code's requirements. Note that compliance with these codes is not legally mandatory. In other words, if a paralegal does not abide by a particular ethical standard of a paralegal association's code of ethics, the association cannot initiate state-sanctioned disciplinary proceedings against the paralegal. The association can, however, expel the paralegal from the association, which may have significant implications for the paralegal's future career.

EXHIBIT 4.1

Rules from Section 1 of NFPA's *Model Code of Ethics and Professional Responsibility and Guidelines for Enforcement*

Only the disciplinary rules are shown in this exhibit. The ethical considerations, which are important to a paralegal's understanding of these rules, can be read in Appendix C of this book.

Reprinted by permission of the National Federation of Paralegal Associations, Inc. (NFPA ©) www.paralegals.org.

---

§1. NFPA MODEL DISCIPLINARY RULES AND ETHICAL CONSIDERATIONS

1.1   A paralegal shall achieve and maintain a high level of competence.

1.2   A paralegal shall maintain a high level of personal and professional integrity.

1.3   A paralegal shall maintain a high standard of professional conduct.

1.4   A paralegal shall serve the public interest by contributing to the improvement of the legal system and the delivery of quality legal services, including *pro bono publico* services and community service.

1.5   A paralegal shall preserve all confidential information provided by the client or acquired from other sources before, during, and after the course of the professional relationship.

1.6   A paralegal shall avoid conflicts of interest and shall disclose any possible conflict to the employer or client, as well as to the prospective employers or clients.

1.7   A paralegal's title shall be fully disclosed.

1.8   A paralegal shall not engage in the unauthorized practice of law.

EXHIBIT 4.2
NALA's *Code of Ethics and Professional Responsibility*

Preamble: A paralegal must adhere strictly to the accepted standards of legal ethics and to the general principles of proper conduct. The performance of the duties of the paralegal shall be governed by specific canons as defined herein so justice will be served and goals of the profession attained.

The canons of ethics set forth hereafter are adopted by the National Association of Legal Assistants, Inc., as a general guide intended to aid paralegals and attorneys. The enumeration of these rules does not mean there are not others of equal importance although not specifically mentioned. Court rules, agency rules and statutes must be taken into consideration when interpreting the canons.

Definition: Legal assistants, also known as paralegals, are a distinguishable group of persons who assist attorneys in the delivery of legal services. Through formal education, training and experience, legal assistants have knowledge and expertise regarding the legal system and substantive and procedural law which qualify them to do work of a legal nature under the supervision of an attorney.

CANON 1.

A paralegal must not perform any of the duties that attorneys only may perform nor take any actions that attorneys may not take.

CANON 2.

A paralegal may perform any task which is properly delegated and supervised by an attorney, as long as the attorney is ultimately responsible to the client, maintains a direct relationship with the client, and assumes professional responsibility for the work product.

CANON 3.

A paralegal must not:

    (a) engage in, encourage, or contribute to any act which could constitute the unauthorized practice of law; and

    (b) establish attorney-client relationships, set fees, give legal opinions or advice or represent a client before a court or agency unless so authorized by that court or agency; and

    (c) engage in conduct or take any action which would assist or involve the attorney in a violation of professional ethics or give the appearance of professional impropriety.

CANON 4.

A paralegal must use discretion and professional judgment commensurate with knowledge and experience but must not render independent legal judgment in place of an attorney. The services of an attorney are essential in the public interest whenever such legal judgment is required.

CANON 5.

A paralegal must disclose his or her status as a legal assistant at the outset of any professional relationship with a client, attorney, a court or administrative agency or personnel thereof, or a member of the general public. A paralegal must act prudently in determining the extent to which a client may be assisted without the presence of an attorney.

CANON 6.

A paralegal must strive to maintain integrity and a high degree of competency through education and training with respect to professional responsibility, local rules and practice, and through continuing education in substantive areas of law to better assist the legal profession in fulfilling its duty to provide legal service.

CANON 7.

A paralegal must protect the confidences of a client and must not violate any rule or statute now in effect or hereafter enacted controlling the doctrine of privileged communications between a client and an attorney.

CANON 8.

A paralegal must disclose to his or her employer or prospective employer any pre-existing clients or personal relationships that may conflict with the interests of the employer or prospective employer and/or their clients.

CANON 9.

A paralegal must do all other things incidental, necessary, or expedient for the attainment of the ethics and responsibilities as defined by statute or rule of court.

CANON 10.

A paralegal's conduct is guided by bar associations' codes of professional responsibility and rules of professional conduct.

Guidelines for the Utilization of Paralegals

As mentioned earlier, the reason attorneys are regulated by the state is to protect the public from the harms that could result from incompetent legal advice and representation. While licensing requirements may help to protect the public, they also give lawyers something of a monopoly over the delivery of legal services. The increased use of paralegals stems, in part, from the legal profession's need to reduce the cost of legal services. The use of paralegals to do substantive legal work benefits clients because the hourly rate for paralegals is lower than that for attorneys.

For this reason, bar associations (and courts, when approving fees) encourage attorneys to delegate work to paralegals to lower the costs of legal services for clients—and thus provide the public with greater access to legal services. In fact, some courts, when determining awards of attorneys' fees, have refused to approve fees at the attorney's hourly rate for work that could have been performed by a paralegal at a lower rate.

NALA, the ABA, and many states have adopted guidelines for the utilization of paralegal services. These were created in response to questions concerning the role and function of paralegals within the legal arena that had arisen in earlier years, including the following: What are paralegals? What kinds of tasks do they perform? What are their professional responsibilities? How can attorneys best utilize paralegal services? What responsibilities should attorneys assume with respect to their assistants' work?

NALA's *Model Standards and Guidelines*

NALA's *Model Standards and Guidelines for the Utilization of Paralegals* provides guidance on several important issues. The document begins by listing the minimum qualifications that legal assistants should have and then, in a series of guidelines, indicates what paralegals may and may not do. We will examine these guidelines in more detail shortly. (See Appendix B for the complete text of the annotated version of NALA's *Model Standards and Guidelines,* as revised in 2007.)

The ABA's *Model Guidelines*

In 1991, the ABA adopted its *Model Guidelines for the Utilization of Legal Assistant Services.* The ABA Standing Committee on Paralegals revised these guidelines in 2003 by basing them on the ABA's *Model Rules of Professional Conduct.* The revised document consists of ten guidelines, each followed by a lengthy comment on the origin, scope, and application of the guideline. The guidelines indicate, among other things, the types of tasks that a lawyer may not delegate to a paralegal and, generally, the responsibilities of attorneys with respect to paralegal performance and compensation. For further detail on what is included in the revised guidelines, now entitled *Model Guidelines for the Utilization of Paralegal Services,* go to **www.americanbar.org/groups/paralegals** and select the publications menu.

State Guidelines

Most states have adopted some form of guidelines concerning the use of legal assistants by attorneys, the respective responsibilities of attorneys and legal assistants in performing legal work, the tasks paralegals may perform, and other ethically challenging areas of legal practice. Although the guidelines of some states reflect the influence of NALA's standards and guidelines, the state guidelines focus largely on state statutory definitions of the practice of law, state codes of ethics regulating the responsibilities of attorneys, and state court decisions. As a paralegal, make sure that you become familiar with your state's guidelines.

The Increasing Scope of Paralegal Responsibilities

The ethical standards and guidelines just discussed, as well as court decisions concerning paralegals, all support the goal of increasing the use of paralegals in the delivery of legal services. Today, paralegals can perform almost any legal task as

ON THE web

NALA's *Model Standards and Guidelines* are online at **www.nala.org**. From the "About Paralegals" menu, select "Model Standards and Guidelines for the Utilization of Paralegals."

long as the work is supervised by an attorney and does not constitute the unauthorized practice of law (to be discussed shortly).

Wide Range of Responsibilities

Paralegals working for attorneys may interview clients and witnesses, investigate legal claims, draft legal documents for attorneys' signatures, attend will executions (in some states), appear at real estate closings (in some states), and undertake numerous other types of legal work, as long as the work is supervised by attorneys. When state or federal law allows it, paralegals can also represent clients before government agencies. Paralegals may perform freelance services for attorneys and, depending on state law and the type of service, perform limited independent services for the public.

Legal assistants may also give information to clients on many matters relating to a case or other legal concern. When arranging for client interviews, they let clients know what kind of information is needed and what documents to bring to the office. They inform clients about legal procedures and what clients should expect to experience during the progress of a legal proceeding. As a paralegal, you will be permitted to give clients all kinds of information. Nonetheless, you must make sure that you know where to draw the line between giving permissible types of advice and giving "legal advice"—advice that only licensed attorneys are permitted to give under state laws.

Follow ABA Guidelines

The tasks that paralegals are legally permitted to undertake are described throughout this book. As stated in the ABA's guidelines, paralegals may not perform tasks that only attorneys can legally perform. If they do so, they risk liability for the unauthorized practice of law—an important topic to which we now turn.

The Unauthorized Practice of Law

State statutes prohibit the unauthorized practice of law (UPL). Although the statutes vary, they all aim to prevent nonlawyers from providing legal counsel. These statutes do not apply only to paralegals. Rather, they apply to all persons—including real estate agents, bankers, insurance agents, and accountants—who might provide services that are typically provided by licensed attorneys. For example, an insurance agent who offers advice to a client on a personal-injury claim might be liable for UPL.

UPL statutes are not always clear about what constitutes the practice of law. Consequently, courts decide whether a person has engaged in UPL on a case-by-case basis. This may make it difficult to know exactly what activities constitute UPL. To avoid violating UPL laws, a person must be aware of the state courts' decisions on UPL. As we will see below, some states are addressing this problem.

Paralegals, of course, can also refer to the general guidelines for their profession provided by NALA. Guideline 2 in NALA's *Model Standards and Guidelines* prohibits a paralegal from engaging in any of the following activities:

- Establishing attorney-client relationships.
- Setting legal fees.
- Giving legal opinions or advice.
- Representing a client before a court, unless authorized to do so by the court.
- Engaging in, encouraging, or contributing to any act that could constitute the unauthorized practice of law.

State UPL Statutes

Because of the difficulty in predicting with certainty whether a court would consider a particular action to be UPL, some states have made efforts to clarify what is meant by the "practice of law." About half of the states have a formal definition of what constitutes the practice of law, either by statute or by court ruling. For example, the Texas UPL statute provides, in part:

> the practice of law means the preparation of a pleading or other document incident to an action or special proceeding or the management of the action or proceeding on behalf of a client before a judge in court as well as a service rendered out of court, including the giving of advice or the rendering of any service requiring the use of legal skill or knowledge, such as preparing a will, contract, or other instrument, the legal effect of which under the facts and conclusions involved must be carefully determined.[2]

The Texas statute also states that this definition is not exclusive and that the state courts have the authority to determine that other activities, which are not listed, also constitute UPL. Other states' definitions focus on various factors, such as appearing in court or drafting legal papers, pleadings, or other documents in connection with a pending or prospective court proceeding. The enforcement of UPL statutes also varies widely among the states. In some states, the attorney general prosecutes violators; in others, a local or state prosecutor enforces UPL statutes; and in some states, the state bar association is in charge of enforcement.

In the following pages, we discuss some of the activities that are considered to constitute UPL in most states. But it must be emphasized that a paralegal should know the details of the UPL statute in the state in which she or he works. Avoiding UPL problems is also discussed in the *Developing Paralegal Skills* feature below.

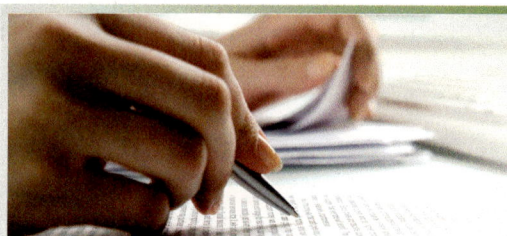

DEVELOPING
paralegal skills

THE DANGERS OF THE UNAUTHORIZED PRACTICE OF LAW

Every state restricts the "practice of law" to licensed attorneys. State bar associations take this restriction seriously, and they aggressively enforce unauthorized practice of law rules against anyone the bar suspects is infringing on attorneys' control of the practice of law.

Unfortunately, the definition of the "practice of law" is unclear, making it a trap for the unwary. The ABA defines it as "the rendition of services for others that call for the professional judgment of a lawyer." In essence, "practicing" law includes giving legal advice, preparing legal documents, and representing a client in court.

Of course, paralegals routinely do the first two of these. Each is perfectly legal as long as these activities are done under the supervision of a licensed attorney. For example, you will often have to relay legal advice from the attorney to the client. To protect yourself, you must make clear that the advice comes from the lawyer, not you. You can avoid unauthorized practice problems by:

- Being clear that everyone understands you are a paralegal in all communications and meetings by:

1. Including your title when signing letters, e-mails, and other documents and on your business cards.

2. Introducing yourself with your title in meetings.

3. Disclosing your status when communicating with a court.

- Ensuring that activities that might be construed to be the "practice of law" are supervised by a licensed attorney by:

1. Making sure that an attorney reviews and signs off on all legal documents you prepare.

2. Explicitly stating that the attorney is the source of any legal advice when relaying advice to a client by stating, "I asked Attorney Smith about that and she said . . . ."

- Informing yourself about your state's unauthorized practice rules by:

1. Researching court decisions, regulations, and state bar opinions on the topic.

2. Contacting your state paralegal associations and state bar for information and publications on the topic.

Taking care to follow such guidelines will protect the law firm you work for and will protect you, your career, and your firm's clients.

The Prohibition against Fee Splitting

An important ethical rule related to the unauthorized practice of law is Rule 5.4 of the *Model Rules of Professional Conduct*. For an attorney or a law firm to split legal fees with a non-lawyer is clearly prohibited. For this reason, paralegals cannot become partners in a law partnership (because the partners share the firm's income), nor can they have a fee-sharing arrangement with an attorney.

One of the reasons for this rule is that it protects the attorney's independent judgment concerning legal matters. For example, if an attorney became partners with two or three nonattorneys, the nonattorneys would have a significant voice in determining the firm's policies. In this situation, a conflict might arise between a policy of the firm and the attorney's duty to exercise independent professional judgment in regard to a client's case. The rule against fee splitting also protects against the possibility that nonlawyers would indirectly, through attorneys, be able to engage in the practice of law, which no one but an attorney can do.

Giving Legal Opinions and Advice

Giving legal advice goes to the essence of legal practice. After all, a person would not seek out a legal expert if he or she did not want legal advice on some matter. Although a paralegal can communicate an attorney's legal advice to a client, a paralegal cannot give legal advice.

The Need for Caution

You need to be careful to avoid giving legal advice even when discussing matters with friends and relatives. Although other nonlawyers often give advice affecting others' legal rights or obligations, paralegals should not do so. For example, when a person gets a speeding ticket, a friend or relative who is a nonlawyer might suggest that the person should argue the case before a judge and explain his side of the story. When a paralegal gives such advice, however, she may be accused of engaging in the unauthorized practice of law. Legal assistants are prohibited from giving even simple, common-sense advice because of the greater weight the recipient might give to the advice of someone who has legal training.

Similarly, you need to be cautious in the workplace. Although you may develop expertise in a certain area of law, you must refrain from advising clients with respect to their legal obligations or rights. Suppose you are a bankruptcy specialist and know that a client who wants to petition for bankruptcy has two realistic options to pursue under bankruptcy law. Should you tell the client about these options and their consequences? No. In effect, advising someone of his legal options is dangerously close to advising a person of his legal rights and may therefore—in the view of many courts, at least—constitute the unauthorized practice of law. Also, even though you may qualify what you say by telling the client that he needs to check with an attorney, this does not alter the fact that you are giving advice on which the client might rely.

Be on the Safe Side

What constitutes the giving of legal advice can be difficult to pin down. Paralegals are permitted to advise clients on a number of matters, so drawing the line between permissible and impermissible advice may be difficult. To be on the safe side—and avoid potential liability for the unauthorized practice of law—never advise anyone regarding any matter if the advice may alter that person's legal position or legal rights.

Whenever you are pressured to render legal advice—as you surely will be at one time or another by your firm's clients or others—say that you cannot give legal advice because it is against the law to do so. Offer to find an attorney who can answer the client's questions. Paralegals usually find that a frank and honest approach provides the best solution to the problem.

Representing Clients in Court

The rule that only attorneys can represent others in legal matters has a long history. There are two limited exceptions to this rule. First, in 1975 the United States Supreme Court held that people have a constitutional right to represent themselves in court.[3] Second, paralegals are allowed to represent clients before some federal and state government agencies, such as the federal Social Security Administration. Hence, as a paralegal you should know that you are not allowed to appear in court on behalf of your supervising attorney—although local courts in some states have made exceptions to this rule for limited purposes.

Disclosure of Paralegal Status

Because of the close working relationship between an attorney and a paralegal, a client may have difficulty perceiving that the paralegal is not also an attorney. For example, a client's call to an attorney may be transferred to the attorney's paralegal. The paralegal may assume that the client knows who she is and may speak freely with the client about a legal matter, advising the client that the attorney will be in touch with the client shortly. The client, however, may assume that the paralegal is an attorney and may make inferences based on the paralegal's comments that result in actions with harmful consequences—in which event the paralegal might be charged with the unauthorized practice of law. To avoid such problems, make sure that clients or potential clients know that you are a paralegal and, as such, are not permitted to give legal advice.

Similarly, in correspondence with clients or others, you should indicate your nonattorney status by adding "Paralegal" or "Legal Assistant" after your name. If you have printed business cards, or if your name is included in the firm's letterhead or other literature, also make sure that your nonlawyer status is clearly indicated.

Guideline 1 of NALA's *Model Standards and Guidelines* emphasizes the importance of disclosing paralegal status by stating that all legal assistants have an ethical responsibility to "disclose their status as legal assistants at the outset of any professional relationship with a client, other attorneys, a court or administrative agency or personnel thereof, or members of the general public." Disciplinary Rule 1.7 of NFPA's *Model Code of Ethics and Professional Responsibility* also stresses the importance of disclosing paralegal status. Guideline 4 of the ABA's *Model Guidelines* places on attorneys the responsibility for disclosing the nonattorney status of paralegals.

Attorneys are responsible for the work product of their offices, including the work done by paralegals. Hence, attorneys are required to ensure that clients and other relevant parties, including other attorneys and the courts, know when work has been performed by a paralegal.

Paralegals Freelancing for Attorneys

Some paralegals work on a freelance basis, as discussed in Chapter 2. In a landmark decision in 1992, the New Jersey Supreme Court stated that it could find no reason why freelance paralegals could not be just as adequately supervised by the attorneys for whom they worked as those paralegals working in attorneys' offices. Since that decision, courts in other states and ethical opinions issued by various state bar associations have held that freelance paralegals who are adequately supervised by attorneys are not engaging in the unauthorized practice of law. As the *Practice Focus* feature on the facing page discusses, there are new ways for paralegals to freelance.

Legal Technicians (Independent Paralegals) and UPL

As mentioned in Chapter 2, legal technicians (also called independent paralegals) provide "self-help" legal services directly to the public. The courts have had to wrestle with questions such as the following: If an independent paralegal advises a client on what forms are necessary to obtain a simple, uncontested divorce, how to

social MEDIA TODAY

Google Chairman Eric Schmidt notes, "If you have something that you don't want anyone to know, maybe you shouldn't be doing it in the first place."

PRACTICE focus

PROFESSIONAL RESPONSIBILITY AND VIRTUAL PARALEGALS

One growing area for paralegals is "virtual paralegals." Unlike paralegals employed directly by law firms, virtual paralegals contract their services to attorneys, law firms, corporations, agencies, and others as independent contractors. Paralegals in virtual careers cite the increased flexibility in their schedules as a major benefit, as well as the ability to work from home. Lauren Hidden of the International Virtual Assistants Association believes virtual positions will increase as firms seek to reduce costs, saying, "The future is very bright" for virtual paralegals.

Like more traditional paralegals, virtual paralegals can only work under the direct supervision of a licensed attorney. The attorney's responsibility to supervise the virtual paralegal's work is no different from his or her responsibility to supervise a paralegal employed by the same firm. What is different is that the virtual paralegal typically works with greater independence.

One important step you can take to address potential ethics issues while working as a virtual paralegal is to draft your own ethics policy, including procedures and processes to ensure that you do not violate state ethics rules for the state in which your supervising attorney is licensed. This requires paralegals working in different states to be able to assure an attorney elsewhere that they are familiar with the appropriate rules.

Draft such a policy conservatively, ensuring that you avoid any action that might put an attorney in violation of state ethics rules or even create the appearance of professional impropriety. Look carefully at the ABA's *Model Guidelines for the Utilization of Legal Assistant Services* for guidance in drafting a policy. Also, review specific guidelines from the bar association in any state in which you may provide services.

---

file those forms with the court, how to schedule a court hearing, and the like, do those activities constitute the practice of law?

Generally, the mere dissemination of legal information does not constitute the unauthorized practice of law. There is a fine line, however, between disseminating legal information (by providing legal forms to a customer, for example) and giving legal advice (which may consist of merely selecting the forms that best suit the customer's needs), and the courts do not always agree on just where this line should be drawn.

An Ongoing Problem

Legal technicians continue to face UPL allegations brought against them primarily by UPL committees and state bar associations. In one case, an Oregon appellate court upheld the conviction of Robin Smith for engaging in UPL. The bar association complained that Smith provided consumers with various legal forms, advised them on which forms to use, and assisted them in completing the documents. The court reasoned that by drafting and selecting documents and giving advice with regard to their legal effect, Smith was practicing law.[4]

Some legal technicians were facing UPL charges in California when the legislature authorized nonlawyers to provide certain types of legal services directly to the public. Under that law, a person who qualifies and registers with the county as a "legal document assistant" (LDA) may assist clients in filling out legal forms but cannot advise clients which forms to use.[5] After the LDA law passed, the case was settled.

The Controversy over Legal Software

Even publishers of self-help law books and computer software programs have come under attack for the unauthorized practice of law. For example, a Texas Court held that the legal software program *Quicken Family Lawyer* violated Texas's UPL statute.[6]

The program provided a hundred different legal forms (including contracts, real estate leases, and wills), along with instructions on how to fill out these forms.

The Texas legislature then amended the UPL statute to reverse the court's ruling. The new law explicitly authorizes the sale of legal self-help software, books, forms, and similar products to the public.[7] Note, however, that the Texas law authorizes these products to be used *only* for "self-help." The law does not permit persons who are not licensed to practice law (such as legal technicians) to use these programs to give legal advice to others.

Do Paralegals Who Operate as Legal Technicians Engage in UPL?

Debate continues as to whether it is legal, at least in some situations, for legal technicians to operate without a lawyer's supervision. Generally, unless a state statute or rule specifically allows paralegals to assist the public directly without the supervision of an attorney, paralegals would be wise not to engage in such practices. Most state courts are much more likely to find that a paralegal is engaging in UPL than that a publisher of legal software is doing so. This is because of the relationship of trust that develops between the paralegal and the client and the potential for abuse. The consequences of violating state UPL statutes can be serious. Any paralegal who contemplates working as a legal technician (independent paralegal) therefore must thoroughly investigate the relevant state laws and court decisions on UPL before offering any services directly to the public and must rigorously abide by the letter of the law.

Should Paralegals Be Licensed?

A major issue facing legal professionals is whether paralegals should be subject to direct regulation by the state through licensing requirements. Unlike certification, which was discussed in Chapter 1, licensing involves direct and mandatory regulation, by the state, of an occupational or professional group. When licensing requirements are established for a professional group, such as for attorneys, a member of the group must have a license to practice his or her profession.

Movements toward regulation of paralegals have been motivated in large part by the activities of legal technicians, or independent paralegals—those who provide legal services directly to the public without attorney supervision. Many legal technicians call themselves paralegals even though they have little, if any, legal training, background, or experience. Yet at the same time, those who cannot afford to hire an attorney can benefit from the self-help services provided by legal technicians who do have training and experience.

General Licensing

A number of states have considered implementing a **general licensing** program. A general licensing program would require all paralegals to meet certain educational requirements and other specified criteria before being allowed to practice their profession.

For example, after five years of study, the New Jersey Supreme Court Committee on Paralegal Education and Regulation recommended that paralegals be licensed. The committee's report proposed that paralegals be subject to state licensure based on demonstrated educational requirements and knowledge of the ethical rules governing the legal profession. The New Jersey Supreme Court, however, declined to follow the committee's recommendations. The court concluded that direct oversight of paralegals is best accomplished through attorney supervision rather than through a state-mandated licensing system.

Paralegal Registration

Florida requires registration of paralegals who wish to become a Florida Registered Paralegal (FRP). Initially, experienced paralegals were allowed to register without meeting an educational requirement. Since 2011, however, to be registered an

general licensing
Licensing in which all individuals within a specific profession or group (such as paralegals) must meet licensing requirements imposed by the state in order to legally practice their profession.

applicant must provide proof of educational qualification as well as meet certain personal requirements, such as not to have engaged in the unauthorized practice of law. All FRPs are listed on the Florida Bar Web site.

Paralegals must meet the continuing education (CE) requirement of 30 hours every three-year reporting cycle. At least five of the hours must be in ethics or professionalism. Failure to complete the CE requirement means loss of FRP status. CE courses specifically authorized are provided by the NALA, the NFPA, and the Florida Bar. Other states are investigating a similar procedure.

Education and Certification

The law in California defines a paralegal or legal assistant as someone who works under the supervision of an attorney, meets certain educational criteria, and completes required continuing education requirements. Paralegals do not have to register, but an independent paralegal not working under the supervision of an attorney cannot call himself or herself a paralegal in California. These independent paralegals can register with the state as a "legal document assistant" (LDA). They prepare documents at the direction of their clients and assist clients in a wide range of areas, from family law to incorporation of businesses. They cannot provide legal advice.

The Louisiana Certified Paralegal Program illustrates another approach. Paralegals who successfully complete the NALA's Certified Legal Assistant (CLA) exam and the Louisiana Certified Paralegal (LCP) exam are certified as a Louisiana Certified Paralegal. The CLA exam tests knowledge of the American legal and judicial systems and four areas of substantive law. The LCP exam focuses on the Louisiana legal and judicial system, ethics, civil procedure, and four areas of substantive Louisiana law.

Direct Regulation—The Pros and Cons

A significant part of the debate over direct regulation has to do with the issue of who should do the regulating. Certainly, state bar associations and government authorities want to have a say in the matter. Yet paralegal organizations and educators, such as NALA, NFPA, and the American Association for Paralegal Education (AAfPE), also want to play a leading role in developing the education requirements, ethical standards, and disciplinary procedures required by a licensing program should one be implemented. The problem is, NALA, NFPA, and the AAfPE have expressed differing views on these matters.

NFPA's Position

NFPA endorses the regulation of the paralegal profession on a state-by-state basis. Given that lower-cost legal services are in great demand, NFPA asserts that widescale regulation of paralegals would improve consumers' access to quality legal services. NFPA favors establishing minimum education requirements to protect the public and to weed out the "bad apples" in the profession—those who call themselves paralegals but who do not have the necessary education or training to perform paralegal work competently.

NFPA proposes a two-tiered system of licensing: general licensing and specialty licensing. General licensing by a state board or agency would require all paralegals within the state to satisfy education, experience, and continuing education requirements; it would also subject practicing paralegals to disciplinary procedures by the licensing body. (As mentioned, NFPA has already developed a set of model enforcement guidelines—see Appendix C.) Specialty licensing would require paralegals who wish to practice in a specialized area to demonstrate, by an examination (see the discussion of the PACE examination in Chapter 1), their proficiency in that area.

NALA's Position

NALA supports voluntary certification (self-regulation) but opposes licensing requirements for paralegals. It takes the position that state licensing would only serve to control entry into the profession and would not improve the quality of the

ON THE web

You can see details of the FRP process and application form by going to **www.floridabar.org** and typing "paralegal" in the search box.

services that paralegals provide. Because a license grants a paralegal permission to work, NALA believes that licensing criteria would be kept at the lowest level of professional competency.

According to NALA, there is no need to regulate paralegals at this time. Most paralegals work under the supervision of attorneys, who are regulated by state ethical codes. NALA believes that regulation would increase the cost of paralegals to employers. This increase would be passed on to consumers, resulting in higher-cost legal services. NALA therefore considers licensing an unnecessary burden to employers, paralegals, and the public.

The AAfPE's Position

The American Association for Paralegal Education (AAfPE) does not take a position on paralegal licensing. The AAfPE recommends that states adopt AAfPE's minimum educational standards in any regulatory plan they enact. It is the view of the AAfPE that paralegals (through associations such as NALA and NFPA) and paralegal educators should put aside their differences and present a united front in influencing licensing proposals. Otherwise, by default, the decision will not be theirs to make.

Other Considerations

While the positions taken by NFPA, NALA, and the AAfPE outline the main contours of the debate over regulation, other groups emphasize some different considerations. For example, one of the concerns of lawyers is that if legal technicians are licensed—through limited licensing programs—to deliver low-cost services directly to the public, the business (and profits) of law firms would suffer. Many lawyers are also concerned that if paralegals are subject to mandatory licensing requirements, law firms will not be able to hire and train persons of their choice to become paralegals.

Some paralegals and paralegal associations are concerned that mandatory licensing would require all paralegals to be "generalists." As it is, a large number of paralegals specialize in particular areas, such as bankruptcy or family law, and do not need to have the broad knowledge of all areas of paralegal practice that licensing might require.

A Final Note

As a professional paralegal, you will have an opportunity to voice your opinion on whether paralegals should be regulated by state governments and, if so, what qualifications should be required. Whatever the outcome of the licensing debate, keep in mind that all of the issues discussed in this chapter are directly relevant to your paralegal career. The most important point to remember as you embark on a paralegal career is that you need to think and act in a professionally responsible manner. Although this takes time and practice, in the legal arena there is little room for learning ethics by "trial and error." Therefore, you need to be especially attentive to the ethical rules governing attorneys and paralegal practice discussed in this chapter.

The *Ethics Watch* features throughout this book offer further insights into some of the ethical problems that can arise in various areas of paralegal performance. Understanding how violations can occur will help you anticipate and guard against them as you begin your career. Once on the job, you can continue your preventive tactics by asking questions whenever you are in doubt and by making sure that your work is adequately supervised.

social
MEDIA TODAY

Social media experts David Thomas and Mike Barlow explain that if you want people to follow your social media activities, you need to gear your efforts toward what your audience cares about, not what you care about.

KEY TERMS AND CONCEPTS

Chapter Summary

Ethics and Professional Responsibility

THE REGULATION OF ATTORNEYS

Attorneys are regulated by licensing requirements and by the ethical rules of their state. The purpose of attorney regulation is to protect the public against incompetent legal professionals and unethical attorney behavior.

1. *Who are the regulators?*—Lawyers establish the majority of rules governing their profession through state bar associations and the American Bar Association (ABA), which has established model rules and guidelines relating to professional conduct. Other key participants in the regulation of attorneys are state supreme courts, state legislatures, and (occasionally) the United States Supreme Court.

2. *Licensing requirements*—Licensed attorneys generally must be graduates of a law school and have passed a state bar examination and an extensive personal background check.

3. *Ethical Codes and Rules*—Most states have adopted a version of either the 1969 *Model Code of Professional Responsibility* or the 1983 revision of the *Model Code,* called the *Model Rules of Professional Conduct,* both of which were published by the ABA. The *Model Rules* are often amended by the ABA to keep up-to-date with the realities of modern law practice. Most states have adopted laws based on the *Model Rules.*

4. *Sanctions for violations*—The *Model Code* and *Model Rules* spell out the ethical and professional duties governing attorneys and the practice of law. Attorneys who violate these duties may be subject to reprimand, suspension, or disbarment. Additionally, attorneys (and paralegals) face potential liability for malpractice or for violations of criminal statutes.

ATTORNEY ETHICS AND PARALEGAL PRACTICE

Some of the ethical rules governing attorney behavior pose difficult problems for paralegals, so paralegals should consult their state's ethical code to learn the specific rules for which they will be accountable. The following rules apply in most states.

1. *Duty of competence*—This duty is violated whenever a client suffers harm as a result of the attorney's (or paralegal's) incompetent action or inaction.

   a. Breaching the duty of competence may lead to a lawsuit against the attorney (and perhaps against the paralegal) for negligence. This may arise from faulty research, missed deadlines, or mistakes in documents.

   b. Attorneys must adequately supervise a paralegal's work to ensure that this duty is not breached.

2. *Confidentiality of information*—All information relating to a client's representation must be kept in confidence and not revealed to third parties who are not authorized to know the information.

   a. Paralegals should be careful both on and off the job not to discuss client information with third parties. Breaches of confidentiality can include unauthorized persons overhearing telephone conversations or personal comments, or faxes being sent to parties not intended to see them.

Continued

b. Client confidences can be revealed only in certain circumstances, such as when a client gives informed consent to the disclosure, when disclosure is necessary to represent a client or to prevent harm to persons or property, or when a court orders an attorney to reveal the information.

3. *Confidentiality and the attorney-client privilege*—Some client information is regarded as privileged information under the rules of evidence and receives even greater protection by attorneys and paralegals subject to rules of confidentiality.

4. *Conflict of interest*—This occurs when representing a client injures the interests of another client.

  a. An attorney may represent both sides in a legal proceeding only if the attorney believes that neither party's rights will be injured and only if both clients are aware of the conflict and have given informed consent to the representation. Paralegals also fall under this rule.

  b. When a firm is handling a case and one of the firm's attorneys or paralegals cannot work on the case because of a conflict of interest, that attorney or paralegal must be "walled off" from the case—that is, prevented from having access to files or other information relating to the case.

  c. Normally, whenever a prospective client consults with an attorney, a conflicts check is done to ensure that if the attorney or firm accepts the case, no conflict of interest will arise.

THE INDIRECT REGULATION OF PARALEGALS

Paralegals are regulated indirectly by attorney ethical rules, by ethical codes created by NFPA and NALA, and by guidelines on the utilization of paralegals, which define the status and function of paralegals and the scope of their authorized activities. The ABA and several states have adopted guidelines on the utilization of paralegals.

These codes and guidelines provide paralegals, attorneys, and the courts with guidance on the paralegal's role in the practice of law. The general rule is that paralegals can perform almost any legal task that attorneys can (other than represent a client in court) as long as they work under an attorney's supervision.

THE UNAUTHORIZED PRACTICE OF LAW

State laws prohibit nonlawyers from engaging in the unauthorized practice of law (UPL). Violations of these laws can have serious consequences.

1. *State UPL Statutes*—Determining what constitutes UPL is complicated by the fact that many state laws give vague or broad definitions. Some states have made efforts to address this problem.

2. *The prohibition against fee splitting*—Paralegals working for attorneys and legal technicians (independent paralegals) need to be careful not to engage in activities that the state will consider UPL, such as a direct fee-sharing arrangement with an attorney.

3. *Prohibited acts*—Paralegals should always make clear their professional status so clients are not confused.

While paralegals work under the supervision of an attorney, one can be an independent or freelance paralegal and need not be a full-time employee of an attorney. The consensus is that paralegals should not engage in the following acts:

a. Establish an attorney-client relationship.

b. Set legal fees.

c. Give legal advice or opinions.

d. Represent a client in court (unless authorized to do so by the court).

e. Encourage or contribute to any act that could constitute UPL.

SHOULD PARALEGALS BE LICENSED?

An issue for legal professionals is whether paralegals should be directly regulated by the state through licensing requirements.

1. *General licensing*—General licensing would establish minimum standards that every paralegal would have to meet in order to practice as a paralegal in the state.

2. *Registration*—Some states, such as Florida, encourage registration of paralegals. While not mandated, it does provide more visibility and professional recogni-

tion. Other states, such as California, have education requirements that must be met before one can claim to be a paralegal.

3. *Direct regulation*—The pros and cons of direct regulation through licensing are being debated vigorously by the leading paralegal and paralegal education associations, state bar associations, state courts, state legislatures, and public-interest groups.

QUESTIONS FOR REVIEW

1. Why is the legal profession regulated? Who are the regulators? How is regulation accomplished?

2. How is the paralegal profession regulated by attorney ethical codes? How is it regulated by paralegal codes of ethics?

3. What does the duty of competence involve? How can violations of the duty of competence be avoided?

4. What is the duty of confidentiality? What is the attorney-client privilege? What is the relationship between the duty of confidentiality and the attorney-client privilege? What are some potential consequences of violating the confidentiality rule?

5. What is the practice of law? How is the unauthorized practice of law (UPL) defined? How might paralegals violate state statutes prohibiting UPL? What types of tasks can legally be performed by paralegals?

ETHICAL QUESTIONS

1. Norma Sollers works as a paralegal for a small law firm. She is a trusted, experienced employee who has worked for the firm for twelve years. One morning, Linda Lowenstein, one of the attorneys, calls from her home and asks Norma to sign Linda's name to a document that must be filed with the court that day. Norma had just prepared the final draft of the document and had placed it on Linda's desk for her review and signature. Linda explains to Norma that because her child is sick, she does not want to leave home to come into the office. Norma knows that she should not sign Linda's name—only the client's attorney can sign the document. She mentions this to Linda, but Linda says, "Don't worry. No one will ever know that you signed it instead of me." How should Norma handle this situation?

2. The law firm of Dover, Cleary and Harper decides to store all of its data in the cloud and enters into a contract with Cloud Service Provider for data storage. The firm does not mention its conversion to cloud storage to any of its clients. Six months later an employee of the Cloud Service Provider notices that one of the firm's clients, a local celebrity, has declared bankruptcy and broadcasts this fact on Facebook, causing significant embarrassment to the client. The client is able to track the disclosure of her confidential information on Facebook to Cloud Service Provider, which obtained the client's file from Dover, Cleary and Harper. Is the law firm guilty of an ethical violation?

3. The BigLaw firm in New York outsources the standard mortgage agreements that it prepares for one if its clients, US Bank, to a firm in a foreign country. The mortgage agreements that are prepared by the lawyers in the foreign country are poorly drafted, so when the lawyers for US Bank review the agreements, they decide they cannot use them and refuse to pay the bill from BigLaw. When BigLaw threatens to sue US Bank, the bank threatens to file a grievance against BigLaw. What ethical violation(s) would form the basis for the bank's grievance?

PRACTICE QUESTIONS AND ASSIGNMENTS

1. Peter Smith, a paralegal, is using a county register of deeds Web site to find property tax records for a client who wants to buy a parcel of property. The client wants to make sure that the property taxes have been paid. Peter locates the property and notes that, according to the information on the Web page, the taxes have been paid. He prints the page and writes a brief memo to the attorney. The attorney then advises the client that the taxes have been paid and that it is okay to go ahead and purchase the property. The client does so, but several weeks later he receives a notice that he owes $6,500 in back taxes. The client, who is understandably upset, complains to Peter's boss. Peter is sent to the county office of the register of deeds to look up the records relating to the property. Peter finds that the correct information was in the county's records but was not on the Web site. He makes a copy of what he finds and returns to the office. What ethical rule has been violated here? What do these "facts" reveal about the reliability of information posted on the Internet?

2. In which of the following instances may confidential client information be disclosed?

   a. A client's daughter calls to find out whether her mother has left her certain property in her will. The mother does not want the daughter to know until the will is read after the mother's death that the daughter has been disinherited.

b. The client in a divorce case threatens to hire a hit man to kill her husband because she believes that killing her husband is the only way that she can stop him from stalking her. It is clear that the client intends to do this.

c. A former client sues her attorney for legal malpractice in the handling of a breach-of-contract case involving her cosmetics home-sale business. The attorney discloses that the client is having an affair with her next-door neighbor, a fact that is unrelated to the malpractice case or the breach-of-contract case.

3. According to this chapter's text, which of the following tasks can a paralegal legally perform?

a. Provide legal advice to clients in the course of helping them prepare divorce pleadings.

b. Interview a witness to a car accident.

c. Represent a client in court.

d. Set legal fees.

e. Work as a freelance paralegal for attorneys.

f. Work as a legal technician providing legal services directly to the public.

QUESTIONS FOR CRITICAL ANALYSIS

1. What could happen if the legal profession were not regulated? What might happen if, for example, there were no rule governing competence in the profession? Does this explain why ethical rules are needed? Why or why not?

2. The material in the chapter indicates that lawyers are largely responsible for regulating their own conduct. What do you think of a system in which members of a profession regulate themselves? Is this a good system? Can you think of a better alternative?

3. An experienced legal secretary opened a business, Northside Secretarial Services, to provide certain legal services directly to the public. She prepared legal documents—and provided detailed instructions for filing the documents with the court and for service of process—in divorce and adoption cases. She held briefing sessions during which she gave detailed instructions about trials and hearings, including the types of questions that the court would ask and the responses that her "clients" should give to the court. The secretary advertised her services in a newspaper, calling herself an "expert in family law." She also sold "do-it-yourself" divorce kits. She charged $50 for her services, and many of her "clients" were indigent and illiterate.

The state bar association charged her with the unauthorized practice of law. A former client testified that when he had found out that his wife was abusing the children, he had been advised by the secretary that he should not try to change the petition for divorce to seek custody of the minor children, but should leave it to the state agency to handle abuse and custody issues.

What was the likely result of the state bar association's filing of unauthorized-practice-of-law charges against the legal secretary? How might she have responded to these charges? What would happen if she was prohibited by court order from engaging in these activities and continued to do so anyway?

4. Compare the activities that constitute the unauthorized practice of law with the activities in which paralegals can lawfully engage under the guidelines for the utilization of legal assistants. Why do you think that the activities that constitute the unauthorized practice of law are prohibited for nonlawyers? Could someone with training as a legal assistant competently handle some of these activities? If so, which ones?

5. If the licensing of paralegals were to be made a requirement, what type of license should they be granted—general or limited? What impact would this have on paralegals and on the legal profession as a whole?

PROJECTS

1. Access your state's rules online to find out the requirements for becoming licensed to practice law in your state. Do your state's rules differ from the requirements mentioned in the text? If so, how?

2. Go to **www.law.com** and enter "unauthorized practice" in the search box. List five cases that discuss unauthorized practice of law and see what the major reasons were for such cases.

GROUP PROJECT

This project involves the review of your state's version of one of the ethical rules of competence, conflict of interest, or client confidentiality as assigned by your instructor. Students one, two, and three will locate your state's version of the rule using online sources, your school's library, or a local law library. Students one, two, and three will summarize the assigned sections of the rule. The group will determine which rule is the law in your state. Student four will compare the summarized sections of the state rule to the ABA Model Rule discussed in this chapter and will present the comparison to the class.

USING INTERNET RESOURCES

1. Go to **www.paralegals.org**, the home page for the National Federation of Paralegal Associations (NFPA). Select "Positions & Issues," and then "Ethics," and then "Opinions." This will take you to a page that lists, among other things, NFPA's ethics opinions. Then do the following:

    a. List five issues that NFPA has addressed in these opinions.

    b. Choose one opinion and write a paragraph explaining why the issue dealt with in the opinion is important for paralegals.

    c. Choose a different opinion, read it carefully, and write a paragraph summarizing NFPA's advice on the issue being addressed in the opinion.

END NOTES

1. Even this mildest sanction can seriously damage an attorney's reputation within the legal community. In some states, state bar associations publish in their monthly journals the names of violators and details of the violations for all members of the bar to read.

2. Title 2 of the Texas Government Code, Section 81.101.

3. *Faretta v. California,* 422 U.S. 806 (1975).

4. *Oregon State Bar v. Smith,* 942 P.2d 793 (1997).

5. This law is codified in California Business and Professions Code, Sections 6400–6416.

6. *In re Nolo Press/Folk Law, Inc.,* 991 S.W.2d 768 (1999).

7. Texas Government Code Section 81.101(c) (Vernon Supp. 2000).

CourseMate The available CourseMate for this text has an interactive eBook and interactive learning tools, including flash cards, quizzes, and more. To learn more about this resource and access free demo CourseMate resources, go to **www.cengagebrain.com**, and search for this book. To access CourseMate materials that you have purchased, go to **login.cengagebrain.com**.

Sources of American Law

Chapter Outline

After completing this chapter, you will know:

- The meaning and relative importance in the American legal system of case law, constitutional law, statutory law, and administrative law.

- How English law influenced the development of the American legal system.

- What the common law tradition is and how it evolved.

- The difference between remedies at law and equitable remedies.

- Some of the terms that are commonly found in case law.

- How national law and international law differ and why these bodies of law sometimes guide judicial decision making in U.S. courts.

Introduction

The first English colonists brought the law of England with them to the New World. Over time, American law developed its own unique characteristics. As Americans adopted the law in their new environment and as the nation grew, they absorbed ideas from the Spanish, French, and Mexican legal systems. We open this chapter with a discussion of the nature of law and then examine traditional law and its significance in the American legal system. Next, we focus on other sources of American law, including constitutional, statutory, and administrative. We also explain how the law of other countries and international law affect decision making in American courts. Another major part of the American legal structure—the court system—will be examined in Chapter 6.

ON THE web

The University of Michigan maintains a useful site with links to almost all U.S. government Web sites and many foreign government Web sites at **www.umich.edu**, search "library documents center."

The Framework of American Law

The law means different things to different people. Before beginning your study of American law, it is useful to have an understanding of what law is and some of the different approaches to law that influence courts' decisions. These topics are covered in the following subsections.

What Is the Law?

How a person defines *law* frequently depends on the person's views on morality, ethics, and truth. Generally, though, we define **law** as a body of rules of conduct established and enforced by the government of a society. These "rules of conduct" may consist of written principles of behavior, such as those established by ancient societies. They may be set forth in a comprehensive code, as used in many European nations. They may consist of a combination of legislatively enacted statutes and court decisions, as in the United States. Regardless of how the rules are created, they establish rights, duties, and privileges for the citizens they govern.

law
A body of rules of conduct established and enforced by the controlling authority (the government) of a society.

One of the most important functions of law in any society is to provide stability, predictability, and continuity so that people can arrange their affairs. If a democratic society is to be credible, its citizens must be able to determine what is legally right and wrong. ◆ **EXAMPLE 5.1—**   Citizens must know what penalties will be imposed on them if they commit wrongful acts. If people suffer harm as a result of others' wrongful acts, they need to know whether and how they can receive compensation for their injuries. ◆   By setting forth the rights, obligations, and privileges of citizens, the law enables people to go about their business and personal lives with confidence and a certain degree of predictability.

Primary Sources of American Law

American law has numerous sources. **Primary sources of law**, or sources that establish the law, include the following:

1. Case law and common law doctrines.

2. The U.S. Constitution and the constitutions of the various states.

3. Statutes—including laws passed by Congress, state legislatures, and local governing bodies.

4. Regulations created by administrative agencies, such as the U.S. Food and Drug Administration (FDA) or state insurance commissions.

primary source of law
In legal research, a document that establishes the law on a particular issue, such as a case decision, legislative act, administrative rule, or presidential order.

We describe each of these important sources of law in the following pages. Note that treaties with other nations are also a primary source of law, although most legal practitioners do not deal with them directly but instead retain an attorney from the foreign jurisdiction to assist. We discuss international law near the end of the chapter.

secondary source of law
In legal research, any publication that indexes, summarizes, or interprets the law, such as a legal encyclopedia, a treatise, or an article in a law review.

case law
Rules of law announced in court decisions.

common law
A body of law developed from custom or judicial decisions in English and U.S. courts and not by a legislature.

precedent
A court decision that furnishes authority for deciding later cases in which similar facts are presented.

stare decisis
The doctrine of precedent, under which a court is obligated to follow earlier decisions of that court or higher courts within the same jurisdiction. This is a major characteristic of the common law system.

binding authority
Any source of law that a court must follow when deciding a case. Binding authorities include constitutions, statutes, and regulations that govern the issue being decided, as well as court decisions that are controlling precedents within the jurisdiction.

persuasive precedent
A precedent decided in another jurisdiction that a court may either follow or reject but that is entitled to careful consideration.

Secondary sources of law are books and articles that summarize, synthesize, and explain the primary sources of law. Examples include legal encyclopedias, treatises, articles in law reviews, and compilations of law, such as the *Restatements of the Law* (which will be discussed later in this chapter). Courts often refer to secondary sources of law for guidance in interpreting and applying the primary sources of law discussed here. They are often useful research tools that aid in locating primary sources.

Case Law and the Common Law Tradition

An important source of law consists of the decisions rendered by judges in cases that come before the courts. Lawyers call this **case law**. As mentioned earlier, because of our colonial heritage, much of American law is based on the English legal system, and our reliance on reports of court decisions is a key part of our English heritage.

The English **common law** was a body of general rules that applied throughout the English realm. In deciding common law cases, judges attempt to be consistent by basing their decisions on principles from earlier cases. By doing this, they seek to ensure that they decide similar cases in similar ways. Each decision becomes part of the law on the subject and serves as a legal **precedent**. Later cases that involve similar legal principles or facts can be decided with reference to precedents. The courts are thus guided by legal doctrines that evolve over time.

The Doctrine of Stare Decisis

The practice of deciding new cases with reference to former decisions, or precedents, is a cornerstone of the English and American judicial systems. It forms a doctrine called *stare decisis*[1] ("to stand by things decided"). Under this doctrine, judges are obligated to follow the precedents established by their own courts or by higher courts within their jurisdictions (the areas over which they have authority—see Chapter 6). These controlling precedents are referred to as binding authorities.

A **binding authority** is any source of law that a court must follow when deciding a case. Binding authorities include constitutions, statutes, and regulations that govern the issue being decided, as well as court decisions that are controlling precedents within the jurisdiction. When no binding authority exists, courts will often review **persuasive precedents**, which are precedents decided in similar cases in other jurisdictions. The court may either follow or reject persuasive precedents, but these decisions are entitled to respect and careful consideration.

The doctrine of *stare decisis* performs many useful functions. It helps the courts to be more efficient because if other courts have carefully reasoned through similar cases, their legal reasoning and opinions can serve as guides. *Stare decisis* also makes the law more stable and predictable. If the law on a given subject is well settled and there are numerous precedents, someone bringing a case to court can predict what law will apply.

Departures from Precedent

Sometimes a court will depart from the rule of precedent. If a court decides that a ruling precedent is wrong or that technological or social changes have made the precedent inappropriate, the court might overrule the precedent. These cases often receive a great deal of publicity. ◆ **EXAMPLE 5.2—** In *Brown v. Board of Education of Topeka*,[2] decided in 1954, the United States Supreme Court expressly overturned prior precedent when it held that separate schools for whites and African Americans, which had been upheld as constitutional in numerous previous cases, were unequal and in violation of the Constitution. The Supreme Court's departure from precedent in *Brown* received tremendous publicity as people began to realize the impact of this change in the law. It helped to launch the civil rights movement, which led to further lawsuits involving racial discrimination. ◆

IN THE office

DAILY CLEANUP

A neat office is important. For one thing, a messy desk presents a less-than-professional appearance. But beyond that, staying neat forces us to stay organized. When papers are piled up on a desk or in a file cabinet, files might be lost even though we may not realize it. The only work item that should be on a desk is what you are working on that day. At the end of every day, the desk should be cleared. As a part of that, all papers must be filed in their proper files (and copies made if they are needed). Don't presume you will do it tomorrow. Have everything put away where it belongs so you can start fresh the next work day.

Cases of First Impression

Sometimes, there is no precedent on which to base a decision, as when a case involves a new technology. (See this chapter's *Technology and Today's Paralegal* feature on the following page for a case of this kind involving a threat made by a posting on YouTube.) ◆ **EXAMPLE 5.3—** In 1986, a New Jersey court had to decide whether a surrogate-parenting contract should be enforced against the wishes of the surrogate parent (the natural mother).[3] This was the first such case to reach the courts, and there was no precedent in any jurisdiction to which the court could look for guidance. ◆

Cases with no precedents are called **cases of first impression**. In these cases or when precedents conflict, courts may consider a number of factors, including legal principles and policies underlying previous court decisions or existing statutes, fairness, social values and customs, **public policy** (a governmental policy based on widely held societal values), and data and concepts drawn from the social sciences. Which of these sources receives the greatest emphasis will depend on the nature of the case being considered and the particular judge hearing the case.

Judges try to be free of personal bias in deciding cases. Each judge, however, has a unique personality, values or philosophical leanings, personal history, and intellectual attributes—all of which frame the decision-making process.

Remedies at Law versus Remedies in Equity

The early English courts could grant only limited **remedies**. If one person wronged another in some way, the court could award as compensation land, items of value, or money. The courts that awarded these things became known as **courts of law**, and the three remedies awarded by these courts became known as **remedies at law**.

This system helped to standardize the ways in which disputes were settled, but parties who wanted a remedy other than economic compensation could not be helped. Sometimes these parties petitioned the king for relief. Most petitions were decided by an adviser to the king, called a *chancellor*, who was said to be the "keeper of the king's conscience." When the chancellor thought that the claim was a fair one for which there was no adequate remedy at law, he would fashion a different remedy, called a **remedy in equity**. In this way, a new body of rules and remedies came into being and eventually led to the establishment of formal courts of chancery, or **courts of equity**.

Equity is the branch of law, founded on what might be described as notions of justice and fair dealing, that seeks to supply a remedy when there is no adequate remedy available at law. Once the courts of equity were established, plaintiffs could bring claims in either courts of law (if they sought money damages) or courts of

---

case of first impression
A case presenting a legal issue that has not yet been addressed by a court in a particular jurisdiction.

public policy
A governmental policy based on widely held societal values.

remedy
The means by which a right is enforced or the violation of a right is prevented or compensated for.

court of law
A court in which the only remedies were things of value, such as money. Historically, in England, courts of law were different from courts of equity.

remedy at law
A remedy available in a court of law. Money damages and items of value are awarded as a remedy at law.

remedy in equity
A remedy allowed by courts in situations where remedies at law are not appropriate. Remedies in equity are based on rules of fairness, justice, and honesty.

court of equity
A court that decides controversies and administers justice according to the rules, principles, and precedents of equity.

TECHNOLOGY AND
today's paralegal

CASES OF FIRST IMPRESSION AND THE INTERNET

The Internet has led to cases of first impression. Here, we look at a Connecticut case involving a claim of a threat of physical harm. The question raised was whether a person threatened by an Internet posting could get help from a court.[a]

Cases involving the Internet can raise jurisdictional questions. *Jurisdiction* is an important legal concept that relates to the authority of a court to hear and decide a case. (You will read more about jurisdiction in Chapter 6.) In the United States, jurisdiction over individuals and businesses located in other states is based on the requirement of minimum contacts. This means that a defendant in a lawsuit or other action must have a certain level of contact with a resident of another state for that state's courts to exercise jurisdiction over the defendant. The principle of minimum contacts forms the basis for *long arm statutes*—state statutes permitting courts to exercise jurisdiction over nonresidents.

DOES THE COURT HAVE JURISDICTION?

Stacy Rios, who lives in Connecticut, sought a restraining order (a form of court-ordered protection that will be discussed in Chapter 17) against Christopher Fergusan, a resident of North Carolina who is the father of Rios's child. When Rios brought the action, she provided the court in Connecticut with proof that she had served Fergusan with appropriate documents (discussed in Chapter 10) informing him that he should appear in court to defend himself. He did not appear, and the court took testimony from Rios. Rios established that Fergusan had posted a video on YouTube in which he carried a gun while performing a rap song in which he said he wanted to shoot her and "put her face on the dirt until she can't breathe no more." Rios filed an application for relief from abuse in the form of a restraining order.

---

a. *Rios v. Fergusan,* 41 Conn.Supp. 212, 978 A.2d 592 (Conn.Super., 2008).

The court noted that this was a case of first impression. It had no Connecticut case law (precedent) to draw on that involved similar circumstances. Fergusan had never been in Connecticut. There was only the video posted on YouTube. Was that sufficient to give the court authority to issue a restraining order?

The court held for Rios. It found authority in cases from Iowa, Massachusetts, and New Jersey involving different facts but similar situations. The court held that even if personal jurisdiction could not be established, as would normally be required, there was a "status exception" in cases involving domestic abuse. Because of this, the state's long arm statute applied. The court found that Fergusan had committed a tort (a wrongful act) in Connecticut by posting a video on the Internet threatening violence. The posting was done in North Carolina, but the threat was intended to be seen by Rios in Connecticut. The court issued the restraining order against Fergusan.

RESEARCHING CASES OF FIRST IMPRESSION

The Internet has posed new issues for the courts in adapting traditional legal principles to cyberspace. Your approach to research thus needs to be flexible. First, see if there is existing law that the judge might determine should apply to your case (or that your supervising attorney can argue should apply). This is important given that new technologies have forced the courts to adapt existing law to meet the needs of modern society. Second, look to see if any other court (in a different state or district, for example) has considered a similar legal issue and what that court concluded. Although cases decided in other jurisdictions are not binding, courts often look at how other courts have handled an issue when deciding matters of first impression.

TECHNOLOGY TIP

Generally, when researching cases of first impression involving Internet transactions, you will need to broaden the scope of your search of the sources of law. A wise paralegal will be creative and adopt a research strategy aimed at discovering both which laws may apply and which laws should apply given the specific facts of the case.

---

equity (if they sought equitable remedies). Plaintiffs had to specify whether they were bringing an "action at law" or an "action in equity," and they chose their courts accordingly. Only one remedy could be granted for a particular wrong. Today, the separate courts have been combined in most states, and both types of remedies can be sought in a single lawsuit. There are also some differences. (See Exhibit 5.1 on the facing page.)

Procedure	Action at Law	Action in Equity
Decision	By judge or jury	By judge (no jury)
Result	Judgment	Decree
Remedy	Monetary damages	Injunction or decree of specific performance

© Cengage Learning 2014

EXHIBIT 5.1
Procedural Differences between an Action at Law and an Action in Equity

Equitable Principles and Maxims

Courts of equity often supplemented the common law by making decisions based on considerations of justice and fairness. Today, courts in the United States can award both legal and equitable remedies, so plaintiffs may request both equitable and legal relief in the same case. Whenever a court orders a party to do or not do something as part of a remedy, such as to stop a discriminatory practice, it is providing an equitable remedy. Yet judges continue to be guided by so-called **equitable principles and maxims** when deciding whether to grant equitable remedies. *Maxims* are propositions or general statements of rules of law that courts often use in arriving at a decision. Some of the most influential maxims of equity are:

- Whoever seeks equity must do equity. (Anyone who wishes to be treated fairly must treat others fairly.)

- Equity requires clean hands. (The plaintiff must have acted fairly and honestly.)

- Equity will not suffer a right to exist without a remedy. (Equitable relief will be awarded when there is a right to relief and there is no adequate legal remedy.)

- Equity values substance over form. (It is more concerned with fairness and justice than with legal technicalities.)

- Equity aids the vigilant, not those who sleep on their rights. (Individuals who fail to assert their legal rights within a reasonable time will not be helped.)

equitable principles and maxims Propositions or general statements of rules of law that are frequently involved in equity jurisdiction.

Doctrine of Laches

The last maxim listed above has evolved into the equitable doctrine of **laches** to encourage people to bring lawsuits while the evidence is still fresh. The idea is that if a party waits too long, the party has "slept on his rights" and lost the ability to bring a claim. What constitutes a reasonable time depends on the circumstances of the case. ◆ **EXAMPLE 5.4—** The Nature Conservancy (TNC) contracted to buy land from Wilder Corporation in 2000. Wilder promised there were no storage tanks on the property. In 2006, having discovered such tanks, TNC sued. Wilder claimed that laches barred the suit—TNC had waited too long to sue. In 2011, the appeals court held that laches did not apply, as there was no unreasonable delay by TNC in bringing the litigation.[4] ◆ The time period for pursuing a particular claim against another party is now usually fixed by a statute of limitations (see Chapter 3 on page 66). After the time allowed under the statute of limitations has expired, further action on that claim is barred. (See *Ethics Watch* on the next page.)

laches An equitable doctrine that bars a party's right to legal action if the party has neglected for an unreasonable length of time to act on his or her rights.

For civil wrongs (torts), the statute of limitations varies, typically ranging from two to five years. For contracts involving the sale of goods, it is normally four years. For criminal prosecutions, the duration is related to the seriousness of the offense. For example, the statute of limitations for petty theft (the theft of an item of insignificant value) may be a year, while the statute of limitations for armed robbery might be twenty years. For the most serious crimes involving first degree murder, there is no statute of limitations.

Equitable Remedies

As mentioned previously, equitable remedies are normally granted only if the court concludes that the remedy at law (monetary damages) is inadequate. The most important equitable remedies—specific performance and injunction—are briefly discussed here.

**social
MEDIA TODAY**

Just as it is critical to manage your online reputation, it is critical for your firm to manage its online reputation. Be careful when posting material that might be linked back to your firm.

ETHICS WATCH

THE STATUTE OF LIMITATIONS AND THE DUTY OF COMPETENCE

The duty of competence requires, among other things, that attorneys and paralegals be aware of the statute of limitations governing a client's legal matter. For example, if a client of your firm, a restaurant owner, wanted to sue a restaurant-supply company for breaking a contract for the sale of dishes, the first thing you should check is your state's statute of limitations covering contracts for the sale of goods. If the time period is about to expire, then you and your supervising attorney need to act quickly to make sure that the complaint (the document that initiates a lawsuit) is filed before the claim is time barred.

Of course, the attorney is responsible to the client, but it is normal for an attorney to rely on a paralegal to check such details. This example reflects the NFPA *Model Code of Ethics and Professional Responsibility,* Section 1.1(a), "A paralegal shall achieve competency through education, training, and work experience," and Section 1.1(c), "A paralegal shall perform all assignments promptly and efficiently."

specific performance
An equitable remedy requiring the performance that was specified in a contract; usually granted only when money damages would be an inadequate remedy and the subject matter of the contract is unique (for example, real property).

SPECIFIC PERFORMANCE.   A judge's decree of **specific performance** is an order to do what was promised. This remedy was, and still is, only available when the dispute before the court concerns a contractual transaction involving something unique and money damages are inadequate. Contracts for the sale of goods that are readily available on the market rarely qualify for specific performance. Monetary damages ordinarily are adequate in such situations because substantially identical goods can be bought or sold in the market.

If the goods are unique, however, a court of equity may grant specific performance. For example, paintings, sculptures, and rare books and coins are so unique that money damages will not enable a buyer to obtain substantially identical substitutes in the market. The same principle applies to disputes relating to interests in land because each parcel is unique. Specific performance is rarely granted in cases involving personal services, but see *Developing Paralegal Skills* on the facing page for a practical example of how the issue arises.

injunction
A court decree ordering a person to do or to refrain from doing a certain act.

INJUNCTION.   An **injunction** is a court order in equity directing the defendant to do or to refrain from doing a particular act. For example, an injunction may be obtained to stop a neighbor from burning trash in his yard or to prevent an estranged husband from coming near his wife. Persons who violate injunctions are typically held in *contempt of court* (see Chapter 4) and punished with a jail sentence or a fine.

The Common Law Today

The common law—which consists of the rules of law announced in previous court decisions—plays a significant role in the United States today, particularly in state courts. The rules governing tort law (civil wrongs) are largely common law. Even

DEVELOPING
paralegal skills

REQUIREMENTS FOR SPECIFIC PERFORMANCE

Louise Lassen, a wealthy heiress, buys a painting from an artist in New York for $275,000. The artist agrees to ship the painting to Louise's home in Chicago within two weeks. After Louise returns home, she learns from the artist that he has changed his mind—he is no longer interested in selling the painting and is returning her payment.

Louise contacts the firm of Murdoch & Larson to have the contract enforced. Kevin Murdoch, one of the firm's partners, asks paralegal Ling Humboldt to assist him in determining whether the remedy of specific performance, which would require the artist to provide the painting, can be sought. Ling is to research case law on specific performance and prepare a research memorandum summarizing his results. Ling lets the attorney know that he will have the memorandum on the attorney's desk by the next morning.

CHECKLIST FOR ANALYZING A LEGAL PROBLEM

- Gather the facts involved in the problem.
- Determine whether unique or rare articles are involved.
- Find out what type of remedy the client wants.
- Determine whether a remedy at law, such as money damages, will compensate the client.
- Apply the law to the client's facts to reach a conclusion regarding the appropriate remedy.

where there is a statute, court decisions often play an important role by clarifying ambiguous statutory language. Federal and state courts frequently must interpret and enforce constitutional provisions, statutes enacted by legislatures, and regulations created by administrative agencies.

To summarize and clarify common law rules and principles, the American Law Institute (ALI) has published a number of *Restatements of the Law.* The ALI, which was formed in the 1920s, is a group of highly regarded practicing attorneys, legal scholars, and judges. The *Restatements* generally summarize and explain the common law rules that are followed in most states with regard to a particular area of law, such as contracts or torts. Although the *Restatements* do not have the force of law unless adopted by a state's highest court, they are important secondary sources of legal analysis on which judges often rely in making their decisions. You will read more about the *Restatements of the Law* in Chapter 7, in the context of legal research.

The Terminology of Case Law

Throughout this text, you will encounter various terms that have traditionally been used to describe parties to lawsuits, case titles, and the types of decisions that judges write. Although details on how to research case law will be given in Chapter 7, it is worthwhile at this point to explain some of the terminology of case law.

Case Titles

The title of a case, sometimes referred to as the *style* of the case or the *case name,* indicates the names of the parties to the lawsuit. Note that a case title, such as *Baranski v. Peretto,* includes only the parties' surnames, not their first names. The *v.* in the case title stands for *versus,* which means "against." In the trial court (the court in which a lawsuit is first brought and tried), Baranski is the plaintiff, so Baranski's name appears first in the case title.

If the case is appealed to a higher court for review, the appeals court sometimes places the name of the party appealing the decision first, so that the case may be

social
MEDIA TODAY

When uploading links to social media, use the controls provided to direct content to the interested audience. Both your friends and professional network will be interested in learning about your career developments. Only your friends and family will want to see photos of your dog or your vacation.

Why is the common law important even in areas that are primarily governed by statutory law?

© Nico Tucci/www.Shutterstock.com

called *Peretto v. Baranski*. Because some appeals courts retain the trial court order of names, it is often impossible to distinguish the plaintiff from the defendant in the title of a reported decision. You must read the facts of the case to identify the parties.

When attorneys or paralegals refer to a court decision, they give not only the title of the case but also the case citation. The **citation** indicates the reports or reporters in which the case can be found (reports and reporters are volumes in which cases are published, or "reported"). For example, a citation to 251 Kan. 728 following a case title indicates that the opinion (the court decision) is found in volume 251 of the Kansas reports on page 728. You will read more about how to read case citations and locate case law in Chapter 7.

The Parties

citation
A reference that indicates where a particular constitutional provision, statute, reported case, or article can be found.

The **parties** to a lawsuit are the plaintiff, who initiates the lawsuit, and the defendant, against whom the lawsuit is brought. Lawsuits frequently involve multiple parties—that is, more than one plaintiff or defendant. For example, a person who is injured by a defective product might sue both the manufacturer of the product and the retailer from whom the product was bought to try to obtain compensation for injuries caused by the product. In this situation, the manufacturer and the retailer would be *co-defendants*. On appeal, the party asking for review is often called the *appellant* and the other party is called the *appellee*.

party
With respect to lawsuits, the plaintiff or the defendant. Some cases involve multiple parties (more than one plaintiff or defendant).

Judges and Justices

The terms *judge* and *justice* are usually synonymous and represent two designations given to judges in various courts. All members of the United States Supreme Court are referred to as justices. Justice is also the formal title usually given to judges of appeals courts, although this is not always the case. Different states use different terms. Justice is commonly abbreviated as J., justices as JJ, and Chief Justice as C.J. A Supreme Court case might refer to Justice Sotomayor as Sotomayor, J., or to Chief Justice Roberts as Roberts, C.J.

In a trial court, a case is heard by one judge. In an appeals court, normally a panel of three or more judges (or justices) sits on the bench. Most decisions reached by appeals courts are explained in written court opinions.

ON THE web

To learn about the justices of the United States Supreme Court, go to the Legal Information Institute, sponsored by Cornell University, at **www.law.cornell.edu**, go to "Court opinions," then go to "US Supreme Court Opinions."

Decisions and Opinions

The **opinion** typically contains a brief procedural history of the case, a summary of the relevant facts, the court's reasons for its decision, the rules of law that apply, and the judgment. There are five types of opinions. When all judges or justices agree on an opinion, the opinion is written for the entire court and is called a *unanimous opinion*. When there is not a unanimous opinion, a *majority opinion* is written, explaining the views of the majority of the judges deciding the case. Sometimes a majority agrees on the result but not on the reasoning. The opinion joined by the largest number of judges, but less than a majority, is called a *plurality opinion*.

Often, a judge who feels strongly about making or emphasizing a point that was not made or emphasized in the majority opinion writes a *concurring opinion*. In a concurring opinion, the judge agrees (concurs) with the decision given in the majority opinion but for different reasons. When an opinion is not unanimous, a *dissenting opinion* may also be written by a judge who does not agree with the majority. The dissenting opinion is important because it may form the basis of the arguments used later in overruling the majority opinion. The names of the judges authoring opinions are indicated at the beginning of those opinions.

opinion
A statement by the court setting forth the applicable law and the reasons for its decision in a case.

The Adversarial System of Justice

U.S. courts, like English courts, follow the **adversarial system of justice**, in which the parties act as adversaries, or opponents. Parties to a lawsuit come before the court as contestants, both sides presenting the facts of their cases in the light most favorable to themselves, in an attempt to "win" the "battle." The parties do not come together in the courtroom with the idea of working out a compromise solution to their problems or of looking at the dispute from each other's point of view. Rather, they take sides, present their best case to the judge or jury (if it is a jury trial), and hope that this impartial decision maker rules in their favor. Because each side's presentation is tested by the other side during trial, in theory the strongest case wins.

adversarial system of justice
A legal system in which the parties to a lawsuit are opponents, or adversaries, and present their cases in the light most favorable to themselves. The impartial decision maker (the judge or jury) determines who wins based on an application of the law to the evidence presented.

The Goal Is to Win

The role of the attorney is to discover and present the strongest legal argument on behalf of a client, regardless of personal feelings about the client or the client's case. Because of the adversarial nature of our system, you may be asked to work on cases that you do not believe in or for clients you do not like.

Criticisms of the Adversarial System

The adversarial nature of proceedings frames the practice of law in many respects. Lawyers are under pressure to win cases. Lawyers may be pressured by the other attorneys in a law firm to win a particular client's case. Additionally, others who work in the lawyer's firm will likely be affected by the lawyer's success or failure in court.

Some people criticize our adversarial system of justice, believing that it contributes to a lack of integrity in the legal profession. After all, the idea is that a trial is supposed to lead to justice. Some attorneys actually make higher incomes by prolonging disputes and obscuring the truth. The public may even view a lawyer who has successfully defended a criminal client as unethical because the client was found not guilty due to a "technicality."

Although our system is not perfect, most Americans agree that everyone should be allowed her or his "day in court" and should be given the opportunity to have legal advice and guidance in presenting her or his case. These are the foundations of the concept of due process of law (which you will read more about in Chapter 13). The adversarial system is basic to what we consider to be justice in the United States.

Constitutional Law

We turn next to another primary source of law. The federal government and the states have separate written constitutions that set forth the general organization, powers, and limits of their respective governments. **Constitutional law** is the law made up of the text of a constitution and court decisions interpreting that text.

constitutional law
Law based on the U.S. Constitution and the constitutions of the states.

The Federal Constitution

The U.S. Constitution is often called the nation's highest law. This principle is set forth in Article VI of the Constitution, which states that the Constitution, laws, and treaties of the United States are "the supreme Law of the Land." This provision is commonly referred to as the **supremacy clause**. A law in violation of the Constitution (including its amendments), no matter what its source, will be declared unconstitutional if it is challenged. For example, if a state legislature enacts a law that conflicts with the federal Constitution, a person or business firm that is subject to that law may challenge its validity in a court action. If the court agrees with the complaining party that the law is unconstitutional, it will declare the law invalid and refuse to enforce it.

supremacy clause
The provision in Article VI of the U.S. Constitution that declares the Constitution, laws, and treaties of the United States "the supreme Law of the Land."

The U.S. Constitution consists of seven articles. These articles, which are summarized in Exhibit 5.2 below, set forth the powers of the three branches of government and the relationships among the three branches.

Constitutional Rights

Soon after the Constitution had been ratified by the states, the first Congress of the United States submitted amendments to the Constitution to the states for approval.

BILL OF RIGHTS. Ten amendments, commonly known as the **Bill of Rights**, were adopted in 1791 and provide protections for individuals—and in some cases, business entities—against various types of government interference. Summarized

Bill of Rights
The first ten amendments to the U.S. Constitution.

EXHIBIT 5.2
The Articles of the U.S. Constitution

Article I creates and empowers the legislature. It provides that Congress is to consist of a Senate and a House of Representatives and fixes the composition of each house and the election procedures, qualifications, and compensation for senators and representatives. Article I also establishes the procedures for enacting legislation and the areas of law in which Congress has the power to legislate.

Article II establishes the executive branch, the process for electing and removing a president from office, the qualifications to be president, and the powers of the president.

Article III creates the judicial branch and authorizes the appointment, compensation, and removal of judges. It also sets forth the jurisdiction of the courts and defines *treason*.

Article IV requires that all states respect one another's laws. It requires each state to give citizens of other states the same rights and privileges it gives its own citizens. It requires that persons accused of crimes be returned to the state in which the crime was committed.

Article V governs the process for amending the Constitution.

Article VI establishes the Constitution as the supreme law of the land. It requires that every federal and state official take an oath of office promising to support the Constitution. It specifies that religion is not a required qualification to serve in any federal office.

Article VII required the consent of nine of the original thirteen states to ratify the Constitution.

Chapter 5   SOURCES OF AMERICAN LAW   133

below are the protections mentioned by the Bill of Rights. The full text of the Constitution, including its amendments (there are now twenty-seven), is presented in Appendix I at the end of the book.

1. The First Amendment guarantees the freedoms of religion, speech, and the press and the rights to assemble peaceably and to petition the government.

2. The Second Amendment guarantees the right to keep and bear arms.

3. The Third Amendment prohibits, in peacetime, the lodging of soldiers in any house without the owner's consent.

4. The Fourth Amendment prohibits unreasonable searches and seizures of persons or property.

5. The Fifth Amendment guarantees the rights to indictment by grand jury and to due process of law and prohibits compulsory self-incrimination and double jeopardy. (These terms and concepts will be defined in Chapter 13, which deals with criminal law and procedures.) The Fifth Amendment also prohibits the taking of private property for public use without just compensation.

6. The Sixth Amendment guarantees the accused in a criminal case the right to a speedy and public trial by an impartial jury and the right to counsel. The accused has the right to cross-examine witnesses against him or her and to solicit testimony from witnesses in his or her favor.

7. The Seventh Amendment guarantees the right to a trial by jury in a civil case involving at least twenty dollars.[5]

8. The Eighth Amendment prohibits excessive bail and fines, as well as cruel and unusual punishment.

9. The Ninth Amendment establishes that the people have rights in addition to those specified in the Constitution.

10. The Tenth Amendment establishes that those powers neither delegated to the federal government nor denied to the states are reserved for the states.

APPLICATION TO STATE GOVERNMENTS.   Originally, the Bill of Rights limited only the powers of the national government. That changed after the adoption of the Fourteenth Amendment to the Constitution. That amendment, passed in 1868 after the Civil War, provides in part: "No State shall . . . deprive any person of life, liberty, or property, without due process of law." Starting in 1925, the Supreme Court began to define various rights and liberties guaranteed in the national Constitution as "due process of law," which it then required of state governments under the Fourteenth Amendment. Today, most of the rights set forth in the Bill of Rights—such as the freedoms of speech and religion guaranteed by the First Amendment—apply to state governments as well as to the national government.

The Courts and Constitutional Law

The rights secured by the Bill of Rights are not absolute. The principles outlined in the Constitution are given form and substance by the courts. Courts often have to balance the rights and freedoms stated in the Bill of Rights against other rights, such as the right to be free from the harmful actions of others. Ultimately, it is the United States Supreme Court, as the final interpreter of the Constitution, that gives meaning to our constitutional rights and determines their boundaries.

COURTS BALANCE THE RIGHT TO FREE SPEECH.   An instance of how the courts must balance the rights and freedoms granted by the Constitution can be found by looking at our right to free speech. Even though the First Amendment guarantees the right to free speech, we are not, in fact, free to say anything we want. ◆ **EXAMPLE 5.5—** In interpreting the meaning of the First Amendment, the Supreme Court has made it clear that certain speech will not be protected. Speech that harms the good reputation of another, for instance, is commonly considered to be a tort, or civil wrong. If the speaker is sued, she may be ordered by a court to pay damages to the harmed person (as you will read in Chapter 14). ◆

FREE SPEECH AND THE INTERNET. The Internet has raised new problems for the courts in determining how to define and apply the protections conferred by the Constitution, particularly with regard to free speech. For example, the Supreme Court has ruled that obscene speech, though difficult to define, is not entitled to complete First Amendment protection. Regulating obscene speech in the online environment, however, has proved to be difficult. ◆ **EXAMPLE 5.6—** Congress first attempted to prohibit *online obscenity* in the Communications Decency Act (CDA) of 1996, which made it a crime to make available to minors online any "obscene or indecent" message.[6] Civil rights groups claimed the CDA was an unconstitutional restraint on speech. The Supreme Court held that portions of the act were unconstitutional in *Reno v. American Civil Liberties Union*.[7] Congress then passed the Child Online Protection Act (COPA).[8] That law was struck down by a federal appeals court as being unconstitutional because it was too vague.[9] In 2009, the Supreme Court agreed with that ruling.[10] ◆

State Constitutions

Each state has a constitution that sets forth the general organization, powers, and limits of the state government. The Tenth Amendment to the U.S. Constitution, which defines the powers and limitations of the federal government, reserves all powers not granted to the federal government to the states. Unless they conflict with the U.S. Constitution, state constitutions are supreme within the states' borders. State constitutions are thus important sources of law. Many are much more detailed than the federal Constitution. Alabama's is 40 times longer than the U.S. Constitution.

Statutory Law

Statutes, which are laws enacted by legislative bodies at any level of government, make up a major source of law. The body of written laws created by the legislature is generally referred to as **statutory law**.

Federal Statutes

statute
A written law enacted by a legislature under its constitutional lawmaking authority.

statutory law
The body of written laws enacted by the legislature.

Federal statutes are laws that are enacted by the U.S. Congress. As mentioned, any law—including a federal statute—that violates the U.S. Constitution will be struck down. Areas of federal statute law include protection of intellectual property rights (see Chapter 15), regulation of the purchase and sale of corporate stock (see Chapter 18), prohibition of employment discrimination (see Chapter 18), protection of the environment (see Chapter 19), and protection of consumers (discussed in Chapter 14). As is discussed in the *Featured Contributor* box on pages 136–137, paralegals will see the interplay of the many different areas of law in practice.

The Federal Government's Constitutional Authority to Enact Laws

federal system
The system of government established by the Constitution, in which the national government and the state governments share sovereign power.

In the **federal system** of government established by the Constitution, the national government (usually called the federal government) and the state governments *share* sovereign power. The Constitution specifies, however, that certain powers can be exercised only by the national government. For example, the national government was authorized to regulate domestic and foreign commerce (trade).

The president of the United States was declared to be the nation's chief executive and commander in chief of the armed forces. And, as already noted, the

Constitution made it clear that laws made by the national government take priority over conflicting state laws. At the same time, the Constitution provided for certain states' rights, including the right to control commerce within state borders and to exercise powers to protect public health, safety, morals, and general welfare.

To protect citizens from the national government using its power arbitrarily, the Constitution divided the national government's powers among three branches:

- The legislative branch, or Congress, which makes the laws.

- The executive branch, which enforces the laws.

- The judicial branch, which interprets the laws.

Each branch performs a separate function, and no branch may exercise the authority of another branch. Each branch, however, has some power to limit the actions of the other two branches. Congress, for example, can enact legislation relating to spending and commerce, but the president can veto that legislation. The executive branch is responsible for foreign affairs, but treaties with foreign governments require approval by the Senate. Although Congress determines the jurisdiction of the federal courts, the federal courts have the power to hold acts of the other branches of the federal government unconstitutional. With this system of **checks and balances**, no one branch of government can accumulate too much power.

The Federal Lawmaking Process

Each law passed by Congress begins as a *bill,* which may be introduced either in the House of Representatives or in the Senate. Often, similar bills are introduced in both chambers of Congress. In either chamber, the House or the Senate, the bill is then referred to a committee and its subcommittees for study, discussion, hearings, and rewriting. If the committee does not approve the bill, it "dies" and goes no further. If approved, it is scheduled for debate by the full House or Senate. Finally, a vote is taken, and the bill is either passed or defeated. If the two chambers pass similar, but not identical, bills, a *conference committee* is formed to write a compromise bill, which must then be approved by both chambers before it is sent to the president to sign. Once the president signs the bill, it becomes law.

During the legislative process, bills are identified by a number. A bill in the House of Representatives is identified by a number preceded by "HR" (such as HR 212). In the Senate, the bill's number is preceded by an "S" (such as S 212). When both chambers pass the bill and it is signed into law by the president, the statute is initially published in the form of a pamphlet or a single sheet, known as a *slip law.* The slip law is assigned a **public law number**, or P.L. number (such as P.L. 5030).

At the end of the two-year congressional term, or session, the statute is published in the term's *session laws,* which are collections of statutes contained in volumes and arranged by year or legislative session. Ultimately, the statute is included in the *United States Code,* in which all federal laws are codified (systematized, or arranged in topical order). You may need to locate a statute by bill number, public law number, or U.S. Code section number in the course of your research. (See Chapter 7 for further details on how federal statutes are published.)

State Statutes

State statutes are laws enacted by state legislatures. Any state law that is found by a court to conflict with the U.S. Constitution or with the state's constitution will be deemed unconstitutional. State statutes include state laws governing real property and insurance (see Chapter 16), estates and family law (discussed in Chapter 17), the formation of corporations and other business entities (see Chapter 18), and certain crimes (see Chapter 13), along with state versions of the Uniform Commercial Code (to be discussed shortly).

GOING green

RECYCLE ELECTRONIC JUNK

Don't put old electronics equipment in the garbage bin. Send it to the electronics recycling center. Most cities have centers where you can take used equipment such as computers and printers no longer needed at the office. Some major electronics makers, such as HP and Dell, are also willing to take old equipment. The U.S. Environmental Protection Agency maintains a list of recycling locations at **www.epa. gov/osw**. In the "Wastes Quick Finder" list, select "Electronics Recycling (eCycling)."

checks and balances
A system in which each of the three branches of the national government—executive, legislative, and judicial—exercises a check on the actions of the other two branches.

public law number
An identification number assigned to a statute.

ON THE web

A good starting point to access state statutes online is **www.law. cornell.edu**. From the "Law by source or jurisdiction" menu, select "State law." Then select "state list."

Featured Contributor

THE INTERRELATIONSHIP OF THE VARIOUS AREAS OF LAW

S. Whittington Brown

BIOGRAPHICAL NOTE

S. Whittington Brown earned a B.A. from Rhodes College and a law degree from the University of Arkansas. He is licensed to practice in the state of Arkansas, the United States District Court, and the United States Court of Appeals. He has served as an attorney and an attorney supervisor for the Arkansas Department of Human Services. He is currently the chief investigator for Developmental Disabilities Services and a licensed polygraph examiner.

At Pulaski Technical College, Brown taught American national government, legal terminology, legal research and writing, legal environment of business, business organizations, and torts. He is also the author of *Legal Terminology*, published by Delmar Cengage Learning. Brown was recognized as an "Outstanding Citizen" of the state of Arkansas by then-governor Bill Clinton.

Law is divided into many different subject areas. An attorney may specialize in personal-injury, property, employment, or contract law, for example. None of these areas, however, exists in a vacuum. One legal principle may apply to many different areas of the law, and one subject area may influence others. An important skill that a paralegal must develop is the ability to see the relationships among areas of law that may appear to be totally unrelated. Consider just one example: the application of constitutional law concepts to criminal law and employment law. At first, it would appear that these fields have nothing in common, but there are provisions of constitutional law that apply to both areas.

DUE PROCESS OF LAW

One of the main principles of constitutional law is due process of law. According to the Fifth and Fourteenth Amendments to the Constitution,

no person shall be deprived of life, liberty, or property, without due process of law. The concept of due process has two parts, substantive due process and procedural due process. *Substantive due process* means that the law itself, that which is being enforced, must be fair. The law must be applied the same way to every person and must not discriminate against anyone. *Procedural due process* means that the method used to enforce the law must be fair; it must be applied the same way to every person. One such element of due process of law is contained in the Fourth Amendment—the prohibition against unreasonable searches and seizures.

APPLICATION TO CRIMINAL LAW

In criminal law a person, because of an alleged violation of the law, faces the loss of property, liberty, or even life, depending upon the seriousness

Conflicts between Federal and State Laws

If a state statute is found to conflict with a federal statute, the state law is invalid. Because some powers are shared, however, it is necessary to determine which law governs in a particular circumstance. *Concurrent powers* are those shared by the federal government and the states, such as the power to impose taxes or to establish courts.

Preemption occurs when Congress chooses to act exclusively in a concurrent area. In this circumstance, a valid federal law or regulation in the preempted area will take precedence over a conflicting state or local law or regulation. Often, it is not clear whether Congress, in passing a law, intended to preempt an entire area of law. In these situations, the courts must determine Congress's intention. No single factor determines whether a court will find preemption.

Generally, congressional intent to preempt will be found if a federal law regulating an activity is so comprehensive or detailed that the states have little or no

preemption
A doctrine under which a federal law preempts, or takes precedence over, conflicting state and local laws.

of the offense. The accused is entitled to due process of law. This includes the right to be represented by an attorney, the right to a trial by a jury, the right to know the charges, the right to confront accusers, and the right to present evidence in his or her defense. Also, any evidence seized in violation of the Fourth Amendment cannot be used against the defendant. A paralegal working in the area of criminal law must be aware not only of the crimes and what makes up each element of them, but also of the due process rights guaranteed by the U.S. Constitution.

APPLICATION TO EMPLOYMENT LAW

Principles of constitutional law also apply to employment. Fourth Amendment limitations on unreasonable searches and seizures apply to the workplace in combination with the right to privacy. The Supreme Court has stated that there are zones of privacy that apply to a person regardless of the situation in which a person may find himself or herself, including the workplace.

An employer may have several reasons for wanting to conduct employee searches: to protect itself against employee theft, to protect sensitive material, and to ensure that illegal conduct is not occurring at the work site. An employee, however, is protected against unreasonable searches and seizures by the Fourth Amendment and has an expectation of privacy, even in the workplace. For a workplace search to take place, certain criteria must be met.

The United States Supreme Court case of *O'Connor v. Ortega*[a] helped set out the criteria for when a search of an employee can take place. First, the employee's expectation of privacy must be reduced. To lessen the expectation, the employer is required to implement a policy establishing when and under what circumstances a search of the workplace may take place. Also, the search must be reasonable and based on allegations made against the employee, the purpose of the search should be clearly established, and the search should be limited in scope. The principles established by the limitation on searches and seizures and the right to privacy have also been applied to the use of lie-detector tests, drug tests, background checks, references, and credit checks in employment situations.

These are just two examples of how one area of law may interact with other areas. A basic principle of constitutional law applies to both criminal law and employment law. Employment law not only involves elements of constitutional law but also contains elements of contract law and agency law. A paralegal must be able to see how the different areas of the law interact with one another and realize that no area of the law exists in a vacuum.

---

a.   480 U.S. 708 (1987).

"An important skill that a paralegal must develop is the ability to see the relationships among areas of law that may appear to be totally unrelated."

room to regulate in that area. Also, when a federal statute creates an agency—such as the National Labor Relations Board—to enforce the law, matters that come within the agency's jurisdiction will likely preempt state laws. Congress has recognized that the states regulate some areas of business, such as insurance. In those areas, Congress generally does not preempt state law. As the *Developing Paralegal Skills* feature on the next page discusses, federal preemption of state law can be a critical issue.

The State Lawmaking Process

When passing laws, state legislatures follow procedures similar to those followed in Congress. All of the states except one have bicameral (two-chamber) legislatures. (Nebraska has a unicameral, or one-chamber, legislature.) Typically, bills may be introduced in either chamber, or both chambers, of the legislature. As in the U.S.

DEVELOPING
paralegal skills

STATE VERSUS FEDERAL REGULATION

Stephanie Wilson works as a paralegal in the legal department of National Pipeline, Inc., whose business is transporting natural gas to local utilities, factories, and other sites around the country. Last month, one of National's pipelines, which ran under a residential street in Minneapolis, Minnesota, exploded, resulting in several injuries and one death.

The federal government has regulated pipeline safety and maintenance since 1968, under the Natural Gas Pipeline Safety Act. As a result of the explosion, the state of Minnesota wants to regulate pipeline safety as well. Stephanie's boss, the general counsel of the company, and several other executives believe that the federal act preempts this field of law, preventing the state from enacting another layer of safety legislation. Stephanie is assigned the task of researching the statute and relevant case law to determine if the federal law does in fact preempt the state's regulation.

TIPS FOR DETERMINING FEDERAL PREEMPTION

- Read through the statute to see if it expressly states that Congress intended to preempt (or not) the relevant field (in this case, pipeline safety).

- If there is no express provision, look for indications that Congress has impliedly occupied the field: Is the federal regulatory scheme pervasive? Is federal occupation of the field necessitated by the need for national uniformity? Is there a danger of conflict between state laws and the administration of the federal program?

- Locate and read cases discussing the issue of federal preemption in this area. Brief any cases that are relevant to this issue. (See Chapter 7 for instructions on how to brief a case.)

Congress, if the two chambers pass similar bills that differ from one another in any respect, a conference committee works out a compromise, which must then be approved by both chambers before being sent to the state's governor to sign into law.

Local Ordinances

Statutory law also includes local governments' ordinances. An **ordinance** is an order, rule, or law passed by a city, county, or special district government to govern matters not covered by federal or state law. As local governments are created by state governments, ordinances may not violate the state or federal Constitution, or go beyond what is allowed by state law. Local ordinances often have to do with land use (zoning ordinances), building and safety codes, construction and appearance of housing, and other matters affecting a local area. Persons who violate ordinances may be fined, jailed, or both.

ordinance
An order, rule, or law enacted by a municipal or county government to govern a local matter as allowed by state or federal legislation.

Uniform Laws

Many areas of state law vary from state to state. The differences were particularly notable in the 1800s, when conflicting statutes created problems for the rapidly developing trade among the states. To counter these problems, a group of legal scholars and lawyers formed the National Conference of Commissioners on Uniform State Laws (NCCUSL) in 1892 to draft uniform statutes for adoption by the states. The NCCUSL continues to issue uniform statutes, often in conjunction with the American Law Institute.

Adoption of uniform laws is a state matter, and a state may reject all or part of proposed uniform laws or rewrite them as the state legislature wishes. Hence, even when a uniform law is said to have been adopted in many states, the laws may not be entirely "uniform." Once adopted by a state legislature, a uniform act becomes a part of the statutory law of that state. ◆ **EXAMPLE 5.7—** A uniform law that has been adopted (at least in part) by all fifty states is the Uniform Commercial Code (UCC) (discussed in Chapter 15). First published in 1962, it provides a set of rules governing commercial transactions and sales contracts. It helps harmonize terms of sales across state lines and sets rules for bank checks and other standard financial instruments. ◆

Administrative Law

Another important source of American law is **administrative law**. It consists of the rules, orders, and decisions of administrative agencies. An **administrative agency** is a federal, state, or local government agency established to perform a specific function, such as the regulation of food sold to consumers. Rules issued by administrative agencies affect most aspects of a business's operation, including the firm's financing, its hiring and firing procedures, its relations with employees and unions, and the way it manufactures and markets its products.

At the federal level there are many administrative agencies with a variety of missions. ◆ **EXAMPLE 5.8—** The federal Environmental Protection Agency coordinates and enforces federal environmental laws. The federal Food and Drug Administration enforces federal laws relating to the safety of food and drugs. The Securities and Exchange Commission regulates purchases and sales of securities (corporate stocks and bonds). ◆

There are administrative agencies at the state and local levels as well. Some state agencies work with a federal agency to regulate an area. State environmental agencies, for example, often play important roles in implementing the regulations issued by the federal Environmental Protection Agency. Other state agencies, such as those dealing with workers' compensation, mostly operate under state law. Just as federal statutes take precedence over conflicting state statutes, so do federal agency regulations take precedence over conflicting state regulations. Because the rules of state and local agencies vary widely, we focus here exclusively on federal administrative law. Notice that some administrative agencies allow paralegals to practice before them, as discussed in the *Practice Focus* feature on the next page.

Agency Creation

Because Congress cannot possibly oversee the actual implementation of all the laws it enacts, it must delegate such tasks to others, particularly when the issues relate to technical areas, such as air and water pollution. Congress creates an administrative agency by passing **enabling legislation**, which specifies the name, composition, purpose, and powers of the agency being created. ◆ **EXAMPLE 5.9—** The Federal Trade Commission (FTC) was created in 1914 by the Federal Trade Commission Act. This act prohibits unfair and deceptive trade practices. It also describes the procedures the agency must follow to charge persons or organizations with violations of the act, and it provides for judicial review (review by the courts) of agency orders. Other portions of the act grant the agency powers to "make rules and regulations for the purpose of carrying out the Act," to conduct investigations of business practices, to obtain reports from interstate corporations concerning their business practices, to investigate possible violations of the act, to publish findings of its investigations, and to recommend new legislation. The act also empowers the FTC to hold trial-like hearings and to **adjudicate** certain kinds of trade disputes that involve FTC regulations. ◆

Note that the FTC's grant of power incorporates functions associated with the legislative branch of government (rulemaking), the executive branch (investigation and enforcement), and the judicial branch (adjudication). Taken together, these functions constitute *administrative process*.

---

administrative law
A body of law created by administrative agencies in the form of rules, regulations, orders, and decisions in order to carry out their duties and responsibilities.

administrative agency
A federal or state government agency established to perform a specific function. Administrative agencies are authorized by legislative acts to make and enforce rules relating to the purpose for which they were established.

🖰 ON THE web

The *United States Government Manual* describes the origins, purposes, and administrators of every federal department and agency. You can access this publication online at **www.usgovernmentmanual.gov/**

enabling legislation
A statute enacted by a legislature that authorizes the creation of an administrative agency and specifies the name, purpose, composition, and powers of the agency being created.

adjudicate
To resolve a dispute using a neutral decision maker.

PRACTICE focus

PRACTICING ADMINISTRATIVE LAW: DISABILITY CLAIMS

Paralegals may work in administrative law, such as preparing Social Security disability claims. The Social Security Administration (SSA) pays more than $100 billion in disability benefits to over nine million Americans each year. Paralegals may represent clients before the SSA. [See **www.ssa.gov/representation** and the National Organization of Social Security Claimants' Representatives (**www.nosscr.org**) for more information.] Paralegals are involved in all aspects of disability claims. They may work for a law firm or review claims for the SSA.

DEVELOPING MEDICAL EXPERTISE

Disability claims often turn on medical evidence, requiring paralegals to organize and review medical evidence. Medical records are filled with technical terms, so to be successful you will have to learn this vocabulary. Medical records come in many forms and include scans, blood tests, prescription records, physicians' notes, and hospital forms. In addition, some cases turn on the availability of work for a claimant with a specific disability and level of work experience and education. Witnesses may testify about limitations the claimant has in daily life and vocational experts may provide evidence on the ability to work.

ROLE OF THE PARALEGAL

If you help represent a claimant, you will have to organize the evidence into a narrative that supports your client's claim, translating medical documents into clear English. If you are assisting the SSA in evaluating claims, you will need to be able to search out the critical facts in the record, often from hundreds of pages of documents. In either case, your job will require you to be part detective, part medical investigator, and part legal expert.

KEY STEPS IN DISABILITY ANALYSIS

This material must be used in the five-step sequential evaluation process:

1. Is the individual working? If so, the claimant is not eligible.

2. Is the condition "severe"? If not, the claimant is not eligible.

3. Does the claimant have a disability described in the SSA Listing of Impairments? The list includes 14 major limitations so severe that an applicant with one is automatically considered disabled.

4. If not, can the individual do the work she previously did? If so, the claimant is not disabled.

5. Can the claimant do other work? If not, then there is a disability.

Rulemaking

rulemaking
The actions undertaken by administrative agencies when formally adopting new regulations or amending old ones.

One of the major functions of an administrative agency is **rulemaking**—creating or modifying rules, or regulations. The Administrative Procedure Act of 1946 imposes strict procedural requirements that agencies must follow in their rulemaking and other functions.

The most common rulemaking procedure involves three steps:

1. The agency must give public notice of the proposed rulemaking proceedings, where and when the proceedings will be held, the agency's legal authority for the proceedings, and the terms or subject matter of the proposed rule. The notice must be published in the *Federal Register*, a daily publication of the U.S. government.

2. Following this notice, the agency must allow time for interested parties to comment in writing on the proposed rule. After the comments have been reviewed, the agency takes them into consideration when drafting the final version of the regulation.

3. The last step is the writing of the final rule and its publication in the *Federal Register*. (See Chapter 7 for an explanation of how to find agency regulations.)

Investigation and Enforcement

Many agencies have both investigatory and prosecutorial powers. When conducting an investigation, an agency can request that individuals or organizations hand over specific papers, files, or other documents. In addition, agencies may conduct on-site inspections, although a search warrant is normally required for inspections. Sometimes, a search of a home, an office, or a factory is the only way to obtain evidence needed to prove a regulatory violation. ◆ **EXAMPLE 5.10—** The Environmental Protection Agency employs Special Agents, authorized to carry firearms, who investigate environmental crimes such as illegal dumping of untreated wastewater into a sewer system or disposing of toxic wastes in a municipal landfill. ◆

After investigating a suspected rule violation, an agency may take administrative action against an individual or a business. Most actions are resolved through negotiated settlements, without the need for formal adjudication. If a settlement cannot be reached, the agency may issue a formal complaint against the suspected violator, and the case may proceed to adjudication.

Adjudication

Agency adjudication usually involves a trial-like hearing before an **administrative law judge (ALJ)**. The ALJ presides over the hearing and has the power to administer oaths, take testimony, rule on questions of evidence, and make determinations of fact. Although the ALJ works for the agency prosecuting the case, he or she is required by law to be an unbiased adjudicator (judge). Hearing procedures vary from agency to agency. They may be informal meetings conducted at a table in a conference room, or they may be formal hearings resembling trials. Some agencies allow paralegals to represent clients at these hearings.

After the hearing, the ALJ issues a decision. The ALJ may compel the charged party to pay a fine or may prohibit the party from carrying on a certain activity. Either side may appeal the ALJ's decision through an internal agency review process. Once the agency has completed its procedures, a dissatisfied party may appeal to a federal court. If no party appeals the case, or if the commission and the court decline to review the case, the ALJ's decision becomes final.

National and International Law

Because business and other activities are increasingly global in scope, many cases now brought before U.S. courts relate to issues involving foreign parties or governments. The laws of other nations and international doctrines or agreements may affect the outcome of these cases. Many paralegals, particularly those who work for law firms with clients operating in foreign countries, may need to become familiar with the legal systems of other nations during the course of their careers.

For example, if you work in a firm in Arizona, California, New Mexico, or Texas, you may assist in the representation of clients who are citizens of Mexico. In this situation, you will want to have some familiarity with Mexican law and any international agreements that regulate U.S.-Mexican relations, such as the North American Free Trade Agreement (NAFTA).

National Law

The law of a particular nation is referred to as **national law**. The laws of nations differ because each country's laws reflect that nation's own unique cultural, historical, economic, and political background. Broadly speaking, however, there are two types of legal systems used by the various countries of the world. We have already discussed one of these systems—the common law system of England and the United States. Generally, countries that were once colonies of Great Britain retained their English common law heritage after they achieved their independence. Today,

administrative law judge (ALJ)
One who presides over an administrative agency hearing and who has the power to administer oaths, take testimony, rule on questions of evidence, and make determinations of fact.

ON THE web

The Library of Congress offers extensive information on national and international law at **www.loc.gov**.

national law
Law that relates to a particular nation (as opposed to international law).

common law systems exist in several countries, including Australia, Canada, India, Ireland, and Nigeria.

In contrast to Great Britain and the common law countries, most European nations base their legal systems on Roman *civil law,* or "code law." The term *civil law,* as used here, refers not to civil as opposed to criminal law but to *codified law*—which is an ordered grouping of legal principles enacted into law by a legislature or governing body. In a **civil law system**, the primary source of law is a statutory code, and case precedents are not judicially binding, as they normally are in a common law system. This is not to say that precedents are unimportant in a civil law system. Judges in such systems do refer to previous decisions as sources of legal guidance. The difference is that judges in a civil law system are not obligated to follow precedent to the extent that judges in a common law system are; in other words, the doctrine of *stare decisis* does not apply.

Today, the civil law system is followed in most of the continental European countries, as well as in the Latin American, African, and Asian countries that were once colonies of the continental European nations. China, Japan, and Thailand also have civil law systems. Ingredients of the civil law system are also found in the Islamic courts of predominantly Muslim countries. In the United States, the state of Louisiana, because of its historical ties to France, has in part a civil law system. The legal systems of Puerto Rico, Québec, and Scotland also have elements of a civil law system.

International Law

Relationships among countries are regulated to an extent by international law. **International law** can be defined as a body of written and unwritten laws observed by independent nations and governing the acts of individuals as well as governments. The key difference between national law and international law is the fact that national law can be enforced by government authorities, whereas international law is enforced primarily for reasons of courtesy or expediency.

In essence, international law is the result of centuries-old attempts to reconcile the traditional need of each nation to be the final authority over its own affairs with the desire of nations to benefit economically from trade and good relations with one another. Although no independent nation can be compelled to obey a law external to itself, nations can and do voluntarily agree to be governed in certain respects by international law for the purpose of facilitating international trade and commerce and civilized discourse.

Treaties

Traditional sources of international law include the customs that have been historically observed by nations in their dealings with one another. Other sources are treaties and international organizations and conferences. A **treaty** is an agreement between two or more nations that creates rights and duties binding on the parties to the treaty, just as a private contract may be used to create rights and duties binding on the parties to the contract. To give effect to a treaty, the supreme power of each nation that is a party to the treaty must ratify it. For example, the U.S. Constitution requires approval by two-thirds of the Senate before a treaty executed by the president will be binding on the U.S. government.

Bilateral agreements, as their name implies, occur when two nations form an agreement that will govern their relations with each other. *Multilateral agreements* are formed by several nations. The European Union, for example, which regulates commercial activities among its European member nations, is the result of a multilateral treaty. Other multilateral agreements have led to the formation of regional trade associations. ◆ **EXAMPLE 5.11—** In 1993 Congress approved the North American Free Trade Agreement (NAFTA), which includes Canada, Mexico, and the United States. It gradually eliminates many of the trade barriers among those nations. Its legal texts are provided at **www.nafta-sec-alena.org**. ◆

---

civil law system
A system of law based on a code rather than case law, often originally from the Roman Empire; the predominant system of law in the nations of continental Europe and the nations that were once their colonies.

international law
The law that governs relations among nations. International customs and treaties are generally considered to be two of the most important sources of international law.

treaty
An agreement, or compact, formed between two independent nations.

🖱 **ON THE** web

To find information on the laws governing other nations, including constitutions around the world, go to **confinder.richmond.edu**.

International Organizations

International conferences and organizations also play an important role in the international legal arena. They adopt resolutions, declarations, and other types of standards that often require a particular behavior of nations. The General Assembly of the United Nations, for example, has adopted numerous resolutions and declarations that embody principles of international law and has sponsored conferences that have led to the formation of international agreements. The United States is a member of more than one hundred multilateral and bilateral organizations, including at least twenty through the United Nations.

KEY TERMS AND CONCEPTS

Chapter Summary

Sources of American Law

THE FRAMEWORK OF AMERICAN LAW

1. *What is the law?*—The law has been defined variously over time, yet all definitions rest on the assumption that law consists of a body of rules of conduct established and enforced by the controlling authority (the government) of a society.

2. *Primary sources of American law*—There are four primary sources of American law: the common law

doctrines developed in cases; the U.S. Constitution and the constitutions of various states; statutory law, including laws passed by Congress, state legislatures, and local governing bodies; and regulations created by administrative agencies.

CASE LAW AND THE COMMON LAW TRADITION

Case law consists of the decisions issued by judges in cases that come before the court. Case law evolved through the common law tradition, which originated in England and was adopted in America during the colonial era.

1. *The doctrine of* stare decisis—*Stare decisis* means "to stand by things decided" and is the doctrine of precedent, which is a major characteristic of the common

Continued

law system. Under this doctrine, judges are obligated to follow the earlier decisions of that court or a higher court within their jurisdiction if the same points arise again in litigation.

a. A court will depart from precedent if the court decides that the precedent should no longer be followed, such as if the ruling was incorrect or does not apply in view of changes in the social or technological environment.

b. If no precedent exists, the court considers the matter as a case of first impression and looks to other areas of law and public policy for guidance.

2. *Remedies at law versus remedies in equity*—In medieval England, two types of courts emerged: courts of law and courts of equity. Courts of law granted remedies at law (such as money damages). Courts of equity arose in response to the need for other types of relief. In the United States today, the same court can typically grant either legal or equitable remedies.

3. *Remedies in equity*—Remedies in equity, which are normally available only when the remedy at law (money damages) is inadequate, include the following:

a. **SPECIFIC PERFORMANCE**—A court decree ordering a party to perform a contractual promise.

b. **INJUNCTION**—A court order directing someone to do or refrain from doing a particular act.

4. *The common law today*—The common law governs all areas of law not covered by statutory law. As the body of statutory law grows to meet different needs, the common law covers fewer areas. Even if an area is governed by a statutory law, however, the common law plays an important role because statutes are inter-preted and applied by the courts, and court decisions may become precedents that must be followed by lower courts within the jurisdiction.

5. *The terminology of case law*—

a. **CASE TITLES**—A case title consists of the surnames of the parties, such as *Baranski v. Peretto*. The citation itself (such as 12 P.3d 385) indicates the volume and page number of the reporter in which the case can be found.

b. **PARTIES**—The plaintiff or the defendant. Some cases involve multiple parties—that is, more than one plaintiff or defendant.

c. **JUDGES AND JUSTICES**—These terms are often used synonymously. Usage of the terms varies among courts. The term *justice* is traditionally used to designate judges who sit on the bench of the United States Supreme Court.

d. **DECISIONS AND OPINIONS**—A document containing the court's reasons for its decision, the rules of law that apply, and the judgment. If the opinion is not unanimous, a majority opinion—reflecting the view of the majority of judges or justices—will be written. Concurring and dissenting opinions may also be written.

6. *The adversarial system of justice*—American courts, like English courts, follow a system of justice in which the parties to a lawsuit are opponents, or adversaries, and present their cases in the light most favorable to themselves. The impartial decision maker (the judge or jury) then determines who wins and who loses based on the evidence presented.

CONSTITUTIONAL LAW

Constitutional law is all law that is based on the provisions in the U.S. Constitution, as amended, and the various state constitutions. The U.S. Constitution creates and empowers the three branches of government, sets forth the relationship between the states and the federal government, and establishes procedures for amending the Constitution.

1. *The federal Constitution*—The U.S. Constitution is the supreme law of the land. A law in violation of the Constitution or one of its amendments, no matter what its source, will be declared unconstitutional and will not be enforced. A state constitution, so long as it does not conflict with the U.S. Constitution, is the supreme law within the state's borders.

2. *Constitutional rights*—The first ten amendments to the federal Constitution are known as the Bill of Rights. These amendments embody a series of protec-tions for individuals—and in some instances, business entities—against certain government actions. The Bill of Rights originally limited only the powers of the federal government. After the Fourteenth Amendment was passed, the Supreme Court began to apply the protections of the Bill of Rights against state government actions.

3. *The courts and constitutional law*—The rights secured by the Constitution are not absolute. The courts, and ultimately the Supreme Court, interpret and define the boundaries of the rights guaranteed by the Constitution.

4. *State constitutions*—Each state has a constitution that defines and limits the powers of state government. Most state Constitutions are much longer and more detailed than the U.S. Constitution.

STATUTORY LAW

Statutory law consists of all laws enacted by the federal Congress, a state legislature, a municipality, or some other governing body.

1. *Federal statutes*—Laws passed by Congress are called *statutes*. Congress has supreme power over areas declared in the Constitution to be within federal jurisdiction. The power of Congress is subject to checks and balances as the judicial branch interprets the laws and the executive branch helps to enforce the laws. Public laws must pass both branches of Congress and then be signed by the president to become part of the U.S. Code.

2. *State statutes*—Laws enacted by state legislatures under the powers granted by the state constitution.

If a state statute conflicts with federal law, it will be stricken as unconstitutional, as federal law preempts state law.

3. *Local ordinances*—Laws passed by local governing units (cities and counties) are called *ordinances*. Such laws may not violate either the federal or state constitution or conflict with laws at the state or federal levels.

4. *Uniform laws*—While laws vary in detail from state to state, many states have adopted uniform statutes, such as the Uniform Commercial Code, to reduce confusion as businesses operate across state lines.

ADMINISTRATIVE LAW

Administrative law consists of the rules, regulations, and decisions of administrative agencies at all levels of government.

1. *Agency creation*—Congress creates administrative agencies by passing enabling legislation, which specifies the name, purpose, function, and powers of the agency being created.

2. *Administrative process*—Administrative agencies exercise three basic functions:

   a. **RULEMAKING**—Agencies make rules governing activities within the areas of their authority. Typically, rulemaking procedure involves publishing notice of the proposed rulemaking, allowing a comment period, and then drafting the final rule.

   b. **INVESTIGATION AND ENFORCEMENT**—Agencies conduct investigations of regulated entities both to gather information and to monitor compliance with agency rules. When a regulated entity fails to comply with agency rules, the agency can take administrative action. Most violations are resolved through negotiated settlements.

   c. **ADJUDICATION**—If a settlement cannot be reached, the agency may issue a formal complaint, and an administrative law judge (ALJ) conducts a hearing and decides the issue. Either party can appeal the ALJ's order to the board or commission that governs the agency if dissatisfied. Most agency decisions can also then be appealed to a court.

NATIONAL AND INTERNATIONAL LAW

1. *National law*—The law of a particular nation. National law differs from nation to nation because each country's laws have evolved from that nation's unique customs and traditions. Most countries have one of the following types of legal systems:

   a. **THE COMMON LAW SYSTEM**—Great Britain was the originator of common law. Countries that were once colonies of Great Britain retained at least part of their English common law heritage after achieving independence. Under the common law, case precedents are judicially binding.

   b. **THE CIVIL LAW SYSTEM**—Many of the continental European countries and the nations that were formerly their colonies have civil law systems.

   Often based on Roman codified law, civil law (or code law) is an ordered grouping of legal principles enacted into law by a governing body. The primary source of law is a statutory code. Although important, case precedents are not judicially binding.

2. *International law*—A body of laws that govern relationships among nations. International law allows nations to enjoy good relations with one another and to benefit economically from international trade. Sources of international law include international customs and traditions developed over time, treaties among nations, and international organizations and conferences.

QUESTIONS FOR REVIEW

1. Define *stare decisis*. Why is the doctrine of *stare decisis* the cornerstone of American common law?

2. What is the difference between binding and persuasive authority? May courts depart from precedent? What is a case of first impression?

3. What remedies were originally available from courts of law? Courts of equity? Why did courts of equity evolve? Are the courts of law and equity still separate?

4. What is a statute? How is statutory law created? What is the difference between a statute and an ordinance? What happens when a state statute conflicts with a federal statute?

5. What is the supremacy clause and where is it located? Briefly describe each article of the United States Constitution. What is the Bill of Rights?

ETHICAL QUESTIONS

1. Paralegal Nanette is asked by her supervising attorney to do some research. Nanette is to review a new state statute exempting certified, ill persons from prosecution for medical marijuana use, in order to find out what the requirements are for becoming a certified medical marijuana user. Nanette looks up the relevant state statute and finds the requirements. Nanette conveys this information to John, her supervising attorney. Nanette has neglected to research the federal drug laws and fails to tell the attorney that there is not an exemption for the medical use of marijuana under federal law. The attorney, relying on Nanette's conclusion, advises the client that once she is a certified medical user, she will be exempt from prosecution. Have John and Nanette violated any ethical rules? Explain.

2. Marilyn works as a paralegal for a small general law practice. At work one day, she receives a telephone call from her Uncle Bill, who is in distress. He owns a commercial fishing business and much of the fish he catches come from the Great Lakes. Uncle Bill has just learned that Asian carp DNA has been found 10 miles from an electrical barrier erected by the U.S Army Corps of Engineers to keep Asian carp out of the Great Lakes. Asian carp grow to be four feet long, weighing 100 pounds, and they can jump 10 feet in the air, often landing in fishermen's boats and injuring them. In addition, due to their size, large appetites, and rate of reproduction, Asian carp threaten the entire Great Lakes ecosystem. If the fish get into the Great Lakes, Uncle Bill's business will be destroyed. Uncle Bill asks Marilyn if he would be subject to criminal penalties if he were to put poison in the water near the electrical barrier to kill any carp that might get through. How should Marilyn answer this question?

PRACTICE QUESTIONS AND ASSIGNMENTS

1. In the following hypothetical situations, identify the type of case (criminal or civil), the remedy being sought, and whether it is a remedy at law or a remedy in equity:

   a. Brianna files a petition with the court. She is seeking compensation from Travis, who failed to deliver new furniture as promised.

   b. Juan sues Bob, seeking to be compensated for the cost of replacing several new trees that Bob's dog destroyed.

   c. Laurie seeks to have a contract enforced for the sale of an antique Mercedes automobile.

   d. Sam files a petition seeking to prevent the electric company from cutting down a large tree on his property.

2. Identify the type of law (common law, constitutional law, statutory law, or administrative law) that applies in each of the following scenarios:

   a. Jean Gorman strongly disagrees with the U.S. government's decision to declare war on a foreign country. She places an antiwar sign in the window of her home. The city passes an ordinance that bans all such signs.

   b. An official of the state department of natural resources learns that the Ferris Widget Company has violated the state's Hazardous Waste Management Act. The official issues a complaint against the company for not properly handling and labeling its toxic waste.

   c. Mrs. Sams was walking down a busy street when two teenagers on inline skates crashed into her because they weren't watching where they were going. As a result of the teenagers' conduct, Mrs. Sams broke her hip, and according to her doctor, she will never walk normally again. She sues the teenagers for damages.

d. Joseph Barnes is arrested and charged with the crime of murder.

3. Identify the constitutional amendment being violated in the following hypothetical situations:

    a. A state imposes the death penalty on a 17-year-old.

    b. The federal government suppresses political speech based on the speaker's identity as a corporation.

c. The police decide that because a house is located in a poor neighborhood, it must be a crack house. The police burst in, tear the house apart looking for drugs, and find nothing.

d. A local government bans handgun possession in the home.

QUESTIONS FOR CRITICAL ANALYSIS

1. Where is the commerce clause found in the U.S. Constitution and what does it say? How has it been used to expand the federal government's regulatory powers? The federal Affordable Care Act of 2010 contains a minimum coverage provision requiring Americans to buy health insurance. The United States Supreme Court heard an appeal of the constitutionality of this requirement. Does Congress have the authority under the commerce clause to require citizens to purchase health insurance?

2. The rights guaranteed by the U.S. Constitution would be of little significance if they were not enforced by the government. In view of this fact, is a written constitution really necessary? Would the rights and privileges enjoyed by Americans be any different if we did not have a written constitution?

3. Laws in the United States come primarily from four sources: the federal Constitution and state constitutions, statutes, administrative agencies, and the courts. Why are there so many different sources? What might happen if there were not? How could the law be changed if only courts made the law?

PROJECTS

1. Look at the U.S. Constitution in Appendix I of this text. Identify the amendment and quote the relevant language in the Bill of Rights that gives U.S. citizens the following rights and protections:

    a. The right to freely exercise one's speech.

    b. Protection against cruel and unusual punishment.

c. Protection against self-incrimination.

d. The right to counsel in criminal prosecutions.

e. The right to keep and bear arms.

2. Find out if law and equity have been merged in your state's courts.

GROUP PROJECT

This chapter describes uniform laws that were created to alleviate conflicting laws that hindered rapidly developing trade among the states. One such uniform law that was created was the Uniform Commercial Code (UCC), a core provision of which regulates the sales of goods. Trade problems also arose among nations. For this project, the group should search the Internet to locate a uniform international law similar to the UCC. Student one will research the source of law to determine what entity created it and what form the law takes (case law, statutory law, treaty, etc.). Student two will research the law and provide an overview of its main provisions. Student three will research the role of the U.S. government and U.S.-based businesses: how they are, or are not, governed by this law and why. Student four will prepare a two-page written summary of this particular law on behalf of the group and submit it to the instructor.

USING INTERNET RESOURCES

1. Go to the Legal Information Institute at **www.law.cornell.edu**. This site offers links to many of the federal and state sources of law that you have read about in this chapter. In this exercise, you will be examining state laws, so select "State Law Resources" from the "Legal Resources" tab near the bottom of the page. Next, select "Listing by Jurisdiction" to locate your state. Browse through the state sources of law that can be accessed online, and then answer the following questions:

    a. Were you able to access the text of your state's constitution?

b. Did the site include your state's code (compilation of statutes) and administrative regulations? Were you able to access your state legislature's Web site and proposed legislation?

c. What other primary materials were included in the site?

d. Now, browse through the site for another state. How does your state's site compare with those of other states in terms of content?

2. The Web site of the United States Supreme Court, located at **www.supremecourt.gov**, contains a description of the Court's role in interpreting the Constitution. Go to this Web site, select "About the Supreme Court," and then select "The Court and Constitutional Interpretation." What is judicial review? What role did the case *Marbury v. Madison* have in shaping the Supreme Court's power of judicial review? Can the Supreme Court give "advisory opinions"? Why or why not?

END NOTES

1. Pronounced *stahr*-ee dih-*si*-ses.

2. 347 U.S. 483, 74 S.Ct. 686, 98 L.Ed. 873 (1954).

3. *In re Baby M,* 217 N.J.Super. 313, 525 A.2d 1128 (1987).

4. *Nature Conservancy v. Wilder Corporation of Delaware,* 656 F.3d 646 (2011).

5. Twenty dollars was forty days' pay for the average person when the Bill of Rights was written.

6. 47 U.S.C. Section 223(d)(1)(B). Specifically, the CDA prohibited any obscene or indecent message that "depicts or describes, in terms patently offensive as measured by contemporary community standards, sexual or excretory activities or organs."

7. 521 U.S. 844, 117 S.Ct. 2329, 138 L.Ed.2d 874 (1997).

8. 47 U.S.C. Section 231. COPA made it a criminal act to post "material that is harmful to minors" on the Web.

9. *American Civil Liberties Union v. Mukasey,* 534 F.3d 181 (3d Cir. 2008).

10. *Cert.* denied, 129 S.Ct. 1032 (2009).

CourseMate The available CourseMate for this text has an interactive eBook and interactive learning tools, including flash cards, quizzes, and more. To learn more about this resource and access free demo CourseMate resources, go to **www.cengagebrain.com**, and search for this book. To access CourseMate materials that you have purchased, go to **login.cengagebrain.com**.

The Court System and Alternative Dispute Resolution

Chapter Outline

Introduction

Basic Judicial Requirements

State Court Systems

The Federal Court System

Alternative Dispute Resolution

After completing this chapter, you will know:

- The requirements that must be met before a lawsuit can be brought in a particular court by a particular party.

- The difference between jurisdiction and venue.

- The types of courts that make up a typical state court system and the different functions of trial courts and appellate courts.

- The organization of the federal court system and the relationship between state and federal jurisdiction.

- How cases reach the United States Supreme Court.

- The various ways in which disputes can be resolved outside the court system.

Introduction

As explained in Chapter 5, American law is based on the case decisions and legal principles that form the common law, the federal Constitution and state constitutions, statutes passed by federal and state legislatures, administrative law, and, in some instances, the laws of other nations and international law.

Paralegals, and particularly litigation paralegals, need to understand the different types of courts in the American system. There are fifty-two court systems—one for each of the fifty states, one for the District of Columbia, and the federal system. And even though there are many similarities among these systems, there are differences as well.

In the first part of this chapter, we examine the structure of the American courts. In addition to the public courts, there is also a system of private dispute resolution mechanisms. Because of the costs, in time and money, and the publicity that can come from court trials, many parties are turning to these alternative methods of dispute resolution to resolve disputes outside of court. In some cases, parties are required by the courts to try to resolve their disputes by one of these methods. In the second part of this chapter, we provide an overview of these alternative methods of dispute resolution and the role that attorneys and paralegals play in facilitating them.

Basic Judicial Requirements

Before a lawsuit can be brought before a court, certain requirements must be met. We begin with these important requirements and some of the key features of the American system of justice.

Standing to Sue

standing to sue
A sufficient stake in a controversy to justify bringing a lawsuit. To have standing to sue, the plaintiff must demonstrate an injury or a threat of injury.

To bring a lawsuit before a court, a party must have **standing to sue**, or a sufficient "stake" in a matter to justify seeking relief through the court system. In other words, a party must have a legally protected, genuine interest at stake in the litigation to have standing. The party bringing the lawsuit must have suffered a harm as a result of the action about which he or she complained. ◆ **EXAMPLE 6.1—** Assume that a friend of one of your firm's clients was injured in a car accident caused by defective brakes. The client's friend would have standing to sue the automobile manufacturer for damages. The client, who feels horrible about the accident, would not have standing because the client was not injured and has no legally recognizable stake in the controversy. ◆

Note that in some cases, a person has standing to sue on behalf of another person. ◆ **EXAMPLE 6.2—** Suppose that a child suffered serious injuries as a result of a defectively manufactured toy. Because the child is a minor, a lawsuit could be brought on his behalf by another person, such as the child's parent or legal guardian. ◆

justiciable controversy
A controversy that is real and substantial, as opposed to hypothetical or academic.

Standing to sue also requires that the controversy at issue be justiciable. A **justiciable**[1] **controversy** is one that is real and substantial, as opposed to hypothetical or academic. ◆ **EXAMPLE 6.3—** In the scenario discussed in Example 6.2, the child's parent could not sue the toy manufacturer merely on the ground that the toy was defective and the parent feared that the toy could cause injury. The issue would become justiciable only if the child had actually been injured due to a defect in the toy as marketed. In other words, the parent normally could not ask the court to determine what damages might be obtained *if* the child might be injured in the future, because this would be a hypothetical question. ◆

Types of Jurisdiction

jurisdiction
The authority of a court to hear and decide a specific case.

In Latin, *juris* means "law," and *diction* means "to speak." Thus, "the power to speak the law" is the literal meaning of the term—**jurisdiction**. Before any court can hear a case, it must have jurisdiction over the person against whom the suit is brought or over the property involved in the suit as well as over the subject matter.

Jurisdiction over Persons

Generally, a court can exercise personal jurisdiction (*in personam* jurisdiction) over residents of a certain geographic area. A state trial court, for example, normally has jurisdictional authority over residents within the state or within a particular area of the state, such as a county or district. A state's highest court (often called the state supreme court[2]) has jurisdictional authority over all residents within the state.

In some cases, under the authority of a **long arm statute**, a state court can exercise personal jurisdiction over certain nonresident defendants based on activities that took place within the state. Before a court can exercise jurisdiction over a nonresident under a long arm statute, though, it must be demonstrated that the nonresident had sufficient contacts *(minimum contacts)* with the state to justify the jurisdiction. ◆ **EXAMPLE 6.4—** If a California citizen caused an injury in a car accident in Arizona, an Arizona state court usually could exercise jurisdiction over the California citizen in a suit by the Arizona victim. Similarly, a state may exercise personal jurisdiction over a nonresident defendant who is sued for breaching a contract that was formed within that state. ◆

For corporations, the minimum-contacts requirement boils down to whether the corporation does business within the state. ◆ **EXAMPLE 6.5—** A Maine corporation that has a branch office or warehouse in Georgia has sufficient minimum contacts with the state to allow a Georgia court to exercise jurisdiction over the Maine corporation. If someone from Georgia simply buys a product from a Maine company while vacationing in Maine, and the Maine company does no business in Georgia, that would not be enough contact to allow the Georgia court to exercise jurisdiction. ◆

A state court may also be able to exercise jurisdiction over a corporation in another country if it can be demonstrated that the alien (foreign) corporation has met the minimum-contacts test. ◆ **EXAMPLE 6.6—** Suppose a Chinese corporation markets its products through an American distributor. If the corporation knew that its products would be distributed to local markets throughout the United States, it could be sued in any state by a plaintiff who was injured by one of the products. ◆

Jurisdiction over Property

A court can also exercise jurisdiction over property that is located within its boundaries even if the people involved do not. This kind of jurisdiction is known as *in rem* jurisdiction, or "jurisdiction over the thing." ◆ **EXAMPLE 6.7—** Suppose a dispute arises over the ownership of a boat docked in Fort Lauderdale, Florida. Ownership is claimed by residents of both Ohio and Nebraska, over whom a Florida court normally cannot exercise personal jurisdiction. In this situation, a lawsuit concerning the boat could be brought in a Florida state court on the basis of the court's *in rem* jurisdiction. ◆

Jurisdiction over Subject Matter

Jurisdiction over subject matter is another limitation on the types of cases a certain court can hear, such as civil or criminal cases, or cases involving bankruptcy, probate, or torts. In both the state and federal court systems, there are courts of *general jurisdiction* and courts of *limited jurisdiction*. The basis for the difference is the subject matter of cases heard. A **probate court**—a state court that handles only matters relating to the transfer of a person's assets and obligations on that person's death—is an example of a court with limited subject-matter jurisdiction. One type of federal court of limited subject-matter jurisdiction is a bankruptcy court. **Bankruptcy courts** handle only proceedings governed by bankruptcy law (a federal law that allows debtors to obtain relief from their debts when they owe more than their assets are worth). In contrast, a court of general jurisdiction can decide almost any type of case.

The subject-matter jurisdiction of a court is usually defined in the statute or constitution creating the court. In both the state and federal court systems, a court's subject-matter jurisdiction can be limited not only by the subject of the lawsuit but also by the amount in controversy, by whether the case is a felony (more serious crimes) or a misdemeanor (less serious crimes), or by whether the proceeding is a trial or an appeal.

long arm statute
A state statute that permits a state to obtain jurisdiction over nonresidents. The nonresidents must have certain "minimum contacts" with that state for the statute to apply.

probate court
A court having jurisdiction over proceedings concerning the settlement of a person's estate.

bankruptcy court
A federal court of limited jurisdiction that hears only bankruptcy proceedings.

Original and Appellate Jurisdiction

original jurisdiction
The power of a court to take a case, try it, and decide it.

trial court
A court in which cases begin and in which questions of fact are examined.

The distinction between courts of original jurisdiction and courts of appellate jurisdiction normally lies in whether the case is being heard for the first time or not. Courts having **original jurisdiction** are courts of the first instance and are usually **trial courts**—that is, courts in which lawsuits begin, trials take place, and evidence is presented.

In the federal court system, the *district courts* are trial courts. In a few instances, such as appeals of agency rules, the court of original jurisdiction is the federal circuit court of appeals. There are a few rare instances in which cases begin in the United States Supreme Court. In the state court systems, the trial courts are known by different names for historical reasons. For example, New York's trial courts are confusingly known as the "Supreme Court," and its highest court as the "Court of Appeals." Make sure you know the proper name of the courts when researching case law. The key point is that normally a court having original jurisdiction is known as a trial court.

appellate jurisdiction
The power of a court to hear and decide an appeal; the authority of a court to review cases that have already been tried in a lower court and to make decisions about them without holding a trial.

Courts having **appellate jurisdiction** act as reviewing courts, or **appellate courts**. In general, cases can be brought before them only on appeal from an order or a judgment of a trial court or other lower court. State and federal trial and appellate courts will be discussed more fully later in this chapter.

Jurisdiction of the Federal Courts

appellate court
A court that reviews decisions made by lower courts, such as trial courts; a court of appeals.

Because the federal government is a government of limited powers, the jurisdiction of the federal courts is also limited. Article III of the U.S. Constitution establishes the boundaries of federal judicial power. Section 2 of Article III states that "the judicial Power shall extend to all Cases, in Law and Equity, arising under this Constitution, the Laws of the United States, and Treaties made, or which shall be made, under their Authority."

Federal Questions

federal question
A question that pertains to the U.S. Constitution, acts of Congress, or treaties. It provides a basis for jurisdiction by the federal courts as authorized by Article III, Section 2, of the Constitution.

Whenever a plaintiff's cause of action is based, at least in part, on the U.S. Constitution, a treaty, or a federal law, then a **federal question** arises, and the federal courts have subject-matter jurisdiction. Any lawsuit involving a federal question can originate in a federal district (trial) court. ◆ **EXAMPLE 6.8—** J-H Computers, a California company, sues Ball Computers, a Texas company, for patent infringement. J-H claims that some parts Ball used in its new laptop computers are based on J-H inventions. J-H contends that it has exclusive rights to these inventions and that Ball has used them without permission. Because patent law is federal law and the federal courts have exclusive jurisdiction over such suits, J-H must file suit against Ball in federal court. ◆

Diversity Jurisdiction

diversity of citizenship
Under the Constitution, a basis for federal district court jurisdiction over a lawsuit between (1) citizens of different states, (2) a foreign country and citizens of a state or states, or (3) citizens of a state and citizens of a foreign country. The amount in controversy must be more than $75,000 before a federal court can exercise jurisdiction in such cases.

Federal district courts can also exercise original jurisdiction over cases involving **diversity of citizenship**. Such cases may arise between (1) citizens of different states, (2) a foreign country and citizens of a state or of different states, or (3) citizens of a state and citizens or subjects of a foreign country. The amount in controversy must be more than $75,000 before a federal court can take jurisdiction in such cases. For purposes of diversity-of-citizenship jurisdiction, a corporation is a citizen of the state in which it is incorporated and of the state in which its principal place of business is located.

◆ **EXAMPLE 6.9—** Maria Ramirez, a citizen of Florida, was walking near a busy street in Tallahassee, Florida, when a crate fell off a passing truck and hit and seriously injured her. She incurred medical expenses and could not work for six months. She wants to sue the trucking firm for $500,000 in damages. The firm's headquarters are in Georgia, although the company does business in Florida. Maria could bring suit in a Florida court because she is a resident of Florida, the trucking firm does business in Florida, and that is where the accident occurred. She could also bring suit in a Georgia court, because a Georgia court could exercise jurisdiction over the trucking firm, which is headquartered in that state. Maria could also sue in a federal court because the requirements of diversity jurisdiction have been met—the lawsuit involves parties from different states, and the amount in controversy (the damages Maria is seeking) exceeds $75,000. ◆

Note that in a case based on a federal question, a federal court will apply federal law. In a case based on diversity of citizenship, however, a federal court will normally apply state law. This is because cases based on diversity of citizenship generally do not involve claims based on federal law.

Exclusive versus Concurrent Jurisdiction

When both federal and state courts have the power to hear a case, as is true in suits involving diversity of citizenship (such as Maria's case described in Example 6.9), **concurrent jurisdiction** exists. When cases can be tried only in one or the other, **exclusive jurisdiction** exists. Federal courts have exclusive jurisdiction in cases involving federal crimes, bankruptcy, patents, trademarks, and copyrights; in most class-action lawsuits;[3] and in suits against the United States. States also have exclusive jurisdiction in certain subject matters—for example, in divorce and adoptions.

The concepts of concurrent and exclusive jurisdiction are illustrated in Exhibit 6.1 below. In the general area called business law, which encompasses different specific areas of law, there are some matters, such as federal bankruptcy law, that are under the exclusive jurisdiction of the federal courts. Other matters, such as banking regulation, can fall under state or federal jurisdiction, and other legal issues, such as corporate law, would fall under state jurisdiction.

When concurrent jurisdiction exists, a party has a choice of whether to bring a suit in a federal or a state court. As described in *Developing Paralegal Skills* on the following page, the party's lawyer will consider several factors in counseling the party as to which choice is preferable. The lawyer may prefer to litigate the case in a state court, perhaps because of familiarity with the state court's procedures, or in federal court because of the larger geographic area from which juries are drawn. It is also possible that the **docket** of the state court may be more crowded than that of the federal court. Other considerations include the law in an available jurisdiction, how that law has been applied in the jurisdiction's courts, and what the results have been in that jurisdiction.

Jurisdiction in Cyberspace

The Internet makes it easier to interact with people in other jurisdictions and complicates jurisdiction issues. As already discussed, for a court to compel a defendant to come before it, there must be at least minimum contacts with the jurisdiction

concurrent jurisdiction
Jurisdiction that exists when two different courts have the power to hear a case. For example, some cases can be heard in either a federal or a state court.

exclusive jurisdiction
Jurisdiction that exists when a case can be heard only in a particular court, such as a federal court.

docket
The list of cases entered on the court's calendar and scheduled to be heard by the court.

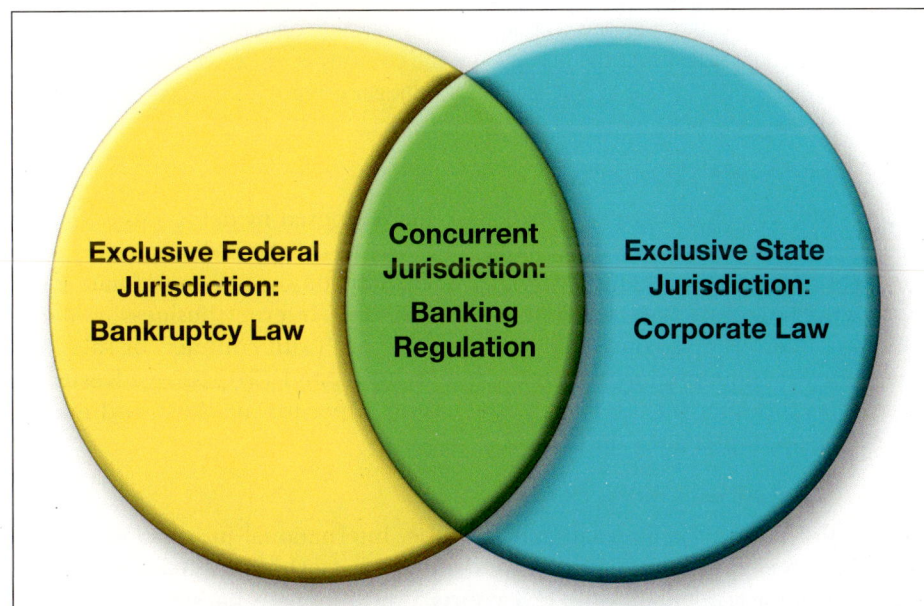

EXHIBIT 6.1
Exclusive and Concurrent Jurisdiction in Business Law

Exclusive Federal Jurisdiction: Bankruptcy Law

Concurrent Jurisdiction: Banking Regulation

Exclusive State Jurisdiction: Corporate Law

© Cengage Learning 2014

DEVELOPING
paralegal skills

CHOICE OF COURTS: STATE OR FEDERAL?

Susan Radtke, a lawyer specializing in employment discrimination, and her legal assistant, Joan Dunbar, are meeting with a new client. The client wants to sue her former employer for gender discrimination. The client complained to her employer when she was passed over for a promotion. She was fired, she claims, as a result of her complaint. The client appears to have a strong case, because several of her former co-workers have agreed to testify that they heard the employer say that he would never promote a woman to a managerial position.

Because both state and federal laws prohibit gender discrimination, the case could be brought in either state or federal court. The client tells Susan that because of Susan's experience, she wants her to decide whether the case should be filed in a state or federal court. Joan will be drafting the complaint, so Susan and Joan discuss the pros and cons of filing the case in each court. Joan reviews a list of considerations with Susan.

TIPS FOR CHOOSING A COURT

- Review the jurisdiction of each court.
- Evaluate the strengths and weaknesses of the case.
- Evaluate the remedy sought.
- Evaluate the population from which the jury will be selected in each court.
- Evaluate the likelihood of winning in each court.
- Evaluate the length of time it will take each court to decide the case.
- Review the costs and procedural rules involved in filing in each court.
- Evaluate the types of discovery available in each court.
- Evaluate the personalities and records of the judges sitting in each court.

---

within which the court sits—the presence of a company's salesperson within the state, for example. Are there sufficient minimum contacts if the only connection to a jurisdiction is an ad on the Web originating from a remote location?

◆ **EXAMPLE 6.10—** Tom, who lives in Idaho, orders $20,000 worth of merchandise from Juanita's On-Line Emporium, a New Mexico company that operates on the Internet. After paying for and receiving the merchandise, Tom claims Juanita's goods are not of the quality described on the company's Web site. Tom sues Juanita's in state court in Idaho. Does the Idaho state court have jurisdiction over the matter? Yes. The company offers to sell goods around the country, and it did make a sale to Tom, so it has sufficient contacts with Idaho to give Idaho courts jurisdiction. ◆

The "Sliding-Scale" Standard

To cope with the challenges to jurisdiction analysis posed by doing business over the Internet, the courts are developing a standard—called a "sliding-scale" standard—for determining when the exercise of jurisdiction over an out-of-state party is proper. The courts have identified three types of Internet business contacts: (1) substantial business conducted over the Internet (with contracts or sales, for example), (2) some interactivity through a Web site, and (3) passive advertising. Jurisdiction is proper for the first category, is improper for the third, and may or may not be appropriate for the second.

International Jurisdictional Issues

Because the Internet is international in scope, international jurisdictional issues arise. What seems to be emerging is a standard that echoes the requirement of minimum contacts applied by the U.S. courts. Courts in many nations indicate that minimum contacts—such as doing business within the jurisdiction—are enough

social
MEDIA TODAY

Be sure to invest time in understanding the privacy, security, automatic notification, and user interface of the social media tools you use.

to compel a defendant to appear and that the defendant's physical presence is not required for the court to exercise jurisdiction. The effect of this standard is that a company may have to comply with the laws of any jurisdiction in which it targets customers for its products. This has been a problem for online auction sites such as eBay, because countries have different rules on what may be offered for sale. Germany, for example, prohibits advertising Nazi memorabilia.

◆ **EXAMPLE 6.11—**   A Minneapolis company requested bids from cell phone makers. A company in Singapore won the bid to supply the phones. All discussions between the companies took place by e-mail, telephone, and fax. The Singapore supplier delivered the goods to the buyer at the port in Singapore. When the phones arrived in Minneapolis, the buyer claimed they did not meet the terms of the contract and sued the Singapore company. Did the federal court in Minnesota have jurisdiction over the Singapore company? No, held the court. The Singapore company had no business presence in the U.S. It sold the goods to the Minneapolis company in Singapore, so it would have to file suit in court in Singapore. ◆

Venue

While jurisdiction has to do with whether a court has authority to hear a case, **venue**[4] is concerned with the most appropriate location for a trial. For example, two state courts may both have the authority to exercise jurisdiction over a case, but it may be more appropriate or convenient to hear the case in one court because all the witnesses live near there.

The concept of venue reflects the policy that a court trying a suit should be in the geographic area (usually the county) in which the parties involved in the lawsuit reside or in which the incident leading to the lawsuit occurred. Pretrial publicity or other factors may require a change of venue to another community, especially in criminal cases in which the defendant's right to a fair and impartial jury has been impaired. ◆ **EXAMPLE 6.12—**   A bomb was set off at a federal building in Oklahoma City, killing 168 persons and injuring hundreds of others. Timothy McVeigh was indicted in connection with the bombing and scheduled for trial in an Oklahoma federal court. The defense attorneys argued—and the court agreed—that McVeigh could not receive a fair trial in Oklahoma because an impartial jury could not be chosen. Although the federal court in Oklahoma had jurisdiction, the court ordered a change of venue to a federal court in Denver for trial. ◆

venue
The geographic district in which an action is tried and from which the jury is selected.

Judicial Procedures

From beginning to end, litigation follows specifically designated procedural rules. As the *Practice Focus* feature on the following page discusses, courts are increasingly moving to fulfill procedure via electronic processes.

The general procedural rules for federal civil court cases are set forth in the Federal Rules of Civil Procedure. For criminal cases they are in the Federal Rules of Criminal Procedure. Each federal court also has its own local rules. State rules, which are often similar to the federal rules, vary from state to state, and even from court to court within a given state. Rules of procedure also differ in criminal and civil cases. Paralegals who work for trial lawyers need to be familiar with the procedural rules of the relevant courts (this includes complying with deadlines—see the *In the Office* feature on the next page). Because judicial procedures will be examined in detail in Chapters 10 through 13, we do not discuss them here.

🖱 ON THE web

The Federal Rules of Civil Procedure are available online at **www. law.cornell.edu**. Select "Federal Rules," which provides Federal Rules of Civil Procedure and other federal rules.

State Court Systems

Each state has its own system of courts, and no two state systems are the same. As Exhibit 6.2 on page 157 indicates, there may be several levels, or tiers, of courts within a state court system: (1) state trial courts of general jurisdiction and limited jurisdiction, (2) appellate courts, and (3) the state's highest court (often called the state supreme court). Judges in the state court system are sometimes elected by the voters for a specified term and sometimes appointed.

PRACTICE focus

MOVING TO MORE ELECTRONICS IN COURTS

More and more, courts are adopting e-filing systems, accepting and serving documents in all types of cases over the Internet. For example, New York uses the New York State Courts Electronic Filing System (NYSCEF) in many counties. Cases can be initiated or documents filed 24 hours a day. The system provides an e-mailed notice of filing. Some counties require e-filing in certain types of cases. Attorneys must consent to use e-filing in nonmandatory cases. Only parties who have consented may use the system.

Once a party consents to the use of the e-filing system, he or she may not file hard copies in a given case except in unusual circumstances. Attorneys may also authorize paralegals to e-file a document using the attorney's login and password, but the attorney remains the filer of record. If the system breaks down, hard copy filing is allowed and many deadlines are extended by a day. Filing fees are paid by credit card.

Texas has a different system. Its eFiling for Courts system requires use of an approved Electronic Filing Service Provider (such as CaseFileXpress). The service provider e-mails a receipt. Once the document is accepted by the courts, a confirmation message and file-stamped copy are e-mailed to the filing attorney. Texas also allows "eService" of documents for cases in which parties have consented to it. Unlike in New York, both the state Web site and the service providers charge fees in Texas, with the average cost being $10.

Systems such as those used in Texas and New York are becoming increasingly common as courts move to more efficient document handling procedures. Paralegals need to become familiar with software such as Adobe's Acrobat system that produces PDF files suitable for e-filing.

Generally, any person who is a party to a lawsuit has the opportunity to plead the case before a trial court and then, if she loses, before at least one level of appellate court. Finally, if a federal statute or federal constitutional issue is involved in the decision of a state supreme court, that decision may be further appealed to the United States Supreme Court.

IN THE office

WATCH THOSE DEADLINES!

One of the paralegal's most important responsibilities is making sure that court deadlines are met. Suppose that your supervising attorney asks you to file with the court a motion to dismiss, which is a document requesting the court to dismiss a lawsuit for a specific reason. You know that the deadline for filing the motion is in three days. After you prepare the document and have it reviewed by your attorney, you put it in the client's file. You plan to deliver the motion to the court the next day.

As soon as you get to work the next morning, you are called to help with a rush matter on another case. Busy with that, you forget about the motion to dismiss until the next week. Too late! Court deadlines are hard rules. To prevent such things from happening, *always* enter every deadline on the office calendaring system, and *always* check your calendar several times a day no matter what else is happening. Missed deadlines can be the basis for malpractice suits by clients against attorneys. If you are using electronic filing, as some courts now require, be sure to allow time for technical difficulties and have a backup plan ready if computer problems occur.

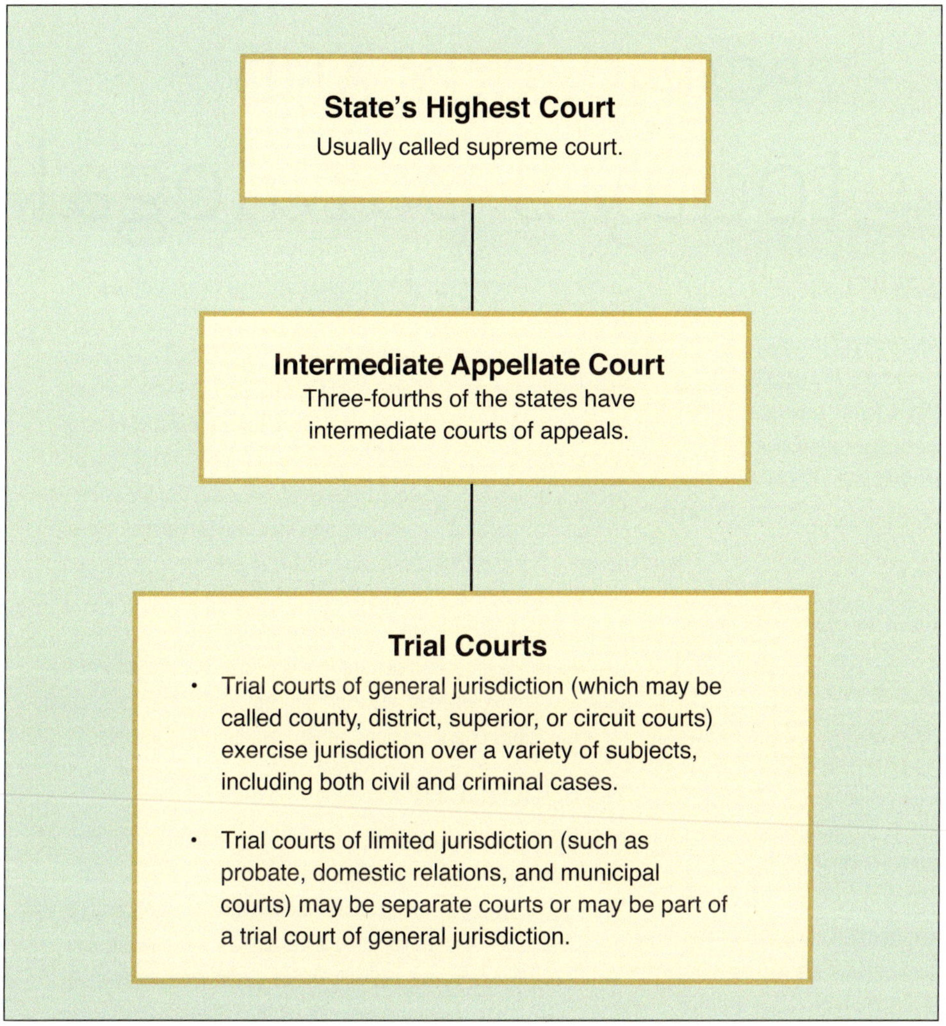

EXHIBIT 6.2
Levels in a State Court System

State's Highest Court
Usually called supreme court.

Intermediate Appellate Court
Three-fourths of the states have intermediate courts of appeals.

Trial Courts

- Trial courts of general jurisdiction (which may be called county, district, superior, or circuit courts) exercise jurisdiction over a variety of subjects, including both civil and criminal cases.

- Trial courts of limited jurisdiction (such as probate, domestic relations, and municipal courts) may be separate courts or may be part of a trial court of general jurisdiction.

© Cengage Learning 2014

Trial Courts

Trial courts are exactly what their name implies—courts in which trials are held and testimony taken. You will read about trial procedures in Chapter 12, where we follow a hypothetical case through the various stages of a trial. (The *Technology and Today's Paralegal* feature on the following page explains some of the changes occurring in the courts as they adapt to Web-based tools.)

Briefly, a trial court is presided over by a judge, who controls the proceedings and issues a decision on the matter before the court. If the trial is a jury trial (many are held without juries), the jury decides the outcome of factual disputes, and the judge issues a judgment based on the jury's conclusion. During the trial, the attorney for each side introduces evidence (such as relevant documents, exhibits, and testimony of witnesses) in support of his or her client's position. Each attorney is given an opportunity to cross-examine witnesses and challenge evidence offered by the opposing party.

General Jurisdiction Courts

State trial courts have either general or limited jurisdiction. Trial courts that have general jurisdiction as to subject matter may be called county, district, superior, or circuit courts.[5] State trial courts of general jurisdiction have jurisdiction over a wide variety of subjects, including both civil disputes (such as landlord-tenant matters or contract claims) and criminal prosecutions. In some states, trial courts of general jurisdiction may hear appeals from courts of limited jurisdiction.

TECHNOLOGY AND
today's paralegal

COURTS IN THE INTERNET AGE

Most courts have sites on the Web. Some courts display only the names of court personnel, office phone numbers, and general information. Others add judicial decisions, electronic forms, court rules, filing guidelines and fees, legal resources, and employment opportunities within the court system. Here are some useful Web sites for paralegals.

FEDERAL, STATE, AND LOCAL COURT STRUCTURES

It is important for paralegals to understand the structures of federal and state court systems so they know which types of cases are tried in which courts. You will find a description of the types of federal courts and links to all federal courts at the Federal Judiciary Web site, accessible at **www.uscourts.gov**.

Each state's court system is structured uniquely. The National Center for State Courts (NCSC), a nonprofit organization dedicated to improving state courts, presents flowcharts depicting the structure of each state court system at **www.ncsc.org**. At the NCSC site, you can find links to state court Web sites, state court statistics, articles about state court trends, and job announcements. Many state judicial systems have centralized Web sites with links to circuit and trial courts' Web sites. For example, the Web site for Michigan courts offers a directory of trial courts, maps of local court jurisdictions, and local trial court links at **courts.michigan.gov**.

COURT DECISIONS

Paralegals are often called on to find court decisions on topics related to current or pending cases. Most state courts include judicial decisions (often referred to as opinions) on their Web sites, and the majority of state courts provide case archives dating back several years. Decisions by the United States Supreme Court are posted on the Court's official Web site at **www.supremecourt.gov** within hours after the decisions are rendered.

Even decisions that are designated as unpublished opinions by the appellate courts are often published online. "Unpublished" decisions generally do not contain the same detailed recital of facts or comprehensive legal analysis as published opinions. Many courts permit unpublished decisions to be cited, although usually as persuasive rather than binding authority. You may also sometimes cite slip opinions. A slip opinion (discussed further in Chapter 7) is the second version of an opinion. It may contain corrections not appearing in the initial opinion, but it is still not the final version.

As a paralegal, it is important that you specify to the attorneys you are assisting whether any court opinions you refer to are unpublished decisions or slip opinions rather than published opinions.

TECHNOLOGY TIP

Paralegals should be comfortable gathering court information through the Internet, and regular practice is the way to achieve such comfort. Use the links mentioned above to find Web sites for courts in your area, review various courts' rules, examine court dockets, and check out what forms are available online. As an example, use the NCSC Web site to locate the Web site for the California courts. (On the home page, select "Information & Resources," then "Browse by State," then "Court Web Sites.") At the California site, browse the docket for the California Supreme Court. A paralegal should be comfortable finding, filling out, and submitting court forms online. Click on "Forms & Rules" from the menu at the top of the California Courts Web site, read the instructions, choose a form from the list, and fill out the form. Then search the Web site to locate the specific procedures that are required for filing the documents with the court. You will find valuable court information through such exercises and be on the road to becoming the technology expert of your legal team.

Limited Jurisdiction Courts

Courts with limited subject-matter jurisdiction are often called "inferior" trial courts or minor courts. Courts of limited jurisdiction include:

- Small claims courts, which hear only civil cases involving claims of less than a certain amount, such as $5,000;

- Domestic relations courts, which handle only divorce actions, paternity suits, and child-custody and support cases;

- Municipal courts, which mainly handle traffic violations; and

- Probate courts, which, as previously mentioned, handle the administration of wills, estate-settlement problems, and related matters.

Appellate, or Reviewing, Courts

After a trial, the parties have the right to file an appeal to a higher court if they are unsatisfied with the trial court's ruling. Practically speaking, parties are unlikely to file an appeal unless a reversible error was committed by the trial court that would cause the appellate court to overturn the trial court's decision. A **reversible error** is a legal error at the trial court level that is significant enough to have affected the outcome of the case. For example, the judge may have given improper instructions about the law to the jury. Usually, appellate courts do not look at questions of *fact* (such as whether a party did, in fact, commit a certain action, such as burning a flag) but at questions of *law* (such as whether the act of flag-burning is a form of speech protected by the First Amendment to the Constitution). Only a judge, not a jury, can rule on questions of law.

Appellate courts normally defer to a trial court's findings on questions of fact because the trial court judge and jury were in a better position to evaluate testimony by directly observing witnesses' gestures, demeanor, and nonverbal behavior during the trial. When a case is appealed, an appellate panel of three or more judges reviews the record (including the written transcript of the trial) of the case on appeal, and the record does not include these nonverbal elements.

Intermediate Appellate Courts

About three-fourths of the states have intermediate appellate courts (IAC), or courts of appeals. The subject-matter jurisdiction of these courts is limited to hearing appeals. Usually, IACs review the records, read appellate briefs filed by the parties, and listen to the oral arguments presented by the parties' attorneys. Then the panel of judges renders (issues) a decision. If a party is unsatisfied with the IAC's ruling, that party can appeal to the highest state court.

Highest State Courts

The highest appellate court in a state is usually called the supreme court but may be called by some other name. For example, in both New York and Maryland, the highest state court is called the court of appeals. Texas and Oklahoma have two high courts, one for civil cases and one for criminal cases. The decisions of each state's highest court on all questions of state law are final. Only when issues of federal law are involved can a decision made by a state's highest court be overruled by the United States Supreme Court.

The Federal Court System

The federal court system is basically a three-tiered model consisting of (1) U.S. district courts (trial courts of general jurisdiction) and various courts of limited jurisdiction, (2) U.S. courts of appeals (intermediate courts of appeals), and (3) the United States Supreme Court, located in Washington, D.C. Exhibit 6.3 on the next page shows the organization of the federal court system.

According to Article III of the U.S. Constitution, there is only one national Supreme Court. All other courts in the federal system are considered "inferior." Congress has the power to create inferior courts. The courts that Congress has created include those on the first and second tiers in our model—the district courts and courts of limited jurisdiction, as well as the U.S. courts of appeals.

Unlike state court judges, who are often elected, federal court judges—including the justices of the United States Supreme Court—are appointed by the president of the United States and confirmed by the U.S. Senate. Federal judges receive lifetime appointments (because under Article III they "hold their Offices during good Behavior").

reversible error
A legal error at the trial court level that is significant enough to have affected the outcome of the case. It is grounds for reversal of the judgment on appeal.

social MEDIA TODAY
Create a "living document" listing the sources you will use to keep up to date on social media trends. Update it regularly to keep it "alive."

ON THE web
The Web site for the federal courts offers information on the federal court system and links to all federal courts at **www.uscourts.gov**

EXHIBIT 6.3
The Organization of the Federal Court System

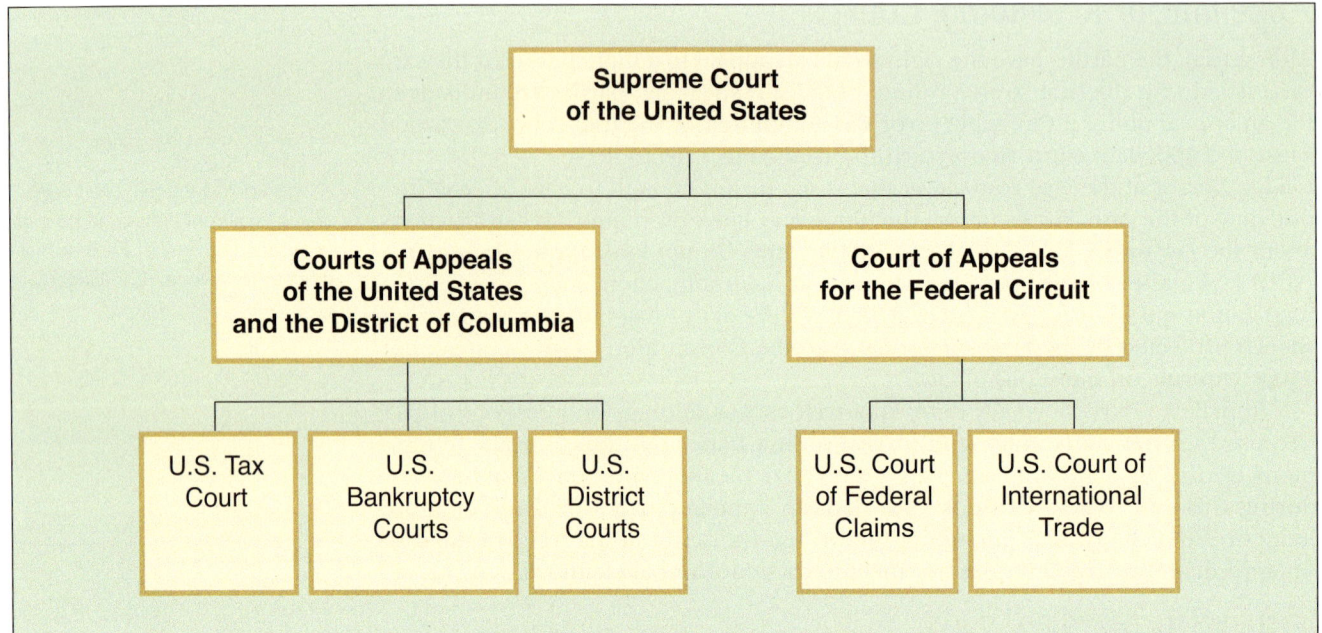

U.S. District Courts

At the federal level, the equivalent of a state trial court of general jurisdiction is the district court. There is at least one federal district court in every state. The number of judicial districts varies over time, primarily owing to population changes and caseloads. Currently, there are ninety-four judicial districts.

U.S. district courts have original jurisdiction in matters of federal law. There are other trial courts with original but special (or limited) jurisdiction, such as the federal bankruptcy courts and others shown in Exhibit 6.3 above. The *Developing Paralegal Skills* feature on page 162 discusses some considerations in federal jurisdiction.

U.S. Courts of Appeals

In the federal court system, there are thirteen U.S. courts of appeals—also referred to as U.S. circuit courts of appeals. The federal courts of appeals for twelve of the circuits (including the District of Columbia Circuit) hear appeals from the federal district courts located within their respective judicial circuits. The court of appeals for the thirteenth circuit, called the Federal Circuit, has national appellate jurisdiction over certain types of cases, such as cases involving patent law and cases involving contract claims against the U.S. government.

A party who is dissatisfied with a federal district court's decision on an issue may appeal that decision to a federal circuit court of appeals. The judges on the court review decisions made by trial courts for any errors of law. The judges generally defer to a district court's findings of fact. The decisions of the circuit courts of appeals are final in most cases, but review by the United States Supreme Court is possible. Exhibit 6.4 on the facing page shows the geographic boundaries of the U.S. circuit courts of appeals and the boundaries of the U.S. district courts within each circuit.

The United States Supreme Court

The highest level of the three-tiered model of the federal court system is the United States Supreme Court. The Supreme Court consists of nine justices. Although the Supreme Court has original, or trial, jurisdiction in rare instances (set forth in Article III, Section 2, of the Constitution—see Appendix I), most of its work is as an appeals

ON THE web

An excellent site for information on the United States Supreme Court—including its cases, functions and procedures, biographies and photographs of the justices, and even the history of the Supreme Court building—is at **www. supremecourt.gov** court. The Supreme Court can review any case decided by any of the federal courts of appeals, and it also has appellate authority over some cases decided in the state courts.

How Cases Reach the Supreme Court

Many people are surprised to learn that there is no absolute right of appeal to the United States Supreme Court. Thousands of cases are filed with the Supreme Court each year but in recent years it has heard about eighty cases each year.

To bring a case before the Supreme Court, a party requests the Court to issue a writ of *certiorari*. A **writ of *certiorari*** [6] is an order issued by the Supreme Court to a lower court requiring the lower court to send it the record of the case for review. The Court will issue a writ only if at least four of the nine justices vote to do so. The vast majority of petitions for writs are denied. A denial is not a decision on the merits of a case, nor does it indicate agreement with the lower court's opinion. It simply means that the Supreme Court declines to grant the request (petition) for appeal. Furthermore, denial of the writ has no value as a precedent.

Types of Cases Reviewed by the Supreme Court

Typically, petitions are granted by the Court in cases that raise important constitutional questions or where lower court decisions conflict with other state or federal courts' decisions. Similarly, if federal appellate courts issue inconsistent opinions on an issue, the Supreme Court may review a case involving that issue and generate a decision to settle the issue.

◆ **EXAMPLE 6.13—** Suppose that an employer fires an employee who refuses to work on Saturdays for religious reasons. The fired employee applies for unemployment benefits from the state unemployment agency, and the agency, concluding that the employer had good reason to fire the employee, denies unemployment benefits. The fired employee sues the state

writ of *certiorari*
A writ from a higher court asking a lower court to send it the record of a case for review. The United States Supreme Court uses *certiorari* to review most of the cases it decides to hear.

EXHIBIT 6.4
Boundaries of the U.S. Courts of Appeals and U.S. District Courts

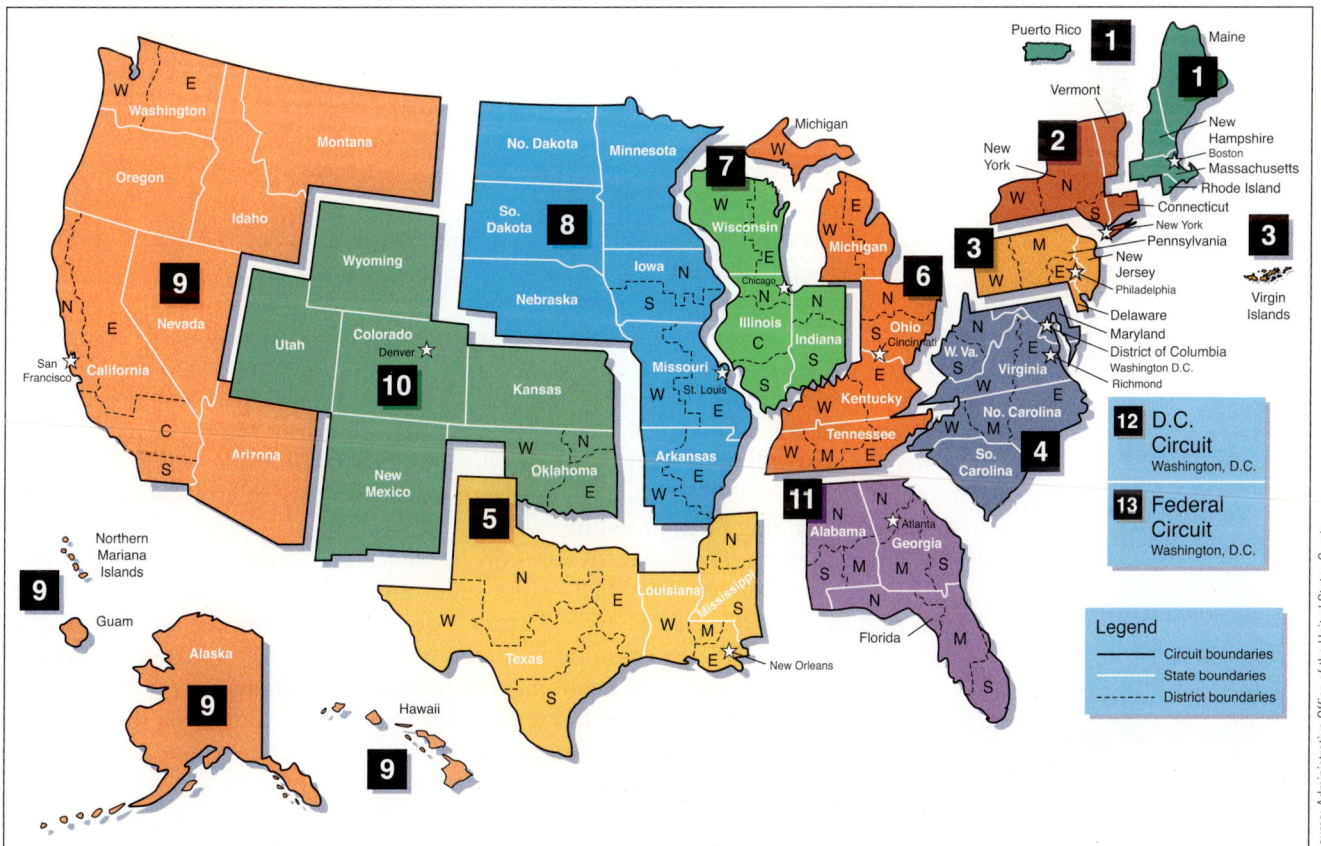

Source: Administrative Office of the United States Courts

DEVELOPING
paralegal skills

FEDERAL COURT JURISDICTION

Mona, a new client, comes to the law offices of Henry, Jacobs & Miller in Detroit, Michigan. She wants to file a lawsuit against a New York hospital where she had emergency gallbladder surgery. Mona contracted an infection as a result of the surgery and nearly died. She was so sick that she missed several months of work and lost wages of $18,000. She also has medical expenses exceeding $60,000. Jane Doyle, a paralegal, is asked to review the case to determine if it can be filed in federal court.

CHECKLIST FOR DETERMINING FEDERAL COURT JURISDICTION

- Is the case based, at least in part, on the U.S. Constitution, a treaty, or other question of federal law?

- If the case does not involve a question of federal law, does it involve more than $75,000 and one of the following:

  1. Citizens of different states?

  2. A foreign country and citizens of a state or different states?

  3. Citizens of a state and citizens or subjects of a foreign country?

If the case involves a combination of more than $75,000 and one of the citizenship requirements above, then diversity jurisdiction exists.

---

unemployment agency on the ground that the employee's right to freely exercise her religion—a constitutional right—was violated. The case is ultimately appealed to a state supreme court, which decides the issue in a way that is contrary to several recent federal appellate courts' interpretations of freedom of religion in the employment context. If the losing party petitions the Supreme Court for a writ of *certiorari,* the Court is more likely to grant the petition and review the case than if all the lower court decisions were consistent. ◆

Alternative Dispute Resolution

Litigation is expensive, adversarial, and time consuming. For these and other reasons, more and more individuals are turning to **alternative dispute resolution (ADR)** as a means of settling their disputes.

Methods of ADR range from neighbors sitting down over a cup of coffee in an attempt to work out their differences to huge multinational corporations agreeing to resolve a dispute through a formal hearing before a panel of experts. The great advantage of ADR is its flexibility. Normally, the parties themselves decide the method that will be used to settle the dispute, what procedures will be used, and whether the decision reached (either by themselves or by a neutral third party) will be legally binding or nonbinding.

Today, about 95 percent of cases are settled before trial, often through some form of ADR. Indeed, over half of the states either require or encourage parties to undertake ADR prior to trial. Several federal courts have instituted ADR programs as well. Here, we examine various forms of ADR. Keep in mind that new methods of ADR—and new combinations of existing methods—are being devised and employed. Additionally, ADR services are now being offered via the Internet. Paralegals who develop expertise in the area of ADR can expand their career opportunities (by becoming mediators, for example). Paralegals can also help attorneys to clarify the issues for clients who must decide whether to take a case to court or choose ADR, as described in *Developing Paralegal Skills* on the facing page.

alternative dispute resolution (ADR)
The resolution of disputes in ways other than those involved in the traditional judicial process. Negotiation, mediation, and arbitration are forms of ADR.

🖱 ON THE web

You can find publications pertaining to ADR by accessing the Federal Judicial Center at **www.fjc.gov**.

DEVELOPING
paralegal skills

TO SUE OR NOT TO SUE

Millie Burke, a paralegal, works for a sole practitioner. She has just been asked by the firm's owner, attorney Jim Wilcox, to draw up a checklist. It is to consist of questions that clients should consider before initiating a lawsuit. Wilcox wants to have the checklist on hand when he first interviews clients who come to him for advice on whether to bring a lawsuit or to settle a dispute by some alternative means. Millie drafts a checklist for Wilcox's review.

CHECKLIST FOR DECIDING WHETHER TO SUE

- Now that you have a rough idea of what it might cost to litigate your dispute, are you still interested in pursuing a trial? If so, you will need to pay a retainer now from which I will draw the initial filing fees and court costs. You will also need to sign an agreement that you will pay me hourly rates if the costs exceed the amount of the retainer.

- What is your goal for the litigation? What do you want to accomplish? What could the other party do to settle the case now?

- Do you have the time and patience to follow a court case through the judicial system, even if it takes several years?

- Is there a way to settle your grievance without going to court? Even if the settlement is less than you think you are owed, you may be better off settling now for the smaller figure. An early settlement will save the cost of litigation and prevent the time loss and frustration associated with litigation.

- Can you use some form of alternative dispute resolution (negotiation, mediation, or arbitration) to settle the dispute? Before you say no, let's review these dispute-settlement methods and discuss the pros and cons of each alternative. Is it important for you to be able to work with or have a relationship with the other party after the case is resolved?

Negotiation

Negotiation is one alternative means of resolving disputes. Attorneys frequently advise their clients to try to negotiate a settlement of their disputes voluntarily before they proceed to trial. During pretrial negotiation, the parties and/or their attorneys may meet to see if a mutually satisfactory agreement can be reached.

◆ **EXAMPLE 6.14—** Assume that Katherine Baranski is suing Tony Peretto for damages. Peretto ran a stop sign. His van crashed into Baranski's car, causing her to suffer injuries and damages exceeding $100,000. After pretrial investigations into the matter, both plaintiff Baranski and defendant Peretto realize that Baranski has a good chance of winning the suit. At this point, Peretto's attorney may make a settlement offer on behalf of Peretto. Baranski may be willing to accept a settlement offer for an amount lower than the amount of damages she claimed in her complaint simply to avoid the time, trouble, expense, and uncertainty involved in taking the case to trial.

To facilitate an out-of-court settlement, Baranski's attorney may ask his paralegal to draft a letter to Baranski pointing out the strengths and weaknesses of her case against Peretto, the ADR options for settling the case before trial, and the advantages and disadvantages associated with each ADR option. Additionally, the paralegal may be asked to draft a letter to Peretto's attorney indicating the strengths of Baranski's case against him and the advantages to Peretto of settling the dispute out of court. ◆ As a result of pretrial negotiations, such as those just described in Example 6.14, a settlement agreement may be reached. In a **settlement agreement**, one party gives up the right to initiate or continue litigation in return for a sum to be paid by the other party. Exhibit 6.5 on the following page shows an example of a settlement agreement. Settlements must usually be approved by the court, and if a party does not live up to its agreement, that can be the basis for a lawsuit to enforce the settlement.

negotiation
A process in which parties attempt to settle their dispute voluntarily, with or without attorneys to represent them.

settlement agreement
An out-of-court resolution to a legal dispute, which is agreed to by the parties in writing. A settlement agreement may be reached at any time prior to or during a trial.

EXHIBIT 6.5
A Sample Settlement Agreement

SETTLEMENT AGREEMENT

THIS AGREEMENT is entered into this twelfth day of May, 2014, between Katherine Baranski and Tony Peretto.

WITNESSETH

WHEREAS, there is now pending in the U.S. District Court for the District of Nita an action entitled *Baranski v. Peretto*, hereinafter referred to as "action."

WHEREAS, the parties hereto desire to record their agreement to settle all matters relating to said action without the necessity of further litigation.

NOW, THEREFORE, in consideration of the covenants and agreements contained herein, the sufficiency of which is hereby mutually acknowledged, and intending to be legally bound hereby, the parties agree as follows:

1. Katherine Baranski agrees to accept the sum of seventy-five thousand dollars ($75,000) in full satisfaction of all claims against Tony Peretto as set forth in the complaint filed in this action.

2. Tony Peretto agrees to pay Katherine Baranski the above-stated amount, in a lump-sum cash payment, on or before the first day of July, 2014.

3. Upon execution of this agreement and payment of the sum required under this agreement, the parties shall cause the action to be dismissed with prejudice.

4. When the sum required under this agreement is paid in full, Katherine Baranski will execute and deliver to Tony Peretto a release of all claims set forth in the complaint filed in the said action.

Katherine Baranski
Katherine Baranski

Tony Peretto
Tony Peretto

Sworn and subscribed before me this twelfth day of May, 2014.

Leela M. Shay
Leela M. Shay
Notary Public
District of Nita

mediation
A method of settling disputes outside of court by using the services of a neutral third party, who acts as a communicating agent between the parties; a method of dispute settlement that is less formal than arbitration.

Mediation

Another alternative to a trial is mediation. In the **mediation** process, the parties attempt to negotiate an agreement with the assistance of a neutral third party, a mediator. In mediation, the mediator typically talks with the parties separately as

A paralegal mediates a dispute by emphasizing the common ground shared by the parties as she proposes possible solutions. Is mediation binding on both parties? Why or why not?

Courtesy of © Brand X Pictures

well as jointly. The mediator emphasizes points of agreement, helps the parties evaluate their positions, and proposes solutions. The mediator, however, does not make a binding decision on the matter being disputed.

The parties may select a mediator on the basis of expertise in a particular field or a reputation for fairness and impartiality. The mediator need not be a lawyer. The mediator may be one person, such as a paralegal, an attorney, or a volunteer from the community, or a panel of mediators may be used. Usually, a mediator charges a fee, which can be split between the parties. Many state and federal courts now require that parties mediate their disputes before being allowed to resolve the disputes through trials. In this situation, the mediators may be appointed by the court.

A Nonadversarial Forum

Mediation is not adversarial in nature, as lawsuits are. In litigation, the parties "do battle" with each other in the courtroom, while the judge serves as the neutral referee. The adversarial nature of the trial process may inflame tensions between the parties. Because of its nonadversarial nature, the mediation process tends to reduce the hostility between the parties and may allow them to resume their former relationship. For this reason, mediation is often the preferred form of ADR for disputes involving business partners, employers and employees, family members, or other long-term relationships.

◆ **EXAMPLE 6.15—** Suppose that two business partners have a dispute over how the profits of their firm should be distributed. If the dispute is litigated, the parties will be adversaries, and their attorneys will emphasize how the parties' positions differ, not what they have in common. In contrast, if the dispute is mediated, the mediator will emphasize the common ground shared by the partners and help them work toward agreement. If the partners will still be doing business together after the case is over, mediation may be preferred to litigation. ◆

Paralegals as Mediators

Because a mediator need not be a lawyer, this field is open to paralegals who acquire appropriate training and expertise. If you are interested in becoming a mediator, you can check with your local paralegal association or with one of the national paralegal associations to find out how you can pursue this career goal. You can also check with a county, state, or federal court in your area to see how to qualify as a mediator for court-referred mediation (to be discussed shortly).

Generally, any paralegal aspiring to work as a mediator must have excellent communication skills. This is because, as a mediator, it will be your job to listen

social
MEDIA TODAY

Most social media are just new ways to have conversations that you are already having—just not as easily or effectively as the new tools make possible. Look at the conversations you are already involved in to find opportunities to use the new tools.

Featured Contributor

WHY MEDIATION MAY BE THE BEST LEGAL ALTERNATIVE

P. Darrel Harrison

BIOGRAPHICAL NOTE

P. Darrel Harrison is a trained mediator who holds an MBA in organizational development and a JD degree. He is an instructor and the program director for the ABA-approved paralegal program at San Diego Miramar College. Mr. Harrison is also vice president and chief grievance/arbitration officer for the San Diego Chapter of the American Federation of Teachers (AFT), Local 1931. He was appointed as a board member to the Mayor's Citizen Review Board, which reviews citizen complaints filed against the San Diego Police Department.

© Cengage Learning 2014

Litigated cases can be costly. Mediation is a cost-effective method of resolving many disputes because it avoids the expense of going to court. Mediation is satisfying because it allows a client the ability to negotiate a compromised outcome rather than a simple win or loss in court.

Mediation is a process for resolving conflicts, in which a neutral, skilled mediator assists the parties to discuss and negotiate their issues and reach a mutually acceptable resolution.

Because many state and federal courts around the United States have provided alternative dispute resolution services, various forms of mediation specialties have developed over the years, such as Parent/Teen Mediation, Family Mediation, Business Mediation, Employment Mediation, Elder Care Mediation, and Guardianship Mediation, to name a few.

THE MEDIATION PROCESS

Despite the specialty areas, mediation basics are universally applied. First there must be willing participants. The commitment to mediation creates an atmosphere of good faith and the positive momentum that leads to a negotiated conclusion.

Once the parties have joined the process, it is essential that the mediator—the third party neutral to the conflict—has the ability to

carefully to each party's complaints and communicate possible solutions to a dispute in a way that is not offensive to either party. (See this chapter's *Featured Contributor* article above for further details on the functions performed by mediators and the role played by paralegals in the mediation process.)

Arbitration

arbitration
A method of settling disputes in which a dispute is submitted to a disinterested third party (other than a court), who issues a decision that may or may not be legally binding.

A more formal method of ADR is **arbitration**, in which an arbitrator hears a dispute and determines the outcome. The key difference between arbitration and the forms of ADR just discussed is that in arbitration, the third party hearing the dispute makes the decision for the parties—a decision that may be legally binding. In negotiation and mediation, in contrast, the parties decide for themselves, although a third party assists them. In a sense, the arbitrator acts as a private judge, even though the arbitrator is not required to be a lawyer. Often, a panel of experts arbitrates disputes.

In some respects, formal arbitration resembles a trial, although the procedural rules are much less restrictive than those governing litigation. In the typical hearing format, the parties present facts and arguments to the arbitrator and describe the outcome they want. Witnesses may be called but the format is less formal than in court. The arbitrator then issues a decision.

engage the parties and help navigate them through the issues to come to a common solution. Unlike arbitration, where the intermediary listens to the arguments of both sides and makes a decision for the disputants, a mediator assists the parties to develop a solution themselves.

Although mediators may provide ideas or even formal proposals for settlement, the mediator is primarily a "process person." The mediator helps the parties define the agenda, identify and reframe the issues, communicate more effectively, find areas of common ground, negotiate fairly, and reach an agreement. A successful mediation has an outcome that is accepted and owned by the parties themselves.

THE MEDIATOR'S SKILLS

No license is required to be a mediator, but nonprofit organizations and universities offer certificates and degrees for mediation training. The National Conflict Resolution Center (NCRC) headquartered in San Diego, California, provides a training program for paralegals, attorneys, mental health professionals, managers, educators, law enforcement professionals, and others who want to complete the certification or credentialing process.

Training programs note that a successful mediator:

- is a good listener,
- has the discipline to resist taking sides,
- can comprehend facts and repeat them accurately,
- is diligent in keeping the parties engaged at all times, and
- possesses the writing skills needed to draft the final agreement.

Additionally, mediators must exercise political skill and use persuasion to get people to soften hard-line positions. Although many mediators are highly trained and experienced, many are not full-time mediators. They work in a variety of professions.

WHEN AND HOW TO ENGAGE A MEDIATOR

When parties have difficulties resolving a dispute:

- It may help to give the other party information about mediation. Provide a link to a mediator's Web site for information about the process.
- Consider asking the other party to suggest a mediator to help resolve the dispute.
- Some mediators will call the other side, explain mediation to them, and encourage them to mediate the dispute.
- You can ask the other side to mediate your dispute *before* or *after* a case is filed.

Preparing for mediation is a lot like preparing to go to a court hearing. Identify and organize the facts relevant to the dispute and make sure you know the facts that support the other side too. If the parties are willing, and the mediator provides good facilitation skills, the benefits of the process and outcome can far outweigh the cost and stress of litigation.

". . . mediation basics are universally applied."

Depending on the parties' circumstances and preferences, the arbitrator's decision may or may not be legally binding on the parties. In nonbinding arbitration, the parties submit their dispute to a third party but remain free to reject the third party's decision. Nonbinding arbitration is more similar to mediation than to binding arbitration. As will be discussed later in this chapter, arbitration that is mandated by the courts usually is not binding on the parties. If, after mandatory arbitration, the parties are not satisfied with the results of arbitration, they may ignore the arbitrator's decision and have the dispute litigated in court. Even if the arbitrator's decision is binding, a party can sometimes appeal the decision to a court for judicial review—as will be discussed next.

Arbitration Clauses and Statutes

Commercial matters are often submitted to arbitration both for speed and because the parties may wish to preserve their relationship. When a dispute arises, parties can agree to settle their differences through arbitration rather than through the court system.

CONTRACTUAL OBLIGATION.   Frequently disputes are arbitrated because of an arbitration clause in a contract entered into before the dispute arose. An **arbitration clause** provides that any disputes arising under the contract will be resolved by

arbitration clause
A clause in a contract providing that, in case of a dispute, the parties will determine their rights through arbitration rather than the judicial system.

arbitration, and generally explains how the arbitration will be handled. For example, an arbitration clause in a contract for the sale of goods might provide that "any controversy or claim arising under this contract will be referred to arbitration before the American Arbitration Association."[7] Most international business contracts require arbitration, often in an international business center such as London or Stockholm.

STATUTORY BACKING.   Most states have statutes (often based on the Uniform Arbitration Act) under which arbitration clauses will be enforced, and some state statutes compel arbitration of certain disputes, such as those involving public employees. At the federal level, the Federal Arbitration Act (FAA) enforces arbitration clauses in contracts involving interstate commerce. Because of the wide scope of the commerce clause in the Constitution (see Appendix I), even business activities that have only minimal effects on commerce between two or more states are regarded as interstate commerce. Thus, arbitration agreements involving transactions only slightly connected to interstate commerce may fall under the FAA.

The FAA does not establish a set arbitration procedure. The parties themselves must agree on the manner of resolving their disputes. The FAA provides only that if the parties have agreed to arbitrate disputes arising in relation to their contract, through an arbitration clause, the arbitration clause will be enforced by the courts. In other words, arbitration must take place before a party can attempt to take a dispute to the courts.

The Arbitration Process

submission agreement
A written agreement to submit a legal dispute to an arbitrator or arbitrating panel for resolution.

The first step in the arbitration process is the **submission agreement**, in which the parties agree to submit their dispute for arbitration. If an arbitration clause was included in a contract, the clause serves this function. Most states require that an agreement to submit a dispute to arbitration must be in writing. The submission agreement typically identifies the parties, the nature of the dispute, the monetary amounts in the dispute, the place of arbitration, and the powers that the arbitrator will exercise. Frequently, the agreement includes a signed statement that the parties intend to be bound by the arbitrator's decision.

THE HEARING.   The next step in the process is the *hearing*. Normally, the parties agree prior to arbitration—in an arbitration clause or in a submission-to-arbitrate agreement—on what procedural rules will govern the proceedings. This includes the method to be used to select an arbitrator or a panel of arbitrators. In a typical hearing, the parties begin as they would at a trial by presenting opening arguments and stating what remedies should or should not be granted.

After the opening statements, evidence is presented. Witnesses may be called and examined by both sides. Once all evidence has been presented, the parties give their closing arguments. Although arbitration is in some ways similar to a trial, the rules (such as those regarding what kinds of evidence may be introduced) are usually much less restrictive than those involved in formal litigation.

award
In the context of ADR, the decision rendered by an arbitrator.

THE AWARD.   After each side has had an opportunity to present its case, the arbitrator reaches a decision. The decision of the arbitrator is called an **award**, even if no monetary award is conferred as a result of the proceedings. The award is usually announced within thirty days of the close of the hearing.

A paralegal may become involved in preparations for arbitration, just as he or she would in preparing for a trial. The paralegal will assist in obtaining and organizing evidence relating to the dispute, may interview witnesses and prepare them for the hearing, and generally will help with other tasks commonly undertaken prior to a trial (see Chapter 10).

The Role of the Courts in Prearbitration

The role of the courts in arbitration is limited. One important role is at the prearbitration stage. When a dispute arises as to whether the parties have agreed in an arbitration clause to submit a particular matter to arbitration, one party may file suit to force arbitration. The court before which the suit is brought will not decide the underlying substantive controversy but must decide whether the dispute is *arbitrable*—that is, whether the matter is one capable of being resolved through arbitration and whether the parties have actually agreed to the arbitration. ◆ **EXAMPLE 6.16—** Suppose that a dispute involves a claim of employment discrimination on the basis of age. If the issue of arbitrability reaches a court, the court will have to decide whether the Age Discrimination in Employment Act (which protects persons forty years of age and older against employment discrimination on the basis of age) permits such claims brought under this act to be arbitrated. ◆

COMPEL ARBITRATION. If the court finds that the subject matter in controversy is covered by the agreement to arbitrate, then a party is likely to be compelled to arbitrate the dispute. Even when a claim involves a violation of a statute passed to protect a certain class of people, such as a statute prohibiting age discrimination against employees in the workplace, a court may determine that the parties must nonetheless abide by their agreement to arbitrate the dispute. ◆ **EXAMPLE 6.17—** In the employment discrimination Example 6.16, suppose the "agreement to arbitrate" is a paragraph in small print within a 300-page employee handbook. The court will have to decide whether there was actually an agreement between the parties to arbitrate their disputes. Generally courts expect arbitration agreements to be clearly stated. ◆ Usually, a court will allow the claim to be arbitrated if the court, in interpreting the statute, can find no legislative intent to the contrary and the parties clearly agreed to arbitration.

FAIRNESS ISSUE. The courts will not compel arbitration if the arbitration rules and procedures are inherently unfair to one of the parties. ◆ **EXAMPLE 6.18—** Suppose that an employer's arbitration agreement with an employee states that the employer establishes the rules for the arbitration. In this situation, the court is likely to conclude that the rules are unfair and thus refuse to enforce the arbitration agreement. ◆

The Postarbitration Role of the Courts

Courts may play an important role at the postarbitration stage. After arbitration produces an award, one of the parties may appeal the award or may seek a court order compelling the other party to comply with the award. In determining whether an award should be enforced, a court conducts a review that is much more restricted in scope than an appellate court's review of a trial court decision. The general view is that because the parties were free to frame the issues and set the powers of the arbitrator at the outset, they cannot complain about the result. An arbitration award may be set aside, however, if the award resulted from the arbitrator's misconduct or "bad faith," or if the arbitrator exceeded his or her powers in arbitrating the dispute. Setting aside an award does not happen very often.

Other ADR Forms

The three forms of ADR just discussed have been the most commonly used forms to date. In recent years, a variety of new types of ADR have emerged. Some of them combine elements of mediation and arbitration. For example, in **binding mediation**, a neutral mediator tries to facilitate agreement between the parties, but if no agreement is reached, the mediator issues a legally binding decision on the matter. In one version of this approach, known as mediation arbitration (med-arb), an arbitrator first attempts to help the parties reach an agreement, just as a mediator would. If no agreement is reached, then formal arbitration is undertaken, and the arbitrator issues a legally binding decision.

Another ADR form is referred to as "assisted negotiation" because it involves a third party in what is essentially a negotiation process. For example, in **early neutral case evaluation**, the parties select a neutral third party (generally an expert in the subject matter of the dispute) to evaluate their respective positions. The parties explain their positions to the case evaluator however they wish. The case evaluator then assesses the strengths and weaknesses of the parties' positions, and this evaluation forms the basis for negotiating a settlement.

social MEDIA TODAY

Find the groups on Facebook and LinkedIn in which people are discussing your areas of practice and participate in the discussions.

binding mediation
A form of ADR in which a mediator attempts to facilitate agreement between the parties but then issues a legally binding decision if no agreement is reached.

early neutral case evaluation
A form of ADR in which a neutral third party evaluates the strengths and weaknesses of the disputing parties' positions; the evaluator's opinion forms the basis for negotiating a settlement.

mini-trial
A private proceeding that assists disputing parties in determining whether to take their case to court. Each party's attorney briefly argues the party's case before the other party and (usually) a neutral third party, who acts as an adviser. If the parties fail to reach an agreement, the adviser issues an opinion as to how a court would likely decide the issue.

The mini-trial is a form of assisted negotiation that is often used by business parties. In a **mini-trial**, each party's attorney briefly argues the party's case before representatives of each firm who have the authority to settle the dispute. Typically, a neutral third party (usually an expert in the area being disputed) acts as an adviser. If the parties fail to reach an agreement, the adviser renders an opinion as to how a court would likely decide the issue. The proceeding assists the parties in determining whether they should negotiate a settlement of the dispute or take it to court. It is a useful way for the parties to assess the strength of each side's case.

Collaborative Law

Still another method of resolving disputes is the collaborative law approach, which is increasingly being used during marital separation procedures. In *collaborative law,* both parties, their attorneys, and any professionals working with the parties agree to meet to resolve all of their issues without litigation. Sometimes a single attorney handles the matter for both sides. The lawyers act as negotiators and communication moderators while advising their clients about their legal rights, entitlements, and obligations. Both parties promise to take a reasoned stand on every issue, to keep discovery cooperative and informal, and to work together to craft an agreement. Any abusive communications are identified, discussed, and eliminated.

Because the attorneys agree not to take part in any litigation that may occur if an agreement is not reached, the attorneys focus only on settlement rather than on preparing documents or presentations for court. If either party seeks court intervention, all attorneys must withdraw from representation. The Uniform Collaborative Law Act, adopted in 2009 by the Uniform Law Commission, has been adopted in several states.

Court-Referred ADR

Today, most states require or encourage parties to undergo mediation or arbitration prior to trial. Generally, when a trial court refers a case for arbitration, the arbitrator's decision is not binding on the parties. If the parties do not agree with the arbitrator's decision, they can go forward with the lawsuit.

The types of court-related ADR programs in use vary widely. In some states, such as Missouri, ADR is completely voluntary. In other states, such as Minnesota, parties are required to undertake ADR before a court will hear their cases. Some states offer a menu of options. Other states, including Florida (which has a statewide, comprehensive mediation program), offer only one alternative.

summary jury trial (SJT)
A settlement method in which a trial is held but the jury's verdict is not binding. The verdict acts as a guide to both sides in reaching an agreement during mandatory negotiations that follow the trial. If a settlement is not reached, both sides have the right to a full trial later.

Courts experiment with a variety of ADR alternatives to speed up justice and reduce its cost. Some federal and state courts now hold **summary jury trials (SJTs)**, in which the parties present their arguments and supporting evidence (other than witness testimony—witnesses are not called in an SJT). The jury renders a verdict, but unlike the verdict in an actual trial, the jury's verdict is not binding. The verdict acts as a guide to both sides in reaching an agreement during mandatory negotiations that immediately follow the SJT. If no settlement is reached, both sides have the right to a full trial later.

Other alternatives being employed by the courts include summary procedures for commercial litigation and the appointment of special masters to assist judges in deciding complex issues.

Providers of ADR Services

American Arbitration Association (AAA)
The major organization offering arbitration services in the United States.

ADR services are provided by both government agencies and private organizations. A major provider of ADR services is the **American Arbitration Association (AAA)**. Most of the nation's largest law firms are members of this nonprofit association. Hundreds of thousands of disputes are submitted to the AAA for resolution each year in the United States and internationally. Cases brought to the AAA are heard by an expert or a panel of experts in the area relating to the dispute and are usually settled quickly. Generally, about half of the panel members are lawyers. To cover its costs, the AAA charges a fee, paid by the party filing the claim. In addition, each party to the dispute pays a specified amount for each hearing day. An additional fee is charged for cases involving personal injuries or property loss.

Many for-profit firms around the country also provide ADR services. Some firms hire retired judges to conduct arbitration hearings or assist parties in settling their disputes. Private ADR firms normally allow the parties to decide on the date of the hearing, the presiding judge, whether the judge's decision will be legally binding, and the site of the hearing—which may be a conference room, a law school office, or a leased courtroom. The judges follow procedures similar to those of the federal courts and use similar rules. Usually, each party to the dispute pays a filing fee and a designated fee for a hearing session or conference.

As mentioned, courts also have ADR programs in which disputes are resolved by court-appointed attorneys or paralegals who are qualified to act as arbitrators or mediators in certain types of disputes. Paralegals have found that becoming a mediator or an arbitrator is an especially rewarding career option. See the *Ethics Watch* feature below regarding the paralegal's role in ensuring that the arbitration process is proper.

ON THE web

To obtain information on the services offered by the American Arbitration Association (AAA), as well as forms used to submit a case for arbitration, go to the AAA's Web site at **www.adr.org**.

ETHICS WATCH

POTENTIAL ARBITRATION PROBLEMS

When individuals and business firms prefer to arbitrate disputes rather than take them to court, they include arbitration clauses in their contracts. These clauses specify who or what organization will arbitrate the dispute and where the arbitration will take place. To safeguard a client's interests when drafting and reviewing arbitration clauses in contracts, the careful paralegal will be alert to the possibility that those who arbitrate the dispute might not be truly neutral or that the designated place of arbitration may pose a great inconvenience and expense for the client. The paralegal should call any such problems to his or her supervising attorney's attention. The attorney can then discuss the problem with the client and help the client negotiate a more favorable arbitration clause.

This is necessary to be consistent with the NFPA *Model Code of Ethics and Professional Responsibility,* Section 1.6(a): "A paralegal shall act within the bounds of the law, solely for the benefit of the client." It is also consistent with the ABA *Model Guidelines for the Utilization of Paralegal Services.* The *Guidelines* state that lawyers may assign legal work to paralegals, but the lawyers remain responsible for the work product. Hence, paralegals should be sure their work is reviewed by supervising attorneys. Paralegals may not perform work for attorneys that may only be performed by licensed attorneys by the rules of a court, the bar association, a statute, or other controlling authority.

Online Dispute Resolution

A number of companies and organizations offer **online dispute resolution (ODR)** conducted on the Internet. Disputes resolved in online forums often involve disagreements over the right to use a certain Web site address or disputes involving sales over the Internet. Those who do business in cyberspace (and the attorneys who represent them) should be aware of this ADR option.

Most online forums do not automatically apply the law of a specific jurisdiction but use general, universal legal principles. As with traditional methods of dispute resolution, a party normally may appeal to a court at any time. Negotiation, mediation, and arbitration services are all available to disputants over the Internet.

Online Negotiation

Several firms offer online forums for negotiating monetary settlements. Typically, one party files a complaint, and the other party is notified by e-mail. Password-protected access to the online forum site is made available. Fees are generally low (often 2 to 4 percent, or less, of the disputed amount). The parties can drop the negotiations at any time. For example, the Web-based firm Smartsettle offers a unique blind-bidding system to help resolve disputes.

Online Arbitration

A number of organizations, including the American Arbitration Association, offer online arbitration services. For instance, Resolution Forum, Inc. (RFI), a nonprofit organization, offers arbitration services through its conferencing system. Using software and an RFI password, the parties to a dispute access an online conference room. When multiple parties are involved, private communications and breakout sessions are possible through private messaging facilities. RFI also offers mediation services.

KEY TERMS AND CONCEPTS

Chapter Summary

The Court System and Alternative Dispute Resolution

BASIC JUDICIAL REQUIREMENTS

1. *Standing to sue*—A legally protected and real interest in a matter sufficient to justify seeking relief through the court system. The controversy at issue must also be a justiciable controversy—one that is real and substantial, not hypothetical or academic.

2. *Types of jurisdiction*—Before a court can hear a case, it must have jurisdiction over the person against whom the suit is brought (*in personam* jurisdiction) or the property involved in the suit (*in rem* jurisdiction), as well as jurisdiction over the subject matter.

   a. **JURISDICTION OVER PERSONS AND PROPERTY**—Courts have jurisdiction over persons, including businesses, who reside in the geographic area of the court. Businesses that have a certain level of minimum contacts in a state may be subject to court jurisdiction under a long arm statute. Similarly, courts have jurisdiction over property located within the geographic boundaries of the court.

   b. **JURISDICTION OVER SUBJECT MATTER**—Limited jurisdiction exists when a court is limited to a specific subject matter, such as probate or divorce. General jurisdiction exists when a court can hear any kind of case. State and federal statutes often define the power of courts to hear matters relating to statutory law.

   c. **ORIGINAL AND APPELLATE JURISDICTION**—Courts that have authority to hear a case for the first time (trial courts) have original jurisdiction. Courts of appeals, or reviewing courts, have appellate jurisdiction; generally, these courts do not have original jurisdiction.

3. *Jurisdiction of federal courts*—Is limited to powers of the national government that arise from the Constitution.

   a. **FEDERAL QUESTIONS**—Jurisdiction exists in federal court when a federal question is involved (when the plaintiff's cause of action is based, at least in part, on the U.S. Constitution, a treaty, or a federal law).

   b. **DIVERSITY JURISDICTION**—May arise for a federal court when a case involves diversity of citizenship (as in disputes between citizens of different states, between a foreign country and citizens of a state or states, or between citizens of a state and citizens of a foreign country) and the amount in controversy exceeds $75,000.

   c. **EXCLUSIVE VERSUS CONCURRENT JURISDICTION**—Concurrent jurisdiction exists when two different courts have authority to hear the same case. Exclusive jurisdiction exists when only state courts or only federal courts have authority to hear a case.

4. *Jurisdiction in cyberspace*—Because the Internet does not have physical boundaries, traditional jurisdictional concepts have been difficult to apply. The courts are developing standards to use in determining when jurisdiction over a Web owner or operator in another state is proper.

5. *Venue*—Venue has to do with the most appropriate location for a trial, which is usually the geographic area where the event leading to the dispute took place or where the parties reside.

6. *Judicial procedures*—Rules of procedure prescribe the way in which disputes are handled in the courts. The Federal Rules of Civil Procedure govern all civil litigation in federal courts. Each state has its own procedural rules (often similar to the federal rules), and each court within a state has specific court rules that must be followed.

STATE COURT SYSTEMS

1. *Trial courts*—Courts of original jurisdiction, in which legal actions are initiated. State trial courts have either general jurisdiction or limited jurisdiction.

2. *Appellate or reviewing courts*—After a trial there is a right of appeal in the federal and state court systems. The focus on appeal is for reversible errors in law made at trial.

   a. **INTERMEDIATE APPELLATE COURTS**—Many states have intermediate appellate courts that review the proceedings of the trial courts; generally, these courts do not have original jurisdiction. Appellate courts ordinarily examine questions of law and procedure while deferring to the trial court's findings of fact.

   b. **HIGHEST STATE COURTS**—Each state has a supreme court, although it may be called by some other name. Decisions of the state's highest court are final on all questions of state law. If a federal question is at issue, the case may be appealed to the United States Supreme Court.

THE FEDERAL COURT SYSTEM

1. *U.S. district courts*—The federal district court is the equivalent of the state trial court. The district court exercises general jurisdiction over claims arising under federal law or based on diversity of citizenship. Federal courts of limited jurisdiction include the U.S. Tax Court, the U.S. Bankruptcy Court, and the U.S. Court of Federal Claims.

2. *U.S. courts of appeals*—There are thirteen intermediate courts of appeals (or circuit courts of appeals) in the federal court system. Twelve of the courts hear appeals from the district courts within their circuits. The thirteenth court has national appellate jurisdiction over certain cases, such as cases involving patent law and cases in which the U.S. government is a defendant.

3. *United States Supreme Court*—The United States Supreme Court is the highest court in the land and the final arbiter of the Constitution and federal law. There is no absolute right of appeal to the Supreme Court, and the Court hears only a fraction of the cases that are filed with it each year.

ALTERNATIVE DISPUTE RESOLUTION

The costs and time-consuming character of litigation, as well as the public nature of court proceedings, have caused many to turn to various forms of alternative dispute resolution (ADR) for settling disagreements. The methods of ADR include the following:

1. *Negotiation*—The simplest form of ADR, in which the parties come together, with or without attorneys to represent them, and try to reach a settlement without the involvement of a third party.

2. *Mediation*—A form of ADR in which the parties reach an agreement with the help of a neutral third party, called a mediator, who proposes solutions and emphasizes areas of agreement.

3. *Arbitration*—The most formal method of ADR, in which the parties submit their dispute to a neutral third party, the arbitrator (or panel of arbitrators), who issues a decision. The decision may or may not be legally binding, depending on the circumstances.

   a. **ARBITRATION CLAUSES AND STATUTES**—Arbitration clauses that are voluntarily agreed on in contracts require the parties to resolve their disputes in arbitration (rather than in court). Federal and state laws encourage the courts to uphold arbitration agreements.

   b. **THE ARBITRATION PROCESS**—First a submission agreement is submitted to the arbiter outlining the dispute. A hearing is held before a single arbiter or a panel who listen to facts and arguments presented by the two sides. After proceedings less formal than in a court, an award is issued to declare the results of the matter.

   c. **ROLE OF THE COURTS IN PREARBITRATION**—A court may be asked to determine if a matter is, in fact, subject to arbitration rather than a court proceeding.

   a. **HOW CASES REACH THE SUPREME COURT**—The Supreme Court has original jurisdiction in a few cases, but it functions primarily as an appellate court. It accepts a tiny fraction of the appeals made to it when at least four justices agree to issue a *writ of* certiorari requiring the lower court to send it the record of the case for review.

   b. **TYPES OF CASES REVIEWED**—As a rule, only petitions that raise the possibility of important constitutional questions are granted. The Court may also review matters where the lower courts are split in their interpretation of a legal issue.

   d. **POSTARBITRATION ROLE OF THE COURTS**—Awards, even when binding, may be appealed to the courts for review. The court's review is much more restricted than an appellate court's review of a trial court record.

4. *Other ADR forms*—Include binding mediation, mediation arbitration (med-arb), early neutral case evaluation, mini-trials, and summary jury trials; generally, these are forms of "assisted negotiation."

5. *Collaborative law*—A form of ADR in which both parties, their attorneys, and any professionals working with the parties meet to resolve their issues without litigation. The lawyers act as negotiators and communication moderators while advising their clients about their legal rights, entitlements, and obligations. If either party seeks court intervention, both attorneys must withdraw from representation.

6. *Court-referred ADR*—In some jurisdictions, courts require parties to undergo some form of ADR so as to help resolve disputes prior to trial. One form for more complicated matters is the summary jury trial, where a jury hears a shortened form of a full trial and issues a nonbinding verdict.

7. *Providers of ADR services*—The leading nonprofit provider of ADR services is the American Arbitration Association. Many for-profit firms also provide ADR services domestically and internationally.

8. *Online dispute resolution*—A number of organizations and firms offer negotiation and arbitration services through online forums. These forums have been a practical alternative for the resolution of disputes over the right to use a certain Web site address or the quality of goods purchased over the Internet.

QUESTIONS FOR REVIEW

1. Define *jurisdiction*. Define *venue*. What is the difference between personal jurisdiction and subject-matter jurisdiction? What is a long arm statute?

2. Over what types of cases can federal courts exercise jurisdiction?

3. How do original and appellate jurisdictions differ? The relationship between state and federal jurisdiction is an example of what type of jurisdiction?

4. How do the functions of a trial court differ from the functions of an appellate court?

5. Describe the procedure for cases to reach the United States Supreme Court.

6. Describe the various methods of alternative dispute resolution.

ETHICAL QUESTIONS

1. Aaron is a paralegal with a law firm that specializes in intellectual property law. Aaron's supervising attorney asks him to e-mail a letter to the client that the attorney has prepared. The letter and its attachments discuss a patent application and contain drawings and plans for a heated steering wheel that the client plans to sell to automobile manufacturers. Aaron does so without encrypting the letter or the attachments, which contain confidential information. A temporary employee working at the client's office accesses the unencrypted e-mail and steals the information. Have any ethical rules been violated by Aaron? By his supervising attorney? If so, which rules? What could Aaron and his supervising attorney have done differently to better protect the client's interests?

2. Suzanne works as a paralegal for a general practice firm. Her supervising attorney, Amy, works occasionally as a mediator for family law cases in the local courts. Today, Amy has mediated a divorce case involving the property settlement of a wealthy businessperson, who also happens to be a defendant in another lawsuit in which Amy represents the plaintiff. As a result of today's mediation, Amy has learned some confidential financial information about this man that could benefit her significantly in the other case. Amy has come to Suzanne and has asked her to use this information to the disadvantage of the wealthy businessman in the other lawsuit. How should Suzanne handle this situation?

PRACTICE QUESTIONS AND ASSIGNMENTS

1. Identify each of the following courts. If not indicated, specify whether it is a state or federal court.

   a. This state court has general jurisdiction over civil cases exceeding $20,000 and takes testimony from witnesses and receives evidence.

   b. This court has appellate jurisdiction and is part of a court system that is divided into geographic units called *circuits*.

   c. This state court only hears issues related to wills and estates. It has original jurisdiction.

   d. This court can exercise federal question and diversity-of-citizenship jurisdiction, and receives testimony and other evidence.

   e. The decisions of this court are usually final. It is the highest appellate court in its limited geographic area.

   f. This federal court has nine justices. It has original jurisdiction over a few types of cases but functions primarily as an appellate court. There is no automatic right to appeal cases to this court.

2. Look at Exhibit 6.4 on page 161. How many federal circuits are there? Which states are included in the 12th Circuit? In which federal circuit is your state located? How many federal judicial districts are located in your state? In which federal district is your community located?

3. Marcella, who is from Toledo, Ohio, drives to Troy, Michigan, and shops at a popular mall. When leaving the parking lot, Marcella causes a car accident when she runs a stop sign. On what basis could a Michigan court obtain jurisdiction over Marcella? If the damages in the lawsuit exceed $75,000, could a federal court in Michigan have jurisdiction over this case? On what jurisdictional basis? What type of jurisdiction would exist if both the courts or the state of Michigan and the federal court have jurisdiction over this case?

4. A plaintiff and defendant are involved in an auto accident. Both are residents of the county and state in which the accident takes place. The plaintiff files a negligence lawsuit in the county circuit court

where the trial will occur. What types of jurisdiction does the court have? (The types to be considered include *in personam* jurisdiction, *in rem* jurisdiction, subject-matter jurisdiction, limited jurisdiction, general jurisdiction, original jurisdiction, appellate jurisdiction, concurrent jurisdiction, and exclusive jurisdiction.)

5. Using the materials presented in the chapter, identify the following methods of alternative dispute resolution:

   a. The parties to a divorce meet with a neutral third party who emphasizes points of agreement and proposes solutions to resolve their dispute. After several hours, the parties come to a solution.

   b. The parties to a contract dispute submit it to a neutral third party for a legally binding resolution. The neutral third party is not a court.

   c. The plaintiff and defense attorneys in a personal-injury case propose settlement figures to one another and their clients in an effort to resolve the lawsuit voluntarily.

   d. The attorneys from the personal-injury example above are able to reach an acceptable settlement figure of $100,000. They draft an agreement whereby the plaintiff gives up her right to sue in exchange for a payment of $100,000 by the defendant.

   e. A commercial dispute involving $95,000 in damages is filed in a federal court. The judge requires the parties' attorneys to present their arguments and supporting evidence, excluding witnesses, to the jury. The jury then renders a nonbinding verdict. Once the nonbinding verdict is rendered, the parties reach a settlement.

QUESTIONS FOR CRITICAL ANALYSIS

1. The federal courts have jurisdiction primarily over civil cases involving diversity of citizenship and questions of federal law. State courts have jurisdiction over matters such as wills, divorces, and property concerns. What is the constitutional basis of this division? What would happen if federal courts decided divorce cases, for example? What would happen if state courts decided cases between a citizen of the state and a foreign citizen?

2. Since 2005, the United States Supreme Court has granted fewer than 100 petitions for *certiorari* per year. As a result, in most cases there is no right to appeal to the United States Supreme Court. Is it fair that citizens should have to petition for *certiorari* to be heard by the Supreme Court? What does the requirement of a grant of *certiorari*, coupled with the limited number of cases that the Supreme Court hears, tell you about the role and purpose of the Supreme Court?

PROJECTS

1. Paralegals frequently assist in ADR proceedings and may serve as mediators. To learn more about opportunities to work as a mediator and the requirements that must be met in order to do so, run an Internet search for the training and other qualifications needed to serve as a mediator in your state. Run another search for opportunities to serve as a nonlawyer mediator in your state. Write a one-page paper summarizing your findings on opportunities and qualifications for serving as a nonlawyer mediator in your state.

2. Go to the federal court locator Web site at: **www.uscourts.gov/court_locator/CourtLocatorSearch.aspx**. Select advanced search and locate the address for the U.S. District Court and Court of Appeals for your geographic location. Does the court have a Web site? If so, go to it and see if electronic filing is available. Does the court give tours? If so, ask your instructor if you can take a tour for extra credit.

GROUP PROJECT

This project asks students to compare the current federal court system to the early federal court system. Article III of the Constitution places the judicial power of the federal government in "one supreme Court, and in such inferior Courts" as the Congress might decide to establish. In 1789 Congress established "inferior courts."

Student one will create a PowerPoint diagram of the current federal court system, complete with the jurisdiction of each court. This information can be found on the Federal Judicial Center's Web site at: **www.uscourts.gov/EducationalResources/FederalCourtBasics/CourtStructure/InsideTheFederalCourts.aspx**.

Student two will create a PowerPoint diagram, including jurisdiction, of the United States Supreme Court beginning in 1789 from the history of the federal judiciary found at **www.fjc.gov/history/home.nsf/page/index.html**.

Student three will create a PowerPoint diagram, including jurisdiction, of the district and circuit courts from the same Web site.

Student four will ascertain from the same Web site when the U.S. Court of Appeals was established and will combine the historic court diagrams into one PowerPoint slide with a separate slide for the current federal court system. Student four will present PowerPoint slides of the group's findings to the class.

USING INTERNET RESOURCES

1. The American Arbitration Association (AAA) is the largest provider of alternative dispute resolution services in the country. To learn more about ADR procedures, go to **www.adr.org**, the home page for the American Arbitration Association. Browse through the site's offerings and find the answers to the following questions:

    a. What types of services does the AAA offer? Does the AAA engage in arbitration outside the United States?

    b. Are you required to use a regional office to file a case? If so, locate the one closest to you.

    c. Are filing fees charged for filing a case with the AAA? What things should you consider before filing a claim for arbitration?

    d. Are arbitration forms available to download from this site? Is there any cost for downloading these forms? Do states provide state-specific forms on this site? If so, what types of forms are provided?

2. Go to the Court Statistics Project at **www.courtstatistics.org** and locate information on your state court system. From that site or another you find, answer these questions: (1) How many levels of trial courts are there in your state? Which courts are on each level? (2) Where would a civil lawsuit be filed? Does the selection of the court in which to file your case depend on the amount you are seeking in damages? (3) Where would a divorce case be filed? A probate case? (4) How many appellate courts are there in your state? Do you have a right to appeal to all of them, or do you have to request an appeal?

END NOTES

1. Pronounced jus-*tish*-a-bul.

2. A state's highest court is often referred to as the state supreme court, but there are exceptions. For example, in New York, what is called the supreme court is a trial court.

3. Under the Class Action Fairness Act (CAFA) of 2005, it is likely that most class-action lawsuits will not qualify for state court jurisdiction.

4. Pronounced *ven*-yoo.

5. The name in Ohio is Court of Common Pleas; the name in New York is Supreme Court; the name in Florida, Illinois, and Missouri is Circuit Court.

6. Pronounced sur-shee-uh-*rah*-ree.

7. As discussed later in the chapter, the American Arbitration Association is a leading provider of arbitration services in the United States.

CourseMate The available CourseMate for this text has an interactive eBook and interactive learning tools, including flash cards, quizzes, and more. To learn more about this resource and access free demo CourseMate resources, go to **www.cengagebrain.com**, and search for this book. To access CourseMate materials that you have purchased, go to **login.cengagebrain.com**.

Legal Research and Analysis

Chapter Outline

After completing this chapter, you will know:

- How primary and secondary sources of law differ and how to use each of these types of sources in the research process.

- How court decisions are published and how to read case citations.

- How to analyze case law and summarize, or brief, cases.

- How federal statutes and regulations are published, and the major sources of statutory and administrative law.

- How to interpret statutory law and understand what kinds of resources are available for researching the legislative history of a statute.

Introduction

For many paralegals, legal research is a central and fascinating part of their jobs. They find it interesting to read the actual words of a court's opinion on a legal question or the text of a statute. Additionally, they acquire firsthand knowledge of the law and how it applies to real people and events. The ability to conduct research thoroughly yet efficiently enhances a paralegal's value to the legal team.

As a paralegal, you may be asked to perform a variety of research tasks. Some tasks will be simple, such as locating and printing out a court case. Other tasks may take days or weeks to complete. In all but the simplest tasks, legal research overlaps with legal analysis. To find relevant case law, for example, you need to be able to analyze the cases you find to ensure that they are actually relevant.

Many paralegals conduct research without entering a law library. Computerized subscription services such as Westlaw and Lexis are the leading providers of research services for legal professionals needing access to legal documents. Many free sources also can be located via Google and other search engines. (See Chapter 8 for a discussion of online legal research.) Further, as the *Practice Focus* feature below discusses, there are rapid changes taking place in how clients deal with potential legal representation. Regardless of how or where you conduct legal research, it is essential to know what sources to consult for different types of information.

Researching Case Law— The Preliminary Steps

To illustrate how to research case law, we use a hypothetical case. One of your firm's clients, Trent Hoffman, is suing Better Homes Store for negligence. During the initial client interview, Hoffman explained to your supervising attorney and you that

social MEDIA TODAY

Don't neglect traditional networking. Social networking is important, but lunches with coworkers, catching up with an acquaintance from a former job, or doing a former classmate a favor are also important.

PRACTICE focus

NEW INFORMATION STRATEGIES

Some new technology threatens law firms' traditional business models. For example, consider "crowd-sourcing," the technique used by some Web-based organizations to distribute a problem to large numbers of people to solve. Web sites such as *LawPivot,* a legal Q&A site, allow potential clients to receive low-cost, crowd-sourced legal answers from a group of participating lawyers. The expansion of this kind of enterprise may undermine traditional fee structures.

LawPivot users enter a confidential legal question and assign it to a category such as "tax" or "immigration." The Web site then suggests member lawyers to whom the user can send the question. Most users receive answers to their question from several lawyers. *LawPivot* suggests that the advantages of this method include low cost, fast answers, and opportunities to meet "qualified relevant

lawyers" whom the user can then hire. Lawyers participate to build their reputations and market themselves.

Among the investors in *LawPivot* is Google's investment arm, which suggests that the approach is believed to have significant promise. Other Web sites are aimed at the consumer market as well. *Rocket Lawyer* and *LegalZoom* both offer access to forms that individuals can complete themselves and then have reviewed by a lawyer.

As firms such as *Rocket Lawyer* and *LawPivot* grow, so too will opportunities for paralegals. The key to these new approaches to technology and the law is to reduce cost for the consumers of legal services. As other firms begin to offer such services, expect opportunities to grow for paralegals to be part of bringing the information revolution to the practice of law.

he had gone to the store to buy a large mirror. As he was leaving the store through a side entrance, carrying the mirror, he ran into a large pole just outside the door. He did not see the pole because the mirror blocked his view. When he hit the pole, the mirror broke, and a piece of glass went into his left eye, causing permanent loss of eyesight. Hoffman claims that the store was negligent in placing a pole so close to the door and wants to sue the store for millions of dollars in damages.

You have already done a preliminary investigation and have obtained evidence supporting Hoffman's account of the facts. Your supervising attorney now asks you to research case law to find other cases with similar fact patterns and see what the courts decided in those cases.

Before you begin, you need to define the issue to be researched and determine your research goals. We look now at these two preliminary steps in researching case law.

Defining the Issue

In defining the legal issue that you need to research, your first task is to examine the facts of Hoffman's case to determine the nature of the legal issue involved. (An example is provided in *Developing Paralegal Skills* below.) Based on his description of the circumstances (verified through your preliminary investigation) and on his allegation that Better Homes Store should not have placed a pole just outside one of the store's entrances, you know that the legal issue relates to the tort of negligence. As a starting point, you should therefore review what you know about negligence theory.

Background Research

If you are unfamiliar with negligence law or any other legal subject, you can start by doing background research to familiarize yourself with the topic, as described in the section on legal encyclopedias later in this chapter.

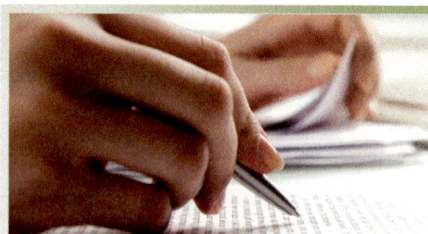

DEVELOPING
paralegal skills

DEFINING THE ISSUES TO BE RESEARCHED

Federal agents observed David Berriman in his parked car talking on his cell phone. Other cars were seen driving up to Berriman's car and stopping. The drivers received brown paper bags in exchange for money. The agents then questioned Berriman, and his car was searched. Cocaine was found in the car. He was arrested for transporting and distributing cocaine, and the police took his car and cell phone. His lawyer is arguing that the government agents did not have the authority to seize the car and cell phone and force him to forfeit this property.

Natalie Chen, a legal assistant with the U.S. attorney's office, has been assigned to research the federal statutes and cases on this issue. Natalie can begin her research project only if she first frames the issues critical to the case. She must thoroughly review the case to determine what specific issues need to be researched.

Using a checklist method, she breaks the facts of the case down into five categories and inserts the relevant facts from her assignment. Now Natalie is ready to begin her research.

CHECKLIST FOR DEFINING RESEARCH ISSUES

- **Parties:** Who are the people involved in the action or lawsuit?
- **Places and things:** Where did the events take place, and what items are involved in the action or lawsuit?
- **Basis of action or issue:** What is the legal claim or issue involved in the action or lawsuit?
- **Defenses:** What legal justification did the police have for seizing David's car and cellular phone? Will this justification still exist if David is found not guilty of the underlying charges, or will the police be required to return the forfeited property?
- **Relief sought:** What is the legal remedy or penalty sought in the case?

Although today most legal research is carried out using online resources, some paralegals still consult printed legal volumes when conducting legal research. How could you use printed resources to confirm some of your online research results?

The tort of negligence is defined as the failure to exercise reasonable care. (Chapter 14 will discuss negligence in detail.) To succeed in a negligence action, a plaintiff must establish four elements:

1. The defendant had a duty of care to the plaintiff.
2. The defendant breached that duty.
3. The plaintiff suffered a legally recognizable injury.
4. The injury was caused by the defendant's breach of the duty of care.

Focus on the Legal Issues

These elements help you determine the issue that needs to be researched. There is little doubt that the third requirement has been met—Hoffman's loss of sight is a legally recognizable injury for which he can be compensated—*if* he succeeds in proving the other three elements of negligence. Proving the fourth element, causation, depends largely on proving the first two elements. In your research, you will therefore focus on the first two elements. Specifically, you need to answer the following questions:

- Did Better Homes Store owe a duty of care to its customer, Hoffman? You might phrase this question in more general terms: Do business owners owe a duty of care to **business invitees**—customers and others invited onto their premises?

- If so, what is the extent of that duty, and how is it measured? In other words, are business owners always liable when customers are injured on their premises? Or must some condition be met before store owners will be liable? For example, must a customer's injury be a *foreseeable* consequence of a condition on the premises, such as the pole right outside the store's door, for the store owner to be liable for the injury?

business invitee
A person, such as a customer or client, who is invited onto business premises by the owner of those premises for business purposes.

- If the injury must be a foreseeable consequence of a condition, would a court find that Hoffman's injury in this case was a foreseeable consequence of the pole's placement just outside the store's door?

These are the issues you need to research. Notice that there is more than one issue. This is common in legal research—only rarely will you be researching a single legal issue.

Determining Your Research Goals

Once you have defined the issues to be researched, you will be in a better position to determine your research goals. Remember that you are working on behalf of a client, who is paying for your services (see the *In the Office* feature below). Your overall goal is to find legal support for Hoffman's claim, but you must also locate legal authority that could be a problem for his claim. To do so, you want to find cases on point and cases that are binding authority. Depending on what you find, you may also need to look for persuasive authorities.

Cases on Point

case on point
A case involving factual circumstances and issues that are similar to those in the case being researched.

One of your research goals is to find cases on point in which the court held for the plaintiff. A **case on point** is a previous case involving fact patterns and legal issues similar to those in the case you are researching. For Hoffman's negligence claim, a case on point would be one in which the plaintiff alleged that he was injured while on a store's premises because of a dangerous condition on those premises.

The ideal case on point would be one in which all four elements (the parties, the circumstances, the legal issues involved, and the remedies sought by the plaintiff) are as similar as possible to those in your case. Such a case is called a case on "all fours." Here, a **case on "all fours"** would be a case in which the plaintiff-customer did not expect a condition (such as an obstacle in her path) to exist and was prevented from seeing the condition by some action that a customer would reasonably undertake (such as carrying a large box out of a store). The parties and the circumstances of the case would thus be similar to those in Hoffman's case. In addition, the plaintiff would have sustained a permanent injury, as Hoffman did, and sought damages for negligence.

case on "all fours"
A case in which all four elements (the parties, the circumstances, the legal issues involved, and the remedies sought) are very similar to those in the case being researched.

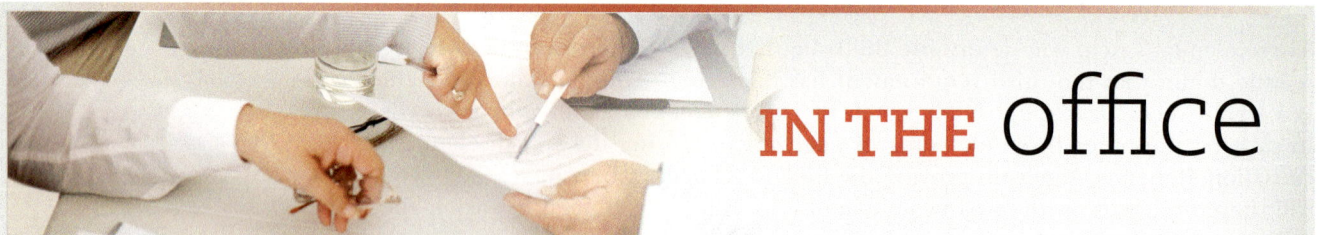

Binding Authorities

Another research goal is to find cases that are binding authorities. As discussed in Chapter 5, a *binding authority* is one that the court must follow in deciding an issue. A binding authority may be a statute, regulation, or constitution that governs

IN THE office

EFFICIENCY IN RESEARCH

Attorneys have a duty to charge their clients reasonable fees. As a paralegal, you help fulfill this duty by working efficiently so as to minimize the number of hours you spend working on the client's matter. Legal research can be extremely time consuming, as every paralegal knows. To reduce the time spent researching an issue, start your quest with a clear idea of your research task. After all, your time is expensive not only for the client (who pays for it), but also for your supervising attorney (who may need your assistance on other cases as well).

By knowing as precisely as possible what the goal of your research is, you can reach that goal more quickly and thus better serve the interests of both the client and your supervising attorney.

the issue, or it may be a previously decided court case that is controlling in your jurisdiction.

BE ON POINT.   For a case to serve as binding authority, it must be on point and must have been decided by a higher court in the same jurisdiction. A higher court can be either an intermediate court of appeals or a court of final appeal, such as a state supreme court or the United States Supreme Court. For example, on an issue of negligence, a state trial court would be bound by the decisions of the intermediate appellate court above it and the state supreme court. If a federal question were involved, the state courts would also be bound by the decisions of the United States Supreme Court.

SOURCE OF PRECEDENT.   A lower court is bound to follow the decisions set forth by a higher court in the same jurisdiction. An appellate court's decision in a case involving facts and issues similar to a case brought in a trial court in the same jurisdiction would thus be a binding authority. A higher court is not required to follow an opinion written by a lower court in the same jurisdiction. When you are performing research, look for cases on point decided by the highest court in your jurisdiction, because those cases carry the most weight.

State courts generally have the final say on state law, and federal courts have the final say on federal law. Thus, except in deciding an issue that involves federal law, state courts do not have to follow the decisions of federal courts. In deciding issues that involve federal law, state courts must abide by the decisions of the United States Supreme Court or the U.S. Courts of Appeals if the Supreme Court has not ruled on the matter. In diversity cases, federal courts must follow the relevant state courts' rulings on matters of state law.

Published and Unpublished Opinions

Some court opinions are "published," while others, despite being readily available on the Internet or in commercial databases such as Westlaw and Lexis, are "unpublished." This distinction is an important one. A published decision is one that has been declared by the court that issued it to be binding precedent. For example, California defines published opinions as those opinions that are "certified for publication or ordered published and may be cited or relied on by courts and parties." A published decision appears in the official reporter for the jurisdiction. For example, published opinions by the U.S. Circuit Courts of Appeals appear in the *Federal Reporter*.

UNPUBLISHED OPINIONS CAN SOMETIMES BE CITED.   An unpublished decision is generally *not* binding precedent, but may be both persuasive to a court and some indication of how a court is likely to rule in the future. The terminology can be confusing. Opinions appearing in West's *Federal Appendix* reporter are formally considered unpublished and are often not citable as precedent, but they do appear in a reporter that lawyers and paralegals can cite.

LOOK FOR STATEMENT BY THE COURT.   Sometimes unpublished opinions include a statement noting that they are not formally published. For example, the federal Second Circuit Court of Appeals provides that its unpublished "summary disposition" opinions "shall not be cited or otherwise used before this or any other court." In contrast, the federal District of Columbia Circuit Court of Appeals explicitly allows citation of its unpublished opinions.

Many courts issue large numbers of unpublished decisions. Each court has its own rules about the citation of unpublished decisions. Some courts forbid citing these decisions. Others require that an attorney citing an unpublished opinion note that it is not published, or perhaps provide the court and opposing counsel with a copy of the opinion. Be sure to check the rules of the jurisdiction in which a legal document is going to be filed to ensure that any reference to an unpublished decision is done properly.

For example, California defines an unpublished opinion as "opinions not certified for inclusion in the Official Reports that are not generally citable as precedent." California has a practice of "depublishing" appellate court opinions that its Supreme Court dislikes. When citing California appellate decisions, it is thus important to verify that they have not been depublished.

Persuasive Authorities

A **persuasive authority** is not binding on a court. In other words, the court is not required to follow that authority in making its decisions. Examples of persuasive authorities include:

- Persuasive precedents—previous court opinions from other jurisdictions, as discussed in Chapter 5 on page 124.

- Legal periodicals, such as law reviews, in which the issue at hand is discussed by legal scholars.

- Encyclopedias summarizing legal principles or concepts relating to a particular issue.

- Legal dictionaries that describe how the law has been applied in the past.

Often, a court refers to persuasive authorities when deciding a *case of first impression,* which is a case involving an issue that has never been specifically addressed by that court before. For example, if in researching Hoffman's claim you find that no similar cases have ever reached a higher court in your jurisdiction, you will look for similar cases decided by courts in other jurisdictions. Decisions by these courts may help guide the court deciding Hoffman's case. Your supervising attorney will want to know about these persuasive authorities so that she can present them to the court for consideration.

Finding Relevant Cases

When conducting legal research, you need to distinguish between two basic categories of legal sources: primary sources and secondary sources. As discussed in Chapter 5, *primary sources of law* include court decisions, statutes enacted by legislative bodies, rules and regulations created by administrative agencies, presidential orders, and generally any documents that *establish* the law. *Secondary sources of law* consist of books and articles that summarize, systematize, compile, explain, and interpret the law.

Generally, when beginning research projects, paralegals use secondary sources of law to help them find relevant primary sources and to educate themselves on topics of law with which they are unfamiliar. For this reason, secondary sources of law are often referred to as *finding tools.* Consider the research project involving the Hoffman claim. How can you find cases on point and binding authorities on this issue? American case law consists of millions of court decisions, and more than forty thousand new decisions are added each year. Finding relevant precedents would be a terrible task if not for secondary sources of law that classify decisions according to subject. Two important finding tools that are helpful in researching case law are legal encyclopedias and case digests, which we describe next. We also look at some other secondary sources that may be helpful.

Legal Encyclopedias

In researching Hoffman's claim, you might look first at a legal encyclopedia to learn more about negligence and the duty of care that businesses owe to business invitees. A popular legal encyclopedia is *American Jurisprudence,* Second Edition, commonly referred to as *American Jurisprudence 2d* or, more briefly, as Am. Jur. 2d. (An excerpt from this encyclopedia is shown in Exhibit 7.1 on the facing page. It is also available online from Westlaw and LexisNexis.)

EXHIBIT 7.1
Excerpt from *American Jurisprudence 2d*

PREMISES LIABILITY

by

Irwin J. Schiffres, J.D. and Sheila A. Skojec, J.D.

Scope of topic: This article discusses the principles and rules of law applicable to and governing the liability of owners or occupants of real property for negligence causing injury to persons or property by reason of defects therein or hazards created by the activities of such owners or occupants or their agents and employees. Treated in detail are the classification of persons injured as invitees, licensees, or trespassers, and the duty owed them, as well as the rules applicable in those jurisdictions where such status distinctions are no longer determinative of the duty owed the entrant; the effect of "recreational use" statutes on the duty owed persons using the property for such purposes; the greater measure of duty owed by the owner to children as compared to adult licensees and trespassers, including the attractive nuisance doctrine; and the specific duties and liabilities of owners and occupants of premises used for business or residential purposes. Also considered is the effect of the injured person's negligence on the plaintiff's right to recover under principles of contributory or comparative negligence.

Federal aspects: One injured on premises owned or operated by the United States may seek to recover under general principles of premises liability discussed in this article. Insofar as recovery is sought under the Federal Torts Claims Act, see 35 Am Jur 2d, FEDERAL TORTS CLAIMS ACT § 73.

Treated elsewhere:

Mutual obligations and liabilities of adjoining landowners with respect to injuries arising from their acts or omissions, see 1 Am Jur 2d, ADJOINING LANDOWNERS AND PROPERTIES §§ 10, 11, 28 et seq., 37 et seq.

Liability for the acts or omissions of the owners or occupants of premises abutting on a street or highway which cause injury to those using the way, see 39 Am Jur 2d, HIGHWAYS, STREETS, AND BRIDGES §§ 517 et seq.

Liability for violation of building regulations, see 13 Am Jur 2d, BUILDINGS §§ 32 et seq.

Liability of employer for injuries caused employees on the employer's premises, see 53 Am Jur 2d, MASTER AND SERVANT §§ 139 et seq.

Liability for injuries caused by defective products on the premises, see 63 Am Jur 2d, PRODUCTS LIABILITY

Respective rights and liabilities of a landlord and tenant where one is responsible for an injury suffered by the other, or by a third person, on leased premises or on premises provided for the common use of tenants, see 49 Am Jur 2d, LANDLORD AND TENANT §§ 761 et seq.

Liability of a receiver placed in charge of property for an injury sustained thereby or thereon by someone other than the persons directly interested in the estate, see 66 Am Jur 2d, RECEIVERS § 364

Duties and liabilities of occupiers of premises used for various particular types of businesses or activities, see 4 Am Jur 2d, AMUSEMENTS AND EXHIBITIONS §§ 51 et seq.; 14 Am Jur 2d, CARRIERS §§ 964 et seq.; 38 Am Jur 2d, GARAGES, AND FILLING AND PARKING STATIONS §§ 81 et seq.; 40 Am Jur 2d, HOSPITALS AND ASYLUMS § 31; 40 Am Jur 2d, HOTELS, MOTELS, AND RESTAURANTS §§ 81 et seq.; 50 Am Jur 2d, LAUNDRIES, DYERS, AND DRY CLEANERS §§ 21, 22; 54 Am Jur 2d, MOBILE HOMES, TRAILER PARKS, AND TOURIST CAMPS § 17; 57 Am Jur 2d, MUNICIPAL, COUNTY, SCHOOL, AND STATE TORT LIABILITY; AND 59 AM JUR 2D, PARKS, SQUARES, AND PLAYGROUNDS §§ 43 et seq.

Duties and liabilities with respect to injuries caused by particular agencies, such as

317

Major Legal Encyclopedias

American Jurisprudence covers hundreds of topics in more than 140 volumes. The topics are presented alphabetically, and each topic is divided into subtopics describing rules of law that have emerged from generations of court decisions. The encyclopedia also provides cross-references to specific court cases, statutory law, and relevant secondary sources of law. Additionally, each volume includes an index, and a separate index covers the entire encyclopedia.

Traditional printed volumes are kept current through supplements called **pocket parts**. Pocket parts, so named because they slip into a pocket (sleeve) in the front or back of the volume, contain changes and additions to various topics and subtopics. Updates to the online services are added regularly. Online services such as Westlaw and Lexis include the date of the most recent update of particular

pocket part

A pamphlet containing recent cases or changes in the law that is used to update legal encyclopedias and other legal authorities. It is called a "pocket part" because it slips into a pocket, or sleeve, in the front or back binder of the volume.

statutory and regulatory provisions. When a legislature or Congress is in session, it is necessary to check more than one online database to get the most up-to-date information on a statutory provision.

A similar encyclopedia is *Corpus Juris Secundum,* or C.J.S. Like Am. Jur. 2d, this encyclopedia provides detailed information on most areas of the law and includes indexes for each volume as well as for the entire set. Its 164 volumes cover 433 topics, which are presented alphabetically and divided into subtopics. Like *American Jurisprudence,* this encyclopedia is available on Westlaw.

Other Sources

Still another tool (published by West) is *Words and Phrases,* which offers definitions and interpretations of legal terms and phrases. Each term or phrase in this 132-volume set is followed by brief summary statements from federal or state court decisions in which the word or phrase has been interpreted or defined. The summary statements also indicate the names of the cases and the reporters in which they can be located. **Reporters** are publications containing the actual text of court cases, as will be discussed later.

When beginning your research into the Hoffman claim, you could use any of these secondary sources, or finding tools, to lead you to the primary sources (cases) that you will need to read and analyze. You can also search some free online sources, such as FindLaw (**lp.findlaw.com**) or Justia US Law (**law.justia.com**) for ideas. Sources may be searched for such terms as *premises liability, business invitees, duty of care,* and *landowners,* for example. Remember, though, that legal encyclopedias do not include specific rules of law from your state, which you will need to locate.

Case Digests

In researching Hoffman's case against Better Homes Store, you might want to check a case digest as well as a legal encyclopedia for references to relevant case law. **Digests,** which are produced by various publishers, are helpful research tools because they provide indexes to case law—from the earliest recorded cases through the most current opinions. (There are also some free online digests that may be worth searching). Case digests arrange topics alphabetically and provide information to help you locate referenced cases, but they do not offer the detail found in legal encyclopedias. Digests are available in both hard copy and online. The online versions are usually included in legal databases such as Westlaw and Lexis.

Collected under each topic heading in a case digest are annotations. **Annotations** are comments, explanatory notes, or case summaries. In case digests, annotations consist of very short statements of relevant points of law in reported cases. The digests published by West offer the most comprehensive system for locating cases by subject matter. Exhibit 7.2 on the facing page shows some excerpts from one of West's federal digests on the standard of care that is owed to an invitee.

The West Key-Number System

West's key-number system has simplified the task of researching case law. The system divides all areas of American law into specific categories, or topics, arranged in alphabetical order. The topics are further divided into many subtopics, each designated by a **key number**, which is accompanied by the West key symbol: ⚷. You can see the use of this key symbol in Exhibit 7.2. Exhibit 7.3 on page 190 shows some of the key numbers used for other subtopics under the general topic of negligence.

USING KEY NUMBERS.   The key-number system organizes millions of case summaries under specific topics and subtopics. For example, in researching the Hoffman claim, suppose that you locate a negligence case on point decided by a court in your state five years ago. Your goal is to find related—and perhaps more recent—cases that support Hoffman's claim. Here is how the key-number system can help. When

---

reporter
A book in which court cases are published, or reported.

digest
A compilation in which brief summaries of court cases are arranged by subject and subdivided by jurisdiction and court.

annotation
A brief comment, an explanation of a legal point, or a case summary found in a case digest or other legal source.

key number
A number (accompanied by the symbol of a key) corresponding to a specific topic within West's key-number system to facilitate legal research of case law.

EXHIBIT 7.2

Excerpts from *West's Federal Practice Digest 4th* on Negligence

77A F P D 4th—173

NEGLIGENCE ☞ 1037(4)

For references to other topics, see Descriptive-Word Index

E.D.Mich. 1998. Under Michigan law, a property owner is not an absolute insurer of the safety of invitees.

Meyers v. Wal-Mart Stores, East, Inc., 29 F.Supp.2d 780.

E.D.Mich. 1995. under Michigan law, property owner is not insurer of safety of invitees.

Bunch v. Long John Silvers, Inc., 878 F.Supp. 1044.

E.D.Mich. 1994. Under Michigan law, property owner is not insurer of safety of invitees.

Dose v. Equitable Life Assur. Soc., 864 F.Supp. 682.

E.D.N.C. 1993. Premises owner does not automatically insure safety of invitees and is not liable in absence of negligence.

Faircloth v. U.S., 837 F.Supp. 123.

E.D.Va. 1999. Under Virginia law, owner of premises is not insurer of his invitees safety; rather, owner must use ordinary care to render premises reasonably safe for invitee's visit.

Sandow-Pajewski v. Busch Entertainment Corp., 55 F.Supp.2d 422.

☞ **1037(4). Care required in general.**

C.A.7 (Ill.) 1986. Under Illinois law, landowner is liable for physical harm to his invitees caused by condition on his land: where landowner could by exercise of reasonable care have discovered condition; where landowner should realize that condition involves unreasonable risk to harm to invitees; where landowner should expect that invitees will not discover danger or will fail to protect against it; and where landowner fails to exercise reasonable care to protect invitees.

Higgins v. White Sox Baseball Club, Inc., 787 F.2d 1125.

C.A.7 (Ind.) 1994. Under Indiana law, landowner's duty to invitee while that invitee is on premises is that of reasonable care.

Salima v. Scherwood South, Inc., 38 F.3d 929.

Under indiana law, landowner is liable for harm caused to invitee by condition on land only if landowner knows of or through exercise of reasonable care would discover condition and realize that it involves unreasonable risk of harm to such invitees, should expect the invitee will fail to discover or realize danger or fail to protect against it, and fails to exercise reasonable care in protecting invitee against danger.

Salima v. Scherwood South, Inc., 38 F. 3d 929.

Under Indiana law, landowner is not liable for harm caused to invitees by conditions whose

For cited U.S.C.A. sections and legislative hist

danger is known or obvious unless landowner could anticipate harm despite obviousness.

Salima v. Scherwood South, Inc., 38 F.3d 929.

C.A.6 (Mich.) 1998. Under Michigan law, where invitor has reason to expect that, despite

NEGLIGENCE

77A F P D 4th—542

XVI. DEFENSES AND MITIGATING CIRCUMSTANCES.—Continued.

570. ____ Professional rescuers; "firefighter's rule."
575. Imputed contributory negligence.

XVII. PREMISES LIABILITY.

(A) IN GENERAL.
☞ 1000. Nature.
1001. Elements in general.
1002. Constitutional, statutory and regulatory provisions.
1003. What law governs.
1004. Preemption.

(B) NECESSITY AND EXISTENCE OF DUTY.
☞ 1010. In general.
1011. Ownership, custody and control.
1012. Conditions known or obvious in general.
1013. Conditions created or known by defendant.
1014. Foreseeability.
1015. Duty as to children.
1016. ____ In general.
1017. ____ Trespassing children.
1018. Duty to inspect or discover.
1019. Protection against acts of third persons in general.
1020. Duty to warn.
1021. Duty of store and business proprietors.
1022. ____ In general.
1023. ____ Duty to inspect.
1024. ____ Protection against acts of third persons.
1025. Duty based on statute or other regulation.

(C) STANDARD OF CARE.
☞ 1030. In general.
1031. Not insurer or guarantor.
1032. Reasonable or ordinary care in general.
1033. Reasonably safe or unreasonably dangerous conditions.
1034. Status of entrant.
1035. ____ In general.
1036. ____ Care dependent on status.
1037. ____ Invitees.
(1). In general.
(2). Who are invitees.
(3). Not insurer as to invitees.
(4). Care required in general.
(5). Public invitees in general.
(6). Implied invitation.
(7). Persons working on property.
(8). Delivery persons and haulers.
1040. ____ Licensees.
(1). In general.
(2). Who are licensees.

EXHIBIT 7.3
Subtopics and Key Numbers
in a West Digest

NEGLIGENCE

SUBJECTS INCLUDED

General civil negligence law and premises liability, including duty, standards of care, breach of duty, proximate cause, injury, defenses, and comparative fault, whether based on the common law or statute, as well as procedural aspects of such actions

General civil liabilities for gross negligence, recklessness, willful or wanton conduct, strict liability and ultrahazardous instrumentalities and activities

Negligence liabilities relating to the construction, demolition and repair of buildings and other structures, whether based on the common law or statute

General criminal negligence offenses and prosecutions

SUBJECTS EXCLUDED AND COVERED BY OTHER TOPICS

Accountants or auditors, negligence of, see ACCOUNTANTS ⚷ 8,9

Aircraft, accidents involving, see AVIATION ⚷ 141–153

Attorney's malpractice liability, see ATTORNEY AND CLIENT ⚷ 105–129.5

Banks, liabilities of, see BANKS AND BANKING ⚷ 100

Brokers, securities and real estate, liabilities of, see BROKERS

Car and highway accidents, see AUTOMOBILES

Common carriers, liabilities to passengers, see CARRIERS

Domestic animals, injuries by or to, see ANIMALS

Dram Shop liability and other liabilities for serving alcohol, see INTOXICATING LIQUORS ⚷ 282–324

*   *   *   *

For detailed references to other topics, see Descriptive-Word Index

_____

Analysis

 I.   IN GENERAL, ⚷ 200–205.
 II.   NECESSITY AND EXISTENCE OF DUTY, ⚷ 210–222.
 III.   STANDARD OF CARE, ⚷ 230–239.
 IV.   BREACH OF DUTY, ⚷ 250–259.
 V.   HEIGHTENED DEGREES OF NEGLIGENCE, ⚷ 272–276.
 VI.   VULNERABLE AND ENDANGERED PERSONS; RESCUES, ⚷ 281–285.
 VII.   SUDDEN EMERGENCY DOCTRINE, ⚷ 291–295.
 VIII.   DANGEROUS SITUATIONS AND STRICT LIABILITY, ⚷ 301–307.

headnote
A note, usually a paragraph long, near the beginning of a reported case summarizing the court's ruling on an issue.

you read through any case in a West's case reporter, you will find that a series of **headnotes** precedes the court's actual opinion. Each headnote summarizes one portion of the opinion. West editors create each headnote and assign it to a particular topic with a key number.

FINDING WHAT YOU NEED.   Key numbers correlate the headnotes in cases to the topics in digests and can be useful in finding cases on a particular subject. Once you find the key number in a case that discusses the issue you are researching, you can find every other case in your state that discusses this issue. You go to the West case digest and locate the particular key number and topic. Beneath the key number, the digest provides case summaries, titles, and citations to cases discussing the issue in the area covered by the digest. When you find a case that seems on point, you know where to find it because you have the citation. (In the next chapter, we will see how this works using *KeyCite* offered by West and *Shepard's* offered by Lexis.)

Types of Digests

As mentioned, West offers a comprehensive system of digests. West publishes digests of both federal court opinions and state court opinions, as well as regional digests and digests that correspond with its reporters covering specialized areas, such as bankruptcy. For example, the *Supreme Court Digest* corresponds to decisions published in West's *Supreme Court Reporter*.

Other sources, available online and sometimes free, publish various digests (for example, **lawdigest.uslegal.com**). Some digests are specific to individual states. Note that other publishers' digests do not use the key-number system.

Annotations: American Law Reports

The *American Law Reports* (A.L.R.) and *American Law Reports Federal* (A.L.R. Federal), published by West, are also useful resources for legal researchers. These multivolume sets present the full text of selected cases in many areas of the law. They are helpful in finding cases from jurisdictions around the country with similar facts and legal issues.

There are six different series of *American Law Reports* covering case law since 1919. The first and second series contain separate digests that provide references to cases and also have word indexes to assist the researcher in locating specific areas. The remaining sets of A.L.R. volumes use a different approach, called a *Quick Index*, which lets the user access cases and information on a particular topic. The cases in these reporters are followed by annotations—that is, references to articles that explain or comment on the specific issues involved in the cases. These reporters can be a good source to turn to for an overview of a specific area of law or current trend in the law.

When using any of the volumes of A.L.R., be sure to update your results. A.L.R. annotations are periodically updated by the addition of relevant cases. For the first series, the annotations are updated in a set of books called the *A.L.R. Blue Book of Supplemental Decisions*. The second series is updated in the *A.L.R. Later Case Service*, and the remaining series are made current by pocket-part supplements located in the front of each volume. In addition, you can consult the annotation history table at the end of the Quick Index to see whether any new annotations supplement or change an earlier annotation. (Of course, most of these services are now available online.)

Other Secondary Sources

A number of other secondary sources are useful in legal research. We look here at three of these sources: treatises, *Restatements of the Law*, and legal periodicals. Like other secondary sources of law, these sources do not have the force of law. Nevertheless, they are important sources of legal analysis and opinion and are often cited as persuasive authorities.

Treatises

A **treatise** is a formal scholarly work by a law professor or other legal professional that treats a particular subject systematically and in detail. Some treatises are published in multivolume sets, while others are contained in a single book.

Single-volume treatises that synthesize the basic principles of a given legal area are known as **hornbooks**. Some, but not all, hornbooks are available online. These texts are useful to paralegals who want to familiarize themselves with a particular area of the law, such as torts or contracts. For example, in researching the issues in Hoffman's negligence case, you might want to locate the treatise entitled *Prosser and Keeton on the Law of Torts*, Fifth Edition, which is included in West's Hornbook

---

social MEDIA TODAY

Research shows that the best way to learn to do things is to actually do them. You can't learn to use social media by reading a book—you need to use the tools.

---

treatise
In legal research, a work that provides a systematic, detailed, and scholarly review of a particular legal subject.

hornbook
A single-volume scholarly discussion, or treatise, on a particular legal subject.

Series, and read the sections on negligence. (Exhibit 7.4 below shows the book open to the chapter on defenses to negligence.) Hornbooks such as *Prosser and Keeton on the Law of Torts* present many examples of case law and references to cases that may be helpful to a researcher.

Restatements of the Law

The *Restatements of the Law* are also a helpful resource, and one on which judges often rely as a persuasive authority when making decisions. They are available online via Lexis and Westlaw. There are *Restatements* in the areas of contracts, torts, agency, trusts, property, restitution, security, judgments, and conflict of laws. Each section in the *Restatements* contains a statement of the principles of law that are generally accepted by the courts or embodied in statutes, followed by a discussion of those principles. The discussions present cases as examples and also discuss variations.

Legal Periodicals

Legal periodicals, such as law reviews and law journals, are also important secondary sources of law that can be helpful. If an article in a legal periodical deals with the specific area that you are researching, the article will likely include footnotes citing cases relating to the topic. These references can save you hours of research time in finding relevant case law.

ON THE web

You can learn more about the American Law Institute (ALI) and its publications, including information on *Restatements of the Law,* by accessing the ALI's Web site at **www.ali.org**

EXHIBIT 7.4

A Page from the *Hornbook on the Law of Torts*

Chapter 11

NEGLIGENCE: DEFENSES

Table of Sections

§ 65. Contributory Negligence

The two most common defenses in a negligence action are contributory negligence and assumption of risk. Since both developed at a comparatively late date in the development of the common law,[1] and since both clearly operate to the advantage of the defendant, they are commonly regarded as defenses to a tort which would otherwise be established. All courts now hold that the burden of pleading and proof of the contributory negligence of the plaintiff is on the defendant.[2]

Contributory negligence is conduct on the part of the plaintiff, contributing as a legal cause to the harm he has suffered, which falls below the standard to which he is required to conform for his own protection.[3] Unlike assumption of risk, the defense does not rest upon the idea that the defendant is relieved of any duty toward the plaintiff. Rather, although the defendant has violated his duty, has been negligent, and would oth-

---

§ 65

1. The earliest contributory negligence case is Butterfield v. Forrester, 1809, 11 East 60, 103 Eng.Rep. 926. The first American case appears to have been Smith v. Smith, 1824, 19 Mass. (2 Pick.) 621. Assumption of risk first appears in a negligence case in 1799. See infra, § 68 n. 1.

2. E.g., Wilkinson v. Hartford Accident & Indemnity Co., La.1982, 411 So.2d 22; Moodie v. Santoni, 1982, 292 Md. 582, 441 A.2d 323; Addair v. Bryant, 1981, ___ W.Va. ___, 284 S.E.2d 374; Pickett v. Parks, 1981, 208 Neb. 310, 303 N.W.2d 296; Hatton v. Chem-Haulers, Inc., Ala.1980, 393 So.2d 950; Sampson v. W. F. Enterprises, Inc., Mo.App.1980, 611 S.W.2d 333; Howard v. Howard, Ky.App.1980, 607 S.W.2d 119; cf. Reuter v. United States, W.D.Pa.1982, 534 F.Supp. 731 (presumption that person killed or suffering loss of memory was acting with due care).

Illinois and certain other jurisdictions held to the contrary for some time. See West Chicago Street Railroad Co. v. Liderman, 1900, 187 Ill. 463, 58 N.E. 367; Kotler v. Lalley, 1930, 112 Conn. 86, 151 A. 433; Dreier v. McDermott, 1913, 157 Iowa 726, 141 N.W. 315. See Green, Illinois Negligence Law II, 1944, 39 Ill.L.Rev. 116, 125–130.

3. Second Restatement of Torts, § 463. See generally, Malone, The Formative Era of Contributory Negligence, 1946, 41 Ill.L.Rev. 151; James, Contributory Negligence, 1953, 62 Yale L.J. 691; Bohlen, Contributory Negligence, 1908, 21 Harv.L.Rev. 233; Lowndes, Contributory Negligence, 1934, 22 Geo.L.J. 674; Malone, Some Ruminations on Contributory Negligence, 1981, 65 Utah L.Rev. 91; Schwartz, Contributory and Comparative Negligence: A Reappraisal, 1978, 87 Yale L.J. 697; Note, 1979, 39 La.L.Rev. 637.

451

The Case Reporting System

The primary sources of case law are the cases themselves. Once you have learned which cases are relevant to the issue you are researching, you need to find the cases and examine the court opinions. (See the *Featured Contributor* article on the following pages for tips on conducting legal research.)

Assume, for example, that in researching Hoffman's case, you learn that your state's supreme court issued a decision a few years ago on a case with a similar fact pattern. In that case, the state supreme court upheld a lower court's judgment that a retail business owner had to pay damages to a customer who was injured on the store's premises. You know that the state supreme court's decision is a binding authority, and, to your knowledge, the decision has not been overruled or modified. Therefore, the case will likely provide weighty support to your attorney's arguments in support of Hoffman's claim.

At this point, however, you have only read *about* the case in secondary sources. To locate the case itself and make sure it is applicable (the *Ethics Watch* below explains why this is important), you must understand the case reporting system and the legal "shorthand" employed in referencing court cases.

ETHICS WATCH

USING SECONDARY SOURCES

When rushing to meet a deadline, you may be tempted to avoid a critical step in the research process—checking primary sources. For example, suppose a firm's client complains that a publisher of his novels is now publishing the novels online, as e-books. The client wants to know if online publication is copyright infringement. At issue is whether the publisher, which has the right to publish the printed texts, also has the right to publish the books online. An attorney for the firm asks Sarah, a paralegal, to research case law to see how the courts have dealt with this issue.

Sarah has just read an article in a law journal about a similar case recently decided by the United States Supreme Court. Without taking the time to read the case itself, she relies on the author's conclusions in the article. She prepares a memo to the attorney presenting her "research" results.

Based on Sarah's memo, the attorney advises the client that the publisher had no right to publish the client's works online. The client decides to sue the publisher. Later, during more extensive pretrial research, Sarah reads the case. Unfortunately for her (and the client and the attorney), the author of the article did not discuss an important qualification made by the Court in its ruling relating to the terms of the publishing contract. The Court's decision does not apply to the client's situation, and the case is not a binding authority.

While the attorney is responsible for the work product for the client, Sarah's failure to rely on primary sources is likely seen as a failure to produce competent work. Such a failure could injure the position of the client and violate the NFPA Model Disciplinary Rule 1.1, "A paralegal shall achieve and maintain a high level of competence."

Featured Contributor

TIPS FOR EFFECTIVE LEGAL RESEARCH

E. J. Yera

BIOGRAPHICAL NOTE

E. J. Yera graduated from the University of Miami School of Law. After clerking for the U.S. District Court for the Southern District of Florida, he served as corporate counsel for Holmes Regional Medical Center in Melbourne, Florida. Yera then worked for the Health Care Task Force in the Antitrust Division of the U.S. Department of Justice in Washington, D.C., and later became a member of the U.S. Attorney's Office in the Southern District of Florida. He has taught and lectured in various paralegal programs and has published several articles.

© Cengage Learning 2014

If you perform legal research frequently, you will develop a routine. The purpose of this article is not to give you ironclad rules but to set out nine guidelines that will help you find the routine that is most comfortable for you. Think about how you can use the tips in your future research tasks.

1. **Before You Start, Make Sure You Know the Exact Legal Issue You Will Be Researching.**   It is not uncommon for paralegals and lawyers to research a question for hours only to discover they were not researching the correct legal question. Before you start your research, determine the legal issue that needs to be researched. You might learn this from reviewing information already available, such as a summary of a client interview. Ask questions of the attorney giving you a research assignment. What counts is coming back with the correct answers, not appearing to understand the research task completely when you first hear about it.

2. **Understand the Language of the Issue.**   Often, the researcher cannot find the answer because the legal terms used in defining the problem are unfamiliar. Legal terms, or "terms of art," are as unfamiliar to many people as a foreign language. If you are uncertain about the meaning of any term or phrase, look it up in a law dictionary or encyclopedia to get an idea of its meaning. You may want to read a hornbook on the topic to give you a basic understanding.

3. **Be Aware of the Circular Nature of Legal Research and Use It to Your Advantage.**   Students often ask whether primary or secondary sources should be researched first. The answer is that it does not matter, as long as you research both types of sources. By researching primary and secondary sources on a topic, you can be assured that you are almost always double-checking your own work. For example, in a case (primary source of law) on a particular issue,

State Court Decisions and Reporters

Written decisions of state appellate courts are published chronologically in volumes called *reports* or *reporters,* which are numbered consecutively. State appellate court decisions are found in the state reporters of that particular state. The reporters may be either the "official" reporters, designated as such by the state legislature, or "unofficial" reporters, published by West. Although some states still have official reporters (and a few states, such as New York and California, have more than one official reporter), many states have eliminated their own official reporters in favor of West's National Reporter System, discussed next. Most state trial court decisions are not published.

Regional Reporters

State court opinions also appear in regional units of West's National Reporter System. Many lawyers and libraries have the West reporters because they report cases more quickly and are distributed more widely than the state-published reports.

the judge writing the opinion will discuss pertinent statutes on the issue. The reason you check both sources is to make sure you have found all of the relevant materials.

4. **Until You Submit the Assignment, Always Assume There Are Additional Relevant Materials to Find.** Always assume that further relevant materials must be located to help complete your research. Of course, there comes a point when you have to assume that you have covered the research territory, and knowing when to stop doing research is one of the hardest things to learn. The intent of this tip, though, is to encourage you not to cut corners when conducting research.

5. **Keep a List of What Sources You Have Found and Where They Have Led You.** You do not want to spend valuable time wondering if you have already checked certain sources. Therefore, it is important to construct a "road map" of where you have been and where you are going.

6. **Take the Time to Become Familiar with the Sources You Are Using.** It seems obvious that you need to be familiar with your sources, yet this requirement is sometimes overlooked. For example, a case digest (a volume summarizing cases) may indicate on its spine that the digest covers the years "1961 to Date." "To Date," however, does not mean that it is the most current digest. It only means that the digest covers cases up to the date of publication. This is true generally for any source you are using—look it over carefully before assuming it contains the sources you need.

7. **Be Aware of the Jurisdiction and the Time Frame You Are Researching.** If you are researching an issue that will be resolved by a Florida state court, then your emphasis should be on Florida cases. Of course, there are times when no case law is available, and you must then find cases on point from other states to use as persuasive authorities. Be aware when researching any area of the law that very often there is either a loose-leaf service or a pamphlet or pocket part containing newer information. Ask yourself the following question: Where can the most up-to-date material be found? If you don't know, ask a law librarian.

8. **Always Refer to *Shepard's* to Make Sure the Cases You Are Using Are Up to Date.** *Shepard's Citations* (and West's *KeyCite*) helps the researcher of case law in two ways. First, it lists cases that have cited the cases you have found. This is helpful because if another case has cited a case you have found, that other case may also be relevant to your issue, and thus you may be able to use it. Also, cases that cite your case are more recent and may be advantageous. Second, *Shepard's* tells you whether the cases that you have found are still "good law"—that is, whether the cases have been overruled, reversed, or the like. Knowing this information is crucial.

9. **Use Computerized Legal Research Services to Update Your Research Results.** Online databases such as Westlaw and Lexis allow you to update your research results by using citators. Also, these services allow you to search the case law for words or phrases. Additionally, the Internet is a great source for legal materials. Many state and federal courts, government agencies, law schools, and bar associations have Web sites containing different primary and secondary legal materials.

"What counts is coming back with the correct answers . . . ."

The National Reporter System divides the states into the following geographic areas: *Atlantic* (A. or A.2d), *South Eastern* (S.E. or S.E.2d), *North Eastern* (N.E. or N.E.2d), *North Western* (N.W. or N.W.2d), *Pacific* (P., P.2d, or P.3d), *South Western* (S.W., S.W.2d, or S.W.3d), and *Southern* (So. or So.2d). The *2d* and *3d* in the abbreviations refer to *Second Series* and *Third Series*. The states included in each of these regional divisions are indicated in Exhibit 7.5 on the following page, which illustrates West's National Reporter System. The names of the areas may not be the same as what we commonly think of as a geographic region. For example, the *North Western* reporter does not include the Pacific Northwest but does include states, such as Iowa, that people do not think of as being in the Northwest. Similarly, Oklahoma is in the Pacific Reporter.

Citation Format

To locate a case, you must know where to look. After a decision has been published, it is normally referred to (cited) by the name of the case, the volume number and the abbreviated name of the book in which the case is located, the page number

EXHIBIT 7.5

West's National Reporter System—Regional and Federal

Regional Reporters	Coverage Beginning	Coverage
Atlantic Reporter (A. or A.2d)	1885	Connecticut, Delaware, Maine, Maryland, New Hampshire, New Jersey, Pennsylvania, Rhode Island, Vermont, and District of Columbia.
North Eastern Reporter (N.E. or N.E.2d)	1885	Illinois, Indiana, Massachusetts, New York, and Ohio.
North Western Reporter (N.W. or N.W.2d)	1879	Iowa, Michigan, Minnesota, Nebraska, North Dakota, South Dakota, and Wisconsin.
Pacific Reporter (P., P.2d, or P.3d)	1883	Alaska, Arizona, California, Colorado, Hawaii, Idaho, Kansas, Montana, Nevada, New Mexico, Oklahoma, Oregon, Utah, Washington, and Wyoming.
South Eastern Reporter (S.E. or S.E.2d)	1887	Georgia, North Carolina, South Carolina, Virginia, and West Virginia.
South Western Reporter (S.W., S.W.2d, or S.W.3d)	1886	Arkansas, Kentucky, Missouri, Tennessee, and Texas.
Southern Reporter (So. or So.2d)	1887	Alabama, Florida, Louisiana, and Mississippi.

Federal Reporters		
Federal Reporter (F., F.2d, or F.3d)	1880	U.S. Circuit Court from 1880 to 1912; U.S. Commerce Court from 1911 to 1913; U.S. District Courts from 1880 to 1932; U.S. Court of Claims (now called U.S. Court of Federal Claims) from 1929 to 1932 and since 1960; U.S. Court of Appeals since 1891; U.S. Court of Customs and Patent Appeals since 1929; and U.S. Emergency Court of Appeals since 1943.
Federal Supplement (F.Supp. or F.Supp.2d)	1932	U.S. Court of Claims from 1932 to 1960; U.S. District Courts since 1932; and U.S. Customs Court since 1956.
Federal Rules Decisions (F.R.D.)	1939	U.S. District Courts involving the Federal Rules of Civil Procedure since 1939 and Federal Rules of Criminal Procedure since 1946.
Supreme Court Reporter (S.Ct.)	1882	U.S. Supreme Court since the October term of 1882.
Bankruptcy Reporter (Bankr.)	1980	Bankruptcy decisions of U.S. Bankruptcy Courts, U.S. District Courts, U.S. Courts of Appeals, and U.S. Supreme Court.
Military Justice Reporter (M.J.)	1978	U.S. Court of Military Appeals and Courts of Military Review for the Army, Navy, Air Force, and Coast Guard.

NATIONAL REPORTER SYSTEM MAP

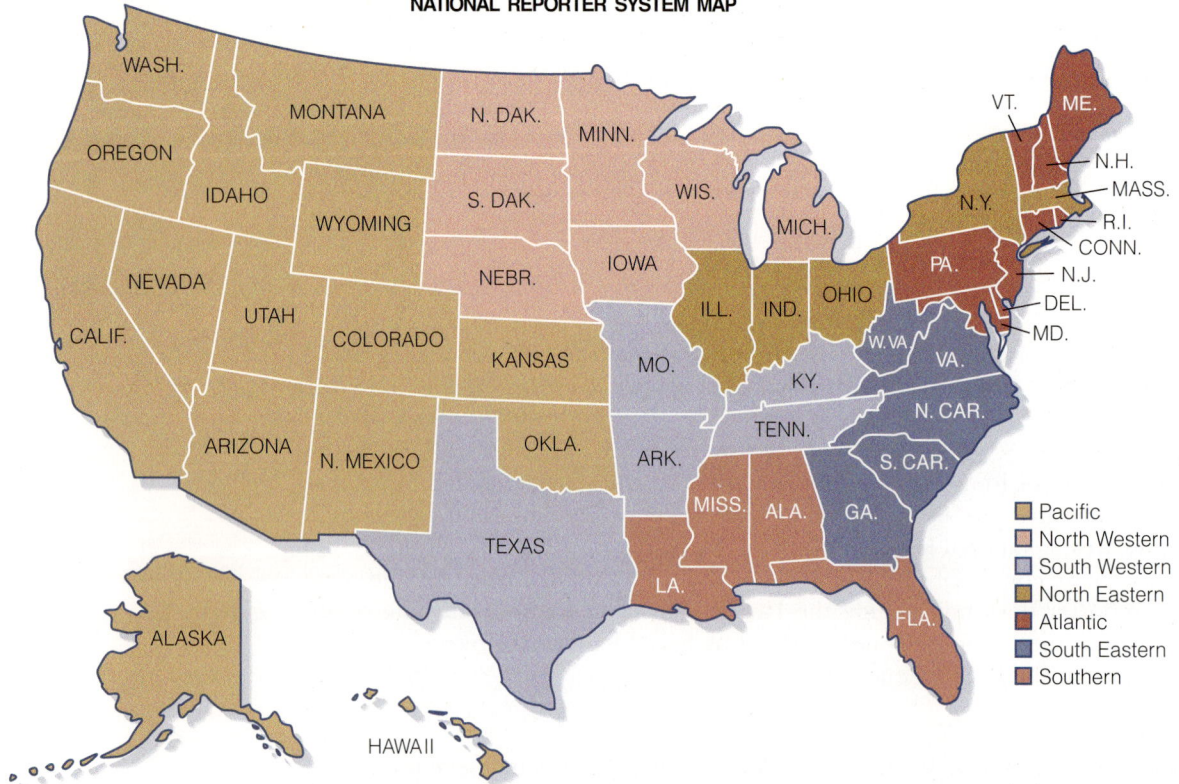

Legend: Pacific, North Western, South Western, North Eastern, Atlantic, South Eastern, Southern on which the case begins, and the year. In other words, there are five parts to a standard **citation**:

Case name	Volume number	Name of book	Page number	(Year)

citation
In case law, a reference to a case by the name of the case, the volume number and name of the reporter in which the case can be found, the page number on which the case begins, and the year. In statutory and administrative law, a reference to the title number, name, and section of the code in which a statute or regulation can be found.

This basic format is used for every citation regardless of whether the case is published in an official state reporter or a regional reporter (or both). When more than one reporter is cited for the same case, each reference is called a **parallel citation** and is separated from the next citation by a comma. The first citation is to the state's official reporter (if there is one), although the text of the court's opinion will be the same (parallel) at any of the listed locations.

parallel citation
A second (or third) citation for a given case. When a case is published in more than one reporter, each citation is a parallel citation to the other(s).

AN EXAMPLE. To illustrate how to find case law from citations, suppose you want to find the following case: *Goldstein v. Lackard*, 81 Mass.App.Ct. 1112, 961 N.E.2d 163 (2012). You can see that the opinion in this case can be found in Volume 81 of the official *Massachusetts Appellate Court Reports*, on page 1112. The parallel citation is to Volume 961 of the *North Eastern Reporter, Second Series*, page 163. In some cases, additional information may appear in parentheses at the end of a citation, usually indicating the court that heard the case (if that information is not clear from the citation alone). Exhibit 7.6 on pages 198 through 200 further illustrates how to read case citations.

PROPER FORM. When conducting legal research, you should write down the citations to the cases or other legal sources that you have consulted, quoted, or want to refer to in a written summary of your research results. Several guides have been published on how to cite legal sources.

Traditionally, the most widely used guide has been *The Bluebook: A Uniform System of Citation*, published by the Harvard Law Review Association. This book explains the proper format for citing cases, statutes, constitutions, regulations, and other legal sources. It is a good idea to memorize the basic format for citations to cases and statutory law because these legal sources are frequently cited in legal writing.

An alternative guide is a booklet entitled *ALWD Citation Manual: A Professional System of Citation*, which is published by the Association of Legal Writing Directors. Legal practitioners should check the rules of their jurisdiction for guidelines on the proper format for citations in documents submitted to a court.

Federal Court Decisions

Court decisions from the U.S. district courts (federal trial courts) are published in West's *Federal Supplement* (F.Supp. or F.Supp.2d), and opinions from the courts of appeals are reported in West's *Federal Reporter* (F., F.2d, or F.3d). These are both unofficial reporters (there are no official reporters for these courts). Both the *Federal Reporter* and the *Federal Supplement* incorporate decisions from specialized federal courts. West also publishes separate reporters, such as its *Bankruptcy Reporter*, that contain decisions in certain specialized fields under federal law. All of these reporters are published online.

United States Supreme Court Decisions

Opinions from the United States Supreme Court are published in several reporters, including the *United States Reports*, West's *Supreme Court Reporter*, and the *Lawyers' Edition of the Supreme Court Reports*, each of which we discuss below. A sample citation to a Supreme Court case is also included in Exhibit 7.6 on the bottom of the next page. Note that there is free access to Supreme Court materials at the Court's Web site and also at Oyez (**www.oyez.org**).

The *United States Reports*

The *United States Reports* (U.S.) is the official edition of all decisions of the United States Supreme Court for which there are written opinions. Published by the federal government, the series includes reports of Supreme Court cases dating from the

EXHIBIT 7.6
How to Read Citations

STATE COURTS

282 Neb. 990, 808 N.W.2d 48 (2012)[a]

N.W. is the abbreviation for West's publication of state court decisions rendered in the *North Western Reporter* of the National Reporter System. *2d* indicates that this case was included in the *Second Series* of that reporter. The number 808 refers to the volume number of the reporter; the number 48 refers to the page in that volume on which this case begins.

Neb. is an abbreviation for *Nebraska Reports,* Nebraska's official reports of the decisions of its highest court, the Nebraska Supreme Court.

204 Cal.App.4th 112, 138 Cal.Rptr.3d 519 (2012)

Cal.Rptr. is the abbreviation for West's unofficial reports—titled *California Reporter*—of the decisions of California courts.

93 A.D.3d 493, 940 N.Y.S.2d 75 (2012)

N.Y.S. is the abbreviation for West's unofficial reports—titled *New York Supplement*—of the decisions of New York courts.

A.D. is the abbreviation for *Appellate Division*, which hears appeals from the New York Supreme Court—the state's general trial court. The New York Court of Appeals is the state's highest court, analogous to other states' supreme courts.

313 Ga.App. 804, 723 S.E.2d 39 (2012)

Ga.App. is the abbreviation for *Georgia Appeals Reports,* Georgia's official reports of the decisions of its court of appeals.

FEDERAL COURTS

___ U.S. ___,   132 S.Ct. 1201, 182 L.Ed.2d 42 (2012)

L.Ed. is an abbreviation for *Lawyers' Edition of the Supreme Court Reports*, an unofficial edition of decisions of the United States Supreme Court.

S.Ct. is the abbreviation for West's unofficial reports—titled *Supreme Court Reporter*—of decisions of the United States Supreme Court.

U.S. is the abbreviation for *United States Reports*, the official edition of the decisions of the United States Supreme Court. The blank lines in this citation (or any other citation) indicate that the appropriate volume of the case reporter has not yet been published and no page number is available.

a. The case names have been deleted from these citations to emphasize the publications. It should be kept in mind, however, that the name of a case is as important as the specific page numbers in the volumes in which It Is found. If a citation is incorrect, the correct citation may be found in a publication's index of case names. In addition to providing a check on errors in citations, the date of a case is important because the value of a recent case as an authority is likely to be greater than that of older cases from the same court.

EXHIBIT 7.6
How to Read Citations—Continued

FEDERAL COURTS (Continued)

668 F.3d 1148 (9th Cir. 2012)

9th Cir. is an abbreviation denoting that this case was decided in the U.S. Court of Appeals for the Ninth Circuit.

839 F.Supp.2d 985 (S.D. Ohio 2012)

S.D. Ohio is an abbreviation indicating that the U.S. District Court for the Southern District of Ohio decided this case.

ENGLISH COURTS

9 Exch. 341, 156 Eng.Rep. 145 (1854)

Eng.Rep. is an abbreviation for *English Reports, Full Reprint,* a series of reports containing selected decisions made in English courts between 1378 and 1865.

Exch. is an abbreviation for *English Exchequer Reports*, which includes the original reports of cases decided in England's Court of Exchequer.

STATUTORY AND OTHER CITATIONS

18 U.S.C. Section 1961(1)(A)

U.S.C. denotes *United States Code*, the codification of *United States Statutes at Large.* The number 18 refers to the statute's U.S.C. title number and 1961 to its section number within that title. The number 1 in parentheses refers to a subsection within the section, and the letter A in parentheses to a subsection within the subsection.

UCC 2–206(1)(b)

UCC is an abbreviation for *Uniform Commercial Code*. The first number 2 is a reference to an article of the UCC, and 206 to a section within that article. The number 1 in parentheses refers to a subsection within the section, and the letter b in parentheses to a subsection within the subsection.

Restatement (Third) of Torts, Section 6

Restatement (Third) of Torts refers to the third edition of the American Law Institute's *Restatement of the Law of Torts*. The number 6 refers to a specific section.

17 C.F.R. Section 230.505

C.F.R. is an abbreviation for *Code of Federal Regulations*, a compilation of federal administrative regulations. The number 17 designates the regulation's title number, and 230.505 designates a specific section within that title.

Continued

EXHIBIT 7.6
How to Read Citations—Continued

WESTLAW® CITATIONS[b]

2012 WL 164930

WL is an abbreviation for Westlaw. The number 2012 is the year of the document that can be found with this citation in the Westlaw database. The number 164930 is a number assigned to a specific document. A higher number indicates that a document was added to the Westlaw database later in the year.

UNIFORM RESOURCE LOCATORS (URLs)

http://www.westlaw.com[c]

The suffix *com* is the top level domain (TLD) for this Web site. The TLD *com* is an abbreviation for "commercial," which usually means that a for-profit entity hosts (maintains or supports) this Web site.

westlaw is the host name—the part of the domain name selected by the organization that registered the name. In this case, West registered the name. This Internet site is the Westlaw database on the Web.

www is an abbreviation for "World Wide Web." The Web is a system of Internet servers that support documents formatted in *HTML* (hypertext markup language) and other formats as well.

http://www.uscourts.gov

This is "The Federal Judiciary Home Page." The host is the Administrative Office of the U.S. Courts. The TLD *gov* is an abbreviation for "government." This Web site includes information and links from, and about, the federal courts.

http://www.law.cornell.edu/index.html

This part of a URL points to a Web page or file at a specific location within the host's domain. This page is a menu with links to documents within the domain and to other Internet resources.

This is the host name for a Web site that contains the Internet publications of the Legal Information Institute (LII), which is a part of Cornell Law School. The LII site includes a variety of legal materials and links to other legal resources on the Internet. The TLD *edu* is an abbreviation for "educational institution" (a school or a university).

http://www.ipl2.org/div/news

This part of the URL points to a static *news* page at this Web site, which provides links to online newspapers from around the world.

div is an abbreviation for "division," which is the way that ipl2 tags the content on its Web site as relating to a specific topic.

The site *ipl2* was formed from the merger of the Internet Public Library and the Librarians' Internet Index. It is an online service that provides reference resources and links to other information services on the Web. The site is supported chiefly by the *iSchool* at Drexel College of Information Science and Technology. The TLD *org* is an abbreviation for "organization" (normally nonprofit).

b. Many court decisions that are not yet published or that are not intended for publication can be accessed through Westlaw, an online legal database.

c. The basic form for a URL is "service://hostname/path." The Internet service for all of the URLs in this text is *http* (hypertext transfer protocol). Because most Web browsers add this prefix automatically when a user enters a host name or a hostname/path, we have generally omitted the *http://* from the URLs listed in this text.

slip opinion
A judicial opinion published shortly after the decision is made and not yet included in a case reporter or advance sheets.

August term of 1791. Soon after the Supreme Court issues a decision, the official slip opinion is published by the U.S. Government Printing Office. (It is published online more quickly at the Supreme Court's Web site. Go to **www.supremecourt. gov**, and select "Opinions," then "Latest Slip Opinions.") The **slip opinion** is the first authoritative text of the opinion and is later printed in what the Supreme

Court notes is the "official version." The full text of all opinions is on the Court's Web site.

After a number of slip opinions have been issued, the advance sheets of the official *United States Reports* appear. These are issued in pamphlet form to provide a temporary resource until the official bound volume is finally published.

The *Supreme Court Reporter*

Supreme Court cases are also published in West's *Supreme Court Reporter* (S.Ct.), which is an unofficial edition of Supreme Court opinions dating from the Court's term in October 1882. In this reporter, the case report—the formal court opinion— is preceded by a **syllabus** (summary of the case) and headnotes with key numbers (used throughout the West reporters and digests) prepared by West editors. This reporter, like the others, can be accessed through online legal search services, as discussed later in the chapter.

The *Lawyers' Edition of the Supreme Court Reports*

The *Lawyers' Edition of the Supreme Court Reports* (L.Ed. or L.Ed.2d) is an unofficial edition of the entire series of the Supreme Court reports containing many decisions not reported in early official volumes. It is published online on LexisNexis. The advantage offered to the legal researcher by the *Lawyers' Edition* is its research tools. In its second series, it precedes each case report with a summary of the case and discusses in detail selected cases of special interest to the legal profession. Also, the *Lawyers' Edition* is the only reporter of Supreme Court opinions that provides summaries of the briefs presented by counsel. (You can find the *Lawyers' Edition* online.)

syllabus
A brief summary of the holding and legal principles involved in a reported case, which is followed by the court's official opinion.

Analyzing Case Law

Attorneys often rely heavily on case law to support a position or argument. One of the difficulties all legal professionals face in analyzing case law is the length and complexity of many court opinions. While some opinions may be only two or three pages long, others can be hundreds of pages in length. Understanding the components of a case—that is, the basic format in which cases are presented—can simplify your task of reading and analyzing case law. Over time, as you acquire experience, case analysis becomes easier. This section focuses on how to read and analyze cases, as well as how to summarize, or *brief,* a case.

social MEDIA TODAY

Keep up to date by regularly checking the "Alerts and Security Tips" section of the **US-CERT.gov** (United States Computer Emergency Readiness Team) Web page.

The Components of a Case

Reported cases contain much more than just the court's decision. Cases have different parts, and you should know why each part is there and what information it communicates. To illustrate the various components of a case, we present an annotated sample court case in Exhibit 7.7 starting on the next page. This exhibit shows an actual case that was decided by the Supreme Court of Nebraska.

Important sections, terms, and phrases in the case are defined or explained in the margins. You will note also that triple asterisks (* * *) and quadruple asterisks (* * * *) frequently appear in the exhibit. The triple asterisks indicate that we have deleted a few words or sentences from the opinion for the sake of readability or brevity. Quadruple asterisks mean that an entire paragraph (or more) has been omitted. Also, when the opinion cites another case or legal source, the citation to the referenced case or source has been omitted to save space and to improve readability.

Following Exhibit 7.7, we discuss the various parts of a case. As you read through the descriptions of these parts, refer to the exhibit, which illustrates most of them. Remember, though, that the excerpt presented in Exhibit 7.7, because it has been pared down for illustration, may be much easier to read than many court opinions that you will encounter.

EXHIBIT 7.7   A Sample Court Case

This section contains the case citation—the name of the case, the name of the court that heard the case, the year of the court's decision, and the reporters in which the court's decision can be found.

→ Thomas & Thomas Court Reporters, L.L.C., appellee,

v.

Douglas Switzer, an individual, and Hathaway Switzer, L.L.C., appellants.

Supreme Court of Nebraska, 2012

810 N.W.2d 677, 283 Neb. 19 (Neb.)

The *docket number* assigned by the Supreme Court of Nebraska.

→ No. S-11-029

The *syllabus*—a brief summary of proceedings. Most reported cases will provide more detail than is seen here.

→ Appeal from the District Court for Douglas County: Gregory M. Schatz, Judge.

Affirmed in part, and in part reversed and remanded with directions.

Names of counsel for defendant-appellants and for plaintiff-appellee. *Pro se* means the defendant, Switzer, is representing himself and his firm.

→ Douglas Switzer and Richard P. Hathaway, of Hathaway Switzer, L.L.C., *pro se*.

Ronald E. Reagan, of Reagan, Melton & Delaney, L.L.P., for appellee.

Names of members of the Supreme Court of Nebraska.

→ Heavican, C.J., Wright, Connolly, Gerrard, Stephan,

McCormack, and Miller-Lerman, JJ.

Name of the member of the Supreme Court of Nebraska who authored the opinion of the court.

→ GERRARD, J.

Brief overview provided by the court.

→ Thomas & Thomas Court Reporters, L.L.C. (Thomas & Thomas), sued Douglas Switzer, an attorney, and his law firm, Hathaway Switzer, L.L.C. (Hathaway Switzer), for failure to pay for court reporting services. The primary issue presented in this appeal is whether Hathaway Switzer is liable to Thomas & Thomas for its fees or whether Hathaway Switzer's clients are. We conclude that Hathaway Switzer is liable.

The court divides the opinion into parts, beginning with the facts of the case that were developed at trial.

→ FACTS

Thomas & Thomas sued Switzer and Hathaway Switzer for failure to pay for court reporting services provided in five cases between January 28 and October 14, 2009. * * * Thomas & Thomas alleged that it was owed a total of $5,992. * * *

In an answer, Switzer individually and Hathaway Switzer denied that they requested services from Thomas & Thomas. * * * Hathaway Switzer alleged that it acted as an agent for its clients in its interactions with Thomas & Thomas. As an affirmative defense, Switzer asserted that Thomas & Thomas had no claim against

EXHIBIT 7.7   A Sample Court Case—Continued

him as an individual because he interacted with Thomas & Thomas only as a member of a limited liability company. * * *

A bench trial was held. At trial, one of the owners of Thomas & Thomas, John Thomas, testified that he had been a court reporter for 35 years and that his wife and co-owner had been a court reporter for 33 years. Thomas explained the procedure used to retain Thomas & Thomas' services. In most cases, a law firm telephones Thomas & Thomas to schedule a deposition. Thomas & Thomas asks the law firm to send it a notice. The deposition request is entered in Thomas & Thomas' billing and scheduling software, which generates a confirmation sheet. The confirmation is faxed or e-mailed to the law firm that requested the services.

Thomas stated that if he had been advised that Hathaway Switzer would not be responsible for services provided for its clients, he would have either demanded cash on delivery, obtained payment before the deposition, or declined the assignment. * * *

The district court entered judgment for Thomas & Thomas. The court noted Thomas & Thomas' evidence that the industry standard in the local community is that the attorney is primarily responsible for the cost of court reporting services, absent an agreement to the contrary. The court found no evidence that Hathaway Switzer had informed Thomas & Thomas that the clients would be responsible for payment until after all the invoices were presented to Hathaway Switzer. * * * The court entered judgment against Switzer and Hathaway Switzer in the amount of $5,992, along with costs . . . .

| Major section laying out the complaint on appeal. |

ASSIGNMENTS OF ERROR

Switzer and Hathaway Switzer assign * * * that the district court erred in finding (1) that Hathaway Switzer was a party to a contract with Thomas & Thomas and therefore liable for payment, when Thomas & Thomas had notice that Hathaway Switzer was acting as an agent for a disclosed principal and Hathaway Switzer had disclaimed contractual liability by its prior course of dealing with Thomas & Thomas, and (2) that Switzer was liable to Thomas & Thomas although it presented no evidence to pierce Hathaway Switzer's company veil. * * *

| Major section noting the focus of the court in an appeal. |

STANDARD OF REVIEW

A suit for damages arising from breach of a contract presents an action at law. In a bench trial of a law action, the trial court's factual findings have the effect of a jury verdict and will not be disturbed on appeal unless clearly wrong. * * * When

Continued

EXHIBIT 7.7   A Sample Court Case—Continued

reviewing questions of law, however, we have an obligation to resolve the questions independently of the conclusion reached by the trial court. * * *

Major section that summarizes the issues before the court on appeal.

ANALYSIS

There is no dispute in this case that someone owes Thomas & Thomas money. The question is, who? Hathaway Switzer contends that its clients are the real debtors. And Switzer contends that even if Hathaway Switzer is liable, he is not liable, in an individual capacity, for the company's debt. We address each argument in turn.

Discussion of the first major issue before the court on appeal.

HATHAWAY SWITZER'S LIABILITY

Hathaway Switzer's argument rests upon basic principles of agency law. The general rule is that when a party contracts with a known agent acting within the scope of his or her authority for a disclosed principal, the contract is that of the principal only and the agent cannot be held personally liable thereon, unless the agent purports to bind himself or herself, or has otherwise bound himself or herself, to performance of the contract. * * *

There is little question that the relationship between attorney and client is one of agency and that the general agency rules of law apply to the relation of attorney and client. Thus, a client may be liable for the acts of the client's attorney when such was within the attorney's scope of authority. But, while general agency rules apply to the attorney-client relationship, there is much more involved than mere agency. The attorney, not the client, is responsible for performing the details of litigation.

Thus, the *Restatement (Third) of the Law Governing Lawyers* provides that unless a lawyer or third person disclaims such liability at the time of contracting, a lawyer is subject to liability to third persons on contracts entered into on behalf of a client if "the contract is between the lawyer and a third person who provides goods or services used by lawyers and who, as the lawyer knows or reasonably should know, relies on the lawyer's credit." * * *

As a practical matter, in today's legal system, an attorney dealing with those who provide legal support services acts less as an agent who relies on the client for authority to manage the case, and more as a "general contractor," albeit a professional, who is responsible for supervising the various aspects of litigation. In that context, it is appropriate that the attorney, with superior legal knowledge and familiarity with the case and client, should bear the burden of clarifying his or her intent regarding payment. It is, in fact, a relatively simple matter for an attorney to

EXHIBIT 7.7   A Sample Court Case—Continued

disclaim liability with a clear statement to that effect. And an attorney's liability for (and payment of) expenses of litigation is consistent with our ethical rules. * * *

| Discussion of the second major issue before the court on appeal. | → | SWITZER'S LIABILITY |

SWITZER'S LIABILITY

Switzer also argues that the court erred in holding him individually liable, essentially piercing Hathaway Switzer's "corporate veil," or company veil in this case. We find more merit to this point.

Thomas & Thomas specifically alleged that Hathaway Switzer is a limited liability company, and that fact is undisputed. Thomas & Thomas also alleged that Switzer was the party "personally engaging the services" of Thomas & Thomas, but this allegation was denied by Switzer. And Switzer repeatedly alleged that he had not, in his individual capacity, retained Thomas & Thomas' services. Switzer also raised an affirmative defense based on his allegation that he interacted with Thomas & Thomas only in his capacity as a member of Hathaway Switzer. * * * Nonetheless, without specifically discussing the issue, the court entered judgment against both Hathaway Switzer and Switzer individually.

But the individual members and managers of a limited liability company are generally not liable for a debt, obligation, or liability of the company. And a court will disregard such a company's identity only where the company has been used to commit fraud, violate a legal duty, or perpetrate a dishonest or unjust act in contravention of the rights of another. * * *

No such proof was presented here. * * * In short, the record does not contain sufficient evidence (or, indeed, any evidence) to support the court's judgment against Switzer in an individual capacity. So, we find merit to this assignment of error. * * * *

| Last major section of the opinion. The court states its conclusion and issues its order. | → | CONCLUSION |

CONCLUSION

We find no merit to Hathaway Switzer's claim that it was not liable for the services provided by Thomas & Thomas. * * * But we find that the court erred in entering judgment against Switzer individually. The court's judgment, to the extent that it holds Hathaway Switzer liable in the sum of $5,992, is affirmed. The judgment is reversed to the extent that it holds Switzer personally liable, and the cause is remanded to the district court with directions to dismiss Thomas & Thomas' claim against Switzer as an individual.

Affirmed in part, and in part reversed and remanded with directions.

Case Title

The title of a case indicates the names of the parties to the lawsuit, and the *v.* in the case title stands for *versus,* or "against." In the trial court, the plaintiff's last name appears first, and the second name is the defendant's. If the case is appealed, however, the appellate court will *sometimes* place the name of the party appealing the decision first, so the parties' names may be reversed. Because some appellate courts retain the trial court order of names, it is often impossible to distinguish the plaintiff from the defendant in the title of a reported appellate court decision. One must carefully read the facts of each case to identify the parties.

Case Citation

Typically, the citation to the case is found just above or just below the case title (and often at the tops of consecutive printed or online pages). If the citation appears on Westlaw and one of the parallel citations is not yet available, the citation may include underlined spaces for the volume and page numbers to be filled in once they become available (such as "___ U.S. ___").

Docket Number

The docket number immediately follows the case title. A docket number is assigned by the court clerk when a case is initially filed. The number serves as an identifier for all papers submitted in connection with the case. A case published in a reporter should not be cited by its docket number, but the number may serve as a valuable tool in obtaining background information on the case.

Cases appearing in slip-opinion form (decisions that have been decided but not yet published in a reporter) are usually identified, filed, and cited by docket number. After publication of the decision, the docket number may continue to serve as an identifier for appellate records and briefs (appellate briefs will be discussed in Chapter 9). There may be changes to correct typographical mistakes made between the initial slip opinion and the reported decision, or the court may change its mind on a matter of substance and withdraw the opinion. Always check to see whether there is a later, reported version of a slip opinion you find during your research to ensure you are citing the correct version of the opinion.

Dates Argued and Decided

An important component of a case is the date on which it was decided by the court. Usually, the date of the decision immediately follows the docket number. In addition to the date of the court's decision on the matter, the date on which the case was argued before the court (in appellate court cases) may also be included here.

Syllabus

Following the docket number is the *syllabus*—a brief synopsis of the facts of the case, the issues analyzed by the court, and the court's conclusion. In official reporters, the courts usually prepare the syllabi. In unofficial reporters, the publishers of the reporters usually prepare them. The syllabus is often a helpful research tool. It provides an overview of the case and points out legal issues discussed by the court. In a few states, such as Ohio, the official syllabus has precedential value. In most states, the syllabus is not binding. In all cases, you should always keep in mind that reading the syllabus is not a substitute for reading the case if the case is relevant.

Headnotes

Often, unofficial reporters, such as those published by West, make extensive use of case *headnotes.* As discussed earlier, headnotes are short paragraphs that highlight and summarize specific rules of law mentioned in the case. In reporters published by West, they are correlated to the comprehensive West key-number system. In Exhibit 7.7, the headnotes were deleted for reasons of space.

social
MEDIA TODAY

You can set Google Alerts to check for mentions of your name on the Web.

Names of Counsel

The published report of the case usually contains the names of the lawyers (counsel) representing the parties. The attorneys' names are typically found just following the syllabus (and headnotes, if any).

Name of Judge or Justice Authoring the Opinion

The name of the judge or justice who authored the opinion in the case will also be included in the published report of the case, just before the court's opinion. In some cases, instead of the name of a judge or justice, the decision will be authored *per curiam* (Latin for "by the court"), which means that the opinion is that of the whole court and not the opinion of any one judge or justice. Sometimes the phrase is used to indicate that the chief justice or presiding judge wrote the opinion. The phrase also may be used for an announcement of a court's disposition of a case that is not accompanied by a written opinion.

Opinion

As you may have noticed, the term *opinion* is often used loosely to refer to a court case or decision. In fact, the term has a precise meaning. The opinion of the court contains the analysis and decision of the judge or judges who heard and decided the case. Most opinions contain a brief statement of the facts of the case, a summary of the legal issues raised by the facts, and the remedies sought by the parties.

In appellate court cases, the court summarizes the errors of the lower court, if any, and the impact of these errors on the case's outcome. The main body of the opinion is the application of the law to the particular facts. The court often mentions case precedents, relevant statutes, and administrative rules to support its reasoning. Additionally, court opinions may contain discussions of policy and other factors that clarify the reason for the court's decision. The various kinds of opinions that may be issued by an appeals court are noted in Exhibit 7.8 below.

The Court's Conclusion

In the opinion, the judges indicate their conclusion, or decision, on the issue or issues before the court. If several issues are involved, as often happens, there may be a conclusion at the end of the discussion of each issue. Often, at the end of the opinion, the conclusions are briefly summarized.

EXHIBIT 7.8
Types of Appellate Court Decisions

Concurring: When one or more judges deciding a case agree with the decision of the majority, they may provide different reasons to support the decision or wish to emphasize a particular point.

Dissenting: When one or more judges disagree with the decision of the majority, the dissenters may write an explanation of why the result should have been different. These can be important as persuasive authority later should the holding in the case be limited or overturned. They are also important as signals that the law in a particular area may not be completely settled.

Majority: An opinion that represents the views of the majority of the judges who decide a case, either affirming or reversing the decision of the lower court.

Memorandum: An opinion in a case that does not create precedent.

Plurality: When there is no single opinion that receives the support of a majority of the judges on a court, the plurality is the opinions receiving the most votes. This often happens when a majority agrees on the outcome but for incompatible reasons.

Unanimous: When all judges on a court (or the panel of judges assigned to hear an appeal) agree on the legal reasoning and decision.

© Cengage Learning 2014

An appellate court also specifies what the *disposition* of a case should be. If the court agrees with a lower court's decision, it will *affirm* that decision, which means that the decision of the lower court remains unchanged. If the appellate court concludes that the lower court erred in its interpretation of the law, the court may *reverse* the lower court's ruling.

Sometimes an appellate court concludes that further factual findings are necessary or that a case should be retried and a decision made that is consistent with the appellate court's conclusions of law. Then, the appellate court will *remand* the case to the lower court for further proceedings consistent with its opinion. In the sample case presented in Exhibit 7.7 on pages 202 through 205, the Nebraska Supreme Court affirmed part of the lower court's decision, reversed a part, and remanded the case to the court for further disposition.

Analyzing Cases

When you are researching case law, your main focus should be on the opinion—the words of the court itself. Some opinions are easier to understand than others. Some judges write more clearly and logically than do others. You may need to reread a case (or a portion of a case) to understand what is being said, why it is being said at that point in the case, and what the judge's legal reasoning is.

Some cases contain several pages describing facts and issues of previous cases and how those cases relate to the one being decided by the court. You might want to reread these discussions several times to distinguish between comments made in the previous case and comments that are being made about the case at bar (before the court).

Look for Guideposts in the Opinion

Often, the judge writing the opinion provides some guideposts, perhaps by indicating sections and subsections within the opinion by numbers, letters, or subtitles. Note that in Exhibit 7.7 on pages 202 through 205, subheadings are used to divide the opinion into basic sections. Scanning through the opinion for these types of indicators can help orient you to the opinion's format.

In cases that involve dissenting or concurring opinions, make sure that you identify these opinions so that you do not mistake one of them for the majority opinion. Generally, you should scan through the case a time or two to identify its components and then read the case (or sections of the case) until you understand the facts and procedural history of the case, the issues involved, the applicable law, the legal reasoning of the court, and how the reasoning leads to the court's conclusion on the issues.

Distinguish the Court's Holding from *Dicta*

holding
The binding legal principle, or precedent, that is drawn from the court's decision in a case.

dicta
A Latin term referring to nonbinding (nonprecedential) judicial statements that are not directly related to the facts or issues presented in the case and thus are not essential to the holding.

When analyzing cases, you should determine which statements of the court are legally binding and which are not. Only the **holding** (the legal principle to be drawn from the court's decision) is binding. Other views expressed in the opinion are referred to as **dicta** and are not binding.

Dicta is the plural of *dictum*. *Dictum* is an abbreviated form of the Latin term *obiter dictum*, which means "a remark by the way." *Dicta* are statements made in a decision that go beyond the facts of the case or that do not directly relate to the facts or to the resolution of the issue being addressed. *Dicta* include comments used by the court to illustrate an example and statements concerning a rule of law not essential to the case. You can probably assume that statements are *dicta* if they begin with "If the facts were different" or "If the plaintiff had . . ." or some other "if/then" phrase.

Summarizing and Briefing Cases

After you have read and analyzed a case, you may decide that it is on point and that you want to include a reference to it in your research findings. If so, you will summarize in your notes the important facts and issues in the case, as well as the court's decision, or holding, and the reasoning used by the court. This is called **briefing a case**.

briefing a case
Summarizing a case. A case brief gives the full citation, the factual background and procedural history, the issue or issues raised, the court's decision, the court's holding, and the legal reasoning on which the court based its decision. It may also include conclusions or notes concerning the case made by the one briefing it.

There is a fairly standard procedure for briefing court cases. First, read the case opinion carefully. When you feel you understand the case, begin to prepare the brief. Typically, a brief presents the essentials of the case under headings such as those listed below. Many researchers conclude their briefs with an additional section in which they note their own comments or conclusions about the case.

1. **Citation.** Give the full citation for the case, including the name of the case, the date it was decided, and the court that decided it.

2. **Facts.** Briefly indicate (a) the reasons for the lawsuit (who did what to whom) and (b) the identity and arguments of the plaintiff(s) and defendant(s).

3. **Procedure.** Indicate the procedural history of the case in a sentence or two. What was the lower court's decision? What did the appellate court do (affirm, reverse, remand)? How did the matter arrive before the present court?

4. **Issue.** State, in the form of a question, the essential issue before the court. (If more than one issue is involved, you may have two—or even more—questions here.)

5. **Decision.** Indicate here—with a "yes" or "no," if possible—the court's answer to the question (or questions) that you noted in the *Issue* section.

6. **Reasoning.** Summarize as briefly as possible the reasons given by the court for its decision (or decisions) and the case or statutory law relied on by the court in arriving at its decision.

7. **Holding.** State the rule of law for which the case stands.

Exhibit 7.9 on the following page presents a briefed version of the sample court case presented in Exhibit 7.7. This brief illustrates the typical format used in briefing cases.

IRAC: A Method for Briefing Cases

Besides the example just provided, another standard format for briefing cases is called the *IRAC method*, referring to *issue, rule, application,* and *conclusion*. This method, which will be discussed more in Chapter 9, involves the following steps:

1. First, decide what legal *issues* are involved in the case. For the case presented in Exhibit 7.7 on pages 202 through 205, these are identified under "Issues" in the case briefing in Exhibit 7.9 on the next page.

2. Next, determine the *rule of law* that applies to the issues. In Exhibit 7.9, the rule of law is discussed under "Reasoning."

3. After identifying the applicable law, determine the *application* of the law to the facts of the case. In Exhibit 7.9, the "Holding" section deals with the court's application of the law.

4. Finally, draw a *conclusion*. Exhibit 7.9 calls that the "Decision." It is the determination of the court after it has applied the law to the case.

Different lawyers and law offices have different preferences for the format to be used in briefing cases. What is most important is accuracy in explaining the key facts, the issues under consideration, the rule of law or legal reasoning used by the court, the application of the law, and the conclusion resulting from that application.

Researching Constitutional and Statutory Law

Up to this point, we have been discussing case law, which is sometimes called *judge-made* law because it is made by the judges in the state and federal court systems. Judge-made law is also known as the common law, as explained in Chapter 5 on

EXHIBIT 7.9
A Briefed Version of the
Sample Court Case

THOMAS & THOMAS COURT REPORTERS, L.L.C., v. DOUGLAS SWITZER AND HATHAWAY SWITZER

283 Neb. 19, 810 N.W.2d 677 (Sup. Ct. Neb., 2012)

FACTS Thomas & Thomas performed court reporting services for the law firm of Hathaway Switzer, L.L.C., and billed it $5,992 for its services. Hathaway Switzer alleged it never requested services from Thomas & Thomas. In contrast, its clients had requested the services and they should be liable. Hathaway Switzer claimed it was merely an agent acting on behalf of its clients. It also claimed that due to pervious dealings, Thomas & Thomas was aware of its agency relationship with clients. Hathaway Switzer did not pay the outstanding bill.

PROCEDURE Thomas & Thomas Court Reporters, L.L.C., sued Douglas Switzer and his law firm, Hathaway Switzer, L.L.C., for failure to pay court reporting services and for attorney's fees. The District Court entered judgment against Switzer and Hathaway Switzer in the amount of $5,992, along with costs. Switzer and Hathaway Switzer appealed to the Supreme Court of Nebraska.

ISSUES (1) Was Hathaway Switzer liable to Thomas & Thomas for its fees or were Hathaway Switzer's clients liable? (2) Was Douglas Switzer personally liable for the fees owed by his law firm, Hathaway Switzer?

DECISION (1) Hathaway Switzer, L.L.C., is liable and not its clients. (2) Douglas Switzer is not personally liable.

REASONING Under the *Restatement (Third) of the Law Governing Lawyers,* unless a lawyer or third person disclaims liability at the time of contracting, a lawyer is subject to liability to third persons on contracts entered into on behalf of a client. This is so if "the contract is between the lawyer and a third person who provides goods or services used by lawyers and who, as the lawyer knows or reasonably should know, relies on the lawyer's credit." Individual members and managers of a limited liability company are generally not liable for a debt, obligation, or liability of the company. A court will disregard a company's identity only where the company has been used to commit fraud, violate a legal duty, or perpetrate a dishonest or unjust act in contravention of the rights of another.

HOLDING The attorney, not the client, is responsible for performing the details of litigation; therefore, Hathaway Switzer is liable to Thomas & Thomas for the court reporting services. There was not sufficient evidence to support the court's judgment against Switzer in an individual capacity.

page 124. Another primary source of law is *statutory law*—the statutes and ordinances enacted by legislative bodies, such as the U.S. Congress, state legislatures, and town governments.

Congress draws its authority to enact federal legislation from the U.S. Constitution. A state legislature draws its authority from the state constitution. In some legal disputes, the constitutionality of a statute or government action may be an issue. In such instances, you may have to go behind the statutes to the relevant constitution, so we look at constitutional law before going into detail about statutes.

Finding Constitutional Law

The federal government and all fifty states have constitutions describing the powers, responsibilities, and limitations of the various branches of government. Constitutions, especially state constitutions, are amended over time. All are available online.

A useful source of federal constitutional law is *The Constitution of the United States of America,* published under the authority of the U.S. Senate and available through the Library of Congress. It includes the U.S. Constitution, corresponding annotations concerning United States Supreme Court decisions interpreting the Constitution, and a discussion of each provision, including background information on its history and interpretation.

Additional constitutional sources are found in the *United States Code Annotated* and the *United States Code Service,* which contain the text of the Constitution and its amendments as well as citations to cases discussing particular constitutional provisions. We discuss these publications shortly, and they are available online. Annotated state codes provide a similar service for state constitutions. Constitutional annotations are updated through supplementary pocket parts. State constitutions are usually included in the publications containing state statutes.

Finding Statutory Law

Some statutes supplement the common law, while other statutes replace it. State legislatures and the U.S. Congress have broad powers in establishing law. If a common law principle conflicts with a statutory provision, the statute will normally take precedence. Additionally, a legislature may create statutes that deal with areas, such as age discrimination, that are not covered by the common law.

Statutes are often published in compilations referred to as **codes**, which arrange materials by topic. Most statutory codes are updated through the issuance of supplemental pocket parts or by loose-leaf services. Paralegals conducting research on statutory law should begin by reviewing the index for the relevant statutory code. Familiarize yourself with the dates the relevant legislature is in session, as you will want to investigate whether or not a relevant statute has been amended. Online legal research services such as Westlaw and Lexis include a note about how up-to-date their coverage is. Printed services are also available.

code
A systematic and topically organized presentation of laws, rules, or regulations.

Federal Statutes

Federal statutes are contained in the *United States Code,* or U.S.C. This official compilation of federal statutes is published by the U.S. government every six years and is updated annually. The U.S.C. is divided into fifty topic classifications. As shown in Exhibit 7.10 on the following page, each of these topics, called *titles,* carries a descriptive name and a number.

For example, laws relating to commerce and trade are in Title 15. Laws concerning the courts and judicial procedures are in Title 28. Titles are divided into chapters (sections) and subchapters. A citation to the U.S.C. includes title and section numbers. Thus, a reference to "28 U.S.C. Section 1346" means that the statute can be found in Section 1346 of Title 28. "Section" may also be designated by the symbol §, and "Sections" by §§.

NAMES OF STATUTES. Statutes are listed in the U.S.C. by their official names. Many legislative bills enacted into law are commonly known by a popular name, however. Some have descriptive titles reflecting their purpose. Others are named after their sponsors.

Sometimes a researcher may know the popular name of a legislative act but not its official name. In this situation, the researcher can consult the U.S.C. volume entitled *Popular Name Table,* which lists statutes by their popular names. For example, suppose you have learned that the Landrum-Griffin Act governs an issue that you are researching. This is the popular name for the act, not the official name. You can consult the *Popular Name Table* to find the act's official title, which is the Labor-Management Reporting and Disclosure Act of 1959. In online searches on Google, Bing, and other search engines, you would want to use both names.

UNOFFICIAL VERSIONS OF U.S. CODE. There are also two unofficial versions of the federal code, each of which contains additional information that is helpful to researchers. West's *United States Code Annotated* (U.S.C.A.) contains the full text of the U.S.C., the U.S. Constitution, the Federal Rules of Evidence, and various

EXHIBIT 7.10

Titles in the *United States Code*

TITLES OF UNITED STATES CODE

*1. General Provisions.	27. Intoxicating Liquors.
2. The Congress.	*28. Judiciary and Judicial Procedure; and Appendix.
*3. The President.	
*4. Flag and Seal, Seat of Government, and the States.	29. Labor.
	30. Mineral Lands and Mining.
*5. Government Organization and Employees; and Appendix.	*31. Money and Finance.
	*32. National Guard.
†6. [Surety Bonds.]	33. Navigation and Navigable Waters.
7. Agriculture.	
8. Aliens and Nationality.	‡34. [Navy.]
*9. Arbitration.	*35. Patents.
*10. Armed Forces; and Appendix.	36. Patriotic Societies and Observances.
*11. Bankruptcy; and Appendix.	*37. Pay and Allowances of the Uniformed Services.
12. Banks and Banking.	
*13. Census.	*38. Veterans' Benefits.
*14. Coast Guard.	*39. Postal Service.
15. Commerce and Trade.	40. Public Buildings, Property, and Works.
16. Conservation.	41. Public Contracts.
*17. Copyrights.	42. The Public Health and Welfare.
*18. Crimes and Criminal Procedure; and Appendix.	43. Public Lands.
	*44. Public Printing and Documents.
19. Customs Duties.	45. Railroads.
20. Education.	*46. Shipping; and Appendix.
21. Food and Drugs.	47. Telegraphs, Telephones, and Radiotelegraphs.
22. Foreign Relations and Intercourse.	
*23. Highways.	48. Territories and Insular Possessions.
24. Hospitals and Asylums.	*49. Transportation; and Appendix.
25. Indians.	50. War and National Defense; and Appendix.
26. Internal Revenue Code.	

*This title has been enacted as law. However, any Appendix to this title has not been enacted as law.
†This title was enacted as law and has been repealed by the enactment of Title 31.
‡This title has been eliminated by the enactment of Title 10.

Page III

other rules, including the Rules of Civil Procedure and the Rules of Criminal Procedure. This useful set of approximately two hundred volumes includes historical notes relating to the text of each statute, along with any amendments to the act. Annotations offer additional assistance by listing cases that have analyzed, discussed, or interpreted the particular statute.

The other unofficial version of the code is the *United States Code Service* (U.S.C.S.), also published by West. The U.S.C.S. and the U.S.C.A. provide somewhat different research tools. For example, the U.S.C.S. contains references and citations to some sources, such as legal periodicals and the legal encyclopedia *American Jurisprudence*, that are not included in the U.S.C.A. Both codes are available on Westlaw and Lexis.

State Statutes

State codes follow the U.S.C. pattern of arranging statutes by subject. Depending on the state, they may be called codes, revisions, compilations, consolidations, general statutes, or statutes.

In some codes, subjects are designated by number. In others, they are designated by name. For example, "13 Pennsylvania Consolidated Statutes Section 1101" means that the statute can be found in Section 1101 of Title 13 of the Pennsylvania code. "California Commercial Code Section 1101" means that the statute can be found in Section 1101 under the heading "Commercial" in the California Code. Abbreviations may be used. For example, "13 Pennsylvania Consolidated Statutes Section 1101" may be abbreviated to "13 Pa.C.S. § 1101," and "California Commercial Code Section 1101" may be abbreviated to "Cal. Com. Code § 1101."

In many states, official codes are supplemented by annotated codes published by private publishers. Annotated codes follow the numbering scheme set forth in the official state code but provide outlines, explanations, and indexes to assist in locating information. These codes also provide references to case law, legislative history sources, and other documents in which the statute has been considered or discussed.

Analyzing Statutory Law

Because of the tremendous growth in statutory and regulatory law in the last century, the legal issues dealt with by attorneys are often governed by statutes and administrative agency regulations. Paralegals must understand how to interpret and analyze this body of law. Although we use the terms *statute* and *statutory law* in this section, the following discussion applies equally well to regulations issued by administrative agencies.

Two Steps in Statutory Analysis

To determine how well a statute applies to the legal issues in your case, you must understand the statute. The first step in statutory analysis is therefore to read the language of the statute.

As with court cases, some statutes are more difficult to read than others. Some are extremely wordy or lengthy or difficult to understand for some other reason. By carefully reading a statute, however, you can usually determine:

- the reasons for the statute's enactment,
- the date on which it became effective,
- the class of parties to which the statute applies,
- the kind of conduct regulated by the statute, and
- the circumstances in which that conduct is prohibited, required, or permitted.

You can also learn whether the statute allows for exceptions and, if so, in what circumstances.

The second step in statutory analysis is to interpret the meaning of the statute. Generally, when trying to understand the meaning of statutes, you should do as the courts do. We therefore now look at some of the techniques used by courts when faced with the task of interpreting the meaning of a given statute or statutory provision. Some practical tips for reading statutes are provided in the *Developing Paralegal Skills* feature on the following page.

Previous Judicial Interpretation

Researching statutory law also involves researching case law to see how the courts have interpreted and applied statutory provisions. As discussed, courts are obligated to follow the precedents set by higher courts in their jurisdictions. A statutory interpretation made by a higher court therefore must be accepted as binding by lower courts in the same jurisdiction. You can find citations to court cases relating to specific statutes by referring to annotated versions of state or federal statutory codes, such as the U.S.C.A., both in print and online.

Legislative Intent

Another technique used in statutory interpretation is learning the intent of the legislature. A court relying on this method determines the meaning of the statute by attempting to find out why the legislators chose to word the statute as they did or,

DEVELOPING
paralegal skills

READING STATUTORY LAW

Statutes are a major source of law at both the state and federal level. Being able to read statutes properly is a crucial skill for paralegals (and lawyers!). Reading and understanding a statute, however, is not the same as reading a court decision. It takes application of special techniques (called principles of statutory interpretation) to properly interpret a statute. Here are five of the most important principles:

1. **The Plain Meaning Rule.** If the language of a statute is clear, the court applies the language as written. While this rule seems obvious and easy to employ, it is not, because courts and agencies often stumble over how to interpret particular words in a statute.

2. **Read a Statute as a Whole.** Provisions in different parts of a statute should be interpreted to fit together, not conflict. As a result, understanding a statute will usually require you to look at all of the statute, not just a single section. A good first stop is to skim the statute quickly, noting the organizational structure, location of definition sections, and other key elements.

3. **Statutory Definitions Govern.** When a statute includes a specific definition, or an area of law uses a word as a term of art, that meaning will be used in interpreting the statute.

Dictionary definitions are guides when there is no statutory definition, but dictionaries differ and the meaning of words can shift over time.

The Supreme Court has relied on dictionaries in more than 600 cases. Dictionaries are becoming increasingly important in decisions. You should check to see if a particular dictionary is recognized as authoritative by the court involved, and should use an edition of the dictionary that was current at the time legislation was drafted. *Just Googling a word is not acceptable research technique.*

4. **Distinguish between "and" and "or."** When a list of requirements in a statute uses "and," all of the things in the list must be satisfied. When the list in a statute uses "or," only one of the items in a list must be satisfied.

5. **"Shall" does not mean "may" and "may" does not mean "shall."** When a statute uses the word "shall," it will be interpreted as requiring a particular action. When a statute uses the word "may," it will be interpreted as allowing discretion.

Like any area of the law, learning how to do statutory interpretation takes practice and effort. The most important concept to remember is that you must read statutes carefully and look at the entire statute, not just one provision.

---

more generally, what the legislators sought to accomplish by enacting the statute. To learn the intent of the legislators who wrote a particular law, it is often necessary to investigate the legislative history of the statute. This can be done by researching such sources as committee reports and records of congressional hearings and other proceedings.

Committee Reports

Committee reports provide the most important source of legislative history. Congressional committees produce reports for each bill, and these reports often contain the full text of the bill, a description of its purpose, and the committee's recommendations. Several tables are also included to set out dates for certain actions. The dates can help the researcher locate floor debates and committee testimony in the *Congressional Record* and other publications. Committee reports are published according to a numerical series and are available through the U.S. Government Printing Office, which is accessible online.

Other Sources of Legislative History

The two tools most frequently used in conducting research on legislative history are the *United States Code Congressional and Administrative News* (U.S.C.C.A.N.) and the Thomas Web site.

The U.S.C.C.A.N., a West publication, contains reprints of statutes and sections describing the statutes' legislative history, including committee reports. Statutes in the U.S.C.A. are followed by notations directing the researcher to the corresponding legislative history in the U.S.C.C.A.N. The Library of Congress's Thomas site (**thomas.loc.gov**) provides access to committee reports, the text of Congressional bills, and the *Congressional Record*, which is published daily while Congress is in session. This publication contains the text of congressional debates and proceedings.

While our focus here has been on existing statutes and related materials, there are times when we need to know what may be coming. Resources devoted to new developments are reviewed in *Technology and Today's Paralegal* below.

Researching Administrative Law

Administrative rules and regulations constitute a growing source of American law. As discussed in Chapter 5, Congress frequently delegates authority to administrative agencies through enabling legislation. For example, in 1914 Congress passed the Federal Trade Commission Act, which established the Federal Trade Commission, or FTC. The act gave the FTC the authority to issue and enforce

TECHNOLOGY AND
today's paralegal

LOOKING AHEAD

Every day, it seems, legislatures propose or pass new laws, administrative agencies propose or issue new regulations, and new cases begin to work their way through the court system. A few of these may reach the nation's highest court. As a paralegal, you can perform a valuable service for your supervising attorney by keeping up with new developments in the legal arena or in your specialty area.

WHAT NEW FEDERAL STATUTES ARE LIKELY TO BE ENACTED?

You can keep up to date on what bills are pending in Congress by subscribing to e-newsletters published by law firms, think tanks, and interest groups.

Washington-based think tanks often follow specific areas, and their e-newsletters and blogs include useful information on the progress of pending legislation. There are no guarantees that the information on such sites is up-to-date or accurate, so be careful to read the actual legislation rather than relying on a third-party account. Law firms with specific practice areas also monitor legislation. Use a legal directory to identify major Washington firms in the practice area you are interested in and then explore their firm Web site for free newsletters. Finally, as noted above, the Library of Congress's Web site, Thomas, tracks pending legislation

(**thomas.loc.gov/home/thomas.php**). Web searches (using a service such as Google, Yahoo!, or Bing) can also help you spot the mention of legislative proposals in the news media.

ARE ANY NEW UNIFORM LAWS BEING DEVELOPED?

To find out about new uniform laws being developed by the National Conference of Commissioners on Uniform State Laws (NCCUSL), you can visit its Web site at **www.nccusl.org**. There, you will find the text of all uniform acts, including every draft of the final uniform act. You can also find out which states have adopted an act and which states have legislation pending, as well as the status of the legislation.

TECHNOLOGY TIP

You can find out what cases are pending before the Supreme Court from online sources. For example, at **www.oyez.org**, you will find a list of cases that the Supreme Court has heard recently or is scheduled to hear in the current term. If you are aware of a case pending before the Court, or want to search for cases on a particular issue, you can find the case name and a brief description at this site. That way you will know if it is relevant to your search. All details of cases, including briefs, can be found at **www.supremecourt.gov**, as well as through online research services, including Westlaw and Lexis.

rules and regulations relating to unfair and deceptive trade practices in the United States. There are, of course, many other federal administrative agencies. The orders, regulations, and decisions of such agencies are legally binding and, as such, are primary sources of law.

The *Code of Federal Regulations* (C.F.R.) is a government publication containing all federal administrative agency regulations. The regulations are compiled from the *Federal Register,* a daily government publication consisting of executive orders and administrative regulations, in which regulations are first published.

The C.F.R. uses the same titles as the *United States Code* (shown previously in Exhibit 7.10 on page 212). This subject-matter organization allows the researcher to determine the section in the C.F.R. in which a regulation will appear. Each title of the C.F.R. is divided into chapters, subchapters, parts, and sections.

The C.F.R. is revised and formally republished four times a year. Recent regulations appear in the *Federal Register* until they are incorporated into the C.F.R. The online version is updated continuously. The C.F.R. is available online at the Government Printing Office's Web site (**www.gpo.gov/fdsys**).

KEY TERMS AND CONCEPTS

annotation 188	*dicta* 208	persuasive authority 186
briefing a case 209	digest 188	pocket part 187
business invitee 183	headnote 190	reporter 188
case on "all fours" 184	holding 208	slip opinion 200
case on point 184	hornbook 191	syllabus 201
citation 197	key number 188	treatise 191
code 211	parallel citation 197	

Chapter Summary

Legal Research and Analysis

RESEARCHING CASE LAW—THE PRELIMINARY STEPS

1. *Defining the issue*—The first step in research is to identify the legal question, or issue, to be researched. Often, more than one issue is involved.

2. *Determining your research goals*—In researching case law, the goal is to find cases that are on point and are binding authorities. Binding authorities are all legal authorities (statutes, regulations, constitutions, and cases) that courts must follow in making their decisions. Courts are not bound to follow persuasive authorities (such as cases decided in other jurisdictions), although courts often consider such authorities, particularly when deciding cases of first impression.

FINDING RELEVANT CASES

Primary sources of law include all documents that establish the law, including court decisions, statutes, regulations, constitutions, and presidential orders. *Secondary sources of law* are publications written about the law, such as legal encyclopedias, digests, treatises, and periodicals.

1. *Legal encyclopedias*—Legal encyclopedias provide detailed summaries of legal rules and concepts and are useful for finding background information on issues being researched. These books arrange topics alphabetically and contain citations to cases and statutes relating to the topic. Two popular legal encyclopedias are *American Jurisprudence,* Second Edition (Am. Jur. 2d), and *Corpus Juris Secundum* (C.J.S.). A third encyclopedia, *Words and Phrases,* covers legal

terms and phrases and cites cases in which the terms or phrases appear.

2. *Case digests*—Digests are compilations in which brief summaries of court cases are arranged by subject and subdivided by jurisdiction and court. They are major secondary sources of law and helpful finding tools. Digests using the West system of topic classification and key numbers provide cross-references to other West publications. Digests arrange topics alphabetically with annotations to cases on each topic but are not as detailed as encyclopedias.

3. *Annotations:* American Law Reports—The *American Law Reports* are multivolume sets that present leading cases, each followed by an annotation that discusses the key issues in the case and that refers the researcher to other sources on the issues.

4. *Other secondary sources*—Other secondary sources of law include treatises, which are scholarly publications that discuss specific areas of law. They summarize, evaluate, or interpret the law, either in a single volume or in multivolume sets. Hornbooks are single-volume treatises. *Restatements of the Law* are respected scholarly compilations of the common law. They present particular cases as examples. Legal periodicals, such as law reviews, contain articles on specific areas of law.

THE CASE REPORTING SYSTEM

The primary sources of case law are the cases themselves. Cases are published in various case reporters.

1. *State court decisions and reporters*—Most state trial court decisions are not published in printed volumes. State appellate court (including supreme court) opinions are normally published in official state reporters. Many states eliminated their own reporters in favor of West's National Reporter System, which reports state cases in its regional reporters. To locate a case in a reporter, you use the case citation. There are five parts: the case name, the volume number, the abbreviated name of the book (volume), the page number on which the decision begins, and the year the case was decided. A parallel citation may appear after the first citation when the case is reported in more than one reporter.

2. *Federal court decisions*—Federal trial court opinions are published unofficially in West's *Federal Supplement,* and opinions from the federal circuit courts of appeals are published in West's *Federal Reporter.*

3. *United States Supreme Court decisions*—Supreme Court opinions are published officially in the *United States Reports,* published by the federal government, and unofficially in West's *Supreme Court Reporter* and the *Lawyers' Edition of the Supreme Court Reports.*

ANALYZING CASE LAW

Case law is often relied upon to support positions taken in court.

1. *Components of a case*—Reported cases contain more information than just the court's decision. Typically, case formats include the following components:
   - The case title (usually plaintiff versus defendant);
   - The name of the court that decided the case;
   - The case citation;
   - The docket number assigned by the court;
   - The dates on which the case was argued and decided;
   - The syllabus (a brief summary of the facts, issues, and ruling);
   - The headnotes (short paragraphs that summarize the rules of law discussed in the case; in West's reporters, headnotes correlate with the key-number system);
   - The names of counsel;
   - The name of the judge who authored the opinion;
   - The opinion (the court's own words on the matter); and
   - The conclusion (holding, ruling).

2. *Analyzing cases*—Legal professionals often brief, or summarize, the cases they research. Knowing how to read, analyze, and summarize cases makes it easier to compare cases and bring together research results accurately and efficiently. One must distinguish holdings from *dicta.*

3. *Summarizing and briefing cases*—Although the format of briefs varies, the following headings are typical: citation, facts, procedure, issue, decision, reasoning, and holding.

4. *IRAC: A method for briefing cases*—Another format for briefing cases is IRAC, which refers to issue, rule, application, and conclusion.

RESEARCHING CONSTITUTIONAL AND STATUTORY LAW

Statutory and constitutional law are primary sources of law. Statutes are based on the constitutional authority of a legislature to enact laws in particular areas.

1. *Finding constitutional law*—The U.S. Constitution can be found in a number of publications, including *The Constitution of the United States of America* (available through the Library of Congress). Annotated versions of state constitutions are also available.

2. *Finding statutory law*—Bills and ordinances passed by legislative bodies (federal, state, and local) become statutory law. Statutes are eventually published in codes, which are updated by supplemental pocket parts and loose-leaf services and are also available online. Federal laws are published officially in the *United States Code* (U.S.C.). The U.S.C. organizes statutes into fifty subjects, or titles, and divides each title into chapters (sections) and subchapters. The *United States Code Annotated* (U.S.C.A.) and the *United States Code Service* (U.S.C.S.) are unofficial publications of federal statutes. They are useful because they provide annotations (comments) and citations to other resources. State codes follow the U.S.C. pattern of arranging statutes by subject. They may be called codes, revisions, compilations, general statutes, or statutes. In many states, official codes are supplemented by annotated codes published by private publishers.

ANALYZING STATUTORY LAW

Statutory law is often difficult to understand, so careful reading and rereading are often required to understand the meaning.

1. *Previous judicial interpretation*—To interpret statutory law, one can turn to several helpful guidelines, including how courts have interpreted the statutes in previous holdings.

2. *Legislative intent*—The legislative history of a statute can reveal what the legislature intended a statute to accomplish in practice and thus help to establish the relevance of the statute to the issue being researched. Sources include transcripts of committee reports and hearings, transcripts of congressional proceedings, and the wording of statutes as first published.

RESEARCHING ADMINISTRATIVE LAW

Regulations issued by federal administrative agencies are primary sources of law. Agency regulations are published in the *Code of Federal Regulations* (C.F.R.). The C.F.R. follows a format similar to that of the *United States Code* (U.S.C.), and the subject classifications (titles) of the C.F.R. correspond to the titles in the U.S.C.

QUESTIONS FOR REVIEW

1. What is the difference between a case on point and a case on "all fours"? Why is finding either of these important when researching case law? What is binding authority? Persuasive authority?

2. What is the definition of a primary source of law? A secondary source of law? How are these sources used in legal research?

3. List and identify the various parts of a case citation. How do citations help you locate a case? What is the West key-number system, and how does it simplify the legal research process?

4. List and briefly describe the components of a reported case. Which part should you focus on when analyzing a case? How do you brief a case? What is the purpose of briefing a case? What should be included in a case brief?

5. Describe how statutes are published. What government bodies create statutes and regulations? What is the name of the official code containing the statutes of the U.S. government? What are some points to consider when reading and interpreting statutory law?

ETHICAL QUESTION

1. Krystee Connolly, a paralegal in a litigation firm, has finished reading a brief that the opposing side submitted to the court in support of a motion for summary judgment. In the brief, she notices a citation to a state supreme court case of which she is unaware. She is experienced in the field and keeps current with new cases as they are decided. She wants to look at the case because it gives the other side a winning edge. She checks in case digests and state encyclopedias, as well as on Westlaw. She checks the state supreme court's Web site and sees no record of such a case. She asks the legal assistant for the opposing counsel to give her a copy of the case. When she does not receive it, she decides that the case is probably fictional. What should Krystee do?

PRACTICE QUESTIONS AND ASSIGNMENTS

1. Identify the case name, volume number, reporter abbreviation, page number, and year of decision for each of the following case citations, including the parallel citations:

   a. *Towe v. Sacagawea, Inc.*, 246 Or.App. 26, 264 P.3d 184 (2011).

   b. *Miranda v. Arizona*, 384 U.S. 436, 86 S.Ct. 1602, 16 L.Ed.2d 694 (1966).

2. Identify the title number, code abbreviation, and section number for the following statutory citations:

   a. 42 U.S.C. Section 1161(a).

   b. 20 C.F.R. 404.101(a).

3. The three bears return home to find that their house has been ransacked by Goldilocks. Their food has been taken, their chairs have been broken, their beds have been slept in, and their bedroom is so filthy that it will require professional cleaning to be usable. The three bears have come to your firm for legal advice on pursuing a claim against Goldilocks. Using the Developing Paralegal Skills feature, *Defining the Issues to be Researched* on page 182, create a checklist for defining the research issues for the case of *The Three Bears v. Goldilocks*.

4. Mr. John D. Consumer bought a new car eight months ago. The car frequently stalls. The problem began the first week after he purchased the vehicle. It stalled late at night on an expressway while he was returning home from a business trip. It has stalled at least monthly since then, often in potentially dangerous areas. Not only has he taken the car to the dealer, who has repeatedly attempted to repair the problem without success, but he has also notified the manufacturer in writing of the problem.

   Most states have a lemon law that requires manufacturers to replace vehicles that cannot be repaired, even if the warranty has expired. Does your state have a lemon law? If so, would the lemon law help Mr. Consumer?

   Your assignment is to research this question and try to find the answer to Mr. Consumer's rights under the law.

   a. Begin by analyzing the facts. Make a list of relevant legal terms to look up in an index.

   b. Select a secondary legal resource—such as *American Jurisprudence* or *Corpus Juris Secundum*— to use in your research. Record the name of the source. Consult the general index volumes.

   c. List the index topics from the general index volumes under which you found relevant information. (If you have difficulty locating relevant information, try checking the topic indexes in the individual volumes.) Many primary and secondary sources have tables of abbreviations near the front of the book that you should consult about the meaning of abbreviations.

   d. Record the citations to sections containing relevant information that you will consult. These sections will be located in the individual volumes of the secondary sources.

   e. Look up these citations in the appropriate volumes of the secondary sources to find an answer to Mr. Consumer's legal issues. According to the secondary source, what is an appropriate response to John D. Consumer's problem? List the citations to the volumes, topics, and sections where you found the possible answers. Be sure to check the pocket part for more current citations if using hard copy.

5. After analyzing the facts of Mr. Consumer's legal dilemma and making a list of legally and factually relevant terms, as described in the preceding question, locate the index to the annotated version of your state statutes. Do the following:

   a. Using your list of terms, look in the index for citations to relevant statute sections. Make a list of citations to sections that appear relevant and that you will consult.

b. Now that you have a list of relevant citations, go to the volume of the statute containing the cited sections and read those sections. How does the statute in your state relate to Mr. Consumer's legal problem?

c. Is the answer given in the secondary source you selected the same as the answer for the preceding question? If not, how do the answers differ? Compare how you found the citations in the index to your state statutes with how you found them in the legal secondary source that you selected. Under what topics did you look in each situation?

6. Using the annotated version of your state statutes, look for relevant case law annotations on Mr. Consumer's legal problem in the notes of decisions following the relevant statutory sections. If no anno-tated version of your state statute exists or if no cases appear there—or if you want to learn to use another source—use a state digest. Once you find relevant case annotations you will want to locate the cases that interpret the statute and that are as similar to Mr. Consumer's situation as possible.

a. Write down the citations to no more than three relevant cases. Now look up those cases in the case reporters.

b. Read through the summary and headnotes of each case. Do the cases still appear to be relevant? If not, go back to the annotated statute or digest and look for more relevant cases.

c. What did you find? Did the courts' application of the statute change in any way your answer to the legal problem facing Mr. Consumer?

QUESTIONS FOR CRITICAL ANALYSIS

1. Think about the differences between primary and secondary sources. Why do attorneys generally cite only primary sources in documents filed with the courts?

2. Why is the distinction between binding and persuasive authority important to the courts? Which source is preferable to find when doing legal research? Why?

3. Which source is it preferable to locate—a case on point or a case on "all fours"? How do these cases fit into the research goals? How likely is it that you might find either a case on point or on "all fours"?

4. Briefly explain the West key-number system. What is its purpose? Is its use limited to digests? How can the key-number system be of assistance to a researcher?

5. What is West's National Reporter System? What geographic units does it include? Is it widely used? Why or why not? How might the West key-number system tie into it?

6. What is the difference between case law and statutory law? Why is the difference significant?

PROJECTS

1. Using a state bar directory or other type of legal directory, find out which law libraries in your area are open to the public. Make arrangements to visit a law library. If tours of the library are offered, try to take a tour.

2. Find the Web site for the *ALWD Citation Manual*. Look up the citation formats for your state court reporters and statutes.

GROUP PROJECT

This project will involve creating a case brief of the *Thomas & Thomas Court Reporters, LLC v. Switzer and Hathaway Switzer* case in Exhibit 7.7.

Student one will write the facts section of the case brief. Student two will write the procedure section of the case brief. Student three will write the issues and answers section and the holding. Student four will write the reasoning section.

The group members will then compare the brief that they have prepared to the sample case brief in Exhibit 7.9 and will critique their brief by making a list of the differences between their case brief and the sample case brief.

USING INTERNET RESOURCES

1. Go to the Cornell University Law School's Legal Information Institute Web site at **www.law.cornell.edu**. Browse through the page that opens, and then answer the following questions:

a. Scroll down to "Legal Resources." What types of primary sources can you access? Are there any secondary sources that are accessible from this page?

b. Under "Legal Resources" click on Wex legal dictionary and encyclopedia and answer these questions:

- What is Wex?
- Locate the definition of a limited liability company and record it.
- Do the same for the definition of limited liability.
- Using these two definitions, explain why Switzer (see Exhibit 7.7) was not personally liable for the debt of the law firm in *Thomas & Thomas Court Reporters, L.L.C. v. Douglas Switzer and Hathaway Switzer.*

CourseMate The available CourseMate for this text has an interactive eBook and interactive learning tools, including flash cards, quizzes, and more. To learn more about this resource and access free demo CourseMate resources, go to **www.cengagebrain.com**, and search for this book. To access CourseMate materials that you have purchased, go to **login.cengagebrain.com**.

Contemporary Online Legal Research

Chapter Outline

After completing this chapter, you will know:

- Strategies for planning and conducting research on the Internet.

- How you can find people and investigate companies using Internet search tools and databases.

- How to find some of the best legal resources available on the Internet.

- The advantages of the major fee-based online programs.

Introduction

Computers and online databases have simplified and improved the ability of paralegals to do high-quality legal research. One of the great benefits of computer technology for legal practitioners is computer-assisted legal research. As you learned in Chapter 7, thorough and up-to-date legal research requires access to a huge volume of source materials, including state and federal court decisions and statutory law. Today, attorneys and paralegals can access most of these materials online.

An obvious advantage of online research is that you can locate, download, and print out court cases, statutory provisions, and other legal documents within minutes without leaving your desk. Another advantage is that new case decisions and changes in statutory law are entered almost immediately into certain online legal databases, especially Westlaw and Lexis. This means that you can find out quickly whether a case decided three months ago is still "good law" today.

In this chapter, we describe various forms of online research. By the time you read the chapter, some of what we say will have changed, particularly with respect to Internet resources. Some of these resources may have improved, others may have been removed, and new ones may have been added. (See this chapter's *Featured Contributor* article on the following pages for tips on conducting research online.) The general approach to conducting research online will not have altered, however. If you master the basic principles of online research discussed in this chapter, you will be able to conduct research on the Internet no matter how much its content changes.

Going Online—An Internet Primer

The Internet is a global communication network. Business computers, university computers, government computers, and personal computers comprise the "network of networks" that constitute cyberspace. Here we discuss many ways in which you can use the Internet to conduct legal and fact-based research. We begin by looking at Internet tools and navigation methods. You may be familiar with many of these tools and methods. If so, consider this section a review of the basics of the mechanics of Internet access, use, and terminology.

Expanded online access to legal resources has changed the nature of legal research. Today, paralegals conduct most of their legal research online. How does online legal research benefit your clients?

© Kristian Sekulic/www.Shutterstock.com

Featured Contributor

TIPS FOR DOING ONLINE LEGAL RESEARCH

Matt Cornick

BIOGRAPHICAL NOTE

Matthew Cornick is a graduate of SUNY at Buffalo and the Emory University School of Law. He has been teaching legal research, family law, and introduction to law and ethics to paralegal students for over twenty years. He frequently speaks to paralegal associations and law firms on the topic of technology in the law office. Cornick has served on the Approval Commission to the American Bar Association's Standing Committee on Paralegals. He is the author of *A Practical Guide to Family Law* and *Using Computers in the Law Office,* Sixth Edition (Delmar Cengage Learning).

© Cengage Learning 2014

Online legal research can make research easier, more efficient, and more thorough. But for some students, and some practicing legal professionals, online legal research offers the prospect of the inherent difficulties of legal research combined with the frustration of working with computers.

I have been in your shoes, and I can assure you that everything is going to be all right. In that spirit, here is some advice for completing your online legal research with a minimum of hassle and distress.

1. **Think before you begin the research.** Much of the frustration that students feel when researching online is due to the lack of proper preparation. Make sure you know precisely which terms you will use in your search query. Prepare a list of alternative terms. For example, if you are researching an issue relating to divorce, it might be found under "Divorce" or "Dissolution" or "Marriage, Termination of" or "Husband and Wife."

Internet Tools

Two of the most widely used applications of the Internet are for e-mail and searching the World Wide Web. Getting around on the World Wide Web requires the use of uniform resource locators (URLs).

Navigating the Internet

Using the Internet to conduct legal research involves navigating through vast numbers of Internet resources until you find the information you are seeking. The Internet is similar to an enormous library, but there is a key difference—the Internet has no centralized, comprehensive card catalog. In place of a card catalog, a researcher uses browsers, guides, directories, and search engines.

Browsers

The Web is accessed through a program called a *browser*. Browsers such as Internet Explorer, Firefox, Opera, Safari, and Google Chrome enable computers to roam the content of the Web. They also make it possible to copy text from Web sites and paste it into a word-processing document. With a browser, you can download images, software, and documents to your computer. You can also use your browser to search through a single Web page and find particular words. This last feature is most helpful when the document is long and your time is short.

2. **There is no need to reinvent the wheel.**   By searching in legal encyclopedias, law journals, treatises, and the like, you can tap into a world of useful information. This is especially true if you review the footnotes. This is where you will find specific references to cases, statutes, and administrative regulations.

3. **Both Westlaw and Lexis offer online training lessons.**   A list of Lexis online tutorials is available at **www.lexisnexis.com/support/training**. Search **store.westlaw.com** for links to online Westlaw training.

4. **There is more to online legal research than Westlaw, Lexis, and other similar services.**   You can use a general-purpose search engine, such as Google, to search for information about a specific area of law. Sometimes, you can jump-start your legal research by "Googling" your query. For example, if you enter "Georgia negligence statute of limitations" in a search engine, you will find the relevant Georgia code sections.

5. **When using online legal research services, time may literally be money.**   Make sure you know whether the tool you plan to use permits unlimited use or charges by the minute. While in paralegal school, you may have free access to Westlaw or Lexis. Rest assured, in the real world there is no "free access." Make sure you have permission to use Westlaw or Lexis and keep an eye on the clock. Use common sense; do not use $500 worth of time to solve a $100 problem.

6. **Keep track of your research.**   Making mistakes during legal research is unavoidable. Making the same mistakes twice (or more) is completely avoidable. Making a list of all the cases, statutes, articles, and other sources you have reviewed will save you time and aggravation.

7. **Perhaps the most valuable online legal research skill you can develop is the ability to cite check primary authorities.**   Be sure you take the time in school to gain the expertise employers will value.

8. **Know when to walk away.**   Once you start seeing the same cases and statutes over and over again, you have probably found everything worth finding.

9. **Don't worry.**   You are not going to break the Internet. Make mistakes, but learn from them.

" . . . everything is going to be all right . . . You are not going to break the Internet."

Search Engines

Next to browsers, the most important tools for conducting research on the Web are search engines. A search engine scans the Web for words and phrases that a researcher has entered, and then generates a list of Web pages that contain them. This means that the results are limited by the researcher's ability to phrase a query within the constraints of the search engine's capabilities. It's recommended that a researcher run several searches using different words when looking for material on the Web. Furthermore, because each search engine works a bit differently, running the same search in different browsers may produce different results. You can experiment to see how results differ by running the same search on Bing, Dogpile, Google, and Yahoo to see the differences.

Search Operators

In response to a search query, a Web search engine will return many irrelevant results. Sometimes, a researcher can eliminate irrelevant sites only by going to the sites and scrolling through them. The use of certain *operators* can greatly refine search results and help you to avoid this problem.

Quotation marks are one of the most useful operators available in most search engines. Placing quotation marks around words or phrases that must appear together in a specific order will effectively narrow search results. For example, a

Google search using the key words "Arizona Music Educators" in quotation marks may return about three thousand results. A Google search using the same key words but without the quotation marks around the phrase may return a half-million results.

There are many different operators that will help you construct an efficient search. You can easily find a guide to these operators online by running a search on Google on phrases such as "google search guide."

Advanced Search

Google has an advanced search feature (**www.google.ca/advanced_search**), as do other search engines. These advanced search options make it easy to run searches that contain all the words in your search or that eliminate certain words from your search results. Perhaps you might want to find all the Web pages that contain a particular phrase such as *music educators*, but you don't want any of those pages to contain the word *Arizona*. You might want to find all pages that contain the word *dog* but not the phrase *cocker spaniel*. Searches of this sort are easy to construct using the Google or Yahoo advanced search screens.

The Internet: The Most Used Research Tool

The Internet has come to dominate most research efforts. Before starting a project, ask yourself the following questions: What sources are needed? Are they online? Are they available elsewhere? Either way, what is the cost? How much time do I have to produce results? As the *Developing Paralegal Skills* feature on the facing page discusses, there are a number of things to take into account to help ensure accuracy.

If the Internet is the right tool for your research, you will have much at your disposal. The fee-based Lexis and Westlaw services are the dominant legal research resources on the Internet, and we discuss them later in the chapter. First, we consider some free services available online.

Free Legal Resources on the Internet

We have already noted a number of legal resources on the Internet, but now let us focus on legal research sites. Most public documents, such as statutes and cases, are available to the public. If these documents are on the Internet, they may be accessible through various Web sites, but some sites have evolved to maintain lead positions in legal research. Here, we look at leading free legal information sites. Later we look at subscription-based sites.

General Legal Resources

There are several commonly used legal sites for those who are not using fee-based services. The Justia site (**www.justia.com**) provides access to a massive amount of legal information, such as case law, codes, law reviews, and other legal materials, as does FindLaw for Legal Professionals (**lp.findlaw.com**). Justia also provides a way to search for information about federal court cases at **dockets.justia.com**). At the docket site, you can quickly find information about lawsuits recently filed in federal court. The Law Library of Congress (**www.loc.gov/law**) provides links to many domestic and foreign sources of law. Its "Guide to Law Online" provides an annotated guide to legal sources, including a list of online law reviews. For matters regarding the Supreme Court, see **www.oyez.org**.

Another major legal resource site is provided by the Legal Information Institute (LII) at Cornell University Law School (**www.law.cornell.edu**). Besides legal documents, this site provides other useful information, such as a guide to legal citations, a legal encyclopedia (a good place to start a project), and a dictionary of legal terms. The Washburn University Law School maintains a popular site at **www.washlaw.edu**. As you will see, it has a plain, no-nonsense menu that provides easy access to certain categories of legal information.

DEVELOPING
paralegal skills

INTERNET-BASED RESEARCH

Many legal materials are available on the Internet, with both fee-based (Westlaw, Lexis, Loislaw, Fastcase, Casemaker, VersusLaw) and free (Cornell Law School's Legal Information Institute, Google Scholar) services providing court opinions, statutes, and agency materials. Courts, legislatures, and agencies also operate their own Web sites, which are often useful resources. Interest groups and law firms maintain specialized collections of key materials as well.

With all that information at your fingertips, often the most important problem is winnowing it down to what is really useful. Here are five questions you should ask about any legal resource you find on the Internet.

- *Who created it, and why did they post it on the Internet?* Does the information come from a neutral source or an interest group? From someone with experience and credentials or a crank? Before you rely on the results of a Web search, check to make sure your results have a legitimate pedigree.

- *Is it accurate?* Joe's Legal Blog may be fun to read, but has Joe accurately reproduced a court opinion or statute? It is always best to check unofficial materials against either an official Web resource or a commercial service that certifies the accuracy of its materials. A medical study on cancer from a respected hospital's site may be more reliable than a similar report you find on a blog.

- *Is it up to date?* Last year's brilliant Web site on employment law in California might be wrong if there has been a new statute, regulation, or case since it was posted. Attorneys are always concerned with the currency of the information they're reading.

- *Is it easy to use?* Many court Web sites are harder to use than commercial services such as Westlaw. It may save your client a few dollars in search costs, but if it takes you twice as long to find the information, the total bill won't be any less.

- *What is the coverage?* Does the resource cover material only up to a certain date? Can you tell easily? How can you get the most up-to-date information? Your clients are paying for your expertise in research. You must be able to deliver a comprehensive answer to them.

One of the most important skills you must have as a paralegal is the ability to do quality legal research. Your clients and your employer deserve your best efforts, so always make sure you use the best research tools to obtain the best information.

Specific Legal Resources

Besides the general sites just mentioned, which offer access to a broad range of resources, many Web sites provide legal information within specific areas. We discuss just a sampling here.

Secondary Sources of Law

Many secondary sources, such as legal encyclopedias and treatises, are not likely to be found on the Web for free. An increasing number of law review articles are published free on the Internet, however. The Law Library of Congress and Justia both provide guides to online law reviews.

The savvy legal researcher realizes that consulting a relevant secondary source at the beginning of a research project may save time and effort, as the source should provide a good overview of the law in an area and point to leading cases and issues. If you are researching an area of law and want to know what the most relevant books and Web sites are for that subject, try Google Scholar and Zimmerman's Research Guide (**law.lexisnexis.com/infopro/zimmermans**).

Court Opinions

More than a century's worth of Supreme Court opinions are available on FindLaw (**lp.findlaw.com**), and several decades' worth are available through LII at Cornell Law School. You can also find the Supreme Court's opinions on its Web site (**www.supremecourt.gov**). Federal appeals courts began to place opinions on the Internet in the early 1990s. For information about federal courts and cases they release, see **www.uscourts.gov**. FindLaw also provides access to federal district courts, as well as to state courts and other state bodies. Google Scholar also provides access to many opinions.

Other Resources

When you are first looking into an issue, you can check the Law Library Resource Xchange (LLRX) at **www.llrx.com** for discussions or research guides that relate to your topic. LLRX, which is discussed more in *Technology and Today's Paralegal* on the facing page, is a Web site that provides up-to-date information on a wide range of Internet research resources for legal professionals.

Various state resources can be found online. For example, the New York State Library has a useful guide for researching legislative history at **www.nysl.nysed.gov/leghist**. While it focuses on New York, the development of legislation is similar in all states, and the tutorial provided is very helpful. The Indiana University School of Law maintains a site that provides links to all legislative materials for all states (**www.law.indiana.edu/lawlibrary/research/guides/index.shtml**) that is very useful.

Federal Law Starting Points

USA.gov (**www.usa.gov**), the official portal to U.S. government information, provides links to every branch of the federal government. The A-Z List of Agencies on that site provides helpful links to federal agencies. The U.S. Government Printing Office (**www.gpo.gov/fdsys**) also provides links to the *Code of Federal Regulations,* the *Congressional Record,* the *Federal Register,* all bills introduced in Congress, the *United States Code,* and other government publications. The Library of Congress's Thomas site (**thomas.loc.gov**) provides a daily congressional digest, a link to the Law Library of Congress, and the full text of laws passed by Congress, as well as summaries of bills. Thomas is a good place to find information about the status of a bill before Congress. The U.S. Department of Justice (**www.justice.gov**) provides information on federal criminal prosecutions and the enforcement of the federal laws of civil rights, employment discrimination, and immigration.

Federal Legislative Home Pages

The U.S. House of Representatives Web site at **www.house.gov** provides links to representatives' roll-call votes, the Congressional schedule, current debates on the House floor, and Web sites of representatives. The Web site of the U.S. Senate at **www.senate.gov** hosts a Virtual Reference Desk with Senate procedures explained via Web links arranged according to topic. The Senate site also provides roll-call votes, information about recent legislative activity, and links to the Web sites of senators.

Business Information

The Web site of the U.S. Department of Commerce (**www.commerce.gov**) provides a wealth of business and economic statistical data and other information. Some of it is available only for a fee. The U.S. Patent and Trademark Office provides many educational resources regarding patents and trademarks at **www.uspto.gov**. Information on copyrights and a searchable database of copyright records is provided by the U.S. Copyright Office at **www.copyright.gov**. The Equal Employment Opportunity Commission (EEOC) posts information on employment discrimination, EEOC regulations, compliance, and enforcement at **www.eeoc.gov**.

Numerous resources to help in forming, financing, and operating small businesses are offered by the Small Business Administration at **www.sbaonline.sba.gov**. The Securities and Exchange Commission maintains public companies' electronic filings at **www.sec.gov** (see the "Filings & Forms" menu). Fedstats (**www.fedstats.gov**) provides access to the statistical information compiled by federal agencies, including information about population, crime statistics, and income.

TECHNOLOGY AND
today's paralegal

STOPPING PROBLEMS BEFORE THEY START

Legal research is easier than ever, thanks to Internet-based research tools. You can quickly find a long list of cases through online databases. But research requires more than turning on a computer, connecting to Lexis or Westlaw, and pressing "print." Your attorneys need *relevant* cases, and it takes skill to winnow a list of search results down to the important cases. Moreover, technical problems can disrupt even a careful research strategy, and there are budget constraints to consider, so here are some tips to help deal with the realities of life as a legal researcher.

Rule 1: Never put off research to the last minute. What seems like a simple research question can turn out to be complicated. Your server may fail at a crucial time. Be prepared—if your firm's Internet connection goes out, don't panic. Know how to switch your research to a smartphone or tablet Internet connection. Nearby alternative locations are often available, from libraries to coffee shops. And always start your research early enough to allow for being thorough, as well as following up on unexpected leads you discover.

Rule 2: Be familiar with low-cost and free alternatives to commercial legal research databases. Westlaw and Lexis are great tools, but sometimes clients cannot afford the cost of their use. **LLRX.com** provides free access to court rules and forms as well as links to useful sources of legal information on the Web. As we see numerous times throughout this text, Cornell Law School's Legal Information Institute (LII) has free and reliable access to court opinions, statutes, and more. Google Scholar (**scholar.google.com**) allows researchers to run key word searches for cases and legal articles. These resources can help you get research done on the cheap. But keep in mind that "cheap" is not always less expensive. If you spend twice as long on research from a free site as you would on a paid site, the "free" one may be more expensive in the long run.

Rule 3: Have a backup system and use it. Make sure you regularly archive your research on a server or other location. Your firm will likely have a backup system for computers. Find out how it works and what steps you need to take to keep your research files securely backed up. Your work should be regularly backed up during the day in case your computer crashes. If your firm allows it, use a cloud backup service to ensure key materials are also stored off-site—but make sure the cloud service offers adequate security. Be equally sure you are not putting sensitive materials on portable media, such as a flash drive, that could be lost.

Rule 4: Download and archive. Don't rely on being able to find that crucial document on the Web again. Web sites vanish, are reorganized, and change their content. Download and store crucial information on your computer or print it out, but make sure you can find what you need quickly. Tools such as X1 (**x1.com**), Copernic Desktop Search (**desktop.copernic.com**), and Instant File Find (**popusoft.com**) make finding files stored on your computer quick and easy. Free-form databases, such as **DevonThink** (for Macs) or **AskSam** (for both PCs and Macs), allow you to create sets of information of varied materials for quick retrieval. Find a tool that works for you and master it.

Rule 5: Plan ahead. As you plan your work on a case, think about what resources you must have to accomplish each task. What documents will you need so you can keep working on the project if your office is closed? Are there any things that cannot be done off-site? Do you have all the relevant passwords and login information needed to access Web sites to continue researching off-site? Which deadlines are coming up?

TECHNOLOGY TIP

As a paralegal, you will likely be working on projects where a missed deadline can mean that your client loses her case. Making sure you can respond to the challenges of everything from malfunctioning technology to natural disasters is a crucial part of your job.

Lexis and Westlaw

Most legal researchers use Lexis and Westlaw. They are the dominant fee-based providers in the legal research business. The services are comprehensive, and once one becomes familiar with them, they are user friendly. Subscribers pay for the use of these services, and they are expensive. Different law firms pay different rates depending on their contracts with the providers.

We will review several other online sites, in part because the use of those services can reduce the amount of time spent on Westlaw or Lexis and thereby keep down research costs. Doing initial work on free sites, and organizing materials in advance, will enable you to be more efficient in the use of these costly resources. Your employer will set the rules for use of the fee-based research sites so you will know what is expected.

While we focus on Lexis and Westlaw, there are lower-cost competitors that are making inroads. Competitors get a share of the market by offering lower prices for similar, if less comprehensive, services. After examining Westlaw and Lexis, we discuss some of these alternatives.

Westlaw and Lexis both include searchable versions of federal and state cases, statutes, and regulations. Additionally, they both contain many law reviews, treatises, legal encyclopedias, legal forms, public records, newspapers and magazines, and other sources. Both services are particularly popular for their *KeyCite* and *Shepard's* citator services (discussed below). Westlaw's key-number service, which arranges the issues in case law into categories, is a fundamental part of many legal research projects, as we discussed in the previous chapter. *KeyCite* builds upon that service.

Accessing Westlaw or Lexis

A subscriber can access Westlaw and Lexis via **www.westlaw.com** and **www.lexis.com**, respectively. To use most of the legal research tools offered by these services, you must subscribe to them and obtain a password. Once you have a password, when you sign on to the service, a welcome page is displayed. (The opening page of Westlaw is shown in Exhibit 8.1 on the facing page.) You can then begin your research. You can conduct a search, check citations, review documents related to a case or topic, set up alerts, and track previous research trails.

Conducting a Search

Both Westlaw and Lexis allow subscribers to locate documents using various search and browse methods. If you have the citation for a document, such as a court case or statute, you can enter the number and quickly call up the document. If you do not know the citation number, you can search according to legal topic, by case or party name, or by publication. Furthermore, you can run word searches, much as you would on Google or another Web browser, within one of the databases.

Westlaw also allows researchers to choose a second platform for searching, WestlawNext. The initial screen of WestlawNext is shown in Exhibit 8.2 on page 232. WestlawNext (which has an app for the iPad) is designed in many ways to provide the sort of searching that is familiar to users of Google and Yahoo. Natural language searching is encouraged. Note that a researcher could enter a search query at the initial screen, and then narrow down the results by jurisdiction, date, type of material, etc., for the results that appear on the left-hand side of the screen. All the features of Westlaw (searching cases, statutes, regulations, *KeyCite*, etc.) are also available on WestlawNext.

Checking Citations

citator

A book or online service that provides the history and interpretation of a statute, regulation, or court decision and a list of the cases, statutes, and regulations that have interpreted, applied, or modified a statute or regulation.

All paralegals should become familiar with citators. A **citator** provides a list of legal references that have cited or interpreted a case, statute, or regulation. A *case citator* provides, in addition, a history of the case. The primary purpose of a case citator is to determine the validity of a case. Secondarily, the purpose is to locate additional sources. A case decided a year ago may now be "bad law" if it has been reversed or modified on appeal. A statute may have been amended or held unconstitutional after its passage by Congress or a state legislature. So whether you are looking at cases, regulations, or statutes, you want to know if your findings are up to date and still considered "good law."

EXHIBIT 8.1

Opening Screen of Westlaw

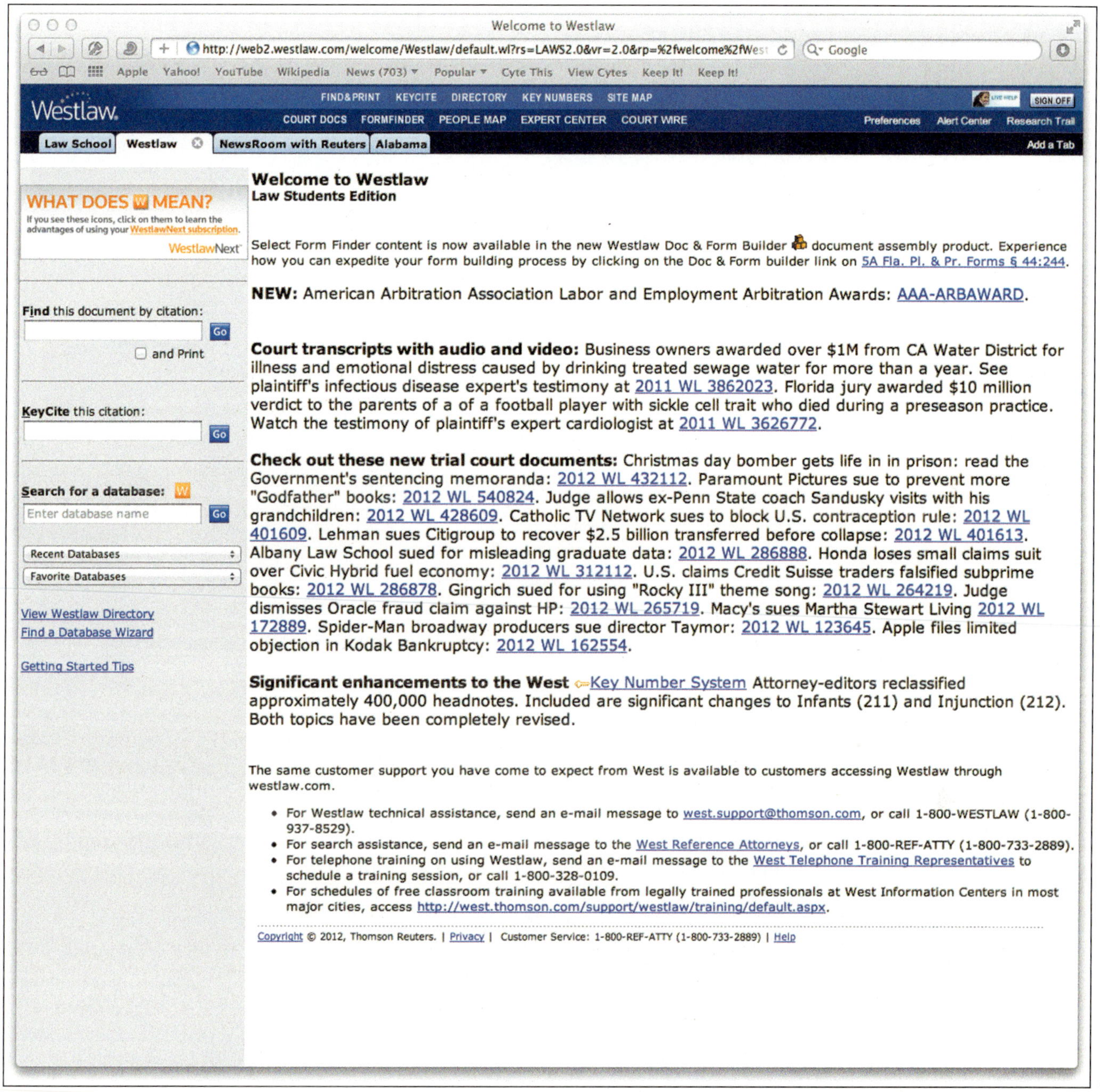

The tools provided by *KeyCite* and *Shepard's* allow you to access updated law within seconds. As emphasized in Chapter 7, a crucial part of legal research is making sure your findings are accurate and up to date. If your supervising attorney is preparing for trial, for example, the attorney will want to base a legal argument on current authorities. A precedential case that may have been good law last month may not remain so today.

Both Westlaw and Lexis provide online citators. In Lexis, the primary citator is *Shepard's*. Westlaw provides a similar service, called *KeyCite*. For practical purposes, you can think of *Shepard's* and *KeyCite* as performing much the same functions. The *Developing Paralegal Skills* feature on page 233 discusses some extra points about *KeyCite*.

KeyCite

An online citator on Westlaw that can trace case history, retrieve secondary sources, categorize legal citations by legal issue, and perform other functions.

Shepard's

An online citator on LexisNexis that provides a list of all the authorities citing a particular case, statute, or other legal authority.

EXHIBIT 8.2
Opening Screen of WestlawNext

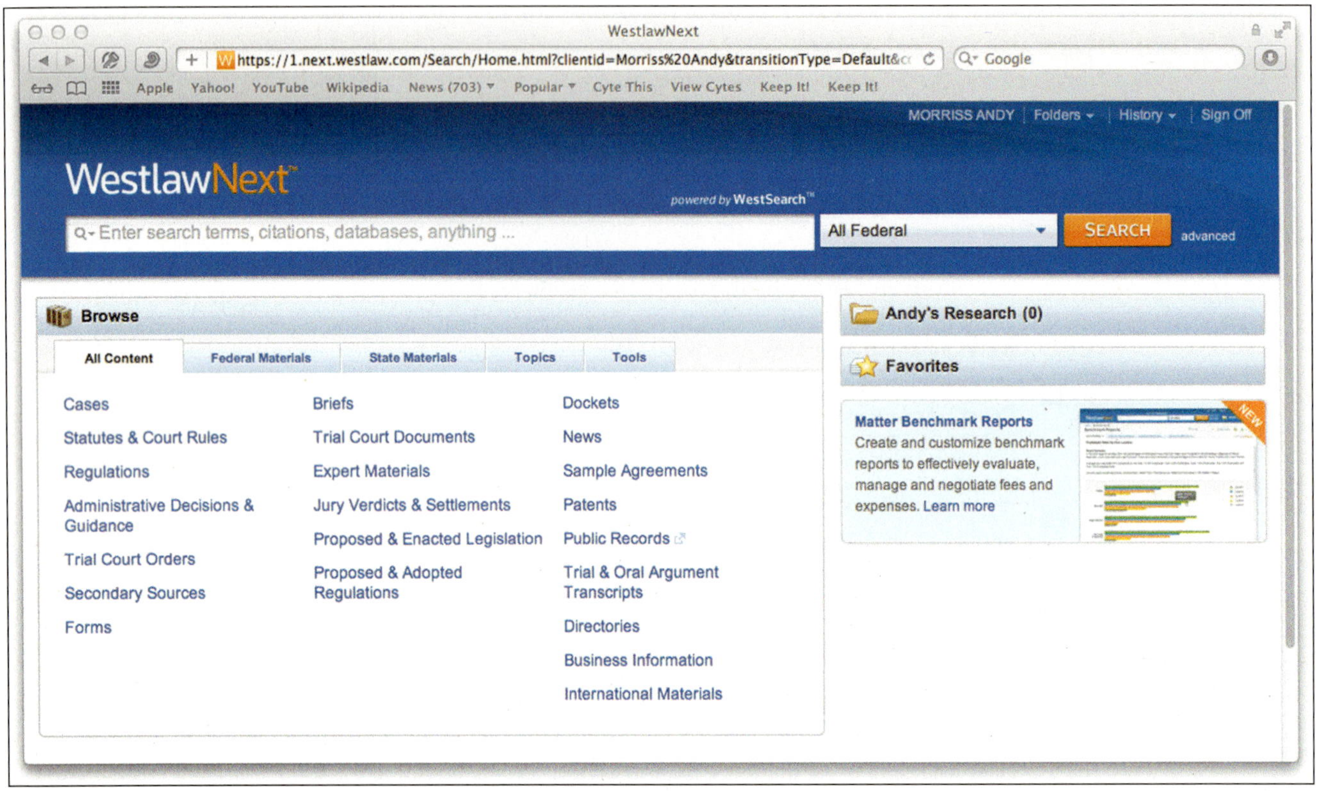

Reprinted from Westlaw with permission of Thomson Reuters.

Shepard's Citations

Shepard's Citations is available both in print format and online. The popularity of the print version has declined over the years. Most libraries no longer subscribe to the print citators, and most attorneys prefer to use the online version. Understandably, the print version isn't updated as quickly as the online version (which tends to be updated daily). The function is the same nonetheless.

Information Provided by *Shepard's* and *KeyCite*:

Paralegals use *Shepard's* and *KeyCite* citators to accomplish several research objectives:

- **Parallel citations**—On occasion, a court's opinion may be published in several different sets of books. Cases that have multiple citations are referred to as having parallel citations. Both *Shepard's* and *KeyCite* list those parallel citations.

- **Other cases**—When you check a case or other law in a citator, you will find a list of cases. These are **citing cases**; that is, they are cases that cite the case you looked up in the citator ("the cited case"). Because they are citing the case you are researching, these citing cases may deal with the same issue, and therefore may be of interest to an attorney.

- **References to periodicals, treatises, and *American Law Reports* annotations**—If you are researching a case on point, *Shepard's* and *KeyCite* may include references to periodicals and treatises that cite that case. A book or article that references the cited case may provide a valuable discussion of the issues in the cited case, as well as referring to other, related cases.

- **Case history**—As mentioned, the citators provide a history of the cited case. For example, they will tell you if the decision in your case on point has been overturned on appeal (or if any further action has been taken).

citing case
A case listed in a citator, which cites the case being researched.

DEVELOPING
paralegal skills

CITE CHECKING ON WESTLAW

Katia, a paralegal, needs to check a citation quickly for a case from the court of appeals to see if it is still good law. Her supervising attorney wants to use the case in a brief that must be filed within a few hours. Katia accesses Westlaw. She enters her password and client-identifying information. Once she has gained access, she clicks on the "KeyCite this citation" box and enters the case citation. The search turns up a red flag, which means that at least part of the case has been reversed or overruled and is no longer good law.

Katia clicks on the red flag, which takes her to the decision in which the case was reversed or overruled. It turns out that part of the case was reversed on grounds that were not related to the rule of law for which her supervising attorney wants to cite the case. Katia and her supervisor can use the case in their brief after all, because the issue they are researching is still good law.

TIPS FOR USING *KEYCITE*

- A red flag means that a case has been reversed or overruled for at least one point of law and must be reviewed.

- A yellow flag means that the case has been questioned or criticized and should be checked.

- Never cite a case without verifying that it is still good law.

- Always read a citing case (discussed on the previous page) to find out why your case has a red or yellow flag, and to determine what issue in your case has been questioned, reversed, or overruled. A red flag doesn't always mean that the entire case has been reversed. The case may provide the support you need for a particular issue.

Use of Symbols

Shepard's uses an elaborate abbreviation system to provide information on how the cited case has been used or treated in the citing case. See Exhibit 8.3 on the next page for a list of the abbreviations. For example, if the ruling in the cited case has been followed by a citing case, the symbol *f* (for "followed") will appear. So if a paralegal is Shepardizing a state appellate court opinion (the cited case) and finds that a subsequent appellate court (citing case) has followed the decision in the cited case being Shepardized, the symbol *f* will appear before the citation to the citing case.

Both online citators use a series of color-coded symbols to indicate a law's status. Red stop signs or flags next to a case name, for instance, will indicate that the case is no longer good law for at least one of its points. A yellow stop sign or flag will indicate that a case has been questioned, distinguished, or criticized by a later court decision. Free user guides, which explain more about the symbols used in *KeyCite* and *Shepard's*, are available at **store.westlaw.com** and at **law.lexisnexis.com/shepards/brochures**.

You can use *Shepard's* or *KeyCite* for almost any legal citation. If you have a regulation, a law review article, or a code section, you can always use a citator to try to find other materials that cite it. If, for instance, you are trying to interpret a code section, you might want to look at the materials that cite it in order to get an idea of how courts have interpreted the code.

Selecting a Database

The legal research materials available through Westlaw and Lexis draw from thousands of databases, so a search by case name or legal topic can easily return an overwhelming number of documents. As a result, paralegals often need to limit their searches to specified databases. To do this, you first select a database that you want to search. If you are using Westlaw, for example, you click on the box labeled "Search for a Database" and enter a database identifier (for example, "ca-cs" to

EXHIBIT 8.3
Abbreviations Used in *Shephard's*

ABBREVIATIONS—ANALYSIS

History of Case

a	(affirmed)	Same case affirmed on rehearing.
cc	(connected case)	Different case from case cited but arising out of same subject matter or intimately connected therewith.
m	(modified)	Same case modified on rehearing.
r	(reversed)	Same case reversed on rehearing.
s	(same case)	Same case as case cited.
S	(superseded)	Substitution for former opinion.
v	(vacated)	Same case vacated.
US cert den		*Certiorari* denied by U.S. Supreme Court.
US cert dis		*Certiorari* dismissed by U.S. Supreme Court.
US reh den		Rehearing denied by U.S. Supreme Court.
US reh dis		Rehearing dismissed by U.S. Supreme Court.

Treatment of Case

c	(criticized)	Soundness of decision or reasoning in cited case criticized for reasons given.
d	(distinguished)	Case at bar different either in law or fact from case cited for reasons given.
e	(explained)	Statement of import of decision in cited case. Not merely a restatement of the facts.
f	(followed)	Cited as controlling.
h	(harmonized)	Apparent inconsistency explained and shown not to exist.
j	(dissenting opinion)	Citation in dissenting option.
L	(limited)	Refusal to extend decision of cited case beyond precise issues involved.
o	(overruled)	Ruling in cited case expressly overruled.
p	(parallel)	Citing case substantially alike or on all fours with cited case in its law or facts.
q	(questioned)	Soundness of decision or reasoning in cited case questioned.

search all California cases). If you do not know the abbreviation for the database you wish to search, you can choose "Directory."

Searching for Databases

For example, suppose your supervising attorney has asked you to research case law on the liability of tobacco products manufacturers for cancer caused by the use of those products. To do a thorough investigation, you will need to search the databases containing decisions from all state courts as well as from all federal courts. By working your way through Westlaw directories, you will be able to find the databases containing decisions from all state courts and all federal courts.

After you become familiar with the database identifiers on whatever service you are using, you can access that database more directly. For example, on the opening page of Westlaw, you can click on "Find a Database Wizard" at the bottom left of the screen. From the list provided, you select the information you wish to research, such as "Case, statute, or legal text or periodical." Next you can select the specific database you want, such as "Cases—Federal" and then "ALLFEDS."

WestlawNext

On WestlawNext, it's not necessary to choose a database at the beginning of your search. Users can run a broad search across all the materials on Westlaw, or all the cases, and then narrow down the results using the frame that appears on the left-hand side of the results screen. (See Exhibit 8.4 on the facing page.)

EXHIBIT 8.4
Results of Search on WestlawNext

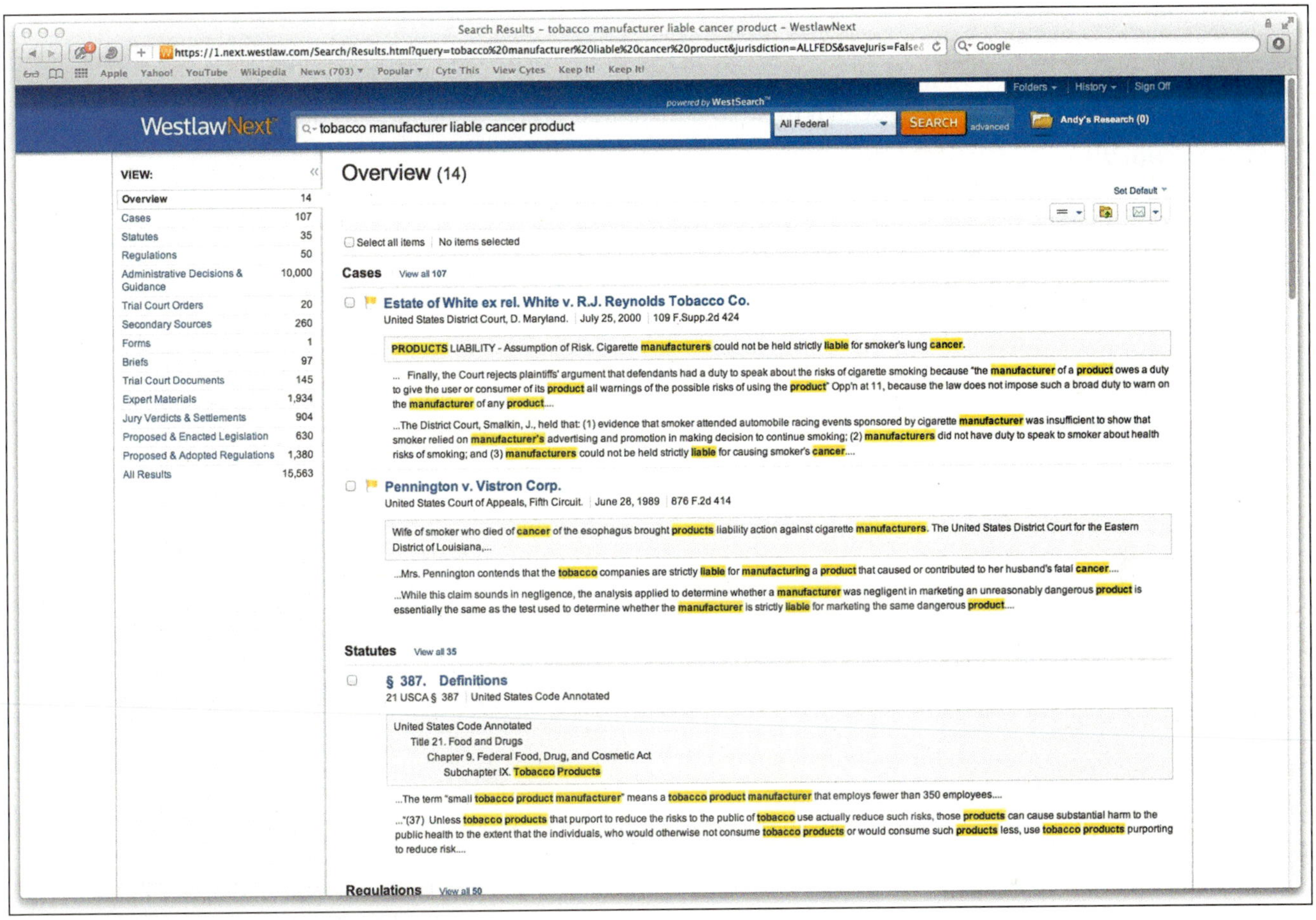

Searching a Database

Once you have chosen a specific database, such as "ALLFEDS," a search box will open on the screen. You will enter your *search query* in this box. In addition to the "Terms and Connectors" (called Boolean) method of searching, both Lexis and Westlaw allow users to draft search queries using "Natural Language" (or plain English). Before beginning your search, you should indicate in the search box which method you will use.

The Terms and Connectors Method

In a search employing terms and connectors, you use numerical and grammatical connectors to specify the relationships of the terms. For example, to find cases on the liability of tobacco products manufacturers for cancer caused by the use of those products, you could type the following terms and connectors in the query box:

liability /p cancer /s tobacco

This would retrieve all cases in which the term *liability* is in the same paragraph ("/p") as the term *cancer,* with the term *cancer* in the same sentence ("/s") as the term *tobacco.* To restrict the scope of your search, you can add a field restriction. For example, you might want to retrieve only court opinions rendered after 2011. If you are using Westlaw, you could add the following to your query to restrict the search results to cases decided after 2011:

& added date (after 12/31/2011)

Exhibit 8.4 above illustrates the results of running a search with these terms on Westlaw.

Many other grammatical and numerical connectors can be used to efficiently search a database. These are listed in the instructions provided to Lexis and Westlaw subscribers.

Generally, when drafting queries, make sure your query is not too broad. If you entered just the term *liability*, for example, your search would be futile because so many thousands of documents contain that term. At the same time, you do not want your search to be so narrow that no cases will be retrieved.

The Natural Language Method

The natural language method allows you to type a description of an issue without the use of terms and connectors in order to retrieve the most relevant documents. In searching for cases relating to the topic in the previous example, your query might read as follows:

Is a tobacco manufacturer liable for cancer caused by the use of its products?

This query would retrieve the documents most closely matching your description. You could also write a query that consisted only of the most important key words:

tobacco manufacturer liable cancer products

Including synonyms in the search may sometimes be necessary to produce more comprehensive results. A thesaurus feature on Westlaw (and a "Suggest Terms for My Search" function on Lexis) can suggest additional terms for your search.

Searching within Results

Often, once you have retrieved your search results, you would like to quickly locate certain key information. For example, suppose that your search resulted in a list of twenty cases relevant to your topic. At this point, Westlaw's "Locate in Results" tool allows you to scan the documents in your search result for terms that were not included in your query. Assume that your original request was, in natural language,

ETHICS WATCH

FINDING ETHICS OPINIONS ON THE WEB

Suppose that your supervising attorney is defending a client in court, and the attorney learns that the client has given testimony that the attorney knows is false. What is the attorney's ethical responsibility in this situation? Should the attorney disclose the client's perjury to the court? Would this be a violation of the attorney-client privilege? Or suppose the attorney learns that the client intends to testify falsely in court. Must the attorney inform the court of the client's intention?

In such situations, the attorney may ask you to find out if the state bar association or the ABA has issued an ethical opinion on this issue. You can find this information by accessing **www.americanbar.org**, where the ABA posts summaries of its ethical opinions. The ABA also posts ethical opinions issued by state bar associations on its Web site. On the site, select "Resources for Lawyers" and then pick "Ethics/Professional Conduct."

"Is a tobacco manufacturer liable for cancer caused by the use of its products?" If you want to know whether "death" is discussed in any of your search-result documents, you can use the "Locate" tool. On Lexis, the "Focus" feature will accomplish the same thing. On WestlawNext, there will be a "Search within Results" option available in the frame to the left of the search results that will allow you to scan through your results.

When browsing through your search results, remember that the time you spend using the service online is costly. If you have found cases that appear to be on point, you can print them out or download them for further study. In some plans, you may be charged for printing documents, so check with your supervisor before you print out that long law review article.

Is Lexis or Westlaw Better?

Because Lexis and Westlaw compete head on, they provide similar services. The formats are somewhat different, and there are differences in the specialty publications offered. Some users prefer one to the other, but that may be largely a matter of which program they have learned to use. A survey done by the law library at Stanford University showed that most large law firms subscribe to both services, allowing research staff to choose the one they prefer. Asked which system they would pick if allowed only one service, 245 respondents said Westlaw, and 89 picked Lexis.

By similar margins, however, respondents said that legal researchers could switch between the systems and use *KeyCite* or *Shepard's* to accomplish the same tasks. So while Westlaw appeared to have pulled ahead of Lexis as the dominant seller of premier online services, both do the task well. Respondents to the survey also noted that it is desirable to learn about other, less costly, programs. So we now turn to some of those offerings.

Alternative Online Programs

Several fee-based online programs offer services more limited but less expensive than those of Westlaw and Lexis. All take advantage of public-access databases, such as those for federal cases. Some have extra search features, usually for higher subscription fees. None is as comprehensive as Westlaw and Lexis, but many can perform some research.

PACER

Public Access to Court Electronic Records (PACER) (**www.pacer.gov**) is an easy-to-use Internet service that allows users to obtain court cases and docket information from federal circuit, district, and bankruptcy courts. PACER is run by the federal judiciary, and its prices are based on the cost of supplying the system. While PACER does contain court opinions, its chief purpose is to provide a site where attorneys and other court personnel can view the documents filed in federal litigation. A typical user might access PACER in order to view a complaint filed in a lawsuit, or to read a judge's ruling.

Fastcase

Fastcase (**www.fastcase.com**) provides access to all Supreme Court decisions, federal appeals decisions back to 1924, and federal district court decisions back to 1932. For most research, that is adequate. Fastcase also has bankruptcy court decisions, as well as decisions of state supreme courts and appeals courts back to about 1950. All federal and state statutes, constitutions, and administrative codes are included.

A feature of Fastcase is that it provides "Authority Check," which looks to see if a case is still good law and provides links to relevant cases. For an extra fee, a user can double-check by linking with *Shepard's* or *KeyCite*. Annual and monthly subscription fees are lower than those of Lexis and Westlaw, which has added to the system's popularity. Some state bar associations, such as those in Illinois and Ohio, have arranged for members to have access to Fastcase as part of membership, so it is becoming more widely used.

Loislaw

Loislaw (**www.loislaw.com**) is a part of Wolters Kluwer, a business and law publishing company. Loislaw has large federal and state case, statutory, and regulatory databases, but it also allows subscribers access to its specialized databases of secondary sources. Wolters Kluwer is the publisher of CCH, which publishes major tax treatises, and it owns Aspen Publishers, a provider of specialized treatises in various areas of law including bankruptcy, construction, employment, estates, family law, and tax.

When doing topical searches, Loislaw uses an application known as "Key Words in Context." This feature highlights the key words in your search documents, making it easier to review the documents by pinpointing the terms. Loislaw also offers "GlobalCite," a research citation tool. When you use this feature, you view the federal or state cases within the results of your search. GlobalCite also retrieves rules, regulations, treatises, and other documents that have cited a case or other document of interest. "LawWatch" is a feature that tracks trends in areas you have identified.

Casemaker

Casemaker Legal Research (**www.casemakerx.com**) is provided by state bar associations to their members as a part of their bar membership. Casemaker provides essentially the same set of federal and state case reports, statutes, and regulations as most other services. In some states, it provides state-specific documents, such as opinions of attorneys general, jury instructions, links to court forms, local federal rules, and other helpful materials. Casemaker has been undergoing expansion of its capabilities, so it is worth reviewing its latest capabilities.

VersusLaw

VersusLaw (**www.versuslaw.com**) is a low-cost service that includes Supreme Court and U.S. Court of Appeals cases and current federal district court cases, as well as state appellate court cases and cases of some specialized courts. A higher-level subscription plan includes federal district court opinions back to about 1950, along with state statutes and regulations. The highest-level plan includes the *United States Code* and the *Code of Federal Regulations* and provides added search features. VersusLaw has limited access to publications that are not in the public domain, so it primarily offers a reasonably priced means to access cases.

Google Scholar

Google Scholar (**scholar.google.com**) is a free service provided by Google. It allows users to run basic key word searches on state and federal case law, as well as search a limited number of law reviews and journals. After accessing scholar.google.com, it's important that you select the link for "advanced scholar search." Choosing that option will allow you to have access to the full range of search features offered by Google Scholar.

Conducting Online Research

As we have seen, the Internet offers many sources of information for paralegals doing legal research. Paralegals often research other matters as well. They may need to locate people, investigate companies, and conduct other practical, fact-based research into matters not directly related to legal issues. There are numerous online databases that make it possible to perform such research quickly and efficiently.

Your goal when conducting any online research is to find accurate, up-to-date information on the topic you are researching in a minimum amount of time. As anyone who has used the Internet knows, it is possible to spend hours navigating through cyberspace looking for specific information. Planning your research in advance and using a variety of research strategies, such as those discussed in this section, can help you achieve your goal of conducting thorough online research efficiently.

Plan Ahead—Analyze the Facts and Identify the Issues

Once you have been given a particular research project, you should plan your research steps before going online. The first step is to know what you are seeking. To avoid wasting time and money, outline your objectives clearly and be sure you understand your goals. To narrow the scope of your research, you may need to know the reason for the research or how the results will be used.

Online Research Strategies

Once online, you can use many strategies to find what you are looking for. We discuss some of those strategies here (see *Developing Paralegal Skills* below for tips on medical research).

Starting Points

Sometimes, a research session begins with one of the online directories or guides discussed earlier in this chapter. For example, if the object of your search is to find a law firm that practices in a specialized area of the law, start at the Martindale-Hubbell Web site (**www.martindale.com**) or with Yahoo's "Law" menu. You can find this menu by going to **dir.yahoo.com** and selecting "Law" from the "Government" menu. On this page, you will see submenus, including "Law Firms and Legal Services."

A search engine can be used to compile a list of Web sites containing certain key words. Keep in mind the limitations of search engines, however. Your search may locate many irrelevant sources and may not spot every site that you would find helpful. In addition, different search engines will yield different results or order the results differently.

DEVELOPING
paralegal skills

MEDICAL RESEARCH ON THE INTERNET

Thom Shannon needs to locate information on bipolar disorder. Thom's supervising attorney is trying to prove that the defendant in a case has this mental disorder. Thom runs a Google search on "bipolar disorder" and finds a reference to the Mayo Clinic's Web site (www.mayoclinic.com). He searches within the Mayo Clinic's site for articles describing this disorder. Thom finds several citations to articles, along with summaries of the articles, but the full text of the articles is not online. He goes to the library at the local medical school to obtain the full text of the articles for those he cannot find by Google Scholar or other search services.

TIPS FOR PERFORMING MEDICAL RESEARCH ONLINE

- Become familiar with medical terminology.
- Search the appropriate medical categories on the Web site.
- Locate appropriate articles and summaries.
- If the full text of the articles is not available online, go to the nearest medical school's library to obtain the articles.
- Make sure that your information is taken from a reputable Web site.

You may have to try several searches before you retrieve the right Web sites. Most search engines contain an advanced search feature that will help you refine your search. For instance, Google's advanced search will let you limit your search to particular phrases, eliminate unwanted words from your results, or find Web pages that were added to the Web after a particular date.

From the preliminary results of a general search, you can click on the links to the sites and determine which are useful. Many sites include their own links to other sources you may find helpful. Some Web sites attempt to collect links to all online resources about particular topics. These sites include directories, which were discussed earlier, as well as other sites, such as **USA.gov**, which provides links to federal offices and agencies.

Discovering Available Resources

Despite your best intentions and attempts to focus your research, you may have to approach a project without a clear objective regarding what you need to find. Your initial research goal may be to discover the extent of resources available online, with your ultimate goal being to obtain more precise results.

CHECK THE LAW LIBRARIES.   Keep in mind that there are several different approaches you can take to find legal resources on the Web. Many law school libraries provide subject guides to legal issues on their Web pages. These subject guides typically discuss the basic sources used for research in a particular field, and on occasion will provide information about the best approaches for researching particular issues. For instance, Georgetown Law Library has an extensive list of the major books available for a particular legal field in its online legal treatise finder (**www.ll.georgetown.edu/ guides/treatisefinder.cfm**). Most law schools will have a guide to searching Google or another search engine for words such as *tax law treatise* or *tax law research* and will retrieve a list of relevant Web sites.

Zimmerman's Research Guide, discussed on page 227, provides information about the appropriate resources to consult when researching a particular legal issue. Many libraries provide access to their catalogs online (see, for example, the New York Public Library's Web site at **catalog.nypl.org** or Yale Law School's catalog (**morris.law.yale.edu**). You can search these catalogs on the Internet just as you would search them in the library. This can save the time that you otherwise might spend in a futile trip to the library. Often, you can arrange to have source material from a distant library delivered to a closer library or directly to you.

BLOGS.   Another way to find out what resources are available is to begin with a blog. These can also be used to update your research. Millions of people generate blogs on a regular basis. A *blog*, short for "Weblog," is essentially an online journal. Some blogs are well established, while others disappear as the authors tire of them. Some of the best-recognized blogs in law include the general Am Law Daily (**amlawdaily.typepad. com**) and Legal Times (**legaltimes.typepad.com**). The American Bar Association's *ABA Journal* site maintains a list of legal blogs (**www.abajournal.com/blawgs**). The Law Library of Congress (**www.loc.gov/law**) has a searchable archive of law blogs arranged by subject. There are also blogs that contain information and opinions about new legal issues, such as **volokh.com**, which is hosted by a UCLA law professor and has several other law professors as contributors.

Blogs can be useful in legal research because they often provide information about recent developments in an area of law and are typically written by law professors and attorneys. If, for instance, you had a problem that focused on a new issue in immigration law, you might want to check the ImmigrationProf Blog (**lawprofessors. typepad.com/immigration**) to see if the issue had been discussed there. Stanford Law School's Legal Research Plus blog (**legalresearchplus.com**) focuses on legal research skills and provides useful information about new research techniques and technology.

Browsing the Links

As you browse through the links that could be useful for your research, you will need to keep track of the Web sites you visit. Marking a site as a "Favorite" (Internet Explorer) or adding a "Bookmark" (Firefox, Safari, or Chrome) for the site is an electronic substitute for keeping a book on your desk. With these, you can create an automatic link to any point on the Web. Once you have added a bookmark, you can return to that site again without searching for it. For example, you might want an automatic link to the site at which you begin your research: a directory, a search engine, or a site that has many links that relate to what you need.

Narrowing Your Focus

Once you find a Web site that could be useful, you will probably need to zero in on specific data within that site. One way to do this, of course, is to use the links within the site.

Remember that your browser also has the ability to search a Web page that you are viewing. This can be particularly helpful when you are attempting to review a long document on the Web for a particular word or phrase. Assume that you found the text of a bill being considered by Congress at the Library of Congress's Thomas site (**thomas.loc.gov**). Your browser's "Find" tool will let you search through that bill—which might be very lengthy—for a particular phrase. You might also use your find tool to search a company's document in the Electronic Data Gathering, Analysis, and Retrieval (EDGAR) database of the Securities and Exchange Commission (SEC) (go to **www.sec.gov/edgar.shtml** and select "Filings"). EDGAR is an indexed collection of documents and forms that public companies and others are required to file with the SEC. Exhibit 8.5 on the following page presents the first page of the EDGAR online collection. Alternatively, you can access EDGAR's private-sector competitor, EDGAR Online, at **www.edgar.com**.

Evaluating What You Find

After you have found what appears to be exactly what you are looking for, you need to consider its reliability and credibility. Ask yourself whether the source of the information is a primary, a secondary, or a tertiary source. Primary sources include company Web sites, experts, and persons with firsthand knowledge. For example, the inventor of a product would be a primary source for information about the invention.

Publicly filed documents are also primary sources. For example, the legal forms that companies are required to file with the Securities and Exchange Commission are good primary sources for the information that they contain (see the discussion of company investigations later in this chapter).

Secondary sources include books and periodicals (such as law journals, newspapers, and magazines) and their online equivalents that contain "secondhand" information.

Tertiary sources are any other sources that might be used in research (*tertiary* means "third" or "thirdhand"). It is always a good idea to find and interpret primary sources yourself before forming conclusions based on secondary or tertiary sources.

A researcher also needs to be aware of whether a source is reputable. A reputable source might be an organization that has established itself in a particular field. A less reputable source might be a personal, self-serving home page. Was the information placed on the Web by a source that may be biased in a certain way? Some people providing information on the Internet may not even be who they represent themselves to be. Online resources are available to help you evaluate Web sites. For instance, The Ohio State University's Web site includes an interactive tutorial and checklist for evaluating Web sites. You can access this tutorial by going to **liblearn. osu.edu/tutor/les1**.

EXHIBIT 8.5

The Securities and Exchange Commission's EDGAR Database

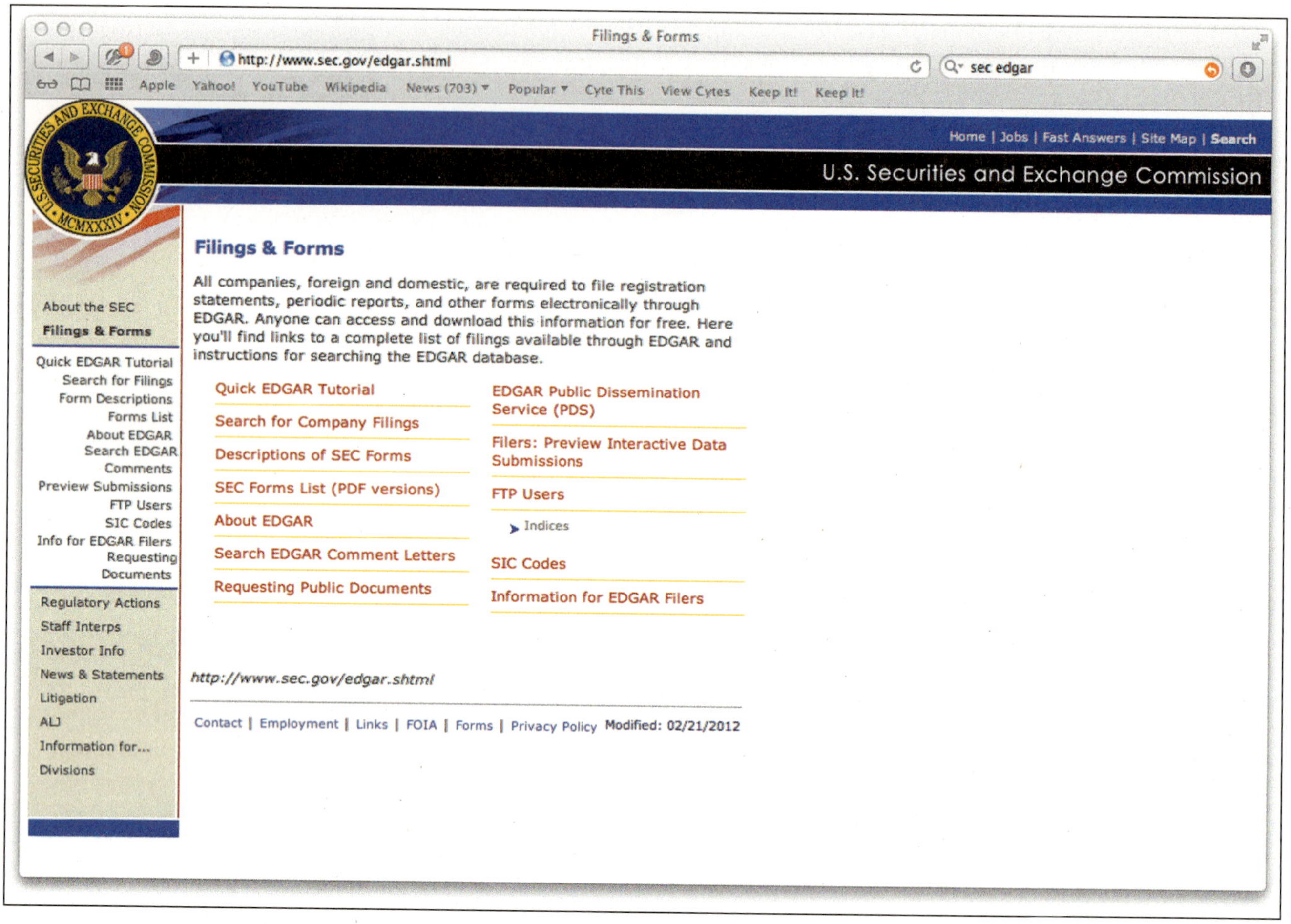

Updating Your Results

Staying current with events in the law and in other areas that relate to your research is important. One way to confirm whether your research results represent the most recent data available is by going online. News sites abound on the Internet. There are general sites sponsored by news organizations, as well as sources such as Google's news search feature (**news.google.com**). Corporate press releases—both current and from archives—can be reviewed at PRNewswire's site, **www.prnewswire.com**. You can also subscribe to e-mailed newsletters and bulletins from various sites. FindLaw offers many free legal news e-mail services at **newsletters.findlaw.com**. Cornell Law School's Legal Information Institute will e-mail subscribers bulletins about Supreme Court cases and arguments. Remember that after you have taken such pains to conduct exhaustive research, you do not want to lose your work. *In the Office* on the facing page suggests ways to organize and keep track of your results.

Locating People and Investigating Companies

As mentioned earlier, paralegals often need to locate people or find information about specific companies, and the Internet can be especially useful in searching for this type of information. There are numerous search services. The comprehensive services charge for their searches.

IN THE office

PROTECT AND ORGANIZE YOUR RESEARCH RESULTS

Almost all work is now stored in computer files. For security, a computer should be connected to an external hard drive in case the computer crashes. Offices should also have secure off-site backup systems so copies of files can be accessed in case of fire. Many firms organize files by specific practice area, such as personal-injury litigation. Within a given area, there may be files for clients' cases, research by topic, memoranda of law, and so forth.

Besides following procedure about filing and backup, make sure your computer is well organized so your supervisor could go into it and find files if necessary. Files are a law firm's work products, not your personal property, so they should always be professionally maintained.

Finding People

A paralegal may need to find particular persons to assist a lawyer in collecting debts, administering an estate, preparing a case for court, and so on. (We will discuss this topic more in Chapter 11.) Public records are helpful in looking for people, but some of these records (including many historic records) are not on the Internet. Despite this limitation, Web searches can be useful, and they can also be cheaper and faster than going to a government office or a library. Sometimes, using a commercial locator service or database can also be less costly than a trip out of the office to the local courthouse or state archives.

BROAD SEARCHES.   On the Web, a researcher can run a broad search with a general search engine such as Yahoo, Bing, Dogpile, or Google. A researcher might also narrow the focus of a search to, for example, all U.S. telephone books. There are several phone book Web sites. Some of these sites, such as the Yahoo People Search at **people.yahoo.com**, provide e-mail addresses. Some include business listings (for example, **www.superpages.com**). Some can conduct a reverse lookup search with a telephone number or an e-mail address to reveal a name and a street address (for example, **www.iaf.net**). Other online search services include iSearch and ZabaSearch.

NARROW SEARCHES.   If you know something about a person, such as an employer or a profession, you can use that information to narrow the search. For example, if you are looking for an attorney, you can link to the *West Legal Directory* in Westlaw, a comprehensive compilation of lawyers in the United States, or conduct a free search on **lawyers.findlaw.com**. The Martindale-Hubbell directory also provides attorneys' contact information.

If you are looking for a professor at a particular university or an employee at a certain company, you can often search the staff directory of the school or business firm online.

SPECIALTY SEARCH TOOLS.   With the right database, you can verify a person's business license, access information about a federal prison inmate, and find a military member or veteran. (For the latter, see **www.gisearch.com**.) Information can also be obtained about persons who contribute to federal election campaigns (see Political MoneyLine at **http://pml.cq.com**). Adoptees and their birth parents can be located through databases such as **www.adoption.com** and **www.omnitrace.com**. For genealogy searches, there are huge databases of facts about family trees and historical events (see, for example, **www.ancestry.com**). Many local tax assessors' databases (see, for instance, the Mobile, Alabama, County Revenue Office's site at **www.mobilecopropertytax.com**) provide information about local property owners and property values.

FEE-BASED SEARCHES.   Some commercial services provide access to their information for a price. For example, possible aliases, home value and property ownership, bankruptcies, tax liens, and small claims civil judgments can be searched through US Search at **www.ussearch.com**. Through a service with access to states' incorporation data and other information, people can be located based on their ownership interest in business organizations. Real property records, bankruptcy filings, and documents relating to court dockets, lawsuits, and judgments can be searched through such sites as KnowX at **www.knowx.com**.

Social Security numbers can also be verified through the Veris database at **veris. info**. Similarly, the public records databases on Westlaw and Lexis can provide a great deal of background information, such as past addresses, marriage and divorce records, criminal history and arrest records, professional licenses, and other such information. Social Security numbers can be verified through these sites as well.

Investigating Companies

Lawyers often need to know about their clients' companies and the companies of their clients' competitors. For example, if a client has suffered an injury caused by a defectively designed product, a lawyer will need to identify the defendant manufacturer, find out whether the manufacturer is a subsidiary of a larger company, and learn the defendant's address. If a client wants to acquire or invest in a particular business firm, research into the firm's background may be vital. There are many ways to find some of this information on the Web.

FINDING COMPANY NAMES AND ADDRESSES.   A researcher can run a search using a telephone number to find a company's name and address (for example, see **www. superpages.com**). Without a telephone number, a company's name and address can be found with the help of a directory that searches by industry and state (see **www. switchboard.com**, for example). A search with such a directory can also help determine whether a specific firm name is in use anywhere in the United States. You can find out who owns a domain name by using the domain lookup tool at **www.whois.com**.

UNCOVERING DETAILED INFORMATION ABOUT COMPANIES.   You can find company information on company Web sites, which may contain annual reports, press releases, and price lists. Some companies put their staff directories online.

Information about publicly held companies may be available through the sites of government agencies. For example, the Securities and Exchange Commission (SEC) regulates public companies and requires them to file documents and forms reporting certain information. This material can be accessed through the SEC's EDGAR database, as already mentioned.

Other information about public companies can be found at free sites as well as fee-based sites. Some free sites provide data on the companies and links to the companies' home pages and other sources of information, such as news articles. The *Wall Street Journal*, at **www.wsj.com**, often includes archives of information that may span decades and may cover companies in other countries. Some of this information is free; some must be purchased.

ADDITIONAL SOURCES.   Another source of both free and for-a-fee information on public companies is **www.corporateinformation.com**. The BizTech Network maintains **www.brint.com**, which provides extensive links to U.S. and international businesses. The newspaper databases on Westlaw and Lexis are good sources of information about companies featured in the media.

Data on privately held companies is more difficult to find because these firms are not subject to the SEC's disclosure requirements. Much of the information available includes only what the companies want to reveal. There are a few sites that compile some data on private companies, associations, and nonprofit organizations. For example, Hoover's Online at **www.hoovers.com** provides brief profiles of many companies, with links to other sites, including search engines. For a fee, Hoover's will provide expanded profiles. Many of the Hoover's databases are available through Lexis.

There are many guides to online business research available through the Web. A search on Google, Safari, or Yahoo for a phrase such as *business research guide online* will retrieve many of them.

Associations and Organizations

When gathering information about a person or a company, you may find it useful to check various professional organizations and associations. The Internet Public Library provides lists of associations by category at **www.ipl.org** (select "Special Collections" and then "Associations on the Net"). Yahoo also provides a directory of business and professional organizations at **dir.yahoo.com** (select "Business and Economy," then "Organizations," then "Professional").

Private business organizations are listed at **www.nvst.com** (select "Resources," and then select "Professional Associations" from the "Venture" menu). Access to lists of many nonprofit organizations can be found at **www.idealist.org**. As the review of sources indicates, paralegals are increasingly sophisticated at Internet-based searches to track down needed information efficiently. The rapid evolution of technology also means new opportunities in law practice, as the *Practice Focus* feature below discusses.

PRACTICE focus

EVOLUTION AND COMPETITION

New technologies can disrupt traditional law practices but create new opportunities for lawyers, paralegals, and other professionals able to identify and use them. New packages enabling document assembly and contract standardization are revolutionizing some areas of law practice.

For example, KIIAC, LLP, provides tools on its **www. contractstandards.com** Web site to help analyze legal documents. The goal is "to openly share contract standards—transaction analysis, checklists, and clause libraries—in an effort to establish global contract norms." The company's software "can analyze any set of agreements and automatically determine what clauses the agreement contains, how those clauses are organized, and the range of standard and non-standard language used in each clause." The software then "generates an outline or checklist of the standard deal terms and all deal-specific variations" and builds "a clause library for each deal term, identifies the core, non-negotiated language and the full range of alternatives." The initial library was built by analyzing publicly available documents in different categories.

USING TECHNOLOGY TO BYPASS LAW FIRMS

Some new technology threatens law firms' traditional business models. For example, consider "crowdsourcing," the technique used by some Web-based organizations to distribute a problem to large numbers of people to solve. Web sites such as LawPivot, a legal Q&A Web site, allows clients to receive low-cost, crowdsourced legal answers from a group of participating lawyers. This model may undermine traditional fee structures. Users enter a confidential legal question and assign it to a category such as "tax" or "immigration."

The Web site then suggests member lawyers to whom the user can send the question; these lawyers each provide an answer. The Web site suggests that the advantages of its method include low cost, fast answers, and opportunities to meet "qualified relevant lawyers" who can then be hired by the user. Lawyers participate to build their reputations and market themselves. Google's investment arm, Google Ventures, is a major investor in LawPivot, suggesting that the approach has substantial promise.

It is hard to know how technological developments will affect your career as a paralegal. What is certain is that as more and more routine tasks are shifted to automated tools or outsourced to lower-cost locations, paralegals and other legal professionals will have to constantly improve their skills so they can find the areas of legal practice in which they can add value for clients. Keeping on top of technological developments is an important step in that direction.

KEY TERMS AND CONCEPTS

citator   230
citing case   232

KeyCite   231

Shepard's   231

Chapter Summary

Contemporary Online Legal Research

GOING ONLINE—AN INTERNET PRIMER

Today's legal professionals can access a vast amount of information using the Internet. Many online resources are available for free, while others charge a fee for accessing their databases.

1. *Internet tools*—Commonly used Internet tools include e-mail and the World Wide Web, a data network that is accessed through a browser such as Firefox or Chrome. Uniform resource locators (URLs) are Internet addresses.

2. *Search engines*—Search engines scan the Web for words entered by a researcher and provide lists of Web sites. Search operators allow you to refine results and reduce the number of irrelevant hits produced. Advanced search features allow further refinement.

FREE LEGAL RESOURCES ON THE INTERNET

A great deal of legal information, especially public documents such as statutes and cases, is accessible through free Internet sites.

1. *General legal resources*—Some free legal sites act as portals, giving access to a broad range of free information. Major sites include FindLaw and Justia. Another is the Legal Information Institute at Cornell University Law School. Other law schools provide research source assistance, too.

2. *Specific legal resources*—Secondary sources are generally not found at free sites. However, an increasing number of law review articles are available. One can also find court opinions and various other legal resources at free sites.

3. *Federal law starting points*—All federal government organizations have Internet sites.

LEXIS AND WESTLAW

For serious legal research, legal professionals often use online commercial legal research services, particularly Lexis and Westlaw.

1. *Accessing Westlaw or Lexis*—Subscribers to these fee-based services can access the services' databases.

2. *Conducting a search*—Lexis and Westlaw provide users with access to an extensive collection of legal, business, and other resources. Using these services, paralegals can access specific documents, update the law, and search hundreds of databases.

3. *Checking citations*—For citation checking, Lexis provides *Shepard's Citations* and Westlaw provides *KeyCite*. Both services enable researchers to make sure their research results are still valid. Both Lexis and Westlaw allow users to search databases with queries using terms and connectors or natural language.

4. *Shepard's Citations*—Previously, *Shepard's* citation work was done with the print version; most research is now done using the online edition. Both *Shepard's* and Westlaw's *KeyCite* enable checking the status of a case for citation purposes.

5. *Selecting a database*—Because of the mass of data found in many searches, researchers learn to restrict searches to specific databases to be more efficient and precise.

6. *Searching a database*—Within a given database, many searches can be done in natural language using terms and connectors that are peculiar to that database.

7. *Searching within results*—Westlaw and Lexis allow a researcher to keep refining results to zero in on relevant documents and cases.

8. *Is Lexis or Westlaw better?*—Both services offer similar features; researchers tend to develop personal preferences.

ALTERNATIVE ONLINE PROGRAMS

Since Westlaw and Lexis are costly to use, less expensive and less comprehensive alternatives have become more popular. Examples include PACER, Fastcase, Loislaw, Casemaker, VersusLaw, and Google Scholar. Such services may be adequate for some projects and may also be used for preliminary research.

CONDUCTING ONLINE RESEARCH

Searching can be costly in time and access fees, so paralegals must learn to become proficient in conducting extensive research as efficiently as possible. The following tips will help you as you learn to make full use of Internet resources:

1. *Plan ahead by analyzing the facts and identifying the issues*—To avoid wasting time, define what you are seeking and determine which sources are most likely to lead you to the desired results.

2. *Develop online research strategies*—Once online, you can use various search tools and other resources (such as listservs, newsgroups, and blogs) to locate information relevant to your topic. Often, researchers need to "browse the links" for a time before finding a site that is particularly relevant. Once you find a useful site, you can use your browser or the site's internal search tool to look for specific information within the site.

3. *Evaluate what you find*—In evaluating your research results, it is especially important to consider the reliability of any information obtained online. Discriminate among primary sources, secondary sources, and tertiary sources.

4. *Update your results*—To update results, you can access online news sites to look for articles or press releases concerning recent developments in the area you are researching.

5. *Locate people and investigate companies*—Paralegals often engage in online research to locate people and obtain their contact information, and to gather data about companies. Sometimes, a person can be located through a broad search of the Web using a search engine such as Yahoo. Narrow searches can be conducted by accessing—for free or for a fee—specialized databases, such as compilations of physicians, lawyers, or expert witnesses. Searches for persons may also be conducted based on defining characteristics such as place of employment. Numerous online sites contain information about both private and public companies.

QUESTIONS FOR REVIEW

1. What should you do before going online to conduct a research session?

2. List five free legal resources that can be accessed via the Internet.

3. What kinds of legal resources can be accessed at various government sites?

4. What is *KeyCite*? How can Westlaw be used to stay current on the law? Does Lexis have an online citator? Describe two ways in which you can search databases on Lexis and Westlaw.

5. List and briefly describe the two dominant fee-based online legal research database services. Do the same for the alternative online legal research databases.

ETHICAL QUESTIONS

1. Anna has been offered a paralegal internship, which is a graduation requirement for her paralegal degree, by a sole practitioner. The job requires Anna to spend the majority of her time doing legal research. The sole practitioner has made Anna's hiring contingent on her using her school-issued Westlaw password to perform the research. Is this ethical? Is it legal? How should Anna handle the situation?

2. Tony is doing research for his supervising attorney to include in a brief that has to be filed with the court of appeals by 5 p.m. today. He finds a case that is on point and provides the exact support needed for their argument. In his haste to summarize the case and get it into the brief, Tony fails to update the case using *Shepard's* or *KeyCite*. As a result, he does not inform the attorney that the case was reversed on appeal and is no longer good law. What ethical rule has Tony violated? What impact might Tony's neglect have on the client's case? On Tony's supervising attorney?

PRACTICE QUESTIONS AND ASSIGNMENTS

1. Which of these research sources—a law library, Web resources, and Westlaw or Lexis—would you use to locate the information described below? Why?

   a. To determine if a case cited in a motion is still good law.

   b. To locate a psychiatric expert witness.

   c. To locate a statutory provision that is up to date.

   d. To locate a witness to a car accident.

   e. To find an heir who is to inherit $500,000.

2. If you did the research assignment in the Chapter 7 Practice Questions and Assignments question 1, Shepardize one of the cases that you found, using *Shepard's* in print. Is the case still good law, or has it been reversed or overruled? How can you tell? How many citing cases are there? If you have access to Westlaw, Lexis, or any of the alternative legal research sites, update the same case using one of the online sources. Print out the results. Explain the differences between *Shepard's* print and online versions.

3. Do a Google Scholar search for tobacco products manufacturers' liability when cancer results from the use of their products. How many items did your search retrieve? How many cases were found on the first two pages? How many articles? Print the first two pages of your result to submit to your instructor.

4. You are working as a paralegal for a probate and estate planning law firm. One of the firm's clients died and now you have to locate all of the heirs. One is a 28-year-old nephew, whose last known address is a college dorm, according to the records that you have. This nephew was orphaned at the age of 17 when his parents died in a car accident, so there are no close relatives to help you find him. You reach an aunt who tells you that she believes the nephew is in graduate school in Chicago. Using the material on finding people, which Web sites would you use in your search to locate the missing nephew? If the free Web sites do not return any contact information for him, would you use fee-based sites? If so, which ones would you consult?

QUESTIONS FOR CRITICAL ANALYSIS

1. Why is it necessary to evaluate the credibility of the Web sites you locate when doing factual research on the Internet? Would this be necessary for government Web sites as well? What might happen if a researcher does not evaluate the credibility of Web sites?

2. Why is it necessary to check citations in a citator? What types of information does *Shepard's* provide?

Which is the most important? Does *KeyCite* provide the same information?

3. How do you draft a terms and connectors search? A natural language search? Can you think of a situation in which a terms and connectors search might be more useful than a natural language search? Explain why.

PROJECT

Using **tumblr.com**, create a blog of your favorite free sites to find people and to conduct research on legal issues. Invite your classmates to submit their favorite sites to be included on your blog.

GROUP PROJECT

This project has you investigate the alternative legal research databases. Students one, two, and three will go online and find information about what state and federal case and statutory law databases, forms databases, citators, and other services are offered by Loislaw, Casemaker, VersusLaw, and Fastcase. Each student should write a summary of what is offered and describe the strengths and weaknesses for doing research with each one. Student four will collect and organize the summaries and submit them to the instructor.

USING INTERNET RESOURCES

Using the facts and information in questions 4, 5, and 6 of Chapter 7 Practice Questions and Assignments, go to **www.justia.com** and click on "US States" and then click on your state. In the search box, type in "automobile or motor vehicle lemon law." Answer the following questions:

1. Are you able to locate the state statute governing defective motor vehicles? If so, what remedy does it offer to Mr. Consumer?

2. Does the search retrieve case law on the lemon law? Does the case law have any effect on the applicability of the statute?

3. If you did Chapter 7 Practice Questions and Assignments questions number 4, 5, and 6 in the library, how do your search results from **www.justia.com** compare to your search results from the print sources? Which do you prefer and why?

CourseMate   The available CourseMate for this text has an interactive eBook and interactive learning tools, including flash cards, quizzes, and more. To learn more about this resource and access free demo CourseMate resources, go to **www.cengagebrain.com**, and search for this book. To access CourseMate materials that you have purchased, go to **login.cengagebrain.com**.

Legal Writing: Form and Substance

Chapter Outline

Introduction

Receiving a Writing Assignment

Writing Well

Pleadings, Discovery, and Motions

General Legal Correspondence

The Legal Memorandum

After completing this chapter, you will know:

- What to consider when accepting a writing assignment.

- What to consider when drafting a legal document.

- Some techniques for improving your writing.

- Some basic guidelines for drafting effective paragraphs and sentences.

- The format for legal correspondence and the most common kinds of letters.

- How to write a legal memorandum.

Introduction

As a paralegal, you will likely draft many kinds of documents, including letters, internal legal memoranda, and pleadings and motions. Legal writing is often closely related to legal research and analysis. Once your research identifies the law that governs an issue, you need to understand the law and, through legal analysis, determine how it applies to a client's case. And if your supervising attorney asks you to draft a memorandum, you will need to explicitly summarize your research and analysis in writing. Of course, many writing assignments are not directly related to legal research. For example, you would not need to do any research to write a letter to a client recapping recent developments in her or his case.

Many of the same writing principles apply regardless of the kinds of documents you draft. This chapter discusses (1) what to consider when receiving a writing assignment, (2) how to present a well-written product, and (3) the kinds of documents commonly prepared by paralegals.

Receiving a Writing Assignment

Before we explain how to draft different kinds of documents, we need to explain what to do when you receive a writing assignment.

When a supervising attorney gives you a writing assignment, you must learn the nature of the assignment, when it needs to be completed, and what kind of writing approach it calls for. We will address each in turn.

Understanding the Assignment

The practice of law can be hectic, and paralegals are often expected to research and write about issues within a short time. When you receive a writing assignment, make sure you understand its exact nature so that you can work as efficiently as possible. If you do not understand the assignment, you will likely waste time doing unnecessary work. Each writing project is a little different, and your approach will vary depending on the kind of document you are drafting, the complexity of the subject matter, and the reader's needs. If you are uncertain about any aspect of the assignment, you

---

social MEDIA TODAY

Be aware of your e-mail address/screen name/login name and what these identifiers represent. Stay away from nicknames. Use a professional and unique name or address to represent yourself consistently across social media platforms.

Much of a paralegal's work involves legal writing, whether it be a research memorandum, a letter to a client, or a pleading or motion to be filed with a court. Excellent writing skills are a must for the professional paralegal. Assess your own writing skills. Think of ways that you can become a better writer and start putting them into practice now.

need to ask questions until the assignment is clear in your mind. As the old saying goes, there is no such thing as a stupid question.

Time Constraints and Flexibility

Knowing the deadline for a writing assignment and adhering to it is essential. Clients and supervising attorneys often need quick answers to questions, and you may need to file a document with a court by a specific date. Being late could have serious consequences.

As a paralegal, you must be flexible and prepared to deal with changing circumstances. For example, you may discover an urgent issue in the middle of a trial or just as a transaction is being finalized. Similarly, your supervising attorney may change an assignment because the client has suddenly demanded a new course of action. If possible, budget extra time for the unexpected. You will be in a better position to take your work in new directions if necessary.

Writing Approaches

When you get a writing assignment, you must also determine what kind of writing approach is appropriate. Some documents call for objective analysis, meaning that you should present a balanced discussion of an issue or a neutral summary of facts. For a persuasive document, in contrast, you will need to advocate for the client by presenting the law, issues, and facts in a favorable light.

A supervising attorney may ask you to consider whether certain clauses in two lease agreements create different legal obligations. Your assignment is not to argue that one agreement is better. Rather, you need to compare the documents objectively, pointing out which clauses lead to which obligations. Objective analysis may also be required when a document will help an attorney advise a client.

For instance, a client may ask an attorney whether he or she has a claim that justifies filing a lawsuit. In this situation, the attorney may ask you to research the issue and draft a memorandum summarizing your analysis. Although you may be tempted to advocate for the client, it would be better to present an unbiased discussion. If the client does not have a claim, the client would probably prefer to learn that before spending time and money on a hopeless lawsuit. You would not do the client any favors by predicting a favorable outcome that is ultimately unlikely.

If you are directly advocating for a client, in contrast, you will need to write persuasively. For example, persuasive analysis is essential if you are drafting a motion asking a court to exclude certain evidence from a trial. Rather than analyze the issue objectively, you need to argue for the client. When writing persuasively, you should present an analysis that clearly favors the client without misrepresenting anything. You therefore need to develop supportive legal arguments and present the matter in the light most favorable to the client.

Writing Well

The law is a communication-intensive profession, and writing is particularly important. For paralegals and attorneys alike, good writing skills go hand in hand with successful job performance. You will spend a lot of time writing, and you are more likely to please your supervising attorneys by writing well. Also keep in mind that some of your written work, such as correspondence, represents your employer to the outside world. A well-written document reflects positively on the organization and enhances its reputation in the community. See the *Developing Paralegal Skills* feature on the facing page for additional tips on quality document creation.

In this section, we will cover some general principles of good legal writing. As you work on specific writing assignments, you may also consider consulting a dictionary, a thesaurus, a style manual (such as *The Chicago Manual of Style),* and perhaps a book on English grammar. As discussed in the *Practice Focus* feature on page 254, there are a number of useful tools of the trade you can use.

GOING green

DON'T WORK SO OFTEN!

Law firms may be able to offer four-day workweeks to some employees and still provide needed coverage in the office for clients. Ten-hour workdays are increasingly popular, as they give employees more flexibility and one less day of commuting and burning gas.

DEVELOPING
paralegal skills

CREATING A USER-FRIENDLY DOCUMENT

Rianna Barnes works as a paralegal for a large law firm. A partner of the firm asks her to draft a policy on sexual harassment for a corporate client. The attorney gives Rianna several sheets of hand-written instructions and some notes on what the document should include. Rianna writes a draft and begins to proofread it.

She realizes that although she used plain English when possible and followed general principles of good writing, the document is somewhat daunting in its appearance. She decides to add a series of headings and subheadings to break up the "fine print" and make the document more inviting to readers.

TIPS FOR CREATING A USER-FRIENDLY DOCUMENT

• Format the document attractively. For example, add enough margin space to make the text more inviting.

• Divide the document into sections with headings to make the organization immediately clear to the reader.

• Add subheadings to further divide large blocks of text. If you use subheadings, always create at least two.

• Make sure the relationships between sections and subsections are clear. You can often do this by drafting an introduction or using transitional sentences at the beginning of each section or subsection.

• Use short sentences, but do not overdo it. Too many short sentences in a row can make the writing choppy and interrupt the flow of the text.

• Use the active voice unless the situation calls for a passive construction (discussed on pages 256 and 257).

• Use plain English whenever appropriate, especially when writing for readers who lack legal training.

• Be stylistically consistent. For example, do not hyphenate a phrase in one place but not others, and be sure to use the same line spacing between paragraphs throughout the document.

Choice of Format

A legal document's formatting can often be quite important. Rather than simply using your document-creation program's default settings for margin widths, paragraph indentations, line spacing, and so forth, you need to confirm that you are using the right formatting for the kind of document you are drafting. If you are drafting a document to be filed in court, you will need to check that court's formatting rules, which are often available online. Your employer will probably also have special formats and even templates for other types of documents, such as letters and legal memoranda. If your employer has a format or template for the kind of document you are drafting, you should use it.

Write for Your Reader

Paralegals write for a wide audience. When you draft a legal document, keep in mind that the document is not an end in itself. Rather, you are writing for a particular reader, such as a judge, an attorney, a client, or a witness. To communicate information or ideas effectively, you need to write with the reader's needs in mind. For example, you may use legal terms and concepts in a letter to an attorney, but the same terms and concepts may confuse someone who lacks legal training. Similarly, a motion filed in court need not explain legal concepts in great detail because your primary reader is the judge or the judge's legal clerk. A judge knows, for instance, that he or she is obligated to follow a governing statute or a binding precedent of a higher court. Adding unnecessary background writing in such a document could distract or even annoy the judge, which will be unfavorable to your client's case.

In addition to the reader's legal knowledge, a paralegal should consider the reader's understanding of the subject matter. You cannot assume that the reader

PRACTICE focus

TOOLS TO HELP LEGAL WRITING

Excelling at legal writing is a key way to ensure success as a paralegal. Good writing includes four key elements.

1. Legal writing requires accurate use of legal terminology. Words such as "trusts" or "consideration" have specific meanings that are not necessarily the same as their meaning in ordinary speech. Use a legal dictionary regularly to ensure you have the right word. *Black's Law Dictionary* is the standard reference. Fortunately, electronic access is available including iPhone and Android app versions, saving you from carrying the full 1,920-page version around with you.

2. Legal writing has quite specific rules about how to refer to sources. These citation rules are quite complex, specifying everything from typeface to specific punctuation rules. The rules are set out in *The Bluebook: A Uniform System of Citation* (www.legalbluebook.com) and the Association of Legal Writing Directors' *Citation Manual* (www.alwd.org). There is not yet an app version of either, but there are online versions accessible via the Web.

3. Legal writing requires clarity and organization. Legal writing guru (and editor of *Black's Law Dictionary*) Bryan Garner publishes *The Redbook: A Manual on Legal Style,* which provides guidance. One of Garner's most important tips is to read good writing (he recommends *The New Yorker* magazine, for example).

4. Legal writing requires specific organizational features. Some courts have explicit formats that must be followed, so you must learn any particular rules that apply. In general, appellate briefs typically must include a table of authorities, listing all sources cited and the page on which they are cited. Fortunately, electronic tools can both relieve the tedium of creating these and improve accuracy. Document-creation programs include tools to assist with these. There are also specialized programs such as Best Authority and CiteIt! to help.

knows as much as you do, especially in cases involving complicated issues. In fact, you should normally assume that the reader lacks expertise in the area and is unfamiliar with the key facts and concepts. To help the reader, make the document understandable on its own terms. Be explicit about how everything fits together, leading the reader from Point A to Point B, from Point B to Point C, and so on. Write in a way that would have made sense to you before you began working on the matter.

Outline the Material

Once you know what you want to demonstrate, discuss, or prove to your reader, you must decide how to organize the material. Organization is essential to effective legal writing, so you should have a framework in mind before you begin writing. Most people find that writing is easier if they have an outline. Of course, what works best will vary from one writing project to another. For a simple writing assignment, you may need only sketch a rough outline on a notepad. If you are drafting a complicated analysis of a legal issue, on the other hand, you may use a document creator to develop a detailed outline, complete with numbers, letters, and bullet points.

Regardless of how detailed your outline is, it should help you write more effectively and efficiently. With a good outline, your first draft will be better organized, and you will spend less time moving material around.

When creating an outline, your first task is to decide the sequence in which topics should be discussed. Your goal is to organize the points you want to make in a logical fashion. Similar topics should be addressed together, and different topics should generally be addressed separately. Lawyers also often begin with their best points, especially when making arguments. As a matter of logic, however, you may need to work your way up to your best point by first establishing other things.

As you outline, think about the advantages and disadvantages of different ways of organizing your information, paying special attention to the document's purpose and the reader's needs.

Organize the Material Logically

Once you begin writing, you need to divide the document into manageable blocks of information. As in an outline, similar topics should generally be addressed together. Also, when analyzing a topic that consists of several elements that must be proved, it is a good idea to address each element in the order in which the elements are required to be proved. For example, in order to have a valid contract, there must be (1) an offer, (2) an acceptance, (3) an exchange of consideration, (4) legal subject matter, and (5) contractual capacity. As such, it would be logical to organize the material by first listing the elements to be proved and then analyzing each element in the order listed.

Purpose of a Paragraph

The most basic device for organizing ideas in a document is the paragraph. A paragraph is a group of sentences that develops a particular idea. A well-written paragraph often begins with a topic sentence that indicates what the paragraph is about. The paragraph's remaining sentences should help develop the topic, leading the reader from one point to another. If a sentence does not relate to the topic of the paragraph, consider moving it to another part of the document or simply deleting it.

When you write, be conscious of why and when you begin new paragraphs. In general, you should start a new paragraph whenever you begin discussing a new topic. If possible, however, you should also keep paragraphs relatively short. Long paragraphs are often hard to follow, and some topics are complicated enough that they deserve multiple paragraphs. As with outlining, you might try using different approaches to organization, seeing what works best given your writing objectives.

Be sure to take your reader with you as you move from one paragraph to another. Although the connections between paragraphs may be clear to you, they may not be clear to your reader. In places, you will need to provide transitional words and phrases to show the reader how different paragraphs relate to each other. Exhibit 9.1 below gives some examples of words and phrases that you can use to establish smooth transitions.

EXHIBIT 9.1
Examples of Transitional Words and Phrases

1. **Indicating a series of ideas**
   first, second, third, next, then, finally

2. **Indicating a continuation of an idea**
   also, moreover, further, additionally

3. **Indicating a causal relationship**
   thus, therefore, hence, as a result, so, because

4. **Indicating a sequence of events**
   before, earlier, meanwhile, at the same time, next, later, then, afterward, eventually

5. **Indicating a contrast**
   although, however, nevertheless, in contrast, though

6. **Indicating a similarity**
   similarly, likewise, for the same reason

7. **Indicating a conclusion**
   in summary, in conclusion, to conclude, finally, in short

© Cengage Learning 2014

Use of Headings

In a longer document, you may also lead the reader through the discussion by adding descriptive headings and subheadings for different parts of the text. For example, if you are writing about a complex legal research project involving several issues, you may devote a separate section to each issue. You might also make the document more reader friendly by providing an introductory "road map" that orients the reader by briefly identifying the issues. In places, you might also use bulleted or numbered lists to highlight key points or make complicated material more approachable. Try to write with the reader's needs in mind.

Proper Sequence

chronologically

In a time sequence; naming or listing events in the time order in which they occurred.

If your document discusses various events, it may help to arrange them **chronologically** —that is, in a time sequence. A chronologically structured discussion is often clearest, especially when you are describing a factual background leading to a lawsuit. You may also consider using a chronological organization even when you are discussing legal issues. For example, you would probably need to structure a discussion chronologically if you are writing about how a particular rule has developed over time.

Write Effective Sentences

Most good writers prefer short, concrete sentences because they are easier to understand. Good writers also write forcefully by using active verbs in place of nominalizations, which are verbs that have been transformed into nouns. For example, it is better to say that "the plaintiff decided to settle" than that "the plaintiff made a decision to settle." Similarly, you could change "make a statement" to "state," "take into consideration" to "consider," and "reach an agreement" to "agree." Strive to write concisely in every writing project. Wordy writing often obscures your points, and concise writing is clearer, more forceful, and more persuasive. See Exhibit 9.2 below for additional examples of how to write more concisely.

Active, Not Passive

You can also often improve sentences by using the active voice rather than the passive voice. The subject of an active-voice sentence is a person or thing that is *acting* ("The plaintiff filed a motion to exclude evidence"). The subject of a passive-voice sentence, in contrast, is a person or thing that is *being acted upon* ("A motion to exclude evidence was filed by the plaintiff"). The active voice is more direct and concise, and it enlivens your writing by emphasizing who did what. In some cases, however, you may use the passive voice to avoid referring to something inappropriate that your client may have done. For example, if your firm represents a

EXHIBIT 9.2
Writing Concisely

Wordy	Concise
a period of five years	five years
as well as	and
at that point in time	then
due to the fact that	because
for the purpose of	for
in order to	to
in spite of the fact that	although
in the event that	if
it may be argued that	arguably
it seems probable that	probably
take into consideration	consider
whether or not	whether

defendant who has been accused of stealing a car, you may consider saying "the car was stolen" instead of "the defendant allegedly stole the car."

Finally, it should go without saying, but be sure to write neatly. Typographical errors and punctuation mistakes can reflect poorly on you, your employer, and the client. Here are some examples:

- *Incorrect:* The plaintiff should *of* told the defendant.
- *Correct:* The plaintiff should *have* told the defendant.
- *Incorrect: You're* hearing will be on December 15.
- *Correct: Your* hearing will be on December 15.
- *Incorrect:* The *plaintiffs* allegations are vague.
- *Correct:* The *plaintiff's* allegations are vague.

When proofreading, set aside time to check for basic writing mistakes. You must avoid them to produce acceptable, professional work.

Limit Legalese: Use Plain English

As discussed above, you should always write with the reader's needs in mind. If you are writing for a person without legal training, you should therefore minimize **legalese**, which consists of legal terms and phrases that may be unfamiliar to laypeople. Some novice legal writers assume that using legalese will impress the reader, but plain English will generally impress the reader more. When writing to someone without legal training, you should either define legal terms or avoid them altogether. For instance, you may refer to *"voir dire"* as simply "jury selection." You should also generally avoid outdated words like "hereof," "therein," and "thereto."

Legal documents, especially contracts, also often contain a lot of unnecessary language. Consider a contractual provision that applies where a borrower makes a representation that is "false or erroneous or incorrect." What is the difference between being "false," being "erroneous," and being "incorrect"? These terms are interchangeable, and it is hard to imagine that something could be false without also being erroneous and incorrect. The provision would therefore be equally effective if it applied to only false misrepresentations.

Although you should minimize legalese, you must also be careful to convey the right meaning. If you do not understand the purpose of specific language in a contract or pleading, ask your supervising attorney. For more information about writing in plain English, see the *Technology and Today's Paralegal* feature on page 258.

Do Not Quote Heavily

Just as you should minimize legalese, you should limit quotations. Quotations can be effective if you use them sparingly, but numerous quotations create stylistic problems and rob a document of your voice and ideas.

When writing about the law, use quotations for the language that matters most and put everything else into your own words. If there is a statute on point, for example, you should probably quote it because its precise language matters. Similarly, you might quote a court's requirements for a claim or defense. But if the language itself does not matter, you should probably paraphrase it. Even when quoting an important rule, you usually need not quote the entire sentence. Instead, quote only the phrase or word that you want to emphasize, and weave it into your own sentence.

Avoid Sexist Language

Legal writing has traditionally used masculine pronouns to refer to both males and females, but there is a definite trend toward using gender-neutral language. Take special care to avoid sexist language in your own writing. For example, if you see a word with "man" or "men" in it (such as "policeman," "fireman," or "workmen's compensation"), use a gender-neutral substitute (such as "police officer,"

legalese
Legal language that is hard for the general public to understand.

social MEDIA TODAY

Learning to write clear and concise posts online will improve your communication skills offline as well.

"firefighter," or "workers' compensation"). In the past few decades, writers have devised various ways to avoid sexist language, including the following:

- Use "he or she" rather than "he."

- Alternate between masculine and feminine pronouns.

- Make the noun plural so that a gender-neutral plural pronoun ("they," "their," or "them") can be used.

- Repeat the noun rather than using a pronoun.

Edit and Proofread Your Document

When you receive a writing assignment, budget time for editing and proofreading. Accuracy and precision are important for paralegal work, and a writer can rarely turn out an error-free document on the first try. Proofreading helps you discover typographical errors, improve your document's organization, and confirm that the document says what it should. Do not expect your document-creation program's spell checker and grammar checker to catch everything. There is no substitute for printing out hard copies and reviewing them several times.

TECHNOLOGY AND
today's paralegal

ONLINE "PLAIN ENGLISH" GUIDELINES

The ability to write clearly and effectively is a valuable asset to any paralegal, because almost every paralegal's job requires writing. As mentioned elsewhere, clear and effective writing means keeping legalese—legal terminology typically understood only by legal professionals—to a minimum or even eliminating it entirely. The problem is how to convert traditional legal language into clear and understandable prose. Today's paralegals can find helpful instruction at many online locations on the art of writing in plain English.

GOVERNMENT PUBLICATIONS

The U.S. government publishes some of the best online plain English guides. *A Plain English Handbook*, put out by the Securities and Exchange Commission (SEC), is available at **www.sec.gov/pdf/handbook.pdf**. Although the handbook was intended to help individuals create clearer and more informative SEC disclosure documents, the booklet's guidelines also apply to other kinds of writing. For guidelines on legal writing, see the Office of the Federal Register's booklet *Drafting Legal Documents* at **www.archives.gov**. (Search for "Drafting Legal Documents.")

The U.S. government has an official Web site dedicated to the use of plain language (**www.plainlanguage.gov**) where you can

search for the Plain Language Action and Information Network's *Federal Plain Language Guidelines*.

GLOBAL CAMPAIGN FOR CLARITY

Since the 1970s, the plain English movement, which is fighting to have public information (such as laws) written in plain English, has received worldwide attention. A British organization called the Plain English Campaign is one of the most prominent groups in this movement. The Plain English Campaign has worked to promote the use of plain English in many nations, including the United States. You can find several helpful guides at its Web site (**www.plainenglishcampaign.com**), including *How to Write in Plain English* and *The A-Z of Alternative Words*.

Another campaign, called Fight the Fog, is directed at institutions in the European Union (EU). Search for "Fight the Fog Europa" to get to the EU Web site that offers a booklet called *How to Write Clearly*, as well as other news and publications in several languages.

TECHNOLOGY TIP

Paralegals interested in improving their plain English writing skills have many Internet resources to which they can turn. The guides mentioned above provide practical information. In addition, paralegals can take online writing courses and use programs that help edit writing.

Writing is a process, and the best writers go through several drafts before filing a document in court or sending a letter to a client. When reviewing drafts, look for gaps in content. Confirm that points are fully developed and well organized, and ask yourself whether the document says what you intended. It is often helpful to read the document aloud or solicit feedback from someone who is unfamiliar with the case or topic. Another technique is to take a break and work on another project, then come back to review the document with fresh eyes.

When editing later drafts, you can pay more attention to paragraph construction, sentence formation, word choice, and so forth. You might find it helpful to prepare a checklist to remind you of specific things to do or avoid—particularly if there is a required format for the kind of document you are drafting. Remember that creating a polished product takes time, and you should spend much of that time proofreading and revising. (Additional editing tips are offered in *Developing Paralegal Skills* below and in this chapter's *Featured Contributor* on pages 260–261.)

Pleadings, Discovery, and Motions

Many paralegal writing tasks involve forms that must be submitted to courts or opposing counsel in connection with lawsuits or criminal prosecutions. These documents will be covered in detail in Chapters 10, 12, and 13. You can see those chapters for explanations and illustrations of specific pretrial forms (pleadings,

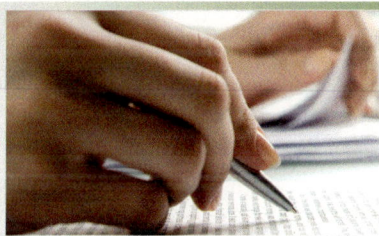

DEVELOPING
paralegal skills

EFFECTIVE EDITING

A supervising attorney asks paralegal Dixie Guiliano to draft a letter to an insurance company demanding it settle a dispute with a client. The client, Nora Ferguson, is an eighty-year-old woman who will never walk again because of a failed hip-replacement operation involving alleged malpractice by her surgeon. The attorney wants to settle the case out of court because of Nora's age and declining health.

Dixie creates the first draft using a settlement letter from another case as a sample. She then uses her document-creation program's spell-check and grammar-check features to look for errors. Dixie knows, however, that using these features is only a preliminary step in proofreading the document. She also knows that careful editing will improve the quality and persuasiveness of her letter.

TIPS FOR EDITING

- Always edit from a printed copy of the document. It is much easier to proofread and revise on paper than on a computer screen.

- If you use another document as a sample or if you cut and paste text from another document, double check that you have changed the names, dates, and other information accurately.

- Allow some time to pass (preferably a day) before editing the first draft so that you can review your writing more critically. Examine each draft in its entirety.

- Edit the content first. Ensure that the document is complete and says what you intended. Look for gaps in your reasoning. Make sure you have discussed all the points that you planned to discuss (including cases or statutes). Confirm that the document is well organized and progresses logically from one idea to another.

- Next, review for stylistic issues. Make sure the document is aimed at the appropriate audience and that you have omitted unnecessary words. Change passive voice into active voice, if possible. Make sure that the document is stylistically consistent.

- Check your grammar and spelling. For all sentences, confirm that verbs agree with subjects and that you use proper verb tenses. Check for punctuation problems with plurals, possessives, and commas.

Featured Contributor

TIPS FOR MAKING LEGAL WRITING EASIER

William Putman

BIOGRAPHICAL NOTE

William Putman received his Juris Doctor degree from the University of New Mexico School of Law and has been a member of the New Mexico Bar since 1975. For ten years, he was an instructor in the Paralegal Studies programs at Central New Mexico Community College in Albuquerque, New Mexico, and Santa Fe Community College in Santa Fe, New Mexico.

Putman is the author of the *Pocket Guide to Legal Writing* and the *Pocket Guide to Legal Research*. He also wrote the textbooks *Legal Analysis and Writing*; *Legal Research, Analysis, and Writing*; and *Legal Research*. He authored the legal writing column in *Legal Assistant Today* for two years and published several articles in that magazine on legal analysis and writing.

© Cengage Learning 2014

UNDERSTAND THE ASSIGNMENT

A legal-writing assignment may seem to be a daunting task. But all writing assignments are made easier if you answer some preliminary questions before you begin to conduct research or start writing.

What is the purpose of the assignment? An important step in the writing process is to be sure that you understand the task you have been assigned. If you have any questions concerning the general nature or specifics of the assignment, ask. Most attorneys welcome inquiries and prefer that a paralegal ask questions rather than proceed in a wrong direction. Misunderstanding the assignment can result in wasting a great deal of time performing the wrong task or addressing the wrong issue.

What type of legal writing (document) is required? Before you begin, determine what type of legal writing the assignment requires—a legal research memorandum, correspondence, the rough draft of a court brief, and so on. This is important because each type of legal writing serves a different function and has its own required elements and format.

Who is the audience? When assessing the requirements of an assignment, identify the intended audience. The intended reader may be a judge, an attorney, or a client. You should ensure that the writing meets the needs of that reader. A legal writing designed to inform a client or other layperson of the legal analysis of an issue is drafted differently than a writing designed to convey the same information to an attorney.

What are the constraints on the assignment? Most assignments have time and length constraints. Assignments usually have a time deadline. Most assignments have a length constraint—that is, they should not exceed a certain number of pages. These constraints govern the amount of research you will conduct and require that you allocate sufficient time for both research and writing.

discovery procedures, and pretrial motions) and for motions made during trials. Keep in mind that most documents submitted to courts should be written persuasively because they directly advocate for clients.

Form books and electronic forms are often helpful, but you should always know the rules of the specific court in which a document is being filed. If you cannot find a copy of a court's rules, ask your supervising attorney for help. It is critical that you use the correct formats and include all the right information.

General Legal Correspondence

Paralegals often draft letters to clients, witnesses, opposing counsel, and others. Even when a message has already been conveyed orally to a party by phone or in person, a paralegal may write a letter confirming the discussion in writing. In fact,

What is the format for the type of document being prepared?
Most law offices have rules or guidelines that govern the organization and format of most types of legal writing, such as case briefs, office memoranda, and correspondence. Courts have formal rules governing the format and style of briefs and other documents submitted for filing. Because the assignment must be drafted within the constraints of the required format, identify the format at the beginning of the process.

These preliminary questions are often overlooked or not given sufficient attention by beginning writers, resulting in headaches later. The task is made easier if you answer these questions.

SOME WRITING TIPS

Many paralegals assigned a legal-writing task find it difficult to make the transition from the research stage to the drafting stage. Here are some guidelines to help make the writing process easier.

Select the right time and place for your writing.   Write during the time of day when you do your best work. For example, if you are a "morning person," write in the morning and save other tasks for later in the day. Also, make sure that the work environment is pleasant and physically comfortable. Have available all of the resources you will need—writing paper, a computer, research materials, and so on. Legal writing requires focus and concentration. Therefore, select a writing time and an environment that allow you to be as free from interruptions and distractions as possible.

Begin writing—do not procrastinate.   Often, one of the most difficult steps in writing is starting to write. Do not put it off. The longer you put it off, the harder it will become to start your writing project. Start writing anything that has to do with the project. Do not expect what you start with to be great—just start. Once you begin writing, it will get easier.

Begin with a part of the assignment about which you feel confident.   You do not have to write in the sequence of the outline. Write the easiest material first, especially if you are having trouble starting.

Do not try to make the first draft the final draft.   The goal of the first draft should be to translate the research and analysis into organized paragraphs and sentences, not to produce a finished product. Just write the information in rough form. It is much easier to polish a rough draft than to try to make the first draft a finished product.

Do not begin to write until you are prepared.   Do all the research and analysis before you begin to write. It is much easier to write a rough draft if you have completed the research and if the research is thorough.

If you become stuck, move to another part of the assignment.
If you are stuck on a particular section, leave it. The mind continues to work on a problem when you are unaware of it. That is why solutions to problems often seem to appear in the morning. Let the subconscious work on the problem while you move on. The solution to the difficulty may become apparent when you return to the problem.

Establish a timetable.   Break the project into logical units and allocate your time accordingly. This helps you avoid spending too much time on one section of the writing and running out of time. Do not become fanatical about the time schedule, however. You created the timetable, and you can break it. It is there as a guide to keep you on track and alert you to the overall time constraints.

> *"All writing assignments are made easier if you answer some preliminary questions."*

paralegals and lawyers often document communications. A letter helps prevent future problems by confirming that the conversation took place and resolving any ambiguities.

Most law firms and legal departments have official letterheads and stationery. The letterhead contains basic information about the firm or department, including its name, address, phone and fax numbers, and perhaps an e-mail address. Some law firms have more detailed letterheads that include the names of partners or the locations of various offices. You should always use your firm's or department's letterhead when representing your organization or writing a letter for an attorney. Put the correspondence's first page on letterhead paper and additional pages on plain, matching, numbered sheets.

In this section, you will read about some common formats and types of legal correspondence. Keep in mind, though, that your employer will probably have its own forms, procedures, and requirements. If so, you should follow them.

General Format for Legal Correspondence

There are many types of legal correspondence, but most include the following components. See Exhibit 9.3 below for a labeled example.

Date

Legal correspondence must be dated. The date appears below the official letterhead, and it should also be part of the file name on your computer. Typing the wrong date could have serious consequences, so make sure that the date is right. Be especially careful at the beginning of a calendar year, when you might type the preceding year simply out of habit.

EXHIBIT 9.3
Components of a Legal Letter

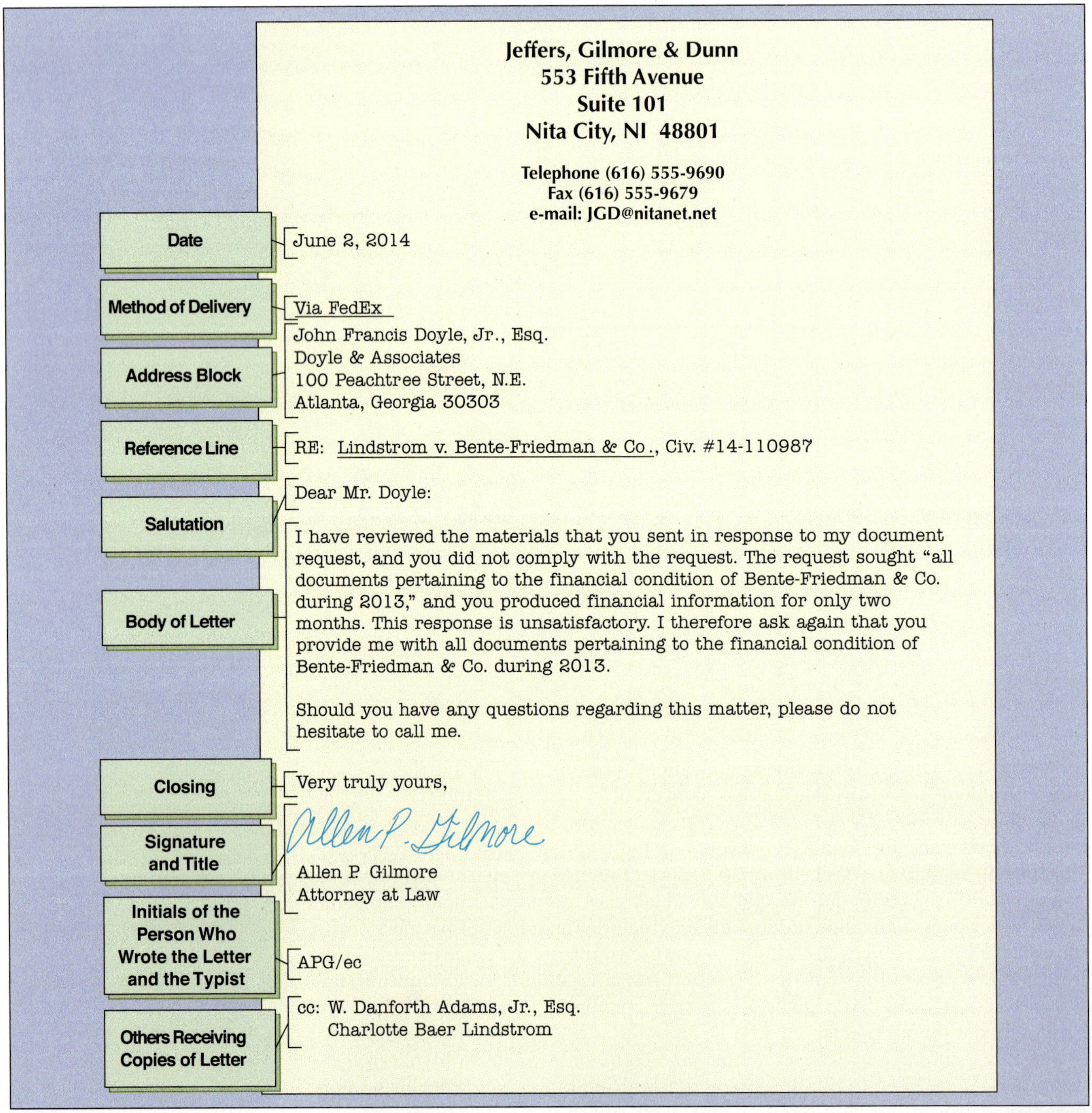

Jeffers, Gilmore & Dunn
553 Fifth Avenue
Suite 101
Nita City, NI 48801

Telephone (616) 555-9690
Fax (616) 555-9679
e-mail: JGD@nitanet.net

Date	June 2, 2014
Method of Delivery	Via FedEx
Address Block	John Francis Doyle, Jr., Esq. Doyle & Associates 100 Peachtree Street, N.E. Atlanta, Georgia 30303
Reference Line	RE: Lindstrom v. Bente-Friedman & Co., Civ. #14-110987
Salutation	Dear Mr. Doyle:
Body of Letter	I have reviewed the materials that you sent in response to my document request, and you did not comply with the request. The request sought "all documents pertaining to the financial condition of Bente-Friedman & Co. during 2013," and you produced financial information for only two months. This response is unsatisfactory. I therefore ask again that you provide me with all documents pertaining to the financial condition of Bente-Friedman & Co. during 2013. Should you have any questions regarding this matter, please do not hesitate to call me.
Closing	Very truly yours,
Signature and Title	*Allen P. Gilmore* Allen P. Gilmore Attorney at Law
Initials of the Person Who Wrote the Letter and the Typist	APG/ec
Others Receiving Copies of Letter	cc: W. Danforth Adams, Jr., Esq. Charlotte Baer Lindstrom

© Cengage Learning 2014

Dates serve important functions in legal matters. For example, the date of a letter may be critical to establish that someone had legal notice of a particular event. Additionally, legal correspondence is normally filed chronologically. Without any record of the date, accurately filing a letter would be difficult if not impossible. As a general rule, you should place a date on every written item that you create, including telephone messages, memos to file, and personal reminders.

Address Block and Method of Delivery

Below the date, you should give an **address block**, which indicates the name of the person to whom the letter is addressed. The address block should contain the person's name and title, and the name and address of the person's firm or place of business. If the letter is sent other than by U.S. mail, you should also indicate the method of delivery in the line above the address block. If the letter is to be sent by FedEx, the line should read "Via FedEx." Similarly, hand-delivered correspondence should say "By Hand Delivery," and fax communications can use the words "By Fax" or "By Facsimile."

address block
The part of a letter that indicates to whom the letter is addressed. The address block is placed in the upper left-hand portion of the letter, above the salutation (and reference line, if one is included).

Reference Line and Salutation

Following the address block, a writer may include a **reference line** identifying the matter discussed in the letter. In a letter regarding a pending lawsuit, the reference line may contain the name of the case, its case file (or docket) number, and a brief notation about the nature of the dispute. Many attorneys also include the firm's file number for the case. In an informative letter (which will be discussed below), the reference line may take the form of a title. For example, for a letter concerning the closing procedures for a financing transaction, the reference line may read "RE: Closing Procedures for ABC Company's $4,000,000 Financing Package."

Immediately below the reference line, you should provide the **salutation**, which is a greeting to the addressee. Because legal correspondence is a professional means of communication, you should generally call the person "Mr." or "Ms.," followed by the person's last name and a colon. Of course, it may be appropriate to address the person by his or her first name if you are writing to a friend or close acquaintance. Use your discretion to determine the appropriate level of formality, erring on the side of being too formal.

reference line
The portion of the letter that indicates the matter to be discussed, such as "RE: Summary of Cases Applying the Family and Medical Leave Act of 1993." The reference line is placed just below the address block and above the salutation.

salutation
In a letter, the formal greeting to the addressee. The salutation is placed just below the reference line.

Body, Closing, and Signature

The main part of the letter is the body. The body's content varies depending on the letter's purpose, but it should always be written formally and communicate information effectively. If, for example, you are asking the recipient of your letter to respond in some way, be sure you are clear about what is expected and when a response is needed. A paralegal must carefully proofread all outgoing correspondence and confirm that it is accurate, well written, and free of grammatical and spelling errors. A poorly written letter or e-mail reflects poorly on your employer and you.

The last part of the body will typically consist of one or two concluding sentences. These final sentences are usually courteous statements, like "Thank you for your time and attention to this matter" or "Should you have any questions or comments, please do not hesitate to contact me."

Finally, the last substantive part of a letter is the **closing**, which is followed by the writer's signature, name, and title. Closings in legal correspondence should be formal—for example, "Sincerely" or "Very truly yours." When you write a letter using your own signature, you should always include your title ("Paralegal" or "Legal Assistant") immediately after your name. Similarly, you may include a line saying "Attorney at Law" when you write a letter to be signed by an attorney.

closing
In a letter, an ending word or phrase placed above the signature, such as "Sincerely" or "Very truly yours."

E-Mail Correspondence

Increasingly, legal professionals communicate by e-mail rather than by letter or telephone. E-mail often may be used for the same purposes as traditional correspondence with less formal content. For example, you might use e-mail to tell a client about recent developments in a case, to send electronic copies of documents to a witness, or to confirm the details of a conversation. Nevertheless, it is still generally better to send hard copies of more formal legal documents, such as demand letters to opposing parties and formal opinion letters to clients. As always, follow your supervising attorney's preferences, being sure to include a standard confidentiality notice if your employer has one.

Most e-mails from a law office should be written formally. After all, e-mails represent your employer and you to the outside world, and they almost never disappear. You should generally follow the same writing conventions that you would when drafting a letter. The salutation, for example, should generally address the recipient as "Mr." or "Ms.," and you should also write formally in the subject line, body, and closing. No matter how short the e-mail, always proofread before clicking "send." As with letters, professionalism is of the utmost importance.

Also, before clicking on "send," reconfirm that the recipients are truly the ones who are supposed to receive the e-mail. It's easy to have added an incorrect recipient in the "To" line and in the "Cc" line (which comes from "carbon copy") or the "Bcc" line (which comes from "blind carbon copy").

Types of Legal Letters

There are several types of legal correspondence, and each one serves a different purpose. The types of legal letters that you should be familiar with include informative letters, confirmation letters, opinion (or advisory) letters, and demand letters.

Informative Letters

informative letter
A letter that conveys information to a client, a witness, an adversary's counsel, or some other person regarding a legal matter (such as the date, time, place, and purpose of a meeting) or a cover letter that accompanies other documents being sent to a person or court.

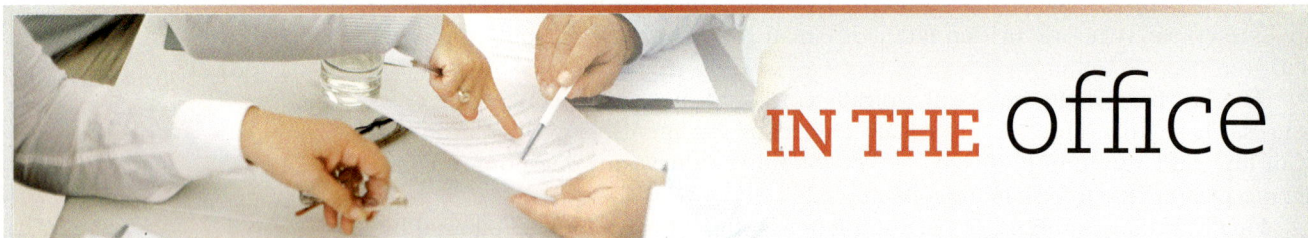

An **informative letter** conveys information to another party. As a paralegal, you will likely write many such letters, and a lot of them will probably be to clients. You might write an informative letter to advise a client about recent developments in a case, to tell him or her about an upcoming meeting or filing, to provide general background on a legal issue, or simply to break down the firm's bill. Write an informative letter in a way that is understandable to the client, given his or her education and experience.

Informative letters are also sent to opposing counsel and others. For example, law firms often send scheduling information to opposing counsel, witnesses, and other people involved in trials, and Exhibit 9.4 on the facing page is a sample letter to a witness in an arbitration proceeding. An informative letter may also serve as a cover letter when you send someone documents.

IN THE office

TIME MANAGEMENT

Many paralegals learn the hard way—through trial and error—that managing time effectively is an essential part of doing a good job. It is easy to forget that good writing takes time and that you may need to revise a document several times before you are satisfied with its quality. When you receive a writing assignment, always give yourself enough time to revise and polish the final document. You have a duty to do the best work possible for your employer, your supervising attorney, and the client. To serve them well, you must manage your time effectively.

EXHIBIT 9.4
A Sample Informative Letter

Jeffers, Gilmore & Dunn
553 Fifth Avenue
Suite 101
Nita City, NI 48801

Telephone (616) 555-9690
Fax (616) 555-9679
e-mail: JGD@nitanet.net

June 25, 2014

Bernadette P. Williams
149 Snowflake Drive
Irving, TX 75062

RE: Kempf/Joseph Arbitration Proceedings

Dear Ms. Williams:

The arbitration will resume on Wednesday, August 6, 2014. Please arrive at the offices of
the American Arbitration Association (the AAA) before 8:30 A.M. The offices of the AAA are
located at 400 West Ferry Boulevard in Dallas. You will be called as a witness sometime
before 12:00 noon.

Should you have any questions or concerns regarding your responsibilities as a witness,
please do not hesitate to contact me.

Sincerely,

Elena Lopez

Elena Lopez
Paralegal

Confirmation Letters

Paralegals also often write confirmation letters. Like informative letters, **confirmation letters** communicate information to the reader. Confirmation letters differ, however, in that they mostly summarize conversations that have already occurred. By providing attorneys with permanent records of earlier conversations, confirmation letters safeguard against any misinterpretation or misunderstanding of what was said. If there is any disagreement about a conversation's details, an attorney can use a confirmation letter to support his or her account. See Exhibit 9.5 on the following page for a sample confirmation letter.

confirmation letter
A letter that summarizes an oral conversation to provide a permanent record of the discussion.

Opinion Letters

The purpose of an **opinion letter**, or **advisory letter**, is to provide both information and advice. Unlike an informative letter, an opinion letter actually gives a legal opinion about the matter discussed. An attorney sending an opinion letter is required to provide a detailed analysis of the law and to bring the analysis to a definite conclusion that states a formal opinion.

An opinion letter may also advise a client about the legality of a course of action. For example, a company planning to establish operations in a foreign country may seek a lawyer's opinion on whether certain conduct would be permissible. The attorney (or a paralegal) will research the issue and then draft an advisory letter to the client. Opinion letters are commonly quite long and include detailed explanations of how the law applies to the client. Sometimes, the attorney simply summarizes his or her conclusion in the opinion letter and attaches a detailed legal memorandum explaining the supporting law and analysis. For an example, see the sample opinion letter in Exhibit 9.6 on page 267.

opinion (advisory) letter
A letter from an attorney to a client containing a legal opinion on an issue raised by the client's question or legal claim. The opinion is based on a detailed analysis of the law.

EXHIBIT 9.5
A Sample Confirmation Letter

Jeffers, Gilmore & Dunn
553 Fifth Avenue
Suite 101
Nita City, NI 48801

Telephone (616) 555-9690
Fax (616) 555-9679
e-mail: JGD@nitanet.net

August 4, 2014

Pauline C. Dunbar
President
Minute-Magic Corporation
7689 Industrial Boulevard
San Francisco, CA 80021

RE: Purchase of real estate from C. C. Barnes, Inc.

Dear Ms. Dunbar:

As we discussed on the phone today, the Minute-Magic Corporation will purchase real estate located at 2683 Millwood Ave., Nita City, NI, from C. C. Barnes for $800,000. The purchase will be financed by a mortage with Citiwide Bank at an interest rate of 5.5 percent.

I look forward to seeing you next week. If you have any questions or comments before then, please give me a call.

Very truly yours,

Allen P. Gilmore

Allen P. Gilmore
Attorney at Law

APG/ec

© Cengage Learning 2014

A firm's opinion letter reflects legal expertise and advice on which a client can rely. As will be discussed in the *Ethics Watch* feature on page 268, an opinion letter must be signed by an attorney. Should a client suffer a loss in a legal matter due to poor-quality legal advice or improper action by an attorney, the client may sue the firm for malpractice. An attorney's signature represents his or her acceptance of responsibility for the document's content.

Demand Letters

demand letter
A letter in which one party explains its legal position in a dispute and requests that the recipient take some action, such as paying money owed.

Another basic type of letter is the demand letter. In a **demand letter**, one party explains its legal position in a dispute and demands that the recipient take some action. Typically, an attorney will send a demand letter before filing a lawsuit against a person or company. In fact, sending a demand letter may even be required, such as in many cases involving consumer-protection violations. Suppose your supervising attorney asks you to draft a letter demanding that a company pay a debt it owes to a client. Your demand letter would summarize the relevant facts, demand payment by a certain date, and say that the client will sue if the company does not pay the debt.

The demand letter should adopt a serious and forceful tone, and the client's demand must not be frivolous. Although the letter should be insistent and adversarial, it should not come across as unreasonable or harassing. After all, a demand letter seeks to accomplish something. For a sample demand letter, see Exhibit 9.7

EXHIBIT 9.6
A Sample Opinion Letter

Jeffers, Gilmore & Dunn
553 Fifth Avenue
Suite 101
Nita City, NI 48801

Telephone (616) 555-9690
Fax (616) 555-9679
e-mail: JGD@nitanet.com

December 10, 2014

J. D. Joslyn
President and Chief Executive Officer
Joslyn Footwear, Inc.
700 Kings Avenue, Suite 4000
New City, NI 48023

Dear Ms. Joslyn:

After careful consideration, I have concluded that Joslyn Footwear, Inc., would risk significant liability by expanding into Latin American markets. The biggest problem concerns the proposed shoe-manufacturing plants. Due to their size, the plants would violate industrial regulations in Mexico, Uruguay, and Argentina.

The enclosed legal memorandum explains in detail how the law applies to your situation and the reasons for my conclusion. Please call me if you have any questions.

Very truly yours,

Allen P. Gilmore

Allen P. Gilmore
Attorney at Law

APG/ec

Enclosure

© Cengage Learning 2014

on page 269. It covers the common situation of demanding that an adversarial party respond to a settlement offer in a lawsuit.

The Legal Memorandum

A legal memorandum is prepared for internal use within a law firm, legal department, or other organization. Generally, a memo presents a thorough analysis of one or more specific legal issues.

As a paralegal, you may be asked to draft a legal memorandum for your supervising attorney. The attorney may need the memo for a number of reasons. For example, the attorney may be preparing an opinion letter or brief, either of which would require detailed legal analysis. To help your supervising attorney represent or advise a client more effectively, a memo should be thorough, well reasoned, and clearly written. Your primary reader is an attorney, so you need not explain basic legal concepts or define common legal terms. Instead, assume that your reader has general knowledge of the law but lacks expertise in the specific area you are discussing.

ETHICS WATCH

LETTERS AND THE UNAUTHORIZED PRACTICE OF LAW

As this text has stressed, engaging in the unauthorized practice of law is unlawful and unethical. To avoid liability for the unauthorized practice of law, never sign opinion or advisory letters with your own name, and when you sign other types of letters, always indicate your status as a paralegal. Even if you are sending a letter to a person who knows you well and knows that you are a paralegal, indicate your status on the letter itself. By doing so, you will prevent both potential confusion and potential legal liability. Even if your name and status are included in the letterhead, as some state laws allow, always type your title below your name as a precaution.

Here are some relevant rules and guidelines:

- NALA *Code of Ethics,* Canon 3: "A paralegal must not . . . give legal opinions or advice."

- NALA *Code of Ethics,* Canon 5: "A paralegal must disclose his or her status as a paralegal at the outset of any professional relationship with a client, an attorney, a court or administrative agency or personnel thereof, or a member of the general public."

- ABA *Model Guidelines* state that attorneys may not grant paralegals the authority to give legal opinions to clients.

- ABA *Model Guidelines* make clear that attorneys have a duty to be sure that clients and any other relevant parties, such as other lawyers, know that paralegals working with attorneys are not authorized to practice law.

- NFPA *Model Code of Ethics,* EC 1.7(a): "A paralegal's title shall clearly indicate the individual's status and shall be disclosed in all business and professional communications to avoid misunderstandings and misconceptions about the paralegal's role and responsibilities."

As with all legal documents, attention to detail is important. A memo must be accurate and neat. As the *Developing Paralegal Skills* feature on page 270 notes, you may be able to help improve the quality of documents drafted by attorneys.

Format

A legal memorandum must be well organized. There is no "right" way to structure a legal memo, but most are divided into sections that serve different purposes. The following sections are very common:

- a heading,
- the question(s) presented,
- brief answers to the questions presented,
- a statement of facts,

EXHIBIT 9.7
A Sample Demand Letter

Jeffers, Gilmore & Dunn
553 Fifth Avenue
Suite 101
Nita City, NI 48801

Telephone (616) 555-9690
Fax (616) 555-9679
e-mail: JGD@nitanet.com

June 13, 2014

Christopher P. Nelson, Esq.
Nelson, Johnson, Callan & Sietz
200 Way Bridge
Philadelphia, PA 40022

RE: *Fuentes v. Thompson*

Dear Mr. Nelson:

This morning, I met with my clients, Eduardo and Myrna Fuentes, the plaintiffs in the lawsuit against your client, Laura Thompson. Mr. and Mrs. Fuentes expressed a desire to withdraw their complaint and settle with Ms. Thompson. The Fuentes' settlement demand is $50,000, payable by certified check no later than July 15, 2014. We think that you and Ms. Thompson will find this offer quite reasonable. After all, given the strength of the Fuentes' claims, a jury award exceeding $200,000 is quite possible.

If you plan to take advantage of the Fuentes' settlement offer, please contact me by the close of business on Friday, June 20, 2014. If we do not hear from you by that date, we will assume that you have rejected our demand and we will proceed with litigation.

Very truly yours,

Allen P. Gilmore

Allen P. Gilmore
Attorney at Law

APG/ec

© Cengage Learning 2014

- a discussion of how the law applies to the facts, and
- a conclusion.

Of course, if your employer or supervising attorney prefers a particular format, you should follow it. Similarly, check for sample documents that your firm uses so that you can make use of them in preparing new memos.

Heading

The heading of a legal memorandum contains four types of information:

- The date on which the memo is submitted.
- The name of the person for whom the memo was prepared.
- The name of the person submitting the memo.
- A brief description of the matter, usually in the form of a reference line.

Exhibit 9.8 on the next page illustrates a sample heading for a legal memorandum.

Questions Presented

The questions-presented section identifies the main legal issues that you discuss in the memorandum. Depending on how complicated the memo is, you may present one simple question or several more complicated questions. Often, a supervising

DEVELOPING
paralegal skills

REVIEWING ATTORNEY-GENERATED DOCUMENTS

Ashana Carroll works as a paralegal for Jeremy O'Connell, a sole practitioner who owns a small general law practice. Jeremy frequently drafts motions and other legal documents because Ashana has her hands full with other writing tasks and general legal work. Typically, Jeremy e-mails his documents to Ashana, instructing her to send letters to recipients and file pleadings and motions in court. Ashana usually takes time to quickly review Jeremy's documents. Even though Jeremy has practiced law for years, Ashana occasionally finds errors in his documents, some of which could have serious consequences.

TIPS FOR REVIEWING AN ATTORNEY'S DOCUMENTS

- Confirm that all names and addresses are current and correct. The attorney may have forgotten that a client recently moved, for example, and mistakenly used an old address.

- If you are filing a document with a court, confirm that you have the most recent version of the court's rules. Court rules change, and it is important to ensure that the correct court rules are referenced in the document filed.

- Confirm that a document to be filed with a court complies with the court's rules concerning format, style, content, and deadlines. Also confirm that the document complies with the specific judge's preferences if you have them on file.

- Check with your supervising attorney if you have any question about how a particular document should be delivered.

attorney will identify the issues for you when asking you to write a memorandum. If so, you can use the attorney's request as a starting point for drafting this section of the memo.

Questions presented help bring the main issues into focus, and they should be case specific based on the facts. Each question should identify the governing law, briefly identify the issue, and explain the most important facts for that issue. See Exhibits 9.9 and 9.10 on the facing page for some examples.

Brief Answers

Brief answers respond to questions presented, and they should follow the same order. An answer's length will depend on the issue's complexity, but each answer should probably be only a few sentences long. Try to begin with a one- or two-word answer to the question, like "yes," "no," "probably," or "probably not." After giving a short answer, explain your reasoning in one to three sentences. Your goal is to

EXHIBIT 9.8
Legal Memorandum—Heading

MEMORANDUM

DATE: August 6, 2014

TO: Allen P. Gilmore, Partner

FROM: Elena Lopez, Paralegal

RE: Neely, Raquel: Emotional Distress—File No. 00-2146
Neely, Raquel, and D'andrea: Emotional Distress—File No. 00-2147

EXHIBIT 9.9
Legal Memorandum—
Statement of Facts

STATEMENT OF FACTS

Raquel Neely ("Neely") and her 11-year-old daughter, D'andrea Neely ("D'andrea"), seek advice in connection with possible emotional distress claims against Miles Thompson.

In October 2012, Neely and D'andrea moved from San Francisco to Union City, where Neely began working for an investment firm. At the firm, Neely worked for Thompson, and the two initially had a friendly, professional relationship. After about six months, however, their relationship soured when Thompson expressed romantic interest in Neely.

On April 1, 2014, Thompson visited Neely's house. D'andrea was home alone because Neely had gone to the grocery store, and Thompson invited D'andrea for a ride in his Corvette. Not knowing about her mother's problems with Thompson, D'andrea said yes. When Neely soon returned home to find D'andrea missing, she panicked and called the police.

Thompson drove D'andrea around Union City for approximately 30 minutes. During the drive, Thompson told D'andrea that her mother was a "selfish woman," that she did not care about her, and that she would leave her "once the right man comes along." As Thompson made his way back to Neely's house, an oncoming vehicle hit the car at the corner of Oak Street and Maple Road, where the Neelys live. According to the police report, Thompson had a high blood-alcohol level, indicating that he was drunk.

Neely heard the crash, ran outside, and approached Thompson's car. Neely then saw D'andrea bleeding profusely from head injuries, causing Neely to faint. She had to spend a day in Union City Hospital for extreme anxiety and trauma.

D'andrea spent two days in Union City Hospital, where she was kept under observation for possible internal injuries. D'andrea is also undergoing psychiatric therapy because of Thompson's comments. She is severely depressed and emotionally unstable, and she suffers from frequent nightmares.

© Cengage Learning 2014

give a thumbnail sketch of the discussion section, which will examine the issue in greater detail. See Exhibit 9.10 below for questions to be presented in the memo, and Exhibit 9.11 on the following page for sample answers to those questions.

Statement of Facts

The statement of facts provides a factual background for the reader, focusing primarily on the facts that are relevant to the legal issues discussed in the rest of the memo. Facts are relevant if they have a bearing on your analysis, which will appear in the memo's discussion section. Therefore, you may consider writing the statement of facts after drafting the discussion section, even though the statement of facts will appear earlier in the final document. See which facts are important for your analysis, and then use them as a starting point for drafting the statement of facts. That approach also ensures that the statement of facts is thorough, so that the reader does not learn new details about the facts later in the memo.

EXHIBIT 9.10
Legal Memorandum—
Questions Presented

QUESTIONS PRESENTED

I. Under California common law, may Raquel Neely recover for negligent infliction of emotional distress when she witnessed injuries to her daughter, D'andrea Neely, but was not herself hurt by the car accident that caused the injuries?

II. Under California common law, may D'andrea Neely recover against Miles Thompson for intentional infliction of emotional distress because he made statements to her that have made her emotionally unstable and have caused severe depression?

© Cengage Learning 2014

BRIEF ANSWERS

I. Probably not. California courts require someone not injured physically to have been present at the scene of the injury-producing event at the time of the event. In this case, Neely did not witness the accident itself, merely the aftermath.

II. Probably. To recover for intentional infliction of emotional distress, a plaintiff must prove that the defendant (1) intended to cause emotional distress or was substantially certain it would result, (2) in fact caused severe emotional distress, and (3) engaged in outrageous conduct. In this case, all three requirements are probably satisfied.

STAY OBJECTIVE.   Like other parts of the memo, the statement of facts should be objective. This section should not present an argument for the client. Rather, it should present an objective, dispassionate summary of the key facts. You should never omit facts that are unfavorable to the client's case. To help the client, your supervising attorney needs to know everything.

IMPORTANCE OF ORGANIZATION.   The statement of facts must also be well organized. For example, you can help orient the reader by providing an introductory paragraph that briefly explains the client's issue, as in the sample statement of facts in Exhibit 9.9 on the previous page. After a short introductory paragraph, you should explain the key facts in a logical order. For many memos, a chronological organization will work well, especially if the facts are relatively simple. If the facts are complicated, you might try a more topical organization that devotes different paragraphs to different kinds of facts. Feel free to experiment with different ways of organizing and see what works best, given the subject matter and the reader's needs.

Discussion

The discussion section presents the writer's detailed analysis of how the law applies to the facts. Some memos address only one main issue, but many address multiple issues. If a memo discusses more than one issue, you may need to divide the discussion section into subsections. For example, if a memo discusses a client's potential claims for both negligent and intentional infliction of emotional distress, you may devote a separate subsection to each cause of action, providing a descriptive heading for each. To be consistent, you should follow the discussion section's organization in other sections of the memo. Thus, if you address negligent infliction first in the discussion section, you should also address it first in the questions presented, brief answers, statement of facts, and conclusion sections.

The Heart of the Memorandum

The discussion section is the heart of a legal memorandum, and it should explicitly summarize both your research and analysis. A good memorandum should answer the following kinds of questions for each issue:

- What is the probability that the client will succeed? For example, does the client have a claim or defense?

- What law governs the issue?

- Is there a statute on point? If so, how does it apply to the client's case? Are the statute's requirements satisfied?

- Are there any cases on point? If so, how do they apply to the client's case? Are the court's rules satisfied? How is the client's case similar to the precedents? How does it differ?

Your analysis should be objective because the memo's purpose is to help an attorney represent or advise a client. The discussion section should candidly evaluate both the strengths and weaknesses of the client's position. If there is a problem with

---

the client's position, you should address it. After all, the supervising attorney can deal with the problem much more effectively if he or she knows about it early on. Remember that your goal is to help the attorney.

IRAC

Like other kinds of legal writing, the discussion section must be well organized. You can keep the discussion clear by using IRAC, which stands for *issue, rule, application, conclusion*. As discussed in Chapter 7, IRAC is an organizational device that helps you present your analysis in a logical order. If you analyze multiple issues or rules of law you should probably present multiple IRACs for each rule you analyze. For each IRAC:

1. Identify the *issue*.
2. Explain the governing *rule*, which may come from statutory provisions, cases on point, or administrative agency regulations.
3. *Apply* the rule to the facts of the client's case.
4. State your *conclusion*.

Then repeat the process until all of the rules from various sources have been applied to the client's case.

Exhibit 9.12 below presents an excerpt from a simple discussion section that uses IRAC. The exhibit identifies the elements of IRAC for illustration purposes, but you would omit them, of course, from a memorandum to a supervising

EXHIBIT 9.12
Legal Memorandum—Discussion (Excerpt Using the IRAC Method)

DISCUSSION (Excerpt)

I. Negligent Infliction of Emotional Distress

Issue
The first issue is whether Neely can recover for negligent infliction of emotional distress because she witnessed injuries to her daughter D'andrea.

Rule
All the relevant events occurred in California, so California law governs this case. There is no statute on point, but California has rejected the "impact rule" that prevents a party from recovering when a plaintiff alleges emotional distress caused by merely witnessing a third party's injuries. *Thing v. La Chusa*, 48 Cal.3d 644, 771 P.2d 814 (Cal. 1989). *Thing* concerned a claim brought by a woman whose child was struck by a car. The mother did not see the accident, but saw her injured child unconscious and bleeding on the road when she arrived on the scene.

Under California's approach, a plaintiff must satisfy three elements to recover for negligent infliction of emotional distress based on injury to another person: (1) the plaintiff must be closely related to the victim; (2) the plaintiff must be present at the scene of the injury-producing event at the time it occurs and be contemporaneously aware that the injury is being caused; and (3) the plaintiff must suffer serious emotional distress as a result.

California adopted this rule, severely limiting the circumstances under which a negligent infliction claim could be brought, out of concern that an expanding "circle of liability" would result unless the law restricted who could bring such claims. *Morton v. Thousand Oaks Surgical Hosp.*, 187 Cal.App.4th 926, 934–935, 114 Cal. Rptr.3d 661, 667 (Cal. App. 2 Dist. 2010). The California courts have held that "The merely negligent actor does not owe a duty the law will recognize to make monetary amends to all persons who have suffered emotional distress on viewing or learning about the injurious consequences of his conduct." *Thing*, 48 Cal.3d 664, 668, 257 Cal.Rptr. 865, 771 P.2d 814.

Application
In this case, Neely did not witness the car crash that injured D'andrea. Rather, she was inside her house when the accident occurred. The facts of her case are thus almost exactly identical to those in *Thing*, in which the California Supreme Court rejected an analogous claim. Moreover, recent California court decisions cite *Thing* approvingly and do not suggest any movement to relax the rule *Thing* announced.

Conclusion
Because Neely did not witness the accident, she probably cannot recover for negligent infliction of emotional distress. The law is well settled in this area, and Neely is unlikely to prevail on that claim.

EXHIBIT 9.13
Legal Memorandum—Conclusion

> ## CONCLUSION
>
> Neely probably does not have a cause of action against Thompson for negligent infliction of emotional distress because she did not witness the accident that caused D'andrea's injuries. However, D'andrea probably has a cause of action for intentional infliction of emotional distress based on Thompson's outrageous comments to her about her mother and convincing her to ride in a car he was driving while drunk.
>
> Neely might also pursue, on her own behalf, a claim that Thompson intentionally inflicted emotional distress by taking D'andrea from her home and making outrageous statements about her mother. I recommend that we talk to Neely about how Thompson's statements affected her. If it can be shown that Thompson intentionally or recklessly caused emotional distress, there may be a claim for Neely.

© Cengage Learning 2014

attorney. Also note that the sample discussion provides citations to legal authorities for various points of law. As mentioned in Chapter 7, there are various citation guides, including *The Bluebook: A Uniform System of Citation* and the *ALWD Citation Manual*. You should use the one that your supervising attorney prefers.

Conclusion

The conclusion is the culmination of the legal memo. The discussion section has examined the issues in detail, evaluating the strengths and weaknesses of the client's position. The conclusion is your opinion of how to resolve the issues. Exhibit 9.13 above gives an example.

The conclusion may acknowledge that research into a particular area bore little fruit. For example, there may be no cases on point addressing one of the issues. The conclusion may also inform the attorney that more facts are needed or suggest that a certain issue needs to be explored more fully. Finally, this section gives you an opportunity to make strategic suggestions. Paralegals should feel comfortable to recommend specific courses of action, especially after conducting a careful analysis. Your judgment will be helpful to your supervising attorney.

KEY TERMS AND CONCEPTS

address block   263

chronologically   256

closing   263

confirmation letter   265

demand letter   266

informative letter   264

legalese   257

opinion (advisory) letter   265

reference line   263

salutation   263

Chapter Summary

Legal Writing: Form and Substance

RECEIVING A WRITING ASSIGNMENT

When receiving a writing assignment, a paralegal should learn the nature of the assignment, when the assignment is due, and what kind of writing approach should be used.

1. *Understanding the assignment*—Getting clear direction about an assignment is important so that you do not waste time working needlessly on something

or taking the wrong approach because you did not receive clear direction about the kind of assignment.

2. *Time constraints and flexibility*—Knowing and adhering to deadlines is essential. Some matters, such as those arising during a trial, will have to be addressed very quickly.

3. *Writing approaches*—Some documents, such as pretrial motions, are persuasive and require the writer to advocate for a particular position. Background material should generally be analytical and not be biased in favor of the client so that the case can be assessed objectively.

WRITING WELL

Good writing skills are essential for preparing legal documents. With experience and practice, you will improve your writing.

1. *Choice of format*—The document should be well organized and in the appropriate format. Most firms use specific templates, and courts often require certain formats in documents submitted to them.

2. *Write for your reader*—Tailor your writing for the intended reader. Documents written for a supervising attorney, a judge, and a client will each have a different style and varying levels of writing.

3. *Outline the material*—Create an outline before you begin writing. To help the reader follow the discussion, write effective paragraphs and provide transitions between ideas.

4. *Organize the material logically*—Large assignments should be broken into manageable blocks that can be organized in logical paragraphs. There should be headings between groups of paragraphs to help frame the presentation in an orderly sequence.

5. *Write effective sentences*—Draft short, concrete sentences with active verbs. Generally use the active voice, in which the sentence's subject is the actor, rather than the passive voice, in which the subject is being acted upon. Limit legalese—it is usually better to use plain English so the reader understands what is being said. Do not quote heavily, and use gender-neutral language.

6. *Edit and proofread your document*—Creating a polished product takes time, and you should spend much of that time proofreading and revising both on the computer and on hard copy. Confirm that the document is thorough, well organized, and neat.

PLEADINGS, DISCOVERY, AND MOTIONS

Paralegals often help draft litigation documents, which should almost always be persuasive. When drafting a document for court, always follow the court's rules concerning formatting and other issues.

GENERAL LEGAL CORRESPONDENCE

Paralegals frequently draft letters to clients, witnesses, opposing counsel, and others.

1. *Format*—Most firms and legal departments have preferred formats for legal correspondence. The first page of a letter is typically printed on the firm's letterhead. Letters should generally be formal in tone and include the following:

   a. The date.

   b. The address block and the method of delivery.

   c. The reference line (including case or file numbers when appropriate) and the salutation.

   d. The body of the letter, the closing, and the signature.

2. *Types of letters*—Paralegals commonly draft the following types of letters:

   a. Informative letters notify clients or others about something, or serve as cover letters when sending someone documents.

   b. Confirmation letters summarize oral conversations that have already occurred.

   c. Opinion letters convey a formal legal opinion about an issue or give formal advice. Only an attorney can sign an opinion letter.

   d. A demand letter explains a party's legal position in a dispute and demands that the recipient take some action, such as paying money owed.

THE LEGAL MEMORANDUM

A legal memorandum is a thoroughly researched analysis of one or more legal issues. A memo's purpose is to inform a supervising attorney about the strengths and weaknesses of a client's position.

1. *Format*—Generally, a legal memo includes the following sections:

   a. Heading

b. Questions presented

c. Brief answers

d. Statement of facts

e. Discussion and conclusion

2. *The heart of the memorandum*—This will clearly state your research and analysis objectively, summa-rizing strengths and weaknesses of a case and the relevant law.

3. *IRAC*—You can make your analysis of an issue clear by using the IRAC method, which stands for *issue, rule, application, conclusion.*

QUESTIONS FOR REVIEW

1. What should you consider when receiving a legal writing assignment?

2. What is the active voice? What is the passive voice? Why is it better to use the active voice in your legal writing?

3. List the components of a typical legal letter. What are the four types of letters discussed in this chapter? What is each letter's purpose?

4. How is a legal memorandum organized? List and describe its components. What is IRAC? How is IRAC used in a legal memorandum?

5. Should a memorandum be objective or persuasive? Why?

ETHICAL QUESTIONS

1. Bill Richardson, a legal assistant, has been asked by his supervising attorney to prepare an internal memorandum analyzing a client's claim. When Bill reviews the facts, he realizes that the client has a very weak case and will probably lose. But Bill thinks that the client was taken advantage of and that she should be given a chance to try to recover at least something. He knows that his supervisor will not take a losing case to court, so he writes the memo in a way that favors the client's position as much as possible. He is not objective in analyzing the potential pitfalls of the case. Is Bill's conduct ethical? Is it professional? How should he have handled the situation?

2. A lawyer filed a complaint with a court that was so badly drafted that after giving the lawyer an addi-tional opportunity to correct and refile it, the court dismissed the complaint with prejudice (meaning that the complaint cannot be revised and refiled). One sentence in the complaint contained 345 words, and more than 20 other sentences contained over 100 words and were unintelligible. On appeal, the appellate court affirmed dismissal of the complaint with prejudice, issued an order to show cause to the attorney instructing him to explain to the court why he should not be barred from practicing law before the court, and directed the court clerk to send its opinion to the state ethics board. What ethics rules did the attorney violate? Would it make a difference if the attorney's writing problems were attributable to him battling cancer during this time?

PRACTICE QUESTIONS AND ASSIGNMENTS

1. Analyze the construction of the following para-graphs. How could they be improved?

> The first is knowing of the danger. The second is voluntarily subjecting oneself to the danger. The defense of assumption of risk has two elements.
>
> She did not voluntarily subject herself to the danger when the stadium assigned seats to season-ticket holders. She knew that balls were often hit into the stands. The plaintiff knew of the danger involved in attending a baseball game.

2. Proofread the following paragraph, circling all of the mistakes. Then rewrite the paragraph.

> The defendent was arested and chrge with drunk driving. Blood alcohol level of .15. He refused to take a breahalyzer test at first. After the police explained to him that he would loose his lisense if he did not take it, he concented. He also has a blood test to verify the results of the breathalyzer.

3. If you did the research required by the *Practice Questions and Assignments* at the end of Chapter 7, prepare a legal memorandum addressing whether your state's lemon law protects Mr. Consumer. Be sure to use the IRAC method to analyze the strength of Mr. Consumer's case using the statutory provisions and cases on point from your state that you located during your research.

4. Prepare an informative letter to a client using the following facts:

    The client, Dr. Brown, is being sued for medical malpractice and is going to be deposed on January 15, 2014, at 1:00 P.M. The deposition will take place at the law offices of Callaghan & Young. The law office address is 151 East Jefferson Avenue, Cincinnati, Ohio. Ask Dr. Brown to call you to set up an appointment, so that you and your supervising attorney, Jeffrey Brilliant, can prepare Dr. Brown for the deposition.

QUESTIONS FOR CRITICAL ANALYSIS

1. Why is it important to tailor your writing to your audience? Explain how writing to a judge is different from writing to a client, and how you would tailor your writing accordingly.

2. Analyze the following hypothetical by applying the IRAC method, and write a one-page paper reporting your results:

    Mr. Damien is a teacher at the Wabash Academy, a private boarding school. He has a twenty-one-year-old son with bipolar affective disorder, formerly called manic-depression, a mood disorder. While visiting Mr. Damien, his son has repeatedly threatened members of the school community. On one occasion, Mr. Damien's son abducted the headmaster's sixteen-year-old daughter and attempted to have her admitted to a psychiatric hospital. Mr. Damien's son also made threaten-ing phone calls to the headmaster. In one call, he claimed to have drained several quarts of his own blood from his body because he was not permitted to communicate with the headmaster's daughter. Mr. and Mrs. Damien refuse to prevent their son from visiting their home on the school's campus. As a result, the school has fired Mr. Damien. Mr. Damien claims that the termination of his employment violates the Americans with Disabilities Act (ADA) of 1990.

    The ADA prohibits an employer from discriminating against a person because he or she is related to a person with disabilities. Under case law interpreting the ADA, employment is not required if a disabled relative poses a direct threat to the health and safety of others.

PROJECTS

1. Review the *Practice Focus* feature *Tools to Help Legal Writing* on page 254 in this chapter. Explain what a table of authorities is and what purpose it serves in an appellate brief. Do an Internet search for the programs CiteIt! or Best Authority mentioned in the feature. From your search, explain how these programs are used to create tables of authority.

2. After seeking advice from your instructor, contact an appellate court in your state. Ask if the court gives tours, has any programs for college students, and what the schedule is to observe oral arguments. If you can, arrange to take a tour and observe an oral argument, reading both sides' briefs first, if possible. Write a one-page paper summarizing your visit. Describe the issues presented to the appellate court during oral argument and some of the questions that the judges asked of the attorneys. How did the oral arguments compare with Chapter 6's description of trial court proceedings?

GROUP PROJECT

Locate the *Federal Rules of Appellate Procedure*, Rule 28, Briefs, on the Cornell University Law School's Legal Information Institute Web site at **www.law.cornell.edu/ rules/frap/rule_28**.

Student one will create a list of the sections that an appellant's brief must contain from Rule 28(a).

Student two will create a list of what an appellee's brief must contain from Rule 28(b).

Student three will summarize how references may be made to the record from Rule 28(e) and whether statutes may be reproduced or included in the brief from Rule 28(f).

Student four will compile and present the work of students one through three in a paper that is submitted to the instructor.

USING INTERNET RESOURCES

1. Go to the Web site **www.theoatmeal.com**.

   a. Scroll down to the icon that says "Ten Words You Need to Stop Misspelling" and open it. Explain the following differences and when each word is used:

   - The different spellings of the word "there."

   - Its and it's.

   - Then and than.

   b. Click on "How to Use an Apostrophe." Explain how an apostrophe is used with possessives.

   Consider bookmarking these Web pages on your computer and iPad.

2. Access the Securities and Exchange Commission's *A Plain English Handbook* at the following site:

   www.sec.gov/pdf/handbook.pdf.

Scroll through the handbook to answer the following questions:

a. Describe the "unoriginal but useful" writing tip given in the handbook's preface. How did the preface's author apply his own advice?

b. How does Chapter 1 of the handbook describe a plain English document?

c. Browse through Chapter 6 of the handbook, titled "Writing in Plain English." Write down two pairs of "before" and "after" examples showing how plain English improved sentences.

d. What is a nominalization? Write a sentence including a nominalization (not one of those listed in Chapter 6 of the handbook), and then rewrite it to convert the nominalization into the sentence's main verb.

CourseMate The available CourseMate for this text has an interactive eBook and interactive learning tools, including flash cards, quizzes, and more. To learn more about this resource and access free demo CourseMate resources, go to **www.cengagebrain.com**, and search for this book. To access CourseMate materials that you have purchased, go to **login.cengagebrain.com**.

Civil Litigation: Before the Trial

Chapter Outline

After completing this chapter, you will know:

- The basic steps involved in the civil litigation process and the types of tasks that may be required of paralegals during each step of the pretrial phase.

- What a litigation file is, what it contains, and how it is organized, maintained, and reviewed.

- How a lawsuit is initiated and what documents and motions are filed during the pleadings stage of the civil litigation process.

- What discovery is and what kinds of information attorneys and their paralegals obtain from parties to the lawsuit and from witnesses when preparing for trial.

Introduction

Every paralegal should be acquainted with the basic phases of civil litigation and the forms and terminology commonly used in the process. The paralegal plays a particularly important role in helping the trial attorney prepare for and conduct a civil trial. Preparation involves a variety of tasks including:

- The relevant law must be carefully researched.
- Evidence must be gathered and documented.
- The litigation file must be created and carefully organized.
- Procedural requirements and deadlines for filing documents with the court must be met.
- **Witnesses**—persons asked to testify at trial—must be prepared in advance and be available to testify at the appropriate time during the trial.
- Any trial exhibits, such as charts, photographs, or video recordings, must be properly prepared, mounted, or scanned into the computer.
- Arrangements must be made to have any necessary equipment, such as a Blu-ray player or laptop and projector, available for use at the trial.

witness
A person who is asked to testify under oath at a trial.

The paralegal's efforts are critically important in preparing for trial, and attorneys usually rely on paralegals to ensure that nothing has been overlooked.

The complexity of even a simple civil trial requires that the paralegal be familiar with the litigation process and courtroom procedures. Much of this expertise can be acquired only through hands-on experience. Attorneys may request that their paralegals assist them during the trial as well. In the courtroom, the paralegal can perform numerous tasks. For example, the paralegal can locate documents or exhibits as they are needed. The paralegal can also observe jurors' reactions to statements made by attorneys or witnesses, check to see if a witness's testimony is consistent with sworn statements made by the witness before the trial, and give witnesses some last-minute instructions outside the courtroom before they are called to testify.

In this chapter, you will learn about the pretrial stages of a civil lawsuit, from the initial attorney-client meeting to the time of trial. In the next chapter, you will read about conducting investigations and interviews prior to trial. The *Featured Contributor* on pages 282 and 283 provides ideas about developing a plan.

Civil Litigation—A Bird's-Eye View

Although civil trials vary greatly in terms of complexity, cost, and detail, they share similar structural characteristics. They begin with an event that gives rise to the legal action, and (provided the case is not settled by the parties at some point during the litigation process—as most cases are) they end with the issuance of a **judgment**, the court's decision on the matter. In the interim, the litigation itself may involve many twists and turns. Even though each case has its own "story line," most civil lawsuits follow some version of the course charted in Exhibit 10.1 on the facing page.

judgment
The court's final decision regarding the rights and claims of the parties to a lawsuit.

Pretrial Settlements

In most cases, the parties reach a *settlement*—an out-of-court resolution of the dispute—before the case goes to trial. Lawsuits are costly in both time and money, and it is usually in the interest of both parties to settle the case out of court. Throughout the pretrial stage of litigation, the attorney will therefore attempt to help the parties reach a settlement. At the same time, the attorney and the paralegal must operate under the assumption that the case will go to trial because all pretrial preparation must be completed prior to the trial date.

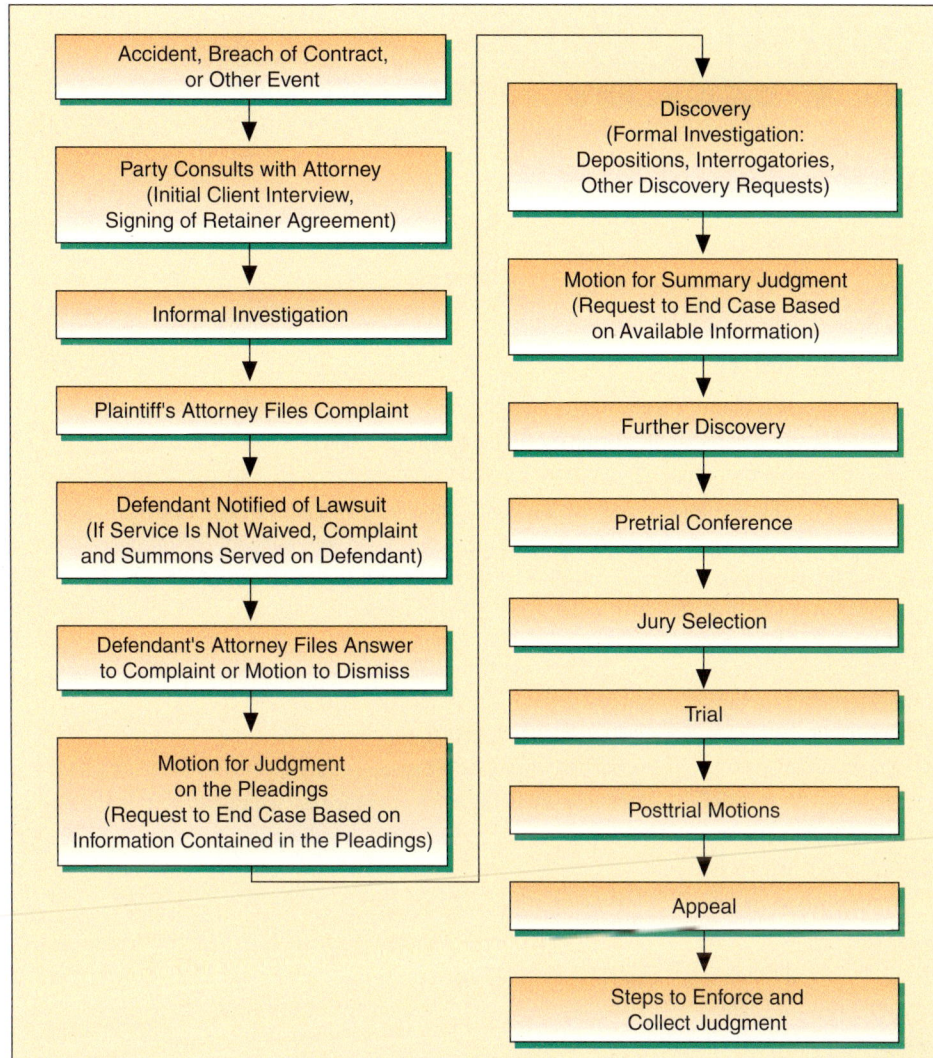

EXHIBIT 10.1
A Typical Case Flowchart

Procedural Requirements

Understanding and meeting procedural requirements are essential in the litigation process. These requirements are set out in the procedural rules of the court in which a lawsuit is brought. Civil trials held in federal district courts are governed by the **Federal Rules of Civil Procedure (FRCP)**. These rules specify what must be done during the various stages of the federal civil litigation process. For example, Rule 4 of the FRCP describes the procedures that must be followed in notifying the defendant of the lawsuit.

Each state also has its own rules of civil procedure (which in many states are similar to the FRCP). In addition, many courts have their own rules of procedure that supplement the federal or state rules. The attorney and the paralegal must comply with all of the rules of procedure that apply to the specific court in which the trial will take place.

A Hypothetical Lawsuit

To illustrate the procedures involved in litigation, consider a hypothetical civil lawsuit. The case involves an automobile accident in which a car driven by Tony Peretto collided with a car driven by Katherine Baranski. Baranski suffered injuries and incurred substantial medical and hospital costs. She also lost wages for the five months in which she was unable to work. Baranski has decided to sue Peretto for

Federal Rules of Civil Procedure (FRCP)
The rules controlling all procedural matters in civil trials brought before the federal district courts.

ON THE web

The Federal Rules of Civil Procedure are available online at the Legal Information Institute Web site at **www.law.cornell.edu**. (Select "Federal Rules" from the menu.)

You can also access the rules governing civil procedure in most states. For example, enter "Michigan civil procedure" in a search engine and you will be linked to official sources.

Featured Contributor

CIVIL LITIGATION: BEFORE THE TRIAL

Loretta Calvert

BIOGRAPHICAL NOTE

Loretta Calvert graduated from NYU School of Law in 1998 and worked at Sullivan & Cromwell as a full-time associate doing complex commercial litigation. Ms. Calvert is the Paralegal Studies Director for Volunteer State Community College, an ABA-approved program. She has taken groups of students to Europe for research projects and produced DVDs with titles including *Dutch Cannabis Policy, Criminal Law in the UK,* and *Prostitution: An International Perspective.* She has presented at various conferences in the United States and served as the AAfPE president for 2012–2013.

© Cengage Learning 2014

For some paralegals working in litigation, this can be the fun part of pursuing a claim or defending a client. This idea may seem strange to you. "Fun?" you think. "A person's marriage, job, or freedom is at stake." Keep a careful distance in cases and remember that the client's problem is not your problem. Otherwise, you will be prone to burnout and stress. When representing a client, settlement is always possible at any time before, during, or after trial. However, many cases settle during this phase because of discovery. A paralegal who has taken the time to organize the client's case file and potential evidence during the discovery phase helps the attorney decide what advice to give the client. I was once disappointed when a large case settled before trial. My supervising partner told me to be happy. The reason the case settled was because our litigation team did an excellent job during discovery.

DRAFTING COMPLAINTS

Now, when drafting a complaint there are two schools of thought. One, you throw everything in the complaint. Any reasonable claim that has some legal probability (remember, you can't put in a frivolous claim;

damages. Because Baranski is the person bringing the lawsuit, she is the plaintiff. Peretto, because he must defend against Baranski's claims, is the defendant. The plaintiff and the defendant are referred to as the *parties* to the lawsuit, as discussed in Chapter 5. (Some cases involve several plaintiffs and/or defendants.)

The attorney for the plaintiff (Baranski) is Allen P. Gilmore. Gilmore is assisted by paralegal Elena Lopez. The attorney for the defendant (Peretto) is Elizabeth A. Cameron. Cameron is assisted by paralegal Gordon McVay. Throughout this chapter and the following two chapters, *Case at a Glance* features in the page margins will remind you of the names of the participants in this lawsuit.

case AT A GLANCE

The Plaintiff—
Plaintiff: Katherine Baranski
Attorney: Allen P. Gilmore
Paralegal: Elena Lopez

The Defendant—
Defendant: Tony Peretto
Attorney: Elizabeth A. Cameron
Paralegal: Gordon McVay

The Preliminaries

Katherine Baranski arranges to meet with Allen P. Gilmore, an attorney with the law firm of Jeffers, Gilmore & Dunn, to see if Gilmore will represent her in the lawsuit. Gilmore asks paralegal Elena Lopez to prepare the usual forms and information sheets, including a retainer agreement and a statement of the firm's billing procedures, and to bring them to the initial interview with Baranski. Gilmore also asks Lopez to run a conflicts check (see Chapter 4) to ensure that representing Baranski in this action will not create a conflict of interest.

otherwise, you violate the rules) goes into the complaint in an effort to overwhelm the other side with volume. For example, on a tort claim you may have a clear assault and battery claim, but you throw in negligence just in case all the elements turn out not to be so clear on assault and battery.

The second option is to carefully select only the best claims, ones you know you will be able to establish all the elements on easily. For example, the client may have been discriminated against because of gender and race; however, most of the client's statements lean to gender issues. In that case, the attorney may decide to pursue only gender discrimination. Besides, you could try to amend a complaint later if circumstances change.

DISCOVERY

After the initial pleadings are out of the way, the parties will probably get down to discovery. This is the phase that makes or breaks a case because if you don't have the evidence to prove an element, you run the risk of losing at trial. Paralegals can use software to organize mounds of documentary evidence.

Electronic evidence grows every day in its importance, and there are more options to assist the legal team in gathering relevant evidence for use at trial. It is important to meet with the attorney and discuss how to organize all the evidence gathered from document production, depositions, interrogatories, requests to admit, and subpoenas. If it is a large case, what software will you use? Who will have access to the database? How will items be keyed into the database? Does the firm need a third party provider to assist? If it is a small case, are standard files, binders, and boxes sufficient? What does the attorney prefer? Basically, you need a discovery plan.

A discovery plan allows you to make important decisions including:

- What sort of litigation hold to use so that important evidence is not destroyed by routine business practices;

- Whether to depose a witness or ask for documents first; and

- Whether metadata is important in the case to establish an element such as intent.

In a large case, one paralegal may focus on the privilege log while another paralegal is the database specialist. It is important everyone on the team have the same instructions so that no matter who is reviewing a document, transcript, or other evidence, the item is receiving identical treatment in the way of coding and storage. There is creativity in the law, and this is the part where you have opportunities to creatively problem solve and use critical thinking skills to the advantage of the attorney.

> " . . . *discovery* . . . . *is the phrase that makes or breaks a case* . . . "

The Initial Client Interview

Most often, an initial client interview is conducted by the attorney—for several reasons. First, if attorney Gilmore is interested in taking on a new client, he will want to explain to the client the value of his services and those of his firm. Second, only an attorney can agree to represent a client. Third, only an attorney can set fees, and if Gilmore takes Baranski on as a client, fee arrangements will be discussed, and possibly agreed on, during the initial client interview. Finally, only an attorney can give legal advice, and the initial client interview may involve advising Baranski of her legal rights and options. In short, what transpires during the initial client interview normally falls under the umbrella of "the practice of law," and, as you read in Chapter 4, only attorneys are permitted to practice law.

Because attorney Gilmore and paralegal Lopez will be working together on the case, Gilmore will ask Lopez to sit in on the interview. Gilmore will want Lopez to meet Baranski, become familiar with Baranski's claim, and perhaps make arrangements for follow-up interviews with Baranski should Gilmore take the case.

Collecting Facts

During the initial client interview, Katherine Baranski explains to attorney Gilmore and paralegal Lopez the facts of her case as she perceives them. Baranski tells them that Tony Peretto, who was driving a Dodge van, ran a stop sign and crashed into the driver's side of her Ford Fusion as she was driving through the intersection of Mattis Avenue and Thirty-eighth Street in Nita City, Nita. The accident occurred at 7:45 A.M. on August 4, 2013. Baranski has misplaced Peretto's address, but she knows that he lives in another state, the state of Zero.[1] Baranski claims that as a result of the accident, she has been unable to work for five months and has lost about $20,000 in wages. Her medical and hospital expenses total $95,000, and the damage to her car is estimated to be $15,000. Throughout the initial interview, Lopez takes notes to record the details of the case as relayed by Baranski.

Release Forms

Gilmore agrees to represent Baranski in the lawsuit against Peretto. He explains the fee structure to Baranski, and she signs the retainer agreement. He has Baranski sign forms authorizing Gilmore to obtain relevant medical, employment, and other records relating to the claim. (These *release forms* will be discussed in Chapter 11.) At the end of the interview, Gilmore asks Lopez to schedule a follow-up interview with Baranski. Lopez will conduct that interview and obtain more details from Baranski about the accident and its consequences.

Preliminary Investigation

After Baranski leaves the office, attorney Gilmore asks paralegal Lopez to undertake a preliminary investigation to get as much information as possible concerning the facts of Baranski's accident. Sources of this information will include the police report of the accident, medical records, employment data, and eyewitness accounts of the accident.

You will read in Chapter 11 about the steps in investigating the facts of a client's case, so we will not discuss investigation here. Bear in mind that at this point in the pretrial process, the paralegal may engage in extensive investigation of the facts. Investigation is a key part of pretrial work, and facts discovered (or not discovered) by the investigator may play an important role in determining the outcome of the lawsuit.

Creating the Litigation File

Attorney Gilmore also asks paralegal Lopez to create a litigation file for the case. As the litigation progresses, Lopez will carefully maintain the file to make sure that such items as correspondence, bills, research and investigation results, and all documents and exhibits relating to the litigation are in the file and arranged in an organized manner.

IN THE office

HACKING LEGAL FILES

Hackers work to steal information or destroy computer files. Protecting the privacy and security of client files, and all other office files, from hackers is a major concern. Security failures can affect a law firm's cases and its reputation. Large law firms usually have a specialist assigned to computer and Internet security. Smaller firms may be less formal, but the concerns are the same: Are files safe? Is the transmission of files to courts safe from interception? Could a hacker destroy the contents of the firm's computers? Are files stored off site secure? While you are probably not a security expert, you should be aware of security for the computers you use and be sure to follow the procedure established by your firm.

Litigation files can easily expand into thousands of documents. Part of the paralegal's job is to file and organize these documents in such a way that they can be quickly retrieved when needed. When might you wish to scan file documents and put them onto an external hard drive? How can you make sure that the external drive is secure?

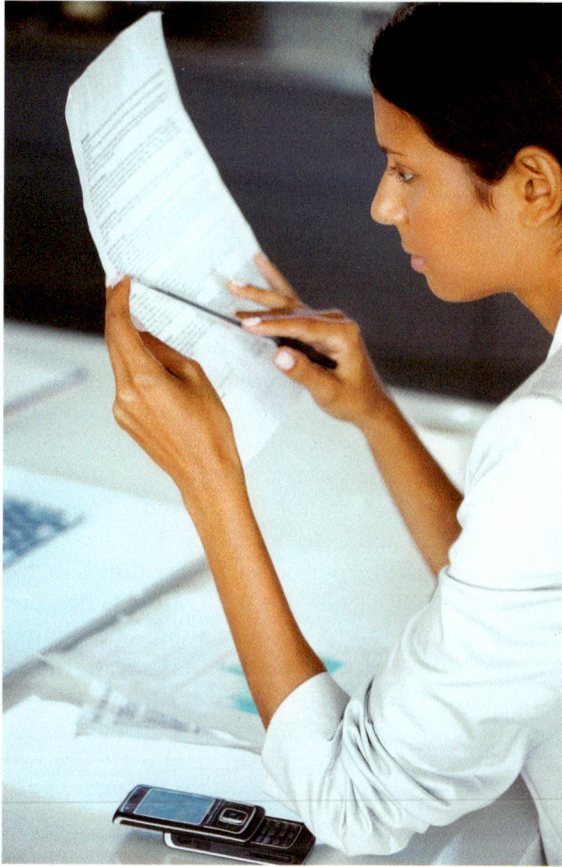

© Yuri Arcurs/www.Shutterstock.com

Organization

Each law firm or legal department has its own organizational scheme to follow when creating and maintaining client files. Recall from Chapter 3 that there are three goals of any law office filing system:

1. to preserve confidentiality,
2. to safeguard legal documents, and
3. to ensure that the contents of files can be easily and quickly retrieved when needed.

Usually it is the paralegal's responsibility to make sure that the litigation file is properly created and maintained.

As a case progresses through the litigation process, subfiles may be created for documents relating to the various stages. For example, at this point in the Baranski case, the litigation file contains notes taken during the initial client interview, the signed retainer agreement, and information and documents gathered by Lopez during her preliminary investigation of the claim. As the lawsuit progresses, Lopez will make sure that subfiles are created for documents relating to the pleadings and discovery stages (to be discussed shortly). Depending on the office filing system, the file folders for these subfiles may be color coded or numbered so that each subfile can be readily recognized and retrieved.

Many firms also scan documents and create electronic copies of the files. Lopez will also prepare an index for each subfile to indicate the documents included. The index will be placed at the front of the folder for easy reference.

Litigation Files

A properly created and maintained litigation file provides a comprehensive record of the case so that others in the firm can quickly acquaint themselves with the progress of the proceedings. Because well-organized files are critical to the success

social MEDIA TODAY

Social media refers to the relatively inexpensive and widely accessible electronic tools that allow anyone to publish and access information, collaborate with others, and build relationships.

of any case, Lopez should take special care to properly maintain the file. The *Developing Paralegal Skills* feature below discusses file organization in more depth.

The Pleadings

The next step is for plaintiff Baranski's attorney, Gilmore, to file a complaint in the appropriate court. The **complaint** (called a *petition* in some courts) is a document that states the claims the plaintiff is making against the defendant. The complaint also contains a statement regarding the court's jurisdiction over the dispute and a demand for a remedy (such as money damages).

The filing of the complaint is the step that begins the formal legal action against the defendant, Peretto. The complaint is one of the **pleadings**, which inform each party of the claims made by the other and specify the issues (disputed questions) involved in the case. We examine here two basic pleadings—the plaintiff's complaint and the defendant's answer.

The complaint must be filed within the period of time allowed by law for bringing legal actions. The allowable period is fixed by state statutes of limitations (discussed in Chapter 5), and this period varies for different types of claims. For example, actions concerning breaches of sales contracts must usually be brought within four years. After the time allowed under a statute of limitations has expired, normally no action can be brought, no matter how strong the case was originally. For instance, if the statute of limitations covering the auto-negligence lawsuit that plaintiff Baranski is bringing against defendant Peretto allows two years for bringing an action, Baranski normally has to initiate the lawsuit within that two-year period or give up forever the possibility of suing Peretto for damages caused by the car accident.

complaint

The pleading made by a plaintiff or a charge made by the state alleging wrongdoing on the part of the defendant.

pleadings

Statements by the plaintiff and the defendant that detail the facts, charges, and defenses involved in the litigation.

DEVELOPING
paralegal skills

FILE WORKUP

Once a litigation file has been created, the paralegal typically "works up" the file. In the Baranski case, after paralegal Lopez has completed her initial investigation into Baranski's claim, she will review and summarize the information that she has amassed so far, including the information that she has gathered through the initial client interview, subsequent client interviews, and any investigation that she has conducted.

Lopez will also identify areas that might require the testimony of an expert witness. For example, if Baranski claimed that as a result of the accident she had broken her hip and would always walk with a limp, Gilmore would want a medical specialist to give expert testimony to support Baranski's claim. (How to locate expert witnesses will be discussed in later chapters.) Lopez would prepare a list of potential experts for Gilmore to review.

Once Lopez has worked up the file, she will prepare a memo to Gilmore summarizing the file. This memo will provide Gilmore with factual information for deciding which legal remedy or strategy to pursue, what legal issues need to be researched, and generally how to proceed with the case.

TIPS FOR PREPARING A FILE WORKUP MEMO

- Summarize the information that has been obtained about the case.
- Suggest a plan for further investigation in the case (you will read about investigation plans in Chapter 11).
- Suggest additional information that might be obtained during discovery (discussed later in this chapter).
- Include a list of expert witnesses to contact, explaining which witnesses might be preferable, and why.

Drafting the Complaint

The complaint itself may be no more than a few paragraphs long, or it may be many pages in length, depending on the complexity of the case. In the Baranski case, the complaint will probably be only a few pages long unless special circumstances require additional details. The complaint will include the following sections, each of which we discuss below:

- Caption.

- Jurisdictional allegations.

- General allegations (the body of the complaint).

- Prayer for relief.

- Signature.

- Demand for a jury trial.

Exhibit 10.2 on the next two pages shows a sample complaint.

Baranski's case is being filed in a federal court, so the Federal Rules of Civil Procedure (FRCP) apply. If the case were being filed in a state court, paralegal Lopez would need to review the appropriate state rules of civil procedure. The rules for drafting pleadings in state courts differ from the FRCP. The rules also differ from state to state and even from court to court within the same state. Lopez could obtain pleading forms from "form books" available in the law firm's files or library (or on DVD, servers, or online) or from pleadings drafted previously in similar cases litigated by the firm.

The Caption

All documents submitted to the court or other parties during the litigation process begin with a caption. The caption is the heading, which identifies the name of the court, the title of the action, the names of the parties, the type of document, and the court's file number. Note that the court's file number may also be referred to as the case number or *docket number*, depending on the jurisdiction. (A **docket** is the official schedule of proceedings in lawsuits pending before a court.)

The caption for a complaint leaves a space for the court to insert the number that it assigns to the case. Courts typically assign the case a number when the complaint is filed. Any document subsequently filed with the court in the case will list the file, case, or docket number on the front page of the document. Exhibit 10.2 on the following pages shows how the caption will read in the case of *Baranski v. Peretto*.

docket
The list of cases entered on a court's calendar and thus scheduled to be heard by the court.

Jurisdictional Allegations

Because attorney Gilmore is filing the lawsuit in a federal district court, he will have to include in the complaint an allegation that the federal court has jurisdiction to hear the dispute. (An **allegation** is an assertion, claim, or statement made by one party in a pleading that sets out what the party expects to prove to the court.) Recall from Chapter 6 that federal courts can exercise jurisdiction over disputes involving either a *federal question* or *diversity of citizenship*.

A federal question arises whenever a claim in a civil lawsuit relates to a federal law, the U.S. Constitution, or a treaty executed by the U.S. government. Diversity of citizenship exists when the parties involved in the lawsuit are citizens of different states and the amount in controversy exceeds $75,000. Because Baranski and Peretto are citizens of different states (Nita and Zero, respectively) and because the amount in controversy exceeds $75,000, the case meets the requirements for diversity-of-citizenship jurisdiction. Gilmore thus asserts that the federal court has jurisdiction on this basis, as illustrated in Exhibit 10.2 on the next page.

allegation
A party's statement, claim, or assertion made in a pleading to the court. The allegation sets forth the issue that the party expects to prove.

EXHIBIT 10.2
The Complaint

The caption

Jurisdictional allegations

General allegations

UNITED STATES DISTRICT COURT
FOR THE WESTERN DISTRICT OF NITA

Katherine Baranski)
       Plaintiff,)
)
v.)   CASE NO: _____
)
)
)   COMPLAINT AND
Tony Peretto)   DEMAND FOR JURY TRIAL
)
       Defendant.)

The **court** in which the complaint is filed.

Names of the **parties**

The court will insert the **file (docket) number** here.

Name/type of document

JURISDICTIONAL ALLEGATIONS

1. That Plaintiff, Katherine Baranski, resides in the City of Nita, County of Nita, State of Nita.

2. That Defendant, Tony Peretto, is a resident of the City of Zero, County of Zero, State of Zero.

3. That the cause of action arose in the City of Nita, County of Nita, State of Nita.

4. That the amount in controversy exceeds $75,000.00 and Plaintiff is entitled to relief based on Diversity of Citizenship under 28 U.S.C. Section 1332.*

*This is a reference to the **title and section numbers** in the *United States Code,* which is a compilation of all federal statutes. See Chapter 7 for a further discussion of how to understand citations (references) to statutory law.

GENERAL ALLEGATIONS

5. That on August 4, 2013, at approximately 7:45 A.M., the Plaintiff, Katherine Baranski, was exercising reasonable care in driving her car in a southbound direction on Mattis Avenue when a vehicle driven by the Defendant, Tony Peretto, collided with the Plaintiff's vehicle. The collision occurred as Defendant Peretto attempted to drive his vehicle across Mattis Avenue on Thirty-eighth Street.

6. That the Defendant, Tony Peretto, owed the Plaintiff, Katherine Baranski, the following duties of care:

    A. Duty to stop at the stop sign on Thirty-eighth Street before crossing Mattis Avenue.
    B. Duty to make reasonable observations of vehicles in plain view before crossing Mattis Avenue.
    C. Duty not to drive his motor vehicle in a reckless, careless, or heedless manner with willful and wanton disregard for the safety and rights of others, within the meaning of Section 9.2326(2) of the Nita Statutes Annotated.

7. That the Defendant, Tony Peretto, breached each of the above duties and violated the following statutes of the State of Nita:

    A. That he was guilty of reckless driving within the meaning of Section 9.2326 of the Nita Statutes Annotated.
    B. That he was guilty of careless and negligent driving within the meaning of Section 9.2326(2) of the Nita Statutes Annotated.

8. That at the time of the collision, the weather conditions were clear and it was daylight.

EXHIBIT 10.2
The Complaint—Continued

9. That at the time of the collision, the Plaintiff, Katherine Baranski, was a generally healthy female, twenty-five years of age.

10. That as a result of the collision, the Plaintiff, Katherine Baranski, suffered severe physical injuries, which prevented her from working for five months, and property damage to her vehicle. The costs that the Plaintiff, Katherine Baranski, incurred as a result of the collision included $95,000 in medical bills, $20,000 in lost wages, and $15,000 in automobile-repair costs.

11. That the injuries sustained by the Plaintiff as a result of the collision were solely caused by the negligence of the Defendant, Tony Peretto.

WHEREFORE, the Plaintiff prays for the following relief:

A. That the Plaintiff be awarded appropriate compensatory damages;

B. That the Plaintiff be awarded an amount deemed fair and just by a Jury to compensate the Plaintiff for damages sustained as presented by the evidence in this case;

C. That the Plaintiff be awarded such other further relief as the Court deems proper. Plaintiff Katherine Baranski claims judgment against the Defendant in an amount in excess of $75,000 in actual, compensatory, and exemplary damages together with attorneys' fees, court costs, and other costs as provided by law.

> **The prayer for relief**

Date: 2/10/14

Jeffers, Gilmore & Dunn

Allen P. Gilmore

Allen P Gilmore
Attorney for Plaintiff
553 Fifth Avenue
Suite 101
Nita City, NI 48801

> **The signature of the plaintiff's attorney**

Katherine Baranski, being first duly sworn, states that she has read the foregoing Complaint by her subscribed and that she knows the contents thereof, and the same is true, except those matters therein stated to be upon information and belief, and as to those matters, she believes to be true.

Katherine Baranski

Plaintiff

Sworn and subscribed before me this 10th day of February, 2014.

Leela M Shay

Notary Public, Nita County,
State of Nita

My Commission Expires:

March 10, 2015

> **Affidavit (and plaintiff's signature)**

DEMAND FOR A JURY TRIAL

The Plaintiff demands a trial by jury.

> **Demand for a jury trial**

Date: 2/10/14

Jeffers, Gilmore & Dunn

Allen P. Gilmore

Allen P Gilmore
Attorney for the Plaintiff
553 Fifth Avenue
Suite 101
Nita City, Nita 48801

Certain cases, including those involving diversity of citizenship, may be brought in either a state court or a federal court. (This was discussed in the *Developing Paralegal Skills* feature in Chapter 6 on page 154.) Thus, an attorney in Gilmore's position can advise the client that there is a choice. Gilmore probably considered several factors when advising Baranski on which court would be preferable for her lawsuit. An important consideration is how long it would take to get the case to trial. Many courts are overburdened by their caseloads, and sometimes it can take years before a court will be able to hear a case. If Gilmore knows that the case could be heard two years earlier in the federal court than in the state court, that will be an important factor to consider.

General Allegations (The Body of the Complaint)

The body of the complaint contains a series of allegations that set forth a claim for relief. In plaintiff Baranski's complaint, the allegations outline the factual events that gave rise to Baranski's claims.[2] The events are described in a series of chronologically arranged, numbered allegations so that the reader can understand them easily. As Exhibit 10.2 on page 288 shows, the numbers of the paragraphs in the body of the complaint continue the sequence begun in the section on jurisdictional allegations.

ADVOCATE THE PLAINTIFF'S POSITION. When drafting the complaint, Lopez will act as an advocate. She must present the facts forcefully to support and strengthen the client's claim. The recitation of the facts must demonstrate that defendant Peretto engaged in conduct that entitles plaintiff Baranski to relief. Even though she will want to present the facts in a light most favorable to Baranski, Lopez must be careful not to exaggerate the facts or make false statements. Rather, she must present the facts in such a way that the reader could reasonably infer that Peretto was negligent and that his negligence caused Baranski's injuries and losses.

What if her research into the case had given Lopez reason to believe that a fact was probably true even though she could not verify it? She could still include the statement in the complaint by prefacing it with the phrase, "On information and belief." This language would indicate to the court that the plaintiff, Baranski, had good reason to believe the truth of the statement, but that the evidence for it either had not yet been obtained or might not hold up under close scrutiny.

BE CLEAR AND CONCISE. The most effective complaints are those that are clear and concise. Moreover, brevity and simplicity are required under FRCP 8(a). When drafting the complaint, Lopez should use clear language and favor simple and direct statements over more complex wording. Lopez should also resist the temptation to include facts that are not absolutely necessary for the complaint. By reducing the body of the complaint to the simplest possible terms, Lopez will not only achieve greater clarity but also minimize the possibility of divulging attorney Gilmore's trial strategies or hinting at a possible defense that the opponent might use to defeat the claim.

OUTLINE HARMS SUFFERED AND REMEDY SOUGHT. After telling Baranski's story, Lopez will add one or more paragraphs outlining the harms suffered by the plaintiff and the remedy that the plaintiff seeks. In general, it is preferable that all allegations of damages—such as hospital costs, lost wages, and auto-repair expenses—be included in a single paragraph, as in Exhibit 10.2, Paragraph 10, top of the previous page. Lopez should check the relevant court rules, however, to see whether the court requires that certain types of damages (Baranski's lost wages, for example) be alleged in a separate paragraph.

Prayer for Relief

Paralegal Lopez will include a paragraph at the end of the complaint, similar to that shown in Exhibit 10.2, asking that judgment be entered for the plaintiff and appropriate relief be granted. This **prayer for relief** will indicate that plaintiff Baranski is seeking money damages to compensate her for the harms that she suffered.

---

social MEDIA TODAY

No one is completely safe from digital attacks, so you should take steps to protect your online reputation. Regularly change passwords and use secure passwords (mixing numbers, symbols, and upper and lower case letters). Assume you are exposed, not that you are safe.

---

prayer for relief
A statement at the end of the complaint requesting that the court grant relief to the plaintiff.

Signature

In federal practice, the signature following the prayer for relief certifies that the plaintiff's attorney (or the plaintiff, if not represented by an attorney) has read the complaint and that the facts alleged are true to the best of his or her knowledge. In addition, some state courts require an affidavit signed by the plaintiff verifying that the complaint is true to the best of the plaintiff's knowledge. **Affidavits** are sworn statements attesting to the existence of certain facts. They are acknowledged by a notary public or another official authorized to administer such oaths or affirmations. Exhibit 10.2 on page 289 illustrates an affidavit for the Baranski complaint.

affidavit
A written statement of facts, confirmed by the oath or affirmation of the party making it and made before a person having the authority to administer the oath or affirmation.

Demand for a Jury Trial

The Seventh Amendment to the U.S. Constitution guarantees the right to a jury trial in federal courts in all "suits at common law" when the amount in controversy exceeds $20 (the equivalent of 40 days' salary at that time). Most states have similar guarantees in their own constitutions, although many states put a higher minimum dollar restriction on the guarantee (for example, in Maryland the minimum amount is $10,000). If this threshold requirement is met, either party may request a jury trial.

The right to a trial by jury does not have to be exercised, and many cases are tried without one, with the judge making the findings of fact. In most states and in federal courts, one of the parties must request a jury trial, or the right is presumed to be waived (that is, the court will presume that neither party wants a jury trial). The decision to exercise the right to a jury trial usually depends on what legal theory the party is using and which judge is assigned to the trial. In the Baranski case, Gilmore may advise Baranski to demand a jury trial if he believes that a jury would be sympathetic to her position. If Baranski wants a jury trial, Gilmore will ask Lopez to include a demand for a jury trial (as in Point B of the prayer for relief in Exhibit 10.2 on page 289) with the complaint. More tips for drafting a complaint are presented in the *Developing Paralegal Skills* feature on the next page.

Filing the Complaint

Once the complaint has been prepared, carefully checked for accuracy, and signed by attorney Gilmore, paralegal Lopez will file the complaint with the court in which the action is being brought.

Traditional Method of Filing

Traditionally, a person filing a complaint personally delivers the complaint to the clerk of the court, together with a specified number of copies of the complaint and a check payable to the court in the amount of the required filing fee. Usually, a summons (which will be discussed shortly) is also attached. If Lopez uses this method of filing, she can either deliver the complaint to the court clerk or have someone deliver it for her. If she is not aware of the court's procedures for filing the complaint, she will need to contact the court to verify the amount of the filing fee and how many copies of the complaint need to be filed.

Typically, the original (signed) complaint is filed with at least two copies (the court keeps the original, and the plaintiff and defendant receive a copy), although additional copies may be required, particularly if there are multiple plaintiffs or defendants.

The court clerk files the complaint by:

- stamping the date on the first page of all the documents (original and copies);
- assigning the case a file number, or docket number; and
- assigning the case to a particular judge.

(In some state courts, the file number or judge may not be assigned until later.) The clerk then returns the date-stamped copies to the person who delivered the documents for service on the defendant (to be discussed shortly).

DEVELOPING
paralegal skills

A CHECKLIST FOR DRAFTING A COMPLAINT IN A FEDERAL CIVIL CASE

Civil cases begin when a complaint is filed in court. To draft a complaint, you need to know the facts your client alleges and the law that supports your client's claim for relief. You will need to review any notes from client interviews and meetings with the attorneys, factual materials (e.g., police or hospital reports), and preliminary research. It is also a good idea to review complaints from similar cases handled by your firm in the past, which can give you a feel for the appropriate writing style. Form books also can provide guidance on how to draft particular claims. It is also critical to check the appropriate court's rules for local requirements.

For civil suits in federal court, Federal Rule of Civil Procedure 8 sets out the required elements. State rules have an equivalent provision. Generally, the local rules will cover the typeface, type and size of paper, and other such matters.

A well-drafted complaint contains the information needed to answer the following questions:

- Who is the plaintiff? Use the plaintiff's legal name and include a statement of the jurisdiction where the plaintiff is a legal resident. If the plaintiff is suing as the representative of someone else, identify the relationship.

- Who is the defendant? It is critical to use the defendant's correct legal name so that you sue the proper person or firm. You also need to provide the defendant's legal residence.

- Why is the suit being filed in this court? How does the court have jurisdiction over the case? List the specific statutes involved. For example, list 28 U.S.C. 1331 for federal question jurisdiction,

28 U.S.C. 1332 for diversity-of-citizenship jurisdiction, or 42 U.S.C. 1983 for civil rights violations. Remember, the court must have jurisdiction over both the cause of action and defendants.

- Did any administrative prerequisites have to be satisfied prior to filing suit? If so, how?

- Is the claim timely filed (within the relevant statute of limitations)?

- What are the facts that make up the plaintiff's case? State these accurately, clearly, and briefly. Give names and dates where known.

- What are the legal claims made by the plaintiff? Draft each claim in a separate "count" in the complaint.

- Are there special pleading requirements for particular claims (e.g., fraud)? How has the plaintiff satisfied them?

- What is the plaintiff asking for? Clearly describe the relief the plaintiff wants—is it monetary damages? An injunction? Declaratory relief? Attorneys' fees and costs? Prejudgment interest? Postjudgment interest? Are special damages requested (such as statutory damages or punitive damages)?

- Who is the attorney filing the suit? Include an appropriate signature block for the lawyer to sign, certifying that she has conducted a reasonable inquiry into the facts that support the claim.

- Is a jury requested? Check to see if the claim is one for which a jury is available. Find out whether the attorney overseeing the case wants to request a jury. If so, you will need to include the appropriate language demanding a jury trial.

All parts of the complaint should be written in clear, direct English. Such professionalism is appreciated by a court.

E-Filing

Instead of delivering a paper document to the court, Lopez may be able to file the complaint electronically. Indeed, electronic filing is becoming more and more common. Because of the reduced time and paperwork involved, electronic filing can result in substantial savings for attorneys, their clients, and the courts. With **e-filing**, registered attorneys can file case documents over the Internet twenty-four hours a day, seven days a week, right up to the filing deadline, with no additional filing fees. (Go go **www.pacer.gov** to see the public access service for the federal court system.)

The security of the e-filing process is important. Only registered parties may access a court's e-filing system. As with most secure electronic communications, the registered party has a user ID and a password. An attorney may give a paralegal authority to use the system on his or her behalf. Consent of the parties to use

electronic filing (e-filing) system
An online system that enables attorneys to file case documents with courts twenty-four hours a day, seven days a week.

e-filing may be required. Once parties agree to e-filing, the court assigns a docket number to the case. From that point forward, all documents filed and served by consenting parties must use the system. Often, documents must be formatted as secure PDF (Portable Document Format) files so they cannot be altered. The parties must provide e-mail addresses for notification of service of documents.

A party to an action being handled by e-filing may have the right to request hard copies of documents. When hard copies are used, they are to include a clear notice that they have been filed electronically. Special steps are taken to protect private information, such as Social Security numbers, credit-card information, a minor child's name, or trade secrets. Fees for documents filed are paid electronically. Therefore, in many cases, all paperwork and communications between the parties and the court may be electronic.

ON THE web

For information about the federal judiciary's Case Management/ Electronic Case Files (CM/ECF) system, go to **www.uscourts. gov**. From the menu, select "Federal Courts" and then "Case Management/Electronic Case Files."

Service of Process

Before the court can exercise jurisdiction over the defendant, the court must have proof that the defendant was notified of the lawsuit. Serving the summons and complaint—that is, officially delivering these documents to the defendant in a lawsuit—is referred to as **service of process**.

The Summons

The **summons** identifies the parties to the lawsuit, as well as the court in which the case will be heard, and directs the defendant to respond to the complaint within a specified period of time. In the Baranski case, paralegal Lopez will prepare a summons by filling out a form similar to that shown in Exhibit 10.3 below. Lopez will also prepare a cover sheet for the case (a preprinted form), which is required in the federal courts and in most state courts.

If the case were being brought in a state court, Lopez would deliver the summons to the court clerk at the same time she delivers the complaint. (In federal court cases, as will be discussed, the complaint may already have been filed under the FRCP provisions relating to waiver of notice.)

service of process
The delivery of the summons and the complaint to a defendant.

summons
A document served on a defendant in a lawsuit informing the defendant that a legal action has been commenced against him or her and that the defendant must appear in court or respond to the plaintiff's complaint within a specified period of time.

EXHIBIT 10.3
A Summons in a Civil Action

**UNITED STATES DISTRICT COURT
FOR THE WESTERN DISTRICT OF NITA**

Katherine Baranski)) V. Plaintiff,)) Tony Peretto) Defendant.)	**Civil Action, File Number 14-14335-NI** *Summons*

To the above-named Defendant:

You are hereby summoned and required to serve upon A. P. Gilmore, Jeffers, Gilmore & Dunn, plaintiff's attorney, whose address is 553 Fifth Avenue, Suite 101, Nita City, NI 48801, an answer to the complaint which is herewith served upon you, within 20 days after service of this summons upon you, exclusive of the day of service. If you fail to do so, judgment by default will be taken against you for the relief demanded in the complaint.

C. H. Hynek   February 10, 2014
CLERK   DATE

John Dolan
BY DEPUTY CLERK

© Cengage Learning 2014

After the clerk files the complaint and signs, seals, and issues the summons, attorney Gilmore will be responsible for making sure that the summons and complaint are served on defendant Peretto. The service of the complaint and summons must be effected within a specified time—120 days under FRCP 4(m)—after the complaint has been filed.

Serving the Complaint and Summons

How service of process occurs depends on the rules of the court or jurisdiction in which the lawsuit is brought. Under FRCP 4(c)(2), service of process in federal court cases may be effected "by any person who is not a party and who is at least 18 years of age." Paralegal Lopez, for example, could serve the summons and complaint by personally delivering it to defendant Peretto. Alternatively, she could make arrangements for someone else to do so, subject to approval of attorney Gilmore. Most law firms contract with independent companies that provide process service in the local area. In some cases, the attorney might request that the court have a U.S. marshal or other federal official serve the summons.

Under FRCP 4(e)(1), service of process in federal court cases may also be effected "pursuant to the law of the state in which the district court is located." Some state courts require that the complaint and summons be served by a public officer, such as a sheriff.

ALTERNATIVE SERVICE METHODS.   Although the most common way to serve process on a defendant is through personal service, or actual delivery, as described above, other methods are permissible at times, depending on the jurisdiction. *Substituted service* is any method of service allowed by law in place of personal service, such as service by certified mail, fax, or e-mail. In general, however, substituted service is not favored. The paralegal and attorney thus need to know the types of service authorized by the laws in the relevant state.

PROOF OF SERVICE.   Regardless of how the summons is served, attorney Gilmore will need some kind of proof that defendant Peretto actually received the summons. In federal court cases, unless service is made by a U.S. marshal or other official, proof of service is established by having the process server fill out and sign a form similar to the **return-of-service form** shown in Exhibit 10.4 on the facing page. This form is then submitted to the court as proof of service.

JURISDICTIONS VARY.   Paralegal Lopez must be careful to comply with the service requirements of the court in which plaintiff Baranski's suit has been filed. If service is not properly made, defendant Peretto will have a legal ground (basis) for asking the court to dismiss the case against him. As mentioned earlier, the court will not be able to exercise jurisdiction over Peretto until he has been properly notified of the lawsuit being brought against him.

Serving Corporate Defendants

In cases involving corporate defendants, the summons and complaint may be served on an officer or a *registered agent* (representative) of the corporation. The name of a corporation's registered agent and its business address can usually be obtained from the secretary of state's office in the state in which the company incorporated its business, or in any state in which the corporation does business.

Finding the Defendant

Because some defendants may be difficult to locate, paralegals sometimes have to investigate to locate a defendant so that process can be served. Helpful information sources include telephone directories, banks, former business partners or fellow workers, credit bureaus, Social Security offices, insurance companies, landlords, state and county tax rolls, utility companies, automobile-registration bureaus, bureaus of vital statistics, and the post office. (Chapter 11 discusses these and other possible sources, including various online sources, that the paralegal might consult when trying to locate parties or witnesses involved in lawsuits.)

---

return-of-service form
A document signed by a process server and submitted to the court to prove that a defendant received a summons.

EXHIBIT 10.4
A Return-of-Service Form

RETURN OF SERVICE

Service of the Summons and Complaint was made by me	DATE 2/11/14
NAME OF SERVER Elena Lopez	TITLE Paralegal

Check one box below to indicate appropriate method of service

☒ Served personally upon the defendant. Place where served: _Defendant Peretto's Home: 1708 Johnston Drive, Zero City, Zero 59806_

☐ Left copies thereof at the defendant's dwelling house or usual place of abode with a person of suitable age and discretion then residing therein. Name of person with whom the summons and complaint were left: _____

☐ Returned unexecuted: _____

☐ Other (specify): _____

DECLARATION OF SERVER

I declare under penalty of perjury under the laws of the United States of America that the foregoing information contained in the Return of Service and Statement of Service Fees is true and correct.

Executed on ____2/11/14____   *Elena Lopez*
              Date   *Signature of Server*

308 University Avenue, Nita City, Nita 48804
Address of Server

The Defendant Can Waive Service

In many instances, the defendant is already aware that a lawsuit is being filed (often the plaintiff's attorney has been in contact with the defendant and has indicated that a complaint would be filed). In such cases, a plaintiff can request the defendant to *waive* (give up) her or his right to be formally served with a summons. FRCP 4(d) sets forth the procedure by which a plaintiff's attorney can request the defendant to accept service of the documents through the mail or "other reliable means." Many states have similar rules.

The aim of FRCP 4(d) is to reduce the costs associated with service of process. As an incentive, defendants who agree to waive formal service of process under the federal rules receive additional time to respond to the complaint (sixty days, compared with the twenty days that a defendant normally has to respond to the complaint under FRCP 12). Some state rules of civil procedure provide other types of incentives, such as making a party who will not agree to waive service pay for reasonable expenses thereafter incurred in serving or attempting to serve the party.

The Defendant's Response

Once a defendant receives the plaintiff's complaint, the defendant must respond to the complaint within a specified time (typically twenty days). If the defendant fails to respond within that time, the plaintiff can ask the court to enter a **default judgment** against the defendant. The defendant will then be liable for all damages the plaintiff is claiming and will lose the opportunity to defend against the claim in court.

default judgment
A judgment entered by a clerk or court against a party who has failed to appear in court to answer or defend against a claim that has been brought against him or her by another party.

answer
A defendant's response to a plaintiff's complaint.

affirmative defense
A response to a plaintiff's claim that does not deny the plaintiff's facts but attacks the plaintiff's legal right to bring an action.

counterclaim
A claim made by a defendant in a civil lawsuit against the plaintiff; in effect, a counterclaiming defendant is suing the plaintiff.

cross-claim
A claim asserted by a defendant in a civil lawsuit against another defendant or by a plaintiff against another plaintiff.

In the Baranski case, assume that defendant Peretto consults with an attorney, Elizabeth A. Cameron, to decide on a course of action. Before Cameron advises Peretto on the matter, she will investigate plaintiff Baranski's claim and obtain evidence of what happened at the time of the accident. She may ask her paralegal, Gordon McVay, to call anyone who may have witnessed the accident and any police officers who were at the scene. Cameron will also ask McVay to gather relevant documents, including the traffic ticket that Peretto received at the time of the accident and any reports filed by the police. If all goes well, Cameron and McVay will complete their investigation in a few days and then meet to assess the results.

Most cases are settled out of court before they go to trial. But even if Peretto's attorney suspects that an out-of-court settlement might be financially preferable to a trial, she will draft a response to Baranski's claim. She knows that if Peretto does not respond to the complaint within the proper time period, the court could enter a default judgment against him.

The Answer

A defendant's **answer** must respond to each allegation in the plaintiff's complaint. FRCP 8(b) permits the defendant to admit or deny the truth of each allegation. Peretto's attorney may advise him to admit to some of the allegations in Baranski's complaint, because doing so narrows the number of issues in dispute. Any allegations that are not denied by the defendant will be deemed to have been admitted.

If Peretto does not know whether a particular allegation is true or false, Cameron may indicate that in the answer. This puts the burden of proving the allegation on Baranski. It is not necessary for Peretto's attorney to include in the answer any of the reasons for the denial of particular allegations in Baranski's complaint. These reasons may be revealed during the discovery phase of the litigation process (discussed later in this chapter).

Exhibit 10.5 on the following two pages illustrates the types of responses that Peretto might make in his answer. Like the complaint, the answer begins with a caption and ends with the attorney's signature. It may also include an affidavit signed by the defendant and/or a demand for a jury trial, as in Exhibit 10.5.

ANSWER AND AFFIRMATIVE DEFENSES. A defendant may assert in the answer a reason why he or she should not be held liable for the plaintiff's injuries even if the facts, as alleged by the plaintiff, are true. This is called raising an **affirmative defense**.

For example, Peretto's attorney might also raise the defense of *contributory negligence*. That is, she could argue that even though Peretto's car collided with Baranski's, Baranski was also negligent because she was exceeding the speed limit when the accident occurred and was thus unable to avoid being hit. (As will be discussed in Chapter 14, in a few states, if it can be shown that the plaintiff was contributorily negligent, the plaintiff will be completely barred from recovery.) Although affirmative defenses are directed toward the plaintiff, the plaintiff is not required to file additional pleadings in response to these defenses.

ANSWER AND COUNTERCLAIM. Peretto's attorney may assert one or more counterclaims. A **counterclaim** is like a reverse lawsuit in which the defendant asserts a claim against the plaintiff for injuries that the defendant suffered from the same incident. For example, Peretto might contend that Baranski lost control of her car and skidded into Peretto's car, causing him to be injured. This allegation would be a counterclaim. The plaintiff is then required to reply to any counterclaims made by the defendant.

CROSS-CLAIM. In cases in which a complaint names multiple defendants, the answer filed by one defendant might be followed by a **cross-claim**, in which the defendant asserts a claim against another defendant. (Note that cross-claims may also be filed by one plaintiff against another plaintiff in the same case.) For example, suppose that plaintiff Baranski had been struck by two vehicles, one belonging to defendant Peretto and one belonging to Leon Balfour. If Peretto and Balfour had been named as co-defendants in Baranski's complaint, Peretto's attorney might have filed an answer to Baranski's complaint that included a cross-claim against Balfour. The party against whom the cross-claim is brought is required to reply to (answer) the claim.

Under the federal rules, a defendant who has a claim against the plaintiff related to the same incident is normally required to file a counterclaim within the defendant's pleading. A party who fails to do so may forgo the possibility of asserting the claim at a later date. This requirement is intended to prevent multiple lawsuits between the same parties.

EXHIBIT 10.5
The Answer

UNITED STATES DISTRICT COURT
FOR THE WESTERN DISTRICT OF NITA

Katherine Baranski   )
          Plaintiff,   )
)
v.   )
)
Tony Peretto   )
          Defendant.   )

CASE NO. 14-14335-NI
Honorable Harley M. Larue

ANSWER AND
DEMAND FOR JURY TRIAL

JURISDICTIONAL ALLEGATIONS

1. Defendant lacks sufficient information to form a belief as to the truth of the allegations contained in paragraph 1 of Plaintiff's Complaint.

2. Defendant admits the allegations contained in paragraph 2 of Plaintiff's Complaint.

3. Defendant admits the allegations contained in paragraph 3 of Plaintiff's Complaint.

4. Defendant lacks sufficient information to form a belief as to the truth of the allegations contained in paragraph 4 of Plaintiff's Complaint.

GENERAL ALLEGATIONS

5. Defendant admits the allegations contained in paragraph 5 of Plaintiff's Complaint.

6. Defendant admits the allegations contained in paragraph 6 of Plaintiff's Complaint.

7. Defendant contends that he was operating his vehicle properly and denies the allegations contained in paragraph 7 of Plaintiff's Complaint for the reason that the allegations are untrue.

8. Defendant admits the allegation contained in paragraph 8 of Plaintiff's Complaint.

9. Defendant lacks sufficient information to form a belief as to the truth of the allegation contained in paragraph 9 of Plaintiff's Complaint.

10. Defendant lacks sufficient information on the proximate cause of Plaintiff's injuries to form a belief as to the truth of the averments contained in paragraph 10 of Plaintiff's Complaint.

11. Defendant denies the allegation of negligence contained in paragraph 11 of Plaintiff's Complaint.

Continued

EXHIBIT 10.5
The Answer—Continued

<u>NEW MATTER AND AFFIRMATIVE DEFENSES</u>

Although denying that the Plaintiff is entitled to the relief prayed for in the Plaintiff's Complaint, Defendant further states that the Plaintiff is barred from recovery hereunder by reason of the following:

1. That the Plaintiff's injuries were proximately caused by her own contributory negligence and want of due care under the circumstances prevailing at the time of the accident.

2. That the Plaintiff was exceeding the posted speed limit at the time and place of the accident and therefore was guilty of careless and negligent driving within the meaning of Section 9.2325(1) of the Nita Statutes Annotated.

3. That the Plaintiff failed to exercise that standard of care that a reasonably prudent person would have exercised under the same or similar conditions for her own safety and that her own negligence, contributory negligence, and/or comparative negligence caused or was a contributing factor to the incident out of which the Plaintiff's cause of action arises.

4. The Defendant reserves the right, by an appropriate Motion, to move the Court to amend the Defendant's Answer to the Plaintiff's Complaint, to allege other New Matters and Affirmative Defenses as may be revealed by discovery yet to be had and completed in this case.

WHEREFORE, the Defendant prays for a judgment of no cause of action with costs and attorneys' fees to be paid by the Plaintiff.

Cameron & Strauss, P.C.

Elizabeth A. Cameron

Date: 2/25/14

Elizabeth A. Cameron
Attorney for the Defendant
310 Lake Drive
Zero City, ZE 59802

Tony Peretto, being first duly sworn, states that he has read the foregoing Answer by him subscribed and that he knows the contents thereof, and the same is true, except those matters therein stated to be upon information and belief, and as to those matters, he believes to be true.

Tony Peretto

Defendant

Sworn and subscribed before me this 25th day of February, 2014.

Laura Curtis

Notary Public, Zero County,
State of Zero

My Commission Expires:
December 8, 2015

<u>DEMAND FOR A JURY TRIAL</u>

The Defendant demands a trial by jury.

Cameron & Strauss, P.C.

Elizabeth A. Cameron

Date: 2/25/14

Elizabeth A. Cameron
Attorney for the Defendant
310 Lake Drive
Zero City, Zero 59802

© Cengage Learning 2014

motion
A procedural request or application presented by an attorney to the court on behalf of a client.

Filing a Motion

A **motion** is a request submitted to the court by an attorney on behalf of his or her client. When one party files a motion with the court, that party must also send to, or serve on, the opposing party a *notice of motion*. The notice of motion informs the opposing party that the motion has been filed and indicates when the court will hear the motion. The notice gives the opposing party an opportunity to prepare for the hearing.

The **motion to dismiss**, as the phrase implies, requests the court to dismiss the case for reasons provided in the motion. Defendant Peretto's attorney, for example, could file a motion to dismiss if she believed that Peretto had not been properly served, that the complaint had been filed in the wrong court, that the statute of limitations for that type of lawsuit had expired, or that the complaint did not state a claim for which relief (a remedy) could be granted. See Exhibit 10.6 below for an example of a motion to dismiss. As we discuss later in the chapter, and as shown by Exhibit 10.13 on page 318, there are a number of pretrial motions that may be filed; here we only note the motion to dismiss.

If Peretto's attorney decides to file a motion to dismiss Baranski's claim, she may want to attach one or more **supporting affidavits**—sworn statements as to certain facts that may contradict the allegations made in the complaint. Peretto's attorney may also have her paralegal draft a **memorandum of law** (which is called a *brief* in some states) to be submitted along with the motion to dismiss and the accompanying affidavits. The memorandum of law will present the legal basis for the motion, citing any statutes and cases that support it. A supporting affidavit gives factual support to the motion to dismiss, while the memorandum of law provides the legal grounds for the dismissal of the claim.

The Scheduling Conference

After the complaint and answer have been filed, the court typically schedules a conference to consult with the attorneys for both sides. (A party who is not represented by an attorney will attend the conference himself or herself.) Following this meeting, the judge enters a *scheduling order* that sets out the time limits within which pretrial events (such as the pleadings, the discovery, and the final pretrial conference) must be completed, as well as the date of the trial. Under FRCP 16(b), the scheduling order should be entered "as soon as practicable but in any event within

motion to dismiss
A motion filed by the defendant in which the defendant asks the court to dismiss the case for a specified reason, such as improper service, lack of personal jurisdiction, or the plaintiff's failure to state a claim for which relief can be granted.

supporting affidavit
An affidavit accompanying a motion that is filed by an attorney on behalf of his or her client. The sworn statements in the affidavit provide a factual basis for the motion.

memorandum of law
A document (known as a *brief* in some states) that delineates the legal theories, statutes, and cases on which a motion is based.

EXHIBIT 10.6
A Motion to Dismiss

UNITED STATES DISTRICT COURT
FOR THE WESTERN DISTRICT OF NITA

Katherine Baranski)
           Plaintiff,)
)   CASE NO. 14-14335-NI
v.   )   Honorable Harley M. Larue
)
)   MOTION TO DISMISS
Tony Peretto)
           Defendant.)

    The Defendant, Tony Peretto, by his attorney, moves the court to dismiss the above-named action because the statute of limitations governing the Plaintiff's claim has expired, as demonstrated in the memorandum of law that is being submitted with this motion. The Plaintiff therefore has no cause of action against the Defendant.

                        Cameron & Strauss, P.C.

                        Elizabeth A. Cameron
Date: 2/20/14   Elizabeth A. Cameron
                        Attorney for the Defendant
                        310 Lake Drive
                        Zero City, ZE 59802

© Cengage Learning 2014

90 days after the appearance of a defendant and within 120 days after the complaint has been served on a defendant." The purpose of this meeting is to enable the court to manage the case efficiently and establish appropriate time restrictions given the facts and circumstances of the case.

Traditional Discovery Tools

Before a trial begins, the parties can use a number of procedural devices to obtain information and gather evidence about the case. Baranski's attorney, for example, will want to know how fast Peretto was driving, whether he had been drinking, and whether he saw the stop sign. The process of obtaining information from the opposing party or from other witnesses is known as **discovery**.

Purpose of Discovery

Discovery serves several purposes. It preserves evidence from witnesses who might not be available at the time of the trial or whose memories will fade as time passes. It can lead to an out-of-court settlement if one party decides that the opponent's case is too strong to challenge. If the case does go to trial, discovery prevents surprises by giving parties access to evidence that might otherwise be hidden. This allows both parties to learn as much as they can about what to expect at a trial before they reach the courtroom. It also serves to narrow the issues so that trial time is spent on the main questions in the case.

The FRCP and similar rules in the states set forth the guidelines for discovery activity. Discovery is intended to give the parties access to witnesses, documents, records, and other evidence that the opposing side has. The rules governing discovery are also designed to make sure that a witness or a party is not unduly harassed, that **privileged information** (communications that ordinarily may not be disclosed in court) is safeguarded, and that only matters relevant to the case at hand are discoverable. The trend today is toward allowing broad discovery so that there are fewer surprises at trial.

Discovery methods include interrogatories, depositions, requests for production and physical examination, and requests for admission. Remember, as with most legal matters, you have an obligation to keep all such information confidential, as discussed in the *Ethics Watch* feature on the facing page.

Interrogatories

Interrogatories are written questions that must be answered, in writing, by the parties to the lawsuit and then signed by the parties under oath. Typically, the paralegal drafts the interrogatories for the attorney's review and approval. In the Baranski case, for example, attorney Gilmore will probably ask paralegal Lopez to draft interrogatories to be sent to defendant Peretto.

Drafting Interrogatories

All discovery documents, including interrogatories, normally begin with a caption similar to the complaint caption illustrated earlier in this chapter. Following the caption, Lopez will add the name of the party who must answer the interrogatories, instructions to be followed by the party, and definitions of certain terms that are used in the interrogatories. The body of the document consists of the interrogatories themselves—that is, the questions that the opposing party must answer. The interrogatories should end with a signature line for the attorney, followed by the attorney's name and address.

REVIEW THE FILE. Before drafting the questions, Lopez will review carefully the contents of the case file (including the pleadings and the evidence and other information she obtained during her preliminary investigation into Baranski's claim). She will want to consult with Gilmore on the litigation strategy he believes should be pursued as the case moves forward. For further guidance, she might consult

---

discovery
Formal investigation prior to trial. Opposing parties use various methods, such as interrogatories and depositions, to obtain information from each other and from witnesses to prepare for trial.

case AT A GLANCE

The Plaintiff—
Plaintiff: Katherine Baranski
Attorney: Allen P. Gilmore
Paralegal: Elena Lopez

The Defendant—
Defendant: Tony Peretto
Attorney: Elizabeth A. Cameron
Paralegal: Gordon McVay

privileged information
Confidential communications between certain individuals, such as an attorney and his or her client, that are protected from disclosure except under court order.

interrogatories
A series of written questions for which written answers are prepared and then signed under oath by a party to a lawsuit (the plaintiff or the defendant).

ETHICS WATCH

KEEPING CLIENT INFORMATION CONFIDENTIAL

As it happens, attorney Gilmore's legal assistant, Lopez, is a good friend of plaintiff Baranski's sister. Lopez learns from the results of Baranski's medical examination that Baranski has a terminal illness. Lopez is sure that the sister, who quarreled with Baranski two months ago and hasn't spoken to her since, is unaware of the illness and would probably be hurt if she learned that Lopez knew of it and didn't tell her. Should Lopez tell her friend about the illness? No. This is confidential information at this point, which Lopez only became aware of by virtue of her job. Should the information be revealed publicly during the course of the trial, then Lopez would be free to disclose it to her friend if the friend still remained unaware of it. In the meantime, Lopez is ethically (and legally) obligated to protect the information from anyone who is not working on the case, including her friend.

This behavior is consistent with the NFPA *Model Disciplinary Rules and Ethical Considerations,* Section EC-1.5(f): "A paralegal shall not engage in any indiscreet communications concerning clients."

form books containing sample interrogatories, as well as interrogatories used in similar cases previously handled by the firm.

COURTS MAY LIMIT THE NUMBER OF INTERROGATORIES.   Depending on the complexity of the case, interrogatories may be few or in the hundreds. Exhibit 10.7 on on the following two pages illustrates the types of interrogatories that have traditionally been used in cases similar to the Baranski-Peretto case. Depending on the rules of the court in which the Baranski lawsuit is being filed, Lopez might draft similar interrogatories for Peretto to answer.

Many state courts limit the number of interrogatories that can be used. FRCP 33 limits the number of interrogatories in federal court cases to twenty-five (unless a greater number are allowed by stipulation of the parties or by court order). Therefore, before drafting interrogatories, the paralegal should always check the rules of the court in which an action is being filed to find out if there are such limits. Interrogatories are particularly useful for ensuring that the defendant's correct legal name has been used or determining whether the defendant has had his or her vision checked recently in a case involving an accident (such as the Baranski case).

Answering Interrogatories

After receiving the interrogatories, Peretto must answer them within a specified time period (thirty days under FRCP 33) in writing and under oath, as mentioned above. Depending on the rules of the court system, answers to interrogatories can often be handled electronically. Very likely, Peretto will have substantial guidance from his attorney and his attorney's paralegal in forming his answers. He must answer each question truthfully, of course, because he is under oath. His attorney and her paralegal will counsel him, though, on how to phrase his answers so that they are both truthful and strategically sound. For example, they will advise him on how to limit his answers to prevent disclosing more information than necessary.

social MEDIA TODAY

Make sure you understand your firm's rules on which employees are allowed to speak for the firm and which are not. Make sure you do not include your employer's name anywhere that is not consistent with firm policy.

EXHIBIT 10.7
Sample Interrogatories

UNITED STATES DISTRICT COURT
FOR THE WESTERN DISTRICT OF NITA

Katherine Baranski   )
          Plaintiff,   )
)   CASE NO. 14-14335-NI
v.   )   Honorable Harley M. Larue
)
)   PLAINTIFF'S FIRST
Tony Peretto   )   INTERROGATORIES
          Defendant.   )   TO DEFENDANT

PLEASE TAKE NOTICE that the following Interrogatories are directed to you under the provisions of Rule 26(a)(5) and Rule 33 of the Federal Rules of Civil Procedure. You are requested to answer these Interrogatories and to furnish such information in answer to the Interrogatories as is available to you.

You are required to serve integrated Interrogatories and Answers to these Interrogatories under oath, within thirty (30) days after service of them upon you. The original answers are to be retained in your attorney's possession, and a copy of the answers is to be served upon Plaintiff's counsel.

The answers should be signed and sworn to by the person making answer to the Interrogatories.

When used in these Interrogatories the term "Defendant," or any synonym thereof, is intended to and shall embrace and include, in addition to said Defendant, all agents, servants and employees, representatives, attorneys, private investigators, or others who are in possession of or who may have obtained information for or on behalf of the Defendant.

These Interrogatories shall be deemed continuing, and supplemental answers shall be required immediately upon receipt thereof if Defendant, directly or indirectly, obtains further or different information from the time answers are served until the time of trial.

1.   Were you the driver of an automobile involved in an accident with Plaintiff on August 4, 2013, at about 7:45 A.M. at the intersection of Mattis Avenue and Thirty-eighth Street, in Nita City, Nita? If so, please state:

    (a) Your name;
    (b) Every name you have used in the past;
    (c) The dates you used each name;
    (d) The date and place of your birth.

2.   Please list your current residence and all residences you occupied in the five years preceding your move to your current residence, including complete addresses, dates of residence, and names of owners or managers.

3.   Please indicate where you are presently employed and where you were employed during the five years preceding the beginning of your current employment. In so doing, please indicate the following:

    (a) The names, addresses, and telephone numbers of each employer or place of business, including the dates during which you worked there;
    (b) How many hours you worked, on average, per week;
    (c) The names, addresses, and telephone numbers of your supervisors (or owners of the business);
    (d) The nature of the work that you performed.

EXHIBIT 10.7
Sample Interrogatories—Continued

4.   At the time of the incident, were you acting as an agent or employee for any person? If so, state:

(a) The name, address, and telephone number of that person;
(b) A description of your duties.

5.   At the time of the incident, did you have a driver's license? If so, state:

(a) The state or other issuing entity;
(b) The license number and type;
(c) The date of issuance and expiration;
(d) Any violations, offenses, or restrictions against your license.

6.   Indicate whether you have ever had your driver's license suspended, revoked, or canceled and whether you have ever been denied the issuance of a driver's license for mental or physical reasons. If you have, please indicate the date and state of such occurrence as well as the reasons for it.

7.   At the time of the incident, did you or any other person have any physical, emotional, or mental disability or condition that may have contributed to the occurrence of the incident? If so, for each person state:

(a) The name, address, and telephone number;
(b) The nature of the disability or condition;
(c) The name, address, and telephone number of any qualified person who treated or diagnosed the condition and the dates of such treatment;
(d) The manner in which the disability or condition contributed to the occurrence of the incident.

8.   Within twenty-four hours before the incident, did you or any person involved in the incident use or take any of the following substances: alcoholic beverage, marijuana, or other drug or medication of any kind (prescription or not)? If so, for each person state:

(a) The name, address, and telephone number;
(b) The nature or description of each substance;
(c) The quantity of each substance used or taken;
(d) The date and time of day when each substance was used or taken;
(e) The address where each substance was used or taken;
(f) The name, address, and telephone number of each person who was present when each substance was used or taken;
(g) The name, address, and telephone number of any health-care provider that prescribed or furnished the substance and the condition for which it was prescribed or furnished.

9.   For each time you have had your vision checked within the last five years, please indicate the following:

(a) The date and reason for the vision examination;
(b) The name, address, and telephone number of the examiner;
(c) The results and/or actions taken.

10.   For each time you have had your hearing checked within the last five years, please indicate the following:

(a) The date and reason for the hearing examination;
(b) The name, address, and telephone number of the examiner;
(c) The results and/or actions taken.

[Additional questions would be asked relating to the accident, including questions concerning road conditions and surface, posted speed limits, shoulders and curbs on the road, general character of the neighborhood, when the defendant noticed the plaintiff's vehicle, where it was located and the speed at which the plaintiff was traveling, whether there were other vehicles between the plaintiff's and the defendant's vehicles, and so forth.]

Dated: 2/15/14 _____   _____
                                            Allen P. Gilmore
                                            Attorney for Plaintiff

Depositions

deposition

A pretrial question-and-answer proceeding, usually conducted orally, in which a party or witness answers an attorney's questions. The answers are given under oath, and the session is recorded.

deponent

A party or witness who testifies under oath during a deposition.

Like interrogatories, **depositions** are given under oath. Unlike interrogatories, however, depositions are usually conducted orally (except in certain circumstances, such as when the party being deposed is at a great distance and cannot be deposed via telephone). Furthermore, unlike interrogatories, they may be taken from witnesses as well as parties.

When an attorney takes a deposition, the attorney is able to question the person being deposed (the **deponent**) *in person* and then follow up with any other questions that come to mind. The attorney is not limited in the number of questions that she or he may ask in a deposition, whereas many courts limit the number of interrogatory questions. Moreover, because the questioning is usually done in person, the deponent must answer the questions without asking an attorney or paralegal how he or she should respond. Thus, the answers to deposition questions are not filtered through counsel in the same way answers to interrogatories are.

When both the defendant and the plaintiff are located in the same jurisdiction, the site of the deposition will usually be the offices of the attorney requesting the deposition. When the parties are located in different jurisdictions, other arrangements may be made. In the Baranski case, attorney Gilmore will travel to Peretto's city, which is in another state, and depose Peretto in the office of Peretto's attorney, Cameron.

Procedure for Taking Depositions

The attorney wishing to depose a party or witness must give reasonable notice in writing to all other parties in the case and to the deposed. This is done by serving the opposing attorney (or attorneys) with a notice of taking deposition, which states the time and place of the deposition and the name of the person being examined (see Exhibit 10.8 below).

EXHIBIT 10.8
Notice of Taking Deposition

UNITED STATES DISTRICT COURT
FOR THE WESTERN DISTRICT OF NITA

Katherine Baranski)
      Plaintiff,)
)   CASE NO. 14-14335-NI
)   Honorable Harley M. Larue
v.   )
)   NOTICE OF TAKING
)   DEPOSITION
Tony Peretto)
      Defendant.)

TO: Elizabeth A. Cameron
      Cameron & Strauss, P.C.
      310 Lake Drive
      Zero City, ZE 59802

    PLEASE TAKE NOTICE that Katherine Baranski, by and through her attorneys, Jeffers, Gilmore & Dunn, will take the deposition of Tony Peretto on Wednesday, April 16, 2014, at 1:30 P M., at the law offices of Cameron & Strauss, P.C., 310 Lake Drive, Zero City, ZE 59802, pursuant to the Federal Rules of Civil Procedure, before a duly authorized and qualified notary and stenographer.

Dated: March 20, 2014   Jeffers, Gilmore & Dunn

                                      Allen P. Gilmore
                                      Allen P Gilmore
                                      Attorney for Katherine Baranski
                                        553 Fifth Avenue, Suite 101
                                        Nita City, NI 48801

If the person scheduled to be deposed will not attend voluntarily, a paralegal may need to prepare a subpoena for deposition and submit it to the court for signature. Generally, a **subpoena** is an order issued by the court clerk directing a party to appear and to testify at trial, as will be discussed in Chapter 12. A *subpoena for deposition* orders the person to appear at a deposition rather than in a court proceeding. A subpoena should also be prepared if the attorney wants the deponent to bring certain documents or tangible things to the deposition (this is called a *subpoena duces tecum*).

Under FRCP 30 and 31, court permission is required for depositions to be taken before the parties have made the initial disclosures required by Rule 26 (discussed later in this chapter). Also, court approval may be required if either party wants to take more than one deposition from the same person or more than a total of ten depositions in the case. Always check the relevant court rules when planning a discovery strategy.

Drafting Deposition Questions

Depositions are conducted by attorneys. Although paralegals may attend depositions, they do not ask questions. Deposition questions are often drafted by paralegals, however. In the Baranski case, for example, attorney Gilmore might ask paralegal Lopez to draft questions for a deposition of defendant Peretto or someone else, such as an eyewitness to the accident. For Peretto's deposition, Lopez might draft questions similar to those presented in Exhibit 10.9 on page 306. Gilmore can then use Lopez's questions as a checklist during the deposition. Note, though, that Gilmore's questions will not be limited to the questions included in the list. Other, unforeseen questions may arise as Gilmore learns new information during the deposition. Also, the deponent's answer to one question may reveal the answer to another, so not all the questions on the checklist will need to be asked.

Preparing the Client for a Deposition

No attorney can predict a deponent's answers beforehand. Spontaneous and sometimes contradictory statements can seriously damage the deponent's case. For this reason, the deposed party and his or her lawyer will want to prepare for the deposition by formulating answers to anticipated questions. For example, if defendant Peretto's attorney plans to depose plaintiff Baranski, attorney Gilmore and paralegal Lopez might have Baranski come into their office for a run-through of possible questions that Peretto's attorney might ask her during the deposition.

This kind of preparation does not mean that the lawyer tells the deponent what to say. Instead, the lawyer offers suggestions as to how the answers to certain questions should be phrased. The answers must be truthful, but the truth can be presented in many ways.

A practice deposition can also help laypeople become accustomed to the unfamiliar format and can reduce stress. This lessens the chances that the witness will make an error during the deposition due to nervousness. For example, Gilmore would caution Baranski to limit her responses to the questions and not engage in speculative answers that might prejudice her claim. If Baranski was asked whether she had ever been involved in an automobile accident before, for example, Gilmore would probably caution her to use a simple (but truthful) "yes" or "no" answer. Attorney Gilmore normally would permit Baranski to provide additional information only in response to precisely phrased questions.

The Role of the Deponent's Attorney

The deponent's attorney will attend the deposition, but the attorney's role is limited. Under FRCP 30, the attorney may instruct a deponent to not answer a question only when necessary to preserve a privilege, to enforce a limitation directed by the court, or to present a motion to terminate the deposition. In other words, if Baranski was being deposed by Peretto's attorney, Cameron, she would have to answer Cameron's questions even if the questions were not clearly relevant to the

subpoena
A document commanding a person to appear at a certain time and place to give testimony concerning a certain matter.

ON THE web

To see an example of the subpoena process, enter "Alaska court form subpoena" in a search engine and you will be taken to the official Alaska court site for a description of "How to Subpoena a Witness" and a link to the relevant forms.

case AT A GLANCE

The Plaintiff—
  Plaintiff: Katherine Baranski
  Attorney: Allen P. Gilmore
  Paralegal: Elena Lopez
The Defendant—
  Defendant: Tony Peretto
  Attorney: Elizabeth A. Cameron
  Paralegal: Gordon McVay

EXHIBIT 10.9
Sample Deposition Questions

DEPOSITION QUESTIONS

1. Please state your full name and address for the record.
2. Please state your age, birth date, and Social Security number.
3. What is your educational level, and what employment position do you hold?
4. Do you have a criminal record, and if so, for what?
5. Have you been involved in previous automobile accidents? What driving violations have you had? Has your driver's license ever been suspended?
6. What is your medical history? Have you ever had health problems? Are you in perfect health? Were you in perfect health at the time of the accident?
7. Do you wear glasses or contact lenses? If so, for what condition? Were you wearing your glasses or contacts at the time the accident occurred?
8. Do you take medication of any kind?
9. Do you have any similar lawsuits or any claims pending against you?
10. Who is your automobile insurer? What are your policy limits?
11. Were there any passengers in your vehicle at the time of the accident?
12. Describe your vehicle. What was the mechanical condition of your vehicle at the time of the accident? Do you do your own mechanical work? If so, what training do you have in maintaining and repairing automobiles? Had you taken your vehicle to a professional mechanic's shop prior to the accident?
13. Please state the date on which the accident occurred.
14. Where were you prior to the accident, for at least the six hours preceding the accident?
15. Where were you going when the accident occurred, and for what purpose?
16. What were you doing during the last few moments before the accident? Were you smoking, eating, drinking, or chewing gum?
17. What were you thinking about just before the accident occurred?
18. What route did you take to reach your destination, and why did you take this particular route?
19. Describe the weather conditions at the time of the accident.
20. Please recite the facts of how the accident occurred.
21. Please describe the area in which the accident occurred. Were there many cars and pedestrians on the streets? Were there traffic controls, obstructions, or the like?
22. What was your location, and in what direction were you going?
23. When did you see the plaintiff's automobile approaching?
24. How far away were you when you first saw the auto? What was your rate of speed?
25. Did your vehicle move forward or was it pushed backward by the impact?
26. When did you first apply your brakes? Were your brakes functioning properly?
27. Did you attempt to avoid the accident? If so, how?
28. Did you receive a traffic ticket as a result of the accident?
29. Do you own the vehicle that you were driving at the time of the accident?
30. Were you acting within the scope of your employment when the accident occurred?
31. What were the conditions of the parties affected by the accident just after the accident occurred?
32. Did you attempt to provide first aid to any party?
33. How did the plaintiff leave the scene, and what was the plaintiff's physical condition?
34. What was the damage to your vehicle, and has it been repaired?

issues of the case—unless the court had previously limited this line of questioning. The deponent's attorney, Gilmore, could object only to questions that called for privileged information to be disclosed. Under Rule 30, that attorney is also required to state objections concisely, in a nonargumentative and nonsuggestive manner.

The deponent's attorney or the other party's attorney may also ask questions during the deposition to clarify a point or to establish facts needed for a motion. These questions are asked after the attorney conducting the deposition has finished. After the deponent's attorney has asked questions, the attorney conducting the deposition has another chance to ask questions. This continues until everyone is done.

As will be discussed shortly, deposition proceedings are recorded. If both attorneys agree to do so, however, they can go "off the record" to clarify a point or discuss a disputed issue. Depositions are stressful events, and tempers often flare. In the event that the deposition can no longer be conducted in an orderly fashion, the attorney conducting the deposition may have to terminate it.

ON THE web

If you are interested in court reporting, visit the Web site of the National Court Reporters Association at **www.ncra.org**.

The Deposition Transcript

Every utterance made during a deposition is recorded. A court reporter usually records the deposition proceedings and creates an official **deposition transcript**. Methods of recording a deposition include stenographic recording (a traditional method that involves the use of a shorthand machine or written shorthand), digital audio recording, digital video recording, or some combination of these methods. Rule 30(b)(2) of the FRCP states that unless the court orders otherwise, a deposition "may be recorded by sound, sound-and-visual, or stenographic means."

The deposition transcript may be used by either party during the trial to prove a particular point or to **impeach** (call into question) the credibility of a witness who says something during the trial that is different from what he or she stated during the deposition. For example, a witness in the Baranski case might state during the deposition that Peretto *did not* stop at the stop sign before proceeding to cross Mattis Avenue. If, at trial, the witness states that Peretto *did* stop at the stop sign before crossing Mattis Avenue, Baranski's attorney (Gilmore) could challenge the witness's credibility on the basis of the deposition transcript. Exhibit 10.10 on page 308 shows a page from a transcript of a deposition conducted by Gilmore in the Baranski case. The deponent was Julia Williams, an eyewitness to the accident. On the transcript, the letter "Q" precedes each question asked by Gilmore, and the letter "A" precedes each of Williams's answers.

Summarizing and Indexing the Deposition Transcript

Typically, the paralegal summarizes the deposition transcript. The summary, which along with the transcript will become part of the litigation file, allows the members of the litigation team to review quickly the information obtained from the deponent during the deposition.

In the Baranski case, assume that Lopez is asked to summarize the deposition transcript of Julia Williams. Typically, the transcript is summarized sequentially—that is, in the order in which it was given during the deposition—as shown in Exhibit 10.11 on page 309. Notice that the summary includes the page and line numbers in the deposition transcript where the full text of the information can be found.

Often, in addition to summarizing the transcript, the paralegal provides an index to the document. The index consists of a list of topics (such as education, employment status, injuries, and medical costs) followed by the relevant page and line numbers of the deposition transcript. Together, the summary and the index allow anyone involved in the case to locate information quickly. More tips for summarizing a deposition are provided in the *Developing Paralegal Skills* feature on page 310.

Requests for Production and Physical Examination

Another method of discovery is the request for the production of documents or tangible things or for permission to enter on land or other property for inspection and other purposes. FRCP 34 authorizes each party to request evidence from any other party. If the item requested is large or cannot be "produced" for some reason (Peretto's van for example), then the party can request permission to enter on the other party's land to inspect, test, sample, and digitally photograph the item. In federal courts, the duty of disclosure under FRCP 26 (to be discussed shortly) has greatly decreased the need to file such production requests.

When the mental or physical condition of a party is in controversy, the opposing party may also request the court to order the party to submit to a physical or mental examination by a licensed examiner. For example, if Peretto claims that Baranski's injuries were the result of a preexisting medical condition rather than the collision, defense attorney Cameron may file a request to have Baranski examined by a licensed physician. Because the existence, nature, and extent of Baranski's injuries are important in calculating the damages that she might be able to recover from Peretto, the court may grant the request.

---

deposition transcript
The official transcription of the recording taken during a deposition.

impeach
To call into question the credibility of a witness by challenging the truth or accuracy of his or her trial statement.

GOING green

TOWARD THE PARERLESS OFFICE

Today, in many instances, the preferred mode of communication is e-mail. Communicating electronically is faster than waiting for written or printed pages, and it saves paper and benefits the environment. You can help your office stay as paper free as possible by printing out only communications and documents that are requested in paper form. Of course, some legal documents must be on paper. Nevertheless, most can be stored in electronic format on hard drives, DVDs, or flash drives.

EXHIBIT 10.10

A Deposition Transcript (Excerpt)

67	Q: Where were you at the time of the accident?
68	A: I was on the southwest corner of the intersection.
69	Q: Are you referring to the intersection where Thirty-eighth Street crosses Mattis Avenue?
70	A: Yes.
71	Q: Why were you there at the time of the accident?
72	A: Well, I was on my way to work. I usually walk down Mattis Avenue to the hospital.
73	Q: So you were walking to work down Mattis Avenue and you saw the accident?
74	A: Yes.
75	Q: What did you see?
76	A: Well, as I was about to cross the street, a dark green van passed within three feet of me and ran the
77	stop sign and crashed into another car.
78	Q: Can you remember if the driver of the van was a male or a female?
79	A: Yes. It was a man.
80	Q: I am showing you a picture. Can you identify the man in the picture?
81	A: Yes. That is the man who was driving the van.
82	Q: Do you wear glasses?
83	A: I need glasses only for reading. I have excellent distance vision.
84	Q: How long has it been since your last eye exam with a doctor?
85	A: Oh, just a month ago, with Dr. Sullivan.

page 4

Requests for Admission

During discovery, a party can also request that the opposing party admit the truth of matters relating to the case. For example, Baranski's attorney can request that Peretto admit that he owned the car involved in the accident. Such admissions save time at trial because the parties will not have to spend time proving admitted facts. Any matter admitted under such a request is established as true for the trial. FRCP 36 permits requests for admission but requires that a request for admission cannot be made, without the court's permission, prior to the prediscovery meeting of the attorneys.

The Duty to Disclose under FRCP 26

Each party has a duty to disclose to the other party specified types of information prior to the discovery stage of litigation. Under FRCP Rule 26(f), once a lawsuit is brought, the parties (the plaintiff and defendant and/or their attorneys, if the parties are represented by counsel) must schedule a prediscovery meeting to discuss the nature of the lawsuit, any defenses that may be raised against the claims being brought, and possibilities for promptly settling or otherwise resolving the dispute. The meeting should take place as soon as practicable but at least fourteen days before a scheduling conference is held or a scheduling order issued.

Either at this meeting or within ten days after it, the parties must also make the initial disclosures described below and submit to the court a plan for discovery. As

EXHIBIT 10.11
A Deposition Summary (Excerpt)

Case:	Baranski v. Peretto Plaintiff 15773	Attorney: Allen P. Gilmore Legal Assistant: Elena Lopez
Deponent:	Julia Williams 3801 Mattis Avenue Nita City, Nita 48800	Date: March 17, 2014

Page	Line(s)	
		* * * *
4	72–77	Williams stated that she was on the way to work at the time of the accident. She was about to cross the street when Peretto's car ("a dark green van") passed within three feet of her, ran the stop sign, and crashed into Baranski's car.
4	80–81	When shown a picture of Peretto, she identified him as the driver of the green van.
4	82–83	Williams has excellent distance vision and does not require corrective lenses. She does need reading glasses for close work.
		* * * *

© Cengage Learning 2014

the trial date approaches, the attorneys must make subsequent disclosures relating to witnesses, documents, and other relevant information.

These rules do not replace the methods of discovery discussed in the preceding section. Rather, they impose a duty on attorneys to disclose specified information automatically to opposing counsel early in the litigation process so that the time and costs of traditional discovery can be reduced. Attorneys may still use discovery tools (depositions and interrogatories, for instance) to obtain information, but they cannot use these methods until the prediscovery meeting has been held and initial disclosures have been made.

Initial Disclosures

FRCP 26(a)(1) requires each party to disclose the following information to the other party either at an initial meeting of the parties or within ten days following the meeting:

- The name, address, and telephone number of any person who is likely to have "discoverable information" and the nature of that information.

- A copy or "description by category and location" of all documents, data, and other "things in the possession, custody, or control of the party" that are relevant to the dispute.

- A computation of the damages being claimed by the disclosing party. The party must make available to the other party for inspection and copying the documents and other materials on which the computation is based.

- Copies of any insurance policies that cover the injuries or harms alleged in the lawsuit and that may pay part or all of a judgment resulting from the dispute.

In the Baranski case, attorney Gilmore and paralegal Lopez must work quickly to assemble all relevant information, documents, and other evidence that Lopez has gathered during client interviews and during her preliminary investigation. Lopez will prepare copies of the documents or other information—or a description of them—for Gilmore's review and signature. The copies or descriptions will then be filed with the court and delivered to Peretto's attorney.

social
MEDIA TODAY

Creating a valuable flow of information requires regular updates. Set goals for regular postings in the social media tools you use.

DEVELOPING
paralegal skills

DEPOSITION SUMMARIES

After a deposition is taken, each attorney orders a copy of the deposition transcript. Copies may be obtained in printed form or in an electronic file. When the transcript is received, the legal assistant's job is to prepare a summary of the testimony that was given. The summary is typically only a few pages in length.

The legal assistant must be very familiar with the lawsuit and the legal theories that are being pursued so that he or she can point out inconsistencies in the testimony or between the testimony and the pleadings. The paralegal might also give special emphasis to any testimony that will help to prove the client's case in court.

After the deposition summary has been created, the paralegal places the summary in the litigation file, usually in a special discovery folder or binder within the larger file. The deposition summary will be used to prepare for future depositions, to prepare pretrial motions, and to impeach witnesses at the trial, should they give contradictory testimony.

TIPS FOR SUMMARIZING A DEPOSITION

- Find out how the deposition is to be summarized—by chronology, by legal issue, by factual issues, or otherwise.
- Read through the deposition transcript and mark important pages.
- Be sure to include a reference to the page and line that is being summarized.
- Take advantage of software that can assist in summarizing the deposition transcript.

Note that in the information disclosed to Peretto's attorney, Lopez must include even information that might be damaging to Baranski's position. Lopez need not disclose *privileged information,* however, such as confidential discussions between Baranski and Gilmore.

Failure to Disclose

A party will not be excused from disclosing relevant information simply because the party has not yet completed an investigation into the case or because the other party has not yet made its disclosures. FRCP 37(c) makes it clear that the failure to make these initial disclosures can result in serious sanctions.

If a party fails to make required disclosures, that party will not be able to use the information as evidence at trial. In addition, the court may impose other sanctions, such as ordering the party to pay reasonable expenses, including attorneys' fees, created by the failure to disclose. In sum, Gilmore and Lopez need to make sure that all relevant information (that is not privileged) is disclosed, or Gilmore will not be able to use it in court (and may face other sanctions as well).

Discovery Plan

discovery plan

A plan formed by the attorneys litigating a lawsuit, on behalf of their clients, that indicates the types of information that will be disclosed by each party to the other prior to trial, the testimony and evidence that each party will or may introduce at trial, and the general schedule for pretrial disclosures and events.

As mentioned above, at the initial meeting of the parties, the attorneys must work out a **discovery plan** and submit a report describing the plan to the court within ten days of the meeting. The type of information to be included in the discovery plan is illustrated in Exhibit 10.12 on the facing page, which shows Form 35, a form created for this purpose. As indicated by the form, Rule 26(f) allows the attorneys substantial room to negotiate the details of discovery, including the time schedules to be followed.

In the Baranski case, paralegal Lopez will make sure that attorney Gilmore takes a copy of Form 35 with him to the initial prediscovery meeting of the parties to use as a checklist, along with tentative dates by which she and Gilmore believe they can have completed their discovery. After the attorneys decide on the details of the plan to be proposed to the court, Gilmore will probably have Lopez draft a final version of the plan for his review and signature.

Subsequent Disclosures

In addition to the initial disclosures just discussed, each party must make other disclosures prior to trial. All subsequent disclosures must also be made in writing, signed by the attorneys, and filed with the court. These include information relating to expert witnesses, other witnesses, and exhibits that may be used at trial.

EXHIBIT 10.12

Form 35—Report of Parties' Planning Meeting (Discovery Plan)

[Caption and Names of Parties]

1. Pursuant to Fed. R. Civ. P. 26(f), a meeting was held on _____(date)_____ at _____(place)_____ and was attended by:

_____(name)_____ for plaintiff(s) _____(party name)_____
_____(name)_____ for defendant(s) _____(party name)_____
_____(name)_____ for defendant(s) _____(party name)_____

2. Pre-Discovery Disclosures. The parties [have exchanged] [will exchange by _____(date)_____] the information required by [Fed. R. Civ. P. 26(a)(1)] [(local rule _____)].

3. Discovery Plan. The parties jointly propose to the court the following discovery plan: [Use separate paragraphs or subparagraphs as necessary if parties disagree.]

Discovery will be needed on the following subjects:
_____(brief description of subjects on which discovery will be needed)_____
All discovery commenced in time to be completed by __(date)__. [Discovery on__(issue for early discovery)__
to be completed by _____(date)_____.]
Maximum of ____ interrogatories by each party to any other party. [Responses due ____ days after service.]
Maximum of ____ requests for admission by each party to any other party. [Responses due ____ days after service.]
Maximum of ____ depositions by plaintiff(s) and ____ by defendant(s).
Each deposition [other than of _____] limited to maximum of ____ hours unless extended by agreement of parties.
Reports from retained experts under Rule 26(a)(2) due:
  from plaintiff(s) by _____(date)_____.
  from defendant(s) by _____(date)_____.
Supplementations under Rule 26(e) due __(time(s) or intervals(s))__.

4. Other Items. [Use separate paragraphs or subparagraphs as necessary if parties disagree.]

The parties [request] [do not request] a conference with the court before entry of the scheduling order.
The parties request a pretrial conference in_____(month and year)_____.
Plaintiff(s) should be allowed until __(date)__ to join additional parties and until ___(date)___ to amend the pleadings.
Defendant(s) should be allowed until __(date)__ to join additional parties and until ___(date)___ to amend the pleadings.
All potentially dispositive motions should be filed by__(date)__.
Settlement [is likely] [is unlikely] [cannot be evaluated prior to ___(date)___] [may be enhanced by use of the following alternative dispute resolution procedure: _____].
Final lists of witnesses and exhibits under Rule 26(a)(3) should be due
  from plaintiff(s) by ___(date)___.
  from defendant(s) by ___(date)___.
Parties should have _____ days after service of final lists of witnesses and exhibits to list objections under Rule 26(a)(3).
The case should be ready for trial by _____(date)_____ [and at the time is expected to take approximately _____(length of time)_____].
[Other matters.]

Date: _____

Expert Witnesses

Under FRCP 26(a)(2), each party must disclose to the other party the names of any expert witnesses who may be called to testify during the trial. Additionally, the following information about each expert witness must be disclosed in a report signed by the expert witness:

- A statement by the expert witness indicating the opinions that will be expressed, the basis for the opinions, and the data or information considered by the witness when forming the opinions.

- Any exhibits that will be used to summarize or support the opinions.

- The qualifications of the expert witness, including a list of all publications authored by the witness within the preceding ten years.

- The compensation to be paid to the expert witness.

- A list of any other cases in which the witness has testified as an expert at trial or by deposition within the preceding four years.

These disclosures must be made at times set by the court. If the court does not indicate any times, then they must be made at least ninety days prior to the trial date.

Other Pretrial Disclosures

Under revised FRCP 26(a)(3), each party must also disclose to the other party the following information about witnesses who will testify at trial or any exhibits that will or may be used:

- A list containing the names, addresses, and telephone numbers of other witnesses who may or will be called during the trial to give testimony. The witness list must indicate whether the witness "will" or "may" be called.

- A list of any witnesses whose deposition testimony may be offered during the trial and a transcript of the relevant sections of the deposition testimony, if the testimony was not taken stenographically.

- A list of exhibits that indicates which exhibits will and may be offered.

These disclosures must be made at least thirty days before trial, unless the court orders otherwise. Once the disclosures have been made, the opposing party has fourteen days to file with the court any objections to the use of any deposition or exhibit. If objections are not made, they are deemed to be waived (unless a party can show good cause why he or she failed to object to the disclosures within the fourteen-day time period).

An attorney's duty to disclose relevant information is ongoing throughout the pretrial stage. Any time an attorney learns about relevant supplemental information concerning statements or responses made earlier, that information must be disclosed to the other party. An important task for many paralegals is keeping track of the opposing parties' discovery requests so she or he can alert the attorney if a supplemental filing is necessary.

Discovery of Electronic Evidence

Electronic evidence, or e-evidence, consists of all computer-generated or electronically recorded information, such as e-mail, voice mail, Facebook, Google+, or Twitter postings on social media sites, blog posts, spreadsheets, documents, and other data. E-evidence has become increasingly important because it can reveal significant facts that are only found in electronic format, such as e-mail. The Federal Rules of Civil Procedure and state rules (as well as court decisions) specifically allow discovery of electronic "data compilations." As in other areas of the practice of law, electronic tools are playing a growing part of discovery, as discussed in the *Practice Focus* feature on the facing page.

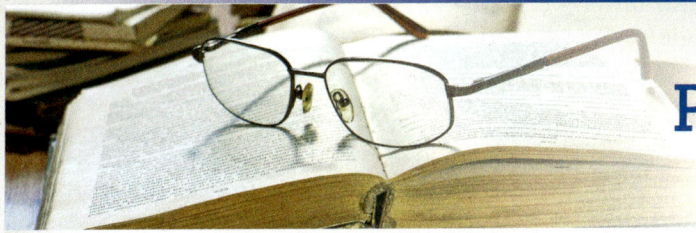

PRACTICE focus

EFFECTIVE E-DISCOVERY

"E-discovery" is on the cutting edge of pretrial practice. One important feature of many e-discovery tools is putting in place a records management system before litigation arises to minimize the burden of responding to discovery requests. Since litigation is a virtual certainty for many businesses, the up-front investment is often worthwhile.

The key to an e-discovery-ready records-management system is to ensure that older records are properly categorized and stored and that records not required by business needs or legal requirements are destroyed and purged from the system. In a recent survey, more than two-thirds of corporate legal departments sought a records-management system that covered everything from data preservation to production of documents.

The most important issues for many clients are controlling costs and reducing risks. Among the most costly aspects of document production is review for relevance and privilege, a process that often consumes more than half of a litigation budget. Automated processes can help reduce costs by excluding documents based on criteria such as file type, dates, storage location, or the presence or absence of key words.

Risk control refers to the measures used to identify, preserve, and organize documents. Errors can lead to fines or other penalties. Among the most difficult issues is how to handle e-mail and calendar archives. Not only must the e-mails themselves be saved, but also the "metadata" about the e-mails, such as storage location, creation dates and times, path information, and so on. Becoming familiar with e-discovery tools can increase your value as a paralegal.

The Advantages of Electronic Evidence

People and businesses use computers to store and communicate enormous amounts of data. Most information stored on computers is never printed on paper. In addition, whenever a person is working on a computer, information is being recorded on the hard drive without being saved by the user. This information, called **metadata**, is the hidden data kept by the computer about a file, including location, path, creator, date created, date last accessed, hidden notes, earlier versions, passwords, and formatting. It reveals information about how, when, and by whom a file was created, accessed, modified, and transmitted. This information can only be obtained from the file in its electronic format—not from printed versions.

E-Mail Communications

Billions of e-mail messages are sent each year. Because e-mail is so widespread, it has become a fertile ground for gathering evidence in litigation. In fact, e-mail has proved to be the "smoking gun" in many cases. This is because many people converse freely and informally in their e-mail communications, as if talking to a close friend or business associate. This makes e-mail believable and compelling evidence—evidence that can be damaging if discovered by outsiders.

In addition, in its electronic form, e-mail contains information that provides links to other e-mails, e-mail attachments, erased files, and metadata. These metadata reveal the identity of any person who received copies of an e-mail message (even "blind" copies). Thus, e-evidence can be used to trace a message to its true originator, reconstruct an e-mail conversation, and establish a timeline of the events in dispute (who knew what, when). Attorneys also use it to verify clients' claims or discredit the claims of the opposition. Whether it is evidence of adultery, sexual harassment, employment discrimination, fraud, or the theft of trade secrets, e-mail often contains the most compelling evidence in a case.

metadata
Embedded electronic data recorded by a computer in association with a particular file, including location, path, creator, date created, date last accessed, hidden notes, earlier versions, passwords, and formatting. Metadata reveal information about how, when, and by whom a document was created, accessed, modified, and transmitted.

E-discovery may also include examination of blog posts, Facebook accounts, Twitter accounts, Google+ accounts, and cloud-based services.

Deleted Files Can Be Retrieved

A major advantage of e-evidence is that even deleted files can often be retrieved from within a computer. This is because deleting a file does not actually destroy the data, but simply makes the space occupied by the file available to be overwritten by new information. Until that space is actually used for new data (which may be in weeks, in months, or never), the deleted record can be retrieved by use of special software.

Backup tools such as Apple's Time Machine mean that there are often copies of "deleted" files on servers or networked hard drives in homes and offices. The growing use of cloud storage makes it even less likely that simply erasing a file actually deletes it. Online cloud storage servers are often themselves backed up in ways that make it possible to locate copies of files deleted from individual computers. Postings on blogs or other Web sites may be accessed using backups of a Web-hosting service. Never assume that a file from a computer connected to a network is truly gone just because it was erased from that computer.

The same is true of e-mails and other forms of messages. Many people believe that when they delete a record or e-mail and empty the recycle bin, the message is gone from their computer. That belief increases the probability of candid e-mail communications. As just described, however, deleted data remain on the computer until overwritten by new data (or wiped out by utility software). Similarly, tweets may have been "re-tweeted," blog posts may have been distributed through networks of servers, and so forth.

In fact, experts have even been able to retrieve data, in whole or in part, from computers that have been damaged by water, fire, or severe impact. Furthermore, all transmissions on the Internet are stored in a server somewhere at various points in their transmission. Therefore, do not assume that e-evidence is not available just because a file was deleted, a computer was damaged, or a utility program was run. Technical issues in discovery are growing ever more complex, as discussed in *Technology and Today's Paralegal* on the facing page.

The Sources of Electronic Evidence

The key to conducting electronic discovery is developing an understanding of the kinds of information that computers can provide so that you will know where to look for particular kinds of information. Generally, computer data can be located in active files, in backup files, or as residual data. Active files are those currently accessible on the computer (documents, e-mail, and spreadsheets, for example). Backup files are those that have been copied to removable media such as flash drives or DVDs or to remote servers. Residual data are data that appear to be gone but are still recoverable from somewhere on the computer system. Residual data no longer have pointers to indicate their location and can only be retrieved by special software.

Backup Data

Backup files can be a source of hidden treasure for the legal team. Reviewing backup copies of documents and e-mail provides useful information about how a particular matter progressed over several weeks or months.

Companies vary in their policies about backing up data. Most companies back up files at routine intervals (daily or weekly), but some have no formal backup schedule. Some companies have backup routines for word-processing documents but not for e-mail. Because the current location of the data depends on the backup policy (or practice) in use, you need to find out what the policy is as soon as you can during discovery. See the *Developing Paralegal Skills* feature on page 316 for more tips on e-discovery.

social
MEDIA TODAY

Have a person who is not one of your Facebook friends search for you to see what your page looks like to the public, then adjust your settings accordingly to correct any issues you have with your profile.

TECHNOLOGY AND
today's paralegal

WHO BEARS THE COSTS OF ELECTRONIC DISCOVERY?

Traditionally, the party responding to a discovery request has had to pay the expenses involved in obtaining the requested materials. If compliance would be too burdensome or too costly, however, the judge could either limit the scope of the request or shift some or all of the costs to the requesting party. How do these traditional rules governing discovery apply to requests for electronic evidence?

WHY COURTS MIGHT SHIFT THE COSTS OF ELECTRONIC DISCOVERY

Electronic discovery has dramatically increased the costs associated with complying with discovery requests. It is no longer simply a matter of photocopying paper documents. Now the responding party may need to hire computer forensics (qualified scientific) experts to make "image" copies of desktop, laptop, and server hard drives, as well as removable storage media (such as DVDs and flash drives), backup drives and server-based systems, voice mail, smartphones, tablet devices, and any other form of digitally stored data.

In cases involving multiple parties or large corporations with many offices and employees, the electronic discovery process can easily run into hundreds of thousands—if not millions—of dollars.

COSTLY DISCOVERY

For example, Viacom, which owns Comedy Central and other television channels, sued YouTube, owned by Google, for more than $1 billion. Viacom claimed that YouTube had committed copyright violations by allowing clips from Viacom's television shows to be posted on YouTube without Viacom's permission.[a] Viacom hired a company, BayTSP, to watch for possible violations on YouTube. BayTSP identified more than 150,000 clips posted on YouTube, and Viacom claimed losses from each such posting.

YouTube demanded to see evidence of the violations. BayTSP estimated that it had gathered more than 1 million documents, all electronic, related to the clip postings. It protested to the court that the document request was unreasonable. BayTSP spent 2,000 hours over six months searching and reviewing the documents. By using electronic filters, it narrowed the list to 650,000 potentially relevant

documents. The court allowed YouTube's request for these documents to go forward. Given the amount at stake in the litigation, YouTube was within its rights, and BayTSP had to provide those documents. The cost of document production would be borne by BayTSP or, the court noted, probably by Viacom because BayTSP worked for it. The court held, however, that when costs are burdensome, a court may order the costs to be split between defendant and plaintiff.

WHAT FACTORS DO COURTS CONSIDER IN DECIDING TO SHIFT COSTS?

When is it appropriate for a court to shift cost from one party to another in discovery? The Federal Rules of Civil Procedure advisory committee lists seven factors:

1. the specificity of the discovery request;

2. the quantity of information available from other and more easily accessed sources;

3. the failure to produce relevant information that seems likely to have existed but is no longer available on more easily accessed sources;

4. the likelihood of finding relevant responsive information that cannot be obtained from other, more easily accessed sources;

5. predictions as to the importance and usefulness of the further information;

6. the importance of the issues at stake in the litigation; and

7. the parties' resources.[b]

TECHNOLOGY TIP

Paralegals should keep in mind not only the high costs of some electronic discovery requests but also the possibility that the court may shift some of these costs to the party requesting discovery. Suppose, for example, that you are assisting a corporate defendant in a product liability lawsuit brought by a plaintiff who was seriously harmed by one of the defendant's products. If the plaintiff requests extensive electronic evidence during discovery, the defendant corporation may be required to pay a significant portion of the costs of the requested discovery.

---

a.   *Viacom International v. YouTube, Inc.,* 2009 WL 102808 (N.D.Cal. 2009).

b.   Fed.R.Civ.P. 26(b)(2).

DEVELOPING
paralegal skills

ELECTRONIC DISCOVERY

Paralegals need to be prepared to deal with electronic discovery. This means not only formulating electronic discovery plans but also making sure to preserve the integrity of any electronic evidence acquired. It is important, too, to remember that e-evidence is fragile. Although—as discussed in the chapter text—it may be difficult to permanently delete files from a computer system, it is not impossible. Every time a user enters new data, loads new software, or performs routine maintenance procedures, the data on the computer are permanently altered.

Firms with careful data retention policies regularly perform procedures to eliminate such files (do you?). Just booting up a computer can change dates and times on numerous files. The following are some general guidelines to follow in conducting e-discovery.

TIPS FOR CONDUCTING E-DISCOVERY

- Immediately write a preservation-of-evidence letter to all parties involved, including your own client, at the outset of the case. This letter informs the parties that they have a duty to take immediate action to preserve any potential electronic evidence.

- Use interrogatories to gather information about the opposing party's computer system so that you can learn as much as possible about the system with which you are dealing.

- Follow up with depositions. Once you know the names of the parties who oversee the system or have special knowledge of it, take depositions from them.

- After you have found out the details of where electronic evidence is located, draft a request for production of the evidence.

- When the e-evidence is acquired, determine how best to manage, review, and interpret the data, which may involve using the services of an outside company that specializes in this field. Special software can help manage files of millions of e-mails or large amounts of other e-evidence.

Note that backup files contain not only e-mail messages and word-processing documents, but also other embedded information that can be useful. For example, when computers are networked, computer logs and audit trails that keep track of network usage may be available. An audit trail will tell you who accessed the system, when it was accessed, and whether those who accessed the system copied, downloaded, modified, or deleted any files. In addition, backup data files include certain nonprinting information, such as the date and time the files were created. Some word-processing software allows users to insert hidden comments or track changes while drafting and revising documents. These comments and revisions can also be accessed from the electronic version of the backup file.

Other Sources of E-Evidence

It is important to remember that electronic evidence is not limited to the data found on computer systems. As stated, e-evidence includes *all* electronically recorded information, such as voice mail, backup voice mail, video, electronic calendars, and phone logs, on iPhones, BlackBerries, iPads, tablets, laptops, and other devices that digitally store data. You should not overlook any possible sources of e-evidence during discovery. Use traditional discovery tactics (such as interrogatories and depositions) to find out about other sources of potential e-evidence. Consider all possible sources that might prove fruitful, but such requests must be reasonable and in good faith.

The Special Requirements of Electronic Evidence

While courts allow discovery of electronic evidence, judges know that electronic evidence can be manipulated. To ensure that the evidence you obtain during discovery will be admissible as evidence in court, you must do two things. First, make sure that you obtain an exact image copy of the electronic evidence. Second, make sure that you can prove that nothing has been altered or changed from the time the image copy was made. Keeping a backup copy of the material as received from the other party is one way to do this. Your law firm will likely have policies on how to handle e-evidence. Be sure to familiarize yourself with these and follow them carefully.

Acquiring an Image Copy

To use any evidence in court, you must convince the court that the evidence is authentic. In the case of electronic evidence, you must show that the electronic version of the evidence that you have acquired is exactly the same as the version that was present on the target system. The way to do this is to have an image copy made.

Suppose the target system is a computer hard drive. Making an image copy would involve creating an electronic image of the drive being copied. The image copy would capture all data, including residual data. This is different from the usual file-by-file copying method.

Making an image copy of a computer drive is complicated and is best left to an expert in computer forensics. Computer forensics experts collect, preserve, and analyze electronic evidence and testify in court if needed. Unskilled attempts to acquire an image of a computer's drive can easily lead to disaster, wrecking the evidence and making it inadmissible at trial.

Preserving the Chain of Custody

Once you have acquired an exact copy of the electronic evidence, you must establish and maintain a chain of custody to avoid any claims that the evidence has been tampered with. The phrase **chain of custody** refers to the movement and location of evidence from the time it is obtained to the time it is presented in court.

It is crucial when dealing with electronic evidence to make sure that you can track the evidence from its original source to its submission to the court. Trackability will provide the court with the assurance that nothing has been added, changed, or deleted. The original image copy should be write-protected so that it is tamperproof, labeled as the original, and kept in a secure location. Typically, a forensic specialist will make copies of the original data that are write-protected and scanned for viruses. You should always use the copies when reviewing e-evidence. You may need to review the evidence only on a secure computer not connected to the Internet to protect the data integrity.

chain of custody
A series describing the movement and location of evidence from the time it is obtained to the time it is presented in court. The court requires that evidence be preserved in the condition in which it was obtained if it is to be admitted into evidence at trial.

Federal Rule of Evidence 502

The use of electronic evidence can result in a huge number of documents being made available to an opposing party. Such availability has increased the number of documents accidentally released. In a number of cases, for example, a party had the right to access e-mails of the opposing party relating to a particular matter. While attempts were made to filter out nonrelevant e-mails, some e-mails that should have been protected by attorney-client confidentiality rules were accidentally among the thousands of e-mails seen by the opposing party.

To deal with this problem, Congress changed Federal Rule of Evidence 502 in 2008. Under it, if there is an accidental release of material that should have been protected, the court may rule that protection was not waived by accidental disclosure. The courts consider the following factors in deciding if a privileged document has been lost to the opposing party or is still protected:

1. the reasonableness of precautions taken to prevent inadvertent disclosure in view of the extent of document production,

2. the number of inadvertent disclosures,

3. the extent of the disclosures,

4. the promptness of steps taken to remedy the disclosure, and

5. whether interests of justice would be served by relieving the party of its error of disclosing a protected document.

Paralegals often play a key role in organizing documents, so they must be alert to such issues. In complex cases involving a huge number of electronic documents, firms that are experts in such matters can be hired to help filter and sort documents. Because e-mails are often the center of such information releases, problems can be headed off in advance by using software that flags, sorts, and preserves e-mail.

Pretrial Motions

As we discussed earlier in the chapter, and as shown in Exhibit 10.13 below, there are a number of motions that may be made before trial. In Chapter 6 we noted that many conflicts are settled by some form of alternative dispute resolution before trial. When that happens, and the parties reach a settlement agreement, the court is informed and, after reviewing the agreement, usually approves it and dismisses the case.

Summary Judgment

If there is no settlement, one of the last substantive motions likely to be filed before trial is a **motion for summary judgment**. The party filing the motion is asking the court to grant a judgment in his or her favor without a trial because there is no real

---

motion for summary judgment
A motion that may be filed by either party in which the party asks the court to enter judgment in his or her favor without a trial. A motion for summary judgment can be supported by evidence outside the pleadings, such as witnesses' affidavits, answers to interrogatories, and other evidence obtained prior to or during discovery.

EXHIBIT 10.13
Pretrial Motions

MOTION TO DISMISS

A motion filed by the defendant in which the defendant asks the court to dismiss the case for a specified reason, such as improper service, lack of personal jurisdiction, or the plaintiff's failure to state a claim for which relief can be granted. A plaintiff would file a motion to dismiss against a counterclaim or cross-claim.

MOTION TO STRIKE

A motion filed by a party in which the party asks the court to strike (delete) material from another party's filing. Motions to strike help to clarify the underlying issues by removing paragraphs that are redundant or irrelevant to the action.

MOTION TO MAKE MORE DEFINITE AND CERTAIN

A motion filed by the defendant to compel the plaintiff to clarify the basis of the plaintiff's cause of action. The motion is filed when the defendant believes that the complaint is too vague or ambiguous for the defendant to respond to it in a meaningful way. Similarly, a plaintiff might file such a motion about a counterclaim or cross-claim.

MOTION TO COMPEL DISCOVERY

A motion that may be filed by either party in which the party asks the court to compel the other party to comply with a discovery request. If a party refuses to allow the opponent to inspect and copy certain documents, for example, the party requesting the documents may make a motion to compel production of the documents.

MOTION FOR JUDGMENT ON THE PLEADINGS

After all pleadings have been filed, either party may file this motion. It may be used when there are no facts in dispute, only a question of how the law will apply to the undisputed facts.

MOTION FOR SUMMARY JUDGMENT

A motion that may be filed by either party in which the party asks the court to enter judgment in his or her favor without a trial. Unlike a motion for judgment on the pleadings, a motion for summary judgment can be supported by evidence outside the pleadings, such as witnesses' affidavits, answers to interrogatories, and other evidence obtained prior to or during discovery.

disagreement about the relevant facts. Once discovery is complete, the parties can argue that no material (relevant) facts are in dispute and the only question is how the law applies to undisputed facts.

Considerations by the Court

When the court considers a motion for summary judgment, it takes into account the evidence the parties have gathered to use at trial. To support the motion, a party submits evidence obtained, such as depositions and interrogatories, and argues that, given the facts, the other party cannot prevail at trial. The court must review the evidence in the light most favorable to the nonmoving party. That is, the court must be satisfied that it has drawn all permissible inferences in that party's favor in interpreting the evidence. This motion is more likely to be successfully used by the defendant, but in about a quarter of cases in which the motion is used, it is successful for the plaintiff.

Motion by Defendant

In the Baranski case, for example, suppose it has been established that Peretto was in another state at the time of the accident. Peretto's attorney could make a motion for summary judgment in Peretto's favor and attach to the motion a witness's sworn statement that Peretto was in the other state at the time of the accident. Unless Baranski's attorney could bring in other evidence to show that Peretto was at the scene of the accident, Peretto's motion for summary judgment would be granted.

A motion for summary judgment would also be appropriate if Baranski had previously signed a release waiving her right to sue Peretto on the claim. In that situation, Cameron would attach a copy of the release to the motion before filing the motion with the court. Cameron would also prepare a memorandum of law in support of the motion. When the motion was heard by the court, Cameron would argue that the execution of the waiver barred Baranski from pursuing her claim against Peretto.

Burden of Proof

The burden would then shift to Baranski's attorney, Gilmore, to demonstrate that the release was invalid or otherwise not binding on Baranski. If the judge believed that the release had been voluntarily signed by Baranski, then the judge would grant the motion. If Gilmore convinced the judge that there was an issue concerning the validity of the release, such as evidence that the release signed by Baranski had been procured by coercive or fraudulent practices, then the judge would deny the motion for summary judgment and permit the case to go to trial. The validity of the release would then be determined at trial by the fact finder.

KEY TERMS AND CONCEPTS

affidavit 291	discovery 300	motion to dismiss 299
affirmative defense 296	discovery plan 310	pleadings 286
allegation 287	docket 287	prayer for relief 290
answer 296	electronic filing (e-filing) system 292	privileged information 300
chain of custody 317	Federal Rules of Civil Procedure (FRCP) 281	return-of-service form 294
complaint 286	impeach 307	service of process 293
counterclaim 296	interrogatories 300	subpoena 305
cross-claim 296	judgment 280	summons 293
default judgment 295	memorandum of law 299	supporting affidavit 299
deponent 304	metadata 313	witness 280
deposition 304	motion 298	
deposition transcript 307	motion for summary judgment 318	

Chapter Summary

Civil Litigation—Before the Trial

CIVIL LITIGATION—A BIRD'S-EYE VIEW

1. *Pretrial settlements*—Throughout the pretrial stage of litigation, the attorney and paralegal attempt to help the parties reach a settlement at the same time as they are preparing the case for trial.

2. *Procedural requirements*—Although civil lawsuits vary from case to case in terms of complexity, cost, and detail, all civil litigation involves similar procedural steps, as described in Exhibit 10.1 on page 281.

The Federal Rules of Civil Procedure (FRCP) govern all civil cases heard in federal courts and specify what must be done during the various stages of litigation. Each state has adopted its own rules of civil procedure, which in many states are similar to the FRCP. Many courts also have (local) rules of procedure that supplement the federal or state rules.

THE PRELIMINARIES

1. *The initial client interview*—The first step in the civil litigation process occurs when an attorney initially meets with a client who wishes to bring a lawsuit against another party or parties. Before the meeting, the paralegal will conduct a conflicts check to ensure that representing the client would not create a conflict of interest. The attorney normally conducts the initial client interview, although the paralegal often attends the interview and may make arrangements with the client for subsequent interviews.

2. *Preliminary investigation*—Once the attorney agrees to represent the client in the lawsuit and the client

has signed the retainer agreement, the attorney and the paralegal undertake a preliminary investigation to ascertain the facts alleged by the client and gain other factual information relating to the case.

3. *Creating the litigation file*—A litigation file is created to hold all documents and records pertaining to the lawsuit. Each law firm or legal department has its own specific procedures for organizing and maintaining litigation files. Generally, the file will expand as the case progresses to include subfiles for the pleadings, discovery, and other documents and information relating to the litigation.

THE PLEADINGS

The pleadings inform each party of the claims of the other and detail the facts, charges, and defenses involved in the litigation. Pleadings typically consist of the plaintiff's complaint, the defendant's answer, and any counterclaim or cross-claim.

1. *Drafting the complaint*—A complaint states the claim or claims that the plaintiff is making against the defendant. A lawsuit in a federal or state court normally is initiated by the filing of a complaint with the clerk of the appropriate court.

    a. The complaint includes a caption, jurisdictional allegations, general allegations (body of the complaint) detailing the cause of action, a prayer for relief, a signature, and, if appropriate, a demand for a jury trial.

    b. A complaint can be filed either by personal delivery of the papers to the court clerk or, if the court permits, by electronic filing. The procedural requirements of courts that allow electronic filing

vary and should be researched prior to any electronic filing.

2. *Filing the complaint*—The document is filed in paper or electronically. E-filing is becoming more common; some states have statewide systems, and some courts require e-filing.

3. *Service of process*—Typically, the defendant is notified of a lawsuit by delivery of the complaint and a summons (which is called service of process). The summons identifies the parties to the lawsuit, identifies the court in which the case will be heard, and directs the defendant to respond to the complaint within a specified time period.

    a. Although often the complaint and summons are personally delivered to the defendant, other methods of service are allowed in some cases, depending on the jurisdiction.

    b. In federal cases and in many states, the defendant can waive, or give up, the right to be personally served with the summons and complaint (and accept service by mail, for example).

   c. Under FRCP 4, if the defendant waives service of process, the defendant receives additional time to respond to the complaint.

4. *The defendant's response*—On receiving the complaint, the defendant has several options.

   a. The defendant may submit an answer. The answer may deny wrongdoing or assert an affirmative defense against the plaintiff's claim, such as the plaintiff's contributory negligence. The answer may be followed by a counterclaim, in which the defendant asserts a claim against the plaintiff arising out of the same incident; or it may be followed by a cross-claim, in which the defendant makes claims against another defendant named in the complaint.

   b. The defendant may make a motion to dismiss the case. That motion asserts that, even assuming that the facts of the complaint are true, the plaintiff has failed to state a cause of action or there are other grounds for dismissal of the suit.

5. *The scheduling conference*—The court may hold a conference to consult attorneys on both sides for case management purposes.

TRADITIONAL DISCOVERY TOOLS

In preparing for trial, the attorney for each party undertakes a formal investigative process called discovery to obtain evidence helpful to his or her client's case.

1. *Interrogatories*—Interrogatories are written questions that the parties to the lawsuit must answer, in writing and under oath. The FRCP and some states' rules limit the number of questions that may be asked, as well as the total number of interrogatories that may be filed.

2. *Depositions*—Like interrogatories, depositions are given under oath, but unlike interrogatories, depositions may be taken from witnesses as well as from the parties to the lawsuit. Also, the attorney is able to question the deponent (the person being deposed) in person. There is no limit on the number of questions that may be asked. Usually, a court reporter records the official transcript of the deposition.

3. *Requests for production and physical examination*—During discovery, the attorney for either side may request that another party produce documents or other tangible things, or allow the attorney access to them for inspection and other purposes. When the mental or physical condition of a party is in controversy, the opposing party may request the court to order the party to submit to an examination by a licensed examiner.

4. *Requests for admission*—A party can request that the opposing party admit the truth of matters relating to the case. Such admissions save time at trial because the parties do not have to spend time proving facts on which they agree.

THE DUTY TO DISCLOSE UNDER FRCP 26

In federal court cases, FRCP 26 requires that the attorneys cooperate in forming a discovery plan early in the litigation process. The rule also requires attorneys to disclose relevant information *automatically*. Under FRCP 26, only after initial disclosures have been made can attorneys resort to the use of traditional discovery tools. An attorney's duty to disclose relevant information under FRCP 26 is ongoing throughout the pretrial stage.

1. *Initial disclosures*—Each party must disclose information about persons likely to have discoverable information, a copy of relevant information or descriptions of it, information about the damages requested, and information about insurance that may apply.

2. *Failure to disclose*—Should a party fail to disclose relevant information, court sanctions may be imposed.

3. *Discovery plan*—Must be reported within ten days of the initial meeting of the attorneys.

4. *Subsequent disclosures*—After the initial disclosure, parties in civil litigation must tell each other before trial about expert witnesses to be used and the names of witnesses and the evidence to be presented at trial.

DISCOVERY OF ELECTRONIC EVIDENCE

Electronic evidence consists of all computer-generated or electronically recorded information, such as e-mail, voice mail, spreadsheets, and word-processing documents. The federal rules and state rules allow discovery of evidence in electronic form. E-evidence has significantly changed discovery in civil litigation because it can reveal facts not discoverable by other means.

1. *Advantages of e-evidence*—Electronic evidence often provides more information than paper discovery, because many data that are on the computer are never printed out. In addition, the computer records hidden data (called metadata) about documents and e-mail, which can be very useful. Even files that were deleted by the user can be retrieved from the residual data within the computer.

2. *Sources of e-evidence*—E-evidence may be located in computers, in the backup data copied to removable media or remote servers, or in the residual data that appear to be gone from the computer. Not all

e-evidence is located on computers, and you should investigate other potential sources, such as voice mail, phone logs, personal digital assistants, and so forth.

3. *Special requirements of e-evidence*—To ensure that e-evidence will be admissible as evidence in the trial, you must obtain an exact image copy of the original data and preserve the chain of custody until trial, making sure to do nothing that will alter the evidence.

PRETRIAL MOTIONS

There are a number of motions that may be filed by either party during or after the discovery stage of litigation. A motion for summary judgment is common. This motion asks the court to enter judgment without a trial. It can be

supported by evidence outside the pleadings (including affidavits, depositions, and interrogatories). The motion will not be granted if key facts are in dispute.

QUESTIONS FOR REVIEW

1. What takes place during the initial client interview? Who conducts this interview, the attorney or the paralegal? Why?

2. Describe the pleadings in a civil lawsuit. What is the effect of each type of pleading on the litigation?

3. What is service of process? Why is it important?

4. When does discovery take place, and what does it involve? List three discovery devices that can be used to obtain information prior to trial.

5. What is the duty to disclose under FRCP 26? How has it changed the discovery process in federal court cases?

6. What pretrial motions are discussed in this chapter? What is the purpose of each motion?

ETHICAL QUESTIONS

1. A client who is suing her employer for employment discrimination calls paralegal DeShawn from her employer-issued smartphone to discuss her case against her employer. Later, the client e-mails documents that may be used as evidence in her upcoming trial to DeShawn from her office computer. What ethical issues do the client's actions raise? What are DeShawn's ethical obligations in this situation? The law firm's obligations?

2. Paralegal Susan works as a paralegal and office manager for a sole practitioner, who is closing her law practice in Georgia and opening a new practice in Florida. The attorney is relying on Susan to close the Georgia law firm and place the files in storage. The

attorney is not going to notify the clients that she is leaving the state because she feels it will upset them and might cause them to post negative reviews about her on the Internet, which could hurt her new law practice in Florida.

Two years after moving to Florida, the attorney is contacted by the Georgia Attorney Grievance Commission because two of her former clients' automobile accident cases were settled without her knowledge and neither of the clients received their settlement proceeds. What ethical violations were committed by the attorney? Were there ethical violations committed by Susan?

PRACTICE QUESTIONS AND ASSIGNMENTS

1. Assume that you work for attorney Tara Jolans of Adams & Tate, 1000 Town Center, Suite 500, White Tower, Michigan. Jolans has decided to represent Sandra Nelson in her lawsuit against David Namisch. Based on the following information and the material in the chapter, draft a complaint to be filed in the U.S. District Court for the Eastern District of Michigan.

Sandra Nelson is the plaintiff in a lawsuit resulting from an automobile accident. Sandra was turning left at a traffic light at the intersection of Jefferson and Mack Streets, while the left-turn arrow was green, when she was hit from the side by a car driven by David Namisch, who failed to stop at the light. The accident occurred on June 3, 2014, at 11:30 P.M. David lives in New York, was visiting his family in Michigan, and just prior to the accident had been out drinking with his brothers. Several witnesses saw the accident. One of the witnesses called the police.

Sandra was not wearing her seat belt at the time of the accident, and she was thrown against the windshield, sustaining massive head injuries. When the police and ambulance arrived, they did not think that she would make it to the hospital alive, but she survived. She wants to claim damages of $500,000 for medical expenses, $65,000 for lost wages, and $55,000 for property damage to her Rolls Royce. The accident was reported in the local newspaper, complete with photographs.

2. Using Exhibit 10.3, A Summons in a Civil Action, on page 293, draft a summons to accompany the complaint against David Namisch. David's address is 1000 Main Street, Apartment 63, New York, NY 10009. The court clerk's name is David T. Brown.

3. Locate your federal district court's Web site and determine the requirements and procedures for electronically filing the complaint and summons drafted in Questions 1 and 2 above. Write a three-paragraph summary of the requirements.

4. Draft the first ten questions for a set of interrogatories to be directed to the plaintiff, Sandra Nelson, based on the facts given in Question 1 above.

QUESTIONS FOR CRITICAL ANALYSIS

1. What are the methods of serving a complaint on a defendant in a federal court lawsuit? What happens if the defendant is not properly served? Is this a fair result? Why or why not?

2. If a defendant fails to respond to the plaintiff's complaint within a specified time period, what can happen? Is this a fair rule? Why or why not?

3. What is the difference between interrogatories and depositions? Which is more efficient? Which is more cost-effective? Which would you prefer to use?

4. A litigation firm is involved in a lawsuit where the majority of the evidence is deleted e-mail and deleted word-processing documents. Is it possible to recover deleted documents? Would the rules of evidence allow these discovered documents to be introduced in court? What procedures would have to be followed?

5. What is the difference between a motion to dismiss and a motion for summary judgment? What type of evidence is each motion based on? When in the pretrial process is each motion used?

PROJECTS

1. Visit the county court clerk's office (or the clerk's office of a local court) and obtain the following: local court rules, summons and return-of-service forms, and a filing-fee schedule. (Check first to see if this information is available online.)

2. Open a word-processing document. Find the properties tab and open it. The document properties contain the document's metadata. Find and write down the document's author, creation date, date last revised, and the name of the person who did so. Write down one way in which metadata could be used in a trial.

GROUP PROJECT

This project addresses the issue of the discoverability of social networking information.

Student one will do an Internet search on whether information on social networking sites is discoverable.

Student two will assume it is discoverable, and will research who has to provide it—the user of a social networking account, or the social networking site itself.

Student three will research whether penalties apply if the postings on a social networking site are removed (known as spoliation of evidence) after a lawsuit begins. If the information is removed, is the removal permanent?

Student four will present the group's findings in a one-page paper.

USING INTERNET RESOURCES

1. Locate the complaint in the *Viacom, Inc. v. YouTube* case discussed in the *Technology and Today's Paralegal* feature on p. 315 by going to the cnet.com news Web site at **http://news.cnet.com/pdf/ne/2007/ViacomYouTubeComplaint3-12-07.pdf?tag=mncol;txt**. Read the complaint and answer these questions:

   a. In what court was the complaint filed?

   b. Who were the plaintiffs?

   c. Where were the defendants?

   d. What established the court's jurisdiction?

   e. What was the nature of the cause of action—that is, what legal claim was asserted?

   f. What remedies did the plaintiffs request?

2. There are numerous legal blogs (blawgs) that discuss legal issues. Several discuss the use of technology, such as iPhones and iPads, in litigation. Jim Calloway's blawg entitled "Law Practice Tips" has a very useful suggestion on how to use Google maps during a deposition. The blawg gives a snapshot of what happens during a deposition and how technology may be used during a deposition by either a lawyer or paralegal. Go to **http://jimcalloway.typepad.com/lawpracticetips/2012/01/ipad-for-litigators-is-a-hot-topic.html** and click on "iPads" under "Categories." Scroll down until you locate the article, "New Ideas for Lawyers and Google Maps." Explain in one to two paragraphs how to have a witness at a deposition use an iPad to mark exactly where he and other parties were located at the time in question with the help of Google maps "Streetview." Explain how this image can be e-mailed to the other attorneys who are present at the deposition. Can this photograph be saved on a laptop? Print out the page from the blawg and attach it to your summary.

END NOTES

1. Nita and Zero are fictitious states invented for the purpose of this hypothetical example.

2. The body of the complaint described in this section is a *fact pleading*, in which sufficient factual circumstances must be alleged to convince the court that the plaintiff has a cause of action. State courts often require fact pleadings, whereas federal courts only require *notice pleading*. FRCP 8(a) requires only that the complaint have "a short and plain statement of the claim showing that the pleader is entitled to relief." Fact pleading and notice pleading are not totally different—that is, the same allegation of facts could be in the body of a complaint submitted to either a federal or a state court. Federal courts simply have fewer requirements in this respect, and therefore they are often more attractive to litigants.

CourseMate The available CourseMate for this text has an interactive eBook and interactive learning tools, including flash cards, quizzes, and more. To learn more about this resource and access free demo CourseMate resources, go to **www.cengagebrain.com**, and search for this book. To access CourseMate materials that you have purchased, go to **login.cengagebrain.com**.

Conducting Interviews and Investigations

Chapter Outline

After completing this chapter, you will know:

- How to prepare for an interview and the kinds of skills employed during the interviewing process.

- The common types of client interviews paralegals may conduct and the different types of witnesses paralegals may need to interview during a preliminary investigation.

- How to create an investigation plan.

- The variety of sources that you can use to locate information or witnesses.

- Rules governing the types of evidence that are admissible in court.

- How to summarize investigation results.

Introduction

Paralegals frequently interview clients and witnesses. After the initial interview (which is usually conducted by the supervising attorney), the paralegal may conduct additional interviews to obtain detailed information. How the paralegal relates to the witness (including the client) has an important effect on the witness's attitude toward the attorney or legal team handling the case.

Learning how to conduct interviews and investigations is thus an important part of preparing for your career as a paralegal. In this chapter, you will read about the basic skills and concepts used when interviewing clients or witnesses and conducting investigations.

Planning the Interview

Planning an interview involves organizing many details. As a paralegal, you may be responsible for locating a witness, scheduling the interview, determining where the interview should take place, arranging for the use of one of the firm's conference rooms or other office space for the interview, and managing additional details. Crucial to the success of any interview is how well you prepare for it.

Know What Information You Want

interviewee
The person who is being interviewed.

Before any interview, you should have clearly in mind the information you want to obtain from the client or witness being interviewed—the **interviewee**. If possible, discuss with your supervising attorney the goal of the interview and the type of information the attorney hopes to obtain. This will ensure that you and the attorney share an understanding of what topics need to be covered in the interview. Once you know the questions that you want to ask, prepare a checklist or outline in advance so that you can refer to it during the interview. As the *Practice Focus* feature on the facing page explains, it is most productive to think through what may happen in an investigation before proceeding.

Standardized Interview Forms

Many law firms have preprinted or computerized forms indicating the kinds of information that should be gathered during client interviews relating to particular types of claims. Firms that frequently handle personal-injury claims, for example, often use a personal-injury intake sheet such as that shown in Exhibit 11.1 on pages 328 and 329. Client intake forms are also available as part of many legal software programs and from a variety of online sources. They may be completed electronically. Using standardized forms helps to ensure that all essential information will be obtained, especially for the beginning interviewer.

In some cases, the information needed will be clear from the legal forms or documents that may eventually be filed with the court. For example, a paralegal interviewing a client who is petitioning for bankruptcy or divorce can look at the bankruptcy or divorce court forms during the interview to make sure all required information is obtained.

Remain Flexible

The prepared questions and preprinted forms should only be used as guidelines during the interview. Do not simply read the questions word for word from a prepared list or stay rigidly to a planned outline of topics. If you do, you lose an opportunity to interact with the interviewee and gain the interviewee's trust, and he or she will probably not disclose any information other than what is specifically asked for.

The interviewer should be flexible, listen carefully to the interviewee's responses, and let those responses guide the questioning. (Remember that you can

PRACTICE focus

THINKING THROUGH A FRAUD INVESTIGATION

As a paralegal, you may be asked to help conduct an internal investigation in which someone suspects fraud has occurred in a business. Suppose a client is concerned that sensitive documents may have been taken by an employee. Here are some key questions that need to be considered:

- **Is an internal investigation the appropriate step?** In some cases, an internal investigative report may simply serve as a road map for a later investigation by law enforcement agencies. The main reasons to conduct an internal review are to send a clear signal that fraud is not tolerated and to stop the fraud.

- **Who is being defrauded?** If the harm is to someone not working for the company, outside legal advice is usually advised, and a key question will be whether the company is liable for fraud committed by an employee.

- **What steps are being taken to avoid defaming individuals accused of fraud?** A costly defamation suit (discussed in Chapter 14) is possible if an individual is falsely accused.

- **Should an employee suspected of fraud have known that his or her conduct was fraudulent or against company policy?** Answering this question will require reviewing company policies and education and training procedures.

- **How will the investigation be documented?** Usually the investigating paralegal will take notes and, with permission, record the interview. You should sign your notes. An attorney may ask an interviewee to prepare a written statement.

- **How will the results be evaluated?** Any report should be solidly based on the facts uncovered during the investigation, not on speculation or assumptions.

- **What statutes are relevant to the possible fraud?** Regulations from state and federal governments increasingly dominate many businesses.

always ask the interviewee to return to a certain topic later on in the interview.) By focusing too much on your own role and on what your next question will be, you can overlook the importance of what the client or witness is saying. Make sure that you listen to the interviewee's responses and modify your questions accordingly. Effective listening techniques are discussed later in this chapter.

Plan to Ask Follow-Up Questions

Another important point to remember is to ask for details and clarification after the interviewee has made a statement. Find out who, what, when, where, and how. If an interviewee says, for example, that he saw someone hit Jane in the face, you will need to ask for more specifics, such as:

- How far away was the interviewee at the time?

- What exactly did he see?

- How many times was Jane hit and with what (open hand, fist, weapon)?

- Who else was present?

- Was it light or dark? Inside or outside?

- From what angle did the interviewee view the incident?

- Does he know Jane or her assailant? How?

- What were Jane and the assailant doing before and after the incident?

- What was the witness doing before the incident?

Also, although you should read the case file thoroughly before the interview, try to set aside what you have read or heard about the case. Let the interviewee

EXHIBIT 11.1
Personal-Injury Intake Sheet

PERSONAL-INJURY INTAKE SHEET

Prepared for Clients of
Jeffers, Gilmore & Dunn

1. **Client Information:**

   Name: Katherine Baranski

   Address: 335 Natural Blvd.

   Nita City, NI   48802

   Social Security No.: 206-15-9858

   Marital Status: Married   Years Married: 3

   Spouse's Name: Peter Baranski

   Children: None

   Phone Numbers: Home (616) 555-2211   Work (616) 555-4849

   Employer: Nita State University

   Mathematics Department

   Position: Associate Professor of Mathematics

   Responsibilities: Teaching

   Salary: $58,000

2. **Related Information:**

   Client at Scene: Yes

   Lost Work Time: 5 months

   Client's Habits: Normally drives south on Mattis Avenue on way to university each morning at about the same time.

tell you the story from his or her own perspective and avoid preconceived notions about what the person will say.

One approach is to pretend that you know nothing about the case and let the interviewee tell you her or his version of the facts. Then, as the interview unfolds, think about what the person is saying from the perspective of your opponent—why should anyone believe that story? Ask follow-up questions aimed at establishing what makes the person's story more or less believable. If a witness says a car was going sixty miles per hour, for example, ask how he or she could tell the speed. If it turns out the witness has been racing cars for the past fifteen years, this fact can be used to help make the witness's testimony more credible.

Recording the Interview

Some interviewers record their interviews. Before you record an interview, obtain permission to do so from both your supervising attorney and the person being

EXHIBIT 11.1
Personal-Injury Intake Sheet—
Continued

3. Incident/Accident:

Date: August 4, 2013   Time: 7:45 A.M.

Place: Mattis Avenue and 38th Street, Nita City, Nita

Description: Mrs. Baranski was driving south on Mattis Avenue
when a car driven by Tony Peretto, who was
attempting to cross Mattis at 38th Street, collided
with Mrs. Baranski's vehicle.

Witnesses: None known by Mrs. Baranski

Defendant: Tony Peretto

Police: Nita City

Action Taken: Mrs. Baranski was taken to City Hospital
by ambulance (Nita City Ambulance Co.).

4. Injuries Sustained:

Nature: Multiple fractures to left hip and leg; lacerations
to left eye and left side of face; multiple contusions
and abrasions

Medical History: No significant medical problems prior to the
accident

Treating Hospital: Nita City Hospital

Treating Physician: Dr. Swanson

Hospital Stay: August 4, 2013   to September 20, 2013

Insurance: Southwestern Insurance Co. of America

Policy No: 00631150962-B

Interview Conducted by:

Allen P. Gilmore   January 30, 2014
Attorney   Date

Elena Lopez   January 30, 2014
Paralegal/Witness   Date

© Cengage Learning 2014

interviewed. When you are using a digital recorder, you should state or include at the beginning of the recording the following identifying information:

- The name of the person being interviewed and any other relevant information about the interviewee.

- The name of the person conducting the interview.

- The names of other persons present at the interview, if any.

- The date, time, and place of the interview.

- On the record, the interviewee's consent to having the interview recorded.

If more than one recording file is used, you should indicate at the end of each file that the interview will be continued on the next file in the series, and each subsequent file should contain identifying information. Secure copies of the interview should be stored electronically.

Benefits of Recording

There are several advantages to recording an interview. For one thing, having a digital audio record of the interview reduces the need to take extensive notes during the interview. You can either have the audio file transcribed for future reference or listen to the file later (when creating an interview summary, for example, as discussed later) to refresh your memory of how the interviewee responded to certain questions.

You may want to have other members of the legal team read the transcript or listen to the file. Sometimes, what seemed insignificant to you may seem significant to someone else working on the case. Also, as a case progresses, a remark made by an interviewee that did not seem important at the time of the interview may take on added significance in view of evidence gathered later.

Down Side of Recording

There are also some disadvantages to recording interviews. If clients and witnesses know everything they are saying is being recorded, they may feel uncomfortable and be less willing to disclose information freely. Such reluctance is understandable in view of the fact that the interviewee does not know what exactly will happen during the interview or how the recording may later be used.

When asking an interviewee for permission to record an interview, you should evaluate how the interviewee responds to this question. Depending on the interviewee's response, you might consider taking notes instead of recording the session. Another option is to go through the questions you will ask with the interviewee once before asking permission to turn on the recorder.

Interviewing Skills

Interviewing skills include interpersonal and communication skills that help you to conduct a successful interview. In this section, you will learn how the use of such skills can help you establish a comfortable relationship with the interviewee. Then, you will read about specific questioning and listening techniques that can help you control the interview and elicit information.

Interpersonal Skills

In conducting an interview, your primary goal is to obtain information. Although some people communicate information readily, others may need prompting and encouragement. If people feel comfortable in your presence and in the interviewing environment, they will generally be more willing to disclose information.

Remember that the interviewee may be nervous or uncomfortable. You should put that person at ease as quickly as possible. A minute or two spent chatting casually is time well spent. Also, saying or doing something that shows your concern for the interviewee's physical comfort helps to make the interviewee feel more relaxed. For example, you might offer a cup of coffee or other beverage.

Using language that the interviewee understands is essential in establishing a good working relationship. If you are interviewing a client with only a grade-school education, for example, do not use the phrase "facial lacerations" when talking about "cuts on the face." If you are interviewing a witness who does not speak English well, and you are not fluent in the witness's language, have an interpreter present. Because most clients and witnesses are not familiar with legal terminology, avoid using legal terms that will not be clearly understood. If you must use a legal term, be sure that you define the term clearly.

Questioning Skills

When questioning witnesses or clients, remain objective at all times and gather as much relevant information as possible. Sometimes, you may find it hard to remain objective when questioning witnesses because you sympathize with the client and may not want to hear about facts contrary to the client's position. But you need

social
MEDIA TODAY

For your profile photo, stick with a close-up, business-appropriate photo in which you are smiling and wearing something you would wear at the office. Avoid symbols, party photos, long-distance shots, or baby pictures.

to uncover details that could weaken the client's case as well as those that support it. Indeed, your supervising attorney must know *all* of the facts, especially any that might damage the client's case in court.

Mask Your Emotions

In some situations, it may be difficult to remain objective not because of your sympathy *for* the client but because of your own personal biases *against* the client, the witness, or the case. Interviewers must be careful to evaluate their feelings prior to conducting an interview. If you feel a person's conduct is morally wrong, you may convey those feelings during the interview. You may even communicate your feelings nonverbally through unspoken signals such as gestures and facial expressions. Nonverbal communication can be powerful. Once the interviewee senses your disapproval, he or she is likely to limit the information disclosed.

Suppose, for example, you are interviewing Sandra, a client who is trying to regain custody of her children. The state took Sandra's children away because she abused drugs and failed to properly care for the children. You have read through the file and strongly disapprove of Sandra's past conduct and have doubts about whether she has recovered from her drug problem. If you do not set aside your personal feelings before meeting with Sandra, they may affect your interaction and limit the success of the interview.

The experienced legal interviewer uses certain questioning techniques to prompt interviewees to communicate. There are several types of questions, including open-ended, closed-ended, leading, and hypothetical questions. Exhibit 11.2 below provides some examples of the types of questions discussed in the following subsections.

EXHIBIT 11.2
Types of Interview Questions

Type of Question	Open-Ended Question	Closed-Ended Question	Leading Question	Hypothetical Question
Definition	A broad, exploratory question that may elicit a lengthy response.	A question phrased in such a way that it elicits a "yes" or "no" response.	A question phrased in such a way that it suggests the desired answer.	A question that asks the interviewee to assume certain facts in forming an answer.
Typical Uses	Mostly with friendly witnesses and clients.	To clarify a witness's statement or to keep her or him on track. With adverse or reluctant witnesses.	At times with adverse witnesses in interviews. By attorneys to cross-examine witnesses at trial (see Chapter 12).	Primarily with expert witnesses in interviews and during trial.
Examples	• Describe the morning of the accident. What did you do that morning? • What did you see before entering the intersection? • When did you first see the defendant's car, and where was it? • How fast was the defendant going at the time of the accident?	• Were you late for work that morning? • Was there anyone in the car with you at the time? • Were you already in the intersection at the time you first saw the plaintiff's car? • Were you exceeding the speed limit at the time the accident occurred?	• You were running late for work that morning, correct? • You saw that the light had turned red before you entered the intersection, didn't you? • Isn't it true that you were driving over the speed limit at the time of the accident? • Isn't it true that you had been out drinking at a bar until late on the night before the accident?	• If a full-sized van is going 60 miles per hour, how far before an intersection must the driver apply the brakes in order to stop the vehicle? • If a 200-pound man drank 14 beers in six hours, how long would it take before the alcohol was out of his system so that it would not affect his ability to drive?

Open-Ended Questions

The **open-ended question** is a broad, exploratory question that invites any number of possible responses. It can be used when you want to give the interviewee an opportunity to talk at some length about a given subject. "What happened on the night of October 28—the night of the murder?" and "What did you see as you approached the intersection?" are open-ended questions. When you ask a question of this kind, be prepared for a lengthy response. If a witness has difficulty narrating the events he or she observed or if a lull develops during the explanation, you need to encourage the witness to continue by using prompting responses (which will be discussed shortly in the context of listening skills).

Open-ended questions are useful in interviewing clients or friendly witnesses (witnesses who favor the client's position). These interviewees are usually forthcoming, and you will be able to gain information from them by indicating in broad terms what you want them to describe. Open-ended questions are also a good way for the interviewer to evaluate whether the interviewee's behavior and overall effectiveness would make him or her a good witness at trial. Someone who speaks clearly and confidently is likely to be a more persuasive witness than someone who hems and haws.

Closed-Ended Questions

The **closed-ended question** is intended to elicit a "yes" or "no" response. "Did you see the murder weapon?" is an example of a closed-ended question. Although closed-ended questions tend to limit communication, they can be useful. For example, if an interviewee tends to wander from the topic being discussed, using closed-ended questions can help keep him or her on track. Closed-ended questions, because they invite specific answers, also may be useful to clarify the interviewee's previous response and to relax the interviewee in preparation for more difficult questions that follow. In addition, closed-ended questions may help to draw information from adverse witnesses (those who are not favorable to the client's position), who may be reluctant to volunteer information.

Leading Questions

The **leading question** is one that suggests to the listener the answer to the question. "Isn't it true that you were only ten feet away from where the murder took place?" is a leading question. Leading questions can be effective for drawing information out of eyewitnesses or clients, particularly when they are reluctant to disclose information. They can be useful for interviewing adverse witnesses who are hesitant to communicate information that may be helpful to the client's position. (In fact, they are the primary method of questioning used by attorneys when cross-examining witnesses at trial, as you will read in Chapter 12.)

When used with a client or friendly witnesses, however, leading questions have a major drawback. They may lead to distorted answers because the client or witness may tailor the answer to fit his or her perception of what the interviewer wants to know. For this reason, leading questions should be used cautiously in interviews and only when the interviewer is aware of the possible distortions that might result.

Hypothetical Questions

You may be asked to interview an expert witness to gather information about a case or to evaluate whether that person would be an effective expert witness at trial (expert witnesses will be discussed later in this chapter). The **hypothetical question** is frequently used with expert witnesses. Hypothetical questions allow you to obtain an answer to an important question without giving away the facts (and confidences) of a client's case. For example, you might invent a hypothetical situation involving a certain type of knee injury (the same injury as that sustained by a client) and then ask an orthopedic surgeon what kind of follow-up care would ordinarily be undertaken for that type of injury.

Listening Skills

The interviewer's ability to listen is one of the most important communication skills. When conducting an interview, you will want to absorb completely the interviewee's verbal answers, as well as any nonverbal messages. Before the interview, you should make sure that the room in which it is to be held will be free of noises, phone calls, visitors, and other interruptions or distractions. Turn off your cell phone (or put it on silent) and ask the witness to do the same. During the interview, you can use several listening techniques to maximize communication and guide the interviewee toward the fullest disclosure.

Passive Listening

As mentioned earlier, the interviewer should listen attentively to the interviewee. It is critical that the client or witness get the impression that the interviewer is interested in what he or she is saying. If the interviewee pauses briefly or there is a lull in the conversation, the interviewer can use **passive listening** techniques, which are verbal or nonverbal cues that encourage the speaker to continue. For example, the interviewer might say, "I'm listening; please go on" or "And what happened then?" A nonverbal cue can be any facial expression or body language that shows you are interested in what is being said. Nodding positively, for example, is an effective nonverbal way to convey your interest. Maintaining eye contact is another nonverbal cue to indicate your interest.

passive listening
The act of listening attentively to the speaker's message and responding to the speaker by providing verbal or nonverbal cues that encourage the speaker to continue; in effect, saying, "I'm listening, please go on."

Active Listening

For communication to be truly interactive, the listener must engage in active listening. **Active listening** involves not only paying close attention to what the speaker is saying but also providing appropriate feedback to show that you understand and may have sympathy for what is being said. Because people do not always say what they mean to say—or what they think they are saying—active listening is the key to a productive interview. Active listening allows the interviewer to clarify and confirm the interviewee's statements throughout the interview.

active listening
The act of listening attentively to the speaker's message and responding by giving appropriate feedback to show that you understand what the speaker is saying; restating the speaker's message in your own words to confirm that you accurately interpreted what was said.

REFLECTING BACK.   One effective active listening technique is for the interviewer to "reflect back," or "mirror," what the interviewee has already said. For example, after the interviewee has expressed her or his thoughts on a particular topic, you might say, "Let me see if I understand you correctly" and then summarize your impression of what was said. If your interpretation is incorrect, the interviewee now has the opportunity to make you understand what she or he meant to say. This technique is useful for clarifying the person's statement. In addition, it reinforces the idea that you are listening carefully and are interested in what the interviewee has to say.

CONTROLLING THE FLOW OF THE INTERVIEW.   Active listening enables the interviewer to put the person's statements into the context of the larger picture and facilitates smooth transitions between interview topics. For example, suppose you are interviewing a client who is suing her former employer. After telling you about the rude and offensive behavior of her co-workers, she says she just couldn't go back to work and starts to cry. By restating what she has told you, you can make the client feel you support and identify with her: "I understand that you did not return to work because of the hostility of your co-workers toward you." You might then move into a discussion of damages by saying, "It sounds as if you've been through a lot. Did you go see a counselor or get help from anyone during that time?"

The interviewer who engages in active listening can direct the flow of the interview according to the reactions and responses of the person being interviewed. As the *Featured Contributor* notes on the next two pages, using effective techniques increases the amount and quality of information you can gain through interviews and investigations.

Featured Contributor

TEN STRATEGIES FOR EFFECTIVE INTERVIEWS AND INVESTIGATIONS

Jennifer J. Allen

BIOGRAPHICAL NOTE

Jennifer Allen received her B.A. in English, cum laude, from Wake Forest University in 1983. She received her J.D. from Wake Forest University School of Law in 1986. She has been a licensed attorney in North Carolina since 1986. Allen has been a faculty member at Davidson County Community College in Lexington, North Carolina, for 23 years. She primarily teaches paralegal, criminal justice, and in-service training for law enforcement officers. In addition, she has taught pre-curricular courses in English, reading, and study skills. She is a recipient of the Excellence in Teaching Award from the National Institute for Staff and Organizational Development (NISOD) located at the University of Texas at Austin.

© Cengage Learning 2014

Paralegals are frequently called upon to investigate various aspects of the cases in which they are involved. Many times this investigation requires that they interview a vast array of people, from clients and witnesses to experts in their field. These ten strategies will help your interviews be more efficient and effective.

1. **Keep an open mind.**   In legal practice, as well as in most areas of life, remember that there are two sides to every story. Don't jump to conclusions or determine who the good guys and bad guys are until you have all the facts. Even then, you will find that people are complicated and no one is all good or bad.

2. **Focus on the facts.**   Focus on information that can be verified. In an interview, you will often get a mix of facts and opinions. You will also find that some "facts" will be disputed by the other side. By focusing on facts, the person being interviewed is less likely to go off on a tangent.

3. **Verify the facts.**   The hard truth is that people lie for any number of reasons. Often, it is because they want the person interviewing them to think well of them. All of us slant the facts somewhat in our favor when we are discussing conflicts in our own lives. There are some facts that can't be verified. If that's the case, just note the

REMEMBER DIGITAL SHADOWS.   When planning an interview, do not neglect the "digital shadow" of the person being interviewed. Part of your preparation for any interview, whether of a client or a potential witness, should include investigating their online presence. You should look for information about the person being interviewed and what the person may have posted about events related to the case. For example, a witness to a car accident may have sent a tweet about the crash or posted a photo or video. The timeline of events provided by an interviewee may be confirmed or contradicted by social media posts.

Frequent social media users may not recall having used social media to discuss a topic unless you prompt them. "Did you post anything about this to Facebook or another Web site?" should be added to your standard set of interview questions.

Interviewees' digital shadows may also tell you a great deal about their potential reliability as a witness. A person with multiple photos of drinking contests may not be as reliable a witness as someone whose online profile focuses on his or her interest in accounting. By preparing in advance, you can avoid surprises later if such information comes out. Use search tools to check whether an interviewee regularly uses public social media. Follow up with questions at the interview.

different versions of the facts. People are not always lying when they report different things; they may process the information differently or not all have the same information.

4. **Acknowledge emotions without inviting them to overwhelm the interview.** People often seek legal assistance during the difficult times of their lives—the death of a loved one, divorce, bankruptcy, etc. Most people feel embarrassed when emotion overtakes them. Have tissues handy, but help the person being interviewed get back under control by asking questions that won't stir up emotions.

5. **Demonstrate compassion with professional boundaries.** You will often feel empathy, especially for clients who are in a tough spot. Remember that your role is to help them with their legal troubles. You can't help with financial, emotional, or psychological troubles.

6. **Have a checklist of questions, but don't be bound by it.** It's a great idea to create checklists of information needed for clients in a variety of legal situations. It's also a great idea to make a list of questions you want to ask witnesses, experts, etc. However, listen carefully. If the questions take you in another relevant direction, be sure to get the information you need there.

7. **Redirect wandering statements.** Regardless of who you are interviewing, remember that some people talk more than others. If you find the interview wandering, gently but firmly bring it back to the important issues.

8. **Inform and educate without giving legal advice.** One of the most important roles that paralegals serve is to help a client navigate the often baffling process of litigation. Clients and witnesses will feel less anxious if they know what to expect. It's fine to answer questions such as, "What will my child custody hearing be like?" It's moving away from education and into giving legal advice to answer a question such as, "Do you think I will get custody of my child?"

9. **Be hospitable.** Be a good host when interviewing people in your office and a good guest when interviewing people at their home or at work. Offering a drink and directions to the bathroom helps relax people. When interviewing people outside the office be mindful of their time and take as little as you can.

10. **Keep confidences.** This is the most important rule of all. Remember that not only the information you gather is to be kept confidential, but also the very identity of the client is confidential. If you work for an attorney who does only criminal law and you mention that a person in the community came to the office, you are revealing a client confidence.

"Don't jump to conclusions . . ."

Interviewing Clients

Here, we first look at client interviews and then discuss witness interviews. The various types of client interviews include the initial interview, subsequent interviews to obtain further information, and informational interviews, or meetings, to inform the client of the case's status and to prepare the client for various legal proceedings.

The Initial Client Interview

As discussed in previous chapters, when a client seeks legal advice from an attorney, the attorney normally holds an initial interview with the client. During this interview, the client explains his or her problem so that the attorney can advise the client on possible legal options and potential legal fees. Either then or later, the client and the attorney will agree on the terms of the representation, if the attorney decides to take the case.

Paralegals often attend initial client interviews. Although the attorney normally conducts this first interview, the paralegal plays an important role. Usually, you observe the client and take notes on what the client is saying. And you provide the client with forms, statements explaining the firm's fees, and other prepared information normally given to new clients. Following the interview, you and the attorney may compare your impressions of the client and of what the client said during the interview.

All people present at the interview should be introduced to the client, their titles given, and the reason for their presence at the interview made known. In introducing you to the potential client, the attorney will probably stress that you are not a lawyer and cannot give legal advice. If your supervising attorney does not indicate your nonattorney status to the client, you should do so. If a firm takes a client's case, the client should be introduced to all members of the legal team working on the case.

A follow-up letter, such as the one shown in Exhibit 11.3 on the facing page, will be sent or e-mailed to the client after the interview. The letter will state whether the attorney has decided to accept the case or, if the attorney orally agreed during the initial client interview to represent the client, will confirm the oral agreement in writing.

Subsequent Client Interviews

Paralegals are often asked to conduct additional client interviews once cases are accepted. For example, assume that a client seeks a divorce. After the initial interview, your supervising attorney may ask you to arrange for an interview to get the information necessary to prepare the divorce pleadings. Paralegals often take responsibility for this. When scheduling the interview, you should tell the client what kinds of documents or other data to bring to the interview. Then send the client a letter confirming the date and time of the interview and listing the items you want the client to bring. During the interview, you will fill out the form that the firm uses to record client information in divorce cases.

When conducting a client interview, the paralegal should disclose his or her nonlawyer status if this fact was not made clear earlier. Remember, even if you have been introduced to the client as a legal assistant, the client may not realize that a paralegal is not an attorney. To protect yourself against potential claims that you have engaged in the unauthorized practice of law, clearly state that you are not an attorney and cannot give legal advice.

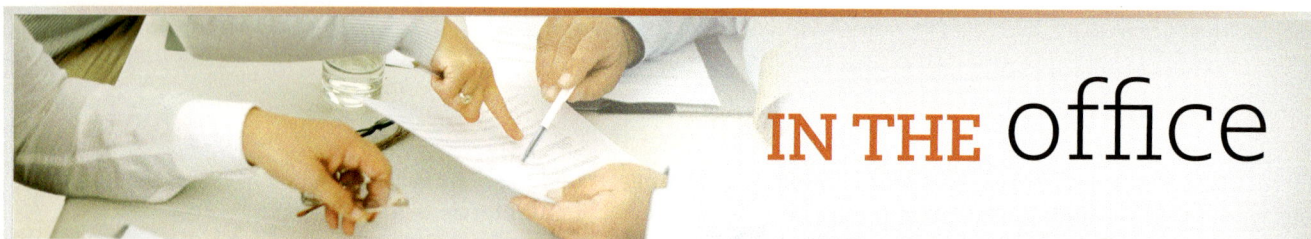

IN THE office

HANDLING CLIENT DOCUMENTS

Clients frequently give paralegals important documents during interviews. A client might, for example, give you the only copy she has of her divorce agreement. States impose strict requirements on attorneys about the safekeeping of clients' funds and other property, including documents. You should never rely on memory when it comes to client documents. Instead, immediately after the conclusion of the interview, record the receipt of any documents or other items received from the client. The information may be recorded in an evidence log (discussed later in this chapter) or as required by the procedures established by your firm to govern the receipt and storage of such property. An evidence log or its equivalent provides you with evidence—should it be necessary—of what you did (or did not) receive from a client. In addition, paper documents should be scanned into electronic case files so backup copies exist.

EXHIBIT 11.3
A Sample Follow-Up Letter
E-Mailed to a Client

From: Allen P. Gilmore, Attorney at Law <allen.p.gilmore@jgd.com>
To: Ms. Katherine Baranski <k.baran@nitamail.net>
Cc: Ms. Elena Lopez <elena.lopez@jgd.com>
Subject: Case Involving Tony Peretto

February 2, 2014
Ms. Katherine Baranski
335 Natural Blvd.
Nita City, Nita 48802

Dear Ms. Baranksi:

It was a pleasure to meet and talk with you on January 30. Jeffers, Gilmore & Dunn will be pleased to act as your representative in your action against Tony Peretto to obtain compensation for your injuries.

Attached is a copy of a fee agreement for your review. A copy of this letter and the agreement are being sent to you by mail. The mailing will contain a self-addressed, stamped envelope for your convenience. As soon as I receive the completed agreement, we will begin investigating your case.

As I advised during our meeting, to protect your rights, please refrain from speaking with the driver of the vehicle, Mr. Peretto; his lawyer; or his insurance company. If they attempt to contact you, simply tell them that you have retained counsel and refer them to me. I will handle any questions that they may have.

If you have any questions, please do not hesitate to call me or my paralegal, Ms. Elena Lopez.

Sincerely,

Allen P. Gilmore, Attorney at Law
Jeffers, Gilmore & Dunn
553 Fifth Avenue, Suite 101
Nita City, NI 48801
Telephone: (616) 555-9690
Fax: (616) 555-9679

----

1 Attachment
Baranski Agreement.doc
194K View as HTML Download

The Informational Interview

The informational interview, or meeting, is an interview in which the client is brought in to discuss upcoming legal proceedings. Most clients know little about the procedures involved in litigation, and firms often use paralegals to explain procedures or prepare clients for the trial experience. For example, the paralegal can describe to clients what takes place during the trial, how to dress and conduct themselves appropriately for trial, where to look when they testify, and so forth. The informational interview helps clients understand why proceedings are taking place and their role in those proceedings.

Summarizing the Interview

The interviewing process does not end with the close of the interview. A crucial step in the process involves summarizing the results of the interview for the legal team working on the case. As a paralegal, you are likely to create an intake memorandum following each initial client interview. If the firm has a prepared intake form for particular types of cases, such as the personal-injury intake sheet referred to earlier and illustrated in Exhibit 11.1 on pages 328 and 329, the completed form might serve as the interview summary. Information obtained during subsequent interviews with a client should be analyzed and summarized in a memo for your supervising attorney or other team members to review and for inclusion in the client's file.

Do It Now

Your interview summary should be created immediately after the interview, while the session is fresh in your mind. When summarizing a client interview, carefully review your notes and, if the session was recorded, review the recording. Never rely only on your memory of the statements made during the interview. It is easy to forget the client's specific words, and it may be important later to know exactly how the client phrased a response. Relying on memory is also risky because, as mentioned earlier, sometimes a statement that seemed irrelevant at the time of the interview may turn out to be important to the case. Make sure that the facts are accurately recorded. Also note your impressions of the client and the client's nonverbal behaviors.

Visual Evidence

Depending on the nature of the legal claim being made by the client, you may want to include a visual element or two in your summary. For example, if the claim concerns an automobile accident, you might consider creating a graphic depiction of the accident to attach to the summary. (For a further discussion of the value of visual communications, see this chapter's *Technology and Today's Paralegal* feature on the facing page.)

Interviewing Witnesses

Witnesses play a key role in establishing the facts of an event. As a legal investigator, your goal is to elicit as much relevant and reliable information as possible from each witness about the event that you are investigating. Interviewing witnesses is similar to interviewing clients, and many of the interviewing skills that we have already discussed also apply. A major difference is that witnesses may not always be friendly to the client's position. Here we describe the various types of witnesses as well as some basic skills and principles particularly relevant to investigative interviews.

Types of Witnesses

Witnesses include expert witnesses, lay witnesses, and eyewitnesses. Witnesses are also sometimes classified as friendly witnesses or hostile (adverse) witnesses.

Expert Witnesses

An **expert witness** has professional training, advanced knowledge, or substantial experience in a specialized area, such as medicine, computer technology, ballistics, or construction techniques. Paralegals often arrange to hire expert witnesses to testify in court or to render an opinion on some matter relating to the client's case. Expert witnesses are often used in cases involving medical malpractice and product liability to establish the duty, or standard of care, that the defendant owed to the plaintiff. For example, if a client is suing a physician for malpractice, your

expert witness
A witness with professional training or substantial experience qualifying him or her to testify as to his or her opinion on a particular subject.

TECHNOLOGY AND
today's paralegal

COMMUNICATING THROUGH GRAPHICS

If a picture is worth a thousand words, a bad picture can do as much damage as a thousand badly chosen words. Information may be easier to convey through a chart or diagram than in a narrative. Unfortunately, it is also easy to confuse people with cluttered graphics and badly designed diagrams. Learning to communicate graphically is an important skill for paralegals, because they may be called upon to help design courtroom graphics and can use graphic skills in developing the facts.

DIAGRAMS AND INTERVIEWS

Diagrams can help you when you are interviewing witnesses. For example, if you are talking to a car accident victim or witness, sketching the scene can help the person you are interviewing remember crucial details. Creating an accurate diagram of the accident scene can help you uncover potential contradictions in witnesses' testimony or discover missing information. Diagrams may be critical to communicating information to a jury about your case. In an accident case, a diagram can show the jury where the witnesses and parties were, helping the jury members to understand the testimony.

GRAPHICS SOFTWARE

There are many graphics packages to help you produce diagrams and charts. SmartDraw Legal Edition provides business graphics as well as templates for crime scene diagrams, accident reconstruction diagrams, patent drawings, and other legal uses. There are many other programs (such as High Impact) available that help produce accident or crime scene reconstructions and other useful graphics. Skills in graphics will give you an edge in creating value for a law firm.

DESIGN PRINCIPLES

One of the best resources for visual display of information is the work of Edward Tufte, dubbed the "Minister of Information" by *New York* magazine and the "Leonardo da Vinci of data" by the *New York Times*. Tufte's books (*The Visual Display of Quantitative Information, Envisioning Information, Visual Explanations,* and *Beautiful Evidence*) have been cited as influencing everything from the iPhone to the *New York Times*. Tufte regularly offers seminars on presenting information at various locations around the country (**www.edwardtufte.com**).

An example of the impact of the misleading nature of some visual presentations occurred in NASA's PowerPoint™ presentation to senior management on the damage to the Space Shuttle *Columbia*. Tufte's critique of the presentation was included in the final report of the Columbia Accident Investigation Board as part of its explanation of why NASA made the bad decisions that led to *Columbia's* explosion.

TECHNOLOGY TIP

To practice your graphic skills, watch director Errol Morris's award-winning documentary film *The Thin Blue Line,* which shows a crime scene repeatedly, based on different witnesses' testimony in a criminal trial. The film pioneered modern methods of crime scene reconstruction. To improve your graphic skills, make crime scene diagrams based on each witness's testimony as you listen to each one, and then use your diagrams to illustrate the inconsistencies among the testimonies.

---

supervising attorney might arrange to have another physician testify as to the standard of care owed by a physician to a patient in similar circumstances.

Lay Witnesses

Most witnesses in court are lay witnesses. In contrast to expert witnesses, **lay witnesses** do not possess any particular skill or expertise relating to the matter before the court. They are people who happened to observe or otherwise have factual knowledge about an event. A physician involved in a financial fraud case, for example, might give testimony about the fraud as a lay witness but not as an expert witness.

lay witness
A witness who can truthfully and accurately testify on a fact in question without having specialized training or knowledge; an ordinary witness.

Eyewitnesses

Eyewitnesses are lay witnesses who may testify in court about an event they observed or experienced firsthand. The term *eyewitness* is deceiving. A better term might be "sense" witness. This is because an eyewitness's firsthand knowledge of an event

eyewitness
A witness who testifies about an event that he or she observed or experienced firsthand.

need not have been derived from the sense of sight—that is, from actually seeing the event. An eyewitness may be someone who listened in on a telephone conversation between an accused murderer and an accomplice. A blind man may have been an eyewitness to a car crash, because he heard it.

In interviews, eyewitnesses are ordinarily asked to describe an event in their own words and as they recall it. Eyewitness accounts may be lengthy, and the paralegal may want to record the interview session to ensure accuracy. The experienced paralegal may also find that different eyewitnesses to the same event give contradictory accounts of what took place because people's perceptions of reality differ. You will deal with many kinds of witnesses and, as the *Ethics Watch* feature below reminds us, caution is always in order.

ETHICS WATCH

INTERVIEWING CLIENTS AND THE UNAUTHORIZED PRACTICE OF LAW

Paralegals must be especially careful not to give legal advice when interviewing clients. Suppose that you are interviewing a client, Collins, who was injured in a car accident and is suing the other driver for negligence. Collins previously told your supervising attorney and you that the accident was the result of the other driver's negligence. During your follow-up interview, however, Collins says to you, "What would happen, in a lawsuit such as mine, if the plaintiff was looking in the backseat to see why her baby was crying? Could the plaintiff still expect to win in court?"

You know that under the laws of your state, contributory negligence on the part of the plaintiff (to be discussed in Chapter 14) could bar recovery of damages. Should you explain this to Collins? No. Even though the question is phrased as a hypothetical, it is possible that your answer could affect Collins's actions. Tell Collins that you are not permitted to give legal advice but that you will relay the "hypothetical" question to your supervising attorney.

This action would be consistent with the following codes and guidelines:

- NFPA *Model Code of Ethics and Professional Responsibility*, Section EC-1.8: "A paralegal shall comply with the applicable legal authority governing the unauthorized practice of law in the jurisdiction in which the paralegal practices."
- The *ABA Model Guidelines for the Utilization of Paralegal Services* advises that it is improper for attorneys allow paralegals to take responsibility for giving legal opinions to clients.
- NALA *Code of Ethics and Professional Responsibility*, Canon 4: "A paralegal must use discretion and professional judgment commensurate with knowledge and experience but must not render independent legal judgment in place of an attorney."

Friendly Witnesses

Some witnesses to an event may be the client's family members, friends, co-workers, or other persons who know the client and who want to be helpful in volunteering information. These witnesses are regarded as **friendly witnesses**. You may think that friendly witnesses are the best kind to interview, and they often are. They may also be biased in the client's favor, however, so the paralegal should look closely for the actual facts (and not the witness's interpretation of the facts) when interviewing friendly witnesses.

friendly witness
A witness who is biased against your client's adversary or sympathetic toward your client in a lawsuit or other legal proceeding.

Hostile Witnesses

Witnesses who may be prejudiced against your client or friendly to your client's adversary are regarded as **hostile witnesses** (or *adverse witnesses*). Interviewing hostile witnesses can be challenging. Sometimes the witness has an interest in the outcome of the case and would be in a better position if your client lost in court. For example, if the client is a tenant who refuses to pay rent until the landlord repairs the roof, then the paralegal interviewing the landlord's building manager should be prepared to deal with that person as a potentially hostile witness.

hostile witness
A witness who is biased against your client or friendly toward your client's adversary in a lawsuit or other legal proceeding; an adverse witness.

Some hostile witnesses refuse to be interviewed. On learning that the alternative might be a subpoena, however, a hostile witness may consent to at least a limited interview. If you plan to interview hostile witnesses, contact and interview them early in your investigation. The longer you wait, the greater the chance that they may be influenced by the opposing party's attorney or the opinions of persons sympathetic to the opposing party.

When interviewing hostile witnesses, be especially careful to be objective, fair, and unbiased in your approach. This does not mean that you have to ignore your client's interests. On the contrary, you will best serve those interests by doing all you can to keep from further alienating a witness whose information might ultimately help your client's case. Be careful not to disclose confidential or important information that the hostile witness might report back to the opposing attorney.

Questioning Witnesses

When you are asking questions as a legal investigator, you should phrase your questions so that they lead to the most complete answer possible. Investigative questions should thus be open ended. Compare, for example, the following two questions:

1. "Did you see the driver of the green van run the stop sign?"

2. "What did you see at the time of the accident?"

The first question calls for a "yes" or "no" answer. The second question, in contrast, invites the witness to explain fully what he or she actually saw. Something else that the witness saw could be important to the case—but unless you allow room for the witness's full description, you will not learn this information.

Notice that the first question also assumes a fact—that the driver of the green van ran the stop sign. The second question makes no assumptions and conveys no information to the witness that may influence the answer. Generally, the less the witness knows about other witnesses' descriptions, the better, because other descriptions could influence the witness's perception. You want to find out exactly what the witness observed, in his or her own words.

social MEDIA TODAY

"Sticky" messages are more useful. In the book *Made to Stick*, Chip and Dan Heath define "stickiness" as embodying six principles: simplicity, unexpectedness, concreteness, credibility, emotions, and stories. Try to adhere to these principles in your social media postings.

Checking a Witness's Qualifications

When interviewing a witness during the course of an investigation, you often will not know whether the testimony of that witness will be needed in court or even whether the claim you are investigating will be litigated. Nonetheless, you should operate under the assumption that each witness is a potential court witness. Thus, you should make sure that the witness is competent to testify, and is reliable and credible.

As part of a factual investigation into a client's legal claim, a paralegal may contact witnesses or other sources for information. Although a restaurant is not an ideal setting for discussing confidential information, sometimes it is not possible to meet a witness or other information source in an office environment. What are the benefits of meeting in a public location? What are some potential problems with such a meeting place?

© Stephen Coburn/www.Shutterstock.com

Competence

Under the Federal Rules of Evidence, any person is competent to be a lay witness as long as the individual has personal knowledge of the matter. Thus, only if a potential witness did not actually see, hear, or perceive the events in some way (because of a disability, for example) will that person be judged incompetent to testify. Although state rules of evidence vary, most states also define competence for lay witnesses broadly. Expert witnesses are qualified only if they possess special knowledge, skill, experience, training, or education.

Credibility

Because it is easy to establish competence for most witnesses, the primary issue is generally not whether a witness can testify but whether the testimony will be credible, or believable. The parties to a lawsuit can attack the credibility of an opponent's witness and try to show that the witness is not telling the truth or is unreliable. In federal courts and most state courts, the credibility or reliability of a witness's testimony can be called into question by evidence that points to the witness's character for truthfulness or untruthfulness. Thus, the paralegal investigating the case should inquire into any matters that tend to show whether the witness is honest.

For example, does the witness abuse drugs or have a reputation in the community as a troublemaker or liar? Has the witness been convicted of a crime? If so, was it a felony, or did it involve any dishonesty or false statement? How long ago was the conviction? Under the federal rules, a witness's credibility can be attacked by evidence of a conviction for a crime punishable by incarceration for over one year or a conviction for any crime involving dishonesty or false statements that occurred within the last ten years.

Bias

The paralegal should also investigate the witness's possible bias. Does the witness have an interest in the claim being investigated that would tend to make his or her testimony less credible? Is the witness a relative or close friend of someone (including another witness or a party) involved in the claim? Does the witness hold a grudge against someone involved? If the answer to any of these questions is yes, the witness's testimony may be discredited in court and will probably not be as convincing as testimony given by a neutral, unbiased witness.

Winding Up the Interview

At the conclusion of an interview, the paralegal should ask if there is anything else the witness would like to add. This gives the witness the opportunity to expand on areas not previously discussed or explain an answer previously given. Does the witness have a Web site, a blog, a Facebook and Twitter account? The paralegal should verify the witness's complete mailing address, physical address, e-mail address, and telephone number. It is also a good idea to get the name and telephone number of a friend or relative living in the immediate area whom you can contact to locate the witness if he or she moves before the trial.

Whenever you interview a witness, take thorough and accurate notes and prepare a memo to your supervising attorney. Include in the memo your evaluation of the witness's credibility and a description of any nonverbal communication that you thought was relevant (if the witness seemed uncomfortable with some aspect of the interview or became nervous when asked questions about a particular topic, for example).

Witness Statements

You may also prepare a formal witness statement. Check with your supervising attorney before preparing such a statement, because formal witness statements may have to be given to the opposing party under applicable discovery rules (as discussed in Chapter 10). A **witness statement** is a written document setting forth what the witness said during the interview. The witness is given an opportunity to review the contents of the statement and then signs the statement to verify its contents. Exhibit 11.4 below shows the type of information normally contained in a witness statement, and Exhibit 11.5 on the next page presents excerpts from a sample witness statement.

Statutes and court rules vary as to the value of witness statements as evidence. Usually, statements made by witnesses during interviews cannot be introduced as evidence in court to prove the truth of what the witness said, but can be used for other purposes. For example, if a hostile witness's testimony in court contradicts something he or she said during your interview, the witness statement may be used to impeach the witness—that is, to call into question the witness's testimony or demonstrate that the witness is unreliable. Witness statements also can be used to refresh a witness's memory at trial or in depositions.

witness statement
The written record of the statements made by a witness during an interview, signed by the witness.

---

1. **Information about the Witness**
   —Name, address, and phone number.
   —Name, address, and phone number of the witness's employer or
     place of business.
   —Interest, if any, in the outcome of the claim being investigated.

2. **Information about the Interview**
   —Name of the interviewer.
   —Name of the attorney or law firm for which the claim is
     being investigated.
   —Date, time, and place of the interview.

3. **Identification of the Event Witnessed**
   —Nature of the action or event observed by the witness.
   —Date of the action or event.

4. **Witness's Description of the Event**

5. **Attestation Clause**
   —Provision or clause at the end of the statement affirming the truth of the witness's
     description as written in the statement.

[Witness's Signature]

EXHIBIT 11.4
Information Contained
in a Witness Statement

© Cengage Learning 2014

STATEMENT OF JULIA WILLIAMS

I, Julia Williams, am a thirty-five-year-old female. I reside at 3765 Mattis Avenue, Nita City, Nita 48800, and my home telephone number is (616) 555-8989. I work as a nurse at the Nita City Hospital & Clinic, 412 Hospital Way, Nita City, Nita 48802. My work telephone number is (408) 555-9898. I am making this statement in my home on the afternoon of February 8, 2014. The statement is being made to Elena Lopez, a paralegal with the law firm of Jeffers, Gilmore & Dunn.

In regard to the accident on the corner of Mattis Avenue and Thirty-eighth Street on August 4, 2013, at approximately 7:45 A.M. on that date, I was standing at the southwest corner of that intersection, waiting to cross the street, when I observed . . .

* * * *

I affirm that the information given in this statement is accurate and true to the best of my knowledge.

Julia Williams
Julia Williams

© Cengage Learning 2014

Planning and Conducting Investigations

Because the facts are often crucial to the outcome of a legal problem, investigation is an important part of legal work. Attorneys often rely on paralegals to conduct investigations, and you should be prepared to accept the responsibility for making sure that an investigation is conducted thoroughly and professionally. In the following pages, you will read about the basics of legal investigation—how to plan and undertake an investigation, how the rules of evidence shape the investigative process, and how important it is to carefully document the results of your investigation.

Of course, you have already read about one aspect of investigations—interviewing witnesses. A preliminary investigation, however, can involve much more. For one thing, before witnesses can be interviewed, they must be located. Information relating to the case may also have to be obtained from a police department, weather bureau, or other source.

Where Do You Start?

Assume that you work for Allen Gilmore, the attorney representing the plaintiff in the hypothetical case discussed in Chapter 10. Recall that the plaintiff in that case, Katherine Baranski, is suing Tony Peretto for negligence. Peretto ran a stop sign at an intersection, and his car collided with Baranski's. Further assume that the case is still in its initial stages. Attorney Gilmore has just met with Katherine Baranski for the initial client interview. You sat in on the interview, listened to Baranski's description of the accident and of the damages she sustained as a result (medical expenses, lost wages, and so on), and took thorough notes.

After the interview, Gilmore asks you to do a preliminary investigation into Baranski's claim. It is now your responsibility to find the answers to a number of questions. Did the accident really occur in the way perceived by Baranski? Exactly where and when did it happen? (See the *Developing Paralegal Skills* feature on the facing page.) How does the police report describe the accident? Were there any witnesses? Was Peretto insured, and if so, by what company? What other circumstances (such as weather) are relevant? Your supervising attorney will want to know the answers to such questions before advising Baranski as to what legal action should be pursued.

As in any legal investigation, your point of departure is the information you already have about the matter. Begin with the statements made by Baranski during

DEVELOPING
paralegal skills

CHECKING THE ACCIDENT SCENE

Gina Hubbard, a paralegal, and her supervising attorney, Juan Calpert, have just concluded an intake interview with a new client. The client was involved in an automobile accident, and the driver of the other car, who sustained serious injuries, is suing the client for damages. The client maintains he was not at fault and has asked Calpert to defend him in the lawsuit. The attorney asks Gina to obtain a copy of the police report on the accident to verify the exact location of the accident, along with other pertinent information, such as photographs taken by police officers. Then Gina should go to the accident site to learn what she can about the site.

Both Gina and the attorney know that this case may be settled early on, and therefore it may be too soon to hire a private investigator to investigate the accident scene. Even if the case is not settled before trial and an investigator is hired later, months may pass and the scene may have changed. Road repairs may alter the area, new signs may be installed, or the street may be widened. It is therefore important that Gina visit the site right away. She makes a list of the equipment she needs to take with her to use when checking the site.

TIPS FOR CHECKING AN ACCIDENT SCENE

- Take a digital camera or your cell phone that has a camera with you at all times so you can include the photos in the file.
- Take a digital camcorder and digital audio recorder as well. You may want to dictate notes about your observations or record an interview with an eyewitness should you encounter someone at the site who saw the accident.
- Use an iPad, laptop, or smartphone so you can create a Google map of the location.
- Take a pencil and pad of paper to create sketches of the area, and be sure to include in the sketches any obstacles that could interfere with visibility.
- Include a tape measure or other measuring device in the tool kit as well. This will allow you to obtain precise measurements so that you can create a scale for your photographs and sketches.

the initial client interview and summarized in your notes. Baranski described what she remembered about the accident, including the date and time it occurred. She said she thought that the police investigator had the names of some persons who had witnessed the accident. Baranski also stated that she was employed as an associate professor in the math department at Nita State University, earning approximately $58,000 a year. Using this information, you can map out an investigation plan.

Creating an Investigation Plan

An **investigation plan** is a step-by-step list of the tasks that you must complete to verify factual information you need to obtain relating to a legal problem. In the Baranski case, the steps in your investigation plan would include those summarized in Exhibit 11.6 on the following two pages and discussed next. Make sure that your supervising attorney approves the investigation plan. Throughout the investigation, keep in close touch with your supervising attorney about progress being made.

investigation plan
A plan that lists each step involved in obtaining and verifying facts and information relevant to the legal problem being investigated.

Contacting the Police Department

The initial step in your plan should be to contact the police department. You will want to look at a copy of the police report of the accident, view any photographs taken at the scene, get the names of persons who may have witnessed the accident, and, if possible, talk to the investigating officer.

Contacting and Interviewing Witnesses

Next, you will want to contact and interview any known witnesses and document their descriptions of what took place at the time of the accident. Known witnesses include the driver (Tony Peretto) of the vehicle that hit Katherine Baranski, the

EXHIBIT 11.6
An Investigation Plan

INVESTIGATION PLAN
File No. 15773

	Date Requested	Date Received

1. Contact Police Department
 —To obtain police report
 —To ask for photographs of accident scene
 —To talk with investigating officer

 —SOURCE: Nita City Police Dept.
 —METHOD: Request in person or by mail

2. Contact Known Witnesses
 —Tony Peretto, van driver
 —Michael Young, police officer at accident scene
 —Julia Williams, witness at accident scene
 —Dwight Kelly, witness at accident scene

 —SOURCE: Police report
 —METHOD: Contact witnesses by initial phone
 call and personal interview when possible

3. Obtain Employment Records
 —To learn Baranski's employment status and income

 —SOURCE: Nita State University
 —METHOD: Written request by mail with
 Baranski's release enclosed

4. Obtain Hospital Records
 —To learn necessary information about
 Baranski's medical treatment and costs

 —SOURCE: Nita City Hospital
 —METHOD: Written request by mail with
 Baranski's release enclosed

© Cengage Learning 2014

police officer at the scene, and the other witnesses noted in the police investigation report. If Peretto is aware of Baranski's intention to sue him, he will probably have retained an attorney. If he has, then you are not permitted to contact him directly—you may communicate with him only through his attorney.

Obtaining Medical and Employment Records

To justify a claim for damages, you will need to determine the nature of the injuries suffered by Baranski as a result of the accident, the medical expenses that she incurred, and her annual or monthly income (to determine the amount of wages she lost as a result of the accident). To get this information, you will need copies of her medical and employment records.

The institutions holding these records will not release them to you unless Baranski authorizes them to do so. Therefore, you will need to arrange with Baranski to sign release forms to include with your requests for copies. A sample authorization form to release medical records is shown in Exhibit 11.7 on page 348. If possible, make sure that Baranski signs these forms before she leaves the office after the initial interview, since waiting for her to return the signed forms may delay your investigation. In addition to obtaining medical records, you may be asked to do some research on the type of injury sustained by Baranski and related information. Typically this requires consulting medical texts and specialized resources on medicine for lawyers.

EXHIBIT 11.6
An Investigation Plan—Continued

	Date Requested	Date Received
5. Contact National Weather Service		
—To learn what the weather conditions were on the day of the accident	_____	_____
—SOURCE: National Weather Service or newspaper		
—METHOD: Phone call or written request		
6. Obtain Title and Registration Records		
—To verify Peretto's ownership of the vehicle	_____	_____
—SOURCE: Department of Motor Vehicles		
—METHOD: Order by mail		
7. Contact Peretto's Insurance Company		
—To find out about insurance coverage		
—To check liability limits	_____	_____
—SOURCE: Insurance company		
—METHOD: Written request by mail		
8. Use a Professional Investigator		
—To contact such witnesses as		
–ambulance attendants	_____	_____
–doctors		
–residents in neighborhood of accident scene		
—To inspect vehicle		
—To take photos of accident site	_____	_____
—To investigate accident scene, and so on	_____	_____
—SOURCE: Regular law firm investigator		
—METHOD: In person		

© Cengage Learning 2014

Contacting the National Weather Service

Weather conditions at the time of the accident may be consequential. If it was raining, for example, Peretto's attorney may argue that Peretto did not see the stop sign or that water on the road prevented him from stopping. You will therefore want to determine what the weather conditions were at the time of the accident by contacting the National Weather Service and consulting other official records. When you interview eyewitnesses, ask them about weather conditions at the place and time of the accident.

Obtaining Vehicle Title and Registration Records

To verify that Tony Peretto owns the vehicle that he was driving at the time of the accident, you will need to obtain title and registration records. Usually, these can be acquired from the state department of motor vehicles, although in some states the secretary of state's office handles such records. The requirements for obtaining such information vary from state to state and may include the submission of special forms and fees. As the *On the Web* feature alongside indicates, you can go online to the relevant state office to obtain what you need.

Contacting the Insurance Company

Once you learn the name of Peretto's insurance company from Baranski or from the police report, you will contact that company to find out what kind of insurance coverage Peretto has and the limits of his liability under the insurance policy.

ON THE web

Relevant driving and vehicle registration records may be on the Web. See, for example, a list of licensed drivers for many states at **www.publicdata.com**. To find the home pages of your state's government agencies, go to **www.usa.gov** and enter the name of your state in the "Search" box.

EXHIBIT 11.7
Authorization to
Release Medical Records

TO: Nita City Hospital & Clinic
      Nita City, NI 48803

PATIENT: Katherine Baranski
             335 Natural Boulevard
             Nita City, NI 48802

      You are hereby authorized to furnish and release to my attorney, Allen P. Gilmore of Jeffers, Gilmore & Dunn, all information and records relating to my treatment for injuries incurred on August 4, 2013. Please do not disclose information to insurance adjusters or to other persons without written authority from me. The foregoing authority shall continue in force until revoked by me in writing, but for no longer than one year following the date given below.

Date: January 30, 2014   *Katherine Baranski*
                               Katherine Baranski

Please attach your invoice for any fee or photostatic costs and send it with the information requested above to my office.

Thank you,

Allen P. Gilmore

Allen P. Gilmore
Jeffers, Gilmore & Dunn
Attorneys at Law
553 Fifth Avenue
Suite 101
Nita City, NI 48801

Helena Moritz
Helena Moritz
Notary Public State of Nita
Nita County
My Commission Expires: November 12, 2015

© Cengage Learning 2014

Insurance companies usually are reluctant to give this information to anyone other than the policyholder. They sometimes cooperate with such requests, however, because they know that if they do not, the information can be obtained during discovery, should a lawsuit be initiated.

Using a Professional Investigator's Services

Depending on the circumstances, your supervising attorney may decide to use a professional investigator for certain tasks, including those just described. An experienced investigator will often have developed many useful contacts with law enforcement officers, subject-matter experts, and other sources. These contacts can speed up the investigation and may give the investigator access to information that others could not easily get. In addition, access to some government and private databases is restricted to government agents and licensed investigators. Attorneys also sometimes hire professional licensed investigators to obtain facts omitted from police reports, search public records, serve subpoenas, evaluate trial presentations, and conduct surveillance on parties important to the case.

You may work with the investigator. For example, your supervising attorney may ask you to arrange for the investigator to inspect and take photographs of the accident scene. You may also work with the investigator to determine the credibility and effectiveness of certain witnesses. In addition, you may meet with the investigator to review discovery documents to provide additional insight or generate investigative leads.

GOING green

GETTING TO THE OFFICE

When the price of gas rises, more people begin to carpool or to take the bus or light rail to the office. Some people then realize that, at least sometimes, they could walk or bicycle to work. Regardless of the current price of gas, consider using alternative transportation to get to work. Walking or bicycling will reduce your energy consumption and your carbon "footprint"—and it's better for your health.

Locating witnesses can be difficult and time consuming, and attorneys sometimes use investigators for this task. As discussed next, however, paralegals today can find people online much more easily than was once possible, potentially reducing the need for outside assistance.

Locating Witnesses

A challenging task for a legal investigator can be locating a witness whose address is unknown. Suppose, for example, that in the Baranski case the police investigation report lists the name, address, and telephone number of Edna Ball, a witness to the accident. When you call her number, you learn that the phone has been disconnected. You go to her address, and the house is vacant. What is your next step? A good starting point is to visit other homes in the neighborhood. Perhaps someone living nearby knows Edna Ball and can give you some leads as to where she is or what happened to her. Other sources are discussed below.

Finding People

One important role paralegals play in many law practices is locating witnesses and other relevant people. Prior to the development of modern search tools, the first place most paralegals looked was an old-fashioned telephone directory or city directory. Although these can still be a source of information, most searching has moved online.

Searches today take advantage of Internet search tools that both simplify and complicate the search. These tools streamline the search process because they allow fast searches of large databases. They also make things more complex because the results may include information about multiple people with the same or similar names. With practice, you will be able to develop relatively straightforward online search methods that will aid you greatly in locating people.

SERVICES. For example, many paralegals use Internet people-finding services to locate witnesses (and witnesses' assets, if needed). Some online services charge a small fee for each search, depending on the type of report requested (simple address record, background check, e-mail address, assets). The services check public records, telephone directories, court and criminal records, and a variety of other sources and provide results quickly and efficiently. (For an example, go to **www. whitepages.com**.) Both of the largest online legal research services (Westlaw and Lexis, discussed in Chapter 8) offer people-finding services as well.

SOCIAL MEDIA SEARCH ENGINES. There are also important search engines that focus on social media sites and so-called "deep web" information from Web pages that search engines like Google do not index. For example, Spokeo looks for data across more than forty social media sites and seeks information from e-mails as well. It can find personal photos on Flickr or profile data on Facebook. Another approach is taken by services such as PeekYou, which finds associations between individuals and Web addresses. While it uses the same information as is used by Google, it packages the data in a way that is more useful for finding out about a person. Try these tools out using your own name to get an idea of how they work.

Other Information Sources

Other sources of information include:

- media reports (newspaper articles and television videos covering the event being investigated);
- court records (probate proceedings, lawsuits, and the like);
- deeds to property (usually located in the county courthouse);
- birth, marriage, and death certificates and voter-registration lists;
- the post office (at which a witness may have left a forwarding address);

- consumer reporting agencies;
- the tax assessor's office; and
- utilities, such as the electric or water company.

Professional organizations may be useful sources as well. For example, if you have learned from one of Edna Ball's neighbors that she is a paralegal, you can check with state and local paralegal associations to see if they have current information on her. You might also check with federal, state, or local governmental agencies (discussed in the following section) to see if information contained in public records will be helpful in locating Edna Ball.

Accessing Government Information

Records and files acquired and stored by government offices and agencies can be a tremendous resource for the legal investigator. Public records are available at local government buildings or offices (such as the county courthouse), as mentioned above. As shown in Exhibit 11.8 below, you can also often find these records on the

EXHIBIT 11.8
Public Records Search Home Page for Dallas County, Texas

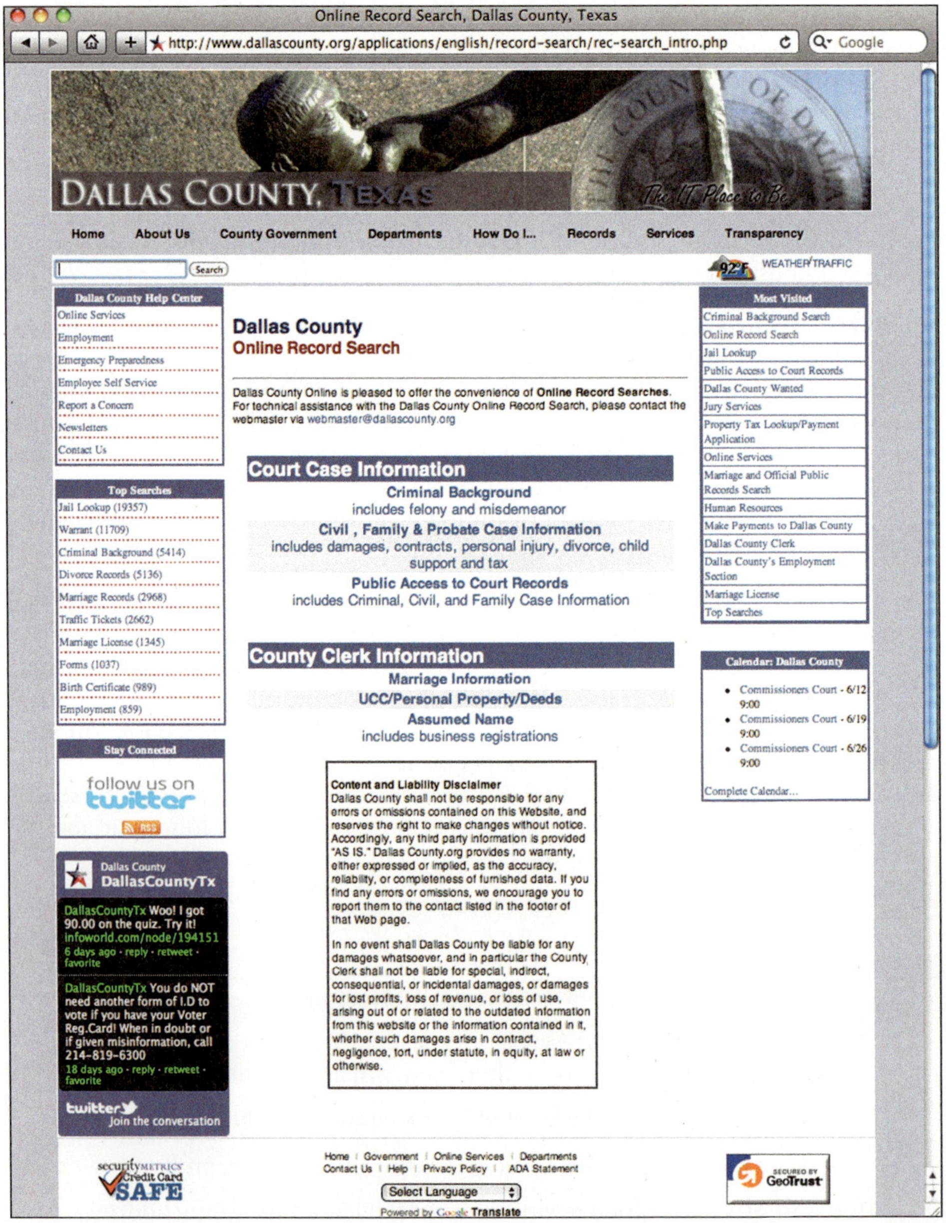

Source: With permission from www.dallascounty.org

Web site of the agency that maintains them. Additionally, it is possible to obtain information from federal agencies, such as the Social Security Administration, and from state agencies, such as the state revenue department or the secretary of state's office.

If you wish to obtain information from any government files or records, check with the specific agency or department to see what rules apply. The *Developing Paralegal Skills* feature below provides more tips on obtaining public information.

The Freedom of Information Act (FOIA) requires the federal government to disclose certain records to any person on request. A request that complies with the FOIA procedures need only contain a reasonable description of the information sought. The FOIA exempts some types of information from the disclosure requirement, including classified information (information concerning national security), confidential material dealing with trade secrets, government personnel rules, and personal medical files. Requesting information through the FOIA is usually a slow process and should be used only when there is no other choice.

Investigation and the Rules of Evidence

Because an investigation is conducted to obtain information and verify facts that may be introduced as evidence at trial, you should know what kind of evidence will be admissible in court before undertaking your investigation.

Evidence is anything that is used to prove the existence or nonexistence of a fact. Whether evidence can be used in court is determined by the **rules of evidence**—rules that explain what types of evidence are admissible and how to have evidence admitted. The Federal Rules of Evidence govern the admissibility of evidence in federal

ON THE web

For further information on how to make an FOIA request, go to **www.nist.gov/admin**, and select "Freedom of Information Act (FOIA)." Also see **www. firstamendmentcenter.org** and search for "FOIA request."

evidence
Anything that is used to prove the existence or nonexistence of a fact.

rules of evidence
Rules governing the admissibility of evidence in trial courts.

DEVELOPING
paralegal skills

ACCESSING GOVERNMENT INFORMATION

Ellen Simmons works for Smith & Case, a law firm that handles environmental cases (see Chapter 19). Ellen is to request copies of documents from the Environmental Protection Agency (EPA). She calls Chris Peter, a paralegal with the EPA. She identifies herself as a paralegal from Smith & Chase, which is representing a client involved at the Suburban Landfill Superfund site. Ellen is greeted with silence and wonders what she might have said to offend Chris. She asks if the EPA has the waste-in/waste-out report that gives the total volume of hazardous waste at the site and lists the potentially responsible parties.

He responds, in a sarcastic voice, that the EPA has the documents. "Are you new?" asks Chris. "Is it that obvious?" jokes Ellen. Chris responds that it's not really that obvious and explains that her predecessor always just sent in FOIA requests for everything that the EPA had in its files and that it took months to respond to these requests. "Believe me, your firm has quite a reputation around here," says Chris. Ellen smiles to herself as she

promises to submit the FOIA request for only the waste-in/waste-out report.

TIPS FOR WORKING WITH GOVERNMENT AGENCIES

- Before you call the agency, review the file to familiarize yourself with the case, and go online to the agency Web site to search for as much background information as possible.
- Review the agency's regulations to ascertain which documents the agency prepares in specific types of cases, such as Superfund cases.
- Make a list of the various documents.
- Determine in advance (from the list) which documents you will be requesting.
- Develop a list of alternatives to use in the event that the documents that you request have not been prepared or are not available.
- Make reasonable requests from the agency.
- Cultivate good working relationships with agency staff members.

courts. State rules of evidence apply in state courts. (Many states have adopted evidence rules patterned on the federal rules.) You do not need to become an expert in evidentiary rules, but a basic knowledge of how evidence is classified and what types of evidence are admissible in court will greatly assist your investigative efforts. For you to know something is not enough. You must have admissible evidence to prove the fact in court.

Direct versus Circumstantial Evidence

Two types of evidence may be brought into court—direct evidence and circumstantial evidence. **Direct evidence** is any evidence that, if believed, establishes the truth of the fact in question. For example, bullets found in the body of a shooting victim provide direct evidence of the type of gun that fired them. **Circumstantial evidence** is indirect evidence that, even if believed, does not establish the fact in question but only the degree of likelihood of the fact. In other words, circumstantial evidence can create an inference that a fact exists.

For example, suppose that your firm's client owns the type of gun that shot the bullets found in the victim's body. This circumstantial evidence does not establish that the client shot the victim. Combined with other circumstantial evidence, however, it could help to convince a jury that the client committed the crime. For instance, if other circumstantial evidence indicates that your firm's client had a motive for harming the victim, that the client was at the scene of the crime at the time the crime was committed and had recently fired his gun, a jury might conclude that the client committed the crime even if the victim's body or the bullets were not found.

Relevance

Evidence will not be admitted in court unless it is relevant. **Relevant evidence** is evidence that tends to prove or disprove the fact in question. For example, evidence that the gun belonging to your firm's client was in the home of another person when the victim was shot would be relevant, because it would tend to prove that the client did not shoot the victim.

Even relevant evidence may not be admitted in court if its probative (proving) value is substantially outweighed by other important considerations. For example, even though evidence is relevant, it may not be necessary—the fact at issue may have been sufficiently proved or disproved by previous evidence. In that situation, the introduction of further evidence would be a waste of time and would cause undue delay in the trial proceedings. Relevant evidence may also be excluded if it would tend to distract the jury from the main issues of the case, mislead the jury, or cause the jury to decide the issue on an emotional basis. Particularly gruesome photos of a murder victim are sometimes excluded on this basis.

Authentication of Evidence

At trial, an attorney must lay the proper foundation for the introduction of certain evidence, such as documents, exhibits, and other objects, and must demonstrate to the court that the evidence is what the attorney claims it is. The process by which this is accomplished is referred to as **authentication**. The authentication requirement relates to relevance, because something offered in evidence becomes relevant to the case only if it is authentic, or genuine. As a legal investigator, you need to make sure that the evidence you obtain is not only relevant but also capable of being authenticated if introduced at trial.

Commonly, evidence is authenticated by the testimony of witnesses. For example, if an attorney wants to introduce an autopsy report as evidence in a case, he or she can have the report authenticated by the testimony of the medical examiner who signed it. Generally, an attorney must offer enough proof of authenticity to convince the court that the evidence is, in fact, what it seems to be.

The Federal Rules of Evidence provide for the self-authentication of specific types of evidence. In other words, certain documents or records need not be authenticated by testimony. Certified copies of public records, for example, are

---

direct evidence
Evidence directly establishing the existence of a fact.

circumstantial evidence
Indirect evidence offered to establish, by inference, the likelihood of a fact that is in question.

relevant evidence
Evidence tending to prove or disprove the fact in question. Only relevant evidence is admissible in court.

authentication
The process of establishing the genuineness of an item that is to be introduced as evidence in a trial.

automatically deemed authentic. Other self-authenticating evidentiary documents include official publications (such as a report issued by the federal EPA), documents containing a notary public's seal or the seal of a public official, and manufacturers' trademarks or labels.

Hearsay

When interviewing witnesses, keep in mind that the witness's testimony *in court* must be based on the witness's own knowledge and not hearsay. **Hearsay** is defined as testimony that is given in court by a witness who relates not what he or she knows personally but what another person said. Literally, it is what someone heard someone else say. Hearsay is generally not admissible in court when offered to prove the truth of the matter asserted.

Hearsay is generally not allowed because the person who made the out-of-court statements was not under oath. Also, the witness reporting the statement may have misunderstood what the person was saying. Furthermore, there is no opportunity to cross-examine the person who actually made the statements.

PERSONAL OBSERVATION. For example, a witness in the Baranski case cannot testify in court that she heard an observer say, "That van is going ninety miles per hour"— even if the other observer was a police officer. Such testimony would be inadmissible under the hearsay rule. The witness can only testify about what she personally observed regarding the accident. Of course, during the investigation, witnesses often tell you what other people said (and you should not discourage them from doing so). If you wish to use information obtained this way as evidence in court, however, you need to find an alternative method of proving it (such as by the testimony of the people who made the original statements).

EXCEPTIONS. The hearsay rule provides exceptions in specific circumstances, often for statements made in situations that indicate a high degree of reliability. For example, a witness is usually allowed to testify about what a dying person said concerning the cause or circumstances of his or her impending death. This is because the courts have concluded that a person facing death will usually not lie about who or what caused that death.

Similarly, if a person makes an excited statement at the time of a stressful or startling event (such as "Oh no! That woman has just dropped her baby out the window"), a witness can usually testify as to that statement in court. If one of the parties to a lawsuit makes an out-of-court admission (for example, if defendant Peretto in the Baranski case admits to his friends that he was driving too fast at the time of the accident), a witness's testimony about what the party said may be admissible, although the rules on out-of-court admissions vary among jurisdictions. Exhibit 11.9 on the next page describes some of the traditional exceptions to the hearsay rule.

Summarizing Your Results

The final step in any investigation is summarizing the results. Your investigation report should provide an overall summary of your findings, a summary of the facts and information gathered from each source that you investigated, and your general conclusions and recommendations based on the information obtained.

Overall Summary

The overall summary should thoroughly describe all of the facts you have gathered. This section should be written so that someone not familiar with the case could read it and become adequately informed about the case's factual background.

Source-by-Source Summaries

You should also create a list of your information sources, including witnesses, and summarize the facts gleaned from each of these sources. Each "source section" should contain all of the information gathered from that source, including direct quotes from witnesses.

---

hearsay
Testimony that is given in court by a witness who relates not what he or she knows personally but what another person said. Hearsay is generally not admissible as evidence.

---

case AT A GLANCE

The Plaintiff—
Plaintiff: Katherine Baranski
Attorney: Allen P. Gilmore
Paralegal: Elena Lopez

The Defendant—
Defendant: Tony Peretto
Attorney: Elizabeth A. Cameron
Paralegal: Gordon McVay

EXHIBIT 11.9
Some Exceptions to the Hearsay Rule

Present Sense Impression—A statement describing an event or condition made at the time the declarer perceived the event or condition or immediately thereafter [FRE 803(1)].* *Example: "I smell smoke."*

Excited Utterance—A statement relating to a startling event or condition made while the declarer was under the stress or excitement caused by the startling event or condition [FRE 803(2)]. *Example: "Oh no! The brakes aren't working!"*

State of Mind—A statement of the declarer's then-existing state of mind, emotion, sensation, or physical condition (such as intent, plan, motive, design, mental feeling, pain, or bodily health). Such statements are considered trustworthy because of their spontaneity [FRE 803(3)]. *Example: "My leg is bleeding and hurts terribly."*

Recorded Recollection—A memorandum or record indicating a witness's previous statements concerning a matter that the witness cannot now remember with sufficient accuracy to testify fully about the matter. If admitted in court, the memorandum or record may be read into evidence but may not itself be received as an exhibit unless offered by an adverse party [FRE 803(5)]. *Example: An employer's memo to one of his or her employees in which the employer responds to the employee's complaint about safety violations in the workplace.*

Former Testimony—Testimony that was given at another hearing or deposition by a witness who is now unavailable, if the party against whom the testimony is now offered was a predecessor in interest and had an opportunity to examine the witness in court during the previous hearing or deposition [FRE 804(b)(1)]. *Example: An employee's testimony about his or her employer that was introduced at a trial brought by the employee's co-worker against that employer for sexual harassment. The employer is now being sued by another employee for sexual harassment, and the employee who testified in the previous trial is out of the country. The employee's testimony in the previous trial may be admissible.*

Business Records—A document or compilation of data made in the course of a regularly conducted business activity, unless the source of the information or the method or circumstances of the document's preparation indicate that it is not trustworthy as evidence. The source of information must be from a person with firsthand knowledge, although this person need not be the person who actually made the entry or created the document [FRE 803(6)]. *Example: Financial statement of a business firm.*

Dying Declarations—In a prosecution for homicide or in a civil proceeding, a statement made by a person who believes that his or her death is impending about the cause or circumstances of his or her impending death [FRE 804(b)(2)]. *Example: Derek said just before he died, "Jethro stabbed me."*

Statement against Interest—A statement that was made by someone who is now unavailable and that was, at the time of its making, so far contrary to the declarer's financial, legal, or other interests that a reasonable person in the declarer's position would not have made the statement unless he or she believed it to be true [FRE 804(b)(3)]. *Example: Sanchez says that Jackson, who is now missing, made the following statement to Sanchez just before leaving town: "I committed the perfect crime!"*

Miscellaneous Exceptions—Miscellaneous exceptions include records of vital statistics [FRE 803(9)]; records of religious organizations [FRE 803(11)]; marriage, baptismal, or similar certificates [FRE 803(12)]; family records (including charts, engravings on rings, inscriptions on family portraits, and engravings on tombstones) [FRE 803(13)]; and statements offered as evidence of a material fact that are trustworthy because of the circumstances in which they were uttered [FRE 804(b)(5) and FRE 803(24)].

*Federal Rules of Evidence.

Each source section should also contain a subsection giving your personal comments on that particular source. You might comment on a witness's demeanor, for example, or on whether the witness's version of the facts was consistent or inconsistent with the versions of other witnesses. Your impressions of the witness's competence or reliability could be noted. If the witness provided you with further leads to be explored, this information could also be included.

Conclusions and Recommendations

In the final section, you will present your overall conclusions about the investigation, as well as any suggestions that you have on the development of the case. Attorneys rely heavily on their investigators' impressions of witnesses and evaluations of investigative results because the investigators have firsthand knowledge of the sources. Your impression of a potentially important witness, for example, may help the attorney decide whether to arrange for a follow-up interview with the witness. Usually, the attorney will want to interview only the most promising witnesses, and your impressions and comments serve as a screening device. Based on your findings during the investigation, you might also suggest to the attorney what further information can be obtained during discovery, if necessary, and what additional research needs to be done.

KEY TERMS AND CONCEPTS

Chapter Summary

Conducting Interviews and Investigations

PLANNING THE INTERVIEW

Paralegals often interview clients and witnesses. Before the interview, the paralegal should prepare the interview environment to ensure that interruptions, noises, and delays will be minimized, that the client will be comfortable, and that any necessary supplies, forms, and equipment are at hand.

1. *Know what information you want*—The interviewer should have in mind the kind of information being sought from the interviewee.

2. *Standardized interview forms*—Preprinted interview forms provide helpful guidelines, but the interviewer should remain flexible during the interview, tailor questions to the interviewee's responses, and ask follow-up questions.

3. *Recording the interview*—Some paralegals record their interviews for future reference. If you do, make sure to obtain permission from your supervising attorney and the person being interviewed before recording. Keep in mind that some clients and witnesses will be less willing to disclose information freely when being recorded. If the interviewee appears hesitant, consider taking notes instead.

INTERVIEWING SKILLS

Interviewing skills include interpersonal skills, questioning skills, and communication skills, particularly listening skills.

1. *Interpersonal skills*—The interviewer should put the interviewee at ease, use language that the person will understand, and avoid using legal terms.

2. *Questioning skills*—Types of questions used during the interviewing process include open-ended, closed-ended, leading, and hypothetical questions.

The questioning technique will depend on the person being interviewed and the type of information sought (see Exhibit 11.2 on page 331).

3. *Listening skills*—The ability to listen is perhaps the most important skill for an interviewer to develop. Passive listening involves listening attentively to the speaker and using either verbal or nonverbal cues to encourage him or her to continue. Active listening

involves giving feedback that indicates to the speaker that you understand what he or she is saying. One effective active listening technique is for the interviewer to "reflect back," or restate, what the interviewee has said. This gives the speaker an opportunity to clarify or correct previous statements. Active listening enables the interviewer to control the flow of the interview. It allows the interviewer to put the interviewee's statements into the larger context and facilitates smooth transitions between topics.

INTERVIEWING CLIENTS

There are three types of client interviews: initial, subsequent, and informational. Interviews are often summarized. The paralegal may play a role in all phases.

1. *Initial client interview*—In setting up an interview, the paralegal should tell the client what documents to bring and follow up with a confirmation letter giving the date and time of the interview and listing the items the client is to bring.

2. *Subsequent client interviews*—Paralegals often conduct interviews after the initial interview, which is more likely to be conducted by the attorney. Always specify that you are not an attorney.

3. *Informational interview*—This kind of interview brings the client up to date on progress in a legal matter and prepares the client for further steps in the process.

4. *Summarizing the interview*—Soon after an interview is concluded, the paralegal should summarize in a written memorandum the information gathered in the interview. The memorandum should include impressions of the client's statements and nonverbal behaviors.

INTERVIEWING WITNESSES

1. *Types of witnesses*—Witnesses include expert witnesses (who have specialized training that qualifies them to testify as to their opinion in a given area), lay witnesses (ordinary witnesses who have factual information about the matter being investigated), eyewitnesses (who have firsthand knowledge of an event—because they saw it happen, for example), friendly witnesses (who are favorable to the client's position), and hostile witnesses (who are biased against the client, are friendly to the opponent, or resent being interviewed for other reasons).

2. *Questioning witnesses*—Investigative questions should be open ended to elicit the most complete answers. Additional questions should ascertain whether the witness is competent, credible, and reliable and whether the witness has any bias relevant to the case.

3. *Winding up the interview*—The paralegal should ask the witness at the end of the interview if the witness would like to add anything to her or his statement. This gives the witness an opportunity to explain an answer or expand on the areas discussed.

4. *Witness statements*—Following an interview, the paralegal should prepare a memo to the supervising attorney relating what the witness said and asking if the attorney wants a formal witness statement prepared. That statement identifies the witness, discloses what was discovered during the interview, and is signed by the witness.

PLANNING AND CONDUCTING INVESTIGATIONS

Factual evidence is crucial to the outcome of a legal problem, and paralegals are often asked to conduct investigations to discover any factual evidence that supports (or contradicts) a client's claims.

1. *Where do you start?*—Before starting an investigation, the paralegal should create an investigation plan—a step-by-step list of which sources will be investigated to obtain specific types of information.

2. *Creating an investigation plan*—A plan will note sources that need to be contacted for key information (police reports, medical and employment records, insurance companies, and so forth). The paralegal should discuss the plan with his or her supervising attorney before embarking on the investigation.

3. *Locating witnesses*—Sources of information regarding witnesses include directories; online people finders; media reports; court records; utility companies; professional organizations; and information recorded, compiled, or prepared by federal, state, and local government entities. Much of this information is available online.

4. *Accessing government information*—Some government records are public and are available in local offices or online. The Freedom of Information Act requires federal agencies to disclose certain records

on request, provided that the form of the request complies with the procedures mandated by the act. Obtaining such records is usually a slow process.

5. *Investigation and rules of evidence*—Evidence is anything that is used to prove the existence or non-existence of a fact. Rules of evidence established by the federal and state courts spell out what types of evidence may or may not be admitted in court.

   a. Direct evidence is any evidence that, if believed, establishes the truth of the fact in question.

   b. Circumstantial evidence is evidence that does not directly establish the fact in question but that establishes, by inference, the likelihood of the fact.

   c. Only relevant evidence, which tends to prove or disprove a fact in question, is admissible as evidence in court.

   d. For evidence to be admitted at trial, the attorney must prove to the court that the evidence is what it purports to be. This is called *authentication*.

   e. Hearsay is testimony given in court by a witness who relates not what he or she knows personally, but what someone else said. Generally, hearsay evidence is not admissible in court. Exceptions are made in circumstances that indicate a high degree of reliability—for example, a dying person's statement about who caused his or her impending death.

6. *Summarizing your results*—When the investigation is complete, the paralegal should summarize the results. This report should include an overall summary, source-by-source summaries, and a final section giving the paralegal's conclusions and recommendations.

QUESTIONS FOR REVIEW

1. What are the different types of questions that can be used in an interview? Explain when you would use each type.

2. What are the different types of interviews described in this chapter? What is the purpose of each type? What is the paralegal's role in each?

3. List the various types of witnesses discussed in the chapter. Describe the type of testimony each witness would give.

4. Describe how you would locate a witness. Give five sources you would consult. Which would be the most useful? Which would be the least useful? Explain why.

5. Define and give examples of the following types of evidence: direct evidence, circumstantial evidence, relevant evidence, authenticated evidence, and hearsay.

ETHICAL QUESTIONS

1. Paralegal Leah's boss has asked her to arrange for a private investigator to place a GPS tracking device, the size of a deck of cards, on the company car of a salesperson of one of the firm's clients. The client suspects the salesperson of playing golf instead of working and wants to investigate his whereabouts. Is it legal? Ethical?

2. Kirsten works as an in-house paralegal for a debt-collection company. She has been given a list of people who have defaulted on their car loans and cannot be located. Kirsten has been told by her supervising attorney to try to locate the debtors on Facebook and other social media sites. If she finds a missing debtor, she is to post a message on the social networking site to contact the collection agency about the debt. If Kirsten cannot locate a debtor, she has been instructed to try to locate the debtor's family members and post the same message. Would this be legal? Ethical? How should Kirsten handle this situation?

PRACTICE QUESTIONS AND ASSIGNMENTS

1. Review the Baranski-Peretto hypothetical case discussed in Chapter 10. Write sample questions that you would ask when interviewing eyewitnesses to the accident. Phrase at least one question in each of the question formats discussed in this chapter.

2. Using the information in this chapter on questioning skills, identify the following types of questions:

   a. "Did you go on a cruise in the Bahamas with a woman who was not your wife, Mr. Johnson?"

   b. "Isn't it true, Mr. Johnson, that a woman other than your wife accompanied you on a cruise in the Bahamas?"

   c. "Mr. Johnson, please describe where you were between January 10 and January 17, 2013?"

3. Using the format in Exhibit 11.4 on page 343, *Information Contained in a Witness Statement,* and Exhibit 11.5 on page 344, *A Sample Witness Statement (Excerpt),* draft a witness statement based on the following facts:

   a. You work for the law firm of Thomas & Snyder. On April 1, 2014, you are interviewing a witness to a car-train accident that happened a few hours ago. The interview takes place at the police station. The witness's name is Henry Black. Henry is retired and lives at 2002 Stephens Road, Clinton Township, Pennsylvania. His telephone number is (123) 456-7890.

   b. Henry was in his Cadillac, stopped in front of the railroad tracks on Jefferson Avenue in Clinton Township, Pennsylvania, at approximately 10:00 A.M., when a red Ford Flex sped past him and across the tracks. He was surprised that the Ford did not stop at the tracks because the train was only about thirty feet away and was blowing its whistle. There were no gates or guard rails in front of the tracks. Henry looked over at the driver of the Ford and saw that she was texting while she was driving. She did not appear to hear the train. As her vehicle crossed the tracks, the train struck it on the passenger side. Fortunately, there appeared to be no one else in the vehicle.

4. Determine whether each of the following statements is a statement of fact or a statement of opinion, and explain why:

   a. "I am sure that the driver was drunk because he pulled up next to me at the stoplight, then threw the car into reverse and backed a quarter of a mile down the one-way street."

   b. "The driver who was arrested for drunk driving ran a stop sign, then made a U-turn so that he could enter the highway. When arrested for erratic driving, his breathalyzer reading was 0.19."

QUESTIONS FOR CRITICAL ANALYSIS

1. Why would you need to obtain the client's or witness's permission to record an interview? Would it be ethical to record an interview without permission? What might happen if you did not obtain permission?

2. How do leading questions tend to cause distorted answers? Why would an attorney want to use this type of question?

3. Several types of witnesses were described in this chapter (expert witnesses, lay witnesses, eyewitnesses, friendly witnesses, hostile witnesses). Do any of these categories overlap—that is, could one witness fall into more than one of the categories? Explain.

4. Clients are often required to sign releases authorizing an entity (such as a hospital) to turn over information to a particular party (such as an attorney). Why is this? What might happen if releases were not required?

5. Rules of evidence govern the admissibility of evidence in court, but do not always apply in various forms of alternative dispute resolution. Why are rules needed in court but are not always used in ADR proceedings? What is the difference in outcome between these proceedings?

PROJECTS

1. Watch an interview on television. Write a two-page, double-spaced paper describing the interview. Include in your description the following information:

   a. The names of the interviewer and the interviewee.

   b. The subject of the interview.

   c. The date and time of the interview and the television channel over which it was broadcast.

   d. The different types of questions (open-ended, closed-ended, and so forth) used by the interviewer and the types of responses elicited by the different kinds of questions.

   e. The ways in which the interviewer and interviewee communicated nonverbally.

   f. Your overall evaluation of the interviewer's skill at interviewing this particular interviewee.

2. Using an advanced Google search, you can restrict your search to a specific Web site. This will allow you to locate information about witnesses, parties to a lawsuit, other attorneys, judges, and so forth on social networking sites, such as LinkedIn and Facebook. Go to **www.google.ie/advanced_search**. Then enter the name of the classmate sitting next to you to see if she or he has a social media site. Make sure that you type the Web site URL, such as www.facebook.com, into the box labeled, "Search within a site or domain."

GROUP PROJECT

Working in groups of three, role-play the initial client interview described in Chapter 10 between Katherine Baranski and the legal team—attorney Allen Gilmore and paralegal Elena Lopez. Attorney Gilmore will need to prepare a list of questions and will ask most of the questions during the interview. Paralegal Lopez will take notes during the interview, provide the retainer agreement and release forms, and schedule the follow-up interview. Change roles if time allows.

USING INTERNET RESOURCES

1. **KnowX.com** is a public records Web site. Much of the information that can be located at this site is information that a private investigator (or a paralegal) might want to find when investigating a case. Access the site at **www.knowx.com** and select "Site Map" from the menu at the top of the screen. Based on the information contained on the site map, what can you find using **KnowX**?

    a. Click on the tab "KnowX Standard." Then click "How It Works." What is the "Ultimate People Finder"? What databases does KnowX search to find people?

    b. Click on the tab "KnowX Professional" under "Location Tools" and select "The Ultimate Business Finder." What databases does KnowX search for business information?

    c. What other categories of information are available? Select two and explain how they might be used by a law firm.

    d. Now click on "How It Works." What is required to open a professional account? What does professional access provide? Is this a service that a law firm might consider using? Explain why or why not.

CourseMate The available CourseMate for this text has an interactive eBook and interactive learning tools, including flash cards, quizzes, and more. To learn more about this resource and access free demo CourseMate resources, go to **www.cengagebrain.com**, and search for this book. To access CourseMate materials that you have purchased, go to **login.cengagebrain.com**.

Trial Procedures

Chapter Outline

After completing this chapter, you will know:

- How attorneys prepare for trial and how paralegals assist in this task.

- How jurors are selected and the roles of attorneys and their legal assistants in the selection process.

- The various phases of a trial and the kinds of trial-related tasks that paralegals often perform.

- The options available to the losing party after the verdict is in.

- How a case is appealed to a higher court for review.

Introduction

Trials cost both time and money, so parties to lawsuits often try to avoid going to trial. Pretrial negotiations between the parties and their attorneys often lead to an out-of-court settlement. Using the pretrial motions discussed in Chapter 10, the parties may try to end the litigation after the pleadings are filed or while discovery takes place. In many cases, parties opt for alternative dispute resolution, such as mediation or arbitration. Recall from Chapter 6 that alternative dispute resolution is not always optional. Some state and federal courts *mandate* that a dispute be mediated or arbitrated before the parties are permitted to bring the dispute before a court. If the parties fail to settle their dispute through any of these means, the case will go to trial.

To illustrate how attorneys and paralegals prepare for trial, we continue using the hypothetical scenario developed in Chapter 10, in which Katherine Baranski (the plaintiff) is suing Tony Peretto (the defendant) for negligence. In the Baranski-Peretto case, Allen P. Gilmore is the attorney for plaintiff Baranski, and Gilmore's legal assistant is Elena Lopez. Defendant Peretto's attorney is Elizabeth A. Cameron, and Cameron's legal assistant is Gordon McVay. In preparing for trial, paralegals use a wide range of skills—including visual presentation skills, as discussed in the *Developing Paralegal Skills* feature below.

case AT A GLANCE

The Plaintiff—
Plaintiff: Katherine Baranski
Attorney: Allen P. Gilmore
Paralegal: Elena Lopez

The Defendant—
Defendant: Tony Peretto
Attorney: Elizabeth A. Cameron
Paralegal: Gordon McVay

Preparing for Trial

As the trial date approaches, the attorneys for the plaintiff and the defendant and their paralegals complete trial preparations. The paralegals collect and organize the documents and other evidence relating to the dispute. They may find it useful

DEVELOPING
paralegal skills

POWERPOINT PRESENTATIONS

Joanna Newcomb, a paralegal manager, works for a large law firm. The paralegals under her supervision often assist attorneys in trial preparations, and Joanna has decided to host workshops for the paralegals on trial presentation techniques. She has decided that the focus of the first workshop will be on the basics of PowerPoint presentations. She prepares a list of suggestions to hand out to the paralegals during the workshop.

TIPS FOR POWERPOINT PRESENTATIONS

- Plan your PowerPoint presentation carefully. Keep in mind that the display should clarify your presentation, not muddle it.

- Use the "four-by-four rule"—limit the text on each slide to four lines of no more than four words of text. This will keep your message simple and focused.

- The audience cannot hear your main points if you turn and talk to the screen, so be sure to talk toward the audience. Print out the slides for your reference while speaking.

- The background color should be geared to your audience. Some studies have shown that dark blue is a favorite color, so consider using that color for a background.

- The color of the text should be easy to read from afar.

- Simple fonts such as Arial, Tahoma, or Verdana are best. Avoid fancy fonts that distract from the substance of your message.

- Images and graphics can enhance your presentation, but do not "paste" images into your PowerPoint file. Instead, from the "Insert" menu, select "Picture" and then "From File" to insert a graphic.

- Rehearse your PowerPoint presentation ahead of time *on the equipment that you will be using.* Nothing will make you look less professional than a sloppy presentation. Audiences understand equipment breakdowns but are not as kind when it comes to poor preparation. Practice until you are comfortable with the timing of the presentation.

- Bring copies of the slides or other handouts to distribute in case for some reason you cannot use the PowerPoint presentation that you prepared.

to create a trial-preparation checklist similar to the one in Exhibit 12.1 below. Settlement negotiations often continue before and throughout the trial; however, both sides must assume that the trial court will decide the issue. Hence, they must be prepared for trial.

At this point in the litigation, plaintiff Baranski's attorney, Gilmore, will focus on legal strategy and how he can best use the information learned during the pleadings and discovery stages when presenting Baranski's case to the court. He will meet with his client and with his key witnesses to make last-minute preparations for trial. He might also meet with defendant Peretto's attorney to try once more to settle the dispute. Gilmore's legal assistant, Elena Lopez, will notify witnesses of the trial date and help Gilmore prepare for trial. For example, she will make sure that all exhibits to be used during the trial are ready and verify that the trial notebook (to be discussed shortly) is in order.

Contacting and Preparing Witnesses

Typically, the paralegal is responsible for ensuring that witnesses are available and in court on the day of the trial. As mentioned in previous chapters, a witness is any person asked to testify at trial. The person may be an eyewitness, an official witness (such as a police officer), an expert witness, or anyone with knowledge relevant to the lawsuit.

Several types of negligence lawsuits require expert witnesses. As discussed in Chapters 10 and 11, an expert witness is one who has specialized knowledge in a

EXHIBIT 12.1
Trial-Preparation Checklist

TWO MONTHS BEFORE THE TRIAL

____ Review the status of the case and inform the attorney of any depositions, interrogatories, or other discovery procedures that need to be completed before trial.
____ Interview witnesses and prepare witness statements.
____ Review deposition transcripts/summaries, answers to interrogatories, witness statements, and other information obtained about the case. Inform the attorney of any further discovery that should be undertaken prior to trial.
____ Begin preparing the trial notebook.

ONE MONTH BEFORE THE TRIAL

____ Make a list of the witnesses who will testify at the trial for the trial notebook.
____ Prepare a subpoena for each witness, and arrange to have the subpoenas served.
____ Prepare any exhibits that will be used at trial and reserve any special equipment (such as for a PowerPoint presentation) that will be needed at the trial.
____ Draft *voir dire* (jury selection) questions and perhaps prepare a jury profile.
____ Prepare motions and memoranda.
____ Continue assembling the trial notebook.

ONE WEEK BEFORE THE TRIAL

____ Check the calendar and call the court clerk to confirm the trial date.
____ Complete the trial notebook. Keep electronic copies of everything.
____ Make sure that all subpoenas have been served.
____ Prepare the client and witnesses for trial.
____ Make the final arrangements (housing, transportation, and the like) for the client or witnesses, as necessary.
____ Check with the attorney to verify how witnesses should be paid (for lost wages, travel expenses, and the like).
____ Make final arrangements to have all equipment, documents, and other items in the courtroom on the trial date.

ONE DAY BEFORE THE TRIAL

____ Meet with others on the trial team to coordinate last-minute efforts.
____ Have a final pretrial meeting with the client.

particular field. Such witnesses are often called to testify in negligence cases, because one element to be proved in a negligence case is the reasonableness of the defendant's actions. In medical-malpractice cases, for example, it takes someone with specialized knowledge in the defendant physician's area of practice to establish the reasonableness of the defendant's actions.

Contacting Witnesses and Issuing Subpoenas

In the Baranski case, attorney Gilmore and paralegal Lopez will have lined up witnesses to testify on behalf of their client. Lopez will inform the witnesses that the trial date has been set and that they will be expected to appear at the trial to testify. A *subpoena* (an order issued by the court clerk directing a person to appear in court—see Chapter 10) will be served on each of the witnesses to ensure the witness's presence in court. A subpoena to appear in a federal court is shown in Exhibit 12.2 on the next page. Although not shown in the exhibit, a return-of-service form, similar to the one illustrated in Chapter 10 on page 295, will be attached to the subpoena to verify that the witness received it.

Unless already familiar with the court's requirements, paralegal Lopez will check with the court clerk to learn what fees and documents she needs to take to the court to obtain the subpoena. The subpoena will then be served on the witness. Most subpoenas to appear in federal court can be served by anyone eighteen years of age or older. Paralegals often serve subpoenas. Subpoenas to appear in state court are often served by the sheriff or other process server.

When contacting *friendly* witnesses (those favorable to Baranski's position), Lopez should take care to explain that all witnesses are served with subpoenas, as a precaution, and to tell each witness when he or she can expect to receive the subpoena. Otherwise, a friendly witness might believe that Gilmore and Lopez did not trust the witness to keep a promise to appear in court and be offended.

Preparing Witnesses for Trial

No prudent attorney ever puts a nonhostile witness on the stand unless the attorney has discussed the testimony beforehand with that person. Good advance preparation can make a tremendous difference to the testimony that a witness provides. The amount of time spent preparing a witness will vary depending on the size of the case, the importance of the witness's testimony, and whether the attorney believes the witness will be able to communicate clearly and effectively in court. Additional time will be needed to prepare witnesses who are relatively inexperienced, are not very articulate, or are especially nervous about testifying.

TELL WITNESSES WHAT TO EXPECT.   Prior to trial, attorney Gilmore and paralegal Lopez will meet with each witness to prepare her or him for trial. Gilmore will discuss the types of questions that he intends to ask the witness in court and the questions that he expects the opposing attorney to ask. He will also tell the witness that during cross-examination opposing counsel will ask leading questions and may try to confuse the witness or attack his or her statements. Gilmore may recommend, for example, that the witness answer the opponent's questions in as few words as possible while not appearing to be overly defensive. The attorney may not, of course, tell the witness what to say in response to questions.

Gilmore will also review with the witness any statements the witness has made about the case, particularly if the statements were given under oath (such as during a deposition). It is important that a witness understand that during the trial, he or she may be asked about any inconsistencies between statements previously given or between trial testimony and prior statements. Additionally, Gilmore may want to review the substantive legal issues involved in the case and discuss how the witness's testimony will affect the outcome of those issues. As the *In the Office* feature on page 365 notes, remember that you are often dealing with confidential information that must be protected.

EXHIBIT 12.2
A Subpoena

AO 88 (Rev. 2/06) Subpoena in a Civil Case

Issued by the
UNITED STATES DISTRICT COURT

———— WESTERN DISTRICT OF NITA ————

Katherine Baranski
V.
Tony Peretto

SUBPOENA IN A CIVIL CASE

CASE NUMBER   14-14335-NI

TO: Julia Williams
3765 Mattis Avenue
Nita City, NI 48803

[X] YOU ARE COMMANDED to appear in the United States District Court at the place, date, and time specified below to testify in the above case.

PLACE OF TESTIMONY	COURT ROOM
4th and Main Nita City, NI	B
	DATE AND TIME 8/4/14 10:00 A.M.

[ ] YOU ARE COMMANDED to appear at the place, date, and time specified below to testify at the taking of a deposition in the above case.

PLACE OF DEPOSITION	DATE AND TIME

[ ] YOU ARE COMMANDED to produce and permit inspection and copying of the following documents or objects at the place, date, and time specified below (list documents or objects):

PLACE	DATE AND TIME

[ ] YOU ARE COMMANDED to permit inspection of the following premises at the date and time specified below.

PREMISES	DATE AND TIME

Any organization not a party to this suit that is subpoenaed for the taking of a deposition shall designate one or more officers, directors, or managing agents, or other persons who consent to testify on its behalf, and may set forth, for each person designated, the matters on which the person will testify. Federal Rules of Civil Procedure, 30(b)(6).

ISSUING OFFICER SIGNATURE AND TITLE (INDICATE IF ATTORNEY FOR PLAINTIFF OR DEFENDANT)	DATE
Allen P. Gilmore, Attorney for the Plaintiff	July 13, 2014

ISSUING OFFICER'S NAME, ADDRESS AND PHONE NUMBER
Allen P. Gilmore, Jeffers, Gilmore & Dunn,
553 Fifth Avenue, Suite 101, Nita City, NI 48801   (616) 555-9690

(See Rule 45, Federal Rules of Civil Procedure, Parts C & D on Reverse)
If action is pending in district other than district of issuance, state district under case number.

IN THE office

PROTECTING CONFIDENTIAL INFORMATION

Some of the materials related to cases are confidential. To protect the interests of clients, help to make sure that information is not exposed to visitors to the office or to other employees who do not have a need to know information related to a particular case. Keep materials put away when you are not working on them. Because most work is done on computers, close files on your computer when you leave your desk so other people cannot read what is there. Computers can be easily locked. Entering your password returns you to the same point, so you do not have to close all files or turn off the computer.

Be particularly careful with laptops, iPads, and flash drives outside of the office. Losing a computer or drive with confidential documents can be disastrous. Also, notice that many people talk on the phone as if no one around them is listening. You must be cautious when talking about legal matters. Be discrete in your cell phone use.

ROLE-PLAYING.   If the witness needs additional preparation, Gilmore or Lopez may engage in some role-playing with the witness. This type of rehearsal is often valuable in helping the witness to understand more fully how the questioning will proceed and what tactics may be involved in the opposing attorney's questions. It also may alleviate some of the witness's fears. In addition, Lopez might take the witness to the courtroom in which the trial will take place to familiarize the witness with the trial setting. Testifying can be a stressful experience. Anything that the paralegal can do to reduce a witness's discomfort will help the witness to better control his or her responses when testifying and thus will ultimately benefit the client.

NUMEROUS DETAILS.   Paralegals are often responsible for handling all the details involved in preparing witnesses for court. For example, Lopez might recommend appropriate clothing and grooming or tell the witness where to look and how to remain calm and composed when speaking to the court. If the witness will be asked about any exhibits or evidence (such as photographs or documents), Lopez will show these items to the witness. Lopez will continually update the witness as to when he or she will probably be called to testify.

Exhibits and Displays

Paralegals frequently prepare exhibits or displays that will be presented at trial. Attorney Gilmore may wish to show the court a photograph of plaintiff Baranski's car taken after the accident occurred, a diagram of the intersection, an enlarged document (such as a police report), or other relevant evidence. Paralegal Lopez will be responsible for making sure that all exhibits are properly prepared and ready to introduce at trial. If any exhibits require special equipment, such as an easel, projector, or laptop computer, Lopez must also make sure that these will be available in the courtroom and properly set up when they are needed. Increasingly, law firms are using high-tech equipment to prepare their trial presentations, as the *Practice Focus* feature on the following page discusses.

The Trial Notebook

To present Baranski's case effectively, Gilmore will need to have all of the relevant documents in the courtroom. He will also need to be able to locate them quickly. To accomplish these goals, Lopez will prepare a trial notebook and set up computer

ON THE web

For complex cases that involve a massive number of documents, a law firm may want assistance in managing and reviewing the documents. Firms that provide this service include Providus, at **www.providusgroup.com**

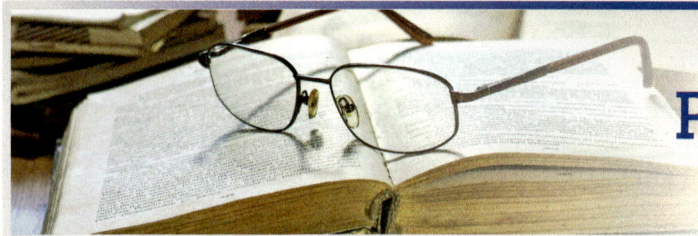

PRACTICE focus

NEW TOOLS IN TRIAL PREPARATION

Attorneys' trial tactics are evolving to include more sophisticated presentations, creating a greater need for paralegals with design and technology skills. Exhibits are no longer simply copies of documents blown up to larger sizes, but also include elaborate video presentations.

In addition, technology is changing how litigation is being conducted outside the courtroom. For example, Web research on opposing witnesses may uncover valuable information to use in discrediting them. You must do thorough Internet-based research about your witnesses before you present them. Otherwise, some facts about your witnesses that you do not know, because they did not tell you embarrassing information, may be known and revealed by opposing counsel.

Some of the less sophisticated work formerly done by paralegals is now automated, creating a demand for paralegals with higher skill levels. For example, electronic indexing makes document retrieval faster and more accurate, enhancing cross-examination. Some courtrooms even allow for real-time transmission of transcribed testimony outside the courtroom, allowing paralegals back in the office to be scouring a witness's testimony for inconsistencies as they occur.

One of the impacts of these changes is a need for paralegals reviewing electronic evidence to be familiar with the programs used to create records. This knowledge enables them to explore issues such as documents' metadata (electronic data on document creation and revision) within records, which might provide additional evidence beyond the text of the document itself. For instance, documents created with document creators such as Microsoft Word include a record showing the person who created it, when it was created, and when it was altered. Such information can be crucial in cases where the parties disagree about the sequence of events.

---

trial notebook
Traditionally, a binder that contains copies of all the documents and information that an attorney will need to have at hand during the trial.

case AT A GLANCE

The Plaintiff—
Plaintiff: Katherine Baranski
Attorney: Allen P. Gilmore
Paralegal: Elena Lopez

The Defendant—
Defendant: Tony Peretto
Attorney: Elizabeth A. Cameron
Paralegal: Gordon McVay

files. Traditionally, the **trial notebook** has been one or more three-ring binders containing trial-related materials separated by tabbed divider sheets. Most lawyers today rely primarily on documents kept in computers, but paper copies are also still common. The discussion here applies to both.

Key Materials

Lopez meets with Gilmore to discuss what he wants to include in the trial notebook for Baranski's case and how the notebook should be organized. Gilmore tells Lopez that the organization of the notebook should make it possible to find quickly whatever documents they may need during the trial. Lopez should include the following materials in the notebook:

- Copies of the pleadings.
- Interrogatories.
- Deposition transcripts and summaries.
- Pretrial motions and any recent rulings on them.
- A list of exhibits and a case outline indicating when they will be used.
- A witness list, the order in which the witnesses will testify, and the questions that will be asked of each witness.
- Relevant cases or statutes that Gilmore plans to cite.
- Any additional documents or information that will be important to have close at hand during the trial.

Note that many of the above materials will be scanned and saved in a file or files on a laptop or server or elsewhere.

Lopez will create a general index to the notebook or computer file's contents and place this index at the front of the notebook. She may also create an index for each section of the binder or computer file and place those indexes at the beginnings of the sections. Paralegals sometimes use a notebook computer and a software retrieval system to help them quickly locate documents, especially in complicated cases involving thousands of documents. Careful, consistent organization of computer files is critical.

Protect Original Documents

When preparing a traditional trial notebook, remember that the notebook should not contain the original documents but copies of them from when they were scanned. The original documents (unless they are needed as evidence at trial) should remain in the firm's files, for reasons of security (should the trial notebook be misplaced) and so those in the office will have access to the documents while the notebook is in court.

Lopez will not wait until the last minute to prepare the trial notebook and electronic files. Rather, at the outset of the lawsuit, she will make copies of the pleadings and other documents as they are generated to include in the notebook. That way, she will not have to spend time just before the trial, when there are other pressing needs, to do work that could have been done earlier. As noted throughout this chapter, high-tech presentations are changing the paralegal's trial-preparation tasks, as discussed in the *Technology and Today's Paralegal* feature on the following pages.

Pretrial Conference

Before the trial begins, the attorneys usually meet with the trial judge in a **pretrial conference** to explore the possibility of resolving the case and, if a settlement is not possible, to determine how the trial will be conducted. In particular, the court or the parties may attempt to clarify the issues in dispute and establish ground rules to restrict such matters as the admissibility of certain types of evidence. For example, Gilmore might have Lopez draft a **motion *in limine***[1] (a motion to limit evidence) to submit to the judge at this time. The motion will request the judge to order that certain evidence not be brought out at trial.

To illustrate: Suppose that Baranski had been arrested in the past for illegal drug possession. Gilmore knows that evidence of the arrest, if introduced by the defense at trial, might prejudice the jury against Baranski. Because Baranski's past arrest is not relevant to the case and potentially prejudicial, Gilmore might submit a motion *in limine* to keep the defense from presenting evidence of the arrest. Exhibit 12.3 on page 369 presents a sample motion *in limine*. Note that with the motion Gilmore would include affidavits and/or a memorandum of law (a brief)— these documents were discussed in Chapter 10—to convince the judge that the motion should be granted.

Once the pretrial conference has concluded, both parties turn their attention to the trial itself. Assuming that the trial will be heard by a jury, however, one more step is necessary before the trial begins: selecting the jurors who will hear the trial and render a verdict on the dispute.

Jury Selection

Before the trial gets under way, a panel of jurors must be assembled. The clerk of the court usually notifies local residents by mail that they have been selected for jury duty. The process of selecting prospective jurors varies, depending on the court, but often they are randomly selected by the court clerk from lists of registered voters or those to whom driver's licenses have been issued. The persons selected then report to the courthouse on the date specified in the notice (unless

social MEDIA TODAY

Before using social media tools at the office, check your firm's policy. The firm should have guidelines on when these are appropriate to use with clients and what private use is appropriate during the workday. If your firm doesn't have a policy, volunteer to help develop the guidelines.

pretrial conference
A conference prior to trial in which the judge and the attorneys litigating the suit discuss settlement possibilities, clarify the issues in dispute, and schedule forthcoming trial-related events.

motion *in limine*
A motion requesting that certain evidence not be brought out at the trial, such as prejudicial, irrelevant, or legally inadmissible evidence.

ON THE web

Numerous firms offer trial consulting services, including assistance in jury selection. You can access the Web site of one such firm, Jury Research Institute, at **www.jri-inc.com**.

TECHNOLOGY AND
today's paralegal

COURTROOM TECHNOLOGY

In the past, attorneys and paralegals involved in complex litigation had to carry boxes of papers into the courtroom and then, during trial, search through them for key documents and exhibits. Visual presentations were usually limited to enlarged photographs or text displayed on an easel. Today, advances in technology give paralegals and attorneys numerous other options.

DIGITAL RECORDS AND VIDEO

A major challenge for the paralegal in complex litigation is keeping the mountains of evidence organized, cross-referenced, and easily accessible during the trial. Suppose, for example, that a witness is making statements on the stand and the paralegal wishes to compare them with statements on the same topic made by that witness in a deposition prior to trial. Finding these earlier statements quickly can be difficult. If the documents have been scanned into a computer, however, the paralegal using litigation support software can search all the documents in the case in a matter of seconds. This means that counsel will not need to bring deposition transcripts, records, and reports to court. Instead, one laptop or iPad can access thousands of documents quickly.

Other technologies being utilized in courts today involve digital video recording and court reporting. For example, when depositions in the case are digitally recorded and loaded on a computer, that video file can be combined on a split screen with the transcript of the written words. This can be an effective way for the lawyer to demonstrate inconsistencies in a witness's statements. Rather than simply reading the deposition transcript in court (as traditionally has been done), the jurors are able to watch the deposition and see the person's face and body language.

In addition, "real-time" court reporting is available. When real-time court reporting is used, the transcript appears on the computer screen as the person is speaking. Real-time videoconferencing can also be used to bring into the courtroom the "live" testimony of experts and other witnesses who cannot be physically present. A judge's permission is usually required to use these technologies in the courtroom.

TRIAL PRESENTATION SOFTWARE

Using trial presentation software can help the legal team to create a more effective, persuasive, and visually stimulating presentation of its case. Most people absorb and retain information better when it is presented visually as well as verbally. Visual information is also more engaging for jurors than long recitations of detailed facts by witnesses (and attorneys). By providing visual displays, then, the legal team's presentation can have a greater impact on juries.

For example, the legal team can create a mixed-media presentation (including video and sound) for use at trial. The order and elements of the presentation can be manipulated in a variety of ways to maximize effectiveness. A person preparing digital images to be included in a presentation, for instance, could highlight certain portions of an image and dim others to help the jury focus on the desired part. He or she could also zoom in on part of an image, insert a box containing an enlargement of part of the image, or add arrows, labels, titles, or symbols to an image.

Be aware that courtroom media systems are often less advanced than those in use in the private sector, so check in advance about what type of media the presentation is stored on. A courtroom system may require a CD-ROM, for example, while the firm's computers all use flash drives or DVDs. Always bring backup equipment and spare copies of presentations on multiple media in case of equipment malfunctions.

Presentation software also makes it easy to create diagrams of an accident scene, graphic illustrations of scientific evidence, medical models and diagrams to help explain medical procedures and injuries, and schematics of mechanical or physical evidence. Rather than simply telling the jury how a particular product or machine caused a client's injuries, for example, an attorney can show how the injury occurred. The legal team can also create flow charts to indicate the relationships between events and bulleted lists to highlight the strengths of its case or the weaknesses of the opponent's case. These exhibits can be modified easily if necessary during the trial.

TECHNOLOGY TIP

Computers and courtroom technologies can make a litigation paralegal's job easier, especially in cases that involve extensive documentation. Make sure to obtain the court's permission, if required, to use a specific technology in the courtroom. Make sure, too, that all presentations and diagrams are accurate and comply with the rules of evidence. Keep a backup copy of all documents, cross-referenced the old-fashioned way, in the event the computer crashes. Finally, if you are working with an outside vendor to provide support or presentation services, be careful not to breach confidentiality rules.

EXHIBIT 12.3
Motion *in Limine*

A. P. Gilmore
Jeffers, Gilmore & Dunn
553 Fifth Avenue
Suite 101
Nita City, NI 48801
(616) 555-9690

Attorney for Plaintiff

UNITED STATES DISTRICT COURT
FOR THE WESTERN DISTRICT OF NITA

Katherine Baranski)	
Plaintiff,)	CASE NO. 14-1433S-NI
)	Honorable Harley M. Larue
v.)	
)	MOTION IN LIMINE
)	
Tony Peretto)	
Defendant.)	

The Plaintiff respectfully moves the Court to prohibit counsel for the Defendant from directly or indirectly introducing or making any reference during the trial to the Plaintiff's arrest in 2005 for the possession of illegal drugs.

The grounds on which this motion is based are stated in the accompanying affidavits and memorandum.

Date: 6/18/14

Allen P. Gilmore
Allen P. Gilmore
Attorney for the Plaintiff

they are granted exceptions or waivers). At the courthouse, they are gathered into a single pool of jurors, and the process of selecting those jurors who will actually hear the case begins. Although some types of trials require twelve-person juries, civil matters can be heard by a jury of as few as six persons in many states. Federal court juries are usually chosen from a wider geographic area than are state court juries. The different demographics are a reason an attorney might prefer one court rather than the other.

Voir Dire

Both the plaintiff's attorney and the defendant's attorney have some input into the ultimate makeup of the jury. Each attorney will question prospective jurors in a proceeding known as *voir dire*.[2] Experienced litigators know the importance of the *voir dire* process. It helps to pick the right jury, but also is a time for attorneys to introduce themselves and their clients to the jury before the trial even begins.

Legal assistants may work with their attorneys to write up the questions that will be asked of jurors during *voir dire*. Because all of the jurors will have previously filled out forms giving basic information about themselves, the questions can be tailored accordingly. The idea is to uncover any biases on the part of prospective jurors and to find persons who might identify with the plights of their respective clients.

voir dire

A proceeding in which attorneys for the plaintiff and the defendant ask prospective jurors questions to determine whether any potential juror is biased or has any connection with a party to the action or with a prospective witness.

Typically, the legal team for each side has already developed an idea of what kind of person would be most sympathetic toward or most likely to vote in favor of its client. Indeed, sometimes experts are hired to help create a juror profile. The paralegals and attorneys then formulate questions based on this notion of the ideal juror in the case.

Jury selection may last an hour or many days, depending on the complexity of the case and the rules and preferences of the particular court or judge. In some courts, the judge questions prospective jurors using queries prepared and submitted by the attorneys. In other courts, the judge has each juror answer a list of standard questions and then gives each attorney a small amount of time to ask follow-up questions. When large numbers of prospective jurors are involved, the attorneys (or the judge) may direct their questions to groups of jurors as opposed to individual jurors in order to reduce the time spent choosing a jury.

Jury Selection Experts and Tools

Picking a jury is a critical step in a trial. The famous litigator Clarence Darrow claimed that "almost every case is won or lost when the jury is sworn." Picking a jury is often done by instinct, with experienced trial lawyers gauging whether a juror is likely to be sympathetic to their clients based on gut reactions, on stereotypes about marital status, race, religious affiliation, or occupation, or on similarly unscientific factors. Today, jury selection is becoming a big business when the stakes are high. Now, significant sums are spent on jury consultants who promise to use science to help lawyers pick a jury. Consultants helped pick juries in the O.J. Simpson criminal trial and the $253 million Vioxx products liability cases, for example.

Not everyone can afford an expensive jury-selection consultant, however. By using online search tools, paralegals and others assisting attorneys can discover valuable information about prospective jurors from their online "digital shadow." A prospective juror may appear in court dressed professionally, but his Facebook profile may feature wild partying. Spotting such information may help a lawyer defending a DWI case decide to keep the party animal on the jury, reasoning that he is more likely to sympathize with the defendant. As the amount of information available online about people increases, having the skills necessary to quickly find revealing information is an ever more valuable skill for the paralegal.

Challenges during Voir Dire

During *voir dire*, the attorney for each side will decide if there are any individuals he or she would like to prevent from serving as jurors in the case. The attorney may then exercise a **challenge** to exclude a particular person from the jury. There are two types of challenges available to both sides in a lawsuit: challenges for cause and peremptory challenges.

Challenges for Cause

The attorney can exercise a **challenge for cause** if the prospective juror is biased against the client or case for some reason. For example, if a juror states during *voir dire* that he or she hates immigrants and the client is foreign born, the attorney can exercise a challenge for cause. Each side's attorney can exercise an *unlimited* number of challenges for cause. Because most people are not forthcoming about their biases, the attorney must be able to prove sufficiently to the court that the person cannot be an objective juror in the case. Often, the judge will ask the challenged juror follow-up questions and then determine that the juror can be objective after all.

Peremptory Challenges

Both attorneys may exercise a *limited* number of **peremptory challenges** without giving any reason to the court as to why they object to a particular juror. In most cases, peremptory challenges are the only challenges exercised (because there is no proof that any juror is biased). A juror may thus be excused from serving on the jury for any

challenge
An attorney's objection, during *voir dire,* to the inclusion of a particular person on the jury.

challenge for cause
A *voir dire* challenge to exclude a potential juror from serving on the jury for a reason specified by an attorney in the case.

peremptory challenge
A *voir dire* challenge to exclude a potential juror from serving on the jury without any supporting reason or cause. Peremptory challenges based on racial or gender criteria are illegal.

reason, including his or her facial expressions or nonverbal behavior during the questioning. Peremptory challenges based on racial criteria or gender, however, are illegal.

Because the number of peremptory challenges is limited (a court may allow only three, for example), attorneys must exercise peremptory challenges carefully. Experienced litigators try to conserve their peremptory challenges so that they can eliminate the prospective jurors who appear the most hostile.

Procedure for Challenges

Typically, *voir dire* takes place in the courtroom, and the attorneys question the six to twelve prospective jurors who are seated in the jury box. Other prospective jurors may be seated in the audience area of the courtroom, so that as one person is excused, another person can walk up to take his or her place in the jury box. The procedure varies depending on the jurisdiction.

Often, rather than making challenges orally in front of the jury, the attorneys write down on a piece of paper which juror they wish to challenge, and the paper is given to the judge. The judge thanks and dismisses the prospective juror, and the process starts over again with the next individual. When this method is used, the remaining prospective jurors do not know which side dismissed the individual and so are less likely to make guesses about the underlying reasons.

The Paralegal's Role during Voir Dire

As mentioned, paralegals help develop a jury profile and draft questions that will be asked during *voir dire*. In addition, a paralegal can assist an attorney by providing another pair of eyes and ears during the jury selection process. Attorneys frequently rely on the observations of other members of the legal team who are present during the questioning.

If paralegal Lopez attends *voir dire* with attorney Gilmore in the Baranski case, for example, she will watch all of the jurors as the attorneys question them. Lopez, because she is not participating in the questioning, is free to observe the prospective jurors more closely than Gilmore. She will report to Gilmore any verbal or nonverbal response she observed that Gilmore might not have noticed. For example, suppose that as Gilmore is questioning one juror, another juror is staring at plaintiff Baranski and frowning with disapproval. Gilmore might not notice this behavior, and Lopez can bring it to his attention. As the *Ethics Watch* feature on the following page notes, you must limit contact with jurors.

Alternate Jurors

Because unforeseeable circumstances or illness may necessitate that one or more of the sitting jurors be dismissed, the court often seats several *alternate jurors*. Depending on the rules of the particular jurisdiction, a court might have two or three alternate jurors present throughout the trial. If a juror has to be excused in the middle of the trial, then an alternate can take his or her place without disrupting the proceedings. Unless they replace jurors, alternate jurors do not participate in jury deliberations at the end of the trial and are dismissed when deliberations begin.

The Trial

Once the jury members are seated, the judge swears in the jury, and the trial begins. During the trial, the attorneys, Allen Gilmore and Elizabeth Cameron, will present their cases to the jury. Because the attorneys will be concentrating on the trial, it will fall to their paralegals to coordinate the logistical aspects of the trial and observe the trial proceedings. Because paralegal Lopez is thoroughly familiar with the case and Gilmore's legal strategy, she will be a valuable ally during the trial. She will anticipate Gilmore's needs and provide appropriate reminders or documents as Gilmore needs them.

social
MEDIA TODAY

A good test for whether posting something is a good idea is to imagine that 1 million people will see it. If you don't want something shared that widely, don't post it online.

case AT A GLANCE

The Plaintiff—
Plaintiff: Katherine Baranski
Attorney: Allen P. Gilmore
Paralegal: Elena Lopez

The Defendant—
Defendant: Tony Peretto
Attorney: Elizabeth A. Cameron
Paralegal: Gordon McVay

ETHICS WATCH

COMMUNICATING WITH JURORS

Suppose that you are the paralegal working on the Baranski case with attorney Allen Gilmore, and you run into one of the jurors in the grocery store. The juror approaches you and says, "You know, I didn't really understand what that witness, Williams, was saying. Did she really see the accident? Also, is it true that Mrs. Baranski will never be able to walk normally again?" You know the answers to these questions, and you would like the juror to know the truth. You also know that it would enhance Baranski's chances of winning the case if this juror were as familiar with the factual background as you are.

What should you do?

1. Explain to the juror that neither you nor a juror is permitted to discuss a case they are hearing with anyone.
2. Inform your neighbor that as a paralegal, you have an ethical duty to abide by the professional rules of conduct governing the legal profession. One of these rules prohibits *ex parte* (private) communications with jurors about a case being tried.
3. Report the conversation to attorney Gilmore, who may decide to tell the judge about it.

These actions are consistent with NFPA's *Model Code of Ethics and Professional Responsibility,* Section EC-1.2(a), "A paralegal shall not engage in any *ex parte* communications involving the courts or any other adjudicatory body [a person or panel that makes a legal decision] in an attempt to exert undue influence or to obtain advantage or the benefit of only one party," and Section EC-1.5(f), "A paralegal shall not engage in any indiscreet communications concerning clients." They are also consistent with the NALA *Code of Ethics,* Canon 9, "A paralegal must do all other things incidental, necessary, or expedient for the attainment of the ethics and responsibilities as defined by statute or rule of court."

The Paralegal's Duties

Prior to each trial day, for example, Lopez will assemble the documents and materials that will be needed in court. During the court proceedings, Lopez will make sure that attorney Gilmore has within reach any documents or exhibits that he needs for questioning parties or witnesses. At the end of the day, Lopez will organize the documents and materials, decide what will be needed for the next day, and file the documents that can remain in the office.

Lopez will also monitor each witness's testimony to ensure that it is consistent with previous statements made by the witness. Lopez will have the relevant deposition transcript (and summary) at hand when a witness takes the stand. She will follow the deposition transcript (or summary) of each witness as that witness testifies. This way, she can pass a note to Gilmore if he misses any inconsistencies in the testimony.

Lopez will also observe how the jury is responding to witnesses and their testimony or to the attorneys' demeanor and questions. She will take notes during the trial on these observations as well as on the points being stressed and the types of evidence introduced by the opposing counsel. At the end of the day, Lopez and Gilmore may review the day's events, and Lopez's "trial journal" will provide a ready reference to what happened in the courtroom.

Opening Statements

The trial both opens and closes with attorneys' statements to the jury. In their **opening statements**, the attorneys give a brief version of the facts and the supporting evidence that they will use during the trial. Because some trials can take weeks or even months, it is helpful for jurors to hear a summary of the story that will unfold during the trial. Otherwise, they may be left wondering how a particular piece of evidence fits into the dispute.

The opening statement is a kind of "road map" that describes the destination that each attorney hopes to reach and outlines how he or she plans to reach it. Plaintiff Baranski's attorney, Gilmore, will focus on such things as his client's lack of fault and the injuries that she sustained when she was hit by defendant Peretto's car. Peretto's attorney, Cameron, will highlight the points that weaken Baranski's claim (for example, Cameron might point out that Baranski was speeding) or otherwise suggest that Peretto did not commit any wrongful act. Note that the defendant's attorney has the right to reserve her or his opening statement until after the plaintiff's case has been presented.

> **opening statement**
> An attorney's statement to the jury at the beginning of the trial. The attorney briefly outlines the evidence that will be offered during the trial and the legal theory that will be pursued.

The Plaintiff's Case

Once the opening statements have been made, Gilmore will present the plaintiff's case first. Because he is the plaintiff's attorney, he has the burden of proving that defendant Peretto was negligent.

Direct Examination

Gilmore will call several eyewitnesses to the stand and ask them to tell the court about the sequence of events that led to the accident. This form of questioning is known as **direct examination**. For example, Gilmore will call Julia Williams, an eyewitness who saw the accident occur, and ask her questions such as those presented in Exhibit 12.4 on the next page. He will also call other witnesses, including the police officer who was summoned to the accident scene and the ambulance driver. Gilmore will try to elicit responses from these witnesses that strengthen Baranski's case—or at least that do not weaken it.

> **direct examination**
> The examination of a witness by the attorney who calls the witness to the stand to testify on behalf of the attorney's client.

During direct examination, attorney Gilmore usually will not be permitted to ask *leading questions,* which are questions that lead the witness to a particular desired response (see Chapter 11). A leading question might be something like the following: "So, Mrs. Williams, you noticed that the defendant ran the stop sign, right?" If Mrs. Williams answers "yes," she has, in effect, been "led" to this answer by Gilmore's leading question. Leading questions discourage witnesses from telling their stories in their own words.

When Gilmore is dealing with *hostile witnesses* (uncooperative witnesses or those who are testifying on behalf of the other party), however, he is normally permitted to ask leading questions. This is because hostile witnesses may be uncommunicative and unwilling to describe the events they witnessed. If Gilmore asked a hostile witness what he or she observed on the morning of August 4 at 7:45 A.M., for example, the witness might respond, "I saw two trucks driving down Mattis Avenue." That answer might be true, but it has nothing to do with the Baranski-Peretto accident. Therefore, to elicit information from this witness, Gilmore would be permitted to use leading questions, which would force the witness to respond to the question at issue.

EXHIBIT 12.4
Direct Examination—
Sample Questions

ATTORNEY:	Mrs. Williams, please explain how you came to be at the scene of the accident.
WITNESS:	Well, I was walking north on Mattis Avenue toward Nita City Hospital, where I work as a nurse.
ATTORNEY:	Please describe for the court, in your own words, exactly what you observed when you reached the intersection of Mattis Avenue and Thirty-eighth Street.
WITNESS:	I was approaching the intersection when I saw the defendant run the stop sign on Thirty-eighth Street and crash into the plaintiff's car.
ATTORNEY:	Did you notice any change in the speed at which the defendant was driving as he approached the stop sign?
WITNESS:	No. He didn't slow down at all.
ATTORNEY:	Mrs. Williams, are you generally in good health?
WITNESS:	Yes.
ATTORNEY:	Have you ever had any problems with your vision?
WITNESS:	No. I wear reading glasses for close work, but I see well in the distance.
ATTORNEY:	And how long has it been since your last eye examination?
WITNESS:	About a month or so ago, I went to Dr. Sullivan for an examination. He told me that I needed reading glasses but that my distance vision was excellent.

© Cengage Learning 2014

Cross-Examination

cross-examination

The questioning of an opposing witness during the trial.

After attorney Gilmore has finished questioning a witness on direct examination, defendant Peretto's attorney, Cameron, will begin her **cross-examination** of that witness. During her cross-examination, Cameron will be primarily concerned with reducing the witness's credibility in the eyes of the jury and the judge. Attorneys typically use leading questions during cross-examination (because the witness is hostile). Generally, experienced trial attorneys ask only questions to which they know the answers—because otherwise a question might elicit testimony from the witness that further supports the opponent's case.

MAKE THE QUESTIONS RELEVANT. Cameron will formulate questions for Gilmore's witnesses based on the witnesses' previous answers in depositions and interrogatories. Discovery usually provides attorneys with a fairly good idea as to what areas of questioning may prove fruitful. Moreover, if a witness's testimony on the witness stand differs materially from the answers previously given, or contradicts some other item of evidence (some physical evidence or the testimony of another witness), the attorney can use this discrepancy to attack the witness's credibility.

FOCUS ON CREDIBILITY. The defendant's attorney, Cameron, must generally confine her cross-examination to matters that were brought up during direct examination or that relate to a witness's credibility. This restriction is not followed in all states, however, and ultimately both the nature and extent of the cross-examination are subject to the discretion of the trial judge. In any event, Cameron's interrogation may not extend to matters unrelated to the case. She normally may not introduce evidence that a witness for the plaintiff is a smoker or dislikes children, for example, unless she can demonstrate that such facts are relevant to the case.

In general, Cameron will try to uncover relevant physical infirmities of the plaintiff's witnesses (such as poor eyesight or hearing), as well as any evidence of bias (such as a witness's habit of playing a friendly round of golf with plaintiff Baranski every Saturday). Some questions that Cameron might ask Julia Williams, Gilmore's eyewitness, are presented in Exhibit 12.5 below.

Redirect and Recross

After defendant Peretto's attorney, Cameron, has finished cross-examining each witness, plaintiff Baranski's attorney, Gilmore, will try to repair any damage done to the credibility of the witness's testimony—or, indeed, to the case itself. Gilmore will do this by again questioning the witness and allowing the witness to explain his or her answer. This process is known as **redirect examination**.

If Cameron's cross-examination revealed that one of Gilmore's eyewitnesses to the accident had vision problems, for example, Gilmore could ask the witness whether he or she was wearing glasses or contact lenses at the time of the accident. Gilmore might also have the witness demonstrate to the court that he or she has good vision by having the witness identify a letter or object at the far end of the courtroom. Because redirect examination is primarily used to improve the credibility of cross-examined witnesses, it is limited to matters raised during cross-examination. (If Cameron chooses not to cross-examine a particular witness, then, of course, there can be no redirect examination by Gilmore.)

Following Gilmore's redirect examination, defendant Peretto's attorney, Cameron, will be given an opportunity for **recross-examination**. Gilmore would then have another opportunity for more direct examination and so on until both sides are done. When both attorneys have finished with the first witness, Gilmore will call the succeeding witnesses in plaintiff Baranski's case, each of whom will be subject to cross-examination (and redirect and recross, if necessary).

redirect examination
The questioning of a witness following the adverse party's cross-examination.

recross-examination
The questioning of an opposing witness following the adverse party's redirect examination.

EXHIBIT 12.5
Cross-Examination—Sample Questions

ATTORNEY:	You have just testified that you were approaching the intersection when the accident occurred. Isn't it true that you stated earlier, under oath, that you were at the intersection at the time of the accident?
WITNESS:	Well, I might have, but I think I said that I was close to the intersection.
ATTORNEY:	In fact, you said that you were at the intersection. Now, you say that you were approaching it. Which is it?
WITNESS:	I was approaching it, I suppose.
ATTORNEY:	Okay. Exactly where were you when the accident occurred?
WITNESS:	I think that I was just in front of the Dairy Queen when the accident happened.
ATTORNEY:	Mrs. Williams, the Dairy Queen on Mattis Avenue is at least seventy-five yards from the intersection of Mattis Avenue and Thirty-eighth Street. Is it your testimony today that you noticed the defendant's car from seventy-five yards away as it was approaching the intersection on Mattis Avenue?
WITNESS:	Well, no, I guess not.
ATTORNEY:	Isn't it true that there were a lot of other cars driving on the road that morning?
WITNESS:	Yes.
ATTORNEY:	And you had no reason to be paying particular attention to the defendant's car, did you?
WITNESS:	Not really.
ATTORNEY:	In fact, you did not see the defendant's car until after the collision occurred, did you, Mrs. Williams?

© Cengage Learning 2014

At trial, attorneys and paralegals must have close at hand all of the documents and information that they may need to refer to during the proceedings. Typically, these materials are contained in the trial notebook, which may consist of several binders. Increasingly, for complex litigation, attorneys and paralegals retrieve necessary documents from offline or online databases using laptop computers. When might it be preferable to have physical documents rather than scanned documents in a digital file?

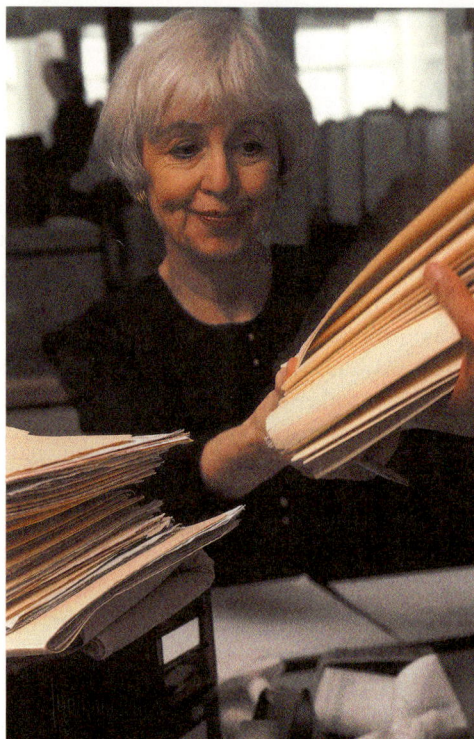

Courtesy of © PhotoDisc®

Motion for a Directed Verdict

motion for a directed verdict
A motion (also known as a *motion for judgment as a matter of law* in the federal courts) requesting that the court grant a judgment in favor of the party making the motion on the ground that the other party has not produced sufficient evidence to support his or her claim.

After attorney Gilmore has presented his case for plaintiff Baranski, then Cameron, as counsel for defendant Peretto, may decide to make a **motion for a directed verdict** (now also known as a *motion for judgment as a matter of law* in federal courts). Using this motion, Cameron will be arguing to the court that the plaintiff's attorney has not offered enough evidence to support a claim against Peretto. If the judge agrees and grants the motion, then judgment will be entered for Peretto, the case will be dismissed, and the trial will be over. A sample motion for judgment as a matter of law is shown in Exhibit 12.6 on the facing page.

The motion for a directed verdict (judgment as a matter of law) is seldom granted because only cases that involve genuine factual disputes are permitted to proceed to trial in the first place. If the judge had believed that Baranski's case was that weak before the trial started, then the judge would probably have granted a pretrial motion to dismiss the case, thereby avoiding the expense of a trial. Occasionally, however, the witnesses' testimony unexpectedly leaves a crucial element unproven. In that event, the court may grant the defendant's motion for a directed verdict, or judgment as a matter of law.

The Defendant's Case

Assuming that the motion for a directed verdict (motion for judgment as a matter of law) is denied by the court, the two attorneys, Gilmore and Cameron, now reverse their roles. Attorney Cameron begins to present evidence demonstrating the weaknesses of plaintiff Baranski's claims against defendant Peretto. She will essentially follow the same procedure used by Gilmore when he presented Baranski's side of the story. Cameron will call witnesses to the stand and question them. After Cameron's direct examination of each witness, that witness will be subject to possible cross-examination by Gilmore, redirect examination by Cameron, recross-examination by Gilmore, and so on.

In her presentation of the defendant's case, Cameron will attempt to counter the points made by Gilmore during his presentation. To that end, Cameron and

EXHIBIT 12.6
Motion for Judgment
as a Matter of Law

Elizabeth A. Cameron
Cameron & Strauss, P.C.
310 Lake Drive
Zero City, ZE 59802
(616) 955-6234

Attorney for Defendant

**UNITED STATES DISTRICT COURT
FOR THE WESTERN DISTRICT OF NITA**

Katherine Baranski   )
                 Plaintiff,)   CASE NO. 14-14335-NI
)   Honorable Harley M. Larue
v.   )
)
)   MOTION FOR JUDGMENT
Tony Peretto   )   AS A MATTER OF LAW
                 Defendant.)

The Defendant, Tony Peretto, at the close of the Plaintiff's case, moves the court to withdraw the evidence from the consideration of the jury and to find the Defendant not liable.

As grounds for this motion, Defendant Peretto states that:

(1) No evidence has been offered or received during the trial of the above-entitled cause of action to sustain the allegations of negligence contained in Plaintiff Baranski's complaint.

(2) No evidence has been offered or received during the trial proving or tending to prove that Defendant Peretto was guilty of any negligence.

(3) The proximate cause of Plaintiff Baranski's injuries was not due to any negligence on the part of Defendant Peretto.

(4) By the uncontroverted evidence, Plaintiff Baranski was guilty of contributory negligence, which was the sole cause of the Plaintiff's injuries.

Date: 7/21/14

Elizabeth A Cameron
Elizabeth A. Cameron
Attorney for the Defendant

© Cengage Learning 2014

her paralegal, Gordon McVay, may have to prepare exhibits and memoranda of law in addition to those originally prepared. The need to prepare additional exhibits and memoranda sometimes arises when the plaintiff's attorney pursues a strategy different from the one anticipated by the defense team. Depending on Cameron's preference or strategy, she may choose to begin by exposing weaknesses in the plaintiff's case (by asserting that the plaintiff was speeding, for example) or by presenting Peretto's version of the accident. In either case, paralegal McVay, like paralegal Lopez, will have to keep track of the materials brought to court each day.

Once Cameron has finished presenting her case, Gilmore will be permitted to offer evidence to *rebut* (refute) evidence introduced by Cameron in Peretto's behalf. After Gilmore's rebuttal, if any, both attorneys will make their closing arguments to the jury.

Closing Arguments

closing argument
The argument made by each side's attorney after the cases for the plaintiff and defendant have been presented. Closing arguments are made prior to the jury charge.

In their **closing arguments**, the attorneys summarize their presentations and argue in their clients' favor. A closing argument should include all of the major points that support the client's case. It should also emphasize the shortcomings of the opposing party's case. Jurors will view a closing argument with some skepticism if it merely recites the central points of a party's claim or defense without also responding to the unfavorable facts or issues raised by the other side. Of course, neither attorney wants to focus too much on the other side's position, but the elements of the opposing position do need to be acknowledged and their flaws highlighted.

Both attorneys will want to organize their presentations so they can explain their arguments and show the jury how their arguments are supported by the evidence. Once both attorneys have completed their remarks, the case will be submitted to the jury, and the attorneys' role in the trial will be finished.

Jury Instructions

charge
The judge's instruction to the jury setting forth the rules of law that the jury must apply in reaching its decision, or verdict.

Before the jurors begin their deliberations, the judge gives the jury a **charge**, in which the judge sums up the case and instructs the jurors on the rules of law that apply. (In some courts, jury instructions are given prior to closing arguments and may even be given at some other point during trial proceedings.) These often include definitions of legal terms relevant to the case and standard instructions on deliberations. In addition, the charge usually contains a request for findings of fact, typically phrased in an "if, then" format.

For example, in the portion of the charge presented in Exhibit 12.7 on the facing page, the jury is first asked to decide if the defendant was negligent. *If* the jury decides that the defendant was negligent, *then* the jury must decide whether the defendant's negligence caused the plaintiff's injuries. This format helps to channel the jurors' deliberations.

Each side typically submits a proposed charge to the court before the trial begins, and an attorney's trial strategy will likely be linked to the charges. The paralegal may draft proposed instructions for the attorney's review. There are useful standard form charges in most jurisdictions and both court opinions and your firm's case files may have helpful examples of language from similar cases. Because errors in the charge can lead an appellate court to reverse a judgment, it is critical to get the charge right. The judge, however, has the final decision as to what instructions will be submitted to the jury.

The Verdict

verdict
A formal decision made by a jury.

Following its receipt of the charge, the jury begins its deliberations. Once it has reached a decision, the jury issues a **verdict** in favor of one of the parties. If the jury finds a party owes damages on a claim or counterclaim, the jury will specify the amount to be paid to the other party. Following the announcement of the verdict, the jurors are discharged.

Usually, immediately after the verdict has been announced and the jurors discharged, the party in whose favor the verdict was issued makes a motion asking the judge to issue a *judgment*—which is the court's final word on the matter—consistent with the jury's verdict. For example, if the jury in the Baranski case finds that Peretto was negligent and awards Baranski damages in the amount of $85,000, the judge will order Peretto to pay the plaintiff that amount.

ON THE web

To find information on jury verdicts in assorted trials throughout the country, including the amount of damages awarded, go to **www.jvra.com**

Posttrial Motions and Procedures

Every trial must have a winner and a loser. Although civil litigation is an expensive and cumbersome process, the losing party may wish to pursue the matter further after the verdict.

The jury is requested to answer the following questions:

(1) Do you find by a preponderance of the evidence that the defendant was negligent?

Answer: (yes or no) _____

If your answer to question (1) is "yes," go on to question (2).
If your answer to question (1) is "no," stop here.

(2) Do you find by a preponderance of the evidence that the defendant's negligence was a proximate (direct) cause of the plaintiff's injuries?

Answer: (yes or no) _____

If your answer to question (2) is "yes," go on to question (3).
If your answer to question (2) is "no," stop here.

(3) Do you find that the plaintiff was negligent?

Answer: (yes or no) _____

If your answer to question (3) is "yes," go on to question (4).
If your answer to question (3) is "no," then skip down to question (6).

(4) Do you find that the plaintiff's negligence was a proximate (direct) cause of the accident and injuries that she suffered?

Answer: (yes or no) _____

If your answer is "yes," go on to question (5).
If your answer is "no," skip to question (6).

(5) Taking 100% as the total fault causing the accident and injuries, what percentage of the total fault causing the accident and injuries do you attribute to:

the defendant _____

the plaintiff _____

(If you find that a party has no fault in causing the accident, then attribute 0% of the fault to that party.)

(6) Disregarding any negligence or fault on the part of the plaintiff, what sum of money would reasonably compensate the plaintiff for her claimed injury and damage?

Answer: $ _____

EXHIBIT 12.7
Jury Charge—Request for Findings of Fact

case AT A GLANCE

The Plaintiff—
Plaintiff: Katherine Baranski
Attorney: Allen P. Gilmore
Paralegal: Elena Lopez

The Defendant—
Defendant: Tony Peretto
Attorney: Elizabeth A. Cameron
Paralegal: Gordon McVay

motion for judgment notwithstanding the verdict
A motion (also referred to as a *motion for judgment as a matter of law* in federal courts) requesting that the court grant judgment in favor of the party making the motion on the ground that the jury verdict against him or her was unreasonable or erroneous.

Assume that plaintiff Baranski wins at trial and is awarded $85,000 in damages. Cameron, as defendant Peretto's attorney, may file a posttrial motion or appeal the decision to a higher court. Note that even though Baranski won the case, she could also appeal the judgment. For example, she might appeal the case on the ground that she should have received $130,000 in damages instead of $85,000, arguing that the latter amount inadequately compensates her for the harms that she suffered as a result of Peretto's negligence.

Motions after the Trial

Assume that defendant Peretto's attorney, Cameron, believes that the verdict for plaintiff Baranski is not supported by the evidence. In this situation, she may file a **motion for judgment notwithstanding the verdict** (also known as a *motion for judgment as a matter of law* in the federal courts). By filing this motion, Cameron asks the judge to enter a judgment in favor of Peretto on the ground (basis) that the jury verdict in favor of Baranski was unreasonable and erroneous. Cameron may file this motion only if she previously filed a motion for a directed verdict (or judgment as a matter of law) during the trial. If she decides to file this motion, she must file it within ten days following the entry of judgment against Peretto.

Supporting Affidavit

Similar to virtually all motions in federal court, this motion must be accompanied by a supporting affidavit or a memorandum of law, or brief (these documents were discussed in Chapter 10). The judge will then determine whether the jury's verdict was reasonable in view of the evidence presented at trial. Such motions are rarely granted.

Motion for a New Trial

motion for a new trial

A motion asserting that the trial was so fundamentally flawed (because of error, newly discovered evidence, prejudice, or other reason) that a new trial is needed to prevent a miscarriage of justice.

Rule 50 of the Federal Rules of Civil Procedure permits either party to file a **motion for a new trial**. Such a motion may be submitted along with a motion for judgment notwithstanding the verdict. A motion for a new trial is a far more drastic tactic because it asserts that the trial was so pervaded by error or so otherwise fundamentally flawed that a new trial should be held. For a motion for a new trial to have a reasonable chance of being granted, the motion must allege such serious problems as jury misconduct, prejudicial jury instructions, excessive or inadequate damages, or the existence of newly discovered evidence (but not if the evidence could have been discovered earlier through the use of reasonable care).

Similar to other posttrial motions in federal courts, the motion for a new trial must be filed within ten days following the entry of the judgment. Exhibit 12.8 on the facing page illustrates a motion for judgment as a matter of law or, in the alternative, for a new trial.

Appealing the Verdict

appeal

The process of seeking a higher court's review of a lower court's decision for the purpose of correcting or changing the lower court's judgment or decision.

If attorney Cameron's posttrial motions are unsuccessful or if she decides not to file them, she may still file an **appeal**. The purpose of an appeal is to have the trial court's decision either reversed or modified by an appellate court. As discussed in Chapter 6, appellate courts, or courts of appeals, are *reviewing* courts, not trial courts. In other words, no new evidence will be presented to the appellate court, and there is no jury.

The appellate court will review the trial court's proceedings to decide whether the trial court erred in applying the law to the facts of the case, in instructing the jury, or in administering the trial generally. Appellate courts rarely tamper with a trial court's findings of fact because the judge and jury were in a better position than the appellate court to evaluate the credibility of witnesses, the nature of the evidence, and the like.

As grounds for the appeal, defendant Peretto's attorney, Cameron, might argue that the trial court erred in one of the ways mentioned in the preceding paragraph. Unless she believes that a reversal of the judgment is likely, however, she will probably advise Peretto not to appeal the case, as an appeal will simply add to the costs and expenses already incurred by Peretto in defending against Baranski's claim.

Notice of Appeal

appellant

The party who takes an appeal from one court to another; sometimes referred to as the *petitioner*.

appellee

The party against whom an appeal is taken—that is, the party who opposes setting aside or reversing the judgment; sometimes referred to as the *respondent*.

When the appeal involves a federal district court decision, as in the Baranski case, the **appellant** (the party appealing the decision) must file a notice of appeal with the district court that rendered the judgment. The clerk of the court then notifies the **appellee** (the party against whom the appeal is taken) as well as the court of appeals. The clerk also forwards to the appellate court a transcript of the trial court proceedings, along with any related pleadings and exhibits. These materials

EXHIBIT 12.8
Motion for Judgment as a
Matter of Law or for a New Trial

Elizabeth A. Cameron
Cameron & Strauss, P.C.
310 Lake Drive
Zero City, ZE 59802
(616) 955-6234

Attorney for Defendant

**UNITED STATES DISTRICT COURT
FOR THE WESTERN DISTRICT OF NITA**

Katherine Baranski   )   CASE NO. 14-14335-NI
                Plaintiff,   )   Honorable Harley M. Larue
)
v.   )
)   MOTION FOR JUDGMENT AS
)   A MATTER OF LAW OR, IN
)   THE ALTERNATIVE,
Tony Peretto   )   MOTION FOR A NEW TRIAL
                Defendant.   )

The Defendant, Tony Peretto, moves this Court, pursuant to Rule 50(b) of the Federal Rules of Civil Procedure, to set aside the verdict and judgment entered on August 15, 2014, and to enter instead a judgment for the Defendant as a matter of law. In the alternative, and in the event the Defendant's motion for judgment as a matter of law is denied, the Defendant moves the Court to order a new trial.

The grounds for this motion are set forth in the attached memorandum.

Date: 8/18/14

                                            Elizabeth A. Cameron
                                            Elizabeth A. Cameron
                                            Attorney for the Defendant

© Cengage Learning 2014

---

together constitute the **record on appeal**. Paralegals often play an important role in selecting the portions of the record to be used on appeal.

The Appellate Brief and Oral Arguments

When a case is appealed, the attorneys for both parties submit written *briefs* that present their positions on the issues to be reviewed by the appellate court. The briefs outline each party's view of the proper application of the law to the facts. In preparing the briefs, the attorneys will have to cite the relevant pages of the court records. Paralegals play a key role in indexing and summarizing the record to assist in the brief writing. These tasks are similar to the organization and summarizing of discovery materials done before trial.

After the appellate court has reviewed the briefs, the court usually sets a time for both attorneys to argue their positions before the panel of judges. The attorneys will then present their arguments and answer any questions that the judges might have. Generally, the attorneys' arguments before an appellate court are limited in terms of both the time allowed for argument and the scope of the argument. Following the oral arguments, the judges decide the matter and issue a formal written opinion, which normally is published in the relevant reporter (see Chapter 7 for a discussion of how court opinions are published).

record on appeal
The items submitted during the trial (pleadings, motions, briefs, and exhibits) and the transcript of the trial proceedings that are forwarded to the appellate court for review when a case is appealed.

The Appellate Court's Options

Once they have reviewed the record and heard oral arguments, if any, the judges have several options. For example, in the Baranski case, if the appellate court decided to uphold the trial court's decision, then the judgment for Baranski would be **affirmed**. If the judges decided to **reverse** the trial court's decision, however, then Peretto would no longer be obligated to pay the damages awarded to Baranski by the trial court. The court might also affirm or reverse a decision *in part*. For example, the judges might affirm the jury's finding that Peretto was negligent but **remand** the case—that is, send it back to the trial court—for further proceedings on another issue (such as the extent of Baranski's damages). An appellate court can also *modify* a lower court's decision. If, for example, the appellate court decided that the jury awarded an excessive amount in damages, the appellate court might reduce the award.

The decision of the appellate court may sometimes be appealed further. A state intermediate appellate court's decision, for example, may be appealed to the state supreme court. A federal appellate court's decision may be appealed to the United States Supreme Court. It will be up to these higher courts to decide whether they will review the case. In other words, these courts normally are not *required* to review cases. Recall from Chapter 6 that although thousands of cases are submitted to the United States Supreme Court each year, it hears fewer than ninety. (An action decided in a state court has a somewhat greater chance of being reviewed by the state supreme court.)

Enforcing the Judgment

The uncertainties of the litigation process are compounded by the lack of guarantees that any judgment will be enforceable. *Developing Paralegal Skills* on the facing page discusses this practical problem. It is one thing to have a court enter a judgment in your favor; it is another to collect the funds to which you are entitled from the opposing party. Even if the jury awarded Baranski the full amount of damages requested ($130,000), for example, she might not, in fact, "win" anything at all. Peretto's auto insurance coverage might have lapsed, in which event the company would not cover any of the damages. Alternatively, Peretto's insurance coverage might be limited to $30,000, meaning that Peretto would have to pay the remaining $100,000 personally.

If Peretto did not have that amount available, then Baranski would need to go back to court and request that the court issue a **writ of execution**—an order, usually issued by the clerk of the court, directing the sheriff to seize (take temporary ownership of) and sell Peretto's assets. The proceeds of the sale would then be used to pay the damages owed to Baranski. Any excess proceeds of the sale would be returned to Peretto.

Judgment Creditor

Even as a **judgment creditor** (one who has obtained a court judgment against a debtor), Baranski may not be able to obtain the full amount of the judgment from Peretto. Laws protecting debtors provide that certain property (such as a debtor's home up to a specific value and tools used by the debtor in his or her trade) is *exempt* from seizure. Exempt property cannot be seized and sold to pay debts owed to judgment creditors.

Similar exemptions would apply if Peretto declared bankruptcy. Thus, even though Baranski won at trial, she, like many others who are awarded damages, might not be able to collect what she is owed. Realize, though, that judgments constitute liens (legal claims) for significant time periods. If the financial circumstances of the debtor—such as Peretto—change in the future, recovery may be possible. There are many roles for paralegals in collecting judgments, including

---

affirm
To uphold the judgment of a lower court.

reverse
To overturn the judgment of a lower court.

remand
To send a case back to a lower court for further proceedings.

writ of execution
A writ that puts in force a court's decree or judgment.

judgment creditor
A creditor who is legally entitled, by a court's judgment, to collect the amount of the judgment from a debtor.

DEVELOPING
paralegal skills

LOCATING ASSETS

Paralegal Myra Cullen works for a firm that represented Jennifer Roth in a lawsuit brought against Best Eatery, a restaurant. Roth won $100,000 in a lawsuit for damages she suffered when she fell and broke her leg in the restaurant's lobby on a rainy morning. Best Eatery's insurance coverage is a small liability policy that will only pay a portion of Roth's award.

Myra has been assigned the task of investigating Best Eatery's assets to determine how the judgment can be collected. Myra learned through pretrial discovery that John Dobman owns Best Eatery as a sole proprietor, which means that he is personally liable for the debts of the business. Myra contacts the county register of deeds to research the value of the property on which Best Eatery is located and any other property owned by John Dobman. In Myra's county, the county clerk's deed records can be searched via the Internet. She knows, however, that after conducting an online search she will need to verify the information obtained. She therefore writes down the document numbers provided online so that she can quickly access the information at the clerk's office.

Myra determines that Dobman's equity (market value minus mortgage outstanding) in the property on which Best Eatery is located is at least $200,000, which could cover any shortfall in the damages. Because the equity in the restaurant is sufficient to cover the award, Myra simply notes the record number of Dobman's other real property (his house) in the client's file.

TIPS FOR LOCATING ASSETS

- Ask what property the defendant owns during discovery, such as in interrogatories.
- Locate the address of the property (you can do this on the Internet).
- Go to the register of deeds (usually online) to learn about any liens filed against the property and the amount of any mortgage loan.
- Check with a real estate agent or an appraiser as to the market value of the property. Tax appraisal values can be accessed online.
- Deduct the liens and the mortgage debt from the market value to determine the defendant's equity.

researching defendants' assets, filing liens, and so on. Many of the same skills used in pretrial investigations are useful here.

Social Media Tools at Work

The difficulty of enforcing court judgments, coupled with the high costs accompanying litigation (including attorneys' fees, court costs, and the litigants' time costs), is a major reason why most disputes are settled out of court, either before or during the trial.

Enforcing judgments is another area where a paralegal's social media skills can pay dividends. Use search engines and other tools to look for social media postings that make reference to valuable assets. Does a judgment debtor have pictures on his or her Facebook page showing expensive jewelry? Has he or she sent tweets about using a new boat or vacation home? People often reveal important clues about their lifestyles in social settings that can help locate assets that could be used to satisfy a judgment.

Judgment debtors' digital shadows may be a useful source of information for developing questions that can be used in a postverdict deposition taken in the search for assets. Be sure to check out their spouses, children, and other relatives as well. If a husband or wife tweets about the generous gift he or she received just before trial, the asset may be able to be recaptured through collection proceedings.

Finally, the *Featured Contributor* reminds us, on pages 384 and 385, of the roles the paralegal plays in the litigation process.

social
MEDIA TODAY

Be careful about sharing passwords or access to your computer. One young professional discovered her ex-boyfriend had installed a keyboard logger on her computer. He had access to all her e-mail and social media accounts. He sent insulting e-mails from her account to her coworkers.

Featured Contributor

THE COMPLEX ROLES IN LITIGATION

Regina G. Dowling, Esq.

BIOGRAPHICAL NOTE

Regina G. Dowling serves the Paralegal Studies Program at the University of Hartford in Connecticut as both director and instructor. She received her law degree from Villanova University. She is co-chair of the Paralegals Committee of the Connecticut Bar Association and a member of the Committee on Insurance Programs for the Bar of the Connecticut Bar Association.

Ms. Dowling has been a member of the greater Hartford legal community for over 20 years, beginning her career as a litigation paralegal in a major Hartford law firm where she specialized in large-case management. As an attorney, she focuses on the representation of regulated industrial, financial, and commercial establishments, as well as a small number of citizen plaintiffs in state and federal court, especially in environmental law.

© Cengage Learning 2014

CIVIL LITIGATION

While litigators are often viewed poorly, litigation plays an important role in our society. It is the method by which disputes are settled in a civilized manner.

When parties cannot resolve a dispute on their own, they take it to the courthouse. A trier of fact (jury) and a trier of law (judge) apply precedent to the facts of the matter and reach a decision that is consistent with prior decisions that are similar unless there is a substantive reason for not applying precedent. As citizens and practitioners, we know (or are able to determine) what the law is—what the consequence for a specified behavior is or what the compensation is for an injury.

PRACTICE

Civil litigation requires patience, an appreciation of strategy, and attention to detail. The litigation process is about strategy: which parties will be sued, in which court, and under which causes of action. Each of those decisions is strategic. The plaintiff must determine whether to file the complaint in state court or federal court, and must analyze the benefits

KEY TERMS AND CONCEPTS

affirm   382

appeal   380

appellant   380

appellee   380

challenge   370

challenge for cause   370

charge   378

closing argument   378

cross-examination   374

direct examination   373

judgment creditor   382

motion for a directed verdict   376

motion for a new trial   380

motion for judgment notwithstanding the verdict   379

motion *in limine*   367

opening statement   373

peremptory challenge   370

pretrial conference   367

record on appeal   381

recross-examination   375

redirect examination   375

remand   382

reverse   382

trial notebook   366

verdict   378

voir dire   369

writ of execution   382

and detriments of filing in each court, and ultimately select the one that is most beneficial to the matter.

Once discovery is entered, consideration is given as to which discovery tools will be used. Tools are selected on the basis of which will yield the most valuable results. Cost may also be a criterion. Depositions are expensive and a client may not be able to afford them; we must determine how else to best obtain the information needed. When faced with a request to produce documents, the scale of the request must be determined, as it possibly could range from millions of pages to a single document.

There is an art to drafting interrogatories, requests for production, and requests for admission. The key is what information is needed to prove the plaintiff's cause of action, or to break down the plaintiff's case (as a defendant). All reports, statements, tests, and documents must be reviewed to ascertain what facts are known and what evidence is needed to meet the burden of proof. Once that determination is made, the interrogatories, requests for production, or requests for admission are crafted narrowly and precisely to elicit the necessary information. Discovery is like a large puzzle. Each party has some pieces, but needs more to determine what the picture is. As the picture is developed, a party may realize that its case is not as strong as it first appeared, and settlement may be desirable.

Preparing for trial can be daunting. A good paralegal has the ability to organize the documents and create a trial notebook for the attorney's use during trial. The notebook contains the important documents and pleadings that have been filed during the course of the litigation, among other documents.

The value of a paralegal in litigation does not end with the preparation for trial. A paralegal plays a significant role during the trial as well and may operate electronic media that are used to present exhibits to the jury. Most likely, the paralegal created the product that is viewed by the jury. The days of bringing a trifold display or an enlarged copy of a document are gone; we use electronic methods. A paralegal may also be charged with note taking during the testimony of witnesses, in preparation for cross-examination or rebuttal. The paralegal may also watch jurors during testimony to try to read their expressions.

PARALEGAL'S ROLE

A successful litigation paralegal is highly motivated, pays attention to detail, possesses strong written and oral skills, is curious, and is competent with technology.

The litigation paralegal is invaluable to the attorney. One may undertake many tasks under the supervision of an attorney. Aside from providing legal advice to the client, signing documents that require an attorney's signature, appearing in court, and asking questions at a deposition, the paralegal can do most any other litigation task. From conducting research on the causes of action to drafting the complaint to assembling the trial notebook, the paralegal is an important and invaluable member of the litigation team.

"Discovery is like a large puzzle."

Chapter Summary

Trial Procedures

PREPARING FOR TRIAL

Before the trial, attorneys for both sides and their paralegals gather and organize evidence, documents, and other materials relating to the case. It is helpful to create a checklist to ensure that nothing is overlooked during this stage.

1. *Contacting and preparing witnesses*—Paralegals often assist in contacting and issuing subpoenas to witnesses, as well as in preparing witnesses for trial.

2. *Exhibits and displays*—Paralegals assume responsibility for making sure that all exhibits and displays are ready by trial; technology in this area is changing rapidly.

3. *Trial notebook*—A comprehensive trial notebook is critical when preparing for trial and at trial, and often afterward. Paralegals are responsible for obtaining and organizing copies of all relevant documents.

PRETRIAL CONFERENCE

Before trial, the attorneys for both sides meet with the trial judge in a pretrial conference to decide whether a settlement is possible or, if not, to decide how the trial will be conducted and what types of evidence will be admis-sible. It is not uncommon for one or both of the attorneys to make a motion *in limine,* which asks the court to keep certain evidence from being offered at the trial.

JURY SELECTION

1. Voir dire—During the *voir dire* process, attorneys for both sides question potential jurors to determine whether any potential jurors should be excluded from the jury.

2. *Challenges during* voir dire—Attorneys for both sides can exercise an unlimited number of challenges for cause on the basis of prospective jurors' bias against the client or case. Both attorneys can exercise a lim-ited number of peremptory challenges without giv-ing any reason to the court for excluding a potential juror.

3. *Paralegals' role during* voir dire—Paralegals may help prepare jury profiles and often observe prospective jurors to gain insights into the potential jurors' views of the case.

4. *Alternate jurors*—In case of illness or other problem during a trial, an alternate juror may be called to step in so the trial may proceed.

THE TRIAL

Once the jury has been selected and seated, the trial begins. The paralegal, if he or she attends the trial, coor-dinates witnesses' appearances, tracks the testimony of witnesses and compares it with sworn statements that the witnesses made before the trial, and provides the attorney with appropriate reminders or documents when necessary.

1. *Opening statements*—The trial begins with opening statements in which the attorneys briefly outline their versions of the facts of the case and the evidence they will offer to support their views.

2. *Plaintiff's case*—Following the attorneys' opening statements, the plaintiff's attorney presents evidence supporting the plaintiff's claims, including the testi-mony of witnesses.

   a. The attorney's questioning of a witness whom he or she calls is referred to as direct examination.

   b. Following direct examination by the plaintiff's attorney, the defendant's attorney may cross-examine the witness.

   c. If the witness was cross-examined, the plaintiff's attorney may question the witness on redirect examination, after which the defendant's attorney may question the witness on recross-examination.

3. *Motion for a directed verdict*—After the plaintiff's attorney has presented his or her client's case, the defendant's attorney may make a motion for a directed verdict, also called a motion for judgment as a matter of law. This motion asserts that the plain-tiff has not offered enough evidence to support the plaintiff's claim against the defendant. If the judge grants the motion, the case will be dismissed.

4. *Defendant's case*—The attorneys then reverse their roles, and the defendant's attorney presents evidence and testimony to refute the plaintiff's claims. Any wit-nesses called to the stand by the defendant's attorney will be subject to direct examination by that attorney, cross-examination by the plaintiff's attorney, and pos-sible redirect examination and recross-examination.

5. *Closing arguments*—After the defendant's attorney has finished his or her presentation, both attorneys give their closing arguments. A closing argument summarizes all the major points that support the cli-ent's case and emphasizes shortcomings in the oppos-ing party's case.

6. *Jury instructions*—Following the attorneys' closing arguments (or, in some courts, at some other point in the proceedings), the judge instructs the jury in a charge—a document that includes statements of the applicable law and a review of the facts as they were presented during the trial. The jury must not disregard the judge's instructions as to what the applicable law is and how it should be applied to the facts of the case as interpreted by the jury.

7. *Verdict*—Once the jury reaches a decision, it issues a verdict in favor of one of the parties and is dis-charged. The court then enters a judgment.

POSTTRIAL MOTIONS AND PROCEDURES

After the verdict has been pronounced and the trial concluded, the losing party's attorney may file a posttrial motion or an appeal.

1. *Posttrial motions*—A motion for judgment notwithstanding the verdict (also called a motion for judgment as a matter of law) asks the judge to enter a judgment in favor of the losing party in spite of the verdict because the verdict was not supported by the evidence or was otherwise in error. A motion for a new trial asserts that the trial was so flawed—by judge or juror misconduct or other pervasive errors—that a new trial should be held.

2. *Appealing the verdict*—The attorney may, depending on the client's wishes, appeal the decision to an appellate court for review. Appeals are usually filed only when the attorney believes that a reversal of the judgment is likely.

   a. If an appeal is pursued, the appellant must file a notice of appeal with the court that rendered the judgment. Then the clerk will forward the record on appeal to the appropriate reviewing court.

   b. The parties then file appellate briefs arguing their positions. Later, they are given the opportunity to present oral arguments before the appellate panel.

   c. The appellate court decides whether to affirm, reverse, remand, or modify the trial court's judgment.

   d. The appellate court's decision may sometimes be appealed further (to the state supreme court, for example).

ENFORCING THE JUDGMENT

Even though a plaintiff wins a lawsuit for damages, it may be difficult to enforce the judgment against the defendant, particularly if the defendant has few assets. The paralegal is often involved in locating assets so that the attorney can request a writ of execution (court order to seize property) in an attempt to collect the amount the client is owed.

QUESTIONS FOR REVIEW

1. What role does the paralegal play in pretrial preparation of witnesses, exhibits, and displays for trial? How are the trial notebooks prepared?

2. Describe the juror selection process. What is the difference between a peremptory challenge and a challenge for cause?

3. What are the different steps or phases of a trial? How are witnesses examined during trial? List the different types of examination that witnesses may go through. What is the difference between direct examination and cross-examination? Define "jury charge."

4. Describe the procedure for filing an appeal. What factors does an attorney consider when deciding whether a case should be appealed? Can the jury decide matters of law?

5. What is a writ of execution? What is a judgment creditor?

ETHICAL QUESTIONS

1. Anthony Paletti, a paralegal, is attending a trial with his supervising attorney. Anthony leaves the courtroom to meet a witness. On his way down the hall, he runs into the defendant in the case. The defendant says to Anthony, "You work for the plaintiff's attorney, don't you? I have a question for you about that contract that your attorney offered into evidence." Should Anthony answer the defendant's question? Why or why not?

2. During the course of a products liability trial, a juror consulted the Web site **www.howstuffworks.com** to

better understand components in the piece of equipment involved in the case. Aaron, a paralegal for the defense attorney, overheard two jurors discussing the information as they left the jury box. The information that the juror had learned would be beneficial to the defendant, whom Aaron's boss is defending in the case. What should Aaron do in this situation?

PRACTICE QUESTIONS AND ASSIGNMENTS

1. Using the material from this chapter, identify the different phases of a trial in the hypothetical situations below:

   a. The plaintiff's attorney asks the witness, "Mrs. Wong, could you explain what you observed at the scene of the accident on January 17, 2014?"

   b. The defense attorney makes a motion saying that the plaintiff's attorney has not offered enough evidence to support a claim against the defendant.

   c. The defense attorney asks the witness, "Mr. Bashara, isn't it true that you were drinking alcohol immediately before you were involved in the car accident?"

   d. The plaintiff's attorney gives her version of the facts and supporting evidence that she will use to prove her case during the trial.

2. Paralegal Patricia Smith is assisting her supervising attorney, who has received a trial date for an auto accident case. The trial is set to begin in ten weeks. Discovery has been completed in the case. The depositions of the plaintiff and defendant have been taken, along with those of two eyewitnesses plus a police officer and Dr. Black, the plaintiff's physician. Additionally, the plaintiff and the defendant have answered interrogatories. Patricia's firm represents the plaintiff, and her supervising attorney plans to call not only the client but also the defendant, an eyewitness (Mr. Sams), and the police officer to testify. All of the witnesses are local. The case file contains police reports, newspaper articles about the accident, and medical records in addition to the deposition and interrogatory materials. Using the material presented in Exhibit 12.1 on page 362, *Trial-Preparation Checklist*, prepare a checklist for Patricia to complete.

3. Using Exhibit 12.2 on page 364, draft a subpoena for a friendly witness using the following facts:

   Simon Kolstad, whose address is 100 Schoolcraft Road, Del Mar, California, is a witness to be subpoenaed in *Sumner v. Hayes*, a civil lawsuit filed in the U.S. District Court for the Eastern District of Michigan, case number 13–123492. He is being subpoenaed by the plaintiff's attorney, Marvin W. Green, whose office is located at 300 Penobscot Building, 705 Premier Ave., Detroit, Michigan. Kolstad is to appear in room number 6 of the courthouse, which is located at 231 Lafayette Boulevard, Detroit, Michigan, at 2:30 P.M. on January 10, 2014.

4. Indicate what action the appellate court has taken in each hypothetical below (affirmed, modified, or reversed the trial court's decision or remanded the case for further proceedings):

   a. A trial court finds for the plaintiff in the amount of $150,000 in a case in which the plaintiff slipped and fell in a grocery store. The court of appeals finds that while the plaintiff is entitled to damages, the damages awarded by the jury are excessive. The appellate court sends the case back to the trial court for reevaluation of the amount of damages awarded.

   b. A trial court finds that the plaintiff was slandered by the defendant. On appeal, the court of appeals finds that the trial court admitted evidence that it should not have allowed and holds that without this evidence, there was no slander.

   c. A trial court finds that the defendant breached a contract and owes the plaintiff $1,000,000 in damages. The defendant appeals, claiming that the damages are not supported by the evidence. The court of appeals agrees with the trial court's decision.

QUESTIONS FOR CRITICAL ANALYSIS

1. Why are all witnesses—even friendly witnesses—called to appear at a trial typically served with subpoenas? What might happen if they were not subpoenaed? How can the service of subpoenas be handled with friendly witnesses so that they are not offended?

2. Why is so much preparation and organization done before a trial, such as preparing witnesses and trial notebooks, drafting questions, and creating exhibits and displays? What impact do these preparations have on a jury? What impact would (or do) disorganization and lack of preparation have on a jury?

3. Are leading questions allowed during direct examination? If so, when? Why are leading questions allowed during cross-examination? Is the use of leading questions fair to the witness being cross-examined?

4. How is a judgment paid when there is no insurance or other cash assets available to pay the judgment? Is all of a defendant's property subject to the judgment? If not, what property is exempt? Is it fair to the plaintiff not to have all of the defendant's property be subject to the judgment? Would your answer change if the plaintiff had become a paraplegic as a result of the defendant's drunk driving?

PROJECTS

1. Look up your state's court rules and find out how many challenges for cause are allowed during *voir dire*. How many peremptory challenges are permitted during *voir dire*?

2. Find a civil trial in a local court and observe the proceedings for two to three hours. Write a summary of what you learned and observed, including the phase of the trial, the types of evidence being presented, and any motions made. Be sure to include the name of the court you visited, the date, and the judge's name.

3. Draft jury instructions informing the jurors that they may not use Twitter or other forms of social media to communicate about the trial. Also, include an instruction not to conduct any research about the case on the Internet or through other means. You may wish to refer to actual court rules that prohibit the use of these forms of communication by jurors.

GROUP PROJECT

The group should research how a paralegal might use social media sites to find information about jurors.

Student one will use online sources (and library sources, if necessary) to find out what kinds of information are available online about potential jurors. Student one should summarize how this information could be used during *voir dire*.

Students two and three will research whether investigation of this nature is ethical, and if so, under what circumstances it might become unethical.

Student four will create a wiki to share the group's results with the rest of the class.

USING INTERNET RESOURCES

1. Go to the Jury Research Institute Web site at **www.juryresearchinstitute.com** and browse through the Web site.

   a. Write a one-page summary of the services that each company provides.

   b. Go to "Browse our Experience," click on "Notable Cases," and review the verdicts. After doing so, do you think that it is worthwhile to hire a jury consultant? From the information found in "Notable Cases," who tends to hire jury consultants?

END NOTES

1. Pronounced in *lim*-uh-nay.

2. Pronounced vwahr *deer*. These old French words mean "to speak the truth." In legal language, the phrase refers to the process of questioning jurors to learn about their backgrounds, attitudes, and similar attributes.

CourseMate The available CourseMate for this text has an interactive eBook and interactive learning tools, including flash cards, quizzes, and more. To learn more about this resource and access free demo CourseMate resources, go to **www.cengagebrain.com**, and search for this book. To access CourseMate materials that you have purchased, go to **login.cengagebrain.com**.

13

Criminal Law and Procedures

Chapter Outline

After completing this chapter, you will know:

- The difference between crimes and other wrongful acts.

- The two elements that are required for criminal liability and some of the most common defenses that are raised in defending against criminal charges.

- Major categories of crimes and some common types of crimes.

- The constitutional rights of persons accused of crimes.

- The basic steps involved in criminal procedure from the time a crime is reported to the resolution of the case.

- How and why criminal litigation procedures differ from civil litigation procedures.

Introduction

Each year, more than 10 million people are arrested on criminal charges and enter the criminal justice system. Therefore, it is no wonder that many attorneys and paralegals work on criminal law cases. In fact, about one in every five paralegals spends most of her or his work time on criminal law.

Criminal cases are prosecuted by **public prosecutors**, who are employed by the government. The chief public prosecutor in federal criminal cases is called a U.S. attorney. Most trials are conducted by assistant U.S. attorneys. In cases tried in state or local courts, the public prosecutor may be referred to as a *prosecuting attorney, state prosecutor, district attorney, county attorney,* or *city attorney*. Defendants in criminal cases may hire private attorneys to defend them. If a defendant cannot afford to hire an attorney, the court will appoint one for him or her. Everyone accused of a crime that may result in a jail sentence has a right to counsel, and this right is ensured by court-appointed attorneys. Some court-appointed defense lawyers work for organizations funded by the states. These are usually called **public defenders**. Others are private attorneys appointed to represent a particular defendant.

In this chapter, we provide an overview of criminal law and procedure. We begin by explaining the nature of crime and the key differences between criminal law and civil law. We then discuss the elements of criminal liability and some of the many types of crime. Throughout the chapter, we emphasize the constitutional protections that come into play when a person is accused of a crime, and focus on how and why criminal procedures differ from civil procedures. As the *Featured Contributor* notes on the following two pages, paralegals need certain talents to be effective in the criminal justice arena.

public prosecutor
An individual, acting as a trial lawyer, who initiates and conducts criminal cases in the government's name and on behalf of the people.

public defender
Court-appointed defense counsel. A lawyer appointed by the court to represent a criminal defendant who is unable to pay to hire private counsel.

What Is a Crime?

What is a crime? To answer that question, we begin by distinguishing crimes from other wrongs, such as torts—and, hence, criminal law from tort, or civil, law. Major differences between civil law and criminal law are summarized in Exhibit 13.1 on page 394. After discussing these differences, we explain how one act can qualify as both a crime and a tort. We then describe classifications of crimes and jurisdiction over criminal acts.

Key Differences between Civil Law and Criminal Law

A **crime** can be distinguished from other wrongful acts, such as torts, in that a crime is an *offense against society as a whole*. Criminal defendants are prosecuted by public officials on behalf of the state, as mentioned above, not by their victims or other private parties. In practice, however, the cooperation of the victim is usually important. The prosecutor can file criminal charges even if the victim does not wish to cooperate, but that makes a successful prosecution less likely. In addition, those who have committed crimes are subject to penalties, including fines, imprisonment, and, in some cases, death.

crime
A broad term for violations of law that are punishable by the state and are codified by legislatures. The objective of criminal law is to protect the public.

As will be discussed in Chapter 14, tort remedies—remedies for civil wrongs—are generally intended to compensate the injured party (by awarding money damages, for example). Criminal law, however, is concerned with punishing the wrongdoer in an attempt to deter others from similar actions.

Statutory Basis

Another factor distinguishing criminal law from tort law is that criminal law is primarily statutory law. Essentially, a crime is whatever a legislature has declared to be a crime. Although federal crimes are defined by the U.S. Congress, most crimes are defined by state legislatures.

Featured Contributor

PARALEGALS AND CRIMINAL LITIGATION

Steven C. Kempisty, Esq.

BIOGRAPHICAL NOTE

Steven Kempisty is a graduate of the State University of New York at Fredonia and the Massachusetts School of Law at Andover. A licensed attorney, he joined Bryant & Stratton College in 1999 and has served as program director for the two-year paralegal program at the Liverpool, New York, campus since 2009. Mr. Kempisty also is a member of the Financial Industry Regulatory Authority (FINRA), where he is an arbitration panelist. His main fields of interest are contract and corporations work.

© Cengage Learning 2014

One of the most important things I tell new students is: "*Law & Order* is a nice program; please understand that it is fiction. The practice of law, especially criminal law and procedure, is not how Hollywood portrays it."

Our legal system can be very complex and cumbersome. The criminal court system often has "logjammed" dockets. Criminal law professionals are often overworked and may have more cases than can be handled by even the most skilled individual. Three important rules for those who wish to become part of the legal profession are: be available, be organized, and be prepared.

BE AVAILABLE

Criminal law provides vital protections to the accused. Government officials take their jobs seriously, and skilled defense attorneys are just as committed as they represent their clients. Being available could mean doing anything from:

1. Reviewing files.
2. Reading old affidavits over and looking at all information.
3. Reading and organizing deposition statements.
4. Looking over police reports.
5. Looking over many different records that may be germane to a case, ranging from old tax records to old indictments.
6. Answering the phone.
7. Rereading the initial interview of a client.

Standards of Proof

The standards of proof required in criminal and civil cases are another difference. Because the state has extensive resources at its disposal when prosecuting criminal cases, there are procedural safeguards to protect the rights of defendants. One of these safeguards is the higher standard of proof that applies in a criminal case. In a civil case, the plaintiff usually must prove his or her case by a *preponderance of the evidence*. Under this standard, the plaintiff must convince the court that, based on the evidence presented by both parties, it is more likely than not that the plaintiff's allegation is true.

In a criminal case, in contrast, the state must prove its case **beyond a reasonable doubt**—that is, normally every juror in a criminal case must be convinced, beyond a reasonable doubt, of the defendant's guilt. The higher standard of proof in criminal cases reflects a fundamental social value—a belief that it is worse to convict an innocent individual than to let a guilty person go free. We will look at other safeguards later in the chapter, in the context of criminal procedure.

beyond a reasonable doubt
The standard used to determine the guilt or innocence of a person charged with a crime. To be guilty of a crime, a suspect must be proved guilty "beyond and to the exclusion of every reasonable doubt."

8. Reviewing numerous pages of statutes, cases, and footnotes.

9. Researching on Westlaw or Lexis.

Some of these tasks may seem mundane, but finding information that is helpful to a case, whether for a prosecutor or defense counsel, is important.

Being available to weed through and organize endless paperwork is hugely valuable to a legal team. It needs to be done. Being available to complete this task, although it appears thankless, will be valued and appreciated.

BE ORGANIZED

Organization is never overrated. Every legal textbook will mention the importance of discovery, document production, and organizing information. Becoming organized is especially important for deposition testimony, for material evidence that may be challenged under hearsay rules, and for keeping the order of your case flowing logically so as to best represent your side in an issue.

Colleagues have told me more than once that they missed an opportunity at some point in a case simply because they were not organized on a particular issue of evidence or procedure. Work together on the organization of a file and case so as to avoid confusion among the team members. The fundamental importance of organization on a legal team is everyone understanding the system and the legal team's goals.

BE PREPARED

Being prepared would appear to be common sense. What I mean is, be prepared for the unexpected since we must "expect the unexpected." With evidentiary disclosure there should never be any surprises or cliff-hanging elements of a case that magically appear the day of trial. Witnesses get cold feet, unorganized people lose important documents, people leave, and subpoenas are defied.

During the many hours that a legal team puts into a case, there can be shifts. When a curveball is thrown, one must seek assistance, seek a continuance or adjournment, but remain calm and carry on. There is no such thing as the perfect plan in law, but being prepared for all problems means they can be handled properly. Panicking will not get the job done.

CONCLUSION

In my very first case I had a client who did not speak English. I had to hire an interpreter for myself and for court appearances with the client. One time the interpreter was late. I was in a panic. A veteran colleague of mine was in court and talked me through the problem. I had forgotten that the client could read and write some in English, so we could progress. My interpreter eventually showed up and we proceeded. My colleague taught me a valuable lesson: Remain focused and calm. To do so, we must be organized and prepared with all relevant information to assist our clients properly.

"The practice of law, especially criminal law and procedure, is not how Hollywood portrays it."

Victimless Crimes

Yet another factor that distinguishes criminal law from tort law is the fact that a criminal act does not necessarily involve a victim, in the sense that the act directly and physically harms another. If Marissa grows marijuana in her backyard for her personal use, she may not be physically or directly harming another's interests, but she is nonetheless committing a crime (in most states and under federal law). Why? Because she is violating a rule of society that has been enacted into law by elected representatives of the people.

Civil Liability for Criminal Acts

Note that those who commit crimes may be subject to both civil and criminal liability. For example, suppose Joe is walking down the street, minding his own business, when suddenly a person attacks him. In the struggle, the attacker stabs Joe several times, seriously injuring him. A police officer restrains and arrests the wrongdoer.

EXHIBIT 13.1
Civil Law and
Criminal Law Compared

Issue	Under Civil Law	Under Criminal Law
Area of concern	Rights and duties between individuals and between persons and government	Offenses against society as a whole
Wrongful act	Harm to a person or to a person's property	Violation of a statute that prohibits a certain activity
Party who brings suit	Person who suffered harm	The state
Standard of proof	Preponderance of the evidence	Beyond a reasonable doubt
Remedy	Damages to compensate for the harm or a decree to achieve an equitable result	Punishment (fine, removal from public office, imprisonment, or death)

In separate legal actions, the attacker may be subject both to criminal prosecution by the state and to a tort (civil) lawsuit brought by Joe. Exhibit 13.2 on the facing page illustrates how the same act can result in both a tort action and a criminal action against the wrongdoer.

Classifications of Crimes

Crimes are generally divided into two broad classifications: felonies and misdemeanors.

Felonies

felony
A crime—such as arson, murder, assault, or robbery—that carries the most severe sanctions. Sanctions range from one year in a state or federal prison to life imprisonment or (in some states) the death penalty.

A **felony** is a serious crime that may be punished by imprisonment for more than one year. In some states, certain felonies are punishable by death. Examples of felonies include murder, rape, robbery, arson, and grand larceny. (You will read more about these and other crimes later in the chapter.)

Felonies are commonly classified by degree. The Model Penal Code,[1] for example, provides for four degrees of felony:

1. *capital offenses,* for which the maximum penalty is death,
2. *first degree felonies,* punishable by a maximum penalty of life imprisonment,
3. *second degree felonies,* punishable by a maximum of ten years' imprisonment, and
4. *third degree felonies,* punishable by up to five years' imprisonment.

Misdemeanors

misdemeanor
A crime less serious than a felony, punishable by a fine or incarceration for up to one year in jail (not a state or federal penitentiary).

A **misdemeanor** is a crime that may be punished by incarceration for not more than one year. If incarcerated, the guilty party goes to a local jail instead of prison. A misdemeanor, by definition, is not a serious crime. Under federal law and in most states, a misdemeanor is any crime that is not defined by law as a felony. State legislatures specify what crimes are classified as felonies or misdemeanors and what the potential punishment for each type of criminal act may be. Examples of misdemeanors include prostitution, disturbing the peace, and public intoxication.

Petty Offenses

petty offense
In criminal law, the least serious kind of wrong, such as a traffic or building-code violation.

Certain types of criminal or quasi-criminal actions, such as violations of building codes, are termed **petty offenses**, or *infractions*. In most jurisdictions, such actions are considered a subset of misdemeanors. Some states, however, classify them separately.

Jurisdiction over Crimes

Most crimes are defined in state statutes, and the states have jurisdiction in cases involving these crimes. Federal jurisdiction extends to thousands of crimes. If a federal law defines a certain action as a crime, federal jurisdiction exists. Generally, federal criminal jurisdiction applies to crimes that:

EXHIBIT 13.2
Tort (Civil) Lawsuit and Criminal
Prosecution for the Same Act

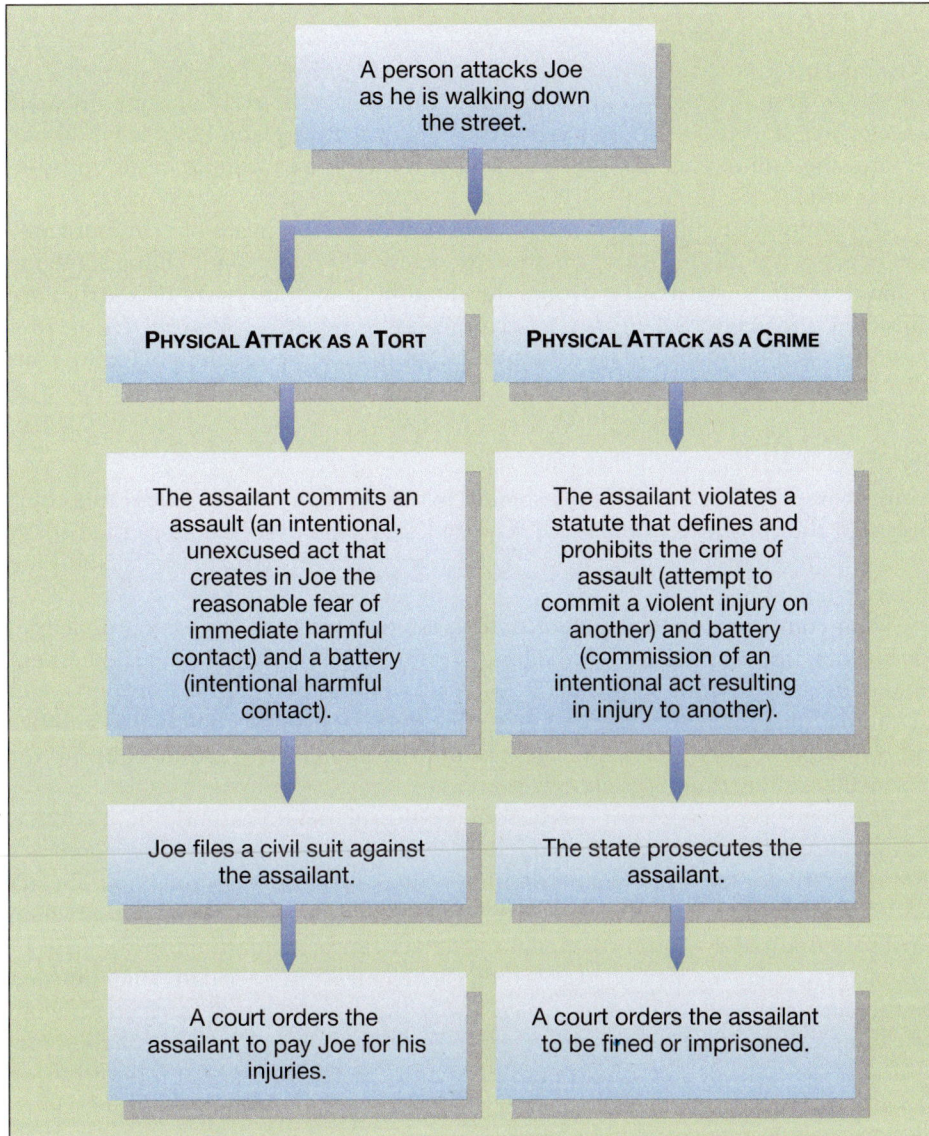

A person attacks Joe as he is walking down the street.

PHYSICAL ATTACK AS A TORT

The assailant commits an assault (an intentional, unexcused act that creates in Joe the reasonable fear of immediate harmful contact) and a battery (intentional harmful contact).

Joe files a civil suit against the assailant.

A court orders the assailant to pay Joe for his injuries.

PHYSICAL ATTACK AS A CRIME

The assailant violates a statute that defines and prohibits the crime of assault (attempt to commit a violent injury on another) and battery (commission of an intentional act resulting in injury to another).

The state prosecutes the assailant.

A court orders the assailant to be fined or imprisoned.

© Cengage Learning 2014

1. occur outside the jurisdiction of any state,

2. involve interstate commerce or communications,

3. interfere with the operation of the federal government or its agents, or

4. are directed at citizens or property located outside the United States.

Consider just one example: burning down a person's home in Dallas is arson under Texas law. Burning down a post office, which is federal property, or a warehouse used by Amazon.com—a building used in interstate commerce—would be a federal crime. A challenging legal issue today concerns how a state or the federal government can exercise jurisdiction over criminal acts that are committed via the Internet, which knows no geographical borders.

Elements of Criminal Liability

For a person to be convicted of a crime, two elements must normally exist simultaneously: (1) the performance of a criminal act and (2) a specified state of mind, or intent. This section describes these two elements of criminal liability and some of the defenses that can be used to avoid liability for crimes.

social MEDIA TODAY

When people Google you, they typically won't click past the first page of the results. Check regularly to see what material appears when you search on your own name.

The Criminal Act

actus reus
A guilty (prohibited) act. The commission of a prohibited act is one of the two essential elements required for criminal liability; the other element is the intent to commit a crime.

A criminal act is known as the *actus reus*,[2] or guilty act. Most crimes require an act of *commission*. That is, a person must *do* something to be accused of a crime. In some cases, an act of *omission* can be a crime, but only when a person has a legal duty to perform the omitted act. Failure to file a tax return is an example of an omission that is a crime.

The guilty-act requirement is based on one of the premises of criminal law—that a person is punished for harm done to society. Thinking about killing someone or about stealing a car may be wrong, but the thoughts do no harm unless they are translated into action. Of course, a person can be punished for *attempting* murder or robbery, but normally only if substantial steps toward the criminal objective have been taken.

State of Mind

mens rea
A wrongful mental state, or intent. A wrongful mental state is a requirement for criminal liability. What constitutes a wrongful mental state varies according to the nature of the crime.

Even a completed act that harms society is not legally a crime unless the court finds that the second element—the required state of mind—was present. Usually a wrongful mental state, or *mens rea*,[3] is necessary as a wrongful act in establishing criminal liability.

What constitutes such a mental state varies according to the wrongful action. For murder, the criminal act is the taking of a life, and the mental state is the intent to take life. For theft, the guilty act is the taking of another person's property, and the mental state involves both the knowledge that the property belongs to another and the intent to steal that property. Without the mental state required by law for a particular crime, there is generally no crime.

The same criminal act can result from varying mental states, and how a crime is defined and punished depends on the degree of "wrongfulness" of the defendant's state of mind. For example, taking another's life is *homicide,* a criminal act. The act can be committed coldly, after premeditation, as in *murder in the first degree,* which carries the most severe criminal penalty. The act can be committed in the heat of passion, as in *voluntary manslaughter,* which carries a less severe penalty than murder. Or the act can be committed as a result of criminal negligence (reckless driving, for example), as in *involuntary manslaughter.* In each of these situations, the law recognizes a different degree of wrongfulness, and the harshness of the punishment depends on the degree to which the act of killing another was an *intentional* act.

Corporate Criminal Liability

responsible corporate officer doctrine
A common law doctrine under which the court may impose criminal liability on a corporate officer for actions of employees under her or his supervision regardless of whether she or he participated in, directed, or even knew about those actions.

A corporation may be held liable for crimes committed by its agents and employees within the course and scope of their employment. Obviously, corporations cannot be imprisoned, but they can be fined or denied certain legal privileges.

Corporate directors and officers are personally liable for the crimes they commit, regardless of whether the crimes were committed for their personal benefit or on the corporation's behalf. Additionally, corporate directors and officers may be held liable for the actions of employees under their supervision. Under what has become known as the **responsible corporate officer doctrine**, a court may impose criminal liability on a corporate officer regardless of whether she or he participated in, directed, or even knew about a given criminal violation.

For example, in one case the chief executive officer of a supermarket chain was held personally liable for sanitation violations in corporate warehouses, in which the food was exposed to contamination by rodents. The case was eventually heard by the United States Supreme Court, which held that the corporate officer was personally liable not because he intended the crime or even knew about it but because he was in a "responsible relationship" to the corporation and had the power to prevent the violation.[4] Courts have used similar reasoning to impose criminal liability on corporate managers whose negligence causes harm to the environment in violation of federal law, such as the Clean Water Act (discussed in Chapter 19).

Defenses to Criminal Liability

A person accused of a crime will typically offer a **defense**—a reason why he or she should not be found guilty. Asserting that a defendant lacks the required criminal intent for a specific crime is one way of defending against criminal liability. This defense and others are discussed below. No one charged with a crime is obligated to offer a defense. The government must prove guilt beyond a reasonable doubt even if the defendant does not offer any particular defense but simply tries, at trial, to poke holes in government claims and evidence.

defense
The evidence and arguments presented in the defendant's support in a criminal action or lawsuit.

The Required Mental State Is Lacking

Proving that a defendant did or did not possess the required mental state for a given crime is difficult because a person's state of mind cannot be known. For example, assume that Jackson shot and killed Avery. Jackson is arrested and charged with the crime of murder. Jackson contends that he did not commit murder because he was too drunk to know what he was doing and thus lacked the required mental state for murder—intent to kill. Jackson claims that, at most, he committed the crime of involuntary manslaughter. There will have to be some facts in evidence tending to show that Jackson was indeed so drunk that he could not have intended to kill Avery.

Criminal defendants may assert that they lacked the required degree of criminal intent for other reasons, including:

- *insanity* (the inability to distinguish between right and wrong due to diminished mental capacity),

- *duress* (which exists when one is forced to commit a specific act), or

- *mistake* (for example, taking someone else's property, such as a briefcase, thinking that it is one's own).

Protection of Persons or Property

We all have the right to protect ourselves from physical attacks by others. This is the right of **self-defense**. In most states, the force we use to protect ourselves must be reasonable under the circumstances, though. The force used must be justified by the degree of threat posed in a given situation. If someone is about to take your life, the use of *deadly force* (shooting that person with a gun, for example) might be deemed reasonable. If, however, someone in a shopping mall tries to steal a bag you are carrying, you normally do not have a right to shoot the thief, because there was no physical threat to your person.

self-defense
The legally recognized privilege to protect oneself or one's property against injury by another. The privilege of self-defense protects only acts that are reasonably necessary to protect oneself or one's property.

DEFENSE OF OTHERS. Similarly, we have the right to use force in **defense of others** if they are threatened with imminent harm. If you and a friend are walking down a city street one night and someone attacks and threatens to kill your friend, you are justified in responding with reasonable force to protect your friend. As with self-defense, the reasonableness of the force used is judged in view of the nature of the threat.

defense of others
The use of reasonable force to protect others from harm.

DEFENSE OF PROPERTY. We also have the right to use reasonable force in the **defense of property**. In particular, if someone is trespassing on our property or is stealing our property, we have the right to use force to stop the trespassing or prevent the theft. Again, the amount of force used must be reasonable. Because human life has a higher value than property, deadly force is normally not allowed in the protection of property unless the thief or trespasser poses a threat to human life.

Depending on the situation, the *castle* (or *stand your ground*) *doctrine* may come into play. This doctrine is based on the common law concept that you have a right to defend your home (your castle), yourself, your property, or an innocent person from the illegal acts of another. In general, if an intruder is in a home, the legal residents of the home do not have a *duty to retreat*. Rather, they have an express right to *stand their ground*. About half the states have expressed this principle in legislation, but the details of how the principle is applied vary across the states.

defense of property
The use of reasonable force to protect one's property from harm threatened by another. The use of deadly force in defending one's property is seldom justified.

Statutes of Limitations

With some exceptions, such as for the crime of murder, statutes of limitations apply to crimes. In other words, criminal cases must be prosecuted within a certain number of years. If a criminal action is brought after the statutory time period has expired, the accused person can raise the statute of limitations as a defense.

Other Defenses

Further defenses include *mistaken identity,* and a defendant may offer an *alibi* (proof that the defendant was somewhere else at the time of the crime, for example).

Because criminal law brings the force of the state to bear against the individual, law enforcement authorities must abide by the letter of procedural law when arresting and prosecuting a person accused of a crime. If they do not, the defendant may be able to use the prosecution's violations of procedural laws as a defense, depending on the nature of the right that was violated and the degree of violation.

Types of Crimes

The number of acts defined as criminal is nearly endless. Federal, state, and local laws provide for the classification and punishment of thousands of different criminal acts. Traditionally, though, crimes have been grouped into five broad categories, or types: violent crime (crimes against persons), property crime, public order crime, white-collar crime, and organized crime.

Violent Crime

Crimes against persons, because they cause others to suffer harm or death, are referred to as *violent crimes.* Murder is a violent crime. So are sexual assault, rape, and assault and battery (discussed further in Chapter 14). **Robbery**—defined as the taking of money, personal property, or any other article of value from a person by means of force or fear—is another violent crime. Typically, states have more severe penalties for *aggravated robbery*—robbery with the use of a deadly weapon—than for simple robbery. Many crimes carry greater penalties if a deadly weapon is involved.

Each violent crime is further classified by degree, depending on the circumstances surrounding the criminal act. These include the intent of the person committing the crime, whether a weapon was used, and the level of pain and suffering experienced by the victim. For example, traditionally, killing another human being could result in one of three different offenses, depending on the defendant's intent: murder (if the killing was intentional), voluntary manslaughter (if intentional but provoked), or involuntary manslaughter (if the killing was unintentional but resulted from criminal negligence or an unlawful act, such as drunk driving).

Most states follow these basic classifications of homicide but add degrees of murder to provide penalties of different severity. For example, deliberate and premeditated killing is usually first degree murder (a *capital offense*—a crime possibly punishable by death). First degree murder may also include killings committed during certain types of felonies, such as arson, burglary, rape, or robbery. When a person is killed during other types of felonies, the charge is likely to be second degree murder, which is typically not punishable by death.

Property Crime

The most common type of criminal activity is property crime—a crime in which the goal of the offender is some form of economic gain or damage to property. Robbery is a form of property crime, as well as a violent crime, because the offender seeks to gain the property of another by use of force or the threat of force (which creates fear). Other property crimes are discussed next.

---

robbery
The taking of money, personal property, or any other article of value from a person by means of force or fear.

Burglary

Burglary usually involves breaking and entering onto the property of another with the intent to commit a felony. A burglary does not necessarily involve theft. The defendant may have intended to commit some other felony and still be guilty of burglary.

Larceny

Any person who wrongfully or fraudulently takes and carries away another person's personal property is guilty of **larceny**. In other words, larceny is "stealing." To be guilty of larceny, the person must have intended to deprive the owner permanently of the property. Larceny does not involve force or fear (as in robbery) or breaking into a building (as in burglary). Taking company products and supplies home for personal use, if one is not authorized to do so, is larceny. Many states have expanded the definition of larceny to include thefts of computer files, computer time, and electricity.

Obtaining Goods by False Pretenses

It is a criminal act to obtain goods by means of false pretenses—for example, buying groceries with a check, knowing that there are insufficient funds to cover it. Statutes dealing with such illegal activities vary widely from state to state.

Receiving Stolen Goods

It is a crime to receive stolen goods. The recipient of such goods need not know the true identity of the owner or the thief. All that is necessary is that the recipient knew or *should have known* that the goods were stolen (which implies the intent to deprive the owner of those goods). In other words, if someone sells you a new laptop for ten dollars from the back of a truck full of laptops, you may be guilty of receiving stolen property.

Arson

The willful and malicious burning of a building (and, in some states, personal property) owned by another is the crime of **arson**. Every state also has a special statute that covers burning a building for the purpose of collecting insurance.

Forgery

The fraudulent making or altering of any writing in a way that changes the legal rights and liabilities of another is **forgery**. If, without authorization, Tyler signs Ben's name to the back of a check made out to Ben, Tyler is committing forgery. Forgery also includes changing trademarks, falsifying public records, counterfeiting, and altering a legal document.

Public Order Crime

Historically, societies have always outlawed activities considered to be contrary to public values and morals. Today, the most common public order crimes include public drunkenness, prostitution, gambling, and illegal drug use. These crimes are sometimes referred to as victimless crimes because they potentially could harm only the offender. Nevertheless, legislatures have deemed these acts as detrimental to society as a whole because these acts are thought to create an environment that gives rise to property and violent crimes or to damage society in some other way.

Some of these crimes can result in property forfeitures. For example, someone who sells illegal drugs from his or her house may lose the house to the government as well as suffer a prison term.

White-Collar Crime

Crimes that typically occur in the business context are commonly referred to as **white-collar crimes**. One of today's most famous white-collar criminals is Bernard Madoff, who pleaded guilty in 2009 to defrauding clients of his failed investment firm and who lost tens of billions of dollars. Although there is no official definition

---

burglary
Breaking and entering onto the property of another with the intent to commit a felony.

larceny
The wrongful or fraudulent taking and carrying away of another person's personal property with the intent to deprive the person permanently of the property.

arson
The willful and malicious burning of a building (and, in some states, personal property) owned by another; arson statutes have been extended to cover the destruction of any building, regardless of ownership, by fire or explosion.

forgery
The fraudulent making or altering of any writing in a way that changes the legal rights and liabilities of another.

white-collar crime
A crime that typically occurs in a business context; popularly used to refer to an illegal act or series of acts committed by a person or business entity using nonviolent means.

of white-collar crime, the term is popularly used to mean an illegal act or series of acts committed by a person or business entity using some nonviolent means. Usually, this kind of crime is committed in the course of a legitimate occupation. Many, but not all, corporate crimes fall into this category.

Embezzlement

When a person entrusted with another person's property fraudulently takes it, **embezzlement** occurs. Typically, embezzlement involves an employee who steals funds. Banks face this problem, and so do a number of businesses in which corporate officers or accountants "cook" the books to cover up the fraudulent taking of funds for their own benefit. Embezzlement is not larceny, because the wrongdoer does not physically take the property from the possession of another, and it is not robbery, because force or fear is not used.

Mail and Wire Fraud

One of the most potent weapons against white-collar criminals is the Mail Fraud Act. Under this act, it is a federal crime (mail fraud) to use the mails, which includes e-mail, to defraud the public. Illegal use of the mails must involve (1) mailing or causing someone else to mail (or e-mail) something written, printed, or photocopied for the purpose of executing a scheme to defraud and (2) a contemplated or an organized scheme to defraud by false pretenses. If, for example, Johnson advertises by mail the sale of a cure for cancer that he knows to be fraudulent because it has no medical validity, he can be prosecuted for fraudulent use of the mails.

Federal law also makes it a crime (called *wire fraud*) to use the telephone to defraud. Under the same statute, it is a crime to use almost any means of public communication, such as radio, television, or the Internet, to defraud.

Bribery

Basically, three types of bribery are considered crimes: bribery of public officials, commercial bribery, and bribery of foreign officials. The attempt to influence a public official to act in a way that serves a private interest is a crime. As an element of this crime, intent must be present and proved. The bribe can be anything the recipient considers to be valuable. Realize that *the crime of bribery occurs when the bribe is offered.* It does not matter whether the bribe is accepted. *Accepting a bribe* is a separate crime.

Typically, people make commercial bribes to obtain information, cover up an inferior product, or secure new business. For example, a person in one business may offer an employee in a competing business some type of payoff in exchange for trade secrets or pricing schedules. So-called *kickbacks*, or payoffs for special favors or services, are a form of commercial bribery in some situations. Bribing foreign officials to obtain favorable business contracts is also a crime under U.S. law, as well as possibly under the officials' home countries' laws.

Bankruptcy Fraud

Today, federal bankruptcy law allows many individuals and businesses to be relieved of oppressive debt through bankruptcy proceedings, as will be explained in Chapter 19. Criminal violations may occur, however, during various stages of bankruptcy. A creditor, for example, may file a false claim against a debtor, which is a crime. Also, a debtor may fraudulently transfer assets to favored parties before or after the petition for bankruptcy is filed. For example, a company-owned automobile may be "sold" at a bargain price to a trusted friend or relative. It is also a crime for the debtor to fraudulently conceal property during bankruptcy, such as by hiding gold coins.

Theft of Trade Secrets

As will be discussed in Chapter 15, trade secrets constitute a form of intellectual property that for many businesses can be extremely valuable. The Economic Espionage Act made the theft of trade secrets a federal crime. The act also made it a federal crime to buy or possess trade secrets, knowing that the trade secrets were stolen or otherwise acquired without the owner's authorization. Conviction can result in prison sentences and large fines.

Additionally, the law provides that any property acquired as a result of the violation, and any property used in the commission of the violation, are subject to criminal *forfeiture*—meaning that the government can take the property. A theft of trade secrets conducted via the Internet, for example, could result in the forfeiture of every computer or other device used to facilitate the violation.

Insider Trading

An individual who obtains "inside information" about the plans or financial status of a corporation with publicly traded stock can make profits by using the information to guide decisions about the purchase or sale of the stock. **Insider trading** is a violation of securities law that subjects the violator to criminal penalties. One who possesses inside information and who has a duty not to disclose it to outsiders may not profit from the purchase or sale of securities based on that information until the information is available to the public. Thus, a paralegal who knows that a client of the law firm is about to announce a merger—which will increase the price of the company's stock—cannot buy the stock prior to the announcement.

Organized Crime

As mentioned, white-collar crime takes place within the confines of the legitimate business world. *Organized crime,* in contrast, operates *illegitimately* by, among other things, providing illegal goods and services. For organized crime, the traditional preferred markets are gambling, prostitution, illegal narcotics, and loan sharking (lending funds at higher-than-legal interest rates), along with more recent ventures into counterfeiting and credit-card scams.

Money Laundering

The profits from illegal activities, particularly illegal drug transactions, amount to billions of dollars a year. Under federal law, banks and other financial institutions are required to report currency transactions involving more than $10,000 or which are otherwise suspicious. Consequently, those who engage in illegal activities face difficulties in depositing their cash profits from illegal transactions.

As an alternative to simply storing cash from illegal transactions in a safe-deposit box, wrongdoers and racketeers have invented ways to launder "dirty" money to make it "clean." This **money laundering** is done through legitimate businesses. For example, suppose that Matt, a successful drug dealer, becomes a partner with a restaurant owner. Little by little, the restaurant shows an increasing profit because Matt falsely reports income obtained through drug dealing as restaurant income. As a partner in the restaurant, Matt is able to report the "profit" as legitimate income on which he pays federal and state taxes. He can then spend that after-tax income without worrying that his lifestyle may exceed the level possible with his reported income.

The Racketeer Influenced and Corrupt Organizations Act (RICO)

To curb the entry of organized crime into the legitimate business world, Congress passed the Racketeer Influenced and Corrupt Organizations Act (RICO). The act makes it a federal crime to (1) use income obtained from racketeering activity to purchase any interest in an enterprise, (2) acquire or maintain an interest in an enterprise through racketeering activity, (3) conduct or participate in the affairs of an enterprise through racketeering activity, or (4) conspire to do any of the preceding activities. Today, RICO is used more often to attack white-collar crime than organized crime.

Racketeering activity is not a new type of crime created by RICO. Rather, RICO incorporates by reference many federal crimes and state felonies and declares

insider trading
Trading in the stock of a publicly listed corporation based on inside information. One who possesses inside information and has a duty not to disclose it to outsiders may not profit from the purchase or sale of securities based on that information until the information is available to the public.

money laundering
Falsely reporting income that has been obtained through criminal activity, such as illegal drug transactions, as income obtained through a legitimate business enterprise to make the "dirty" money "clean."

that if a person commits *two* of these offenses, he or she is guilty of "racketeering activity." Any individual found guilty of a violation is subject to a fine of up to $25,000 per violation, imprisonment for up to twenty years, or both. Additionally, the statute provides that those who violate RICO may be required to forfeit any assets, in the form of property or cash, that were acquired as a result of the alleged illegal activity or that were "involved in" or an "instrumentality of" the activity.

Cyber Crimes

cyber crime
A crime that occurs online, in the virtual community of the Internet, as opposed to the physical world.

Many crimes are committed with computers and occur in cyberspace. These crimes fall under the broad label of **cyber crime**. Most cyber crimes are not "new" crimes. Rather, they are existing crimes in which the Internet is the instrument of wrongdoing. The challenge for law enforcement is to apply traditional laws—which were designed to protect persons from physical harm or to safeguard their physical property—to new methods of committing crime. Here, we look at several types of cyber crimes against persons and property.

Cyber Theft

In cyberspace, thieves are not subject to the physical limitations of the "real" world. A thief with Internet access could, in theory, steal data stored in a networked computer anywhere on the globe. Cyber theft is a growing problem.

ON THE web

The FBI has a "cyber mission" that focuses on various aspects of cyber crime. To learn more, go to **www.fbi.gov** and enter "Cyber crime" in the search box.

Financial Crimes

Computer networks provide opportunities for employees to commit crimes that involve serious economic losses. For example, employees of a company's accounting department can transfer funds among accounts with little effort and often with less risk than would be involved in paper transactions. The dependence of businesses on computer operations has left many companies vulnerable to sabotage, fraud, embezzlement, and the theft of proprietary data, such as trade secrets or other intellectual property.

Identity Theft

identity theft
The theft of a form of identification, such as a name, date of birth, or Social Security number, which is then used to access the victim's financial resources.

A form of cyber theft that has become particularly troublesome is **identity theft**. Identity theft occurs when the wrongdoer steals a form of identification—such as a name, date of birth, or Social Security number—and uses the information to access the victim's financial resources. This crime existed to a certain extent before the widespread use of the Internet. The Internet, however, turned identity theft into a fast-growing financial crime. The Internet provides not only another way to steal personal information but also a way for those who steal information to use items such as stolen credit-card numbers while protected by anonymity. Millions of Americans are victims of identity theft each year.

Cyberstalking

California passed the first antistalking law in 1990, in response to the murders of six women by stalkers. The law made it a crime to harass or follow a person while making a "credible threat" that puts the person in reasonable fear for her safety or the safety of her immediate family. Most states and the federal government followed with similar antistalking legislation.

cyberstalking
The crime of stalking in cyberspace. The cyberstalker usually finds the victim through Internet chat rooms, newsgroups, bulletin boards, or e-mail and proceeds to harass that person or put the person in reasonable fear for his or her safety or the safety of his or her immediate family.

Later, it became clear that these laws, which required a "physical act" such as following the victim, were insufficient. They could not protect persons against **cyberstalking**, in which the perpetrator harasses the victim using the Internet, e-mail, Facebook, Twitter, or some other electronic communication. In 1998, California amended its stalking statute to include threats made through an electronic communication device. The federal government and most states now have legislation to criminalize cyberstalking.

Hacking

Persons who use one computer to break into another are sometimes referred to as **hackers**. Hackers who break into computers without authorization often commit cyber theft. Sometimes, however, the principal aim of hackers is to cause random data errors on others' computers or otherwise disrupt the target's business.

It is difficult to know how frequently hackers succeed in breaking into databases across the United States. The FBI has estimated that only 25 percent of all corporations that suffer such security breaches report the incident to a law enforcement agency. After all, corporations do not want it to become publicly known that the security of their data has been breached. Admitting to a breach would be admitting to a certain degree of incompetence, which could damage their reputations.

Prosecuting Cyber Crimes

The Internet has raised new issues in the investigation of crimes and the prosecution of offenders. As discussed in Chapter 6, the issue of jurisdiction presents difficulties in cyberspace. Identifying the wrongdoers can be difficult. Cyber criminals do not leave physical traces, such as fingerprints or DNA samples, as evidence of their crimes. Even electronic "footprints" can be hard to find and follow, and many are located in foreign countries.

Perhaps the most significant federal statute specifically addressing cyber crime is the Counterfeit Access Device and Computer Fraud and Abuse Act. This act provides, among other things, that a person who accesses or attempts to access a computer online, without authority, to obtain classified, restricted, or protected data is subject to criminal prosecution. Such data could include financial and credit records, medical records, legal files, military and national security files, and other confidential information in government or private computers.

The crime has two elements: accessing a computer without authority and taking the data. This theft is a felony if it is committed for a commercial purpose or for private financial gain or if the value of the stolen data (or computer time) exceeds $5,000. Penalties include fines and imprisonment for up to twenty years. In addition, a victim of computer theft can bring a civil suit against the violator to obtain damages, an injunction, and other relief.

Social Media and Criminal Justice

Both law enforcement officers and criminals are using social media tools, and paralegals working regularly in criminal law will need to keep up with the latest developments. Some law enforcement social media is open only to police department employees, such as Law Officer Connect. But other sites are open to anyone interested in the issues. Follow sites such as **ConnectedCOPS.net** to keep up with the latest developments in social media and criminal law.

Use of Social Media

Criminals are using social media to seek out victims and to organize group criminal activity. In Britain, flash mobs have been organized over Blackberry networks to create opportunities to "grab and snatch" items from jewelry stores. As a result, law enforcement officials are taking more interest in obtaining records from smartphones or social media sites as part of their investigations.

Law enforcement agencies are expanding their use of social media in solving crimes. For example, the FBI has created a popular YouTube channel featuring videos describing wanted criminals. The FBI's 30-second YouTube video on former mob boss and fugitive James "Whitey" Bulger was part of a social media campaign that ultimately led to the tip that Bulger was living in an apartment in California. Bulger's capture came after a 20-year manhunt, showing the power of social media campaigns.

hacker
A person who uses one computer to break into another.

ON THE web

For information on identity theft, see the Department of Justice at **www.ojp.usdoj.gov** and the Federal Trade Commission at **www.ftc.gov**. Enter "Identity Theft" in the search boxes.

Similarly, police in Tacoma, Washington, used social media evidence to confirm that victims and suspects in a triple homicide knew each other. Utah police discovered photos on a convicted sex offender's MySpace account that showed forbidden contact with two youths. A Colorado detective created a photo lineup from social networking profile photos, helping victims to identify the suspects.

Proper Evidence

Paralegals assisting in criminal defenses will need to determine whether their clients have a presence on such sites and, if so, whether or not the information about them can be protected from police investigators. The law in this area is not settled, so the courts have to consider the following factors, in addition to the usual requirements of relevance and reliability, in determining if evidence from social media sites deserves privacy protection:

1. Was the information protected by a password or other form of privacy protection?

2. Did the affected party have a reasonable expectation of privacy even if no password protection was applied (e.g., was the material readily accessible to outsiders)?

3. Did the police have a reasonable suspicion or probable cause to investigate the social networking site, or were they simply engaged in a "fishing expedition"?

4. Is there a reason to believe the evidence is a reliable representation of what the person posted, or might it have been hacked?

Social media are also having an impact in the courtroom. A juror in a Pennsylvania criminal case posted updates on the case on Twitter and Facebook. In a Florida criminal case, several jurors used Google to look up definitions of terms and to discover evidence that had been excluded by the judge. That led to a mistrial. An alert paralegal watches the jury for signs of use of smartphones or tablets during trial, because such activities can be highly prejudicial to either side.

Paralegals working in both criminal defense and criminal prosecution need to keep up to date on the latest developments in social media technology to do their jobs. Not only will they need this knowledge to do their own jobs, they will need it to anticipate what the other side in the case is going to do next.

Constitutional Safeguards

From the moment a crime is reported until the trial concludes, law enforcement officers and prosecutors must follow specific criminal procedures that protect an accused person's constitutional rights. Before allowing a case to go to trial, the prosecutor and paralegals assigned to the case review all pretrial events closely to make sure that requirements have been properly observed. Defense attorneys and their legal assistants also investigate and review the actions of arresting and investigating police officers in an attempt to obtain grounds for a dismissal of the charges against their clients.

Safeguards in the Bill of Rights

The U.S. Constitution provides specific procedural safeguards to protect persons accused of crimes against the potentially arbitrary or unjust use of government power. These safeguards are spelled out in the Fourth, Fifth, Sixth, and Eighth Amendments to the U.S. Constitution and are summarized below. (The full text of the Constitution is presented in Appendix I.)

1. The Fourth Amendment prohibits unreasonable searches and seizures and requires a showing of probable cause (which will be discussed shortly) before a search or an arrest warrant may be issued.

2. The Fifth Amendment requires that no one shall be deprived of "life, liberty, or property without due process of law." **Due process of law** means that the government must follow a set of reasonable, fair, and standard procedures (that is, criminal procedural law) in any action against a citizen.

3. The Fifth Amendment prohibits **double jeopardy** (trying someone twice for the same criminal offense).

4. The Fifth Amendment guarantees that no person shall be "compelled in any criminal case to be a witness against himself." This is known as the privilege against compulsory **self-incrimination**.

5. The Sixth Amendment guarantees a speedy and public trial, a trial by jury, the right to confront witnesses, and the right to a lawyer at various stages in some proceedings.

6. The Eighth Amendment prohibits excessive bail and fines, as well as cruel and unusual punishment.

The Exclusionary Rule

Under what is known as the **exclusionary rule**, all evidence obtained in violation of the constitutional rights spelled out in the Fourth, Fifth, and Sixth Amendments normally is excluded from the trial, along with all evidence derived from the improperly obtained evidence. Evidence derived from illegally obtained evidence is known as the "fruit of the poisonous tree." For example, if drugs are discovered during an illegal search, the search is "the poisonous tree," and the drugs are the "fruit," which normally will be excluded from evidence if the case is brought to trial.

The purpose of the exclusionary rule is to deter police from conducting warrantless searches and from engaging in other misconduct. The rule is sometimes criticized because it can lead to injustice. Some defendants have "gotten off on a technicality" because law enforcement personnel failed to observe procedural requirements. Even though a defendant may be obviously guilty, if the evidence of that guilt was obtained improperly (without a valid search warrant, for example), it normally cannot be used against the defendant in court.

The Miranda Rule

In *Miranda v. Arizona*,[5] a case decided in 1966, the United States Supreme Court established the rule that individuals who are arrested must be informed of certain constitutional rights, including their Fifth Amendment right to remain silent and their Sixth Amendment right to counsel.

These rights, which have come to be called the *Miranda* **rights**, are listed in Exhibit 13.3 on the next page. If the arresting officers fail to inform a criminal suspect of these constitutional rights, any statements the suspect makes normally are not admissible in court. It is important to note that the police are not required to give *Miranda* warnings until the individual is placed in custody. Thus, if a person who is not in custody makes voluntary admissions to an officer, these statements are admissible.

The exact meaning of the *Miranda* rule is subject to frequent tests in the courts. The Supreme Court has held that a confession need not be excluded even though the police failed to inform a suspect in custody that his attorney had tried to reach him by telephone. Furthermore, the Court has stated that a suspect's conviction will not be overturned solely on the ground that the suspect was coerced into making a confession by law enforcement personnel. If other, legally obtained evidence admitted at trial is strong enough to justify the conviction without the confession, then the fact that the confession was obtained illegally can, in effect, be ignored.

---

due process of law
Fair, reasonable, and standard procedures that must be used by the government in any legal action against a citizen. The Fifth Amendment to the U.S. Constitution prohibits the deprivation of "life, liberty, or property without due process of law."

double jeopardy
To place at risk (jeopardize) a person's life or liberty twice. The Fifth Amendment to the Constitution prohibits a second prosecution for the same criminal offense.

self-incrimination
The act of giving testimony that implicates oneself in criminal wrongdoing. The Fifth Amendment to the Constitution states that no person "shall be compelled in any criminal case to be a witness against himself."

exclusionary rule
In criminal procedure, a rule under which any evidence obtained in violation of the accused's constitutional rights, as well as any evidence derived from illegally obtained evidence, will not be admissible in court.

Miranda **rights**
Certain constitutional rights of accused persons taken into custody by law enforcement officials, such as the right to remain silent and the right to counsel, as established by the United States Supreme Court's decision in *Miranda v. Arizona*.

EXHIBIT 13.3
The *Miranda* Rights

> On taking a criminal suspect into custody and before any interrogation takes place, law enforcement officers are required to communicate the following rights and facts to the suspect:
>
> 1. **The right to remain silent.**
> 2. **That any statements made may be used against the person in a court of law.**
> 3. **The right to talk to a lawyer and have a lawyer present while being questioned.**
> 4. **If the person cannot afford to hire a lawyer, the right to have a lawyer provided at no cost.**
>
> In addition to being advised of these rights, the suspect must be asked if he or she understands the rights and whether he or she wishes to exercise the rights or waive (not exercise) the rights.

Criminal Procedures Prior to Prosecution

Although the Constitution guarantees due process of law to individuals accused of committing crimes, the actual steps involved in bringing a criminal action vary depending on the jurisdiction and type of crime. In this section, we provide an overview of the basic procedures that take place before an individual is prosecuted for a crime. Exhibit 13.4 on the facing page illustrates a general outline of criminal procedure in both federal and state cases. Because of the many procedural variations, however, a paralegal involved in a criminal case will need to learn the specific procedural requirements that apply to the case.

Arrest and Booking

arrest
To take into custody a person suspected of criminal activity.

booking
The process of entering a suspect's name, offense, and arrival time into the police log (blotter) following his or her arrest.

An **arrest** occurs when police officers take a person into custody and charge that person with a crime. (Note that often the interaction with the police is captured on video.) After the arrest, the police typically search the suspect and take the suspect to a *holding facility* (usually at the police station or a jail), where booking occurs. **Booking** refers to the process of entering a suspect's name, the offense for which the suspect is being held, and the time of arrival into the police log (computer). The suspect is fingerprinted and photographed, told the reason for the arrest, and allowed to make a phone call.

If the crime is not serious, the officer may then release the suspect on personal recognizance—that is, on the suspect's promise to appear before a court at some later date. Otherwise, the suspect may be held in custody pending an initial appearance in court (which generally occurs within a few days).

Law enforcement personnel are in control of the arrest and booking of suspects. Paralegals and attorneys usually are not involved until after an arrest has been made. The defense will, however, look closely to see that the proper procedure was followed in the arrest of the client. An officer can legally arrest a person with or without a warrant, as long as the officer has probable cause to believe that the person committed a crime (discussed shortly). Before an officer questions a suspect who has been arrested, the officer must give the *Miranda* warnings discussed earlier.

Detention Is Not an Arrest

Before we discuss probable cause, it is important to note that an arrest differs from a *stop* or *detention*, such as a traffic stop. Police officers have a right to stop and detain a person if they have a *reasonable suspicion* that the person committed, or is about to commit, a crime. Reasonable suspicion is a much lower standard than probable cause—because stopping a person is much less invasive than arresting the person. That means, for example, that an officer can stop a person who matches the description of an assailant in the neighborhood based on reasonable suspicion. The officer

EXHIBIT 13.4
Major Procedural Steps
in a Criminal Case

ARREST

Police officer takes suspect into custody. Most arrests are made without a warrant. After the arrest, the officer searches the suspect, who is then taken to the police station.

BOOKING

At the police station, the suspect is searched again, photographed, fingerprinted, and allowed at least one telephone call. After the booking, charges are reviewed, and if they are not dropped, a complaint is filed and a magistrate reviews the case for probable cause.

INITIAL APPEARANCE

The suspect appears before the magistrate, who informs the suspect of the charges and of his or her rights. If the suspect requires a lawyer, one is appointed. The magistrate sets bail (conditions under which a suspect can obtain release pending disposition of the case).

GRAND JURY

A grand jury determines if there is probable cause to believe that the defendant committed the crime. The federal government and about half of the states require grand jury indictments for at least some felonies.

PRELIMINARY HEARING

In a court proceeding, a prosecutor presents evidence, and the judge determines if there is probable cause to hold the defendant over for trial.

INDICTMENT

The grand jury formally charges a criminal suspect by issuing an indictment.

INFORMATION

The prosecutor formally charges a criminal suspect by filing an information, or criminal complaint.

ARRAIGNMENT

The suspect is brought before the trial court, informed of the charges, and asked to enter a plea.

PLEA BARGAIN

The prosecutor may offer a plea bargain. A plea bargain is a prosecutor's promise to make concessions (or promise to seek concessions) in return for a suspect's guilty plea. Concessions may include a reduced charge or a lesser sentence.

GUILTY PLEA

In most jurisdictions, most cases that reach the arraignment stage do not go to trial but are resolved by a guilty plea, often as a result of a plea bargain. The judge sets the case for sentencing.

TRIAL

Generally, most felony trials are jury trials, and most misdemeanor trials are bench trials (trials before judges). If the verdict is "guilty," the judge sets the case for sentencing. Everyone convicted of a crime has the right to an appeal.

© Cengage Learning 2014

can even "frisk" the person being detained (pat down the person's clothes) to make sure the person is not carrying a weapon. The officer cannot legally arrest any person, however, without probable cause.

Probable Cause

probable cause
Reasonable grounds to believe the existence of facts warranting certain actions, such as the search or arrest of a person.

The requirement of **probable cause** is a key factor that is assessed repeatedly throughout the various stages of criminal proceedings. The first stage, arrest, requires probable cause. In the context of arrest, probable cause exists if there is a substantial likelihood that both of the following events occurred:

1. A crime was committed.

2. The individual committed the crime.

Note that probable cause involves a *likelihood*—not just a possibility—that the suspect committed the crime. It is not enough that the police officer suspects that the individual has committed a crime. It must be likely. The probable cause requirement stems from the Fourth Amendment, which prohibits unreasonable searches and seizures.

If a police officer observes a crime being committed, the officer can arrest the wrongdoer on the spot without a warrant, because the probable cause requirement is met. If a victim or some other person reports a crime to the police, the police must decide whether there is enough information about the alleged wrongdoer's guilt to establish probable cause to arrest. What is and is not considered probable cause varies across jurisdictions. Usually, if the suspect is at home at the time of the arrest, the police will need to obtain an arrest warrant (unless the police pursued the suspect to the home or some other emergency circumstance exists).

Warrants

arrest warrant
A written order, based on probable cause and typically issued by a judge, commanding that the person named on the warrant be arrested by the police.

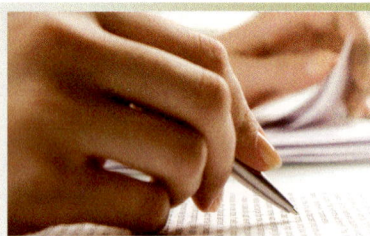

Often, the police try to gather information to help them determine whether a suspect should be arrested. If, after investigating the matter, the police decide to arrest the suspect, they must obtain an **arrest warrant**, which is typically issued by a judge. To obtain this warrant, the police will have to convince the official, usually through supporting affidavits, that probable cause exists. The warrant process is discussed further in the *Developing Paralegal Skills* feature below.

DEVELOPING
paralegal skills

THE PROSECUTOR'S OFFICE—WARRANT DIVISION

Kathy Perello works as a legal assistant in the warrant division of the county prosecutor's office. Officer McCarthy is at her door with a burglary report regarding a suspect they want to arrest. He presents the paperwork from the prosecutor that authorizes the arrest and requests that Kathy prepare an arrest warrant. Officer McCarthy will take the warrant to the court, swear to the truth of its contents, and ask the judge to sign the warrant so that he can make the arrest.

CHECKLIST FOR PREPARING A WARRANT

- Obtain written authorization from a prosecutor before initiating the warrant procedure.

- Obtain a copy of the suspect's criminal history.

- Use the above to prepare the warrant.

- Verify that the criminal history matches the suspect.

- Make sure that the crime and the suspect are both specifically described.

- Review the typed warrant to ensure that it includes any other required terms.

- Call the officer to pick up the warrant and take it to a judge for a determination of probable cause.

SEARCH WARRANTS.   Probable cause is also required to obtain a **search warrant**, which authorizes police officers or other criminal investigators to search specifically named persons or property for evidence and to seize the evidence if they find it (see Exhibit 13.5 on the following two pages). Probable cause requires law enforcement officials to have trustworthy evidence that would convince a reasonable person that the proposed search or seizure is more likely justified than not. Furthermore, the Fourth Amendment prohibits general warrants. It requires a particular description of that which is to be searched or seized. Once a warrant is obtained, the search cannot extend beyond what is described in the warrant.

WHEN WARRANT NOT NEEDED.   There are exceptions to the requirement for a search warrant. For example, if an officer is arresting a person (either with an arrest warrant or sufficient probable cause) and sees drug paraphernalia "in plain view," no search warrant is required to seize that evidence. Another exception exists when it is likely that the items sought will be removed or destroyed before a warrant can be obtained.

Investigation after the Arrest

In most cases the police must find and interview witnesses and conduct searches (of the suspect's home or car, for example) to collect evidence. Witnesses may view the suspect in a *lineup*, in which the suspect appears with a group of several others. In more serious cases, detectives may take charge of the investigation.

As the police review the evidence at hand, they may conclude there is not enough evidence to justify recommending the case for prosecution. If so, the suspect is released, and no charges are filed. The police can still recommend prosecution later if more evidence is obtained. Alternatively, the police may decide to change the offense with which the suspect is being charged. The police may also decide to release the suspect with a warning or a referral to a social-service agency. Unless the suspect is released at this point in the criminal process, control over the case moves from the police to the public prosecutor.

The Prosecution Begins

The prosecution of a criminal case begins when the police inform the public prosecutor of the alleged crime, provide the reports written by the arresting and investigating officers, and turn over evidence relating to the matter. The prosecutor may choose to investigate the case further by personally interviewing the suspect, the arresting and investigating officers, and witnesses, and gathering other evidence. The prosecutor's legal assistants often participate in these tasks. Based on a review of the police file or an investigation, the prosecutor decides whether to take the case to trial or drop the case and allow the suspect to be released.

Major reasons for releasing the suspect include insufficient evidence and unreliable witnesses. If you are working for a client, by now you are keeping close track of all details such as witnesses as *In the Office* discusses on page 412.

Prosecutorial Discretion

Prosecutors have broad discretion. If they decide to pursue a case, they also decide what charges to file. Because prosecutions are expensive and resources are limited, most prosecutors do not go forward with a case unless they are confident that they can prove the case in court. Typically, a prosecutor who decides to file a case will allege as many criminal offenses as could possibly be proved based on the facts. If the defendant is facing numerous charges, the likelihood is greater that the prosecutor will get a conviction on at least one of them (the chances are also greater that the defendant will plead guilty to one or more of the offenses in exchange for having the others dropped).

search warrant
A written order, based on probable cause and issued by a judge or public official (magistrate), commanding that police officers or criminal investigators search a specific person, place, or property to obtain evidence.

social MEDIA TODAY

Things you do in public can end up online in a flash. A member of Congress was filmed on an airplane reading an adult magazine. A fellow passenger quickly posted photos of the congressperson taken with his cell phone.

EXHIBIT 13.5
A Search Warrant

Ch. 89 **SEARCH AND SEIZURE** **§ 7942**
Rule 41

§ 7942. Search Warrant

AO 93 (Rev. 5/85) Search Warrant ⊕

United States District Court

_____ DISTRICT OF_____

In the Matter of the Search of
(Name, address or brief description of person or property to be searched)

SEARCH WARRANT

CASE NUMBER:

TO: _____ and any Authorized Officer of the United States

Affidavit(s) having been made before me by_____ who has reason to
Affiant

believe that ☐ on the person of or ☐ on the **premises known as** (name, description and/or location)

in the _____ District of_____ there is now
concealed a certain person or property, namely (describe the person or property)

I am satisfied that the affidavit(s) and any recorded testimony establish probable cause to believe that the person
or property so described is now concealed on the person or premises above-described and establish grounds for
the issuance of this warrant.

YOU ARE HEREBY COMMANDED to search on or before _____
Date

(not to exceed 10 days) the person or place named above for the person or property specified, serving this warrant
and making the search (in the daytime—6:00 A.M. to 10:00 P.M.) (at any time in the day or night as I find
reasonable cause has been established) and if the person or property be found there to seize same, leaving a copy
of this warrant and receipt for the person or property taken, and prepare a written inventory of the person or property seized and promptly return this warrant to _____
U.S Judge or Magistrate
as required by law.

_____ at _____
Date and Time Issued City and State

_____ _____
Name and Title of Judicial Officer Signature of Judicial Officer [G13950]

http://www.uscourts.gov

If the decision is made to prosecute the case, then the prosecutor must undertake the necessary procedures to formally charge the person before the court.
These procedures vary depending on the court and the type of case. Often, misdemeanor charges are handled somewhat differently than felony charges. Some
prosecutors may file complaints involving misdemeanor charges, but a grand jury
indictment (which will be discussed shortly) is required for felony charges. The way
a criminal case is initiated is one area of criminal procedure that varies substantially
among the states. Keep this in mind as you read the following subsections.

Complaint and Initial Appearance

The criminal litigation process may begin with the filing of a _complaint_ (see
Exhibit 13.6 on page 413). The complaint includes a statement of the charges that
are being brought against the suspect. The suspect now becomes a criminal defen-

EXHIBIT 13.5
A Search Warrant—Continued

§ **7942**
Rule 41

SPECIAL PROCEEDINGS

Ch. 89

AO 93 (Rev. 5/85)   Search Warrant

RETURN		
DATE WARRANT RECEIVED	DATE AND TIME WARRANT EXECUTED	COPY OF WARRANT AND RECEIPT FOR ITEMS LEFT WITH
INVENTORY MADE IN THE PRESENCE OF		
INVENTORY OF PERSON OR PROPERTY TAKEN PURSUANT TO THE WARRANT		

CERTIFICATION

I swear that this inventory is a true and detailed account of the person or property taken by me on the warrant.

_____

Subscribed, sworn to, and returned before me this date.

_____   _____
U.S. Judge or Magistrate   Date

[G13951]

http://www.uscourts.gov

dant. Because the defendant is in the court system, prosecutors must show that they have legal grounds to proceed. They must show probable cause that a crime was committed and that the defendant committed the crime.

Initial Appearance

In most jurisdictions, defendants are taken before a judge or magistrate very soon after arrest. During this *initial appearance,* the judge makes sure that the person appearing is the person named in the complaint, informs the defendant of the charge or charges made in the complaint, and advises the defendant of the right to counsel and the right to remain silent. If a defendant cannot afford to hire an attorney, a public defender or member of the private bar may be appointed to represent the defendant at this time (or the defendant may be asked to fill out an application for appointed counsel).

IN THE office

THE BENEFITS OF GOOD RECORD KEEPING

One of your jobs as a paralegal is to make sure that witnesses are in court at the proper time. This relates to the attorney's duty of competence. Suppose that despite all your efforts a witness fails to appear in court. Your supervising attorney is upset and asks you how it could have happened.

You show the attorney:

- the memorandum of your interview with the client, in which you noted that the witness was willing to testify,
- the receipt from the certified letter that you sent to the witness, which contained the subpoena, indicating that the witness had received it, and
- telephone memos of calls you made to the witness prior to the trial in which the witness agreed to be in court on the date of the trial, as well as follow-up calls you made immediately before and then during the trial to confirm appearance.

Although your documentation is not a cure for the problem presented by the missing witness, it does provide evidence—should it be necessary—that neither you nor the attorney was negligent.

Bail

bail
The amount of money or conditions set by the court to ensure that an individual accused of a crime will appear for further criminal proceedings. If the accused person provides bail, whether in cash or by means of a bail bond, then the person is released from jail.

The judge must also make a decision whether to set bail or release the defendant until the next court date. **Bail** is an amount paid by the defendant to the court as insurance that the defendant will show up for future court appearances. If the defendant shows up as promised, the court returns the funds. Courts often use standard bail schedules, which set the bail for specific kinds of cases, and may deny bail for more serious crimes. The Eighth Amendment prohibits "excessive bail," and a defendant can request a hearing to seek a reduction in bail.

If the court sets bail in an amount that the defendant is unable to pay, the defendant (or the defendant's attorney or paralegal) can arrange with a *bail bondsperson* to post a bail bond on the defendant's behalf. The bail bondsperson promises to pay the bail amount to the court if the defendant fails to return for further proceedings. In return, the bail bondsperson receives a payment from the defendant, usually 10 percent of the bail amount.

Preliminary Hearing

preliminary hearing
An initial hearing in which a judge or magistrate decides if there is probable cause to believe that the defendant committed the crime with which he or she is charged.

The defendant again appears before a magistrate or judge at a **preliminary hearing**. During this hearing, the magistrate or judge determines whether the evidence presented is sufficient to establish probable cause to believe the defendant committed the crime with which he or she is charged. This may be the first adversarial proceeding in which both sides are represented by counsel. Paralegals may become involved in the process at this point by assisting in preparation for the hearing.

The prosecutor may present witnesses, who may be cross-examined by defense counsel (the defense rarely presents its witnesses prior to trial). A defendant who intends to plead guilty usually waives the right to a preliminary hearing to help move things along more quickly. In many jurisdictions, however, the preliminary hearing is required in certain felony cases.

If the magistrate finds the evidence insufficient to establish probable cause, either the charge is reduced to a lesser one or charges are dropped altogether and the defendant is released. If the magistrate believes there is sufficient evidence to

EXHIBIT 13.6
A Complaint

United States District Court

DISTRICT OF _____

UNITED STATES OF AMERICA
V.

CRIMINAL COMPLAINT

CASE NUMBER: _____

(Name and Address of Defendant)

I, the undersigned complainant being duly sworn state the following is true and correct to the best of my

knowledge and belief. On or about _____ in _____ county, in the

_____ District of _____ defendant(s) did, (Track Statutory Language of Offense)

in violation of Title _____ United States Code, Section(s) _____.

I further state that I am a(n) _____ and that this complaint is based on the following
                                        Official Title

facts:

Continued on the attached sheet and made a part hereof: ☐ Yes   ☐ No

_____
Signature of Complainant

Sworn to before me and subscribed in my presence,

_____   at   _____
Date   City and State

_____   _____   [E4706]
Name & Title of Judicial Officer   Signature of Judicial Officer

http://www.uscourts.gov

establish probable cause, the prosecutor issues an information. The **information** is the formal charge against the defendant and binds over the defendant for further proceedings, which usually means that the defendant is arraigned and the case proceeds to trial.

Grand Jury Review

The federal government and about half of the states require a grand jury—not a prosecutor—to make the decision as to whether a case should go to trial in felony cases. In other words, a grand jury's indictment is an alternative to a prosecutor's information to initiate the criminal litigation process.

A **grand jury** is a group of citizens called to decide whether there is probable cause to believe that the defendant committed the crime with which he or she is charged and therefore should go to trial. Even in cases in which grand jury review is not required, the prosecutor may call a grand jury to evaluate the evidence against a suspect, which will indicate to the prosecutor the relative strength or weakness of the case.

information
A formal criminal charge made by a prosecutor without a grand jury indictment.

grand jury
A group of citizens called to decide whether probable cause exists to believe that a suspect committed the crime with which he or she has been charged and thus should stand trial.

At a preliminary hearing, a judge or a magistrate evaluates the evidence against the defendant. If the evidence is sufficient to establish probable cause (reasonable grounds to believe that the defendant committed the crime with which he or she is charged), the prosecutor issues an information, and the defendant is bound over for further proceedings. Paralegals often assist either the defendant or the prosecutor in preparing for preliminary hearings. What might some of the duties of a paralegal be?

© Junian Enterprises/www.Shutterstock.com

The grand jury sits in closed session and hears only evidence presented by the prosecutor—the defendant cannot present evidence at this hearing. Normally, the defendant and the defendant's attorney are not even allowed to attend grand jury proceedings—although in some cases the prosecutor calls the defendant as a witness. The prosecutor presents to the grand jury evidence the state has against the defendant, including photographs, documents, tangible objects, test results, the testimony of witnesses, and other items.

If the grand jury finds that probable cause exists, it issues an **indictment**[6] against the defendant called a *true bill*. Over 97 percent of the cases that prosecutors bring to grand juries result in an indictment. The indictment is filed with the trial court and becomes the formal charge against the defendant. An example of an indictment is shown in Exhibit 13.7 on the facing page.

Arraignment

At the **arraignment**, the defendant is informed of the charges and must respond to the charges by entering a plea. Three possible pleas can be entered: guilty, not guilty, and *nolo contendere*, which is Latin for "I will not contest it" and is often called a no-contest plea. A plea of no contest is neither an admission of guilt nor a denial of guilt—but it operates like a guilty plea in that the defendant is convicted.

The primary reason for pleading no contest is so that the plea cannot later be used against the defendant in a civil trial. For example, if a defendant pleads guilty to assault, the admission of guilt can be used to impose civil liability, whereas with a no-contest plea, the plaintiff in the civil suit must prove the defendant committed the assault. No-contest pleas are thus useful for the defendant who could be sued in a civil action for damages caused to a person or property.

At the arraignment, the defendant can move to have the charges dismissed, which happens in a fair number of cases for a variety of reasons. The defendant may claim, for example, that the case should be dismissed because the statute of limitations for the crime in question has lapsed. Most frequently, however, the defendant

indictment

A charge or written accusation, issued by a grand jury, that probable cause exists to believe that a person has committed a crime for which he or she should stand trial.

arraignment

A court proceeding in which the suspect is formally charged with the criminal offense stated in the indictment. The suspect then enters a plea (guilty, not guilty, or *nolo contendere*) in response.

nolo contendere

Latin for "I will not contest it." A criminal defendant's plea in which he or she chooses not to challenge, or contest, the charges brought by the government. Although the defendant will still be convicted and sentenced, the plea neither admits nor denies guilt.

EXHIBIT 13.7
An Indictment

[Title of Court and Cause]

The Grand Jury charges that:

On or about _____ , 20 __ , at _____ , _____ , in the _____ District of _____ , _____ , having been convicted of knowingly acquiring and possessing a SNAP/Food Stamp EBT card in a manner not authorized by the provisions of Chapter 51, Title 7, United States Code, and the regulations issued pursuant to said chapter, a felony conviction, in the federal district court for the _____ District of _____ , and sentenced on _____ , 20__ , did knowingly possess a firearm that had been transported in and affecting commerce, to wit: an OMC Pistol, Back Up 380 Caliber, serial number _____ ; all in violation of Section 1202(a)(1) of Title 18, United States Code, Appendix.

A True Bill

_____ ,

Foreperson.

_____ ,

United States Attorney.

© Cengage Learning 2014

pleads guilty to the charge or to a lesser charge that has been agreed on through **plea bargaining** between the prosecutor and the defendant. If the defendant pleads guilty, no trial is necessary, and the defendant is sentenced based on the plea. If the defendant pleads not guilty, the case is set for trial.

Pretrial Motions

Defense attorneys and their paralegals will search for and be alert to any violation of the defendant's constitutional rights. Many pretrial motions are based on possible violations of the defendant's rights as provided by the Constitution and criminal procedural law. We discuss here a few of the most common motions filed in a criminal case.

Note, however, that the specific requirements for pretrial motions vary depending on the jurisdiction. Not every jurisdiction allows every type of pretrial motion, and the standards used by judges to evaluate such motions may differ as well. Also keep in mind that a motion is generally accompanied by a separate pleading that sets forth the legal argument in support of the motion. A memorandum of law, a brief, affidavits, or supporting points and authorities may be filed in support of a pleading.

Motions to Suppress

One of the most common and effective motions made by defense attorneys is the **motion to suppress evidence**. A motion to suppress asserts that the evidence against the defendant was illegally obtained and should be excluded (inadmissible). Typically, this motion is filed when an officer performs a search without probable cause, seizes evidence, and then arrests the defendant based on that evidence.

For example, suppose an officer stops the defendant's vehicle because his taillight is out and then searches the contents of the defendant's trunk, finding illegal narcotics. The defendant is subsequently charged with possession. A motion to suppress would be appropriate here (and probably successful) because the officer did not have probable cause to search the trunk when carrying out a traffic stop.

The defense attorney normally prepares the motion and submits a brief in support of the motion. (Often, these motions and memoranda are drafted by paralegals.) Exhibit 13.8 on pages 416 and 417 shows a sample memorandum. Often,

plea bargaining
The process by which the accused and the prosecutor in a criminal case work out a mutually satisfactory disposition of the case, subject to court approval. Usually, plea bargaining involves the defendant's pleading guilty to a lesser offense in return for a lighter sentence.

motion to suppress evidence
A motion requesting that certain evidence be excluded from consideration during the trial.

EXHIBIT 13.8
Memorandum in Support of a Motion to Suppress

[Attorney for Defendant]

SUPERIOR COURT OF THE STATE OF NITA
FOR THE COUNTY OF NITA

THE PEOPLE OF THE STATE OF NITA,	)	Case No.: C45778
Plaintiff,	)	D.A. No.: A39996
	)	
	)	**MEMORANDUM OF LAW IN SUPPORT**
v.	)	**OF MOTION TO SUPPRESS**
	)	
	)	DATE: 10-27-14
Eduardo Jose Mendez,	)	TIME: 1:15
Defendant.	)	Estimated Time: 45 min.
	)	No. of Witnesses: 1

Defendant, Eduardo Jose Mendez, by and through his attorney the Public Defender of the County of Nita, respectfully submits the following memorandum of law in support of his motion to Suppress.

STATEMENT OF FACTS

On or about September 23, 2014, at approximately 02:15, Officer Ramirez observed Mr. Mendez riding his bicycle in the area of 1300 Elm St. and 500 C St. It was drizzling, and few people walked the streets. Officer Ramirez indicated that the area is known for narcotic activity and that he believed Mr. Mendez had been participating or was about to participate in narcotic activity.

Mr. Mendez was on his bicycle at the corner of Elm and C St. when Officer Ramirez approached him. He indicated that Mr. Mendez appeared to be nervous and was sweating profusely. He asked Mr. Mendez what he was doing, and Mr. Mendez responded that he was waiting for his girlfriend. Officer Ramirez conducted a pat-down search for weapons. He felt several hard objects inside Mr. Mendez's pants pockets and asked Mr. Mendez if he had a knife in his pocket. Mr. Mendez consented to a search of his pockets, and Officer Ramirez found only a wooden pencil.

Without asking for permission, and without notice, Officer Ramirez reached for and grabbed Mr. Mendez's baseball cap. The officer took the cap off of Mr. Mendez's head. He felt the outside of the cap and with his fingers manipulated a small soft lump in Mr. Mendez's cap. He went through the cap and moved the side material of the cap. He found a small plastic package burnt on one end. He opened the package. Officer Ramirez found a small amount of an off-white powder substance inside the package.

ARGUMENT

I. MR. MENDEZ'S FOURTH AMENDMENT RIGHT TO PRIVACY WAS VIOLATED BECAUSE THE OFFICER'S DETENTION OF MR. MENDEZ WAS NOT JUSTIFIED BY REASONABLE SUSPICION

A person has been seized within the meaning of the Fourth Amendment if, in view of all the circumstances surrounding the incident, a reasonable person would have believed that he was not free to leave. *United States v. Mendenhall,* 446 U.S. 544, 554 (1980). Here, Officer Ramirez seized Mr. Mendez when he stopped to question him. Mr. Mendez submitted to Officer Ramirez's show of authority when he responded to the questioning. Mr. Mendez's belief that he was not free to leave is evidenced by his actions during the seizure. He appeared nervous and kept looking around in all directions as if looking for someone to help him. A reasonable person such as Mr. Mendez, in view of all of the circumstances, would have believed and in fact did believe he was not free to leave. Therefore, the officer's initial stop was a seizure.

* * * *

the attorney requests the court to allow oral argument on the motion, although in some jurisdictions it is automatic. The court then conducts a hearing on the motion. The attorneys for both sides may call witnesses (police officers and others who were present) to testify, and the judge makes a ruling.

EXHIBIT 13.8
Memorandum in Support of a Motion to Suppress—Continued

Officer Ramirez did not have reasonable suspicion to stop Mr. Mendez. He fails to point to specific facts causing him to suspect criminal activity was afoot. Officer Ramirez notes in his police report that he "felt" that defendant "had been participating or was about to participate in narcotic activity." The officer also indicated that he believed the area was known for narcotic activity. However, "Persons may not be subjected to invasions of privacy merely because they are in or are passing through a high-crime area." *McCally-Bey v. Kirner*, 24 F.Supp.3d 389 (N.D. Nita 2002).

These observations taken as a whole and Officer Ramirez's explanation do not rise to the requisite level of reasonable suspicion necessary to invade the privacy of a citizen.

II. OFFICER RAMIREZ'S PAT-DOWN SEARCH EXCEEDED ITS SCOPE WHEN HE SEARCHED THE BASEBALL CAP AND MANIPULATED ITS CONTENTS

Under the *Terry* doctrine, a search is referred to as a "frisk." *Terry v. Ohio*, 392 U.S. 1 (1968). A *frisk* is justified only if the officer reasonably believes that the person is armed and dangerous. A frisk is a pat-down of a person's outer clothing. It is limited in scope to its purpose, which is to search for weapons. Even slightly lingering over a package because it feels like it contains drugs exceeds the scope of the search. *Minnesota v. Dickerson*, 508 U.S. 366 (1993). An officer cannot manipulate a package or a substance that is clearly not a weapon through an individual's clothing during a *Terry* pat-down search.

* * * *

III. OFFICER RAMIREZ DID NOT HAVE PROBABLE CAUSE TO CONDUCT A WARRANTLESS SEARCH OF MR. MENDEZ

* * * *

IV. ALL EVIDENCE OBTAINED AS A RESULT OF AN UNLAWFUL DETENTION MUST BE SUPPRESSED AS TAINTED EVIDENCE; FRUIT OF THE POISONOUS TREE

* * * *

* * * *

As discussed above, the detention of Mr. Mendez did not meet constitutionally established standards of reasonableness. Hence, all evidence obtained as a result of such unlawful detention is inadmissible. In addition, all evidence seized as a result of the arrest that followed from his unlawful detention is inadmissible as fruit of the poisonous tree.

* * * *

For the above-mentioned reasons, all evidence obtained as a result of Mr. Mendez's detention, illegal search, and subsequent arrest in this case must be suppressed.

Dated:

Respectfully submitted,

_____
Attorney for Defendant

If the judge agrees that the evidence should be excluded and grants the motion, the defendant may be able to avoid trial. This is because frequently, without the evidence, the prosecution will not be able to prove its case against the defendant and will thus drop the charges.

Motions to Dismiss

A motion can be filed to dismiss all or some of the charges pending against the defendant. There are many grounds for filing a motion to dismiss. Motions to dismiss in criminal cases often assert that the defendant's constitutional rights—or criminal procedures stemming from the Constitution—have been violated.

For example, the defense might argue that the prosecution waited too long to prosecute the case in violation of the defendant's Sixth Amendment right to a speedy and public trial (sometimes called a *speedy trial motion*). The defense will file the motion along with a supporting memorandum, which may argue that the defendant has been prejudiced by the delay, that witnesses are no longer available, and that a fair trial cannot be had. If the judge grants the motion, the case is dismissed.

Because it may eliminate charges against a client without subjecting the client to the risks of a jury trial, the motion to dismiss is one of the most useful motions for the defense to file. A paralegal who becomes skilled at writing persuasive motions to dismiss will thus be a valuable asset to the defense team.

Other Common Motions

Just as in civil cases, attorneys in criminal cases often file motions *in limine* (discussed in Chapter 12 on page 367) to keep certain evidence out of the trial. For example, a defense attorney whose client has prior criminal convictions may file a motion *in limine* requesting the court to prevent any evidence of these convictions from being offered by the prosecution. The prosecutor may also file such motions to keep possibly prejudicial evidence from being admitted (concerning a victim's reputation, for example).

In some cases the defense will file motions appropriate to the matter:

- When there is a good deal of pretrial publicity, the defense may make a **motion for a change of venue** asking the court to relocate the trial.

- When the judge has publicly displayed some bias or personally knows the parties or witnesses in a case, the defense may file a **motion to recuse** asking the trial judge to remove himself or herself from the case. If the motion is granted, a different judge will hear the case.

- When a case involves more than one defendant, the defense counsel may file a **motion to sever** (separate) the cases for purposes of trial.

Various other motions—including motions to reduce the charges against the defendant, to obtain evidence during discovery, or to extend the trial date—may also be made prior to the trial. As with motions made during the civil litigation process, each motion must be accompanied by supporting affidavits and/or legal memoranda.

Discovery

In preparing for trial, public prosecutors, defense attorneys, and paralegals engage in discovery proceedings (including depositions and interrogatories), interview and subpoena witnesses, prepare exhibits and a trial notebook, examine documents and evidence, and do other tasks necessary to effectively prosecute or defend the defendant. Although similar to civil litigation in these respects, criminal discovery is generally more limited, and the time constraints are different. The *Developing Paralegal Skills* feature on the facing page gives some useful tips for discovery in criminal cases.

During discovery, defendants are generally entitled to obtain any evidence in the possession of the prosecutor relating to the case, including statements previously made by the defendant, objects, documents, and reports of tests and examinations. The prosecutor must hand over evidence that tends to show the defendant's innocence as well as evidence of the defendant's guilt. Defendants are given this

---

motion for a change of venue
A motion requesting that a trial be moved to a different location to ensure a fair and impartial proceeding, for the convenience of the parties, or for some other acceptable reason.

motion to recuse
A motion to remove a particular judge from a case.

motion to sever
A motion to try multiple defendants separately.

DEVELOPING
paralegal skills

DISCOVERY IN THE CRIMINAL CASE

A law firm is defending Taylor Rogers in a case of attempted murder. He allegedly shot a person in a drive-by shooting on the expressway. Lee Soloman, a paralegal, is working on the case. Today, as the result of a successful discovery motion that his supervising attorney received from the court, Lee has obtained copies of all evidence that the prosecuting attorney has in his file. Lee's job is to create the discovery file and then to work with the material in the file to prepare the case.

TIPS FOR CRIMINAL DISCOVERY

- Create a discovery file containing sections for the defendant's statements, witnesses' statements, police reports, tests, and other evidence.
- Review the evidence and prepare a memo summarizing it.
- Review the memo and/or evidence with your supervising attorney.
- If the supervising attorney agrees, contact witnesses and obtain statements.
- Interview the police officers who were involved in the arrest or who were at the crime scene.

right to offset the fact that the prosecution (the state) has more resources at its disposal than the defendant (an individual citizen).

Some state statutes allow the prosecutor access to materials that the defense intends to introduce as evidence in the trial. Also, in some jurisdictions, when the defense attorney requests discovery of case materials from the prosecutor, the defense is required to disclose similar materials to the prosecutor in return. In the absence of such statutes, courts have generally refused discovery to the prosecution. This judicial restraint is intended to protect the defendant from self-incrimination, as guaranteed by the Fifth Amendment to the U.S. Constitution (see Appendix I). Today, as the *Practice Focus* feature on the next page discusses, criminal trials can involve ever more sophisticated tools of investigation.

The Trial

Only a small fraction of the criminal cases brought by the state actually go to trial. Some defendants are released, or the charges against them are dropped. Most defendants plead guilty to the offense or to a lesser offense prior to trial. Plea bargaining occurs at every stage of criminal proceedings, from the arraignment to the date of trial (even during a trial, defendants can accept a plea bargain). Because a trial is expensive and the outcome uncertain, both sides in criminal cases have an incentive to negotiate a plea and thus avoid the trial—just as both sides in a civil dispute are motivated to reach a settlement.

Although some criminal trials go on for weeks and are highly publicized, most criminal trials last less than one week (often only a few days). The trial itself is conducted in much the same way as a civil trial. The prosecutor and the defense attorney make their opening statements, examine and cross-examine witnesses, and summarize their positions in closing arguments. At some trials, graphics are used for illustration. These are discussed in the *Developing Paralegal Skills* feature on page 421 and in *Ethics Watch* on page 422. Following closing arguments, the jury is instructed and sent to deliberate. When the jury renders a verdict, the trial comes to an end. There are, however, a few major procedural differences between criminal trials and civil trials, including those discussed next.

ON THE web

For a discussion of the steps in a criminal (or civil) trial, go to **www.americanbar.org**, and enter "Steps in a Trial" in the search box.

PRACTICE focus

CSI COMES TO THE COURTROOM

Technology is revolutionizing the practice of criminal law by changing the type of evidence available to police in investigating crimes. Criminal prosecutions today involve not just witness testimony, but evidence collected with the latest scientific techniques. Paralegals working in criminal law need to educate themselves on how these technologies work so they can prepare arguments for and against admissibility of high-tech evidence. Techniques you may have seen on *CSI* are turning up in routine police work.

Some of the technologies moving from science fiction to reality include the following:

- Facial recognition software means that identification isn't just for lineups any more. Facial recognition software works off underlying bone structure, so cosmetic changes to hair styles or beards won't fool it.

- Handheld spectrometers allow investigators in the field to detect drug residues and other substances at levels invisible to the naked eye.

- Fluorescent dyes react to blood and can reveal even tiny droplets of blood otherwise invisible. Once blood spatter data are collected, simulations can suggest the type of weapon used, how a wound was inflicted, and whether the assailant was left- or right-handed.

- Portable lasers are allowing crime scene investigators to locate tiny bits of evidence, such as a fragment from a strand of hair.

- 3-D scanning allows instant re-creation of crime scenes on laptops at the scene, giving police faster access to important information.

- Firearms databases allow police to distinguish bullets fired from different guns as accurately as fingerprints distinguish individual people.

All this technology can help solve crimes, but each piece can also be misused by police or prosecutors. Paralegals on both sides of the case need to understand these technologies to effectively argue their relevance and admissibility in individual cases.

The Presumption of Innocence

In criminal trials, the defendant is innocent until proved guilty. The prosecutor bears the burden of proving the defendant guilty as charged. Defendants do not have to prove their innocence. In fact, they are not required to present any evidence whatsoever to counter the state's accusations (although it is usually in their best interests to provide some defense). Even a defendant who actually committed the crime is innocent in the eyes of the law unless the prosecutor can present sufficient evidence to convince the jury or judge of the defendant's guilt.

Not only does the state bear the burden of proving the defendant guilty, but it also is held to a high standard of proof. The prosecution must prove its case *beyond a reasonable doubt.* It is not enough for the jury (or judge) to think that the defendant is probably guilty. The members of the jury must be firmly convinced of guilt. The jurors receive instructions such as, "If you think there is a real possibility that he is not guilty, you *must* give him the benefit of the doubt and find him not guilty." The presumption of innocence and the high burden of proof are designed to protect the individual from the state.

The Privilege against Self-Incrimination

As mentioned, the Fifth Amendment to the U.S. Constitution states that no person can be forced to give testimony that might be self-incriminating. Therefore, a defendant does not have to testify at trial. Witnesses may also refuse to testify on this ground. For example, if a witness, while testifying, is asked a question and answering the question would reveal her own criminal wrongdoing, the witness may

DEVELOPING
paralegal skills

PREPARING GRAPHIC PRESENTATIONS

Melanie Hofstadter, a paralegal who is about to retire from her job, is training her replacement. Melanie works for a law firm that specializes in criminal law and has assisted the attorneys countless times with trial preparations. Now she is instructing the new paralegal, Keera Mason, on how to prepare graphic presentations for the attorneys' courtroom use.

Melanie explains that trial graphics are classified into three main types: fact graphics, concept graphics, and case graphics.

1. Fact graphics show only the facts on which both parties agree—for example, a time line indicating the order in which events occurred.

2. Concept graphics are used to educate the judge and jury about ideas with which they may not be familiar, such as the general procedures involved in DNA fingerprinting.

3. Case graphics, or analytical graphics, illustrate the basis of the defense or allegation; for example, a flowchart showing how certain facts are related and how they lead to a specific conclusion.

Melanie gives Keera a document that contains a list of tips and suggestions that Keera should keep in mind when preparing trial graphics.

TIPS FOR PREPARING A GRAPHIC PRESENTATION

- Remember that less can be more. A good graphic presentation should be simple and straightforward. Trim excess words and punctuation from charts, lists, and diagrams; using incomplete sentences and simple phrases is acceptable in graphic presentations.

- Use boldfaced text and easy-to-read fonts.

- Keep plenty of "white space" in the graphic displays.

- Know what you want the reader to focus on, and eliminate all distractions.

- Remember that it is your job to make it easy for the jury to see, read, and understand your points. Don't overburden the graphic displays with too much information or detail.

- Keep in mind that the main purpose of trial graphics is to focus attention on the points that you want to emphasize or highlight, not to focus attention on the actual presentation or display.

"take the Fifth" and refuse to testify on the ground that the testimony may incriminate her. It does not prevent defendants from being required to provide physical samples (such as blood); submit to fingerprinting, photography, or measurements; write or speak for identification purposes; appear in court; or make a gesture or assume a particular position.

The Right to a Speedy Trial

The Sixth Amendment requires a speedy and public trial for criminal prosecutions but does not specify what is meant by "speedy." The federal Speedy Trial Act (18 USC §3161-3174) also sets time limits. Federal Rule of Criminal Procedure 48 also gives courts discretion to dismiss cases not brought to trial promptly. Most states have similar statutes and rules.

Generally, criminal cases are brought to trial much more quickly than civil cases. A defendant who remains in custody prior to trial, for example, is often tried within thirty to forty-five days from the date of arraignment. If the defendant (or the defendant's attorney) needs more time to prepare a defense, the defendant may give up the right to be tried within a certain number of days but will still go to trial within a relatively short period of time (a few months, typically). As noted in Chapter 5, the Sixth Amendment also guarantees accused persons the right to confront and cross-examine witnesses against them.

ETHICS WATCH

THE IMPORTANCE OF ACCURACY

In preparing exhibits for trial, especially when creating an exhibit from raw data, it is important that the paralegal ensure that the exhibit is accurate and not misleading. An attorney has a duty not to falsify evidence. If erroneous evidence is introduced in court and challenged by opposing counsel, your supervising attorney may face serious consequences. By preparing an inaccurate exhibit (for example, by miscalculating a column of figures), the paralegal may jeopardize the attorney's professional reputation by causing the attorney to breach a professional duty.

This paralegal responsibility comes from the following codes:

- NALA *Code of Ethics,* Canon 10: "A paralegal's conduct is guided by bar associations' codes of professional responsibility and rules of professional conduct."
- NFPA *Model Code of Ethics and Professional Responsibility,* Section EC-1.3: "A paralegal shall maintain a high standard of professional conduct."

The Requirement for a Unanimous Verdict

Of the criminal cases that go to trial, the majority are tried by a jury. In most jurisdictions, jury verdicts in criminal cases must be *unanimous* for **acquittal** or conviction. In other words, all twelve jurors (some states allow smaller juries; six jurors are common) must agree that the defendant is either guilty or not guilty.

If the jury cannot reach unanimous agreement on whether to acquit or convict the defendant, the result is a **hung jury**. When the jury is hung, the defendant may be tried again (although often the case is not retried). The requirement for unanimity is important because if even one juror is not convinced of the defendant's guilt, the defendant will not be convicted. Thus, the prosecuting attorney must make as strong a case as possible, while the defense attorney can aim at persuading one or more jurors to have doubts. As in all litigation, throughout a trial, a law firm must take steps to maintain the security of its information, as discussed in the *Technology and Today's Paralegal* feature on the facing page.

Sentencing

When a defendant is found guilty by a trial court (or pleads guilty to an offense without a trial), the judge will pronounce a **sentence**, which is the penalty imposed on anyone convicted of a crime. Often, the sentence is pronounced in a separate proceeding.

Limited Role of Jury

Unless the prosecutor is seeking the death penalty, the jury normally is not involved in the sentencing of the defendant. Jurors are dismissed after they return a verdict, and the judge either sentences the defendant on the spot or schedules a future court appearance for sentencing. At the sentencing hearing, the judge usually

---

acquittal
A certification or declaration following a trial that the individual accused of a crime is innocent, or free from guilt, in the eyes of the law and is thus absolved of the charges.

hung jury
A jury whose members are so irreconcilably divided in their opinions that they cannot reach a verdict. The judge in this situation may order a new trial.

sentence
The punishment, or penalty, ordered by the court to be inflicted on a person convicted of a crime.

TECHNOLOGY AND
today's paralegal

EVOLVING TECHNOLOGY, SECURITY, AND EVIDENCE

The many technologies used in law offices change frequently. It is useful to be aware of developments that affect the functioning of a law office and can destroy the security of information sent to other parties. Technology can pose threats to the security of information as well as offer new opportunities in the collection and evaluation of evidence.

PROTECTING SECURITY

A lack of awareness of technological capabilities can mean that documents believed to be secure are not. For example, members of the media were able to read parts of a confidential settlement that had been redacted (blacked out) in the settlement of a lawsuit involving Facebook and ConnectU. The computer codes that supposedly hid some information from public view were bypassed in electronic copies of documents released to the press, allowing reporters to see the private information. The lawyers for ConnectU claimed to have received $65 million from Facebook in the settlement, but the press could see the amount was actually $31 million. ConnectU fired the law firm that made the mistake.

KNOWING WHERE PEOPLE ARE OR WERE

Global positioning system (GPS) devices are now built into many vehicles. The digital information collected by these devices may allow investigators to determine the location of a vehicle at a certain point in time, which can help in criminal investigations. Where a suspect was at a particular time may be revealed by GPS data, for example.

Federal rules now require cell phones to support GPS information so that 911 emergency calls can be pinpointed by location. This can be important in criminal investigations, because it would enable an investigator to find out the location of persons and their cell phones, even if they did not call 911.

USING DIGITAL FORENSIC EXPERTS

The use of digital forensic experts in litigation is increasing. Professionals can assist in the evaluation of digital material and identify when it has been compromised and is no longer trustworthy. Just as the use of DNA evidence has helped to convict some people accused of crimes and free others falsely accused, digital evidence is playing an increasing role in helping to establish guilt or innocence.

TECHNOLOGY TIP

The rapid evolution of technology means that law firms must watch for possibilities not envisioned before. Web sites such as **eLawExchange. com** provide information about innovations affecting law and about how to find experts when needed. Paralegals should use such resources to keep up to date with evolving technologies.

---

listens to arguments from both attorneys concerning the factors in "aggravation and mitigation" (which involve why the defendant's punishment should be harsh or lenient).

Range of Penalties

Most criminal statutes set forth a maximum and minimum penalty that should be imposed for a violation. Thus, judges often have a range of options and a great deal of discretion in sentencing individual defendants. The judge typically sentences the offender to one or more of the following:

- Incarceration in a jail or a prison.
- Probation (formal or informal).
- Fines or other financial penalties.
- Public work service (for less serious offenses).
- Classes (for certain types of offenses, such as domestic violence and alcohol- or drug-related crimes).
- Death (in some states).

ON THE web

The U.S. Sentencing Guidelines can be found online at **www.ussc.gov**

In federal and many state cases, the defense and prosecutor prepare sentencing memoranda, arguing for particular sentences. The federal courts use sentencing guidelines to help judges determine sentences. Paralegals are often involved in helping to draft sentencing memoranda and organize supporting documents, such as letters of support for the defendant or statements from the victim for a prosecutor. In some states, victims have the right to address the sentencing court and may have an attorney or paralegal assist them in preparing their statements.

Incarceration

Defendants sentenced to incarceration will go to a county jail for less serious offenses (involving sentences of less than one year) or a state or federal prison for serious crimes (involving sentences of more than one year).

The judge may consider alternatives to jail time. Defendants may be placed on house arrest (and wear an electronic device that will notify the authorities if they leave a designated area). Defendants who have alcohol or drug problems may sometimes be allowed to satisfy the incarceration portion of a sentence in an inpatient rehabilitation program. In some states, defendants may be allowed to satisfy short periods of custody time (ten to thirty days) by checking into the jail on weekends only or by participating in a supervised release program, which enables them to stay employed.

Probation

probation
When a convicted defendant is released from confinement but is still under court supervision for a period of time.

A part of many sentences is **probation**. Typically, defendants are sentenced to less than the maximum penalty and placed on probation with certain conditions for a set time. In such cases, the sentence imposed is said to be *suspended*. If the person fails to meet the conditions of probation, probation may be revoked, and the person may be sentenced to custody time up to the maximum for the offense.

COMBINATION OF PENALTIES.   If convicted of driving while under the influence, for example, a defendant might be sentenced to two days in jail, three years of informal probation, a fine of $3,000, and ten days of public work service (picking up roadside trash). The court could also require the defendant to attend a first-offenders program (meeting twice a week for six to eight weeks and costing several thousand dollars). If the defendant does not do all of these things, the court can revoke probation and sentence the person to spend up to a year in jail.

TYPES OF PROBATION.   Probation can be either formal or informal. In formal probation, which is typical in felony cases, the defendant is required to meet regularly with a probation officer. The defendant may be required to submit to drug and alcohol testing, to possess no firearms, and to avoid socializing with those who might be engaging in criminal activity, for example.

Defendants on informal probation do not have a probation officer, but they may be required to comply with certain conditions. This could include paying a fine, performing public work service, participating in specified programs (such as attending Alcoholics Anonymous meetings or anger management classes), and not violating the law.

Diversion

diversion program
In some jurisdictions, an alternative to prosecution that is offered to certain felony suspects to deter them from future unlawful acts.

In many states, **diversion programs** are available to defendants charged with certain offenses specified by statute. Diversion is an alternative to prosecution. Generally, these programs suspend criminal prosecution for a certain period of time and require that the defendant complete specified conditions—such as attending special classes and not getting in trouble with the police—during that time. If the person fulfills *all* of the requirements of diversion, the case will be dismissed. If the defendant fails to complete the diversion satisfactorily, the criminal prosecution springs back to life, and the defendant is prosecuted for the crime.

The objective is to deter the defendant from further wrongdoing by offering an incentive—namely, a way to avoid any record of conviction.

Diversion is a good option for defendants who are guilty of the crimes alleged and want to avoid having criminal convictions on their records. Most defendants who are eligible for diversion choose that option at the arraignment or soon after and thus do not proceed to trial. On occasion, however, judges may allow a person to divert even after a trial.

Appeal

Persons convicted of crimes have a right of appeal. Most felony convictions are appealed to an intermediate court of appeal. In some states, however, there is no intermediate court of appeal, so the appeal goes directly to the state's highest appellate court, usually called the supreme court of the state. Most convictions that result in supervised release or fines are not appealed, but a high percentage of the convictions that result in prison sentences are appealed. About 10 percent of such convictions are reversed on appeal. The most common reason for reversal is that the trial court admitted improper evidence, such as evidence obtained by a search that did not meet constitutional requirements.

If a conviction is overturned on appeal, the defendant may or may not be tried again, depending on the reason for the reversal and on whether the case was reversed with or without prejudice. A decision reversed "with prejudice" means that no further action can be taken on the claim or cause. A decision reversed "without prejudice" may be tried again.

social MEDIA TODAY

Social media are specifically designed to make social computing available to anyone with a device capable of connecting to the Internet.

KEY TERMS AND CONCEPTS

Chapter Summary

Criminal Law and Procedures

WHAT IS A CRIME?

1. *Key differences between civil and criminal law*—Crimes are distinguished from civil wrongs, such as torts, in several ways:

   a. Crimes are deemed to be offenses against society as a whole.

   b. Whereas tort (civil) litigation involves lawsuits between private parties, criminal litigation involves the state's prosecution of a wrongdoer.

   c. Crimes are defined as such by state legislatures or the federal government.

   d. In criminal cases the state must prove the defendant's guilt beyond a reasonable doubt. In civil cases, the plaintiff need only prove a case by a preponderance of the evidence.

   e. A criminal act need not involve a victim.

2. *Civil liability for criminal acts*—Those who commit crimes may be subject to both criminal and civil liability, such as when a person commits an assault, but the legal actions are separate matters.

3. *Classification of crimes*—Crimes fall into two basic classifications: felonies and misdemeanors.

   a. Felonies are more serious crimes (such as murder, rape, and robbery) for which penalties may range from imprisonment for a year or longer to (in some states) death.

   b. Misdemeanors are less serious crimes (such as prostitution, disturbing the peace, and public intoxication) for which penalties may include imprisonment for up to a year. Petty offenses, or infractions, such as violations of building codes, are usually a subset of misdemeanors.

4. *Jurisdiction over crimes*—Most crimes fall under state statutes and state prosecution, but there is a long list of federal criminal acts, too.

ELEMENTS OF CRIMINAL LIABILITY

For criminal liability to exist, the state must meet certain standards of proof:

1. *The criminal act*—Most crimes require that the defendant be shown to have committed or attempted to commit an act, *actus reus,* the guilty act.

2. *State of mind*—Even a wrongful act that harms society will not be punished unless the defendant had the required state of mind, *mens rea,* or intent to do a criminal act.

3. *Corporate criminal liability*—Under modern law, corporations may be held liable for crimes, and corporate officers and directors may be held personally liable for the crimes of the corporation.

4. *Defenses to criminal liability*—Criminal liability may be avoided if the state of mind required for the crime was lacking or some other defense against liability can be raised. Defenses include self-defense, defense of others, defense of property, and the running of a statute of limitations.

TYPES OF CRIMES

The number of acts defined as criminal by federal, state, and local laws is lengthy. The five traditional major categories of crimes are as follows:

1. *Violent crime*—Crimes that cause another person to suffer harm or death are violent crimes, such as murder, rape, robbery, and assault and battery.

2. *Property crime*—The most common criminal activities are those in which the offender either takes or damages the property of another. Property crimes include burglary, larceny (stealing), obtaining goods by false pretenses, receiving stolen goods, arson, and forgery.

3. *Public order crimes*—Crimes that do not cause direct harm to others but involve behavior that society has deemed inappropriate, such as public drunkenness and illegal drug use, are public order crimes.

4. *White-collar crime*—Illegal acts committed by individuals or business entities in the course of legitimate business—for example, embezzlement, mail or wire fraud, bribery, theft of trade secrets, and insider trading—are white-collar crimes.

5. *Organized crime*—The criminal enterprises that make up organized crime usually provide illegal goods and

services such as gambling, prostitution, and illegal narcotics. Money from such activities will be made to appear legitimate by money laundering, which

is a focus of regulatory attention. The Racketeer Influenced and Corrupt Organizations Act (RICO) is applied to a wide range of activities.

CYBER CRIMES

Cyber crimes are crimes that are committed with computers and occur in cyberspace. They are not new crimes but existing crimes in which the Internet is the instrument of wrongdoing. Cyber crimes include theft of money or data,

identity theft, cyberstalking, and hacking. Prosecuting cyber crimes presents new challenges to law enforcement and the courts.

SOCIAL MEDIA AND CRIMINAL JUSTICE

Social media tools are being used increasingly by law enforcement authorities, so legal providers must know the appropriate parameters of such use when defending clients.

1. *Use of social media*—Criminals are also making greater use of social media tools, so law enforcement is responding by monitoring transmissions and gathering records of transmissions.

2. *Proper evidence*—Lawyers, when providing assistance to those accused of crimes, will look to see if the rights of clients have been violated in the collection of evidence through investigators' improper exploitation of social media. Improper use in court proceedings is another concern.

CONSTITUTIONAL SAFEGUARDS

Specific procedures must be followed in arresting and prosecuting a criminal suspect to safeguard the suspect's constitutional rights. The Constitution guarantees that persons accused of crimes have rights and protections, including protection against unreasonable searches and seizures, the right to due process of law, protection against double jeopardy, protection against self-incrimination (the right to remain silent), the right to a speedy and public trial, the right to confront witnesses and be represented by an attorney, and protection against excessive bail and cruel and unusual punishment.

1. *Exclusionary rule*—Evidence obtained in violation of a defendant's constitutional rights normally must be

excluded from trial, along with evidence derived from illegally obtained evidence.

2. Miranda *rule*—At the time a criminal suspect is taken into custody, the arresting officers must inform the suspect of his or her rights by reading the *Miranda* warnings. Evidence or confession obtained in violation of the suspect's rights will normally not be admissible in court. The Supreme Court has made numerous exceptions to the *Miranda* rule, such as when public safety is at stake.

CRIMINAL PROCEDURES PRIOR TO PROSECUTION

The initial procedure undertaken by the police after a crime is reported or observed includes steps that must be followed properly in order for a case to proceed.

1. *Arrest and booking*—Officers take a person into custody and charge the person with a crime. The suspect is usually taken to a holding facility (jail) where the person is detained while being booked (entered into

the police log). Police must show probable cause for the accusation made and, in many cases, need an arrest warrant issued by a judge.

2. *Investigation after the arrest*—Police may need to interview witnesses, collect evidence, execute search warrants, and take other steps in making the case that a suspect should be prosecuted.

THE PROSECUTION BEGINS

Police make a report of the alleged crime to a public prosecutor. The prosecutor decides, based on a review of the evidence, if the case should proceed or the accusations be dropped.

1. *Complaint and initial appearance*—A complaint against an accused person includes a statement of charges; upon being served with a complaint, the person formally becomes a defendant. There will be

an initial appearance before a judge or magistrate, and the defendant is usually released on personal recognizance or must post bail.

2. *Preliminary hearing*—Appearance before a judge will determine if there is sufficient evidence to show probable cause so as to allow the matter to proceed.

3. *Grand jury review*—The federal government and many states use a grand jury to obtain an indictment in felony cases; only with such an indictment will the case go to trial.

4. *Arraignment*—The defendant is formally charged in court and enters a plea. Often the parties have agreed to a plea bargain that will terminate proceedings at this point.

5. *Pretrial motions*—If the case proceeds, various motions may be entered, often by the defense, such as a motion to suppress evidence or a motion to dismiss the case.

6. *Discovery*—In criminal cases, the defendant is entitled to obtain any evidence relating to the case possessed by the prosecution, including documents, statements previously made by the defendant, objects, reports of tests or examinations, and other evidence. In some instances, the prosecutor is entitled to obtain certain evidence related to the case possessed by the defense as well.

THE TRIAL

Most criminal cases are settled before they get to trial through plea bargaining or other means. Most criminal trials last less than one week and are similar to civil trials, except in a few major ways.

1. *The presumption of innocence*—The defendant is innocent until the prosecutor proves the defendant's guilt to the jury (or judge) beyond a reasonable doubt. The defendant is not required to present any evidence at the trial.

2. *The privilege against self-incrimination*—The defendant and witnesses cannot be forced to testify if such testimony would be incriminating.

3. *The right to a speedy trial*—Criminal defendants have a right to a speedy and public trial. Even if they waive that right, criminal cases usually go to trial more quickly than civil cases.

4. *The requirement for a* unanimous jury—Most criminal cases are tried by juries. Generally, all of the jurors must reach agreement in order to acquit or convict

the defendant (whereas civil trials typically do not require unanimous agreement).

5. *Sentencing*—The judge sentences a defendant who has been found guilty (or who pleads guilty or no contest), often at a separate proceeding. Most criminal statutes set forth a range of penalties that can be imposed, and judges are free to select the appropriate penalty within that range. Typically, sentences involve fines, imprisonment, and probation (including conditions of probation). In some cases (in some states), the death penalty may be imposed.

6. *Diversion*—Alternatively, the defendant may be sentenced to a diversion program, which will result in a dismissal of the case provided that the defendant complies with all the requirements of diversion (which vary by state).

7. *Appeal*—If the defendant loses at trial, he or she may appeal the case to a higher court. A small percentage of criminal cases are reversed on appeal.

QUESTIONS FOR REVIEW

1. What are the key differences between civil and criminal law?

2. What two elements are required for criminal liability? What are the five traditional types of crime? What defenses can be raised against criminal liability?

3. What are cyber crimes? What role can social media play in these crimes? What are the factors used to determine whether social media evidence is protected from use by prosecutors?

4. What are the constitutional rights of a person accused of a crime? Which constitutional amendments provide those rights? What are *Miranda* rights, and which amendments provide the basis for *Miranda* rights?

5. List and explain the basic steps involved in criminal procedure from the time a crime is reported to the resolution of the case.

6. Explain what happens during sentencing. Describe the different types of penalties and alternatives that exist. What happens during an appeal?

ETHICAL QUESTIONS

1. Raja is a paralegal with a criminal defense law firm. One of her responsibilities, after the attorney accepts a case, is to meet with the client to provide to the client, in writing, the firm's social networking policy. It requires clients to remove any social networking accounts they have on sites such as Facebook or Google+ because postings may provide detrimental evidence. Because Raja is busy, she fails to meet with a new client charged with drunk driving. The client is convicted. During sentencing, the judge notes that his initial inclination had been to give the client the minimum sentence, because it was her first offense. However, the prosecutor presented pictures of the cli-ent's partying lifestyle that occurred after the arrest, so the judge is giving her the maximum sentence. What ethics rules has Raja violated? What might be the outcome for Raja? Her supervising attorney?

2. Lynda Lore is an experienced paralegal who works for a criminal defense firm. The lawyers trust her implic-itly and feel that she is as knowledgeable as they are. One Monday morning, Johnny Dodds, an attorney with the firm, is scheduled to be in court for a motion and, at the same time, at a deposition. Johnny calls Lynda into his office and asks her to take the deposi-tion. Should Lynda take it? Why or why not?

PRACTICE QUESTIONS AND ASSIGNMENTS

1. Identify each of the following crimes by its classification:

   a. Jerry refuses to put his trash out at the curb for the weekly trash pickup. Instead, he lets it collect on the side of his garage, where it is an eyesore and attracts rats to the neighborhood. The police department receives complaints from his neigh-bors and gives Jerry a citation for violating the trash ordinance.

   b. Neehan is arrested for being under the influence of drugs in public. She faces a possible jail sen-tence of six months.

   c. Susanna is arrested for forging Martha's name on the back of a check made out to Martha and then depositing the check into her own bank account. The penalty includes confinement for over one year in prison on conviction.

2. Using the material presented in the chapter on state of mind, identify the type of homicide committed in each of the following situations:

   a. David, while driving in an intoxicated state, crashes into another car and kills its occupants.

   b. David, after pulling up next to his wife at a stoplight and observing her passionately kissing another man, smashes into her car and kills her.

   c. David, who is angry with his boss for firing him, plans to kill his boss by smashing his car into his boss's car, killing his boss and making it look like a car accident. David carries out his plan, kills his boss, and survives the accident.

3. Identify the following criminal procedures:

   a. Ani is charged with the crime of arson. She pleads not guilty and is bound over for trial in the district court.

   b. Reyna is taken to the police station, searched, photographed, fingerprinted, and allowed to make one telephone call.

   c. A jury of Barbara's peers reviews the evidence against her and determines whether probable cause exists and whether the prosecutor should proceed to trial for manslaughter.

   d. Police officers stop Miguel on the street because his description matches that of a reported gas-station robber. He is three blocks from the gas station when they stop him. They question him, search him, and find that he has a pocketful of $20 and $50 bills—the same denominations that were reported by the gas-station attendant as having been stolen. The police read Miguel his rights and take him to the police station.

   e. Andrew is taken before a magistrate, where the charges against him are read and counsel is ap-pointed. His request to be set free on bail is denied.

   f. In exchange for a guilty plea to manslaughter, the prosecutor agrees to drop the more serious mur-der charges against Maria.

4. Mona was laid off from her manufacturing job three years ago. Her unemployment compensation has run out, as has her severance package, and she has few prospects for finding work in the down econ-omy. Mona learns that a former co-worker has died. She thinks that if she can file a tax return using the co-worker's name and Social Security number, she can collect a tax refund. Mona takes the woman's name and looks up her Social Security number on a genealogy Web site. She waits until January 2014 to file the tax return in the deceased's name. She receives a refund check. Mona decides that this is a quick and easy way to make money, so she

continues to take names from obituaries reported in the media and file more false tax returns until she has collected over $100,000. What crimes has Mona committed?

5. The police pick up Larry and take him to the station for questioning in a local murder case. They detain him for three days. After two days of questioning, Larry says, "I want an attorney. You haven't let me call my attorney." It is late, and Larry's attorney does not answer the phone, but she receives the message first thing in the morning on the third day that Larry is in custody and heads directly to the police station, where she secures Larry's release. She confirms that the police failed to tell Larry that he had the right to have an attorney present and did not give him any of his other *Miranda* rights. What will be the result if a prosecutor tries to use the information that Larry gave to the police against him in court?

QUESTIONS FOR CRITICAL ANALYSIS

1. What makes a crime a federal crime? Why is there a difference between state and federal crimes? Should there be?

2. A guilty act is typically required in order for a crime to be committed. Is it ever possible for a crime to be committed without a guilty act? If so, how? Give an example of such a crime.

3. Should cyber crimes include the elements of traditional crimes (*actus reas* and *mens rea*)? Why or why not? Do you think the punishment for crimes committed in cyberspace should be more severe than the punishment for traditional crimes? Why or why not?

4. After answering a few background questions regarding his name and title, a government official took the Fifth Amendment 82 times during the course of a hearing on corruption charges. What does taking the Fifth Amendment 82 times say about guilt or innocence? Does taking the Fifth Amendment protect the official from self-incrimination?

5. Locate a copy of the United States Supreme Court decision in *United States v. Jones*, 132 S.Ct. 945 (2012), available on the Court Web site at **www.supremecourt. gov/opinions/11pdf/10-1259.pdf**. Answer the following questions about the case:

   a. What are the facts of the case?

   b. Which courts heard this case and what did they decide?

   c. Why did the Court say it did not need to decide whether Jones had a reasonable expectation of privacy issue?

   d. If the Court did not decide the case on the reasonable expectation of privacy issue, what did it base its decision on?

   e. What is your opinion of the decision in this case?

PROJECTS

1. Contact your local police department and ask if it gives tours to students. If so, arrange to take a tour of the department and learn, to the extent possible, what procedures are followed in booking and investigation.

2. Review your state's court rules to see how the rules for criminal cases differ from those for civil cases. List and describe the major differences.

GROUP PROJECT

This project involves researching cyberbullying. Google Scholar is the recommended source for your research.

Student one will locate the Lori Drew case on cyberbullying and provide a summary of the facts and legal repercussions.

Student two will locate and summarize an article discussing cyberbullying in the schools. Student three will locate and summarize an article discussing schools' interpretation of the First Amendment.

Student four will locate and summarize an article discussing ways to legally address the cyberbullying problem in the schools.

The group will make a recommendation on how to help schools with the problem of cyberbullying and will submit their recommendation and summaries to the instructor.

USING INTERNET RESOURCES

1. Go to the Famous Trials Web site operated by the University of Missouri–Kansas City School of Law at **http://law2.umkc.edu/faculty/projects/ftrials/ftrials.htm**. Choose one of the famous cases, read it, and then answer the following questions:

   a. Who was the defendant, and with what crime or crimes was he or she charged?

   b. What defenses were raised by the defendant?

   c. What court heard the case?

   d. What was the court's decision?

END NOTES

1. The American Law Institute (mentioned in Chapter 5) issued the Official Draft of the Model Penal Code in 1962. The Model Penal Code was designed to assist state legislatures in reexamining and recodifying state criminal laws. Uniformity among the states is not as important in criminal law as in other areas of the law. Crime varies with local circumstances, and it is appropriate that punishments vary accordingly.

2. Pronounced *ak*-tus *ray*-us.

3. Pronounced menz *ray*-uh.

4. *United States v. Park,* 421 U.S. 658, 95 S.Ct. 1903, 44 L.Ed.2d 489 (1975).

5. 384 U.S. 436, 86 S.Ct. 1602, 16 L.Ed.2d 694 (1966).

6. Pronounced in-*dite*-ment.

CourseMate The available CourseMate for this text has an interactive eBook and interactive learning tools, including flash cards, quizzes, and more. To learn more about this resource and access free demo CourseMate resources, go to **www.cengagebrain.com**, and search for this book. To access CourseMate materials that you have purchased, go to **login.cengagebrain.com**.

Part 3

Key Elements of the Law

Tort Law, Product Liability, and Consumer Law

Chapter Outline

After completing this chapter, you will know:

- What a tort is, the purpose of tort law, and the basic categories of torts.

- The four elements of negligence.

- What is meant by strict liability and the underlying policy for imposing strict product liability.

- What defenses can be raised in product liability actions.

- Some of the ways in which the government protects consumers against unfair business practices and harmful products.

Introduction

Torts are wrongful actions. In fact, the word *tort* is French for "wrong." Through tort law, society seeks to compensate those who have suffered injuries as a result of the wrongful conduct of others. Although some torts, such as trespass, originated in the English common law, the field of tort law continues to expand. As new ways to commit wrongs—such as the use of the Internet to commit wrongful acts—are recognized, the courts extend the principles of tort law to cover these wrongs.

Here, we discuss some of the primary concepts of tort law and how they are being applied today. We also consider *product liability,* which is a major area of tort law under which sellers can be held liable for defective products. In the final pages of the chapter, we look at a growing body of law designed to protect the health and safety and the credit of consumers.

tort
A civil wrong not arising from a breach of contract; a breach of a legal duty that causes harm or injury to another.

The Basis of Tort Law

Two notions serve as the basis of all torts: wrongs and compensation. Tort law recognizes that some acts are wrong because they cause injuries to others. In a tort action, one person or group brings suit against another person or group to obtain compensation (money damages) or other relief for the harm suffered.

Because tort suits involve "private" wrongs, they are distinguishable from criminal actions, which involve "public" wrongs. The state prosecutor brings criminal actions against individuals who commit acts that are considered to be wrongs against society as a whole (crimes are usually defined by statute, as discussed in Chapter 13). Sometimes an act may result in both a tort lawsuit and a criminal prosecution.

Generally, the purpose of tort law is to provide remedies for the invasion of interests or rights—such as people's interests in their physical safety and security, privacy, freedom of movement, and reputation—that society seeks to protect. In this chapter, we first discuss two broad categories of torts: *intentional torts* and *negligence.* The classification of a particular tort depends largely on how the tort occurs (intentionally or unintentionally) and the surrounding circumstances. We then examine the concept of *strict liability,* a tort doctrine under which a defendant may be held liable for harm or injury to another regardless of intention or fault, and look at the application of this doctrine in the area of product liability.

When thinking about torts, it is important to focus on the **elements** of a specific tort in question. The elements are the points that a plaintiff must prove to succeed in a tort claimed. These are important, as they will affect your work. In analyzing a client's tort claim you will have to check to make sure there is evidence to prove each element of the tort.

elements
The issues and facts that the plaintiff must prove to succeed in a tort claim.

Intentional Torts

An **intentional tort**, as the term implies, requires *intent.* Hence, intent will be an element of all intentional torts. In tort law, intent does not necessarily mean that the person accused (who is sometimes called the **tortfeasor**) intended to harm someone. Rather, it means that the actor intended the consequences of an act or knew or should have known that certain consequences would result from an act. The law generally assumes that individuals intend the *normal* consequences of their actions. Thus, pushing another—even if done in fun and without any bad intent—is an intentional tort if an injury results, because the person being shoved can be expected to fall down.

Intentional torts fall into two categories: intentional torts against persons and intentional torts against property. Next, we look at both of these categories.

Intentional tort
A wrongful act knowingly committed.

tortfeasor
One who commits a tort.

Intentional Torts against Persons

Intentional torts against persons include assault and battery, false imprisonment, intentional infliction of emotional distress, defamation, invasion of the right to privacy, appropriation, misrepresentation, and wrongful interference.

Assault

assault

Any word or action intended to make another person apprehensive or fearful of immediate physical harm; a reasonably believable threat.

An **assault** is any communication or action intended to make another person apprehensive or fearful of immediate physical harm. In other words, an assault is a threat that a reasonable person would believe. Apprehension is not the same as fear. If a contact is such that a reasonable person would want to avoid it, and if there is a reasonable basis for believing that the contact will occur, then the plaintiff suffers apprehension regardless of whether he or she is afraid.

The interest protected by tort law concerning assault is the freedom from having to expect harmful or offensive contact. The occurrence of apprehension is enough to justify compensation. The elements of assault are:

1. an act intended to cause an apprehension of harmful or offensive contact, and

2. an act that causes apprehension in the victim that harmful or offensive contact is imminent.

Battery

battery

The intentional and offensive touching of another without lawful justification.

The *completion* of the threat, if it results in harm to the plaintiff, is a **battery**, which is defined as harmful or offensive physical contact *intentionally* performed.

◆ **EXAMPLE 14.1—** Suppose that Ivan threatens Jean with a gun, then shoots her. The pointing of the gun at Jean is an assault. The firing of the gun (if the bullet hits Jean) is a battery. ◆

The interest protected by tort law concerning battery is the right to personal security and safety. The contact can be harmful, or it can be merely offensive (such as an unwelcome kiss). Physical injury need not occur. The contact can involve any part of the body or anything attached to it—for example, a hat or other item of clothing, a purse, or a chair or an automobile in which one is sitting. Whether the contact is offensive or not is determined by the *reasonable person standard* (which is discussed later in the chapter). The contact can be made by the defendant or by some force the defendant sets in motion—for example a rock thrown or food poisoned. The elements of battery are:

1. an intent to cause an unwanted contact, and

2. the unwanted harmful contact.

COMPENSATION. If the plaintiff shows that there was offensive contact, or fear of such contact, and the jury agrees, the plaintiff has a right to compensation. There is no need to show that the defendant acted out of malice; the person could have just been playing around. The underlying motive does not matter, only the intent to bring about the harmful or offensive contact to the plaintiff. Proving a motive is not necessary but is often relevant. A plaintiff may be compensated for the emotional harm resulting from a battery, as well as for physical harm.

DEFENSES TO ASSAULT AND BATTERY. A number of legally recognized defenses, or reasons why plaintiffs should not obtain compensation they are seeking, can be raised by defendants in tort actions. Later in the chapter, we review defenses that can be raised in many tort cases. The following defenses may be used by a defendant who is sued for assault, battery, or both:

- *Consent.* When a person consents to the act that damages her or him, there is generally no liability (legal responsibility) for the damage done. For instance, if Sue consents to being kissed, Bryan can raise this as a defense if she sues for battery.

- *Self-defense.* An individual who is defending her life or physical well-being can claim self-defense. In situations of both *real* and *apparent* danger, a person may use whatever force is *reasonably* necessary to prevent harmful contact. Thus, if Simon is assaulting Linda with a knife, she can claim this defense if Simon sues her for hitting him with a baseball bat.

- *Defense of others.* A person can act in a reasonable manner to protect others who are in real or apparent danger. If Fred offensively grabs Rafic's wife and Rafic hits Fred, Rafic can raise this as a defense if Fred tries to sue him for battery.

- *Defense of property.* People can use reasonable force in attempting to remove intruders from their homes (but also see the discussion of the castle doctrine in Chapter 13 on page 397). Generally, force that is likely to cause death or great bodily injury should not be used just to protect property. For instance, if you catch someone in the act of breaking into your garage, you can use nondeadly force to stop that person without being liable for battery.

Note that the defendant bears the burden of proving the facts necessary to be able to rely on these defenses. The plaintiff must, of course, respond to such defenses when they are raised.

False Imprisonment

False imprisonment is defined as the intentional confinement or restraint of another person's activities without justification. The elements of false imprisonment are:

1. intent to confine or restrain a person, and

2. actual confinement in boundaries not of the plaintiff's choosing.

False imprisonment interferes with the freedom to move without restraint. The confinement can be accomplished through the use of physical barriers, physical restraint, or threats of physical force. It is essential that the person being restrained not comply with the restraint willingly, but one does not have to resist physically to be subject to restraint.

Stores are often sued for false imprisonment after they have attempted to confine a suspected shoplifter for questioning. (An example is provided in the *Developing Paralegal Skills* feature on the next page.) Under the "privilege to detain" granted to merchants in some states, a merchant can use the defense of *probable cause* to justify delaying a suspected shoplifter. Probable cause exists when the evidence to support the belief that a person is guilty outweighs the evidence against that belief. Although laws governing false imprisonment vary from state to state, generally they require that any detention be conducted in a *reasonable* manner and for only a *reasonable* length of time.

Intentional Infliction of Emotional Distress

The tort of **intentional infliction of emotional distress** (or mental distress) can be defined as an intentional act that amounts to extreme and outrageous conduct resulting in severe emotional distress to another. The elements of intentional infliction of emotional distress are:

1. outrageous conduct by the defendant

2. intent

3. severe emotional distress by the plaintiff

4. with the emotional distress being caused by the defendant's conduct.

◆ **EXAMPLE 14.2—** Suppose a prankster calls Erica and says that her husband has just been in a horrible accident. As a result, Erica suffers intense mental pain or anxiety. The caller's behavior is extreme and outrageous conduct that exceeds the bounds of decency accepted by society and is therefore **actionable** (capable of serving as the basis for a lawsuit). ◆ Courts in some jurisdictions require that the emotional distress be evidenced by some physical symptom or illness or some emotional disturbance that can be documented by a psychiatric consultant or other medical professional.

---

social MEDIA TODAY

Consider setting up personal and professional Facebook pages or Twitter accounts and keeping your posts separated. Remember that just because material is on your "personal" page or account, it still may be seen by others outside your network.

---

false imprisonment
The intentional confinement or restraint of a person against his or her will.

intentional infliction of emotional distress
Intentional, extreme, and outrageous conduct resulting in severe emotional distress to another.

actionable
Capable of serving as the basis of a lawsuit. An actionable claim can be pursued in a lawsuit or other court action.

DEVELOPING
paralegal skills

A CLAIM OF FALSE IMPRISONMENT

Julie Waterman works for a small law firm. She has just been asked to interview a new client. The client detained a customer in his store for suspected shoplifting, and now he is facing a lawsuit brought by the customer for false imprisonment. Julie will conduct the interview with the client, gather as much information as she can about the incident, and summarize what she learns in a memorandum for the attorney to review later. Before the interview, Julie checks the relevant state law governing false imprisonment. During the interview, Julie makes sure that she covers the topics on her checklist for determining false imprisonment.

CHECKLIST FOR DETERMINING FALSE IMPRISONMENT

- Did the client have cause to believe that the customer was shoplifting? What made the client suspect that the customer took merchandise without paying for it?
- Did the customer resist the detention?
- How long did the client detain the customer? Fifteen minutes? An hour? Was the duration of the detention reasonable?
- Was the customer in a reasonably comfortable environment during the detention? Was he prevented from leaving the store?
- Was the customer subjected to abusive or accusatory words or to any indignity while being confined?
- Were all procedures used to detain the customer reasonable?

---

defamation
Anything published or publicly spoken that causes injury to another's good name, reputation, or character.

slander
Defamation in oral form.

libel
Defamation in writing or other published form (such as videotape).

Defamation

Wrongfully harming a person's good reputation constitutes the tort of **defamation**. The law imposes a general duty on all persons to refrain from making false, damaging statements about others. Breaching this duty orally involves the tort of **slander**. Breaching it in writing involves the tort of **libel**. The tort of defamation also arises when a false statement is made about a person's product, business, or title to property.

The common law defines four types of false utterances that are considered defamation *per se* (meaning that no proof of injury or harm is required for these false statements to be actionable):

- A statement that another has a loathsome communicable disease.
- A statement that another has committed improprieties while engaging in a profession or trade.
- A statement that another has committed or has been imprisoned for a serious crime.
- A statement that an unmarried woman is unchaste.

THE PUBLICATION REQUIREMENT.   The basis of the tort of defamation is the publication of a statement or statements that hold an individual up to contempt, ridicule, or hatred. Publication here means simply that the defamatory statements are communicated to persons other than the defamed party. ◆ **EXAMPLE 14.3—**   If Crystal writes Andrew a private letter accusing him of embezzling funds, the action does not constitute libel. If John calls Rita dishonest and incompetent when no one else is around, the action does not constitute slander. In neither case was the message communicated to a third party. ◆

The courts have generally held that even dictating a letter to a secretary constitutes publication, although the publication may be privileged (the meaning of privileged communications in defamation law will be discussed shortly). Moreover, if a third party overhears defamatory statements by chance, the courts usually hold that this also constitutes publication. Defamatory statements made via the Internet are actionable as well. Note further that anyone who republishes or repeats defamatory statements is liable even if that person reveals the source of the statements.

DEFENSES AGAINST DEFAMATION. Truth is normally an absolute defense against a defamation charge. In other words, if the defendant in a defamation suit can prove that his allegedly defamatory statements were true, the defendant will not be liable.

Another defense that is sometimes raised is that the statements were **privileged** communications and thus the defendant is immune from liability. Privileged communications are of two types: absolute and qualified. Only in judicial proceedings and certain legislative proceedings is an *absolute* privilege granted. For example, statements made in the courtroom by attorneys and judges during a trial are absolutely privileged, as are statements made by legislators during debate in a legislature. A *qualified*, or *conditional*, privilege applies when a statement is related to a matter of public interest or when the statement is necessary to protect a person's private interest and is made to another person with an interest in the same subject matter.

In general, false and defamatory statements that are made about *public figures* (public officials and any persons in the public limelight) and that are published in the press are privileged if they are made without **actual malice**. To be made with actual malice, a statement must be made *with either knowledge of falsity or a reckless disregard of the truth*. Statements made about public figures, especially when they are made through the media, are usually related to matters of general public interest. Furthermore, public figures usually have access to the media to respond to defamatory statements. Hence, public figures have a greater burden of proof in defamation cases (they must prove actual malice) than do private individuals.

Invasion of the Right to Privacy

A person has a right to solitude and freedom from prying public eyes—in other words, to privacy. The United States Supreme Court has held that a fundamental right to privacy is implied by various amendments to the U.S. Constitution. Some state constitutions explicitly provide for privacy rights. In addition, a number of federal and state statutes protect individual rights in specific areas. Tort law also safeguards these rights through the tort of *invasion of privacy*. Four acts qualify as an invasion of privacy:

- *The use of a person's name, picture, or other likeness for commercial purposes without permission.* This tort, which is usually referred to as the tort of appropriation, will be examined shortly.

- *Intrusion into a person's affairs or seclusion.* For example, invading someone's home or illegally searching someone's briefcase is an invasion of privacy. The tort has been held to extend to eavesdropping by wiretap, hacking into a computer, the unauthorized viewing of a bank account, compulsory blood testing, and window peeping.

- *Publication of information that places a person in a false light.* This could be a story attributing to the person ideas not held or actions not taken. (Publishing such a story could involve the tort of defamation as well.)

- *Public disclosure of private facts about an individual that an ordinary person would find objectionable.* A newspaper account of a private citizen's sex life or financial affairs could be an actionable invasion of privacy.

The Electronic Privacy Information Center (EPIC) is a good resource on privacy issues. Go to **epic.org** for more information. How privacy issues are relevant at work is discussed in the *In the Office* feature on the following page.

---

privilege
In tort law, the ability to act contrary to another person's right without that person's having legal redress for such acts. Privilege may be raised as a defense to defamation.

actual malice
Real and demonstrated evil intent. In a defamation suit, a statement made about a public figure normally must be made with actual malice (with either knowledge of its falsity or a reckless disregard of the truth) for liability to be incurred.

ON THE web

For information about debt-collection practices and links to many information sources, visit the Privacy Rights Clearinghouse at **www. privacyrights.org**. Select "Fact Sheets," and open item 27, "Debt Collection Practices: When Hardball Goes Too Far."

IN THE office

ONLINE PRIVACY

A pressing issue in the online world has to do with the privacy rights of Internet users, especially in the employment context. Law firms routinely provide their paralegals and other employees with computers and smartphones with which to access e-mail and the Internet. What if a paralegal uses his work computer and e-mail to make sexually explicit or unprofessional comments about other employees? Can a paralegal claim a right to privacy in the personal e-mail sent from his or her office computer? Does it matter if the paralegal used a personal e-mail address from a work-provided device?

Most courts that have considered the question have concluded that employees have no reasonable expectation of privacy in e-mails sent from their office computers. This is true even when employees were not informed that their e-mails could be read by the employer. After all, the employer has both a legal and an ethical obligation to prevent harassment and discrimination in the workplace. Although employers who provide Internet access to employees can usually monitor or access their employees' e-mail messages without liability for invasion of privacy, they would not be allowed by most courts to publicly disclose the contents of an employee's personal e-mail. Always assume work e-mail and a history of your Web activity can be seen by your employer, and avoid using employer-provided electronic devices for personal purposes.

Appropriation

The use by one person of another person's name, likeness, or other identifying characteristic, without permission and for the benefit of the user, constitutes the tort of **appropriation**. Under the law, an individual's right to privacy normally includes the right to the exclusive use of her or his identity.

◆ **EXAMPLE 14.4—** An example of appropriation can be found in the case brought by Vanna White, the hostess of the popular television game show *Wheel of Fortune*, against Samsung Electronics. Without White's permission, Samsung included in an advertisement for its videocassette recorders a depiction of a robot dressed in a wig, gown, and jewelry, posed in a scene that resembled the *Wheel of Fortune* set, in a stance for which White is famous. The court held in White's favor, holding that the tort of appropriation does not require the use of a celebrity's name or likeness. The court stated that Samsung's robot ad left "little doubt" as to the identity of the celebrity whom the ad was meant to depict. ◆

appropriation
In tort law, the use by one person of another person's name, likeness, or other identifying characteristic without permission and for the benefit of the user.

Misrepresentation (Fraud)

Misrepresentation leads another to believe in a condition that is different from the condition that actually exists. This is often accomplished through a false or an incorrect statement. The tort of **fraudulent misrepresentation**, or fraud, involves intentional deceit for personal gain—not misrepresentations innocently made by someone who is unaware of the facts.

ELEMENTS OF FRAUD. The tort of fraudulent misrepresentation includes several elements:

- Misrepresentation of facts or conditions with knowledge that they are false or with reckless disregard for the truth.

- Intent to induce another to rely on the misrepresentation.

- Justifiable reliance by the deceived party.

- Damages suffered as a result of the reliance.

- Causal connection between the misrepresentation and the harm suffered.

fraudulent misrepresentation
Any misrepresentation, either by misstatement or omission of a material fact, knowingly made with the intention of deceiving another and on which a reasonable person would and does rely to his or her detriment.

Fraud exists only when a person represents as a fact something he knows is untrue. It is fraud to claim that a roof does not leak when one knows it does. Facts can be objectively determined, unlike *seller's talk* or hype. ◆ **EXAMPLE 14.5—** If Harry says, "I am the best accountant in town," that is seller's talk, not fraud. The speaker is not trying to represent something as fact, because the term *best* is subjective (open to interpretation) and because a "reasonable person" would not rely on Harry's statement. ◆

FACT VERSUS OPINION.   Normally, the tort of misrepresentation or fraud occurs only when there is reliance on a *statement of fact*. Sometimes, however, reliance on a *statement of opinion* may involve the tort of misrepresentation if the person making the statement of opinion has a superior knowledge of the subject matter. ◆ **EXAMPLE 14.6—**   When a lawyer makes a statement of opinion about the law in a state in which the lawyer is licensed to practice, a court would hold reliance on such a statement to be equivalent to reliance on a statement of fact. ◆

Wrongful Interference

Today, many lawsuits involve situations in which a person or business is accused of wrongfully interfering with the business of another. These **business torts** are generally divided into two categories: wrongful interference with a contractual relationship (contract law will be discussed in Chapter 15) and wrongful interference with a business relationship.

business tort
Wrongful interference with another's business rights.

WRONGFUL INTERFERENCE WITH A CONTRACTUAL RELATIONSHIP.   The area of tort law relating to intentional interference with a contractual relationship has expanded in recent years. Three elements are necessary to establish the tort of wrongful interference with a contractual relationship:

1. A valid, enforceable contract exists between two parties,
2. A third party knows that this contract exists, and
3. The third party *intentionally* causes either of the two parties to breach the contract.

The contract may be between a firm and its employees or a firm and its customers. Sometimes, for example, a competitor of a firm draws away one of the firm's key employees. If the original employer can show (1) that the competitor induced the employee to leave in breach of a contract and (2) that the employee would not otherwise have broken the contract, then the employer may be entitled to compensation from the competitor.

WRONGFUL INTERFERENCE WITH A BUSINESS RELATIONSHIP.   Wrongful interference with a business relationship occurs when a party unreasonably interferes with another's business in an attempt to gain a larger share of the market. The elements of a wrongful interference with a business relationship are:

1. defendant knew or had reason to know that a third party and the plaintiff are in a business relationship, and
2. defendant intentionally interfered in the relationship.

There is a difference between competitive methods that do not give rise to tort liability and **predatory behavior**—actions undertaken with the intention of unlawfully driving competitors completely out of the market. The distinction usually depends on whether a business is attempting to attract customers in general or to solicit only those customers who have shown an interest in a similar product or service of a specific competitor. ◆ **EXAMPLE 14.7—** If a shopping center contains two shoe stores, an employee of Store A cannot be sent to the entrance of Store B to divert customers to Store A. This type of activity constitutes the tort of wrongful interference with a business relationship, which is commonly considered to be an unfair trade practice. ◆

predatory behavior
Business behavior that is undertaken with the intention of unlawfully driving competitors out of the market.

DEFENSES TO WRONGFUL INTERFERENCE.   A person will not be liable for the tort of wrongful interference with a contractual or business relationship if it can be shown that the interference was justified, or permissible. Good faith competitive behavior is a permissible interference even if it results in the breaking of a contract.

◆ **EXAMPLE 14.8—** If Antonio's Meats advertises so effectively that Beverly's Supermarket breaks its contract with Otis Meat Company, Otis Meat will be unable to recover against Antonio's Meats on a wrongful interference theory. Public policy favors free competition through honest advertising. ◆

Intentional Torts against Property

Intentional torts against property include trespass to land, trespass to personal property, and conversion. These torts are wrongful actions that interfere with individuals' legally recognized rights to their land or personal property. The law distinguishes real property from personal property (see Chapter 16). *Real property* is land and things "permanently" attached to the land. *Personal property* consists of movable items. Thus, a house is real property, whereas the furniture inside the house is personal property. Money and stocks and bonds are also personal property. (See this chapter's *Technology and Today's Paralegal* feature on the facing page for a discussion of how spam can constitute the tort of interference with personal property.)

Trespass to Land

trespass to land
The entry onto, above, or below the surface of land owned by another without the owner's permission.

A **trespass to land** occurs whenever a person, without permission, enters onto land that is owned by another, causes anything to enter onto the land, remains on the land, or permits anything to remain on it. The elements are:

1. plaintiff has lawful possession of the property at the time of the trespass,
2. there is an unauthorized entry by defendant, and
3. there is damage suffered by the plaintiff.

Actual harm to the land is not an essential element of this tort because the tort is designed to protect the right of owners to exclusively possess their property. Common trespasses include walking or driving on the land, shooting a gun over the land, throwing rocks at a building that belongs to someone else, causing water to back up on someone else's land, and placing part of one's building on an adjoining landowner's property.

TRESPASS CRITERIA, RIGHTS, AND DUTIES. The owner of the real property must show that a person is a trespasser. For example, a person who ignores "private property" signs and enters, uninvited, onto the property is clearly a trespasser. A guest in your home is legally an invitee, not a trespasser—unless she has been asked to leave but refuses. Any person who enters onto your property to commit an illegal act (such as a thief) is a trespasser, with or without posted signs. Normally, a trespasser must pay for any damage caused to the property and can be removed from the premises through the use of reasonable force without the owner being liable for assault and battery.

Further, a property owner owes no duty of care to a trespasser. If a trespasser sneaks across your backyard and breaks a leg when he steps in a hole in your lawn, he cannot sue you for having a hole in the lawn.

DEFENSES AGAINST TRESPASS TO LAND. The most common defense to trespass is that the trespass was justified. For example, when a trespasser enters to assist someone in danger, a defense exists. Another defense exists when the trespasser can show that he had permission to come onto the land for a specified purpose, such as to read an electric meter. Note that the property owner can revoke such permission. If the property owner asks a meter reader to leave and the meter reader refuses, the meter reader at that point becomes a trespasser.

TECHNOLOGY AND
today's paralegal

IDENTITY THEFT, SPAM, AND RELATED LEGAL ISSUES

The Internet offers a wide range of valuable services, from shopping to filing legal documents. As you know, its popularity means that deceptive and destructive practices constantly evolve and cause problems. These problems can have legal dimensions. As a paralegal, you should be aware of problems, efforts to control them, and resources that can provide assistance.

IDENTITY THEFT

Identity theft causes much grief and at least $50 billion in financial losses annually. We hear horror stories about individuals having their accounts drained and their credit ruined. Most of the losses, however, fall on businesses victimized by the use of stolen credit-card information and other valuable data.

One type of identity theft involves *phishing.* A perpetrator "fishes" for financial data and passwords by posing as a legitimate bank, PayPal, the IRS, a credit-card company, or other reputable source. The *phisher* sends an official looking e-mail asking the recipient to "update" or "confirm" vital information. Once those data are received, the phisher quickly drains accounts.

Various government agencies provide information about identify theft and advice about preventing it or dealing with its effects:

- The Federal Trade Commission offers information at **www.ftc.gov**. Enter "Identity Theft" in the search box.
- At the Department of Justice Web site, **www.justice.gov**, enter "Identify Theft" in the search box.
- The Social Security Administration offers advice about stolen Social Security numbers at **www.ssa.gov**.

Private sources include the Identity Theft Resources Center at **www.idtheftcenter.org** and the Privacy Rights Clearinghouse at **www.privacyrights.org**.

You should give out personal information such as credit-card or bank account numbers only when you are certain the person you are speaking with is who they claim to be, or the Web site you are using is secure.

THE FEDERAL CAN-SPAM ACT

Bulk, unsolicited e-mail, or *spam,* imposes a burden on an Internet service provider's equipment as well as on e-mail recipients. Spam accounts for a high percentage of all e-mail. When dealing with clients who market goods or services through commercial e-mails, paralegals need to understand laws regulating spam. An important federal law in this area is the Controlling the Assault of Non-Solicited Pornography and Marketing (CAN-SPAM) Act. You can find information about it at the Federal Trade Commission's Web site. Go to **www.ftc.gov** and enter "CAN-SPAM" in the search box.

SPAMMING AS A TORT

Spamming may also constitute a tort if it interferes with a computer system's functioning. A number of plaintiffs have successfully sued, under tort law, when spam overloaded a business's computer system or impaired a business's computer equipment. In these cases, spamming was held to constitute unauthorized interference with the use of the personal property of another, which is a trespass to personal property. Because a great deal of spam comes from other countries, however, tort actions are limited in their effectiveness.

TECHNOLOGY TIP

Paralegals in consumer law need to keep up to date on issues such as identity theft. Paralegals should also be familiar with the resources available to those with complaints and be familiar with laws regulating spam, such as the CAN-SPAM Act.

Trespass to Personal Property

Whenever any individual unlawfully harms the personal property of another or otherwise interferes with the owner's right to exclusively possess that personal property, **trespass to personal property** occurs. The elements of trespass to personal property are:

1. lawful possession of the property by the plaintiff and
2. unauthorized entry on the property by the defendant.

trespass to personal property
The unlawful taking or harming of another's personal property; interference with another's right to the exclusive possession of his or her personal property.

◆ **EXAMPLE 14.9—** Suppose a student takes another student's paralegal book as a practical joke and hides it so that the owner is unable to find it for several days before a final examination. In this situation, the student has engaged in a trespass to personal property. ◆

If it can be shown that trespass to personal property was warranted, then a complete defense exists. Most states, for example, allow automobile repair shops to hold a customer's car (under what is called an *artisan's lien*) when the customer refuses to pay for repairs already completed. Not all service providers can do this, however. Veterinarians are generally not permitted to keep a pet until the bill owed for pet treatment has been paid.

Conversion

Whenever personal property is wrongfully taken from its owner, the act of **conversion** occurs. The elements of conversion are:

1. the plaintiff has rightful possession of personal property,
2. the defendant intentionally interferes with that right, and
3. the interference deprives the plaintiff of the possession or use of the property.

Conversion is any act depriving an owner of personal property without that owner's permission and without just cause. When conversion occurs, the lesser offense of trespass to personal property usually occurs as well. If the initial taking of the property was unlawful, there is trespass. Keeping the property is conversion. Even if the owner permitted the initial taking of the property, failure to return it may still be conversion. Conversion is the civil side of crimes related to theft. A store clerk who steals merchandise from the store commits a crime and engages in the tort of conversion at the same time.

Even if a person mistakenly believed that she was entitled to the goods, a tort of conversion may occur. ◆ **EXAMPLE 14.10—** Someone who buys stolen goods may be guilty of conversion even if she did not know that the goods were stolen. If the true owner brings a tort action against the buyer, the buyer must either return the property to the owner or pay the owner the full value of the property (despite having already paid the thief). If the person accused of conversion can show that the purported owner did not in fact own the property, however, a defense exists. ◆

Negligence

The tort of **negligence** occurs when someone suffers injury because of another's failure to live up to a required *duty of care*. The elements of the tort of negligence are:

1. the defendant owed a duty of care to the plaintiff,
2. the defendant breached that duty,
3. the plaintiff suffered a legally recognizable injury, and
4. the defendant's breach caused the injury suffered.

In contrast to intentional torts, in torts involving negligence, the one committing the tort did not wish to commit the initial act or to bring about the consequences of the act. Rather, the actor's conduct creates a *risk* of such consequences. If no risk is created, there is no negligence. The risk must also be foreseeable—that is, it must be such that a reasonable person engaging in the same activity would anticipate the risk and guard against it.

Many of the actions discussed in the section on intentional torts constitute negligence if the element of intent is missing. ◆ **EXAMPLE 14.11—** If Juan intentionally shoves Naomi, who falls and breaks an arm as a result, Juan will have committed the intentional tort of battery. If Juan carelessly bumps into Naomi on the stairway because he is running down the stairs, and she falls and breaks an arm as a result, Juan's action will constitute negligence. In either situation, Juan has committed a tort. ◆

Next, we elaborate on each of the four elements of negligence.

---

conversion
The act of wrongfully taking or retaining a person's personal property and placing it in the service of another.

social MEDIA TODAY

Being invisible online is better than being mentioned negatively, but not as good as being visible in a positive way. Your reputation will be good, bad, or invisible. Create a strategy for enhancing your online presence.

negligence
The failure to exercise the standard of care that a reasonable person would exercise in similar circumstances.

The Duty of Care and Its Breach

Central to the tort of negligence is the concept of a **duty of care**. This concept arises from the belief that if we are to live in society with other people, some actions can be tolerated and some cannot. Some actions are right and some are wrong. Some actions are reasonable and some are not. The basic principle underlying the duty of care is that people are free to act as they please so long as their actions do not infringe on the interests of others.

Reasonable Person Standard

The law of torts defines and measures the duty of care by the **reasonable person standard**. In determining whether a duty of care has been breached, the courts ask how a reasonable person would have acted in the same circumstances. The reasonable person standard is not necessarily how a particular person would act. That is, it is how a judge or jury thinks a person of ordinary sense should have acted under circumstances, whether criminal or civil, similar to those in the matter in question. That individuals are required to exercise a reasonable standard of care in their activities is a pervasive concept in the law. Many of the issues dealt with in subsequent chapters of this text have to do with this duty.

In negligence cases, the degree of care to be exercised varies depending on the defendant's occupation or profession, relationship with the plaintiff, and other factors. Generally, whether an action constitutes a breach of the duty of care is determined on a case-by-case basis. The outcome depends on how the trial court judge (or jury, if it is a jury trial) decides a reasonable person in the position of the defendant would have acted in the circumstances of the case. In the following subsections, we examine the degree of care typically expected of property owners and professionals.

The Duty of Property Owners

Property owners are expected to exercise reasonable care to protect persons coming onto their property from harm. Owners who rent or lease property to tenants are expected to exercise reasonable care to ensure that the tenants and their guests are not harmed in common areas, such as stairways and laundry rooms, by keeping them in safe condition.

DUTY TO BUSINESS INVITEES.   Retailers and other firms that invite persons to come onto their premises have a duty to exercise reasonable care to protect those persons, who are considered **business invitees**. ◆ **EXAMPLE 14.12—** If you entered a supermarket, slipped on a wet floor from a spilled product, and suffered injuries, the owner of the supermarket would be liable for damages if, when you slipped, there was no sign warning that the floor was wet. A court would hold that the business owner was negligent because the owner failed to exercise a reasonable degree of care in protecting the store's customers against foreseeable risks about which the owner knew or *should have known*. That a patron might slip on the wet floor and be injured as a result was a foreseeable risk, and the owner should have taken care to avoid this risk or to warn the customer of it. ◆ The owner also has a duty to discover and remove any hidden dangers that might injure a customer or other invitee.

OPEN AND OBVIOUS RISKS.   Some risks, of course, are so obvious that the owner need not warn of them. For instance, a business owner does not need to warn customers to open a door before attempting to walk through it. Other risks, however, even though they may seem obvious to a business owner, may not be so in the eyes of another, such as a child. ◆ **EXAMPLE 14.13—** A hardware store owner may not think it is necessary to warn customers that a stepladder leaning against the back wall of the store could fall down and harm them. It is possible, though, that a child could tip the ladder over or climb on it and be hurt as a result. In that case, the store could be held liable. ◆

The Duty of Professionals

If a person has special knowledge or skill, the person's conduct must be consistent with that status. Professionals—including physicians, psychiatrists, architects, engineers, accountants, contractors, lawyers, and others—are required to have a

---

duty of care
The duty of all persons, as established by tort law, to exercise reasonable care in dealings with others. Failure to exercise due care, which is normally determined by the reasonable person standard, is the tort of negligence.

reasonable person standard
The standard of behavior expected of a hypothetical "reasonable person"; the standard against which negligence is measured and that must be observed to avoid liability for negligence.

business invitee
A person, such as a customer or a client, who is invited onto business premises by the owner of those premises for business purposes.

Featured Contributor

IS THERE A PLACE FOR PARALEGALS IN THE FIELD OF MEDICAL MALPRACTICE?

Beth Walston-Dunham

BIOGRAPHICAL NOTE

Beth Walston-Dunham has been publishing legal texts since 1990. She earned a B.S. degree in psychology and business from Central Missouri State University in 1981 and a J.D. degree from the Saint Louis University School of Law in 1984. She has been licensed in the states of Illinois, Missouri, Nebraska, and Texas, where her practice included plaintiffs' medical malpractice litigation. Ms. Walston-Dunham has also held the position of administrative partner in a private medical practice and has worked as a consultant on risk management issues for health-care professionals. She served as the first director of paralegal studies, legal administration, and prelaw programs at the College of Saint Mary in Omaha, Nebraska.

© Cengage Learning 2014

The role of the paralegal in the justice system, and specifically the field of tort law, is filled with opportunities for development and advancement. Civil litigation has grown exponentially in recent years. As a result, a wide variety of doors have opened for paralegals both within and outside the traditional law office setting.

One particularly large area of growth has been that of medical malpractice law. Medical malpractice is nothing new. It has been a part of civil litigation in this country for nearly two hundred years. But today,

variables such as rapidly developing technology, new health-care professions, scientific advances, changes in insurance, and even the baby boom following World War II have contributed to a virtual explosion in the number of patients and treatments. These developments have resulted in a corresponding increase in the possibility of professional malfeasance and legal claims by those allegedly injured.

Without question, the paralegal has become an invaluable part of the legal team in the field of medical malpractice. Because of the high per-

standard minimum level of special knowledge and ability. In determining what is reasonable care in the case of professionals, their training, standards of the profession, and expertise are taken into account. In other words, an accountant cannot defend against a lawsuit for negligence by stating, "But I was not familiar with that principle of accounting." Furthermore, a business is held to the standard of care expected of knowledgeable people in that line of work. Thus, an auto repair shop cannot deny knowledge of the proper procedures for an oil change.

If a professional violates her or his duty of care toward a client, the professional may be sued for malpractice. For example, a patient might sue a physician for *medical malpractice*. Thus, a surgeon who did not follow standard procedures and thereby injured a patient would have negligently committed medical malpractice. The *Featured Contributor* feature above further discusses malpractice. A client might sue an attorney for *legal malpractice* (discussed in Chapter 4).

The Injury Requirement and Damages

To recover damages (receive compensation), the plaintiff in a tort lawsuit must prove that she or he suffered a *legally recognizable* injury—some loss, harm, wrong, or invasion of a legally protected interest. This is generally true in lawsuits for centage of settled claims, a great deal of the work required to successfully litigate or defend a malpractice case comes in the pretrial stages. Of course, the qualified paralegal in the law firm can be a valuable asset in nearly every element of trial and pretrial preparation, with the exception of giving legal advice and advocacy. Common duties include, but are not limited to, the following:

- Gathering information about the incident that allegedly caused injury.
- Interviewing potential witnesses.
- Preparing and responding to discovery materials such as interrogatories and requests for production, inspection, and physical examination.
- Securing expert witnesses.
- Preparing for depositions (both witness preparation and preparation of questions to be asked).
- Conducting legal research.
- Drafting pleadings, motions, discovery materials, and memoranda.
- Assembling evidence and preparing trial exhibits.

In addition to working in a law firm setting, paralegals have many opportunities within the health-care industry to participate in areas related to medical malpractice. A primary example is the field of risk management. In recent years, this relatively new profession has become deeply embedded in the field of health care. Whether risk management is conducted by an independent risk assessment company that works on a contract basis with providers, by an in-house risk management department for a health-care provider, or by a corporate legal department for providers of insurance, health care, or related products, the goal is the same: to identify vulnerable areas and to react accordingly. The response may range from changing policies and procedures, to providing employee education and training, to collecting information about an incident that has already occurred. All of these are areas in which a paralegal can effectively function to meet the needs of the employer.

Clearly, the doors open to paralegals in tort law, and specifically medical malpractice, are boundless. The key is to have a thorough understanding of the legal system, and particularly the process of litigation.

Additionally, a paralegal should have the ability to examine the broad aspects of a case, think "outside the box," and use organizational skills to address issues related to litigation involving professional malfeasance.

"Clearly, the doors open to paralegals in tort law, and specifically medical malpractice, are boundless. The key is to have a thorough understanding of the legal system, and particularly the process of litigation."

intentional torts as well as lawsuits for negligence. The facts of the case must clearly establish a basis for recovery.

Essentially, the purpose of tort law is to compensate for legally recognized injuries resulting from wrongful acts. If no harm or injury results from a given negligent action, there is nothing to compensate. ◆ **EXAMPLE 14.14—** If you carelessly bump into a passerby, who stumbles and falls as a result, you may be liable in tort if the passerby is injured in the fall. If the person is unharmed, however, there normally could be no suit for damages, because no injury was suffered. ◆

Compensatory Damages

The purpose of tort law is to compensate injured parties for damages suffered, not to punish people for the wrongs that they commit. **Compensatory damages** are intended to compensate, or reimburse, a plaintiff for actual losses—to make the plaintiff "whole." Occasionally, however, punitive damages are also awarded in tort lawsuits.

Punitive Damages

Punitive damages are intended to punish the wrongdoer and deter others from similar wrongdoing. Punitive damages are rarely awarded in lawsuits for ordinary negligence. They usually are given only in cases involving intentional torts. They

compensatory damages
A money award equivalent to the actual value of injuries or damages sustained by the aggrieved party.

punitive damages
Money damages awarded to a plaintiff to punish the defendant and deter future similar conduct.

Paralegals who work in the area of tort law often assist in litigation involving automobile accidents. Investigating the facts of the accident and preparing sketches are usually an important aspect of the paralegal's job. What is the relationship between fact investigation and preparation of sketches for trial?

Courtesy of © Digital Vision Ltd.

may be awarded, however, if the defendant's negligent conduct was particularly reckless or willful. For example, in a case over the *Exxon Valdez* oil spill, a jury awarded $5 billion in punitive damages against Exxon in addition to $287 million in actual damages. (This award was later reduced to $507.5 million on appeal.)

Causation

Another element necessary to a tort is *causation*. If a person fails in a duty of care and someone suffers injury, the wrongful activity must have caused the harm for a tort to have been committed. In deciding whether there is causation, the court must address two questions:

causation in fact
Causation brought about by an act or omission without which an event would not have occurred.

- *Is there causation in fact?* Did the injury occur because of the defendant's act, or would it have occurred anyway? If an injury would not have occurred without the defendant's act, then there is causation in fact. **Causation in fact** can usually be determined by the use of the *but for* test: "but for" the wrongful act, the injury would not have occurred. For example, Arnie runs a red light and hits another car. The accident would not have occurred but for Arnie's running the red light.

proximate cause
Legal cause; exists when the connection between an act and an injury is strong enough to justify imposing liability.

- *Was the act the proximate cause of the injury?* **Proximate cause**, or legal cause, exists when the connection between an act and an injury is strong enough to justify imposing liability. ◆ **EXAMPLE 14.15—** Arnie runs a red light and hits Nicki's car. Her car has explosives in the trunk, and they explode when the car is hit. The explosion hurts bystanders. The injured bystanders cannot sue Arnie. His negligence was the cause in fact of the accident, but it was not the proximate cause of the bystanders' injuries. They may be able to sue Nicki, however, because it may not be reasonable to transport explosives in the trunk of a car. ◆

Both questions must be answered in the affirmative for liability in tort to arise. If a defendant's action constitutes causation in fact but a court decides that the action is not the proximate cause of the plaintiff's injury, the causation requirement has not been met—and the defendant normally will not be liable to the plaintiff.

Defenses to Negligence

Defendants often defend against negligence claims by asserting that the plaintiffs have failed to prove the existence of one or more of the required elements for negligence. Additionally, there are three basic *affirmative* defenses to negligence claims that defendants can use to avoid or reduce their liability even if the facts are as the plaintiff claims: (1) assumption of risk, (2) superseding cause, and (3) contributory or comparative negligence.

Assumption of Risk

A plaintiff who voluntarily enters into a risky situation, knowing the risk involved, will not be allowed to recover. This is the defense of **assumption of risk**. The requirements of this defense are (1) knowledge of the risk and (2) voluntary assumption of the risk. Remember, the defendant has the burden of proof of establishing these.

The risk can be assumed by express agreement, or the assumption of risk can be implied by the plaintiff's knowledge of the risk and subsequent conduct. For instance, a driver entering a NASCAR race knows that there is a risk of being killed or injured in a crash. Of course, the plaintiff does not assume a risk different from or greater than the risk normally carried by the activity. In the scenario just mentioned, the race driver does not assume the risk that the banking in the curves of the racetrack will give way during the race because of a construction defect.

In emergency situations, risks are not considered assumed. Neither are they assumed when a statute protects a class of people from harm and a member of the class is injured by the harm. ◆ **EXAMPLE 14.16—** Employees are protected by statute from harmful working conditions and therefore do not assume the risks associated with the workplace. An employee who is injured will generally be compensated regardless of fault under state workers' compensation statutes (to be discussed in Chapter 18). ◆

Superseding Cause

An unforeseeable intervening event may break the connection between a wrongful act and an injury to another. If so, it acts as a *superseding cause*—that is, it relieves a defendant of liability for injuries caused by the intervening event. ◆ **EXAMPLE 14.17—** Suppose that Derrick keeps a plastic container of gasoline in the trunk of his car. The presence of the gasoline creates a foreseeable risk and is a negligent act. If Derrick's car skids and crashes into a tree, causing the gasoline can to explode, Derrick will be liable for injuries sustained by passing pedestrians because of his negligence. If lightning striking the car causes the explosion, however, the lightning supersedes Derrick's original negligence as a cause of the damage, because the lightning strike was not foreseeable. ◆

Contributory and Comparative Negligence

All individuals are expected to exercise a reasonable degree of care in looking out for themselves. In a few jurisdictions, recovery for injury resulting from negligence is prevented if the plaintiff was also negligent. This is the defense of **contributory negligence**. Under the common law doctrine of contributory negligence, no matter how insignificant the plaintiff's negligence is relative to the defendant's negligence, the plaintiff will not recover any damages.

Most states apply the doctrine of **comparative negligence**. Here, the plaintiff's negligence and the defendant's negligence are computed and the liability for damages distributed accordingly. Some jurisdictions have adopted a "pure" form of comparative negligence that allows the plaintiff to recover, even if the extent of his or her fault is greater than that of the defendant. For example, if the plaintiff was 80 percent at fault and the defendant 20 percent at fault, the plaintiff may recover 20 percent of her damages. Many states' comparative negligence statutes, however, contain a "50 percent" rule by which the plaintiff recovers nothing if he was more than 50 percent at fault.

assumption of risk
Voluntarily taking on a known risk; a defense against negligence that can be used when the plaintiff has knowledge of and appreciates a danger and voluntarily exposes himself or herself to the danger.

GOING **green**

FLIP THAT SWITCH

Often, people working at a computer for much of the day have needless overhead lights turned on, running up the electric bill and generating more carbon for the atmosphere. Make sure unnecessary light fixtures and other electronic equipment are turned off while working, and especially when leaving the office.

contributory negligence
A theory in tort law under which a complaining party's own negligence contributed to his or her injuries. Contributory negligence is an absolute bar to recovery in some jurisdictions.

comparative negligence
A theory in tort law under which the liability for injuries resulting from negligent acts is shared by all persons who were guilty of negligence (including the injured party) on the basis of each person's proportionate carelessness.

Special Negligence Doctrines and Statutes

There are a number of special doctrines and statutes relating to negligence. We examine only a few of them here.

Negligence *Per Se*

negligence *per se*
An action or failure to act in violation of a statutory requirement.

Certain conduct, whether it consists of an action or a failure to act, may be treated as **negligence *per se*** (*per se* means "in or of itself"). Negligence *per se* may occur if an individual violates a statute or an ordinance providing for a criminal penalty and that violation causes another to be injured. The injured person must prove:

1. that the statute clearly sets out what standard of conduct is expected, when and where it is expected, and of whom it is expected,

2. that he or she is in the class intended to be protected by the statute, and

3. that the statute was designed to prevent the type of injury that was suffered.

The standard of conduct required by the statute is the duty that the defendant owes to the plaintiff, and a violation of the statute is the breach of that duty.

◆ **EXAMPLE 14.18—**   A statute may require a property owner to keep a building in safe condition and may also subject the owner to a criminal penalty, such as a fine, if the building is not kept safe. The statute is meant to protect those who are rightfully in the building. Thus, if the owner, without a sufficient excuse, violates the statute and a tenant is injured as a result, then a majority of courts will hold that the owner's unexcused violation of the statute conclusively establishes a breach of a duty of care—that is, that the owner's violation is negligence *per se.* ◆

Special Negligence Statutes

Good Samaritan statute
A state statute stipulating that persons who provide emergency services to others in peril—unless they do so recklessly, thus causing further harm—cannot be sued for negligence.

A number of states have enacted statutes prescribing duties and responsibilities in certain circumstances. For example, most states have what are called **Good Samaritan statutes**. Under these statutes, persons who receive voluntary aid from others cannot turn around and sue the "Good Samaritans" for negligence. These laws were passed largely to protect physicians and medical personnel who volunteer their services in emergency situations to those in need, such as individuals hurt in car accidents.

dram shop act
A state statute that imposes liability on the owners of bars, as well as those who serve alcoholic drinks to the public, for injuries resulting from accidents caused by intoxicated persons when the sellers or servers of alcoholic drinks contributed to the intoxication.

Many states have also passed **dram shop acts**. Under such acts, a bar owner or bartender may be held liable for injuries caused by a person who became intoxicated while drinking at the bar or who was already intoxicated when served by the bartender. In some states, statutes impose liability on *social hosts* (persons hosting parties) for injuries caused by guests who became intoxicated at the hosts' homes. Under these statutes, it is unnecessary to prove that the bar owner, bartender, or social host was negligent.

Cyber Torts: Defamation Online

cyber tort
A tort committed by use of the Internet.

Who should be held liable for **cyber torts**, or torts committed in cyberspace? For example, who should be held liable when someone posts a defamatory message online? Should an Internet service provider (ISP) that provides access to the Internet be liable for the remark if the ISP was unaware that it was being made?

Cyber torts (like cyber crimes, discussed in Chapter 13) are not new torts as much as they are new ways of committing torts that present special issues of proof. How, for example, can it be proved that an online defamatory remark was "published" (which requires that a third party see or hear it)? How can the identity of the person who made the remark be discovered? We explore some of these questions in this section. Generally, determining what tort duties apply in cyberspace and at what point one of those duties is breached is not an easy task for the courts.

Liability of Internet Service Providers

Online forums allow anyone—customers, employees, or crackpots—to complain about a business firm's personnel, policies, practices, or products. Regardless of whether the complaint is justified or whether it is true, it might have an impact on the business. One question that created problems for the courts was whether providers of such forums could be held liable for defamatory statements. Congress responded with the Communications Decency Act, which states that Internet service providers, or "interactive computer service providers," are not liable for such material.[1]

Piercing the Veil of Anonymity

A problem for anyone who seeks to sue for online defamation is discovering the identity of the person who posted the defamatory message. ISPs can disclose personal information about their customers only when ordered to do so by a court. Because of this, businesses and individuals have resorted to lawsuits against unidentified "John Does." Then, using the authority of the courts, they can obtain from the ISPs the identities of the persons responsible for the messages.

◆ **EXAMPLE 14.19—**   In one case, Eric Hvide, a former chief executive of a company called Hvide Marine, sued a number of "John Does" who had posted allegedly defamatory statements about his company on various online message boards. Hvide, who eventually lost his job, sued the John Does for libel in a Florida court. The court ruled that Yahoo and AOL had to reveal the identities of the defendant Does. Hvide was then able to amend his complaint to substitute the names of the actual individuals for the "John Does" listed in his original complaint. ◆

In some cases, the rights of plaintiffs in such situations have been balanced against the defendants' rights to free speech. For example, some courts have concluded that more than a bare allegation of defamation is required to outweigh an individual's right to anonymity in the exercise of free speech.

> **social MEDIA TODAY**
>
> Make sure you understand your firm's rules on which employees are allowed to speak for the firm and which are not. Do not include your employer's name anywhere on social media that is not consistent with firm policy.

Strict Liability

Intentional torts and torts of negligence involve acts that depart from a reasonable standard of care and cause injuries. Under the doctrine of **strict liability**, liability for injury is imposed for reasons other than fault. Traditionally, strict liability was imposed for damages proximately caused by an abnormally dangerous or exceptional activity.

Abnormally dangerous activities have three characteristics:

1. The activity involves potential harm, of a serious nature, to persons or property.

2. The activity involves a high degree of risk that cannot be completely guarded against by the exercise of reasonable care.

3. The activity is not commonly performed in the community or area.

The primary basis of liability is the creation of an extraordinary risk. Even if blasting with dynamite in construction is performed with all reasonable care, for instance, there is still a risk of injury. Balancing that risk against the potential for harm, the person engaged in the activity will pay for any injury it causes. Knowing that they will be liable for any injuries, those engaged in such activities have strong incentives to use extreme caution.

The most significant application of strict liability is in the area of *product liability*—liability of manufacturers and sellers for harmful or defective products. This is a newer application of the doctrine of strict liability. Because of the importance of product liability in tort litigation, we discuss this liability in the following section.

> **strict liability**
> Liability regardless of fault. In tort law, strict liability may be imposed on a merchant who introduces into commerce a good that is so defective as to be unreasonably dangerous.

Product Liability

product liability
The legal liability of manufacturers, sellers, and lessors of goods to consumers, users, and bystanders for injuries or damages that are caused by the goods.

Those who manufacture, sell, or lease goods can be held liable for injuries and damages caused by defective goods under the law of **product liability**. Liability here is a matter of social policy. It is based on the notion that manufacturers are better able to bear the cost of injury than innocent victims. In addition, requiring producers to pay for injuries caused by their products encourages them to make safer products. How paralegals may work in this area of law is discussed in the *Practice Focus* feature below.

Theories of Product Liability

A party who is injured by a defective product can bring a suit against the product's seller or manufacturer under several theories. These theories include negligence, misrepresentation, and strict product liability.

Product Liability Based on Negligence

If a manufacturer fails to exercise due care to make a product safe, *any person* who is injured by the product can sue the manufacturer for negligence. The plaintiff does not have to be the person who bought the product. The manufacturer must use due care in designing the product, selecting the materials, producing and assembling the product, testing and inspecting the product for safety, and placing adequate warnings on the label to inform users of dangers.

Product Liability Based on Misrepresentation

When a manufacturer or seller misrepresents the quality, nature, or appropriate use of a product, and the user is injured as a result, the basis of liability may be the tort of fraud. Generally, the misrepresentation must have been made knowingly or

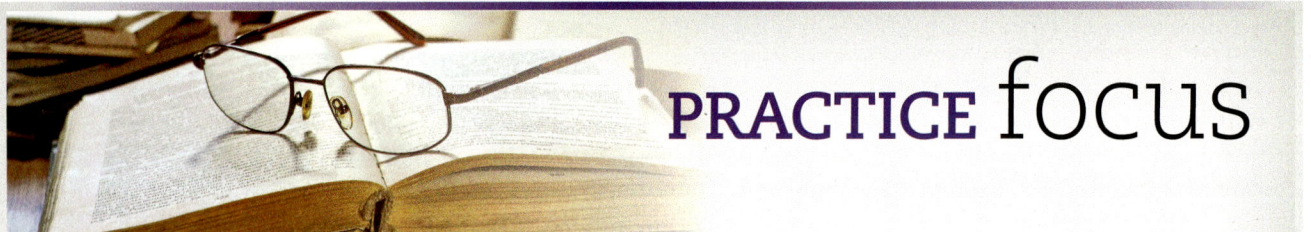

PRACTICE focus

HANDLING PRODUCT-RELATED CLAIMS

Product liability cases make up almost 7% of personal injury cases in the United States. These affect products used in every American home, from cars to toys. For example, there are over 200,000 toy-related injuries annually. Product-related injuries can be caused by anything from choking on a small part in a toy to an electric vehicle's battery catching fire.

If a client brings a product liability case to your firm, there are a number of important steps you will need to take in the course of the investigation of the claim. You must attempt to locate and preserve the product that allegedly caused the injury. This may require quick action. If an individual is injured in a car accident in which you suspect there may be a product defect as a cause, you will need to contact the owner (if different from your client), garage,

towing company, or police impound lot that has possession of the vehicle and ask them to refrain from any work on or disposal of the vehicle. You will also want to inspect it as soon as possible. You will need photographs, a secure chain of custody for the product, and an expert inspection of it.

If an injury led to an ambulance or police call, you will want to secure authenticated copies of any tapes of the calls or records created. If anyone saw a doctor as a result of the product's malfunction, you will need his or her medical records. If someone died, you will want his or her death certificate and autopsy report (if any). Getting these records and any witness statements quickly is important to your supervising attorney's evaluation of the case.

Product liability cases often involve considerable technical evidence. Knowing the scientific and engineering terms and being able to interact with experts in these areas will make you a more effective paralegal.

with reckless disregard for the facts, and the party must have intended the user to rely on the statement.

Strict Product Liability

Under the doctrine of strict liability, a manufacturer that has exercised reasonable care can still be held liable if a product is defective and injures someone. Strict product liability reflects the general principle that the law should protect consumers from unsafe and dangerous products. The rule of strict liability is also applicable to the suppliers of component parts that are used in the final product.

Strict liability will be imposed if the plaintiff can establish the following six requirements:

1. The product must be in a defective condition when the defendant sells it.

2. The defendant must normally be engaged in the business of selling the product.

3. The product must be unreasonably dangerous to the user or consumer because of its defective condition (in most states).

4. The plaintiff must incur physical harm to self or property by use or consumption of the product.

5. The defective condition must be the proximate cause of the injury or damage.

6. The goods must not have been substantially changed from the time the product was sold to the time the injury was sustained.[2]

Note that the plaintiff is not required to show why or how the product became defective. The plaintiff must only prove that the **unreasonably dangerous product** caused the injury and that the condition of the product was essentially the same as when it was sold. A product may be unreasonably dangerous due to a flaw in the manufacturing process, a design defect, or an inadequate warning.

MANUFACTURING DEFECTS.   A product that departs from its intended design, even though all possible care was exercised in the preparation and marketing of the product, has a manufacturing defect. Liability is imposed on the manufacturer (and on the wholesaler and retailer) regardless of whether the manufacturer acted "reasonably."

DESIGN DEFECTS.   A product has a design defect if the foreseeable risks of harm posed by the product could have been reduced or avoided by adopting an economically feasible, reasonable alternative design. The *Ethics Watch* feature on the next page discusses how work and personal life can conflict even in this area of law.

WARNING DEFECTS.   A product may also be deemed to be defective because of inadequate instructions or warnings in situations in which the risk of harm was foreseeable and could have been avoided if a proper warning had been given.

In evaluating the adequacy of warnings, courts consider the risks of the product and whether the content of the warning was understandable to the expected user.[3] For example, children would likely respond better to bright, bold, simple warning labels, whereas adults may benefit from more detailed information.

Sellers must warn those who purchase their products of harms that can result from the *foreseeable misuse* of the product. The key is the foreseeability of the misuse. Sellers are not required to take precautions against every possible unusual use of their products.

Defenses to Product Liability

There is no duty to warn about risks that are obvious or commonly known. Gas stations do not have to warn consumers to avoid drinking gasoline. Knives are supposed to be sharp. Warnings about *obvious risks* do not add to the safety of a product and could even detract from it by making other warnings seem less significant.

unreasonably dangerous product
A product that is defective to the point of threatening a consumer's health and safety. A product will be considered unreasonably dangerous if it is dangerous beyond the expectation of the ordinary consumer or if a less dangerous alternative was economically feasible for the manufacturer, but the manufacturer failed to produce it.

ETHICS WATCH

CONFIDENTIALITY AND PRODUCT LIABILITY

Paralegals who work in the area of product liability may find themselves in a sticky situation. For example, suppose your firm represents a particular toy manufacturer. The toy firm sells a toy that is popular for young children. The toy, however, is apparently defective and has injured a few children. It has not been recalled. Everything you know about this toy you have learned from the work you have done on the case.

Should you talk to your attorney about the possibility of discussing with the client the possibility of a voluntary recall? Suppose some of your friends have children around that age. Can you warn your friends about the defective toy? If you tell one person, you may violate the ethical rule of confidentiality. What if you don't warn someone and that person's child is injured?

This is just one example of ethical dilemmas that may arise for paralegals who work in the area of product liability. In circumstances such as these, it is advisable to consult your supervising attorney for direction.

The issue discussed here is related to the NALA *Code of Ethics and Professional Responsibility,* Canon 4: "A paralegal must use discretion and professional judgment commensurate with knowledge and experience but must not render independent legal judgment in place of an attorney." It is also related to the NFPA *Model Code of Ethics,* Section EC 1.5: "A paralegal shall preserve all confidential information provided by the client or acquired from other sources before, during, and after the course of the professional relationship."

To avoid liability under any theory of product liability, the defendant can show that there is no basis for the plaintiff's claim or that the plaintiff has not met the requirements for liability. For example, if the suit alleges a product caused an injury and the defendant proves that the product did not cause the plaintiff's injury, the defendant will not be liable. Defendants may also assert the affirmative defenses discussed next.

Assumption of Risk

The obviousness of a risk and a user's decision to proceed in the face of that risk may be a defense in a product liability suit. For example, if a buyer ignored a product recall by the seller, a court might conclude that the buyer had assumed the risk. To establish this defense, the defendant must show that:

1. the plaintiff knew and appreciated the risk created by the product defect, and

2. the plaintiff voluntarily assumed the risk, even though it was unreasonable to do so.

Product Misuse

Defendants can also claim that the plaintiff misused the product. This defense is similar to claiming that the plaintiff has assumed the risk. Here, however, the use was not the one for which the product was designed. If the misuse is reasonably foreseeable, the seller must take measures to guard against it, such as by warning consumers, but if a consumer does something dangerous, such as use a chain saw to trim their toenails, the chainsaw maker is not liable.

Comparative Negligence

Developments in the area of comparative negligence (discussed earlier in this chapter) have affected the doctrine of strict liability—the most extreme theory of product liability. Most jurisdictions consider the negligent or intentional actions of both the plaintiff and the defendant when apportioning liability and damages.

Consumer Law

Since the 1960s, many laws have been passed to protect the health and safety of consumers. A **consumer** is a person who purchases, for private use, goods or services from business firms. Sources of consumer protection exist at all levels of government. Exhibit 14.1 below indicates some of the areas of consumer law regulated by statutes that are expanded by regulations. Nearly every agency and department of the federal government has an office of consumer affairs, and most states have one or more such offices, including the offices of state attorneys general, to assist consumers.

All statutes, agency rules, and common law judicial decisions that serve to protect the interests of consumers are classified as **consumer law**. Because of the wide variation among state consumer protection laws, our primary focus here is on federal legislation—specifically, on legislation governing deceptive advertising, labeling and packaging, sales, health protection, product safety, and credit protection. However, as Exhibit 14.1 shows, state laws often provide broad protection for business practices that can injure consumers.

Deceptive Sales Practices

Under the common law, if a seller misrepresented the quality, price, or availability of a certain product, the consumer's recourse was to sue the seller for fraud or for breach of contract. Fraud requires proof of *intent* to misrepresent the product's

consumer
A person who buys products and services for personal or household use.

consumer law
Statutes, agency rules, and judicial decisions protecting consumers of goods and services.

EXHIBIT 14.1
Selected Areas of Consumer Law Regulated by Statutes

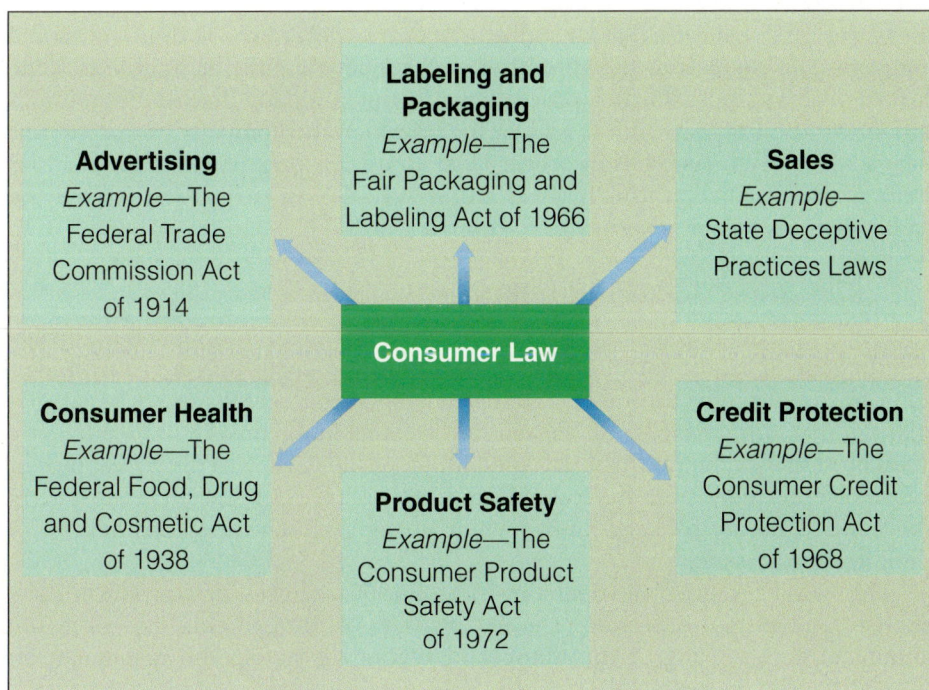

Advertising
Example—The Federal Trade Commission Act of 1914

Labeling and Packaging
Example—The Fair Packaging and Labeling Act of 1966

Sales
Example—State Deceptive Practices Laws

Consumer Law

Consumer Health
Example—The Federal Food, Drug and Cosmetic Act of 1938

Product Safety
Example—The Consumer Product Safety Act of 1972

Credit Protection
Example—The Consumer Credit Protection Act of 1968

© Cengage Learning 2014

ON THE web

A good source for information on the FTC, its regulations protecting consumers, and other government sites dealing with consumer issues is the FTC home page at **www.ftc.gov**

deception

In consumer law, a material misrepresentation or omission in information that is likely to mislead a reasonable consumer to his or her detriment.

usefulness to the buyer. Frequently, the burden of having to prove intent was too great, and consumers were left with little or no legal recourse against deceptive practices. Whether the claim is fraud or breach of contract, litigation is costly, so consumers rarely pursue actions involving relatively small losses, even if they would be likely to win the cases.

Today, various agencies, both federal and state, are empowered to protect consumers from deceptive business practices. At the federal level, the most important agency is the Federal Trade Commission (FTC). The Federal Trade Commission Act of 1914 authorizes the FTC to determine what constitutes a deceptive practice.

The FTC policy on **deception** holds that a practice is deceptive and subject to agency action if:

1. there is misrepresentation or omission of information in a communication to consumers,

2. the deception is likely to mislead a reasonable consumer, and

3. the deception is material—it is likely to be misleading to the detriment of consumers.

This broad definition allows the FTC to attack a wide variety of business practices, as do statutes such as the California Civil Code, Chapter 3, which concerns deceptive practices. Besides such general regulations, there are more specific areas of regulation, as we see next.

Deceptive Advertising

deceptive advertising

Advertising that misleads consumers, either by unjustified claims concerning a product's performance or by failure to disclose relevant information concerning the product's composition or performance.

Over the past several decades, consumers have received increased protection against **deceptive advertising**. Deceptive advertising comes in many forms. Deception may arise from a false statement or claim about a company's own products or a competitor's products. Some advertisements contain "half-truths," meaning that the information presented is true but incomplete, leading consumers to a false conclusion.

◆ **EXAMPLE 14.20—** The makers of Campbell's soups advertised that most Campbell's soups were low in fat and cholesterol and thus were helpful in fighting heart disease. What the ads did not say was that Campbell's soups are high in sodium and that high-sodium diets may increase the risk of heart disease. The FTC ruled that Campbell's claims were thus deceptive. ◆ Generally the test for whether an ad is deceptive is *whether a reasonable consumer would be deceived by the ad.*

If the FTC believes that an advertisement is deceptive, it drafts a formal complaint and sends it to the alleged offender. The company may agree to settle the complaint without further proceedings. If the company does not agree to a settlement, the FTC can conduct a hearing, at which the company can present its defense. If the FTC succeeds in proving that a business practice, such as an advertisement, is deceptive, it usually issues a **cease-and-desist order** requiring that the challenged practice or advertising be stopped.

cease-and-desist order

An administrative or judicial order prohibiting a person or business firm from conducting activities that an agency or court has deemed illegal.

Labeling and Packaging Laws

A number of federal and state laws deal with the information on labels and packages. In general, labels must be accurate and must use words that are easily understood by the ordinary consumer. For instance, a box of cereal cannot be labeled "giant" if that would exaggerate the amount of cereal in the box. In some instances, labels must specify the raw materials used in the product, such as the percentage of cotton or other fiber used in clothing. In other instances, the product must carry a warning. Cigarette packages must include warnings about the health hazards of smoking, for example.

The Fair Packaging and Labeling Act of 1966 requires that products carry labels that identify the product; the net quantity of the contents, as well as the amount in each serving, if the number of servings is stated; the manufacturer;

and the packager or distributor. The act also establishes requirements concerning words used to describe packages, disclosure of ingredients of nonfood products, and the partial filling of packages.

Food products must bear labels detailing nutritional content, including how much fat the food contains and what kind of fat it is. The federal Food and Drug Administration (FDA) has guidelines to standardize nutritional information on packaged foods, and the FTC plays a key role in enforcing the restrictions. The Nutrition Labeling and Education Act of 1990 requires standard nutrition facts (including fat content) on food labels, regulates the use of such terms as *fresh, low fat,* and *organic,* and, subject to FDA approval, authorizes certain health claims.

Sales Transactions

Many laws that protect consumers require the disclosure of terms in sales transactions and provide rules governing certain sales, such as door-to-door sales, mail-order sales, and the receipt of unsolicited merchandise. One FTC regulation, for example, requires sellers to give consumers three days to cancel any door-to-door sale. In addition, the FTC requires that consumers be notified in Spanish of this right if the oral negotiations for the sale were in Spanish. The FTC also has rules requiring sellers of some goods and services (such as used cars and funeral services) to disclose particular information to consumers. Most states have enacted laws specifically governing consumer sales transactions or broad consumer deception that apply to a wide range of practices.

Consumer Health and Safety

Regulating the labeling and packaging of products helps to promote consumer health and safety. But there is a difference between regulating information about a product and regulating the content of the product. ◆ **EXAMPLE 14.21—** Tobacco products have not been altered by regulation or banned despite their obvious hazards. What has been regulated are the warnings that producers are required to give consumers about the hazards of tobacco. As the law stands today, if people choose to use tobacco products with knowledge of the risks to their health, that is their choice. ◆ We now look at several laws that regulate the actual products made available to consumers.

In 1906, Congress passed the Pure Food and Drug Act, which was the first legislation aimed at protecting consumers against impure and misbranded food and drug products. In 1938, the Federal Food, Drug and Cosmetic Act was passed to strengthen the 1906 legislation. These acts and later amendments established standards for foods, specified safe levels of food additives, and regulated some aspects of food advertising. They also required that drugs must be proved effective as well as safe before they could receive permission to be sold. Most of the statutes involving food and drugs are enforced by the Food and Drug Administration, but the Department of Agriculture and other agencies have jurisdiction in certain areas.

Still other statutes, categorized as product-safety acts, regulate the distribution of hazardous or defective products. One example is the Consumer Product Safety Act, enacted to protect consumers from dangerous products. The Consumer Product Safety Commission, which was created by the act, conducts research on the safety of products and maintains a clearinghouse on the risks associated with various products. The commission sets standards for consumer products and bans the sale of products it deems hazardous to consumers. Products banned by the commission include unsafe fireworks, cribs, and toys, as well as many products containing asbestos, lead, or vinyl chloride.

Consumer Credit Protection

Because of the extensive use of credit by American consumers, credit protection has become an important area regulated by consumer protection legislation. One of the most significant statutes regulating the credit and credit-card industry is the Truth-in-Lending Act (TILA), the name commonly given to Title 1 of the Consumer Credit Protection Act, which was passed by Congress in 1968 and greatly expanded since then.

The Truth-in-Lending Act

The TILA is basically a *disclosure law*. It is administered by the Federal Reserve Board and requires sellers and lenders to disclose credit terms or loan terms so that borrowers can shop around for the best financing arrangements. TILA requirements apply only to persons and entities that, in the ordinary course of business, lend money, sell on credit, or arrange for the extension of credit. Sales or loans made between two consumers do not come under the act. Additionally, the act only protects persons (not businesses). Under the provisions of the TILA, terms of a credit instrument must be clearly and conspicuously (obviously) disclosed and follow regulations. The TILA provides that a consumer can cancel a contract if a creditor fails to follow exactly the required procedures.

EQUAL OPPORTUNITY.   Congress enacted the Equal Credit Opportunity Act (ECOA) as an amendment to the TILA. The ECOA prohibits the denial of credit solely on the basis of race, religion, national origin, color, gender, marital status, or age. The act also prohibits discrimination on the basis of whether an individual receives certain forms of income, such as public-assistance benefits. Creditors may not collect information about any of these characteristics from an applicant and may not require the signature of an applicant's spouse, other than as a joint applicant.

CREDIT CARDS.   The TILA also contains provisions regarding credit cards. One provision limits the liability of a cardholder to $50 per card for unauthorized charges made before the creditor is notified that the card has been lost. Another provision prohibits a credit-card company from billing a consumer for any unauthorized charges on a credit card that was improperly issued by the company. Further provisions of the act concern billing disputes related to credit-card purchases. The act outlines specific procedures and time deadlines for both the consumer and the credit-card company to follow in settling a dispute.

Fair Credit Reporting

Lenders use *credit reports* to decide whether and how much to lend to prospective borrowers. To protect consumers against inaccurate credit reporting, Congress enacted the Fair Credit Reporting Act. It provides that consumer credit reporting agencies—such as Equifax, TransUnion, and Experian—may issue credit reports only for specified purposes. Authorized purposes include the extension of credit, the issuance of insurance policies, and compliance with a court order. A report may also be issued in response to a consumer's request for a copy of his or her own credit report. Any time a consumer is denied credit or insurance on the basis of the credit report, the consumer must be notified of that fact and of the name and address of the credit reporting agency that issued the credit report.

Under the act, consumers may request the source of any information being given out by a credit agency, as well as the identity of any party that received an agency's report. Consumers also have access to the information contained about them in a credit reporting agency's files. If a consumer discovers that these files contain inaccurate information, the agency, on the consumer's written request, must investigate. If the investigation reveals that the information is unverifiable or inaccurate, the agency must delete it within a reasonable period of time.

Fair and Accurate Credit Transactions Act

To help combat identity theft, Congress passed the Fair and Accurate Credit Transactions (FACT) Act. It established a fraud alert system so that consumers who suspect that they have been victimized by identity theft can place an alert on their credit files. The act also requires the major credit reporting agencies to provide consumers with free copies of their own credit reports every twelve months. Since 2008, the act has required that financial institutions work with the Federal Trade Commission to identify "red flag" indicators of identity theft and to develop rules on how to dispose of sensitive credit information.

The FACT Act gives consumers who have been victimized by identity theft some assistance in rebuilding their credit reputations. For example, credit reporting agencies must stop reporting allegedly fraudulent account information once the consumer establishes that identify theft has occurred. Business owners and creditors are required to provide consumers with copies of any records that can help the consumer prove that a particular account or transaction is fraudulent (a forged signature, for example).

Fair Debt-Collection Practices

Congress passed the Fair Debt Collection Practices Act (FDCPA) in an attempt to curb perceived abuses by collection agencies. The act applies to debt-collection agencies that, usually for a percentage of the amount owed, regularly attempt to collect debts on behalf of someone else.

The act prohibits such debt-collection practices as contacting consumers at their place of employment if the employers object, contacting consumers at inconvenient times, and contacting consumers if they are represented by attorneys. The act also prohibits debt-collection agencies from contacting most third parties about a debt unless authorized to do so by a court, using harassment and intimidation (such as abusive language), using false or misleading information, and communicating with the consumer after receipt of a notice that the consumer is refusing to pay the debt (except to advise the consumer of legal action to be taken by the collection agency). ◆ **EXAMPLE 14.22—** West Asset Management, a debt collector, was sued for harassment under the FDCPA for repeatedly calling a widow and trying to convince her to pay a debt owed by her deceased husband to Bank of America. The widow had no obligation to repay the debt, as Bank of America and the debt collector knew. A Florida court held that both Bank of America and the debt collector could be liable for improper debt-collection tactics. ◆

Garnishment Proceedings

Creditors have numerous remedies available to them when consumers fail to pay their debts. Among these remedies is garnishment. **Garnishment** occurs when a creditor, after complying with procedures mandated by state law, legally seizes a portion of a debtor's property (such as wages) in the possession of a third party (such as an employer). The creditor must first obtain an *order of garnishment* from the court, which allows the creditor to have access to the debtor's wages while they are still in the control of the employer. Laws governing garnishment vary considerably from state to state.

Both federal and state laws limit the amount that can be taken from a debtor's take-home pay. The federal Consumer Credit Protection Act provides that a debtor can keep either 75 percent of the net earnings per week or a sum equivalent to the pay for thirty hours of work at federal minimum wage rates, whichever is greater. State laws also provide dollar exemptions, and these amounts are often larger than those provided by federal law.

Employers dislike garnishment proceedings. After all, such proceedings impose time costs on employers (possible appearance at court hearings, record-keeping costs, and the like). To protect the job security of employees whose wages are subject to garnishment, federal law provides that garnishment of an employee's wages usually cannot be grounds for that employee's dismissal. The *Developing Paralegal Skills* feature on the following page discusses this issue further with respect to the role that may involve a paralegal.

garnishment
A proceeding in which a creditor legally seizes a portion of a debtor's property (such as wages) that is in the possession of a third party (such as an employer).

ON THE web

The U.S. Department of Labor provides details about wage garnishment procedures at **www.dol.gov**. Enter "garnishment" in the advanced search box.

DEVELOPING
paralegal skills

DISCHARGED FOR GARNISHMENT

Eva White works as a paralegal for a firm that specializes in employment law. A business client has called Eva's supervising attorney to ask for advice concerning garnishment. Basically, the client wants to know if he can fire an employee so that he can avoid having to comply with garnishment proceedings that have been initiated against the employee. The attorney has asked Eva to research recent case law and current statutes and regulations on the question of whether an employer may fire an employee for this reason.

Eva goes online to research garnishment and locates a case in which an employee was fired two days after his employer received notice of the garnishment. The case turned on whether the employer had notice that the garnishment proceedings had already been initiated against the employee. She reads through the case and finds a citation to the statute. Eva's next step is to check the statute itself to ensure that she has up-to-date knowledge of how the statute is being applied.

CHECKLIST FOR LEGAL RESEARCH

- Locate statutes and regulations issued under the statutes.

- Locate case law to see how the statute and regulations have been interpreted and applied and whether the statute has been found to be unconstitutional.

- Update your case law findings by checking a citator (see Chapter 8) to make sure that the holding in the case is still good law.

- Update the statute by checking the pocket part or using a citator to see if the statute has been amended or repealed.

KEY TERMS AND CONCEPTS

Chapter Summary

Tort Law, Product Liability, and Consumer Law

THE BASIS OF TORT LAW

Two notions serve as the basis of all torts: wrongs and compensation. Tort law recognizes that some acts are wrong because they cause injuries to others. A *tort* is a civil wrong. In a tort action, one person or group brings a personal-injury suit against another person or group to obtain compensation (money damages) or other relief for the harm suffered. Generally, the purpose of tort law is to provide remedies for the invasion of various interests, such as physical security, privacy, freedom of movement, and reputation. Torts fall into two broad classifications: *intentional torts* and *negligence*.

INTENTIONAL TORTS

A general category of torts where the actor intended to perform an act that resulted in an injury to a protected right of another party.

1. *Intentional torts against persons*—Intentional acts that violate protected interests that people have under the common law.

   a. An assault is an intentional act that causes another person to be apprehensive or fearful of immediate harm. A battery is an assault that results in physical contact. Defenses to such actions include consent, self-defense, and the defense of others and of property.

   b. False imprisonment is the intentional confinement or restraint of another person's movement without justification.

   c. An intentional act that amounts to extreme and outrageous conduct that results in severe emotional distress to another can be the basis of a suit for intentional infliction of emotional (mental) distress.

   d. A false statement, not made under privilege, that is communicated to a third person and that causes damage to a person's reputation may be defamation. If spoken it is slander; if in print, it is libel. Defenses include the privilege to relay the information, such as in the news, or to protect another interest.

   e. Invasion of the right to privacy is the use of a person's name or likeness for commercial purposes without permission, wrongful intrusion into a person's private activities, publication of information that places a person in a false light, or disclosure of private facts that an ordinary person would find objectionable.

   f. The use of another person's name, likeness, or other identifying characteristic without permission and for the benefit of the user is the intentional tort of appropriation.

   g. Misrepresentation or fraud is a false representation made by one party, through misstatement of facts or by conduct, with the intention of deceiving another and on which the other reasonably relies to his or her detriment, thereby suffering a loss.

   h. Knowing, intentional interference by a third party with an enforceable contractual relationship or an established business relationship between other parties for the purpose of advancing the economic interests of the third party is the tort of wrongful interference.

2. *Intentional torts against property*—Intentional acts by a party that violate interests of others protected at common law.

   a. Trespass to land is the invasion of another's real property without consent or privilege.

   b. Unlawfully damaging or interfering with the owner's right to use, possess, or enjoy personal property is the tort of trespass to personal property.

   c. Conversion is a tort in which personal property is taken from its rightful owner.

NEGLIGENCE

Negligence is the careless performance of a legally required duty or the failure to perform a legally required act. Elements that must be proved are that a legal duty of care existed to another party, that the defendant breached that duty, and that the breach caused damage or injury to another.

1. *The duty of care and its breach*—Negligence involves the failure to exercise the duty of care expected of all parties. We are held to the standard of a reasonable person under the circumstances. For businesses, this means an obligation to provide safe premises for clients. Professionals must meet the standards expected of knowledgeable members of the area of expertise.

2. *The injury requirement and damages*—A plaintiff in a negligence suit must have sustained an injury that produced legally recognized damages. Most commonly, plaintiffs receive compensatory damages, but when the actions of a defendant are particularly offensive, punitive damages may be added.

3. *Causation*—The injury must be logically attributable to the violation of a protected interest by the defen-

dant because there is a cause in fact or proximate cause.

4. *Defenses to negligence*—A defendant may plead an affirmative defense in negligence cases: assumption of risk, superseding cause, and contributory negligence by the plaintiff.

5. *Special negligence doctrines and statutes*—Negligence *per se* is a type of negligence that may occur if a person violates a statute or an ordinance providing for a criminal penalty and the violation causes another to be injured. There are special negligence statutes such as dram shop acts and Good Samaritan laws that prescribe duties and responsibilities in certain circumstances. The violation of such statutes will impose civil liability or help protect a party accused of negligence.

CYBER TORTS: DEFAMATION ONLINE

General tort principles are extended to cover cyber torts, or torts that occur in cyberspace, such as online defamation. Cyber torts often present special issues of proof. Federal and state statutes may also apply to certain forms of cyber torts.

1. *Liability of Internet service providers*—ISPs are generally protected from suit when they have been the

method of transmission of damaging information, as long as they have taken reasonable steps to protect against abuse of their services.

2. *Piercing the veil of anonymity*—ISPs may be required to provide the names of their clients who have been accused of torts. The law is still evolving on this point.

STRICT LIABILITY

The doctrine of strict liability is old but has been expanded over time to apply to more areas of tort law. Under it, a person or company may be held liable, regardless of the degree of care exercised, for damages or injuries caused by a product or activity.

1. *Abnormally dangerous activities*—Strict liability applies to those engaged in particularly dangerous activities, such as with toxic chemicals and explosives.

All burden is placed on those who engage in such activities or use such materials, so they have strong incentives to protect others against injury and will be held liable for any injuries related to such activities.

2. *Other applications of strict liability*—The most important application of the doctrine of strict liability is in the area of defective products. This is a major part of product liability law.

PRODUCT LIABILITY

The makers of products can be liable in tort to injuries and damages caused by defective products. This is an old doctrine that has evolved over time.

1. *Theories of product liability*—Suits for product liability may be based on negligence, in which it is alleged that due care was not used by the manufacturer in designing, producing, or testing the product before selling it, or there was a failure to place adequate warnings on the label or product. It may be based on misrepresentation, which is when the seller misrepresents the quality, nature, or appropriate use of the product, and the user is injured as a result. Strict product liability occurs when it is shown that even though

a manufacturer has exercised a reasonable degree of care, the product was defective and injured someone. Most such suits claim that either there was a defect in the production process, or there was a design defect that caused the product to be more dangerous than it should have been, or there was a failure to warn of dangers in the product.

2. *Defenses to product liability*—If sued, a producer can offer several defenses: assumption of risk—the user or consumer knew of the risk of harm and voluntarily assumed it; product misuse—the user or consumer misused the product in a way unforeseeable by the manufacturer; comparative negligence—the plaintiff

and the defendant should share liability under the doctrine of comparative negligence if the plaintiff's misuse of the product contributed to the risk of injury; and commonly known dangers. If a defendant suc-ceeds in convincing the court that a plaintiff's injury resulted from a commonly known danger, such as the danger associated with using a sharp knife, the defendant will not be liable.

CONSUMER LAW

Statutes, agency rules, and common law judicial decisions that serve to protect the interests of consumers are classified as consumer law. There are many federal consumer protection statutes, in addition to a wide variety of state consumer protection statutes. Some state statutes provide more protection than that afforded by the federal laws discussed below.

1. *Deceptive sales practices*—The Federal Trade Commission (FTC) has authority to investigate and sue firms engaged in deceptive business practices that could injure a reasonable consumer. The agency also issues regulations to define certain deceptive practices. State attorneys general have broad powers to attack deceptive practices.

2. *Deceptive advertising*—Advertising that misleads consumers or that is based on false claims is prohibited by the FTC. Generally, the test for whether an ad is deceptive is whether a reasonable consumer would be deceived by the ad. The FTC can require the advertiser to stop the challenged advertising, often by getting a court to issue a cease-and-desist order.

3. *Labeling and packaging*—Manufacturers must comply with labeling or packaging requirements for their specific products. In general, labels must be accurate and not misleading. Food products must bear labels detailing their nutritional content, and standards must be met before a product can use terms like *fresh* and *organic* on the label.

4. *Sales transactions*—Many federal laws regulate the disclosure of terms to consumers in sales transactions, particularly in door-to-door and mail-order sales. The FTC conducts most of the federal regulation of sales. States have broad statutes that allow them to sue firms for harmful sales practices that cover a wide range of activities.

5. *Consumer health and safety*—Laws protecting the health and safety of consumers regulate the content of a food, drug, or other item. The Federal Food, Drug and Cosmetic Act protects consumers against impure and misbranded foods and drugs. The act establishes food standards, specifies safe levels of food additives, and regulates some aspects of food advertising. The Consumer Product Safety Act seeks to protect consumers from risk of injury from hazardous products. The Consumer Product Safety Commission has the power to remove products that are deemed hazardous from the market and to ban the manufacture and sale of hazardous products.

6. *Consumer credit protection*—Credit protection has become an important area regulated by federal consumer protection legislation. Among the most important is the Truth-in-Lending Act (TILA). It is a disclosure law requiring sellers and lenders to disclose credit terms or loan terms so that individuals can shop around to compare terms. This law also provides for the following:

   a. *Equal credit opportunity*—Prohibits creditors from discriminating on the basis of race, religion, national origin, color, gender, marital status, or age.

   b. *Credit-card protection*—Limits the liability of cardholders for unauthorized charges made on unsolicited credit cards.

   c. *Credit-card rules*—TILA provides detailed rules that apply in case of a dispute between a credit-card holder and the bank that issued the card.

   The Fair Credit Reporting Act protects consumers against inaccurate credit reporting and provides that credit reports can only be issued for certain purposes. Consumers are entitled to receive a copy of their credit report on request and to be notified any time they are denied credit or insurance based on the report. The reporting agency must conduct an investigation if the consumer contests any information on the credit report.

   The Fair and Accurate Credit Transactions Act helps protect against identity theft by establishing a national fraud alert system for credit users; by requiring major credit reporting agencies to provide consumers with free copies of their credit reports every twelve months; by requiring that account numbers on credit-card receipts be shortened; and by assisting victims of identity theft in reestablishing their credit reputations.

   The Fair Debt Collection Practices Act prohibits debt collectors from using unfair debt-collection practices, such as contacting debtors at their place of employment if their employers object, contacting debtors at unreasonable times, contacting third parties about the debt unless authorized to do so by a court, and harassing debtors.

   Garnishment is when a creditor has the right to seize a portion of the debtor's property (such as wages) in the possession of a third party (such as an employer) to satisfy a debt. The creditor must comply with specific procedures mandated by state law.

QUESTIONS FOR REVIEW

1. Define tort. What is the underlying purpose of tort law? What are the main categories of torts, and how do they differ?

2. What is an intentional tort? List the elements of assault, battery, intentional infliction of emotional distress, and defamation. How do intentional torts against persons differ from cyber torts?

3. What are the four elements of negligence? Why is the duty of care for professionals different from the duty of an ordinary person? What are the affirmative defenses to a negligence action?

4. What is product liability? What are the three legal theories for product liability suits? List and define the affirmative defenses to a product liability suit.

5. List and describe the six areas of federal consumer law discussed in the chapter. Do states have consumer protection laws? If so, what level of consumer protection do state laws provide?

ETHICAL QUESTIONS

1. Sang Juan is a paralegal for a bank. He has been trying to get a debtor, a 45-year-old man who is behind on his loan payments, to respond to his calls and attempts to collect the loan. Sang Juan poses as an attractive 18-year-old girl, complete with bikini photos, on Facebook and flirts with the debtor in an effort to get in contact with him. When the debtor responds to Sang Juan's "flirtations," Sang Juan exposes his true identity with a posting that says "pay your debts DEADBEAT!" Has Sang Juan violated any ethical rules? Any laws?

2. Chloee is a new legal assistant interviewing a client who wants to sue the manufacturer of an allegedly defective elliptical training machine. The client claims that while using the machine, it stopped suddenly, causing him to fall off and seriously injure his hip. Near the end of the interview, the client asks Chloee whether she thinks he has a good case. Chloee responds, "Well, as you know, I'm a paralegal, and I cannot give legal advice. Personally, though, I think that you do have a good case." Has Chloee violated her ethical duties? How would you have handled the situation?

PRACTICE QUESTIONS AND ASSIGNMENTS

1. Bob is driving to work for his morning shift at the plant when he encounters strikers who are picketing and blocking the entrance to the factory. Bob cannot afford to lose his job, so he decides to cross the picket line. When he attempts to drive through, the picketers surround his car and begin to rock and push it. Bob's car is spun around and ends up in oncoming traffic. Bob suffers a panic attack and his anxiety disorder is aggravated so that he cannot work. Does Bob have a tort claim against the picketers? If so, which torts were committed?

2. Kayanna and Draymond are divorced. While they were married, Draymond continually accused Kayanna of being "unfaithful" to him and sexually promiscuous. Now that the divorce is final, Kayanna learns that Draymond is sending e-mails to their mutual friends claiming that she is promiscuous. Can Kayanna sue Draymond for defamation? Could she have brought a defamation action prior to the divorce? What would happen to Kayanna's claim if Draymond could prove that she was, in fact, promiscuous?

3. In which of the following situations will the acting party be liable for the tort of negligence? Explain fully.

   a. Mary goes to the golf course on Sunday morning, eager to try out a new set of golf clubs she has just purchased. As she tees off on the first hole, the head of her club flies off and injures a nearby golfer.

   b. Mary's doctor gives her some pain medication and tells her not to drive after she takes it, as the medication induces drowsiness. In spite of the doctor's warning, Mary decides to drive to the store while on the medication. Owing to her lack of alertness, she fails to stop at a traffic light and crashes into another vehicle, injuring a passenger.

4. Carmen buys a television set manufactured by AKI Electronics. She is going on vacation, so she takes the set to her mother's house for her mother to use. Because the set is defective, it explodes, causing considerable damage to her mother's house. Carmen's mother sues AKI for the damage to her house. Discuss the product liability theories under which Carmen's mother can recover from AKI.

QUESTIONS FOR CRITICAL ANALYSIS

1. Ricardo is a paralegal with the city attorney's office. He learns that the student body president of his college has taken a position on open student housing that Ricardo is opposed to. He follows the student body president both virtually—from his office computer—and physically by attending every public forum held on campus. Ricardo starts a Facebook page discussing the student body president's activities. Some of the statements that Ricardo makes on Facebook are true, but others are not. Ricardo calls the state senator for whom the student body president is interning to tell her that hiring him would not be a good idea because of his politics. Ricardo makes this call from his employer-issued cell phone. Finally, the student body president hires an attorney to sue Ricardo. What torts might they allege? If Ricardo's employer wants to know whether the allegations are true, can Ricardo prevent his employer from accessing his computer and cell phone records? Should employees have a right to privacy in employer-owned computers and cell phones?

2. A law school has an open admissions policy. Once admitted, students must earn a grade of "C" or better in all courses to stay enrolled. Many students flunk out. Several disgruntled students started a blog, where they complain about the law school's policies. Over time, more students post on the blog and some of the statements are untrue. The law school sues for online defamation, naming the defendants as John Does. Will the Internet service provider have to reveal the identities of the defendant Does? How do the rights of the plaintiff balance against the defendants' First Amendment rights to free speech?

3. A plaintiff in a negligence case must prove proximate cause, also known as legal cause, to succeed in the action. Foreseeability is one commonly used test of proximate cause. What impact does foreseeability have on the issue of causation? What might happen without such a test?

4. Product liability is imposed on manufacturers based on the notion that they are better able to bear the cost of injury than innocent victims, and that requiring producers to pay for injuries caused by their products encourages them to make safer products. Is this good social policy? What impact does it have on victims of defective products? On manufacturers?

5. Many consumer laws have been enacted over time. Are these consumer laws needed? What could be done to encourage businesses to behave differently and reduce the need for consumer protection laws?

PROJECTS

1. Find an article online or in a print newspaper on a serious-injury accident. Read the article carefully, and write a two-page memo evaluating the potential negligence claim and indicating what you think is needed to "work up" the case. For example, you might make a list of any witnesses who need to be interviewed, any police reports or other records (such as medical records) that should be obtained. Make sure to attach the article, or a copy of it, to the memo you prepare.

2. Contact a credit reporting agency and obtain a credit report on yourself, if one exists. Does the report contain any inaccurate information about your credit transactions? If so, and if a denial of credit, employment, or insurance might have been based on the report, you can and should have it corrected, as permitted under the Fair Credit Reporting Act.

GROUP PROJECT

This project asks you to research tobacco litigation. Go to the University of California–San Francisco Web site on this subject at www.library.ucsf.edu/tobacco. (It is also available at http://oag.ca.gov/tobacco/msa.)

Student one will locate the summary of the Master Tobacco Settlement Agreement and summarize it.

Student two will obtain a list of cigarette ingredients and provide it to the group.

Student three will provide the state lawsuit chart showing the names of cases and filing dates of tobacco suits in 42 states.

Student four will organize and present the material to the class.

USING INTERNET RESOURCES

Go to FindLaw's Injury and Tort Law Web Guide at **www.findlaw.com/01topics/index.html**. Under "Practice Areas," go to "Injury & Tort Law" to find answers to the following questions:

1. Under "Web Guide by Resource Type," select "Databases and Statistics." What kind of information generally is available at this location? How might this information be used in a tort lawsuit? Which government agencies' data can you access?

2. Return to "Web Guide by Resource Type." Under the heading "Publications—Journals, Newsletters and Articles," you can find many articles on tort law.

Select and read an article that interests you and write a one-page summary. Print the article and attach a copy to your summary.

3. Now select "Web Sites" under "Web Guide by Resource Type" and browse through the listings. How many of the listings are related to defective products and product liability actions? How many provide information about consumer law? Explore one of the Web sites provided, and write a short synopsis of what you found at that site. Include the Web site's URL in your synopsis.

END NOTES

1. 47 U.S.C. Section 230.
2. *Restatement (Second) of Torts*, Section 402A.
3. *Restatement (Third) of Torts: Products Liability*, Section 2, Comment h.

CourseMate   The available CourseMate for this text has an interactive eBook and interactive learning tools, including flash cards, quizzes, and more. To learn more about this resource and access free demo CourseMate resources, go to **www.cengagebrain.com**, and search for this book. To access CourseMate materials that you have purchased, go to **login.cengagebrain.com**.

Contracts and Intellectual Property Law

After completing this chapter, you will know:

- The requirements for forming a valid contract and the circumstances under which contracts are not enforceable.

- The remedies available when a contract is breached, or broken.

- The nature and legal validity of an electronic signature.

- The nature and forms of intellectual property.

- What conduct gives rise to a violation of intellectual property.

Introduction

The law governs virtually every transaction or activity that individuals engage in across the nation. Simple, everyday transactions—such as buying a gallon of milk at a convenience store or installing a new app on your smartphone—are subject to laws that define the rights and duties of the parties involved. In this chapter, you will learn about two of the most important areas of law—contracts and sales. Paralegals routinely help attorneys deal with disputes involving contract and sales law. Because such disputes often deal with complicated issues, paralegals need a thorough understanding of the basic principles of these substantive law areas.

Another area of law that has become increasingly important involves intellectual property, such as patents, trademarks, and copyrights. As you will learn later in the chapter, the value of intellectual property has increased because of the massive flow of ideas and innovations throughout the world. Attorneys and their paralegals are frequently called on to help their clients register and protect various forms of intellectual property.

Requirements to Form a Valid Contract

promise
An assurance that one will or will not do something in the future.

Contract law deals with, among other things, the keeping of promises. A **promise** is an assurance that one will or will not do something in the future. As mentioned in Chapter 2, a *contract* is any agreement (based on a promise or an exchange of promises) that can be enforced in court.

Bilateral and Unilateral Contracts

Two basic terms used in discussing types of contracts are *bilateral* and *unilateral*. Most contracts are bilateral. People make a bilateral contract when they exchange a promise for a promise: Yvonne offers to sell Sean her car for $10,000, and he accepts, saying he will have the money tomorrow. When people make a unilateral contract, they exchange a promise for an act: Yvonne tells Devon she will pay him $50 if he will wax her car. He says nothing but later he waxes the car. Because he completed the requested act, Yvonne owes him $50. Both types of contracts are valid, although they may be referred to by different names. Some states do not use the term *unilateral contract*.

Contract Validity

If a client alleges that a party has breached (failed to perform) a contract, the first issue that your supervising attorney and you need to examine is whether a *valid contract* (a contract that will be enforced by a court) was ever formed. To form a valid contract, four basic requirements must be met:

- **Agreement.** An agreement includes an offer and an acceptance. One party must offer to enter into a legal agreement, and another party must accept the terms of the offer.

- **Consideration.** Any promises made by parties must be supported by legally sufficient and bargained-for consideration (which is something of value that is received or promised to convince a person to make a deal, as you will read shortly).

- **Contractual capacity.** Both parties entering into the contract must have the contractual capacity to do so. The law must recognize them as possessing characteristics that qualify them as competent parties.

- **Legality.** The contract's purpose must be to accomplish some goal that is legal and not against public policy.

If any of these four elements is lacking, no contract will have been formed. We look more closely at these requirements in the following subsections. It is important that you understand as you read these discussions that each requirement is separate and independent.

Agreement

A contract is, in essence, an **agreement** between two or more parties. Therefore, if the parties fail to reach an agreement on the terms of the contract, no contract exists. Ordinarily, agreement is evidenced by two events: an *offer* and an *acceptance*. One party offers a certain bargain to another party, who then accepts that bargain. When contracts are drafted with the assistance of an attorney, it is possible that both parties to the agreement will want to use the same attorney. That raises special issues, as noted in the *Ethics Watch* feature below.

Offer

An **offer** is a promise or commitment to do or refrain from doing some specified thing in the future. Three elements are necessary for an offer to be effective:

- The **offeror** (the party making the offer) must have the *intent to be bound* by the offer.

agreement
A meeting of the minds, and a requirement for a valid contract. Agreement involves two distinct events: an offer to form a contract and the acceptance of that offer by the offeree.

offer
A promise or commitment to do or refrain from doing some specified thing in the future.

offeror
The party making the offer.

ETHICS WATCH

POTENTIAL CONFLICTS OF INTEREST

Many times in a law office, two parties come in together and want the attorney (and paralegal) to write a contract that represents their oral agreement. This raises an obvious conflict-of-interest issue. Can the attorney represent both parties in a contract? Conflict rules prevent an attorney from simultaneously representing adverse parties in a legal proceeding. On the one hand, the parties could write up a legally binding contract without an attorney. On the other hand, should a dispute arise over the contract, assisting one party will necessarily be adverse to the other. In this situation, there should be careful research on the rules on waiving conflicts in their state.

If the state has adopted the 2002 Revision of the Model Rules (discussed in Chapter 4), the attorney must obtain the informed consent of each party in writing. This means the attorney must explain the risks of having one attorney draw up a contract for two people and also must discuss the alternatives. Then the two parties must sign a consent form.

Paralegals often have a role to play in these interactions, such as conducting an initial interview with the parties. The position of a paralegal in such circumstances is covered by the NALA Code of Ethics and Professional Responsibility, Canon 2: "A paralegal may perform any task which is properly designated and supervised by an attorney, as long as the attorney is ultimately responsible to the client, maintains a direct relationship with the client, and assumes professional responsibility for the work product."

- The terms of the offer must be *reasonably certain*, or *definite*, so that the parties and the court can determine the terms of the contract. (Note that in contracts for the sale of goods, discussed later in this chapter, the requirement of definiteness is relaxed somewhat so that a contract can exist even if certain terms are left "open," or unspecified.)

- The offer must be communicated to the **offeree** (the party to whom the offer is made).

offeree
The party to whom the offer is made.

Offers made in jest, in undue excitement, or in obvious anger do not meet the intent requirement. ◆ **EXAMPLE 15.1—** Al and Sue ride to work together each day in Sue's car, which she bought for $18,000 six months ago. One cold morning, Al and Sue get into the car, but Sue cannot get it started. Angry, she yells, "I'll sell you this stupid car for $600!" Al writes Sue a check for $600. Has a contract to sell the car been formed? If Al consulted with your supervising attorney, claiming that Sue had breached a contract because she had refused to give him the car, what would the attorney say? The attorney would tell Al that a reasonable person would have recognized under the circumstances that Sue's offer was not serious—she did not intend to be bound but was simply frustrated. Therefore, no valid contract was formed. ◆

Similarly, an offer will not be effective if it is too ambiguous in its terms. ◆ **EXAMPLE 15.2—** Kim wants to sell her set of legal encyclopedias but has not mentioned a price. Jamal says to Kim, "I'll buy your encyclopedias and pay you some money for them next week." In this situation, no contract will result, because "some money" is not a definite term. ◆

Note that when considering a dispute, the courts evaluate it from the standpoint of a reasonable person. ◆ **EXAMPLE 15.3—** Jeff has been attempting to buy some land from Raul for months. One night, while drinking together at a bar, Jeff offers Raul $20,000 for the land. Raul agrees and the two sign a simple agreement while in the bar. Raul later claims it was a joke and refuses to sell. Because a reasonable person would think this was an agreement to sell, Raul has agreed to sell despite his mental reservation. ◆

Advertisements

Advertisements are generally not offers but are invitations to make an offer. When an ad is "clear, definite, and explicit" and leaves nothing open for negotiation, however, it may be an offer. One of the most well-known advertisement cases concerned a Pepsi ad encouraging consumers to accumulate "Pepsi Points" by buying Pepsi products.

A real estate paralegal reviews the terms of a purchase offer with a potential home buyer to ensure that all of the contract's terms are clear. What is the role of the paralegal during real estate transactions?

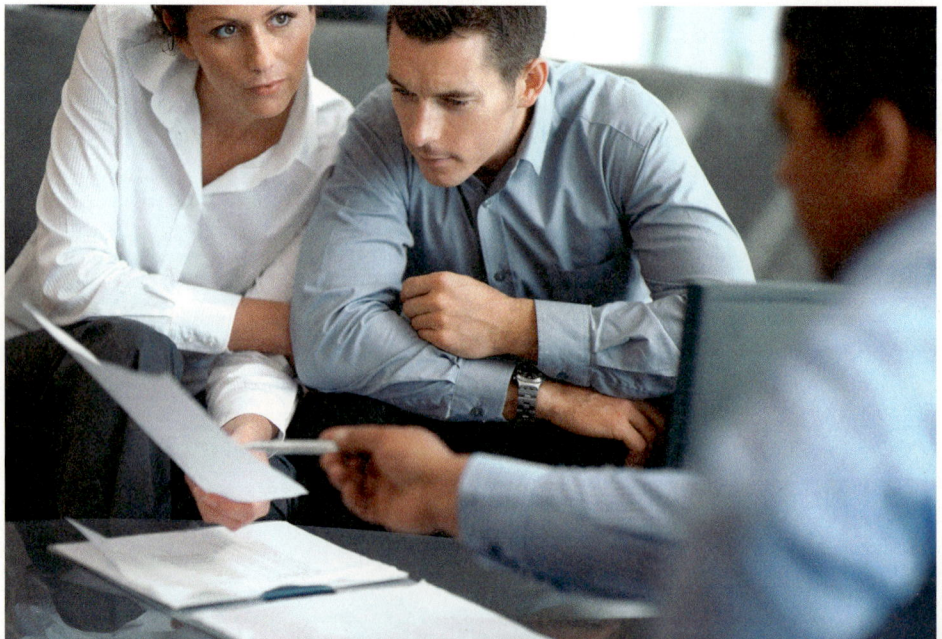

The ad showed many items, from sunglasses to hats, that the consumer could acquire. The final item was a military fighter jet, listed for 700,000 points. When someone attempted to order the jet, and Pepsi refused to deliver it, the consumer sued. The court ruled that the advertisement was not an offer because an objective, reasonable person would not have considered the commercial to be an offer. (You can find the commercial on YouTube by searching for "Harrier Jet Pepsi." There are two versions—one from before the lawsuit and one from after it. What are the differences?)

Termination of the Offer

Once an offer has been communicated, the party to whom the offer was made can accept the offer, reject the offer, or make a counteroffer. If a party accepts the offer, a contract is formed (provided all the other requirements to form a contract are met). If the party rejects the offer, the offer is terminated. In other words, the offer no longer stands (and the offeree cannot take the offeror up on the offer later). The offeree also has the option of rejecting the offer and simultaneously making another offer—called a counteroffer.

COUNTEROFFER.   In a counteroffer, the offeree becomes the offeror—offering to form a contract with different terms.   ◆ **EXAMPLE 15.4—**   Dilan offers to perform work for Wayne for $50,000 a year. Wayne responds, "Your price is too high. I'll hire you for $40,000." Wayne's response is a counteroffer, because it terminates Dilan's offer and creates a new offer by Wayne. ◆

Both a rejection of the offer and the making of a counteroffer terminate the original offer. The original offer can also be terminated if the party making the offer withdraws the offer before it has been accepted (which is called *revoking* the offer). If the offer has already been accepted, however, then both parties are bound in contract.

OTHER BASES FOR TERMINATION.   An offer also terminates automatically in some circumstances, such as when the specific subject matter of the offer is destroyed, one of the parties dies or becomes incompetent, or a new law is passed that makes the contract illegal. Additionally, an offer terminates if a period of time is specified in the offer and the offer is not accepted within that period. If no time for acceptance is specified in the offer, the offer expires when a *reasonable* period of time has passed. What constitutes a reasonable period of time in the eyes of the court varies, depending on the circumstances.

Acceptance

As mentioned, a party's **acceptance** of the offer results in a legally binding contract if all of the other elements of a valid contract are present. The acceptance must be *unequivocal*—that is, the terms of the offer must be accepted exactly as stated by the offeror. This principle of contract law is known as the **mirror image rule**—the terms of the acceptance must be the same as ("mirror") the terms of the offer. If the acceptance is subject to new conditions or if the terms of the acceptance materially change the original offer, the acceptance may be deemed a counteroffer that implicitly rejects the original offer.

PROPER COMMUNICATION.   Another requirement, for most types of contracts, is that the acceptance be communicated to the offeror. A significant problem in contract formation has to do with the timeliness of acceptances. The general rule is that acceptance of an offer is timely if it is made before the offer is terminated.

Problems arise, however, when the parties involved are not dealing face-to-face. In such cases, acceptance takes effect at the time the acceptance is communicated via the mode expressly or impliedly authorized by the offeror. This is the **mailbox rule**. Under this rule, if the offer states that it must be accepted by mail, the acceptance becomes valid the moment it is deposited in the mail (even if it is never received by the offeror).

acceptance
In contract law, the offeree's indication to the offeror that the offeree agrees to be bound by the terms of the offeror's offer, or proposal to form a contract.

mirror image rule
A common law rule that requires that the terms of the offeree's acceptance adhere exactly to the terms of the offeror's offer for a valid contract to be formed.

mailbox rule
A rule providing that an acceptance of an offer takes effect at the time it is communicated via the mode expressly or impliedly authorized by the offeror, rather than at the time it is actually received by the offeror. If acceptance is to be by mail, for example, it becomes effective the moment it is placed in the mailbox.

REASONABLENESS STANDARD.   Most of the time, the party making the offer does not indicate the preferred method of acceptance. In those cases, acceptance of an offer may be made in any manner that is *reasonable under the circumstances*. Several factors determine whether the acceptance is reasonable: the nature of the circumstances at the time the offer was made, the means used to transmit the offer, and the reliability of the offer's delivery. ◆ **EXAMPLE 15.5—** An offer is sent by FedEx overnight delivery because an acceptance is urgently required. In this situation, the offeree's acceptance by fax or e-mail will be deemed reasonable. ◆ In contracts formed on the Internet, the issues of timeliness and method of acceptance usually do not arise. This is because persons often accept online offers simply by clicking on a box stating "I agree" or "I accept." Such **click-on agreements** are widely used in the formation of contracts online (as discussed later in this chapter).

Consideration

Another requirement for a valid contract is consideration. **Consideration** is usually defined as something of value—such as money or the performance of an action not otherwise required—that is given in exchange for a promise. No promise is enforceable without consideration. ◆ **EXAMPLE 15.6—** You give your friend $1,000 in exchange for her promise to take care of your house and garden for six months. This promise normally will be enforceable, because consideration has been given. Your consideration is $1,000. Your friend's consideration is the assumption of an obligation (taking care of the house and garden) that she otherwise would not assume. ◆ Note that both parties to the contract must give consideration for the contract to be enforced. Many disputes result when one party argues there is a lack of consideration. Consideration is a requirement of the common law. In contrast, most civil law countries, such as Germany and France, do not require consideration for a contract to be valid.

Elements of Consideration

Often, consideration is broken down into two parts: (1) something of *legal value* must be given in exchange for the promise, and (2) there must be a *bargained-for exchange*. The "something of legal value" may consist of a return promise that is bargained for. It may also consist of performance, which may be an act, a forbearance, or the creation, modification, or destruction of a legal relationship. Forbearance involves not doing something one has a legal right to do. ◆ **EXAMPLE 15.7—** When you are twenty-one, your grandfather promises to pay you $10,000 if you agree not to smoke any cigarettes before the age of twenty-five. Your consideration in this situation is refraining from smoking cigarettes. ◆

Contract Change Requires New Consideration

Once a contract has been formed, the general common law rule is that the terms of the contract cannot be modified without further consideration. For instance, after making the deal in the example just given, your grandfather cannot modify the terms by requiring you not to drink alcohol for the same $10,000—you would have to get additional consideration for this new agreement.

Legal Sufficiency of Consideration

For a binding contract to be created, consideration must be *legally sufficient*. To be legally sufficient, consideration for a promise must be either *legally detrimental to the promisee or legally beneficial to the promisor*. A party can incur legal detriment either by promising to give legal value (such as the payment of money) or by a forbearance or a promise of forbearance.

The requirement of consideration is what distinguishes contracts from gifts. ◆ **EXAMPLE 15.8—** You promise to give your friend $1,000 as a gift, and she promises to accept your gift. In this situation, no contract results, because your friend has given no legally sufficient consideration. ◆

---

click-on agreement
An agreement that arises when a buyer, engaging in a transaction on a computer, indicates his or her assent to be bound by the terms of an offer by clicking on a button that says, for example, "I agree"; sometimes referred to as a click-on license or a click-wrap agreement.

consideration
Something of value, such as money or the performance of an action not otherwise required, that motivates the formation of a contract. Each party must give consideration for the contract to be binding.

social MEDIA TODAY

Get regular training on online security issues. The threats online are constantly evolving. You need to stay on top of best practices for keeping your employer's computers, network, reputation, and information secure.

Adequacy of Consideration

Adequacy of consideration refers to the fairness of the bargain. In general, a court will not question the adequacy of consideration if the consideration is legally sufficient. Parties are normally free to bargain as they wish. If people could sue merely because they had entered into a bad bargain, the courts would be overloaded with frivolous suits. In other words, Alonzo is free to sell his 2013 Mercedes Benz, which is in perfect condition, to Herb for $3,000, even if the car is worth more (the court normally will not invalidate the contract).

In extreme cases, a court may consider the adequacy of consideration in terms of its amount or worth because inadequate consideration may indicate fraud, duress, undue influence, or a lack of bargained-for exchange. It may also reflect a party's incompetence (for example, an individual might have been too intoxicated or simply too young to make a contract).

Promissory Estoppel

In some circumstances, contracts will be enforced even though consideration is lacking. Under the doctrine of **promissory estoppel**, a person who has reasonably and substantially relied on the promise of another may be able to obtain some measure of recovery. The following elements are required:

- There must be a clear and definite promise.
- The promisee must justifiably rely on the promise.
- The reliance normally must be of a substantial and definite character.
- Justice will be better served by enforcement of the promise.

If these requirements are met, a promise may be enforced even though it is not supported by consideration. In essence, the promisor will be *estopped* (prevented) from asserting the lack of consideration as a defense. ◆ **EXAMPLE 15.9—**   Your uncle tells you, "I'll pay you $500 a week so you won't have to work anymore." In reliance on your uncle's promise, you quit your job, but your uncle refuses to pay you. Under the doctrine of promissory estoppel, you may be able to enforce such a promise. ◆

Contractual Capacity

For a contract to be deemed valid, the parties to the contract must have **contractual capacity**—the legal ability or competence to enter into a contractual relationship. Courts generally presume the existence of contractual capacity, but there are some situations in which capacity is lacking or questionable. In many instances, a party may have the capacity to enter into a valid contract but also have the right to avoid liability under it.

Minors

Minors usually are not legally bound by contracts. Subject to certain exceptions, the contracts entered into by a minor are *voidable* (they can be canceled, or avoided) at the option of that minor. The minor has the option of *disaffirming* (renouncing) the contract and setting aside the contract and all legal obligations arising from it. An adult who enters a contract with a minor, however, cannot avoid his or her contractual duties on the ground that the minor can do so. Unless the minor exercises the option to set aside the contract, the adult party is bound by it.

Intoxication and Mental Capacity

Intoxication is a condition in which a person's normal capacity to act or think is inhibited by alcohol or some other drug. Under the common law rule, if the person was sufficiently intoxicated to lack mental capacity, the transaction is voidable at the option of the intoxicated person even if the intoxication was purely voluntary. In spite of the common law rule, most courts today rarely permit contracts to be avoided because of a party's intoxication.

ON THE web

To learn more about consideration in the context of small businesses, go to **smallbusiness.findlaw.com**.

promissory estoppel
A doctrine under which a promise is binding if the promise is clear and definite, the promisee justifiably relies on the promise, the reliance is reasonable and substantial, and justice will be better served by enforcement of the promise.

contractual capacity
The threshold mental capacity required by law for a party who enters into a contract to be bound by that contract.

If a person has been adjudged mentally incompetent by a court of law and a guardian has been appointed, any contract made by the mentally incompetent person is *void*—no contract exists. Only the guardian can enter into binding legal duties on the incompetent person's behalf. Even if the court has not previously ruled that the person is mentally incompetent, the contract may be avoided if incompetence is proved. ◆ **EXAMPLE 15.10—** Rita, who suffers from Alzheimer's disease, signs a contract to buy ten new vacuum cleaners. If the contract is challenged and it can be proved that Rita did not understand what she was doing at the time she signed the contract, the contract will not be valid. ◆ The issue of contractual capacity is discussed further in the *Developing Paralegal Skills* feature below.

Legality

A contract to do something that is prohibited by federal or state statutory law is illegal and, as such, void from the outset and unenforceable. For example, a contract to buy a kidney from another person is void because it is illegal. No court would enforce the contract if a lawsuit were brought for breach of contract. Any contract to commit an illegal act is unenforceable.

In some instances, the subject matter of the contract is not illegal, but one of the parties is not legally authorized to perform the contract. Consider an illustration. All states require that members of certain occupations—including physicians, lawyers, real estate brokers, architects, electricians, contractors, and stockbrokers—obtain licenses allowing them to practice. When a person enters into a contract with an unlicensed individual, the contract may still be enforceable, depending on the nature of the licensing statute.

DEVELOPING
paralegal skills

ASSESSING CONTRACTUAL CAPACITY

You are a legal assistant for Jeff Barlow. He asks you to draft a contract for Margaret Klaus, a seventy-six-year-old widow. In the contract, Margaret will convey all of her shares in NAPO Corporation to her nephew Jeremy. In return, Jeremy promises to take care of Margaret for the rest of her life. Barlow is leaving on vacation and asks you to have the document completed and to arrange a meeting with the client and her nephew to sign the contract when he returns.

You learn that the stock being conveyed is worth a great deal of money. Also, you begin to have doubts about Margaret's mental status. You have talked to her at least once a day for the past week. During conversations, she often calls you by different names, repeats herself, and does not remember what you just told her. Although Jeremy has been living with Margaret for the past six months, whenever Margaret calls, she is alone and seems to be frightened. Now that you have finished the contract, you wonder if Margaret is capable of consenting to it and whether Jeremy has exerted too much influence over her. What should you do?

TIPS FOR DEALING WITH SUSPICIONS OF INCOMPETENCE

- Document everything. Keep a record of all the conversations you had with the client that led you to suspect a lack of contractual capacity, as well as any other facts that contributed to your suspicions (if you discovered the person was taking medication for mental illness, for example).

- Do not discuss your suspicions with *anyone* except your supervising attorney. Making such statements about a person can be damaging to his or her reputation, and you may even be held liable for defamation.

- Remember, it is the attorney's job to take into consideration the client's contractual capacity, not yours. You just want to make Barlow aware of the situation in an effort to protect the client's best interests.

Some states expressly provide that the lack of a license in certain occupations bars the enforcement of work-related contracts. If there is no express provision, one must look to the underlying purpose of the licensing requirements for a particular occupation. If the purpose is to protect the public from unauthorized practitioners, a contract involving an unlicensed individual normally is unenforceable. If the underlying purpose of the statute is to raise government revenues, however, a contract entered into with an unlicensed practitioner generally is enforceable—although the unlicensed person may be fined.

Additionally, some contracts are not enforced because the court deems them to be contrary to public policy. For example, contracts that restrain trade (anticompetitive contracts) and contracts that are so oppressive to innocent parties that they are deemed *unconscionable* (unconscionable contracts will be discussed shortly) are not enforceable owing to the negative impact they would have on society.

Defenses to Contract Enforceability

Two competent parties have entered into a contract for a legal purpose. The agreement is supported by consideration. The contract thus meets the four requirements for a valid contract. Nonetheless, the contract may be unenforceable if the parties have not genuinely assented (agreed) to its terms, if the contract is so oppressive to one of the parties that a court will refuse to enforce it, or if the contract is not in the proper form—such as in writing, if the law requires it to be in writing.

Concern about enforceability means that at least part of a contract is likely to come from an existing contract known to contain the necessary elements. As the *Technology and Today's Paralegal* feature on the following page notes, there are many sources for form contracts that paralegals can consult.

Genuineness of Assent

Lack of **genuineness of assent** can be used as a defense to the contract's enforceability. Genuineness of assent may be lacking because of a mistake, fraudulent misrepresentation, undue influence, or duress.

Mistake

It is important to distinguish between *mistakes of fact* and *mistakes of value or quality*. If a mistake concerns the future market value or quality of the object of the contract, the mistake is one of *value*, and either party normally can enforce the contract. Each party is considered to have assumed the risk that the value would change or prove to be different from what he or she thought. Without this rule, almost any party who did not receive what he or she considered a fair bargain could argue mistake.

MISTAKE OF FACT. Only a mistake of fact allows a contract to be avoided. Mistakes of fact occur in two forms—*unilateral* and *mutual (bilateral)*. A **unilateral mistake** occurs when one party to the contract makes a mistake as to some **material fact**—that is, a fact important to the subject matter of the contract. The general rule is that a unilateral mistake does not give the mistaken party any right to relief from the contract. There are some exceptions to this rule, however. ◆ **EXAMPLE 15.11—** A contractor's bid was extremely low because he made a mistake in addition when totaling the estimated costs. In this situation, any contract resulting from the bid normally can be rescinded. (**Rescission** is the act of canceling, or nullifying, a contract.) ◆

MUTUAL MISTAKE. When *both* of the parties are mistaken about the same material fact, a **mutual mistake** has occurred, and either party can cancel the contract. ◆ **EXAMPLE 15.12—** At Perez's art gallery, Diana buys a painting of a landscape. Both Diana and Perez believe that the painting is by the famous artist Vincent van Gogh. Later, Diana discovers that the painting is a clever fake. Because neither Perez nor Diana was aware of this material fact when they made their deal, Diana can rescind (cancel) the contract and recover the purchase price of the painting. ◆

genuineness of assent
Knowing and voluntary assent to the contract terms. If a contract is formed as a result of mistake, misrepresentation, undue influence, or duress, genuineness of assent is lacking, and the contract will be voidable.

unilateral mistake
Mistake as to a material fact on the part of only one party to a contract. In this situation, the contract is normally enforceable against the mistaken party, with some exceptions.

material fact
A fact that is important to the subject matter of the contract.

rescission
A remedy in which the contract is canceled and the parties are returned to the positions they occupied before the contract was made.

mutual mistake
Mistake as to the same material fact on the part of both parties to a contract. In this situation, either party can cancel the contract.

TECHNOLOGY AND
today's paralegal

CONTRACT FORMS

Before the printing press was invented, every contract form had to be handwritten. Since the advent of printing, many standard contract forms have been readily available at low cost. With the Internet, preprinted forms are unnecessary, as attorneys and paralegals can customize contract forms for each situation.

ONLINE CONTRACT FORMS

A large variety of contract forms, as well as other legal and business forms, is available online. For example, at **forms.lp.findlaw.com**, you can access over 25,000 legal forms for lawyers, businesses, and the public. The contracts range from basic sales contracts to sample software licensing agreements. Many are available free of charge. PublicLegal also offers a number of free contract forms and links to other online resources at **www.ilrg.com**.

Yet another source for contract forms is 'Lectric Law Library's collection of forms at **www.lectlaw.com**. (Select "Free Legal Forms," and then "Business & General Forms.") This site includes forms for the assignment of a contract, a contract for the sale of a business, and many others (some free, some for purchase).

There are many other sources for contract forms on the Internet. For example, **www.uslegalforms.com** has numerous forms available in many areas of practice. Not only can you search for contracts by topic (such as corporate or employment), but you can look up state-specific forms (separation agreements, for example). Most forms are available for a nominal fee. Similar types of services are available at many other sites, including **www.legal-forms-now.com**, **www.findforms.com**, and **www.allaboutforms.com**.

TECHNOLOGY TIP

Online contract forms are a great resource for paralegals. Thousands of forms can be easily accessed and customized for use in particular transactions. Keep in mind, though, that the contracts you find online will not necessarily be valid for your state or situation. You must always research the contract requirements in your state to verify that you are using the appropriate form.

Fraudulent Misrepresentation

When an innocent party is fraudulently induced to enter into a contract, the contract usually can be avoided because that party has not *voluntarily* consented to its terms. Normally, the innocent party can either rescind (cancel) the contract and be restored to his or her original position or enforce the contract and seek damages for any injuries resulting from the fraud.

You read about the tort of fraud in Chapter 14. In the context of contract law, fraudulent misrepresentation occurs when one party to a contract misrepresents a material fact to the other party, with the intention of deceiving the other party, and the other party justifiably relies on the misrepresentation. To collect damages, a party must also have been injured. A party may still be able to avoid the contract in some states without proving that he or she was injured by the fraud, however.

Note that the misrepresentation may be based on conduct as well as oral or written statements. ◆ **EXAMPLE 15.13—** Gene is contracting to buy Rachelle's horse for racing. While showing Gene the horse, Rachelle skillfully keeps the horse's head turned away so that Gene does not see that the horse is blind in one eye. Rachelle's conduct constitutes fraud. ◆

Undue Influence

Undue influence arises from special kinds of relationships in which one party can greatly influence another party, thus overcoming that party's free will. As was illustrated in *Developing Paralegal Skills* on page 474, elderly people may be unduly influenced by their caretakers. In addition, clients may be unduly influenced by their attorneys, and children may be unduly influenced by their parents. The essential feature of undue influence is that the party being taken advantage of does not, in reality, exercise free will in entering into a contract. A contract entered into under excessive or undue influence lacks genuine assent and is therefore voidable.

Duress

Assent to the terms of a contract is not genuine if one of the parties is *forced* into the agreement. Forcing a party to do something, including entering into a contract, through fear created by threats is legally defined as *duress*. In addition, blackmail or extortion to induce consent to a contract constitutes duress. Duress is both a defense to the enforcement of a contract and a ground for the rescission of a contract.

Unconscionable Contracts or Clauses

Ordinarily, a court does not look at the fairness or equity of a contract. For example, a court normally will not inquire into the adequacy of consideration. Persons are assumed to be reasonably intelligent, and the court does not come to their aid just because they have made unwise or foolish bargains.

In certain circumstances, however, a bargain is so oppressive to one of the parties that the court will refuse to enforce the contract. Such a bargain is called an **unconscionable contract** (or **unconscionable clause**). Contracts entered into because of one party's vastly superior bargaining power may be deemed unconscionable. These situations usually involve an **adhesion contract**, which is a contract drafted by the dominant party and then presented to the other—the adhering party—on a "take-it-or-leave-it" basis.

> **unconscionable contract or unconscionable clause**
> A contract or clause that is so oppressive to one of the parties that the court will refuse to enforce the contract.

> **adhesion contract**
> A contract drafted by the dominant party and then presented to the other—the adhering party—on a "take-it-or-leave-it" basis.

The Statute of Frauds

An otherwise valid contract may be unenforceable if it is not in the proper form. To ensure that there is reliable proof of the agreement, certain types of contracts are required to be in writing. If a contract is required by law to be in writing and there is no written evidence of the contract, it may not be enforceable.

Every state has a statute (or more than one statute) that specifies what types of contracts must be in writing (or be evidenced by a written document). This statute is commonly referred to as the **Statute of Frauds**. Although the state statutes vary slightly, the following types of contracts are normally required to be in writing:

> **Statute of Frauds**
> A state statute that requires certain types of contracts to be in writing to be enforceable.

- Contracts involving interests in land or anything attached to land, such as buildings, plants, minerals, or timber.

- Contracts that cannot by their terms be performed within one year from the day after the date of formation.

- Collateral, or secondary, contracts, such as promises to answer for the debt or duty of another.

- Promises made in consideration of marriage, such as prenuptial agreements (which will be discussed in Chapter 17).

- Contracts for the sale of goods priced at $500 or more. (This is a rule under the Uniform Commercial Code, not the common law.)

Note that the test for determining whether an oral contract is enforceable under the "one-year rule" stated in the second item is not whether an agreement is *likely* to be performed within one year but whether performance is *possible* within one year. Also, the one-year period begins to run the day *after* the contract is formed. Exhibit 15.1 on the next page illustrates the one-year rule.

> **Uniform Commercial Code**
> Statutes adopted by all states, in part or in whole, that contain uniform laws governing business transactions as defined in the code.

Sales Contracts and Warranties

The principles we have been discussing come from the common law of contracts. Recall from Chapter 5 that legislatures can pass laws that replace common law principles. That is what happened in the case of the **Uniform Commercial Code (UCC)**. **Sales contracts**—or, more specifically, contracts for the sale of goods—are governed by state statutes based on Article 2 of the UCC. The UCC is one of the

> **sales contract**
> A contract for the sale of goods, as opposed to a contract for the sale of services, real property, or intangible property. Sales contracts are governed by Article 2 of the Uniform Commercial Code.

EXHIBIT 15.1
The One-Year Rule

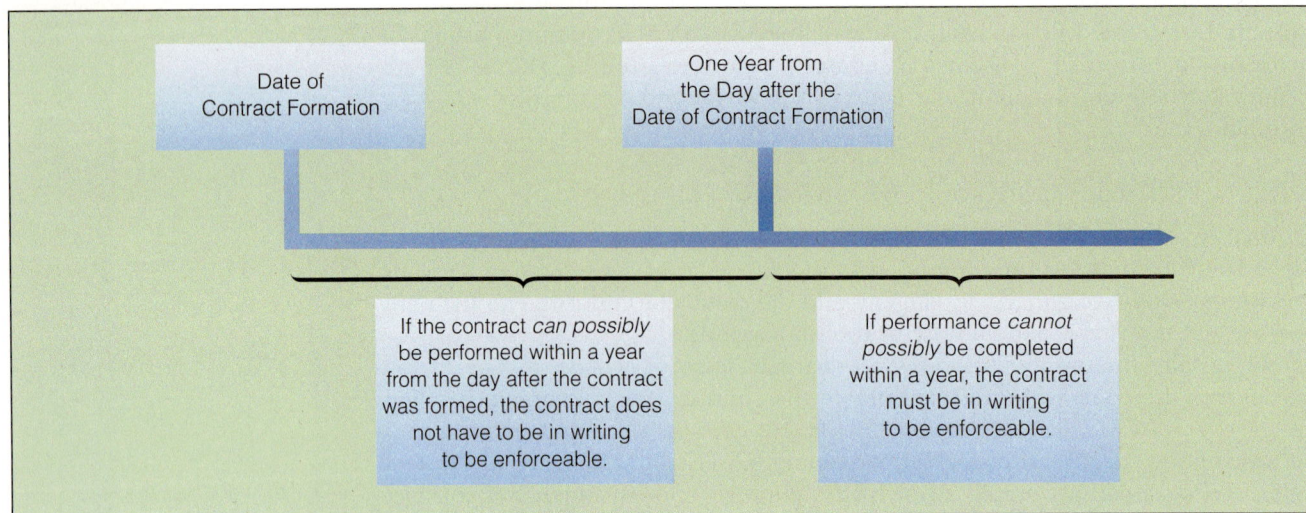

Date of
Contract Formation

One Year from
the Day after the
Date of Contract Formation

If the contract *can possibly* be performed within a year from the day after the contract was formed, the contract does not have to be in writing to be enforceable.

If performance *cannot possibly* be completed within a year, the contract must be in writing to be enforceable.

© Cengage Learning 2014

many—and one of the most significant—uniform laws created by the American Law Institute and the National Conference of Commissioners on Uniform State Laws. The UCC was first issued in 1952 and has since been revised to reflect the changing customs and needs of business and society. The UCC has been adopted, in whole or in part, by all of the states. State statutory codes are not necessarily called the Uniform Commercial Code, however. In Ohio, for example, UCC provisions are incorporated into the Ohio Commercial Code.

Researching matters involving the sale of goods usually requires using specialized legal resources because UCC provisions are generally the same (uniform) across states. Decisions from other states are more persuasive authority than in other areas of law. Commentary by the Uniform Law Commission on the UCC provisions is also important.

The Scope of UCC Article 2

In regard to Article 2 of the UCC, two things should be kept in mind. First, Article 2 deals with the sale of *goods*, not real property (real estate), services, or intangible property. Second, the rules may vary quite a bit, depending on whether the buyer or seller is a merchant. You should always note the subject matter of a dispute and the people (merchants or consumers) involved when you are dealing with cases involving contractual disputes. If the subject is goods, then the UCC will likely govern. If it is real estate or services, then the common law principles discussed earlier will apply.

What constitutes a "good" is not always clear. Courts have disagreed over whether software downloaded from the Internet is a "good" since there is no physical object being sold.

As under the common law, the parties to sales contracts are free to fashion the terms of their contracts as they wish. The UCC normally comes into play only when a dispute arises over ambiguous or missing terms. Note also that the UCC does not replace the common law of contracts. A contract for the sale of goods is also subject to the common law requirements of agreement, consideration, contractual capacity, and legality. Similarly, the common law defenses against contract formation or enforceability also apply to sales contracts. If the UCC has not modified a common law principle, then the common law governs. In other words, the general rule is that when the UCC addresses a particular matter, the UCC governs. When the UCC is silent, then the common law of contracts applies.

ON THE web

You can access the Uniform Commercial Code (UCC), including Article 2, at the Web site of the Legal Information Institute. Go to **www.law.cornell.edu**, select "U.C.C."

Warranties under the UCC

The UCC provides that a **warranty** of title arises in any sale of goods—that is, a seller automatically warrants (promises) to a buyer that the seller has good title to (legitimate ownership rights in) the goods being sold and can transfer that good title to the buyer. If the goods turn out to be stolen, for example, and the buyer has to return the goods to the real owner, the seller will be liable to the buyer for the value of the goods.

Express Warranty

The UCC also contains provisions on express and implied warranties as to the quality or nature of the goods being sold. An *express warranty* is an oral or written promise made by a seller concerning the nature of the goods being sold. ◆ **EXAMPLE 15.14—** The statement, "This is a new Black & Decker lawn mower" is an express warranty, or promise, that the lawn mower is indeed a Black & Decker lawn mower and that it is new. If you purchase the lawn mower and learn that it is used, the seller has breached an express warranty. ◆

Implied Warranties

Under the UCC, implied warranties arise in all sales transactions. Every merchant makes an *implied warranty of merchantability* when goods are sold. The goods must be merchantable—that is, they must be "reasonably fit for the ordinary purposes for which such goods are used." Some examples of unmerchantable goods are a light bulb that explodes when switched on, hamburger meat that contains fragments of glass, and a new boat that leaks. Goods sold by merchants must also be fit for the particular purpose for which they are sold. For this *implied warranty of fitness for a particular purpose* to arise, the buyer must rely on the seller's skill or judgment in selecting suitable goods.

◆ **EXAMPLE 15.15—** Suppose Kathleen indicated to the sellers of a horse, who were knowledgeable horse dealers, that she planned to use the horse for breeding. In this case, the horse was to be used for a particular, nonordinary purpose. When Kathleen later discovered the horse was incapable of reproducing, she could rely on the implied warranty of fitness to recover the purchase price. ◆

Disclaimers

The UCC permits express and implied warranties to be disclaimed, provided that the buyer is made aware of the disclaimers at the time the sales contract is formed. To disclaim an implied warranty of fitness for a particular purpose, the disclaimer must be in writing and be conspicuous (printed in larger or contrasting type or in a different color, for example). A merchantability disclaimer must mention the word *merchantability*, but it need not be in writing. If it is made in writing, the writing must be conspicuous.

Generally speaking, unless circumstances indicate otherwise, the implied warranties are disclaimed by the expression "as is," "with all faults," or similar language that is commonly understood by both parties as meaning that there are no implied warranties. An example of the application of these issues in the practice of contract law is presented in the *Developing Paralegal Skills* on the next page.

Contract Performance and Remedies

A party's contractual duties, under a common law contract or a contract formed under the UCC, can be terminated in several ways. The most common way to terminate contractual duties, however, is by the **performance** of those duties. Failure to perform contractual duties as promised results in a **breach of contract**. When one party breaches a contract, the other party (the nonbreaching party) can seek remedies.

---

warranty
An express or implied promise by a seller that specific goods to be sold meet certain criteria, or standards of performance, on which the buyer may rely.

social MEDIA TODAY

Practice writing in your firm's style before posting anything online that could be linked to the firm. Volunteer to write for firm newsletters or internal blogs as a way to test whether your style is appropriate.

performance
In contract law, the fulfillment of duties arising under a contract; the normal way of discharging contractual obligations.

breach of contract
The failure, without legal excuse, of a contractual party to perform the obligations assumed in a contract.

DEVELOPING
paralegal skills

CONTRACT REVIEW

Sam Thompson works as a paralegal for a corporation. One of his jobs is to review contracts between the corporation and outside vendors. He is reviewing a contract for the corporation's purchase of fifty new tablet devices from an outside vendor.

The contract, which is a preprinted form contract, was submitted by the vendor and consists of thirty paragraphs of "fine print." The blanks in the form, for such terms as price and quantity, have been filled in by the vendor. As Sam reads the contract, he comes across a warranty disclaimer provision. Sam realizes that this contract provision means that there will be no warranty of merchantability or fitness for a particular purpose for the new tablet devices. He makes a note to tell his supervising attorney about this provision. The attorney will want to inform management of this limitation on warranties.

TIPS FOR REVIEWING A CONTRACT

- Find out which contract provisions are acceptable to the client.
- Obtain the original copy of the contract.
- Read each provision carefully.
- Be certain you understand the meaning of each provision. If you are uncertain, find out what a provision means. Do not rely on the formulaic language in standard contract forms.
- Prepare a memo explaining the client's rights and liabilities under the contract.
- In the memo, mention any contract terms and provisions that the client might find objectionable.

Contract Performance

Conditions expressly stated in a contract must be fully satisfied for complete performance to take place. A party who in good faith performs substantially all of the terms of a contract, however, can usually enforce the contract against the other party under the doctrine of *substantial performance*. Generally, performance that provides a party with the important and essential benefits of a contract, in spite of any omission or deviation from the terms, is substantial performance. Because substantial performance is not perfect, the other party is entitled to damages to compensate for the failure to comply with the contract.

Impossibility of Performance

After a contract has been made, performance may become impossible in an objective sense ("it can't be done," rather than "I can't do it"). For example, the subject matter of the contract may be destroyed, one of the parties to a personal contract may die prior to performance, or performance may become illegal because of a change in the law. In these situations, the law excuses parties from their contractual performance duties under what is known as the doctrine of *impossibility of performance*.

Commercial Impracticability

Under the doctrine of *commercial impracticability*, courts may excuse parties from their performance obligations when the performance becomes much more difficult or expensive than contemplated at the time the contract was formed. For someone to invoke this doctrine successfully, however, the anticipated performance must become *extremely* difficult or costly. ◆ **EXAMPLE 15.16—** Delbert's Trucking agreed to carry a load of freight each day for a year from Molly's Factory to a train station four miles away. Delbert's and Molly's agreed that the price would be $40 per day. Two months later, the road Delbert's used was torn out by highway crews to enable reconstruction work expected to take six months. As a result, Delbert's must travel thirty miles to get to the train station. Molly's cannot expect Delbert's to fulfill the contract at the original price. Unexpected cost conditions have greatly changed, making fulfillment of the contract impracticable. ◆

Contract Remedies

A *remedy* is the relief provided for an innocent party when the other party has breached the contract. It is the means employed to enforce a right or to redress an injury. The most common remedies available to a nonbreaching party include damages, rescission, restitution, reformation, and specific performance.

Damages

A breach of contract entitles the nonbreaching party to sue for money damages (see Chapter 4). Damages are designed to compensate a party for the loss of the bargain. Generally, innocent parties are to be placed in the position they would have occupied had the contract been fully performed.

COMPENSATORY DAMAGES.   Damages compensating the nonbreaching party for the loss of the bargain are known as *compensatory damages*. These damages compensate the injured party only for damages actually sustained and proved to have arisen directly from the loss of the bargain caused by the breach of contract. They simply replace what was lost because of the breach.

The amount of compensatory damages is the difference between the value of the breaching party's promised performance and the value of his or her actual performance. This amount is reduced by any loss that the injured party has avoided. In addition, the injured party may be able to recover *incidental damages*—expenses resulting directly from the breach of contract, such as those incurred to obtain performance from another source. ◆ **EXAMPLE 15.17—** You are hired to perform certain services during August for $3,000, but the employer breaches the contract and you find another job that pays only $500. You can recover $2,500 as compensatory damages. In addition, as incidental damages, you can recover any expenses you incurred in finding the other job. ◆

Damages in contracts cases must be reasonably certain, not based on mere speculation. This often comes up in cases where the plaintiff is alleging that the defendant's breach of the contract caused lost profits for the plaintiff. Lost future profits may be established based on past profits, which raises difficulties for new businesses that have no track record. The requirement of reasonable certainty also generally bars mental distress damages in contracts cases.

IN THE office

LISTEN UP

Hearing is not the same as listening. Many people are not good listeners. We often hear what we want to hear as we filter information through our own experiences and interests. When clients talk, focus carefully on what they say, as they may reveal information you had not anticipated. Observing their body language is also important. Showing empathy and interest encourages clients to share more information, which may prove useful in handling legal issues. Taking an active interest in what others say, whether clients or co-workers, can increase your productivity and earn you recognition as a person who helps solve problems.

CONSEQUENTIAL DAMAGES.   *Consequential damages,* or *special damages,* are a type of compensatory damages. Consequential damages are caused by special circumstances beyond the contract itself. They flow from the consequences, or results, of a breach. For consequential damages to be awarded, the breaching party must have known (or have had reason to know) that special circumstances would cause the nonbreaching party to suffer an additional loss.   ◆ **EXAMPLE 15.18—**   Glenda contracts with Eric to ship an item that she needs to repair her printing press. The contract clearly states that Glenda must receive the item by Monday or she will not be able to print her paper and will lose $1,000. If Eric is late in shipping the item, Glenda normally can recover the consequential damages caused by the delay (that is, the $1,000 in losses). ◆

LIQUIDATED DAMAGES.   When writing a contract, the parties may specify an amount to be paid in the event of a future breach of the contract. This amount, called *liquidated damages,* must be reasonably related to the damages that may be suffered if the contract is not fulfilled. Liquidated damages are a form of compensatory damages. They may not be designed to serve as a *penalty* to deter a party from breaching a contract.   ◆ **EXAMPLE 15.19—**   Shondra is planning to open a new store on June 1 in a shopping center. The owner of the center assures her the store space will be ready. But what if it is not? Shondra will be stuck with inventory she will have to put in storage, employees who cannot work, and so forth. The parties may agree that if the store space is not ready when promised, the shopping center will pay Shondra $500 a day in liquidated damages to compensate her for her expenses. That would be reasonable, but if the contract had stated the damages were to be $50,000 a day, it would be a penalty that could not be enforced. ◆

PUNITIVE DAMAGES.   *Punitive damages* are not available in an action for breach of contract. Punitive damages are intended to punish guilty parties, and contract law is not concerned with establishing or punishing guilt. Its intention is to compensate a party for the loss of a bargain, no more and no less. In some situations, if a tort such as fraud or negligence is involved, punitive damages may be appropriate. In such situations, a tort claim may be added.

Rescission, Restitution, and Reformation

As already discussed, *rescission* is essentially an action to undo, or terminate, a contract—to return the contracting parties to the positions they occupied prior to the transaction. When fraud, a mistake, duress, undue influence, misrepresentation, or lack of contractual capacity is present, rescission is available. The failure of one party to perform entitles the other party to rescind the contract.

Generally, to rescind a contract, the parties must make **restitution** to each other by returning goods, property, or funds previously conveyed. If physical property or goods can be returned, they must be. If the property or goods have been consumed, the restitution must be made in an equivalent dollar amount.

When the parties have imperfectly expressed their agreement in writing, the equitable remedy of **reformation** may also be available. In cases involving breach of contract, this remedy occurs when the court revises a contract to reflect the true intention of the parties—if a mutual mistake occurred, for example.

Specific Performance

The equitable remedy of **specific performance** calls for the performance of the act promised in the contract. Normally, specific performance is not granted unless the party's legal remedy (money damages) is inadequate. For this reason, contracts for the sale of goods rarely qualify for specific performance—substantially identical goods can be bought or sold in the market. If the contract involves unique goods, however, such as a painting or a rare book, a court will grant specific performance.

Generally, courts refuse to grant specific performance of contracts for personal services—contracts that require one party to work personally for another party. This is because public policy strongly discourages involuntary servitude, and ordering one party to perform personal services against his or her will amounts to a type of servitude. Moreover, the courts do not want to monitor personal-service contracts.

---

restitution
An equitable remedy under which a person is restored to his or her original position prior to loss or injury, or placed in the position that he or she would have been in had the breach not occurred.

reformation
An equitable remedy granted by a court to correct, or "reform," a written contract so that it reflects the true intentions of the parties.

specific performance
An equitable remedy requiring exactly the performance that was specified in a contract; usually granted only when money damages would be an inadequate remedy and the subject matter of the contract is unique (for example, real property).

◆ **EXAMPLE 15.20—**   If you contract with a brain surgeon to perform brain surgery on you and the surgeon refuses to perform, the court will not compel (and you certainly would not want) the surgeon to perform under these circumstances. The court cannot assure meaningful performance in such a situation. ◆

Remedies for Breach of Sales Contracts

Remedies for breach of a contract for the sale of goods are designed to put the aggrieved party in as good a position as if the other party had fully performed. The seller's remedies for breach include the right to stop or withhold delivery of the goods and the right to recover damages or the purchase price of the goods from the buyer.

The buyer's remedies include:

1. the right to reject *nonconforming goods* (goods that do not conform to those specifically agreed on in the contract) or improperly delivered goods,

2. the right to *cover* (buy goods elsewhere and recover from the seller the extra cost of obtaining the substitute goods),

3. the right to recover damages, and

4. in certain circumstances, the right to obtain specific performance of the sales contract.

Electronic Contracting and Electronic Signatures

Today, many contracts are formed over the Internet. In general, the courts apply the traditional principles of contract law in cyberspace. Most disputes concerning contracts formed online tend to center on the specific terms of the contract and whether the parties voluntarily agreed to those terms. Paralegals working for firms advising clients engaged in online sales play an important role in helping to review the client's Web site to ensure it conforms to the rules discussed in this section.

Online Offers and Acceptances

Generally, the terms of an online offer should be just as comprehensive as the terms in an offer made in a written (paper) document. All possible contingencies should be anticipated and provided for in the offer. Because jurisdictional issues often arise with online transactions, dispute-settlement provisions, such as arbitration clauses, are frequently used in electronic contracts. The offer should be displayed on the screen in such a way as to be easily readable and clear. An online offer should also include some mechanism, such as providing an "I agree" or "I accept" box, by which the customer can accept the offer.

Click-On Agreements

As described earlier, a click-on agreement (also sometimes called a *click-on license, click-through agreement,* or *click-wrap agreement*) arises when a buyer, completing a transaction on a computer, indicates assent to be bound by the terms of an offer by clicking on a button that says "I agree" or "I accept." The terms may be contained on a Web site through which the buyer is obtaining goods or services, or they may appear on a computer screen when software is loaded. The courts have normally enforced click-on agreements.

◆ **EXAMPLE 15.21—** Aaron is downloading a new software program from the Internet. A message pops up on the screen with a small window through which Aaron can read the terms of the *licensing agreement.* (Note that a contract involving software usually grants a *license* by which a party is given the right to use the software but does not own the software.) Even if Aaron clicks on the "I agree" box below the window without reading the terms, he will nonetheless be bound by the terms of that agreement. ◆

social
MEDIA TODAY

Social media expert Scott Klososky says that increasingly the ability to grasp social tech tools and apply them quickly will make a big difference in how those around you view your performance. He thinks social tech literacy will be as much a requirement for jobs in the future as Internet literacy is today.

Shrink-Wrap Agreements

shrink-wrap agreement

An agreement whose terms are expressed in a document located inside the box in which the goods (usually software) are packaged.

A **shrink-wrap agreement** is an agreement whose terms are expressed inside the box in which the goods are packaged. (The term *shrink-wrap* refers to the plastic that covers the box.) Usually, the party who opens the box is told that she or he agrees to the terms by keeping whatever is in the box. ◆ **EXAMPLE 15.22—** Abdul orders a new computer program to be sent via FedEx. When he receives the program, he finds that the box also contains an agreement setting forth the terms of the sale, including what remedies are available. The document also states that Abdul's use of the program for longer than thirty days will be construed as an acceptance of the terms. ◆

In most cases, a shrink-wrap agreement is an agreement between the manufacturer of the hardware or software and the ultimate buyer-user of the product (not between a retailer and a buyer). Thus, the terms typically concern warranties, remedies, and other issues associated with the use of the product.

Generally, the courts have enforced the terms of shrink-wrap agreements with one exception: If a court finds that the buyer learned of the shrink-wrap terms *after* the parties entered into a contract, the court may conclude that those terms were proposals for additional terms and were not part of the contract unless the buyer expressly agreed to them.

◆ **EXAMPLE 15.23—** When Abdul, in Example 15.22, entered into the contract to purchase the program, he was not informed that any dispute regarding his purchase had to be arbitrated. He installed the program when it arrived, and it ruined his computer. He then discovered that the shrink-wrap agreement included an arbitration clause. In that situation, a court may conclude that the arbitration clause—which Abdul did not know about or consent to—was a proposal rather than part of the agreement. ◆

E-Signatures

In some instances, a contract cannot be enforced unless it is signed by the party against whom enforcement is sought. A significant issue in the context of Internet transactions has to do with how electronic signatures, or **e-signatures**, can be created and verified on e-contracts.

e-signature

An electronic sound, symbol, or process attached to or logically associated with a record and executed or adopted by a person with the intent to sign the record, according to the Uniform Electronic Transactions Act.

In the days when many people could not write, documents were often signed with an "X." Then handwritten signatures become common, followed by typed signatures, printed signatures, and, most recently, digital signatures, which are transmitted electronically. Throughout the evolution of signature technology, the question of what constitutes a valid signature has arisen again and again, and with good reason—without some consensus on what constitutes a valid signature, little business or legal work could be accomplished.

Today, several technologies allow electronic documents to be signed. Because paralegals are frequently responsible for obtaining the necessary signatures on legal documents, some knowledge of digital signatures and alternative technologies is useful.

State Laws Governing E-Signatures

Most states have laws governing e-signatures. In an attempt to create uniformity among these laws, the National Conference of Commissioners on Uniform State Laws and the American Law Institute issued the Uniform Electronic Transactions Act (UETA) in 1999. To date, the UETA has been adopted, at least in part, by forty-seven states. Among other things, the UETA states that a signature or a contract may not be denied legal effect or enforceability solely because it is in electronic form.

Under the UETA, an *e-signature* is broadly defined as "an electronic sound, symbol, or process attached to or logically associated with a record and executed or adopted by a person with the intent to sign the record." In other words, the signature does not have to be created by any specific technology and can be simply a person's name typed at the end of an e-mail message. The parties do have to agree to conduct their business electronically for the UETA provisions to apply, however. Also, the UETA states that it does not apply to (or change) the provisions of the Uniform Commercial Code (discussed earlier in this chapter) and does not apply to wills and trusts (see Chapter 17).

Federal Law on E-Signatures and E-Documents

In 2000, Congress enacted the Electronic Signatures in Global and National Commerce Act (E-SIGN Act) to provide that no contract, record, or signature may be "denied legal effect" solely because it is in an electronic form. In other words, under this law, an electronic signature is as valid as a signature on paper, and an electronic document can be as enforceable as a paper one. For an electronic signature to be enforceable, the contracting parties must have agreed to use electronic signatures. For an electronic document to be valid, it must be in a form that can be retained and accurately reproduced.

The E-SIGN Act does not apply to all types of documents. Contracts and documents that are exempt include court papers, divorce decrees, evictions, foreclosures, health-insurance terminations, prenuptial agreements, and wills. Also, only certain agreements governed by the Uniform Commercial Code fall under this law.

The E-SIGN Act has significantly expanded the possibilities for contracting online. From a remote location, a person can now open an account with a financial institution, obtain a mortgage or other loan, buy insurance, retain an attorney, and purchase real estate over the Internet. Payments and transfers of funds can be done entirely online. By using e-contracts, a person can thus avoid the time and costs associated with producing, delivering, signing, and returning paper documents.

Intellectual Property Law

The contract law just discussed had its origins hundreds of years ago. Much of it is based on concepts developed in England. Now we move on to an area of law that, although it has existed for some time, has become a major concern in recent years. It has to do with the wealth created by people's minds. Most people think of wealth in terms of houses, land, cars, stocks, and bonds. Wealth, however, also includes **intellectual property**, which consists of the products that result from intellectual, creative processes. As the *Practice Focus* feature on the following page notes, complex strategic issues involving intellectual property (IP) are becoming more important in law practice.

Although it is an abstract term for an abstract concept, intellectual property is nonetheless wholly familiar to virtually everyone. *Trademarks, service marks, copyrights, trade secrets,* and *patents* are all forms of intellectual property. The book you are reading is copyrighted. If you drink a Coke™, you consume a product with a trademarked name, made by a formula that is a trade secret, advertised using copyrighted material, and manufactured with equipment that has been patented. The apps you use, the movies you see, and the music you listen to are all forms of intellectual property.

The need to protect creative works was voiced by the framers of the U.S. Constitution more than two hundred years ago: Article I, Section 8, of the Constitution authorized Congress "[t]o promote the Progress of Science and useful Arts, by securing for limited Times to Authors and Inventors the exclusive Right to their respective Writings and Discoveries." Laws protecting patents, trademarks, and copyrights are designed to protect and reward inventive and artistic creativity. Exhibit 15.2 on page 487 summarizes the forms of intellectual property, how they are acquired, and what remedies are available for *infringement,* or unauthorized use.

intellectual property
Property resulting from intellectual, creative processes.

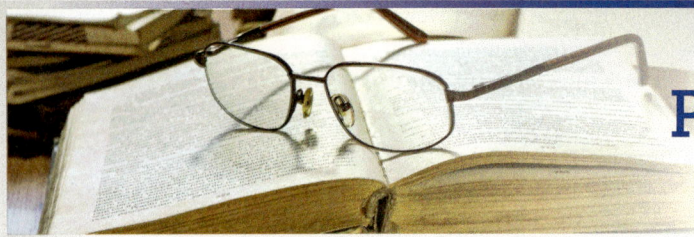

PRACTICE focus

NEW STRATEGIES IN INTELLECTUAL PROPERTY

A growing area of practice in intellectual property (IP) law involves licensing agreements between owners of patents, copyrights, and trademarks. Not only do IP owners often license rights to other businesses, but strategies to reduce taxes often lead firms to put their collection of IP rights in a subsidiary in the Netherlands, as the band U2 did with their song royalties. Similarly, Google used what is called the "double Irish" strategy. It licensed the European rights to its search and advertising business to Google Ireland Holdings, based in Bermuda, where taxes are low. It operates the business through Google Ireland Limited, which passes the revenue to the Bermuda-based company.

A key part of any licensing or IP-based tax strategy is proper valuation of the intellectual property rights involved. Paralegals are often involved in documenting the value of the IP rights. For patents, you might be asked to research the following:

- Is the patent in force in the relevant jurisdiction and have all fees been paid?
- Are there related patents listed in the foreign or domestic patent applications? If so, who owns them?
- What is the scope of the patent claim? Were there any amendments that narrow or broaden the scope made during the application process?
- Is there any past or pending litigation involving the patent?
- Are there any "blocking" patents, i.e., patents on which this patent infringes?
- Is the patent protected in relevant foreign jurisdictions?

By researching these types of questions and documenting the answers, a paralegal can assist in establishing a fair valuation for IP rights that will enable firms to negotiate the sale of rights or to claim appropriate tax benefits.

ON THE web

A good source for information on patents is the U.S. Patent and Trademark Office at **www.uspto.gov**. Another source is **www.patents.com**, a free patent search site.

patent
A government grant that gives an inventor the exclusive right or privilege to make, use, or sell an invention for a limited time period.

Growing Value of Intellectual Property

The study of intellectual property law is important because intellectual property has taken on increasing significance, not only in the United States but globally as well. In today's information age, it should come as no surprise that the value of the world's intellectual property exceeds the value of physical property, such as machines and houses. Ownership rights in intangible intellectual property are more important to the prosperity of U.S. companies than are their tangible assets. Because of the importance of obtaining and protecting intellectual property rights, attorneys and paralegals with specialized knowledge in this area are in great demand in law firms and in corporations. (See this chapter's *Featured Contributor* article on pages 488 and 489 for information on how to protect intellectual property.)

Patents

A **patent** is a grant from the government that gives an inventor the exclusive right to make, use, and sell an invention for a period of twenty years from the date of filing the application for a patent. Patents for designs, as opposed to inventions, are given for a fourteen-year period. To secure a patent, the applicant must demonstrate to the satisfaction of the U.S. Patent and Trademark Office that the invention, discovery, process, or design is genuine, novel, useful, and not obvious in light of current technology. A patent holder gives notice to all that an article or design is patented by placing on it the word *Patent* or *Pat.* and the patent number. As of 2013, under the America Invents Act, patent law in the U.S. will be as it is in other countries. The law gives patent protection to the first to file for a patent on a product or process, even if another person may have been the first to invent.

EXHIBIT 15.2
Forms of Intellectual Property

	Definition	How Acquired	Duration	Remedy for Infringement
Patent	A grant from the government that gives an inventor exclusive rights to an invention.	By filing a patent application with the U.S. Patent and Trademark Office and receiving its approval.	For inventions, 20 years from the date of application; for design patents, 14 years from the date of application.	Money damages, including royalties and lost profits, *plus* attorneys' fees. Damages may be tripled for intentional infringements.
Copyright	The right of an author or a creator of a literary or artistic work or other production (such as a computer program) to have the exclusive use of that work for a given period of time.	Automatic (once the work or creation is put in tangible form). Only the *expression* of an idea (and not the idea itself) can be protected by copyright.	For authors: the life of the author plus 70 years. For publishers: 95 years after the date of publication or 120 years after creation.	Actual damages plus profits received by the party who infringed or statutory damages under the Copyright Act, *plus* costs and attorneys' fees in either situation.
Trademark	A distinctive word, name, symbol, or device that an entity uses to distinguish its goods or services from those of others. The owner has the exclusive right to use that mark.	1. At common law, created by use of the mark. 2. Registration with the U.S. Patent and Trademark Office; mark must already be in use or be placed in use within the following six months.	Unlimited, as long as the mark is in use. To continue notice by registration, holder must renew between the fifth and sixth years and, thereafter, every ten years.	1. Injunction prohibiting future use of mark. 2. Actual damages plus profits received by the party who infringed. 3. Destruction of articles that infringed. 4. *Plus* costs and attorneys' fees.
Trade Secret	A business secret that makes a company or product unique and that would be of value to a competitor. Trade secrets include customer lists, plans, and research and development.	Through the development of the information and processes that constitute the business secret.	Unlimited, so long as not revealed to others (once a trade secret is revealed to others, it is no longer secret).	Money damages for misappropriation (the Uniform Trade Secrets Act also permits punitive damages if willful), *plus* costs and attorneys' fees.

If a firm makes, uses, or sells another's patented design, product, or process without the patent owner's permission, it commits the tort of patent infringement. Patent infringement may exist even though the patent owner has not put the patented product in commerce. Patent infringement may also occur even though not all features or parts of an invention are copied. (With respect to a patented process, however, all steps or their equivalent must be copied for infringement to exist.)

Copyrights

Literary or artistic productions (including computer software) are protected under copyright law. A **copyright** gives the creator of a work the right to the exclusive use of that work for a given period of time. Copyrights are governed by the Copyright Act of 1976, as amended. Works created after January 1, 1978, are automatically given statutory copyright protection for the life of the author plus 70 years. For copyrights owned by publishing houses, the copyright expires 95 years from the

copyright

The exclusive right of an author (or other creator) to publish, print, or sell an intellectual production for a statutory period of time.

Featured Contributor

STRATEGIES FOR PROTECTING INTELLECTUAL PROPERTY: THE INTELLECTUAL PROPERTY AUDIT

Deborah E. Bouchoux

BIOGRAPHICAL NOTE

Deborah E. Bouchoux is an attorney licensed to practice in the District of Columbia. She has been involved in paralegal education for more than twenty years. Bouchoux teaches in the Paralegal Studies Program at Georgetown University in Washington, D.C., and serves as a member of the advisory board for the program.

Ms. Bouchoux is a frequent lecturer for the National Capital Area Paralegal Association and is the author of *Intellectual Property: The Law of Trademarks, Copyrights, Patents, and Trade Secrets,* as well as *Protecting Your Company's Intellectual Property: A Practical Guide to Trademarks, Copyrights, Patents, and Trade Secrets.*

© Cengage Learning 2014

Because clients are often unaware of the value of their intangible assets or intellectual property, many law firms conduct intellectual property audits for their clients. The audit will identify the intellectual property owned by the client, and the legal team and the client will then develop a strategy to protect that property.

Audits are also conducted when a company sells its assets or merges with another entity. The buyer will want to know what type of intellectual property assets the company possesses so that it will know what assets it is acquiring, and to ensure that it will not be inheriting infringement lawsuits. This type of audit is often referred to as a *due-diligence review.*

THE NEED FOR INTELLECTUAL PROPERTY AUDITS

Clients may not understand the value of their intellectual property portfolios and the need to protect their rights. They may be using unique marketing materials that should be copyrighted, slogans that should be trademarked, and confidential information that should be protected as trade secrets. Without protection, valuable rights may be lost.

For example, the disclosure of confidential information will lead to a loss of trade secret rights and result in declining profits. Moreover, once companies realize what intellectual property they own, they can use that intellectual property to create revenue. Trademarks, copyrights, patents, and trade secrets can all be licensed to others for fees to generate a continuing revenue stream for the company, or perhaps pledged as collateral when obtaining financing from lenders.

STRATEGIES FOR CONDUCTING AN INTELLECTUAL PROPERTY AUDIT

There are several steps in conducting a successful intellectual property audit. These steps are explored in the following subsections.

Designating the Team.   The law firm should designate an attorney and paralegal to serve as representatives of the firm, and the company should select an individual who will serve as the company's team leader. Together, these individuals will be primarily responsible for conducting the audit and can answer any questions that may arise in the course of the audit. The team should have a preliminary meeting to discuss the scope and nature of the audit. For example, the client will need to determine whether only U.S. materials will be reviewed or whether consideration will be given to seeking protection in foreign countries for certain trademarks and patents. The involvement of legal counsel ensures that any matters discussed are subject to the attorney-client privilege and remain confidential.

date of publication or 120 years from the date of creation, whichever is first. For works by more than one author, the copyright expires 70 years after the death of the last surviving author.

Copyrights can be registered with the U.S. Copyright Office in Washington, D.C. (but registration is not required). A copyright owner also no longer needs to place a © or *Copyright* on the work to have the work protected against infringement. Chances are that if somebody created it, somebody owns it.

Preparing the Audit Questionnaire.   The legal team should prepare a worksheet or questionnaire for the client that is designed to elicit information from the client about its intellectual property assets. Paralegals play a significant role in drafting the audit questionnaire. The audit questionnaire will typically ask the following:

- Does the client use any specific names, logos, or slogans in advertising its products and services?

- Are any written materials used in marketing (such as brochures, newspaper or Web-based advertisements, and materials used for presentations)?

- Has the client developed any products, software, or processes?

- Does the client use any software or products owned by another entity?

- Does the client use any confidential methods or processes in developing and marketing its products and services, including financial forecasts, marketing plans, and customer lists?

- Has the company ever been sued for or accused of infringing another party's intellectual property rights?

- How does the company control access to its valuable and proprietary materials?

- Do employment, confidentiality, nondisclosure, and noncompete contracts exist to protect proprietary materials?

The questionnaire should be tailored to the needs of the client. For example, companies engaged in telecommunications services or software development will need detailed sections designed to obtain information on software products and proprietary information. In contrast, companies engaged in consulting will likely have no "products" that need protection but will have a wealth of written materials that should be protected as trade secrets or registered as copyrights.

Conducting the Audit.   On receiving the questionnaire, the client should begin gathering the materials that are responsive to the questionnaire. The legal team will then review the materials that the client has assembled to determine which materials can be protected under intellectual property law. If the client has a Web site, it should be carefully reviewed to ensure not only that the site is protected under copyright law but also that it does not infringe on the rights of another party. Paralegals often coordinate the time and manner of the audit by scheduling the audit date, arranging for a conference room, and ensuring that a photocopy machine is available to copy documents that are responsive to the questionnaire. Generally, the audit is conducted at the client's office because this is where the pertinent materials and documents are located.

Writing the Audit Report.   After conducting the audit, the legal team prepares a written report for the client summarizing the results of the audit. The report identifies all of the intellectual property owned by the client and makes recommendations for its continued protection and maintenance. For example, the audit may disclose that the client uses a distinctive slogan in its advertising materials. The legal team will then recommend that the slogan be registered as a trademark.

POSTAUDIT ACTIVITY

After the audit is complete, the legal team, and particularly the paralegal, will begin preparing applications to register trademarks, copyrights, and patents and will develop written policies to protect the client's trade secrets. Contracts will need to be drafted for the client to use when it hires independent contractors to develop certain products, such as software. Such contracts will clarify that the company will own all rights to any work products produced by those independent contractors. License agreements may need to be drafted so that the company can license its intellectual property to others to use. An Internet use policy may be needed so that all employees are aware of the confidential nature of the company's electronic communications.

The company will be advised to review materials used by its competitors to ensure that its competitors do not infringe on the company's valuable intellectual property rights—by using a trademark that is confusingly similar to one owned by the company, for example. Finally, the paralegal will implement a docketing system to ensure that the client's intellectual property rights are maintained. For example, the paralegal should calendar the dates for maintenance and renewal of company trademarks. The paralegal should also schedule the date of the next intellectual property audit.

> *"Paralegals play a significant role in drafting the audit questionnaire."*

What Can Be Copyrighted?

Note that it is not possible to copyright an *idea*. Others may freely use the underlying ideas embodied in a work. What is copyrightable is the way in which an idea is *expressed*. Whenever an idea and an expression are inseparable, the expression cannot be copyrighted. Generally, anything that is not an original expression of an idea does not qualify for copyright protection. Facts widely known to the public are not

ON THE web

For information on copyrights, go to the U.S. Copyright Office at **www.copyright.gov**.

copyrightable. Page numbers normally are not copyrightable because they follow a sequence known to everyone. Mathematical calculations are not copyrightable. The key requirement to obtain copyright protection is originality.

Copyright Infringement

Whenever the form or expression of an idea is copied, an infringement of copyright occurs. The reproduction does not have to be exactly the same as the original, nor does it have to reproduce the original in its entirety.

Penalties or remedies can be imposed on those who infringe copyrights. These range from actual damages (damages based on the actual harm caused to the copyright holder by the infringement) or statutory damages (damages provided for under the Copyright Act, not to exceed $150,000) to criminal proceedings for willful violations (which may result in fines and/or imprisonment).

An exception to liability for copyright infringement is made under the "fair use" doctrine. Under the Copyright Act, a person or organization can in certain situations reproduce copyrighted material without paying royalties (fees paid to the copyright holder for the privilege of reproducing the copyrighted material). Generally, the courts determine whether a particular use is fair on a case-by-case basis.

Trademarks and Related Property

trademark

A distinctive mark, motto, device, or emblem that a manufacturer stamps, prints, or otherwise affixes to the goods it produces so that they can be identified on the market and their origins made known. Once a trademark is established (under the common law or through registration), the owner is entitled to its exclusive use.

A **trademark** is a distinctive mark, motto, device, or emblem that a manufacturer stamps, prints, or otherwise affixes to the goods it produces so that those goods can be distinguished from the goods of other manufacturers and merchants. Examples of trademarks are brand-name labels on jeans, luggage, and other products. Generally, to be protected under trademark law, a mark must be distinctive. A distinctive mark might consist of an uncommon word (such as *Xerox* or *Google*) or words used in an uncommon or fanciful way (such as *English Leather* for an aftershave lotion instead of for leather processed in England).

At common law, the person who used a symbol or mark to identify a business or product was protected in the use of that trademark. Today, trademarks are usually registered with the federal government. Federal registration provides stronger protections for trademark owners. A mark can be registered with the Trademark Office (1) if it is already in commerce or (2) if the applicant intends to put the mark into commerce within six months.

Trade Names

trade name

A term that is used to indicate part or all of a business's name and that is directly related to the business's reputation and goodwill. Trade names are protected under the common law (and under trademark law, if the business's name is the same as its trademark).

Trademarks apply to *products*. The term **trade name** is used to indicate part or all of a business's name, such as McDonald's. Unless the trade name is also used as a trademark (as with Xerox and Coca-Cola, for example), the name is not protected under federal trademark law. Trade names are protected under the common law, however. Holiday Inns, Inc., for example, could sue a motel owner who used that name or a portion of it (such as "Holiday Motels") without permission. As with trademarks, words must be unusual or fanciful if they are to be protected as trade names. The word *Safeway,* for example, was considered by a court to be sufficiently fanciful to obtain protection as a trade name for a chain of food stores.

Trademark Infringement

Registration of a trademark with the U.S. Patent and Trademark Office gives notice on a nationwide basis that the trademark belongs exclusively to the registrant. The registrant is also allowed to use the symbol ® to indicate that the mark has been registered. Whenever that trademark is copied to a substantial degree or used in its entirety by another party (intentionally or unintentionally), the trademark has been infringed and the owner can sue.

A person need not have registered a trademark in order to sue for trademark infringement, but registration does furnish proof of the date the owner began using the trademark. Only those trademarks that are deemed sufficiently distinctive from all competing trademarks will be protected.

Trademark Dilution

Historically, federal trademark law prohibited the unauthorized use of the same mark on competing or "related" goods or services only when such use would be likely to confuse consumers. The federal Trademark Dilution Act extends that protection.

Trademark *dilution* occurs when a trademark is used, without authorization, in a way that diminishes the distinctive quality of the mark. Unlike trademark infringement, a dilution cause of action does not require proof that consumers are likely to be confused by a connection between the unauthorized use and the mark. For this reason, the products (or services) involved do not have to be similar. In addition, a famous mark may be diluted not only by the use of an *identical* mark but also by the use of a *similar* mark.

Trade Secrets

Some business processes and information that are not (or cannot be) patented, copyrighted, or trademarked are nevertheless protected against appropriation by a competitor as trade secrets. **Trade secrets** consist of customer lists, plans, research and development, pricing information, marketing techniques, production techniques, and generally anything that makes an individual company unique and that would have value to a competitor. Trade secrets are often protected by confidentiality agreements.

What Is Protected?

Unlike copyright and trademark protection, protection of trade secrets extends both to ideas and to their expression. (For this reason, and because a trade secret involves no registration or filing requirements, trade secret protection may be well suited for software.) Of course, the secret formula, method, or other information must be disclosed to some persons, particularly to key employees. Businesses generally attempt to protect their trade secrets by having all employees who use the process or information agree in their contracts, or in confidentiality agreements, never to divulge it and by carefully limiting who has access to the secret in the company.

As the *Developing Paralegal Skills* feature on the following page discusses, there are multiple situations in which protection is needed.

Misappropriation of Trade Secrets

One who discloses or uses another's trade secret, without a privilege to do so, is liable to the other if (1) he or she discovered the secret by improper means or (2) the disclosure or use constitutes a breach of confidence. The theft of confidential business data through industrial espionage, such as when a business taps into a competitor's computer, is a theft of trade secrets and is actionable.

At one time, virtually all law with respect to trade secrets was common law. In an effort to reduce the unpredictability of the law in this area, the Uniform Trade Secrets Act (UTSA) was proposed. Today, it has been adopted in forty-three states. Some major commercial states, including New York, New Jersey, and Texas, have not adopted it though. Under the UTSA, a plaintiff can also recover punitive damages for willful misappropriation of business secrets.

A federal statute, the Economic Espionage Act, also addresses trade secret theft. While its focus is on the theft of trade secrets that are sold to foreign powers, it also applies to domestic theft. Violations of the statute can result in a prison term and significant fines.

trade secret
Information or processes that give a business an advantage over competitors who do not know the information or processes.

DEVELOPING
paralegal skills

DRAFTING CONFIDENTIALITY AGREEMENTS

The law protects trade secrets indefinitely, but a business may need to disclose secret information. For example, a company may need to hire a consultant to revamp a computer system or a marketing firm to implement a sales program. Such parties may need access to some company trade secrets. One way to protect against the unauthorized disclosure of such information is through confidentiality agreements.

WHAT IS A CONFIDENTIALITY AGREEMENT?

In a confidentiality agreement, one party promises not to divulge or use trade secret information. Such agreements are often included in licensing and employment contracts, but they can also be separate contracts. The key is to make sure that the agreement protects the trade secrets and applies to any related transactions between the parties.

For instance, assume that a business executes a confidentiality agreement with a marketing firm. It is important that the agreement refer to any other contracts that the business has with the marketing firm. Also, subsequent contracts with the marketing firm should refer back to the confidentiality agreement or include a new confidentiality provision.

THE SCOPE OF A CONFIDENTIALITY AGREEMENT

Confidentiality agreements must be reasonable. When drafting one, be clear about what information needs to be protected, and for how long. Also, make certain that the client defines what is meant by *confidential information* and that this is included in the agreement. Does the client want to protect just a customer list or all nonpublic financial and technical information? The agreement must specify clearly what secrets are to be protected and must be realistic about what is called a trade secret.

The duration of the agreement usually depends on the nature of the information. Important secret information should remain confidential longer than less important secrets. In a marketing campaign, the time for confidentiality may be six months, the length of the campaign.

The agreement should be tailored to the client's needs. If the party to whom the client is disclosing information will no longer need the information after a certain date—such as when the project is completed—include a provision requiring the return of confidential information after that date. This will reduce concerns that the client's confidential trade secrets might later fall into the hands of a stranger and show that the firm has taken specific steps to protect the information.

Key Terms and Concepts

Chapter Summary

Contracts and Intellectual Property Law

REQUIREMENTS TO FORM A VALID CONTRACT

A contract is any agreement (based on a promise or an exchange of promises) that can be enforced in court. To form a valid contract, four basic requirements must be met.

1. *Agreement*—An agreement includes an offer and an acceptance. One party must offer to enter into a legal agreement, and another party must accept the terms of the offer.

   a. An offer is a promise to do or to refrain from doing some specified thing in the future.

   b. The offeror must have the intent to be bound, the terms must be reasonably certain or definite, and the offer must be communicated to the offeree.

   c. Both a rejection of the offer and the making of a counteroffer terminate the original offer. The offer is also terminated if the party making the offer withdraws the offer before it has been accepted. Otherwise, the offer expires after a reasonable period of time has passed.

   d. An offer may automatically terminate by law if the subject matter is destroyed, one party dies or becomes incompetent, or the contract becomes illegal.

   e. The terms of the acceptance must be the same as ("mirror") the terms of the offer.

   f. Acceptance of an offer is timely if it is made before the offer is terminated. Acceptance takes effect at the time the acceptance is communicated via the mode expressly or impliedly authorized by the offeror. This is called the *mailbox rule*.

   g. If the contract does not specify the method of acceptance, an offer may be accepted by any means that is reasonable under the circumstances.

2. *Consideration*—Consideration is usually defined as "something of value"—such as money or the performance of an action—given in exchange for a promise.

   a. To be legally sufficient, consideration must involve a legal detriment to the promisee, a legal benefit to the promisor, or both.

   b. In general, a court will not question the adequacy of consideration (fairness of the bargain). Courts will inquire into the adequacy of consideration only when fraud, undue influence, duress, or incompetence is involved.

   c. Some contracts may be enforced (or partially enforced) under the doctrine of promissory estoppel even though consideration is lacking.

3. *Contractual capacity*—The parties to the contract must have the legal ability to enter into a contractual relationship. Courts generally presume contractual capacity unless one party is a minor, intoxicated, or mentally incompetent.

4. *Legality*—A contract to do something that is prohibited by federal or state statutory law is illegal and, as such, void from the outset and thus unenforceable.

   a. Contracts entered into by persons who do not have a license, when one is required by statute, may not be enforceable.

   b. Some contracts are not enforced because the court deems them to be contrary to public policy.

DEFENSES TO CONTRACT ENFORCEABILITY

A contract that meets all the above requirements may not be enforceable if (1) the parties have not genuinely assented (agreed) to its terms, (2) the contract is so oppressive to one of the parties that a court will refuse to enforce it, or (3) the contract is not in the proper form.

1. *Genuineness of consent*—A contract can be avoided if there was a lack of real consent. This may be on the basis of mistake if the mistake was one of material fact (not value) and only when both parties are mistaken (mutual mistake). Lack of consent could also be based on fraudulent misrepresentation in the making of the contract, or be a result of undue influence (when free will is overcome by another party) or duress (making a contract under fear or a threat).

2. *Unconscionable contracts or clauses*—When a contract (or clause in a contract) is so oppressive to one of the parties that a court will refuse to enforce it, the oppressed party will be excused from performance. These situations usually involve an adhesion contract, which is a contract drafted by the dominant party and presented on a "take-it-or-leave-it" basis.

3. *Statute of Frauds*—Every state has a Statute of Frauds, which is a statute that specifies what types of contracts must be in writing (or be evidenced by a written document). The following types of contracts are normally required to be in writing:

   a. Contracts involving interests in land.

   b. Contracts that cannot by their terms be performed within one year from the day after the date of formation.

   c. Collateral, or secondary, contracts, such as promises to answer for the debt or duty of another.

   d. Promises made in consideration of marriage.

   e. Contracts for the sale of goods priced at $500 or more.

SALES CONTRACTS AND WARRANTIES

States have statutes to replace common law contracts in certain areas of commerce.

1. *The scope of UCC Article 2*—The Uniform Commercial Code (UCC) governs contracts for the sale of goods (as opposed to real property or services). The UCC primarily comes into play when disputes arise over ambiguous or missing terms and when the buyer or seller is a merchant.

2. *Warranties under the UCC*—The UCC contains provisions on express and implied warranties that arise when goods are sold. For example, under the UCC, every merchant warrants that the goods are reasonably fit for the ordinary purpose for which such goods are used.

CONTRACT PERFORMANCE AND REMEDIES

The most common way to terminate contractual duties under a common law contract or UCC-based contract is by the performance of those duties. Failure to perform contractual duties as promised results in a breach of the contract.

1. *Contract performance*—Performance that provides a party with the important and essential benefits of a contract, in spite of deviations from the terms, is substantial performance. Because substantial performance is not in full compliance with the contract, the other party is entitled to damages to compensate for the failure to comply with the contract. However, if, after a contract has been made, performance becomes objectively impossible (the subject matter is destroyed, for example), then performance is excused because of impossibility or commercial impracticability.

2. *Contract remedies*—When there is a breach, remedies can include:

   a. Money damages are a legal remedy designed to compensate a party for the loss of the bargain.

      1. Compensatory damages compensate the injured party only for damages actually sustained. Incidental damages are for expenses caused directly by a breach of contract, such as the cost of obtaining performance from another source.

      2. Consequential damages flow from the party's breach and were foreseeable at the time the contract was formed.

      3. Liquidated damages are an amount specified in the contract in case of a failure to perform.

   b. The following equitable remedies are available only in limited circumstances:

      1. Rescission is an action to undo or cancel the contract. When a contract is rescinded, restitution must be made.

      2. Reformation is an action in which the court rewrites the contract to reflect the parties' true agreement.

      3. Specific performance, which requires a party to perform the contract, is available only when money damages are inadequate and the contract is not for personal services.

3. *Remedies for breach of sales contracts*—The UCC may provide additional remedies to buyers and sellers (such as the buyer's right to reject nonconforming goods).

ELECTRONIC CONTRACTING AND ELECTRONIC SIGNATURES

Many contracts are formed over the Internet. How the courts apply the traditional rules of contract law is an increasingly important issue. Generally, the terms of the offer should be just as comprehensive as in written documents. The method of acceptance should also be specified.

1. *Online offers and acceptances*—As with regular contracts, it is best to have clear terms to reduce grounds for later disputes. The courts enforce click-on agreements where the buyer accepts the offer by clicking "I agree" or something similar. Similarly, shrink-wrap agreements, when the terms are expressed inside or on the box in which the goods are packaged, are agreed to by keeping the goods. Courts enforce such agreements unless the buyer learned of the terms after entering the contract.

2. *E-signatures*—Digital signatures verify the identity of parties to a contract. A party's signature can be electronically encoded onto a key or card that is veri-fied by a third party or can be digitally captured and attached to the electronic document.

3. *State laws governing e-signatures*—The Uniform Electronic Transactions Act (UETA), which governs e-signatures, has been adopted, at least in part, by forty-seven states.

4. *Federal law on e-signatures and e-documents*—The Electronic Signatures in Global and National Commerce Act (E-SIGN Act) gave validity to e-signatures by providing that no contract, record, or signature may be "denied legal effect" solely because it is in electronic form.

INTELLECTUAL PROPERTY LAW

Intellectual property—the products that result from intellectual, creative processes—is becoming increasingly valuable. The following are the four basic types of intellectual property rights. If a party infringes on these rights, the owner of the property can file suit and possibly obtain damages.

1. *Patent*—A grant from the government that gives an inventor the exclusive right to make, use, and sell an invention.

2. *Copyright*—The right of an author or a creator of a literary or artistic work or other production (such as a computer program) to have the exclusive use of that work for a given period of time.

3. *Trademarks and related property*—A distinctive mark or motto that a manufacturer stamps, prints, or affixes to goods so that its products are distinguishable from those of others. Trademarks apply to products, whereas trade names apply to business names. Infringements and dilution of marks are bases for suit for unauthorized use of the property.

4. *Trade secret*—A business secret that makes a particular company or product unique and that would be of value to a competitor (such as customer lists, plans, and research and development).

QUESTIONS FOR REVIEW

1. What are the four basic requirements for forming a valid contract? Are there any circumstances in which the court will enforce the parties' agreement even though it lacks consideration? What defenses can be used against a claim of breach of contract?

2. What is the Uniform Commercial Code (UCC), and to what types of contracts does it apply? How does the UCC affect the common law of contracts? What warranties are presumed to exist under the UCC?

3. Describe the remedies that are available when a contract is breached. What is specific performance, and in what circumstances is it available?

4. What kinds of electronic contracts do the courts enforce? What constitutes an electronic signature, and what is the legal validity of such a signature? What are the state and federal laws that govern electronic signatures and contracts?

5. List the four major forms of intellectual property and describe what intellectual property is. Why is it an important topic in the law today?

ETHICAL QUESTIONS

1. Shayna is a paralegal at a bank. She reviews a package of loan documents for a complex commercial transaction that has been submitted by the lawyers for the borrower. She does not fully understand one provision in the documents that eliminates the need for a guarantor. A guarantor promises that the loan will be repaid in the event that the borrower fails to do so, an important protection for the bank. Shayna does not include this provision in her summary to her supervising attorney, and the loan goes through without

the guarantee. Later the borrower defaults on the loan and the bank is out several million dollars. What ethics rules have been violated? What might be the outcome for Shayna? For her supervising attorney?

2. Cole works as a paralegal for an oil company. The attorney he works for is responsible for negotiating franchise contracts with people who want to buy gas-station franchises. Most of those applying for franchises have lawyers who negotiate for them. Bob Little is applying for a franchise without a lawyer to represent him. It is apparent that Little does not have much education or experience. He has, however, recently inherited some money, and he wants to achieve his dream of owning a gas station.

He has been sent a copy of the standard-form franchise agreement. The standard-form contract is one sided against the franchisee (the person buying the franchise). Little calls and says that he is ready to buy his franchise from the oil company and asks Cole to set up a telephone conference for that purpose. Cole would like to tell Little that he really should have a lawyer represent his interests. Can he recommend to Little that he retain a lawyer? Should he give Little any tips about how to negotiate a franchise arrangement? What might happen if Cole does either of these things? What might happen if he does nothing?

PRACTICE QUESTIONS AND ASSIGNMENTS

1. Using the material on contract law in this chapter, identify which contract below is a bilateral contract and which is a unilateral contract:

   a. Juanita offers to sell Mier her laptop for $200. Mier agrees and tells her he will meet her in the cafeteria at noon the next day with cash.

   b. Jonah e-mails Michael and offers Michael $5,000 to paint his house green during the first week of June. Michael does not respond to Jonah's e-mail, but arrives at Jonah's house on June 1st and begins painting it green.

2. Bernie, the sole owner of a small business, has a large piece of used farm equipment for sale. He offers to sell the equipment to Hank for $10,000. Discuss what happens to the offer in the following situations:

   a. Bernie dies prior to Hank's acceptance; at the time he accepts, Hank is unaware of Bernie's death.

   b. The night before Hank accepts, a fire destroys the equipment.

3. Using the material on acceptances presented in this chapter, identify which situation below will result in a contract:

   a. Kelly offers to sell her used algebra textbook to Patrick for $50. Patrick responds, "Maybe—if I have enough money once I get my book refund later this week."

   b. Kirk offers Kristina $50 for her textbook. Kristina says, "Sure. I'll drop it off in the morning."

4. Using the material on contract law presented in this chapter, identify which defenses the defendants in the following hypothetical cases might use in an action for breach of contract:

   a. Mrs. Martinez, a Spanish-speaking immigrant, buys a washing machine and signs a financing agree-

ment that allows her to pay for it in monthly installments. The agreement contains a clause that allows the store to repossess the appliance if she misses a payment. Mrs. Martinez misses the next-to-the-last payment. The store notifies Mrs. Martinez that she has breached her contract and that it intends to repossess the washing machine. How might Mrs. Martinez defend against the store's action?

   b. Sally orally agrees to purchase a farm from her lifelong friend, Fred. She promises to pay Fred $120,000 for the farm. She trusts Fred, so she does not put the deal in writing. A few days later, Fred sells the same property to Nell for $140,000. Fred and Nell put their agreement in writing. When Sally learns of Fred's contract with Nell, she sues Fred for breach of contract. What is Fred's defense?

   c. Rob enters into a contract with Tom to sell Tom fifty sweaters in Christmas colors and featuring Christmas designs. The first shipment of sweaters is due on October 1, 2013. When the sweaters are not delivered, Tom calls Rob and learns that the factory where the sweaters were to be produced has burned down. Tom, who is upset because he needed the sweaters for his Christmas catalog sales, sues Rob for breach of contract. What is Rob's defense?

5. Joel goes to an expensive restaurant in New York for lunch. He orders the special, pasta with white truffles. The price is not given, and he does not ask the waiter how much it costs. When the bill arrives at the end of the meal, Joel is flabbergasted—he was charged $175 for his entrée. Does a dinner meet the definition of a sale of goods under the UCC? If so, does the UCC rule that where the buyer and seller have agreed to a contract but have not agreed on the price, the price must be a reasonable price for the goods, and not the price that the seller demands?

6. Based on the material on intellectual property law presented in the chapter, in which of the following situations would a court likely hold Maruta liable for copyright or trademark infringement?

   a. At the library, Maruta photocopies ten pages from a scholarly journal relating to a topic on which she is writing a term paper.

   b. Maruta makes leather handbags and sells them in her small leather shop. She advertises her hand-bags as "Vutton handbags," hoping that customers might mistakenly assume that they were made by Vuitton, the well-known maker of high-quality luggage and handbags.

   c. Maruta owns a video store. She purchases one copy of all the latest DVDs from various DVD manufacturers. Then, using blank discs, she makes copies to rent or sell to her customers.

QUESTIONS FOR CRITICAL ANALYSIS

1. Consideration, a requirement for a valid contract, is defined as *something of value*. What items, other than money, meet this definition? Explain how consideration distinguishes a contract from a gift.

2. Why are minors allowed to avoid contractual obligations by canceling or disaffirming contracts? Are there contracts that minors should be unable to avoid? Discuss what type of contracts it would be fair or unfair for minors to avoid.

3. Generally, courts hold that gambling contracts are illegal and thus void. Do you think that the advent of legalized forms of gambling, such as state-operated lotteries, is consistent with a continued public policy against the enforcement of gambling contracts? Why or why not?

4. Many of our day-to-day transactions, such as buying a can of cola from a vending machine or purchasing groceries with a debit card, involve contracts. Explain how these contracts meet the requirements of a valid contract. Do they meet the requirements of the Statute of Frauds? Would a court enforce these contracts?

5. Rosalia works as a paralegal in a firm specializing in appellate law practice. She prepares many legal briefs along with her supervising attorney, and sometimes her supervising attorney just reviews and then signs and files the briefs. Recently, it has come to the firm's attention that several fee-based online legal research databases have been reproducing the firm's legal briefs in their databases and selling access to them. Rosalia's supervising attorney has obtained copyright registration over many of their briefs and is considering suing for copyright infringement. Analyze whether Rosalia and her supervising attorney have a case, or whether the reproduction of the briefs represents fair use.

PROJECTS

1. Using the requirements for an offer that were stated in the chapter, draft a simple offer to purchase a used Kindle reader from a classmate. Make sure that the offer is definite and certain. Next, write an explanation (in one or two paragraphs) of how you would communicate the offer to the person, how long the offer would remain open, and what method of acceptance you would prefer.

2. Interview a paralegal who works in an intellectual property firm. Find out what his or her day-to-day work entails. Draft an outline covering the topics you discussed, and then give an oral presentation to the class.

GROUP PROJECT

In this project, each group will analyze advertisements to determine if they can be offers.

Students one and two will review the Pepsi Harrier Jet commercials (numbers one and two) on **YouTube.com** to determine the differences between the two ads. (These ads are discussed on pages 470 and 471.)

Student three should locate the U.S. Second Circuit Court of Appeals opinion in this case on Google Scholar and create a list of the reasons that the court gave for finding that the first ad was held not to be enforceable.

Student four will play the two commercials for the class, explaining how they differ and offering support for the court's opinion that no legal offer was made.

USING INTERNET RESOURCES

1. Go to the list of contract provisions found on the Ask the Lawyer Web site at **askthelawyer.info/what-are-some-key-contract-provisions**. How many different types of clauses are discussed? Record the types of clauses or print a list of the provisions.

2. Go to FindLaw's site on business contracts, at **contracts.corporate.findlaw.com**. There, you can access contracts listed by industry, by type, or by company name, or you can browse through the most recent contracts added to the site. Select a contract to view. Note the name of the contract and its general purpose. Does the contract use all of the clauses (reflecting typical contract provisions) that you noted in question 1? Does it use any? If so, which of the typical clauses are used?

CourseMate The available CourseMate for this text has an interactive eBook and interactive learning tools, including flash cards, quizzes, and more. To learn more about this resource and access free demo CourseMate resources, go to **www.cengagebrain.com**, and search for this book. To access CourseMate materials that you have purchased, go to **login.cengagebrain.com**.

Real Property and Insurance Law

Chapter Outline

Introduction

Real Property

Insurance Law

After completing this chapter, you will know:

- The difference between real property and personal property.

- How one acquires, holds, and transfers ownership rights in property and what procedures are involved in the sale of real estate.

- The terminology used in insurance contracts and the various classifications of insurance.

- What an insurable interest is and the difference between an insurance agent and an insurance broker.

- The provisions that are typically included in an insurance contract and the rights and duties of the parties under insurance contracts.

Introduction

As you study the major areas of substantive law, keep in mind that although the topics are covered separately, as if they existed in isolation from one another, there is in fact a great deal of overlap among them. For example, in tort and product liability cases, which you read about in Chapter 14, the defendant's insurance coverage—or lack of it—is often an important factor in how litigation proceeds. Property owners also depend on insurance to protect themselves from liability, because torts or crimes could occur on their property for which they will be held responsible.

The first part of this chapter investigates property law. About a quarter of all paralegals specialize in this area. After that, we look at insurance law, an area of specialization for about 20 percent of paralegals. While these are distinct areas of law, they are connected in practice. Most property owners insure their property against possible losses due to fires, accidents, or other perils. Further, mortgage companies and banks that make loans to finance property purchases require that insurance be carried.

Real Property

For centuries, the law has divided property into two classifications: real property and personal property. **Real property**, or *real estate*, is land and all things attached to the land, such as trees and buildings, as well as the minerals below the surface of the land plus the air above the land.

Personal property is all other property. Personal property can be either tangible or intangible. *Tangible* personal property, such as an iPhone or a car, has physical substance. *Intangible* personal property represents a set of rights and interests but has no real physical existence. Stocks, bonds, and intellectual property rights (discussed in Chapter 15) are examples of intangible personal property.

Ownership Rights in Property

Property ownership is often viewed as a "bundle of rights." One who owns the entire bundle—ownership rights to the greatest degree possible—is said to own the property in **fee simple absolute**. An owner in fee simple absolute (sometimes just called fee simple) is entitled to use, possess, or dispose of the real or personal property (by sale, gift, or other means) however he or she chooses during his or her lifetime. On the owner's death, the interests in the property descend to the owner's heirs.

Government Restrictions on Property

Of course, those who own real property even in fee simple absolute may be subject to certain restrictions on their right to use the property as they choose. For example, zoning laws may prohibit an owner of property in a given area from conducting certain activities (such as running a business) on the property.

Also, under its power of **eminent domain**, the government has a right to take private property for public use (for a highway, for example), as long as the government fairly compensates the owner for the value of the land taken.

Easements

Property owned in fee simple absolute may also be subject to an **easement**, which is the right of another to use the owner's land for a limited purpose. Easements are said to "run with the land." That is, they usually pass with title to real property as its ownership changes over time. There are many kinds of easements:

- An easement may allow utility companies to maintain gas pipelines and electricity cables that cross the property.

- A right-of-way easement may allow people to cross the property to get to other property.

---

real property
Immovable property consisting of land and the buildings and plant life thereon.

personal property
Any property that is not real property. Generally, any property that is movable or intangible is classified as personal property.

fee simple absolute
Ownership rights entitling the holder to use, possess, or dispose of the property however he or she chooses during his or her lifetime.

eminent domain
The power of a government to take land for public use from private citizens for just compensation.

easement
The right of a person to make limited use of another person's real property without taking anything from the property.

- A solar easement may be granted to a neighbor to guarantee that trees will not be allowed to grow so as to block sunlight from hitting solar panels on the neighbor's roof.

- A historic preservation easement may promise that the appearance of a house will not be changed.

Concurrent Ownership

Persons who share the bundle of ownership rights to either real or personal property are said to be concurrent owners. There are two principal types of concurrent ownership: tenancy in common and joint tenancy.

TENANCY IN COMMON.   A *tenancy in common* is a form of co-ownership in which two or more persons own undivided interests in certain property. The interest is undivided because each tenant has rights in the whole property. Although the ownership is in common, tenants may have equal or unequal shares. ◆ **EXAMPLE 16.1—** Rosa and Chao own a rare stamp collection together as tenants in common. This does not mean that Rosa owns certain stamps and Chao others. Rather, it means that each of them has rights in the *entire* collection. (If Rosa owned some of the stamps and Chao owned others, then the interest would be *divided*.) ◆ If a tenant in common dies, the tenant's ownership rights pass to his or her heirs.

JOINT TENANCY.   A *joint tenancy* is also a form of co-ownership in which two or more persons own undivided interests in property. The key feature of a joint tenancy is the "right of survivorship." When a joint tenant dies, that tenant's interest passes to the surviving joint tenant or tenants and not to the deceased tenant's heirs, as it would with a tenancy in common. ◆ **EXAMPLE 16.2—** Suppose that Rosa and Chao from the previous example held their stamp collection in a joint tenancy. If Rosa died before Chao, the entire collection would become the property of Chao. Rosa's heirs would receive no interest in the collection. ◆

If a joint tenant transfers his or her interest in the property, the transfer terminates the joint tenancy. The new co-owner (the one to whom the rights were transferred) and the other tenant or tenants become tenants in common.

OTHER TENANCIES.   Two other types of concurrent ownership are tenancy by the entirety and community property. A *tenancy by the entirety* is a form of co-ownership by husbands and wives that is similar to a joint tenancy, except that the spouses cannot separately transfer their interests in the property during their lifetimes. Not all states recognize tenancies by the entirety. In ten states, husbands and wives generally hold property as *community property*. In those states, community property is all property acquired during the marriage. Each spouse technically owns an undivided interest in the property. Usually each owns one-half, but courts may decide otherwise when there is a divorce.

Life Estates

A *life estate* is an interest in real property that is transferred to another for the life of that individual. A conveyance "to Allison for her life" creates a life estate. In a life estate, the life tenant cannot do anything to the property that would reduce its value for the owner of the future interest in it. The person with a life interest in property does not have to occupy the property. It may be used for rental income.

Future Interests

When someone who owns real property in fee simple conveys the property to another conditionally or for a limited time, the original owner still retains an interest in the land. This interest is called a *future interest* because it will only arise in the future. The holder of a future interest may transfer it to another during his or her lifetime. If the interest is not transferred, it will pass to the owner's heirs on his or her death. The law has complex rules governing future interests that vary from state to state.

---

tenancy in common
A form of co-ownership of property in which each party owns an undivided interest that passes to his or her heirs at death.

joint tenancy
The joint ownership of property by two or more co-owners in which each co-owner owns an undivided portion of the property. On the death of one of the joint tenants, his or her interest automatically passes to the surviving joint tenant or tenants.

social MEDIA TODAY

As someone who understands social media, you often have to explain it to others. This can be difficult. Keep explanations simple. Try to show people that social media are tools to be used to do tasks they are already familiar with. Facebook, Twitter, Tumblr, and a smartphone or tablet device all provide different ways of communicating.

The Transfer and Sale of Real Property

The ownership of property, or the right to use it, can be transferred in numerous ways. Property can be given to another as a gift or transferred to another by inheritance, leased to another, or sold. Most commonly, property is transferred by sale. The sale of tangible personal property (goods) is covered by the common law of contracts, as modified by Article 2 of the Uniform Commercial Code, which we discussed in Chapter 15. Rights in certain types of intangible property (such as checks and money orders) are covered by other articles of the UCC. The sale of real property is governed by the common law of contracts as well as state (and, to a limited extent, federal) statutory law.

Here we look at some of the basic steps and procedures involved in the sale of real estate. These steps and procedures are summarized in Exhibit 16.1 below.

Contract Formation—Offer and Acceptance

The common law contractual requirements discussed in Chapter 15 all apply to real estate contracts. Because the Statute of Frauds applies to contracts for the sale of real property, they must be in writing.

When a buyer wishes to purchase real estate, he submits an offer to the seller. The offer specifies all of the terms of the proposed contract—a description of the property, the price, and any other conditions that the buyer wishes to include. Often, a buyer conditions the offer on the buyer's ability to obtain financing. The offer might also specify which party will bear the cost of any repairs that need to be made. Typical provisions included in a real estate sales agreement are illustrated in Exhibit 16.2 on the following page. When signed by the buyer and the seller, the offer constitutes a contract for the sale of land that is binding on the parties.

EXHIBIT 16.1

Steps Involved in the Sale of Real Estate

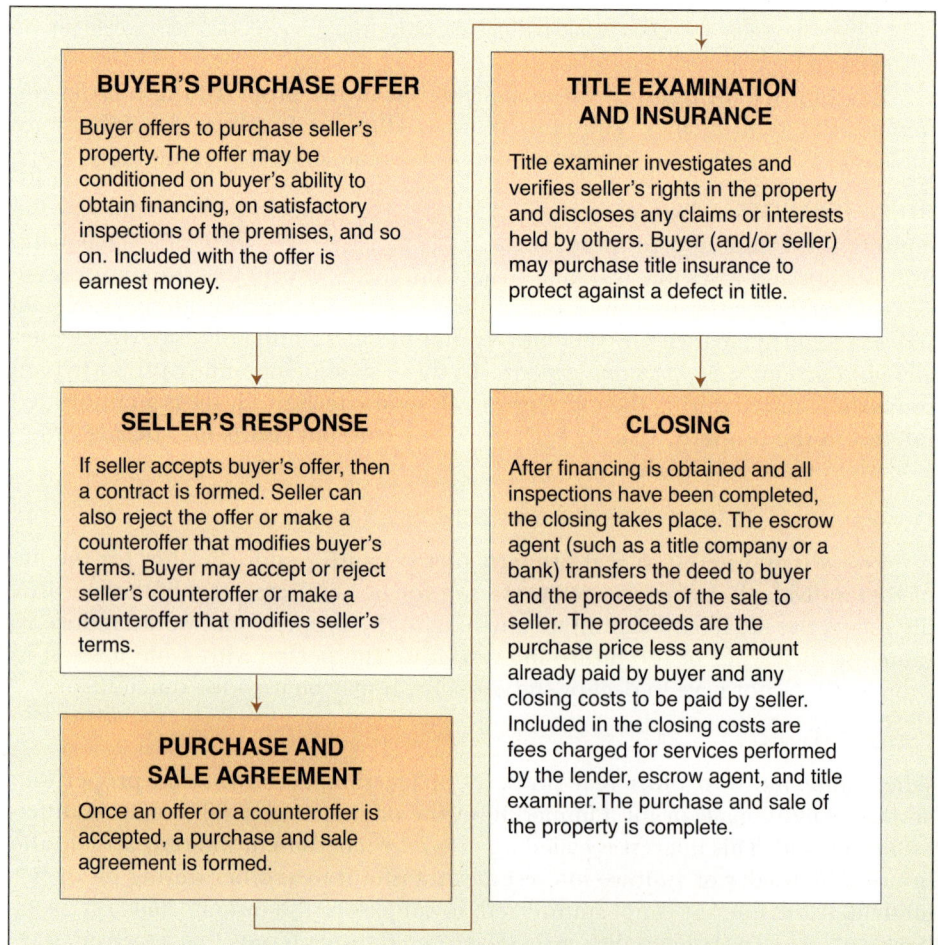

BUYER'S PURCHASE OFFER

Buyer offers to purchase seller's property. The offer may be conditioned on buyer's ability to obtain financing, on satisfactory inspections of the premises, and so on. Included with the offer is earnest money.

TITLE EXAMINATION AND INSURANCE

Title examiner investigates and verifies seller's rights in the property and discloses any claims or interests held by others. Buyer (and/or seller) may purchase title insurance to protect against a defect in title.

SELLER'S RESPONSE

If seller accepts buyer's offer, then a contract is formed. Seller can also reject the offer or make a counteroffer that modifies buyer's terms. Buyer may accept or reject seller's counteroffer or make a counteroffer that modifies seller's terms.

CLOSING

After financing is obtained and all inspections have been completed, the closing takes place. The escrow agent (such as a title company or a bank) transfers the deed to buyer and the proceeds of the sale to seller. The proceeds are the purchase price less any amount already paid by buyer and any closing costs to be paid by seller. Included in the closing costs are fees charged for services performed by the lender, escrow agent, and title examiner. The purchase and sale of the property is complete.

PURCHASE AND SALE AGREEMENT

Once an offer or a counteroffer is accepted, a purchase and sale agreement is formed.

EXHIBIT 16.2
Typical Provisions in Real
Estate Sales Agreements

- Names of parties and/or real estate agents.
- Date of agreement and how long seller has to accept agreement.
- Legal description of the property's location and size.
- Amount of the purchase offer.
- Amount of cash to be paid at the time of sale.
- Amount of earnest money deposit.
- Type of loan or financing the buyer plans to use.
- Whether the sale is contingent on the buyer's obtaining financing.
- Condition of the title and debt that buyer will assume.
- Warranties of title (restrictions, rights, or limitations).
- Condition of property and zoning or use rights.
- Prorations of taxes, insurance, or other obligations.
- Description of any fixtures, appliances, and furnishings that will be included in sale and any warranty as to the condition of such items.
- Inspection rights given to buyer (for example, water, well, mechanical, structural, electrical, termite), who will pay the costs of inspections, and whether the sale is contingent on inspector's approval.
- Statement of who will bear the cost for such items as transfer fees, abstracts of title, and closing costs.
- Conditions under which the offer may be canceled.

© Cengage Learning 2014

EARNEST MONEY.   The buyer normally puts up a sum of money, called *earnest money,* along with the offer to buy the property. By paying earnest money, the buyer indicates that he is making a serious offer. Normally, the offer provides that if the seller accepts the offer (and forms a contract with the buyer), the buyer will forfeit this money if he breaches the contract. Other damages for breach might also be specified in the agreement. If the deal goes through, the earnest money is usually applied to the purchase price of the real estate.

RESPONDING TO AN OFFER.   Once the offer is submitted to the seller, the seller has three options: accept the offer, reject it, or modify its terms—thus creating a counteroffer. The buyer, in turn, can then accept, reject, or modify the terms of the counteroffer—thus creating yet another counteroffer for the seller to consider. In real estate transactions, bargaining over price and other conditions of the sale frequently involves the exchange of one or more counteroffers.

  When one of the parties accepts an offer or counteroffer, a contract is formed by which both parties normally must abide. As the *Ethics Watch* on the next page discusses, paralegals must be sure real estate paperwork is accurate.

The Role of the Escrow Agent

The sale of real property normally involves three parties: the seller, the buyer, and the escrow agent. Frequently, both the buyer and the seller are assisted by real estate agents, attorneys, and paralegals. Some states require participation by an attorney. The *escrow agent*, which may be a title company, bank, or special escrow company, acts as a neutral party in the transaction and facilitates the sale by allowing the buyer and the seller to complete the transaction without having to exchange documents and funds directly with each other.

  To understand the vital role played by the escrow agent, consider the problems that might otherwise arise. Essentially, in the sale of property, the buyer gives the

GOING green

WHAT AM I BREATHING?
Although we think about outdoor
air quality, most of us spend 90 to
95 percent of our time indoors.
What is the air quality there? Many
people have allergies to the strong
chemicals used to clean carpets
and for other purposes. Check to
see what kind of cleaning supplies
are used in your office. There are
usually green alternatives that can
do the job but are not as potent
and are less likely to cause breathing problems for some employees.

ETHICS WATCH

ACCURATE PAPERWORK AND REAL ESTATE TRANSACTIONS

Arlie Song, a paralegal, was drafting a real estate offer for one of the firm's clients. Instead of entering $90,000 as the amount being offered for a piece of land, he accidentally entered $900,000. The document was sent to the seller, who recognized the obvious mistake and returned the paperwork unsigned. Before the paperwork could be redone, another buyer offered the seller $100,000, and that offer was accepted. The client then bought another piece of property for $105,000 and sued Song's supervising attorney for $15,000 in damages. The chance to buy the property for $90,000 had been missed due to the mistake. As with all legal documents, a paralegal must be sure that real estate transaction documents are accurate, because the law firm could be liable for errors.

The duty to use care in preparing work products arises from the NALA *Code of Ethics,* Canon 2: "A paralegal may perform any task which is properly delegated and supervised by an attorney, as long as the attorney is ultimately responsible to the client . . . and assumes professional responsibility for the work product."

seller funds, and the seller conveys (transfers) to the buyer a deed, representing ownership rights in the property (deeds will be discussed shortly). Neither the buyer nor the seller wishes to part with the funds or the deed until all conditions of the sale and purchase have been met.

The solution is the use of an escrow agent. The escrow agent holds the deed until the buyer pays the seller for the property at the *closing* (the final step in the sale of real estate). The escrow agent also holds any funds paid by the buyer, including the earnest money mentioned above, until the sale is completed. At the closing, the escrow agent receives funds from the buyer, the buyer is given the deed, and the seller is given the money. The triangular relationship among the buyer, the seller, and the escrow agent is depicted in Exhibit 16.3 on the facing page.

Financing

Because few buyers want to, or can, pay cash for real property, buyers generally need to secure financing. Commonly, a buyer of real property finances the purchase by obtaining a loan (called a **mortgage**) from a bank, a mortgage company, or some other party. When a buyer obtains a mortgage, the bank or mortgage company takes a security interest in the property—that is, the bank or mortgage company secures the right to claim ownership of the property if the buyer fails to make the scheduled payments.

Inspection of the Premises

In addition to obtaining financing, buyers may have the premises inspected to see if there are any major electrical or plumbing problems, structural defects, termite or insect infestations, or other concerns. Often, the contract of sale is conditioned on the outcome of these inspections. If problems surface during the inspections, the

mortgage
A written instrument giving a creditor an interest in the debtor's property as security for a debt.

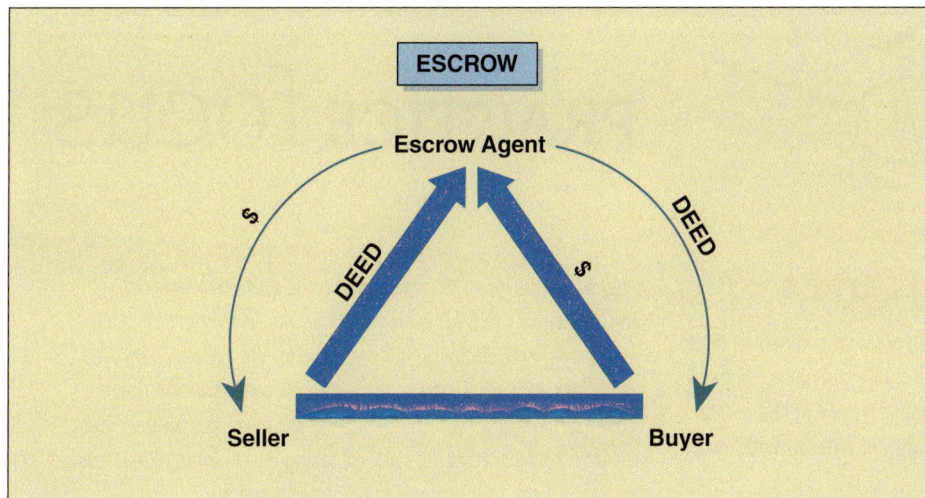

EXHIBIT 16.3

The Concept of Escrow

This exhibit illustrates the triangular relationship among the escrow agent, the seller, and the buyer in a transfer of real estate. The seller gives the escrow agent the deed, the buyer gives the escrow agent the funds, and at the time of the closing, the escrow agent gives the seller the funds and the buyer the deed.

buyer and seller may negotiate (or may have included in the contract) arrangements specifying which party will pay what portion of the costs of any necessary repairs.

As *the Practice Focus* feature on the following page discusses, inspection for environmental issues of property being considered for purchase can be an important issue. A search of the list of previous owners and users of property may give clues as to potential contamination issues.

Title Examination and Insurance

Whenever title to property is transferred from one party to another, the transfer is recorded by the county recording office. A *title examination* involves checking these records carefully to make sure that the seller is actually the owner of the property described in the purchase offer and to determine whether claims (such as for overdue taxes) on the property exist that were not disclosed by the seller. The title examination is an important task to be accomplished prior to the purchase of real estate. Most of this work is done online today, but visits to a county courthouse may be required in some instances.

The title examination may be undertaken by the buyer or the buyer's attorney (paralegals frequently assume this responsibility) or by the lending institution, a title insurance company, or another party.

Normally, the history of past ownership and transfers of the property is already summarized in a document called an abstract, which may be in the possession of the seller (or the holder of the seller's mortgage or other company or institution). After examining the abstract, the title examiner gives an opinion as to the validity of the title. Title examinations are not foolproof, though, and buyers of real property often buy title insurance to protect their interests in the event that some defect in the title was not discovered during the examination.

The Closing

One of the terms specified in the contract is when the closing will take place. The closing—also called the *settlement* or the closing of escrow—is coordinated by the escrow agent. At the closing, several events are likely to happen at once:

- the buyer signs the mortgage note (if the purchase was financed by a mortgage),

- the buyer obtains title insurance,

- the seller receives the proceeds of the sale (the purchase price less the amount previously paid by the buyer and less closing costs), and

- the buyer receives the deed to the property.

ON THE web

If you are interested in learning about the Real Estate Settlement Procedures Act and what it requires of lending institutions, go to **www.hud.gov,** and enter "RESPA" in the search box.

PRACTICE focus

COMMERCIAL COMPLEXITIES

Real estate transactions can be difficult, creating a variety of openings for paralegals. Mortgage companies, title companies, banks, title insurance companies, and businesses involved in real estate employ paralegals. Two particularly important areas are title issues and financing.

COMPLEX TITLES

Because of the wide range of uses of commercial properties, title examination may be more complex than in a residential real estate deal. Approval of local government zoning authorities may be needed, or an environmental regulator may need to sign off on the use. Careful investigation of previous property uses is necessary if there is any possibility of contamination from earlier occupants. Paralegals are often involved in tracing the history of a commercial or industrial site, including identifying all previous owners and tenants.

Armed with such a list, you may then need to consult industry publications and do online research to learn what sorts of

chemicals were used on a property in the past. Before modern environmental laws, for example, it was not uncommon for floor drains to simply discharge into the ground. If machinery was used in a room with such a drain, there may be contamination that is costly to remedy. As a result of such possibilities, the contract must include complicated contingencies, taking into account all approvals needed for the buyer to make use of the property.

COMPLEX FINANCING

Financing commercial real estate deals is also often more complex than residential transactions. Because commercial properties are frequently remodeled to suit a buyer's needs, it is also important to check for claims filed by previous workers. Commercial lenders may require waiver of homestead claims or demand limits on the property's use to prevent environmental hazards from destroying the value of the collateral. Paralegals are often involved in monitoring compliance of such conditions.

deed
A document by which title to property is transferred from one party to another.

DEEDS. A **deed** is the instrument of conveyance (transfer) of real property. As indicated on the sample deed in Exhibit 16.4 on the facing page, a deed gives the names of the seller *(grantor)* and buyer *(grantee),* describes the property being transferred, evidences the seller's intent to convey (for example, "I hereby bargain, sell, grant, or give") the property, and contains the seller's signature.

CLOSING COSTS. *Closing costs* comprise fees for services, including those performed by the lender, escrow agent, and title company. These costs can range from several hundred to several thousand dollars, depending on the amount of the mortgage loan and other conditions of the sale, and must be paid, in cash, at the closing. Usually, the buyer and seller can learn in advance what the closing costs will be by checking (or having their attorneys or real estate agents check) with the escrow agent handling the closing.

Also, under the federal Real Estate Settlement Procedures Act, lending institutions must notify—within a specified time period—each mortgage loan applicant of the precise costs that must be paid at the closing. Paralegals are often involved in this process, as illustrated in the *Developing Paralegal Skills* feature on page 508.

lease
In real property law, a contract by which the owner of real property (the landlord) grants to a person (the tenant) an exclusive right to use and possess the property, usually for a specified period of time, in return for rent or some other form of payment.

Leases

An owner of either personal or real property can lease, or rent, the property to another person or a business firm. A **lease** is a contractual agreement under which a property owner (the *lessor*) agrees to rent his or her property to another (the *lessee*) for a specified period of time. Leases of personal property (cars or equipment) are covered by the Uniform Commercial Code, which spells out the rights and duties of lessors and lessees.

EXHIBIT 16.4
A Sample Deed

Date: May 31, 2014

Grantor: RAYMOND A. GRANT AND WIFE, JOANN H. GRANT

Grantor's Mailing Address (including county):
                   4106 North Loop Drive
                   Austin, Travis County, Texas
Grantee: DAVID F. HOGAN AND WIFE, RUTH E. HOGAN, AS
                   JOINT TENANTS WITH RIGHT OF SURVIVORSHIP
Grantee's Mailing Address (including county):
                   5929 Fuller Drive
                   Austin, Travis County, Texas

Consideration:
For and in consideration of the sum of Ten and No/100 Dollars ($10.00) and other
valuable consideration to the undersigned paid by the grantees herein named, the receipt
of which is hereby acknowledged, and for which no lien is retained, either express or
implied.

Property (including any improvements):
Lot 23, Block "A", Northwest Hills, Green Acres Addition, Phase 4, Travis County, Texas,
according to the map or plat of record in volume 22, pages 331-336, of the Plat Records
of Travis County, Texas.

Reservations from and Exceptions to Conveyance and Warranty:

This conveyance with its warranty is expressly made subject to the following:
Easements and restrictions of record in volume 7863, page 53, volume 8430, page 35,
volume 8133, page 152, of the Real Property Records of Travis County, Texas; and to
any other restrictions and easements affecting said property which are of record in
Travis County, Texas.

   Grantor, for the consideration and subject to the reservations from and exceptions to conveyance and
warranty, grants, sells, and conveys to Grantee the property, together with all and singular the rights and
appurtenances thereto in any wise belonging, to have and hold it to Grantee, Grantee's heirs, executors,
administrators, successors, or assigns forever. Grantor binds Grantor and Grantor's heirs, executors,
administrators, and successors to warrant and forever defend all and singular the property to Grantee and
Grantee's heirs, executors, administrators, successors, and assigns against every person whomsoever
lawfully claiming or to claim the same or any part thereof, except as to the reservations from and exceptions
to conveyance and warranty.

When the context requires, singular nouns and pronouns include the plural.

                              BY: *Raymond A. Grant*
                                  Raymond A. Grant
                              BY: *JoAnn H. Grant*
                                  JoAnn H. Grant

STATE OF TEXAS
COUNTY OF TRAVIS
   This instrument was acknowledged before me on the   31st   day of   May 2014
by   Raymond A. and JoAnn H. Grant

                              Rosemary Potter
                              Notary Public, State of Texas
                              Notary's name (printed): ROSEMARY POTTER

Notary Seal

                              Notary's commission expires: 1/31/2015

© Cengage Learning 2014

Leases of real property are governed by the common law of contracts and by
state statutory law. Although under the common law an oral lease is valid, a party
who seeks to enforce an oral lease may have difficulty proving its existence. In most
states, statutes mandate that leases exceeding one year's duration must be in writing. When real property is leased, the lessor (landlord) retains ownership rights to
the property, but the lessee (tenant) obtains the right to the exclusive possession
of the property. Most leases, however, give the landlord the right to come onto the
property for certain purposes—to make repairs, for example.

   Paralegals frequently draft or review lease agreements for clients (or for corporate employers). You should be familiar with the types of terms that are typically

DEVELOPING
paralegal skills

REVIEWING THE CLOSING PACKAGE

Addie Casmir, a paralegal, is reviewing a closing package for her supervising attorney, a sole practitioner. Addie's job is to request the closing package from the lender and review it before the closing takes place. The closing package consists of the purchaser's requirements, closing statement, settlement statement, deed, bill of sale, mortgage documents, and title insurance policy. Addie needs to make sure that there are no mistakes in the closing documents.

CHECKLIST FOR
REVIEWING A CLOSING PACKAGE

- Order the closing package as far in advance as possible.
- Set aside uninterrupted time for reviewing the closing package.

- Review for accuracy the address and legal description of the property in the mortgage note and the deed.
- Using a calculator, review the purchaser's requirements sheet, the closing statement, the bill of sale, and the mortgage documents to make sure that there are no numerical errors.
- Review each document to make sure that the parties' names are listed and spelled correctly.
- Review the deed to ensure that the ownership rights are listed accurately and that the names are correct.
- Contact the client and remind him or her of the items that must be brought to the closing.

---

included in a lease agreement, or contract. Normally, a lease contract will specify the names of the lessor and lessee, the location of the premises being leased, the amount of rent to be paid by the lessee, the duration of the lease, and the respective rights and duties of the parties in regard to the use and maintenance of the leased premises. Exhibit 16.5 on the facing page illustrates the kinds of provisions that are commonly included in lease agreements.

Commercial Leases

Leases for commercial or business property are usually much more detailed than residential leases, so special expertise is needed to work with them. The terminology describing the building generally follows industry practices and terms used by the Building Owners and Managers Association International. In a residential lease, the house or apartment is usually identified by address. In a commercial lease, terms such as *gross leasable* or *net leasable square footage* are used.

Specific discussion of common areas and responsibilities for them is included. Such leases also often discuss inspection rights, what signage will be allowed, liability waivers, damage provisions, how alterations are to be handled, responsibility for repairs, and other issues usually peculiar to commercial property.

Property Law and the Paralegal

Paralegals frequently perform tasks that require an understanding of the law governing real property. In a small legal practice, work may involve assisting your supervising attorney in handling real estate transactions. If you work for a law firm (or a department within a law firm) that specializes in real estate transactions, you will have extensive contact with buyers and sellers of real property, as well as with real estate agents, title companies, banking institutions that finance real estate purchases, and the attorneys and paralegals who work on behalf of the other parties in real estate sales.

EXHIBIT 16.5
Typical Lease Terms

Term of lease: Indicates the duration of the lease, including the beginning and ending dates.

Rental: Indicates the amount of the rent payments and the intervals (monthly or yearly, for example) at which rent will be paid.

Maintenance and use of leased premises: Describes which areas will be repaired and maintained by the landlord and which by the tenant.

Utilities: Stipulates which utilities (electricity, water, and so forth) will be paid by the landlord and which by the tenant.

Alterations: Normally states that no structural alterations to the property will be made by the tenant without the landlord's consent.

Assignment: States whether the tenant's rights in the lease can be assigned (transferred) by the tenant to a third party.

Insurance: Indicates whether the landlord or the tenant will insure the premises against damage. (Normally, the landlord secures insurance coverage for the building, and the tenant obtains a "renters policy" for his or her own personal property—furniture and other possessions—that will be housed in the building.)

Taxes: Designates which party will be liable for taxes or special assessments on the property. (Normally, the landlord assumes this responsibility, but in some commercial leases, the tenant agrees to take on this obligation.)

Destruction: States what will happen in the event that the premises are totally destroyed by fire or other casualty.

Quiet enjoyment: A covenant (promise) by the landlord that the tenant shall possess and enjoy the premises without interference by any third party.

Termination: Usually specifies that the tenant's right to possession of the premises ends when the lease expires.

Renewal: Indicates that the tenant has an option to renew the lease if the landlord is notified of the intent to renew within a certain period of time (such as one month or three months) before the lease expires.

© Cengage Learning 2014

See this chapter's *Featured Contributor* article on the next two pages for a discussion of the role of a legal due-diligence team in purchases of real estate.

Here are just some of the types of tasks that you might perform as a real estate paralegal working for a law firm:

- Interview a client who wants to buy or sell property and identify potential issues regarding the property and financing.

- Assist the client with the preliminary negotiations (offers and counteroffers) leading up to the purchase contract.

- Draft the offers and counteroffers, as well as other documents necessary to the sale.

- Conduct a title examination by going online, or perhaps to the county courthouse, to examine records of previous property transfers.

- Obtain or create a title abstract.

- Contact the title company to arrange for the closing.

**social
MEDIA TODAY**

Seek guidance from your supervising attorney before responding to negative online comments about your organization. No firm wants a "flame war." Flame wars make you look immature or unprofessional.

Featured Contributor

PROTECTING THE REAL ESTATE PURCHASER: THE LEGAL DUE-DILIGENCE TEAM

Daniel F. Hinkel

BIOGRAPHICAL NOTE

Daniel F. Hinkel earned a J.D. degree from the University of Illinois School of Law and a B.S. from Eastern Illinois University. He is vice president and corporate counsel for ING Investment Management, LLC, in Atlanta, Georgia.

Mr. Hinkel has taught in paralegal programs for years. He is also the author of a number of books, including *Practical Real Estate Law* and *Essentials of Practical Real Estate Law,* both published by Delmar Cengage Learning.

Home ownership is highly desired by many families, and commercial real estate is a preferred asset for many investors. Whether the purchaser is acquiring a home for a residence or purchasing a shopping center as an investment, the transaction will be governed by the common law doctrine of *caveat emptor,* "let the buyer beware." This doctrine provides that a seller, absent an express warranty, is not liable to a buyer for any existing defects regarding the title to the land or any physical defects in the improvements located on the land. Even misrepresentations made by a seller concerning the property are generally not recoverable in an action for fraud if the purchaser could have discovered the truth from proper due diligence, such as a thorough inspection of the home or a title examination.

THE LEGAL DUE-DILIGENCE TEAM

A legal due-diligence team can save a real estate purchaser money and future headaches. Paralegals are important members of the legal due-diligence team. The extent of the team's work will depend on the nature of the property being purchased. A home may require only a title and survey review. An investment property may require a review of title, survey, government regulations, leases, and other contracts that affect the use of the property.

TITLE DUE DILIGENCE

One of the main responsibilities of the legal due-diligence team is to determine that when the sale has been completed, the purchaser will have good title of ownership to the real property. The legal due-diligence team should require that the public real property title records be examined and the examination carefully reviewed to determine the title's marketability.

Local government title registry offices are using electronic data technology for their deed and title records. A title search of the title indices can now be conducted from a computer, and recorded instruments can be viewed online. Many local governments also have Web pages where, for a reasonable fee, a person can access the real property records online. A title search is possible in some instances without a trip to the courthouse.

It is common in many communities for a title insurance company to examine the public records and provide the legal due-diligence team with a title report or commitment to issue title insurance and copies of all the recorded documents listed in the title report. The team's paralegal will review this report and, in consultation with the team's attorney, determine if the title matters affect the marketability and the purchaser's proposed use of the property. The legal due-diligence team will also

- Handle the escrow account.
- Attend the closing. (In some states, paralegals are allowed to represent clients at closings.)

Corporations also purchase and sell property, and some larger firms have real estate groups within their legal departments. If you work for a business that buys and sells a significant amount of property, your employer will be the "client" and you will perform similar tasks on the corporation's behalf.

arrange for a title insurance policy insuring the purchaser's ownership to be issued at the time of purchase.

SURVEY DUE DILIGENCE

The legal due-diligence team should require a survey of the property. Most surveys are "as built," meaning the survey locates all physical improvements on the land in relation to the boundary lines of the land. The surveyor will locate all fences, walls, driveways, pavements, building structures, and natural features, such as streams and ponds. The survey will also indicate if the property is in a flood hazard area, which may require flood insurance.

The team's paralegal may review the survey. A survey is usually reviewed in conjunction with the title commitment. This review will determine that all matters that would have a physical presence on the property, such as easements or building setback lines, are shown on the survey. The review will confirm that the description of the real property matches the description offered by the seller and that the description can be insured by the title insurance company. If there are differences between the description shown on the survey and in the title report, the legal due-diligence team will investigate the matter and determine why the differences exist and how they can be resolved.

In addition, the survey reviewer will note the location of improvements on the property and look for encroachments onto (or by) the property, or encroachments of buildings over easements. The reviewer will also determine if there is proper access to the property from a public street and if the necessary utilities, such as electricity, gas, and water, are available.

GOVERNMENT REGULATION DUE DILIGENCE

For an investment property, the legal due-diligence team will inquire into government regulations that affect the property. The team will obtain confirmation of the property's zoning status and determine if the pur-

chaser's use or intended use of the property will comply with the uses permitted by zoning regulations.

LEASE REVIEW

The legal due-diligence team may review leases in connection with an investment property. The leases provide income to the purchaser, and the price of the property may be based on assumptions regarding the rental income contained in the leases. The team's paralegal may review the leases and prepare an abstract, or summary, of the leases. The summary review will verify the terms of the lease, such as rental terms, the duration of the lease, and the various obligations and responsibilities of both the landlord and the tenant. A lease will also be reviewed to determine if the tenant has an option to purchase the property. If the lease contains an option to purchase, the team attorney will carefully discuss the option with the purchaser to verify that it is acceptable.

The legal due-diligence team may prepare and require each tenant to sign an estoppel certificate. An estoppel certificate signed by the tenant generally confirms the basic facts regarding the lease, such as rental terms and duration and payment of security deposits. Also, it will state that there is no default under the lease and that the tenant has no defenses, setoffs, recoupments, claims, or counterclaims of any nature against the landlord.

THE LEGAL DUE-DILIGENCE TEAM PROVIDES VALUE

A legal due-diligence team made up of attorneys and paralegals performs an important role in protecting a purchaser from the harsh effects of the *caveat emptor* rule. A legal team's thorough investigation and competent review and analysis of supporting documents provide good value for the real property purchaser-client.

> *"One of the main responsibilities of the legal due-diligence team is to determine that when the sale has been completed, the purchaser will have good title of ownership to the real property."*

Insurance Law

As mentioned in Chapter 2, *insurance* is a contract in which the insurance company (the *insurer*), in return for consideration, promises to pay a sum of money to another (either the *insured* or the *beneficiary*) if the insured suffers harm or loss from a particular, stated peril. Basically, insurance is an arrangement for *transferring and*

risk
A prediction concerning potential loss based on known and unknown factors.

risk management
Planning that is undertaken to reduce the risk of loss from known and unknown events. In the context of insurance, risk management involves transferring certain risks from the insured to the insurance company.

allocating risk. In many instances, **risk** can be described as a prediction concerning potential loss based on known and unknown factors.

Risk management normally involves the transfer of certain risks from the insured party to the insurance company by a contractual agreement. The insurance contract and its provisions will be examined shortly. First, however, we look at the different types of insurance that can be obtained, insurance terminology, and the concept of insurable interest.

Classifications of Insurance

Insurance is classified according to the nature of the risk involved. For instance, fire insurance, automobile insurance, and life insurance apply to different types of risk and protect against different types of loss. Exhibit 16.6 below lists and describes a number of insurance classifications.

EXHIBIT 16.6
Selected Insurance Classifications

Type of Insurance	Coverage
Automobile	May cover damage to automobiles resulting from specified hazards or occurrences (such as fire, vandalism, theft, or collision); normally provides protection against liability for personal injuries and property damage resulting from the operation of the vehicle.
Casualty	Protects against losses incurred by the insured as a result of being held liable due to negligence for personal injuries or property damage sustained by others.
Fidelity or Guaranty	Provides indemnity against losses in trade or losses caused by the dishonesty of employees, the insolvency of debtors, or breaches of contract. May also be called a surety bond.
Fire	Covers losses incurred by the insured as a result of fire.
Group	Provides individual life, medical, or disability insurance coverage but is obtainable through a group of persons, usually employees; the policy premium is paid either entirely by the employer or partially by the employer and partially by the employee.
Health	Covers expenses incurred by the insured as a result of physical injury or illness and other expenses relating to health and life maintenance.
Homeowners'	Protects homeowners against some or all risks of loss to their residences and the residences' contents or liability arising from the use of the property.
Key-Person	Protects a business in the event of the death or disability of a key employee.
Liability	Protects against liability imposed on the insured as a result of injuries to the person or property of another. May also cover product liability actions.
Life	Covers the death of the policyholder. On the death of the insured, an amount specified in the policy is paid by the insurer to the insured's beneficiary.
Malpractice	Protects professionals (physicians, lawyers, and others) against malpractice claims brought against them by their patients or clients; a form of liability insurance.
Mortgage	Covers a mortgage loan; the insurer pays the balance of the mortgage to the creditor on the death or disability of the debtor.
Title	Protects against any defects in title to real property and any losses incurred as a result of existing claims against or liens on the property at the time of purchase.
Umbrella	Provides additional coverage beyond other policies. It is a means of protecting against catastrophic losses.

Insurance Terminology

An insurance contract is called a **policy**, the consideration paid to the insurer is called a **premium**, and the insurance company is sometimes called an **underwriter**. The parties to an insurance policy are the insurer (the insurance company) and the insured (the person covered by its provisions or the holder of the policy).

Insurance contracts are usually obtained through an *agent,* who ordinarily works for the insurance company, or through a *broker,* who is ordinarily an *independent contractor.* When a broker deals with an applicant for insurance, the broker may be the applicant's agent and not an agent of the insurance company. In contrast, an insurance agent is an agent of the insurance company, not of the applicant. As a general rule, the insurance company is bound by the acts of its insurance agents when they act within the agency relationship (agency relationships will be discussed in Chapter 18). In most situations, state law determines the status of all parties writing or obtaining insurance.

Insurable Interest

People can insure anything in which they have an **insurable interest**. Without an insurable interest, there can be no enforceable contract. For real and personal property, an insurable interest exists when the insured derives a pecuniary (monetary) benefit from the continued existence of the property, such as a car, a home, business premises, or computer data. Put another way, a person has an insurable interest in property when she would sustain a financial loss from its damage or destruction. In regard to life insurance, a person must have a reasonable expectation of benefit from the continued life of another in order to have an insurable interest in that person's life.

The Insurance Contract

An insurance contract is governed by the general principles of contract law, although the insurance industry is regulated by each state and, in some areas, such as health insurance, by federal law as well. In this section, we consider several aspects of the insurance contract, including the application for insurance, the date when the contract takes effect, and some of the important provisions typically found in insurance contracts. In addition, we discuss the cancellation of an insurance policy and defenses that insurance companies can raise against payment on a policy.

Application

The filled-in application form for insurance is usually attached to the policy and made a part of the insurance contract. Thus, an insurance applicant is bound by any false statements that appear in the application (subject to certain exceptions). Because the insurance company evaluates the risk factors based on the information included in the insurance application, misstatements or misrepresentations can void a policy, especially if the insurance company can show that it would not have extended insurance if it had known the true facts. In some instances there can be a criminal prosecution for fraud.

Effective Date

The effective date of an insurance contract—that is, the date on which the insurance coverage begins—is important. In some instances, the insurance applicant is not protected until a formal written policy is issued. In other situations, the applicant is protected between the time the application is received and the time the insurance company either accepts or rejects it. The following facts should be kept in mind:

- A broker is usually the agent of an applicant. Therefore, until the broker obtains a policy from the insurer, the applicant normally is not insured.

- A person who seeks insurance from an insurance company's agent will usually be protected from the moment the application is made, provided that some form of premium has been paid. Between the time the application is

---

policy
In insurance law, a contract for insurance coverage. The policy spells out the precise terms and conditions as to what will and will not be covered under the contract.

premium
In insurance law, the price paid by the insured for insurance protection for a specified period of time.

underwriter
In insurance law, the insurer, or the one assuming a risk in return for the payment of a premium.

insurable interest
An interest either in a person's life or well-being or in property that is sufficiently substantial to justify insuring against injury to or death of the person or damage to the property.

🖱 ON THE web

The Web site of the Insurance Information Institute provides a wealth of information on insurance-related issues, including statistical data and a glossary of insurance terms. Go to **www.iii.org**

Executives of a newly formed corporation consult with an attorney concerning the types of insurance they should purchase for the business. Many paralegals work in the area of insurance law and assist with tasks relating to insurance claims. What types of such claims arise in an insurance context?

© Yuri Arcurs/www.Shutterstock.com

binder
A written, temporary insurance policy.

received and either rejected or accepted, the applicant is covered (possibly subject to a medical examination for life insurance). Usually, the agent will write a memorandum, or **binder**, indicating that a policy is pending and stating its essential terms.

- If the parties agree that the policy will be issued and delivered at a later time, the contract is not effective until the policy is issued and delivered or sent to the applicant, depending on the agreement. Thus, any loss sustained between the time of application and the delivery of the policy is not covered.

- The parties may agree that a life insurance policy will be binding at the time the insured pays the first premium or that the policy may be expressly contingent on the applicant's passing a physical examination. If the applicant pays the premium and passes the examination, the policy coverage is continuously in effect. If the applicant pays the premium but dies before having the physical examination, then in order to collect, the applicant's estate must show that the applicant *would have passed* the examination had he or she not died.

Coinsurance Clauses

Often, when taking out fire insurance policies, property owners insure their property for less than full value because most fires do not result in a total loss. To encourage owners to insure their property for an amount close to full value, fire insurance policies commonly include a coinsurance clause. Typically, a *coinsurance clause* provides that if owners insure the property up to a specified percentage of its replacement value—usually 80 percent—they will be fully reimbursed for any loss. If the insurance is for less than the required percentage, the owners are responsible for a proportionate share of the loss.

◆ **EXAMPLE 16.3—** Assume that a property is valued at $100,000 and the owner insures this property for $80,000, satisfying the insurer's 80 percent coinsurance requirement. When the property suffers $50,000 in fire damages, the owner recovers the full $50,000. If the owner had insured the same property for only $40,000—half of the usual 80 percent ($80,000) coinsurance requirement—then the owner would have recovered only half of the $50,000 in fire damages, or $25,000. ◆

Indemnity Clauses

The term *indemnity* refers to a duty to make good on any loss, damage, or liability claims incurred by another. The term is used frequently in insurance law and insurance contracts because it involves the duty to compensate for loss. Under the principle of indemnity, indemnified parties are restored to the financial position that they were in before the loss or accident.   Indemnity clauses are frequently found in rental contracts.

◆ **EXAMPLE 16.4—**   Martinez is seeking to lease a building that is suitable for operating a dry-cleaning business. Commercial Property, Inc., a rental agency, has such a building for rent in the area in which Martinez wishes to locate. Martinez signs a lease agreement with Commercial that contains an indemnity clause. Under the indemnity clause, if an employee is injured while using the dry-cleaning equipment, he or she cannot sue Commercial Property. In effect, Martinez has agreed to hold the rental agency harmless for any damages caused by use of the equipment. ◆ Because indemnity clauses protect specified parties from suffering financial loss due to lawsuits, they are sometimes referred to as *hold-harmless clauses.*

Corporations often indemnify their directors and officers for any legal costs and fees that they might incur if they become involved in lawsuits by virtue of their positions. (Corporate directors and officers will be discussed in Chapter 18.)

◆ **EXAMPLE 16.5—**   Patricia Harding files a product liability lawsuit against Repp, Inc., and its chief executive officer, James Kerr. If Kerr's employment contract includes an indemnity clause, Repp will assume responsibility for any costs that Kerr incurs in defending himself against this lawsuit. ◆

Subrogation Clauses

In simple terms, *subrogation* is the right to pursue another party's claim. In insurance, subrogation deals with the right of the insurer to be put in the position of the insured to pursue recovery from a third party who is legally responsible to the insured for a loss paid by the insurer to the insured. If the insurance company has compensated the insured for a loss sustained, and then later receives recovery from a third party in the name of the insured, the company can ask a court to order reimbursement from the proceeds.

◆ **EXAMPLE 16.6—**   Rian owns a building that she leases out to several businesses. A third party negligently causes a fire on the premises, which burns down the building. Rian can sue the third party for damages. If Rian does not file a claim against the party who caused the fire, a subrogation clause allows the insurance company to step into Rian's shoes and file a negligence claim against the third party on Rian's behalf. Rian may be fully compensated for the damages by the fire insurance company. If so, and if the lawsuit is successful, the insurer is entitled to be reimbursed from the proceeds in the amount it paid to Rian to cover her loss. ◆

Most insurance contracts contain explicit subrogation clauses, which often require the insured party to cooperate with the insurance company by providing documents, records, and whatever else is necessary for the company to pursue claims on behalf of the insured. Even if the contract does not contain a subrogation clause or does not use the word *subrogation,* however, courts often hold that insurance companies have a right to subrogation unless this right is explicitly waived (given up).

Other Provisions and Clauses

Some other important provisions and clauses in insurance contracts are defined in Exhibit 16.7 on the next page. Paralegals are often responsible for analyzing the various insurance clauses and summarizing the contract terms for their employers or clients. The courts are aware that most people do not have the special training necessary to understand the intricate terminology used in insurance policies. Thus, the words used in an insurance contract have their ordinary meanings, not

social
MEDIA TODAY

Follow carefully. Choose carefully whom to follow on services such as Twitter so you don't overwhelm yourself with too much information and miss important developments.

EXHIBIT 16.7
Insurance Contract Provisions and Clauses

Incontestability Clause	An incontestability clause provides that after a policy has been in force for a specified length of time—usually two or three years—the insurer cannot contest statements made in the application.
Appraisal Clause	Insurance policies frequently provide that if the parties cannot agree on the amount of a loss covered under the policy or the value of the property lost, an appraisal, or estimate, by an impartial and qualified third party can be demanded.
Arbitration Clause	Many insurance policies include clauses that call for arbitration of disputes that may arise between the insurer and the insured concerning the settlement of claims.
Antilapse Clause	An antilapse clause provides that the policy will not automatically lapse if no payment is made on the date due. Ordinarily, under such a provision, the insured has a *grace period* of thirty or thirty-one days within which to pay an overdue premium before the policy is canceled.
Multiple Insurance	Many insurance policies include a clause providing that if the insured has multiple insurance policies that cover the same property and the amount of coverage exceeds the loss, the loss will be shared proportionately by the insurance companies.

© Cengage Learning 2014

a technical meaning specific only to insurance. They are interpreted by the courts in light of the nature of the coverage involved. (For some online sources relating to policy interpretation and analysis, as well as sources relating to other aspects of insurance-related legal work, see this chapter's *Technology and Today's Paralegal* feature on the facing page.)

When there is an ambiguity in the policy, the provision generally is interpreted against the insurance company. Also, when it is unclear whether an insurance contract actually exists because the written policy has not been delivered, the uncertainty normally is resolved against the insurance company. The court presumes that the policy is in effect unless the company can show otherwise. Similarly, an insurer must notify the insured of any change in coverage under an existing policy.

Cancellation

The insured can cancel a policy at any time, and the insurer can cancel under certain circumstances. When an insurance company can cancel its insurance contract, the policy or a state statute usually requires that the insurer give advance written notice of the cancellation to the insured. The same requirement applies when only part of a policy is canceled. Any premium paid in advance may be refundable on the policy's cancellation. The insured may also be entitled to a life insurance policy's cash surrender value.

The insurer can cancel an insurance policy for various reasons, depending on the type of insurance. ◆ **EXAMPLE 16.7—** Automobile insurance can be canceled for nonpayment of premiums or suspension of the insured's driver's license. Property insurance can be canceled for nonpayment of premiums or for other reasons, including the insured's fraud or misrepresentation, conviction for a crime that increases the hazard insured against, or gross negligence that increases the hazard insured against. Life and health policies can be canceled because of false statements made by the insured in the application, but cancellation can only take place before the effective date of an incontestability clause. ◆

An insurer cannot cancel—or refuse to renew—a policy for discriminatory reasons or other reasons that violate public policy or because the insured has appeared as a witness in a case against the company.

Good Faith Obligations

Both parties to an insurance contract are responsible for the obligations that they assume under the contract. In addition, both the insured and the insurer have an implied duty to act in good faith. Good faith requires the party who is applying

social
MEDIA TODAY

The average American is exposed to large amounts of data daily. As data are flowing into your devices, data about you are constantly flowing out—and not always to harmless places.

TECHNOLOGY AND
today's paralegal

ONLINE RESOURCES CONCERNING INSURANCE CLAIMS

When a dispute arises between an insurance company and a policyholder regarding an insurance claim, attorneys are often consulted. In these situations, paralegals fulfill functions for both sides, including analyzing insurance policies, researching the facts involved in the claim, and locating experts. Here, we provide some practical Internet resources.

ANALYZING CLAUSES IN INSURANCE POLICIES

Paralegals who deal with insurance law must know how to read and analyze an insurance policy. FindLaw offers "a step by step method that insurance professionals and attorneys use to analyze a policy" at **library.findlaw.com**. Search for "Primer on Insurance Law" as well as clicking on the "Insurance" title on the main page. Insurance policies are sometimes written in terms that laypersons don't understand. A glossary of insurance terms is offered by the Insurance Information Institute at **www.iii.org**.

INSURANCE COMPLAINTS AND INSURANCE FRAUD

A paralegal assisting a client with an insurance claim may need to research related complaints against the client's insurance company. The Web site of the National Association of Insurance Commissioners (NAIC) offers a good starting point for such research. NAIC's home page, at **www.naic.org**, furnishes an online fraud reporting system and links to state insurance department Web sites.

To assist in the prevention and discovery of fraudulent insurance claims, the Coalition Against Insurance Fraud (CAIF) presents many resources at **www.insurancefraud.org**. Through CAIF's Web site, you can access state regulations related to insurance fraud and links to many antifraud associations, state fraud bureaus, and investigation tools. CAIF also posts many reports related to insurance fraud offenses.

LOCATING ADJUSTERS AND APPRAISERS

When a policyholder files a claim, the policyholder's insurance company may employ an insurance adjuster. The adjuster inspects the damaged property, analyzes the insurance policy, and estimates the amount of loss. Paralegals sometimes assist attorneys in locating adjusters. The National Association of Independent Insurance Adjusters (NAIIA) represents independently owned claims-adjusting companies that have been approved by insurance carriers. Through the NAIIA's Web site, **www.naiia.com**, a claim can be assigned to an NAIIA adjuster in your area. This Web site also offers many industry links.

Another resource is the National Association of Public Insurance Adjusters (NAPIA), **www.napia.com**. It accredits public insurance adjusters, who are hired to assist consumers. The NAPIA Web site offers a search engine to locate local public insurance adjusters.

In the case of an automobile insurance claim, it may be beneficial to use the online appraiser locator available through the Independent Automotive Damage Appraisers (IADA) Web site at **www.iada.org**. IADA is an association of automotive appraisers organized to protect insurance consumers from overpaying for auto body repairs.

TECHNOLOGY TIP

The Internet has given voice to disgruntled employees and customers, some of whom create Web sites to document why they are upset with particular companies. In *The Taubman Company v. Webfeats,* the federal Sixth Circuit Court of Appeals held that disgruntled consumers have the right to use companies' names and trademarks in Web domain names with the suffix "sucks" to criticize the companies (search YouTube for "Taubman Sucks"). Search for blogs, tweets, and other online material critical of businesses. These may contain useful information about problems at the companies and potential witness names.

for insurance to reveal everything necessary for the insurer to evaluate the risk. In other words, the applicant must disclose all material facts, including all facts that an insurer would consider in determining whether to charge a higher premium or to refuse to issue a policy altogether. Once the insurer has accepted the risk, and some event occurs that gives rise to a claim, the insurer has a duty to investigate to determine the facts.

When a policy provides insurance against third party claims, the insurer is obligated to make reasonable efforts to settle such a claim. If a settlement cannot be reached, then regardless of the claim's merit, the insurer must defend any suit against the insured. Usually, a policy provides that in this situation the insured must cooperate. A policy provision may expressly require the insured to attend hearings and trials, to help in obtaining evidence and witnesses, and to assist in reaching a settlement.

Defenses against Payment

If an insurance company can show that a policy was obtained by fraud, it may have a valid defense for not paying on a claim. A defense also exists if the insurer can show that the insured lacked an insurable interest—thus rendering the policy void from the beginning. Improper actions, such as those that are against public policy or are otherwise illegal, can also give the insurance company a defense against the payment of a claim or allow it to rescind the contract.

An insurance company can be prevented from asserting some defenses that are normally available, however. ◆ **EXAMPLE 16.8—** Suppose that a company tells an insured that information requested on a form is optional, and the insured provides it anyway. The company cannot use the information to avoid its contractual obligation under the insurance contract. Similarly, an insurance company normally cannot escape payment on the death of an insured on the ground that the person's age was stated incorrectly on the application. ◆

Self-Insurance

Sometimes firms and individuals *self-insure* against risks. That means they set aside money to cover risks rather than buy insurance. For example, some large employers can predict their employees' total health care costs even if they cannot predict which individual employees will need benefits. Rather than pay an insurance company, the company sets aside the amount of money necessary to pay the claims it predicts will occur. Paralegals are often involved in administering self-insurance plans on behalf of corporate legal departments. Since the company is engaged in an insurance function, it may need to follow some insurance laws.

Captive Insurance

Increasingly, companies with large insurance needs are considering establishing their own insurance companies, called *captive insurers*. When a company owns its own insurance company, it has three advantages.

1. It can determine the type of coverage it will carry. Instead of being limited to insurance policies available in the marketplace, it can design its own coverage.

2. It can deduct the premiums it pays its captive insurer from its profits before paying taxes, a significant advantage over self-insurance.

3. It can control the investment policy the captive insurer uses for its reserves.

Most captive insurance companies in the United States are registered in Vermont, which has special laws making it easier to run a captive insurance company. Many hospitals and other medical firms use captive insurance based in the Cayman Islands, which also has such laws. Paralegals at companies using captives are often involved in the record keeping and administration of the captive.

IN THE office

CLARIFYING INSTRUCTIONS

Attorneys and paralegals are usually busy. Often, attorneys give instructions to paralegals quickly and briefly, assuming that the instructions are understood as intended. Problems arise if the instructions are not clear to the paralegal.

You must make sure that you understand the instructions. For example, suppose that your supervising attorney asks you to draft a letter to an insurance company, using as a model a letter recently sent to another insurance company on behalf of a client named Jane Lattimore. The name doesn't ring a bell with you, but you assume that you can find that letter quickly in the files. The attorney then leaves the office for the rest of the day, and you waste time searching in vain through the files for "Jane Lattimore."

The next morning, you explain the problem to the attorney and learn that Jane Lattimore is, in fact, the married name of a client whose files are under her maiden name, Jane Calvin. You are upset, the attorney is displeased, and the sending of the letter is delayed—all of which could have been avoided if you had asked "Who is Jane Lattimore?" when the attorney was giving you instructions.

The Paralegal and Insurance

A paralegal working for an insurance company may be asked to assist in drafting insurance policies or amendments to policies, and to investigate the facts behind claims filed by policyholders. As the *In the Office* feature above discusses, careful review of documents is critical. A paralegal working for a real estate investment firm may analyze insurance policies related to commercial property investments. Additionally, a paralegal might work for a state insurance regulatory agency. In this context, a paralegal may assist in drafting administrative procedures, investigating insurance fraud and licensing issues, and responding to consumers' insurance claims and questions—such as claims for workers' compensation (to be discussed in Chapter 18).

Paralegals who assist in insurance-related litigation involving torts will likely be involved in many of the same types of work that are required in the area of tort law (discussed in Chapter 14). Here is just a sampling of tasks related to insurance law that paralegals commonly manage:

- Research insurance clauses in relation to specific claims.

- Interact with experts, witnesses, and clients to obtain factual information about events giving rise to insurance claims.

- Work with representatives of an insurance company in defending an insured against a lawsuit brought against the insured.

- Obtain medical records concerning a client who needs assistance in obtaining payment from the insurer. (This involves issues covered in the *Developing Paralegal Skills* feature on the following page.)

- Create, review, or prepare insurance application forms or insurance policies.

- Schedule medical appointments for health-insurance claimants.

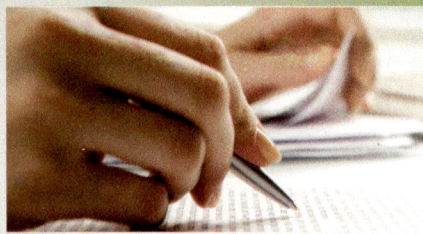

DEVELOPING
paralegal skills

MEDICAL RECORDS

Derek Busset is a legal assistant for the small personal-injury firm of McNair and Iverson. McNair is handling a case in which Blanche Rosenthal's car was struck by an automobile driven by Daniel Gomez, who is insured by Reliable Insurance. The police report indicates that at the time of the accident, Gomez was speeding through a yellow light at the intersection when his car collided with Rosenthal's 2013 Hyundai, which had just entered the intersection on a green light.

The insurance company has compensated Rosenthal for the damage to her vehicle but disputes the amount she is claiming for medical expenses. The insurance company believes that Rosenthal's back injury was a preexisting condition. That is, it was not caused by the accident. After speaking with a representative from the insurance company, attorney McNair asks paralegal Derek to contact Rosenthal and acquire the medical records to support her claims. McNair also wants Derek to write up a summary of what the records show.

TIPS FOR OBTAINING AND EVALUATING MEDICAL RECORDS

- Obtain a list from the client of all of the physicians who treated the client and the hospitals or other facilities in which the client received medical care.

- Prepare—and have the client sign—medical release forms, which authorize the treating physicians to provide the patient's medical records directly to the law firm.

- Keep a log of the records as they are received.

- If a claim involves the possibility of a preexisting condition, make certain to request the client's complete medical history (from before the injury as well as after it). These records will be needed to determine whether a preexisting condition might have caused or contributed to the plaintiff's injury.

- Use a medical dictionary or reference book so that you can decipher the terminology and abbreviations frequently used by medical personnel in charts and records.

KEY TERMS AND CONCEPTS

binder   514
deed   506
easement   500
eminent domain   500
fee simple absolute   500
insurable interest   513

joint tenancy   501
lease   506
mortgage   504
personal property   500
policy   513
premium   513

real property   500
risk   512
risk management   512
tenancy in common   501
underwriter   513

Chapter Summary

Real Property and Insurance Law

REAL PROPERTY

Real property (also called real estate or realty) includes land and all things attached to the land (such as buildings and plants), as well as subsurface and air rights. All other types of property, both tangible and intangible, are personal property.

1. *Ownership rights in property*—Fee simple absolute is the most complete form of ownership, entitling the holder to use, possess, or dispose of the property however he or she chooses during his or her lifetime. Restrictions on property use can be imposed by ease-

ments, which can also grant to others limited rights to use property. While property rights are strong, the government has the right to use the power of eminent domain to take property with compensation. Co-ownership in which each party owns an undivided interest in the property that passes to his or her heirs at death is called tenancy in common. Joint tenancy is co-ownership in which each party owns an undivided interest in the property that automatically passes to the surviving joint tenant(s) on the death of one of them.

2. *The transfer and sale of real property*—Real property can be transferred as a gift, by inheritance, by lease, or by sale. Usually, real property is transferred by sale, which typically involves the following steps.

    a. The buyer makes a purchase offer, often conditioned on obtaining financing, and pays an earnest money deposit.

    b. If the seller accepts the offer, a contract is formed. Real estate agents may assist both the buyer and the seller in negotiating the terms.

    c. An escrow agent acts as a neutral party in the transaction, holding the deed and any money paid by the buyer until the sale is completed.

    d. Most buyers obtain a mortgage loan to finance the purchase. The holder of the mortgage then has a security interest in the property.

    e. Often, the sale is contingent on certain inspections of the property.

    f. A title examination is performed to ensure that the seller is actually the owner of the property and that no liens exist of which the buyer was not aware.

    g. At the closing, the buyer signs the mortgage note (if the sale is financed) and obtains title insurance, the seller is paid the purchase price (less any closing costs), and the buyer is given the deed to the property.

3. *Leases*—The owner of real property (the lessor) may agree (contract) to rent the property out to another (the lessee) for a specified period of time. The lessee has the exclusive right to use the property. Leases are governed by contract law and by state statutes. Leases are usually in writing and must be written if the lease period exceeds one year.

4. *Commercial leases* are usually more detailed than residential leases and contain more specialized terminology.

INSURANCE LAW

1. *Classifications*—See Exhibit 16.6 on page 512.

2. *Terminology*—

    a. *Policy*—The insurance contract.

    b. *Premium*—The consideration paid to the insurer for the policy.

    c. *Underwriter*—The insurance company.

    d. *Insurer*—The insurance company.

    e. *Insured*—The person or property covered by the insurance.

    f. *Insurance agent*—A representative of the insurance company.

    g. *Insurance broker*—Ordinarily, an independent contractor.

    h. *Beneficiary*—A person to receive payment under the policy.

3. *Insurable interest*—An insurable interest exists whenever an individual or entity benefits from the preservation of the property to be insured or the continued health or life of the person to be insured.

4. *The insurance contract*—The general principles of contract law are applied; the insurance industry is also regulated by the states.

    a. An insurance applicant is bound by any false statements that appear in the application (subject to certain exceptions), which is part of the insurance contract.

    b. Misrepresentations may be grounds for voiding the policy.

    c. Coverage on an insurance policy can begin when a binder (a written memorandum indicating that a formal policy is pending and stating its essential terms) is written; when the policy is issued; at the time of contract formation; or, depending on the terms of the contract or specific state law, when certain conditions are met.

    d. See Exhibit 16.7 on page 516 for a review of major provisions in insurance contracts. Words are given their ordinary meanings. Any ambiguity in the policy will be interpreted against the insurance company. When it is unclear whether an insurance contract actually exists, the uncertainty generally will be resolved against the insurance company. The court will presume that the policy is in effect unless the company can show otherwise.

    e. Defenses against payment to an insured include fraud, lack of an insurable interest, and improper actions on the part of the insured.

5. *Self-insurance*—Some parties prefer to self-insure against risk of loss by setting aside funds for such possibilities.

6. *Captive insurance*—Sometimes employed by large companies that form their own insurance company to handle insurance needs.

QUESTIONS FOR REVIEW

1. Explain the difference between real property and personal property. What is a fee simple? List and define the other ways in which ownership rights in property can be held.

2. Explain what law governs the sale of real property. Describe the basic steps involved in the sale of real estate. What role does an escrow agent play?

3. What are the various classifications of insurance? Define an insurable interest. How does an insurable interest arise in property? In another's life?

4. What is the difference between an insurance agent and an insurance broker? Why is this difference significant for people seeking insurance coverage?

ETHICAL QUESTION

1. Joanne Dorman works as a paralegal in the claims department of an automobile insurance company. She is asked to review a claim brought by Derek Farmer, her nephew. Derek is a college student with few financial resources. Joanne's sister (Derek's mother) told Joanne that Derek broke his windshield recently when he accidentally ran into a mailbox beside the road leading to their rural home. In the claim that she is reviewing, however, Derek states that a rock hit his windshield. Joanne understands immediately what Derek is trying to do. Derek's policy states that his collision coverage (which would apply to the mailbox accident) has a $500 deductible. His comprehensive coverage (which would apply if a rock had hit his windshield) has a deductible of only $50. Derek is obviously trying to avoid having to pay the full $500 deductible, which he can ill afford. In contrast, the insurance company could easily absorb the extra cost. What should Joanne do in this situation?

PRACTICE QUESTIONS AND ASSIGNMENTS

1. Review the diagram in Exhibit 16.3 on page 505. Explain the relationship among the parties to an escrow agreement, and explain each party's responsibility.

2. Using the material presented in Exhibit 16.4 on page 507, *A Sample Deed*, and the following facts, draft a deed to real property.

- At a closing on January 22, 2014, Roberto Alvarez and Paloma Alvarez, husband and wife, of 987 Packard Street, Galveston, Texas, transfer their beachfront condo to Javier and Eduardo Gomez, brothers, for consideration of $250,000 cash. Javier Gomez lives at 10101 Summit Place, New City, Texas. Eduardo Gomez's address is 99901 Hill Street, Casper, Texas. The Gomez brothers will own the condo as tenants in common.

- The legal description of the property is Lot 91 of Whiteacre Subdivision, Galveston County, Texas, according to the plat map contained in volume 89, pages 123–129, of the Plat Records of Galveston County, Texas.

- The conveyance with a warranty is expressly made subject to the Easements and Restrictions of Record in volume 7877, page 456, and volume 9988, page 431, of the Real Property Records of Galveston County, Texas, and to any other restrictions and easements affecting the property that are of record in Galveston County, Texas.

- The notary public who will acknowledge the deed is Rosemary Potter, and her commission expires January 31, 2015.

3. Identify the types of ownership rights described in the following statements.

a. John and Linda, a brother and a sister, jointly own a cottage that they inherited from their mother. They have rights of survivorship.

b. Ja'neen conveys her townhouse to her mother for as long as her mother lives. On her mother's death, the property is to go to Ja'neen's daughter.

c. Alya Abboud owns her home, and she can use, possess, or dispose of it as she pleases. On Alya's death, the property will descend to her heirs.

d. John Tully and Sam Marsh jointly own a large farm in Iowa. If either of them dies, the heirs of the deceased owner will inherit that owner's share of the farm.

4. Identify the following steps in a real estate sales transaction:

a. An offer or counteroffer is accepted.

b. Title to the property is reviewed to determine the seller's ownership interest and to determine if any liens against the property exist.

c. The buyer applies for financing at a bank or mortgage company.

d. A house is inspected to see if it needs repairs exceeding $1,000, such as roof repairs or basement waterproofing.

e. The buyer tenders a sum of money along with an offer.

QUESTIONS FOR CRITICAL ANALYSIS

1. Why is property ownership described as a "bundle of rights"? What is one called who owns the entire bundle? Is it ever possible to own less than the entire bundle? How? Give an example. Is it possible to share the bundle of rights? How? Give examples.

2. Assume that John submits an offer to Lisa to purchase Lisa's home for $150,000. Lisa responds to John's offer with a counteroffer: she will sell John her home for $175,000. John then offers to purchase the home for $165,000, so long as he can obtain a mortgage and the house does not have termites. Lisa accepts the offer. In each of these transactions, who is the offeror, and who is the offeree? At what point is a contract for the sale of the home formed?

3. "When people obtain insurance to protect them against certain risks, they become more careless with respect to protecting against those risks themselves." Do you agree with this statement? Why or why not?

4. Statistics show that the extent of risk assumed by insurance companies varies depending on the gender of the insured. Many people contend that laws prohibiting gender-based insurance rates are thus fundamentally unfair. Do you agree with this contention? Explain your reasoning.

PROJECT

Locate a homeowners' or renters' insurance policy. Find the effective date, and determine whether a binder was initially issued. Also, try to locate coinsurance, cancellation, appraisal, antilapse, and multiple insurance clauses. (Note that not all policies have the same coverage, so it is possible that not all of these clauses will be present in the insurance policy.) Write a one-page description of the clauses that are included in the policy, including the effective date.

GROUP PROJECT

This project requires students to review leases of real property, such as houses or apartments. Students one, two, and three should each select a lease to examine. They may find a lease online, buy one at a local office supply store, or use their own lease if they prefer. The leases should contain state-specific provisions. Each student will summarize the provisions in the lease he or she selected. Student four will create a chart comparing the provisions of the three leases and present it to the class.

USING INTERNET RESOURCES

1. Go to the Web site of the Insurance Information Institute at **www.iii.org**. Follow the links to auto insurance and to homeowners' and renters' insurance. Browse through the information, or watch videos on the topics if available, and then answer the following questions:

   a. What six types of coverage may be included in a basic auto policy?

   b. What is comprehensive coverage? What types of losses does this coverage protect against? What is uninsured or underinsured motorist coverage, and when does it come into play?

   c. What is covered by a standard homeowners' insurance policy? In the context of homeowners' insurance, what does liability coverage protect against?

   d. What does renters' insurance cover? What are the types of renters' insurance policies that can be purchased? What are the differences among these types of policies with respect to coverage? What is a floater policy?

CourseMate The available CourseMate for this text has an interactive eBook and interactive learning tools, including flash cards, quizzes, and more. To learn more about this resource and access free demo CourseMate resources, go to **www.cengagebrain.com**, and search for this book. To access CourseMate materials that you have purchased, go to **login.cengagebrain.com**.

Family Law and Estates

Chapter Outline

Introduction

Family Law

Wills, Trusts, and Estates

After completing this chapter, you will know:

- The legal rights and obligations of parents and children.

- How marital property and debts are divided when a marriage is dissolved.

- What estate planning is and why it is important.

- The various devices that are used in estate planning.

- The requirements for a valid will and the laws that govern property distribution when a person dies without a valid will.

Introduction

The legal relationships of people within a family are governed by *family law*, the subject of the first part of this chapter. Family law describes how we create families, who can create a family, and the legal obligations owed to family members, such as parents' duties to provide for the medical needs of their children. It also governs the dissolution of families through divorce, which is a major area of work for paralegals. There is property to be distributed at the end of a marriage. Matters can be complicated by issues regarding child custody, child support, and alimony. Such complications can lead to ongoing conflicts that involve legal support.

Whether property is distributed before or during a marriage, or when one ends, property must be transferred when a person dies. For that reason, the laws governing the succession of property are a necessary extension to the laws concerning the ownership of property. In the latter part of the chapter, we examine various legal devices (procedures or techniques), including wills and trusts, that are often used to transfer a person's real and personal property, or *estate*, after death.

Family Law

Marriage, divorce, adoption, child support and custody, child and spousal abuse, and parental rights and duties are all areas of family law. Much of the legal work relating to family law has to do with marriage dissolution. Marriage is a status conferred by state law. Thus, when marriage ends, the state, through the court system, must become involved. Because of the high divorce rate in this country, many attorneys and paralegals deal with divorce cases. Such cases may include child-support and child-custody issues. In addition, the property owned by a divorcing couple must be divided between the spouses.

In this section, you will read about some important legal concepts and doctrines governing family matters, including the matters surrounding marriage dissolution. (For a discussion of the important role that paralegals can play in the area of family law, see this chapter's *Featured Contributor* article on pages 526 and 527.)

Marriage Requirements

Despite the fact that many couples today live together (cohabit) without marrying, most Americans marry at least once during their lifetimes. Marriage confers certain legal and practical advantages. The marriage establishes the rights and duties of the spouses, as well as of any children born during the marriage. Married couples may also have an easier time obtaining insurance and credit and adopting children. Additionally, many companies offer health insurance to spouses but not to unmarried partners.

States place some limitations on who can marry. The betrothed must be man and woman (except in a few states, as you will read shortly), currently unmarried, not closely related by blood, and over a certain age—usually eighteen years. State laws vary, and some states prohibit marriage between those who are closely related even if the relation is only by marriage. Persons who are under the required age can marry with parental consent or if they are emancipated from their parents. **Emancipation** normally occurs when a child leaves home to support himself or herself. Below a certain age, such as fourteen or sixteen, marriage may be absolutely prohibited by state law except with court approval.

Procedural Requirements

Certain procedures are generally required for a legally recognized marriage to take place. The parties must first obtain a *marriage license* from the state government, usually through the county clerk's office. About half of the states also require a *blood test* to check for certain diseases. Some states require couples to go through a short

emancipation
The legal relinquishment by a child's parents or guardian of the legal right to exercise control over the child. Usually, a child who moves out of the parents' home and supports himself or herself is considered emancipated.

Featured Contributor

PARALEGALS IN FAMILY LAW PRACTICE

Nancy R. Gallo

BIOGRAPHICAL NOTE

Nancy R. Gallo is a professor and the coordinator of legal studies programs at Sussex County Community College in Newton, New Jersey. She is the author of the textbook *Introduction to Family Law* and a frequent public speaker. A graduate of William Paterson University, Ms. Gallo worked as a paralegal before earning her J.D. and being licensed to practice law in Florida and New Jersey. She has volunteered as an early-settlement panel member for the Sussex County Superior Court, and her practice has included family mediation. Gallo is a member of the Family Law Syllabus Task Force (2003) of the American Association for Paralegal Education, the Family Law Section of the American Bar Association, and the Elder Law Section of the New Jersey Bar.

© Cengage Learning 2014

An interesting development of late-twentieth-century legal practice was the creation of the *boutique* law firm. Boutique legal practices left behind the concept of a lone general practitioner handling the A to Z of a client's legal issues and instead moved toward the goal of having individual attorneys and their paralegals become specialists in one or two areas of practice.

VALUE OF SPECIALISTS

Family law is a good example of an area of the law that has flourished under specialist experts. Paralegals in this area are integral team members working with their employers toward a common goal of building and maintaining a respected and lucrative legal practice. Indeed, a new client's

waiting period before getting the license or between the time of acquiring the license and getting married.

In most states, some form of *marriage ceremony* is also required. The parties must present the license to someone authorized by the state to perform marriages, such as a justice of the peace, a judge, or a member of the clergy. The marriage ceremony must involve a public statement of the agreement to marry. After the ceremony, the *marriage license must be recorded* with a government official. That provides notice to those who deal with the couple that they are indeed married. Because marriage can affect property rights or the ability to pay debts, this is an important role of the law.

Same-Sex Couples

One of the most controversial family law topics today involves the ability of gay or lesbian couples to marry. Many states expressly prohibit such marriages. In 2004, Massachusetts became the first state to allow same-sex marriages.

In addition, some states have passed laws allowing same-sex couples to form "civil unions" or "domestic partnerships." Like a marriage, these include the right to inherit a partner's property, to divorce, to be granted child custody, to receive alimony or child support, and to decide on medical treatment for an incapacitated partner. They are legally a marriage in all but name. Some of the most difficult legal issues in family law now involve same-sex couples who marry where it is permissible but later move to a state that does not recognize such unions. Exhibit 17.1 on page 528 provides a summary of the law in states with such provisions as of 2012.

first contact with a law firm may be with one of the firm's paralegals. This is an important first step in client relations, because there is truth in the maxim, "There's no second chance to make a good first impression."

The most typical comment about a family law practice is that there seldom is a typical day. Indeed, paralegals working with family law practitioners will find themselves dealing with cases reflecting a wide range of human experiences. Such a practice very often delves into a client's most personal issues. For example, a family law practice may involve the seemingly convoluted machinations of divorce and separation or the necessity of filing a restraining order. The drafting of prenuptial agreements, settlement agreements, and adoption paperwork may all occur in a typical day.

STEADY AREA OF WORK

The statistical truth is that today, in the United States, about half of all marriages end in divorce. The high divorce rate may be good for business, but attorneys and paralegals practicing family law, more than those in most other areas of the law, must balance the client's legal needs with sensitivity to the client's emotional state. A well-trained paralegal can have a vital and important role in assisting the attorney with this dual responsibility. In fact, a paralegal may often be a client's closest link to a law firm during a very emotional time. The special emotional needs of family law clients will often inspire a paralegal to call on previously unknown reserves of patience and sensitivity.

One thing that is absolutely true is that law firms handling matters involving family law will heavily depend on paralegals to soothe often agitated clients and to keep a virtual mountain of paperwork moving efficiently. Paralegal work in a family law practice is seldom dull, usually involves very personal relationships with clients, and can result in life-changing benefits to clients. One cannot say that about too many areas of the law.

"The most typical comment about a family law practice is that there seldom is a typical day."

Common Law Marriages

A **common law marriage** is one in which the parties become married solely by mutual consent and without a license or ceremony. At one time, common law marriages were frequent. Today, in the United States, only fifteen states and the District of Columbia recognize common law marriage.

There are four general requirements for a common law marriage. The parties:

1. must be eligible to marry,
2. must have a present and continuing intention and implied agreement to be husband and wife,
3. must live together as husband and wife, and
4. must hold themselves out to the public as husband and wife.

Note that cohabitation alone does not normally produce a common law marriage. The parties must additionally hold themselves out to others as husband and wife.

Once a couple is legally regarded as married, they have all of the rights and obligations of a traditionally married couple—including the obligation to support each other and their children. Furthermore, while most states do not recognize common law marriages, they acknowledge the validity of a common law marriage that was formed in one of the states that do permit common law marriages. Once a couple is regarded as married by common law, they must obtain a court decree

common law marriage
A marriage that is formed by mutual consent and without a marriage license or ceremony. The couple must be eligible to marry, have a present and continuing agreement to be husband and wife, live together as husband and wife, and hold themselves out to the public as husband and wife. Many states do not recognize common law marriages.

© Cengage Learning 2014

EXHIBIT 17.1
State Law Provisions for
Non-traditional Relationships

Same-Sex Marriage, Civil Union, and Domestic Partnership Provisions	States
Issues marriage licenses to same-sex couples	California, Connecticut, District of Columbia, Iowa, Massachusetts, New Hampshire, New York, Vermont
Recognizes same-sex marriages from other states	Maryland, New York
Allows civil unions, providing state-level spousal rights to same-sex couples	Delaware, Hawaii, Illinois, New Jersey, Rhode Island
Grants nearly all state-level spousal rights to unmarried couples (domestic partnerships)	California, Nevada, Oregon, Washington
Provides some state-level spousal rights to unmarried partners (domestic partnerships)	District of Columbia, Hawaii, Maine, Wisconsin

to dissolve the marriage. There is no legal meaning to the notion of a "common law divorce." Many people not trained in law do not understand common law marriages. Hence, it is important for paralegals to ask questions in situations in which one may exist so that the supervising attorney can properly advise the client.

Marital Duties

In the old days, marriages were arranged between families through private contracts. Part of the contractual arrangement was that the husband would support and provide for his wife and children. The wife, in turn, had certain duties in the home. Although we still hear the term *marriage contract,* in fact, marriage represents a special type of contract that is governed not by contract law but by the state. In the United States, each state has laws that govern marriage and divorce and establish the spousal obligations of married partners and their obligations toward any children.

Financial Support

Generally, spouses are allowed to arrange their own affairs however they see fit. Nonetheless, the law still holds that one spouse has a duty to support the other spouse and children financially by providing such basics as food, shelter, and medical care—insofar as the spouse is able to do so. In many states, this duty lasts throughout the marriage, even if the spouses are living apart. Failure to provide support for a child may be a criminal violation. Additional duties may be created by a separate agreement between the spouses.

Spousal Abuse

Each state creates its own definition of domestic violence through legislation and court decisions. In all states, however, it is a criminal act to batter a spouse. Unlawful abuse has been extended to include extreme cases of harassment (such as stalking) and threats of physical beating or confinement. In some cases, an emergency restraining order may be necessary. A **restraining order** is a court order that requires one person (such as an abusing spouse) to stay away from another (such as the victim of spousal abuse). Shelters are sometimes available to assist abused spouses and their children.

Domestic Abuse

Domestic abuse often remains unrecognized in family relationships. Injurious behavior happens in many ways, not only physical. American law started taking notice of domestic abuse only in recent decades, so it is a "new" area of law by the standards of most legal concepts. Paralegals should expect as many legal questions as answers when they encounter domestic abuse situations.

restraining order
A court order that requires one person (such as an abusing spouse) to stay away from another (such as an abused spouse).

Domestic abuse is a complex topic and one for which paralegals with social work training often are particularly valuable. Among the issues that victims of domestic abuse encounter are problems of threats, financial abuse, fear of losing custody of their children, isolation, mental illness, shame and embarrassment, and prior negative experiences with the courts or police. Law firms are not equipped to handle all the problems surrounding domestic abuse, but paralegals who may encounter such situations can help clients with referrals to social service agencies such as The Hotline (**www.thehotline.org**).

Parental Rights and Obligations

Legally, a child is defined as an unmarried minor (under the age of eighteen) who is not emancipated. Prior to a child's emancipation, parents have certain rights of control over the child. Parents can direct the upbringing of their children and control where they live, what school they attend, and even what religion they practice. Parents also generally control the medical care to be given, although a parent's refusal to provide for such care in life-threatening situations (for religious reasons, for example) can be a crime. Parents have broad legal authority to control the behavior of their children and even physically punish them—so long as the punishment does not constitute child abuse (to be discussed shortly).

Parents also have obligations toward their children. Parents must provide food, shelter, clothing, medical care, and other necessities. Parents must also ensure that their children attend school (normally until the age of sixteen or eighteen). If a couple is married, the law presumes that any newborn child was fathered by the husband, and the husband must support the child unless he can prove that he is not the biological father. (Some states do not allow the husband an opportunity to prove his lack of paternity, however.) Although parental duties to a child generally end when the child reaches the age of eighteen, these duties may continue for a longer period if the child is seriously disabled.

Liability for Children's Wrongful Acts

Parents are sometimes held liable for the wrongful actions of their children. Although state laws vary considerably, parents are most likely to be held liable when they have knowledge of prior, similar behavior by the child. They may be liable if they have improperly assisted a child in procuring a driver's license or provided the child with a vehicle when the child should not be driving. Parents have been held liable for giving their children access to firearms and when their children have vandalized property.

In some states, greater liability is provided by statute. In California, for example, parents can be liable for up to $25,000 per incident of property defacement, while Illinois provides for liability of $2,500 for willful and malicious acts by children. ◆ **EXAMPLE 17.1—** Vanessa Purdy permits her fourteen-year-old son, Jeremy, to drive the family car to the grocery store by himself, without supervision, although he has no driver's license. En route to the store, Jeremy causes an accident in which Thomas Boone, a passenger in the other car, is seriously injured. Boone would probably succeed in a negligence suit against Vanessa Purdy in this situation. ◆

Child Abuse and Neglect

All states allow parents to physically punish their children within reason. A parent, for example, may slap or spank a child without violating the laws prohibiting child abuse. Some states allow corporal (physical) punishment in the schools (under the doctrine of *in loco parentis,* or "in the place of the parents"). In all states, however, laws prohibit sexual molestation and extreme punishment of children by anyone. For punishment to constitute physical child abuse, the punishment normally must result in injuries—such as broken skin or bones, excessive bruising, or swelling.

Child neglect is also a form of child abuse. Child neglect occurs when parents or legal guardians fail to provide for a child's basic needs, such as food, shelter,

ON THE web

The Child Welfare Information Gateway provides links to information about child abuse, foster care, and related topics at **www.childwelfare.gov**.

clothing, and medical treatment. Child abuse may even extend to emotional abuse, as when a person publicly humiliates a child in an extreme way.

Children Born out of Wedlock

A large number of children are born to unmarried parents, and the law provides rights and protections for these children. One important right is the right of the child to be supported by the biological father. The biological father (and mother) has a legal obligation to contribute to the support for the child that is identical to that of a married father. The obligation usually lasts until the child is no longer a minor. The mother's subsequent marriage to another man does not necessarily extinguish the obligation of the biological father to support the child.

In most states, the eventual marriage of the parents of a child born out of wedlock "legitimizes" the child. Unmarried men can also take legal responsibility for their children by formally acknowledging paternity.

paternity suit

A lawsuit brought by an unmarried mother to establish that a certain person is the biological father of her child. DNA testing or a comparable procedure is often used to determine paternity.

PATERNITY SUITS. An unmarried mother may file a **paternity suit** to establish that a certain person is the biological father of her child. If the unwed mother is on public-welfare assistance, the government may file a paternity suit on the mother's behalf to obtain reimbursement for welfare payments given to the mother even if she does not want it to do so. Fathers may also file paternity actions in order to obtain visitation rights or custody of the child. The paternity of a child can be proved scientifically. DNA testing or comparable procedures that check for genetic factors can determine, with almost 100 percent accuracy, whether a person parented a particular child. In a few states, grandparents also have certain legal rights, such as visitation.

INHERITANCE RIGHTS. Under the common law, a child born out of wedlock (an illegitimate child) had no right to inherit. Today, inheritance laws governing illegitimate children vary from state to state. Generally, an illegitimate child is treated as the child of the mother and can inherit from her and her relatives. The child is usually not regarded as the legal child of the father unless paternity is established through some legal proceeding.

Many state statutes permit the illegitimate child to inherit from the father if paternity has been established prior to the father's death. Even if paternity has been established, however, the illegitimate child will not necessarily have inheritance rights identical to those of legitimate children. Generally, the courts have upheld state probate statutes that discriminate between legitimate and illegitimate children for valid state purposes.

Adoption

In contrast to children born out of wedlock, adopted children normally have the same legal rights as the biological children of a married couple, including the right to inherit property from their adoptive parents on the parents' deaths. **Adoption** is a procedure in which persons become the legal parents of a child who is not their biological child. Once an adoption is formally completed, the adoptive parents have all the responsibilities of biological parents. Should they divorce, each adoptive parent has all the child-support obligations of a biological parent. Note that adoption is not the same as **foster care**, which is a temporary arrangement in which a family is paid by the state to care for a child for a limited period of time, often pending adoption.

adoption

A procedure in which persons become the legal parents of a child who is not their biological child.

foster care

A temporary arrangement in which a family is paid by the state to care for a child for a limited period of time, often pending adoption.

Requirements for Adoptions

Adoptions are governed by state laws, and these laws vary substantially from state to state. Generally, however, there are three minimum requirements for an adoption to be legal. First, the child's biological parents must give up their legal rights (either by consent, by death, or by order of the court). The adopting parents must then follow all procedures required by the state in which the adoption occurs. Finally, the adoption must be formally approved by a judge. There may be additional requirements in specific circumstances. For example, adopting a child above a certain age generally requires the child's official consent.

All states permit single persons to adopt children, but married couples are generally preferred. Although some courts have approved adoptions by same-sex couples, generally such couples find it legally difficult to adopt children. Several states have enacted laws that explicitly prohibit same-sex couples from adopting children.

Agency Adoptions

Adoption is often carried out through social-service agencies that are licensed by the state to place children for adoption. The biological parents terminate their parental rights, essentially giving up these rights to the agency and authorizing the agency to find legal parents for their child. Traditionally, in agency adoptions, the identities of the biological and the adoptive parents were kept confidential. Increasingly, though, state laws are allowing for the disclosure of this information in certain circumstances. In some states, for instance, if an adopted child wants to meet with his or her birth parent or vice versa, the court will contact the child or parent to see if he or she will agree to such a meeting.

Independent Adoptions

Prospective adoptive parents may also pursue independent adoption. An **independent adoption** is one that is arranged privately, as when a physician, lawyer, or other person puts a couple seeking to adopt a child in contact with a pregnant woman who has decided to give up her child for adoption. These parties make their own private arrangements. Usually, the adopting parents pay for the legal and medical expenses associated with the childbirth and adoption. The intermediary may also receive a fee. Because this method of adoption has the potential for abuse, it is prohibited by most states.

Stepparent Adoptions

Many adoptions today are stepparent adoptions, which occur when a married partner adopts his or her spouse's children from a former marriage. Usually, in such adoptions, the parental rights of the children's other biological parent are terminated either by consent or through a court proceeding.

Surrogacy

Couples having difficulty conceiving a child sometimes use a surrogate mother. That is a woman who carries an embryo implanted into her womb and has contracted to give the child to someone else after its birth. The child is then adopted by the people who hired the surrogate. Surrogacy contracts are heavily regulated by the states and requirements vary considerably.

Court Approval and Probation

All adoptions must be approved in court. The primary standard for approving an adoption is the "best interests of the child." Because this standard is so vague, the courts have a great deal of leeway in deciding whether to place children with prospective adoptive parents. The court considers the financial resources of the adopting parents, their family stability and home environment, their ages, their religious and racial compatibility, and other factors relevant to the child's future health and welfare.

After the adoption, many states place the new parents on "probation" for a time—usually from six months to one year. The agency or court appoints an individual to monitor developments in the home to ensure that the adoptive parents are caring appropriately for the child's well-being. If not, the child may be removed and returned to an agency for placement in another home.

ON THE web

Information on adoption laws and links to state statutes can be found at **www.law.cornell.edu**. In the "Search Box" enter "Adoption." A discussion of international adoption can be found at **adoption.state.gov**.

---

independent adoption
A privately arranged adoption, as when a doctor, lawyer, or other person puts a couple seeking to adopt a child in contact with a pregnant woman who has decided to give up her child for adoption.

Marriage Termination

A marriage can only be terminated by the state. In other words, even though partners want to end their marriage, and even though they separate and live apart, they will continue to have the legal rights and obligations of spouses until their marriage is legally terminated. Paralegals involved in family law practice have an important role to play in gathering accurate information on a divorcing client's finances. The other spouse may be affecting your client by disposing of joint assets or by continuing to incur debt for which your client may be liable in part. There are two ways in which a marriage can be terminated: by annulment or by divorce.

Annulment

annulment

A court decree that invalidates (nullifies) a marriage. Although the marriage itself is deemed nonexistent, children of a marriage that is annulled are deemed legitimate.

An **annulment** is a court decree that invalidates (nullifies) a marriage. This means that the marriage never took legal effect in the first place. Today, annulments are not common. Many seeking annulments do so because their religion does not condone divorce. In such situations, an annulment allows a subsequent marriage to be recognized as valid in the eyes of the church.

An annulment may be granted on various grounds. For example, lack of genuine consent, fraud, and bigamy may be grounds for annulment. **Bigamy** is the act of marrying one person while already legally married to another.

bigamy

The act of entering into marriage with one person while still legally married to another.

Even though a marriage is deemed invalid through annulment, children born during the marriage are considered legitimate in the eyes of the law. Also, as in a divorce, when a marriage is annulled, issues involving child support, spousal support, child custody, and property settlement must be decided by the couple or by the court.

Divorce

divorce

A formal court proceeding that legally dissolves a marriage.

The most common way to end a marriage is divorce. A **divorce** is a formal court proceeding that legally dissolves a marriage. Divorce laws vary among the states, with some states having simpler divorce procedures than others.

FAULT-BASED VERSUS NO-FAULT DIVORCES.   Until the 1960s, to obtain a divorce, a petitioning party had to allege reasons for the divorce. Adultery, desertion, cruelty, or abuse were among the acceptable grounds for divorce under state law. This is called *fault-based divorce*. Unless the petitioning party could prove that his or her partner was "at fault" for the breakdown of the marriage in one of these ways, a divorce would not be granted. Eventually, changing economic and social conditions in America led to new attitudes toward divorce, which resulted in less stringent requirements for divorce. Thus arose the **no-fault divorce**—a divorce in which neither party is deemed to be at fault for the breakdown of the marriage.

no-fault divorce

A divorce in which neither party is deemed to be at fault for the breakdown of the marriage.

Today, all states allow no-fault divorces. Generally, a no-fault divorce may be based on one of three grounds:

- Irreconcilable differences (the most common ground).
- Living separately for a period of time specified by state statute (ranging from six months to three years).
- Incompatibility.

No-fault divorces effectively make it impossible for one spouse to prevent a divorce desired by the other. Even in no-fault divorces, however, fault may be taken into consideration by the court in determining a couple's property settlement or spousal support arrangements.

The majority of the states permit *both* fault-based and no-fault divorces. Sometimes, a party may seek a fault-based divorce in an attempt to gain a more favorable property settlement (to be discussed shortly) than he or she could get in a no-fault divorce.

petition for divorce

The document filed with the court to initiate divorce proceedings. The requirements governing the form and content of a divorce petition vary from state to state.

DIVORCE PROCEDURES.   The first step in obtaining a divorce is to file a **petition for divorce** with the appropriate state court. Although the form and content of the petition vary, generally the petition includes:

- The names and addresses of both spouses.

- The date and place of their marriage.

- The names and addresses of any minor children and whether the wife is currently pregnant.

- The reasons for the divorce.

- A summary of any arrangements made by the divorcing couple as to support, custody, or visitation.

- The relief sought.

The petition is served on the other spouse, who must file an answer to the petition within the number of days specified by state law. If the couple cannot agree on certain matters while the divorce is pending—such as who obtains custody of the children or who pays the mortgage—the court will hold a hearing to decide which partner should assume what responsibilities temporarily. Unless the case is settled through mediation or negotiation, a trial will be conducted, and the judge will decide the terms of the parties' final divorce decree. Working on divorce matters is, of course, sensitive, as the *In the Office* feature below discusses.

Religious couples may also seek a divorce or annulment from religious authorities in addition to a legal divorce. Because such proceedings insisted upon by one party can affect the other, civil law practitioners need to be alert to possible issues that can complicate matters.

NEGOTIATION AND MEDIATION.   Few divorces actually go to trial. Usually, the parties settle their differences prior to trial—though often only after lengthy negotiations, which are facilitated by their attorneys. If the parties agree to a settlement concerning contested issues, the agreement will be put in writing and presented to the court for its approval.

Divorcing spouses increasingly use mediation to settle disagreements, and in many states, mediation is mandatory in divorce cases. The mediator typically meets with the parties in the absence of lawyers and tries to guide the parties into agreeing on a mutually satisfactory settlement. As we noted in Chapter 6, some paralegals are trained mediators and conduct mediation proceedings.

social MEDIA TODAY

Learn and follow the rules about using your title and organization name in your profile, as an identifier on content, or elsewhere online.

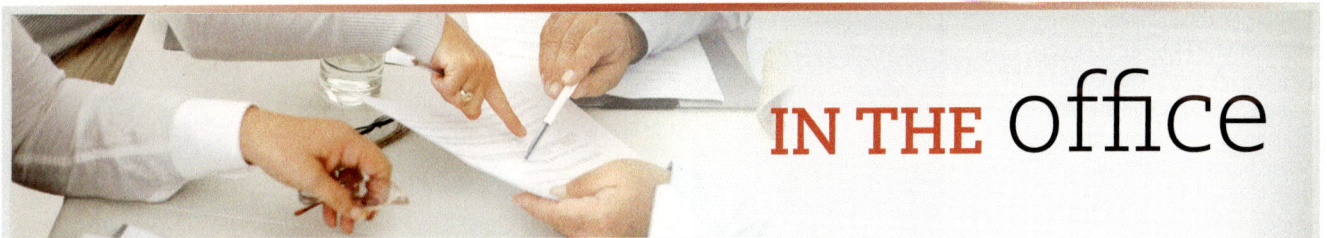

IN THE office

PROTECTING CLIENT INFORMATION AND CLIENT INTERESTS

Paralegals who specialize in divorce law normally have frequent contact with divorcing clients. If you are a specialist in this area, you will probably come to know some of your clients quite well. You will also learn all kinds of personal information from them—about their lives, their spouses, and other things. What do you do with this information? Do you make a note of everything that a client tells you? Do you only record what you think is relevant to the case? How do you decide what is or is not relevant?

Many paralegals have solved this problem by taking thorough notes during interviews and writing notes after casual conversations with clients. Some paralegals even digitally record interviews. What seems irrelevant now may, in light of later developments, be an important fact. If you keep good notes on a case and review the notes as the case progresses, you can help to ensure that your supervising attorney will know the desires of the client.

Child Custody

In many divorces, the issue of child custody—the right to live with and to care for the children on an everyday basis—is the most contentious issue to be resolved. In some cases, a court may appoint a guardian *ad litem* for the child. A **guardian *ad litem*** is a person appointed by the court (often an attorney) to represent the interests of a child or a mentally incompetent person before the court.

guardian *ad litem*

A person appointed by the court to represent the interests of a child or a mentally incompetent person before the court.

Factors Considered in Determining Child Custody

Traditionally, the mother almost always received child custody. Mothers still usually receive primary custody, but courts now explicitly consider a number of factors when awarding custody. These factors include the following:

- The nature of the relationship and emotional ties with each parent.
- The ability of each parent to provide for the child's needs and education, and each parent's interest in doing so.
- The ability of each parent to provide a stable environment for the child.
- The mental and physical health of each parent.
- The wishes of the child—especially older children.

In determining custody, courts may also consider other relevant factors, such as whether one parent is a smoker. Custodial arrangements are not permanent and may be changed by a court in view of the parents' changing circumstances.

ON THE web

Some attorneys and paralegals provide *pro bono* assistance in child-custody cases by acting as guardians *ad litem*. For an example of the program in Florida, see **www.guardianadlitem.org**

Types of Custodial Arrangements

The parent who has **legal custody** of a child has the right to make major decisions about the child's life without consulting the other parent. Often, the parent who has legal custody also has physical custody.

Many states now provide for **joint custody**—shared custody—of the children of divorcing parents. Joint *legal* custody means that both parents together make major decisions about the child. Some procedures, such as mediation, are usually available in the event of disagreement. In some states, including California, mediation is mandatory in child-custody disputes. Joint legal custody may also involve joint *physical* custody, in which both parents maintain a home for the child and have

legal custody

Custody of a child that confers on the parent the right to make major decisions about the child's life without consulting the other parent.

joint custody

Custody of a child that is shared by the parents following the termination of a marriage.

A divorcing couple meets with a mediator in an attempt to resolve their dispute over child-custody arrangements. Couples are often required to mediate their disputes before being allowed to litigate them in court. What are the benefits of such mediation?

Courtesy of © image 100 ltd.

physical custody of the child for roughly comparable time periods. Joint physical custody usually works best if both parents live in the same school district or if the child attends a private school to which both parents have access.

Divorced parents may take turns living in a home where the child resides, moving out when it is the other parent's turn to have physical custody. Courts are looking at creative arrangements such as this to provide the child with the best environment. Paralegals involved with family law will need expertise ranging from social work and psychology to property law and tax law to assist in such cases.

Grandparents can petition the court to obtain custody of their grandchildren as well. In some situations, such as when a parent is disabled or when parents are not taking proper care of their children, a court may decide that grandparents should be granted custody.

Visitation Rights

Typically, the noncustodial parent receives **visitation rights**—the right to have contact with the child. The parent may get to spend weekends, holidays, or other time periods with the child. The times and duration of the noncustodial parent's visits are often stated in the divorce settlement, and state statutes may set standards. In some situations, the court may order supervised visitation to ensure the child's safety. This means that the noncustodial parent's visits will take place in the presence of a third party. Only in extreme situations—such as when child abuse is involved—will a court completely deny visitation rights to the noncustodial parent.

In most states, courts can grant visitation rights to grandparents, although these laws vary from state to state. Many such laws require the visitation to be in the best interest of the child, and many require the grandparent to have an established relationship with the child. If the state's requirements are met, a court may set a schedule specifying the time that grandchildren are to spend with their grandparents.

visitation rights
The right of a noncustodial parent to have contact with his or her child. Grandparents and stepparents may also be given visitation rights.

Child Support

Regardless of the custody arrangements, a court must make some provision for **child support**—the financial support necessary to provide for the child's needs. States now have official, standardized guidelines determining child-support duties. These guidelines are often percentage formulas based on parental income. Judges must follow the guidelines, unless special circumstances justify a departure or the parents agree to a different arrangement. A child with a disability, for example, may require more support than provided for under the guidelines.

Child-support orders may be revised and adjusted according to the changing needs of the child and incomes of the parents. In cases where a parent evades responsibility, many of the skills necessary to collect judgments or locate assets, as discussed in Chapter 12, are useful.

child support
The financial support necessary to provide for a child's needs. Commonly, when a marriage is terminated, the noncustodial spouse agrees or is required by the court to make child-support payments to the custodial spouse.

Withholding Payment

It is a common misconception that if one former spouse fails to meet his or her obligations under a divorce settlement or other court order (such as by withholding visitation rights), the other party can withhold payment of child support. Child support is a court order—it cannot be withheld because a former spouse does something that the other former spouse does not like. Similarly, a parent cannot withhold visitation rights because the other parent did not pay support. An obligation to the child and to the state is involved, not an obligation to the other parent.

Interstate Enforcement of Child Support Decrees

We discussed uniform laws in Chapter 5. One such law, the Uniform Interstate Family Support Act, has been adopted by every state to help deal with the problem of nonpayment of child support by a parent who has moved to another state. Every state agrees to respect and enforce child-support orders entered by the court of the child's home state. Only the law of the state in which the child and the parent have been living will govern issues regarding child support, so a parent cannot escape that obligation by moving to a state with more lenient rules. The act also allows the parent who is supposed to receive the child-support payments to obligate the employer of the other parent to withhold payments from the other parent's paycheck for the benefit of the child.

Spousal Support

alimony

Financial support paid to a former spouse after a marriage has been terminated. The alimony may be permanent or temporary (rehabilitative).

In some situations, a divorce decree may also require that one spouse provide for the other spouse's support. **Alimony** (sometimes called *maintenance*) is financial support paid to a former spouse. Historically, the husband was the wage earner and was expected to pay alimony to his former wife so that she could maintain her standard of living. Today, the law governing alimony has changed significantly, largely because so many couples are both income earners.

Alimony may be permanent or temporary. If a court orders one spouse to pay *permanent alimony* to the other, the alimony must be paid until the former spouse receiving the alimony remarries or dies (unless the court modifies the order for some reason). A more common form of alimony is temporary. This *rehabilitative alimony* is designed to provide ex-spouses with the education, training, or job experience necessary to support themselves. In deciding whether rehabilitative alimony is appropriate, a court usually considers the recipient's prospects of developing a new career.

◆ **EXAMPLE 17.2—** Rather than seek more education, Janeen worked long, hard hours to help put her husband, Nguyen, through medical school. Soon after finishing school, he filed for divorce. Janeen may be entitled to the resources necessary to help her develop her own skills through more education. ◆ If the recipient is relatively advanced in age, the court may grant permanent rather than rehabilitative alimony.

The amount of alimony awarded usually depends on the specific circumstances of the parties—their age, education, and incomes, for example. In about half the states, courts may also consider the reason for the divorce. If one party was more responsible than the other for the breakdown of the marriage, the alimony paid by that spouse might be higher than it would otherwise have been. Courts will also consider whether one spouse supported the other through college or graduate school in determining alimony awards.

In some states, even if two people who have been living together never married, one of the partners may be awarded support payments, sometimes called *palimony*, after the couple breaks up.

Property Division

property settlement

The division of property between spouses on the termination of a marriage.

When a marriage is terminated, the property owned by the couple (including their debts) must be divided. **Property settlement**—the division of property on divorce—is often a main area of disagreement. Although most divorcing couples eventually settle their financial disputes, the settlement reached is colored by the requirements of state law. As the *Developing Paralegal Skills* feature on the facing page indicates, there is often significant detail work in property-settlement cases.

Marital Property

marital property

All property acquired during the course of a marriage, apart from inheritances and gifts made to one or the other of the spouses.

The way in which any court divides a couple's property depends largely on whether the property is considered marital property or separate property. **Marital property** is all property acquired during the course of a marriage (apart from inheritances and gifts received by one of the spouses). **Separate property** is property that a spouse owned before the marriage, plus inheritances and gifts acquired during the marriage. This property belongs to the spouse personally and not to the marital unit. On dissolution of the marriage, separate property is not divided but is retained by the owner.

separate property

Property that a spouse owned before the marriage, plus inheritances and gifts acquired by the spouse during the marriage.

The ownership right in separate property may be lost, however, if it is combined with marital property. ◆ **EXAMPLE 17.3—** Hannah Olin owns a lot in Bangor, Maine. Hannah marries Mustafa Shamir, and they build a house together after their marriage.

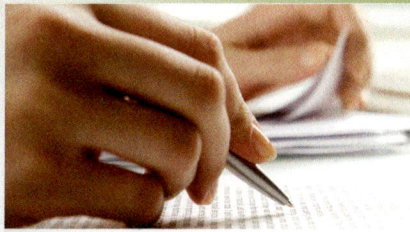

DEVELOPING
paralegal skills

PREPARING FOR PROPERTY-SETTLEMENT NEGOTIATIONS

Lea, a paralegal, works for a small law firm that specializes in family law matters. One of the firm's clients, Mrs. Clark, is seeking a divorce. Tomorrow, her husband and his attorney will meet with Mrs. Clark and Lea's supervising attorney to negotiate a property settlement. Lea is preparing a settlement-agreement checklist for the attorney to take to the settlement meeting.

Lea makes a list of all of the property owned by the Clarks, along with the value of each item and outstanding liens (legal claims—to satisfy debts, for example) on the property. She also leaves blanks after "H" for husband and "W" for wife. After the parties agree to how they will divide the property, the attorney can fill in the appropriate amounts. Lea also includes a list of the debts owed by the Clarks. Again, she leaves blanks so that the attorney can write in how much of each debt will be paid by each spouse.

Property	Value	Amount Owed	Disposition	
Home	$500,000	$200,000	H ___	W ___
Cottage	$193,000	$50,000	H ___	W ___
BMW	$52,000	$27,500	H ___	W ___
Savings Account	$9,500	___	H ___	W ___
Retirement (H)	$2,000,000	___	H ___	W ___
IRA (H)	$800,000	___	H ___	W ___
Life Insurance (H)	$1,000,000	___	H ___	W ___

Debts	Amount	Disposition	
Visa	$7,300	H ___	W ___
MasterCard	$2,500	H ___	W ___
Current Taxes (Due)	$9,456	H ___	W ___
Next Year's Taxes (Estimated)	$13,180	H ___	W ___

Lea goes over the checklist carefully to make sure that all of the Clarks' property and debts are included and that the amounts are accurate. Once she is satisfied that the checklist is accurate and complete, she takes it to her supervising attorney for review.

By building the house on the lot (thus creating marital property), Hannah has lost her separate property rights in the land. ◆ Merely renovating separately held property (sprucing up a vacation home, for instance) may transform the separate property into joint property. Placing separate property (money) into a jointly held bank account may also transform the money into joint property.

Pension Benefits

Dividing pension benefits can be particularly complicated. Suppose one spouse served for twenty years in the military. He or she is entitled to future personal benefits which must be taken into account in a property division, even though no benefits are being collected at the present time.

It is also important to determine if action may be needed immediately to protect a client's interests. ◆ **EXAMPLE 17.4—** Suppose Maria tells you that she and her husband, Julio, who are divorcing, own some property as joint tenants (see Chapter 16). If Maria were to die before the divorce was final, Julio would get title to the property. Action to sever the joint tenancy immediately would be necessary. ◆

Community Property

As discussed in Chapter 16, in some states, mostly in the West, husbands and wives hold property as community property. In those states, **community property** is all property acquired during the marriage (not including inheritances or gifts received by either party during the marriage). Even if only one party supplied all of the income and assets during the marriage, both spouses share equally (half and half) in the ownership of that property. Property owned by either partner before the marriage—and inheritances or gifts that partner received during the marriage—remain the property of that individual, or separate property, however.

There are complex accounting issues when community and separate property are commingled, such as when one spouse deposits money she or he inherited into a joint bank account. Particularly tricky issues arise when couples move from a community property state to a common law property state, or vice versa. Paralegals need to be alert as to where a couple has lived so they can check for such potential complications.

Common Law Marital Property

Common law property states provide for the *equitable distribution* (fair distribution) of property to the divorcing spouses—that is, the marital property is divided according to the equities of the case (not necessarily split evenly). In some of these states, only the marital property is subject to distribution. In other states, all of the property owned by the couple, including separate property, may be factored into the property distribution. While in most settlements, separate property remains with the owner, the courts exercise substantial discretion in deciding which person should receive what property. In deciding how to divide property between divorcing spouses, the courts consider a number of factors, including the following:

- The duration of the marriage.
- The health of the parties.
- The individuals' occupations and vocational skills.
- The individuals' relative wealth and income.
- The standard of living during the marriage.
- The relative contributions to the marriage (both financial and homemaker contributions).
- The needs and concerns of any children.
- Tax and inheritance considerations.

A typical property controversy in divorce cases concerns rights to the marital residence. If there are minor children, the house is usually given to the parent with custody of the children. It may be difficult to balance the grant of the house with other property (many families have few substantial assets other than their homes). Once the children are grown, the court may order the house to be sold and the proceeds divided to ensure that the property distribution is equitable.

Prenuptial Agreements

Increasingly, couples are using prenuptial agreements to avoid problems over property division that may arise in the future. A **prenuptial agreement** (also known as an *antenuptial agreement*) is a contract between the parties that is entered into before marriage and that provides for the disposition of property in the event of a divorce or the death of one of the spouses. Prenuptial agreements must be in writing to be enforceable. They are more likely to be enforceable if consideration was given.

Most states uphold prenuptial agreements, even if the agreements eliminate financial support in the event of divorce. About half of the states have adopted the Uniform Premarital Agreement Act. This act helps to standardize the legal framework governing prenuptial agreements around the country, so there is less

community property
In certain states, all property acquired during a marriage, except for inheritances or gifts received during the marriage by either marital partner. Each spouse has a one-half ownership interest in community property.

prenuptial agreement
A contract formed between two persons who are contemplating marriage to provide for the disposition of property in the event of a divorce or the death of one of the spouses after they have married.

confusion when parties are from different states. Courts do look closely at prenuptial agreements for evidence of unfairness. Courts may find a prenuptial agreement unfair if the parties did not retain independent counsel prior to signing the agreement. To enforce a prenuptial agreement, a party must also show that the agreement was made voluntarily and without threats or unfair pressure.

Family Law and the Paralegal

As this overview of family law indicates, the opportunities for paralegals in the area of family law are extensive. Many paralegals work for law practices that specialize in legal work related to divorces, such as child-custody arrangements and property settlements. However, divorce is just one specialty within the broad area of family law. Paralegals often work in other areas of family law:

- adoptions
- state welfare departments
- publicly sponsored legal aid foundations, or
- groups that assist persons of low income with family-related legal problems.

Because the area of family law involves many special legal areas, paralegals working in family law perform many different types of work. Here are some examples of the kinds of tasks you might perform if you work in this specialty:

- Interview a client who is seeking a divorce to obtain information about the married couple, their property and debts, the reasons for the marriage breakdown, and their children, if any.
- Draft a petition for divorce and file divorce-related documents with the court.
- Assist in pretrial divorce proceedings, negotiations, and mediation.
- Assist in preparing a divorcing client for trial and in other trial-preparation matters.
- Draft a settlement agreement or prenuptial agreement.
- Assist in making arrangements for a private adoption.
- Research state laws governing marriage requirements, divorce procedures, child-custody arrangements, property settlements, and other matters.
- Help battered spouses obtain protection from their abusing spouses.
- Assist in preparing tax documents for a client getting a divorce.
- Help victims of child abuse obtain assistance.

<aside>
social
MEDIA TODAY

Use private tools such as Yammer that limit material to those invited into a group instead of public tools like Twitter for work-related communication.
</aside>

Wills, Trusts, and Estates

As mentioned in the chapter introduction, a person's real and personal property will be transferred to others when the person dies. People usually undertake *estate planning* to control how their property will be transferred. *Wills* and *trusts* are two basic devices used in the estate-planning process. We look at these devices, as well as others, in this section. We also discuss the process of *estate administration*, which involves collecting and transferring a decedent's (deceased person's) property.

Wills

As we noted in Chapter 2, a *will* is the final declaration of how a person wishes to have his or her property disposed of after death. The maker of a will is also called a **testator** (from the Latin *testari*, "to make a will"). A will is referred to as a *testamentary disposition* of property, and one who dies after having made a valid will is said to

testator
One who makes a valid will.

testate
The condition of having died with a valid will.

intestate
The state of having died without a valid will.

intestacy laws
State statutes that specify how property will be distributed when a person dies intestate.

executor
A person appointed by a testator to serve as a personal representative on the testator's death.

administrator
A person appointed by a court to serve as a personal representative for a person who died intestate, who made a will but failed to name an executor, or whose executor cannot serve.

have died **testate**. If no valid will has been executed, a decedent is said to have died **intestate**. When a person dies intestate, state **intestacy laws** govern the distribution of the property among heirs or next of kin.

A will can serve other purposes besides the distribution of property. The will can appoint a guardian for minor children or incapacitated adults. It can also appoint a *personal representative* to settle the affairs of the deceased. An **executor** is a personal representative named in a will. An **administrator** is a personal representative appointed by the court for a decedent who died without a will, who made a will but failed to name an executor for the estate, or whose executor is unable to serve.

When a person dies intestate, the value of having paid a lawyer to prepare a will becomes clear. Because there is no will, the court appoints the administrator, who may not be the person the deceased individual would have chosen. The property is divided according to a schedule created by state law, usually giving it to close relatives or, if none can be found, to the state. The process is usually more costly than had a will existed, and the property of the estate may not be distributed the way the decedent would have preferred. Over half of all people die without a will, leaving an additional burden on their families.

Paralegals often play major roles in preparing wills and must be cautious to follow ethical guidelines, as noted in the *Ethics Watch* feature below.

ETHICS WATCH

WILLS AND PARALEGAL SUPERVISION

Wills must accurately reflect the testator's wishes, so special care must be exercised in preparing a client's will. After all, unless the will is modified or revoked, it is indeed the "final word" on how the testator intends his or her property to be distributed. You will rest easier if you make sure that your supervising attorney reviews carefully any will that you draft, any subsequent modifications that are made, and particularly the document in its final form. Attorneys have a duty to supervise paralegals' work. In regard to wills, you should remind your supervising attorney of this duty, if necessary.

Proper supervision by an attorney is required by the NALA Code of Ethics, Canon 2: "A paralegal may perform any task which is properly delegated and supervised by an attorney, as long as the attorney is ultimately responsible to the client, maintains a direct relationship with the client, and assumes professional responsibility for the work product."

Supervision is also required by the ABA Model Guidelines for the Utilization of Paralegal Services. According to the ABA, attorneys responsible for a work product may assign certain tasks to paralegals that the attorneys would normally perform. However, attorneys may not delegate work that must be performed by lawyers. That would include tasks specifically required by be performed by attorneys by a statute or a court rule or by rules of professional conduct or as mandated by any other legal authority.

Laws Governing Wills

The laws governing wills come into play when a will is probated. To **probate** (prove) a will means to establish its validity and carry the administration of the estate through a process supervised by a *probate court*. When drafting wills for clients, attorneys and paralegals must make sure that the wills meet the specific requirements imposed by state statute.

Probate laws vary from state to state. In 1969, however, the American Bar Association and the National Conference of Commissioners on Uniform State Laws approved the Uniform Probate Code (UPC). The UPC, which has since been significantly revised, codifies general principles and procedures for the resolution of conflicts in settling estates and relaxes some of the requirements for a valid will contained in earlier state laws. About one-third of the states have adopted the UPC. Other states have incorporated some part of the UPC into their own probate codes.

Probate laws vary widely among states, and paralegals should always check the particular laws of the state involved. If your clients own property in several states or in foreign countries, you will need to research the other states' or countries' laws as well when assisting with an estate plan or the administration of an estate.

Requirements for a Valid Will

A will must comply with state statutory requirements and formalities. If it does not, it will be declared void, and the decedent's property will be distributed according to state intestacy laws. Generally, most states uphold the following basic requirements for executing a will:

- *The testator must have testamentary capacity.* In other words, the testator must be of legal age (usually eighteen) and sound mind at the time the will is made.

- *Generally, a will must be in writing.* A will can be handwritten (called a *holographic will*). In a few states, *nuncupative* wills (oral "deathbed" wills made before witnesses) that dispose of personal property are permitted.

- *A will must be signed by the testator.* That is generally at the end of the document.

- *A will must be witnessed.* The number of witnesses (often two, sometimes three), their qualifications, and the manner in which the witnessing must be done are generally determined by state law. Law firm employees are often called on to witness wills. Generally, you should not witness a will you helped to prepare.

- *In some states, a will must be published.* A will is "published" by an oral declaration by the maker to the witnesses that the document they are about to sign is the maker's "last will and testament."

Paralegals can often help in ensuring that wills comply with relevant requirements, as illustrated in the *Developing Paralegal Skills* feature on the following page.

The Probate Process

Probate procedures may vary depending on the size of the decedent's estate. For smaller estates, most state statutes provide for the distribution of assets without formal probate proceedings. Faster and less expensive methods are then used. The intent to transfer property to an heir may be established by *affidavit*, which is a statement of facts written down and sworn to voluntarily in the presence of an official authorized to affirm it. In addition, some state statutes provide that title to cars, savings and checking accounts, and certain other property can be passed to heirs merely by filling out forms. Property held as joint tenants or tenants by the entirety (see Chapter 16) does not go through probate but passes automatically to the other tenants or tenant.

FAMILY SETTLEMENT AGREEMENTS. A majority of states also provide for *family settlement agreements,* which are private agreements among the beneficiaries. Once a

---

probate
To prove and validate a will; the process of proving and validating a will and settling matters pertaining to the administration of a decedent's estate, guardianship of a decedent's children, and similar matters.

DEVELOPING
paralegal skills

DRAFTING A CLIENT'S WILL

Mr. Perkins has come to the law firm of Smith & Hardy to have his will prepared. He has previously met with attorney Jennifer Hardy, who has been assisting him in estate planning. Today, Perkins meets with Hardy's paralegal, James Reese, who will review the information needed to prepare the will.

After the meeting, James returns to his office and begins drafting Perkins's will. Later in the week, after going over the will with Hardy, James will meet with Perkins again so that Perkins can review and sign the will.

CHECKLIST FOR DRAFTING A WILL

- Start with a computerized standard will form.
- Review each provision, or clause, in the standard form.
- Input the client's name, address, and other information.
- Modify the clauses as necessary to fit the client's needs.
- Specifically describe the assets the client wishes to leave to specific heirs.
- Number each page and clause of the will.
- Print out the document and carefully proofread it.
- Make any necessary corrections and print out the final copy to be reviewed by your supervising attorney.

GOING green

STAY HOME

Telecommuting is increasingly popular. It saves gas (and vehicle emissions) and the time otherwise spent getting to and from the office. It may be reasonable for paralegals who normally work in an office to work at home sometimes—for example, when doing research on cases. As the number of independent paralegals rises, so do the chances of working from a home office—and some employers prefer to keep down the office space they must provide for staff.

trust
An arrangement in which property is transferred by one person (the grantor, or settlor) to another (the trustee) for the benefit of a third party (the beneficiary).

will is admitted to probate, the family members can agree to settle among themselves the distribution of the decedent's assets. Although a family settlement agreement speeds the settlement process, a court order is still needed to protect the estate from future creditors and to clear title to the assets involved. The use of these and other types of summary procedures in estate administration can save time and money.

FORMAL PROBATE LIKELY.   For larger estates, formal probate proceedings are normally undertaken, and the probate court supervises the settlement of the decedent's estate. Additionally, in some situations—such as when a guardian for minor children or for an incompetent person must be appointed and a trust has been created to protect the minor or the incompetent person—more formal probate procedures cannot be avoided. Formal probate proceedings may take several months to complete. As a result, a sizable portion of the decedent's assets (up to perhaps 10 percent) may go toward payment of fees charged by attorneys and personal representatives, as well as court costs.

Trusts

Trusts are important estate-planning devices that are being increasingly utilized to avoid the costs associated with probating a will. A **trust** involves any arrangement by which legal title to property is transferred from one person (called the *settlor* or *grantor*) to be administered by another (the trustee) for the benefit of still another party (the *beneficiary*).   ◆ **EXAMPLE 17.5—**   If Mendel conveys (transfers) his farm to Western Bank to be held for the benefit of his daughters, Mendel has created a trust. Mendel is the *settlor* or *grantor*. Western Bank is the *trustee*. Mendel's daughters are the *beneficiaries* (Exhibit 17.2 on the facing page illustrates this trust arrangement).   ◆

There are numerous kinds of trusts, each with its own special characteristics. Increasingly, trusts are being used for family businesses to handle issues relating to ownership and control. Trusts are also used for planning purposes to protect assets from creditors and to avoid forced heirship laws requiring a person to leave a portion of his or her estate to relatives specified by statute. Remembering that the use of trusts is flexible, we now look at some of the most common types of trusts.

EXHIBIT 17.2

A Trust Arrangement

In a trust, there is a separation of interests in the trust property. The trustee takes *legal* title, which appears to be complete ownership and possession but does not include the right to receive any benefits from the property. The beneficiary takes *equitable* title, which is the right to receive all benefits from the property.

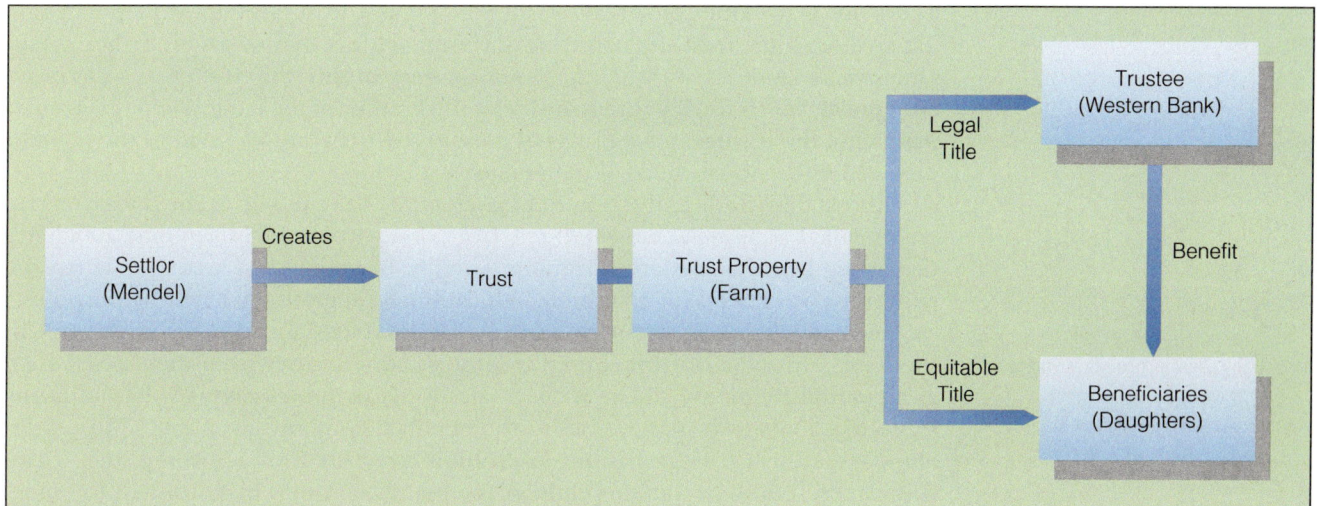

© Cengage Learning 2014

Living Trusts

A living trust—or *inter vivos* **trust** (*inter vivos* is Latin for "between or among the living")—is a trust executed by a grantor during his or her lifetime. A living trust may be a good estate-planning option because living trusts are not included in the property of a probated estate.

REVOCABLE OR IRREVOCABLE. Living trusts can be irrevocable or revocable. The distinction between these two types of living trusts is an important one for estate planners. In an *irrevocable* living trust, the grantor permanently gives up control over the property. In a *revocable* living trust, in contrast, the grantor retains control over the trust property during his or her lifetime.

TRUST ADMINISTRATION. To establish an irrevocable living trust, the grantor executes a trust deed, and legal title to the trust property passes to the named trustee. The trustee has a duty to administer the property as directed by the grantor for the benefit and in the interest of the beneficiaries. The trustee must preserve the trust property by not engaging in speculative schemes with the trust assets. The focus is on investments that are prudent and generate revenue over time. If required by the terms of the trust agreement, the trustee must pay income to the beneficiaries, all in accordance with the terms of the trust. Once an irrevocable *inter vivos* trust has been created, the grantor has, in effect, given over the property for the benefit of the beneficiaries.

To establish a revocable living trust, the grantor deeds the property to the trust but retains the power to amend, alter, or revoke the trust during his or her lifetime. The grantor may also arrange to receive income earned by the trust assets during his or her lifetime. Unless the trust is revoked, the principal of the trust is transferred to the trust beneficiary on the grantor's death.

Testamentary Trusts

A trust created by will to come into existence on the settlor's death is called a **testamentary trust**. Although a testamentary trust has a trustee who maintains legal title to the trust property, actions of the trustee are subject to judicial approval. This trustee can be named in the will or appointed by the court. Thus, a testamentary trust does not fail because a trustee has not been named in the will. The legal responsibilities of the trustee are the same as in an *inter vivos* trust.

inter vivos trust
A trust created by the grantor (settlor) and effective during the grantor's lifetime—that is, a trust not established by a will.

testamentary trust
A trust that is created by will and that does not take effect until the death of the testator.

If a will that establishes a testamentary trust is invalid, then the trust will also be invalid. The property that was supposed to be in the trust will then pass according to intestacy laws, not according to the terms of the trust.

Special Types of Trusts

There are many kinds of special trusts. So long as a trust does not violate state law, the creator of the trust can construct any arrangement that meets his or her needs. One special kind of trust is the *life insurance trust*. In this, the trust owns a life insurance policy, which usually covers the life of the grantor of the trust. When the insured party dies, the life insurance proceeds go into the trust and are used in the manner provided by the instructions of the grantor.

A trust designed for the benefit of a segment of the public or the public in general is called a *charitable trust*. It differs from other types of trusts in that the identities of the beneficiaries are uncertain. Usually, to be deemed a charitable trust, a trust must be created for charitable, educational, religious, or scientific purposes.

In a *spendthrift trust*, the beneficiary has limited right of access to money in the trust. This type of trust is used to protect beneficiaries from themselves, such as a compulsive gambler. The trustee who oversees the trust usually has authority to decide how much money goes to the beneficiary at any given time. Most states allow spendthrift trust provisions to prohibit creditors from attaching such trusts. A divorced spouse or a minor child of the beneficiary may be permitted to obtain alimony or child-support payments, however.

Other Estate-Planning Devices

Commonly, beneficiaries under a will must wait until the probate process is complete—which can take several months if formal probate proceedings are undertaken—to have access to funds or other assets received under the will. For this and other reasons, some persons arrange to have property transferred in ways other than by will and outside the probate process. (For information on finding estate-planning options online, see this chapter's *Technology and Today's Paralegal* feature on the facing page.)

One method of avoiding probate is by establishing a living trust, as has already been discussed. A person can also arrange to hold title to certain real or personal property as a joint tenant with a spouse or other person. Remember from Chapter 16 that, in a joint tenancy, when one joint tenant dies, the other joint tenant or tenants automatically inherit the deceased tenant's share of the property. (This is true even if the deceased tenant has provided otherwise in a will.)

Yet another way of transferring property outside the probate process is by making gifts to children or others while one is still living. Finally, to make sure that a spouse, child, or some other dependent is provided for, many people take out life insurance policies. On the death of the policyholder, the proceeds of the policy go directly to the beneficiary and are not involved in the probate process. Because of the cost and time involved, parties generally wish to avoid probate. The role that a paralegal might play in this process is illustrated in the *Practice Focus* feature on page 546.

Estate Administration

Estate administration is the process of collecting a decedent's assets, settling his or her debts, and distributing all remaining assets. These tasks are undertaken by the decedent's personal representative. In some states, however, a special court, usually called a probate court, oversees the administration of decedents' estates. The rights of both creditors and beneficiaries must be protected during the estate-administration proceedings.

Executor

If a will exists, it probably names a personal representative (executor) to administer the estate. If there is no will, if the will fails to name a personal representative, or if the personal representative named in the will cannot serve, then the court

---

social
MEDIA TODAY

Adapt your presentation skills to the social media era. Read resources such as **www.speakingaboutpresenting. com** to learn more about how to increase the effectiveness of your presentations with audiences likely to engage in social media commentary.

---

estate administration
The process in which a decedent's personal representative settles the affairs of the decedent's estate (collects assets, pays debts and taxes, and distributes the remaining assets to heirs); the process is usually overseen by a probate court.

TECHNOLOGY AND
today's paralegal

ONLINE HELP FOR ESTATE PLANNING

The Internet offers an abundance of estate-planning Web sites. Many of them, however, are aimed at consumers and laypersons. The trick for paralegals and attorneys who specialize in estate planning is to find sites that are useful to professionals. A number of Web sites can help estate planners perform research on tax and probate laws and stay current with legislation and developments in the field. These sites may also provide sample forms or estate plans and estate-tax calculators.

WHERE TO BEGIN

A good place to start your research is at **www.estateplanninglinks. com**. This site offers a comprehensive collection of articles and links to Web sites pertaining to estate planning, probate, trusts, charitable trusts, IRAs (individual retirement accounts), tax law, and elder law. Created and maintained by lawyers, the site is geared toward professionals. Another good starting place is Cornell University's Legal Information Institute. You can access relevant federal and state statutes and agency regulations. You can also read recent estate-planning cases decided by the United States Supreme Court, the federal circuit courts, and many state appellate courts at this site. Go to **www.law.cornell.edu** and enter "Estate Planning" in the "Search" box.

OTHER WEB SITES

Many organizations also have useful Web sites, including the American College of Trust and Estate Counsel at **www.actec.org**. The Society of Trust and Estate Practitioners (STEP) is an international organization dealing with estate planning issues that provides resource at **www.step.org**. Paralegals and attorneys can find practical information at **www.texasprobate.com**. This site has a state focus but presents articles, forms, and links that can be utilized by all.

SOFTWARE TOOLS

Information about software programs that assist estate planning (and many other areas of practice) can be found at the Market Center of FindLaw (**marketcenter.findlaw.com**). Under the "Market Center" heading, select "Legal Software" from the pull-down menu, and enter "Wills" (or other terms) in the "Search" field to browse the products offered.

TECHNOLOGY TIP

Paralegals will find many good estate-planning resources and tools on the Web. Only a few are mentioned here. Once you find the sites that are most helpful to your practice, bookmark them for later reference.

must appoint one (an administrator). The personal representative must inventory and collect the assets of the decedent and, if necessary, have them appraised to determine their value. In addition, the personal representative is responsible for managing the assets of the estate during the administration period and for preventing them from being wasted or unnecessarily depleted. ◆ **EXAMPLE 17.6—** The estate of Barney includes a farm where crops have been planted. The representative would need to arrange for the crops to be harvested and sold so as to make good use of estate assets. ◆

Duties of Personal Representative

The personal representative pays debts owed by the decedent and also arranges for the estate to pay taxes. For larger estates, a federal tax is levied on the total value of the estate after debts and expenses for administration have been deducted and after various exemptions have been allowed. The tax is on the estate itself rather than on the beneficiaries. In some states, a state inheritance tax is imposed on the recipient of a decedent's property rather than on the estate. Some states also have a state estate tax similar to the federal estate tax.

In general, inheritance tax rates are graduated according to the type of relationship between the beneficiary and the decedent. The lowest rates and largest exemptions are applied to a surviving spouse and the children of the decedent.

When the ultimate distribution of assets to the beneficiaries is determined, the personal representative is responsible for distributing the estate pursuant to

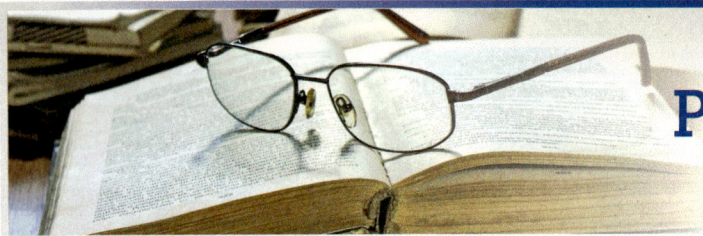

PRACTICE focus

HELPING CLIENTS WITH ESTATE PLANNING

Being an estate planning paralegal can be particularly satisfying if you enjoy helping people. Unlike litigation jobs, estate planning rarely involves adversarial work. Instead, it is a cooperative atmosphere in which the lawyer and paralegal are assisting the client in creating a plan that satisfies the requirements of tax law and state law to accomplish the client's goals.

Clients generally have three different objectives in creating an estate plan.

1. They want to ensure that they have adequately provided for their own future needs. Because end-of-life medical care can be particularly costly, elderly clients in particular worry about preserving their assets in case of an emergency. You may find yourself working with a financial advisee to address these needs.

2. Clients want to minimize their estate tax bills, providing their heirs with as much of the money they have saved and the assets they have purchased as possible. In many cases, estate planning involves sophisticated planning to minimize the tax burden, using trusts, insurance policies, and other techniques for this purpose. For clients who own small businesses or farms of even modest size, estate taxes can be substantial if proper planning is not done. You can have a satisfying experience helping pass a family business or farm from one generation to the next.

3. Clients seek to distribute their assets to provide for loved ones now rather than after the client dies. A reason for this can be so that assets are not exhausted in paying for medical expenses in old age so as to force Medicare to cover more such costs. A paralegal may be called upon to create legal documents that ensure a particular gift is used for the purpose the client wishes, such as to fund a grandchild's education or to pay for a specific charitable activity.

Using a mix of drafting skills, interviewing skills, and legal research skills, you can help people achieve peace of mind about their own financial situation as well as give them the satisfaction of knowing their heirs will be provided for.

---

the court order. Once the assets have been distributed, an accounting is rendered to the court, the estate is closed, and the personal representative is relieved of any further responsibility or liability for the estate.

Wills, Trusts, and Estates and the Paralegal

As this section of the chapter has demonstrated, paralegals are often involved in legal work relating to wills, trusts, other estate-planning devices, and estate administration. If you work for a general law practice, you may be required to assist in handling tasks relating to all of these areas at one time or another. If you specialize in estate planning and administration, you may be employed by a law firm or a probate court and work extensively with probate proceedings. Among other things, you might be responsible for coordinating the efforts of the personal representative with those of the probate court. An increasing number of paralegals specialize in trust law and find career opportunities in trust departments of banking institutions.

Here is a sampling of the tasks paralegals perform in the areas of wills, trusts, and estates:

- Interview clients to obtain information about their assets and liabilities for estate-planning purposes.

- Draft a will for a client.

- Create the necessary documents to establish a trust for a client.

- Monitor a trust fund's investments to ensure that the funds are not unnecessarily depleted.

- Locate beneficiaries named in a will or the next of kin of a person who died intestate.
- File a will with the probate court to initiate probate procedures.
- Research laws governing estate and inheritance taxes to determine how they apply to a decedent's estate.
- Research state laws governing wills and probate procedures.
- Perform asset appraisals.

KEY TERMS AND CONCEPTS

administrator   540

adoption   530

alimony   536

annulment   532

bigamy   532

child support   535

common law marriage   527

community property   538

divorce   532

emancipation   525

estate administration   544

executor   540

foster care   530

guardian *ad litem*   534

independent adoption   531

inter vivos trust   543

intestacy laws   540

intestate   540

joint custody   534

legal custody   534

marital property   536

no-fault divorce   532

paternity suit   530

petition for divorce   532

prenuptial agreement   538

probate   541

property settlement   536

restraining order   528

separate property   536

testamentary trust   543

testate   540

testator   539

trust   542

visitation rights   535

Chapter Summary

Family Law and Estates

FAMILY LAW

1. *Marriage requirements*—Marriage is a status conferred by state law that establishes the rights and duties of spouses to one another and to any children born to them.

   a. Traditionally, the couple must be a man and a woman, currently unmarried, not closely related by blood, and at least eighteen (unless they have parental consent or are emancipated).

   b. Certain procedures may be required by the state for a marriage to be legally recognized, including a marriage license, a blood test, a waiting period, and a marriage ceremony, after which the license must be recorded.

   c. In some states, the law allows marriages between two people of the same sex. Some other states allow same-sex partners to form "civil unions" or "domestic partnerships."

2. *Common law marriage*—A minority of states allow parties who hold themselves out to the world as married to be married without a ceremony or license.

3. *Marital duties*—Spouses have the duty to support the other spouse and children financially by providing basic necessities. Abusing one's spouse is illegal in all states.

4. *Parental rights and obligations*—Parents have the legal right to control the upbringing of their minor children and to punish them within reason. They also provide for the children's necessities and ensure that the children attend school (until a certain age).

a. Generally, parents are not liable for the wrongful actions of their children unless the actions result from the parents' negligence.

b. Child abuse and neglect are prohibited in all states.

c. The biological father of a child born out of wedlock is obligated to support the child once paternity is established. An illegitimate child can usually inherit from the mother but not from the father unless paternity has been established. Even when paternity has been established, an illegitimate child may not have the same inheritance rights as legitimate children.

5. *Adoption*—Adoption is a procedure by which persons become the legal parents of a child who is not their biological child. An adopted child normally has the same legal rights as the biological children of a married couple, including inheritance rights. State law governs adoption, and procedures vary. The court must approve all adoptions.

a. Agency adoptions are done through state-licensed social-service agencies.

b. Independent adoptions are arranged privately, often through lawyers or doctors.

c. Stepparent adoptions are those in which a married partner adopts his or her spouse's children from a prior marriage.

d. A child may be carried by a surrogate mother and then adopted by the parents who sponsored the surrogacy. Strict state regulations apply.

6. *Marriage termination*—A marriage can only be terminated by the state, through annulment or divorce.

a. Annulment is a court order invalidating a marriage; it is no longer common.

b. Divorce is the most common way to end a marriage. Divorce laws vary across states and may provide for fault-based or no-fault divorces. In a fault-based divorce, the petitioner must prove certain grounds for the divorce, such as adultery, cruelty, or abuse. A party may seek a fault-based divorce in the hope of gaining a more favorable property settlement. No-fault divorces are based on the grounds that the partners have irreconcilable differences, have been living separately for the length of time required by state statute, or are incompatible.

c. The first step in obtaining a divorce is to file a petition for divorce with the appropriate state court. The petition is served on the other spouse. If the parties cannot agree on certain matters (child custody, finances) in the interim, the court may hold a hearing to assign temporary responsibility for those matters. Many states require parties to attend mediation before trial.

7. *Child custody*—Which parent the child lives with is often contested in a divorce. The court sometimes appoints a guardian *ad litem* to protect the interests of the child. The court considers a number of factors when deciding custody.

a. Parents granted joint legal custody make major decisions about the child together. Parents with joint physical custody have physical custody of the child for roughly comparable time periods. Many states now provide for joint custodial arrangements.

b. Usually, one parent is awarded legal custody of the child and can make major decisions without consulting the other parent. The noncustodial parent receives visitation rights.

8. *Child support*—The noncustodial parent will likely be required to pay a certain sum monthly (often set according to guidelines) as support for the child. The court will consider the abilities of the parents to provide partial or full custody. Visitation rights are normally determined in divorce proceedings.

9. *Spousal support*—In some situations, one of the spouses is ordered to pay support (alimony) to the other. Alimony can be temporary (rehabilitative) or permanent.

10. *Property division*—

a. Marital property is property acquired during the marriage. It will be divided on divorce. Separate property is anything that a spouse owned prior to the marriage, plus inheritances and gifts received during the marriage. Separate property is usually not divided.

b. In some states, all property acquired during the marriage is considered community property, even if only one party supplied all of the income and assets during the marriage. Each spouse has a one-half ownership interest in community property.

c. Other states divide the divorcing couple's property by equitable (fair) distribution. The court decides how much of the marital property each spouse should receive given the circumstances of the parties and does not necessarily divide the property equally. In some states, only the marital property is divided; in others, separate property may also be included.

11. *Prenuptial agreements*—Agreements (contracts) made before marriage to provide for division of property in the event of divorce or death. Prenuptial agreements must be in writing. Most states enforce such agreements unless they are clearly unfair.

WILLS, TRUSTS, AND ESTATES

A will is the final declaration of how a person desires to have his or her property disposed of after death.

1. *Laws governing wills*—A person who dies without leaving a will is said to have died intestate, and the decedent's property is distributed under state intestacy statutes. A person who makes a will is called a testator. The personal representative named in a will to settle the affairs of the decedent is called an executor. If the court appoints the personal representative, she or he is called an administrator.

2. *Requirements of a valid will*—A will must comply with state statutory requirements, which usually involve the following:

   a. The testator must have testamentary capacity (be of sound mind at the time the will is made).

   b. The will generally must be in writing.

   c. The testator must sign the will.

   d. The will must be witnessed by a specified number of persons (usually two or three).

   e. In some states, the will must be published.

3. *Probate procedures*—To probate a will means to establish its validity and administer the estate through a court process. Probate laws vary from state to state.

Procedures may be formal or informal, depending on the size of the estate and other factors, such as whether a guardian for minor children must be appointed.

4. *Trusts*—A trust is an arrangement by which property is transferred from one person (the grantor, or settlor) to be administered by another (the trustee) for the benefit of a third party (the beneficiary).

   a. A living *(inter vivos)* trust is executed by the grantor during his or her lifetime and can be revocable or irrevocable.

   b. A testamentary trust is created by will and comes into existence on the grantor's death.

   c. Special types of trusts include life insurance trusts, charitable trusts, and spendthrift trusts.

5. *Other estate-planning devices*—Several other strategies may be used to transfer property. These include owning property as joint tenants, giving gifts to children or others while one is still alive, and purchasing life insurance policies.

6. *Estate administration*—The process of collecting a decedent's assets, settling debts, and distributing remaining assets by the executor or representative of the estate under probate court supervision.

QUESTIONS FOR REVIEW

1. What are the rights and duties of parents for their children? What are the legal obligations of parents to children born out of wedlock and adopted children? Can parents be held liable for their children's wrongful acts?

2. What are the requirements for marriage? Can same-sex couples marry? On the termination of a marriage, how is property divided? What is separate property? Community property?

3. List the requirements of a valid will. Why is it important to check the laws of your state for the requirements of a will? What laws govern the distribution of the estate of a person who dies without a valid will?

4. Why and how are wills probated? What are the duties of a personal representative?

5. What is a trust? Name and describe the various types of trusts discussed in this chapter. What are some other estate-planning devices?

ETHICAL QUESTIONS

1. During the course of their twenty-five-year marriage, Mr. and Mrs. Jones have had their family attorney, Mr. Shapiro, prepare their wills, handle their real estate purchases, and assist them with other legal matters. On Monday, Mrs. Jones calls Mr. Shapiro and makes an appointment. She explains that she wants to file a divorce action against Mr. Jones. On Wednesday, Mr. Jones calls Mr. Shapiro. He wants to make an appointment to discuss filing a divorce action against Mrs. Jones. May the attorney, Mr. Shapiro, represent both Mr. Jones and Mrs. Jones in the divorce action?

2. Theft crimes often are committed against clients' estates. Consider the following theft. A paralegal at a California law firm stole a $19,000 check from the

firm, made it payable to herself and her roommate, and changed the amount of the check to $285,000. She deposited the check into a bank account that was jointly held with her roommate. They chartered a jet to New York, rented rooms in a luxury hotel, and went on a shopping spree. The two were also accused of obtaining two cashier's checks in the amounts of $100,000 and $33,000 from the stolen

funds to use as a down payment on a $3.7 million house in California. They were caught when the $285,000 check was rejected by the bank that had initially issued the $19,000 check. What laws and ethics rules have been violated? What might be the outcome for the paralegal in this case? For her roommate? For her law firm?

PRACTICE QUESTIONS AND ASSIGNMENTS

1. Using the no-fault divorce material discussed in the chapter, which of the following are grounds for a no-fault divorce:

   a. Irreconcilable differences

   b. Cruelty

   c. Living separately for a period of time specified by state statute (ranging from six months to three years).

   d. Adultery

2. Identify which of the following factors will generally *not* be considered by the courts when determining child custody:

   a. The mental and physical health of each parent.

   b. The ability of each parent to provide for the child's needs and education.

   c. The ability of the parents of each spouse to support and care for the child if the spouse has a full-time job.

   d. The nature of the relationship and emotional ties between the child and each parent.

3. Identify each of the following types of trusts:

   a. Barbara inserts a trust provision in her will requiring that all of her property be held in trust for her children until they reach the age of thirty.

   b. Steve, who is seventy years old, transfers his home into a trust for the benefit of his children and their spouses.

   c. Kathy creates a trust in her will for cancer research.

4. Identify which of the following types of estate-planning devices allow property to be transferred outside the probate process:

   a. Living trusts.

   b. Life insurance.

   c. Testamentary trusts.

   d. Holding property as joint tenants with rights of survivorship.

   e. Gifts to children.

QUESTIONS FOR CRITICAL ANALYSIS

1. Prior to passage of no-fault divorce laws, to obtain a divorce, a person had to allege grounds for divorce such as adultery, desertion, cruelty, or abuse. Today, all states allow no-fault divorces. Since the 1960s, the divorce rate has continually risen. It has now reached 50 percent—one out of every two marriages ends in divorce. How do the no-fault grounds for divorce compare to the fault grounds when it comes to proving the need for a divorce? How might no-fault divorce laws have affected the divorce rate? Are there other social changes in recent times that might have contributed to the increase in the divorce rate?

2. A woman agrees that in exchange for $10,000, she will be artificially inseminated, conceive a child, carry the child to term, and after delivery of the baby, surrender it to the father and his wife. The mother will terminate her parental rights, and the father's wife

will adopt the child. If the father and his wife contracted with the surrogate mother for the baby and the surrogate mother refused to give up the baby, how might a court use existing custody laws to resolve the dispute? How might the contract be attacked as invalid?

3. Assume your client is recently divorced. His wife has raised the possibility of moving away to Connecticut to be near her family and have the children attend the same elementary school as she did. Your client calls, upset because he has just come home from a business trip and his children did not arrive for their scheduled visit. When he went to his ex-wife's house, it was clear that they had moved out. His ex-wife's cell phone account has been closed, and none of her friends or relations will return his calls. He suspects that his ex-wife has moved to Litchfield, Connecticut.

All you know are the names of the wife and children and the town. Before hiring a private investigator, what online sources would you use to locate her? The children? Would you use social media sites? Explain.

4.   Suppose that a wealthy testator has a son who suffers from a severe disability that requires costly medical monitoring and treatment. Because the son can earn no income and has no independent wealth, the state assumes the costs of his treatment. If the testator's will provides that all of his wealth and property should go to charity, can the son successfully contest the will? Can the state intervene to obtain compensation for the costs associated with the son's medical care? Why or why not?

PROJECTS

1.   Go to FindLaw, the Legal Information Institute at Cornell Law School, or other useful Web sites to locate your state's divorce laws. Answer the following questions in writing and submit them to your instructor:

   a. What are the requirements for divorce in your state?

   b. What procedural requirements are usually involved?

   c. How long must a person live in your state before a court would have jurisdiction over a family law matter such as divorce or child custody?

   d. Must a person use an attorney to file for divorce?

   e. If a person does not have the resources to pay for an attorney to help with family law matters, such as child custody, is there a state program to help?

2.   A paralegal who works in probate law may need to locate the heirs of a person who died without a will (intestate). You can go to International Genealogical Search at **www.heirsearch.com** to search for missing heirs. Go to the Web site and look at the "success stories" posted there and write a summary of the services offered.

GROUP PROJECT

This project requires the class to research the ways that the Internet is used and sometimes abused in divorce cases.

Student one will locate information on the legal status of grandparenting time.

Student two will locate information on illegally spying on a spouse. If there are relevant state laws on this topic, student two should note those laws.

Student three will locate information on Internet tools, such as Facebook, used by couples during and after a divorce to facilitate communication. Each student will write a summary of his or her findings and attach copies of his or her sources to the summary.

Student four will compile the summaries and present them to the class, either orally or on a discussion board or wiki created by the instructor for this assignment.

USING INTERNET RESOURCES

1.   To learn more about intestacy laws, access the Uniform Probate Code (UPC) at the Web site of the Legal Information Institute at **www.law.cornell.edu**. Click on Uniform Laws, then on Uniform Probate Code. Answer the following questions:

   a. How many states have adopted the UPC in its entirety?

   b. How many states have adopted it in part or with modifications? Is your state one of them?

   c. Review the typical state probate code. Make a list of the articles that the typical state probate code contains. Define the terms used in the articles. For example, Article II covers intestate succession and wills.

CourseMate   The available CourseMate for this text has an interactive eBook and interactive learning tools, including flash cards, quizzes, and more. To learn more about this resource and access free demo CourseMate resources, go to **www.cengagebrain.com**, and search for this book. To access CourseMate materials that you have purchased, go to **login.cengagebrain.com**.

Chapter 18

Business Organizations and Employment Law

Chapter Outline

Introduction

Agency Law

Employment Law

Forms of Business Organization

After completing this chapter, you will know:

- The most common forms of business organizations and how each type of business organizational form is created and operated.

- How profits, losses, risks, and liabilities are distributed in each business organizational form.

- What agency relationships are and the significance of agency law for business relationships.

- How the government regulates employer-employee relationships.

Introduction

Paralegals commonly work with people in business as well as being employees of business entities themselves. Knowledge of the various legal forms used by businesses is helpful in understanding legal issues that arise in this environment. In this chapter, we begin by reviewing how a range of business organizations are formed and some of the key features of the different legal structures. Then we turn to agency law, a part of the common law that plays a role in almost all business relationships. Agency is directly related to employment law, which we discuss in the final part of the chapter. Because litigation over the employment relationship is common, it is a subject worth investigation.

Forms of Business Organization

Traditionally, there were three basic forms of business organization: the sole proprietorship, the partnership, and the corporation. These forms continue to be used. In addition, today's business owners and professionals are turning to newer, alternative business organizational forms known as limited liability companies (LLC), limited liability partnerships (LLP), and professional corporations (PC).

Each business form involves different relationships, rights, obligations, and regulatory schemes. In your work as a paralegal, you will want to have some idea of what rights and duties accompany each of these business forms when you work on behalf of clients. ◆ **EXAMPLE 18.1—** Your firm represents a person injured in a traffic accident involving a delivery van. You will need to determine the form of the business entity that owns the van in order to file suit. The van may say "Smith Produce" on it but be owned by "Smith Bros. LLC," which is likely to be the defendant in an action. ◆

Different entities may be appropriate for different purposes. Businesses are often made up of a collection of related entities. A limited partnership may own a building, an LLC may run a business located in the building, and a corporation may hold intellectual property rights related to the enterprise. Paralegals must often do careful investigative work to help unravel the web of entities that may be involved in a case.

Sole Proprietorships

Remember from Chapter 3 that the simplest form of business is the *sole proprietorship*, in which one person—the sole proprietor—owns the business. The sole proprietor is entitled to all of the business's profits and bears personal responsibility for all of the business's debts and other obligations. Sole proprietors can own and manage any type of business, from an informal, home-office undertaking to a large restaurant or construction firm.

There are more than 20 million sole proprietorships in the United States. In fact, they constitute over two-thirds of all American businesses. They are also usually small enterprises—only about 1 percent of the sole proprietorships in the United States earn more than $1 million per year.

Formation of a Sole Proprietorship

The sole proprietorship is easier and less costly to start than any other kind of business, as few legal forms are involved. No partnership agreement need be devised, because there are no partners. No papers need be filed with the state to establish the business. At most, minor paperwork will be required, depending on the law of the city in which the business is located. In the majority of states, if retail sales are involved, the proprietor will also need a tax number to report and remit sales taxes.

Because it is the simplest business form to create, persons first starting up businesses often choose to operate a sole proprietorship. An attorney or a freelance paralegal might begin doing business as a sole proprietor.

Advantages of Sole Proprietorships

A major advantage of the sole proprietorship is that the sole proprietor is entitled to all the profits made by the firm (because she or he takes all the risk). The sole proprietor is also free to make all decisions concerning the business—whom to hire, when to take a vacation, what kind of business to pursue, and the like. Additionally, sole proprietors are allowed to establish tax-exempt retirement accounts. (Law offices are usually not involved in establishing retirement accounts for small businesses.)

Disadvantages of Sole Proprietorships

A major disadvantage of the sole proprietorship is that the proprietor alone, as the firm's sole owner, is personally liable for any losses, debts, and obligations incurred by the business enterprise. As discussed in Chapter 3, *personal liability* means that the personal assets of the business owner (such as a home, car, savings account, or other tangible or intangible property) may be subject to creditors' claims if the business fails.

As a paralegal, if you are asked to do a preliminary investigation of a client's claim against a business entity, one of the first things you should check is the form of the business. ◆ **EXAMPLE 18.2—** Your law firm's client wants to sue a business firm for damages. If you learn that the firm is a sole proprietorship, then you will know that if the firm itself has insufficient assets to pay damages to the client (should the client win in court), the firm's owner will personally be liable for the damages. Depending on what you learn about the firm's financial condition, you may want to investigate the owner's personal financial position as well as the firm's assets. ◆

Another disadvantage of the sole proprietorship is that it may be difficult to obtain capital for expansion. The sole proprietor is dependent on loans made by lending institutions and others. For this reason, sole proprietors sometimes decide to take on partners who will contribute capital to the business, or they may incorporate and sell shares in the business to raise funds.

Taxation and Sole Proprietorships

A sole proprietor must pay income taxes on business profits, but she does not have to file a separate tax return in the name of the business. Rather, the profits are reported on the sole proprietor's personal tax return, usually on Schedule C of the federal tax return, and taxed as personal income.

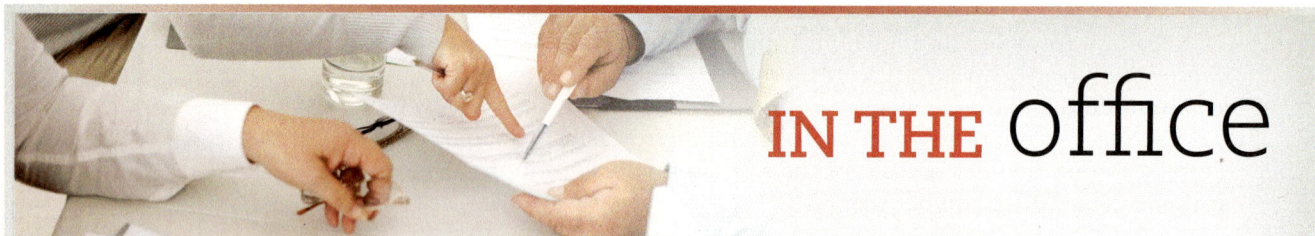

IN THE office

PRODUCTIVE MEETINGS

When working on a case, you may attend team meetings involving several attorneys and paralegals. Of course, you will want to prepare questions to ask at the meeting to help gather information you need to guide your work. But you will not want to be pulled into lengthy discussions about unrelated matters or about cases that are not related to your work. Once your part of the meeting is finished, you can excuse yourself to get back to work unless it is clear you are expected to stay. Most supervisors respect employees who are dedicated to the task at hand.

The sole proprietor on the right has so much business she has decided to form a partnership with her friend on the left. Will the new partner face the same liabilities that were faced by the sole proprietor?

Termination of the Sole Proprietorship

In a sole proprietorship, the owner is the business. For that reason, when the owner dies, the busines is automatically dissolved. If the business is transferred to family members or other heirs, a new entity is created. Similarly, if the proprietor sells the business, whoever buys it must establish either a new sole proprietorship or some other business form, such as a partnership or a corporation. This can involve considerable legal work. ◆ **EXAMPLE 18.3—** A client of your law firm inherited her father's business assets, which include a clothing store. If the business was held as a sole proprietorship, you will need to help her change the title on all real estate and any vehicles owned by the business as well as the names on all licenses used by the business. If the business was organized as a corporation, however, these things may not need to be changed. ◆

Partnerships

As discussed in Chapter 3, some law firms organize their business in the form of a *partnership*, which arises when two or more individuals undertake to do business together as *partners*. Each partner owns a portion of the business and shares jointly in the firm's profits or losses. Partners are personally liable for the debts and obligations of the business if the business fails, just as sole proprietors are. Each partner has—unless otherwise agreed upon and with proper legal formalities observed—decision-making authority involving partnership assets.

The Uniform Partnership Act (UPA) governs the operation of partnerships *unless the partners have expressly agreed otherwise.* Like the Uniform Commercial Code, the UPA is a model that becomes law when adopted by a state legislature. The earliest version of the UPA was issued in 1914. The most recent version was issued in 1997, which most states have adopted.

Partnership Formation

Under the UPA, as is true at common law, a partnership is when two or more people come together to own a business for profit. To create a partnership, two or more persons interested in establishing a profit-making business simply agree to do so, as partners. The partnership agreement can be expressed orally or in writing, or it can be implied by conduct. If the partnership is to continue for over a year, then the agreement must be in writing to satisfy the Statute of Frauds, a state statute that specifies what types of contracts must be in writing to be enforceable (discussed in Chapter 15).

ON THE web

You can review the text and other materials relating to the Uniform Partnership Act by going to the Web site of the Uniform Law Commission at **www.uniformlaw.org**. Search for "Partnership Act."

Rights and Duties of Partners

When two or more persons agree to do business as partners, legally they enter into a special relationship with one another. A partnership is based on a voluntary contract between two or more competent persons who agree to place some or all of their money or other assets, labor, and skill in a business, with the understanding that profits and losses will be proportionately shared.

DEFAULT RULES. The rights of partners are often written into the partnership agreement. If the agreement does not specify these rights, then the UPA comes into play (the state's version of the UPA, as adopted). Some of the important rights of partners are listed in Exhibit 18.1 below.

If two or more people are engaged in a common business enterprise and they do not form a separate legal entity, by default the law will treat them as having formed a partnership. ◆ **EXAMPLE 18.4—** Jameel and Maria decide to open a coffee shop together. They do not consult a lawyer or take any other steps to form a separate business entity. Maria signs a contract to buy six espresso machines at $12,000 each. Should Maria not make the payments, Jameel will be liable on the contract as Maria's partner despite not having signed the contract or even knowing that she made it. ◆

OBLIGATION TO PARTNERS. Partners owe each other a *fiduciary duty*, the highest level of obligation imposed by the law (this concept is discussed in more detail later in the chapter when we discuss agency). This means that the partners must put the interests of the partnership ahead of their own personal interests in any matters related to the purpose of the enterprise. ◆ **EXAMPLE 18.5—** A partner in a real estate investment partnership received a personal offer to buy a building the partnership has been leasing. She cannot buy it for herself without first allowing the partnership the opportunity to do so. ◆

Liability of Partners

Historically, a partnership could not be sued, bring a lawsuit, or own property in its own name. This traditional rule treated all partnerships as aggregates of individuals. Under this rule, which is still followed in some states, only the individual partners—not the partnership—can be sued. Because this approach is so cumbersome, most states today recognize the partnership as a legal entity that can sue or be sued and collect judgments in the partnership's name.

JOINT LIABILITY. A distinguishing feature of the partnership, and one that is often regarded as a disadvantage, is the potentially extensive personal liability faced by partners for partnership obligations and for the actions of the other partners. Partners have **joint liability**, or shared liability. In other words, partners may be held personally liable not only for their own actions and those of the partnership as an entity but also for the actions of other partners.

joint liability
Shared liability. In partnership law, partners incur joint liability for partnership obligations and debts.

EXHIBIT 18.1
Rights of Partners

PARTNERS HAVE THE RIGHT:

- To hold an ownership interest in the firm and to receive a share of the profits.
- To inspect partnership books and records.
- To an accounting of partnership assets and profits (for example, to determine the value of each partner's share in the partnership). An accounting can be performed voluntarily or can be compelled by a court order. Formal accounting occurs by right when a partnership is dissolved.
- To participate in the management of the business operation unless the partnership agreement specifies otherwise.

JOINT AND SEVERAL LIABILITY.   Partners may also be subject to **joint and several liability.** Several liability means *individual* liability. Joint and several liability means that a third party may sue all of the partners (jointly) or one or more of the partners separately (severally). This is true even if one of the partners sued did not participate in, ratify, or know about whatever gave rise to the cause of action.

◆ **EXAMPLE 18.6—**   Suppose that a plaintiff wants to recover for damages allegedly caused by a physician's negligence (medical malpractice). The physician is one of four partners in a medical practice partnership. Because partners are jointly and severally liable, the plaintiff could sue either the physician who allegedly caused the harm, the partnership, one of the other physicians (even if that physician had nothing to do with the plaintiff's treatment), or all of the physicians to recover damages. ◆ The liability faced by partners is a major reason for the rapid growth of a new form of partnership, the limited liability partnership, which will be discussed later.

Taxation of Partnerships

The partnership itself, as an entity, does not pay federal income taxes. The partnership as an entity files an information return with the Internal Revenue Service on which the income received by the partnership is reported. The partners declare their shares of the partnership's profits on their personal income tax returns and pay taxes accordingly. For this reason, a partnership is referred to as a "pass-through" entity. The profits "pass through" to the partners.

Partnership Termination

The partnership agreement may specify the duration of the partnership by indicating that the partnership will end on a certain date or on the occurrence of a certain event. It would be a breach of the partnership agreement for one partner to withdraw from the partnership before the specified date arrived or the specified event occurred. The withdrawing partner would be liable to the remaining partners for any related losses.

DISSOLUTION.   When an agreement does not specify the duration of the partnership, a partner is free to withdraw at any time without incurring liability to the remaining partners. Under the 1994 version of the UPA, withdrawal by a partner results in the **dissolution** (the formal disbanding) of the partnership (although a new partnership may arise among those who stay with the enterprise). Under the revised UPA, however, the withdrawal of a partner causes a partnership to be dissolved only if the withdrawal results in the breakup of the partnership itself and the business cannot continue. The occurrence of certain other events, such as the death or bankruptcy of a partner, results in a process similar to the withdrawal of a partner.

WINDING UP.   Partnership termination is a two-step process. Dissolution is the first step in the process. The second step is the **winding up** of partnership affairs. Once the firm is dissolved, it continues to exist legally until the process of winding up all business affairs (collecting and distributing the firm's assets) is complete.

Limited Partnerships

Ordinary partnerships, such as those just discussed, are often referred to as *general partnerships*. The **limited partnership**, in contrast, is a special form of partnership involving two different types of partners—general partners and limited partners. The **general partners** manage the business and have the rights and liabilities of partners in a general partnership. The **limited partners** are only investors in the business. Investment funds are typically limited partnerships. A limited partnership may be formed, for example, to purchase and develop real estate, oil and gas wells, intellectual property, or other assets. The limited partners play a passive role. Their funds help to finance the venture and they receive a share of the profits in return.

The limited partner may not participate in the management of the partnership and, in return, enjoys limited liability status. Unlike general partners, who

joint and several liability
Shared and individual liability. In partnership law, joint and several liability means that a third party may sue all of the partners (jointly) or one or more of the partners separately (severally). This is true even if one of the partners sued did not participate in, ratify, or know about whatever gave rise to the cause of action.

dissolution
The formal disbanding of a partnership or a corporation.

winding up
The process of winding up all business affairs (collecting and distributing the firm's assets) after a partnership or corporation has been dissolved.

limited partnership
A partnership consisting of one or more general partners and one or more limited partners.

general partner
A partner who participates in managing the business of a partnership and has all the rights and liabilities that arise under traditional partnership law.

limited partner
One who invests in a limited partnership but does not play an active role in managing the operation of the business. Unlike general partners, limited partners are only liable for partnership debts up to the amounts that they have invested.

are personally liable for partnership obligations, limited partners are liable only up to the amounts that they have invested. In other words, if the partnership goes bankrupt, they will lose their investments but cannot be held liable for partnership debts beyond that amount.

In contrast to the informal, private, and voluntary agreement that may create a general partnership, the formation of a limited partnership is a public and formal proceeding that must follow state statutory requirements. The partners must sign a *certificate of limited partnership*. In order to do so, the partners must submit information similar to that found in a corporate charter. The certificate must be filed with the proper state official (usually, the secretary of state). In this respect, the limited partnership resembles the corporation. The formal steps put potential creditors on notice of the limitations on the liabilities of the limited partners. Usually the limited partnership's name must include the initials "L.P." or some other indication of its status.

Corporations

Paralegals frequently work on behalf of corporate clients or on legal matters involving corporations. An increasing number of paralegals work for corporate employers. As a paralegal, you should thus have a basic knowledge of how corporations are formed and operated.

You should also be familiar with the basic rights and responsibilities of corporate participants. These include the **shareholders** (the owners of the business, called shareholders because they purchase corporate **shares**, or stock), the **directors** (persons elected by the shareholders to direct corporate affairs), and the **officers** (persons hired by the directors to manage the day-to-day operations of the corporation). Corporate officers include the corporate president, vice president, secretary, treasurer, and possibly others, such as a chief financial officer and chief executive officer. Corporate officers are employees of the corporation and subject to employment contracts.

Entity Status

Although it is owned by individuals, the corporation is a separate legal entity that is created and recognized by state law. In the eyes of the law, a corporation is a legal "person" that enjoys many of the rights and privileges that U.S. citizens enjoy, such as the right of access to the courts as an entity that can sue or be sued. It also has, among other rights, the right to due process of law and the right to freedom from unreasonable searches and seizures.

The Model Business Corporation Act (MBCA) is a codification of modern corporation law that has been influential in the codification of corporation statutes. Today, most state statutes are guided by the revised version of the MBCA, known as the Revised Model Business Corporation Act (RMBCA). There is, however, considerable variation among the statutes of the states that have based their statutes on the MBCA or the RMBCA, and several states do not follow either act. Because of this, as a paralegal you will need to rely on individual state corporation laws rather than the MBCA or RMBCA.

A corporation may be incorporated in one state but do business elsewhere. For example, many large corporations are incorporated in Delaware. This state has highly regarded corporate law and judges who are experts in corporate legal matters. Similarly, some companies are legally organized in foreign countries. Many insurance firms incorporate in Bermuda but do business in the United States.

Corporate Formation

Generally, forming a corporation involves two steps. The first step consists of preliminary organizational and promotional undertakings—particularly, obtaining capital for the future corporation. Before a corporation becomes a reality, people invest in the proposed corporation as subscribers. The subscribers become the shareholder-owners of the corporation when the corporation becomes a legal entity.

shareholder
One who has an ownership interest in a corporation through the purchase of corporate shares, or stock.

share
A unit of stock; a measure of ownership interest in a corporation.

director
A person elected by the shareholders to direct corporate affairs.

officer
A person hired by corporate directors to assist in the management of the day-to-day operations of the corporation.

ON THE web

To access the "Model Business Corporation Act Annotated," enter that term in the "Search" box at **www.americanbar.org**. Other corporate law materials can be found at **www.law.cornell.edu**.

The second step in forming a corporation is the process of incorporation. Exact procedures for incorporation differ among states, but the basic requirements are similar. The primary document needed to begin the incorporation process is called the **articles of incorporation** (see Exhibit 18.2 below for sample articles of incorporation for a small corporation). The articles include basic information about the corporation and serve as a primary source of authority for its future organization and business functions. Once they have been filed in the appropriate state office, the articles of incorporation become a public record.

Paralegals frequently assist their supervising attorneys in preparing incorporation papers and filing them with the appropriate state office. (See the *Developing Paralegal Skills* feature on the next page for an illustration of how paralegals can help with incorporation tasks.) Also, as a paralegal, you may need to obtain information about a corporation—for example, when you are conducting an investigation. For both of these reasons, you should know what information is generally

articles of incorporation
The document filed with the appropriate state official, usually the secretary of state, when a business is incorporated. State statutes usually prescribe what kind of information must be contained in the articles of incorporation.

EXHIBIT 18.2
Articles of Incorporation

Filed with Secretary of State
_____, 20_____

SHORT FORM
ARTICLES OF INCORPORATION
OF
_____Hiram, Inc._____

ARTICLE I

The name of this corporation _____Hiram, Inc._____

ARTICLE II

The purpose of this corporation is to engage in any lawful act or activity for which a corporation may be organized under the General Corporation Law of New Pacum other than the banking business, the trust company business, or the practice of a profession permitted to be incorporated by the New Pacum Corporation Code.

ARTICLE III

The name and address in the State of New Pacum of this corporation's initial agent for service of process is: _____Hiram Galliard,_____
__8934 Rathburn Avenue, North Bend, New Pacum 98754_____

ARTICLE IV

The corporation is authorized to issue only one class of shares of stock; and the total number of shares that this corporation is authorized to issue is _____10,000_____.

ARTICLE V

The corporation is a close corporation. All the corporation's issued shares of stock shall be held of record by not more than ten (10) persons.

DATED: _June 3, 2014_____

Hiram Galliard   _Martha Bonnell_
_____   _____
[Signature(s) of Incorporator/Directors(s)]

I (we) hereby declare that I (we) am (are) the person(s) who executed the foregoing Articles of Incorporation, which execution is my (our) act and deed.

Hiram Galliard   _Martha Bonnell_

© Cengage Learning 2014

DEVELOPING
paralegal skills

RESERVING A CORPORATE NAME

Jon is a paralegal at a law firm. A local building contractor, Thiess Brown, comes to the law firm for assistance. He believes that his firm is going to grow and that he should incorporate. In a discussion with Jon and his supervising attorney, Brown asks about calling his new corporation Thiess Construction. The attorney says that the availability of the name will be investigated. Jon is assigned to look into the naming issue.

Jon knows that, as in most states, he must contact the secretary of state's office to check on the availability of names for corporations. In Jon's state, the secretary of state's Department of Business Services maintains the database of registered corporate names in the state. A search of the department's Web site reveals that the names Thiess Construction and Thiess Corporation are not in use. Either name could be reserved for Brown's firm. Jon also checks a list of available domain names at Network Solutions (see www.networksolutions.com/whois/index.jsp) to find out whether Brown can purchase the domain name thiessconstruction.com should he want to establish a Web site.

He should also check alternative domains such as .biz and .net. Then Jon goes to the Web site of the U.S. Patent and Trademark Office to check the availability of names for possible trademark use.

TIPS FOR CLAIMING A CORPORATE NAME, DOMAIN NAME, AND TRADEMARK

- Determine if the preferred name and several possible alternatives are available.

- Check on the possibility of registering the company name, or a part of it, as a trademark or service mark. This is especially valuable should the company grow larger.

- Check on the availability of domain names for the client to use today or in the future for a Web site. Buying a domain name and similarly spelled domain names before a firm becomes well known is good strategy.

- Provide the lists of possibilities to your supervising attorney for the client's consideration.

- Once the client has decided what to do, file the appropriate forms.

---

certificate of incorporation or corporate charter
The document issued by a state official, usually the secretary of state, granting a corporation legal existence and the right to function.

bylaws
A set of governing rules adopted by a corporation or other association.

publicly held corporation
A corporation whose shares are eligible to be publicly traded in securities markets, such as the New York Stock Exchange.

included in the articles of incorporation. Exhibit 18.3 on the facing page lists and describes this information.

After the articles of incorporation have been prepared, signed, and authenticated by the incorporators, they are sent to the appropriate state official, usually the secretary of state, along with the appropriate filing fee. In many states, the secretary of state then issues a **certificate of incorporation** representing the state's authorization for the corporation to conduct business. (This may be called the **corporate charter**.) The certificate and a copy of the articles are returned to the incorporators, who then hold the initial organizational meeting that completes the details of incorporation. (How this process is being done online more and more is discussed in the *Technology and Today's Paralegal* feature on page 562.)

At this first organizational meeting, the corporation adopts a set of rules to govern the management of the corporation, called the **bylaws**. These bylaws grant or restrict the powers of the corporation.

Classifications of Corporations

How a corporation is classified depends on its purpose, ownership characteristics, and location. A *private corporation* is, as the term indicates, a corporation that is privately owned. A *public corporation* is formed by the government for a political or governmental purpose, as when a town incorporates. Note that a public corporation is not the same as a publicly held corporation. A **publicly held corporation** is any corporation with shares that are or could be publicly traded in securities markets, such as the New York Stock Exchange.

EXHIBIT 18.3
Information Generally Included
in the Articles of Incorporation

THE NAME OF THE CORPORATION

- The choice of a corporate name is subject to state approval to ensure against duplication or deception. State statutes usually require that the secretary of state run a check on the proposed name in the state of incorporation. Once cleared, a name can be reserved for a short time, for a fee, pending the completion of the articles of incorporation.

THE NATURE AND PURPOSE OF THE CORPORATION

- The intended business activities of the corporation must be specified in the articles, and, naturally, they must be lawful. Stating a general corporate purpose (for example, "to engage in lawful business") is usually sufficient to give rise to all of the powers necessary or convenient for the purpose of the organization. There is no need to give specific details of the planned business.

THE DURATION OF THE CORPORATION

- A corporation can have perpetual existence under most state corporation statutes. A few states, however, prescribe a maximum duration, after which the corporation must formally renew its existence.

THE CAPITAL STRUCTURE OF THE CORPORATION

- The capital structure of the corporation may be set forth in the articles. A few state statutes require a relatively small capital investment (for example, $1,000) for ordinary business corporations but a greater capital investment for those engaged in insurance or banking. The number of shares of stock authorized for issuance, their valuation, the various types or classes of stock authorized for issuance, and other relevant information concerning equity, capital, and credit must be outlined in the articles.

THE INTERNAL ORGANIZATION OF THE CORPORATION

- Whatever the internal management structure of the corporation, it should be described in the articles, although it can be included in bylaws adopted after the corporation is formed.

THE REGISTERED OFFICE AND AGENT OF THE CORPORATION

- The corporation must indicate the location and address of its registered office within the state. Usually, the registered office is also the principal office of the corporation. The corporation must give the name and address of a specific person who has been designated as an agent and who can receive legal documents (including service of process) on behalf of the corporation.

THE NAMES AND ADDRESSES OF THE INCORPORATORS

- Each incorporator must be listed by name and must indicate an address. An incorporator is a person—often the corporate promoter—who applies to the state on behalf of the corporation to obtain its corporate charter. States vary on the required minimum number of incorporators. It can be as few as one or as many as three. Incorporators are required to sign the articles of incorporation when they are submitted to the state. Often, this is their only duty. In some states, they participate at the first organizational meeting of the corporation.

© Cengage Learning 2014

FOR-PROFIT OR NOT-FOR-PROFIT.   Corporations may also be classified as either *for-profit corporations* or *not-for-profit* (or *nonprofit*) *corporations*. A not-for-profit corporation may be formed by a group—such as a charitable association, a hospital, or a religious organization—to conduct its business without exposing the individual owners to personal liability.

TECHNOLOGY AND
today's paralegal

ONLINE INCORPORATION

Today, it is easy to form a corporation or limited liability company for any lawful purpose in any state. The requirements, however, differ from state to state. As a paralegal, your supervising attorney may ask you to assist a client who wishes to incorporate a business. The client may wish to incorporate in the state in which she already does business, in another state, or even in another country. You can assist in the process by learning about the formal requirements and cost of incorporation in various states. In addition, you can find many online providers of company formation and registered agent services. (The *registered agent* acts as the original incorporator, files the articles of incorporation, and may remain the registered agent for the life of the corporation.)

RESEARCHING STATE REQUIREMENTS

State governments have Web sites at which you can find the state rules. Typically, incorporation is handled by the secretary of state's office. It is usually easiest to find state rules through an online search or by using the directory called "State and Local Government on the Net" at **www.statelocalgov.net**. Most state sites post guidelines or instructions on forming corporations (and other business entities), fee schedules, and frequently asked questions (FAQs). Many provide downloadable corporate forms and have searchable databases of corporate names and registered agents.

ONLINE INCORPORATION SERVICES

Some companies provide incorporation services online that will assist you with establishing the corporation or LLC. Although many sites are aimed at persons seeking to incorporate, some target law firms

as clients and provide additional useful services. For example, if your client is interested in forming a corporation in Delaware, Harvard Business Services (**www.delawareinc.com**) offers an efficient way to incorporate. It provides downloadable forms and will act as the corporation's registered agent for a fixed annual fee. Other Web sites offer similar services, such as The Company Corporation (**www.incorporate.com**).

Another useful Web site for corporate attorneys and paralegals is that of the Corporation Service Company (CSC) at **www.cscglobal.com**. CSC offers a range of services, including corporate formation and registered agent services. The company will scan and upload all the documents related to a transaction or litigation into an online database, providing centralized access to important documents for authorized users anywhere in the world and allowing multiple parties to track ongoing negotiations. Useful news and substantive law updates (federal and state) are provided at this site as well.

TECHNOLOGY TIP

The Web provides an efficient means of finding out state requirements, obtaining the proper forms, and keeping on top of current developments affecting corporations and LLCs. The usefulness of a particular site will depend on the paralegal's level of experience and the individual needs of the client or firm.

---

close corporation

A corporation owned by a small group of shareholders, often family members; also called a closely held corporation. Shares in close corporations cannot be publicly traded on the stock market, and often other restrictions on stock transfer apply. Some close corporations qualify for special tax status as S corporations.

CLOSE CORPORATIONS.   Corporations owned by a small group of shareholders, such as family members, are called **close corporations**, or *closely held corporations*. Unlike publicly held corporations, close corporations cannot sell their shares on public securities markets and usually place restrictions on the transfer of corporate shares—to keep the business in the family, for example. State laws may provide more flexibility for close corporations, such as reducing the statutory formalities that must be observed by public corporations.

Also, certain close corporations are permitted to elect a special corporate tax status under Subchapter S of the Internal Revenue Code. These corporations are called *S corporations*.

PROFESSIONAL CORPORATIONS.   Lawyers, physicians, accountants, architects, engineers, and other professionals sometimes incorporate as *professional corporations*. We discuss these organizations later in this chapter.

Directors and Officers

Corporations separate ownership and control. The shareholders own the corporation but the directors have legal control. This structure allows shares to be widely dispersed without overly complicating the decision-making arrangement. The articles of incorporation name the initial board of directors, which is appointed by the incorporators. Thereafter, the board of directors is elected by the shareholders. The board holds formal meetings and records the minutes (formal notes of what transpired at the meetings). Each director has one vote, and generally the majority rules.

RIGHTS AND RESPONSIBILITIES.   The directors' rights include the right to participate in board meetings and the right to inspect corporate books and records. The directors' responsibilities to the corporation and its shareholders include declaring and paying **dividends** (payments to shareholders representing their share of corporate profits), appointing and removing officers, and making significant policy decisions.

The board of directors appoints the corporate officers who manage the day-to-day operations of the firm. As previously mentioned, the officers are employees of the corporation and are subject to employment contracts. Officers are also agents of the corporation. (We discuss agency later in this chapter.)

Directors and officers have fiduciary duties (discussed in detail on pages 569 through 570) to the corporation and its shareholder-owners, including the duty of loyalty and the duty to exercise reasonable care when conducting corporate business. The duty of loyalty is breached when an officer or director uses corporate funds or confidences for personal gain, as when an officer discloses company secrets (such as a proposed merger) to an outsider. The duty of care is breached when a director's or officer's negligence—failure to make informed and reasonable decisions—results in harmful consequences for the corporate entity.

POTENTIAL LIABILITY.   Corporate directors and officers can face criminal penalties, including imprisonment, for their actions or for the actions of employees under their supervision. In addition, a corporation may be held financially liable for any criminal acts or torts committed by its agents or officers within the course and scope of their employment.

The Sarbanes-Oxley Act imposes numerous disclosure requirements on corporate directors and officers of publicly held companies. Chief corporate executives—and the lawyers and accountants who work for them—must take legal responsibility for the accuracy of their financial statements and reports or risk steep penalties for violating the act.

Shareholders

Any person who purchases a share in a corporation becomes an owner of the corporation. Through shareholders' meetings, the shareholders play an important role in the corporate entity—they elect the directors who control the corporation, and they have a right to vote on some decisions that significantly affect the corporation, such as whether to sell the company. They also have a right to share in corporate profits proportionate to the number of shares they hold. Shareholders do not manage the daily affairs of the corporation, nor are they liable for corporate debts or other obligations beyond the amounts of their investments. Corporate owners, or shareholders, thus have *limited liability*—a key advantage of the corporate form of business.

Corporate Taxation

The corporation as an entity pays income taxes on corporate profits. Then, when the profits are distributed to the shareholders in the form of dividends, the shareholders pay personal income taxes on the income they receive out of the already-taxed profits. This double-taxation feature of the corporate form of business is one of its major disadvantages.

dividend
A distribution of profits to corporate shareholders, disbursed in proportion to the number of shares held.

ON THE web

For an example of a site that offers online incorporation services, go to **www.bizfilings.com**. For a government Web site with links to various sources of information on business formation, go to **www.sba.gov**

liquidation

In regard to corporations, the process by which corporate assets are converted into cash and distributed among creditors and shareholders according to specific rules of preference.

Some small (close) corporations are permitted to avoid the double taxation of corporate profits by electing S corporation status under Subchapter S of the Internal Revenue Code. An S corporation, like a partnership, is a "pass-through" entity for tax purposes. This means that the corporation itself does not pay income taxes. Instead, it files an information return only, as a partnership does, indicating the corporation's net profits. The S corporation shareholders declare their proportionate shares of the corporation's net income on their personal tax returns and pay taxes on that income accordingly.

Types of Stock

Corporations may issue different types of stock, each of which grants the owner a different set of rights. Some stock may carry extra voting rights. This is often used in family corporations to preserve family control. *Preferred stock* has greater rights to receive dividends or payments if the company liquidates compared to *common stock*, which typically carries greater voting rights than preferred stock. You may need to read corporate charters and bylaws carefully to determine a corporation's structure.

Corporate Termination

Like partnership termination, corporate termination involves two steps. The first step, dissolution, extinguishes the legal existence of the corporation. The second step, liquidation, involves the winding up of the corporation's business affairs. After creditors have been paid, all remaining assets are distributed to the shareholders. The appropriate state's secretary of state is notified that the corporation no longer exists.

Corporations can be terminated at a time specified in the articles of incorporation or by the agreement of the shareholders and the board of directors. In certain circumstances, a court may dissolve a corporation. For example, if the directors are deadlocked and cannot agree on the management of the corporation, a court may grant a shareholder's petition to dissolve the corporation. A corporation may also be terminated by law if it fails to meet certain statutory requirements, such as the payment of taxes or annual fees.

Limited Liability Organizations

Recall that one of the major tax advantages of a partnership is that the partnership's income passes through to the partners as personal income. Consequently, partners avoid the double taxation of the corporate form of business. But there is a price to pay for this tax advantage: partners face unlimited personal liability. The partners normally can avoid unlimited personal liability by incorporating their business, because corporate owners (shareholders) have limited liability. But again, there is a price to pay: the double taxation of profits characteristic of the corporate form of business.

As mentioned, one way to achieve both goals—limited liability and single taxation of profits—is to elect S corporation status. Certain requirements must be met, however, before a corporation can qualify for S corporation status. One requirement is that the corporation must have one hundred or fewer shareholders, thus excluding large firms. Another requirement is that an S corporation may have only one class of stock (meaning that there is little flexibility in how corporate profits are distributed). Additionally, certain entities (such as partnerships and, with some exceptions, corporations) cannot be shareholders in an S corporation.

Several forms of organization have developed to address these problems. They include the limited liability company, the limited liability partnership, and the professional corporation. The use of these business forms has spread quickly because of the advantages they offer to businesspersons. As noted in the *Practice Focus* feature on the facing page, legal formalities must be met over time for limited liability to be retained.

PRACTICE focus

PROTECTING LIMITED LIABILITY

When a limited liability business organization (such as a corporation or limited partnership) is created, the new entity limits the potential losses for the owners to the amount they have invested in the business. Their personal assets are safe from the business's creditors. To maintain this limit, businesses must keep up to date on a variety of regulatory and tax filings.

Further, they must comply with legal formalities, including keeping regular records of directors' meetings. As a paralegal practicing in the business organizations area, you will often be called upon to verify an entity's status, complete regulatory filings, and maintain business records. You will have to work with a variety of state agencies, including state tax authorities and the secretary of state's office for the state where the business is registered.

When a business entity fails to maintain the appropriate records or file the required documents, the owners risk being held liable by creditors who can pierce the corporate veil. (This doctrine applies even to non-corporate entities with limited liability such as LLCs.) Your role is thus important to safeguarding your client's assets, because a failure might lead to his or her personal assets being seized by a business creditor. If you are involved in business litigation, you will often need to research the tax, regulatory, and business records of any limited liability entities involved in the case.

Business people sometimes are so focused on running their businesses that they pay inadequate attention to filing required documents or keeping records the law requires. Lawyers and paralegals play a vital role in ensuring that these requirements are met and can offer clients services to help them meet their legal requirements on an ongoing basis.

Limited Liability Companies

The **limited liability company (LLC)** is a hybrid form of business enterprise that combines the pass-through tax benefits of S corporations and partnerships with the limited liability of limited partners and corporate shareholders. Like the limited partnership and the corporation, an LLC must be formed and operated in compliance with state law. To form an LLC, *articles of organization* must be filed with a central state agency, such as the secretary of state's office. The business's name must include the words "Limited Liability Company" or the initials "L.L.C."

A major advantage of the LLC is that, as indicated, it does not pay taxes as an entity. Rather, profits are "passed through" the LLC, and taxes are paid personally by the owners of the company, who are called *members* instead of shareholders. Another key advantage is that the liability of members is limited to the amounts of their investments. In an LLC, members are also allowed to participate in management activities, and under some state statutes, the firm's managers need not even be members of the LLC.

Yet another advantage is that corporations and partnerships, as well as foreign investors, can be LLC members. Additionally, in contrast to S corporations, there is no limit on the number of members of the LLC. Finally, part of the LLC's attractiveness to businesspersons is the flexibility it offers. The members can themselves decide how to operate the various aspects of the business through a simple document called the *operating agreement*.

The disadvantages of the LLC are relatively few, so this form of organization has become popular for smaller, privately held companies. Just as Delaware is the premier state for corporate charters, Nevada has become a frequent choice of jurisdiction for LLC formation.

limited liability company (LLC)
A hybrid form of business organization authorized by a state in which the owners of the business have limited liability and taxes on profits are passed through the business entity to the owners.

Limited Liability Partnerships

limited liability partnership (LLP)
A hybrid form of business organization authorized by a state that allows professionals to enjoy the tax benefits of a partnership while limiting in some way the normal joint and several liability of partners.

The **limited liability partnership (LLP)** is similar to the LLC. The difference is that the LLP is designed for professionals, such as attorneys, who normally do business as partners in a partnership. Like LLCs, LLPs must be formed and operated in compliance with state statutes. The appropriate form must be filed with a central state agency, usually the secretary of state's office, and the business's name must include either "Limited Liability Partnership" or the initials "L.L.P."

The major advantage of the LLP is that it allows a partnership to function as a pass-through entity for tax purposes but limits the personal liability of the partners for partnership tort liability. Although LLP statutes vary from state to state, generally each state statute limits in some way the liability of partners. In most states, it is relatively easy to convert a traditional partnership into an LLP because the firm's basic organizational structure remains the same. Additionally, all of the laws governing partnerships still apply (apart from those modified by the LLP statute). Normally, an LLP statute is simply an amendment to a state's already existing partnership law.

A few states provide for a specific type of limited partnership called a *limited liability limited partnership* (LLLP). In an LLLP, the liability of all partners is limited to the amounts of their investments in the firm.

Professional Corporations

professional corporation (PC)
A corporation formed by professionals, such as attorneys or accountants. Each member of the firm is liable for his or her own malpractice, but is generally protected by limited liability as in the corporate form.

Professionals in practice together, such as a group of physicians or lawyers, traditionally formed partnerships or limited partnerships. An alternative to those forms of organization that is used in many states is the **professional corporation (PC)**. While the rules vary from state to state, in general a PC may only be formed by licensed professionals, such as a group of dentists.

A practicing professional can be held personally liable for malpractice, but the existence of the professional corporation limits the liability of the other members. For example, suppose a group of physicians owns a PC through which they offer medical services. If one physician in the group is found liable for monetary damages due to medical malpractice, the other physicians in the professional corporation are not likely to be personally liable for that judgment. The physician who lost the malpractice suit would be personally liable, but other members of the medical practice would be protected.

In general, only the professionals involved in the PC can be owners. In other words, there cannot be outside investors. Only members of the practice can be shareholders in the firm, and all members of the firm must be licensed members of the same profession. So that people who deal with the firm are aware of its legal status, state law requires that the name be followed by the letters "P.C."

The Paralegal and Business Organizations

The discussion in this chapter makes clear the many ways in which paralegals benefit from knowledge of business organizations. Because so much legal work has to do with business clients, it is impossible to summarize the diverse tasks involving business organizations that paralegals carry out. (See the *Featured Contributor* on pages 568 and 569 for further discussion.) The following list, however, will give you an idea of some of the types of work that paralegals frequently perform in this area:

- Reserve a corporate name for an incorporator.

- Draft a partnership agreement and the documents necessary to form a limited partnership or limited liability company and file the required papers with the appropriate state office.

- Prepare articles of incorporation and file them with the appropriate state office.

- Prepare minutes of corporate meetings and maintain a minutes binder.

- Review or prepare documents relating to the sale of corporate securities (stocks and bonds) and assist a supervising attorney in making sure that federal and state requirements relating to the sale of corporate securities are met.

- Assist in the dissolution of a partnership or corporation.

- Assist in litigation relating to a corporation or other form of business.

- Research state laws governing partnerships, corporations, and limited liability organizations.

- Monitor deadlines to ensure regulatory filings are up to date.

Agency Law

The common law of agency involves concepts and principles with which all paralegals should be familiar. Agency is a pervasive concept in our society because little work could get done without agents. An **agency** relationship exists when one party, called the **agent**, agrees to represent or act for another party, called the **principal**. If you are working as a paralegal employee, in essence you are an agent of your employer. Attorneys, because they represent and act for their clients, are agents of those clients. All forms of business organizations involve agents.

Indeed, a business world without agents is hard to imagine. Imagine the late founder of Apple, Steve Jobs, having to design, produce, and sell all of his company's software. Obviously, other people had to be appointed to fill in—act as agents—for the owners of Apple—the principal.

Employees and Independent Contractors

Normally, all employees who deal with third parties are deemed to be agents. ◆ **EXAMPLE 18.7—** A salesperson in a department store is an agent of the store's owner (the principal) and acts on the owner's behalf. Any sale of goods made by the salesperson to a customer is binding on the principal. Similarly, most representations of fact made by the salesperson with respect to the goods sold are binding on the principal. ◆

Agency relationships can also arise between employers and independent contractors (such as real estate agents) who are hired to perform special tasks or services (such as the sale of property). An **independent contractor** is a person who is hired to perform a specific undertaking but who is free to choose how and when to perform the work. ◆ **EXAMPLE 18.8—** Building contractors and subcontractors are independent contractors because the property owner does not control the acts of either of these professionals. Truck drivers who own their equipment and hire themselves out on a per-job basis are independent contractors, but truck drivers who drive company trucks on a regular basis are usually classified as employees. ◆ Generally, courts look at the degree of control and supervision the employer exercised over the work performed to determine if the individual was an employee or an independent contractor. An independent contractor may or may not be an agent.

Agency Formation

Normally, agency relationships come about voluntarily by agreement of the parties. Although the parties often sign a contract (such as an agreement to list a house for sale with a real estate agent), the agreement need not be in writing. ◆ **EXAMPLE 18.9—** If Deborah asks Ling, a gardener, to contract with others to landscape her yard, and Ling agrees, an agency relationship is created. If Ling then enters into a contract with a landscape architect to design Deborah's yard, Deborah, as the principal, is legally bound by that contract. ◆

An agency agreement can also be implied by conduct. ◆ **EXAMPLE 18.10—** Suppose that a hotel allows Dwight to park cars to earn tips, even though Dwight does not have an employment contract there. The hotel's manager tells Dwight when to work, as well as where and how to park the cars. The hotel's conduct implies that Dwight has authority to act as a parking valet, and Dwight will be considered the hotel's agent for that purpose. ◆

agency
A relationship between two persons in which one person (the agent) represents or acts in the place of the other (the principal).

agent
A person who is authorized to act for or in the place of another person (the principal).

principal
In agency law, a person who, by agreement or otherwise, authorizes another person (the agent) to act on the principal's behalf in such a way that the acts of the agent become binding on the principal.

independent contractor
A person who is hired to perform a specific undertaking but who is free to choose how and when to perform the work. An independent contractor may or may not be an agent.

Featured Contributor

GOING CORPORATE

Angela Schneeman

BIOGRAPHICAL NOTE

Angela Schneeman is a freelance paralegal and author who specializes in corporate law. She has been a paralegal since 1984, when she received her legal assistant certificate from the University of Minnesota, where she also earned her BS degree in Business and Legal Studies. Ms. Schneeman has worked as a paralegal for law firms, the legal departments of publicly held corporations, and a major accounting firm. She works with attorneys in Minneapolis and St. Paul, Minnesota. Schneeman is the author of several textbooks for paralegals, including *The Law of Corporations and Other Business Organizations, Sixth Edition,* and *The Pocket Guide to Legal Ethics.*

© Cengage Learning 2014

If you are contemplating a career as a paralegal, or perhaps desire a new focus in your current paralegal employment, you may want to explore a career as a corporate paralegal. Corporate paralegals may work in-house in a corporation's legal department, or they may work for a law firm and specialize in corporate law.

LAW FIRM VERSUS IN-HOUSE

Roughly 20 percent of all paralegals work in-house for corporations. Generally, the paralegals who work in corporate legal departments have relatively high job satisfaction. Often they receive better-than-average salaries and benefits, work less overtime, and are not subject to the billing requirements imposed on their counterparts in law firms.

Many paralegals who work for law firms, however, will tell you they wouldn't consider trading the fast-paced atmosphere of the law firm for an in-house position. Most corporate paralegals who work in law firms assist one or more attorneys who represent a number of corporate clients. These paralegals are usually required to work at least forty hours per week and meet established billing requirements.

Most corporate paralegals have regular contact with the firm's corporate clients and may meet with them either at the law firm or at the client's office. Typically such paralegals report that they enjoy the variety of their work and that they like working for a variety of corporate clients.

WHAT YOU'LL NEED TO KNOW

Corporate paralegals must be familiar with the business corporation act of the state in which they work and with federal law concerning corporations. In addition, paralegals must be familiar with the procedures of the state office, such as the secretary of state, that creates and regulates corporations.

An agency relationship can also arise if the *principal* causes a third person to reasonably believe that another person is his or her agent, thus creating the *appearance* of an agency that does not in fact exist. ◆ **EXAMPLE 18.11—**   Carmen, a sales representative, brings her friend with her to solicit orders from a customer and repeatedly refers to her friend as her assistant. The customer reasonably believes that the friend works with Carmen and proceeds to place orders with the friend. Carmen will not be allowed to deny that the friend is her agent. ◆ Similarly, if a principal approves or affirms a contract after the fact—by filling orders placed with a person who was not truly an agent, for example—an agency relationship is created.

Fiduciary Duties

An important concept in agency law is that an agency is a **fiduciary relationship**— one involving a high degree of trust and confidence. Because of this, certain

fiduciary relationship
A relationship involving a high degree of trust and confidence.

WHAT YOU'LL BE DOING

The work of corporate paralegals is diverse, and it's difficult to generalize about their duties. Paralegals who work in law firms are often responsible for maintaining the corporate minute books of all corporate clients and reviewing those books periodically to make sure annual minutes are prepared and that all documents are kept up to date. In-house paralegals may assist the corporate secretary in keeping the corporate record books up to date for the corporation and any subsidiaries. Corporate paralegals may also perform the following types of duties:

- Draft contracts and corporate documents of all types.
- Assist with incorporation and dissolution of corporations.
- Research state and federal corporate and securities law.
- Assist with mergers and acquisitions.
- Assist with completing and filing periodic reports with the Securities and Exchange Commission and stock exchanges.

CORPORATE SPECIALTIES

Because of the complexities of modern corporate law and transactions, most corporate attorneys and paralegals specialize within this field. One popular corporate paralegal specialty is the area of mergers and acquisitions. Paralegals are essential members of most merger and acquisition teams and are often responsible for much of the related due-diligence work. Due-diligence work involves investigating the financial risks of a merger or acquisition.

Large transactions can include on-site inspections of facilities and inventory, as well as the review of hundreds of documents such as contracts, real estate titles, and patents. Paralegals collect, catalogue, and review the documents the other party is required to produce to close the transaction. They may also be responsible for preparing and producing documentation for the other party's review. Merger and acquisition work can require traveling and, at times, working long hours under pressure, but most paralegals who work in this area find it interesting and rewarding.

Mergers and acquisitions is just one example of a specialty for corporate paralegals. Some other areas corporate paralegals may specialize in include:

- Securities
- International law
- Contracts
- Intellectual property
- Labor
- Business litigation

In-house paralegals may specialize in one or more of the following areas:

- Corporate governance
- Litigation
- Contracts
- Subsidiary maintenance
- Shareholder relations

The opportunities for corporate paralegals are vast and varied. If you are interested in beginning a career as a corporate paralegal, the chances are there is a position with the right specialty, working conditions, and challenges to suit you.

"Because of the complexities of modern corporate law and transactions, most corporate attorneys and paralegals specialize."

fiduciary duties arise whenever an agency relationship comes into existence. Basically, this means that each party owes the other the duty to act honestly and to pursue faithfully the objective of the agency.

Duties Run Both Ways

The principal is obligated to cooperate with the agent, provide safe working conditions for the agent, and reimburse the agent for work performed and for any expenses incurred while working on the principal's behalf. The agent, in turn, must perform his tasks competently and must obey and be loyal to the principal. The duty of loyalty means that the agent's actions must be strictly for the benefit of the principal and must not result in any secret profit for the agent. ◆ **EXAMPLE 18.12—** A real estate agent representing the seller of a house should not tell a prospective buyer that the seller is willing to accept 20 percent less than the asking price and is desperate to sell. ◆

Avoiding Conflicts of Interest

In addition, the agent cannot represent two principals in the same transaction unless both know of the dual capacity and consent to it. ◆ **EXAMPLE 18.13—** A real estate agent who represents both the seller and a buyer in a transaction must secure a written consent from each to effect the dual agency. ◆ The agent also has a duty to notify the principal of all matters that come to her or his attention concerning the subject matter of the agency and to render an accounting to the principal of all property and funds received and paid out on behalf of the principal.

Duties also imply rights. In general, the agent has a right corresponding to every duty owed by the principal, and vice versa. Consider that when an attorney serves as an agent for a client (the principal), the attorney has a duty of loyalty to the client. The client, therefore, has a right to the attorney's loyalty. If you read through your state's ethical rules governing attorneys, you will find that many of the rules governing attorney-client relationships are rooted in these agency concepts.

Agency Relationships and Third Parties

Agency law also comes into play when disputes arise over who should be liable—the principal, the agent, or both—when an agent either forms a contract with a third party or causes injury to a third party. Generally, a principal is liable only for the authorized actions of her agent. Because the principal is frequently an employer or company that has greater resources with which to pay damages (has "deeper pockets") than the employee, the injured party usually seeks to hold the principal liable for the loss or damage caused by an agent.

Contract Liability

If an agent is not authorized to enter into a contract on behalf of the principal, then normally the principal will not be bound by the contract unless he or she voluntarily accepts (ratifies) it. An agent may be clearly authorized, either orally or in writing, to form certain contracts. The agent's authority may also be implied by custom—that is, an agent normally has the authority to do whatever is customary or necessary to fulfill the purpose of the agency. A paralegal office manager, for example, has the implied authority to enter into a contract to purchase office supplies on behalf of the firm because the authority to purchase supplies is necessary to the duties of office manager.

Tort Liability

Obviously, any person, including an agent, is liable for her or his own torts. Whether a principal can also be held liable for an agent's torts depends largely on whether the agent was an employee and whether the agent was acting within the scope of his or her employment at the time of committing the tort.

Under the doctrine of *respondeat superior*,[1] the principal-employer is liable for harm caused to a third party by an agent-employee *acting within the scope of employment*. The doctrine imposes **vicarious liability** on the employer—that is, liability without regard to the personal fault of the employer—for torts committed by an employee in the course or scope of employment. The theory of *respondeat superior* is similar in this respect to the theory of strict liability covered in Chapter 14.

Today's courts consider a number of factors in determining whether a particular act occurred within the course and scope of employment. If the employer authorized the act or had reason to know that the employee would do the act in question, if the injury occurred during work hours, or if the employer furnished the means or tools (for example, a truck or a machine) that caused the injury, that fact would point toward employer liability. In contrast, if the injury occurred after work hours or while the employee was on a "frolic" of his or her own, having substantially abandoned the employer's business, the employer might not be held responsible. These factors are illustrated in the *Developing Paralegal Skills* feature on the next page.

---

respondeat superior
A doctrine in agency law under which a principal-employer may be held liable for the wrongful acts committed by agents or employees acting within the scope of their agency or employment.

vicarious liability
Legal responsibility placed on one person for the acts of another.

DEVELOPING
paralegal skills

A CASE OF *RESPONDEAT SUPERIOR*

Rosie Ball and her son Steven were driving home from the grocery store one evening. They were slowly making their way down an icy street. As they entered an intersection with a stop sign for oncoming traffic, their car was hit broadside. The other driver went through the stop sign at high speed. Steven sustained a severe head injury that resulted in irreparable brain damage. The driver of the other car, who works for a large company, had gone out for several drinks after work with other employees before heading home.

Rosie contacted attorney Jared Mills, who is the supervising attorney for paralegal Thom Mintin. After meeting with Rosie, the attorney asks Thom to research the issue of whether the driver's employer can be held liable for the car accident under a theory of *respondeat superior.*

Thom learns that an employer is liable under *respondeat superior* for the negligent acts of an employee if the acts are committed in the scope of employment. The employer may also be liable for an employee's acts if the acts occur while the employee is on a brief "detour" from the employer's work. The employer is not liable, however, if the employee is on a "frolic" and is not engaged in an activity related to the work that he was hired to perform.

CHECKLIST FOR DETERMINING LIABILITY UNDER THE DOCTRINE OF *RESPONDEAT SUPERIOR*

- Did the employee's act constitute a tort?
- Did the employee commit the act within the course and scope of his employment?
- Was the act committed during work hours or after work hours?
- Did the employer authorize the act or have reason to know that the employee would do the act?
- Did the employer furnish the means by which the injury was inflicted (the car, for example)?
- Was the act committed during a brief detour from the employee's course of employment, or was the employee on a "frolic" of his own when the act occurred?

Liability for Independent Contractors' Torts

Generally, the principal is not liable for physical harm caused to a third person by the negligent act of an independent contractor in the performance of the contract. This is because the employer does not have the right to control the details of an independent contractor's performance. Exceptions to this rule are made in certain situations, however, as when exceptionally hazardous activities are involved or when the employer does in fact exercise a significant degree of control over the contractor's performance.

Employment Law

Whenever a business organization hires an employee, an employment relationship is established. In the United States, employment relationships traditionally have been governed primarily by the common law. Today, though, federal and state statutes regulate the workplace extensively and provide employees with many rights and protections. Common law doctrines apply to areas *not* covered by statutory law.

Because attorneys and paralegals are frequently involved in legal work relating to employment relationships, you should have a basic understanding of employment law. In this section, we look at the common law doctrine governing employment relationships and at some of the ways in which the government regulates today's workplace.

ON THE web

Useful major sources of employment law information you can find easily on the Web include the Department of Labor Employment Law Guide; Nolo's Employment Law Center; and the Employment Law Information Network.

Employment at Will

Traditionally, employment relationships have been governed by the common law doctrine of employment at will, as well as by the common law rules governing contracts, torts, and agency. Under the doctrine of **employment at will**, either party may terminate an employment relationship at any time and for any reason, unless a contract or statute specifically provides otherwise. This continues to be the basic rule, so most workers have the legal status of "employees at will."

Nonetheless, there are many situations in which the doctrine is not applied. Sometimes, an employment contract limits the circumstances under which an employee can be fired. Even in the absence of an express employment contract, some courts have held that an *implied* contract can exist—for example, when an employee manual states that, as a matter of policy, workers will be dismissed only for "good cause." (For this reason, it is often important for a paralegal to read the employee manual when researching an employee's termination.)

Also, as mentioned, federal and state statutes governing employment relationships prevent the at-will doctrine from being applied in a number of circumstances. Today's employer is not permitted to fire an employee if to do so would violate a federal or state employment statute, such as one prohibiting employment termination for discriminatory reasons (to be discussed shortly).

Restrictive Covenants

Many employers seek to restrict employees' ability to compete with them after the employees leave their job by asking the employees to sign **restrictive covenants** (also known as *covenants not to compete*). In these agreements, employees agree not to enter into competing businesses or to solicit the employer's customers for a specified period after the end of their employment. Laws vary from state to state, with some states such as California refusing to enforce such agreements, and others requiring that the limits on the ex-employee be limited to a reasonable time and geographic scope. Paralegals may be asked to research the law to ensure that an employer's proposed restrictive covenant would be valid in all the states where the employer has employees.

Wrongful Discharge

Whenever an employer discharges an employee in violation of an employment contract or a statutory law protecting employees, the employee may bring an action for **wrongful discharge**. For example, most states have a statute prohibiting employers from discharging an employee because the employee has filed a workers' compensation claim, reported for jury duty, performed some other public duty, or refused to commit an illegal act. ◆ **EXAMPLE 18.14—** An employee of a construction company is hit by a falling brick and suffers a serious injury. The employee files a claim for workers' compensation (discussed shortly). The employer then fires the employee. The employee can sue for wrongful discharge. ◆

Common Law Principles Apply

Wrongful discharge can also arise from the violation of a common law principle. ◆ **EXAMPLE 18.15—** Cool Company hired Yvonne to be its representative in Detroit. She was to be paid a 20 percent commission for all business generated. Just before the commission was due to be paid, Cool fired Yvonne and did not pay her a commission on business that she generated. Yvonne can sue for breach of contract and also for wrongful discharge. ◆

Constructive Discharge

Sometimes, employees claim that they were "constructively discharged" from their jobs. **Constructive discharge** occurs when the employer causes the employee's working conditions to be so intolerable that a reasonable person in the employee's position would feel compelled to quit. This issue arises, for example, in some sexual-harassment cases, as we will soon review. ◆ **EXAMPLE 18.16—** Mindy works for Megathon, Inc. Dustin is her supervisor and constantly calls Mindy at home and frequently bothers her at the office, insisting she date him. Even though Mindy complains to the human relations department, nothing is done. If Mindy finally quits to protect herself, she may sue Megathon on the grounds of constructive discharge. ◆

Wage Laws

The Fair Labor Standards Act (FLSA) of 1938 established guidelines regulating overtime pay and minimum hourly wages. The act provided that if in any week an employee works more than forty hours, the hours in excess of the first forty must be compensated at one and a half times the employee's regular hourly rate. As for the minimum hourly wage, it represents the absolute minimum amount that an employer can pay an employee per hour. The federal minimum wage rate, which is set by Congress, is changed periodically.

Many states also have minimum wage laws, which sometimes set higher minimums than exist under federal law. All states also have wage payment statutes that require employers to pay employees promptly and limit what they can deduct from employees' pay.

Family and Medical Leave

In 1993, Congress passed the Family and Medical Leave Act (FMLA) to protect employees who need time off work for family or medical reasons. The FMLA requires employers who have fifty or more employees to provide employees with up to twelve weeks of family or medical leave during any twelve-month period. During the employee's leave, the employer must continue the worker's health-care coverage and guarantee employment in the same position or a comparable position when the employee returns to work.

The act does not apply to employees who have worked less than one year or fewer than twenty-five hours a week during the previous twelve months. (The *Ethics Watch* feature on the following page reminds us that we must be careful when discussing FMLA or other laws with clients.)

Leave Rights

Generally, an employee may take family leave when he or she wishes to care for a newborn baby, a newly adopted child, or a foster child just placed in the employee's care. An employee may also take medical leave when the employee or the employee's spouse, child, or parent has a "serious health condition" requiring care. For most absences, the employee must demonstrate that the health condition requires continued treatment by a health-care provider and includes a period of incapacity of more than three days. Employees suffering from certain chronic health conditions, such as asthma and diabetes, as well as employees who are pregnant, may take FMLA leave for their own incapacities that require absences of less than three days.

Remedies for Violation of FMLA

Remedies for violations of the FMLA include:

1. damages for unpaid wages (or salary), lost benefits, denied compensation, and actual monetary losses (such as the cost of providing for care) up to an amount equivalent to the employee's wages for twelve weeks;

2. job reinstatement; and

3. promotion.

The successful plaintiff is entitled to court costs, attorneys' fees, and—in cases involving bad faith on the part of the employer—double damages. Supervisors may also be subject to personal liability, as employers, for violations of the act.

social MEDIA TODAY

Look for collaborative Web tools such as Basecamp to enable your team to manage projects and share resources. Basecamp can coordinate assignments, keep teams aware of timelines, and facilitate communication. Learning to use such tools can enhance your value as an employee.

ETHICS WATCH

DISPENSING LEGAL ADVICE

Laura, a paralegal, was interviewing a client who was considering petitioning for bankruptcy. The client's right arm was in a sling. Laura asked him about the injury, and he described how it had happened. He said that he had been unable to work at his job for two weeks and that he was worried because his employer was threatening to fire him if he couldn't return to work within another week or two. Laura said, "I'm wondering how you could be fired, because employers are required by law to give their employees medical leave for up to twelve weeks during any one-year period."

Laura said that she would check with her supervising attorney about that matter, and then she continued the interview about bankruptcy. Thinking about what Laura said, the client later confronted his employer and demanded a twelve-week leave. The employer fired him. The employer had only a few employees and was not subject to the leave requirements of the Family and Medical Leave Act.

Laura could be considered to have engaged in the unauthorized practice of law by giving legal advice to a client. That would be a violation of the NFPA *Model Code of Ethics and Professional Responsibility,* Section EC-1.8: "A paralegal shall comply with the applicable legal authority governing the unauthorized practice of law in the jurisdiction in which the paralegal practices." It would also violate the NALA *Code of Ethics,* Canon 4: "A paralegal must use discretion and professional judgment commensurate with knowledge and experience but must not render independent legal judgment in place of an attorney."

State Workers' Compensation Laws

workers' compensation laws
State statutes that establish an administrative procedure for compensating workers for injuries that arise out of or in the course of their employment, regardless of fault.

State **workers' compensation laws** establish an administrative procedure for compensating workers injured on the job. Instead of suing, an injured worker files a claim with the administrative agency or board that administers the local workers' compensation claims. State workers' compensation statutes normally allow employers to purchase insurance from a private insurer or a state fund to pay workers' compensation benefits in the event of a claim. Most states also allow employers to be *self-insured*—that is, employers who show an ability to pay claims do not need to buy insurance.

No Fault

In general, the right to recover benefits is based wholly on the existence of an employment relationship and the fact that an injury was *accidental* and *occurred on the job or in the course of employment,* regardless of fault. Intentionally inflicted self-injury, in contrast, would not be accidental and hence would not be covered. If an injury occurred while an employee was commuting to or from work, it usually would not be considered to have occurred on the job or in the course of employment and hence would not be covered.

The employee must notify the employer promptly of an injury (usually within thirty days of the injury's occurrence). Generally, the employee also must file a workers' compensation claim with the appropriate state agency or board within a certain period (sixty days to two years) from the time the injury is first noticed, rather than from the time of the accident.

No Right to Sue

The existence of workers' compensation benefits bars the employee from suing for injuries caused by the employer's negligence. ◆ **EXAMPLE 18.17—** Jim was hit by a falling brick while working at a construction site. He contacts an attorney who advises him that in his state, workers' compensation benefits will likely total about $200,000, given the nature of the injury. Jim wants to reject those benefits and sue his employer, the construction site operator, for more. That is not an option. Workers' compensation benefits are his exclusive remedy. ◆

By barring lawsuits for negligence, workers' compensation laws also bar employers from raising common law defenses to negligence. For example, an employer can no longer raise such defenses as contributory negligence or assumption of risk (see Chapter 14) to avoid liability for negligence. A worker may sue an employer who *intentionally* injures the worker, but such cases are not common. The *Developing Paralegal Skills* feature below reviews some procedures for workers' compensation claims.

DEVELOPING
paralegal skills

ASSISTING WITH A WORKERS' COMPENSATION CLAIM

Calloway, an employee of GearHead Outlet, was on a ladder arranging tools when a box fell and knocked him to the floor. His wrist was broken in three places. Calloway submitted a workers' compensation claim to GearHead's human relations department two days after the incident. When the cast was removed, his physician prescribed physical therapy to alleviate the pain he experienced and to restore function to the wrist. GearHead's insurance provider, Delacroix Mutual, sent Calloway to another physician, who prescribed pain medication and declared the physical therapy unnecessary. Calloway's wrist continued to be in pain.

Two weeks later, Calloway contacted the law firm of Shapiro and Masters, which specializes in workers' compensation litigation. Attorney Melanie Shapiro conducted an initial interview with Calloway and accepted Calloway's case. After the interview, Shapiro asked paralegal Geena Tulane to gather evidence and prepare for a hearing before a workers' compensation judge.

CHECKLIST FOR A WORKERS' COMPENSATION CLAIM

- Review the employer's workers' compensation insurance policy with the attorney to clarify coverage terms.

- Collect all medical records and compensation claim forms from the client or employer.

- Assemble evidence regarding the medical condition the client has as a result of the work-related injury or illness. If possible, photograph the scene where the injury occurred, as well as any visible injuries that may assist in proving the claim. Gather statements from any witnesses.

- Check with state insurance regulators for a record of prior complaints against the insurer.

- Compile an estimate of all medical costs. Call the offices of the physicians to whom the client has been referred for treatment of the injury or illness to inquire about their fees for specific treatments.

- Keep a log of all communications with the insurer, including e-mails and recorded phone messages. Document when the claim was submitted to the insurer, how and when the insurer responded, what the insurer asked for, and what was provided.

- Draft a request for a workers' compensation hearing with the state commission or court responsible for settling workers' compensation claims.

- Before submitting claim information for the hearing, compile the information in a coherent, organized presentation. A well-documented claim is more likely to be successful.

Employment Discrimination

Federal and state laws prohibiting employment discrimination are key features of today's employment landscape. Some state and local laws protect employees to a greater extent than do federal laws. For example, many states ban employment discrimination based on sexual orientation, which federal law does not. Some cities also ban appearance-based discrimination. The major federal laws prohibiting employment discrimination are the following:

- Title VII of the Civil Rights Act of 1964 (prohibits discrimination based on race, color, national origin, religion, and gender).

- The Age Discrimination in Employment Act of 1967 (prohibits discrimination based on age).

- The Americans with Disabilities Act of 1990 (prohibits discrimination based on disability).

Title VII of the Civil Rights Act of 1964

The most significant federal law prohibiting discrimination is the Civil Rights Act of 1964. One section of the act, known as Title VII, pertains to employment practices. Title VII prohibits employers with fifteen or more full-time employees from discriminating against employees or potential employees on the basis of race, color, national origin, religion, or gender. The Pregnancy Discrimination Act of 1978 amended Title VII to expand the definition of gender-based discrimination to include discrimination based on pregnancy.

Title VII has been interpreted by the courts to prohibit both intentional and unintentional discrimination. The latter occurs when certain employer practices or procedures have a discriminatory effect, even though they were not intended to be discriminatory. Courts call this "disparate impact" discrimination. ◆ **EXAMPLE 18.18—** A city requires all of its firefighters to be at least six feet tall. In effect, that job requirement discriminates against women, because few women are that tall. The effect of the rule is discriminatory, even though the intent in adopting the rule might have been to ensure an able-bodied firefighting crew. ◆ Job qualifications should focus on ability to perform job duties, not measures that can be discriminatory.

SEXUAL HARASSMENT. The courts have also extended Title VII protection to those who are subject to **sexual harassment** in the workplace. There are two types of sexual harassment. *Quid pro quo harassment* occurs when a superior doles out awards (promotions, raises, benefits, or other advantages) to a subordinate in exchange for sexual favors. (*Quid pro quo*, a Latin term, means "this for that" or "something for something.") In contrast, *hostile-environment harassment* occurs when an employee is subjected to offensive sexual comments, jokes, or physical contact in the workplace that make it difficult or impossible for the employee to perform a job satisfactorily.

LIABILITY FOR HARASSMENT. Generally, under the doctrine of *respondeat superior* (discussed earlier in this chapter), an employer may be held responsible (liable) for the conduct of certain employees, such as managers and supervisors. In a sexual-harassment case, if an employee in a supervisory position did the harassing, the employer will usually be held liable *automatically* for the behavior. Under the Supreme Court's decisions in a 1998 case, *Faragher v. City of Boca Raton*, employers can avoid liability for sexual harassment if they can show: "(a) that the employer exercised reasonable care to prevent and correct promptly any sexually harassing behavior, and (b) that the plaintiff employee unreasonably failed to take advantage of any preventive or corrective opportunities provided by the employer or to avoid harm otherwise."

WHAT DID THE EMPLOYER KNOW? If the person who did the harassing was not a supervisor but a co-worker, the employer will be held liable only if the employer knew, or should have known, about the harassment and failed to take immediate

---

sexual harassment

In the employment context, (1) the hiring or granting of job promotions or other benefits in return for sexual favors (*quid pro quo* harassment) or (2) language or conduct that is so sexually offensive that it creates a hostile working environment (hostile-environment harassment).

corrective action. ◆ **EXAMPLE 18.19—** Elena was sexually harassed by a co-worker and complained to her supervisor several times, but nothing was done. If Elena later sued her employer for a Title VII violation, the employer could be held liable because the supervisor did not take steps to deal properly with the complaint. ◆ An employer may even be held liable at times for the actions of nonemployees (customers or clients, for example) if the employer knew about the harassment and let it continue.

Note that Title VII prohibits not only sexual harassment but also the harassment of any employee on the basis of race, color, national origin, religion, age, or disability. In other words, racial or ethnic slurs against an employee may give rise to a hostile work environment claim under Title VII, just as sexually offensive comments would.

THE EQUAL EMPLOYMENT OPPORTUNITY COMMISSION.   The Equal Employment Opportunity Commission (EEOC) is a federal agency that administers and enforces Title VII and the laws prohibiting employment discrimination based on disability or age (to be discussed shortly), as well as some other federal antidiscrimination laws. Claims of Title VII violations must first be filed with the EEOC or the equivalent state agency. The EEOC will either investigate and take action on the claim on behalf of the employee or allow the employee to file a civil suit against the employer. The EEOC also has established guidelines that are often used by the courts to determine if the actions complained of constitute harassment under the law.

EMPLOYERS' LIABILITY UNDER TITLE VII.   An employer's liability under Title VII can be extensive. In general, the court can order injunctive relief against the employer (a judicial order to prevent future discrimination), retroactive promotions that were wrongfully withheld from the employee, and past wages to compensate the employee for any time he or she was wrongfully unemployed. Punitive damages are also available in cases involving *intentional* discrimination.

Discrimination Based on Age

The Age Discrimination in Employment Act (ADEA) of 1967 prevents employers from discriminating against workers who are forty years of age or older on the basis of their age. For the ADEA to apply, an employer must have twenty or more employees. Procedurally, discrimination suits brought under the act are very similar to suits brought under Title VII, and similar remedies are available.

Discrimination Based on Disability

Congress enacted the Americans with Disabilities Act (ADA) in 1990 to strengthen existing laws prohibiting discrimination in the workplace against individuals with disabilities. Employers with fifteen or more employees are obligated to satisfy the requirements of the ADA.

As defined by the 1990 statute, disabilities include heart disease, cancer, blindness, paralysis, acquired immune deficiency syndrome (AIDS), serious emotional illnesses, and learning disabilities.

REASONABLE ACCOMMODATION.   Under the ADA, an employer is not permitted to discriminate against a person with a disability if *reasonable accommodations* can be provided to assist the worker in satisfactorily performing the job. ◆ **EXAMPLE 18.20—** Garrett must use a wheelchair as a result of spinal damage suffered in an auto accident. He cannot use a standard-issue computer desk because it is too high for him. If the desk legs are shortened, he can work at it. Garrett's employer must provide him with a shorter desk as a reasonable accommodation. ◆

HARDSHIP.   An employer is not required to accommodate a worker with a disability if the accommodation would constitute an undue hardship for the employer, however. If the cost of accommodating the employee is extremely high, that high cost might constitute an undue hardship. ◆ **EXAMPLE 18.21—** Aisha has a neuromuscular disease that means she cannot lift more than five pounds. She applies for a job as a package handler at UPS. The company is not obligated to reorganize its method of package sorting so that only light packages would be directed to her. The cost of that accommodation would be very high. ◆ Although enforcement of the ADA falls within the jurisdiction of the EEOC, the worker alleging discrimination in violation of the ADA may also file a civil lawsuit against the employer for violation of the act.

Employment Law and the Paralegal

As a legal professional, you may be involved in tasks relating to employment law. You may work in the corporate counsel's office of a large corporate enterprise, for example. As a paralegal in a law firm or a government agency, you might assist in work relating to claims of employment discrimination, which might require you to interact with the EEOC or a relevant state agency. Here are a few tasks that paralegals commonly undertake in the area of labor and employment law:

- Draft employment contracts for an employer.

- Assist in drafting an employee handbook.

- Prepare for and attend administrative hearings before the EEOC.

- Gather factual information to counter or support a claim of employment discrimination.

- Prepare reports and furnish documentation in response to an EEOC investigation into an employee's claim of employment discrimination.

- Draft a policy manual for a business client concerning what actions constitute discriminatory employment practices.

- Research the EEOC's guidelines on sexual harassment and relevant case law to determine what types of policies and procedures will help a client avoid liability for sexual harassment.

- Prepare notices regarding a firm's employment policies.

- Assist in litigation involving multiple plaintiffs who are suing the same employer.

KEY TERMS AND CONCEPTS

agency   567
agent   567
articles of incorporation   559
bylaws   560
certificate of incorporation   560
close corporation   562
corporate charter   560
constructive discharge   572
director   558
dissolution   557
dividend   563
employment at will   572

fiduciary relationship   568
general partner   557
independent contractor   567
joint and several liability   557
joint liability   556
limited liability company (LLC)   565
limited liability partnership (LLP)   566
limited partner   557
limited partnership   557
liquidation   564
officer   558
principal   567

professional corporation (PC)   566
publicly held corporation   560
respondeat superior   570
restrictive covenants   572
sexual harassment   576
share   558
shareholder   558
vicarious liability   570
winding up   557
workers' compensation laws   574
wrongful discharge   572

Chapter Summary

Business Organizations and Employment Law

FORMS OF BUSINESS ORGANIZATION

1. *Sole proprietorship*—This is the simplest form of business organization. It is used by anyone who does business without creating a separate business entity. The owner is the business, even though he or she may hire employees to run the business.

   a. The owner is personally liable for all business debts and obligations.

   b. The owner pays personal income taxes on all profits.

   c. The proprietorship terminates on the death of the sole proprietor or the sale or transfer of the business.

2. *Partnership*—Created by the written or oral agreement of the parties to do business jointly as partners. All partners share equally in management unless otherwise provided for in the partnership agreement. The partners may hire employees to assist them in running the business.

   a. Partners are personally liable for partnership debts and obligations.

   b. The partnership as an entity does not pay income taxes but files an informational tax return with the Internal Revenue Service each year. Each partner pays personal income tax on his or her share of the profits of the partnership.

   c. Partners have a fiduciary duty that sets a high legal standard for actions related to partnership business. A partnership may be terminated by the agreement of the partners or by the occurrence of certain events, such as the death or bankruptcy of a partner.

   d. A limited partnership is a formal proceeding that must comply with state statutory requirements. Only the general partners may participate in management in a limited partnership. The general partners have unlimited personal liability. The liability of limited partners is limited to the amount of their investments.

3. *Corporation*—A corporation is created by a state-issued charter.

   a. The shareholders elect directors, who set policy and appoint officers to manage day-to-day corporate affairs. A corporation may be publicly held with many shareholders or be a close corporation with stock not freely traded.

   b. Shareholders have limited liability and are not personally liable for the debts of the corporation (beyond the amount of their investments).

   c. The corporation pays income tax on net profits; shareholders again pay income tax on profits distributed as dividends.

   d. A corporation may be terminated at the time specified in the articles of incorporation, by agreement of the shareholders and the board of directors, or by court decree.

4. *Limited liability organizations*—Other forms of business organization are the limited liability partnership (LLP), the limited liability company (LLC), and the professional corporation (PC). Generally, these organizations allow business owners to combine the tax advantages of the partnership with the limited liability of limited partners or corporate shareholders.

AGENCY LAW

An agency relationship arises when one person (called the *agent*) agrees to act for or in the place of another person (called the *principal*).

1. *Employees versus independent contractors*—Employees who deal with third parties are normally considered to be agents of their employers. An independent contractor differs from an employee in that the employer does not control the details of the independent contractor's job performance. The independent contractor may or may not be an agent.

2. *Agency formation*—An agency relationship may be formed by express agreement (oral or written) or implied by conduct. It can also arise if the principal causes a third party to believe the agency existed.

3. *Fiduciary duties*—The parties in an agency are held to certain obligations. The principal must cooperate with the agent, provide safe working conditions for the agent, and reimburse the agent for work performed and for any expenses incurred on the principal's behalf. The agent must perform his or her tasks

competently, obey and be loyal to the principal, notify the principal of matters concerning the agency, and render an accounting to the principal of how and for what purpose the principal's funds were used.

4. *Agency relationships and third parties*—The principal normally is bound by any contract formed by the agent on behalf of the principal, as long as the action was authorized. If the action was not authorized, the principal will not be liable unless he or she voluntarily agrees to be bound by (ratifies) the contract. Agents are personally liable for the torts that they commit. If an agent commits a tort within the scope of his or her employment as an agent, the principal may also be held liable under the doctrine of *respondeat superior*. A principal is not liable for harm caused by an independent contractor's negligence.

EMPLOYMENT LAW

1. *Employment at will*—Traditionally, the employment relationship has been governed by the doctrine of "employment at will"—that is, the relationship can be terminated at any time for any reason by either the employer or the employee—as well as by common law rules relating to contracts, torts, and agency. Most Americans have the legal status of "employees at will," but federal and state statutes prevent the doctrine from being applied in some circumstances.

2. *Restrictive covenants*—Employers may demand that employees limit their competition with the employer in the future. The law varies considerably across states in how such restrictions are viewed.

3. *Wrongful discharge*—Wrongful discharge occurs whenever an employer discharges an employee in violation of the law or of an employment contract.

4. *Wage laws*—The Fair Labor Standards Act imposes minimum wage and hourly work limits on employers. Some states have minimum wage laws that go beyond the rate set by Congress.

5. *Family and medical leave*—The Family and Medical Leave Act of 1993 requires employers with fifty or more employees to provide their employees (except for key employees) with up to twelve weeks of unpaid family or medical leave during any twelve-month period to care for a newborn baby, a newly adopted child, or a foster child just placed in the employee's care, or when the employee or the employee's spouse, child, or parent has a serious health condition requiring care.

6. *State workers' compensation laws*—Every state has an administrative procedure for compensating workers injured on the job.

7. *Employment discrimination*—Both federal and state laws prohibit discrimination against employees in the workplace. State laws sometimes afford greater protection. The major federal laws are:

   a. Title VII of the Civil Rights Act (1964), which prohibits employment discrimination against job applicants and employees on the basis of race, color, national origin, gender, or religion. The courts have interpreted Title VII to prohibit both intentional and unintentional discrimination, as well as pregnancy discrimination and sexual harassment.

   b. The Age Discrimination in Employment Act (ADEA) of 1967, which prohibits employment discrimination against employees who are forty years of age or older.

   c. The Americans with Disabilities Act (ADA) of 1990, which prohibits discrimination on the basis of disability against individuals qualified for a given job. Employers must reasonably accommodate the needs of persons with disabilities.

QUESTIONS FOR REVIEW

1. List and describe the three most common traditional forms of business entities. How is each entity created and terminated?

2. What is a limited liability company? What advantages does this business organizational form offer to businesspersons? How does a limited liability company differ from a limited liability partnership?

3. How does an agency relationship arise? What is the difference between an employee and an independent contractor in an agency relationship? When is a principal liable for the contracts formed by an agent? For the torts of the agent?

4. What is a fiduciary obligation? In which relationships discussed in the chapter does a fiduciary obligation arise?

5. What federal statutes prohibit employment discrimination? What kinds of discrimination are prohibited under these statutes? What federal agency handles claims of employment discrimination?

ETHICAL QUESTIONS

1. Peter works as a legal assistant for a law firm. The firm's client is suing her former employer for wrongful termination of the employment relationship. The client has financial records that prove that her supervisor authorized nondisclosure of income to the Internal Revenue Service. Disclosing these records would seriously affect her supervisor's credibility and would strengthen the client's case. Peter contacts the client to obtain the records. She refuses, fearing the effect it might have on her ability to find another job. Peter's supervising attorney is adamant about the need to obtain these records. The attorney is concerned that the firm might be guilty of malpractice if it fails to introduce this evidence. To whom is Peter obligated, the client or the firm? Why? How should Peter resolve this conflict?

2. Aimee is a paralegal in the legal department of a large corporation. One day, her good friend Sarah, who works in the company's purchasing department, asks Aimee for help. Sarah is being sexually harassed by her boss. Aimee tells Sarah that she cannot give her any legal advice. Sarah asks Aimee to make an appointment for her with Aimee's supervising attorney, so that she can get the legal advice that she needs. May employees of a corporate legal department represent other employees of the corporation? Why or why not?

PRACTICE QUESTIONS AND ASSIGNMENTS

1. Identify whether each of the business firms described below is a sole proprietorship, a partnership, or a corporation, and explain why:

   a. Terrence and Lars have owned a business together for three months. Terrence contributed 60 percent of the capital needed to start the business, and Lars contributed the other 40 percent. Each owner is responsible for a proportionate share of the profits and losses of the business, and each owner participates in managing the business.

   b. Four wealthy individuals create a business for the purpose of funding the construction of a new commerce center to revitalize the downtown business district in their city. Each individual contributes 25 percent of the funds necessary for the project, and each individual is liable for only 25 percent of the firm's losses. They all sign an agreement.

   c. Ana Ing, David Goldberg, and Mike Werner are all certified public accountants. They decide to do business together. By the end of its first year, the firm has become very profitable. As a result, the firm has to pay a substantial amount in income taxes on its profits.

   d. Dr. Menendez practices medicine on his own; he has not incorporated his business.

   e. The Pear Co. is a for-profit business that has a charter issued by the state. The charter provides for the limited liability of the company's owners.

2. Explain why the principal is (or is not) liable for the actions of the agent in each of the following situations:

   a. Attorney Arun Singh tells his paralegal, Aki Cho, to purchase litigation software.

   b. Attorney Jayne Sutterly leaves a written memo to her paralegal, David Hayes, instructing David to solicit bids for a computer network for the law firm from three computer consulting firms. David not only obtains three bids but also hires one of the firms to set up the network at a cost of $10,000.

   c. Paralegal Megan Meldrum works for a sole practitioner and has office management duties in addition to her paralegal responsibilities. When the photocopier no longer functions, she enters into a lease for a new machine without discussing it with her supervising attorney. The cost of the new machine is the same as the cost of the old machine. Would it make any difference if the cost of the new machine were significantly greater than the cost of the old one?

3. Identify what type of employment discrimination, if any, is being practiced in each of the following hypothetical situations:

   a. Lana Ronsky, a legal assistant in an all-male law firm, is the object of frequent sexual jokes and comments and occasional uninvited touching—all of which are offensive to her and make it difficult for her to do her job.

   b. Monica Pierson, a partner in a large law firm, interviews seven potential legal assistants, including an Asian American. Although the Asian American is the best qualified for the job, Monica does not hire him because he speaks English with an accent, which might offend some of the firm's clients.

   c. Diana Bekins, the manager of an insurance agency, makes it clear to Jacky McBride, a new sales representative, that she will promote him only if he provides sexual favors in return.

   d. A police department has a rule that only police officers who have been injured on the job may apply for light duty assignments. Six pregnant police officers, out of 150 on the force, were excluded from light duty assignments.

QUESTIONS FOR CRITICAL ANALYSIS

1. Limited liability entities, especially the limited liability company, have increased in popularity for those going into business. How do limited liability companies differ from corporations? Discuss the advantages of these forms of business organization.

2. Attorneys are agents of their clients and thus are governed by the principles of agency law discussed in this chapter. Do you see any similarities between the duties of agents to their principals and the ethical rules governing attorneys (discussed in Chapter 4)? If so, what are the similarities? In other words, which duties of agents, if any, correspond to the specific ethical rules discussed in Chapter 4?

3. Employers typically want their employees to be bright young people who are dedicated to their work. Some employers do not want to hire people who need to take family or maternity leaves, who are old, or whose racial or ethnic background is dissimilar to theirs. Should employers be allowed to hire only the people they want to hire? Should they be able to limit their employees to certain age groups or ethnic backgrounds? Should they be able to refuse to hire job candidates with disabilities? Why or why not? What laws protect people in these groups from employment discrimination?

PROJECTS

1. One of the oldest companies providing registered agent services is the CT Corporation. Run an Internet search for it. Follow the links through representation services until you find information on the company's registered agent services. Answer the following questions:

   a. Approximately how long has the CT Corporation (part of Wolters Kluwer) been providing registered agent services?

   b. What is its client base?

   c. What services does CT Corporation provide when it acts as a registered agent? Is there an additional fee for these services?

   d. After having reviewed the information in the previous question, write a one-sentence definition of a registered agent.

2. Locate your state employment agency online. From the Web site or a resource such as FindLaw, determine whether your state adheres to the employment-at-will doctrine. Also find out if, and in what circumstances, exceptions to this doctrine are made.

GROUP PROJECT

Students will set up a limited liability company using the hypothetical information below, as well as forms from their state government's Web site, if one is available. If not, consult a state formbook from a law library.

Roberto Hernandez, a 52-year-old mechanical engineer, lost his job. Unable to find similar work, he started a handyman business making repairs on rental properties. Roberto had a friend who owned 38 rental properties and was willing to hire him to make repairs and do remodeling on the properties. Roberto started his business as a sole proprietorship called Roberto's R&R. He has done so well that he needs to hire a couple of carpenters and a painter to work for him. Roberto is concerned about possible liability, so he has consulted your supervising attorney, who has advised Roberto that he should form a single-member, limited liability company.

Student one is responsible for finding out if the name, Roberto's R&R, is available for use. If so, he or she should print (or copy) and prepare the necessary forms to reserve it. If the name is not available, student one should recommend another name.

Student two is responsible for determining if an operating agreement is needed for a single-member, member-managed limited liability company. If so, student two should obtain and prepare such an agreement.

Student three is responsible for learning about the state filing requirements, procedures, fees, and form(s) that Roberto must file to create his LLC, including obtaining the mailing or e-mail address to which the forms should be sent.

Students three and four are responsible for preparing the form(s) and explaining to the class how a limited liability company is established in your state. The purpose of the LLC should be any legal purpose for which a business may be established in your state. The students should use your school's address if an address is required. If a registered agent and duration of the business are required, the students should use Roberto's name as agent, and "perpetual" duration if that designation is allowed under your state's law.

USING INTERNET RESOURCES

1. *Fortune* magazine contains important financial information about businesses. Go to **www.fortune.com**. Locate the Fortune 500 list and answer the following questions:

   a. What is a Fortune 500 company?

   b. Using the tabs marked "full list" and then "near you," determine whether there are any companies from your state on the list. If so, list them. If not, list the name of the first company on the overall list.

END NOTE

1. Pronounced ree-*spahn*-dee-uht soo-*peer*-ee-your.

CourseMate The available CourseMate for this text has an interactive eBook and interactive learning tools, including flash cards, quizzes, and more. To learn more about this resource and access free demo CourseMate resources, go to **www.cengagebrain.com**, and search for this book. To access CourseMate materials that you have purchased, go to **login.cengagebrain.com**.

Bankruptcy and Environmental Law

Chapter Outline

Introduction

The Bankruptcy Code

Liquidation Proceedings

Individual Repayment Plans

Reorganizations

Environmental Law

After completing this chapter, you will know:

- The various types of relief available for debtors under federal bankruptcy law.

- The basic procedures involved in an ordinary, or straight, bankruptcy proceeding.

- How bankruptcy law provides relief for corporate debtors and what basic procedures are involved in corporate reorganizations.

- The major laws regulating environmental pollution.

- The basic purpose and provisions of Superfund.

Introduction

Historically, debtors had few rights. At one time, debtors who could not pay their debts as they came due faced harsh consequences, including imprisonment and involuntary servitude. Today, in contrast, debtors have numerous rights. One of these rights is the right to petition for bankruptcy relief under federal law.

The number of petitions for bankruptcy filed each year in the United States rose dramatically from 1980 until passage of the 2005 Bankruptcy Reform Act, which significantly reduced individual bankruptcy filings. Filings jumped again in the economic downturn that began in 2008 and have since remained relatively high. This means that there will continue to be a demand for paralegals in bankruptcy law.

In this chapter, you will read about the different types of relief offered under federal bankruptcy law and about the basic bankruptcy procedures required for specific types of relief. You will also learn about the major laws regulating environmental pollution. Although bankruptcy and environmental law are quite distinct areas of law, both are based largely on federal legislation, and both are areas in which many paralegals specialize.

The Bankruptcy Code

Bankruptcy relief is provided under federal law. Although state laws play important roles in bankruptcy proceedings, particularly state laws governing property, the governing law is based on federal legislation, as required by the Constitution, and bankruptcy proceedings take place in federal courts.

Bankruptcy law prior to 2005 was based on the Bankruptcy Reform Act of 1978, as amended—hereinafter called the Bankruptcy Code, or more simply, the Code. In 2005, Congress enacted the Bankruptcy Reform Act, which significantly overhauled certain provisions of the Bankruptcy Code. Paralegals may be involved in assisting individuals or firms with filing for bankruptcy to seek relief from their debts. Alternatively, they may help represent clients who are owed money by a debtor that has filed for bankruptcy. Some paralegals work for bankruptcy courts or for U.S. Trustee offices that help recover assets in bankruptcy cases.

Goals of Bankruptcy Law

Modern bankruptcy law is designed to accomplish two main goals. The first is to provide relief and protection to debtors who have "gotten in over their heads." The second is to provide a fair means of distributing debtors' assets among all creditors. Thus, the law attempts to balance the rights of debtors and creditors.

Although the twin goals of bankruptcy remain the same, the balance between them has shifted over time. There was growing criticism after the 1978 act that too many debtors were able to avoid paying their debts. Thus, one of the major goals of the 2005 reform legislation was to require more consumers to pay as many of their debts as they possibly could instead of having those debts fully extinguished in bankruptcy. Nonetheless, debtors remain able to discharge their debts while retaining their *exempt property*. That is, state law allows bankruptcy filers to keep certain property while they have a fresh start.

Bankruptcy Courts

Bankruptcy proceedings are held in federal bankruptcy courts, which are under the authority of U.S. district courts, and rulings from bankruptcy courts can be appealed to the district courts. Essentially, a bankruptcy court fulfills the role of an administrative court for the federal district court concerning matters in bankruptcy. The bankruptcy court holds the proceedings required to administer the estate of the debtor in bankruptcy. Bankruptcy court judges are appointed for terms of fourteen years.

ON THE web

For an overview of the bankruptcy courts and procedures, go to **www.uscourts.gov**, and select "Bankruptcy" from the Federal Courts menu.

ON THE web

Before debtors can begin bankruptcy proceedings, they must receive credit counseling. For a list of approved programs, visit the Web site of the U.S. Trustee Program at **www.usdoj.gov/ust**. Select from the list "Credit Counseling & Debtor Education."

liquidation
A proceeding under Chapter 7 of the Bankruptcy Code (often referred to as *ordinary,* or *straight,* bankruptcy) in which a debtor states his or her debts and turns all assets over to a trustee, who sells the nonexempt assets and distributes the proceeds to creditors. With certain exceptions, the remaining debts are then discharged, and the debtor is relieved of the obligation to pay the debts.

consumer-debtor
A debtor whose debts are primarily consumer debts—that is, debts for purchases that are primarily for household or personal use.

discharge
The termination of an obligation. A discharge in bankruptcy terminates the debtor's obligation to pay the debts discharged by the court.

petition in bankruptcy
An application to a bankruptcy court for relief in bankruptcy; a filing for bankruptcy. The official forms required for a petition in bankruptcy must be completed accurately, sworn to under oath, and signed by the debtor.

A bankruptcy court can conduct a jury trial if the appropriate district court has authorized it and the parties to the bankruptcy consent. Bankruptcy courts follow the Federal Rules of Bankruptcy Procedure rather than the Federal Rules of Civil Procedure (see Chapter 10).

Types of Bankruptcy Relief

The Bankruptcy Code is contained in Title 11 of the *United States Code* (U.S.C.) and has eight chapters.[1] Chapters 1, 3, and 5 of the Code include general definitional provisions and provisions governing case administration, creditors, the debtor, and the estate. These three chapters apply generally to all kinds of bankruptcies. Three chapters of the Code set forth the most important types of relief that debtors can seek:

- Chapter 7 provides for **liquidation** proceedings (the selling of all nonexempt assets and the distribution of the proceeds to the debtor's creditors).
- Chapter 11 governs reorganizations.
- Chapter 13 provides for the adjustment of debts by persons with regular incomes.

In the following pages, we look at the specific type of bankruptcy relief provided under all three chapters. (The *Featured Contributor* on pages 588 and 589 provides an explanation of common terminology in bankruptcy.) To inform a **consumer-debtor** (defined as an individual whose debts are primarily consumer debts) of the types of relief available, the Code requires that the clerk of the court give all consumer-debtors written notice of the general purpose, benefits, and costs of each chapter under which they might proceed. In addition, the clerk must provide consumer-debtors with information on the types of services available from credit counseling agencies. In practice, most of these steps are handled by an attorney, not by court clerks.

Liquidation Proceedings

Liquidation under Chapter 7 of the Bankruptcy Code is probably the most familiar type of bankruptcy proceeding and is often referred to as *ordinary,* or *straight,* bankruptcy. Put simply, a debtor in a liquidation bankruptcy states his or her debts and turns all assets over to a *bankruptcy trustee.* The trustee sells the nonexempt assets and distributes the proceeds to creditors (the trustee's role will be discussed in more detail later in this chapter). With certain exceptions, the remaining debts are then **discharged** (extinguished), and the debtor is relieved of the obligation to pay the debts.

Any "person"—defined as including individuals and business entities—may be a debtor in a liquidation proceeding. A husband and wife may file jointly under a single petition. Insurance companies, banks, savings and loan associations, investment companies licensed by the Small Business Administration, and credit unions *cannot* be debtors in a liquidation bankruptcy, however. Rather, other chapters of the Bankruptcy Code or federal or state statutes apply to them.

A straight bankruptcy can be commenced by the filing of either a voluntary or an involuntary **petition in bankruptcy**—the document that is filed with a bankruptcy court to initiate bankruptcy proceedings. If a debtor files the petition, it is a *voluntary bankruptcy.* If one or more creditors file a petition to force the debtor into bankruptcy, it is an *involuntary bankruptcy.* We discuss both voluntary and involuntary bankruptcy proceedings under Chapter 7 in the following subsections.

Voluntary Bankruptcy

To bring a voluntary petition in bankruptcy, a debtor files official forms designated for that purpose in the bankruptcy court. Before debtors can file a petition, they must receive credit counseling from an approved nonprofit agency within the

180-day period preceding the date of filing. Debtors filing a Chapter 7 petition must include a certificate proving that they have received individual or group counseling from an approved agency within the last 180 days. One of your tasks as a paralegal may be to assist a debtor in locating and completing the required credit counseling course.

The Code requires consumer-debtors who have opted for liquidation bankruptcy proceedings to confirm the accuracy of the petition in bankruptcy that they have filed. They must also state in the petition, at the time of filing, that they understand the relief available under other chapters of the Code and have chosen to proceed under Chapter 7. Attorneys representing consumer-debtors must file an affidavit stating that they have informed the debtors of the relief available under each chapter of the Bankruptcy Code. In addition, attorneys must reasonably attempt to verify the accuracy of consumer-debtors' petitions and schedules (described below).

Chapter 7 Schedules

The voluntary petition must contain the following schedules:

1. A list of both secured and unsecured creditors, their addresses, and the amount of debt owed to each. A **secured creditor** is one who has a security interest in the collateral that secures the debt. For example, a lending institution that finances the purchase of an automobile normally takes a security interest in the automobile—the collateral for the loan.

2. A statement of the financial affairs of the debtor.

3. A list of all property owned by the debtor, including property that the debtor claims is exempt.

4. A listing of current income and expenses.

5. A certificate from an approved credit counseling agency (as discussed previously).

6. Proof of payments received from employers within sixty days prior to the filing of the petition.

7. A statement of the amount of monthly income, itemized to show how the amount is calculated.

8. A copy of the debtor's federal income tax return (or a transcript of the return) for the year ending immediately before the filing of the petition.

secured creditor
A lender, seller, or any other person in whose favor there is a security interest.

A paralegal meets with a couple filing for bankruptcy. What are some of the tasks that this paralegal must undertake to help this couple complete their filing?

Featured Contributor

KEY TERMS IN THE CHAPTER 7 BANKRUPTCY PROCESS

Jo-Christy Brown

BIOGRAPHICAL NOTE

Jo-Christy Brown is a graduate of Texas Tech University. After graduating, she worked as a computer sales representative. She then attended the University of Texas School of Law. Following graduation, she began her practice in Austin as an associate with a large local firm, where she later became a partner.

After practicing in the areas of commercial litigation and environmental law, Ms. Brown decided to form her own firm that would focus on the strengths of women lawyers and provide a positive work environment for legal professionals with family responsibilities. That firm grew to include twelve lawyers. She continues to own and operate her own law firm.

© Cengage Learning 2014

Bankruptcy has terms peculiar to this area of law. Your text focuses on some details of procedure under the Bankruptcy Code. It would be useful to review key terminology that paralegals hear when involved in bankruptcy work. The focus here is on Chapter 7 bankruptcy, but many of the terms are also relevant for Chapter 13 and other types of bankruptcy.

BEGINNING STEPS IN THE BANKRUPTCY PROCESS

A *debtor* is the party, whether a person or a business, liable for debts and the subject of the bankruptcy proceedings. The party owed the debt is a *creditor.* When a debtor owes money or other legal obligations to credi-

tors, such as a bank or credit-card company that made loans, and the debt far exceeds the debtor's ability to repay the amounts owed, a debtor may decide it is wise to file for bankruptcy under *Chapter 7*. Under Chapter 7, the debtor must liquidate his or her nonexempt property and give the proceeds to creditors. To be eligible, the debtor must satisfy the *means test* that compares income to debt. Before filing bankruptcy, the debtor must complete *credit counseling,* a short course on personal financial management.

The party declaring bankruptcy, through an attorney, files a *statement of intention.* This is a declaration made by a debtor concerning plans for

U.S. trustee
A government official who performs administrative tasks that a bankruptcy judge would otherwise have to perform.

The official forms must be completed accurately, sworn to under oath, and signed by the debtor. To conceal assets or knowingly supply false information on these schedules is a federal crime.

Most likely, the debtor must file a tax return at the end of each tax year while the case is pending and provide a copy to the court. This can be forced at the request of the court, or of the **U.S. trustee**, or of any party with a valid interest in the proceedings (such as a creditor). This requirement also applies to Chapter 11 and 13 bankruptcies (discussed later in this chapter).

Means Test

A major focus of the bankruptcy proceeding is the *means test*. The purpose of the test is to keep upper-income people from abusing the bankruptcy process by filing for Chapter 7, as was thought to have happened in the past. The test forces more people to file for Chapter 13 bankruptcy (discussed later), rather than allow liquidation of debts.

INCOME ABOVE OR BELOW MEDIAN?   Debtors wishing to file for bankruptcy must complete the means test to determine whether they qualify for Chapter 7. The debtor's average monthly income in recent months is compared with the median income dealing with consumer debts that are secured by property of the debtor. *Secured debt* is debt that is "backed" by a mortgage, a pledge of collateral, or another lien. This kind of debt gives the creditor, called a *secured creditor*, the right to attempt to get control of property such as a house, a car, or other assets that the debtor originally offered as collateral to the lender to obtain a loan.

All of the debtor's property in a bankruptcy proceeding is called an *estate*. The estate is all of the legal property of the debtor at the time the bankruptcy proceeding begins. In a *statement of financial affairs,* the debtor answers questions on an official form about income, property, and other matters relevant to the proceeding. This statement is part of the debtor's *schedule* of assets, liabilities, and other financial information.

WHO GETS WHAT?

The Bankruptcy Code details the rules about what property the debtor gets to keep (called *exempt assets*) and what obligations the debtor may *avoid* (eliminate or reduce) for certain debts, as well as what assets must be liquidated to meet the debtor's obligations to creditors (called *nonexempt assets*). An *automatic stay* is an injunction that prohibits collections against the debtor because of the bankruptcy. Many times, a bankrupt person will file an automatic stay to "freeze" or protect the estate until the details of a bankruptcy can be finalized.

The Code also determines the *priority* of creditors beyond the secured creditors; that is, the ranking of unsecured claims. If a debtor made a payment to a creditor in the ninety-day period before filing for bankruptcy, this may be held to be a *preferential debt payment* that the creditor must return to the estate. In some cases such payments will be held to be *fraudulent transfers* where the debtor is attempting to evade responsibilities. These funds must also be returned.

The estate of the bankrupt is represented by the *trustee* who is appointed by the court overseeing the bankruptcy to review the debtor's condition and to exercise statutory powers for the benefit of the creditors in sorting out everyone's claims against the bankrupt estate. Some property will be declared to be *exempt* from the estate and will not be available to pay down the claims of the creditors. Certain obligations are considered to be *nondischargeable debts* that are not eliminated in bankruptcy, such as educational loans and child support.

WRAPPING IT UP

In the course of the bankruptcy proceedings, the court decides what debt obligations will be *discharged* (legally eliminated). In some bankruptcies, the court orders a plan for repayment of debts by the debtor, called the *confirmation*. In most bankruptcy cases, the work is done by lawyers representing the parties, and the debtor never appears in court. At the end, the debtor is said to be given a *fresh start*.

> *"In most bankruptcy cases . . .*
> *the debtor is said to be given a fresh start."*

in the geographical area in which the person lives. (The U.S. Trustee Program provides these data on its Web site.) If the debtor's income is below the median income (for the area in which the debtor lives), the debtor is usually allowed to file for Chapter 7 bankruptcy, as there is no presumption of bankruptcy abuse.

The key element of the means test is to see if a person considering bankruptcy is eligible for Chapter 7 or not. If the income of the person, adjusted for family size, is below the median income of households in the area in the last six months, then Chapter 7 is likely available. (As of 2012, the median income of the average American family of three was about $58,000 annually.)

ALLOWANCES. If the debtor's income is above the median income, then further calculations must be made to project the debtor's income and expenses into the future. Recent monthly income is presumed to continue for the next sixty months. From that the debtor subtracts the living expenses allowed by Internal Revenue Service (IRS) formulas. (The U.S. Trustee Program Web site also provides these numbers.) The IRS formula includes allowances for:

- food,

- clothing,

- housekeeping supplies,
- housing (including mortgage payment),
- personal care products,
- transportation (including car payment),
- health care,
- utilities, and
- other necessary expenses.

If the debtor's estimated future disposable income is more than an amount set annually by the U.S. Trustee Program, then debt abuse is presumed, and the debtor must file for Chapter 13, except in unusual circumstances.

Additional Grounds for Dismissal

A debtor's petition for Chapter 7 relief may be dismissed for abuse or for failing to provide the necessary documents (such as schedules and tax returns) within the specified time. In addition, a motion to dismiss a Chapter 7 filing may be granted in two other situations. First, if the debtor has been convicted of a violent crime, the victim can file a motion to dismiss the voluntary petition. Second, if after filing a petition the debtor fails to pay domestic-support obligations (which include child and spousal support), the court may dismiss the petition.

Order for Relief

order for relief
A court's grant of assistance to a complainant.

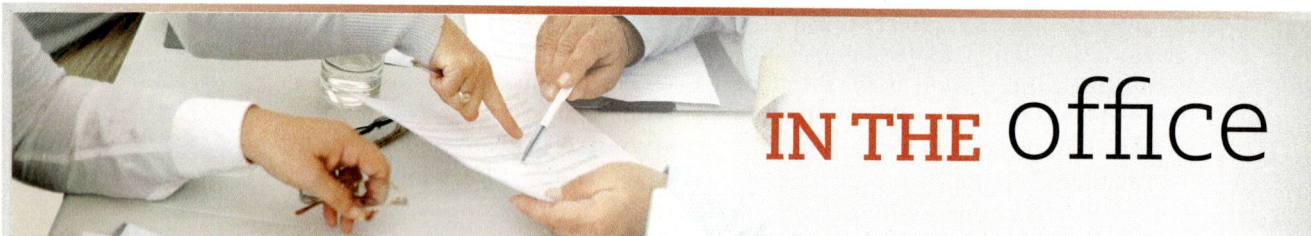

If the voluntary petition for bankruptcy is found to be proper, the filing of the petition will itself constitute an **order for relief**. (An order for relief is a court's grant of assistance to a bankruptcy petitioner.) Once a consumer-debtor's voluntary petition has been filed, the clerk of the court or other appointee must give the trustee and creditors notice of the order for relief by mail not more than twenty days after entry of the order.

Involuntary Bankruptcy

An involuntary bankruptcy occurs when the debtor's creditors force the debtor into bankruptcy proceedings. For an involuntary action to be filed, the following requirements must be met: If the debtor has twelve or more creditors, three or more of these creditors having unsecured claims totaling $14,000 must join in the

IN THE office

DRESS FOR SUCCESS

Fair or not, our appearance can affect how others perceive us. Law offices have a professional air about them, and employees must dress accordingly. Appearance is especially important when interviewing for a job. A number of books and Web sites discuss professional dress, but here are some basic guidelines. Wearing a fresh-looking navy or black suit to an interview with a light-colored blouse or shirt is safe.

Women should wear conservative jewelry, if any, and cover tattoos. Men should remove earrings, and women should remove jewelry from piercings other than ear piercings. On the job itself, you will observe what is expected so that you can dress to show respect for the office and for your position.

petition. If a debtor has fewer than twelve creditors, one or more creditors having a claim of $14,000 may file.

If the debtor challenges the involuntary petition, a hearing will be held, and the bankruptcy court will enter an order for relief if it finds either of the following:

1. The debtor is not paying debts as they become due.

2. A general receiver, assignee, or custodian took possession of substantially all of the debtor's property within 120 days before the filing of the petition.

If the court grants an order for relief, the debtor will be required to supply the same information in the bankruptcy schedules as in a voluntary bankruptcy.

An involuntary petition should not be used as an everyday debt-collection device, and the Code provides penalties for the filing of frivolous petitions against debtors. Judgment may be granted against the petitioning creditors for the costs and attorneys' fees incurred by the debtor in defending against an involuntary petition that is dismissed by the court. If the petition is filed in bad faith, damages can be awarded for injury to the debtor's reputation.

Automatic Stay

The moment a petition in bankruptcy—either voluntary or involuntary—is filed, there exists an **automatic stay**, or suspension, of nearly all litigation and other action by creditors against the debtor or the debtor's property. In other words, once a petition has been filed, creditors cannot contact the debtor by phone or mail or start any legal proceedings to recover debts or to repossess property. In some circumstances, a creditor may petition the bankruptcy court for relief from the automatic stay, however.

Stay on Litigation

Similarly, all lawsuits against a debtor with a pending bankruptcy filing are stayed and the plaintiffs must seek permission from the bankruptcy court to allow their claims to proceed. If a client of yours, for example, has sued her former employer for sex discrimination and the employer files for bankruptcy, your client's suit will be stayed (put on hold) until the bankruptcy court gives permission for the suit to continue.

The Code provides that if a creditor *knowingly* violates the automatic stay (a willful violation), any party injured, including the debtor, is entitled to recover actual damages, costs, and attorneys' fees and may be entitled to recover punitive damages as well.

Exceptions to the Automatic Stay

There are several exceptions to the automatic stay. An exception is created for domestic-support obligations, which include any obligation owed to a spouse, a former spouse, a child of the debtor, the child's parent or guardian, or a governmental unit. In addition, proceedings against the debtor related to divorce, child custody or visitation, domestic violence, and support enforcement are not stayed.

Also excepted are investigations by a securities regulatory agency, proceedings to establish certain claims against real property (including property taxes), eviction actions on judgments obtained prior to the filing of the petition, and withholding from the debtor's wages for repayment of a retirement account loan.

Bankruptcy Estate

At the beginning of a liquidation proceeding under Chapter 7, a **bankruptcy estate** (sometimes called an *estate in property*) is created. The estate consists of all the debtor's interests in property currently held, wherever located. Interests in certain property—such as gifts, inheritances, property settlements (divorce), and life insurance death proceeds—to which the debtor becomes entitled *within 180 days after filing* may also become part of the estate. In contrast, contributions that the debtor has already made to an employee benefit plan are excluded from the estate.

automatic stay
A suspension of all judicial proceedings upon the occurrence of an independent event. Under the Bankruptcy Code, the moment a petition to initiate bankruptcy proceedings is filed, all litigation or other legal action by creditors against a debtor and the debtor's property is suspended.

bankruptcy estate
In bankruptcy proceedings, all of the debtor's interests in property currently held and wherever located, as well as interests in certain property to which the debtor becomes entitled within 180 days after filing for bankruptcy.

Generally, though, the filing of a bankruptcy petition fixes a dividing line: property acquired prior to the filing of the petition becomes property of the estate, and property acquired after the filing remains the debtor's. An important role for paralegals in bankruptcy cases is locating property that should be included in the debtor's bankruptcy estate.

Creditors' Meeting

Within a reasonable time after the order for relief has been granted, the U.S. trustee must call a meeting of the creditors listed in the schedules filed by the debtor. The bankruptcy judge does not attend this meeting. The debtor is required to attend the meeting (unless excused by the court) and to submit to examination under oath by the creditors and the trustee. Failing to appear when required or making false statements under oath may result in the debtor being denied a discharge in bankruptcy. The trustee ensures that the debtor is aware of the potential consequences of bankruptcy and of the ability to file for bankruptcy under a different chapter of the Bankruptcy Code.

Creditors' Claims

proof of claim
A document filed with a bankruptcy court by a creditor to inform the court of a claim against a debtor's property. The proof of claim lists the creditor's name and address, as well as the amount that the creditor asserts is owed to the creditor by the debtor.

To be entitled to receive a portion of the debtor's estate, each creditor normally files a **proof of claim** with the bankruptcy court clerk within ninety days of the creditors' meeting. The proof of claim lists the creditor's name and address, as well as the amount that the creditor asserts is owed to the creditor by the debtor. A creditor need not file a proof of claim if the debtor's schedules list the creditor's claim as liquidated (exactly determined) and the creditor does not dispute the amount of the claim. A proof of claim is necessary if there is any dispute concerning the claim. *Developing Paralegal Skills* below reviews some steps that may be involved in filing a claim.

DEVELOPING
paralegal skills

PREPARING A PROOF OF CLAIM

Alonzo Smith works as a paralegal for a bankruptcy attorney. Alonzo has been assigned the task of preparing a proof-of-claim form to be filed with the bankruptcy court for a client. The client is Bill Peaslee, a farmer who supplies a number of local restaurants with organic produce. One of Peaslee's customers, Ashleigh Burke (the sole owner of Greenleaf Restaurant) owes Peaslee nearly $10,000 for orders placed in the previous nine months.

Three weeks ago, when attempting to collect the past-due balance from Burke, Peaslee learned that Burke had filed for bankruptcy relief. Peaslee, as a creditor of an individual debtor filing for bankruptcy protection, must file a proof of claim with the bankruptcy court to establish the amount of his claim against Burke. After Alonzo's supervising attorney provides the necessary information, Alonzo turns to his computer.

CHECKLIST FOR PREPARING A PROOF-OF-CLAIM FORM

- Retrieve the proof-of-claim form from the firm's forms database.

- Key in the client-creditor's name and address.

- Insert the amount that the debtor owes to the client.

- Enter the date, the debtor's name, and other required data.

- Print out the completed form and proofread it carefully.

- Give the completed form to the supervising attorney to review.

- After the attorney has reviewed the form, make copies of it to send to the court for filing.

Exemptions

As mentioned, the bankruptcy trustee takes control over the debtor's property in a Chapter 7 bankruptcy, but an individual debtor is entitled to exempt (exclude) certain property from the bankruptcy. The Bankruptcy Code exempts (among other things) the following property:

1. Up to $20,200 in equity in the debtor's residence (the *homestead exemption,* which will be discussed shortly).

2. Interest in a motor vehicle up to $3,225.

3. Interest, up to $475 for a particular item, in household goods and furnishings, wearing apparel, appliances, books, animals, crops, and musical instruments (the aggregate total of all items is limited to $9,850).

4. Interest in jewelry up to $1,225.

5. Interest in any other property up to $975, plus any unused part of the $20,200 debtor's residence exemption up to about $10,000.

6. Any tools of the debtor's trade up to $1,850.

7. Any unmatured life insurance contract owned by the debtor.

8. Employee contributions to a qualified pension plan.

9. Social Security and certain public assistance benefits, alimony and support, certain retirement funds and pensions, and education savings accounts held for specific periods of time.

10. The right to receive personal-injury and other awards up to $18,450.

The amounts allowed are changed over time, so you should check to see the current allowances.

Individual states have the power to pass legislation precluding debtors from using the federal exemptions within the state. Most states have done this. In those states, debtors may use only state, not federal, exemptions. In the rest of the states, an individual debtor (or a husband and wife filing jointly) may choose either the exemptions provided under state law or the federal exemptions. In those states, paralegals often help attorneys determine which exemptions are most advantageous for debtors, given their circumstances.

The Homestead Exemption

In some states, among them Florida and Texas, state **homestead exemptions** allow debtors petitioning for bankruptcy to shield unlimited amounts of equity in their homes from creditors. The amount of exemption, though, is limited by federal law. The Bankruptcy Code requires that the debtor must have lived in the state for two years prior to filing the petition to be able to use the state homestead exemption. In addition, if the homestead was acquired within three and a half years before the date of filing, the maximum equity exempted is $125,000, even if the state law would permit a higher amount.

The Bankruptcy Trustee

Promptly after the order for relief in the liquidation proceeding has been entered, an interim, or provisional, **bankruptcy trustee** is appointed by the U.S. trustee. The bankruptcy trustee may be a bankruptcy attorney who is not involved in the case. The basic duty of the bankruptcy trustee is to collect and reduce to cash the property in the bankruptcy estate that is not exempt. The trustee is held accountable for administering the debtor's estate in the interests of *both* the debtor and the creditors.

---

homestead exemption
A law permitting the debtor to retain the family home, either in its entirety or up to a specified dollar amount, free from the claims of unsecured creditors or trustees in bankruptcy.

bankruptcy trustee
A person appointed by the bankruptcy court to administer the debtor's estate in the interests of both the debtor and the creditors. The basic duty of the bankruptcy trustee is to collect and reduce to cash the estate in property and to close up the estate as speedily as is compatible with the best interests of the parties.

Duties for Means Testing

In Chapter 7 cases, the trustee is required to review promptly all materials filed by the debtor. After the first meeting of the creditors, the trustee must file a statement as to whether the case is presumed to be an abuse under the means test. The trustee must provide a copy of this statement to all creditors within five days. Not later than forty days after the first creditors' meeting, the trustee must either file a motion to dismiss the petition (or convert it to a Chapter 13 case) or file a statement setting forth the reasons why the motion would not be appropriate.

Trustee's Powers

The trustee has the power to require persons holding the debtor's property at the time the petition is filed to deliver the property to the trustee. To enable the trustee to implement this power, the Code provides that the trustee occupies a position equivalent in rights to that of certain other parties, such as some types of creditors.

In addition, the trustee has specific *powers of avoidance*—that is, the trustee can set aside (avoid) an earlier sale or other transfer of the debtor's property, taking it back as a part of the debtor's estate. These powers include voidable rights available to the debtor, preferences, and fraudulent transfers by the debtor. Each is discussed in more detail below. Additionally, certain statutory liens (creditors' claims against the debtor's property) may be avoided by the trustee.

The debtor shares most of the trustee's avoidance powers. Thus, if the trustee does not take action to enforce one of the rights just mentioned, the debtor in a liquidation bankruptcy can enforce that right.

VOIDABLE RIGHTS. A trustee steps into the shoes of the debtor. Thus, any reason that a debtor can use to obtain the return of property can be used by the trustee as well. These grounds include fraud, duress, incapacity, and mutual mistake (discussed in Chapter 15).

PREFERENCES. A debtor is not permitted to transfer property or to make a payment that favors—or gives a preference to—one creditor over others. The trustee is allowed to recover payments made by the debtor to one creditor in preference over another.

To have made a preferential payment that can be recovered, a debtor generally must have transferred property, for a preexisting debt, within *ninety days* of the filing of the petition in bankruptcy. The transfer must give the creditor more than the creditor would have received as a result of the bankruptcy proceedings.

If a preferred creditor (one who has received a preference) has sold the transferred property to an innocent third party, the trustee cannot recover the property from the innocent party. The creditor, however, generally can be held accountable for the value of the property sold.

FRAUDULENT TRANSFERS. The trustee can avoid fraudulent transfers or obligations if they were made within two years of the filing of the petition or if they were made with actual intent to hinder, delay, or defraud a creditor. For example, suppose that a debtor who is thinking about petitioning for bankruptcy sells his stamp collection, worth at least $10,000, to a friend for $500. The friend agrees that in the future he will "sell" the collection back to the debtor for the same amount of money. This is a fraudulent transfer that the trustee can undo.

Distribution of Property

In the distribution of the debtor's estate in bankruptcy, secured creditors take priority over unsecured creditors. The Code provides that a consumer-debtor, within thirty days of filing a liquidation petition or before the date of the first meeting of

---

preference

In bankruptcy proceedings, the debtor's favoring of one creditor over others by making payments or transferring property to that creditor at the expense of the rights of other creditors. The bankruptcy trustee is allowed to recover payments made to one creditor in preference over another.

the creditors (whichever is first), must file with the clerk a statement of intention with respect to the secured collateral. The statement must indicate whether the debtor will retain the collateral or surrender the collateral to the secured party. Also, if applicable, the debtor must specify whether the collateral will be claimed as exempt property and whether the debtor intends to redeem the property or reaffirm the debt secured by the collateral. The trustee is obligated to enforce the debtor's statement within forty-five days after it is filed.

Distribution to Secured Creditors

If the collateral is surrendered to the secured party, the secured creditor can enforce the security interest either by accepting the property in full satisfaction of the debt or by selling the collateral and using the proceeds to pay off the debt. Thus, the secured party has priority over unsecured parties as to the proceeds from the disposition of the collateral. Should the collateral be insufficient to cover the secured debt owed, the secured creditor becomes an unsecured creditor for the difference.

Distribution to Unsecured Creditors

Bankruptcy law establishes an order of priority for classes of debts owed to unsecured creditors, and they are paid in the order of their priority. Each class of unsecured creditors must be fully paid before the next class is entitled to any of the remaining proceeds. If there are insufficient proceeds to pay fully all the creditors in a class, the proceeds are distributed proportionately to the creditors in the class, and classes lower in priority receive nothing. There are almost never sufficient funds to pay all creditors. The order of priority among classes of unsecured creditors is as follows (some of these classes involve claims against bankrupt businesses):

1. Claims for domestic-support obligations, such as child support and alimony.

2. Administrative expenses, including court costs, trustee fees, and attorneys' fees.

3. In an involuntary bankruptcy, expenses incurred by the debtor in the ordinary course of business.

4. Unpaid wages, salaries, and commissions earned within ninety days of the filing of the petition. The amount is capped for each claimant.

5. Unsecured claims for contributions to be made to employee benefit plans. The amount is capped for each claimant.

6. Consumer deposits given to the debtor before the petition was filed. The amount is capped for each claimant.

7. Certain taxes and penalties due to government units, such as income and property taxes.

8. Claims for death or personal injury resulting from the unlawful operation of a motor vehicle.

9. Claims of general creditors.

If any amount remains after the priority classes of creditors have been satisfied, it is turned over to the debtor. That is unlikely to happen. If the debtor had sufficient funds to satisfy all debtors, there would likely have been no bankruptcy filing.

Discharge

From the debtor's point of view, the primary purpose of liquidation is to obtain a fresh start through a discharge of debts. Certain debts, however, are not dischargeable in bankruptcy. Also, certain debtors may not qualify to have all debts discharged in bankruptcy. These situations are discussed next.

SOCIAL MEDIA TODAY

Social media are still in the developmental stage. Learning what does not work is often as important as learning what does. Don't be afraid to try new tools or to abandon them if they prove not to be useful.

Exceptions to Discharge

Discharge of a debt may be denied because of the nature of the claim or the conduct of the debtor. Claims that are not dischargeable in a liquidation bankruptcy include the following:

1. Claims for back taxes accruing within two years prior to bankruptcy.

2. Claims for amounts borrowed by the debtor to pay federal taxes or any nondischargeable taxes.

3. Claims against property or funds obtained by the debtor under false pretenses or by false representations.

4. Claims by creditors who were not notified of the bankruptcy. These claims did not appear on the schedules the debtor was required to file.

5. Claims based on fraud or misuse of funds by the debtor while acting in a fiduciary capacity or claims involving the debtor's embezzlement or larceny.

6. Domestic-support obligations and property settlements as provided for in a separation agreement or divorce decree.

7. Claims for amounts due on a retirement account loan.

8. Claims based on willful or malicious conduct by the debtor toward another or the property of another.

9. Certain government fines and penalties.

10. Certain student loans or obligations to repay funds received as an educational benefit, scholarship, or stipend—unless payment of the loans imposes an undue hardship on the debtor and the debtor's dependents.

11. Consumer debts of more than $500 for luxury goods or services owed to a single creditor incurred within ninety days of the order for relief.

12. Cash advances totaling more than $750 that are extensions of open-end consumer credit obtained by the debtor within seventy days of the order for relief.

13. Judgments against a debtor as a result of the debtor's operation of a motor vehicle while intoxicated.

14. Fees or assessments arising from property in a homeowners' association, as long as the debtor retains an interest in the property.

15. Failure of the debtor to provide required or requested tax documents.

Objections to Discharge

In addition to the exceptions to discharge just listed, a bankruptcy court may also deny the discharge based on the debtor's conduct. In such a situation, the assets of the debtor are still distributed to the creditors, but the debtor remains liable for the unpaid portion of all claims. Some grounds for the denial of discharge based on the debtor's conduct follow:

1. The debtor's concealment or destruction of property with the intent to defraud a creditor.

2. The debtor's fraudulent concealment or destruction of financial records.

3. The granting of a discharge to the debtor within eight years prior to the petition filing.

4. Failure of the debtor to complete the required credit counseling course.

5. Proceedings in which the debtor could be found guilty of a felony.

social
MEDIA TODAY

Do not post the same items on all of your social networks.

Effect of Discharge

The primary effect of a discharge is to void, or set aside, any judgment on a discharged debt and prohibit any action to collect a discharged debt. A discharge does not affect the liability of a co-debtor. As this review of bankruptcy procedures makes clear, it is a complicated process that requires attention to detail, as further explained in the *Practice Focus* feature below.

Individual Repayment Plans

As noted earlier, some debtors who file for bankruptcy may prefer liquidation under Chapter 7 but, due to the means test, may be required to file under Chapter 13. Chapter 13 of the Bankruptcy Code provides for "Adjustment of Debts of an Individual with Regular Income." Individuals (not partnerships or corporations) with regular income who owe fixed unsecured debts of less than $340,000 or fixed secured debts of less than $1 million may take advantage of bankruptcy repayment plans. Among those eligible are salaried employees and sole proprietors.

Many small-business debtors have a choice of filing a plan for reorganization (discussed later in this chapter) or for repayment. There are several advantages to repayment plans. One is that they are less expensive and less complicated than reorganization proceedings or liquidation proceedings.

Filing the Petition

A repayment-plan case can be initiated only by the filing of a *voluntary* petition by the debtor. In addition, certain liquidation and reorganization cases may be converted to repayment-plan cases with the consent of the debtor.

PRACTICE focus

SKILLS NEEDED TO ASSIST BANKRUPTCY CLIENTS

Whether representing debtors or creditors, businesses or individuals, paralegals in bankruptcy practice need a mix of detective, accounting, and legal research skills. At the heart of a bankruptcy practice is the effort to negotiate a resolution of claims that exceed the assets available. In some cases, it takes detective skills to track down hidden assets or find flaws in creditors' accounts. Accounting ability is vital, since paralegals have to review the books and financial statements of debtors to sort out claims.

Negotiations, handled by attorneys, resolve most bankruptcy cases, as the creditors recognize that they will have to take less than full payment, and the main issue is how much of a "haircut" (reduced payment) each group will take on its claims.

Working on bankruptcy matters often begins by interviewing the client and assembling his or her financial records to determine eligibility for particular forms of bankruptcy relief. The supervising attorney will review the information you gather and then recommend the appropriate type of bankruptcy filing to the client.

You will then assist in drafting the bankruptcy petition, listing all the debts and assets. The attorney will provide counseling for a client to ensure that she or he takes full advantage of the various exemptions provided by state and federal laws that protect certain assets (such as a home). Once the petition has been filed, paralegals often assist in the negotiations with creditors over the resolution of the claims. Working as a paralegal for a creditor requires similar skills, since an important part of the job is ensuring that the debtor applies the proper amount of assets to help pay debts owed to your client.

Upon the filing of a repayment-plan petition, a trustee, who will make payments under the plan, must be appointed. The automatic stay previously discussed also takes effect. Although the stay applies to all or part of a consumer debt, it does not apply to any business debt incurred by the debtor.

Filing the Plan

Only the debtor may file a repayment plan. This plan may provide either for payment of all obligations in full or for payment of a lesser amount. The duration of the payment plan (three or five years) is determined by the debtor's median family income. If the debtor's income is greater than the state median income under the means test (previously discussed), the proposed time for repayment must be five years. The term may not exceed five years.

The Code requires the debtor to make "timely" payments from the debtor's disposable income, and the trustee is required to ensure that the debtor commences these payments. The debtor must begin making payments under the proposed plan within thirty days after the plan has been filed with the court. If the plan has not been confirmed, the trustee is instructed to hold the payments until the plan is confirmed and then distribute them accordingly. If the plan is denied, the trustee will return the payments to the debtor less any costs. Failure of the debtor to make timely payments or to begin payments within the thirty-day period will allow the court to convert the case to a liquidation bankruptcy or to dismiss the petition.

Confirmation of the Plan

After the plan is filed, the court holds a confirmation hearing, at which interested parties may object to the plan. The hearing must be held at least twenty days, but no more than forty-five days, after the meeting of the creditors. Confirmation of the plan is dependent on the debtor's certification that postpetition domestic-support obligations have been paid in full and all prepetition tax returns have been filed. The court will confirm a plan with respect to each claim of a secured creditor under any of the following circumstances:

1. If the secured creditors have accepted the plan.

2. If the plan provides that secured creditors retain their claims against the debtor's property until payment is made in full or until the debtor receives a discharge.

3. If the debtor surrenders the property securing the claim to the creditors.

Objections to the Plan

Unsecured creditors do not have a vote to confirm a repayment plan, but they can object to it. The court can approve a plan over the objection of the trustee or any unsecured creditor only in the following two situations:

1. When the value of the property to be distributed under the plan is at least equal to the amount of the claims.

2. When all the debtor's projected disposable income to be received during the plan period will be applied to making payments. Disposable income is all income received *less* amounts needed to pay domestic-support obligations and/or amounts needed to meet ordinary expenses to continue the operation of a business.

Modification of the Plan

Prior to completion of payments, the plan may be modified at the request of the debtor, the trustee, or an unsecured creditor. If any interested party objects to the modification, the court must hold a hearing to determine approval or disapproval of the modified plan.

Discharge

After the completion of all payments, the court grants a discharge of the debts provided for by the repayment plan. Not all debts are dischargeable, however. Nondischargeable debts in a Chapter 13 bankruptcy include:

- allowed claims not provided for by the plan,
- certain long-term debts provided for by the plan,
- claims for domestic-support obligations,
- payments on retirement accounts,
- debts for trust fund taxes or taxes for which returns were never filed or filed late (within two years of the bankruptcy filing),
- student loans,
- injury or property damage obligations arising from driving under the influence of alcohol or drugs,
- debts arising from fraudulent tax obligations,
- criminal fines and restitution,
- debts arising from fraud by a person acting in a fiduciary capacity, and
- restitution payments due for willfully and maliciously causing personal injury or death.

If the debtor does not complete the plan, a hardship discharge may be granted if failure to complete the plan was due to circumstances beyond the debtor's control and if the value of the property distributed under the plan was greater than creditors would have received in a liquidation proceeding. A discharge can be revoked within one year if it was obtained by fraud.

Reorganizations

The type of bankruptcy proceedings used most commonly by a corporate debtor is the Chapter 11 *reorganization*. In a reorganization, the creditors and the debtor formulate a plan under which the debtor pays a portion of his or her debts and is discharged of the remainder. The debtor is allowed to continue in business. Although this type of bankruptcy is commonly a corporate reorganization, any debtor (except a stockbroker or a commodities broker) who is eligible for Chapter 7 relief is eligible for relief under Chapter 11. Railroads are also eligible. There is a "fast-track" Chapter 11 procedure for small-business debtors whose liabilities do not exceed $2 million and who do not own or manage real estate. This procedure does not require the appointment of committees and can save time and costs.

The same principles that govern the filing of a liquidation (Chapter 7) petition apply to reorganization proceedings. The case may be brought either voluntarily or involuntarily. The same principles govern the entry of the order for relief. The automatic-stay provision is also applicable in reorganizations. An exception from the automatic stay is triggered in the event that the debtor files for bankruptcy again within two years, and new grounds for dismissal (such as substantial abuse) or conversion of the case are established.

Workouts

In some instances, to avoid bankruptcy proceedings, creditors may prefer private, negotiated adjustments or creditor-debtor relations, also known as **workouts**. Often these out-of-court workouts are much more flexible and more conducive to a speedy settlement. Speed is critical, because delay is one of the most costly elements in any bankruptcy proceeding. Another advantage of workouts is that they avoid the administrative costs of bankruptcy proceedings.

workout
An out-of-court negotiation in which a debtor enters into an agreement with a creditor or creditors for a payment or plan to discharge the debtor's debt.

Best Interests of the Creditors

After a petition for Chapter 11 bankruptcy has been filed, a bankruptcy court, after notice and a hearing, may dismiss or suspend all proceedings at any time if that would better serve the interests of the creditors. The Code also allows a court, after notice and a hearing, to dismiss a case under reorganization "for cause." Cause includes the absence of a reasonable likelihood of rehabilitation, the inability to effect a plan, and an unreasonable delay by the debtor that may harm the interests of creditors.

Debtor in Possession

debtor in possession (DIP)
In Chapter 11 bankruptcy proceedings, a debtor who is allowed, for the benefit of all concerned, to maintain possession of the estate in bankruptcy (the business) and to continue business operations.

On entry of the order for relief, the debtor generally continues to operate the business as a **debtor in possession (DIP)**. The court, however, may appoint a trustee (often referred to as a *receiver*) to operate the debtor's business if mismanagement of the business is shown or if appointing a trustee is in the best interests of the estate.

The DIP's role is similar to that of a trustee in a liquidation. The DIP is entitled to avoid preferential payments made to creditors and fraudulent transfers of assets that occurred prior to the filing of the Chapter 11 petition. The DIP has the power to decide whether to cancel or assume obligations under executory contracts (contracts that have not yet been performed) that were made prior to the filing.

ETHICS WATCH

THE PERILS OF INDEPENDENT PRACTICE

As you read in Chapter 2, independent paralegals provide services directly to the public (without attorney supervision). Some independent paralegals assist debtors by selling them "do-it-yourself" bankruptcy kits, preparing bankruptcy forms, and the like.

Although the Bankruptcy Code allows paralegals to act as bankruptcy petition preparers without attorney supervision, it contains strict requirements that must be followed. The law prohibits petition preparers from advising bankruptcy debtors about numerous issues and from offering legal advice. For example, petition preparers may not tell a debtor whether he or she will be able to retain certain property, such as a house or car, after filing for bankruptcy. They may not say whether a particular debt will or can be discharged. They may not tell debtors how to characterize an interest in property when filling out the forms, whether to reaffirm a particular debt, or what tax consequences might be involved.

Violators may be subject to a fine; may be required to forfeit the fees they received from, or pay damages to, the debtor; and may even be ordered not to prepare bankruptcy petitions in the future. Because of the dangers involved, paralegals who prepare bankruptcy petitions without attorney supervision must be exceedingly careful to avoid pitfalls and potential lawsuits.

Such care is consistent with the NALA *Code of Ethics,* Canon 4: "A paralegal must use discretion and professional judgment commensurate with knowledge and experience but must not render independent legal judgment in place of an attorney."

Creditors' Committees

As soon as practicable after the entry of the order for relief, a creditors' committee of unsecured creditors is appointed. This committee often is composed of the biggest suppliers to the business. The committee may consult with the trustee or the DIP concerning the administration of the case or the formulation of the reorganization plan. Additional creditors' committees may be appointed to represent creditors with special interests. Generally, no orders affecting the estate will be entered without either the consent of the committee or a hearing in which the judge hears the position of the committee.

The Reorganization Plan

A reorganization plan to rehabilitate the debtor is a plan to conserve and administer the debtor's assets in the hope of a return to successful operation and solvency. The plan must be fair and equitable and must do the following:

1. Designate classes of claims and interests.
2. Specify the treatment to be afforded the classes. (The plan must provide the same treatment for each claim in a particular class.)
3. Provide an adequate means for execution.
4. Provide for payment of tax claims over a five-year period.

Filing the Plan

Only the debtor may file a plan within the first 120 days after the date of the order for relief. This period may be extended, but not beyond eighteen months from the date of the order for relief. If the debtor does not meet the 120-day deadline or obtain an extension, and if the debtor fails to obtain the required creditor consent within 180 days, any party may propose a plan. The plan need not provide for full repayment to unsecured creditors. Instead, creditors receive a percentage of each dollar owed to them by the debtor. If a small-business debtor chooses to avoid creditors' committees, the time for the debtor's filing is 180 days.

Acceptance and Confirmation of the Plan

Once the plan has been developed, it is submitted to each class of creditors for acceptance. For the plan to be adopted, each class that is adversely affected by the plan must accept it. A class has accepted the plan when a majority of the creditors, representing two-thirds of the amount of the total claim, vote to approve it.

Even when all classes of creditors accept the plan, the court may refuse to confirm it if it is not "in the best interests of the creditors." The plan can also be modified at the request of the debtor, the trustee, the U.S. trustee, or a holder of an unsecured claim. If an unsecured creditor objects to the plan, specific rules apply to the value of property to be distributed under the plan. Tax claims must be paid over a five-year period.

Even if only one class of creditors has accepted the plan, the court may still confirm the plan under the Code's so-called **cram-down provision**. In other words, the court may confirm the plan over the objections of a class of creditors. Before the court can exercise this right of cram-down confirmation, it must be demonstrated that the plan "does not discriminate unfairly" against any creditors and that the plan is "fair and equitable."

cram-down provision
A provision of the Bankruptcy Code that allows a court to confirm a debtor's Chapter 11 reorganization plan even though only one class of creditors has accepted it. To exercise the court's right under this provision, the court must demonstrate that the plan does not discriminate unfairly against any creditors and is fair and equitable.

Discharge

The plan is binding on confirmation. Confirmation of a plan does not, however, discharge an individual debtor. For individual debtors, execution of the plan must be completed before discharge will be granted, unless the court orders otherwise. For all other debtors, the court may order discharge at any time after the plan is confirmed. The debtor at this time is given a reorganization discharge from all claims not protected under the plan. This discharge does not apply to any claims that would be denied discharge under liquidation.

Bankruptcy Law and the Paralegal

Today, roughly one in every five paralegals spends about half of his or her work time on bankruptcy law. Much of the work previously handled by attorneys can now be done by paralegals with expertise in this area. For example, a debtor-client who wants to petition for bankruptcy relief must provide the court with numerous forms stating in detail the debtor's assets and liabilities. These forms must be filled out accurately and clients must follow procedures properly.

The specific types of work handled by bankruptcy paralegals vary, of course, depending on whether they work on behalf of the debtor, a creditor, or the bankruptcy trustee. Here are a few examples of paralegal tasks that you might be asked to perform if you were assisting a debtor-client (which could be an individual or a corporate representative) in petitioning for bankruptcy relief:

- Conduct an intake interview—and follow-up interviews as necessary—to obtain information concerning the debtor's income, debts, and assets.
- Verify the accuracy of the debtor's financial statements.
- Verify legal title status of property in which the debtor has an interest.
- Make arrangements for the debtor to receive credit counseling from an approved agency.
- Draft the bankruptcy petition based on the information obtained from the client.
- Verify the validity of creditors' claims that have been submitted to the bankruptcy court.
- Prepare the client for bankruptcy proceedings, such as creditors' meetings.
- Assist in work on the debtor's behalf in any legal actions relating to the bankruptcy proceedings.
- Research the Bankruptcy Code to verify that certain provisions are still effective and keep up to date on bankruptcy law.
- Research state statutes governing property exemptions.
- Research case law to see how the courts have applied a certain provision of the Bankruptcy Code or a state law applicable to the bankruptcy proceedings.

Environmental Law

We now turn to a discussion of the various ways in which businesses are regulated by the government in attempting to protect the environment. Remember from Chapter 2 that *environmental law* is defined as all law pertaining to environmental protection.

Environmental law is not new. Indeed, the federal government began to regulate some activities, such as those involving the pollution of navigable waterways, in the late 1800s. In the last few decades, however, the body of environmental law has expanded substantially as the government has attempted to control industrial waste and to protect natural resources. Today, businesses must comply with many environmental regulations. Because of the complexity, firms often need legal assistance to make sure that they meet environmental requirements. For this reason, many attorneys and paralegals specialize in environmental law. In this section, we look at some of the most significant environmental statutes and regulations.

Federal Regulation of the Environment

Congress has passed a number of statutes to control the impact of human activities on the environment. Some of these statutes were passed in an attempt to improve the quality of air and water. Some of them specifically regulate toxic chemicals and hazardous wastes. Exhibit 19.1 below lists the major federal statutes that apply to various areas of the environment. Because regulations change frequently, a paralegal who works in the area will want to keep on top of the changes as the *Developing Paralegal Skills* feature discusses on the following page.

Environmental Regulatory Agencies

Much of the body of federal law governing business activities consists of the regulations issued and enforced by administrative agencies. The most well known of the agencies regulating environmental law is, of course, the Environmental Protection Agency (EPA), which was created by President Richard Nixon in 1970 to coordinate federal environmental responsibilities. Not only the EPA but also other agencies of the federal government must take environmental factors into consideration when making significant decisions.

Many federal environmental laws also provide that citizens can sue to enforce environmental regulations if government agencies fail to do so—or to limit enforcement if agencies go too far in their enforcement actions. Finally, note that although we do not discuss state regulation here, each state has an environmental agency that parallels the EPA. Those agencies are often delegated major responsibilities by the EPA.

Environmental Impact Statements

The National Environmental Policy Act (NEPA) of 1969 requires that for every major federal action that significantly affects the quality of the environment, an **environmental impact statement (EIS)** must be prepared. Construction by a

environmental impact statement (EIS)

A statement required by the National Environmental Policy Act for any major federal action that will significantly affect the quality of the environment. The statement must analyze the action's impact on the environment and explore alternative actions that might be taken.

EXHIBIT 19.1
Federal Regulation of Environmental Pollution

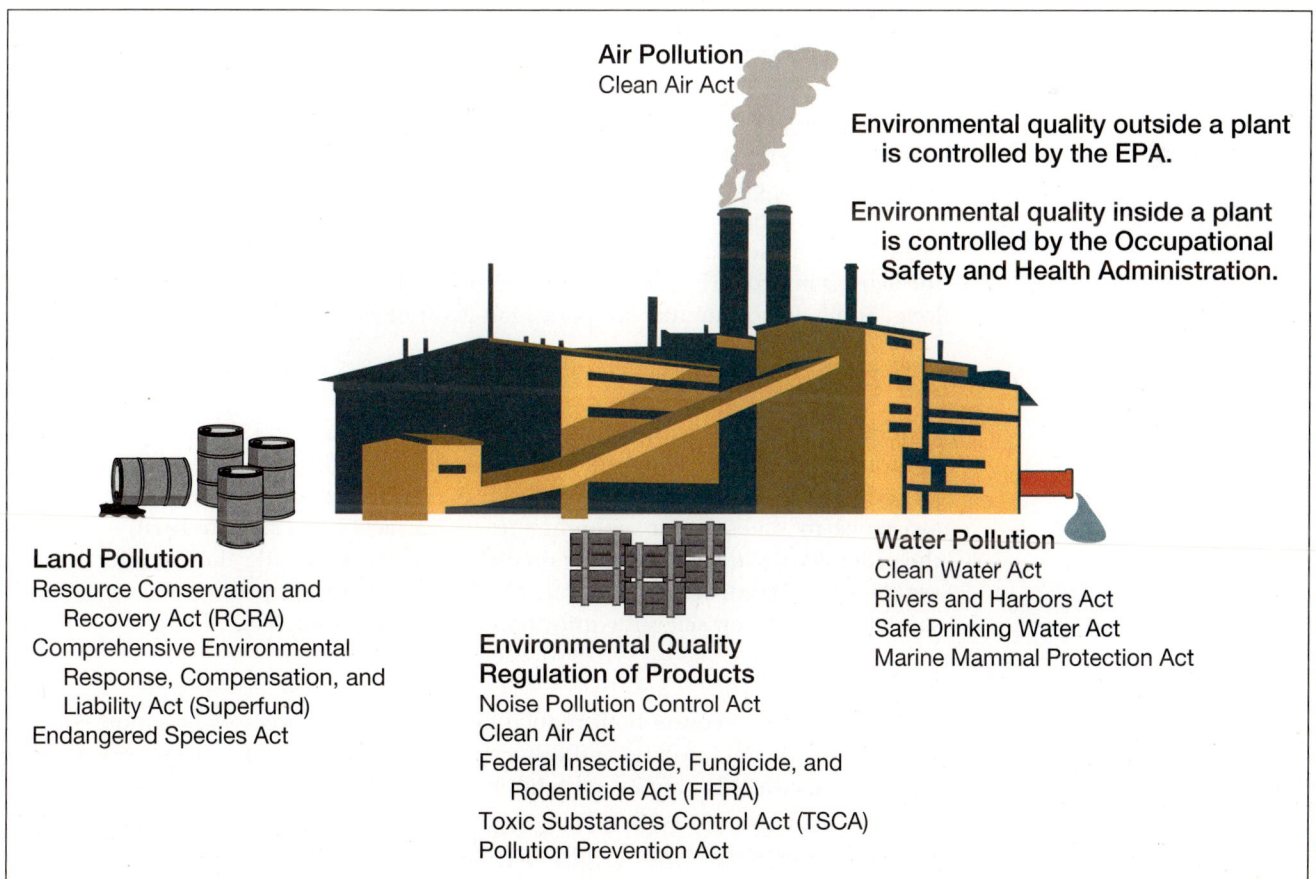

Air Pollution
Clean Air Act

Environmental quality outside a plant is controlled by the EPA.

Environmental quality inside a plant is controlled by the Occupational Safety and Health Administration.

Land Pollution
Resource Conservation and
    Recovery Act (RCRA)
Comprehensive Environmental
    Response, Compensation, and
    Liability Act (Superfund)
Endangered Species Act

Environmental Quality Regulation of Products
Noise Pollution Control Act
Clean Air Act
Federal Insecticide, Fungicide, and
    Rodenticide Act (FIFRA)
Toxic Substances Control Act (TSCA)
Pollution Prevention Act

Water Pollution
Clean Water Act
Rivers and Harbors Act
Safe Drinking Water Act
Marine Mammal Protection Act

From Meiners/Ringleb/Edwards, *The Legal Environment of Business*, 11E. © 2012 Cengage Learning

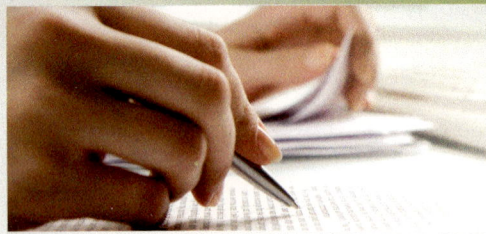

DEVELOPING
paralegal skills

MONITORING THE
FEDERAL REGISTER

Robin Hayes is a legal assistant for CARCO, Inc., a large company that manufactures automobile parts. She works in the environmental law practice group within the corporation's legal department. One of her responsibilities is to monitor online the *Federal Register* regularly for newly proposed environmental regulations and for changes to existing rules. Today, Robin notices a change to the hazardous waste manifest, a form that CARCO is required to use when shipping hazardous waste to a disposal facility. The change requires the company to certify its efforts in reducing the amount of hazardous waste that it generates. Robin prepares a memo to the attorneys in the group, because they will need to inform management of the change.

CHECKLIST FOR
MONITORING THE *FEDERAL REGISTER*

- Review the Federal Register regularly.
- Review the topics and subtopics to determine if notices, rules, or proposed rules have been issued on topics affecting your client.
- Skim through any notices, rules, and proposed rules that may apply to your client.
- Read in detail the relevant notices, rules, and proposed rules that may apply to your client.
- Print out relevant notices, rules, and proposed rules for circulation to the attorneys and others who should be advised of this information.
- Notify the attorneys and others of upcoming deadlines for comments on proposed rules and changes.

private developer of a ski resort on federal land, for example, may require an EIS. Building or operating a nuclear power plant, which requires a federal permit, or constructing a dam as part of a federal project would require an EIS. An EIS must analyze (1) the impact on the environment that the action will have, (2) any adverse effects on the environment and alternative actions that might be taken, and (3) irreversible effects the action might generate.

EISs have become instruments used by private citizens, consumer interest groups, businesses, and others to challenge federal agency actions on the basis that the actions improperly threaten the environment. A typical EIS is hundreds of pages long. Some environmental law paralegals assist in preparing and reviewing EISs.

Air Pollution

Federal involvement with air pollution goes back to the 1950s, when Congress authorized funds for air-pollution research. In 1963, the federal government passed the Clean Air Act, which focused on multistate air pollution and provided assistance to states. Later amendments to the act, especially in 1970, expanded the federal role in regulating air quality. These laws provide the basis for issuing regulations to control air pollution. The EPA attempts to update pollution-control standards when new scientific information becomes available.

Mobile and Stationary Sources of Pollution

The Clean Air Act covers both mobile and stationary sources of pollution. Mobile sources include automobiles and other moving sources. The Clean Air Act of 1970 and its amendments require automobile manufacturers to cut new automobiles' exhaust emissions by a certain percentage by a given date. Every few years, the EPA reviews the standards and usually makes them tougher, so fewer emissions are allowed.

Stationary sources include manufacturing plants, electric utilities, and other nonmoving sources of pollution. The Clean Air Act authorizes the EPA to establish air-quality standards for these sources. The EPA sets the maximum levels of certain pollutants that may be emitted by stationary sources, and the states formulate plans to achieve those standards. Different standards apply to sources of pollution in clean areas and sources in polluted areas. Different standards also apply to existing sources of pollution and major new sources.

Performance standards for major sources require the use of "maximum achievable control technology" to reduce emissions from the combustion of fossil fuels (coal and oil). The EPA issues guidelines as to what equipment meets this requirement.

Penalties for Violating the Clean Air Act

The EPA can assess civil penalties of up to $25,000 per day for violations of emission limits under the Clean Air Act. Additional fines of up to $5,000 per day can be assessed for other violations, such as failing to maintain required records. To penalize those for whom it is more cost-effective to violate the act than to comply with it, the EPA is authorized to obtain a penalty equal to the violator's economic benefits from noncompliance. Persons who provide information about violators may be paid up to $10,000. Private citizens can also sue violators. Those who knowingly violate the act may be subject to criminal penalties, including fines of up to $1 million and imprisonment for up to two years (for false statements or failure to report violations).

Corporate officers are among those who may be subject to these penalties. The threat of penalties is not an empty one, as most years there are more than a hundred criminal indictments. As regulations in this and other areas change constantly and vary across states, one should keep on top of relevant materials as noted in the *Technology and Today's Paralegal* feature on the following page.

Water Pollution

Federal regulations governing water pollution can be traced back to the Rivers and Harbors Act of 1899. These regulations prohibited ships and manufacturers from discharging or depositing refuse in navigable waterways.

Navigable Waters

Navigable waters include coastal waters, freshwater wetlands, and lakes and streams used by interstate travelers and industry. In practice, essentially every body of water and every stream is considered navigable and subject to regulation. In 1948, Congress passed the Federal Water Pollution Control Act (FWPCA), but its regulatory system and enforcement proved inadequate. In 1972, amendments to the FWPCA—known as the Clean Water Act—were enacted to (1) make waters safe for swimming, (2) protect fish and wildlife, and (3) eliminate the discharge of pollutants into the water. The amendments required that polluters apply for permits before discharging wastes into navigable waters.

Focus on Point-Source Emissions

In practice, the Clean Water Act focuses on pollutants that are emitted from *point sources*. These are sources occupying small areas and heavily concentrated outputs. The act, as amended over time, has five main elements:

1. National effluent (pollution) standards set by the EPA for each industry.

2. Water quality standards set by the states under EPA supervision.

3. A *discharge permit* program that sets water quality standards to limit pollution.

4. Special provisions for toxic chemicals and for oil spills.

5. Construction grants and loans from the federal government for *publicly owned treatment works (POTWs),* primarily sewage treatment plants.

TECHNOLOGY AND
today's paralegal

ENVIRONMENTAL COMPLIANCE

Paralegals can quickly find an abundance of information not only on environmental laws but also on what businesses must do to comply with these laws. Here, we look at just a few online resources that paralegals can use to obtain such information.

ENVIRONMENTAL LAWS AND REGULATIONS

A primary source for environmental laws and regulations is, of course, the U.S. Environmental Protection Agency (EPA), which coordinates and enforces many of these laws and regulations. You can visit the EPA's Web site to find a wealth of detailed information on existing law as well as new regulations and proposed rules, proposed environmental legislation in Congress, and an explanation of how the EPA writes regulations.

Another helpful Web site is **enviro.blr.com**. Here, you can find information on environmental laws and regulatory activity. You can also find various tools (such as special forms and checklists) for monitoring and implementing a firm's compliance with regulatory requirements.

COMPLIANCE ASSISTANCE

You can access the EPA's rules at the agency's Web site, **www.epa.gov**. From the home page, click on "Laws & Regulation" and then click on "Compliance" to access the rules in various subject areas.

The Environmental Compliance Assistance Platform, at **www.envcap.org**, is designed to help businesses comply with environmental regulations. This site includes links to compliance assistance for various industries and groups (for example, for the construction, health-care, and automotive recycling industries). You can also access state regulations and other information. The Small Business Environmental home page will also take you to numerous compliance resources (see **www.smallbiz-enviroweb.org**).

ENVIRONMENTAL SOFTWARE

Some firms offer special software to help businesses monitor and comply with environmental regulations. For example, **www.prismsystems.com** offers environmental management tools. Another company, **www.ihs.com**, has products to help manage environmental and health performance and risk.

TECHNOLOGY TIP

When you are searching for government resources and are not sure where to go, remember that **usa.gov** is a gateway to *all* federal agencies and institutions. Offerings by private firms are expanding constantly, so searching to see what is available may reveal interesting results.

DISCHARGE PERMITS. The Clean Water Act makes it illegal for any person, business, or government to dump pollutants into navigable waters without a discharge permit. These permits are issued under the National Pollution Discharge Elimination System. Any point source emitting pollutants into water must have a permit. Non-point-source pollution, such as runoff from farms, is not subject to much regulation.

REQUIRED TECHNOLOGY. As Exhibit 19.2 on the facing page shows, there are two major categories of point-source discharges into the nation's waters. The first are POTWs, most of which are local government sewage treatment plants. They must use the *best conventional technology* for treating waste in order to receive a permit to discharge. The EPA sets that technology standard. Subject to more strict controls are emissions from point sources such as factories. They must use the *best available technology* to treat their waste water before returning the water to a waterway. When a firm shows that it is in compliance with the technology standard, then it can obtain a discharge permit.

Penalties for Violating the Clean Water Act

Because point-source water pollution control is based on a permit system, the permits are the key to enforcement. States have primary responsibility for enforcing the permit system, subject to EPA monitoring.

EXHIBIT 19.2
Primary Sources of Water Effluents

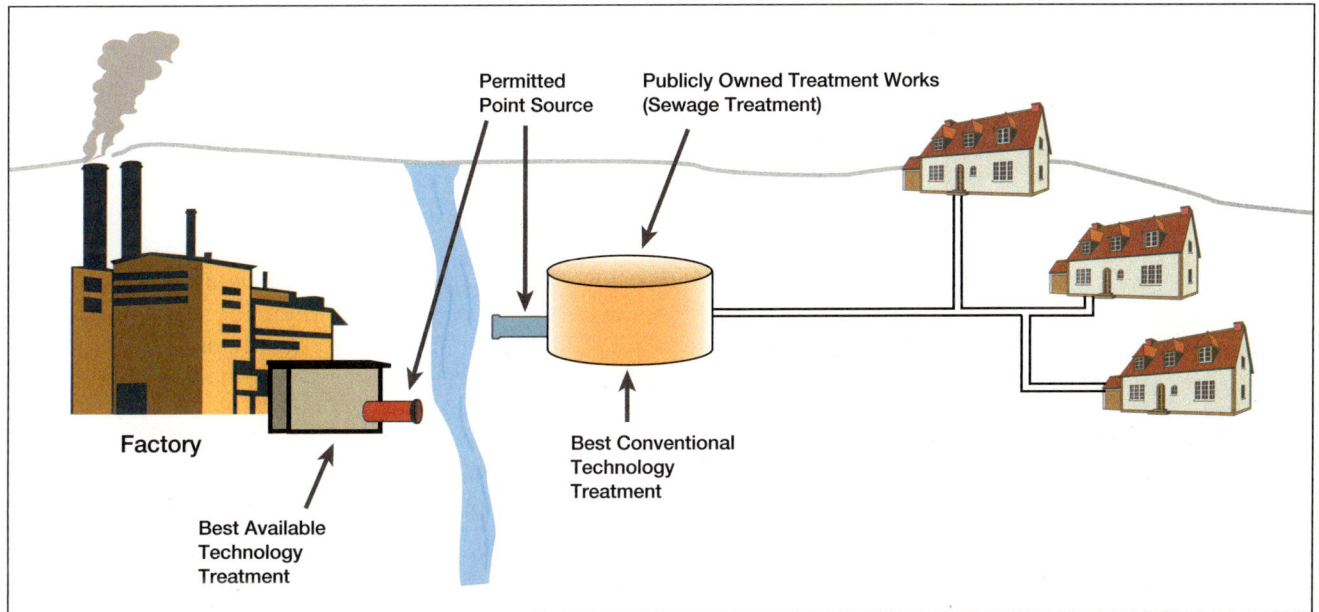

Permitted
Point Source

Publicly Owned Treatment Works
(Sewage Treatment)

Factory

Best Available
Technology
Treatment

Best Conventional
Technology
Treatment

From Meiners/Ringleb/Edwards, *The Legal Environment of Business*, 11E. © 2012 Cengage Learning

Discharging emissions into navigable waters without a permit, or in violation of pollution limits under a permit, violates the Clean Water Act. Firms that have discharge permits must monitor their own performance and file *discharge monitoring reports*. These reports are available for public inspection. Violators must report their violations and are subject to fines. Lying about a violation is more serious than admitting the truth about improper discharges.

Serious violations can result in criminal prosecutions, and every year people are sent to prison for dumping toxic pollutants. As with the Clean Air Act, citizens have the right to bring suits for pollutant violations that the EPA or a state environmental agency has not addressed properly.

Wetlands

Years ago, wetlands were seen as nuisances to be drained and filled with dirt. The Clean Water Act recognizes the ecological value of wetlands and protects them. *Wetlands* are any lands, such as swamps and bogs, that support vegetation adapted to saturated soil conditions. They are protected no matter how large or small they are.

Under the Clean Water Act, anyone wanting to change a wetland, usually for construction purposes, must obtain a permit from the U.S. Army Corps of Engineers. Each year, the Corps of Engineers issues more than 10,000 permits that involve significant wetland impact. The Corps reviews proposals for dredging or filling, and it often limits the work or requires work to be done elsewhere in exchange for the wetland lost to construction. The Corps issues another 75,000 permits annually for activities found to have "minimal adverse environmental effects" to wetlands. The decisions of the Corps are reviewed by the EPA. Violators are subject to fines that can be in the millions of dollars.

Toxic Chemicals

Originally, most environmental cleanup efforts were directed toward reducing smog and making water safe for fishing and swimming. Over time, however, control of toxic chemicals became an important part of environmental law.

Pesticides and Herbicides

The first toxic chemical problem to receive widespread public attention was that posed by pesticides and herbicides. Using these chemicals to kill insects and weeds has increased agricultural productivity, but their residue remains in the environment. In rare instances, accumulations of this residue have killed animals, and scientists have identified potential long-term effects that are detrimental to humans. Under the Federal Insecticide, Fungicide, and Rodenticide Act of 1947 (FIFRA), pesticides and herbicides must be registered before they can be sold. They may be used only for approved applications and in limited quantities when applied to food crops. If a substance is identified as harmful, the EPA can cancel its registration.

For a pesticide to remain on the market, there must be a "reasonable certainty of no harm" to people from exposure to the pesticide. This means that there must be no more than a one-in-a-million risk to people of developing cancer from exposure in any way, including eating food that contains residues from the pesticide.

Penalties for registrants and producers for violating the act include imprisonment for up to one year and a fine of no more than $50,000. Penalties for commercial dealers include imprisonment for up to one year and a fine of no more than $25,000. Farmers and other private users of pesticides or herbicides who violate the act are subject to a $1,000 fine and imprisonment for up to thirty days.

Hazardous Wastes

Some industrial, agricultural, and household wastes pose more serious threats than others. If not properly disposed of, these toxic chemicals may present a substantial danger to human health and the environment. If released into the environment, they may contaminate public drinking water resources.

RESOURCE CONSERVATION AND RECOVERY ACT. RCRA requires the EPA to establish regulations to monitor and control hazardous waste disposal and to determine which forms of solid waste should be considered hazardous and thus subject to regulation. The act authorizes the EPA to issue various technical requirements for some types of facilities for storage and treatment of hazardous waste. The act also requires all producers of hazardous waste materials to label and package properly any hazardous waste that is to be transported.

In practice, RCRA imposes a "cradle-to-grave" system of controls on hazardous substances. As Exhibit 19.3 on the facing page indicates, chemicals, besides being subject to regulatory standards at the point of production and sale, are subject to the use of manifests under RCRA. The hazardous substance producer must attach a *manifest,* or data sheet, to all products that will become hazardous waste. The sellers of those substances must have an EPA permit. The manifests must accompany the substances down the chain of use so parties can be held responsible for use and disposal of the products. Firms that operate *treatment, storage, and disposal (TSD) sites* must meet all regulations regarding the proper handling, use, and destruction of hazardous materials.

Under RCRA, a company may be assessed a civil penalty based on the seriousness of the violation, the probability of harm, and the extent to which the violation deviates from RCRA requirements. The assessment may be up to $25,000 for each violation. Criminal penalties include fines up to $50,000 for each day of violation, imprisonment for up to two years (in most instances), or both. Criminal fines and the time of imprisonment can be doubled for certain repeat offenders.

SUPERFUND. The Comprehensive Environmental Response, Compensation, and Liability Act (CERCLA), commonly known as Superfund, regulates the cleanup of disposal sites in which hazardous waste is leaking into the environment. A special federal fund was created for this purpose.

GOING green

WHAT ARE YOU SITTING ON?

When furniture and other supplies are ordered for the office, look to see if recycled options are available, including furniture that is recyclable at the time of disposal. Many large office furniture makers offer environmentally friendly alternatives.

EXHIBIT 19.3
Regulation of Hazardous Substances

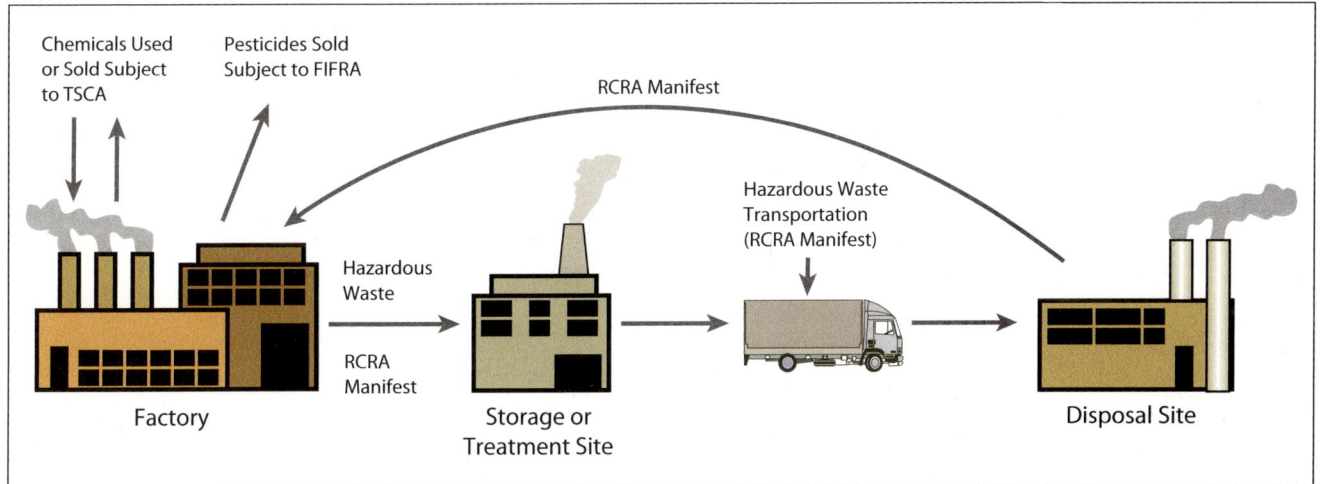

Chemicals Used or Sold Subject to TSCA
Pesticides Sold Subject to FIFRA
RCRA Manifest
Hazardous Waste Transportation (RCRA Manifest)
Factory
Hazardous Waste
RCRA Manifest
Storage or Treatment Site
Disposal Site

Superfund provides that when a release or a threatened release of hazardous chemicals from a site occurs, the following persons are responsible for cleaning up the site:

1. the person who generated the wastes disposed of at the site,
2. the person who transported the wastes to the site,
3. the person who owned or operated the site at the time of the disposal, and
4. the current owner or operator.

A person falling within one of these categories is referred to as a **potentially responsible party (PRP)**. If the PRP does not clean up the site, Superfund authorizes the EPA to clean up the site and recover cleanup costs from the PRP.

Superfund imposes strict liability on PRPs. Also, liability under Superfund is usually joint and several—that is, a PRP who generated only a fraction of the hazardous waste disposed of at the site may nevertheless be liable for all of the cleanup costs. CERCLA authorizes a party who has incurred cleanup costs to bring a "contribution action" against any other person who is liable or potentially liable for a percentage of the costs.

Paralegals in the Practice of Environmental Law

A paralegal specializing in environmental law may work for a federal or state agency, for a law firm or corporate legal department, or with an organization interested in natural resource issues. As we have seen in this chapter, there are complex legal issues. Some of the tasks that you might perform include:

- Draft and file permits with federal, state, or local agencies to use property in compliance with environmental and natural resource rules.
- Draft and file documents necessary to include another company as a potential defendant in an action brought by an agency.
- Monitor the *Federal Register* and state administrative regulations to determine if new environmental requirements have been imposed.
- Research the scope and applicability of a regulation to determine if a client's planned action may violate that rule, whether a permit is required, and any other particular requirements.

potentially responsible party (PRP)
A party who may be liable under the Comprehensive Environmental Response, Compensation, and Liability Act, or Superfund. Any person who generated hazardous waste, transported hazardous waste, owned or operated a waste site at the time of disposal, or currently owns or operates a site may be responsible for some or all of the cleanup costs involved in removing the hazardous substances.

- Prepare for and attend hearings before natural resource control agencies.

- Assist in negotiations between an environmental agency and a firm to settle a dispute over claimed violations of a regulation.

- Coordinate a client's environmental policies and monitor corporate compliance with reporting requirements under various environmental statutes.

- Trace property histories to look for potential contributors to a Superfund site cleanup action.

KEY TERMS AND CONCEPTS

Chapter Summary

Bankruptcy and Environmental Law

FORMS OF BANKRUPTCY RELIEF COMPARED

PURPOSE	CHAPTER 7	CHAPTER 11	CHAPTER 13
	Liquidation.	Reorganization.	Individual repayment plan.
WHO CAN PETITION	Debtor (voluntary) or creditors (involuntary).	Debtor (voluntary) or creditors (involuntary).	Debtor (voluntary) only.
WHO CAN BE A DEBTOR	Any "person" (including partnerships and corporations) except insurance companies, banks, savings and loan institutions, investment companies licensed by the Small Business Administration, and credit unions. Farmers and charitable institutions cannot be involuntarily petitioned. If the court finds the petition to be a substantial abuse of the use of Chapter 7, the debtor may be required to convert to a Chapter 13 repayment plan.	Any debtor (except a stockbroker or a commodities broker) eligible for Chapter 7 relief; railroads are also eligible.	Any individual (not partnerships or corporations) with regular income who owes fixed unsecured debts of less than $340,000 or fixed secured debts of less than $1 million.
PROCEDURE LEADING TO DISCHARGE	Nonexempt property is sold with proceeds to be distributed (in order) to priority groups. Dischargeable debts are terminated.	Plan is submitted; if it is approved and followed, debts are discharged.	Plan is submitted (must be approved if debtor turns over disposable income for a three- or five-year period); if it is approved and followed, debts are discharged.

| **ADVANTAGES** | On liquidation and distribution, most debts are discharged, and the debtor has the opportunity for a fresh start. | Debtor continues in business. Creditors can accept the plan, or it can be "crammed down" on them. Plan allows for reorganization and liquidation of debts over the plan period. | Debtor continues in business or retains possession of assets. If plan is approved, most debts are discharged after the plan period. |

ENVIRONMENTAL LAW

1. *Federal regulation of the environment—*

a. The federal Environmental Protection Agency (EPA) was created in 1970 to coordinate federal environmental programs. The EPA administers most federal environmental policies and statutes.

b. The National Environmental Policy Act of 1969 imposes environmental responsibilities on all federal agencies and requires the preparation of an environmental impact statement (EIS) for every major federal action. An EIS must analyze the action's impact on the environment.

2. *Important areas regulated by federal law—*

a. **AIR POLLUTION**—Regulated primarily by the Clean Air Act of 1970 as amended. The EPA sets allowable emission standards for various pollutants emitted from mobile sources (vehicles) and stationary sources (power plants, factories). Polluters must meet specific technological control standards.

b. **WATER POLLUTION**—Regulated primarily under the Clean Water Act of 1972 as amended. Polluters who dump waste into navigable waters must meet technical standards set by the EPA and enforced primarily by the states. The focus is on point sources such as sewage treatment plants and industrial sites, which must have discharge permits. The act also protects wetlands. Changing a wetland requires a permit from the Army Corps of Engineers.

c. **TOXIC CHEMICALS AND HAZARDOUS WASTE**—The Federal Insecticide, Fungicide, and Rodenticide Act controls pesticides and herbicides. Most chemicals are subject to the Resource Conservation and Recovery Act, which requires sellers, transporters, users, and disposers to use manifests to track the history of the substances from production to destruction. The act also requires cleanup of polluted dump sites (Superfund sites).

QUESTIONS FOR REVIEW

1. What is a liquidation proceeding under Chapter 7? How is one initiated? What is the difference between a voluntary bankruptcy and an involuntary bankruptcy? What is "means testing"?

2. What is an automatic stay? What effect does the filing of a bankruptcy petition have on creditors?

3. How does a Chapter 13 bankruptcy differ from Chapter 7 bankruptcy? What happens if a company files for reorganization under Chapter 11?

4. What is an environmental impact statement (EIS), and when is one required? What factors does an EIS evaluate?

5. What important areas covered in the chapter are regulated by federal environmental laws? List the major laws providing the regulatory framework in each area. What is the Superfund? What parties are responsible for the cleanup of hazardous waste sites?

ETHICAL QUESTIONS

1. Marla, an independent paralegal, provides a variety of services for the public. Among other things, she provides debtors with bankruptcy forms and petitions. Mr. Ford has sought Marla's services in filing for bankruptcy. He takes home a set of Chapter 7 forms, reads through them, and begins to provide the information needed. He is not certain that he qualifies for Chapter 7 liquidation. He calls Marla and asks her if he has any other options. How should Marla answer Mr. Ford's questions?

PRACTICE QUESTIONS AND ASSIGNMENTS

1. Douglas Worth earns a salary of $30,000 a year as a sales representative. In addition to his salary, he is entitled to a 10 percent commission on what he sells. Over the past five years, Douglas earned annual commissions of $80,000 to $100,000. Because the economy was booming and Douglas was making such large commissions, he purchased a $50,000 Cadillac and a $25,000 boat and incurred credit-card debts totaling $35,000. Due to the economic downturn, Douglas has made only $10,000 in commissions in the last six months. He still owes $40,000 on the Cadillac and $20,000 on the boat. In all, he owes $95,000 to creditors. Douglas cannot pay his debts as they become due, and it does not appear that his financial situation will improve over the next two years. As a result, he is thinking about filing for bankruptcy. If the median income in Douglas's state is $35,000 a year, would he be able to obtain a Chapter 7 liquidation? Explain your answer.

2. Identify the environmental law that applies to each of the following situations and explain how it would resolve the problem:

   a. The foreman at a manufacturing plant disposes of a fifty-five-gallon drum of spent solvents, a toxic waste, every week by pouring it on the ground "out back."

   b. An investigation reveals that the local gas utility company has PCBs in its pipeline in excess of those allowed.

   c. An oil company releases oil into a local river, contaminating the river, which is a major source of drinking water for the area.

   d. A manufacturing plant that produces metallic paint for use on motor vehicles releases more pollutants into the air than the allowable emissions limits for its vicinity.

   e. Years ago, five large manufacturing companies disposed of hazardous waste by burying the waste on the property of a farmer forty miles away from the city and its inhabitants. The rural farm is now part of a suburb. The suburb's groundwater and drinking water are found to be contaminated by the waste buried on the site of the former farm. The citizens demand that the site be cleaned up.

QUESTIONS FOR CRITICAL ANALYSIS

1. Do you think that people should be able to avoid paying their debts by filing for bankruptcy? Does a person have a moral responsibility to pay his or her debts, even if it takes years and years to pay them off entirely?

2. Do you think that our bankruptcy laws are too lenient or too harsh for debtors? Do the means testing rules provide greater help for low-income debtors? Do bankruptcy laws adequately balance the needs of debtors "who have gotten in over their heads" with the interests of creditors?

3. The Clean Air Act, the Clean Water Act, and the Resource Conservation and Recovery Act, among others, regulate the amount of pollution allowed into the air, water, and other aspects of the environment. Should any pollution be allowed into the environment? Who should determine how "clean" air or water should be? What might happen if no pollution at all were allowed?

PROJECTS

1. If there is a federal bankruptcy court located near you, attend a bankruptcy proceeding for a day or part of a day. Write a one-page summary of your experience. Include the date and time that you attended the proceeding, the name of the judge whose courtroom you observed, and a detailed summary of the types of proceedings, such as motions, etc., that you observed.

2. Review your state's bankruptcy laws to determine what property is exempt from the debtor's estate in property. Does your state prohibit debtors from using the federal exemptions within the state, or is a debtor allowed to choose between state and federal exemptions? Write a one-page summary of your findings.

GROUP PROJECT

This project involves reviewing the Keystone XL pipeline project as an example of the environmental impact statement (EIS) that is required by the National Environmental Policy Act (NEPA). Students should search for articles from authoritative news Web sites such as the *New York Times, Washington Post,* and *Wall Street Journal* and should not include articles from Wikipedia.

Student one will do an Internet search for articles about the environmental impact statement that was done for the Keystone XL pipeline and will explain what section of NEPA requires an EIS.

Student two will do an Internet search to document the history of the Keystone XL pipeline, its current status, and the projected economic effects of the pipeline.

Student three will do an Internet search for articles about the potential environmental effects of building the Keystone XL pipeline along its originally planned route through the sand hills in Nebraska, as well as the alternative route that has been proposed.

Student four will do an Internet search for statistics on the number of oil pipeline spills that have occurred over the past 10 years and the cost, time, and success rates of cleaning up the environment.

The group will then reach a decision about the advisability of building the Keystone XL pipeline. Using its research as evidence, the group will present its recommendation to the class.

USING INTERNET RESOURCES

1. Go to **www.abiworld.org**, the Web site of the American Bankruptcy Institute. Select "Online Resources" at the top of the page, and then select "Bankruptcy Statistics." Answer the following questions:

    a. What does the statistics page say about consumer debt?

    b. Click on "Filings by State" then go to "Annual Business and Non-business Filings by State." According to this page, which state had the most personal (nonbusiness) bankruptcy filings during the most recent year mentioned? Which state had the fewest?

    c. On the "Filings by State" page, click on "Quarterly Filings by State." How many bankruptcy filings occurred in the most recent quarter? Are most of these filings business filings or nonbusiness filings?

END NOTE

1. There are no Chapters 2, 4, 6, 8, or 10 in Title 11. Such "gaps" are not uncommon in the U.S.C. This is because chapter numbers (or other subdivision unit numbers) are sometimes reserved for future use when a statute is enacted. A gap may also appear if a law has been repealed.

CourseMate The available CourseMate for this text has an interactive eBook and interactive learning tools, including flash cards, quizzes, and more. To learn more about this resource and access free demo CourseMate resources, go to **www.cengagebrain.com**, and search for this book. To access CourseMate materials that you have purchased, go to **login.cengagebrain.com**.

NALA's Code of Ethics and Professional Responsibility

A paralegal must adhere strictly to the accepted standards of legal ethics and to the general principles of proper conduct. The performance of the duties of the paralegal shall be governed by specific canons as defined herein so that justice will be served and goals of the profession attained. (See *Model Standards and Guidelines for Utilization of Legal Assistants*, Section II.)

The canons of ethics set forth hereafter are adopted by the National Association of Legal Assistants, Inc., as a general guide intended to aid paralegals and attorneys. The enumeration of these rules does not mean there are not others of equal importance although not specifically mentioned. Court rules, agency rules, and statutes must be taken into consideration when interpreting the canons.

Canons of Ethics

Definition

Legal assistants, also known as paralegals, are a distinguishable group of persons who assist attorneys in the delivery of legal services. Through formal education, training and experience, legal assistants have knowledge and expertise regarding the legal system and substantive and procedural law which qualify them to do work of a legal nature under the supervision of an attorney.

NALA members also adopted the ABA definition of a legal assistant/paralegal, as follows:

> *A legal assistant or paralegal is a person qualified by education, training or work experience who is employed or retained by a lawyer, law office, corporation, governmental agency or other entity who performs specifically delegated substantive legal work for which a lawyer is responsible. (Adopted by the ABA in 1997)*

Canon 1

A paralegal must not perform any of the duties that attorneys only may perform nor take any actions that attorneys may not take.

Canon 2

A paralegal may perform any task which is properly delegated and supervised by an attorney, as long as the attorney is ultimately responsible to the client, maintains a direct relationship with the client, and assumes professional responsibility for the work product.

Canon 3

A paralegal must not: (a) engage in, encourage, or contribute to any act which could constitute the unauthorized practice of law; and (b) establish attorney-client relationships, set fees, give legal opinions or advice, or represent a client before a court or agency unless so authorized by that court or agency; and (c) engage in conduct or take any action which would assist or involve the attorney in a violation of professional ethics or give the appearance of professional impropriety.

Canon 4

A paralegal must use discretion and professional judgment commensurate with knowledge and experience but must not render independent legal judgment in place of an attorney. The services of an attorney are essential in the public interest whenever such legal judgment is required.

Canon 5

A paralegal must disclose his or her status as a paralegal at the outset of any professional relationship with a client, attorney, a court or administrative agency or personnel thereof, or a member of the general public. A paralegal must act prudently in determining the extent to which a client may be assisted without the presence of an attorney.

Canon 6

A paralegal must strive to maintain integrity and a high degree of competency through education and training with respect to professional responsibility, local rules and practice, and through continuing education in substantive areas of law to better assist the legal profession in fulfilling its duty to provide legal service.

Canon 7

A paralegal must protect the confidences of a client and must not violate any rule or statute now in effect or hereafter enacted controlling the doctrine of privileged communications between a client and an attorney.

Canon 8

A paralegal must disclose to his or her employer or prospective employer any pre-existing client or personal relationship that may conflict with the interests of the employer or prospective employer and/or their clients.

Canon 9

A paralegal must do all other things incidental, necessary, or expedient for the attainment of the ethics and responsibilities as defined by statute or rule of court.

Canon 10

A paralegal's conduct is guided by bar associations' codes of professional responsibility and rules of professional conduct.

NALA's Model Standards and Guidelines for Utilization of Paralegals

NALA's study of the professional responsibility and ethical considerations of paralegals is ongoing. This research led to the development of the NALA *Model Standards and Guidelines for Utilization of Paralegals*. This guide summarizes case law, guidelines, and ethical opinions of the various states affecting paralegals. It provides an outline of minimum qualifications and standards necessary for paralegal professionals to assure the public and the legal profession that they are, indeed, qualified. The following is a listing of the standards and guidelines.

The annotated version of the *Model Standards and Guidelines* was last revised in 2007. It is online at **www.nala.org** (select "Model Standards and Guidelines for Utilization of Paralegals" from the "About Paralegals" menu), where detailed comments are provided about each guideline.

Preamble

Proper utilization of the services of legal assistants contributes to the delivery of cost-effective, high-quality legal services. Legal assistants and the legal profession should be assured that measures exist for identifying legal assistants and their role in assisting attorneys in the delivery of legal services. Therefore, the National Association of Legal Assistants, Inc., hereby adopts these Standards and Guidelines as an educational document for the benefit of legal assistants and the legal profession.

History

The National Association of Legal Assistants adopted this Model in 1984. At the same time the following definition of a legal assistant was adopted:

> Legal assistants, also known as paralegals, are a distinguishable group of persons who assist attorneys in the delivery of legal services. Through formal education, training, and experience, legal assistants have knowledge and expertise regarding the legal system and substantive and procedural law which qualify them to do work of a legal nature under the supervision of an attorney.

Historically, there have been similar definitions adopted by various legal professional organizations. Recognizing the need for one clear definition the NALA membership approved a resolution in July 2001 to adopt the legal assistant definition of the American Bar Association (ABA). This definition continues to be utilized today.

Definition

A legal assistant or paralegal is a person qualified by education, training, or work experience who is employed or retained by a lawyer, law office, corporation, governmental agency, or other entity who performs specifically delegated substantive legal work for which a lawyer is responsible. (Adopted by the ABA in 1997 and by NALA in 2001.)

Standards

A legal assistant should meet certain minimum qualifications. The following standards may be used to determine an individual's qualifications as legal assistant:

Successful completion of the Certified Legal Assistant (CLA)/Certified Paralegal (CP) certifying examination of the National Association of Legal Assistants, Inc.;

1. Graduation from an ABA-approved program of study for legal assistants;

2. Graduation from a course of study for legal assistants which is institutionally accredited but not ABA approved, and which requires not less than the equivalent of 60 semester hours of classroom study;

3. Graduation from a course of study for legal assistants, other than those set forth in (1) and (2) above, plus not less than six months of in-house training as a legal assistant;

4. A baccalaureate degree in any field, plus not less than six months of in-house training as a legal assistant;

5. A minimum of three years of law-related experience under the supervision of an attorney, including at least six months of in-house training as a legal assistant; or

6. Two years of in-house training as a legal assistant.

For purposes of these Standards, "in-house training as a legal assistant" means attorney education of the employee concerning legal assistant duties and these Guidelines. In addition to review and analysis of assignments, the legal assistant should receive a reasonable amount of instruction directly related to the duties and obligations of the legal assistant.

Guidelines

These Guidelines relating to standards of performance and professional responsibility are intended to aid legal assistants and attorneys. The ultimate responsibility rests with an attorney who employs legal assistants to educate them with respect to the duties they are assigned and to supervise the manner in which such duties are accomplished.

Guideline 1

Legal assistants should:

- Disclose their status as legal assistants at the outset of any professional relationship with a client, other attorneys, a court or administrative agency or personnel thereof, or members of the general public;

- Preserve the confidences and secrets of all clients; and
- Understand the attorney's Rules of Professional Responsibility and these Guidelines in order to avoid any action which would involve the attorney in a violation of the Rules, or give the appearance of professional impropriety.

Guideline 2

Legal assistants should not:

- Establish attorney-client relationships;
- Set legal fees, give legal opinions or advice;
- Represent a client before a court, unless authorized to do so by said court;
- Engage in, encourage, or contribute to any act which could constitute the unauthorized practice of law.

Guideline 3

Legal assistants may perform services for an attorney in the representation of a client, provided:

- The services performed by the legal assistant do not require the exercise of independent professional legal judgment;
- The attorney maintains a direct relationship with the client and maintains control of all client matters;
- The attorney supervises the legal assistant;
- The attorney remains professionally responsible for all work on behalf of the client, including any actions taken or not taken by the legal assistant in connection therewith; and
- The services performed supplement, merge with, and become the attorney's work product.

Guideline 4

In the supervision of a legal assistant, consideration should be given to:

- Designating work assignments that correspond to the legal assistant's abilities, knowledge, training, and experience;
- Educating and training the legal assistant with respect to professional responsibility, local rules and practices, and firm policies;
- Monitoring the work and professional conduct of the legal assistant to ensure that the work is substantively correct and timely performed;
- Providing continuing education for the legal assistant in substantive matters through courses, institutes, workshops, seminars, and in-house training; and
- Encouraging and supporting membership and active participation in professional organizations.

Guideline 5

Except as otherwise provided by statute, court rule or decision, administrative rule or regulation, or the attorney's rules of professional responsibility, and within the preceding parameters and proscriptions, a legal assistant may perform any function delegated by an attorney, including but not limited to the following:

- Conduct client interviews and maintain general contact with the client after the establishment of the attorney-client relationship, so long as the client is aware of the status and function of the legal assistant, and the client contact is under the supervision of the attorney.
- Locate and interview witnesses, so long as the witnesses are aware of the status and function of the legal assistant.

- Conduct investigations and statistical and documentary research for review by the attorney.

- Conduct legal research for review by the attorney.

- Draft legal documents for review by the attorney.

- Draft correspondence and pleadings for review by and signature of the attorney.

- Summarize depositions, interrogatories, and testimony for review by the attorney.

- Attend executions of wills, real estate closings, depositions, court or administrative hearings, and trials with the attorney.

- Author and sign letters providing the legal assistant's status is clearly indicated and the correspondence does not contain independent legal opinions or legal advice.

Conclusion

These Standards and Guidelines were developed from generally accepted practices. Each supervising attorney must be aware of the specific rules, decisions, and statutes applicable to legal assistants within his/her jurisdiction.

NFPA's Model Code of Ethics and Professional Responsibility and Guidelines for Enforcement

Preamble

The National Federation of Paralegal Associations, Inc. ("NFPA®"), is a professional organization comprised of paralegal associations and individual paralegals throughout the United States and Canada. Members of NFPA® have varying backgrounds, experiences, education, and job responsibilities that reflect the diversity of the paralegal profession. NFPA® promotes the growth, development, and recognition of the paralegal profession as an integral partner in the delivery of legal services.

In May 1993 NFPA® adopted its Model Code of Ethics and Professional Responsibility ("Model Code") to delineate the principles for ethics and conduct to which every paralegal should aspire.

Many paralegal associations throughout the United States have endorsed the concept and content of NFPA®'s Model Code through the adoption of their own ethical codes. In doing so, paralegals have confirmed the profession's commitment to increase the quality and efficiency of legal services, as well as recognized its responsibilities to the public, the legal community, and colleagues.

Paralegals have recognized, and will continue to recognize, that the profession must continue to evolve to enhance their roles in the delivery of legal services. With increased levels of responsibility comes the need to define and enforce mandatory rules of professional conduct. Enforcement of codes of paralegal conduct is a logical and necessary step to enhance and ensure the confidence of the legal community and the public in the integrity and professional responsibility of paralegals.

In April 1997 NFPA® adopted the Model Disciplinary Rules ("Model Rules") to make possible the enforcement of the Canons and Ethical Considerations contained in the NFPA® Model Code. A concurrent determination was made that the Model Code of Ethics and Professional Responsibility, formerly aspirational in nature, should be recognized as setting forth the enforceable obligations of all paralegals.

The Model Code and Model Rules offer a framework for professional discipline, either voluntarily or through formal regulatory programs.

§1. NFPA® Model Disciplinary Rules and Ethical Considerations

1.1 A Paralegal Shall Achieve and Maintain a High Level of Competence.

Ethical Considerations

EC–1.1(a) A paralegal shall achieve competency through education, training, and work experience.

EC–1.1(b) A paralegal shall aspire to participate in a minimum of twelve (12) hours of continuing legal education, to include at least one (1) hour of ethics education, every two (2) years in order to remain current on developments in the law.

EC–1.1(c) A paralegal shall perform all assignments promptly and efficiently.

1.2 A Paralegal Shall Maintain a High Level of Personal and Professional Integrity.

Ethical Considerations

EC–1.2(a) A paralegal shall not engage in any *ex parte* communications involving the courts or any other adjudicatory body in an attempt to exert undue influence or to obtain advantage or the benefit of only one party.

EC–1.2(b) A paralegal shall not communicate, or cause another to communicate, with a party the paralegal knows to be represented by a lawyer in a pending matter without the prior consent of the lawyer representing such other party.

EC–1.2(c) A paralegal shall ensure that all timekeeping and billing records prepared by the paralegal are thorough, accurate, honest, and complete.

EC–1.2(d) A paralegal shall not knowingly engage in fraudulent billing practices. Such practices may include, but are not limited to: inflation of hours billed to a client or employer; misrepresentation of the nature of tasks performed; and/or submission of fraudulent expense and disbursement documentation.

EC–1.2(e) A paralegal shall be scrupulous, thorough, and honest in the identification and maintenance of all funds, securities, and other assets of a client and shall provide accurate accounting as appropriate.

EC–1.2(f) A paralegal shall advise the proper authority of nonconfidential knowledge of any dishonest or fraudulent acts by any person pertaining to the handling of the funds, securities, or other assets of a client. The authority to whom the report is made shall depend on the nature and circumstances of the possible misconduct (for example, ethics committees of law firms, corporations and/or paralegal associations, local or state bar associations, local prosecutors, administrative agencies, etc.). Failure to report such knowledge is in itself misconduct and shall be treated as such under these rules.

1.3 A Paralegal Shall Maintain a High Standard of Professional Conduct.

Ethical Considerations

EC–1.3(a) A paralegal shall refrain from engaging in any conduct that offends the dignity and decorum of proceedings before a court or other adjudicatory body and shall be respectful of all rules and procedures.

EC–1.3(b) A paralegal shall avoid impropriety and the appearance of impropriety and shall not engage in any conduct that would adversely affect his/her fitness to practice. Such conduct may include, but is not limited to: violence, dishonesty, interference with the administration of justice, and/or abuse of a professional position or public office.

EC–1.3(c) Should a paralegal's fitness to practice be compromised by physical or mental illness, causing that paralegal to commit an act that is in direct violation of the Model Code/Model Rules and/or the rules and/or laws governing the jurisdiction in which the paralegal practices, that paralegal may be protected from sanction upon review of the nature and circumstances of that illness.

EC–1.3(d) A paralegal shall advise the proper authority of nonconfidential knowledge of any action of another legal professional that clearly demonstrates fraud, deceit, dishonesty, or misrepresentation. The authority to whom the report is made shall depend on the nature and circumstances of the possible misconduct (for example, ethics committees of law firms, corporations and/or paralegal associations, local or state bar associations, local prosecutors, administrative agencies, etc.). Failure to report such knowledge is in itself misconduct and shall be treated as such under these rules.

EC–1.3(e) A paralegal shall not knowingly assist any individual with the commission of an act that is in direct violation of the Model Code/Model Rules and/or the rules and/or laws governing the jurisdiction in which the paralegal practices.

EC–1.3(f) If a paralegal possesses knowledge of future criminal activity, that knowledge must be reported to the appropriate authority immediately.

1.4 A Paralegal Shall Serve the Public Interest by Contributing to the Improvement of the Legal System and Delivery of Quality Legal Services, Including Pro Bono Publico Services.

Ethical Considerations

EC–1.4(a) A paralegal shall be sensitive to the legal needs of the public and shall promote the development and implementation of programs that address those needs.

EC–1.4(b) A paralegal shall support efforts to improve the legal system and access thereto and shall assist in making changes.

EC–1.4(c) A paralegal shall support and participate in the delivery of *Pro Bono Publico* services directed toward implementing and improving access to justice, the law, the legal system, or the paralegal and legal professions.

EC–1.4(d) A paralegal should aspire annually to contribute twenty-four (24) hours of *Pro Bono Publico* services under the supervision of an attorney or as authorized by administrative, statutory, or court authority to:

1. persons of limited means; or

2. charitable, religious, civic, community, governmental, and educational organizations in matters that are designed primarily to address the legal needs of persons with limited means; or

3. individuals, groups, or organizations seeking to secure or protect civil rights, civil liberties, or public rights.

The twenty-four (24) hours of *Pro Bono Publico* services contributed annually by a paralegal may consist of such services as detailed in this EC-1.4(d), and/or administrative matters designed to develop and implement the attainment of this aspiration as detailed above in EC-1.4(a) & (c), or any combination of the two.

1.5 A Paralegal Shall Preserve All Confidential Information Provided by the Client or Acquired from Other Sources before, during, and after the Course of the Professional Relationship.

Ethical Considerations

EC–1.5(a) A paralegal shall be aware of and abide by all legal authority governing confidential information in the jurisdiction in which the paralegal practices.

EC–1.5(b) A paralegal shall not use confidential information to the disadvantage of the client.

EC–1.5(c) A paralegal shall not use confidential information to the advantage of the paralegal or of a third person.

EC–1.5(d) A paralegal may reveal confidential information only after full disclosure and with the client's written consent; or, when required by law or court order; or, when necessary to prevent the client from committing an act that could result in death or serious bodily harm.

EC–1.5(e) A paralegal shall keep those individuals responsible for the legal representation of a client fully informed of any confidential information the paralegal may have pertaining to that client.

EC–1.5(f) A paralegal shall not engage in any indiscreet communications concerning clients.

1.6 A Paralegal Shall Avoid Conflicts of Interest and Shall Disclose Any Possible Conflict to the Employer or Client, as Well as to the Prospective Employers or Clients.

Ethical Considerations

EC–1.6(a) A paralegal shall act within the bounds of the law, solely for the benefit of the client, and shall be free of compromising influences and loyalties. Neither the paralegal's personal or business interest, nor those of other clients or third persons, should compromise the paralegal's professional judgment and loyalty to the client.

EC–1.6(b) A paralegal shall avoid conflicts of interest that may arise from previous assignments, whether for a present or past employer or client.

EC–1.6(c) A paralegal shall avoid conflicts of interest that may arise from family relationships and from personal and business interests.

EC–1.6(d) In order to be able to determine whether an actual or potential conflict of interest exists a paralegal shall create and maintain an effective record-keeping system that identifies clients, matters, and parties with which the paralegal has worked.

EC–1.6(e) A paralegal shall reveal sufficient nonconfidential information about a client or former client to reasonably ascertain if an actual or potential conflict of interest exists.

EC–1.6(f) A paralegal shall not participate in or conduct work on any matter where a conflict of interest has been identified.

EC–1.6(g) In matters where a conflict of interest has been identified and the client consents to continued representation, a paralegal shall comply fully with the implementation and maintenance of an Ethical Wall.

1.7 A Paralegal's Title Shall Be Fully Disclosed.

Ethical Considerations

EC–1.7(a) A paralegal's title shall clearly indicate the individual's status and shall be disclosed in all business and professional communications to avoid misunderstandings and misconceptions about the paralegal's role and responsibilities.

EC–1.7(b) A paralegal's title shall be included if the paralegal's name appears on business cards, letterhead, brochures, directories, and advertisements.

EC–1.7(c) A paralegal shall not use letterhead, business cards, or other promotional materials to create a fraudulent impression of his/her status or ability to practice in the jurisdiction in which the paralegal practices.

EC–1.7(d) A paralegal shall not practice under color of any record, diploma, or certificate that has been illegally or fraudulently obtained or issued or which is misrepresentative in any way.

EC–1.7(e) A paralegal shall not participate in the creation, issuance, or dissemination of fraudulent records, diplomas, or certificates.

1.8 A Paralegal Shall Not Engage in the Unauthorized Practice of Law.

Ethical Considerations

EC–1.8(a) A paralegal shall comply with the applicable legal authority governing the unauthorized practice of law in the jurisdiction in which the paralegal practices.

§2. NFPA Guidelines for the Enforcement of the Model Code of Ethics and Professional Responsibility

2.1 Basis for Discipline

2.1(a) Disciplinary investigations and proceedings brought under authority of the Rules shall be conducted in accord with obligations imposed on the paralegal professional by the Model Code of Ethics and Professional Responsibility.

2.2 Structure of Disciplinary Committee

2.2(a) The Disciplinary Committee ("Committee") shall be made up of nine (9) members including the Chair.

2.2(b) Each member of the Committee, including any temporary replacement members, shall have demonstrated working knowledge of ethics/professional responsibility–related issues and activities.

2.2(c) The Committee shall represent a cross section of practice areas and work experience. The following recommendations are made regarding the members of the Committee.

1. At least one paralegal with one to three years of law-related work experience.
2. At least one paralegal with five to seven years of law-related work experience.
3. At least one paralegal with over ten years of law-related work experience.
4. One paralegal educator with five to seven years of work experience, preferably in the area of ethics/professional responsibility.
5. One paralegal manager.

6. One lawyer with five to seven years of law-related work experience.

7. One lay member.

2.2(d) The Chair of the Committee shall be appointed within thirty (30) days of its members' induction. The Chair shall have no fewer than ten (10) years of law-related work experience.

2.2(e) The terms of all members of the Committee shall be staggered. Of those members initially appointed, a simple majority plus one shall be appointed to a term of one year, and the remaining members shall be appointed to a term of two years. Thereafter, all members of the Committee shall be appointed to terms of two years.

2.2(f) If for any reason the terms of a majority of the Committee will expire at the same time, members may be appointed to terms of one year to maintain continuity of the Committee.

2.2(g) The Committee shall organize from its members a three-tiered structure to investigate, prosecute, and/or adjudicate charges of misconduct. The members shall be rotated among the tiers.

2.3 Operation of Committee

2.3(a) The Committee shall meet on an as-needed basis to discuss, investigate, and/or adjudicate alleged violations of the Model Code/Model Rules.

2.3(b) A majority of the members of the Committee present at a meeting shall constitute a quorum.

2.3(c) A Recording Secretary shall be designated to maintain complete and accurate minutes of all Committee meetings. All such minutes shall be kept confidential until a decision has been made that the matter will be set for hearing as set forth in Section 6.1 below.

2.3(d) If any member of the Committee has a conflict of interest with the Charging Party, the Responding Party, or the allegations of misconduct, that member shall not take part in any hearing or deliberations concerning those allegations. If the absence of that member creates a lack of a quorum for the Committee, then a temporary replacement for the member shall be appointed.

2.3(e) Either the Charging Party or the Responding Party may request that, for good cause shown, any member of the Committee not participate in a hearing or deliberation. All such requests shall be honored. If the absence of a Committee member under those circumstances creates a lack of a quorum for the Committee, then a temporary replacement for that member shall be appointed.

2.3(f) All discussions and correspondence of the Committee shall be kept confidential until a decision has been made that the matter will be set for hearing as set forth in Section 6.1 below.

2.3(g) All correspondence from the Committee to the Responding Party regarding any charge of misconduct and any decisions made regarding the charge shall be mailed certified mail, return receipt requested, to the Responding Party's last known address and shall be clearly marked with a "Confidential" designation.

2.4 Procedure for the Reporting of Alleged Violations of the Model Code/Disciplinary Rules

2.4(a) An individual or entity in possession of nonconfidential knowledge or information concerning possible instances of misconduct shall make a confidential written report to the Committee within thirty (30) days of obtaining same. This report shall include all details of the alleged misconduct.

2.4(b) The Committee so notified shall inform the Responding Party of the allegation(s) of misconduct no later than ten (10) business days after receiving the confidential written report from the Charging Party.

2.4(c) Notification to the Responding Party shall include the identity of the Charging Party, unless, for good cause shown, the Charging Party requests anonymity.

2.4(d) The Responding Party shall reply to the allegations within ten (10) business days of notification.

2.5 Procedure for the Investigation of a Charge of Misconduct

2.5(a) Upon receipt of a Charge of Misconduct ("Charge"), or on its own initiative, the Committee shall initiate an investigation.

2.5(b) If, upon initial or preliminary review, the Committee makes a determination that the charges are either without basis in fact or, if proven, would not constitute professional misconduct, the Committee shall dismiss the allegations of misconduct. If such determination of dismissal cannot be made, a formal investigation shall be initiated.

2.5(c) Upon the decision to conduct a formal investigation, the Committee shall:

1. mail to the Charging and Responding Parties within three (3) business days of that decision notice of the commencement of a formal investigation. That notification shall be in writing and shall contain a complete explanation of all Charge(s), as well as the reasons for a formal investigation, and shall cite the applicable codes and rules;

2. allow the Responding Party thirty (30) days to prepare and submit a confidential response to the Committee, which response shall address each charge specifically and shall be in writing; and

3. upon receipt of the response to the notification, have thirty (30) days to investigate the Charge(s). If an extension of time is deemed necessary, that extension shall not exceed ninety (90) days.

2.5(d) Upon conclusion of the investigation, the Committee may:

1. dismiss the Charge upon the finding that it has no basis in fact;

2. dismiss the Charge upon the finding that, if proven, the Charge would not constitute Misconduct;

3. refer the matter for hearing by the Tribunal; or

4. in the case of criminal activity, refer the Charge(s) and all investigation results to the appropriate authority.

2.6 Procedure for a Misconduct Hearing before a Tribunal

2.6(a) Upon the decision by the Committee that a matter should be heard, all parties shall be notified and a hearing date shall be set. The hearing shall take place no more than thirty (30) days from the conclusion of the formal investigation.

2.6(b) The Responding Party shall have the right to counsel. The parties and the Tribunal shall have the right to call any witnesses and introduce any documentation that they believe will lead to the fair and reasonable resolution of the matter.

2.6(c) Upon completion of the hearing, the Tribunal shall deliberate and present a written decision to the parties in accordance with procedures as set forth by the Tribunal.

2.6(d) Notice of the decision of the Tribunal shall be appropriately published.

2.7 Sanctions

2.7(a) Upon a finding of the Tribunal that misconduct has occurred, any of the following sanctions, or others as may be deemed appropriate, may be imposed upon the Responding Party, either singularly or in combination:

1. Letter of reprimand to the Responding Party; counseling;

2. Attendance at an ethics course approved by the Tribunal; probation;

3. Suspension of license/authority to practice; revocation of license/authority to practice;

4. Imposition of a fine; assessment of costs; or

5. In the instance of criminal activity, referral to the appropriate authority.

2.7(b) Upon the expiration of any period of probation, suspension, or revocation, the Responding Party may make application for reinstatement. With the application for reinstatement, the Responding Party must show proof of having complied with all aspects of the sanctions imposed by the Tribunal.

2.8 Appellate Procedures

2.8(a) The parties shall have the right to appeal the decision of the Tribunal in accordance with the procedure as set forth by the Tribunal.

Definitions

APPELLATE BODY   means a body established to adjudicate an appeal to any decision made by a Tribunal or other decision-making body with respect to formally heard Charges of Misconduct.

CHARGE OF MISCONDUCT   means a written submission by any individual or entity to an ethics committee, paralegal association, bar association, law enforcement agency, judicial body, government agency, or other appropriate body or entity, that sets forth non-confidential information regarding any instance of alleged misconduct by an individual paralegal or paralegal entity.

CHARGING PARTY   means any individual or entity who submits a Charge of Misconduct against an individual paralegal or paralegal entity.

COMPETENCY   means the demonstration of: diligence, education, skill, and mental, emotional, and physical fitness reasonably necessary for the performance of paralegal services.

CONFIDENTIAL INFORMATION   means information relating to a client, whatever its source, that is not public knowledge nor available to the public. ("Non-Confidential Information" would generally include the name of the client and the identity of the matter for which the paralegal provided services.)

DISCIPLINARY COMMITTEE   means any committee that has been established by an entity such as a paralegal association, bar association, judicial body, or government agency to: (a) identify, define, and investigate general ethical considerations and concerns with respect to paralegal practice; (b) administer and enforce the Model Code and Model Rules and; (c) discipline any individual paralegal or paralegal entity found to be in violation of same.

DISCIPLINARY HEARING   means the confidential proceeding conducted by a committee or other designated body or entity concerning any instance of alleged misconduct by an individual paralegal or paralegal entity.

DISCLOSE   means communication of information reasonably sufficient to permit identification of the significance of the matter in question.

ETHICAL WALL   means the screening method implemented in order to protect a client from a conflict of interest. An Ethical Wall generally includes, but is not limited to, the following elements: (1) prohibit the paralegal from having any connection with the matter; (2) ban discussions with or the transfer of documents to or from the paralegal; (3) restrict access to files; and (4) educate all members of the firm, corporation, or entity as to the separation of the paralegal (both organizationally and physically) from the pending matter. For more information regarding the Ethical Wall, see the NFPA publication entitled "The Ethical Wall—Its Application to Paralegals."

EX PARTE means actions or communications conducted at the instance and for the benefit of one party only, and without notice to, or contestation by, any person adversely interested.

INVESTIGATION means the investigation of any charge(s) of misconduct filed against an individual paralegal or paralegal entity by a Committee.

LETTER OF REPRIMAND means a written notice of formal censure or severe reproof administered to an individual paralegal or paralegal entity for unethical or improper conduct.

MISCONDUCT means the knowing or unknowing commission of an act that is in direct violation of those Canons and Ethical Considerations of any and all applicable codes and/or rules of conduct.

PARALEGAL is synonymous with "Legal Assistant" and is defined as a person qualified through education, training, or work experience to perform substantive legal work that requires knowledge of legal concepts and is customarily but not exclusively performed by a lawyer. This person may be retained or employed by a lawyer, law office, governmental agency, or other entity or may be authorized by administrative, statutory, or court authority to perform this work.

PRO BONO PUBLICO means providing or assisting to provide quality legal services in order to enhance access to justice for persons of limited means; charitable, religious, civic, community, governmental, and educational organizations in matters that are designed primarily to address the legal needs of persons with limited means; or individuals, groups, or organizations seeking to secure or protect civil rights, civil liberties, or public rights.

PROPER AUTHORITY means the local paralegal association, the local or state bar association, committee(s) of the local paralegal or bar association(s), local prosecutor, administrative agency, or other tribunal empowered to investigate or act upon an instance of alleged misconduct.

RESPONDING PARTY means an individual paralegal or paralegal entity against whom a Charge of Misconduct has been submitted.

REVOCATION means the rescission of the license, certificate, or other authority to practice of an individual paralegal or paralegal entity found in violation of those Canons and Ethical Considerations of any and all applicable codes and/or rules of conduct.

SUSPENSION means the suspension of the license, certificate, or other authority to practice of an individual paralegal or paralegal entity found in violation of those Canons and Ethical Considerations of any and all applicable codes and/or rules of conduct.

TRIBUNAL means the body designated to adjudicate allegations of misconduct.

NALS Code of Ethics and Professional Responsibility

Members of NALS are bound by the objectives of this association and the standards of conduct required of the legal profession.

Every member shall:

- Encourage respect for the law and the administration of justice;

- Observe rules governing privileged communications and confidential information;

- Promote and exemplify high standards of loyalty, cooperation, and courtesy;

- Perform all duties of the profession with integrity and competence; and

- Pursue a high order of professional attainment.

Integrity and high standards of conduct are fundamental to the success of our professional association. This Code is promulgated by the NALS and accepted by its members to accomplish these ends.

Canon 1

Members of this association shall maintain a high degree of competency and integrity through continuing education to better assist the legal profession in fulfilling its duty to provide quality legal services to the public.

Canon 2

Members of this association shall maintain a high standard of ethical conduct and shall contribute to the integrity of the association and the legal profession.

Canon 3

Members of this association shall avoid a conflict of interest pertaining to a client matter.

Canon 4

Members of this association shall preserve and protect the confidences and privileged communications of a client.

Canon 5

Members of this association shall exercise care in using independent professional judgment and in determining the extent to which a client may be assisted without the presence of a lawyer and shall not act in matters involving professional legal judgment.

Canon 6

Members of this association shall not solicit legal business on behalf of a lawyer.

Canon 7

Members of this association, unless permitted by law, shall not perform paralegal functions except under the direct supervision of a lawyer and shall not advertise or contract with members of the general public for the performance of paralegal functions.

Canon 8

Members of this association, unless permitted by law, shall not perform any of the duties restricted to lawyers or do things which lawyers themselves may not do and shall assist in preventing the unauthorized practice of law.

Canon 9

Members of this association not licensed to practice law shall not engage in the practice of law as defined by statutes or court decisions.

Canon 10

Members of this association shall do all other things incidental, necessary, or expedient to enhance professional responsibility and participation in the administration of justice and public service in cooperation with the legal profession.

Paralegal Associations

National Federation of Paralegal Associations (NFPA); please see www.paralegals.org for updates.

NFPA Associations

Region I

Alaska Association of Paralegals
www.alaskaparalegals.org

Hawaii Paralegal Association
www.hawaiiparalegal.org

Oregon Paralegal Association
www.oregonparalegals.org

Paralegal Association of Southern Nevada

Sacramento Valley Paralegal Association
www.svpa.org

San Francisco Paralegal Association
www.sfpa.com

Washington State Paralegal Association
www.wspaonline.org

Region II

Arkansas Paralegal Association
www.arkansasparalegal.org

Dallas Area Paralegal Association
www.dallasparalegals.org

Illinois Paralegal Association
www.ipaonline.org

Kansas Paralegal Association
www.ksparalegals.org

Minnesota Paralegal Association
www.mnparalegals.org

Missouri Paralegal Association
www.missouriparalegalassoc.org

The New Orleans Paralegal Association
www.neworleansparalegals.org

Rocky Mountain Paralegal Association (CO, NE, SD, UT, WY)
www.rockymtnparalegal.org

Region III

Cleveland Association of Paralegals
www.capohio.org

Georgia Association of Paralegals
www.gaparalegal.org

Greater Lexington Paralegal Association
www.lexingtonparalegals.org

Indiana Paralegal Association
www.indianaparalegals.org

Memphis Paralegal Association
www.memphisparalegalassoc.org

Michiana Paralegal Association (IN, MI)
www.michianaparalegals.org

Middle Tennessee Paralegal Association
www.mtpa.memberlodge.org

Northeast Indiana Paralegal Association
www.neindianaparalegal.org

Palmetto Paralegal Association
www.ppasc.org

Paralegal Association of Central Ohio
www.pacoparalegals.org

South Florida Paralegal Association
www.sfpa.info

Tampa Bay Paralegal Association
www.tbpa.org

Region IV

Bucks County Paralegal Association
www.buckscoparalegals.com

Central Pennsylvania Paralegal Association
www.centralpaparalegals.com

Lycoming County Paralegal Association (PA)
www.lycolaw.org/lcpa/main.htm

Maryland Association of Paralegals
www.mdparalegals.org

Montgomery County Paralegal Association (PA)
www.montcoparalegals.org

National Capital Area Paralegal Association
www.ncapa.com

Paralegal Association of Northern
   Virginia
www.panv.org

Philadelphia Association of
   Paralegals
www.philaparalegals.com

Pittsburgh Paralegal Association
www.pghparalegals.org

South Jersey Paralegal
   Association
www.sjpaparalegals.org

Region V

Capital District Paralegal
   Association (NY)
www.cdpa.info

Central Connecticut Paralegal
   Association
www.ctparalegals.org

Central Massachusetts Paralegal
   Association
www.cmpa.net

Connecticut Association of
   Paralegals
www.ct-cap.com

Long Island Paralegal Association

Massachusetts Paralegal
   Association
www.massparalegal.org

New Haven County Association of
   Paralegals
www.nhcap.org

New York City Paralegal
   Association
www.nyc-pa.org

Paralegal Association of New
   Hampshire
www.panh.org

Paralegal Association of Rochester
www.rochesterparalegal.org

Rhode Island Paralegal Association
www.riparalegals.org

Vermont Paralegal Organization
www.vtparalegal.org

Western Massachusetts Paralegal
   Association
www.wmassparalegal.org

Western New York Paralegal
   Association
www.wnyparalegals.org

NALA State and Local Affiliates

This list is current as of the publication date. For updates, please check the NALA web site (www.nala.org).

Alabama

Alabama Association of Paralegals
www.alabamaparalegals.net

Alaska

Fairbanks Association of Legal
   Assistants
www.fairbanksparalegal.org

Arizona

Arizona Paralegal Association
www.azparalegal.org

Maricopa County Association of
   Paralegals
www.mcaparalegals.org

Tucson Paralegal Association
www.tucsonparalegals.org

Arkansas

Arkansas Paralegal Alliance
www.arkansasparalegalalliance.org

California

Fresno Paralegal Association
www.fresnoparalegal.org

Inland Counties Association of
   Paralegals
www.icaponline.org

Los Angeles Paralegal Association
www.lapa.org

Orange County Paralegal
   Association
www.ocparalegal.org

Paralegal Association of Santa
   Clara County
www.pascco.org

San Diego Paralegal Association
www.sdparalegals.org

Santa Barbara Paralegal
   Association
www.sbparalegals.org

Ventura County Paralegal
   Association
www.vcparalegal.org

Colorado

Legal Assistants of the Western
   Slope

Pikes Peak Paralegals
www.pikespeakparalegals.org

Florida

Central Florida Paralegal Association
www.cfpainc.com

Gulf Coast Paralegal Association
www.gcpa.info

Northeast Florida Paralegal
   Association
www.nefpa.org

Northwest Florida Paralegal
   Association
www.nwfpa.com

Paralegal Association of Florida
www.pafinc.org

South Florida Paralegal Association
www.sfpa.info

Southwest Florida Paralegal
   Association
www.swfloridaparalegals.com

Georgia

Southeastern Association of Legal
   Assistants
www.seala.org

Illinois

Central Illinois Paralegal Association
www.ciparalegal.org

Iowa

Iowa Association of Legal Assistants.Paralegals
www.ialanet.org

Western Iowa Technical Community College Legal Assistant Association

Kansas

Heartland Paralegal Association
www.heartlandparalegalassociation.weebly.com

Kansas Association of Legal Assistants
www.accesskansas.org/kala

Kentucky

Western Kentucky Paralegals
www.kypa.org/WKP.htm

Louisiana

Louisiana State Paralegal Association
www.la-paralegals.org

Northwest Louisiana Paralegal Association

Mississippi

Holmes Association of Legal Students

Mississippi Paralegal Association
www.msparalegals.org

Missouri

St. Louis Paralegal Association
www.stlpa.org

Montana

Montana Association of Legal Assistants*Paralegals
www.malanet.org

Nebraska

Nebraska Paralegal Association
www.nebraskaparalegal.org

Nevada

Nevada Paralegal Association
www.nevadaparalegal.org

Sierra Nevada Association of Paralegals
www.snapreno.com

New Jersey

Paralegal Association of New Jersey
www.laanj.org

North Carolina

Metrolina Paralegal Association
www.charlotteareaparalegals.com

North Carolina Paralegal Association
www.ncparalegal.org

North Dakota

Red River Valley Paralegal Association
www.rrvpa.org

Western Dakota Association of Legal Assistants
www.wdala.org

Ohio

Paralegal Association of Northwest Ohio
www.panonet.org

Oklahoma

Central Oklahoma Association of Legal Assistants
www.coala.cc

Oklahoma Paralegal Association
www.okparalegal.org

TCC Student Association of Legal Assistants

Tulsa Area Paralegal Association
www.tulsaparalegals.org

Oregon

Pacific Northwest Paralegal Association
www.pnpa.org

Pennsylvania

Lancaster Area Paralegal Association
www.lapaparalegals.com

South Carolina

Charleston Association of Legal Assistants
www.charlestonlegalassistants.org

South Carolina Upstate Paralegal Association
www.scupa.org

South Dakota

South Dakota Paralegal Association
www.sdparalegals.com

Tennessee

Greater Memphis Paralegal Alliance
www.memphisparalegals.org

Smoky Mountain Paralegal Association
www.smparalegal.org

Tennessee Paralegal Association
www.tnparalegal.org

Texas

Capital Area Paralegal Association
www.capatx.org

El Paso Paralegal Association

Houston Association of Bankruptcy Paralegals
www.houstonbankruptcyparalegals.org

Houston Corporate Paralegal Association
www.hcpa.cc

Houston Paralegal Association
www.hpatx.us

ITT Paralegal Association of Houston-North

ITT Paralegal Association of Houston-West

ITT Paralegal Association of
Webster, TX

J.L. Turner Legal Association
www.jltla.org

Paralegal Association/Permian
Basin
www.paralegalspb.org

North Texas Paralegal Association
www.ntparalegals.org

Northeast Texas Association of
Paralegals
www.ntaparalegals.org

South Texas Organization of
Paralegals
www.stopweb.org

Southeast Texas Association of
Paralegals
www.setap.org

Texas Panhandle Paralegal
Association
www.txtppa.webs.com

Tyler Area Association of Legal
Professionals

West Texas Paralegal Association

Utah

Legal Assistants Association of
Utah
www.laau.info

Virgin Islands

Virgin Islands Association of Legal
Assistants

Virginia

Richmond Paralegal Association
www.richmondparalegals.org

Roanoke Valley Paralegal
Association
www.rvpa.org

Tidewater Paralegal Association

Virginia Peninsula Paralegal
Association
www.vappa.org

West Virginia

Legal Assistants/Paralegals of
Southern West Virginia
www.lapswv.org

Wisconsin

Madison Area Paralegal Association
www.madisonparalegal.org

Wyoming

Legal Assistants of Wyoming
www.lawyo.com

NALS State and Chapter Associations

NALS . . . the association for legal professionals is a multilevel association with state and chapter associations. Following is a list of NALS state and chapter associations. For additional details, please check with the NALS Resource Center at **www.nals.org**.

Alabama

AALS
www.alabama-als.org

Baldwin County Association of
Legal Professionals

BLSA (Birmingham)
www.blsa-al.com

Dallas County Legal Secretaries
Association

Mobile Legal Professionals
Association

MALS
www.malsmontgomery.blogspot.com

Alaska

NALS of Anchorage
www.nalsofanchorage.org

Arizona

NALS of Arizona
www.nalsofarizona.org

NALS of Phoenix
www.nalsofphoenix.org

NALS of Tucson and Southern
Arizona
www.nalsoftucson.org

NALS of Yavapai County

Arkansas

AALS–The Association for
Arkansas Legal Support
Professionals
www.aalsonline.org

Garland County Legal Support
Professional

Greater Little Rock Legal Support
Professionals
www.greaterlittlerocklsp.com

Jefferson County Association of
Legal Support Professionals

Northeast Arkansas Legal Support
Professionals
www.nealsp.org

Northwest Arkansas Legal Support
Professionals

Saline County Legal Support
Professionals

White County Association of Legal
Support Professionals
www.wclsp.com

California

NALS of California

NALS of Orange County
www.nalsoc.org

Port Stockton LSA

Florida

NALS of Central Florida

NALS of the Everglades

NALS of West Coast Florida
www.nalsofwcfl.org

Georgia

NALS of Georgia

NALS of Atlanta
www.nalsofatlanta.org

Cobb County Legal Secretaries
  Association

Hawaii

Hawaii Legal Support Professionals
www.hawaiilsp.org

Idaho

IDALS
www.idals.org

BLSA (Boise)

LLSA (Lewiston)

North Idaho Legal Secretaries
  Association

Illinois

NALS of Illinois
www.nalsofillinois.org

Maine

NALS of Maine
www.nalsofmaine.org

NALS of Central Maine

NALS of Midcoast Maine

NALS of Northeast Maine

NALS of Southern Maine

Michigan

NALS of Michigan
www.nalsofmichigan.org

Berrien Cass LSP

NALS of Calhoun County

NALS of Detroit
www.nalsofdetroit.org

Genessee Association of Legal
  Support Professionals

Grand Traverse County

NALS of Greater Kalamazoo
www.nalsofgreaterkalamazoo.org

Jackson County Legal Support
  Professionals
www.nalsofjacksoncounty.com

NALS of Lansing
www.nalsoflansing.org

Mid Michigan Association of Legal
  Support Professionals

NALS of Northern Michigan

NALS of West Michigan
www.nalsofwmi.org

NALS of Washtenaw County

Minnesota

NALS of Greater Minnesota

NALS Twin Cities

Mississippi

Mississippi Division of NALS, Inc.

Greenwood Legal Professionals
  Association

Gulf Coast Association for Legal
  Support Professionals

Jackson Legal Professionals
  Association

Metro Legal Professionals
  Association

Pinebelt Legal Professionals

Tri-County Legal Support
  Professionals Association
www.tclspa.org

Missouri

NALS of Missouri
www.nalsofmissouri.org

East Central Missouri Legal
  Professionals
www.eastcentralmolegalprofs.org

Heart of America Legal
  Professionals Association
  (Kansas City)

Kansas City Legal Secretaries
  Association
www.kclsa.net

Lakes Area Legal Support
  Association

NALS of Greater St. Louis
www.nalsofgreaterstlouis.org

Springfield Area Legal Support
  Professionals
www.salsp.org

Tri-County ALP

Nevada

NALS of Nevada

Douglas-Carson Legal Professionals

NALS of Las Vegas, a professional
  legal association
www.nalsoflasvegas.org

NALS of Washoe County

New Jersey

NJALS . . . the association for legal
  professionals
www.njals.org

Hunterdon County Legal
  Secretaries Association

Middlesex Legal Professionals
  Association

Monmouth Legal Secretaries
  Association

Somerset County Legal Secretaries
  Association

Union-Essex Legal Professional
  Association

New York

NALS of New York
www.nalsofnewyorkinc.org

Central NY Chapter of NALS
www.nalsofnewyorkinc.org/
onondaga.html

NALS of Nassau County
www.nalsofnewyorkinc.org/nassau.
html

NALS of New York City
www.nalsofnewyorkinc.org/
newyorkcity.html

NALS of Suffolk County
www.nalsofnewyorkinc.org/suffolk.
html

Westchester County Legal
Secretaries Association d/b/a
Lower Hudson Valley Legal
Support Staff
www.nalsofnewyorkinc.org/
lowerhudsonvalley.html

North Dakota

NALS of Fargo-Moorhead

Ohio

NALS of Ohio

NALS of Central Ohio

NALS of Northeast Ohio

Stark County Association for Legal
Professionals

Oklahoma

NALS of Oklahoma
www.nalsofok.org

Oregon

NALS of Oregon
www.nalsor.org

Central Oregon Legal
Professionals
www.nalsor.org/COLP/index.htm

NALS of Lane County
www.nalsor.org/Lane/index.htm

Legal Professionals of Douglas
County
www.nalsor.org/douglas/index.htm

NALS of Mid-Willamette Valley
www.nalsor.org/MWValley/index.
htm

Mt. Hood Legal Professionals
www.nalsor.org/Mt_Hood/index.
htm

NALS of Portland
www.nalsor.org/Portland/index.
htm

NALS of Southern Oregon Coast

Pennsylvania

NALS of Pennsylvania
www.palegal.org

Lehigh-Northhampton Counties
Legal Secretaries Association

Philadelphia Legal Secretaries
Association
www.philalsa.org

Schuylkill County

South Carolina

Legal Staff Professionals of South
Carolina
www.lspsc.org

Hilton Head Legal Staff
Professionals

Legal Staff Professionals of
Greenville
www.lspg.org

Legal Staff Professionals of the
Low Country
www.lsplowcountry.org

Legal Staff Professionals of the
Midlands

Legal Staff Professionals of
Orangeburg

Spartanburg County Legal Staff
Professionals

South Dakota

Black Hills Legal Professionals
Association
www.bhlpa.org

Tennessee

TALS . . . Legal Professionals of
Tennessee
www.talstn.org

Chattanooga Legal Professionals

Knoxville Association of Legal
Professionals

MLSA—Legal Professionals of
Memphis
www.memphislsa.org

NALS of Nashville
www.nalsnashville.com

Rutherford/Canon County LP

Williamson County LP

Texas

Texas Association of Legal
Professionals
www.texasalp.org

NALS of Amarillo

Arlington Legal Secretaries
Association

Austin Legal Professionals
Association
www.austinlsa.org

Corpus Christi Association of Legal
Professionals
www.ccalp.com

Dallas Association of Legal
Professionals
www.dallasalp.org

East Texas Area Legal
Professionals Association

El Paso County Legal Support
Professionals

Fort Worth ALP

Greater Dallas Association of Legal
Professionals

Houston Association of Legal
Professionals
www.houstonalp.org

Lubbock Legal Professionals Association

Midland ALP

San Antonio Legal Secretaries Association
www.sanantoniolsa.org

Waco Legal Professionals Association
www.wacolpa.com

Wichita County Legal Secretaries Association

Virginia

VALS—the Association for Legal Professionals
www.v-a-l-s.org

Charlottesville-Albemarle Legal Secretaries Association

Fredericksburg Area Legal Secretaries Association

New River Valley Legal Secretaries Association

Norfolk-Portsmouth Area Legal Secretaries Association

Northern Virginia Legal Secretaries Association
www.nvlsa.org

Peninsula Association of Legal Support Staff

Prince William County Association for Legal Professionals

RLSA . . . the association for legal professionals

Roanoke Valley Legal Secretaries Association

Virginia Beach Legal Staff Association
www.vblsa.org

Washington

NALS of Washington
www.nalsofwashington.org

NALS of Greater Seattle
www.nalsofgs.org

NALS of Kitsap County
www.nalsofkitsap.org

NALS of Pierce County

NALS of SnoKing

NALS of Spokane

Wisconsin

Bay Area Association for Legal Professionals

Greater Milwaukee Association of Legal Professionals

Lakeshore Area Association for Legal Professionals

Legal Personnel of South Central Wisconsin
www.lpscw.org

St. Croix Valley Legal Professionals

Information on NALA's CP Program

Certification

In the working environment, professional certification is a time honored process respected by both employers and those within the career field. The following is a definition used by many to describe professional certification:

> *Professional certification is a voluntary process by which a nongovernmental entity grants a time-limited recognition to an individual after verifying that the individual has met predetermined, standardized criteria. (Source: Rops, Mickie S., CAE,* Understanding the Language of Credentialing, *American Society of Association Executives, May 2002.)*

The definition hits the high points. Certification is voluntary, not imposed by government. It is time limited, which means that those with the certification must fulfill ongoing educational requirements to keep the certification current, and the criteria for certification [are] recognized in the community. Keep these aspects in mind as you read more about the CP program.

Administration

The NALA Certifying Board for Paralegals is responsible for content, standards and administration of the Certified Paralegal Program. It is composed of paralegals who have received an Advanced Paralegal Certification designation, attorneys and paralegal educators.

In the technical areas of statistical analyses, examination construction, reliability and validity tests, the Board contracts with a professional consulting firm offering expertise in these areas as well as in occupational research. Technical analyses of the Certified Paralegal examination are conducted on an ongoing basis to ensure the integrity of the examination. Content analyses of the test design, accuracy of questions, and topic/subject mix for each exam section are ongoing processes of the Certifying Board. The Board also utilizes the occupational data available through surveys of legal assistants and other means, including review of textbooks and research within the field of paralegal education. Through these analyses and procedures, the Board is assured that the examination reflects and responds to work-place realities and demands.

Background and Numbers

Established in 1976, the CLA (Certified Legal Assistant) program has enabled the profession to develop a strong and responsive self-regulatory program offering a nationwide credential for legal assistants. The Certified Paralegal/Certified Legal Assistant program establishes and serves as a:

- National professional standard for legal assistants.

- Means of identifying those who have reached this standard.

- Credentialing program responsive to the needs of legal assistants and responsive to the fact that this form of self-regulation is necessary to strengthen and expand development of this career field.

- Positive, ongoing, voluntary program to encourage the growth of the legal assistant profession, attesting to and encouraging a high level of achievement.

As of November 2011, there are 16,757 Certified Paralegals and nearly 2500 Advanced Certified Paralegals in the United States. Over 25,000 paralegals have participated in this program. [Go to **www.nala.org**, select "Certification," and find the appropriate links under "Background and Numbers"] to see the distribution of Certified Paralegals across the United States [and] the distribution of Advanced Certified Paralegals. The growth of these programs is impressive.

The Certified Paralegal Credential

Use of the CLA or CP credential signifies that a paralegal is capable of providing superior services to firms and corporations. National surveys consistently show Certified Legal Assistants/Certified Paralegals are better utilized in a field where attorneys are looking for a credible, dependable way to measure ability. The credential has been recognized by the American Bar Association as a designation which marks a high level of professional achievement. The CLA or CP credential has also been recognized by over 47 legal assistant organizations and numerous bar associations.

For information concerning standards of professional credentialing programs, you may want to see the article: "The Certified Legal Assistant Program and the United States Supreme Court Decision in *Peel v. Attorney Registration and Disciplinary Committee of Illinois.*" [It is available at **www.nala.org** under the "Certification" tab.] In this case, the United States Supreme Court addressed the issue concerning the utilization of professional credentials awarded by private organizations. In *Peel v. Attorney Registration and Disciplinary Committee of Illinois,* 110 S.Ct. 2281 (1990), the Court suggested that a claim of certification is truthful and not misleading if it meets certain standards. This article details those standards in terms of the standards of the NALA Certified Paralegal Program.

Is It CLA or CP?

The terms "legal assistant" and "paralegal" are synonymous terms. This is not a choice or opinion of NALA, but a fact. The terms are defined as such throughout the United States in state supreme court rules, statutes, ethical opinions, bar association guidelines and other similar documents. These are the same documents which provide recognition of the paralegal profession and encourage the use of paralegals in the delivery of legal services.

NALA has become increasingly aware that while the terms are the same as "lawyer" and "attorney," a preference in terms is emerging. Different geographic areas use one term more than another. For this reason, we filed for a certification mark "CP" with the U.S. Patent and Trademark Office. The certification mark was successfully registered on July 20, 2004.

Those who are admitted to the Certified Paralegal program, and successfully complete the examination may use either the CLA or CP credential.

CLA is a certification mark duly registered with the U.S. Patent and Trademark Office (No. 113199). CP® is a certification duly registered with the U.S. Patent and Trademark Office (No. 78213275). Any unauthorized use of these credentials is strictly forbidden.

Am I a Certified Paralegal?

Occasionally, paralegals call themselves "certified" by virtue of completing a paralegal training course, or another type of preparatory education. Although a school may award a certificate of completion, this is not the same as earning professional certification by an entity such as NALA. In this instance the school's certificate is designation of completion of a training program.

CP Examination Description

The Certified Paralegal examination is divided into five sections. A minimum passing score of 70% is required on all five sections in order to earn the Certified Paralegal credential.

Examinees are asked to demonstrate knowledge by responding to true/false, multiple choice and matching questions requiring knowledge of the subject and reading comprehension skills. Analytical skills and writing abilities are further tested by essay questions. The sections of the examination are as follows:

Communications

- Word usage and vocabulary
- Grammar/punctuation
- Writing skills
- Nonverbal communications
- General communications related to interviewing and client communications
- General communications related to interoffice office situations

This section contains a writing exercise.

The Elements of Style, Strunk & White, has been adopted by the NALA Certifying Board as the authority for the Communications section.

Ethics

- Ethical responsibilities centering on performance of delegated work including confidentiality, unauthorized practice of law, legal advice, conflict of interest, billing and client communications
- Client/public contact including identification as a non-lawyer, advertising and initial client contact
- Professional integrity/competence including knowledge of legal assistant codes of ethics
- Relationships with co-workers and support staff
- Attorney codes/discipline
- Knowledge of the American Bar Association's *Rules of Professional Conduct* and the NALA *Code of Ethics and Professional Responsibility* is required by this examination.

Legal Research

- Sources of law including primary authority, secondary authority; understanding how law is recorded
- Research skills including citing the law; Shepardizing, updating decisions; procedural rules of citations

- Analysis of research problem including identification of relevant facts and legal issues

A Uniform System of Citation, Harvard Law Review Association, has been adopted by the NALA Certifying Board as the authority for the Legal Research section.

Judgment and Analytical Ability

- Comprehension of data—identifying and understanding a problem
- Application of knowledge—ability to link facts or legal issues from other cases to the problem at hand, recognizing similarities and differences by analogy
- Evaluating and categorizing data
- Organizing data and findings in a written document

This section contains an essay question which requires analysis of a research request, finding applicable law, and writing a responsive memo.

Examinees will be graded on the ability to:

- Identify which facts are relevant and state them concisely and accurately;
- Identify the threshold or main issue and any secondary issue(s);
- Identify the relevant legal authority and apply it to the facts; and
- Draw persuasive logical conclusions.

Substantive Law

The substantive law section of the examination is composed of five sub-sections. The first section, Substantive Law–General, covers concepts of the American legal system. **All examinees are required to take this section.** Subjects covered within this section include:

- Court system[s] including their structure and jurisdiction
- Branches of government, agencies, and concepts such as separation of powers
- Legal concepts and principles including sources of law, judicial decision making, appellate process
- Sources and classifications of law including the constitution, statutes, common law, civil law, statutory law and equity law

The other four sub-sections are selected by the applicants from a list of nine substantive areas of the law. These tests cover general knowledge of the following practice areas:

- Administrative Law
- Bankruptcy
- Business Organizations
- Civil Litigation
- Contracts
- Criminal Law and Procedure
- Estate Planning and Probate
- Family Law
- Real Estate

The skills required by these tests involve recall of facts and principles that form the basis of the specialty practice area. Examinees must also demonstrate an understanding of the structure of the law and procedures to be followed in each specialty practice area.

Examinee Information

If you have made the decision to seek the Certified Paralegal credential, go to **www.nala.org** and open the "Certification" tab and then the "Examinee Information" tab, which provides details on "Application Procedure Overview," "Application Form and Requirements," "ACT Testing Center Information Details," "Non-ACT Testing Centers Detail," "Planning for the Certified Paralegal Examination," and "After the Examination Details—Results and CLE Details."

Advanced Paralegal Certification

Commitment to continued growth and life-long learning is the hallmark of a professional. Once a Certified Paralegal's career is launched, there will be a need for advanced CLE programs as one changes areas of practice, or is met with more challenging assignments. The Advanced Paralegal Certification program is designed to recognize this effort.

Advanced Paralegal Certification is available to those with a current Certified Paralegal certification. The advanced certification programs are written with the understanding that a person seeking advanced certification has already mastered the Certified Paralegal examination and has demonstrated knowledge and skills in areas of written communications, legal research, ethics, judgment and legal analysis, the American legal system, as well as general knowledge of four specialty areas of practice.

[You can go directly to the APC site at **www.nala.org/apc.aspx**.] Below is a summary of the APC program.

Background

The Certified Paralegal certification program offers professional certification for paralegals immediately upon completion of their training. In 1982, NALA instituted the CLA Specialty program, to recognize a Certified Paralegal's specialized knowledge in a specialty area of practice. In 2002, a special task force was appointed to look at the CLA Specialty Certification program and see if changes were needed. The Task Force determined it was time to redesign and restructure the program. The result is the Advanced Paralegal Certification program, a web-based, curriculum based certification program.

APC Program—Curriculum-Based Certification

The curriculum-based certification is an accepted model of certification and professional development programs throughout the United States and across numerous occupations. This is certification based on specific course material.

An assessment component is part of the curriculum-based program. Participants are required to demonstrate mastery of the course material throughout the process. Both the educational and assessment components are on-line.

A curriculum-based model assumes that participants will discuss course material and consult outside sources, including colleagues, reference books, and specialty practice area experts. The focus is on education and learning specific subject matter rather than testing, which has already been done by the Certified Paralegal Examination to ensure that candidates have the requisite analytical, research, and writing skills.

Many years in development, this program increases access to advanced certification for paralegals working in specific practice areas.

Courses

APC courses are developed by the APC board and experienced technical writers. The courses are about 20 hours in length. The length of time spent on the courses will vary based on one's understanding of the material. Also, the courses include additional reading material and cases.

Advanced Paralegal Certification programs are now offered in the following areas: [Go to **www.nala.org/apc.aspx** and click on the appropriate links for details on these APC courses.]

- Contracts Management/Contracts Administration
- Discovery
- Social Security Disability
- Trial Practice
- Alternative Dispute Resolution
- Business Organizations: Incorporated Entities
- Trademarks
- Personal Injury
- Personal Injury—8 Practice Area Courses
- Land Use
- Criminal Litigation
- Commercial Bankruptcy

Programs scheduled to begin include:

- Real Estate Principles
- Business Organization: Non-corporate Entities

APC Board

The Advanced Paralegal Certification program of NALA is administered by a board composed of experienced paralegals, attorneys, paralegal educators, and paralegal managers. The Chair of the APC board is also a member of the NALA Board of Directors. All paralegals on the APC board have received the advanced certification credential. The board relies heavily on the expertise of technical writers and professional testing consultants.

For Certified Paralegals

Paralegals who have a valid Certified Paralegal certification credential from NALA and successfully complete an APC Course are awarded use of the ACP credential to signify this outstanding achievement. In addition, Certified Paralegals may also receive 20 hours of continuing legal education credit for completion of an advanced program. For the Personal Injury program, 20 hours of credit is awarded for completion of the Personal Injury Core Course; 10 hours is awarded for completion of a Personal Injury practice area course.

Paralegals who do not have the Certified Paralegal certification are welcome to participate in these advanced programs. The credential will not be awarded, however.

The Marks

CLA®, CLAS®, and CP® are certification marks duly registered with the U.S. Patent and Trademark Office (No. 113199, No. 1751731, and No. 78213275, respectively). Unauthorized use of these credentials is strictly forbidden.

Source: **www.nala.org**. This information is subject to updates and edits at any time.

Information on NFPA's PCC and PACE® Examinations

For years, the National Federation of Paralegal Associations (NFPA) has sponsored the Paralegal Advanced Competency Exam (PACE) so practicing paralegals can display their ability. Recently, the NFPA began to offer the Paralegal CORE Competency Exam™ (PCCE™). Now early-career and entry-level paralegals can provide employers an assessment of their capabilities.

Paralegal CORE Competency Exam™

First available in late 2011, the PCCE™ is offered around the country at Prometric Test Centers for a fee of $215. Scores are produced four times a year, and reporting takes six to eight weeks. When tried on a pilot basis, seventy-eight percent of the paralegals who took the PCC Exam scored 550 or better, which is the score needed to be a CORE Registered Paralegal™ and allows a paralegal to use the CRP™ credential from NFPA.

About the PCC Exam
- two and one-half hours long
- 125 multiple-choice questions
- computer administered with instant preliminary results
- widely available around the country most days of the week
- 52 percent Paralegal Practice, 48 percent Substantive Areas of Law
- topics include paralegal ethics, legal technology, and key terminology
- draws on paralegal education coursework and skills essential to paralegal competency
- study aids available through NFPA, and an online review course is jointly offered with the Advanced Paralegal Institute

The advantage of the CRP™ designation is that it provides the legal community with an independent, statistically validated measure of ability. To be eligible to take the PCC Exam, a candidate must have a certain level of paralegal education or practical experience. The NFPA Web site discusses the criteria and provides more details about the exam process.

About PACE®

Key Points of PACE

The Paralegal Advanced Competency Exam (PACE) is offered by the National Federation of Paralegal Associations, Inc.,® (NFPA) to test the competency level of experienced paralegals.

Exam for Experienced Paralegals

PACE is offered to paralegals who have a minimum of two years' experience and meet specific educational requirements. PACE is designed for professional paralegals who want to pioneer the expansion of paralegal roles for the future of the profession, not to restrict entry into the profession.

Fair and Independent

PACE has been developed by a PES, a professional testing firm, assisted by an independent task force including paralegals, lawyers, paralegal educators, and content specialists from the general public who are legal advocates. Ongoing administration is handled by the PES.

Voluntary

Paralegals have the option to sit for the exam at more than 200 Sylvan Technology Centers. As activities and proposals for regulation of the profession increase, all paralegals will be encouraged to take the exam.

Credential Maintenance

To maintain the PACE RP® credential, paralegals are required to obtain 12 hours of continuing legal education every two years, including at least one hour in ethics.

PACE = Paralegal Advanced Competency Exam

Offering experienced paralegals an option to:
- validate your experience and job skills
- establish credentials and
- increase your value to your organization and clients.

The only exam of its kind, PACE
- was developed by a professional testing firm
- is administered by an independent test administration company
- tests concepts across practice areas
- offers the profession a national standard of evaluation and
- is offered at multiple locations on numerous dates and at various times.

PACE = Personal Advancement for the Experienced Paralegal

Why Take PACE®?

Paralegals receive two major benefits by taking PACE. The exam

- provides a fair evaluation of the competencies of paralegals across practice areas, and

- creates a professional level of expertise by which all paralegals can be evaluated.

PACE presents a bold opportunity to all paralegals to advance the profession. This exam provides hard facts about the competency of experienced paralegals. While PACE does not address all the issues of regulation, including certification and licensing, it does provide the legal service industry with an option to evaluate the competency level of experienced paralegals.

As members of a self-directed profession, all paralegals should consider the vital role the profession performs within the legal service industry. PACE is independently monitored and well-structured. PACE provides test results across practice areas and, possibly, state-specific laws. While the test is offered on a voluntary basis, all experienced paralegals are encouraged to sit for the exam.

NFPA® is committed to ensuring the paralegal profession responds to the changing needs of the public and legal service industry. In voting to develop PACE, NFPA's membership took a bold step toward addressing the future issues facing the profession.

PACE® Credentialing

Those who pass PACE and maintain the continuing education requirement may use the designation "PACE - Registered Paralegal®" or "RP®."

To maintain the RP credential, 12 hours of continuing legal or specialty education is required every two years, with at least one hour in legal ethics.

Registered Paralegals should review the *Facts Every RP Should Know* to be aware of the ways the PACE credential can be used and information on registration of CLE credits. Also included in the fact sheet is information on non-renewal status, inactive status, suspension and revocation of the use of the RP credential and the appeals process.

Note: This material, and additional material on PACE, is available at the NFPA Web site at **www.paralegals.org**.

Reprinted by permission of the National Federation of Paralegal Associations, Inc. (NFPA®), **www.paralegals.org**.

Information on NALS Certification

NALS offers members and nonmembers the opportunity to sit for three unique certifications dedicated to the legal services profession. The exams are of varying levels and are developed by professionals in the industry. ALS . . . the basic certification for legal professionals and PLS . . . the advanced certification for legal professionals are two certifications dedicated to legal professionals of all types. The third certification is dedicated to those professionals performing paralegal duties. The Professional Paralegal (PP) certification was developed by paralegals for paralegals. Each of the three certifications is developed by NALS and takes advantage of the more than 75 years of experience and dedication to the legal services industry only NALS has to offer.

Accredited Legal Secretary Certification

ALS . . . The Basic Certification for Legal Professionals

One way to demonstrate your preparedness for the demanding field of law is by becoming an ALS. This designation is awarded after passing a four-hour, three-part examination. Attaining this goal demonstrates your commitment and aptitude for succeeding in the ever-changing legal environment.

The ALS Examination:

- demonstrates ability to perform business communication tasks;
- gauges ability to maintain office records and calendars, and prioritize multiple tasks when given real-life scenarios;
- measures understanding of office equipment and related procedures;
- denotes aptitude for understanding legal terminology, legal complexities, and supporting documents;
- assesses recognition of accounting terms to solve accounting problems; and
- appraises knowledge of law office protocol as prescribed by ethical codes.

ALS Examination Eligibility

To sit for the examination, you must have completed one of the following:

- an accredited business/legal course,
- the NALS Legal Training Course, or
- one year of general office experience.

Membership in NALS is not a requirement.

The Exam Covers

The examination covers the following parts:

- PART 1: Written Communications
- PART 2: Office Procedures and Legal Knowledge
- PART 3: Ethics, Human Relations, and Judgment

Examination Guidelines

All three parts of the examination must be taken on the first attempt. If you do not pass the entire examination on the first attempt, you may retake the examination parts you did not pass. All failed parts must be retaken at the same time. You will be charged the full exam fee each time you sit.

Those passing the exam will receive a certificate that is valid for five years.

Certification may be extended through continuing education, based on NALS guidelines, for one year.

Examination Dates and Application Deadlines

- March: First Saturday (Postmarked by January 1)
- June: First Saturday* (Postmarked by April 15)
- September: Last Saturday (Postmarked by August 1)
- December: First Saturday* (Postmarked by October 15)

June and December testing are for those who have completed the Basic or Advanced NALS Legal Training Course.

Examination Fees

- Student/LTC Participant (minimum of 9 credit hours)—$50
- NALS member (not a full-time student)—$75
- Nonmember (not a full-time student)—$100

Professional Legal Secretary Certification

PLS . . . The Advanced Certification for Legal Professionals

How do your skills compare with the hallmark of a professional? PLS® is the designation for lawyer's assistants who want to be identified as exceptional. Certification is received after passing a one-day, four-part examination which demonstrates not only dedication to professionalism but acceptance of the challenge to be exceptional. Personal motivation is necessary to attain such a goal.

The purpose of the examination is to certify a lawyer's assistant as a person who possesses:

- a mastery of office skills;
- the ability to interact on a professional level with attorneys, clients, and other support staff;
- the discipline to assume responsibility and exercise initiative and judgment; and
- a working knowledge of procedural law, the law library, and how to prepare legal documents.

PLS Examination Eligibility

Any person who has had three years' experience in the legal field may take the examination. Membership in NALS is not a requirement. A partial waiver of the three-year legal experience requirement may be granted for postsecondary degrees, successful completion of the ALS exam, or other certifications. The maximum waiver is one year.

The PLS Certification Exam Covers

- PART 1: Written Communications
- PART 2: Office Procedures and Technology
- PART 3: Ethics and Judgment
- PART 4: Legal Knowledge and Skills

Examination Guidelines

All four parts of the examination must be taken on the first attempt. If you do not pass the entire examination on the first attempt, but do pass one or more parts, you may retake the part (or parts) you failed. All failed parts must be retaken at the same time. Those passing the exam will receive a certificate that is valid for five years. Recertification is required every five years and may be achieved through the accumulation of continuing legal education hours and activities.

Examination Dates Each Year and Application Deadlines

- March: First Saturday in March (Postmarked by January 1)
- September: Last Saturday in September (Postmarked by August 1)

Examination Fees

- For the initial examination: Members—$150; Nonmembers—$200
- For part retakes: Members—$40 per part; Nonmembers—$50 per part

Professional Paralegal (PP)

Are you looking for a way to establish your credentials nationwide as a Professional Paralegal? Established in 2004 at our members' request, the Certified PP designation is an attainable goal for paralegals who wish to be identified as exceptional in all areas of law. The certificate is received after passing a one-day, four-part examination.

Successful completion of the PP examination demonstrates:

- A mastery of procedural skills and communication skills.
- An advanced knowledge of procedural law, the law library, and the preparation of legal documents.
- A working knowledge of substantive law and the ability to perform specifically delegated substantive legal work under an attorney's supervision.
- The ability to interact on a professional level with attorneys, clients, and other staff.
- The discipline to assume responsibility and exercise initiative and judgment while adhering to legal ethical standards at all times.

Working under the supervision of a practicing lawyer or a judge, the Certified PP is expected to possess:

- The same high standard of ethical conduct imposed upon members of the Bar.

- Excellent written and verbal communication skills.

- Knowledge and understanding of legal terminology and procedures, as well as procedural and substantive law.

- The ability to assume responsibility, exercise initiative and judgment, and prepare substantive legal documents within the scope of assigned authority.

- Attaining this goal demonstrates dedication to professionalism and acceptance of the challenge to be exceptional. Personal motivation is necessary to attain such a goal.

PP Examination Eligibility

Any person who has five years' experience performing paralegal/legal assistant duties (a candidate may receive a partial waiver of one year if he or she has a post-secondary degree, other certification, or a paralegal certificate; a candidate with a paralegal degree may receive a two-year partial waiver).

The Exam Covers

- PART 1: Written Communications

- PART 2: Legal Knowledge and Skills

- PART 3: Ethics and Judgment Skills

- PART 4: Substantive Law

Examination Guidelines

All four parts of the examination must be taken on the first attempt with the exception of current PLSs, for which only Part 4 in Substantive Law is needed. If you do not pass the entire examination on the first attempt, but do pass one or more parts, you may retake the part (or parts) you failed. All failed parts must be retaken at the same time.

Those passing the exam will receive a certificate that is valid for five years. Recertification is required every five years and may be achieved through the accumulation of continuing legal education hours and activities.

Examination Dates and Application Deadlines

- March: First Saturday (Postmarked by January 1)

- September: Last Saturday (Postmarked by August 1)

Examination Fees

- For current PLSs
  Members: $150
  Nonmembers: $200

- For non-PLSs
  Members: $200
  Nonmembers: $250

- Retake fees:
  Members: $50 per part
  Nonmembers: $60 per part

The Constitution of the United States

Preamble

We the People of the United States, in Order to form a more perfect Union, establish Justice, insure domestic Tranquility, provide for the common defence, promote the general Welfare, and secure the Blessings of Liberty to ourselves and our Posterity, do ordain and establish this Constitution for the United States of America.

Article I

Section 1.   All legislative Powers herein granted shall be vested in a Congress of the United States, which shall consist of a Senate and House of Representatives.

Section 2.   The House of Representatives shall be composed of Members chosen every second Year by the People of the several States, and the Electors in each State shall have the Qualifications requisite for Electors of the most numerous Branch of the State Legislature.

No Person shall be a Representative who shall not have attained to the Age of twenty five Years, and been seven Years a Citizen of the United States, and who shall not, when elected, be an Inhabitant of that State in which he shall be chosen.

Representatives and direct Taxes shall be apportioned among the several States which may be included within this Union, according to their respective Numbers, which shall be determined by adding to the whole Number of free Persons, including those bound to Service for a Term of Years, and excluding Indians not taxed, three fifths of all other Persons. The actual Enumeration shall be made within three Years after the first Meeting of the Congress of the United States, and within every subsequent Term of ten Years, in such Manner as they shall by Law direct. The Number of Representatives shall not exceed one for every thirty Thousand, but each State shall have at Least one Representative; and until such enumeration shall be made, the State of New Hampshire shall be entitled to chuse three, Massachusetts eight, Rhode Island and Providence Plantations one, Connecticut five, New York six, New Jersey four, Pennsylvania eight, Delaware one, Maryland six, Virginia ten, North Carolina five, South Carolina five, and Georgia three.

When vacancies happen in the Representation from any State, the Executive Authority thereof shall issue Writs of Election to fill such Vacancies.

The House of Representatives shall chuse their Speaker and other Officers; and shall have the sole Power of Impeachment.

Section 3. The Senate of the United States shall be composed of two Senators from each State, chosen by the Legislature thereof, for six Years; and each Senator shall have one Vote.

Immediately after they shall be assembled in Consequence of the first Election, they shall be divided as equally as may be into three Classes. The Seats of the Senators of the first Class shall be vacated at the Expiration of the second Year, of the second Class at the Expiration of the fourth Year, and of the third Class at the Expiration of the sixth Year, so that one third may be chosen every second Year; and if Vacancies happen by Resignation, or otherwise, during the Recess of the Legislature of any State, the Executive thereof may make temporary Appointments until the next Meeting of the Legislature, which shall then fill such Vacancies.

No Person shall be a Senator who shall not have attained to the Age of thirty Years, and been nine Years a Citizen of the United States, and who shall not, when elected, be an Inhabitant of that State for which he shall be chosen.

The Vice President of the United States shall be President of the Senate, but shall have no Vote, unless they be equally divided.

The Senate shall chuse their other Officers, and also a President pro tempore, in the Absence of the Vice President, or when he shall exercise the Office of President of the United States.

The Senate shall have the sole Power to try all Impeachments. When sitting for that Purpose, they shall be on Oath or Affirmation. When the President of the United States is tried, the Chief Justice shall preside: And no Person shall be convicted without the Concurrence of two thirds of the Members present.

Judgment in Cases of Impeachment shall not extend further than to removal from Office, and disqualification to hold and enjoy any Office of honor, Trust, or Profit under the United States: but the Party convicted shall nevertheless be liable and subject to Indictment, Trial, Judgment, and Punishment, according to Law.

Section 4. The Times, Places and Manner of holding Elections for Senators and Representatives, shall be prescribed in each State by the Legislature thereof; but the Congress may at any time by Law make or alter such Regulations, except as to the Places of chusing Senators.

The Congress shall assemble at least once in every Year, and such Meeting shall be on the first Monday in December, unless they shall by Law appoint a different Day.

Section 5. Each House shall be the Judge of the Elections, Returns, and Qualifications of its own Members, and a Majority of each shall constitute a Quorum to do Business; but a smaller Number may adjourn from day to day, and may be authorized to compel the Attendance of absent Members, in such Manner, and under such Penalties as each House may provide.

Each House may determine the Rules of its Proceedings, punish its Members for disorderly Behavior, and, with the Concurrence of two thirds, expel a Member.

Each House shall keep a Journal of its Proceedings, and from time to time publish the same, excepting such Parts as may in their Judgment require Secrecy; and the Yeas and Nays of the Members of either House on any question shall, at the Desire of one fifth of those Present, be entered on the Journal.

Neither House, during the Session of Congress, shall, without the Consent of the other, adjourn for more than three days, nor to any other Place than that in which the two Houses shall be sitting.

Section 6. The Senators and Representatives shall receive a Compensation for their Services, to be ascertained by Law, and paid out of the Treasury of the United States. They shall in all Cases, except Treason, Felony and Breach of the Peace, be privileged from Arrest during their Attendance at the Session of their respective Houses, and in going to and returning from the same; and for any Speech or Debate in either House, they shall not be questioned in any other Place.

No Senator or Representative shall, during the Time for which he was elected, be appointed to any civil Office under the Authority of the United States, which shall have been created, or the Emoluments whereof shall have been increased during such time; and no Person holding any Office under the United States, shall be a Member of either House during his Continuance in Office.

Section 7. All Bills for raising Revenue shall originate in the House of Representatives; but the Senate may propose or concur with Amendments as on other Bills.

Every Bill which shall have passed the House of Representatives and the Senate, shall, before it become a Law, be presented to the President of the United States; If he approve he shall sign it, but if not he shall return it, with his Objections to the House in which it shall have originated, who shall enter the Objections at large on their Journal, and proceed to reconsider it. If after such Reconsideration two thirds of that House shall agree to pass the Bill, it shall be sent together with the Objections, to the other House, by which it shall likewise be reconsidered, and if approved by two thirds of that House, it shall become a Law. But in all such Cases the Votes of both Houses shall be determined by Yeas and Nays, and the Names of the Persons voting for and against the Bill shall be entered on the Journal of each House respectively. If any Bill shall not be returned by the President within ten Days (Sundays excepted) after it shall have been presented to him, the Same shall be a Law, in like Manner as if he had signed it, unless the Congress by their Adjournment prevent its Return in which Case it shall not be a Law.

Every Order, Resolution, or Vote, to which the Concurrence of the Senate and House of Representatives may be necessary (except on a question of Adjournment) shall be presented to the President of the United States; and before the Same shall take Effect, shall be approved by him, or being disapproved by him, shall be repassed by two thirds of the Senate and House of Representatives, according to the Rules and Limitations prescribed in the Case of a Bill.

Section 8.   The Congress shall have Power To lay and collect Taxes, Duties, Imposts and Excises, to pay the Debts and provide for the common Defence and general Welfare of the United States; but all Duties, Imposts and Excises shall be uniform throughout the United States;

To borrow Money on the credit of the United States;

To regulate Commerce with foreign Nations, and among the several States, and with the Indian Tribes;

To establish an uniform Rule of Naturalization, and uniform Laws on the subject of Bankruptcies throughout the United States;

To coin Money, regulate the Value thereof, and of foreign Coin, and fix the Standard of Weights and Measures;

To provide for the Punishment of counterfeiting the Securities and current Coin of the United States;

To establish Post Offices and post Roads;

To promote the Progress of Science and useful Arts, by securing for limited Times to Authors and Inventors the exclusive Right to their respective Writings and Discoveries;

To constitute Tribunals inferior to the supreme Court;

To define and punish Piracies and Felonies committed on the high Seas, and Offenses against the Law of Nations;

To declare War, grant Letters of Marque and Reprisal, and make Rules concerning Captures on Land and Water;

To raise and support Armies, but no Appropriation of Money to that Use shall be for a longer Term than two Years;

To provide and maintain a Navy;

To make Rules for the Government and Regulation of the land and naval Forces;

To provide for calling forth the Militia to execute the Laws of the Union, suppress Insurrections and repel Invasions;

To provide for organizing, arming, and disciplining, the Militia, and for governing such Part of them as may be employed in the Service of the United States, reserving to the States respectively, the Appointment of the Officers, and the Authority of training the Militia according to the discipline prescribed by Congress;

To exercise exclusive Legislation in all Cases whatsoever, over such District (not exceeding ten Miles square) as may, by Cession of particular States, and the Acceptance of Congress, become the Seat of the Government of the United States, and to exercise like Authority over all Places purchased by the Consent of the Legislature of the State in which the Same shall be, for the Erection of Forts, Magazines, Arsenals, dock-Yards, and other needful Buildings;—And

To make all Laws which shall be necessary and proper for carrying into Execution the foregoing Powers, and all other Powers vested by this Constitution in the Government of the United States, or in any Department or Officer thereof.

Section 9. The Migration or Importation of such Persons as any of the States now existing shall think proper to admit, shall not be prohibited by the Congress prior to the Year one thousand eight hundred and eight, but a Tax or duty may be imposed on such Importation, not exceeding ten dollars for each Person.

The privilege of the Writ of Habeas Corpus shall not be suspended, unless when in Cases of Rebellion or Invasion the public Safety may require it.

No Bill of Attainder or ex post facto Law shall be passed.

No Capitation, or other direct, Tax shall be laid, unless in Proportion to the Census or Enumeration herein before directed to be taken.

No Tax or Duty shall be laid on Articles exported from any State.

No Preference shall be given by any Regulation of Commerce or Revenue to the Ports of one State over those of another: nor shall Vessels bound to, or from, one State be obliged to enter, clear, or pay Duties in another.

No Money shall be drawn from the Treasury, but in Consequence of Appropriations made by Law; and a regular Statement and Account of the Receipts and Expenditures of all public Money shall be published from time to time.

No Title of Nobility shall be granted by the United States: And no Person holding any Office of Profit or Trust under them, shall, without the Consent of the Congress, accept of any present, Emolument, Office, or Title, of any kind whatever, from any King, Prince, or foreign State.

Section 10.   No State shall enter into any Treaty, Alliance, or Confederation; grant Letters of Marque and Reprisal; coin Money; emit Bills of Credit; make any Thing but gold and silver Coin a Tender in Payment of Debts; pass any Bill of Attainder, ex post facto Law, or Law impairing the Obligation of Contracts, or grant any Title of Nobility.

No State shall, without the Consent of the Congress, lay any Imposts or Duties on Imports or Exports, except what may be absolutely necessary for executing its inspection Laws: and the net Produce of all Duties and Imposts, laid by any State on Imports or Exports, shall be for the Use of the Treasury of the United States; and all such Laws shall be subject to the Revision and Controul of the Congress.

No State shall, without the Consent of Congress, lay any Duty of Tonnage, keep Troops, or Ships of War in time of Peace, enter into any Agreement or Compact with another State, or with a foreign Power, or engage in War, unless actually invaded, or in such imminent Danger as will not admit of delay.

Article II

Section 1.   The executive Power shall be vested in a President of the United States of America. He shall hold his Office during the Term of four Years, and, together with the Vice President, chosen for the same Term, be elected, as follows:

Each State shall appoint, in such Manner as the Legislature thereof may direct, a Number of Electors, equal to the whole Number of Senators and Representatives to which the State may be entitled in the Congress; but no Senator or Representative, or Person holding an Office of Trust or Profit under the United States, shall be appointed an Elector.

The Electors shall meet in their respective States, and vote by Ballot for two Persons, of whom one at least shall not be an Inhabitant of the same State with themselves. And they shall make a List of all the Persons voted for, and of the Number of Votes for each; which List they shall sign and certify, and transmit sealed to the Seat of the Government of the United States, directed to the President of the Senate. The President of the Senate shall, in the Presence of the Senate and House of Representatives, open all the Certificates, and the Votes shall then be counted. The Person having the greatest Number of Votes shall be the President, if such Number be a Majority of the whole Number of Electors appointed; and if there be more than one who have such Majority, and have an equal Number of Votes, then the House of Representatives shall immediately chuse by Ballot one of them for President; and if no Person have a Majority, then from the five highest on the List the said House shall in like Manner chuse the President. But in chusing the President, the Votes shall be taken by States, the Representation from each State having one Vote; A quorum for this Purpose shall consist of a Member or Members from two thirds of the States, and a Majority of all the States shall be necessary to a Choice. In every Case, after the Choice of the President, the Person having the greater Number of Votes of the Electors shall be the Vice President. But if there should remain two or more who have equal Votes, the Senate shall chuse from them by Ballot the Vice President.

The Congress may determine the Time of chusing the Electors, and the Day on which they shall give their Votes; which Day shall be the same throughout the United States.

No person except a natural born Citizen, or a Citizen of the United States, at the time of the Adoption of this Constitution, shall be eligible to the Office of President; neither shall any Person be eligible to that Office who shall not have attained to the Age of thirty five Years, and been fourteen Years a Resident within the United States.

In Case of the Removal of the President from Office, or of his Death, Resignation or Inability to discharge the Powers and Duties of the said Office, the same shall devolve on the Vice President, and the Congress may by Law provide for the Case of Removal, Death, Resignation or Inability, both of the President and Vice President, declaring what Officer shall then act as President, and such Officer shall act accordingly, until the Disability be removed, or a President shall be elected.

The President shall, at stated Times, receive for his Services, a Compensation, which shall neither be increased nor diminished during the Period for which he shall have been elected, and he shall not receive within that Period any other Emolument from the United States, or any of them.

Before he enter on the Execution of his Office, he shall take the following Oath or Affirmation: "I do solemnly swear (or affirm) that I will faithfully execute the Office of President of the United States, and will to the best of my Ability, preserve, protect and defend the Constitution of the United States."

Section 2. The President shall be Commander in Chief of the Army and Navy of the United States, and of the Militia of the several States, when called into the actual Service of the United States; he may require the Opinion, in writing, of the principal Officer in each of the executive Departments, upon any Subject relating to the Duties of their respective Offices, and he shall have Power to grant Reprieves and Pardons for Offenses against the United States, except in Cases of Impeachment.

He shall have Power, by and with the Advice and Consent of the Senate to make Treaties, provided two thirds of the Senators present concur; and he shall nominate, and by and with the Advice and Consent of the Senate, shall appoint

Ambassadors, other public Ministers and Consuls, Judges of the supreme Court, and all other Officers of the United States, whose Appointments are not herein otherwise provided for, and which shall be established by Law; but the Congress may by Law vest the Appointment of such inferior Officers, as they think proper, in the President alone, in the Courts of Law, or in the Heads of Departments.

The President shall have Power to fill up all Vacancies that may happen during the Recess of the Senate, by granting Commissions which shall expire at the End of their next Session.

Section 3. He shall from time to time give to the Congress Information of the State of the Union, and recommend to their Consideration such Measures as he shall judge necessary and expedient; he may, on extraordinary Occasions, convene both Houses, or either of them, and in Case of Disagreement between them, with Respect to the Time of Adjournment, he may adjourn them to such Time as he shall think proper; he shall receive Ambassadors and other public Ministers; he shall take Care that the Laws be faithfully executed, and shall Commission all the Officers of the United States.

Section 4. The President, Vice President and all civil Officers of the United States, shall be removed from Office on Impeachment for, and Conviction of, Treason, Bribery, or other high Crimes and Misdemeanors.

Article III

Section 1. The judicial Power of the United States, shall be vested in one supreme Court, and in such inferior Courts as the Congress may from time to time ordain and establish. The Judges, both of the supreme and inferior Courts, shall hold their Offices during good Behaviour, and shall, at stated Times, receive for their Services a Compensation, which shall not be diminished during their Continuance in Office.

Section 2. The judicial Power shall extend to all Cases, in Law and Equity, arising under this Constitution, the Laws of the United States, and Treaties made, or which shall be made, under their Authority;—to all Cases affecting Ambassadors, other public Ministers and Consuls;—to all Cases of admiralty and maritime Jurisdiction;—to Controversies to which the United States shall be a Party;—to Controversies between two or more States;—between a State and Citizens of another State;—between Citizens of different States;—between Citizens of the same State claiming Lands under Grants of different States, and between a State, or the Citizens thereof, and foreign States, Citizens or Subjects.

In all Cases affecting Ambassadors, other public Ministers and Consuls, and those in which a State shall be a Party, the supreme Court shall have original Jurisdiction. In all the other Cases before mentioned, the supreme Court shall have appellate Jurisdiction, both as to Law and Fact, with such Exceptions, and under such Regulations as the Congress shall make.

The Trial of all Crimes, except in Cases of Impeachment, shall be by Jury; and such Trial shall be held in the State where the said Crimes shall have been committed; but when not committed within any State, the Trial shall be at such Place or Places as the Congress may by Law have directed.

Section 3. Treason against the United States, shall consist only in levying War against them, or, in adhering to their Enemies, giving them Aid and Comfort. No Person shall be convicted of Treason unless on the Testimony of two Witnesses to the same overt Act, or on Confession in open Court.

The Congress shall have Power to declare the Punishment of Treason, but no Attainder of Treason shall work Corruption of Blood, or Forfeiture except during the Life of the Person attainted.

Article IV

Section 1. Full Faith and Credit shall be given in each State to the public Acts, Records, and judicial Proceedings of every other State. And the Congress may by general Laws prescribe the Manner in which such Acts, Records and Proceedings shall be proved, and the Effect thereof.

Section 2. The Citizens of each State shall be entitled to all Privileges and Immunities of Citizens in the several States.

A Person charged in any State with Treason, Felony, or other Crime, who shall flee from Justice, and be found in another State, shall on Demand of the executive Authority of the State from which he fled, be delivered up, to be removed to the State having Jurisdiction of the Crime.

No Person held to Service or Labour in one State, under the Laws thereof, escaping into another, shall, in Consequence of any Law or Regulation therein, be discharged from such Service or Labour, but shall be delivered up on Claim of the Party to whom such Service or Labour may be due.

Section 3. New States may be admitted by the Congress into this Union; but no new State shall be formed or erected within the Jurisdiction of any other State; nor any State be formed by the Junction of two or more States, or Parts of States, without the Consent of the Legislatures of the States concerned as well as of the Congress.

The Congress shall have Power to dispose of and make all needful Rules and Regulations respecting the Territory or other Property belonging to the United States; and nothing in this Constitution shall be so construed as to Prejudice any Claims of the United States, or of any particular State.

Section 4. The United States shall guarantee to every State in this Union a Republican Form of Government, and shall protect each of them against Invasion; and on Application of the Legislature, or of the Executive (when the Legislature cannot be convened) against domestic Violence.

Article V

The Congress, whenever two thirds of both Houses shall deem it necessary, shall propose Amendments to this Constitution, or, on the Application of the Legislatures of two thirds of the several States, shall call a Convention for proposing Amendments, which, in either Case, shall be valid to all Intents and Purposes, as part of this Constitution, when ratified by the Legislatures of three fourths of the several States, or by Conventions in three fourths thereof, as the one or the other Mode of Ratification may be proposed by the Congress; Provided that no Amendment which may be made prior to the Year One thousand eight hundred and eight shall in any Manner affect the first and fourth Clauses in the Ninth Section of the first Article; and that no State, without its Consent, shall be deprived of its equal Suffrage in the Senate.

Article VI

All Debts contracted and Engagements entered into, before the Adoption of this Constitution shall be as valid against the United States under this Constitution, as under the Confederation.

This Constitution, and the Laws of the United States which shall be made in Pursuance thereof; and all Treaties made, or which shall be made, under the Authority of the United States, shall be the supreme Law of the Land; and the Judges in every State shall be bound thereby, any Thing in the Constitution or Laws of any State to the Contrary notwithstanding.

The Senators and Representatives before mentioned, and the Members of the several State Legislatures, and all executive and judicial Officers, both of the United States and of the several States, shall be bound by Oath or Affirmation, to support this Constitution; but no religious Test shall ever be required as a Qualification to any Office or public Trust under the United States.

Article VII

The Ratification of the Conventions of nine States shall be sufficient for the Establishment of this Constitution between the States so ratifying the Same.

Amendment I [1791]

Congress shall make no law respecting an establishment of religion, or prohibiting the free exercise thereof; or abridging the freedom of speech, or of the press; or the right of the people peaceably to assemble, and to petition the Government for a redress of grievances.

Amendment II [1791]

A well regulated Militia, being necessary to the security of a free State, the right of the people to keep and bear Arms, shall not be infringed.

Amendment III [1791]

No Soldier shall, in time of peace be quartered in any house, without the consent of the Owner, nor in time of war, but in a manner to be prescribed by law.

Amendment IV [1791]

The right of the people to be secure in their persons, houses, papers, and effects, against unreasonable searches and seizures, shall not be violated, and no Warrants shall issue, but upon probable cause, supported by Oath or affirmation, and particularly describing the place to be searched, and the persons or things to be seized.

Amendment V [1791]

No person shall be held to answer for a capital, or otherwise infamous crime, unless on a presentment or indictment of a Grand Jury, except in cases arising in the land or naval forces, or in the Militia, when in actual service in time of War or public danger; nor shall any person be subject for the same offence to be twice put in jeopardy of life or limb; nor shall be compelled in any criminal case to be a witness against himself, nor be deprived of life, liberty, or property, without due process of law; nor shall private property be taken for public use, without just compensation.

Amendment VI [1791]

In all criminal prosecutions, the accused shall enjoy the right to a speedy and public trial, by an impartial jury of the State and district wherein the crime shall have been committed, which district shall have been previously ascertained by law, and to be informed of the nature and cause of the accusation; to be confronted with the witnesses against him; to have compulsory process for obtaining witnesses in his favor, and to have the Assistance of Counsel for his defence.

Amendment VII [1791]

In Suits at common law, where the value in controversy shall exceed twenty dollars, the right of trial by jury shall be preserved, and no fact tried by jury, shall be otherwise reexamined in any Court of the United States, than according to the rules of the common law.

Amendment VIII [1791]

Excessive bail shall not be required, nor excessive fines imposed, nor cruel and unusual punishments inflicted.

Amendment IX [1791]

The enumeration in the Constitution, of certain rights, shall not be construed to deny or disparage others retained by the people.

Amendment X [1791]

The powers not delegated to the United States by the Constitution, nor prohibited by it to the States, are reserved to the States respectively, or to the people.

Amendment XI [1798]

The Judicial power of the United States shall not be construed to extend to any suit in law or equity, commenced or prosecuted against one of the United States by Citizens of another State, or by Citizens or Subjects of any Foreign State.

Amendment XII [1804]

The Electors shall meet in their respective states, and vote by ballot for President and Vice-President, one of whom, at least, shall not be an inhabitant of the same state with themselves; they shall name in their ballots the person voted for as President, and in distinct ballots the person voted for as Vice-President, and they shall make distinct lists of all persons voted for as President, and of all persons voted for as Vice-President, and of the number of votes for each, which lists they shall sign and certify, and transmit sealed to the seat of the government of the United States, directed to the President of the Senate;—The President of the Senate shall, in the presence of the Senate and House of Representatives, open all the certificates and the votes shall then be counted;—The person having the greatest number of votes for President, shall be the President, if such number be a majority of the whole number of Electors appointed; and if no person have such majority, then from the persons having the highest numbers not exceeding three on the list of those voted for as President, the House of Representatives shall choose immediately, by ballot, the President. But in choosing the President, the votes shall be taken by states, the representation from each state having one vote; a quorum for this purpose shall consist of a member or members from two-thirds of the states, and a majority of all states shall be necessary to a choice. And if the House of Representatives shall not choose a President whenever the right of choice shall devolve upon them, before the fourth day of March next following, then the Vice-President shall act as President, as in the case of the death or other constitutional disability of the President.—The person having the greatest number of votes as Vice-President, shall be the Vice-President, if such number be a majority of the whole number of Electors appointed, and if no person have a majority, then from the two highest numbers on the list, the Senate shall choose the Vice-President; a quorum for the purpose shall consist of two-thirds of the whole number of Senators, and a majority of the whole number shall be necessary to a choice. But no person constitutionally ineligible to the office of President shall be eligible to that of Vice-President of the United States.

Amendment XIII [1865]

Section 1. Neither slavery nor involuntary servitude, except as a punishment for crime whereof the party shall have been duly convicted, shall exist within the United States, or any place subject to their jurisdiction.

Section 2. Congress shall have power to enforce this article by appropriate legislation.

Amendment XIV [1868]

Section 1. All persons born or naturalized in the United States, and subject to the jurisdiction thereof, are citizens of the United States and of the State wherein they reside. No State shall make or enforce any law which shall abridge the privileges or immunities of citizens of the United States; nor shall any State deprive any person of life, liberty, or property, without due process of law; nor deny to any person within its jurisdiction the equal protection of the laws.

Section 2. Representatives shall be apportioned among the several States according to their respective numbers, counting the whole number of persons in each State, excluding Indians not taxed. But when the right to vote at any election for the choice of electors for President and Vice President of the United States, Representatives in Congress, the Executive and Judicial officers of a State, or the members of the Legislature thereof, is denied to any of the male inhabitants of such State, being twenty-one years of age, and citizens of the United States, or in any way abridged, except for participation in rebellion, or other crime, the basis of representation therein shall be reduced in the proportion which the number of such male citizens shall bear to the whole number of male citizens twenty-one years of age in such State.

Section 3. No person shall be a Senator or Representative in Congress, or elector of President and Vice President, or hold any office, civil or military, under the United States, or under any State, who having previously taken an oath, as a member of Congress, or as an officer of the United States, or as a member of any State legislature, or as an executive or judicial officer of any State, to support the Constitution of the United States, shall have engaged in insurrection or rebellion against the same, or given aid or comfort to the enemies thereof. But Congress may by a vote of two-thirds of each House, remove such disability.

Section 4. The validity of the public debt of the United States, authorized by law, including debts incurred for payment of pensions and bounties for services in suppressing insurrection or rebellion, shall not be questioned. But neither the United States nor any State shall assume or pay any debt or obligation incurred in aid of insurrection or rebellion against the United States, or any claim for the loss or emancipation of any slave; but all such debts, obligations and claims shall be held illegal and void.

Section 5. The Congress shall have power to enforce, by appropriate legislation, the provisions of this article.

Amendment XV [1870]

Section 1. The right of citizens of the United States to vote shall not be denied or abridged by the United States or by any State on account of race, color, or previous condition of servitude.

Section 2. The Congress shall have power to enforce this article by appropriate legislation.

Amendment XVI [1913]

The Congress shall have power to lay and collect taxes on incomes, from whatever source derived, without apportionment among the several States, and without regard to any census or enumeration.

Amendment XVII [1913]

Section 1. The Senate of the United States shall be composed of two Senators from each State, elected by the people thereof, for six years; and each Senator shall have one vote. The electors in each State shall have the qualifications requisite for electors of the most numerous branch of the State legislatures.

Section 2. When vacancies happen in the representation of any State in the Senate, the executive authority of such State shall issue writs of election to fill such vacancies: Provided, That the legislature of any State may empower the executive thereof to make temporary appointments until the people fill the vacancies by election as the legislature may direct.

Section 3. This amendment shall not be so construed as to affect the election or term of any Senator chosen before it becomes valid as part of the Constitution.

Amendment XVIII [1919]

Section 1. After one year from the ratification of this article the manufacture, sale, or transportation of intoxicating liquors within, the importation thereof into, or the exportation thereof from the United States and all territory subject to the jurisdiction thereof for beverage purposes is hereby prohibited.

Section 2. The Congress and the several States shall have concurrent power to enforce this article by appropriate legislation.

Section 3. This article shall be inoperative unless it shall have been ratified as an amendment to the Constitution by the legislatures of the several States, as provided in the Constitution, within seven years from the date of the submission hereof to the States by the Congress.

Amendment XIX [1920]

Section 1. The right of citizens of the United States to vote shall not be denied or abridged by the United States or by any State on account of sex.

Section 2. Congress shall have power to enforce this article by appropriate legislation.

Amendment XX [1933]

Section 1. The terms of the President and Vice President shall end at noon on the 20th day of January, and the terms of Senators and Representatives at noon on the 3d day of January, of the years in which such terms would have ended if this article had not been ratified; and the terms of their successors shall then begin.

Section 2. The Congress shall assemble at least once in every year, and such meeting shall begin at noon on the 3d day of January, unless they shall by law appoint a different day.

Section 3. If, at the time fixed for the beginning of the term of the President, the President elect shall have died, the Vice President elect shall become President. If the President shall not have been chosen before the time fixed for the beginning of his term, or if the President elect shall have failed to qualify, then the Vice President elect shall act as President until a President shall have qualified; and the Congress may by law provide for the case wherein neither a President elect nor a Vice President elect shall have qualified, declaring who shall then act as President, or the manner in which one who is to act shall be selected, and such person shall act accordingly until a President or Vice President shall have qualified.

Section 4. The Congress may by law provide for the case of the death of any of the persons from whom the House of Representatives may choose a President whenever the right of choice shall have devolved upon them, and for the case of the death of any of the persons from whom the Senate may choose a Vice President whenever the right of choice shall have devolved upon them.

Section 5. Sections 1 and 2 shall take effect on the 15th day of October following the ratification of this article.

Section 6. This article shall be inoperative unless it shall have been ratified as an amendment to the Constitution by the legislatures of three-fourths of the several States within seven years from the date of its submission.

Amendment XXI [1933]

Section 1. The eighteenth article of amendment to the Constitution of the United States is hereby repealed.

Section 2. The transportation or importation into any State, Territory, or possession of the United States for delivery or use therein of intoxicating liquors, in violation of the laws thereof, is hereby prohibited.

Section 3. This article shall be inoperative unless it shall have been ratified as an amendment to the Constitution by conventions in the several States, as provided in the Constitution, within seven years from the date of the submission hereof to the States by the Congress.

Amendment XXII [1951]

Section 1. No person shall be elected to the office of the President more than twice, and no person who has held the office of President, or acted as President, for more than two years of a term to which some other person was elected President shall be elected to the office of President more than once. But this Article shall not apply to any person holding the office of President when this Article was proposed by the Congress, and shall not prevent any person who may be holding the office of President, or acting as President, during the term within which this Article becomes operative from holding the office of President or acting as President during the remainder of such term.

Section 2. This article shall be inoperative unless it shall have been ratified as an amendment to the Constitution by the legislatures of three-fourths of the several States within seven years from the date of its submission to the States by the Congress.

Amendment XXIII [1961]

Section 1. The District constituting the seat of Government of the United States shall appoint in such manner as the Congress may direct:

A number of electors of President and Vice President equal to the whole number of Senators and Representatives in Congress to which the District would be entitled if it were a State, but in no event more than the least populous state; they shall be in addition to those appointed by the states, but they shall be considered, for the purposes of the election of President and Vice President, to be electors appointed by a state; and they shall meet in the District and perform such duties as provided by the twelfth article of amendment.

Section 2. The Congress shall have power to enforce this article by appropriate legislation.

Amendment XXIV [1964]

Section 1. The right of citizens of the United States to vote in any primary or other election for President or Vice President, for electors for President or Vice President, or for Senator or Representative in Congress, shall not be denied or abridged by the United States, or any State by reason of failure to pay any poll tax or other tax.

Section 2.　The Congress shall have power to enforce this article by appropriate legislation.

Amendment XXV [1967]

Section 1.　In case of the removal of the President from office or of his death or resignation, the Vice President shall become President.

Section 2.　Whenever there is a vacancy in the office of the Vice President, the President shall nominate a Vice President who shall take office upon confirmation by a majority vote of both Houses of Congress.

Section 3.　Whenever the President transmits to the President pro tempore of the Senate and the Speaker of the House of Representatives his written declaration that he is unable to discharge the powers and duties of his office, and until he transmits to them a written declaration to the contrary, such powers and duties shall be discharged by the Vice President as Acting President.

Section 4.　Whenever the Vice President and a majority of either the principal officers of the executive departments or of such other body as Congress may by law provide, transmit to the President pro tempore of the Senate and the Speaker of the House of Representatives their written declaration that the President is unable to discharge the powers and duties of his office, the Vice President shall immediately assume the powers and duties of the office as Acting President.

Thereafter, when the President transmits to the President pro tempore of the Senate and the Speaker of the House of Representatives his written declaration that no inability exists, he shall resume the powers and duties of his office unless the Vice President and a majority of either the principal officers of the executive department or of such other body as Congress may by law provide, transmit within four days to the President pro tempore of the Senate and the Speaker of the House of Representatives their written declaration that the President is unable to discharge the powers and duties of his office. Thereupon Congress shall decide the issue, assembling within forty-eight hours for that purpose if not in session. If the Congress, within twenty-one days after receipt of the latter written declaration, or, if Congress is not in session, within twenty-one days after Congress is required to assemble, determines by two-thirds vote of both Houses that the President is unable to discharge the powers and duties of his office, the Vice President shall continue to discharge the same as Acting President; otherwise, the President shall resume the powers and duties of his office.

Amendment XXVI [1971]

Section 1.　The right of citizens of the United States, who are eighteen years of age or older, to vote shall not be denied or abridged by the United States or by any State on account of age.

Section 2.　The Congress shall have power to enforce this article by appropriate legislation.

Amendment XXVII [1992]

No law, varying the compensation for the services of the Senators and Representatives, shall take effect, until an election of Representatives shall have intervened.

Spanish Equivalents for Important Legal Terms in English

Abandoned property: bienes abandonados

Acceptance: aceptación; consentimiento; acuerdo

Acceptor: aceptante

Accession: toma de posesión; aumento; accesión

Accommodation indorser: avalista de favor

Accommodation party: firmante de favor

Accord: acuerdo; convenio; arregio

Accord and satisfaction: transacción ejecutada

Act of state doctrine: doctrina de acto de gobierno

Administrative law: derecho administrativo

Administrative process: procedimiento o metódo administrativo

Administrator: administrador (-a)

Adverse possession: posesión de hecho susceptible de proscripción adquisitiva

Affirmative action: acción afirmativa

Affirmative defense: defensa afirmativa

After-acquired property: bienes adquiridos con posterioridad a un hecho dado

Agency: mandato; agencia

Agent: mandatorio; agente; representante

Agreement: convenio; acuerdo; contrato

Alien corporation: empresa extranjera

Allonge: hojas adicionales de endosos

Answer: contestación de la demande; alegato

Anticipatory repudiation: anuncio previo de las partes de su imposibilidad de cumplir con el contrato

Appeal: apelación; recurso de apelación

Appellate jurisdiction: jurisdicción de apelaciones

Appraisal right: derecho de valuación

Arbitration: arbitraje

Arson: incendio intencional

Articles of partnership: contrato social

Artisan's lien: derecho de retención que ejerce al artesano

Assault: asalto; ataque; agresión

Assignment of rights: transmisión; transferencia; cesión

Assumption of risk: no resarcimiento por exposición voluntaria al peligro

Attachment: auto judicial que autoriza el embargo; embargo

Bailee: depositario

Bailment: depósito; constitución en depósito

Bailor: depositante

Bankruptcy trustee: síndico de la quiebra

Battery: agresión; física

Bearer: portador; tenedor

Bearer instrument: documento al portador

Bequest or legacy: legado (de bienes muebles)

Bilateral contract: contrato bilateral

Bill of lading: conocimiento de embarque; carta de porte

Bill of Rights: declaración de derechos

Binder: póliza de seguro provisoria; recibo de pago a cuenta del precio

Blank indorsement: endoso en blanco

Blue sky laws: leyes reguladoras del comercio bursátil

Bond: título de crédito; garantía; caución

Bond indenture: contrato de emisión de bonos; contrato del ampréstito

Breach of contract: incumplimiento de contrato

Brief: escrito; resumen; informe

Burglary: violación de domicilio

Business judgment rule: regla de juicio comercial

Business tort: agravio comercial

Case law: ley de casos; derecho casuístico

Cashier's check: cheque de caja

Causation in fact: causalidad en realidad

665

Cease-and-desist order: orden para cesar y desistir

Certificate of deposit: certificado de depósito

Certified check: cheque certificado

Charitable trust: fideicomiso para fines benéficos

Chattel: bien mueble

Check: cheque

Chose in action: derecho inmaterial; derecho de acción

Civil law: derecho civil

Close corporation: sociedad de un solo accionista o de un grupo restringido de accionistas

Closed shop: taller agremiado (emplea solamente a miembros de un gremio)

Closing argument: argumento al final

Codicil: codicilo

Collateral: garantía; bien objeto de la garantía real

Comity: cortesía; cortesía entre naciones

Commercial paper: instrumentos negociables; documentos a valores commerciales

Common law: derecho consuetudinario; derecho común; ley común

Common stock: acción ordinaria

Comparative negligence: negligencia comparada

Compensatory damages: daños y perjuicios reales o compensatorios

Concurrent conditions: condiciones concurrentes

Concurrent jurisdiction: competencia concurrente de varios tribunales para entender en una misma causa

Concurring opinion: opinión concurrente

Condition: condición

Condition precedent: condición suspensiva

Condition subsequent: condición resolutoria

Confiscation: confiscación

Confusion: confusión; fusión

Conglomerate merger: fusión de firmas que operan en distintos mercados

Consent decree: acuerdo entre las partes aprobado por un tribunal

Consequential damages: daños y perjuicios indirectos

Consideration: consideración; motivo; contraprestación

Consolidation: consolidación

Constructive delivery: entrega simbólica

Constructive trust: fideicomiso creado por aplicación de la ley

Consumer protection law: ley para proteger el consumidor

Contract: contrato

Contract under seal: contrato formal o sellado

Contributory negligence: negligencia de la parte actora

Conversion: usurpación; conversión de valores

Copyright: derecho de autor

Corporation: sociedad anómina; corporación; persona juridica

Co-sureties: cogarantes

Counterclaim: reconvención; contrademanda

Counteroffer: contraoferta

Course of dealing: curso de transacciones

Course of performance: curso de cumplimiento

Covenant: pacto; garantía; contrato

Covenant not to sue: pacto or contrato a no demandar

Covenant of quiet enjoyment: garantía del uso y goce pacífico del inmueble

Creditors' composition agreement: concordato preventivo

Crime: crimen; delito; contravención

Criminal law: derecho penal

Cross-examination: contrainterrogatorio

Cure: cura; cuidado; derecho de remediar un vicio contractual

Customs receipts: recibos de derechos aduaneros

Damages: daños; indemnización por daños y perjuicios

Debit card: tarjeta de dé bito

Debtor: deudor

Debt securities: seguridades de deuda

Deceptive advertising: publicidad engañosa

Deed: escritura; título; acta translativa de domino

Defamation: difamación

Delegation of duties: delegación de obligaciones

Demand deposit: depósito a la vista

Depositions: declaración de un testigo fuera del tribunal

Devise: legado; deposición testamentaria (bienes inmuebles)

Direct examination: interrogatorio directo; primer interrogatorio

Directed verdict: veredicto según orden del juez y sin participación activa del jurado

Disaffirmance: repudiación; renuncia; anulación

Discharge: descargo; liberación; cumplimiento

Disclosed principal: mandante revelado

Discovery: descubrimiento; producción de la prueba

Dissenting opinion: opinión disidente

Dissolution: disolución; terminación

Diversity of citizenship: competencia de los tribunales federales para entender en causas cuyas partes intervinientes son cuidadanos de distintos estados

Divestiture: extinción premature de derechos reales

Dividend: dividendo

Docket: orden del día; lista de causas pendientes

Domestic corporation: sociedad local

Draft: orden de pago; letrade cambio

Drawee: girado; beneficiario

Drawer: librador

Duress: coacción; violencia

Easement: servidumbre

Embezzlement: desfalco; malversación

Eminent domain: poder de expropiación

Employment discrimination: discriminación en el empleo

Entrepreneur: empresario

Environmental law: ley ambiental

Equal dignity rule: regla de dignidad egual

Equity security: tipo de participación en una sociedad

Estate: propiedad; patrimonio; derecho

Estop: impedir; prevenir

Ethical issue: cuestión ética

Exclusive jurisdiction: competencia exclusiva

Exculpatory clause: cláusula eximente

Executed contract: contrato ejecutado

Execution: ejecución; cumplimiento

Executor: albacea

Executory contract: contrato aún no completamente consumado

Executory interest: derecho futuro

Express contract: contrato expreso

Expropriation: expropriación

Federal question: caso federal

Fee simple: pleno dominio; dominio absoluto

Fee simple absolute: dominio absoluto

Fee simple defeasible: dominio sujeta a una condición resolutoria

Felony: crimen; delito grave

Fictitious payee: beneficiario ficticio

Fiduciary: fiduciaro

Firm offer: oferta en firme

Fixture: inmueble por destino, incorporación a anexación

Floating lien: gravamen continuado

Foreign corporation: sociedad extranjera; U.S. sociedad constituída en otro estado

Forgery: falso; falsificación

Formal contract: contrato formal

Franchise: privilegio; franquicia; concesión

Franchisee: persona que recibe una concesión

Franchisor: persona que vende una concesión

Fraud: fraude; dolo; engaño

Future interest: bien futuro

Garnishment: embargo de derechos

General partner: socio comanditario

General warranty deed: escritura translativa de domino con garantía de título

Gift: donación

Gift *causa mortis:* donación por causa de muerte

Gift *inter vivos:* donación entre vivos

Good faith: buena fe

Good faith purchaser: comprador de buena fe

Holder: tenedor por contraprestación

Holder in due course: tenedor legítimo

Holographic will: testamento ológrafo

Homestead exemption laws: leyes que exceptúan las casas de familia de ejecución por duedas generales

Horizontal merger: fusión horizontal

Identification: identificación

Implied-in-fact contract: contrato implícito en realidad

Implied warranty: guarantía implícita

Implied warranty of merchantability: garantía implícita de vendibilidad

Impossibility of performance: imposibilidad de cumplir un contrato

Imposter: imposter

Incidental beneficiary: beneficiario incidental; beneficiario secundario

Incidental damages: daños incidentales

Indictment: auto de acusación; acusación

Indorsee: endorsatario

Indorsement: endoso

Indorser: endosante

Informal contract: contrato no formal; contrato verbal

Information: acusación hecha por el ministerio público

Injunction: mandamiento; orden de no innovar

Innkeeper's lien: derecho de retención que ejerce el posadero

Installment contract: contrato de pago en cuotas

Insurable interest: interés asegurable

Intended beneficiary: beneficiario destinado

Intentional tort: agravio; cuasidelito intenciónal

International law: derecho internaciónal

Interrogatories: preguntas escritas sometidas por una parte a la otra o a un testigo

***Inter vivos* trust:** fideicomiso entre vivos

Intestacy laws: leyes de la condición de morir intestado

Intestate: intestado

Investment company: compañia de inversiones

Issue: emisión

Joint tenancy: derechos conjuntos en un bien inmueble en favor del beneficiario sobreviviente

Judgment *n.o.v.:* juicio no obstante veredicto

Judgment rate of interest: interés de juicio

Judicial process: acto de procedimiento; proceso jurídico

Judicial review: revisión judicial

Jurisdiction: jurisdicción

Larceny: robo; hurto

Law: derecho; ley; jurisprudencia

Lease: contrato de locación; contrato de alquiler

Leasehold estate: bienes forales

Legal rate of interest: interés legal

Legatee: legatario

Letter of credit: carta de crédito

Levy: embargo; comiso

Libel: libelo; difamación escrita

Life estate: usufructo

Limited partner: comanditario

Limited partnership: sociedad en comandita

Liquidation: liquidación; realización

Lost property: objetos perdidos

Majority opinion: opinión de la mayoría

Maker: persona que realiza u ordena; librador

Mechanic's lien: gravamen de constructor

Mediation: mediación; intervención

Merger: fusión

Mirror image rule: fallo de reflejo

Misdemeanor: infracción; contravención

Mislaid property: bienes extraviados
Mitigation of damages: reducción de daños
Mortgage: hypoteca
Motion to dismiss: excepción parentoria
Mutual fund: fondo mutual

Negotiable instrument: instrumento negociable
Negotiation: negociación
Nominal damages: daños y perjuicios nominales
Novation: novación
Nuncupative will: testamento nuncupativo

Objective theory of contracts: teoria objetiva de contratos
Offer: oferta
Offeree: persona que recibe una oferta
Offeror: oferente
Order instrument: instrumento o documento a la orden
Original jurisdiction: jurisdicción de primera instancia
Output contract: contrato de producción

Parol evidence rule: regla relativa a la prueba oral
Partially disclosed principal: mandante revelado en parte
Partnership: sociedad colectiva; asociación; asociación de participación
Past consideration: causa o contraprestación anterior
Patent: patente; privilegio
Pattern or practice: muestra o práctica
Payee: beneficiario de un pago
Penalty: pena; penalidad
Per capita: por cabeza
Per stirpes: por estirpe
Perfection: perfeción
Performance: cumplimiento; ejecución
Personal defenses: excepciones personales
Personal property: bienes muebles
Plea bargaining: regateo por un alegato
Pleadings: alegatos
Pledge: prenda

Police powers: poders de policia y de prevención del crimen
Policy: póliza
Positive law: derecho positivo; ley positiva
Possibility of reverter: posibilidad de reversión
Precedent: precedente
Preemptive right: derecho de prelación
Preferred stock: acciones preferidas
Premium: recompensa; prima
Presentment warranty: garantía de presentación
Price discrimination: discriminación en los precios
Principal: mandante; principal
Privity: nexo jurídico
Privity of contract: relación contractual
Probable cause: causa probable
Probate: verificación; verificación del testamento
Probate court: tribunal de sucesiones y tutelas
Proceeds: resultados; ingresos
Profit: beneficio; utilidad; lucro
Promise: promesa
Promisee: beneficiario de una promesa
Promisor: promtente
Promissory estoppel: impedimento promisorio
Promissory note: pagaré; nota de pago
Promoter: promotor; fundador
Proximate cause: causa inmediata o próxima
Proxy: apoderado; poder
Punitive, or exemplary, damages: daños y perjuicios punitivos o ejemplares

Qualified indorsement: endoso con reservas
Quasi contract: contrato tácito o implícito
Quitclaim deed: acto de transferencia de una propiedad por finiquito, pero sin ninguna garantía sobre la validez del título transferido

Ratification: ratificación
Real property: bienes inmuebles

Reasonable doubt: duda razonable
Rebuttal: refutación
Recognizance: promesa; compromiso; reconocimiento
Recording statutes: leyes estatales sobre registros oficiales
Redress: reporacón
Reformation: rectificación; reforma; corrección
Rejoinder: dúplica; contrarréplica
Release: liberación; renuncia a un derecho
Remainder: substitución; reversión
Remedy: recurso; remedio; reparación
Replevin: acción reivindicatoria; reivindicación
Reply: réplica
Requirements contract: contrato de suministro
Res judicata: cosa juzgada; res judicata
Rescission: rescisión
Respondeat superior: responsabilidad del mandante o del maestro
Restitution: restitución
Restrictive indorsement: endoso restrictivo
Resulting trust: fideicomiso implícito
Reversion: reversión; sustitución
Revocation: revocación; derogación
Right of contribution: derecho de contribución
Right of reimbursement: derecho de reembolso
Right of subrogation: derecho de subrogación
Right-to-work law: ley de libertad de trabajo
Robbery: robo
Rule 10b-5: Regla 10b-5

Sale: venta; contrato de compreventa
Sale on approval: venta a ensayo; venta sujeta a la aprobación del comprador
Sale or return: venta con derecho de devolución
Sales contract: contrato de compraventa; boleto de compraventa
Satisfaction: satisfacción; pago
Scienter: a sabiendas
S corporation: S corporación

Secured party: acreedor garantizado
Secured transaction: transacción garantizada
Securities: volares; titulos; seguridades
Security agreement: convenio de seguridad
Security interest: interés en un bien dado en garantía que permite a quien lo detenta venderlo en caso de incumplimiento
Service mark: marca de identificación de servicios
Shareholder's derivative suit: acción judicial entablada por un accionista en nombre de la sociedad
Signature: firma; rúbrica
Slander: difamación oral; calumnia
Sovereign immunity: immunidad soberana
Special indorsement: endoso especial; endoso a la orden de una person en particular
Specific performance: ejecución precisa, según los términos del contrato
Spendthrift trust: fideicomiso para pródigos
Stale check: cheque vencido
Stare decisis: acatar las decisiones, observar los precedentes
Statutory law: derecho estatutario; derecho legislado; derecho escrito
Stock: acciones
Stock warrant: certificado para la compra de acciones
Stop-payment order: orden de suspensión del pago de un cheque dada por el librador del mismo
Strict liability: responsabilidad uncondicional
Summary judgment: fallo sumario

Tangible property: bienes corpóreos

Tenancy at will: inguilino por tiempo indeterminado (según la voluntad del propietario)
Tenancy by sufferance: posesión por tolerancia
Tenancy by the entirety: locación conyugal conjunta
Tenancy for years: inguilino por un término fijo
Tenancy in common: specie de copropiedad indivisa
Tender: oferta de pago; oferta de ejecución
Testamentary trust: fideicomiso testamentario
Testator: testador (-a)
Third party beneficiary contract: contrato para el beneficio del tercero-beneficiario
Tort: agravio; cuasidelito
Totten trust: fideicomiso creado por un depósito bancario
Trade acceptance: letra de cambio aceptada
Trade name: nombre comercial; razón social
Trademark: marca registrada
Traveler's check: cheque del viajero
Trespass to land: ingreso no authorizado a las tierras de otro
Trespass to personal property: violación de los derechos posesorios de un tercero con respecto a bienes muebles
Trust: fideicomiso; trust

Ultra vires: ultra vires; fuera de la facultad (de una sociedad anónima)
Unanimous opinion: opinión unámine
Unconscionable contract or clause: contrato leonino; cláusula leonino
Underwriter: subscriptor; asegurador

Unenforceable contract: contrato que no se puede hacer cumplir
Unilateral contract: contrato unilateral
Union shop: taller agremiado; empresa en la que todos los empleados son miembros del gremio o sindicato
Universal defenses: defensas legitimas o legales
Usage of trade: uso comercial
Usury: usura

Valid contract: contrato válido
Venue: lugar; sede del proceso
Vertical merger: fusión vertical de empresas
Void contract: contrato nulo; contrato inválido, sin fuerza legal
Voidable contract: contrato anulable
Voir dire: examen preliminar de un testigo a jurado por el tribunal para determinar su competencia
Voting trust: fideicomiso para ejercer el derecho de voto

Waiver: renuncia; abandono
Warranty of habitability: garantía de habitabilidad
Watered stock: acciones diluídos; capital inflado
White-collar crime: crimen administrativo
Writ of attachment: mandamiento de ejecución; mandamiento de embargo
Writ of *certiorari*: auto de avocación; auto de certiorari
Writ of execution: auto ejecutivo; mandamiento de ejecutión
Writ of *mandamus*: auto de mandamus; mandamiento; orden judicial

Glossary

ABA-approved program A legal or paralegal educational program that satisfies the standards for paralegal training set forth by the American Bar Association.

acceptance In contract law, the offeree's indication to the offeror that the offeree agrees to be bound by the terms of the offeror's offer or proposal to form a contract.

acquittal A certification or declaration following a trial that the individual accused of a crime is innocent, or free from guilt, in the eyes of the law and is thus absolved of the charges.

actionable Capable of serving as the basis of a lawsuit. An actionable claim can be pursued in a lawsuit or other court action.

active listening The act of listening attentively to the speaker's message and responding by giving appropriate feedback to show that you understand what the speaker is saying; restating the speaker's message in your own words to confirm that you accurately interpreted what was said.

actual malice Real and demonstrated evil intent. In a defamation suit, a statement made about a public figure normally must be made with actual malice (with either knowledge of its falsity or a reckless disregard of the truth) for liability to be incurred.

actus reus A guilty (prohibited) act. The commission of a prohibited act is one of the two essential elements required for criminal liability; the other element is the intent to commit a crime.

address block The part of a letter that indicates to whom the letter is addressed. The address block is placed in the upper left-hand portion of the letter, above the salutation (and reference line, if one is included).

adhesion contract A contract drafted by the dominant party and then presented to the other—the adhering party—on a "take-it-or-leave-it" basis.

adjudicate To resolve a dispute using a neutral decision maker.

administrative agency A federal or state government agency established to perform a specific function. Administrative agencies are authorized by legislative acts to make and enforce rules relating to the purpose for which they were established.

administrative law A body of law created by administrative agencies in the form of rules, regulations, orders, and decisions in order to carry out their duties and responsibilities.

administrative law judge (ALJ) One who presides over an administrative agency hearing and who has the power to administer oaths, take testimony, rule on questions of evidence, and make determinations of fact.

administrator A person appointed by a court to serve as a personal representative for a person who died intestate, who made a will but failed to name an executor, or whose executor cannot serve.

adoption A procedure in which persons become the legal parents of a child who is not their biological child.

Advanced Paralegal Certification (APC) A credential awarded by the National Association of Legal Assistants to a Certified Paralegal (CP) or Certified Legal Assistant (CLA) whose competency in a legal specialty has been certified based on an examination of the paralegal's knowledge and skills in the specialty area.

adversarial system of justice A legal system in which the parties to a lawsuit are opponents, or adversaries, and present their cases in the light most favorable to themselves. The impartial decision maker (the judge or jury) determines who wins based on an application of the law to the evidence presented.

affidavit A written statement of facts, confirmed by the oath or affirmation of the party making it and made before a person having the authority to administer the oath or affirmation.

affirm To uphold the judgment of a lower court.

affirmative defense A response to a plaintiff's claim that does not deny the plaintiff's facts but attacks the plaintiff's legal right to bring an action.

agency A relationship between two persons in which one person (the agent) represents or acts in the place of the other (the principal).

agent A person who is authorized to act for or in the place of another person (the principal).

agreement A meeting of the minds, and a requirement for a valid contract. Agreement involves two distinct events: an offer to form a contract and the acceptance of that offer by the offeree.

alimony Financial support paid to a former spouse after a marriage has been terminated. The alimony may be permanent or temporary (rehabilitative).

allegation A party's statement, claim, or assertion made in a pleading to the court. The allegation sets forth the issue that the party expects to prove.

alternative dispute resolution (ADR) The resolution of disputes in ways other than those involved in the traditional judicial process. Negotiation, mediation, and arbitration are forms of ADR.

American Arbitration Association (AAA) The major organization offering arbitration services in the United States.

American Association for Paralegal Education (AAfPE) A national organization of paralegal educators; the AAfPE was established in 1981 to promote high standards for paralegal education.

American Bar Association (ABA) A voluntary national association of attorneys. The ABA plays an active role in developing educational and ethical standards for attorneys and in pursuing improvements in the administration of justice.

annotation A brief comment, an explanation of a legal point, or a case summary found in a case digest or other legal source.

annulment A court decree that invalidates (nullifies) a marriage. Although the marriage itself is deemed nonexistent, children of a marriage that is annulled are deemed legitimate.

answer A defendant's response to a plaintiff's complaint.

appeal The process of seeking a higher court's review of a lower court's decision for the purpose of correcting or changing the lower court's judgment or decision.

appellant The party who takes an appeal from one court to another; sometimes referred to as the *petitioner*.

appellate court A court that reviews decisions made by lower courts, such as trial courts; a court of appeals.

appellate jurisdiction The power of a court to hear and decide an appeal; the authority of a court to review cases that have already been tried in a lower court and to make decisions about them without holding a trial.

appellee The party against whom an appeal is taken—that is, the party who opposes setting aside or reversing the judgment; sometimes referred to as the *respondent*.

appropriation In tort law, the use by one person of another person's name, likeness, or other identifying characteristic without permission and for the benefit of the user.

arbitration A method of settling disputes in which a dispute is submitted to a disinterested third party (other than a court), who issues a decision that may or may not be legally binding.

arbitration clause A clause in a contract providing that, in case of a dispute, the parties will determine their rights through arbitration rather than the judicial system.

arraignment A court proceeding in which the suspect is formally charged with the criminal offense stated in the indictment. The suspect then enters a plea (guilty, not guilty, or *nolo contendere*) in response.

arrest To take into custody a person suspected of criminal activity.

arrest warrant A written order, based on probable cause and typically issued by a judge, commanding that the person named on the warrant be arrested by the police.

arson The willful and malicious burning of a building (and, in some states, personal property) owned by another; arson statutes have been extended to cover the destruction of any building, regardless of ownership, by fire or explosion.

articles of incorporation The document filed with the appropriate state official, usually the secretary of state, when a business is incorporated. State statutes usually prescribe what kind of information must be contained in the articles of incorporation.

assault Any word or action intended to make another person apprehensive or fearful of immediate physical harm; a reasonably believable threat.

associate attorney An attorney working for a law firm who is not a partner and does not have an ownership interest in the firm. Associates are usually less experienced attorneys and may be invited to become partners after working for the firm for several years.

assumption of risk Voluntarily taking on a known risk; a defense against negligence that can be used when the plaintiff has knowledge of and appreciates a danger and voluntarily exposes himself or herself to the danger.

attorney-client privilege A rule of evidence requiring that confidential communications between a client and his or her attorney (relating to their professional relationship) be kept confidential, unless the client consents to disclosure.

authentication The process of establishing the genuineness of an item that is to be introduced as evidence in a trial.

automatic stay A suspension of all judicial proceedings upon the occurrence of an independent event. Under the Bankruptcy Code, the moment a petition to initiate bankruptcy proceedings is filed, all litigation or other legal action by creditors against a debtor and the debtor's property is suspended.

award In the context of alternative dispute resolution, the decision rendered by an arbitrator.

bail The amount of money or conditions set by the court to ensure that an individual accused of a crime will appear for further criminal proceedings. If the accused person provides bail, whether in cash or by means of a bail bond, then the person is released from jail.

bankruptcy court A federal court of limited jurisdiction that hears only bankruptcy proceedings.

bankruptcy estate In bankruptcy proceedings, all of the debtor's interests in property currently held and wherever located, as well as interests in certain property to which the debtor becomes entitled within 180 days after filing for bankruptcy.

bankruptcy law The body of federal law that governs bankruptcy proceedings. The twin goals of bankruptcy law are (1) to protect a debtor by giving him or her a fresh start and (2) to ensure that creditors competing for a debtor's assets are treated fairly.

bankruptcy trustee A person appointed by the bankruptcy court to administer the debtor's estate in the interests of both the debtor and the creditors. The basic duty of the bankruptcy trustee is to collect and reduce to cash the estate in property and to close up the estate as speedily as is compatible with the best interests of the parties.

battery The intentional and offensive touching of another without lawful justification.

beyond a reasonable doubt The standard used to determine the guilt or innocence of a person charged with a crime. To be guilty of a crime, a suspect must be proved guilty "beyond and to the exclusion of every reasonable doubt."

bigamy The act of entering into marriage with one person while still legally married to another.

Bill of Rights The first ten amendments to the U.S. Constitution.

billable hours Hours or fractions of hours that attorneys and paralegals spend in work that requires legal expertise and that can be billed directly to clients.

binder A written, temporary insurance policy.

binding authority Any source of law that a court must follow when deciding a case. Binding authorities include constitutions, statutes, and regulations that govern the issue being decided, as well as court decisions that are controlling precedents within the jurisdiction.

binding mediation A form of alternative dispute resolution in which a mediator attempts to facilitate agreement between the parties but then issues a legally binding decision if no agreement is reached.

bonus An end-of-the-year payment to a salaried employee in appreciation for that employee's overtime work, diligence, or dedication to the firm.

booking The process of entering a suspect's name, offense, and arrival time into the police log (blotter) following his or her arrest.

breach To violate a legal duty by an act or a failure to act.

breach of contract The failure, without legal excuse, of a contractual party to perform the obligations assumed in a contract.

briefing a case Summarizing a case. A case brief gives the full citation, the factual background and procedural history, the issue or issues raised, the court's decision, the court's holding, and the legal reasoning on which the court based its decision. It may also include conclusions or notes concerning the case made by the one briefing it.

burglary Breaking and entering onto the property of another with the intent to commit a felony.

business invitee A person, such as a customer or a client, who is invited onto business premises by the owner of those premises for business purposes.

business tort Wrongful interference with another's business rights.

bylaws A set of governing rules adopted by a corporation or other association.

case law Rules of law announced in court decisions.

case of first impression A case presenting a legal issue that has not yet been addressed by a court in a particular jurisdiction.

case on "all fours" A case in which all four elements (the parties, the circumstances, the legal issues involved, and the remedies sought) are very similar to those in the case being researched.

case on point A case involving factual circumstances and issues that are similar to those in the case being researched.

causation in fact Causation brought about by an act or omission without which an event would not have occurred.

cease-and-desist order An administrative or judicial order prohibiting a person or business firm from conducting activities that an agency or court has deemed illegal.

certificate of incorporation (corporate charter) The document issued by a state official, usually the secretary of state, granting a corporation legal existence and the right to function.

certification Formal recognition by a private group or a state agency that a person has satisfied the group's standards of ability, knowledge, and competence; ordinarily accomplished through the taking of an examination.

Certified Legal Assistant (CLA) or **Certified Paralegal (CP)** A legal assistant whose legal competency has been certified by the National Association of Legal Assistants (NALA) following an examination that tests the legal assistant's knowledge and skills.

chain of custody A series describing the movement and location of evidence from the time it is obtained to the time it is presented in court. The court requires that evidence be preserved in the condition in which it was obtained if it is to be admitted into evidence at trial.

challenge An attorney's objection, during *voir dire,* to the inclusion of a particular person on the jury.

challenge for cause A *voir dire* challenge to exclude a potential juror from serving on the jury for a reason specified by an attorney in the case.

charge The judge's instruction to the jury setting forth the rules of law that the jury must apply in reaching its decision, or verdict.

checks and balances A system in which each of the three branches of the national government—executive, legislative, and judicial—exercises a check on the actions of the other two branches.

child support The financial support necessary to provide for a child's needs. Commonly, when a marriage is terminated, the noncustodial spouse agrees or is required by the court to make child-support payments to the custodial spouse.

chronologically In a time sequence; naming or listing events in the time order in which they occurred.

circumstantial evidence Indirect evidence offered to establish, by inference, the likelihood of a fact that is in question.

citation In case law, a reference to a case by the name of the case, the volume number and name of the reporter in which the case can be found, the page number on which the case begins, and the year. In statutory and administrative law, a reference to the title number, name, and section of the code in which a statute or regulation can be found.

citator A book or online service that provides the history and interpretation of a statute, regulation, or court decision and a list of the cases, statutes, and regulations that have interpreted, applied, or modified a statute or regulation.

citing case A case listed in a citator that cites the case being researched.

civil law Law dealing with the definition and enforcement of private rights, as opposed to criminal matters.

civil law system A system of law based on a code rather than case law, often originally from the Roman Empire; the predominant system of law in the nations of continental Europe and the nations that were once their colonies.

click-on agreement An agreement that arises when a buyer, engaging in a transaction on a computer, indicates his or her assent to be bound by the terms of an offer by clicking on a button that says, for example, "I agree"; sometimes referred to as a click-on license or a click-wrap agreement.

close corporation A corporation owned by a small group of shareholders, often family members; also called a closely held corporation. Shares in close corporations cannot be publicly traded on the stock market, and often other restrictions on stock transfer apply. Some close corporations qualify for special tax status as S corporations.

closed-ended question A question phrased in such a way that it elicits a simple "yes" or "no" answer.

closing In a letter, an ending word or phrase placed above the signature, such as "Sincerely" or "Very truly yours."

closing argument The argument made by each side's attorney after the cases for the plaintiff and defendant have been presented. Closing arguments are made prior to the jury charge.

code A systematic and topically organized presentation of laws, rules, or regulations.

common law A body of law developed from custom or judicial decisions in English and U.S. courts and not by a legislature.

common law marriage A marriage that is formed by mutual consent and without a marriage license or ceremony. The couple must be eligible to marry, have a present and continuing agreement to be husband and wife, live together as husband and wife, and hold themselves out to the public as husband and wife. Many states do not recognize common law marriages.

community property In certain states, all property acquired during a marriage, except for inheritances or gifts received during the marriage by either marital partner. Each spouse has a one-half ownership interest in community property.

comparative negligence A theory in tort law under which the liability for injuries resulting from negligent acts is shared by all persons who were guilty of negligence (including the injured party) on the basis of each person's proportionate carelessness.

compensatory damages A money award equivalent to the actual value of injuries or damages sustained by the aggrieved party.

complaint The pleading made by a plaintiff or a charge made by the state alleging wrongdoing on the part of the defendant.

concurrent jurisdiction Jurisdiction that exists when two different courts have the power to hear a case. For example, some cases can be heard in either a federal or a state court.

confirmation letter A letter that summarizes an oral conversation to provide a permanent record of the discussion.

conflict of interest A situation in which two or more duties or interests come into conflict, as when an attorney attempts to represent opposing parties in a legal dispute.

conflicts check A procedure for determining whether an agreement to represent a potential client will result in a conflict of interest.

consideration Something of value, such as money or the performance of an action not otherwise required, that motivates the formation of a contract. Each party must give consideration for the contract to be binding.

constitutional law Law based on the U.S. Constitution and the constitutions of the states.

constructive discharge A termination of employment that occurs when the employer causes the employee's working conditions to be so intolerable that a reasonable person in the employee's position would feel compelled to quit.

consumer A person who buys products and services for personal or household use.

consumer-debtor A debtor whose debts are primarily consumer debts—that is, debts for purchases that are primarily for household or personal use.

consumer law Statutes, agency rules, and judicial decisions protecting consumers of goods and services.

contingency fee A legal fee that consists of a specified percentage (such as 30 percent) of the amount the plaintiff recovers in a civil lawsuit. The fee is paid only if the plaintiff wins the lawsuit (recovers damages).

continuing legal education (CLE) programs Courses through which attorneys and other legal professionals extend their education beyond school.

contract An agreement (based on a promise or an exchange of promises) that can be enforced in court.

contractual capacity The threshold mental capacity or age required by law for a party who enters into a contract to be bound by that contract.

contributory negligence A theory in tort law under which a complaining party's own negligence contributed to his or her injuries. Contributory negligence is an absolute bar to recovery in some jurisdictions.

conversion The act of wrongfully taking or retaining a person's personal property and placing it in the service of another.

copyright The exclusive right of an author (or other creator) to publish, print, or sell an intellectual production for a statutory period of time.

corporate law Law that governs the formation, financing, merger and acquisition, and termination of corporations, as well as the rights and duties of those who own and run the corporation.

counterclaim A claim made by a defendant in a civil lawsuit against the plaintiff; in effect, a counterclaiming defendant is suing the plaintiff.

court of equity A court that decides controversies and administers justice according to the rules, principles, and precedents of equity.

court of law A court in which the only remedies were things of value, such as money. Historically, in England, courts of law were different from courts of equity.

cram-down provision A provision of the Bankruptcy Code that allows a court to confirm a debtor's Chapter 11 reorganization plan even though only one class of creditors has accepted it. To exercise the court's right under this provision, the court must demonstrate that the plan does not discriminate unfairly against any creditors and is fair and equitable.

crime A broad term for violations of law that are punishable by the state and are codified by legislatures. The objective of criminal law is to protect the public.

criminal law Law that governs and defines those actions that are crimes and that subjects persons convicted of crimes to punishment imposed by the government (a fine or incarceration).

cross-claim A claim asserted by a defendant in a civil lawsuit against another defendant or by a plaintiff against another plaintiff.

cross-examination The questioning of an opposing witness during the trial.

cyber crime A crime that occurs online, in the virtual community of the Internet, as opposed to the physical world.

cyberstalking The crime of stalking in cyberspace. The cyberstalker usually finds the victim through Internet chat rooms, newsgroups, bulletin boards, or e-mail and proceeds to harass that person or put the person in reasonable fear for his or her safety or the safety of his or her immediate family.

cyber tort A tort committed by use of the Internet.

damages Money awarded as a remedy for a civil wrong, such as a breach of contract or a tort (wrongful act).

debtor in possession (DIP) In Chapter 11 bankruptcy proceedings, a debtor who is allowed, for the benefit of all concerned, to maintain possession of the estate in bankruptcy (the business) and to continue business operations.

deception In consumer law, a material misrepresentation or omission in information that is likely to mislead a reasonable consumer to his or her detriment.

deceptive advertising Advertising that misleads consumers, either by unjustified claims concerning a product's performance or by failure to disclose relevant information concerning the product's composition or performance.

deed A document by which title to property is transferred from one party to another.

defamation Anything published or publicly spoken that causes injury to another's good name, reputation, or character.

default judgment A judgment entered by a clerk or court against a party who has failed to appear in court to answer or defend against a claim that has been brought against him or her by another party.

defendant A party against whom a lawsuit is brought.

defense The evidence and arguments presented in the defendant's support in a criminal action or lawsuit.

defense of others The use of reasonable force to protect others from harm.

defense of property The use of reasonable force to protect one's property from harm threatened by another. The use of deadly force in defending one's property is seldom justified.

demand letter A letter in which one party explains its legal position in a dispute and requests that the recipient take some action, such as paying money owed.

deponent A party or witness who testifies under oath during a deposition.

deposition A pretrial question-and-answer proceeding, usually conducted orally, in which a party or witness answers an attorney's questions. The answers are given under oath, and the session is recorded.

deposition transcript The official transcription of the recording taken during a deposition.

dicta A Latin term referring to nonbinding (nonprecedential) judicial statements that are not directly related to the facts or issues presented in the case and thus are not essential to the holding.

digest A compilation in which brief summaries of court cases are arranged by subject and subdivided by jurisdiction and court.

direct evidence Evidence directly establishing the existence of a fact.

direct examination The examination of a witness by the attorney who calls the witness to the stand to testify on behalf of the attorney's client.

director A person elected by the shareholders to direct corporate affairs.

disbarment A severe disciplinary sanction in which an attorney's license to practice law in the state is revoked because of unethical or illegal conduct.

discharge The termination of an obligation. A discharge in bankruptcy terminates the debtor's obligation to pay the debts discharged by the court.

discovery Formal investigation prior to trial. Opposing parties use various methods, such as interrogatories and depositions, to obtain information from each other and from witnesses to prepare for trial.

discovery plan A plan formed by the attorneys litigating a lawsuit, on behalf of their clients, that indicates the types of information that will be disclosed by each party to the other prior to trial, the testimony and evidence that each party will or may introduce at trial, and the general schedule for pretrial disclosures and events.

dissolution The formal disbanding of a partnership or a corporation.

diversion program In some jurisdictions, an alternative to prosecution that is offered to certain felony suspects to deter them from future unlawful acts.

diversity of citizenship Under the Constitution, a basis for federal district court jurisdiction over a lawsuit between (1) citizens of different states, (2) a foreign country and citizens of a state or states, or (3) citizens of a state and citizens of a foreign country. The amount in controversy must be more than $75,000 before a federal court can exercise jurisdiction in such cases.

dividend A distribution of profits to corporate shareholders, disbursed in proportion to the number of shares held.

divorce A formal court proceeding that legally dissolves a marriage.

docket The list of cases entered on the court's calendar and scheduled to be heard by the court.

double billing Billing more than one client for the same billable time period.

double jeopardy To place at risk (jeopardize) a person's life or liberty twice. The Fifth Amendment to the U.S. Constitution prohibits a second prosecution for the same criminal offense.

dram shop act A state statute that imposes liability on the owners of bars, as well as those who serve alcoholic drinks to the public, for injuries resulting from accidents caused by intoxicated persons when the sellers or servers of alcoholic drinks contributed to the intoxication.

due process of law Fair, reasonable, and standard procedures that must be used by the government in any legal action against a citizen. The Fifth Amendment to the U.S. Constitution prohibits the deprivation of "life, liberty, or property without due process of law."

duty of care The duty of all persons, as established by tort law, to exercise reasonable care in dealings with others. Failure to exercise due care, which is normally determined by the reasonable person standard, is the tort of negligence.

early neutral case evaluation A form of alternative dispute resolution in which a neutral third party evaluates the strengths and weaknesses of the disputing parties' positions; the evaluator's opinion forms the basis for negotiating a settlement.

easement The right of a person to make limited use of another person's real property without taking anything from the property.

elder law A relatively new legal specialty that involves serving the needs of older clients, such as estate planning and making arrangements for long-term care.

electronic filing (e-filing) systems An online system that enables attorneys to file case documents with courts twenty-four hours a day, seven days a week.

elements The issues and facts that the plaintiff must prove to succeed in a tort claim.

emancipation The legal relinquishment by a child's parents or guardian of the legal right to exercise control over the child. Usually, a child who moves out of the parents' home and supports himself or herself is considered emancipated.

embezzlement The fraudulent appropriation of the property or money of another by a person entrusted with that property or money.

eminent domain The power of a government to take land for public use from private citizens for just compensation.

employment at will A common law doctrine under which employment is considered to be "at will"—that is, either party may terminate the employment relationship at any time and for any reason, unless a contract or statute specifies otherwise.

employment manual A firm's handbook or written statement that specifies the policies and procedures that govern the firm's employees and employer-employee relationships.

enabling legislation A statute enacted by a legislature that authorizes the creation of an administrative agency and specifies the name, purpose, composition, and powers of the agency being created.

environmental impact statement (EIS) A statement required by the National Environmental Policy Act for any major federal action that will significantly affect the quality of the environment. The statement must analyze the action's impact on the environment and explore alternative actions that might be taken.

environmental law All state and federal laws or regulations enacted or issued to protect the environment and preserve environmental resources.

equitable principles and maxims Propositions or general statements of rules of law that are frequently involved in equity jurisdiction.

e-signature An electronic sound, symbol, or process attached to or logically associated with a record and executed or adopted by a person with the intent to sign the record, according to the Uniform Electronic Transactions Act.

estate administration The process in which a decedent's personal representative settles the affairs of the decedent's estate (collects assets, pays debts and taxes, and distributes the remaining assets to heirs); the process is usually overseen by a probate court.

estate planning Making arrangements, during a person's lifetime, for the transfer of that person's property to others on the person's death. Estate planning often involves executing a will or establishing a trust fund to provide for others, such as a spouse or children, on a person's death.

ethical wall A term that refers to the procedures used to create a screen around a legal employee to shield him or her from information about a case in which there is a conflict of interest.

evidence Anything that is used to prove the existence or nonexistence of a fact.

exclusionary rule In criminal procedure, a rule under which any evidence obtained in violation of the accused's constitutional rights, as well as any evidence derived from illegally obtained evidence, will not be admissible in court.

exclusive jurisdiction Jurisdiction that exists when a case can be heard only in a particular court, such as a federal court.

executor A person appointed by a testator to serve as a personal representative on the testator's death.

expense slip A slip of paper on which any expense, or cost, that is incurred on behalf of a client (such as the payment of court fees or long-distance telephone charges) is recorded.

expert witness A witness with professional training or substantial experience qualifying him or her to testify as to his or her opinion on a particular subject.

eyewitness A witness who testifies about an event that he or she observed or experienced firsthand.

false imprisonment The intentional confinement or restraint of a person against his or her will.

family law Law relating to family matters, such as marriage, divorce, child support, and child custody.

federal question A question that pertains to the U.S. Constitution, acts of Congress, or treaties. It provides a basis for jurisdiction by the federal courts as authorized by Article III, Section 2, of the Constitution.

Federal Rules of Civil Procedure (FRCP) The rules controlling all procedural matters in civil trials brought before the federal district courts.

federal system The system of government established by the Constitution, in which the national government and the state governments share sovereign power.

fee simple absolute Ownership rights entitling the holder to use, possess, or dispose of the property however he or she chooses during his or her lifetime.

felony A crime—such as arson, murder, assault, or robbery—that carries the most severe sanctions. Sanctions range from one year in a state or federal prison to life imprisonment or (in some states) the death penalty.

fiduciary relationship A relationship involving a high degree of trust and confidence.

fixed fee A fee paid to the attorney by his or her client for having provided a specified legal service, such as the creation of a simple will.

forgery The fraudulent making or altering of any writing in a way that changes the legal rights and liabilities of another.

forms file A reference file containing copies of the firm's commonly used legal documents and informational forms. The documents in the forms file serve as models for drafting new documents.

foster care A temporary arrangement in which a family is paid by the state to care for a child for a limited period of time, often pending adoption.

fraudulent misrepresentation Any misrepresentation, either by misstatement or omission of a material fact, knowingly made with the intention of deceiving another and on which a reasonable person would and does rely to his or her detriment.

freelance paralegal A paralegal who operates his or her own business and provides services to attorneys on a contract basis. A freelance paralegal works under the supervision of an attorney, who assumes responsibility for the paralegal's work product.

friendly witness A witness who is biased against your client's adversary or sympathetic toward your client in a lawsuit or other legal proceeding.

garnishment A proceeding in which a creditor legally seizes a portion of a debtor's property (such as wages) that is in the possession of a third party (such as an employer).

general licensing Licensing in which all individuals within a specific profession or group (such as paralegals) must meet licensing requirements imposed by the state in order to legally practice their profession.

general partner A partner who participates in managing the business of a partnership and has all the rights and liabilities that arise under traditional partnership law.

genuineness of assent Knowing and voluntary assent to the contract terms. If a contract is formed as a result of mistake, misrepresentation, undue influence, or duress, genuineness of assent is lacking, and the contract will be voidable.

Good Samaritan statute A state statute stipulating that persons who provide emergency services to others in peril—unless they do so recklessly, thus causing further harm—cannot be sued for negligence.

grand jury A group of citizens called to decide whether probable cause exists to believe that a suspect committed the crime with which he or she has been charged and should stand trial.

guardian *ad litem* A person appointed by the court to represent the interests of a child or a mentally incompetent person before the court.

hacker A person who uses one computer to break into another.

headnote A note, usually a paragraph long, near the beginning of a reported case summarizing the court's ruling on an issue.

hearsay Testimony that is given in court by a witness who relates not what he or she knows personally but what another person said. Hearsay is generally not admissible as evidence.

holding The binding legal principle, or precedent, that is drawn from the court's decision in a case.

homestead exemption A law permitting the debtor to retain the family home, either in its entirety or up to a specified dollar amount, free from the claims of unsecured creditors or trustees in bankruptcy.

hornbook A single-volume scholarly discussion, or treatise, on a particular legal subject.

hostile witness A witness who is biased against your client or friendly toward your client's adversary in a lawsuit or other legal proceeding; an adverse witness.

hung jury A jury whose members are so irreconcilably divided in their opinions that they cannot reach a verdict. The judge in this situation may order a new trial.

hypothetical question A question based on hypothesis, conjecture, or fiction.

identity theft The theft of a form of identification, such as a name, date of birth, or Social Security number, which is then used to access the victim's financial resources.

impeach To call into question the credibility of a witness by challenging the truth or accuracy of his or her trial statement.

independent adoption A privately arranged adoption, as when a doctor, lawyer, or other person puts a couple seeking to adopt a child in contact with a pregnant woman who has decided to give up her child for adoption.

independent contractor A person who is hired to perform a specific undertaking but who is free to choose how and when to perform the work. An independent contractor may or may not be an agent.

indictment A charge or written accusation, issued by a grand jury, that probable cause exists to believe that a person has committed a crime for which he or she should stand trial.

information A formal criminal charge made by a prosecutor without a grand jury indictment.

informative letter A letter that conveys information to a client, a witness, an adversary's counsel, or some other person regarding a legal matter (such as the date, time, place, and purpose of a meeting) or a cover letter that accompanies other documents being sent to a person or court.

injunction A court decree ordering a person to do or to refrain from doing a certain act.

insider trading Trading in the stock of a publicly listed corporation based on inside information. One who possesses inside information and has a duty not to disclose it to outsiders may not profit from the purchase or sale of securities based on that information until the information is available to the public.

insurable interest An interest either in a person's life or well-being or in property that is sufficiently substantial to justify insuring against injury to or death of the person or damage to the property.

insurance A contract by which an insurance company (the insurer) promises to pay a sum of money or give something of value to another (either the insured or the beneficiary) to compensate for a specified loss.

intellectual property Property that results from intellectual, creative processes. Copyrights, patents, and trademarks are examples of intellectual property.

intentional infliction of emotional distress Intentional, extreme, and outrageous conduct resulting in severe emotional distress to another.

intentional tort A wrongful act knowingly committed.

international law The law that governs relations among nations. International customs and treaties are generally considered to be two of the most important sources of international law.

interrogatories A series of written questions for which written answers are prepared and then signed under oath by a party to a lawsuit (the plaintiff or the defendant).

interviewee The person who is being interviewed.

inter vivos **trust** A trust created by the grantor (settlor) and effective during the grantor's lifetime—that is, a trust not established by a will.

intestacy laws State statutes that specify how property will be distributed when a person dies intestate.

intestate The state of having died without a valid will.

investigation plan A plan that lists each step involved in obtaining and verifying facts and information relevant to the legal problem being investigated.

joint and several liability Shared and individual liability. In partnership law, joint and several liability means that a third party may sue all of the partners (jointly) or one or more of the partners separately (severally). This is true even if one of the partners sued did not participate in, ratify, or know about whatever gave rise to the cause of action.

joint custody Custody of a child that is shared by the parents following the termination of a marriage.

joint liability Shared liability. In partnership law, partners incur joint liability for partnership obligations and debts.

joint tenancy The joint ownership of property by two or more co-owners in which each co-owner owns an undivided portion of the property. On the death of one of the joint tenants, his or her interest automatically passes to the surviving joint tenant or tenants.

judgment The court's final decision regarding the rights and claims of the parties to a lawsuit.

judgment creditor A creditor who is legally entitled, by a court's judgment, to collect the amount of the judgment from a debtor.

jurisdiction The authority of a court to hear and decide a specific case.

justiciable controversy A controversy that is real and substantial, as opposed to hypothetical or academic.

key number A number (accompanied by the symbol of a key) corresponding to a specific topic within Westlaw's key-number system to facilitate legal research of case law.

KeyCite An online citator on Westlaw that can trace case history, retrieve secondary sources, categorize legal citations by legal issue, and perform other functions.

laches An equitable doctrine that bars a party's right to legal action if the party has neglected for an unreasonable length of time to act on his or her rights.

larceny The wrongful or fraudulent taking and carrying away of another person's personal property with the intent to deprive the person permanently of the property.

law A body of rules of conduct established and enforced by the controlling authority (the government) of a society.

law clerk A law student working as an apprentice with a law firm to gain practical experience.

lay witness A witness who can truthfully and accurately testify on a fact in question without having specialized training or knowledge; an ordinary witness.

leading question A question that suggests, or "leads to," a desired answer. Interviewers may use leading questions to elicit responses from witnesses who otherwise would not be forthcoming.

lease In real property law, a contract by which the owner of real property (the landlord) grants to a person (the tenant) an exclusive right to use and possess the property, usually for a specified period of time, in return for rent or some other form of payment.

legal administrator An administrative employee of a law firm who manages day-to-day operations. In smaller law firms, legal administrators are usually called office managers.

legal-assistant manager or **paralegal manager** An employee in a law firm who is responsible for overseeing the paralegal staff and paralegal professional development.

legal custody Custody of a child that confers on the parent the right to make major decisions about the child's life without consulting the other parent.

legal nurse consultant (LNC) A nurse who consults with legal professionals and others about medical aspects of legal claims or issues. Legal nurse consultants normally must have at least a bachelor's degree in nursing and significant nursing experience.

legal technician, or **independent paralegal** A paralegal who offers services directly to the public without attorney supervision. Independent paralegals assist consumers by supplying them with forms and procedural knowledge relating to simple or routine legal procedures.

legalese Legal language that is hard for the general public to understand.

libel Defamation in writing or other published form (such as videotape).

licensing A government's official act of granting permission to an individual, such as an attorney, to do something that would be illegal in the absence of such permission.

limited liability company (LLC) A hybrid form of business organization authorized by a state in which the owners of the business have limited liability and taxes on profits are passed through the business entity to the owners.

limited liability partnership (LLP) A hybrid form of business organization authorized by a state that allows professionals to enjoy the tax benefits of a partnership while limiting in some way the normal joint and several liability of partners.

limited partner One who invests in a limited partnership but does not play an active role in managing the operation of the business. Unlike general partners, limited partners are liable for partnership debts only up to the amounts that they have invested.

limited partnership A partnership consisting of one or more general partners and one or more limited partners.

liquidation In regard to corporations, the process by which corporate assets are converted into cash and distributed among creditors and shareholders according to specific rules of preference. In regard to bankruptcy, a proceeding under Chapter 7 of the Bankruptcy Code (often referred to as *ordinary,* or *straight,* bankruptcy) in which a debtor states his or her debts and turns all assets over to a trustee, who sells the nonexempt assets and distributes the proceeds to creditors. With certain exceptions, the remaining debts are then discharged, and the debtor is relieved of the obligation to pay the debts.

litigation The process of working a lawsuit through the court system.

litigation paralegal A paralegal who specializes in assisting attorneys in the litigation process.

long arm statute A state statute that permits a state to obtain jurisdiction over nonresidents. The nonresidents must have had certain "minimum contacts" with that state for the statute to apply.

mailbox rule A rule providing that an acceptance of an offer takes effect at the time it is communicated via the mode expressly or impliedly authorized by the offeror, rather than at the time it is actually received by the offeror. If acceptance is to be by mail, for example, it becomes effective the moment it is placed in the mailbox.

malpractice Professional misconduct or negligence—the failure to exercise due care—on the part of a professional, such as an attorney or a physician.

managing partner The partner in a law firm who makes decisions relating to the firm's policies and procedures and who generally oversees the business operations of the firm.

marital property All property acquired during the course of a marriage, apart from inheritances and gifts made to one or the other of the spouses.

material fact A fact that is important to the subject matter of the contract.

mediation A method of settling disputes outside of court by using the services of a neutral third party, who acts as a communicating agent between the parties; a method of dispute settlement that is less formal than arbitration.

memorandum of law A document (known as a *brief* in some states) that delineates the legal theories, statutes, and cases on which a motion is based.

mens rea A wrongful mental state, or intent. A wrongful mental state is a requirement for criminal liability. What constitutes a wrongful mental state varies according to the nature of the crime.

metadata Embedded electronic data recorded by a computer in association with a particular file, including location, path, creator, date created, date last accessed, hidden notes, earlier versions, passwords, and formatting. Metadata reveal information about how, when, and by whom a document was created, accessed, modified, and transmitted.

mini-trial A private proceeding that assists disputing parties in determining whether to take their case to court. Each party's attorney briefly argues the party's case before the other party and (usually) a neutral third party, who acts as an adviser. If the parties fail to reach an agreement, the adviser issues an opinion as to how a court would likely decide the issue.

***Miranda* rights** Certain constitutional rights of accused persons taken into custody by law enforcement officials, such as the right to remain silent and the right to counsel, as established by the United States Supreme Court's decision in *Miranda v. Arizona.*

mirror image rule A common law rule that requires that the terms of the offeree's acceptance adhere exactly to the terms of the offeror's offer for a valid contract to be formed.

misdemeanor A crime less serious than a felony, punishable by a fine or incarceration for up to one year in jail (not a state or federal penitentiary).

money laundering Falsely reporting income that has been obtained through criminal activity, such as illegal drug transactions, as income obtained through a legitimate business enterprise to make the "dirty" money "clean."

mortgage A written instrument giving a creditor an interest in the debtor's property as security for a debt.

motion A procedural request or application presented by an attorney to the court on behalf of a client.

motion for a change of venue A motion requesting that a trial be moved to a different location to ensure a fair and impartial proceeding, for the convenience of the parties, or for some other acceptable reason.

motion for a directed verdict A motion (also known as a *motion for judgment as a matter of law* in the federal courts) requesting that the court grant a judgment in favor of the party making the motion on the ground that the other party has not produced sufficient evidence to support his or her claim.

motion for a new trial A motion asserting that the trial was so fundamentally flawed (because of error, newly discovered evidence, prejudice, or other reason) that a new trial is needed to prevent a miscarriage of justice.

motion for judgment notwithstanding the verdict A motion (also referred to as a *motion for judgment as a matter of law* in federal courts) requesting that the court grant judgment in favor of the party making the motion on the ground that the jury verdict against him or her was unreasonable or erroneous.

motion for summary judgment A motion that may be filed by either party in which the party asks the court to enter judgment in his or her favor without a trial. A motion for summary judgment can be supported by evidence outside the pleadings, such as witnesses' affidavits, answers to interrogatories, and other evidence obtained prior to or during discovery.

motion *in limine* A motion requesting that certain evidence not be brought out at the trial, such as prejudicial, irrelevant, or legally inadmissible evidence.

motion to dismiss A motion filed by the defendant in which the defendant asks the court to dismiss the case for a specified reason, such as improper service, lack of personal jurisdiction, or the plaintiff's failure to state a claim for which relief can be granted.

motion to recuse A motion to remove a particular judge from a case.

motion to sever A motion to try multiple defendants separately.

motion to suppress evidence A motion requesting that certain evidence be excluded from consideration during the trial.

mutual mistake Mistake as to the same material fact on the part of both parties to a contract. In this situation, either party can cancel the contract.

National Association of Legal Assistants (NALA) One of the two largest national paralegal associations in the United States; formed in 1975. NALA is actively involved in paralegal professional development.

National Federation of Paralegal Associations (NFPA) One of the two largest national paralegal associations in the United States; formed in 1974. NFPA is actively involved in paralegal professional development.

national law Law that relates to a particular nation (as opposed to international law).

negligence The failure to exercise the standard of care that a reasonable person would exercise in similar circumstances.

negligence *per se* An action or failure to act in violation of a statutory requirement.

negotiation A process in which parties attempt to settle their dispute voluntarily, with or without attorneys to represent them.

networking Making personal connections and cultivating relationships with people in a certain field, profession, or area of interest.

no-fault divorce A divorce in which neither party is deemed to be at fault for the breakdown of the marriage.

nolo contendere Latin for "I will not contest it." A criminal defendant's plea in which he or she chooses not to challenge, or contest, the charges brought by the government. Although the defendant will still be convicted and sentenced, the plea neither admits nor denies guilt.

offer A promise or commitment to do or refrain from doing some specified thing in the future.

offeree The party to whom the offer is made.

offeror The party making the offer.

office manager An administrative employee who manages the day-to-day operations of a firm. In larger law firms, office managers are usually called legal administrators.

officer A person hired by corporate directors to assist in the management of the day-to-day operations of the corporation.

online dispute resolution (ODR) The resolution of disputes with the assistance of an organization that offers dispute-resolution services via the Internet.

open-ended question A question phrased in such a way that it elicits a relatively unguided and lengthy narrative response.

opening statement An attorney's statement to the jury at the beginning of the trial. The attorney briefly outlines the evidence that will be offered during the trial and the legal theory that will be pursued.

opinion A statement by the court setting forth the applicable law and the reasons for its decision in a case.

opinion (advisory) letter A letter from an attorney to a client containing a legal opinion on an issue raised by the client's question or legal claim. The opinion is based on a detailed analysis of the law.

order for relief A court's grant of assistance to a complainant.

ordinance An order, rule, or law enacted by a municipal or county government to govern a local matter as allowed by state or federal legislation.

original jurisdiction The power of a court to take a case, try it, and decide it.

paralegal, or **legal assistant** A person qualified by education, training, or work experience who is employed or retained by a lawyer, law office, corporation, governmental agency, or other entity and who performs specifically delegated substantive legal work, for which a lawyer is responsible.

parallel citation A second (or third) citation for a given case. When a case is published in more than one reporter, each citation is a parallel citation to the other(s).

partner A person who operates a business jointly with one or more other persons. Each partner is a co-owner of the business firm.

partnership An association of two or more persons to carry on, as co-owners, a business for profit.

party With respect to lawsuits, the plaintiff or the defendant. Some cases involve multiple parties (more than one plaintiff or defendant).

passive listening The act of listening attentively to the speaker's message and responding to the speaker by providing verbal or nonverbal cues that encourage the speaker to continue; in effect, saying, "I'm listening, please go on."

patent A government grant that gives an inventor the exclusive right or privilege to make, use, or sell an invention for a limited time period.

paternity suit A lawsuit brought by an unmarried mother to establish that a certain person is the biological father of her child. DNA testing or a comparable procedure is often used to determine paternity.

peremptory challenge A *voir dire* challenge to exclude a potential juror from serving on the jury without any supporting reason or cause. Peremptory challenges based on racial or gender criteria are illegal.

performance In contract law, the fulfillment of duties arising under a contract; the normal way of discharging contractual obligations.

personal liability An individual's personal responsibility for debts or obligations. The owners of sole proprietorships and partnerships are personally liable for the debts and obligations incurred by their businesses. If their firms go bankrupt or cannot meet debts, the owners will be personally responsible for the debts.

personal property Any property that is not real property. Generally, any property that is movable or intangible is classified as personal property.

persuasive authority Any legal authority, or source of law, that a court may look to for guidance but on which it need not rely in making its decision. Persuasive authorities include cases from other jurisdictions, discussions in legal periodicals, and so forth.

persuasive precedent A precedent decided in another jurisdiction that a court may either follow or reject but that is entitled to careful consideration.

petition for divorce The document filed with the court to initiate divorce proceedings. The requirements governing the form and content of a divorce petition vary from state to state.

petition in bankruptcy An application to a bankruptcy court for relief in bankruptcy; a filing for bankruptcy. The official forms required for a petition in bankruptcy must be completed accurately, sworn to under oath, and signed by the debtor.

petty offense In criminal law, the least serious kind of wrong, such as a traffic or building-code violation.

plaintiff A party who initiates a lawsuit.

plea bargaining The process by which the accused and the prosecutor in a criminal case work out a mutually satisfactory disposition of the case, subject to court approval. Usually, plea bargaining involves the defendant's pleading guilty to a lesser offense in return for a lighter sentence.

pleadings Statements by the plaintiff and the defendant that detail the facts, charges, and defenses involved in the litigation.

pocket part A pamphlet containing recent cases or changes in the law that is used to update legal encyclopedias and other legal authorities. It is called a "pocket part" because it slips into a pocket, or sleeve, in the front or back binder of the volume.

policy In insurance law, a contract for insurance coverage. The policy spells out the precise terms and conditions as to what will and will not be covered under the contract.

potentially responsible party (PRP) A party who may be liable under the Comprehensive Environmental Response, Compensation, and Liability Act, or Superfund. Any person who generated hazardous waste, transported hazardous waste, owned or operated a waste site at the time of disposal, or currently owns or operates a site may be responsible for some or all of the cleanup costs involved in removing the hazardous chemicals.

prayer for relief A statement at the end of the complaint requesting that the court grant relief to the plaintiff.

precedent A court decision that furnishes authority for deciding later cases in which similar facts are presented.

predatory behavior Business behavior that is undertaken with the intention of unlawfully driving competitors out of the market.

preemption A doctrine under which a federal law preempts, or takes precedence over, conflicting state and local laws.

preference In bankruptcy proceedings, the debtor's favoring of one creditor over others by making payments or transferring property to that creditor at the expense of the rights of other creditors. The bankruptcy trustee is allowed to recover payments made to one creditor in preference over another.

preliminary hearing An initial hearing in which a judge or magistrate decides if there is probable cause to believe that the defendant committed the crime with which he or she is charged.

premium In insurance law, the price paid by the insured for insurance protection for a specified period of time.

prenuptial agreement A contract formed between two persons who are contemplating marriage to provide for the disposition of property in the event of a divorce or the death of one of the spouses after they have married.

pretrial conference A conference prior to trial in which the judge and the attorneys litigating the suit discuss settlement possibilities, clarify the issues in dispute, and schedule forthcoming trial-related events.

primary source of law In legal research, a document that establishes the law on a particular issue, such as a case decision, legislative act, administrative rule, or presidential order.

principal In agency law, a person who, by agreement or otherwise, authorizes another person (the agent) to act on the principal's behalf in such a way that the acts of the agent become binding on the principal.

privilege In tort law, the ability to act contrary to another person's right without that person's having legal redress for such acts. Privilege may be raised as a defense to defamation.

privileged information Confidential communications between certain individuals, such as an attorney and his or her client, that are protected from disclosure except under court order.

probable cause Reasonable grounds to believe the existence of facts warranting certain actions, such as the search or arrest of a person.

probate To prove and validate a will and ensure that the instructions in a valid will are carried out. The process of proving and validating a will and settling matters pertaining to the administration of a decedent's estate, guardianship of a decedent's children, and similar matters.

probate court A court having jurisdiction over proceedings concerning the settlement of a person's estate.

probation When a convicted defendant is released from confinement but is still under court supervision for a period of time.

procedural law Rules that define the manner in which the rights and duties of individuals are enforced.

product liability The legal liability of manufacturers, sellers, and lessors of goods to consumers, users, and bystanders for injuries or damages that are caused by the goods.

professional corporation (PC) A corporation formed by professionals, such as attorneys or accountants. Each member of the firm is liable for his or her own malpractice, but is generally protected by limited liability as in the corporate form.

promise An assurance that one will or will not do something in the future.

promissory estoppel A doctrine under which a promise is binding if the promise is clear and definite, the promisee justifiably relies on the promise, the reliance is reasonable and substantial, and justice will be better served by enforcement of the promise.

proof of claim A document filed with a bankruptcy court by a creditor to inform the court of a claim against a debtor's property. The proof of claim lists the creditor's name and address, as well as the amount that the creditor asserts is owed to the creditor by the debtor.

property settlement The division of property between spouses on the termination of a marriage.

proximate cause Legal cause; exists when the connection between an act and an injury is strong enough to justify imposing liability.

public defender Court-appointed defense counsel. A lawyer appointed by the court to represent a criminal defendant who is unable to pay to hire private counsel.

public law number An identification number assigned to a statute.

public policy A governmental policy based on widely held societal values.

public prosecutor An individual, acting as a trial lawyer, who initiates and conducts criminal cases in the government's name and on behalf of the people.

publicly held corporation A corporation whose shares are eligible to be publicly traded in securities markets, such as the New York Stock Exchange.

punitive damages Money damages awarded to a plaintiff to punish the defendant and deter future similar conduct.

real estate Land and things permanently attached to the land, such as houses, buildings, and trees.

real property Immovable property consisting of land and the buildings and plant life thereon.

reasonable person standard The standard of behavior expected of a hypothetical "reasonable person"; the standard against which negligence is measured and that must be observed to avoid liability for negligence.

record on appeal The items submitted during the trial (pleadings, motions, briefs, and exhibits) and the transcript of the trial proceedings that are forwarded to the appellate court for review when a case is appealed.

recross-examination The questioning of an opposing witness following the adverse party's redirect examination.

redirect examination The questioning of a witness following the adverse party's cross-examination.

reference line The portion of a letter that indicates the matter to be discussed, such as "RE: Summary of Cases Applying the Family and Medical Leave Act of 1993." The reference line is placed just below the address block and above the salutation.

reformation An equitable remedy granted by a court to correct, or "reform," a written contract so that it reflects the true intentions of the parties.

Registered Paralegal (RP) A paralegal whose competency has been certified by the National Federation of Paralegal Associations (NFPA) after successful completion of the Paralegal Advanced Competency Exam (PACE).

relevant evidence Evidence tending to prove or disprove the fact in question. Only relevant evidence is admissible in court.

remand To send a case back to a lower court for further proceedings.

remedy The means by which a right is enforced or the violation of a right is prevented or compensated for.

remedy at law A remedy available in a court of law. Money damages and items of value are awarded as a remedy at law.

remedy in equity A remedy allowed by courts in situations where remedies at law are not appropriate. Remedies in equity are based on rules of fairness, justice, and honesty.

reporter A book in which court cases are published, or reported.

reprimand A disciplinary sanction in which an attorney is rebuked for misbehavior. Although a reprimand is the mildest sanction for attorney misconduct, it is serious and may significantly damage the attorney's reputation in the legal community.

rescission A remedy in which the contract is canceled and the parties are returned to the positions they occupied before the contract was made.

respondeat superior A doctrine in agency law under which a principal-employer may be held liable for the wrongful acts committed by agents or employees acting within the scope of their agency or employment.

responsible corporate officer doctrine A common law doctrine under which the court may impose criminal liability on a corporate officer for actions of employees under her or his supervision regardless of whether she or he participated in, directed, or even knew about those actions.

restitution An equitable remedy under which a person is restored to his or her original position prior to loss or injury, or placed in the position that he or she would have been in had the breach not occurred.

restraining order A court order that requires one person (such as an abusing spouse) to stay away from another (such as an abused spouse).

restrictive covenants Agreements between an employer and employee that the employee will not attempt to compete with the employer for a specified period after employment ends.

retainer An advance payment made by a client to a law firm to cover part of the legal fees and/or costs that will be incurred on that client's behalf.

retainer agreement A signed document stating that the attorney or the law firm has been hired by the client to provide certain legal services and that the client agrees to pay for those services.

return-of-service form A document signed by a process server and submitted to the court to prove that a defendant received a summons.

reverse To overturn the judgment of a lower court.

reversible error A legal error at the trial court level that is significant enough to have affected the outcome of the case. It is grounds for reversal of the judgment on appeal.

risk A prediction concerning potential loss based on known and unknown factors.

risk management Planning that is undertaken to reduce the risk of loss from known and unknown events. In the context of insurance, risk management involves transferring certain risks from the insured to the insurance company.

robbery The taking of money, personal property, or any other article of value from a person by means of force or fear.

rulemaking The actions undertaken by administrative agencies when formally adopting new regulations or amending old ones.

rules of evidence Rules governing the admissibility of evidence in trial courts.

sales contract A contract for the sale of goods, as opposed to a contract for the sale of services, real property, or intangible property. Sales contracts are governed by Article 2 of the Uniform Commercial Code.

salutation In a letter, the formal greeting to the addressee. The salutation is placed just below the reference line.

search warrant A written order, based on probable cause and issued by a judge or public official (magistrate), commanding that police officers or criminal investigators search a specific person, place, or property to obtain evidence.

secondary source of law In legal research, any publication that indexes, summarizes, or interprets the law, such as a legal encyclopedia, a treatise, or an article in a law review.

secured creditor A lender, seller, or any other person in whose favor there is a security interest.

self-defense The legally recognized privilege to protect oneself or one's property against injury by another. The privilege of self-defense protects only acts that are reasonably necessary to protect oneself or one's property.

self-incrimination The act of giving testimony that implicates oneself in criminal wrongdoing. The Fifth Amendment to the Constitution states that no person "shall be compelled in any criminal case to be a witness against himself."

self-regulation The regulation of the conduct of a professional group by members of the group. Self-regulation involves establishing ethical or professional standards of behavior with which members of the group must comply.

sentence The punishment, or penalty, ordered by the court to be inflicted on a person convicted of a crime.

separate property Property that a spouse owned before the marriage, plus inheritances and gifts acquired by the spouse during the marriage.

service of process The delivery of the summons and the complaint to a defendant.

settlement agreement An out-of-court resolution to a legal dispute, which is agreed to by the parties in writing. A settlement agreement may be reached at any time prior to or during a trial.

sexual harassment In the employment context, (1) the hiring or granting of job promotions or other benefits in return for sexual favors (*quid pro quo* harassment) or (2) language or conduct that is so sexually offensive that it creates a hostile working environment (hostile-environment harassment).

share A unit of stock; a measure of ownership interest in a corporation.

shareholder One who has an ownership interest in a corporation through the purchase of corporate shares, or stock.

Shepard's An online citator on LexisNexis that provides a list of all the authorities citing a particular case, statute, or other legal authority.

shrink-wrap agreement An agreement whose terms are expressed in a document located inside the box in which the goods (usually software) are packaged.

slander Defamation in oral form.

slip opinion A judicial opinion published shortly after the decision is made and not yet included in a case reporter or advance sheets.

sole proprietorship The simplest form of business organization, in which the owner is the business. Anyone who does business without creating a formal business entity has a sole proprietorship.

specific performance An equitable remedy requiring exactly the performance that was specified in a contract; usually granted only when money damages would be an inadequate remedy and the subject matter of the contract is unique (for example, real property).

staff attorney An attorney hired by a law firm as an employee. A staff attorney has no ownership rights in the firm and will not be invited to become a partner in the firm.

standing to sue A sufficient stake in a controversy to justify bringing a lawsuit. To have standing to sue, the plaintiff must demonstrate an injury or a threat of injury.

stare decisis The doctrine of precedent, under which a court is obligated to follow earlier decisions of that court or higher courts within the same jurisdiction. This is a major characteristic of the common law system.

state bar association An association of attorneys within a state. In most states, an attorney must be a member of the state bar association to practice law in the state.

statute A written law enacted by a legislature under its constitutional lawmaking authority.

Statute of Frauds A state statute that requires certain types of contracts to be in writing to be enforceable.

statute of limitations A statute setting the maximum time period within which certain actions can be brought to court or rights enforced. After the period of time has run, no legal action can be brought.

statutory law The body of written laws enacted by the legislature.

strict liability Liability regardless of fault. In tort law, strict liability may be imposed on a merchant who introduces into commerce a good that is so defective as to be unreasonably dangerous.

submission agreement A written agreement to submit a legal dispute to an arbitrator or arbitrating panel for resolution.

subpoena A document commanding a person to appear at a certain time and place to give testimony concerning a certain matter.

substantive law Law that defines the rights and duties of individuals with respect to each other's conduct and property.

summary jury trial (SJT) A settlement method in which a trial is held but the jury's verdict is not binding. The verdict acts as a guide to both sides in reaching an agreement during mandatory negotiations that follow the trial. If a settlement is not reached, both sides have the right to a full trial later.

summons A document served on a defendant in a lawsuit informing the defendant that a legal action has been commenced against him or her and that the defendant must appear in court or respond to the plaintiff's complaint within a specified period of time.

support personnel Employees who provide clerical, secretarial, or other support to the legal, paralegal, and administrative staff of a law firm.

supporting affidavit An affidavit accompanying a motion that is filed by an attorney on behalf of his or her client. The sworn statements in the affidavit provide a factual basis for the motion.

supremacy clause The provision in Article VI of the U.S. Constitution that declares the Constitution, laws, and treaties of the United States "the supreme Law of the Land."

suspension A serious disciplinary sanction in which an attorney who has violated an ethical rule or a law is prohibited from practicing law in the state for a specified or an indefinite period of time.

syllabus A brief summary of the holding and legal principles involved in a reported case, which is followed by the court's official opinion.

tenancy in common A form of co-ownership of property in which each party owns an undivided interest that passes to his or her heirs at death.

testamentary trust A trust that is created by will and that does not take effect until the death of the testator.

testate The condition of having died with a valid will.

testator One who makes a valid will.

third party A person or entity not directly involved in an agreement (such as a contract), legal proceeding (such as a lawsuit), or relationship (such as an attorney-client relationship).

time slip A record documenting, for billing purposes, the hours (or fractions of hours) that an attorney or a paralegal worked for each client, the date on which the work was done, and the type of work done.

tort A civil wrong not arising from a breach of contract; a breach of a legal duty that causes harm or injury to another.

tortfeasor One who commits a tort.

trade journal A newsletter, magazine, or other periodical that provides a certain trade or profession with information (products, trends, or developments) relating to that trade or profession.

trade name A term that is used to indicate part or all of a business's name and that is directly related to the business's reputation and goodwill. Trade names are protected under the common law (and under trademark law, if the business's name is the same as its trademark).

trade secret Information or processes that give a business an advantage over competitors who do not know the information or processes.

trademark A distinctive mark, motto, device, or emblem that a manufacturer stamps, prints, or otherwise affixes to the goods it produces so that they can be identified on the market and their origins made known. Once a trademark is established (under the common law or through registration), the owner is entitled to its exclusive use.

treatise In legal research, a work that provides a systematic, detailed, and scholarly review of a particular legal subject.

treaty An agreement, or compact, formed between two independent nations.

trespass to land The entry onto, above, or below the surface of land owned by another without the owner's permission.

trespass to personal property The unlawful taking or harming of another's personal property; interference with another's right to the exclusive possession of his or her personal property.

trial court A court in which cases begin and in which questions of fact are examined.

trial notebook Traditionally, a binder that contains copies of all the documents and information that an attorney will need to have at hand during the trial.

trust An arrangement in which title to property is transferred by one person (the grantor, or settlor) to another (the trustee) for the benefit of a third party (the beneficiary).

trust account A bank account in which one party (the trustee, such as an attorney) holds funds belonging to another person (such as a client); a bank account into which funds advanced to a law firm by a client are deposited. Also called an *escrow account.*

unauthorized practice of law (UPL) The performance of actions defined by a legal authority, such as a state legislature, as constituting the "practice of law" without authorization to do so.

unconscionable contract or **unconscionable clause** A contract or clause that is so oppressive to one of the parties that the court will refuse to enforce the contract.

underwriter In insurance law, the insurer, or the one assuming a risk in return for the payment of a premium.

Uniform Commercial Code Statutes adopted by all states, in part or in whole, that contain uniform laws governing business transactions as defined in the code.

unilateral mistake Mistake as to a material fact on the part of only one party to a contract. In this situation, the contract is normally enforceable against the mistaken party, with some exceptions.

unreasonably dangerous product A product that is defective to the point of threatening a consumer's health and safety. A product will be considered unreasonably dangerous if it is dangerous beyond the expectation of the ordinary consumer or if a less dangerous alternative was economically feasible for the manufacturer, but the manufacturer failed to produce it.

U.S. trustee A government official who performs administrative tasks that a bankruptcy judge would otherwise have to perform.

venue The geographic district in which an action is tried and from which the jury is selected.

verdict A formal decision made by a jury.

vicarious liability Legal responsibility placed on one person for the acts of another.

visitation rights The right of a noncustodial parent to have contact with his or her child. Grandparents and stepparents may also be given visitation rights.

voir dire A proceeding in which attorneys for the plaintiff and the defendant ask prospective jurors questions to determine whether any potential juror is biased or has any connection with a party to the action or with a prospective witness.

warranty An express or implied promise by a seller that specific goods to be sold meet certain criteria, or standards of performance, on which the buyer may rely.

white-collar crime A crime that typically occurs in a business context; popularly used to refer to an illegal act or series of acts committed by a person or business entity using nonviolent means.

wiki A Web page that can be added to and modified by anyone or by authorized users who share the site. The most famous example is Wikipedia.

will A document directing how and to whom the maker's property and obligations are to be transferred on his or her death.

winding up The process of winding up all business affairs (collecting and distributing the firm's assets) after a partnership or corporation has been dissolved.

witness A person who is asked to testify under oath at a trial.

witness statement The written record of the statements made by a witness during an interview, signed by the witness.

workers' compensation laws State statutes that establish an administrative procedure for compensating workers for injuries that arise out of or in the course of their employment, regardless of fault.

workout An out-of-court negotiation in which a debtor enters into an agreement with a creditor or creditors for a payment or plan to discharge the debtor's debt.

work product An attorney's mental impressions, conclusions, and legal theories regarding a case being prepared on behalf of a client. Work product normally is regarded as privileged information.

writ of *certiorari* A writ from a higher court asking a lower court to send it the record of a case for review. The United States Supreme Court uses *certiorari* to review most of the cases it decides to hear.

writ of execution A writ that puts in force a court's decree or judgment.

wrongful discharge An employer's termination of an employee's employment in violation of the law.

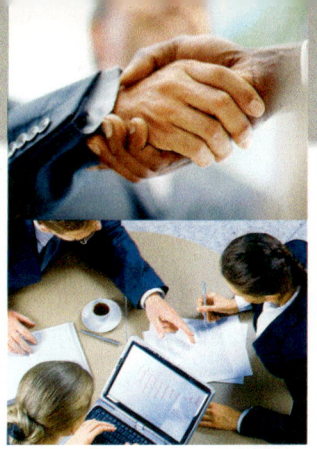

Index